Nineteenth-Century Literature Criticism

Guide to Gale Literary Criticism Series

For criticism on	Consult these Gale series
Authors now living or who died after December 31, 1999	*CONTEMPORARY LITERARY CRITICISM (CLC)*
Authors who died between 1900 and 1999	*TWENTIETH-CENTURY LITERARY CRITICISM (TCLC)*
Authors who died between 1800 and 1899	*NINETEENTH-CENTURY LITERATURE CRITICISM (NCLC)*
Authors who died between 1400 and 1799	*LITERATURE CRITICISM FROM 1400 TO 1800 (LC)* *SHAKESPEAREAN CRITICISM (SC)*
Authors who died before 1400	*CLASSICAL AND MEDIEVAL LITERATURE CRITICISM (CMLC)*
Authors of books for children and young adults	*CHILDREN'S LITERATURE REVIEW (CLR)*
Dramatists	*DRAMA CRITICISM (DC)*
Poets	*POETRY CRITICISM (PC)*
Short story writers	*SHORT STORY CRITICISM (SSC)*
Literary topics and movements	*HARLEM RENAISSANCE: A GALE CRITICAL COMPANION (HR)* *THE BEAT GENERATION: A GALE CRITICAL COMPANION (BG)* *FEMINISM IN LITERATURE: A GALE CRITICAL COMPANION (FL)* *GOTHIC LITERATURE: A GALE CRITICAL COMPANION (GL)*
Asian American writers of the last two hundred years	*ASIAN AMERICAN LITERATURE (AAL)*
Black writers of the past two hundred years	*BLACK LITERATURE CRITICISM (BLC)* *BLACK LITERATURE CRITICISM SUPPLEMENT (BLCS)* *BLACK LITERATURE CRITICISM: CLASSIC AND EMERGING AUTHORS SINCE 1950 (BLC-2)*
Hispanic writers of the late nineteenth and twentieth centuries	*HISPANIC LITERATURE CRITICISM (HLC)* *HISPANIC LITERATURE CRITICISM SUPPLEMENT (HLCS)*
Native North American writers and orators of the eighteenth, nineteenth, and twentieth centuries	*NATIVE NORTH AMERICAN LITERATURE (NNAL)*
Major authors from the Renaissance to the present	*WORLD LITERATURE CRITICISM, 1500 TO THE PRESENT (WLC)* *WORLD LITERATURE CRITICISM SUPPLEMENT (WLCS)*

ISSN 0732-1864

Volume 202

Nineteenth-Century Literature Criticism

Criticism of the
Works of Novelists, Philosophers, and Other
Creative Writers Who Died between 1800
and 1899, from the First Published Critical
Appraisals to Current Evaluations

Kathy D. Darrow
Project Editor

GALE
CENGAGE Learning

Detroit • New York • San Francisco • New Haven, Conn • Waterville, Maine • London

Nineteenth-Century Literature Criticism, Vol. 202

Project Editor: Kathy D. Darrow

Editorial: Dana Barnes, Thomas Burns, Elizabeth Cranston, Kristen Dorsch, Jeffrey W. Hunter, Jelena O. Krstović, Michelle Lee, Thomas J. Schoenberg, Lawrence J. Trudeau

Data Capture: Frances Monroe, Gwen Tucker

Rights and Acquisitions: Mollika Basu, Jermaine Bobbitt, Tracie Richardson

Composition and Electronic Capture: Gary Oudersluys

Manufacturing: Cynde Bishop

Associate Product Manager: Marc Cormier

For product information and technology assistance, contact us at **Gale Customer Support, 1-800-877-4253.**
For permission to use material from this text or product, submit all requests online at **www.cengage.com/permissions.**
Further permissions questions can be emailed to **permissionrequest@cengage.com**

Gale
27500 Drake Rd.
Farmington Hills, MI, 48331-3535

LIBRARY OF CONGRESS CATALOG CARD NUMBER 84-643008

ISBN-13: 978-1-4144-2133-9
ISBN-10: 1-4144-2133-8

ISSN 0732-1864

Printed in the United States of America
1 2 3 4 5 6 7 12 11 10 09 08

Contents

Preface vii

Acknowledgments xi

Literary Criticism Series Advisory Board xiii

Preface

Since its inception in 1981, *Nineteenth-Century Literature Criticism* (*NCLC*) has been a valuable resource for students and librarians seeking critical commentary on writers of this transitional period in world history. Designated an "Outstanding Reference Source" by the American Library Association with the publication of is first volume, *NCLC* has since been purchased by over 6,000 school, public, and university libraries. The series has covered more than 500 authors representing 38 nationalities and over 28,000 titles. No other reference source has surveyed the critical reaction to nineteenth-century authors and literature as thoroughly as *NCLC*.

Scope of the Series

NCLC is designed to introduce students and advanced readers to the authors of the nineteenth century and to the most significant interpretations of these authors' works. The great poets, novelists, short story writers, playwrights, and philosophers of this period are frequently studied in high school and college literature courses. By organizing and reprinting commentary written on these authors, *NCLC* helps students develop valuable insight into literary history, promotes a better understanding of the texts, and sparks ideas for papers and assignments. Each entry in *NCLC* presents a comprehensive survey of an author's career or an individual work of literature and provides the user with a multiplicity of interpretations and assessments. Such variety allows students to pursue their own interests; furthermore, it fosters an awareness that literature is dynamic and responsive to many different opinions.

Every fourth volume of *NCLC* is devoted to literary topics that cannot be covered under the author approach used in the rest of the series. Such topics include literary movements, prominent themes in nineteenth-century literature, literary reaction to political and historical events, significant eras in literary history, prominent literary anniversaries, and the literatures of cultures that are often overlooked by English-speaking readers.

NCLC continues the survey of criticism of world literature begun by Gale's *Contemporary Literary Criticism* (*CLC*) and *Twentieth-Century Literary Criticism* (*TCLC*).

Organization of the Book

An *NCLC* entry consists of the following elements:

- The **Author Heading** cites the name under which the author most commonly wrote, followed by birth and death dates. Also located here are any name variations under which an author wrote, including transliterated forms for authors whose native languages use nonroman alphabets. If the author wrote consistently under a pseudonym, the pseudonym will be listed in the author heading and the author's actual name given in parenthesis on the first line of the biographical and critical information. Uncertain birth or death dates are indicated by question marks. Single-work entries are preceded by a heading that consists of the most common form of the title in English translation (if applicable) and the original date of composition.

- The **Introduction** contains background information that introduces the reader to the author, work, or topic that is the subject of the entry.

- The list of **Principal Works** is ordered chronologically by date of first publication and lists the most important works by the author. The genre and publication date of each work is given. In the case of foreign authors whose works have been translated into English, the list will focus primarily on twentieth-century translations, selecting those works most commonly considered the best by critics. Unless otherwise indicated, dramas are dated by first performance, not first publication. Lists of **Representative Works** by different authors appear with topic entries.

- Reprinted **Criticism** is arranged chronologically in each entry to provide a useful perspective on changes in critical evaluation over time. The critic's name and the date of composition or publication of the critical work are given at the beginning of each piece of criticism. Unsigned criticism is preceded by the title of the source in which it appeared. All titles by the author featured in the text are printed in boldface type. Footnotes are reprinted at the end of each essay or excerpt. In the case of excerpted criticism, only those footnotes that pertain to the excerpted texts are included. Criticism in topic entries is arranged chronologically under a variety of subheadings to facilitate the study of different aspects of the topic.

- A complete **Bibliographical Citation** of the original essay or book precedes each piece of criticism.

- Critical essays are prefaced by brief **Annotations** explicating each piece.

- An annotated bibliography of **Further Reading** appears at the end of each entry and suggests resources for additional study. In some cases, significant essays for which the editors could not obtain reprint rights are included here. Boxed material following the further reading list provides references to other biographical and critical sources on the author in series published by Gale.

Indexes

Each volume of *NCLC* contains a **Cumulative Author Index** listing all authors who have appeared in a wide variety of reference sources published by Gale, including *NCLC*. A complete list of these sources is found facing the first page of the Author Index. The index also includes birth and death dates and cross references between pseudonyms and actual names.

A **Cumulative Nationality Index** lists all authors featured in *NCLC* by nationality, followed by the number of the *NCLC* volume in which their entry appears.

A **Cumulative Topic Index** lists the literary themes and topics treated in the series as well as in *Classical and Medieval Literature Criticism, Literature Criticism from 1400 to 1800, Twentieth-Century Literary Criticism,* and the *Contemporary Literary Criticism* Yearbook, which was discontinued in 1998.

An alphabetical **Title Index** accompanies each volume of *NCLC*, with the exception of the Topics volumes. Listings of titles by authors covered in the given volume are followed by the author's name and the corresponding page numbers where the titles are discussed. English translations of foreign titles and variations of titles are cross-referenced to the title under which a work was originally published. Titles of novels, dramas, nonfiction books, and poetry, short story, or essay collections are printed in italics, while individual poems, short stories, and essays are printed in roman type within quotation marks.

In response to numerous suggestions from librarians, Gale also produces an annual paperbound edition of the *NCLC* cumulative title index. This annual cumulation, which alphabetically lists all titles reviewed in the series, is available to all customers. Additional copies of this index are available upon request. Librarians and patrons will welcome this separate index; it saves shelf space, is easy to use, and is recyclable upon receipt of the next edition.

Citing *Nineteenth-Century Literature Criticism*

When citing criticism reprinted in the Literary Criticism Series, students should provide complete bibliographic information so that the cited essay can be located in the original print or electronic source. Students who quote directly from reprinted criticism may use any accepted bibliographic format, such as University of Chicago Press style or Modern Language Association style.

The examples below follow recommendations for preparing a bibliography set forth in *The Chicago Manual of Style,* 14th ed. (Chicago: The University of Chicago Press, 1993); the first example pertains to material drawn from periodicals, the second to material reprinted from books:

Franklin, J. Jeffrey. "The Victorian Discourse of Gambling: Speculations on *Middlemarch* and *The Duke's Children*." *ELH* 61, no. 4 (winter 1994): 899-921. Reprinted in *Nineteenth-Century Literature Criticism.* Vol. 168, edited by Jessica Bomarito and Russel Whitaker, 39-51. Detroit: Thomson Gale, 2006.

Frank, Joseph. "*The Gambler*: A Study in Ethnopsychology." In *Freedom and Responsibility in Russian Literature: Essays in Honor of Robert Louis Jackson,* edited by Elizabeth Cheresh Allen and Gary Saul Morson, 69-85. Evanston, Ill.: Northwestern University Press, 1995. Reprinted in *Nineteenth-Century Literature Criticism.* Vol. 168, edited by Jessica Bomarito and Russel Whitaker, 75-84. Detroit: Thomson Gale, 2006.

The examples below follow recommendations for preparing a works cited list set forth in the *MLA Handbook for Writers of Research Papers,* 6th ed. (New York: The Modern Language Association of America, 2003); the first example pertains to material drawn from periodicals, the second to material reprinted from books:

Franklin, J. Jeffrey. "The Victorian Discourse of Gambling: Speculations on *Middlemarch* and *The Duke's Children*." *ELH* 61.4 (Winter 1994): 899-921. Reprinted in *Nineteenth-Century Literature Criticism.* Eds. Jessica Bomarito and Russel Whitaker. Vol. 168. Detroit: Thomson Gale, 2006. 39-51.

Frank, Joseph. "*The Gambler*: A Study in Ethnopsychology." *Freedom and Responsibility in Russian Literature: Essays in Honor of Robert Louis Jackson.* Eds. Elizabeth Cheresh Allen and Gary Saul Morson. Evanston, Ill.: Northwestern University Press, 1995. 69-85. Reprinted in *Nineteenth-Century Literature Criticism.* Eds. Jessica Bomarito and Russel Whitaker. Vol. 168. Detroit: Thomson Gale, 2006. 75-84.

Suggestions are Welcome

Readers who wish to suggest new features, topics, or authors to appear in future volumes, or who have other suggestions or comments are cordially invited to call, write, or fax the Associate Product Manager:

Associate Product Manager, Literary Criticism Series
Gale
27500 Drake Road
Farmington Hills, MI 48331-3535
1-800-347-4253 (GALE)
Fax: 248-699-8054

Acknowledgments

The editors wish to thank the copyright holders of the criticism included in this volume and the permissions managers of many book and magazine publishing companies for assisting us in securing reproduction rights. Following is a list of the copyright holders who have granted us permission to reproduce material in this volume of *NCLC*. Every effort has been made to trace copyright, but if omissions have been made, please let us know.

COPYRIGHTED MATERIAL IN *NCLC*, VOLUME 202, WAS REPRODUCED FROM THE FOLLOWING PERIODICALS: ack:entry

Christianity and Literature, v. 54, summer, 2005; v. 55, winter, 2006; v. 56, summer, 2007. Copyright © 2005, 2006, 2007 Conference on Christianity and Literature. All reproduced by permission.—*Journal of the American Academy of Religion*, v. 62, summer, 1994. Copyright © 1994 American Academy of Religion. Reproduced by permission.—*Renascence*, v. LVI, fall, 2003. Copyright © 2003 Marquette University Press. Reproduced by permission.—*Russian Studies in Literature*, v. 40, no. 4, fall 2004 for "Whom Did the Devil Tempt, and Why? Ivan Karamazov: The Enticements of the 'Russian Path'" by Vladimir Kantor. English language translation Copyright © 2004 by M. E. Sharpe, Inc. Used with permission. All rights reserved. Not for reproduction.—*Slavic Review*, v. 66, spring, 2007. Copyright © 2007 by the American Association for the Advancement of Slavic Studies, Inc. Reproduced by permission.—*Studies in English Literature, 1500-1900*, v. 40, autumn, 2000. Copyright © 2000 William Marsh Rice University. Reproduced by permission.—*Studies in Philology*, v. 101, winter, 2004. Copyright © 2004 by the University of North Carolina Press. Used by permission.—*Studies in the Novel*, v. 27, spring, 1995. Copyright © 1995 by the University of North Texas. Reproduced by permission.—*Tennyson Research Bulletin*, v. 8, November, 2005. Reproduced by permission.—*Victorian Newsletter*, fall, 2004 for 'Eternal Honour to His Name': Tennyson's Ode on the Death of the Duke of Wellington and Victorian Memorial Aesthetics" by Anna Jane Barton. Reproduced by permission of *The Victorian Newsletter* and the author.—*Victorian Periodicals Review*, v. 36, fall, 2003. Copyright © 2003 University of Toronto Press. Reproduced by permission of University of Toronto Press Incorporated.—*Victorian Poetry*, v. 38, summer, 2000; v. 39, spring, 2001; v. 40, winter, 2002; v. 40, fall, 2002; v. 41, spring, 2003; v. 43, winter, 2005; v. 43, spring, 2005; v. 44, summer, 2006; v. 45, summer, 2007. Copyright © 2000, 2001, 2002, 2003, 2005, 2006, 2007 West Virginia University. All reproduced by permission.—*Victorian Studies*, v. 43, winter, 2001. Copyright © 2001 Indiana University Press. Reproduced by permission.—*Victorians Institute Journal*, v. 32, 2004. Copyright © 2004 *Victorians Institute Journal*. Reproduced by permission.

COPYRIGHTED MATERIAL IN *NCLC*, VOLUME 202, WAS REPRODUCED FROM THE FOLLOWING BOOKS:

Brown, Susan. From "'A Still and Mute-Born Vision': Locating Mathilde Blind's Reproductive Poetics," in *Victorian Women Poets*. Edited by Alison Chapman. Brewer, 2003. Copyright © verso 2003. Reproduced by permission.—Contino, Paul J. From "'Descend That You May Ascend': Augustine, Dostoevsky, and the Confessions of Ivan Karamazov," in *Augustine and Literature*. Edited by Robert P. Kennedy, Kim Paffenroth, and John Doody. Lexington, 2006. Copyright © 2006 by Rowman & Littlefield Publishers, Inc. All rights reserved. Reproduced by permission.—Justman, Stewart. From *Literature and Human Equality*. Northwestern University Press, 2006. Copyright © 2006 by Northwestern University Press. All rights reserved. Reproduced by permission.—Schönborn, Alexander von. From "Church and State: Dostoevsky and Kant," in *Cold Fusion: Aspects of The German Cultural Presence in Russia*. Edited by Gennady Barabtarlo. Berghahn, 2000. Copyright © 2000 Gennady Barabtarlo. All rights reserved. Republished with permission of Berghahn, conveyed through Copyright Clearance Center, Inc.—Todd, William Mills, III. From "Storied Selves: Constructing Characters in *The Brothers Karamazov*, in *Self and Story in Russian History*. Edited by Laura Engelstein and Stephanie Sandler. Cornell University Press, 2000. Copyright © 2000 by Cornell University. Used by permission of the publisher, Cornell University Press.

Gale Literature Product Advisory Board

The members of the Gale Literature Product Advisory Board—reference librarians from public and academic library systems—represent a cross-section of our customer base and offer a variety of informed perspectives on both the presentation and content of our literature products. Advisory board members assess and define such quality issues as the relevance, currency, and usefulness of the author coverage, critical content, and literary topics included in our series; evaluate the layout, presentation, and general quality of our printed volumes; provide feedback on the criteria used for selecting authors and topics covered in our series; provide suggestions for potential enhancements to our series; identify any gaps in our coverage of authors or literary topics, recommending authors or topics for inclusion; analyze the appropriateness of our content and presentation for various user audiences, such as high school students, undergraduates, graduate students, librarians, and educators; and offer feedback on any proposed changes/enhancements to our series. We wish to thank the following advisors for their advice throughout the year.

Mathilde Blind
1841-1896

(Born Mathilde Cohen, also published under the pseudonym Claude Lake) German-born English poet, biographer, critic, essayist, translator, and novelist.

INTRODUCTION

Mathilde Blind was highly regarded as a woman of letters during the mid-nineteenth century in Europe. Her abilities as a translator, literary critic, and political essayist were greatly esteemed by her contemporaries, and she garnered critical praise as a poet as well. Modern scholars view Blind as a revolutionary feminist and as a daring and thoughtful social and political voice of dissent in the midst of nineteenth-century Victorian culture.

BIOGRAPHICAL INFORMATION

Blind was born in Germany on March 21, 1841. Blind's father, a banker whose last name was Cohen, died while Blind was an infant, and her mother, Friederike Ettlinger, married Karl Blind in 1849. Blind's mother and stepfather were active in the radical political movement for a united, democratic Germany. Due to their involvement in this movement they were exiled from Germany, France, and Belgium before being granted asylum in England. The Blind home in St. John's Wood, near Regent's Park in London, was an influential literary and political salon frequented by many famous political radicals, including Karl Marx. After being expelled from the Ladies Institute in St. John's Wood because of her professed atheism, Blind traveled to Zurich, where she lived with her maternal uncle. Blind attended the University of Zurich, studying German, Gothic, and Latin, and became immersed in a world of radical Swiss intellectuals. When she returned to London, Blind assumed a self-directed program of rigorous study at the British Library and attended lectures and gatherings of various European intellectuals. Blind assumed the stance of a feminist and a revolutionary, questioning religious beliefs and societal norms; she was greatly influenced by the British Romantic poets, the Pre-Raphaelite Brotherhood, and women authors Mary Wollstonecraft, George Sand, George Eliot, Elizabeth Barrett Browning, and Christina Rossetti. Blind established herself as a noted scholar on the works of Percy Bysshe Shelley and other literary figures and her close relationships with Pre-Raphaelite painter Ford Madox Brown and Shelley scholar Richard Garnett have been of particular interest to modern scholars. In the late 1860s, Blind's brother, Ferdinand, hanged himself in a German prison, where he was held following his attempt to assassinate German chancellor Otto von Bismarck. Although her social stature granted her considerable license to express nontraditional views, some of Blind's works, particularly those containing overt references to atheism, women's rights, political oppression, and revolution, sparked controversy within the Victorian literary and intellectual establishment. Near the end of her life, Blind spent a great deal of time with her good friend, Mona Caird, a novelist who published an intensely controversial essay in 1888 in which she denounces marriage and declares that women are not naturally inclined toward chastity. In 1892 Blind became heir to the considerable estate of her stepbrother, Max Cohen, and this financial freedom enabled her to travel extensively throughout Europe, and especially in southern France, Italy, and Egypt, where the warm climates eased the symptoms of her chronic bronchitis. Blind died on November 26, 1896 in London. She stipulated in her will that a great portion of her estate be used by Newnham College, Cambridge to support and develop opportunities for women in higher education.

MAJOR WORKS

The imagery and settings of Blind's poetry, in the British Romantic tradition, are tied to the natural world, and are informed by a radical, reformist spirit. In 1867 Blind published the collection *Poems*—under the pseudonym Claude Lake—that reflects the influence of Romanticism, revolutionary political ambitions, and the poet's own frustration as a woman writing in a male-dominated world. The poems that Blind contributed to the short-lived journal *The Dark Blue,* including her first published poem, "Nocturne" (1872), are politically and socially subversive and represent the ideals of aestheticism, an important artistic and literary movement that departed from the Pre-Raphaelite model and anticipated the "art for art's sake" movement. Blind's *The Prophecy of Saint Oran and Other Poems* (1881) was withdrawn from circulation by the publisher after objections were raised to the pagan, humanist elements of the collection's title poem, which comprises Blind's feminist, free-thinking revision of a Scottish legend. Blind's *The Heather on Fire: A Tale of the Highland*

Clearances (1886) contains a steadfastly critical poetic rendering of the "Highland Clearances" that took place in Scotland during the eighteenth and nineteenth centuries, when native Scots were driven from their land to make room for English and American commerce and sport. In *The Ascent of Man* (1889), Blind seeks to reconcile Charles Darwin's "survival of the fittest" view of humankind with Jean Jacques Rousseau's view of humanity as inherently virtuous, focusing upon the valuable insights and progress that can result from humans' struggles to civilize themselves and to be creative, even when their struggles result in violence. Blind's poetry in her *Dramas in Miniature* (1891) is considered to most accurately portray her personal life and private emotions, and the verses in *Birds of Passage* (1895) reflect the influence of Blind's travels in Egypt and Italy. In addition to her works of poetry and her critical essays, Blind produced the first biography of George Eliot written by a woman in 1883, a biography of Madame Marie-Jeanne Roland in 1886, and translated such works as David Friedrich Strauss's *The Old Faith and the New, a Confession* in 1874 and Marie Bashkirtseff's diary, *The Journal of Marie Bashkirtseff,* in 1890.

CRITICAL RECEPTION

Blind's literary skills and scholarship were widely recognized by her contemporaries. Following the delivery of her lecture on Percy Bysshe Shelley in 1870, and the publication of the memoir Blind composed for her edition of *A Selection from the Poems of Percy Bysshe Shelley* in 1872, Blind was considered by some to have proven herself superior to esteemed Shelley scholar William R. Rossetti. Blind's technical skills as a poet and as a novelist—she authored one novel, *Tarantella,* in 1885—have received mixed responses from critics, but her boldness and innovations in subject matter have been consistently praised. Modern-day scholars have focused primarily on the feminist and radical political content of Blind's works, and have expressed interest in her role as a prominent female, atheist, and anti-establishment intellectual in Victorian society.

PRINCIPAL WORKS

Poems [as Claude Lake] (poetry) 1867
Shelley: A Lecture (lecture) 1870
"Nocturne" (poem) 1872; published in the journal *The Dark Blue*
A Selection from the Poems of Percy Bysshe Shelley [editor and contributor of memoir] (poetry) 1872
The Old Faith and the New, a Confession [translator; from David Friedrich Strauss's *Der alte und der neue Glaube*] (philosophy) 1874

"Mary Wollstonecraft" (essay) 1878; published in the journal *New Quarterly Magazine*
The Prophecy of Saint Oran and Other Poems (poetry) 1881
George Eliot (biography) 1883
Tarantella, A Romance. 2 vols. (novel) 1885
The Heather on Fire: A Tale of the Highland Clearances (poetry) 1886
Madame Roland (biography) 1886
The Letters of Lord Byron [editor and author of introduction] (letters) 1887
"Shelley's View of Nature Contrasted with Darwin's" (essay) 1888
The Ascent of Man (poetry) 1889; revised edition, 1890
The Journal of Marie Bashkirtseff [translator; from Marie Bashkirtseff's *Le journal de Marie Bashkirtseff* and author of introduction] (diary) 1890
Dramas in Miniature (poetry) 1891
Songs and Sonnets (poetry) 1893
Birds of Passage: Songs of the Orient and Occident (poetry) 1895
A Selection from the Poems of Mathilde Blind [edited by Arthur Symons] (poetry) 1897
*The Poetical Works of Mathilde Blind [edited by Symons] (poetry) 1900
Shakespeare Sonnets (poetry) 1902

*This edition includes a memoir of Blind written by Richard Garnett.

CRITICISM

The Unitarian Review and Religious Magazine (review date July 1883)

SOURCE: Review of *George Eliot,* by Mathilde Blind. *The Unitarian Review and Religious Magazine* 20, no. 1 (July 1883): 94.

[*In the following review, the anonymous critic offers a brief, favorable summation of Blind's biography,* George Eliot.]

[*George Eliot*] is the first volume of the Famous Women Series, to be simultaneously published in this country and in England. The initial volume is well written, and adds somewhat to our knowledge of the great novelist. The new information is, however, very limited, and is extended by several letters which are of almost no value. The correct date of the birth of Marian Evans is given as Nov. 22, 1819, and various other important particulars are given from authentic sources. Compared with the very little that was known of her previous to her death, this volume gives a very good idea of her life, and is a valuable help to an understanding of her genius. It also contains a criticism of George Eliot's works, written in a pleasant and sympathetic style. Very little new matter is given concerning her peculiar religious and philosophical opinions, and the criticism adds nothing toward understanding her in these directions. The book is one that it will be difficult for the succeeding writers of the series, who are all to be women, to surpass.

The Critic (review date 14 February 1885)

SOURCE: Review of *Tarantella,* by Mathilde Blind. *The Critic* 3, no. 59 (14 February 1885): 78.

[*In the following brief review, the anonymous critic focuses on the mixture of German and Italian stylistic elements in* Tarantella.]

Tarantella, by Mathilde Blind (Roberts), is a story with more variety in style than is often found in a single novel. The movement is at first rather slow and tedious, though it contains some quiet and pretty studies of German life; then suddenly we are plunged into a perfect whirlwind of swift passion and Italian sentiment; then, again, the German and Italian elements are opposed to each other, with results that are striking, original and interesting. The book is too long, but it contains some exquisite bits of pure and lovely romance, though the sensational, passionate element is too prominent in parts.

Christian Union (review date 19 February 1885)

SOURCE: Review of *Tarantella,* by Mathilde Blind. *Christian Union* 31, no. 8 (19 February 1885): 21.

[*In the following excerpt, the anonymous critic offers a mixed review of* Tarantella.]

Miss Mathilde Blind has done some very good work in other branches of literature, but, if we mistake not, *Tarantella* is her first attempt at fiction. While it has certain distinctly good qualities, including the power of poetical description and intensity of expression, it is, on the whole, unsatisfactory. Beginning with an invocation to Spring, followed by an introduction to the petty details of German domestic life and bread-and-butter German sentimentalism, it suddenly and unexpectedly plunges into a wildly fantastic and impossible plot ending tragically with the death of the heroine. The title, *Tarantella,* is the name of the dance music composed by the hero, Emanuel, by which he saves the life of a beautiful Capri girl, who has been stung by the tarantula, according to the old superstition that one so bitten must die unless tempted by music to dance until from

fatigue she falls to sleep. The girl thus saved he marries, and she proves the evil genius of the story, her passionate Italian wickedness being contrasted very cleverly with the sweet grace and simplicity of Emanuel's second love, whom he finds in a quiet little German village. As we have said, there is strength in the story, but the manner of telling it is overstrained, exaggerated, and at times positively unpleasant. The characters, too, do not impress one as really human; one sees the strings of the puppets move too clearly. In short, the novel is unbalanced in construction and uneven in execution, but it has in it the promise of better things.

The Literary World (review date 21 March 1885)

SOURCE: Review of *Tarantella,* by Mathilde Blind. *The Literary World* 16, no. 6 (21 March 1885): 102.

[*In the following excerpt, the anonymous critic faults Blind's* Tarantella *as formulaic but provides a favorable assessment of the author's talent for description.*]

Miss Blind's mild incursion upon the region of romance, already mentioned by an English correspondent, is productive of many extravagances without very much of genuine imaginative beauty. The most impressive scene takes place on the island of Capri, where a beautiful Italian girl has been bitten by a tarantula, and is saved from death by a German violinist, who, by his wonderful playing (with a fine thunder-storm accompaniment) inspires the maiden to a mad dance that overcomes the effects of the poison. Of course the German falls desperately in love, marries her and takes her to Rome, where she soon rewards his devotion by eloping with a Russian Count. The scene then changes to Germany, and charming little Mina is sacrificed to the machinations of the now proud Countess, who at heart is still supposed to remain faithful to her first love. The great musician emerges from his experiences scarred in spirit but purified by pain; he becomes a famous composer and "strikes out a new vein" in symphonies, to listen to which "you might have thought yourself listening to a picture of Raphael's, if a picture of Raphael's had sound in it."

> Tourists at all bitten with the musical mania, especially if American, would lie in wait for hours to get a sight of his face, or even of his back, being of opinion, no doubt, that to see a celebrity even from behind is a sop to curiosity.

As for the wicked Countess, her estates are confiscated by the Russian government and she becomes a social outcast. Some of the descriptive passages in *Tarantella* lead us to think that Miss Blind could, if she chose, write a very good novel of domestic life in Germany.

***The Dial* (review date April 1885)**

SOURCE: Review of *Tarantella*, by Mathilde Blind. *The Dial* 5, no. 60 (April 1885): 326.

[*In the following excerpt, the anonymous critic regards* Tarantella *as uneven in quality and unbalanced in terms of style and content.*]

Miss Mathilde Blind is another woman whose first novel will be read with great interest by those already familiar with the critical and miscellaneous work in which she has displayed such marked ability. ***Tarantella*** is a much better story than [Vernon Lee's] *Miss Brown*, although not without faults of style. This style is at times too pretentious, both for the subject and for the powers of the writer. In the case of individual words it is lacking in nicety of perception; in its construction it often exhibits a lapse into German idioms, which offends a fine sense of the harmonies of English speech. The story itself is interesting, but long-winded, thereby also betraying its Germanic affinities. Its chief value is psychological, it being a study of a curiously morbid if not apocryphal type of character—that of a Neapolitan woman of rudimentary moral development and of abnormally passionate nature, upon whom in early womanhood the bite of a tarantula produces the peculiar frenzy which tradition claims that it may produce in women of unusually excitable nature. She is roused to the exhibition of this frenzy by the music of a young violinist, whose interposition saves her from the fatal effects of the venom. To this musician she becomes passionately attached, and the attachment serves to blast his entire after-life. In its outcome the story is highly tragic for all the chief actors, and, although very uneven, it is not without real beauty and real strength in its finer passages.

***The Critic* (review date 1 May 1886)**

SOURCE: Review of *Madame Roland*, by Mathilde Blind. *The Critic*, no. 122 (1 May 1886): 216.

[*In the following review, the anonymous critic provides a highly negative assessment of* Madame Roland, *deriding Blind for failing to be objective in her treatment of Roland, and for including too much irrelevant detail.*]

No one should attempt to delineate another's life, unless in all cases he is prepared to give his subject at least the benefit of the doubt. At the same time, 'gush' is to be reprehended. Mathilde Blind, in her ***Life of Madame Roland,*** is unwisely enthusiastic. An inch on Cleopatra's nose might have changed the history of the world; but Miss Blind writes as if the whole course of the French Revolution might have been altered if the little Marie-Jeanne Phlipon, afterwards Madame Ro-

land, had been brought up in her childhood on a different kind of breakfast. The minuteness of unimportant detail weakens the general impression, and to write of Madame Roland almost as of some one supernatural in gifts and attainments, in no way adds to her dignity. When the young girl chronicles a natural interest in her country, Miss Blind exclaims: 'Magnificent humanitarian cry to have burst from the lips of this lovely recluse of twenty!' Everything that she does is extraordinary; nothing that she does is blameworthy. Her biographer is blind to every fault and failing. When Madame Roland tells her husband frankly that she loves 'another,' Miss Blind sees in it only a beautiful unwillingness to indulge in what would have seemed to Madame Roland the treason of loving another without her husband's knowing it. Miss Blind has certainly shown infinite patience in research; but the fact remains that the research was not worth while. It is never worth while to know so much about anybody as the biographer tells us about her heroine. She has thrown herself so completely into her subject, that she actually writes of Madame Roland as of a heroine of fiction, telling us what she thought as she walked along the street when a young girl, with all the *naïveté* of a child herself. It is a pity to find fault with one who has taken such pains, and who is so generous in admiring all that was great in one of the noted women of the world; but the biography as a whole impresses one as too long, too minute, too one-sided to be highly valuable.

***The Leeds Mercury* (review date 15 June 1886)**

SOURCE: Review of *The Heather on Fire*, by Mathilde Blind. *The Leeds Mercury*, no. 15034 (15 June 1886): 6.

[*In the following review, the anonymous critic lauds Blind's talents as a poet—in particular the author's choice of descriptive detail and "exquisitely delicate" touch—in* Heather on Fire.]

A poem remarkable for beauty of expression and pathos of incidents will be found in ***The Heather on Fire,*** by Mathilde Blind. It is a tale of the Highland clearances, embodying facts incident to many of the evictions made by landed proprietors; in some instances only in order that game may supplant human beings; in some attended by cruelty which, if not intended, was none the less real and widespread. The lovely Isle of Arran is the scene of the story told by Miss Blind, and her chief characters are a young couple, Michael and Mary, of the crofter class. The return of fishermen after a long absence, during which they have been fortunate, while relatives left at home have been ill at ease, introduces the lovers thus:—

> But oh, rejoicing most of any there,
> Rejoicing met one fond and faithful pair,

Whose true and tender hearts, tried in love's fire,
Life could not change, howe'er it might conspire
With the revolving, disenchanting years
To turn love's rainbow promises to tears,
And ruthlessly to tear asunder still
What seemed for ever joined by fate and mutual will.

Had not nine Aprils with fleet sun and showers
On wan hill-sides kindled a flame of flowers?
Had not nine harvest moons in sheltered nooks
Seen the shorn fields piled with the barley stooks,
Since these two lovers in their buoyant youth
Exchanged the vows they kept with stainless truth?
Both toiling late and soon, year in, year out,
One louged-for day to bring their marriage morn
   about.

But toil is loug, and oh, man's youth so fleet!
Fleeter love's hours when hands and lips may meet!
Weary the moons when they are wrenched apart.
For hope delayed still maketh sick the heart.
And often when the lashing rain would smite
The lowly hut throughout the moaning night,
Beside her bed the girl fell on her knees,
Praying her God for those in peril of the seas.

But now their nets had drawn great hauls aloft,
And Michael, who had left his inland croft
For female hands to till while he should reap
The fickle harvest of the unsown deep,
Returned not empty-handed to the side
Of her he looked to wed ere Christmas-tide;
And thirstily he met those sea-deep eyes,
Where her long love lay hid, a pearl beyond all price.

A grave, grand Crofter pitted in his pride
Against the niggard soil or veering tide;
Whose natural ruddy fairness wind and sun
Conspired to dye together of a dun
Unchanging umber—much as though he were
Tarred like his sails for equal wear and tear—
Wherein his eyes' unsullied blue seemed isled,
Clear as two crystal springs by foul things ne'er de-
   filed.

Grave, too, the girl that was to be his bride,
Whose dark head, as she stopped out by his side
Brushed his red-bearded chin: supple and frail,
She looked a birch tree awaying with the gale;
And her pale cheeks and shadowy eyes and hair
Seemed veiled by some pathetic brooding care,
But that her ripe lips, with their cranberry red,
A glow of youthful bloom on all her features shed.

Exquisitely delicate are the touches with which the
progress of this tale of true love is delineated up to its
consummation amid the simple rejoicings of the neigh-
bourhood; and the flight of years of married life and
daily toil as numerous as those of their courtship is told
in stanzas full of music and of soul. There were now
"old folk and wee bairns" to be cared for, and in "a
drear autumnal night," when Michael was away at sea
and a sickly boy's fretful cries seemed too much in harmony with the voice of external nature, poor Mary's
heart began to fail. Then came calls to peace and trust.
The child "slumbered more at ease":—

The tempest too lulled suddenly: a swound
As spent forces hushed the wuthering sound
And tumult of the elements; wan and grey
In the eastern heavens broke the irresolute day
Still pale and tearful, as the close-veiled sun
Like one who fears to see the havoc doue
Peered furtively; his first and faltoring ray
Hailed by a lark's clear voice hymning the new-born
   day.

A poor caged lark! But as the exultant note
Burst from the little palpitating throat
Of the imprisoned songster, the dull yoke
Of care that seemed to stifle Mary broke
In a hot flood of tears; yea, hope once more,
Like a tall pillar of fire, shone before
Her groping steps—the bird's voice seemed to tell
Her listening, anxious heart all would be well, be
   well.

The ruin of the poor woman's hope and the destruction
of the entire hamlet through the firing of the heather by
order of the landlord's factor, following on this sense of
security; with all else of wrong and harm done and suffered in the process of "clearing," are described with a
touching minnteness, recalling the less barbarously conducted expulsion of the dwellers in Grand Pré a hundred year ago, as told by Longfellow. We must refrain
from further extracts; but this tale (*which can be had
for a shilling*) is one which, unless we are mistaken,
may so affect public feeling as to be an effectual bar to
similar human clearings in future.

The Pall Mall Gazette (essay date 25 July 1889)

SOURCE: Review of *The Ascent of Man*, by Mathilde
Blind. *The Pall Mall Gazette*, no. 7598 (25 July 1889):
3.

[*In the following excerpt, the anonymous critic offers a
mixed review of* The Ascent of Man.]

Of the volumes of verse before us the most important
exhibit, in various forms, the influence of scientific discoveries or speculations upon the poetic literature of
our time. Prominent among them stands Miss Blind's
new work [*The Ascent of Man*], which will undoubtedly add to her already considerable reputation. The
principal section of the volume, from which it takes its
name, is directly inspired by the evolutionary doctrine
of the "Ascent of Man." Beginning with the era when
the atoms "struck out of dim fluctuant forces flashed
mingling in union primeval," the writer treats successively of the ages previous to the birth of man, of his
advent on this planet "wild-stammering-nameless-
shameless-nude," and of his gradual progress in civilization. The subject is by no means an easy one to treat
in a truly poetical fashion, but, on the whole, Miss
Blind has shown great skill in mastering the difficulties
inherent in her task. Her imagination has evidently been

fired by the mysterious prehistoric vista which researches in various fields have lately opened up, and her descriptions of the early struggle for existence are powerful and picturesque in a high degree. In her versification of actual history the writer is, we think, not so uniformly successful, though in her account of the birth of the arts there are lyric outbursts of great beauty. The section dealing with Love, entitled "The Pilgrim Soul," is original and melodious; but it would seem that it is the problem of pain in the universe which has the chief fascination for Miss Blind, and to this she returns in the concluding portion of the **"Ascent of Man."** She is only redeemed from the despair which the spectacle of the world's misery excites by the vision of a glorious future. This thought finds its principal expression in some very fine verses supposed to be addressed by the "Unknown Force" behind all nature to Humanity, and ending with the assurance—

> From Man's martyrdom in slow convulsion
> Will be born the infinite goodness—God.

The Critic (review date 25 January 1896)

SOURCE: Review of *Birds of Passage,* by Mathilde Blind. *The Critic* 25, no. 727 (25 January 1896): 59.

[*In the following review, the anonymous critic provides a favorable assessment of* Birds of Passage.]

A new volume of poems by Miss Mathilde Blind, bearing the familiar title of **Birds of Passage,** comprises a number of lyrical and descriptive pieces, the greater part of them being inspired by scenes and experiences in the course of a journey into Egypt and through Europe. The author, who is well known in England as being among the foremost women poets, writes with ease and exhibits a somewhat unusual mastery of the mechanism of verse-making. She employs the art of alliteration to good purpose in many of the poems of this conection, and there is a plentiful sprinkling of enticing similes and graceful phrases throughout, all of which gives to her work the qualities of readableness and interest and serves to charm the reader's fancy as well, **"The Tomb of the Kings"** is quite the best of the Oriental pieces, vivid in its picturesqueness, rich in color, smooth and sonorous in its rhythm and written with evident feeling; but it falls short of the standard set by the Oriental verse of Bayard Taylor and Clinton Scollard. The poet's individual gift is shown to a greater advantage in her **"Songs of the Occident,"** and especially in those where the Muse is not so much concerned with geographical and historical matters. Such a lyric as **"The Mirror of Diana,"** suggested by Lake Nemi, is altogether delightful, as may be seen from these stanzas:—

> And all the songs and all the scents,
> The light of glow-worms and the fires
> Of fire-flies in the cypress spires;
> And all the wild wind instruments
> Of pine and ilex, as the breeze
> Sweeps out their mystic harmonies;—
>
> All are but messengers of May
> To that white orb of maiden fire
> Who fills the moth with mad desire
> To die enamored in her ray,
> And turns each dewdrop in the grass
> Into a fairy looking-glass.

Many of these **Birds of Passage** sing as sweetly as this one, and all of them make a harmonious chorus, well suited to maintain the reputation of their poet-leader. The book is a worthy addition to its half-dozen predecessors. If it cannot be called notable, it may justly be called poetical, which is an epithet that rightly belongs to very few volumes of modern verse. We note that the edition is limited to 250 copies.

The Literary World (review date 3 September 1898)

SOURCE: Review of *Selected Poems,* by Mathilde Blind. *The Literary World* 29, no. 18 (3 September 1898): 284.

[*In the following excerpt, the anonymous critic declares that the poetry chosen for inclusion in Arthur Symond's edition of Blind's* Selected Poems *is "probably fairly representative of her genius."*]

The emotional, ardent nature of Mathilde Blind finds its fit expression in a volume of her **Poems** selected by Arthur Symons, probably fairly representative of her genius. Her instincts were religious, her sympathies world wide, her feelings intense. She could hardly have been otherwise than poetic in any written revelation of herself. Her poems are full of fire and tragic suggestion of deeps beyond utterance, of possibilities of love and suffering. They are an embodiment of herself, of her strivings and longings and regrets. They indicate no study for finish, but have the spontaneity of one who was "a poet almost in spite of herself." The editor has shown good judgment and taste in the selection. A fine portrait of Miss Blind fronts the title-page.

Alfred R. Wallace (essay date 1899)

SOURCE: Wallace, Alfred R. Introduction to *The Ascent of Man,* by Mathilde Blind, pp. v-xii. London: T. Fisher Unwin, 1899.

[*In the following essay, Wallace delineates and offers praise for Blind's treatment of social, religious, and scientific aspects of evolution in* The Ascent of Man.]

The subject of Evolution offers grand material for the poet of the future, but hitherto few have taken advantage of it. Tennyson was the first, and still remains unsurpassed in those exquisite verses of "In Memoriam" which deal with it. The late F. T. Palgrave in his poem, "The Voices of Nature," made use of it in special relation to the spiritual nature of man, and in "The Reign of Law," "Vox Dei," and one or two other short poems, he refers to it. But it was reserved for the authoress of this volume to make it the subject of [**"The Ascent of Man"**] an important and lengthy poem, devoted more especially to Man—physical, intellectual, and spiritual—in his relation to the Cosmos, to the lower forms of life, and to the Deity.

Her treatment of the subject, if not altogether satisfactory—and it is doubtful whether any living writer could treat it in a manner and with a power fully worthy of the theme—is undoubtedly poetical, and is imbued with modern ideas, though, as was perhaps inevitable, it deals more with the social and spiritual aspects of the subject than with those which are purely scientific, though these latter are by no means neglected.

She appears to have taken her main inspiration from Darwin's "Descent of Man," and she anticipated Professor Drummond both as to his title and in some of his main conceptions.

A brief outline of the poem in its subject-matter and mode of treatment, with a few illustrative passages, will enable the reader to form some idea of its nature and scope, and to determine whether it in any way comes up to his conception of what such a poem should be. It consists of three main divisions, respectively entitled, "Chaunts of Life," "The Pilgrim Soul," and "The Leading of Sorrow," each with its special versification and treatment. The first and most important of these is that which deals with physical and mental evolution, from inorganic matter to man, and specially with man's development and progress from savagery to civilisation. In the first ten pages the whole course of evolution, from the lowest forms of life up to man, is sketched out with considerable force and beauty, and with due regard to the keynote of the whole poem—that Life, Love, and God are essentially one.

The beginning of life is thus described:—

> And vaguely in the pregnant deep,
>   Clasped by the glowing arms of light
> From an eternity of sleep
>   Within unfathomed gulfs of night,
> A pulse stirred in the plastic slime
> Responsive to the rhythm of Time.
>
> Enkindled in the mystic dark
> Life built herself a myriad forms,
> And, flashing its electric spark

> Through films and cells and pulps and worms,
> Flew shuttlewise above, beneath,
> Weaving the web of life and death.

The geological succession of life is then rapidly indicated with some vivid touches, culminating in the anthropoid apes, whence arose man.

> And lo, 'mid reeking swarms of earth
>   Grim struggling in the primal wood,
> A new strange creature hath its birth:
>   Wild—stammering—nameless—shameless—nude;

His helplessness, and the possession of a hand, sharpen his senses and improve his intellect, till—

> With cunning hand he shapes the flint,
>   He carves the horn with strange device,
> He splits the rebel block by dint
>   Of effort—till one day there flies
> A spark of fire from out the stone;
> Fire which shall make the world his own.

Then follows the development of the various arts; from dreams arises the belief in spirits, demons, and gods; priestcraft soon follows; then chieftainship, sacrifices, conquests, and slavery. Man builds walled cities for protection; vast empires arise with their despotisms, cruelties, and bloodshed, culminating in the giant power and the destruction of Rome. Then the rise of Christianity, of heresies with persecutions and martyrdoms, and the history of Europe is briefly sketched down to the epoch of Napoleon and Waterloo.

There follows a short but effective description of the development of the soul of man—of his intellectual, emotional, and moral nature struggling upwards through superstition and errors towards universal sympathy and love.

The second part—"The Pilgrim Soul"—is an allegory of our modern civilisation in which wealth and pleasure and luxury have to a large extent banished that sympathy and love which can alone secure general happiness and peace. The contrasts of wealth and poverty, of luxury and vice, are painted with a terrible force and plainness. Love is pictured in the form of a child, naked, hungry, and cold, and outcast from the city of wealth and luxury. She who finds him takes him home, shelters and nourishes him, he grows and becomes greater than the lost gods of the cruel city to which he returns for its ultimate salvation.

In the third part—"The Leading of Sorrow"—a veiled phantom conducts the writer through the world to show her the universality of sorrow and death. We have first a vivid picture of the destruction and war ever going on in the animal world, from the lowest to the highest forms. The pessimistic view of the pain and misery thus arising is that taken by the author—one entirely opposed to that of Darwin and the present writer. Hence she says—

Cried I, turning to the shrouded figure—
   'Oh, in mercy veil this cruel strife!
Sanguinary orgies which disfigure
   The green ways of labyrinthine life.
From the needs and greeds of primal passion,
   From the serpent's track and lion's den,
To the world our human hands did fashion,
   Lead me to the kindly haunts of men.'

At first this seems fair and peaceful. The cornfields and orchards, the vineyards and farms with their happy peasants, the town in the valley with its contented citizens are brightly described; but suddenly the sounds and sights of an invading army are brought before us, the country is devastated, the town burnt, and all the horrors of war prevail:—

Fallen lies the fair old town, its houses
   Charred and ruined gape in smoking heaps;
Here with shouts a ruffian band carouses,
   There an outraged woman vainly weeps.

'Hence'—I cried in unavailing pity—
   'Let us flee these scenes of monstrous strife,
Seek the pale of some imperial city
   Where the law rules starlike o'er man's life.'

But this is found to be only going from bad to worse. It is true there is law and order, wealth and luxury, but along with these is the most intense misery, want, and crime, not as occasional incidents at more or less distant intervals, but perpetually present as a part of the regular order of human life. She sees the

Rich folk roll on cushions softly swelling
To the week-day feast and Sunday prayer.

But also the

. . . human rubbish, gaunt and squalid,
Whom their country spurns for lack of room.

Then follow some powerful sketches of the destruction and ruin that so often falls on good and happy lives, calling forth a burst of indignant protest:—

'Hence, ah, hence'—I sobbed in quivering passion—
   'From these fearful haunts of fiendish men!
Better far the plain, carnivorous fashion
   Which is practised in the lion's den.'

Yea, let earth be split and cloven asunder
   With man's still accumulating curse—
Life is but a momentary blunder
   In the cycle of the Universe.

Then she loses consciousness, and sees a vision of the stars and nebulæ, and suns and planets in their complex motions and developments as a mighty whole; and she hears a Voice, saying—

Wilt thou judge me, wilt thou curse me, Creature
   Whom I raised up from the Ocean slime?

And the grand course of evolution is grandly described, culminating in the production of man—

'I have climbed from reek of sanguine revels
   In Cimmerian wood and thorny wild,
Slowly upwards to the dawnlit levels,
   Where I bore thee, oh my youngest Child!

'I have cast my burden on thy shoulder;
   Unimagined potencies have given
That from formless Chaos thou shalt mould her
   And translate gross earth to luminous heaven.'

Then the Voice ceases; the seer awakes; the sun rises—

And beside me in the golden morning
   I beheld my shrouded phantom-guide;
But no longer sorrow-veiled and mourning—
   It became transfigured by my side.
And I knew—as one escaped from prison
   Sees old things again with fresh surprise—
It was Love himself, Love re-arisen
   With the Eternal shining through his eyes.

Many readers will, no doubt, consider this presentation of the subject too fragmentary, too fanciful, and altogether inadequate. But the writer knew her own strength, had her own ideas, and has evidently taken great pains to develop them in the manner and to the extent best adapted to her own genius and powers of expression.

And, if carefully considered as a whole, the poem will be found by many to have a fascination and completeness that does not at first appear, and to express in picturesque and forcible language many of those ideas as to the place of man in the great Cosmos, and as to the fundamental cause of the terrible evils that disgrace our civilisation, which permeate the writings of our greatest modern poets, moralists, and thinkers. These ideas are rapidly spreading, and will lead to that combined effort for social and humanitarian improvement which will, in all probability, be the great and distinguishing feature of the coming century.

James Diedrick (essay date winter 2002)

SOURCE: Diedrick, James. "'My Love Is a Force That Will Force You to Care': Subversive Sexuality in Mathilde Blind's Dramatic Monologues." *Victorian Poetry* 40, no. 4 (winter 2002): 359-86.

[*In the following essay, Diedrick illustrates Blind's unique vision and critique of cultural traditions in* Dramas in Miniature.]

Male reviewers struggled to characterize the poems Mathilde Blind awarded pride of place in her 1891 collection *Dramas in Miniature.* Up to this time Blind was best known as an accomplished writer of sonnets and lyrics, and as a less accomplished but admirably ambitious writer of longer poems on the Highland Clearances (**"The Heather on Fire,"** 1884) and Darwinian theory (**"The Ascent of Man,"** 1889).[1] The eight "dramas" that begin the 1891 volume seemed a departure, and generated considerable interpretive anxiety. Eric Robertson begins his _Academy_ review by confessing his confusion over the title: "Does it promise us real condensed drama—brief stories containing plots that a more diffuse writer might be glad to expand into a novel? Does it rather suggest a kind of toy-drama— stories of which the plots may be sharply articulated, while yet their interests are mock-heroic? Or, again, is it intended to denote nothing more than dramatic episodes?"[2] As he confronts the poems themselves, it becomes clear that Robertson's uneasiness stems more from their subject matter (adultery, prostitution, sexual violence, female sexual aggression, eroticized religious reverie) than from their generic affiliations. Robertson is especially struck by the frankness of **"The Battle of Flowers,"** which he notes "gives us a contrasting picture of the courtesan triumphant, as she drives along the Quai Anglais at Nice":

> Triumphant—without shame or fear
>   You air a thousand graces;
> Though women turn, when you appear,
>   With cold averted faces;
> Though men at sight of you will stop,
>   As if they looked into a shop;
> Shall both for this not doubly pay?
>   Jeanne Ray! Jeanne Ray!

(ll. 81-88)

Blind's own fearlessness in these poems—exemplified here by her disinclination to moralize and her frank representation of commodified sexuality—leads Robertson to caution his audience. Alluding to what he considers their "low" subject matter, he avers that "most of her readers, will indeed, continue to think that Miss Blind is at her highest in the earlier study of that **'Ascent of Man,'**" whose "noble strenuousness" is missing from the "less profound 'dramas' now published" (p. 531).

Arthur Symons, who four years later would feature Blind in the first issue of _The Savoy_, attempts to impose a "noble strenuousness" on **Dramas in Miniature** itself in his _Athenaeum_ review. Asserting that all but one of the dramatic poems are rightly labeled "tragedies," he adds "they are tragedies of the kind which many people are apt to sum up, and, as they imagine, to condemn, in the one word 'painful.'" Later in the review he comes much nearer the mark when he calls them "flowers of evil," suggesting the ways in which Blind, like Baudelaire, provocatively fuses aestheticism and naturalism in several of the poems. Rather than elaborating this important insight, however, Symons ends his review by retreating to a generalization equating female creativity

with artlessness—a generalization designed to reassure many male writers during the gender troubles of the 1890s. "Miss Blind is pre-eminently successful as a writer of lyrics. In her lyrics she is 'simple, sensuous, and passionate': she catches at times the heart's own rhythm in its troubled exquisite moments."[3] Given the fact that the poems under review are predominantly dramatic rather than lyric, Symons' ostensible insight into Blind's poetic "essence" must be viewed as a willful act of critical blindness, a symptom of a larger historical misconstruction of Victorian women's poetry as sentimental and lacking in formal complexity. Symons took a more active role in shaping Blind's poetic legacy a year after she named him her literary executor and a year after her death: he omitted all of her dramatic monologues from **A Selection From the Poems of Mathilde Blind** (1897). This editorial decision made it easier for Symons to misrepresent Blind in his introduction as "a poet, almost in spite of herself . . . it was direct, and not directed, emotion which gave her verse its share of that rapture without which poetry cannot exist."[4]

This form of condescension was common among Blind's male acquaintances. Her long-time correspondent and literary advisor Richard Garnett wrote a "Memoir" of the poet for **The Poetical Works of Mathilde Blind** (1900) that helped entomb her reputation for much of the twentieth century. Garnett praises the person at the expense of the poems, which he claims "are far from expressing the entire force and depth of her nature," and suffer from "an inattention to external polish and finish," sometimes reflecting "negligence of the laws of Art, not less imperative than the laws of Nature."[5] He also claims that Blind's best poems are her lyrics, a judgment rooted in his attitude toward women poets more generally. In his _DNB_ entry on Christina Rossetti, for instance, he concludes that except for _Goblin Market_ "she is, like most poetesses, purely subjective, and in no respect creative."[6] Theodore Watts-Dunton, who like Blind was a poet and a regular reviewer for _The Athenaeum,_ is consistently grudging in his many reviews of her work. Reviewing **Birds of Passage: Songs of the Orient and the Occident** (1895) for _The Saturday Review,_ Watts-Dunton claims that "when Miss Blind aims at least, she attains most. Her true talent is lyrical."[7] Assessing her career in an obituary essay for the December 5, 1896 issue of _The Athenaeum,_ Watts-Dunton tangles himself up in metaphors that suggest at least one source of his criticisms:

> If the truth must be said, she would have been a more completely happy woman had she been more free from the thirst for fame which grew upon her with the passage of time. Just as the loveliest woman palls upon

one the moment that she shows herself to be too conspicuous of her beauty, so the finest poet will pall upon
one the moment he exhibits an undue yearning for
fame.

(p. 797)

More recently, Blind's poetry has been subject to other
forms of misconstruction. Kathleen Hickok's *Representations of Women* (1984) and Isobel Armstrong's *Victorian Poetry: Poetry, Poetics and Politics* (1993) rightly
emphasize Blind's daring in writing about women's experiences in and of the body, but one unintended consequence of their focus on the important sonnet **"Motherhood"** from **"The Ascent of Man"** has been to
associate Blind with the domestic and pietistic strain in
Victorian poetry—an association that would have
puzzled her contemporaries.[8] Although her career and
literary friendships paralleled those of Coventry Patmore's in significant ways, Blind's poetry constitutes a
sustained critique of the gender assumptions inscribed
in Patmore's *The Angel in the House.*[9] Blind was among
other things an outspoken critic of Victorian marriage,
which she joined Goethe in calling "the grave of woman's genius."[10] In her 1878 essay on Mary Wollstonecraft for the *New Quarterly Magazine,* Blind paraphrases William Godwin's "subversive" views on
marriage in terms that indicate her assent: "he considered it wrong, nay immoral, for a person to appropriate
another, as happens in matrimony."[11]

Blind's criticisms of marriage are part of a larger indictment of the Victorian gender system, from the sexual
double standard to the division of intellectual and emotional "labor" that Patmore and others mythologized
during her lifetime. *The Woman Question* (1888), co-authored by Blind's friend Eleanor Marx, argues that
"there is no more a 'natural calling' of woman than
there is a 'natural' law of capitalistic production, or a
'natural' limit to the amount of the labourer's product
that goes to him for means of subsistence. . . . They
are only certain temporary conventions of society, like
the convention that French is the language of diplomacy."[12] Blind's essays, reviews, and poetry embody a
similarly radical view of gender conventions, expressed
with special force in the seven dramatic monologues
she published between 1871 and 1895. By analyzing
several of these poems in the pages that follow, with
special attention to **"The Song of the Willi,"** **"Nocturne,"** and **"A Carnival Episode,"** I seek to rescue
some of Blind's best poetry from the reductive judgments that have dogged her literary legacy. I also want
to reinscribe Blind in the aesthetic movement of the
1860s and 1870s, demonstrating the ways in which her
career illuminates often unacknowledged connections
between what Talia Schaffer has called the "female aesthetes" and the more overtly political New Woman writers of the 1880s and 1890s.[13]

Given their gendered assumptions about Blind's poetic
"essence," it is not surprising that most of Blind's contemporaries were deaf to the subtler intonations and
radical implications of her dramatic monologues.[14] To
believe her male reviewers, and freely paraphrase Robert Browning, the reach of such poems exceeded Blind's
grasp. Yet her dramatic monologues are among her best
poems, at times giving (indirect) voice to her deepest
feelings, at others expressing the skepticism and historical materialism she imbibed as the child of philosophical and political radicals. In **"The Russian Student's
Tale,"** the first poem in **Dramas in Miniature,** Blind
imaginatively inhabits the callow sensibility of a privileged male student who thinks he is taking advantage of
an inexperienced young woman he has just met during
a holiday excursion with his college friend. As the
speaker leads the woman away for a private interlude in
a woodland café, the language of his narrative betrays
his sexual opportunism and his all-too-eager indulgence
in the pathetic fallacy:

> Eye in eye, and hand in hand,
> Awake amid the slumberous land,
> I told her all my love that night—
> How I had loved her at first sight;
> How I was hers, and seemed to be
> Her own to all eternity.
> And through the splendour of the white
> Electrically glowing night,
> Wind-wafted from some perfumed dell,
> Tumultuously there loudly rose
> Above the Neva's surge and swell
> With amorous ecstasies and throes,
> And lyric spasms of wildest wail,
> The love-song of the nightingale.

(ll. 54-67)

By strategic use of the verb "seem" ("I told her . . . /
How I was hers, and seemed to be / Her own to all
eternity"), and by the use of other distancing devices
throughout the poem, Blind invites the reader to treat
the speaker's Keatsian vision skeptically.

In Robert Langbaum's reader-response definition of the
form, the dramatic monologue suspends readers between sympathetic identification with the speaker and
ethical/moral judgment.[15] Dramatic monologues also
emphasize the inherently social, socially contingent nature of knowledge and moral values. Extending Dorothy Mermin's point that the genre creates a representation of the "individual as part of society," Cynthia
Scheinberg adds that "women poets remind us that there
are any number of different kinds of relationships this
individual can have with a given society."[16] Although
she concentrates on Amy Levy in her essay, Scheinberg
notes the "generic neglect" of other women poets who
wrote dramatic monologues: Felicia Hemans, Charlotte
Brontë, Mary A. Robinson, Adelaide Proctor, Augusta
Webster, and Mathilde Blind. Calling for an analysis of

significant dramatic monologues by Victorian women poets, she argues that by doing so "we can see how the dramatic monologue accommodates a wide spectrum of poets from very different subject positions within Victorian culture" (p. 180).

Difference defined Blind's "subject position" from the start. Born Mathilde Cohen in Mannheim in 1841, she quickly became a child of revolution. In 1847 her mother, Friederike Ettlinger, widowed when Mathilde was an infant, joined the movement for a united and democratic Germany with Karl Blind, a radical political writer and activist whom she married in 1849. He had been expelled from Heidelberg University in 1846 for writing an article denouncing the punishment of a free-thinking soldier, and he and Ettlinger were both condemned to prison in Durkheim in 1847 for circulating a pamphlet that the government deemed treasonable. Blind became one of the leaders of the Baden insurrections during the revolutions of 1848; the suppression of this movement by the Prussian military led to his exile from Germany.[17] By 1849 Blind and his new family had also been exiled from France, and in 1852 they were expelled from Belgium under pressure from the reactionary government of Napoleon III. Granted asylum in England, they settled in St. John's Wood, where their household became both a haven for Europe's radical exiles and an influential intellectual salon.

During her teenage years Mathilde Blind attended schools in both London and Zurich (she was expelled from the St. John's School for Girls because of her professed atheism), but the political commitments of her parents, their allies, and frequent visitors—Louis Blanc, Joseph Mazzini, Giuseppi Garibaldi, and Karl Marx—had the most profound influence on her outlook. In his "Memoir" Garnett notes with telling ambivalence that the circumstances of Mathilde's girlhood "conspired to nurture" that "independence which distinguished her for good and ill" (p. 2). In the society of political refugees that formed in St. John's Wood, he continues, "admiration must necessarily be reserved for audacity in enterprise, fortitude in adversity, . . . anything breathing unconquerable defiance of the powers that were" (p. 3). Garnett reports that by age twenty-five Mathilde's militancy regarding the Woman Question was fully developed: "She was in favour of women following all callings, except the military and naval, and when invited by the present writer to consider the consequence of throwing a mass of cheap labour into occupations much overstocked, she rejoined, with decision, that the men might emigrate" (p. 18).[18]

Despite (or perhaps because of) her advanced views on gender, Blind spent her twenties mastering the masculine voice and writing about male writers.[19] Both strategies won her the admiration of influential male artists and writers and helped her gain entry into the London

publishing world. In 1867 she brought out a volume of lyric poems under the pseudonym Claude Lake, dedicated to the Italian revolutionary Joseph Mazzini and heavily in debt to the poetic tropes of Coleridge, Wordsworth, and Shelley.[20] In 1869 she delivered a lecture on Shelley at St. George's Hall and, at the invitation of John Chapman, she wrote a long review-essay of William Michael Rossetti's edition of Shelley's poetry for the *Westminster Review* that established her reputation as a critic.[21] It also earned her the respect of men like Garnett, William Michael Rossetti, *Athenaeum* editor Norman MacColl, and the German-born painter Ford Madox Brown, who became a life-long champion of her poetry (and possibly her lover).[22] In his invaluable *Ford Madox Brown: A Record of his Life and Work* (1896), Brown's grandson Ford Madox Hueffer gives a revealing account of the salons Brown hosted in the late 1860s and early 1870s, where Blind formed the allegiances that launched her career:

> The guests were nearly all of them people of interest. The nickname which was accorded them as a body was 'Pre-Raphaelite,' a better one might have been the 'Aestheticists.' The Aestheticists, at least, formed the nucleus, but there was a 'tail' of occasional visitors of distinction ranging from Turgeneff and Mazzini to Mark Twain.
>
> So many of the *habitués* have since passed on to fame that these gatherings must needs be historic—Rossetti, Burne-Jones, Holman Hunt, William Morris, Algernon Swinburne and Theodore Watts-Dunton, Christina and William Rossetti, Mr. Stephens; Dr. Garnett and the all-too-soon forgotten younger 'Pre-Raphaelite' poets 'B. V.,' Arthur O'Shaughnessy, Philip Marston; and Mr. John Payne.
>
> Music was represented by Theo. Marzials and Dr. Hueffer, who championed the music of the future in those past days. In the younger generation Miss Blind, Miss Spartali, now Mrs. Stillman, and Lucy, Catherine, and Oliver Madox Brown promised much.[23]

Swinburne and Blind may have mingled at Brown's salons, but they had met several years earlier. Their paths first crossed in 1867, when Swinburne made a pilgrimage to the Blind house to meet two of his revolutionary heroes: Karl Blind and Louis Blanc, the French statesman-in-exile who was visiting the Blinds.[24] Mathilde and Swinburne exchanged volumes of verse, Swinburne read and praised her 1870 lecture on Shelley, and the two exchanged letters in the 1870s.[25] In 1871 Blind wrote a glowing review of Swinburne's *Songs Before Sunrise,* although it was never published.[26] They were fellow republicans, atheists, and aesthetes, and for a short period in the 1870s, it seemed to some of their friends that they should become lovers.[27]

The year before they met, Swinburne had published a review of Baudelaire's *Les Fleurs du Mal* that became a seminal document of Victorian aestheticism. His defense of Baudelaire's morality is worth quoting, since it informs the poetry Blind would publish in the aesthetic mode in the early 1870s:

> There is not one of these poems that could have been written in a time when it was not the fashion to dig for moral motives and conscious reasons. . . . There is not one poem . . . which has not a distinct and vivid background of morality to it. Only this moral side of the book is not thrust forward in the foolish and repulsive manner of a half-taught artist.[28]

By "displacing value from subject to treatment," Patricia Clements writes, Swinburne was "laying down in print for the first time in English some of the basic positions of modernism." The association of Swinburne with Baudelaire became complete in 1866 when Swinburne published *Poems and Ballads*. As Swinburne's most recent biographer, Rikky Rooksby, has written, this volume, featuring poems about lesbianism, hermaphroditism, necrophilia, and sadomasochism, struck Victorian poetry "with the force of a tidal wave . . . sent ripples of sexual and religious rebellion far and wide . . . challenged Victorian culture's repressive attitudes to the body, to sex, to the value of sensual life, and struck a blow for artistic expression."[29]

Since Blind was herself in rebellion against Victorian sexual codes, she did not object to Swinburne's transgressive subject-matter—though she was concerned that her association with him might endanger the reception of her own work.[30] In fact, the first poem she published under her own name, **"The Song of the Willi"** ("willi" is derived from the Slovakian word "víly," denoting the ghosts of young women who died on their wedding days) is itself sexually subversive.[31] At the same time, **"The Song of the Willi"** embodies Blind's critique of the masculine privilege and supremacy that Swinburne expresses in his "Notes on Poems and Reviews" (1866), published in response to the attacks leveled against *Poems and Ballads*. His imagery in this essay suggests that the production and consumption of "adult art" is strictly man's work: "It would seem indeed as though to publish a book were equivalent to thrusting it with violence into the hands of every mother and nurse in the kingdom as fit and necessary food for female infancy. . . . No one wishes to force men's food down the throats of babes and sucklings." Adding that "the office of adult art is neither puerile nor feminine, but virile," he warns against allowing "the domestic circle . . . to be for all men and writers the outer limit and extreme horizon of their world of work." It seems that if a purely masculine space is preserved, artistic castration can be prevented and tumescence restored: "Then all accepted work will be noble and chaste in the wider masculine sense, not truncated and curtailed, but outspoken and full-grown."[32]

Blind invaded Swinburne's masculine space with a vengeance in August 1871, when her ballad **"The Song of the Willi"** appeared in the sixth issue of *The Dark Blue*. The speaker is a passionate, outspoken, full-grown woman whose desires not even death can quell. As Blind explained in a headnote accompanying the revised version of the poem published in *Dramas in Miniature*:

> According to a widespread Hungarian superstition— showing the ingrained national passion for dancing— the Willi or Willis were the spirits of young affianced girls who, dying before marriage, could not rest in their graves. It was popularly believed that these phantoms would nightly haunt lonely heaths in the neighbourhood of their native villages till the disconsolate lovers came as if drawn by a magnetic charm. On their appearance the Willi would dance with them without intermission till they dropped dead from exhaustion.
>
> (p. 71)

On the anniversary of the night she would have been wed, the speaker of **"The Song of the Willi"** rises from her bed that "has no feather," wondering of her lover "while I flit restless, a low wailing sprite, / Ah, say, canst thou sleep in thy bed?"[33] She recalls the country dance they attended a week before they were to be married, and she quotes her lover's pledge in the midst of their dancing, when "fleeter than all the fleet dancers we sped / In the rush of the rapturous race" (ll. 55-56):

> Thou'rt light, O my chosen; a bird is not lighter,
>   My dove, my doe!
> I'd dance into death with thee; death would be brighter,
>   My own swift roe!
>
> (ll. 41-44)

Then she recounts in elliptical language how her bridesmaids were transformed into the three fates, and love into death:

> High up in the chambers the maidens together,
>   Ah me, ah me!
> Were piling bleached linen as pure as swan's feather,
>   Ah me, ah me!
> Were weaving and spinning and singing aloud,
>   Were broidering my bride-veil of lace,
> But the lowering three sisters they wove me my shroud
>   As death kissed me cold in the face.
>
> (ll. 89-96)

As she draws nearer to her lover's house, the speaker notices other "pale flitting phantoms" gathering around her, and she becomes their guiding spirit, leading them to their bridegrooms and their own dances of death. She is aroused by the sound of her lover's approach, and in a significant inversion of gender roles her heart "leaps like a stag that is borne as on wings" (l. 125). Reunited with her lover, she overpowers him with her passion: "Round thy face, round thy throat, I roll my dank tresses, / Oh my love, my love!" (ll. 131-132). The poem ends with a duet of love and death, with her lover too inverting conventional norms: "Oh, brighter the night than the fires of the day" he proclaims, as she answers, "When thine eyes shine as stars over me." He responds, "Oh, sweeter thy grave than the soft breath of May—," and she sings the last line: "Down to death then, my love, but with thee" (ll. 149-152).

In her November 1872 *Athenaeum* review of William Morris' *Love Is Enough,* Blind writes that Morris' poem "transports us for the time into a land of mingled romance and faerie," but denies that such poetry is escapist:

> This kind of poetry always produces on our imagination an effect somewhat resembling the impression received on looking at a familiar landscape through the mellow emblazonry of a painted casement. . . . We see reality, not enhanced, but transformed. We behold her through an unfamiliar medium of strange and deceptive splendour.[34]

Writing of Graham Tomson's use of the ballad form, Linda Hughes notes that "the displacement of action to an apparently nonreferential plane not only tapped her most powerful imaginative gifts . . . but also freed many of the emotional restraints she customarily imposed on her poetry."[35] By incorporating a dramatic monologue into a ballad form, Blind created a powerful female voice that spoke more directly of her experiences as a woman and a woman poet than the ostensibly more personal lyrics she published as "Claude Lake." Among other things, **"The Song of the Willi"** implicitly refutes Swinburne's argument that only men can speak of sexual desire, and it does so by creating a woman who shares important qualities with Dolores and Anactoria in *Poems and Ballads,* dominant females who derive and bestow pleasure by giving pain to men. Indeed, the ghostly lover in **"The Song of the Willi"** literally achieves the desire of the speaker of **"Anactoria"**: "I would my love could kill thee; I am satiated / With seeing thee live, and fain would have thee dead" (ll. 23-24). At the same time, Blind's poem participates in the critique of male aestheticism present in many of the poems Christina Rossetti wrote in the late 1840s. What Kathy Psomiades has written about these poems ("Dream-Land," "After Death," "When I am dead, my dearest") applies equally to **"The Song of the Willi"**: "The encounter with a dead woman is described from the perspective not of a distanced masculine onlooker but of the one dead, either through sympathetic speculation on her mental state in the grave or through an account of her view of the living, often in a first-person narrative" (p. 62).[36]

Considering the other Hungarian tales of love and death that were available to her, Blind's choice of the willi legend is significant. In *Hungarian Classical Ballads and their Folklore,* Ninon Leader describes two ballads that share some elements with **"The Song of the Willi,"** the one a classic Hungarian ballad, the other a fragment deriving from the Lenore legend. The first, **"The Girl Who Was Danced to Death,"** which "is still popular in Hungary, especially in the western and in the northeastern parts, . . . tells the story of a girl who rejected her suitor, or loved two young men at the same time, and was therefore punished by a most cruel death: she had to dance with the suitor till she died." The discovery and merciless punishment of female sexual infidelity lies at the ideological heart of this ballad; the most the speaker of **"The Song of the Willi"** can be accused of is unrequited love and sexual longing. In the second, **"The Dead Bridegroom,"** the bridegroom, like the fiancé in Blind's poem, returns after death to seek the fulfillment of vows his lover made. Leader notes that in many versions of this story, most notably the Lenore legend, the bridegroom is the devil in disguise, but that this is "a Christian rationalization of the original form of the story."[37] Devils are conspicuously absent from **"The Song of the Willi"**; the speaker's supernatural existence registers in the poem as a metaphor for deeply human desires, not as a marker of evil. As she would later do in her first long poem, **"The Prophecy of St. Oran,"** Blind freely manipulates legendary material to serve freethinking and feminist ends.

Blind's earliest fame as a creative writer derives from **"The Song of the Willi"** and four other contributions to *The Dark Blue* (including two more poems). Indeed, she was twice singled out as the most distinguished contributor to the short-lived but influential magazine that helped propagate the ideas and ideals of aestheticism. The August 15, 1871 issue of *The Academy* notes that "the two last numbers of *The Dark Blue* show an improvement in the poetical contributions, hitherto not the strongest point of that magazine," crediting **"The Song of the Willi"** for the change, and the August 12 number of *The Illustrated London News,* after complaining that "the magazine seems to encounter great difficulty in getting rid of its amateur character," notes that "there is one contribution, however, far remote from amateurship—Miss Mathilde Blind's vivid and powerful ballad of the Willi, in the Teutonic mythology the ghost of the dead betrothed, who dances her surviving lover into his grave. Miss Blind's version of the myth is no less spirited than Sir Walter Scott's rendering of 'Lenore,' of which it strongly reminds us." And when Blind published the short story **"A Month at the Achensee"** in the October 1872 issue of the magazine, *The Illustrated London News* again effused: "The most remarkable contribution to *The Dark Blue* is Miss M. Blind's **'Month at the Achensee,'** a beautiful story, half tragedy, half idyll, interspersed with charming descriptions of the scenery of the Tyrol."[38]

Blind shared space in *The Dark Blue* with many of the leading writers in Great Britain: William Morris, Swinburne, Dante Gabriel Rossetti, Sheridan LeFanu, Thomas Arnold, Edward Dowden, and W. S. Gilbert. Ford Madox Brown provided two illustrations for Dante Gabriel Rossetti's poem "Down Stream" that appeared in the journal, and the gifted Pre-Raphaelite painter Simeon Solomon illustrated Swinburne's poem "The End of a Month." In his *Autobiography,* W. B. Yeats described the aesthetic revolution effected by the poets represented in *The Dark Blue*:

> The poetry which found its expression in the poems of writers like Browning and of Tennyson, and even of writers, who are seldom classed with them, like Swinburne, and like Shelley in his earlier years . . . tried to absorb into itself the science and politics, the philosophy and morality of its time; but a new poetry, which is always contracting its limits, has grown up under the shadow of the old. Rossetti began it.[39]

In their introduction to the entry on *The Dark Blue* in *The Wellesley Index to Periodicals,* Christine Rose Bradley and Walter E. Houghton effectively describe this aspect of the journal's significance, and they rightly emphasize that many of its contributors were "in conscious revolt against what they called 'Victorianisms.'" But they omit any mention of Blind's contributions (she was one of the few women featured in its pages) and thereby misrepresent the role of women poets in the aesthetic movement.[40] Among other things **"The Song of the Willi"** gives the lie to Vita Sackville-West's claim that the "numerous and prolific" women poets of the 1870s all hewed to "the high Victorian standard of bashfulness," producing "elegant or devotional pieces . . . wordy and portentous moralising . . . dreary narrative poems . . . descriptive pieces which reminded one of nothing so much as a washy and indifferent water-colour."[41] Blind's presence in *The Dark Blue,* and her defiant occupation of poetic territory Swinburne sought to claim solely for men, was anything but bashful. She is presumably one of the women poets E. L. Bryans indicts in his essay "Characteristics of Women's Poetry" for the December 1871 issue of the journal—poets like E. B. Browning, who "have endeavoured to obtain a reputation for masculine power and vigour by attempting descriptions of those feelings and passions which their sex is supposed neither to possess or even be acquainted with" (p. 490).

If, as Michel Foucault has written, the nineteenth century "initiated sexual heterogeneities," *The Dark Blue* played an important role in their cultural circulation. In just two years, the journal featured lesbianism in LeFanu's "Carmilla" (serialized in the journal between 1871 and 1872); homoeroticism in Simeon Solomon's illustration to Swinburne's poem "The End of a Month" (also indirectly celebrated in Swinburne's essay "Simeon Solomon: Notes on His 'Vision of Love' and Other Studies" in the July 1871 issue); and sadomasochism in "The End of a Month" (published in *The Dark Blue* after being rejected by *Fraser's Magazine* for its sexual explicitness).[42] This is in addition to frequent poetic representations of nonmarital heterosexual intimacy, highlighted by a trio of poems that exist in a provocatively dialogic relation to one another: "The End of a Month" (April 1871), D. G. Rossetti's "Down Stream" (October 1871), and Blind's own **"Nocturne"** (March 1872). All three explore the relationship between Eros and death; all three feature couples locked in destructive embraces; all three employ nature imagery to represent sexual experience.

Rossetti's five-stanza poem is the most conventional and sentimental of the three, featuring a seduced and abandoned woman who drowns herself and her infant a year after her lover has left her. Rossetti's imagery and Ford Madox Brown's frontispiece drawing, however, are unusually explicit. In Brown's rendering of the lovers' liaison in a small rowboat, the woman leans back against her lover, who is clasping her right hand and kissing her neck. The male is seen only in profile, but the woman's face and swooning expression directly confront the viewer, as does her left arm, shown gripping a decidedly phallic oar handle.[43] In one stanza Rossetti portrays the rhythm of sexual intercourse, describing the lovers on the river "brimmed with rain," making their way "through close-met banks and parted banks / Now near now far again" (ll. 10-12). Brown's second illustration shows the drowned mother and child lying in the same stream where she was seduced a year earlier, "with lilies meshed in tangled hair, / On this year's first of June" (ll. 31-32).

Swinburne's poem is also concerned with sex and death, but "The End of a Month" emphasizes the psychology of the speaker as he contemplates the wreckage of his affair. He and his lover stand by the sea together for the last time, every detail of the landscape reflecting their situation: "Across, aslant, a scudding sea-mew / Swam, dipped, and dropped, and grazed the sea; / And one with me I could not dream you: / And one with you I could not be" (ll. 37-40).

The dramatic monologue form helps Swinburne render the fevered state of the male lover, who spends thirty-two stanzas obsessing over this failed affair. The concluding stanzas of the poem fearlessly convey the grip the woman still has on his erotic imagination:

> But as to a bee's gilt thighs and winglets,
>   The flower-dust and the flower-smell clings;
> As a snake's mobile rampant ringlets
>   Leave the sand marked with print of rings;
>
> So to my soul in surer fashion
>   Your savage stamp and savour hangs;
> The print and perfume of old passion,
>   The wild-beast mark of panther's fangs.

(ll. 121-128)

"Nocturne" lacks the startling and often sadomasochistic imagery of "The End of a Month," but it still has much in common with Swinburne's poem. Employing alliteration, internal rhyme, and repetition in a dramatic monologue on the frenzy and grief of lost love, Blind creates a speaker for whom all of nature initially limns his passion. Pushing out to sea with his lover "at the dead of night, when the heart beats free" (l. 3), he projects his erotic desire into the ocean itself: "The sea, and the waves in their fall and rise, / Bosomlike heaving with languid sighs / Lifted, and tumbled, and broke with desire, / Licked, and fawned on her with tongues of fire" (ll. 17-20). Unlike "The End of a Month," however, and her own **"The Song of the Willi,"** Blind eschews the familiar abab ballad meter in favor of an aabb pattern reflecting the structure of parallelism and antithesis on which the entire poem is based. Divided in two, just as the speaker feels without his lost lover, **"Nocturne"** begins in the past, when he was at one with his love and with all the natural world. It moves inexorably to its midpoint—the moment in the present when he wakes to discover that his lover has died beside him as they both slept in their boat at sea. The speaker is shocked and unhinged by his lover's death, but the fact that she dies after "her whole life swooned into mine, as swoons / The sunset into the broad lagoons; / Ruddy red radiance of sunset that flows / To the sea, till the sea blossoms like a rose" (ll. 33-36) evokes the familiar Victorian trope equating unmarried female sexual experience with death. Unlike Browning's "Porphyria's Lover," however, which invites the reader to read misogyny and madness in the speaker's words, **"Nocturne"** deflects attention away from the speaker's culpability, focusing instead on his intense grief, culminating at the end of the poem when the speaker asks the ocean to "bury the dead and the quick in one gloom— / One ebbing, and flowing and earth-girdling tomb" (ll. 81-82). Although this ending recalls the lovers' fate in **"The Song of the Willi,"** **"Nocturne"** is a more subjective poem than its predecessor. As in her last dramatic monologue, **"A Fantasy"** (1895), Blind displaces her own feelings onto a male speaker, indirectly expressing the isolation and romantic disappointment that often characterize her lyrics. In this sense, it has a great deal in common with the monodramas favored by the romantic poets—which, as Jeffrey Cox has written, "became a tool in their creation of a tragedy of the self."[44]

"Nocturne" is the last poem Blind published in *The Dark Blue,* and it lacks the gender-inverting suggestiveness of **"The Song of the Willi."** It is tempting to read the poem as Blind's final, chilly embrace of pure aestheticism, since after it appeared she took an eight-year hiatus from publishing poetry (occupied by editing, criticism, and a translation of David Strauss's *The Old Faith and the New*) before she returned with a more explicitly ideological form of verse. The intertextuality of **"Nocturne"** points to the many influences—poetic, pictorial, and theoretical—which shaped this phase of her poetic career. Its very title evokes the belief in the interrelationships among poetry, music, and painting that informed the art of the Pre-Raphaelites and aesthetes. In the June 1871 issue of *The Dark Blue* Edward Dowden wrote that the conception of "the essential unity of art," the idea that "poetry, painting, sculpture, architecture, music, and dance are but various manifestations of one and the same human tendency, is of modern origin" (p. 484). Less than a year before Blind published **"Nocturne,"** James McNeill Whistler exhibited two paintings at the Dudley Gallery in November 1871 as "Harmony in Blue Green—Moonlight," which in 1872 he renamed "Nocturne in Blue and Silver—Chelsea." Blind knew Whistler from Brown's salons, and her own **"Nocturne,"** like Whistler's paintings, is an impressionistic dreamscape, the poetic equivalent of melancholy night-music. The voices of fellow poets echo throughout the poem as well; its subject matter and musical effects are a virtual parody of Swinburne's sexual and stylistic preoccupations, and two passages explicitly evoke Keats and Browning, guiding spirits of the Pre-Raphaelites and aesthetes. "Yea, her whole life swooned into mine, as swoons / The sunset into the broad lagoons" (ll. 33-34) evokes the consummation scene in "The Eve of St. Agnes"; "Her eyes with a wide, blank, lusterless stare / Are fixed upon mine, and the strangling gold / Of her hair coils over me fold upon fold" (ll. 66-68) recalls "Porphyria's Lover."

In **"The Song of the Willi"** both lovers speak, vow, and plead with one another, but in **"Nocturne"** the woman is conspicuously silent—like the women in both "Down Stream" and "The End of a Month." If **"Nocturne"** is in part a critique of the tradition Blind is about to partially disavow, the woman may at one level represent the poet herself, and her fear that continued affiliation with the male members of what she called "the aesthetic school of poetry of our day" would be deathly to her own poetic vocation.[45] Admittedly aestheticism was useful to Blind, granting her license to express subversive views while ostensibly pursuing art for art's sake. But Blind's poetic career was not encouraged or nurtured by the male poets she associated with in the 1870s. D. G. Rossetti was famously distant from Blind and her poetry (despite her close friendship with his brother William and the best efforts of Ford Madox Brown), and Swinburne reserved his enthusiasm for her republican sentiments.[46] By the time she wrote the introduction to her edition of *The Letters of Lord Byron* (1887) Blind had put considerable distance between herself and the doctrine of "art for art's sake":

> Words always stood as signs for things to Byron, his object being to get hold of the one that most adequately expressed the image in his mind: a manner of writing which differs entirely from the aesthetic method, where the luxuriant beauty of expression becomes of such su-

preme importance that it weakens, undermines, and finally destroys the sap and marrow of thought, as the
enlacing ivy the tree that is its stay.[47]

This helps explain why, when Blind returned to the dramatic monologue form in 1891, she eschewed the ahistorical, dreamlike settings of her earliest monologues in
favor of poems with precisely observed social settings.

When Blind came to write ***Dramas in Miniature,*** her
reputation as a woman of letters had grown considerably. In addition to four books of poetry, she had written distinguished criticism for *The Examiner* and *The
Athenaeum,* two biographies (of George Eliot and Madame Roland), an analysis of Mary Wollstonecraft's life
for the *New Quarterly Magazine,* and an essay on Marie
Bashkirtseff for Oscar Wilde's *The Woman's World.*
This essay led to her second major translation, *The
Journal of Marie Bashkirtseff* (1889), which became a
publishing sensation and a touchstone for the New
Woman debate.[48] At the same time Blind had become a
central figure in Bohemian and literary London, a friend
and inspiration to younger women poets.[49] She hosted
and attended many women's literary salons, identifying
closely with those of Mary Robinson and Graham Tomson, which offered a sense of solidarity to women whose
radical views marginalized them from mainstream culture. This was particularly important to the freethinking
Blind, whose ***Prophecy of St. Oran*** was withdrawn by
its publisher in 1884 because of fears about its "atheistic character."[50] Tomson, Blind, Amy Levy, Violet Hunt,
and Mona Caird formed an important community of
women who, as Ana I. Parejo Vadillo has written, shared
"subversive ideas on sexual politics" and "unequivocally negated any form of theist belief." In part because
of her association with equally daring poets like Tomson, Levy, and Edith Nesbit, the dramatic monologues
Blind wrote in the 1890s are more explicitly critical of
prevailing social and gender codes than those she published in the 1870s. They openly address the issues
Sally Mitchell has identified as crucial to New Woman
writing and illustrate Linda Hughes' claim that fin-de-
siècle women poets were as deeply engaged with these
issues as their novelist counterparts.[51]

Several dramatic monologues in ***Dramas in Miniature,***
for instance, assail the sexual double standard in terms
familiar to the New Woman novel. In **"The Russian
Student's Tale,"** the speaker decides to spurn the young
woman he has professed his love for—and had a sexual
liaison with—after discovering that economic need had
earlier forced her into prostitution. The speaker of **"The
Message"** is a nun in a charity hospital who attempts to
convert and bring Christian absolution to a dying prostitute, who is instead recalled to a last outburst of love
and reconciliation by a young girl who brings flowers
to the ward and triggers memories of childhood joy.
The prostitute's name, "Nellie Dean," is almost identi-

cal to that of the housekeeper in *Wuthering Heights,*
whose narration is often unreliable. Her name thus alerts
readers to evaluate carefully the speaker's own potentially self-serving narration. The prostitute is from the
working classes; the speaker is aligned with other
middle-class charity workers whose efforts were often
compromised by paternalism. She narrates the last hours
of Nellie Dean's life to an auditor identified only as
"sir," linking him with the anonymous men the dying
Nellie describes, who "with now a kiss and now a blow"
accosted her when she walked the streets. **"The Message"** forms an important counterpart to D. G. Rossetti's "Jenny," narrated by another "sir" who has purchased a prostitute for the night and who speculates
about her life while she sleeps beside him (she is of
course silenced by this conceit, and never speaks a
word). In **"The Message"** Blind restores speech to the
kind of woman typically demonized or sentimentalized
by her contemporaries. When the speaker quotes her,
Nellie speaks with what the speaker calls "savage
spleen," which led Arthur Symons to complain that the
poem's "brutal vividness" is presented "in perhaps
somewhat too intentionally prosaic language."[52] Symons
compares **"The Message"** unfavorably with "Jenny" on
aesthetic grounds, calling the latter "the one almost
flawless poem of its kind" (659). Like Swinburne, Symons implies that explicit treatment of sexual subjects
is best left to men. He also privileges formal elegance
in terms that align him with those proponents of the
"aesthetic method" Blind criticizes in her introduction
to Byron's letters. Significantly, Symons has little to
say about the poem that follows **"The Message"** in
Dramas in Miniature—a poem that explores sexual
transgression among the upper classes and eschews
"prosaic language."

In 1890, after reading Henrik Ibsen's *Ghosts,* Blind
wrote to Richard Garnett that "our ideals of moral conduct are really undergoing a process of disintegration
and it makes me feel a little giddy, as if the earth were
beginning to rock under one's feet." Blind enacts this
conviction of an epochal shift—and the simultaneously
unsettling and liberating feelings it evokes—in **"A Carnival Episode,"** her most complex meditation in *Dramas in Miniature* on gender and sexuality.[53] From the
licensed sexual libertinism of its opening to the earthquake that brings it to a close, **"A Carnival Episode"**
is an explosive poem, employing the dramatic monologue form to expose the cultural logic of gender relationships under the dominion of patriarchy and empire.
Unlike "Porphyria's Lover," which it echoes at several
points, **"A Carnival Episode"** is less interested in the
individual psychology of the speaker than the ideological structures that shape his speech. Although the three
characters in the poem are French (by displacing the action to a country associated with sexual decadence,
Blind gains a degree of freedom and protection in rendering erotic intrigue that would have been denied her

if they had been British), they are clearly meant to represent the tensions, contradictions, and gender divisions characterizing fin-de-siècle England.

At the beginning of the poem the speaker, a military officer, is standing with a married woman on a balcony in Nice during carnival. They are looking down on the revelers below and contemplating adultery. Blind's imagery vividly conveys the carnivalesque inversion of hierarchy that incites the male speaker's erotic desire. Public and private boundaries have eroded as "houses . . . emptied themselves in the streets"; sexual libertinism prevails as "the pavements were turning the colour of sheets" under the "shower of confetti" (ll. 13, 15-16). As the concluding stanza of the poem makes clear, however, it is not just the male whose passion has been aroused: the woman is given the last words and she acknowledges that she was on the verge of acting on her physical desire when the earthquake struck. It is significant that a poem charting the end of an epoch in "moral conduct" ends with a woman acknowledging her own sexual desire for a man not her husband—even if nature forestalls her adultery. Blind represents the woman's desire even more explicitly earlier in the poem, when the speaker describes how she drops her mask "at the sight / Of my passion now reaching its uttermost height" (ll. 58-59).

Since nineteen of the poem's twenty sestets are given over to the male speaker, however, it is his voice that dominates, and his "mobile army of metaphors," to use Nietzsche's suggestive phrase, that exposes the interdependencies of sexuality, patriarchy, and empire Blind explores in the poem.[54] The speaker is infuriated by his passion for the woman's "fatally fair" beauty, because she is married to his commanding officer, the absent "General," "the man of all men I adored," who "might be fighting for us at the point of his sword; / Might be killing or killed by an African horde, / Afar beneath African skies" (ll. 53-56). His binding relationship to this General, the precise nature of which is rendered ambiguous by his use of the word "adored," leads him to demonize the woman, employing a Medusa trope familiar to fin-de-siècle writers and artists: "We two there together drew back from the glare; / Drew in to the room, and her hood unaware / Fell back from the plaits of her opulent hair, / That uncoiled the brown snakes of its tresses" (ll. 27-30).

Although he richly robes her in metaphor, he identifies this woman only as "the General's wife." As he contemplates acting on his desire, his primary concern is not that he will violate the bond between the woman and her husband, but the one between himself and the General. He says the woman is possessed of a "mutinous mien," and will make him mutinous as well. More cold-blooded than Lady Macbeth, she "would turn to a traitor a man who was true / She could drain him of

love and then break him in two, / And wash her white hands of his shame" (ll. 33, 64-66). When he drops her hand nine stanzas later, it is because "treason is mother to fear" (l. 90). In their combination of military and misogynist language, the speaker's words emphasize the extent to which his consciousness has been shaped by his relationship to the General—and, by extension, to the patriarchy. Gayle Rubin's influential definition of patriarchal heterosexuality as one or another form of the "traffic in women" applies here.[55] If women are symbolic property for the primary purpose of delineating relationships between men, the speaker's language assumes a certain logic. He cannot imagine his relationship with the woman outside the terms dictated by his relationship to the General, which is characterized by a volatile mixture of adoration, subordination, envy, and rivalry. He wants the woman to submit to his power and authority just as he has submitted to the power and authority of her husband. When his anger and passion rise to a murderous pitch he tells her: "My love is a force that will force you to care; / Nay, I'll strangle us both in the ropes of your hair / Should you dream you can drop me at will" (ll. 70-72). The imagined or real death of both lovers, familiar from both **"The Song of the Willi"** and **"Nocturne,"** here registers the speaker's rage to bring the woman under his control—and thereby assert power in his relationship with the General—even if death is the result.

Blind also draws an implicit parallel between the possessive lust of the man for the woman and France's colonial activities in Africa (and, by extension, England's colonial activities in Africa, India, and closer to home). The speaker's insistence that the General's wife has invited his attention is a version of the imperialist argument that justifies colonial aggression on the grounds that colonized people "want" or "need" British intervention—an argument Blind became familiar with while researching English treatment of Scottish peasants during the Highland Clearances for *The Heather on Fire.* In fact the speaker's erotic imagination—his association of love with obsession, coercion, and force—echoes at the personal level the dynamics of an imperial ideology that rationalizes coercion and domination as means to the end of "enlightened," enlightening rule. In her preface to *The Heather on Fire,* Blind writes that "the progress of civilisation . . . has come with a curse to these Highland glens, and turned green pastures and golden harvest-fields once more into a desert," and notes that "the ferocity shown by some of the factors and ground-officers employed by the landlords in evicting their inoffensive tenantry, can only be matched by the brutal excesses of victorious troops on a foreign soil."[56] Given the colonial metaphors woven through **"A Carnival Episode,"** the woman's ultimate rejection of the speaker's domination gestures toward those other forms of resistance Blind enacts in her earlier poem.

Blind critiques Christian ideology along with imperialism and patriarchy in **"A Carnival Episode."** She does so in part with another allusion to "Porphyria's Lover," a poem whose speaker takes God's silence as sanction for his murder ("and yet God has not said a word!"). The speaker in **"A Carnival Episode"** wonders if God has caused the earthquake that ends his liaison with the woman. His interrogative voice shows that he is less certain than Browning's speaker, but he is equally monomaniacal, assuming that his relationship is an affair of state and God:

> Had it come upon us at that magical hour,
>   The judgment of God the Most High?
> The floor 'gan to heave and the ceiling to lower,
> The dead walls to start with malevolent power,
> Till your hair seemed to rise and your spirit to cower,
>   As the very stones shook with a sigh.
>
> (ll. 91-96)

Given Blind's antitheistic perspective, it is not surprising that the speaker's apocalyptic interpretation of the natural disaster is rendered suspect by the remainder of the poem. While the earthquake seems to paralyze him, it inspires the woman to decisive action: "She sprang like a greyhound—no greyhound more fleet— / And ran down the staircase in motion; / And blindly I followed her into the street / All choked up with people in panic retreat" (ll. 103-106). Employing the clichéd language of romantic love one last time, the speaker "implored her with sighing / To fly with me now and for ever" (ll. 113-114), but she has the last word, characterizing their affair as a "Carnival joke" and thanking nature, not God, for parting them: "blest be the terrible earthquake that broke / In between you and me, and has saved at a stroke / Us two in the night there together" (ll. 117-120). The violence of nature ends the poem and the threat to the woman's reputation, but not before Blind has dramatized the historically contingent nature of the "ideals of moral conduct" within patriarchy.

Mathilde Blind's last dramatic monologue, **"A Fantasy,"** appeared in *Birds of Passage: Songs of the Orient and the Occident* (1895). During her travels in the Middle East, Blind learned of the nomadic tribes of Arabs living in the desert, who depended on their fleet war horses for survival—horses famed for their intelligence, powers of endurance, and loyalty to their human owners. The opening lines of this bracingly elliptical poem—"I was an Arab, / I loved my horse; / Swift as an arrow / He swept the course" (ll. 1-4)—are suggestively ambiguous. Is the speaker speaking from beyond the grave, like the speaker in **"The Song of the Willi"**? Is he in exile in some other country? Or is this poem, like W. E. Henley's "When I was a King in Babylon," a fantasy of an earlier life, reflecting the interest in reincarnation that emerged in the 1890s? This ambiguity acts as an invitation, allowing readers wide latitude in

assigning gender to the lovers in the poem. The central "fantasy" in the thirteen-stanza ballad is the story of the Arab's love for "Ibraham's daughter, / Beautiful maid" (ll. 27-28), whom the speaker calls "Sparkling as water / Cool in the shade" (ll. 25-26), bidding her to "Kiss me with kisses, / Buds of thy mouth, / Sweeter than Cassia / Fresh from the South" (ll. 41-44). The speaker's use of present tense in lines 28-48 emphasizes the intensity of erotic desire, and suggests that the speaker may be recasting a current love affair in deliberately exoticizing and fantastic language. **"A Fantasy"** can be read in strictly heterosexual terms, but if it is a reincarnation fantasy, the gender of the speaker could be female, and the poem a coded expression of lesbian passion.[57]

Read in the context of the Commonplace Book Blind kept between 1892 and 1896, the melancholy undertow of **"A Fantasy"** may be interpreted biographically, registering the emotional price Blind sometimes paid for her fierce independence. A year before **"A Fantasy"** appeared in print, Blind wrote: "I have been an exile in this world. Without a God, without a country, without a family."[58] As one interprets the poem's last stanza with this statement in mind, Blind becomes one with the Arab rider, alone and wandering through the "beautiful desert / Boundless and bare":

> I was an Arab
>   Ages ago!
> Hence this home-sickness.
>   And all my woe.
>
> (ll. 49-52)

Although she may have often felt like an exile, Mathilde Blind found a poetic home in the dramatic monologue—furnished with spacious rooms, opening out onto startling vistas.

Notes

I wish to thank the Newberry Library and the British Academy for a travel fellowship enabling me to conduct research for this essay at the British Library, the Bodleian Library, the City University of London *Athenaeum* archives, and the Public Records Office. I also wish to thank Linda Hughes for sharing with me the results of her own research on Graham Tomson and late-century women poets. LeeAnne Richardson read an early draft of this essay and provided many helpful suggestions. This essay was written with the support of the Howard L. McGregor Professorship administered by Albion College.

1. Widely reviewed in the major journals during her lifetime, Blind was also represented in several Victorian anthologies: *Sonnets of Three Centuries: A Selection,* ed. Hall Caine (London, 1882); *Women's Voices: An Anthology of the Most Characteristic Poems by English, Scotch and Irish Women,*

ed. Elizabeth Sharp (London, 1889); *The Poets and the Poetry of the Century,* ed. Alfred H. Miles (London, 1892); and *A Victorian Anthology 1847-1895,* ed. Edmund Clarence Stedman (Boston, 1895).

2. Review of *Dramas in Miniature, The Academy* (December 12, 1891): 531. Robertson, editor of the *Magazine of Art* from 1880-81 and of the "Great Writers" series of biographies, was appointed professor of English at the University of the Punjab, Lahore, in 1887.

3. Arthur Symons, review in *The Athenaeum,* May 21, 1892: 660. Subsequent references to Symons' review will cite page numbers parenthetically.

4. *A Selection from the Poems of Mathilde Blind,* ed. Arthur Symons (London, 1897), p. vi. Edith Nesbit ends her December 3, 1898 *Athenaeum* review of this volume by chastising Symons for omitting one of Blind's dramatic monologues: "Why has he omitted the wonderful wild 'Song of the Willi'?" (p. 784).

5. *The Poetical Works of Mathilde Blind,* ed. Arthur Symons (London: T. Fisher Unwin, 1900), pp. 42-43. Subsequent references to Garnett's Memoir will be cited parenthetically.

6. *The Dictionary of National Biography,* ed. Leslie Stephen and Sidney Lee, vol. 17 (London: Oxford Univ. Press, 1917), p. 283.

7. Theodore Watts-Dunton, review in *The Saturday Review,* August 24, 1895: 243.

8. Kathleen Hickok, *Representations of Women: Nineteenth-Century British Women's Poetry* (Westport.: Greenwood Press, 1984), and Isobel Armstrong, *Victorian Poetry: Poetry, Poetics and Politics* (London: Routledge, 1993). Blind is also discussed in William B. Thesing, *The Dictionary of Literary Biography, vol. 190: Victorian Women Poets* (Detroit: Gale, 1998), pp. 28-39; Helen Groth, "Victorian Women Poets and Scientific Narratives," in *Women's Poetry, Late Romantic to Late Victorian* (London: Macmillan, 1999), pp. 325-351; Ana I. Vadillo Parejo, "New Woman Poets and the Culture of the Salon at the Fin de Siècle," in *Women: A Cultural Review* 10, no. 1 (1999): 22-34; Marysa De Moor, *Their Fair Share: Women, Power and Criticism in the Athenaeum, from Millicent Garrett Fawcett to Katherine Mansfield, 1870-1920* (Burlington: Ashgate, 2000); and Abigail Burnham Bloom, *Nineteenth-Century British Women Writers: A Bio-Bibliographical Critical Sourcebook* (Westport: Greenwood Press, 2000), pp. 41-44. Currently all seven books of Blind's poetry (as well as her groundbreaking biography of George Eliot) are available online at *The Victo-rian Women Writers Project* (http://www.indiana.edu/~letrs/vwwp).

9. The London *Times* inadvertently emphasized Blind's boldly independent and unconventional career in its December 2, 1896 notice of her cremation and memorial service by printing it directly after the funeral notice for Patmore. Patmore was given a high-church funeral, and at the end of the service the Catholic poet Alice Meynell "lowered into the grave a wreath of laurels inscribed 'From the women of England.'" Blind's funeral discourse was pronounced over her remains in a Unitarian Chapel by her long-time friend Moncure Conway, who had been compelled to leave his Unitarian ministry at Harvard in the 1850s for his sermons against slavery. In addition to Conway, Richard Garnett, Ford Madox Ford, Theodore Watts-Dunton, and Mona Caird were members of what Garnett later described as a "large audience of men and women, many of much distinction, who had esteemed and loved and admired her in life" (p. 7, col. f).

10. Review of *Songs of Britain,* by Lewis Morgan in *The Athenaeum* (April 30, 1887), p. 569. I wish to thank the staff of the library at the City University of London for granting me permission to examine the marked files of *The Athenaeum,* which allowed me to identify all of Blind's unsigned contributions to the journal.

11. Mathilde Blind, "Mary Wollstonecraft," *The New Quarterly Magazine* (July 1878), p. 410. Blind's skepticism toward marriage, and her own unconventional relationship with Ford Madox Brown (beginning in the mid 1870s, she spent a good part of each year living in the Brown household), brought her under increasing attack in the 1880s and 1890s. Leslie Stephen, who in the 1880s was a regular visitor at the home of Lucy Clifford, categorized Blind as one "of Lucy [Clifford's] free-thinking friends" and thought of her as a pernicious influence because she wanted Clifford to publish her late husband's criticisms of marriage. See *Selected Letters of Leslie Stephen,* vol. 2, 1882-1904, ed. John W. Bicknell (Columbus: Ohio State Univ. Press, 1996), p. 345.

12. Edward Aveling and Eleanor Marx Aveling, *The Woman Question* (London, 1886), p. 8. For more on the Blind-Eleanor Marx relationship, see Simon Avery, "'Tantalising Glimpses': The Intersecting Lives of Eleanor Marx and Mathilde Blind," in *Eleanor Marx (1855-1898): Life, Work, Contacts,* ed. John Stokes (Burlington: Ashgate, 2001), pp. 173-187.

13. In *The Forgotten Female Aesthetes: Literary Culture in Late-Victorian England* (Charlottesville:

Univ. Press of Virginia, 2000), Talia Schaffer acknowledges that the line separating female aesthetes and New Woman writers "was so thin as to seem sometimes, almost imperceptible." Nonetheless, her book seeks to maintain it: "The difference is that the female aesthetes chose to participate in a high-art tradition rather than a political movement" (p. 25). The example of Mathilde Blind, unaccountably absent from Schaffer's study, suggests that this is a distinction without a difference.

14. I use the term "dramatic monologue" as opposed to "monodrama" because, as A. Dwight Culler has demonstrated, the former was more commonly used than the latter in the second half of the nineteenth century. See "Monodrama and the Dramatic Monologue," *PMLA* 90 (1975): 366-385. In "Augusta Webster: The Social Politics of Monodrama," *Victorian Review* 29 (2000): 75-107, Patricia Rigg argues for the use of "monodrama" in relation to women's poetry, noting that in contrast to Robert Browning's dramatic monologues, "dramatic poetry by women tends to be less specific in defining the speaker, thereby retaining an important attribute of lyric poetry and delineating a rather transparent dramatic 'mask'" (p. 75). While this is true of Blind's earliest dramatic monologues, those collected in *Dramas in Miniature* contain more specifically delineated characters.

15. Robert Langbaum, *The Poetry of Experience* (Chicago: Chicago Univ. Press, 1957).

16. Dorothy Mermin, *The Audience in the Poem* (New Brunswick: Rutgers Univ. Press, 1983), p. 8, and Cynthia Scheinberg, "Recasting 'sympathy and judgment': Amy Levy, Women Poets, and the Victorian Dramatic Monologue," *VP* 35 (1997): 170. Subsequent references to Scheinberg's essay will cite page numbers parenthetically. For more on women writers and the dramatic monologue, see Lucy Brashear, "Emily Dickinson's Dramatic Monologues," *The American Transcendental Quarterly* 56 (March 1985): 65-76; Angela Leighton's discussions of Augusta Webster in *Victorian Women Poets: Writing Against the Heart*, pp. 177-185; Isobel Armstrong, *Victorian Poetry: Poetry, Poetics and Politics*, pp. 325-326; Susan Brown, "Determined Heroines: George Eliot, Augusta Webster, and Closet Drama by Victorian Women," *VP* 33 (1995): 89-109; Kate Flint, ". . . As a Rule, I Does Not Mean I: Personal Identity and the Victorian Woman Poet," in *Rewriting the Self: Histories from the Renaissance to the Present*, ed. Roy Porter (London: Routledge, 1997), pp. 156-166, and Patricia Rigg.

17. Karl Blind wrote about his revolutionary activities (and those of his wife) in "The German Army, With Personal Recollections, 1848-1889" (*North American Review* 149 [August 1889]: 182-195) and a five-part series in *The Cornhill* under the general title "In Years of Storm and Stress" (September 1898: 337-352, June 1898: 780-793, September 1899: 334-347, November 1899: 648-661, and June 1900: 788-813). They provide tantalizing glimpses of Mathilde Blind in childhood, and describe Ettlinger deepening his philosophical radicalism while imprisoned by reading Feuerbach. See also Karl Marx, *Revolution and Counter-Revolution; or Germany in 1848*, ed. Eleanor Marx Aveling (New York, 1896).

18. All of Blind's published statements on the Woman Question are similarly astringent. See especially her (anonymous) review of E. R. Pennell's biography of Mary Wollstonecraft (*The Athenaeum*, July 11, 1885, p. 41) and her introduction to her translation of *The Journal of Marie Bashkirtseff* (London, 1890). In 1889, Blind joined several thousand other women in signing a declaration in favor of women's suffrage, and in her will she bequeathed the greater part of her nearly £10,000 estate to Newnham College, Cambridge, establishing an endowment ("The Mathilde Blind Benefaction") to support women pursuing degrees in "either English or Foreign or Ancient Literature" (Last Will and Testament, October 23, 1896, p. 3).

19. Even at this early stage in her literary career, Blind was forming friendships with radical women. William Michael Rossetti's wife, Ford Madox Brown's daughter Lucy, used Mathilde as a model for several of her paintings and shared Blind's outspoken feminism. See Jan Marsh and Pamela Gerrish Nunn, *Pre-Raphaelite Women Artists* (New York: Thames and Hudson, 1997), pp. 45, 126-129.

20. *Poems*, by Claude Lake (London, 1867). Blind published her "Personal Recollections of Mazzini" in the *Portnightly Review* 55 (May 1891): 702-712.

21. Mathilde Blind, "Shelley," a review-essay of *The Poetical Works of Percy Bysshe Shelley, with Notes and a Memoir* by W. M. Rossetti. 2 vols., *Westminster Review* 38 (July 1870): 75-97.

22. See Helen Rossetti Angeli, *Dante Gabriel Rossetti: His Friends and Enemies* (London: Hamish Hamilton, 1949), p. 49, and Teresa Newman and Ray Watson, *Ford Madox Brown and the Pre-Raphaelite Circle* (London: Chatto and Windus, 1991), pp. 147-196.

23. Ford Madox Hueffer, *Ford Madox Brown: A Record of his Life and Work* (London, 1896), p. 235.

24. See *The Swinburne Letters,* ed. Cecil Y. Lang, 6 vols. (New Haven: Yale Univ. Press, 1959-62), 1:248.

25. Blind wrote to Swinburne on August 2, 1870, enclosing her Shelley lecture and urging him to publish the much-delayed *Songs Before Sunrise* (MS, Richard Garnett Papers, Ransome Humanities Center, University of Texas-Austin), and again on September 7, 1870, praising the success of the Paris Commune (MS, Special Collections, The University of Michigan Special Collections). Most of Swinburne's letters to Blind have been lost, although volume 6 of *The Swinburne Letters* reprints a letter in which Swinburne thanks Blind for sending him her Shelley lecture. Lang erroneously claims the letter was written June 6, 1870, but it was likely written in August or September. In the revised version of his "Notes on the Text of Shelley," originally published in the April 1, 1869 *Fortnightly Review,* Swinburne singles out Blind's *Westminster Review* essay on William Michael Rossetti's edition of Shelley for special praise (*Essays and Studies* [London, 1875], p. 235).

26. See *The Diary of W. M. Rossetti, 1870-1873,* p. 50, and Richard Garnett's March 8, 1871 letter to Blind (MS Correspondence and Papers, 1866-1896, British Library MS Add. Ms. 61927).

27. Edmund Gosse, in his "An Essay (With Two Notes) on Swinburne" (unpublished in his lifetime) sought unsuccessfully to confirm the rumors of an affair with Mathilde Blind; see the appendix to *The Swinburne Letters,* 6:243. See also Donald Thomas, *Swinburne: The Poet in His World* (New York: Oxford Univ. Press, 1979), p. 150.

28. A. C. Swinburne, "Charles Baudelaire: Les Fleurs du Mal," *Spectator* (September 6, 1862): 998-100, repr. in *Swinburne as Critic,* ed. Clyde K. Hyder (Boston: Routledge & Kegan Paul, 1972), pp. 27-36.

29. Patricia Clements, "Swinburne," in *Baudelaire and the English Tradition* (Princeton: Princeton Univ. Press, 1985), p. 15; Rikky Rooksby, *A. C. Swinburne: A Poet's Life* (Hampshire: Scolar, 1997), pp. 133-135.

30. Blind wrote to Richard Garnett on October 14, 1872, thanking him for sending her copies of the *Illustrated London News* and the *London Weekly News,* both of which had praised her story "A Month at the Achensee" that appeared in the October 1872 issue of *The Dark Blue.* But she complains that the notice in the *London Weekly News* "makes one see the full justice of Blake's aphorism 'A fool sees not the same tree that a wise man sees.' . . . I am styled 'a bold admirer of Swinburne,' although how or in what manner that transpires from the story in question I fail to perceive" (MS Correspondence and Papers, 1866-1896, British Library MS Add. Ms. 61927).

31. The word "villi" first appeared in Hungarian in 1821. See Loránd Benkõ, *A magyar nyelv történeti-etimológiai szótára,* 4 vols. (Budapest: Akadémiai Kiadó, 1967). Blind likely encountered the willi legend in the German collection *Magyarische Sagen und Märchen,* written by the Hungarian aristocrat and amateur ethnographer János József Mailáth (1786-1855) and published in Germany (Brünn, 1825); a second, revised and expanded edition titled *Magyarische sagen, mährchen und erzählungen* appeared in 1837 (Stuttgart). Both editions contain a story titled "Der Willi-Tanz," Mailáth's version of the willi legend. In Mailáth's narrative a baron's daughter falls in love with her father's page; when her father banishes him and she hears a false report of his death, she falls into a mortal illness. Her nanny tells her the story of the willi just before her father returns from a trip to announce that he has married her to a nearby lord. She dies shortly after hearing this news, and her lover returns to mourn at her grave. When he arrives one evening in the forest where she is buried he sees a circle of dancing spirits; his lover emerges from the group, embraces him, and he dies as she kisses him. Although this legend became quite popular in Hungary (the first edition of Mailáth's collection was translated into Hungarian by Ferenc Kazinczy and published in 1864), and appears in many Hungarian poems in the first half of the century, the legend itself is Slovakian in origin. Because of Mailáth's collection, Blind was one of many writers—including Hungarian writers—who mistakenly located the origins of the legend in Hungary. I wish to thank Tamás Bényei, professor of English and American Studies at the University of Debrecen, Hungary, for his help in establishing these details.

32. *Swinburne Replies,* ed. Clyde Kenneth Hyder (Syracuse: Syracuse Univ. Press, 1966), pp. 24, 29, 33. For a full discussion of Swinburne's response to criticisms of *Poems and Ballads,* see Allison Pease, "Questionable Figures: Swinburne's *Poems and Ballads,*" *VP* 35 (1996): 43-56.

33. "The Song of the Willi. A Ballad," *The Dark Blue* 1, no. 6 (August 1871): 742, ll. 31-32. Subsequent references will cite this version of the poem. Although the revised version published in *Dramas in Miniature* incorporates several wording improvements, the original retains more of the "noble and nude and antique" quality of the ballad tradition Blind is appropriating.

34. November 23, 1872, p. 657. Blind delivered a lecture on the Volsunga Saga, the Scandinavian counterpart of the Lay of the Nibelungen, at the Assembly Rooms in St. John's Wood on May 26, 1870. See "Metropolitan News," *The Illustrated London News* (May 27, 1870): 543. She wrote a review-essay on "The Lily," a metrical translation of Eystein Asgrimsson's fourteenth-century Icelandic poem, for the June 1871 issue of *The Dark Blue* (pp. 524-528). Ten years later she undertook another poetic transformation of legendary material in *The Prophecy of St. Oran (The Prophecy of St. Oran and Other Poems* (London, 1881).

35. Linda K. Hughes, "'Fair Hymen holdeth hid a world of woes': Myth and Marriage in Poems by Graham R. Tomson," *VP* 32 (1994): 101, repr. in *Victorian Women Poets: A Critical Reader,* ed. Angela Leighton (Oxford: Blackwell, 1995), p. 165.

36. Blind greatly admired certain of Christina Rossetti's poems, especially her ballads and children's verses; see *The Diary of W. M. Rossetti, 1870-1873,* p. 170.

37. Ninon Leader, *Hungarian Classical Ballads and their Folklore* (Cambridge: Cambridge Univ. Press, 1967), pp. 292, 326-327.

38. "Literary Notes," *The Academy* (August 15, 1871), p. 394; "The Magazines," *The Illustrated London News* (August 12, 1871), p. 135; "The Magazines," *The Illustrated London News* (October 13, 1872), p. 358.

39. W. B. Yeats, *Autobiography* (New York: Macmillan, 1924), p. 146.

40. *The Wellesley Index to Victorian Periodicals, 1824-1900,* vol. 4 (Toronto: Univ. of Toronto Press, 1987), p. 181. Blind was the only woman writer whose contributions to the journal advanced the aims of aestheticism. The few other women contributors included Amelia Lewis, the mother of *The Dark Blue* publisher John Christian Freund, who regularly contributed pious essays with titles like "The Marriage of Father Christmas and Sweet Christianity," and Eliza Lynn Linton, notorious later in the century for a series of hyperbolic anti-feminist essays, who contributed a short story. In 1868 Linton published an unsigned essay in the March 14 issue of *The Saturday Review* entitled "The Girl of the Period" that already displays her trademark style; she identifies the emergent New Woman represented by Blind and others as embodying "loud and rampant modernization . . . talking slang as glibly as a man, and by preference leading the conversation to doubtful subjects" (p. 340). For more on *The Dark Blue,* see

George R. Sims, *My Life: Sixty Years' Recollections of Bohemian London* (London: Eveleigh Nash, 1917), pp. 54-56; Alfred Percival Graves, *To Return to All That* (London: Jonathan Cape, 1930), p. 157; and T. Earle Welby, *The Victorian Romantics, 1850-1870* (London: Gerald Howe, 1929), pp. 52-59.

41. Vita Sackville-West, "The Women Poets of the 'Seventies," in *The Eighteen-Seventies: Essays by Fellows of the Royal Society of Literature,* ed. Harley Granville-Barker (New York: Macmillan, 1929), pp. 114, 120. Sackville-West later singles out several women poets of the 1870s for praise, including Blind, writing that "her gift has been slightly underrated," but quickly adds that "I must not dwell too long on Mathilde Blind, for the majority of her publications in verse lie outside the 'seventies" (p. 131).

42. Swinburne discusses his struggle to find a publisher for "The End of a Month" in two letters to Thomas Purnell (see *The Swinburne Letters,* 2:124, 128). This poem was republished as "At a Month's End" in *Poems and Ballads,* Second Series. For a reading of "Carmilla" as a story of lesbian desire, see Elizabeth Signorotti, "Repossessing the Body: Transgressive Desire in 'Carmilla' and *Dracula,*" *Criticism* 38 (Fall 1996): 607-632.

43. In an October 5, 1871 letter to Brown, Rossetti praises this illustration, but expresses some concern abouts its sexual suggestiveness: "By the bye you have certainly not minced the demonstrative matter—but would there perhaps be a slight matter of overbalancing?" *Letters of Dante Gabriel Rossetti,* ed. Oswald Doughty and John Robert Wahl (Oxford: Oxford Univ. Press, 1967), 2:1016.

44. Jeffrey Cox, "Melodrama, Monodrama and the Forms of Romantic Tragic Drama," in *Within the Dramatic Spectrum,* ed. Karelisa V. Hartigan (Lanham: Univ. Press of America, 1986), p. 21. "Nocturne," like "The Song of the Willi," also participates in the romantic tradition that identifies death as the ultimate expression of erotic love—a tradition Blind analyzes in her February 1884 essay "The Tale of Tristram and Iseult" for the *National Review* (pp. 826-837).

45. Review of *The Poetical Works of Frances Anne Kemble, The Athenaeum* (January 12, 1884): 50.

46. For Brown's attempts to win D. G. Rossetti's support for Blind's poetry, see Helen Rossetti Angeli, *Dante Gabriel Rossetti: His Friends and Enemies,* pp. 49-52. Swinburne praised Blind's Shelley criticism but refrained from commenting publicly on her poetry. See *The Swinburne Letters,* 2:116, and 6:267.

47. *The Letters of Lord Byron (Selected),* ed. with an introduction by Mathilde Blind (London, 1887).

48. Bashkirtseff, a Russian-born painter and precocious diarist, lived fast, died young, produced a series of important paintings (many of lower-class street scenes in a vivid, naturalist style), and a journal that galvanized late-century feminists in England and America. Bashkirtseff's untutored, radical feminism, expressed with flashes of brilliance, colloquial wit, and anger, thrilled Blind and her contemporaries, especially in her anti-essentialist view of gender: "I grumble at being a woman because there is nothing of the woman about me but the envelope" (*The Journal of Marie Bashkirtseff,* 2 vols. [London, 1890], 1:6). Blind's own comments about the journal in the first of her two-part *Woman's World* article (June 1888) suggest why it inspired her to return to the dramatic monologue: "Too young to dissemble, the writer unconsciously lays bare her inmost soul, with all its foibles and frailties, its lofty aspirations, its pitiable vanities. It is exactly like seeing some one living in a glass house, or hearing them thinking aloud" (p. 352).

49. The Indian poet Sarojini Naidu, author of *The Golden Threshold,* who came to England in 1895 to attend King's College London, met Blind in January 1896, describing her as "among the most known of living writers just now. We had a delightful chat, and she made me recite some of my poems (she had heard of them) which she praised very much." See Sarojini Naidu, *Selected Letters 1890s to 1940s,* ed. Makarand Paranjape (New Delhi: Kali for Women, 1996), p. 10.

50. In a September 24, 1881 letter to Ford Madox Brown, William Michael Rossetti wrote: "I was sorry to see, in your last letter to Lucy, the bother about Mathilde's book. It looks to me very much as if the Publisher had got frightened by somebody about the atheistic character of the book, and had determined to sell it no more" (*Selected Letters,* p. 400).

51. Ana I. Parejo Vadillo, "New Woman Poets and the Culture of the Salon at the *Fin de Siècle,*" pp. 23, 30. Sally Mitchell identifies political activism on behalf of women's rights, the extension of behaviors and living arrangements previously associated with working-class women to middle-class women, and a new openness about sexual desire as key New Woman themes. See "New Women, Old and New," *VLC* 27 (1999): 579-588. Linda K. Hughes, editor of *New Woman Poets: An Anthology* (London: The 1890s Society, 2000), argues for the value of studying "New Woman novelists, essayists, and poets side by side, using their very differences in genre to chart the pervasiveness of New Woman expression in the 1890s and the social effects of literary form" in "Between 2 (+) Stools: Female Poets as New Woman Writers," paper delivered at the British Women Writers Conference, Kansas City, March 2001.

52. By contrast, Arnold Bennett praised the poem for its use of colloquial diction in his unsigned review of *Dramas in Miniature* in the December 9, 1891 "Book Chat" column of the magazine *Woman,* p. 10.

53. Blind's letter to Garnett is in the Richard Garnett Papers, Ransom Humanities Center, University of Texas—Austin. "A Carnival Episode" originally appeared under the title "The Carnival, Nice" in the journal *Black & White* 1, no. 18 (June 6, 1891): 574 (*Dramas in Miniature* was published in November). The setting of the poem was no doubt inspired by Marie Bashkirtseff's account of Rome during carnival season; see *The Journal of Marie Bashkirtseff,* 2:164.

54. "On Truth and Lies in a Non-Moral Sense," in *The Portable Nietzsche,* trans. Walter Kaufmann (New York: Viking, 1968), p. 46.

55. Gayle Rubin, "The Traffic in Women: Notes Toward a Political Economy of Sex," in *Toward an Anthropology of Women,* ed. Rayna Reiter (New York: Monthly Review Press, 1975), pp. 157-210.

56. Mathilde Blind, *The Heather on Fire: A Tale of Highland Clearances* (London, 1886), pp. 4, 1. I wish to thank Beth Wittbrodt for drawing my attention to this connection, and for her other suggestive comments on "A Carnival Episode."

57. Blind's own sexual orientation remains something of a mystery. While she developed intimate relationships with several men, from Ford Madox Brown to Richard Garnett, she also formed close relationships with unconventional women, including such sexual noncomformists as Vernon Lee and Mona Caird. In 1882 Lee reported that she had become "good friends with Mathilde Blind," and in September 1885 she wrote to her mother that Blind "twice asked me to go & see her in the country" (*Vernon Lee's Letters,* ed. Irene Cooper [London: Privately printed, 1937], pp. 91, 196). In the fall of 1893 Blind and Mona Caird rented a cottage together east of Oxford, and spent several weeks touring the countryside around Wendover. Blind recorded this experience in her Commonplace Book, now at the Bodleian Library.

58. Commonplace Book, 1892-95, Bodleian Library, Oxford (ms. Walpole e.1).

James Diedrick (essay date fall 2003)

SOURCE: Diedrick, James. "A Pioneering Female Aesthete: Mathilde Blind in *The Dark Blue*." *Victorian Periodicals Review* 36, no. 3 (fall 2003): 210-41.

[*In the following essay, Diedrick focuses upon Blind's contributions to the radical journal* The Dark Blue *and argues that such a study offers insights into the author's relationship to the aesthetics espoused in the journal.*]

Late last century, Mathilde Blind began emerging from what E. P. Thompson has called "the enormous condescension of posterity." An accomplished poet, biographer, essayist, translator, and reviewer for *The Athenaeum* and *The Examiner,* the German-born Blind was a central figure in Bohemian London from the 1860s to the 1890s, and her work was widely reviewed in the leading journals. She fell into obscurity in the twentieth century, along with many other important women poets recently rescued from the margins of literary history.[1] Her current resurgence can be measured by her appearance alongside E. B. Browning and Christina Rossetti in a 2001 anthology of thirteen Victorian Women Poets—the fifth anthology in less than ten years to feature her work (Blain).[2] Some of her poetry, especially **"The Ascent of Man,"** has been given serious critical attention, and her career as a critic has recently been highlighted in Marysa DeMoor's *Their Fair Share: Women, Power and Criticism in the "Athenaeum," from Millicent Garrett Fawcett to Katherine Mansfield, 1870-1920.*[3] Her association with the influential journal *The Dark Blue,* however—which decisively shaped her subsequent career—has yet to be analyzed. In their introduction to the entry on *The Dark Blue* in *The Wellesley Index to Victorian Periodicals,* Christine Rose Bradley and Walter E. Houghton emphasize the progressive politics and avant-grade aesthetics that characterized the short-lived journal (1871-73), noting that it advocated the education of women and advanced the cause of aestheticism (181-2).[4] But their list of significant contributors, which included William Morris, Dante Gabriel and William Michael Rossetti, and Swinburne, has room for only one woman: Eliza Lynn Linton, who published a single story ("My Cousin James") in the April 1872 number.[5] Mathilde Blind, who contributed a review-essay, three poems, and a short story, is never mentioned—despite the fact that she went on to become one of the most widely published and anthologized women poets of the late-Victorian era.[6] In the pages that follow, I want to redress this omission, assessing the significance of her publications in *The Dark Blue* and what they reveal about her complex relationship to the aesthetic movement.

* * *

Blind's involvement with *The Dark Blue* resulted from the conditions of her exile. She was born Mathilde Co-

hen in Manheim, Germany in 1841, the second of two children; her father, an elderly retired banker, died while she was still an infant. In 1847, her mother, Friederike Ettlinger, became involved in agitation for a united and democratic Germany with Karl Blind, a radical political writer and activist whom she married in 1849. He had been expelled from Heidelberg University in 1846 for writing an article denouncing the punishment of a free-thinking soldier, and he and Ettlinger were both condemned to prison in Durkheim in 1847 for circulating a pamphlet that the government deemed treasonable. Blind became one of the leaders of the Baden insurrections during the revolutions of 1848; the suppression of this movement led to his exile from Germany. By 1849, Blind and his new family had also been exiled from France, and, in 1851, they were expelled from Belgium under pressure from the reactionary government of Napoleon III. Granted asylum in England, they settled in St. John's Wood, just west of Regent's Park. For the next thirty years their household became both a haven for Europe's radical exiles and an influential intellectual salon. Their location also brought them in contact with a group of London artists and writers that decisively shaped Mathilde Blind's career.

During her teenage years Mathilde Blind attended schools in both London and Zurich (she was expelled from the St. John's School for Girls because of her professed atheism), but the radical ideas and political commitments of her parents, their allies, and frequent visitors—Louis Blanc, Joseph Mazzini, Giuseppi Garibaldi, and Karl Marx—had the most profound influence on her outlook.[7] Even though the 1848 revolutions failed in their political aims, "leaving little behind," in Eric Hobsbawm's words, "except myth and promise," they "marked the end, at least in western Europe, of the politics of tradition, of the monarchies which believed that their people (except for middle-class malcontents) accepted, even welcomed, the rule of divinely appointed dynasties presiding over hierarchically stratified societies, sanctioned by traditional religion, of the belief in the patriarchal rights and duties of social and economic superiors" (24-25). In the "Memoir" of the poet he wrote for *The Poetical Works of Mathilde Blind* (1900), Richard Garnett notes with telling ambivalence that the circumstances of Mathilde's girlhood "conspired to nurture" that "independence which distinguished her for good and ill" (2). In the society of political refugees that formed in St. John's Wood, he continues, "admiration must necessarily be reserved for audacity in enterprise, fortitude in adversity, . . . anything breathing unconquerable defiance of the powers that were" (3). Garnett reports that by age twenty-five Mathilde's views regarding the Woman Question were fully developed: "She was in favour of women following all callings, except the military and naval, and when invited by the present writer to consider the consequence of throwing a mass of cheap labour into occupations much overstocked, she rejoined, with decision, that the men might emigrate" (18).[8] Blind formed close relationships with several men but never married, enjoying a degree of independence and freedom of movement that was rare among Victorian women.[9]

Despite (or perhaps because of) her advanced views on gender, Blind spent her twenties mastering the masculine voice and writing about male writers. Both strategies won her the admiration of influential male artists and writers and helped her gain entry into the London publishing world, including the officers of *The Dark Blue*. In 1867, she brought out a volume of lyric poems under the pseudonym Claude Lake, dedicated to the Italian revolutionary Joseph Mazzini and heavily in debt to the poetic tropes of Coleridge, Wordsworth, and Percy Shelley.[10] In 1869, she delivered a lecture on Shelley at St. George's Hall and, at the invitation of editor John Chapman, wrote a long review-essay of William Michael Rossetti's edition of Shelley's poetry for the *Westminster Review* that established her reputation as a critic.[11] It also earned her the respect of men like Garnett, William Michael Rossetti, William Morris, Swinburne, *Athenaeum* editor Norman MacColl, and the German-born painter Ford Madox Brown, who became a life-long champion of her poetry.

In his invaluable *Ford Madox Brown: A Record of his Life and Work* (1896), Brown's grandson Ford Madox Hueffer (later Ford Madox Ford) gives a revealing account of the salons Brown hosted in the late 1860s and early 1870s, where Blind formed the allegiances that shaped her career:

> The guests were nearly all of them people of interest. The nickname which was accorded them as a body was "Pre-Raphaelite," a better one might have been the "Aestheticists." The Aestheticists, at least, formed the nucleus, but there was a "tail" of occasional visitors of distinction ranging from Turgeneff and Mazzini to Mark Twain.
>
> So many of the *habitués* have since passed on to fame that these gatherings must needs be historic—Rossetti, Burne-Jones, Holman Hunt, William Morris, Algernon Swinburne and Theodore Watts-Dunton, Christina and William Rossetti, Mr. Stephens; Dr. Garnett and the all-too-soon forgotten younger "Pre-Raphaelite" poets "B. V.," Arthur O'Shaughnessy, Philip Marston; and Mr. John Payne.
>
> Music was represented by Theo. Marzials and Dr. Hueffer, who championed the music of the future in those past days. In the younger generation, Miss Blind, Miss Spartali, now Mrs. Stillman, and Lucy, Catherine, and Oliver Madox Brown promised much.
>
> (235)

Swinburne and Blind may have mingled at Brown's salons, but they had met several years earlier. Their paths first crossed in 1867, when Swinburne made a pilgrim-

age to the Blind house to meet two of his revolutionary heroes: Karl Blind and Louis Blanc, the French statesman-in-exile who was visiting the Blinds (*Swinburne Letters* 1: 248). Mathilde and Swinburne exchanged volumes of verse, Swinburne read and praised her 1870 lecture on Shelley, and the two exchanged letters in the 1870s.[12] They were fellow republicans, atheists, and aesthetes, and for a short period in the 1870s, it seemed to some of their friends that they should become lovers.[13]

In early 1871, Blind wrote a glowing review of Swinburne's *Songs Before Sunrise*; although it was never published, it was instrumental in gaining her entry into *The Dark Blue*. William Michael Rossetti recorded the event in his 12 March 1871 diary entry: "Miss Blind has sent me her review of Swinburne's *Songs Before Sunrise*; from a hasty reading I think it uncommonly good; wrote to her to say so and to come to a final understanding as to the magazine it should be offered to" (*The Diary of W. M. Rossetti* 50). Blind had sent the review to Richard Garnett even earlier, and he wrote to her on March 8 with specific advice:

> I have an idea about your essay, unless Rossetti has anticipated me. There is a new magazine called *The Dark Blue* to which Swinburne is to contribute a poem next month. They must therefore be favourable to him, and there might be an opening for an article about him . . . there could be no harm in your writing to the editor yourself, saying that you had written an essay, and asking if he would read it. Say you are a friend of Swinburne's, and wrote the paper in the *Westminster*.
>
> (Correspondence and Papers, Add. ms. 61927)

Garnett, who acted as her informal literary adviser throughout her life, knew that Blind had recently left her family to live on her own and that she was short of money.[14] At the time he recommended she publish with *The Dark Blue,* he was unaware that the magazine was already facing financial difficulties under the editorship of John Christian Freund.

Freund had graduated Oxford in 1868, and in 1870, after publishing a collection of tales under the title *By the Roadside,* he and several Oxford friends determined to found a new kind of Oxford periodical, reflecting its university connection but reaching out to a general readership. *Dark Blue: an Oxford University Magazine* had collapsed after a single issue in 1868, so the title was available. But Freund and his friends dropped the terms "University" and "Oxford," envisioning "a periodical that would appeal" to "the whole English-speaking public, and hence influence their mode of thought," as Freund put it in his "Address to the public" in the February 1872 issue.[15] John Ruskin contributed start-up funds to the enterprise, and early issues—which besides the Rossettis, Morris, and Swinburne featured work by Sheridan La Fanu, Andrew Lang, Thomas Arnold, Edward

Dowden, Simeon Solomon, and W. S. Gilbert—assured the journal an important place in the history of British aestheticism. Bradley and Houghton write that "after *The Oxford and Cambridge Magazine* of 1856, the avant garde, having nowhere else to turn, probably seized on *Dark Blue* in hope of making it its organ" (182). And George Saintsbury noted that "*The Dark Blue* . . . during its short life in the earliest 'Seventies, had a staff [of contributors] not easily surpassable, and almost reminding one of the earlier English *London Magazine* and of the French *Globe*" (507). Freund's vanity and financial incompetence, however, spelled the end of the journal after three short years. As one of the journal's sub-editors put it, "*The Dark Blue* was burdened . . . by a weak novel, composed jointly by Freund and his mother; its life was mismanaged, and its brief life soon ended" (Graves 137-8).

Although Freund declined Blind's review of Swinburne, he did publish another of her reviews in the first volume of the journal, written in the wake of William Morris's revival of interest in Scandinavian literature. When Blind first met Morris at the Browns in the late 1860s, he was immersed in his study of Icelandic language and myth, aided by the Icelandic expatriate Eiríkr Magnússon. Magnússon had moved to England in 1862 after receiving his bachelor's degree at Iceland's clergy school; he was appointed a librarian at Cambridge University in 1871, and became a lecturer in Old Norse philology at the university in 1893. He met Morris in 1868, and the two began reading Icelandic together three times a week (Magnússon also accompanied Morris to Iceland during his first trip to that country in 1871). From this collaboration issued a series of translations that began in 1869 and continued for another twenty years. In 1870, Morris published a prose translation of the Scandinavian epic *The Volsunga Saga,* based on a poetic translation Magnússon had sent him in the summer of 1869, and on May 27, 1870, Mathilde Blind delivered a lecture on the saga which singled out Morris' version for special praise. The 28 May issue of *The Illustrated London News* recorded the event:

> On Wednesday a lecture was delivered at the Assembly Rooms, St. John's-Wood, by Miss Mathilde Blind, on the Volsunga Saga, the Scandinavian counterpart of the Lay of the Niebelungen. After a brief introduction, setting forth the general characteristics of Scandinavian legend, the speaker related the leading *incidences* of the ancient saga, following the noble version recently made by Mr. William Morris. This Old-World story, simply and dramatically narrated, produced a marked effect upon a highly-cultivated audience, by whom the lecture was warmly applauded.
>
> (543)

Less than a year later, Morris published "The Story of Frithiof the Bold" in the first two issues of *The Dark Blue* (re-published in 1875 as part of the collection

Three Northern Love Stories and Other Tales, where Magnússon is credited as co-translator). In contrast to the medieval romances that influenced his earliest art and offered him an escape from the contemporary world, Morris discovered in the Scandinavian sagas a transformative vision of social organization. As E. P. Thompson notes: ". . . there ran through Morris's response to the sagas and to Iceland a continual sense of the contrast between the ideals of the Northern past and those of his own society. Even in the Iceland of the nineteenth-century he found a manliness and independence among the crofters and fisherman lacking in capitalist Britain" (184). In an 1883 lecture to the Fabian Socialists, Morris praised the communal spirit and gender attitudes of old Icelandic Society: "The position of women was good in this society, the married couple being pretty much on an equality: there are many stories told of women divorcing themselves for some insult or offence, a blow being considered enough excuse" (qtd. in Morris I: 450).

Blind, whose 1882 poem ***The Prophecy of St. Oran*** embraces the pagan values of a princess who is unmoved by the proselytizing of Christian missionaries, valued Morris and Magnússon's revival of "antique" styles of poetry not only because they embraced alternative modes of poetic representation but because they implicitly questioned contemporary religious and social assumptions.[16] Blind's freethinking is evident in the first paragraph of her first publication in *The Dark Blue*— her June 1871 review of Magnússon's translation of Eystein Asgrimsson's fourteenth-century Iceland poem *Lilja* (*The Lily*). Before commenting on the quality of Magnússon's translation, or his introductory primer on Icelandic prosody, Blind dwells on the epochal change manifested by this poem and others like it, written at a time when "the specifically Northern forms of religious thought embodied in Eddaic literature had been driven into the background of the popular imagination, now completely filled by the image of the Virgin" (524). As the language of aggression and conquest in this sentence suggests, Blind views the literary consequences of the transformation negatively. In place of the indigenous, pagan poetry of Scandinavia, nascent Christianity produced "countless singers, who, in verse more or less good, tried to embody the ruling sentiment of their time" (524). Even though Blind calls "The Lily" "the one Icelandic poem . . . of enduring value on this subject" (524), this does not mean it is poetry of a high order:

> Though shaped according to the strictest rules of Icelandic prosody it is on the whole remarkably devoid of all true poetical inspiration, so that it would appear that the heathen gods had avenged the oblivion to which they had been condemned by abstracting those dwarf-guarded vats, where, according to the mythic traditions

of the people, that mixture of blood and honey was preserved, of which whosoever drank became a poet. Blood and honey . . . do not flow in the veins of the "Lily."

(527)

Her concluding advice to the translator implicitly conveys a preference for that poetry produced by the "heathen gods": "we would here express the hope that Mr. Magnússon may bring his rare editorial powers to bear on a work of more intrinsic and general interest, and make the English public more fully acquainted with those treasures of folk-lore with which Scandinavian and Icelandic literature are enriched" (528).

Although "The Lily" itself leaves Blind cold, she warms to Magnússon's skill as a translator and his knowledge of prosody: "his command of the English language, the purity, precision, and elegance of his diction are indeed astonishing as the work of a foreigner, being in this respect, we believe, perfectly unique" (528). Magnússon clearly offered models for Blind herself, who strove for command of a language not originally her own, and who would go on to distinguish herself as a translator of both David Friedrich Strauss (*The Old Faith and the New,* 1873) and Marie Bashkirtseff (*The Journal of Marie Bashkirtseff,* 1890). Discussing his "original and truly ingenious etymological explanation of the technical terms of Scandinavian prosody," his "instructive account of the principles of alliteration and assonance" (526), Blind writes as the eager, enthusiastic student of poetry and poetic form she would remain throughout her career. In fact, this review offers a preview of her tenure as a regular staff reviewer for *The Athenaeum,* a position she held from 1872 to 1887. On 23 November 1872, in her second appearance in *The Athenaeum,* Blind reviewed Morris's *Love is Enough.* Although Blind's response to Morris's poem is mixed, she has nothing but praise for its form (an innovative variation on the rhymeless alliterative measure that characterizes both "The Lily" and the medieval English poem "Piers Plowman"). Her analysis of Morris's prosody, technical yet lucid, reveals how much she gained from Magnússon's discussion of alliteration and assonance in Icelandic poetry. It also demonstrates that she associated the aesthetes' revival and adaptation of earlier poetic modes (including Swinburne's embrace of Greek forms) not with escapism or mere stylistic virtuosity, but with the search for new forms of poetic truth. Praising Morris's "innovation on the old system" in *Love is Enough,* which consists of "the rise of a new alliterative wave before the preceding one has completely subsided, and produces an inexpressibly rich and far-reaching echo of sounds," Blind claims that by this means the "sense" of the poem is brought vividly to life in and for the reader. "We not merely realize a scene, or an image, by means of a mental effort, but are brought into an immediate sensuous contact with it. Triumphs of this kind are of the essence of poetry" (657).

Blind herself strove for just this kind of sensuous immediacy in the first poem she published in *The Dark Blue,* **"The Song of the Willi,"** appearing in the August 1871 issue of the journal.[17] It demonstrates Blind's own imaginative adaptation of legendary materials, as well as her desire to achieve for women some of the same freedom of subject-matter and treatment enjoyed by the male aesthetes. As she explained in a headnote accompanying the revised version of the poem published in *Dramas in Miniature* (1891),

> According to a widespread Hungarian superstition—showing the ingrained national passion for dancing—the Willi or Willis were the spirits of young affianced girls who, dying before marriage, could not rest in their graves. It was popularly believed that these phantoms would nightly haunt lonely heaths in the neighbourhood of their native villages till the disconsolate lovers came as if drawn by a magnetic charm. On their appearance the Willi would dance with them without intermission till they dropped dead from exhaustion.[18]

(71)

On the anniversary of the night she would have been wed, the speaker of **"The Song of the Willi"** rises from her bed that "has no feather," wondering of her lover ". . . while I flit restless, a low wailing sprite, / Ah, say, canst thou sleep in thy bed?" (lines 31-32). She recalls the country dance they attended a week before they were to be married, and she quotes her lover's pledge in the midst of their dancing, when "fleeter than all the fleet dancers we sped / In the rush of the rapturous race" (lines 55-56):

> Thou'rt light, O my chosen; a bird is not lighter,
>   My dove, my doe!
> I'd dance into death with thee; death would be brighter,
>   My own swift roe!

(lines 41-4)

Then she recounts in elliptical language how her bridesmaids were transformed into the three fates, and love into death:

> High up in the chambers the maidens together,
>   Ah me, ah me!
> Were piling bleached linen as pure as swan's feather,
>   Ah me, ah me!
> Were weaving and spinning and singing aloud,
> Were broidering my bride-veil of lace,
> But the lowering three sisters they wove me my shroud
> As death kissed me cold in the face.

(lines 89-96)

As she draws nearer to her lover's house, the speaker notices other "pale flitting phantoms" gathering around her, and she becomes their guiding spirit, leading them to their bridegrooms and their own dances of death. She is aroused by the sound of her lover's approach, and in a significant inversion of gender roles her heart "leaps like a stag that is borne as on wings" (line 125). Reunited with her lover, she overpowers him with her passion: "Round thy face, round thy throat, I roll my dank tresses, / Oh my love, my love!" (lines 131-2). The poem ends with a duet of love and death, with her lover too inverting conventional norms. "Oh, brighter the night than the fires of the day," he proclaims, as she answers, "When thine eyes shine as stars over me." He responds, "Oh, sweeter thy grave than the soft breath of May—," and she sings the last line, "Down to death then, my love, but with thee" (lines 149-52).

In her *Athenaeum* review of *Love Is Enough,* Blind writes that Morris' poem "transports us for the time into a land of mingled romance and faerie," but denies that such poetry is escapist: ". . . this kind of poetry always produces on our imagination an effect somewhat resembling the impression received on looking at a familiar landscape through the mellow emblazonry of a painted casement . . . we see reality, not enhanced, but transformed. We behold her through an unfamiliar medium of strange and deceptive splendour . . ." (657). Writing of Graham Tomson's use of the ballad form, Linda Hughes notes that "the displacement of action to an apparently nonreferential plane not only tapped her most powerful imaginative gifts . . . but also freed many of the emotional restraints she customarily imposed on her poetry" ("'Fair Hymen'" 165). Blind's use of a supernatural subject allowed her to create a powerful female voice that spoke more directly of her experiences as a woman and a woman poet than the ostensibly more personal lyrics she published as "Claude Lake."

If the legendary subject-matter of **"The Song of the Willi"** reflects Blind's interest in Morris and Magnússon's literary excavations, it also embodies her willingness to follow the trail blazed by Swinburne's *Poems and Ballads,* published just five years earlier. In this revolutionary volume, as Kathy Psomiades has written, "Art's body, eroticized, becomes a body of political protest because it makes visible what respectable culture tries to hide, brings into language what ought to remain unspoken . . ." (71-2). **"The Song of the Willi"** clearly embraces a version of Swinburnian aestheticism, sharing with *Poems and Ballads* what Swinburne called a "luxurious delight" in all that is "noble and nude and antique" ("Notre-Dame Des Sept Douleurs," *Collected Works* 1; line 150). At the same time, it embodies Blind's critique of the masculine privilege and supremacy Swinburne expresses in his "Notes on Poems and Reviews" (1866), published in response to the attacks leveled against *Poems and Ballads,* which asserts that "the office of adult art is neither puerile nor feminine, but virile" (qtd. in Hyder 29).[19] It does so by creating a woman who shares important qualities with Dolores and Anactoria in *Poems and Ballads,* dominant

females who derive and bestow pleasure by giving pain to men. Indeed, the ghostly lover in **"The Song of the Willi"** literally achieves the desire of the speaker of "Anactoria": "I would my love could kill thee; I am satiated / With seeing thee live, and fain would have thee dead" (lines 23-4). At the same time, Blind's poem participates in the critique of male aestheticism present in many of the poems Christina Rossetti wrote in the late 1840s. Psomiades' analysis of these poems ("Dream-Land," "After Death," "When I am Dead, My Dearest") applies equally to **"The Song of the Willi"**: "the encounter with a dead woman is described from the perspective not of a distanced masculine onlooker but of the one dead, either through sympathetic speculation on her mental state in the grave or through an account of her view of the living, often in a first-person narrative" (62).[20]

Blind's first poem in *The Dark Blue* announced the emergence of an important new voice at the same time that it raised hopes for the future of the journal itself. The 12 August number of *The Illustrated London News,* after complaining that "the magazine seems to encounter great difficulty in getting rid of its amateur character," notes that "there is one contribution, however, far remote from amateurship—Miss Mathilde Blind's vivid and powerful ballad of the Willi, in the Teutonic mythology the ghost of the dead betrothed, who dances her surviving lover into his grave. Miss Blind's version of the myth is no less spirited than Sir Walter Scott's rendering of 'Lenore,' of which it strongly reminds us" (135). Three days later, the 15 August 1871 issue of *The Academy* noted that "the two last numbers of the *Dark Blue* show an improvement in the poetical contributions, hitherto not the strongest point of that magazine," and the anonymous reviewer credited **"The Song of the Willi"** for the change (394). The poem's fame far outlasted the journal in which it first appeared: when Edith Nesbit reviewed Arthur Symons' edition of *A Selection from the Poems of Mathilde Blind* in the 3 December 1898 issue of *The Athenaeum,* she complains about its absence: "Why has he omitted the wonderful wild **'Song of the Willi'**?" (784).

Among other things **"The Song of the Willi"** gives the lie to Vita Sackville-West's claim that the "numerous and prolific" women poets of the 1870s all hewed to "the high Victorian standard of bashfulness," producing "elegant or devotional pieces . . . wordy and portentous moralising . . . dreary narrative poems . . . descriptive pieces which reminded one of nothing so much as a washy and indifferent water-colour . . ." (114, 120). Blind's presence in *The Dark Blue,* and her defiant occupation of poetic territory Swinburne sought to claim solely for men, was anything but bashful. She is presumably one of the women poets E. L. Bryans indicts in his essay "Characteristics of Women's Poetry" for the December 1871 issue of the journal—poets like

E. B. Browning, who "have endeavoured to obtain a reputation for masculine power and vigour by attempting descriptions of those feelings and passions which their sex is supposed neither to possess or even be acquainted with" (490).

If, as Michel Foucault has written, the nineteenth century "initiated sexual heterogeneities" (37), *The Dark Blue* played an important role in their cultural circulation. In just two years, the journal featured lesbianism in Sheridan La Fanu's "Carmilla" (serialized in the journal between 1871 and 1872); homoeroticism in Simeon Solomon's illustration to Swinburne's poem "The End of the Month" (also indirectly celebrated in Swinburne's essay "Simeon Solomon: Notes on His 'Vision of Love' and Other Studies" in the July 1871 issue); and sadomasochism in "The End of a Month" (published in *The Dark Blue* after being rejected by *Fraser's Magazine* for its sexual explicitness).[21] This is in addition to frequent poetic representations of non-marital heterosexual intimacy, highlighted by a trio of poems that exist in a provocatively dialogic relationship to one another: "The End of the Month" (April 1871), D. G. Rossetti's "Down Stream" (October 1871), and Blind's own **"Nocturne"** (March 1872), the second dramatic monologue she published in the journal. All three explore the relationship between Eros and death; all three feature couples locked in destructive embraces; all three employ nature imagery to represent sexual experience. And the date of Blind's poem suggests that it was written at least in part as a response to those of Rossetti and Swinburne.

Rossetti's five-stanza poem is the most conventional and sentimental of the three, featuring a seduced and abandoned woman who drowns herself and her infant a year after her lover has left her. Rossetti's imagery and Ford Madox Brown's frontispiece drawing, however, are unusually explicit. In Brown's rendering of the lovers' liaison in a small row boat, the woman leans back against her lover, who is clasping her right hand and kissing her neck. The male is seen only in profile, but the woman's face and swooning expression directly confront the viewer, as does her left arm, shown gripping a decidedly phallic oar handle. In one stanza, Rossetti portrays the rhythm of sexual intercourse, describing the lovers on the river "brimmed with rain," making their way "through close-met banks and parted banks / Now near now far again" (lines 10-12). Brown's second illustration shows the drowned mother and child lying in the same stream where she was seduced a year earlier, "with lilies meshed in tangled hair, / On this year's first of June" (lines 31-2).[22]

Swinburne's poem is also concerned with sex and death, but "The End of the Month" emphasizes the psychology of the speaker as he contemplates the wreckage of his affair. He and his lover stand by the sea together for the last time, every detail of the landscape reflecting their situation: "Across, aslant, a scudding sea-mew / Swam, dipped, and dropped, and grazed the sea; / And one with me I could not dream you: / And one with you I could not be" (lines 37-40). The dramatic monologue form helps Swinburne render the fevered state of the male lover, who spends 32 stanzas obsessing over this failed affair. The concluding stanzas of the poem fearlessly convey the grip the woman still has on his erotic imagination:

> But as to a bee's gilt thighs and winglets,
>   The flower-dust and the flower-smell clings;
> As a snake's mobile rampant ringlets
>   Leave the sand marked with print of rings;
>
> So to my soul in surer fashion
>   Your savage stamp and savour hangs;
> The print and perfume of old passion,
>   The wild-beast mark of panther's fangs.
>
> (lines 121-28)

Stanzas like these, rendering with uncommon power the unruly nature of erotic desire, earned Swinburne the wrath of contemporary reviewers, who declared similar stanzas in *Poems and Ballads* "a carnival of ugly shapes," displaying "a mind all aflame with the feverish carnality of a schoolboy" (Hyder 31, 23).

"Nocturne" lacks the startling and often sadomasochistic imagery of "The End of the Month," but it still has much in common with Swinburne's poem.[23] Employing alliteration, internal rhyme, and repetition in a dramatic monologue on the frenzy and grief of lost love, Blind creates a speaker for whom all of nature initially limns his passion. Pushing out to sea with his lover "at the dead of night, when the heart beats free" (line 3), he projects his erotic desire into the ocean itself: "The sea, and the waves in their fall and rise, / Bosomlike heaving with languid sighs / Lifted, and tumbled, and broke with desire, / Licked, and fawned on her with tongues of fire" (lines 17-20). Unlike "The End of the Month," however, and her own **"The Song of the Willi,"** Blind eschews the familiar abab ballad meter in favor of an aabb pattern reflecting the structure of parallelism and antithesis on which the entire poem is based. Divided in two, just as the speaker feels without his lost lover, **"Nocturne"** begins in the past, when he was at one with his love and with all the natural world. It moves inexorably to its midpoint—the moment in the present when the he wakes to discover that his lover has died beside him as they both slept in their boat at sea. The speaker is shocked and unhinged by his lover's death, but the fact that she dies after "her whole life swooned into mine, as swoons / The sunset into the broad lagoons; / Ruddy red radiance of sunset that flows / To the sea, till the sea blossoms like a rose" (lines 33-36) evokes the familiar Victorian trope equating unmarried female sexual experience with death. Unlike Browning's "Porphyria's Lover," however, which invites the reader to discern misogyny and madness in the speaker's words, **"Nocturne"** deflects attention away from the speaker's culpability, focusing instead on his intense grief, culminating at the end of the poem when the speaker asks the ocean to "bury the dead and the quick in one gloom—/ One ebbing, and flowing and earth-girdling tomb—" (lines 81-2). Although this ending recalls the lovers' fate in **"The Song of the Willi,"** **"Nocturne"** is a more subjective poem than its predecessor. Blind displaces her own feelings onto a male speaker, indirectly expressing the isolation and romantic disappointment that often characterize her lyrics. Like **"The Song of the Willi,"** **"Nocturne"** participates in the romantic tradition that identifies death as the ultimate expression of erotic love. Discussing the many and varied versions of the Tristram and Iseult legend in an essay for the *National Review,* Blind praises Wagner's opera for having "resolved the complete medieval romance into its simplest elements. . . . The love of Tristan and Isolde is a transcendental passion, reaching beyond time and space—ever tending towards death as the goal of absolute passion where their severed lives, no longer conscious of limitation, shall be 'lost, engulfed, to mingle with the living breath of the universal soul'" (837).

"Nocturne" is the last poem Blind published in *The Dark Blue,* and it lacks the gender-inverting suggestiveness of **"The Song of the Willi."** It is tempting to read the poem as Blind's final, chilly embrace of pure aestheticism, since after it appeared she took an eight-year hiatus from publishing poetry (occupied by editing, criticism, and a translation of David Strauss's *The Old Faith and the New*) before she returned with a more explicitly ideological form of verse (*The Prophecy of St. Oran*). The intertextuality of **"Nocturne"** points to the many influences—poetic, pictorial, and theoretical—which shaped this phase of her poetic career. Its very title evokes the belief in the interrelationship among poetry, music, and painting that informed the art of the Pre-Raphaelites and aesthetes. In the June 1871 issue of *The Dark Blue,* Edward Dowden wrote that the conception of "the essential unity of art," the idea that "poetry, painting, sculpture, architecture, music, and dance are but various manifestations of one and the same human tendency, is of modern origin" (484). Less than a year before Blind published **"Nocturne,"** James McNeill Whistler exhibited two paintings at the Dudley Gallery in November 1871 as "Harmony in Blue Green—Moonlight," which in 1872 he renamed "Nocturne in Blue and Silver—Chelsea" (Spencer 72). Blind knew Whistler from Brown's salons, and her own **"Nocturne,"** like Whistler's paintings, is an impressionistic dreamscape, the poetic equivalent of melancholy night-music. The voices of fellow poets echo throughout the poem as well; its subject matter and musical effects are a virtual parody of Swinburne's sexual and stylistic pre-

occupations, and two passages explicitly evoke Keats and Browning, guiding spirits of the Pre-Raphaelites and aesthetes. "Yea, her whole life swooned into mine, as swoons / The sunset into the broad lagoons" (lines 33-4) evokes the consummation scene in "The Eve of St. Agnes"; "Her eyes with a wide, blank, lusterless stare / Are fixed upon mine, and the strangling gold / Of her hair coils over me fold upon fold" (lines 66-8) recalls "Porphyria's Lover."

In **"The Song of the Willi"** both lovers speak, vow, and plead with one another, but in **"Nocturne"** the woman is conspicuously silent—like the women in both "Down Stream" and "The End of a Month." If **"Nocturne"** is in part a critique of the tradition Blind is about to partially disavow, the woman may at one level represent the poet herself, and her fear that continued affiliation with the male members of what she called "the aesthetic school of poetry of our day" (Review of *The Poetical Works of Frances Anne Kemble* 50) would be deathly to her own poetic vocation. Admittedly aestheticism was useful to Blind, granting her license to express subversive views while ostensibly pursuing art for art's sake. But Blind's poetic career was not encouraged or nurtured by the male poets she associated with in the 1870s. D. G. Rossetti was famously distant from Blind and her poetry (despite her close friendship with his brother William and the best efforts of Ford Madox Brown), and Swinburne reserved his enthusiasm for her republican sentiments.[24] By the time she wrote the introduction to her edition of *The Letters of Lord Byron* (1887), in fact, Blind had put considerable distance between herself and the doctrine of "art for art's sake":

> Words always stood as signs for things to Byron, his object being to get hold of the one that most adequately expressed the image in his mind: a manner of writing which differs entirely from the aesthetic method, where the luxuriant beauty of expression becomes of such supreme importance that it weakens, undermines, and finally destroys the sap and marrow of thought, as the enlacing ivy the tree that is its stay.
>
> (vii)

This may help explain why, when Blind returned to the dramatic monologue form in 1891, she eschewed the ahistorical, dream-like settings of her *Dark Blue* monologues in favor of poems featuring precisely observed social settings.

The one highly-wrought aesthetic form Blind never disavowed was the sonnet. She published over thirty during her career, beginning with **"Winter"** in the January 1872 issue of *The Dark Blue,* and she won high praise from male and female poets alike for her achievements in the genre.[25] Two of Blinds' sonnets were featured in T. Hall Caine's 1882 collection *Sonnets of Three Centuries* alongside examples by D. G. and Christina Rossetti, Swinburne, and Matthew Arnold.[26] In fact, Caine singles out Blind's **"The Dead,"** along with D. G. Rossetti's "Stillborn Love" and "Lost Days" and Swinburne's "Let us go forth" as exemplars of what he calls "Sonnets of Contemporary Structure." Distinct from the Shakespearean and Miltonic sonnet, this form constitutes "a return to the Petrarchan pattern, prompted, however, by other purposes, and achieving other results" (xx). Claiming that the "merit and promise of enduring popularity consist in its being grounded in a fixed law of nature," Caine asserts that "the natural phenomenon it reproduces is the familiar one of the flow and ebb of a wave of the sea" (xxi). He elaborates:

> . . . the "sonnet-wave"—twofold in quality as well as movement—embraces flow and ebb of thought or sentiment, and flow and ebb of music. For the perfecting of a poem on this pattern the primary necessity therefore, is, that the thought chosen be such as falls naturally into unequal parts, each essential to each, and the one answering the other. The first and fundamental part shall have unity of sound no less than unity of emotion, while in the second part the sonnet shall assume a freedom of metrical movement analogous to the lawless ebb of a returning billow. The sonnet-writer who has capacity for this structure may be known by his choice of theme. Instinctively or consciously he alights on subjects that afford this flow and ebb of emotion. Nor does he fail to find in every impulse animating his muse something that corresponds with the law of movement that governs the sea.
>
> (xxii)

Caine lists Wordworth's "It is a beauteous evening" and Blind's **"Death"** as embodying these principles, but he could as well have chosen **"Winter,"** which itself echoes another Wordsworth sonnet, "Composed upon Westminster Bridge, September 3, 1802."

"Winter" embodies the principles Caine identifies in "Sonnets of Contemporary Structure" to a remarkable degree. The octave evokes a world cleansed and quieted by the "inviolate snow," an impression deepened by Blind's use of assonance and alliteration:

> How hushed the world is: how the sea-like sound
> Of multitudinous streets, that shriek and swell
> With life, is muffled, save for some lone bell
> Making the sunless silence more profound.
> The awful whiteness, spread along the ground,
> Of the inviolate snow, seems to compel
> The flames of fire to flash with visible
> Increase of radiance, by drear norlight bound.

As the verb "muffled" suggests, however, unruly passions continue to "swell" under this serene surface, both verbs intimating the "unequal" thoughts that fully emerge in the sestet. While the octave, in Caine's words, "representing a wave," brings "a slow swell of melody," the sestet, "as representing the ebb," introduces a quicker and shorter beat" (xxiii). This occurs as Blind abruptly shifts the emphasis of the sonnet from outer to inner, world to self, harmony to discord, abruptly withdrawing all tranquility in the poem's final lines:

> Thou, too, O heart, sore beat by roar and flow
> Of heavy-weltering, clamorous-tongued desires,
> Liest hush'd, as you shrill streets smooth'd by the
>   snow,
> Each louder wish 'neath fresh-fallen peace expires;
> Yet all the intenser throb thought's quenchless fires,
> Wan Memory rims with tears and years of woe.
>
> (556)

Like the home fires in the octave, burning brighter in the snow-blanketed darkness, the speaker's "quenchless fires" of unsatisfied longing are rendered more intense by the layers of loss under which they burn.

Blind's last publication in *The Dark Blue* was the story **"A Month at the Achensee,"** published in the October 1872 issue.[27] It is simultaneously a distillation of the radicalism implicit in the review-essay and two ballads she published in the journal and the first manifestation of a narrative impulse that would find its fullest expression in her 1884 novel *Tarantella.* Its appearance was greeted enthusiastically; Richard Garnett wrote Blind on 17 October 1872 to report that "everybody seems to like your story extremely," prompted in part by a comment in the 13 October 1872 *The Illustrated London News*: "The most remarkable contribution to the *Dark Blue* is Miss M. Blind's **'Month at the Achensee,'** a beautiful story, half tragedy, half idyll, interspersed with charming descriptions of the scenery of the Tyrol" (358).[28] The reviewer for the *London Weekly News* perceived something more than "charm" and "beauty" in the story, claiming that its author was clearly "a bold admirer of Swinburne." Although Blind objected to this characterization in a letter to Garnett the following day ("how or in what manner that transpires from the story in question I fail to perceive"), **"A Month at the Achensee"** unmistakably combines the ecstatic pantheism and religious skepticism of *Poems and Ballads* with the overtly republican politics in *Songs Before Sunrise.*

During her month at a "Scholastica" in the Austrian Alps, the female narrator of the story experiences both the awesome sublimity of nature and the corrosive nature of class relations (Blind structures the narrative so that the former provides a kind of choric commentary on the latter). The narrator arrives at her destination after a perilous carriage journey over roadways sodden with "weeks of incessant rain," and awakes to a morning in which the world has been re-born. "A curtain seemed to be rent asunder on high, . . . mountain-peaks on mountain-peaks innumerable sprang into light," and they "shone out over mist-drenched wood and valley like a band of colossal cherubim, who, reaching upwards into the intolerable effluence of Deity, stretch out and hand down to the shadowy haunts of men a muffled and mitigated flame" (228).[29] The heterodox nature of this deity becomes clear as the narrator meets and becomes friends with Sebastian, a sixty-year old chaplain whose religious skepticism and concern for the outcast mirrors Blind's own. The son of a poor peasant, and educated for the church, Sebastian tells the narrator that he spent most of his life ministering to the Tyrolese peasants. But his own immersion in the works of Descartes, Spinoza, and Kant has led him away from orthodoxy, and finally "the duality of this life became intolerable to him" (230). Seeking a way out of this dilemma, "he determined to become a chaplain in a lunatic asylum." He explains to the narrator that his preaching there "could do no harm" and would "afford him a capital opportunity for studying human nature." In a sardonic addendum worthy of Swinburne, the narrator adds that Sebastian "gave me to understand, in confidence, that he thought his present abode the fittest sanctuary of the Holy Church" (230).

On an evening soon after her arrival, the narrator is sitting with Sebastian outside the asylum "discussing the different degrees of madness," and "the heart-rending list of poets who had drifted into the shadow-haunted land" (230). Their talk is interrupted, first by a female voice singing a song of complaint against a persistent suitor she no longer loves ("Thou dost beat and bruise my breast / With the sighs of thy unrest"), then by the appearance of Hugo, recently returned from "the wars," where he was awarded a cross of honour for his work as an army surgeon. He embraces Sebastian, tells him that he may soon secure a medical practice in Vienna and asks Sebastian if he thinks Marie will be pleased by this news. Hugo runs off wildly when he recognizes the singer's voice as that of Marie, leaving Sebastian free to tell their story to the narrator. "They are both poor foresters' children, looked down upon in these parts by the rich peasants, who possess their herds and flocks and acres of land," he begins. He adds that "when they ceased to be playmates they became lovers," but while Hugo's love, "whose roots struck into the earliest of memories . . . branched out . . . into his futurity," Marie's affections competed with her ambition, "for a doctor's wife she would be, but not a peasant's or forester's" (231-2). Aware that none of her many other suitors love her with the purity and intensity of Hugo, Marie nonetheless makes a match with a wealthy landowner, and the marriage takes place two weeks after the narrator's arrival. Unwilling to tell Hugo of her plans, she sends him to Innsbruck "on some law errand"—in order, as Sebastian says to the narrator with pointed irony, "that he should be safe out of the way while she marries the big house I bade you look at the other day" (235).

Hugo returns, however, just as the marriage ceremony is concluding. Marie's "yes" is "instantaneously accompanied by a shrill, strident, and horrible laugh." As the narrator observes: "In that laugh there was heart-wreck. It was as if you saw a human soul cloven in twain, and toppling, sheer and sudden, into the dull black gulf of despair" (236). Hugo flees, Sebastian goes in search of him, and the next morning the weather turns. "Mass on mass of inky cloud seemed brewed and boiling up from some cauldron sunk in amongst the shaggy mountains, and they gradually strangled and stamped out the breadth and height of the azure sky" (236). Three days later Hugo is returned on a stretcher, raving: "The devil! The devil! He stands on the White Mountain! He has got me by the throat! His hairs are ropes, flames, chains!" Sebastian despairs of Hugo ever regaining his sanity, and lays all the blame on the spirit of Mammon that has possessed Marie. "He had a heart of gold. Gold! No, let me not compare that heart, full of such devotion, to the miserable metal for which that woman has sacrificed it" (237). Chastened and subdued, the narrator sits in the courtyard of the Scholastica awaiting the coach that will take her away: "The driver's whip and voice sounded still from afar; but the roll of wheels could not be heard, because of the heavy fall of snow during the night. 'Marie' came like a wail of the wind round the house, and then all was still" (238).

Richard Garnett, an ardent supporter of *Tarantella* (he called it a work of genius and compared it to Olive Schreiner's *The Story of an African Farm*), did voice a single objection to the novel: "it may be complained . . . that the action is too much retarded by description."[30] While natural description and poetic effects clearly trump characterization and thematic subtlety in **"A Month at the Achensee,"** this emphasis is in keeping with the story's fable-like quality. As in **"The Song of the Willi,"** where she used the ballad form to challenge the boundaries of gender and sexuality, Blind's "charming" short story, "half tragedy, half idyll," provokes its readers while providing aesthetic pleasure. While Marie is clearly demonized in the story for spurning love and driving Hugo to madness, the logic of her actions derive from a system that is a major source of Blind's enmity. **"A Month at the Achensee,"** reflecting Blind's thorough familiarity with the theories of Karl Marx, starkly dramatizes the observation of her friend Eleanor Marx, writing in *The Woman Question*: "The position of women rests, as everything in our complex modern society rests, on an economic basis. . . . The woman question is one of the organization of society as a whole" (4).[31]

The economic basis of the woman question was not an abstract one for Blind. At the time she wrote **"A Month at the Achensee,"** she was acutely aware of the economic difficulties faced by unmarried women. In 1871, she had left her mother and stepfather's home to live on her own, in part because of conflicts with her stepfather, even though she could scarcely afford to live independently. She struggled much of her life to make a living from her writing and turned down at least one marriage proposal rather than sacrifice her independence.[32] It wasn't until 1892, four years before her death, that Blind became the sole heir to her step-brother's fortune, which brought to an end what Garnett called her "harassing struggle with narrow means, which had counted for much in her adversities" ("Memoir" 37).

* * *

Like the literary friendships she formed in the 1860s, Blind's publications in *The Dark Blue* define her as a woman firmly allied with the politically radical wing of the aesthetic movement. They anticipate her better-known works of ideological engagement like **The Heather on Fire** (an attack on the English treatment of Scottish peasants during the Highland Clearances), and they help explain why she would become an inspiration to many New Woman writers who emerged in the 1880s and early 1890s.[33] Blind ultimately grew frustrated with the piecemeal work of magazine publication, writing to William Michael Rossetti in 1882 that "as far as my taste goes I wish that I had no need to write such articles at all, and if only my novel had got accepted by this time, I would never trouble any magazine again."[34] Her experiences with John Freund, whose treatment of contributors was notoriously unprofessional, undoubtedly contributed to this attitude.[35] Yet Mathilde Blind's brief tenure with *The Dark Blue* was a formative one, earning her early critical acclaim and laying the foundation for a long and important career. Because of the arc and influence of that career, her early successes as a pioneering female aesthete constitute an important chapter in the history of Victorian aestheticism.

Notes

I wish to thank the Newberry Library and the British Academy for a travel fellowship enabling me to conduct research for this essay in London at the British Library, the Public Records Office, and the City University of London *Athenaeum* archives. LeeAnne Richardson read an early draft of this essay and provided many helpful suggestions. This essay was written with the support of the Howard L. McGregor Professorship administered by Albion College.

1. Important recent work on nineteenth-century women writers includes Angela Leighton's *Victorian Women Poets*; Isobel Armstrong's *Victorian Poetry: Poetry, Poetics and Politics*; Dorothy Mermin's *Godiva's Ride*; Kerry McSweeney's *Supreme Attachments*; Yopie Prins' *Victorian Sappho*; Abigail Burnham Bloom's *Nineteenth-Century British Women Writers*; and five anthologies of Victorian women's poetry published since 1994, all of which feature Blind (Breen, Leighton and Reynolds, Armstrong Bristow and Sharrock, Hughes, Blain). Four collections of essays on Victorian women poets have also appeared (Armstrong and Blain, *Women's Poetry, Late Ro-*

mantic to. Late Victorian: Gender and Genre 1830-1900; Bristow, *Victorian Women Poets*; Cosslett, *Victorian Women Poets*; and Leighton, *Victorian Women Poets: A Critical Reader*). The spring 1995 issue of *Victorian Poetry* (vol. 33, no.1) was a special issue on Women Poets, edited by Linda Hughes, and the fall 1999 issue of the same journal (vol. 37, no.3) was a special issue on Women Poets 1880-1910, edited by Bonnie Robinson. Recent studies that contain important discussions of Victorian women poets include Kathy Psomiades, *Beauty's Body: Femininity and Representation in British Aestheticism*; Talia Schaffer, *The Forgotten Female Aesthetes: Literary Culture in Late-Victorian England* (Charlotesville: University Press of Virginia, 2000); Schaffer and Psomiades, ed. *Women and British Aestheticism* (Charlottesville: University Press of Virginia, 1999); and Ana I. Vadillo Parejo, "New Woman Poets and the Culture of the Salon at the Fin de Siécle," *Women: A Cultural Review* 10.1 (1999): 22-34.

2. Currently all seven books of Blind's poetry (as well as her groundbreaking biography of George Eliot) are available online at The Victorian Women Writers Project <http://www.indiana.edu/~letrs/vwwp>.

3. Kathleen Hickok's *Representations of Women* (1984) and Isobel Armstrong's *Victorian Poetry: Poetry, Poetics and Politics* (1993) both discuss "Motherhood," the sonnet that concludes Part 2 of "The Ascent of Man," emphasizing Blind's rejection of the doctrine of original sin. In "Victorian Women Poets and Scientific Narratives," Helen Groth also discusses "The Ascent of Man," incorporating Hickok and Armstrong's claims about the sonnet "Motherhood." I discuss "The Ascent of Man" in "Mathilde Blind," *Nineteenth-Century British Women Writers: A Bio-Bibliographical Critical Sourcebook* (41-44), and in "Mathilde Blind," *Victorian Women Poets: The Dictionary of Literary Biography* (28-39).

In *Their Fair Share*, DeMoor claims that Blind wrote 26 full-length reviews for *The Athenaeum,* but when I studied the editor's "marked file" of the journal, now held by the library of the City University of London, I determined that she wrote just 20. Sixteen of the books she reviewed were volumes of poetry, three were biographies, and one was a novel. Blind also wrote five reviews for *The Examiner* in 1873 and early 1874, but was unceremoniously dismissed when William Minto took over as editor in 1874. In a 22 November 1875 letter to Swinburne, William Michael Rossetti criticized Minto's action: "I wish he had not, on taking possession of the *Examiner* forthwith ousted our good friend and really capable critic Miss Blind from her post of contributor of poetical critiques. He undertook, I believe, to do most of these himself—to which of course no outsider can start the least objection: but I do think it seemed harsh—and ill-judged as well—never to give Mathilde the least further employment of any kind" (*Selected Letters of William Michael Rossetti* 331).

4. For more on *The Dark Blue* by members of its staff, see Graves, *To Return to All That* and Sims, *My Life: Sixty Years' Recollections of Bohemian London*. Sims, whose mother was an activist for women's rights, provides valuable glimpses of the progressive circles in which Mathilde Blind (and her parents) moved: "Among our frequent guests were Augusta Webster, the poetess, Karl and Mathilde Blind, Dr. Anna Kingsford, Mrs. Fenwick-Miller—she was Miss Fenwick-Miller then—Emily Faithfull, Ella Dietz, Dr. Zerffi, Professor Plumtree, Samuel Butler, the author of *Erewhon,* Frances Power Cobbe, and occasionally Lydia Becker" (53).

5. From 1868 on, Linton was publically antagonistic toward the emergent "New Woman." In that year she contributed an unsigned essay to the 14 March issue of *The Saturday Review* entitled "The Girl of the Period," displaying the hyperbolic antifeminism that became her trademark. She identifies "The Girl of the Period" as representing "loud and rampant modernization . . . talking slang as glibly as a man, and by preference leading the conversation to doubtful subjects" (340). In another unsigned essay in the 29 April 1871 issue, she identifies one group of "Modern Man-Haters" as "those restless and ambitious persons who are less than women, greedy of notoriety, indifferent to home life and holding home duties in disdain, with strong passions rather than warm affections, with perverted instincts in one direction, and none worthy of the name in another" (529).

6. Blind was represented in several anthologies: T. Hall Caine's *Sonnets of Three Centuries: A Selection*; Elizabeth Sharp's *Women's Voices: An Anthology of the Most Characteristic Poems by English, Scotch and Irish Women*; Alfred H. Miles' *The Poets and Poetry of the Century*; and Edmund Stedman's *A Victorian Anthology 1847-1895*. She was also one of the few Victorian women poets to be honored with posthumous collections, both edited by Arthur Symons: A Selection from the *Poems of Mathilde Blind* and *The Poetical Works of Mathilde Blind*.

7. Both of her parents were formative influences on Mathilde's thinking. Although she was not herself a writer, Friederike's radicalism is well documented. In the first of his five-part account of their revolutionary activities during the 1848 revolutions, Karl Blind writes that among the books she asked for while imprisoned in Frankenthal were the works of Ludwig Feuerbach, including *The Essence of Christianity* (translated into English by George Eliot). He adds that "she knew the great thinker also personally" ("In Years of Storm and Stress, I: Political Prison Life Before 1848" 348). In London, she and Mathilde often read together at the British Library Reading Room (they both submitted letters requesting reading passes on 2 May 1859; see MS Correspondence and Papers, Add. Ms. 61927).

8. All of Blind's published statements on the Woman Question are similarly astringent. Her (anonymous) review of E. R. Pennell's biography of Mary Wollstonecraft in *The Athenaeum* expresses exasperation with the British for not fully embracing their foremost feminist: "when we find her name omitted from such a treatise as Mr. John Stuart Mill's 'Subjection of Women,' and Mrs. Mill treated as the chief representative of that movement, she appears to have been as hardly dealt with by the supporters of the cause she advocated as by its opponents" (41). In her introduction to her translation of *The Journal of Marie Bashkirtseff*, Blind uses Bashkirtseff's experience to express her own frustration at the pace of change in gender relations: "Did we but know it, the same revolts, the same struggles, the same helpless rage have gone on in many another woman's life for want of scope for her latent powers and faculties" (viii). In 1889, Blind joined several thousand other women in signing a declaration in favor of women's suffrage, and in her will she bequeathed the greater part of her nearly £10,000 estate of to Newnham College, Cambridge, establishing an endowment ("The Mathilde Blind Benefaction") to support women pursuing degrees in "either English or Foreign or Ancient Literature" (Last Will and Testament, 23 October 1896).

9. Her friend and literary adviser Richard Garnett, married when he met her, fell in love with Blind in the 1860s and remained emotionally intimate with her until her death (see McCrimmon 59-71 and note 2 180). In 1871, the American poet Joaquin Miller, who dazzled literary London in the late 1860s with his exotic dress, manner, and poetry, and himself published in *The Dark Blue*, formally proposed marriage to Blind (*The Diary of W. M. Rossetti, 1870-1873* 67, 72). Her most complex relationship was with Ford Madox Brown. Beginning in the mid-1870s, she spent a good part of each year living in the Brown household, and her relationship with the painter was the subject of considerable speculation. In his 15 Janu-

ary 1891 diary entry, William Michael Rossetti reports that when Ford Madox Brown's grandson Ford Hueffer (later Ford Madox Ford) was staying in Paris the previous summer with his uncle, "this uncle made some reference to the intimacy of Math. Blind in Brown's house, and denounced in the strongest terms her family, or some members of her family, and vowed that, if M. B. continued to go to the house, he would have nothing further to do with Ford +c" (*William Michael Rossetti Diaries*, A.1.1.5). In her memoir *Dante Gabriel Rossetti: His Friends and Enemies,* Rossetti's daughter Helen Rossetti Angeli writes that Ford Madox Brown's feelings for Blind in the late 1880s and early 90s "were perhaps more romantic than those of mere friendship. Not long before his death (his wife Emma predeceased him by some four years) there was a rumour in the family that he meant to marry her, even that he actually had married her. This, however, was mere rumor" (49). Blind was present with Brown at his death ("his last quite coherent words must, I think, have been uttered whilst advising some alterations to a work of Miss Blind's") (Ford Madox Hueffer, *Ford Madox Brown: A Record of His Life and Work* 397). For more on the Blind-Brown relationship, see Teresa Newman and Ray Watson, *Ford Madox Brown and the Pre-Raphaelite Circle* (147-96).

10. Blind published her "Personal Recollections of Mazzini" in the *Fortnightly Review* in 1891.

11. Blind consulted and corresponded extensively with fellow Shelley admirer Richard Garnett about her essay, but maintained her critical independence, as is evident in her 26 January 1870 letter thanking Garnett for offering her a "syllabus" of readings on Shelley: "It is really too kind of you to have taken all this trouble to draw up a syllabus of a review for me. I assure you I was quite delighted with it. It will certainly be a great help to me, although of course I must think the subject out for myself and feel at present inclined to go somewhat more into Shelley's own works and character than you seem to think advisable. You say that I may assure the public for which I shall write to be well acquainted with Shelley, but I really have strong doubts on that subject. Men like Mr. Furnivall and Mr. Conway and others with whom I have had occasion to speak of our beloved poet seem to have had little beyond his shorter lyrical pieces, indeed with many great admirers of Shelly's poems, there seems a sort of avoidance of the more obscure and intricate work like 'The Prometheus Unbound,' 'The Triumph of Life' etc." (MS Correspondence and Papers, Add. Ms. 61927).

12. On 2 August 1870, Blind wrote to Swinburne, enclosing her Shelley lecture and urging him to pub-

lish the much-delayed *Songs Before Sunrise*: "It seems to me that the 'Songs before Sunrise,' launched forth at this present moment, heavy with the gloom of impending war, would come upon the world with truly prophetic force and significance. Let us hear that great blast of song, you alone of living English poets can intone" (ALS, Harry Ransom Humanities Research Center). She wrote him again on 7 September 1870, celebrating the success of the Paris Commune and thanking him for his letter: "I should have written before to thank you for your delightful letter and sonnet which gratified me very much if I had not been quite carried away by the torrent of passing events" (ALS, Algernon Charles Swinburne Papers, U of Michigan Special Collections). Most of Swinburne's letters to Blind have been lost, although volume 6 of *The Swinburne Letters* reprints a letter in which Swinburne thanks Blind for sending him her Shelley lecture (267). Lang erroneously claims the letter was written 6 June 1870; it was likely written in August or September.

13. Donald Thomas writes that during the late 1860s, when Swinburne's health and stability were threatened by his appetite for brandy and the flagellation brothels on Circus Road in St. John's Wood, several of his friends looked to Mathilde Blind "as the means of saving Swinburne from the grotesque routines of Circus Road" (150). Edmund Gosse, in his unpublished "An Essay (With Two Notes) on Swinburne," reports on his efforts to confirm the rumors of an affair with Mathilde Blind, though his readiness to employ cliches of female neediness and dependence cast doubt on his claims: ". . . the Jewish poetess Mathilde Blind, from about 1867 onwards, openly 'threw herself at his head,' and gave him every opportunity to propose marriage to her. She complained, in my presence, of his insensibility: 'he comes to tea with me, and does not seem to notice, and he recites poetry, and goes away!' she said" (Qtd. in *The Swinburne Letters* 6: 243).

14. Garnett, who (along with Arthur Symons) became Blind's literary executor, also helped her manage her small savings, even paying her landlady when she was out of town, as he reports in a 27 January 1876 letter (MS Correspondence and Papers, Add. Ms. 61928). Throughout her life Garnett used his professional contacts to help Blind publish her work.

15. *Dark Blue* 2 (February 1872): iii-v. The title also doubtless appealed because of its classical resonance. The Greek Muses too had always been associated with water, and Hesiod writes of them

singing "by the dark blue water / of the spring."
See Hesiod, *Theogony* 2.3-4.

16. Like Feuerbach and Strauss, Blind (as well as her mother and stepfather) viewed Christianity as historically determined myth—potent and profoundly influential, but not necessarily superior to other world religions, or even to pagan belief systems. At the same time, as German expatriates and humanists they were eager to emphasize the ways in which all of northern Europe was united by certain key mythologies. Karl Blind published several essays on Teutonic mythology that trace connections among Greek, Vedic, and Eddaic beliefs; see especially "Freia-Holda, the Teutonic Goddess of Love," "Discovery of Odinic Songs in Shetland," and "Wagner's 'Nibelung' and the Siegfried Tale."

17. The poem was revised and republished in *Dramas in Miniature* (1891), but I quote from the original version. Although the revised version incorporates several wording improvements, the original retains more of the "noble and nude and antique" quality of the ballad tradition Blind is appropriating.

18. The German word "willi" is derived from the Slovakian word "víly," denoting the ghosts of young women who died on their wedding days. The word "villi" first appeared in Hungarian in 1821 (Benko). Blind likely encountered the "villi" legend in the German collection *Magyarische Sagen und Märchen*, written by the Hungarian aristocrat and amateur ethnographer János József Mailáth (1786-1855) and published in Germany in 1825. A second, revised and expanded edition titled *Magyarische sagen, mährchen und erzählungen* appeared in 1837. Both editions contain a story titled "Vilik-tánca," Mailáth's version of the villi legend. Although this legend became quite popular in Hungary (the first edition of Mailáth's collection was translated into Hungarian by Ferenc Kazinczy and published in 1864), and appears in many Hungarian poems in the first half of the century, the legend itself is Slovakian in origin. Because of Mailáth's collection, Blind was one of many writers—including Hungarian writers—who mistakenly located the origins of the legend in Hungary. I wish to thank Tamás Bényei, professor of English and American Studies at the University of Debrecen, Hungary, for his help in establishing these details.

19. Swinburne's imagery in this essay suggests that the production and consumption of "adult art" is strictly man's work: "It would seem as though to publish a book were equivalent to thrusting it with violence into the hands of every mother and nurse in the kingdom as fit and necessary food for fe-

male infancy. . . . No one wishes to force men's food down the throats of babes and sucklings." He warns against allowing "the domestic circle . . . to be for all men and writers the outer limit and extreme horizon of their world of work." If a purely masculine space is preserved, artistic castration can be prevented and tumescence restored: "Then all accepted work will be noble and chaste in the wider masculine sense, not truncated and curtailed, but outspoken and full-grown" (24, 29, 33). For a full discussion of Swinburne's response to criticisms of *Poems and Ballads,* see Pease.

20. Blind greatly admired certain of Christina Rossetti's poems, especially her ballads and children's verses. In a 29 February 1872 diary entry, William Michael Rossetti wrote that "Mathilde Blind is a very intense admirer of Christina's *Sing-Song;* had written a notice of it, which she offered to the *Academy,* but Appleton seemed to think it too fervently expressed, and Colvin wrote an article instead" (*The Diary of W. M. Rossetti, 1870-1873* 170).

21. For a reading of "Carmilla" as a story of lesbian desire, see Signorotti. Swinburne discusses his struggle to find a publisher for "The End of the Month" in two letters to Thomas Purnell (*The Swinburne Letters* 2: 124, 128).

22. Dante Gabriel Rossetti wrote "Down Stream" in the summer of 1871 and sent a copy to the painter William Bell Scott in July under the title "The River's Record." He told Scott, "it's rather out of my usual way, rude aiming at the sort of popular view that Tennyson perhaps alone succeeds in taking." On 10 September 1871, he wrote to his brother William to say the poem was to be published in *The Dark Blue,* with illustrations by Ford Madox Brown: "I'm Dark-Blued at last, owing to Brown, who was asked to illustrate something of mine for them if I would contribute. It's a little sort of ballad I wrote here—to appear in October." On 5 October, he wrote to Ford Madox Brown praising Brown on the quality of his illustrations, but expressing some concern that the first illustration makes the lovers look like "rustics," whereas "I *meant* my unheroic hero for an Oxford swell." He also comments on the sexual suggestiveness of the first illustration: "By the bye you have certainly not minced the demonstrative matter—but would there perhaps be a slight matter of overbalancing?" (*Letters of Dante Gabriel Rossetti* 958, 1013, 1016).

23. "Nocturne" appeared in the March 1872 issue of *The Dark Blue* (25-26). This is the only poem published in the journal that was not reprinted in either *Selections from the Poetry of Mathilde Blind* or *The Poetical Works of Mathilde Blind.*

24. For Madox-Brown's attempts to win D. G. Rossetti's support for Blind's poetry, see Angeli (49-52). Swinburne praised Blind's Shelley criticism but refrained from commenting publicly on her poetry (*The Swinburne Letters,* 2: 116, 6: 267).

25. As her reviews indicate, Blind upheld strict standards of sonnet form. In her review of *The Poetical Works of Frances Anne Kemble,* she writes that Kemble's sonnets can only be called sonnets "by courtesy," adding that they "are often of exceeding beauty in spite of curious anomalies of structure, the poetess serenely ignoring the primary law of the sonnet, and invariably running the octave into the sestet without break or halt anywhere either in the thought or rhyme" (50).

26. Blind is represented in the collection by "Time's Shadow" (237) and "The Dead" (238), the latter originally published in the 1 April 1881 issue of *The Athenaeum* (459). In an 11 February 1882 letter to Blind, Richard Garnett had high praise for "The Dead": "I have got Mr. Hall Caine's book. I sincerely think that the sonnet of yours from the *Athenaeum* is the finest thing in it from any of the modern poets" (MS Correspondence and Papers, Add. Ms. 61928). Blind's penultimate collection of poetry, the 1893 *Songs and Sonnets,* gathered most of her sonnets in a single volume.

27. She originally tried to place it elsewhere, as Richard Garnett's 31 August 1871 letter makes clear: "I am very sorry that your story is not to be in *Fraser.* I have not seen it, you know, but as you have established yourself so well in the *Dark Blue* I should think you could hardly do wrong in sending it there" (MS Correspondence and Papers, Add. Ms. 61928).

28. Garnett encouraged Blind in her fiction-writing efforts, inquiring in his 17 October letter about an additional story she had composed around the same time: "you say nothing about your second story. I hope you are going to: for this, I think, is the most promising field pecuniarily, and your genius will appear to as great advantage as in any other." The "second story" Garnett mentions was a fairy tale which Garnett tried unsuccessfully to help Blind publish. Garnett reports in a 21 February 1870 letter that he has received a note from *Macmillan* editor George Grove declining the story, "as I expected he would." He then counsels Blind to approach J. C. MacDonald, manager of the London *Times,* "and if you succeed with him this disappointment will prove to have been a blessing in disguise." He continues: "I entreat you not to be discouraged at this disappointment, long since foreseen and already provided for. Your genius and perseverance *shall* triumph over the perversity of editors, and you will then have the sat-

isfaction of knowing that they can triumph over anything." Garnett continued to be a champion of Blind's fiction; when her novel *Tarantella* was accepted by T. Fisher Unwin, he read the proofs and personally forwarded them to Unwin. In a 17 September 1884 letter to Blind, he expressed himself "delighted with the book," adding that he had great expectations for its reception: "I shall be disappointed if the book does not attract much attention" (MS Correspondence and Papers, Add. Ms. 61929).

29. Many of the details in this story are based on the period from 1858-59 when Blind was staying with her mother's relatives in Zurich, especially her solitary walking tours in the Swiss Alps. Compare this description to the one found in the fragmentary autobiography Blind wrote nearly twenty years after composing "A Month at the Achensee": "The Alps, aglow like mountains of roses round a heavenly Jerusalem, receding range beyond range into ever airier infinitudes of light, a vision like the last part of Beethoven's Ninth Symphony turned into visible form and beckoning something usually ignored . . . in some depth of being below our habitual consciousness—something latent within leaping up, irresistibly yearning to that glorified region as if they too belonged to each other from everlasting to everlasting—what a sensation, momentary and yet to be kept through life as one of its few treasures" (MS Correspondence and Papers, Add. Ms. 61930, fol. 1r-55r).

30. The *African Farm* comparison appears in a 17 September 1884 letter: "since *The Story of a South African Farm* (I suppose you have read this) it is the only novel I have read that can claim to rank as a work of genius." The concern about excess description is expressed in a 16 April 1886 letter (MS Correspondence and Papers, Add. Ms. 61929).

31. For more on the connections between Mathilde Blind and Eleanor Marx, see Avery.

32. Writing to Shelley Society secretary Thomas James Wise in early 1890, Blind's close friend William Michael Rossetti alludes to Blind's continuing financial straits, nothing that she "can't pay any such extra sums" to help erase the Society's debt (*Selected Letters of William Michael Rossetti* 541). In 1878, Blind approvingly quoted William Godwin's claim that it is "wrong, nay immoral, for a person to appropriate another, as happens in matrimony" ("Mary Wollstonecraft" 410).

33. Sarojini Naidu, who became a noted Indian poet, came to England in 1895 and studied at Girton College Cambridge. In a 19 January 1896 letter she describes meeting Mathilde Blind: "- a most

charming, genial, woman, with an intellectual brow and friendly eyes. You know she is among the most known of living writers just now. We had a delightful chat, and she made me recite some of my poems (she had heard of them) which she praised very much" (10). For more on Blind's association with New Woman writers, see Parejo.

34. MS letter, Princeton University Library, 26 February 1882.

35. Freund overspent his capital on the first half dozen issues of the journal to attract nationally known writers and print commissioned illustrations. As a result, Bradley and Houghton write, "payments to contributors had to be delayed even from the start" (180). The month after Blind's "The Song of the Willi" appeared in the August 1871 issue, Freund shifted publishers from Sampson Low to the unknown British and Colonial Publishing Co. and reduced contributors' rates. Complimenting Blind on the appearance of her story "A Month at the Achensee" in volume 4, Richard Garnett adds, "I hope that wretched Freund has paid you" (MS Correspondence and Papers, Add. Ms. 61927). Dante Gabriel Rossetti reports being paid thirty shillings for his poem "Down Stream"; since Blind was not a well-known writer at the time, it is likely she was paid less for each of her five contributions to the journal (*Letters of Dante Gabriel Rossetti* 996).

Works Cited

Angeli, Helen Rossetti. *Dante Gabriel Rossetti: His Friends and Enemies.* London: Hamish Hamilton, 1949.

Armstrong, Isobel. *Victorian Poetry: Poetry, Poetics, and Politics.* London; New York: Routledge, 1993.

Armstrong, Isobel, Joseph Bristow, and Cath Sharrock, eds. *Nineteenth-Century Women Poets: An Oxford Anthology.* Oxford: Oxford UP, 1996.

Armstrong, Isobel, and Virginia Blain, eds. *Women's Poetry, Late Romantic to Late Victorian: Gender and Genre 1830-1900.* Basingstoke and New York: Macmillan, 1999.

Avery, Simon. "'Tantalising Glimpses': The Intersecting Lives of Eleanor Marx and Mathilde Blind." *Eleanor Marx (1855-1898): Life, Work, Contacts.* Ed. John Stokes. (Aldershot: Ashgate, 2000). 173-187.

Bashkirtseff, Marie. *The Journal of Marie Bashkirtseff.* Trans. Mathilde Blind. 2 vols. London: Cassell, 1890.

Benko, Loránd. *A magyar nyelv történeti-etimológiai szótára,* 4 vols. (Budapest: Akadémiai Kiadó, 1967.

Blain, Virginia. *Victorian Women Poets: An Annotated Anthology.* Longman Annotated Texts. Harlow, England: Longman, 2001.

Blind, Karl. "Freia-Holda, the Teutonic Goddess of Love." *Cornhill* 25 (May 1872): 599-614.

———. "Discovery of Odinic Songs in Shetland." *The Nineteenth Century* 5 (June 1879): 1091-1112.

———. "Wagner's 'Nibelung' and the Siegfried Tale," *Cornhill* 45 (May 1882): 594-609.

———. "In Years of Storm and Stress, I: Political Prison Life Before 1848," *Cornhill* 78 (September 1898): 337-352.

Blind, Mathilde [Claude Lake]. *Poems.* London: Alfred W. Bennett, 1867.

———. "Shelley. A Review of *The Poetical Works of Percy Bysshe Shelley,* edited by William Michael Rossetti." *Westminster Review* 94 July (1870): 75-97.

———. Letter to Algernon Charles Swinburne. 2 August 1870. Harry Ransom Humanities Research Center, U of Texas, Austin.

———. Letter to Algernon Charles Swinburne. 7 September 1870. Algernon Charles Swinburne Papers, 1837-1909. U of Michigan Library Special Collections, Ann Arbor.

———. Review of *Lilja* ("The Lily") by Eystein Asgrimsson, trans. Eiríkr Magnússon. *The Dark Blue* 1 (June 1871): 524-28.

———. "Winter." *The Dark Blue* 2 (January 1872): 556.

———. "Nocturne." *The Dark Blue* 3 (March 1872): 25-26.

———. "A Month at the Achensee." *The Dark Blue* 4 (October 1872): 227-238.

———. Review of *Love is Enough,* by William Morris. *The Athenaeum* (23 November 1872): 657-658.

———. "Mary Wollstonecraft." *The New Quarterly Magazine* (July 1878): 390-412.

———. Letter to William Michael Rossetti. 26 February 1882. Gen. Mss. Misc C0140. Princeton U Library Department of Rare Books and Special Collections, Princeton.

———. "The Tale of Tristram and Iseult." *The National Review* 2 (February 1884): 826-37.

———. *Tarantella, A Romance.* 2 vols. London: T. F. Unwin, 1884.

———. Review of *The Poetical Works of Frances Anne Kemble. The Athenaeum* (12 January 1884): 50-51.

———. Review of *Mary Wollstonecraft Godwin,* by E. R. Pennell. *The Athenaeum* (11 July 1885): 41-2.

———. Introduction. *The Letters of Lord Byron (Selected).* Ed. Mathilde Blind. London: Walter Scott, 1887. v-xvi.

————. "Personal Recollections of Mazzini." *Fortnightly Review* 55 (May 1891): 702-12.

————. *Dramas in Miniature.* London: Chatto & Windus, 1891.

————. *A Selection From the Poems of Mathilde Blind.* Ed. Arthur Symons. London: T. Fisher Unwin, 1897.

————. *The Poetical Works of Mathilde Blind.* Ed. Arthur Symons. London: T. Fisher Unwin Paternoster Square, 1900.

————. Correspondence and Papers, 1866-1896. Add. ms. 61927-61930. British Lib., London.

Bloom, Abigail Burnham. *Nineteenth-Century British Women Writers: A Bio-Bibliographical Critical Sourcebook.* Westport: Greenwood Press, 2000.

Bradley, Christine Rose, and Walter E. Houghton. "The Dark Blue, 1871-1873: Introduction." *Wellesley Index to Periodicals 1824-1900.* Ed. Walter E. Houghton. Vol. 4. Toronto: U of Toronto P, 1987. 178-192.

Breen, Jennifer. *Victorian Women Poets 1830-1901: An Anthology.* London: J. M. Dent, 1994.

Bristow, Joseph. *Victorian Women Poets.* New York: St. Martin's Press, 1995.

Caine, T. Hall, ed. *Sonnets of Three Centuries: A Selection.* London: Elliot Stock, 1882.

Cosslett, ed. *Victorian Women Poets.* London and New York: Longman, 1996.

De Moor, Marysa. *Their Fair Share: Women, Power and Criticism in the Athenaeum, from Millicent Garrett Fawcett to Katharine Mansfield, 1870-1920.* Aldershot, Hampshire: Ashgate, 2000.

Diedrick, James. "'Mathilde Blind.'" *Victorian Women Poets.* Ed. William B. Thesing. The Dictionary of Literary Biography. Detroit: Gale, 1998. 28-39.

————. "Mathilde Blind." *Nineteenth-Century British Women Writers.* Ed. Abigail Burnham Bloom. Westport, Connecticut:: Greenwood, 2000. 41-44.

Dowden, Edward. "Modern Art Science and Art Criticism: An Historical Sketch." *The Dark Blue* (June 1871): 475-86).

Foucault, Michele. *The History of Sexuality, Volume I: An Introduction.* New York: Pantheon Books, 1978.

Furniss, Harry. *My Bohemian Days.* London: Hurst and Blakett, 1919.

Garnett, Richard. "Memoir." *The Poetical Works of Mathilde Blind,* pp. 2-43.

Groth, Helen. "Victorian Women Poets and Scientific Narratives." *Women's Poetry, Late Romantic to Late Victorian.* London: MacMillan, 1999, 325-351.

Hesiod, *Theogony,* Trans. Richard Lattimore. Ann Arbor: University of Michigan Press, 1959.

Hobsbawm, E. J. *The Age of Capital, 1848-1875.* London: Weidenfeld and Nicolson, 1975.

Hueffer, Ford Madox. *Ford Madox Brown: A Record of his Life and Work.* London: Longmans, Green, and Co., 1896.

Hughes, Linda. "A Female Aesthete at the Helm: *Sylvia's Journal* and 'Graham R. Tomson,' 1893-1894." *Victorian Periodicals Review* 29.2 (Summer 1996): 173-92.

————. "'Fair Hymen holdeth hid a world of woes': Myth and Marriage in Poems by Graham R. Tomson." *VP* 32 (1994): 97-120. Rpt. In *Victorian Women Poets: A Critical Reader,* pp. 162-185.

————. *New Woman Poets: An Anthology.* Lost Chords. London: The 1890s Society, 2001.

Hyder, Clyde *Swinburne: The Critical Heritage.* London: Routledge & Kegan Paul, 1970.

Leighton, Angela. *Victorian Women Poets: Writing Against the Heart.* Charlottesville: University Press of Virginia, 1992.

————. *Victorian Women Poets: A Critical Reader.* Oxford: Blackwell, 1996.

Leighton, Angela, and Margaret Reynolds, eds. *Victorian Women Poets: An Anthology.* Oxford, England: Blackwell, 1995.

Levy, Amy. *The Complete Novels and Selected Writings of Amy Levy, 1861-1889.* Ed. Melvyn New. Gainesville, Florida: University Press of Florida, 1993.

Linton, Eliza Lynn. "The Girl of the Period." *The Saturday Review* (14 March 1868): 339-40.

————. "Modern Man-Haters." *The Saturday Review* (29 April 1871): 528-29.

Mailáth, János Nepomuk József. *Magyarische Sagen und Märchen.* Brünn: T. G. Trafsler, 1825.

————. *Magyarische sagen, mährchen und erzählungen.* Stuttgart: J. G. Cotta, 1827.

Marx, Eleanor, and Edward Aveling. *The Woman Question.* London: Routledge/Thoemmes Press, 1886.

McCrimmon, Barbara. *Richard Garnett: The Scholar as Librarian.* Chicago: American Library Association, 1989.

McSweeney, Kerry. *Supreme Attachments: Studies in Victorian Love Poetry.* Aldershot, UK and Brookfield, VT: Ashgate, 1998.

Mermin, Dorothy. *Godiva's Ride: Women of Letters In England, 1830-1880.* Bloomington: Indiana Univ. Press, 1993.

Morris May. *William Morris, Artist, Writer, Socialist.* London: Basil Blackwell, 1936.

Naidu, Sarojini, and Makarand Paranjape. *Selected Letters 1890s to 1940s.* Ed. Makarand Paranjape. New Dehli: Kali for Women, 1996.

Nesbit, Edith. Review of *A Selection from the Poems of Mathilde Blind. The Athenaeum* (3 December 1898): 783-4.

Newman, Teresa, and Ray Watson. *Ford Madox Brown and the Pre-Raphaelite Circle.* London: Chatto & Windus, 1991.

Pease, Allison. "Questionable Figures: Swinburne's Poems and Ballads," *VP* 35 (1996): 43-56.

Prins, Yopie. *Victorian Sappho.* Princeton, N.J.: Princeton University Press, 1999.

Psomiades, Kathy. *Beauty's Body: Femininity and Representation in British Aestheticism.* Stanford: Stanford UP, 1997.

Rossetti, Dante Gabriel, *Letters of Dante Gabriel Rossetti.* 4 vols. Ed. Oswald Doughty and John Robert Wahl. Oxford: Oxford University Press, 1967.

Rossetti, William Michael. *The Diary of W. M. Rossetti, 1870-1873.* Ed. Odette Bornand. Oxford: Oxford University Press, 1977.

———. *Selected Letters of William Michael Rossetti.* Ed. Roger W. Peattie. University Park: Pennsylvania State University Press, 1990.

———. *William Michael Rossetti Diaries, 1886-1893.* Angeli-Dennis Collection A.1.1.5. U of British Columbia, Vancouver.

Sackville-West, Vita. "The Women Poets of the 'Seventies," in *The Eighteen-Seventies: Essays by Fellows of the Royal Society of Literature,* ed. Harley Granville-Barker (New York: MacMillan, 1929), pp. 112-134.

Saintsbury, George. *A History of English Criticism.* Edinburgh: Blackwood & Sons, 1949.

Sharp, Elizabeth. *Women's Voices: An Anthology of the Most Characteristic Poems by English, Scotch and Irish Women.* London: White and Allen, 1889.

Signorotti, Elizabeth. "Repossessing the Body: Transgressive Desire in 'Carmilla' and *Dracula,*" *Criticism* 38 (Fall 1996): 607-632.

Sims, George R. *My Life: Sixty Years' Recollections of Bohemian London.* London: Eveleigh Nash, 1917.

Spencer, Robin. "Whistler, Swinburne and Art for Art's Sake." *After the Pre-Raphaelites: Art and Aestheticism in Victorian Britain.* New Brunswick: Rutgers University Press, 1999, pp. 59-89.

Stedman, Edmund Clarence. *A Victorian Anthology 1847-1895.* Boston: Houghton Mifflin, 1895.

Swinburne, Algernon Charles. *Swinburne's Collected Poetical Works,* 2 vols. (London: William Heinemann, 1924.

———. *The Swinburne Letters.* Ed. Cecil Y. Lang. 6 vols. New Haven: Yale University Press, 1959-62.

———. *Swinburne Replies,* ed. Clyde Kenneth Hyder. Syracuse: Syracuse University Press, 1966.

Thomas, Donald. *Swinburne: The Poet in His World.* New York: Oxford University Press, 1979.

Thompson, E. P. *William Morris: Romantic to Revolutionary.* Stanford: Stanford University Press, 1976.

Vadillo, Ana. "New Woman Poets and the Culture of the Salon." *Women: A Cultural Review* 10.1 (1999): 22-34.

Susan Brown (essay date 2003)

SOURCE: Brown, Susan. "'A Still and Mute-Born Vision': Locating Mathilde Blind's Reproductive Poetics." In *Victorian Women Poets,* edited by Alison Chapman, pp. 123-44. Woodbridge, England: D. S. Brewer, 2003.

[*In the following essay, Brown studies Blind's poetic expression of political ideals in* The Heather on Fire.]

Mathilde Blind suffered a fate common to many Victorian women poets when a strong reputation in her lifetime evaporated after her death. Her somewhat oblique relationship to English intellectual tradition and national identity may partly explain this, but she was ill served by her literary executor Arthur Symons' dubious praise of her as one to whom 'all life was an emotion; and thought, to her, was of the same substance as feeling'. He proclaims 'She was a poet, almost in spite of herself.'[1] This familiar reduction of poetic achievement to a spontaneous effusion of emotion sits particularly oddly with Blind's work, which her contemporaries praised for boldness, mastery, and artistry.[2] She was ambitiously innovative in genres ranging from the ostensibly feminine lyric to the scientific epic. This essay explores one facet of her achievement by considering the poetics Blind evolved for her political poetry, particularly *The Heather on Fire: A Tale of the Highland Clearances.*

Blind was primed to write political poetry. Born in Germany in 1841, she moved to England with her mother and her step-father, Karl Blind, who eventually took political refuge in England after leading an uprising during the 1848-49 insurrections in Baden.[3] Blind's early poetry attests to a strong transnational commitment to nineteenth-century democratic movements. Her first volume, published as 'Claude Lake' in 1867,[4] is dedicated to her intellectual mentor, Italian nationalist Joseph (Guiseppe) Mazzini. Mazzini advised her on her studies and, she recollected, helped with his 'essentially spiritual doctrine to bridge over' the void of despair resulting from her consciousness of 'the preponderance of evil and sorrow, the poor pittance of happiness doled out to the individual'.[5]

The opening poem, **'The Torrent',** one of a pair of 'Poems to J. M.', introduces some characteristics of Blind's verse: bold diction, vivid natural imagery, conceptual ambition, wide-ranging allusion, and unusual yet effective verbal patterns. An initial waterfall image is offered as a handy 'material symbol' (p. 10) for Mazzini, giving way to other liquid imagery:

> Thou hero! for through prejudice's walls,
>   That lock up earth against the quick'ning floods,
> And 'gainst the fresh regenerating falls
>   Of young ideas, that in sprouting mood
> Seethe like new wine, stirred by the grape's hot blood,
>   In the old bottles; thou, oh, brave and bold!
> Didst force thy way.
>
> (p. 10)

Elizabeth Barrett Browning, a major influence on Blind, had employed the image of new wine cracking old wine skins in advocating new poetic forms in *Aurora Leigh*.[6] Blind's version fuses artistic preoccupations to political endeavour as represented both by Mazzini and by her own poetic enterprise, since the poem concludes: 'I will heroic deeds, prophetic words, proclaim' (p. 13). With unflinching self-assertion she aligns herself with the male political revolutionary whom her dedication characterises as a 'Prophet, Martyr and Hero' (prelims). This constitutes a significant proclamation of agency by the female poet, albeit muted by the pseudonymous mode of publication. Blind perceived Mazzini as deeply invested in gender differentiation, recalling his criticism of her scepticism[7] and his dismay that 'women, even women, who should be all compact of faith and devotion, are beginning to question and to analyse!'[8] Yet her poem subtly feminises him by yoking him to fluid images associated with reproductive processes—quickening, regeneration, fermentation—and the fruitful if apparently destructive liberation of the earth from the trammels of prejudice.[9]

Reproductive imagery recurs elsewhere in the volume with positive connotations. **'Invocation, June 1866'** invites the 'Spirit of the time! / Pregnant with the future' to 'Breathe thro' me in music' as the speaker applauds resistance in Venice, Rome, Poland, and Germany to 'imperial chains' and 'tyranny' (pp. 79-80). **'Ode To a Child'** argues that genius receives the greatest gift of nature: participation in 'creation', the highest of activities. Human reproduction represents a kind of poetic fulcrum for Blind, balanced between the present and a fragile and uncertain set of possibilities, which the poet strives to discern and articulate:

> At times, perchance, I seem to see
> The hid existence of far off events,
> Trailing their slumb'rous shadows silently.
> For in the dusky deeps
> Of thy large eyes
> Sometime the veilèd outline of a still
> And mute-born vision sleeps
> As in the hollows of a hill,
> With dim and darksome rents
> The dreamful shadow of the morning lies,
> And softly, slowly, ever down doth roll,
> Till lost in mystic deeps it flees our watchful eyes.
>
> (p. 84)

This prophet discerns, dimly and fleetingly in the eyes of an existing child, a kind of proto-embryo, an obscure possibility for the future in a very tenuous form: that of a sleeping, inarticulate 'vision', an object of the gaze discernible only in a sketchy outline. Perception here is as troubled as the syntax. Even as it asserts that the vision is merely sleeping, the passage suggests through the enjambment which places 'still' prominently at the end of the line, that it may be still-born as well as mute. The poet's role is the more critical, since her glimpse of this evanescent possibility may be all that survives. Reproductive risk is bound up with the difficulty of attaining and sustaining poetic inspiration, while the melding of vision and voice is perhaps an ironic reflection on her own name.

Blind's first collection thus conveys the difficulties of the kind of politically-engaged poetry she desires to produce, a prophetic aesthetic addressing a fervently anticipated but uncertain futurity. Because she was not a Christian who could read in history the gradual unfolding of God's plan but was instead susceptible to the bleak perspective that 'we are ephemeral creatures here to-day and gone to-morrow, that the life in us is as the flame of a candle which burns down to the socket and goes out',[10] she was forced to contemplate the possibility that the changes she envisioned might not come to pass.

In 1886 Mathilde Blind published *The Heather on Fire: A Tale of the Highland Clearances*.[11] Blind herself had no connection to Scotland before visiting there, which she did first in 1873 when she was in her early thirties, when she was deeply impressed by the grandeur of the landscape, particularly in the Hebrides, and the history of the people.[12] And it was a topical subject. The forcible eviction of tenant farmers from their lands in the highlands and islands of Scotland had begun in the late eighteenth century as a result of factors including the suppression of the clans and the desire to increase the profitability of estates. Following the decade of famine which began in 1846, there had been a new wave of Clearances. A growth in radical journalism and cultural nationalism, continued economic strain in crofting regions, and awareness of the militant land struggles in Ireland culminated in 1881 in agitation that marked the beginning of the 'Crofters' War'. A Royal Commission was established to investigate crofters' grievances. Its failure to devise a solution provoked renewed agitation and civil disobedience by crofters and their urban allies, which met with military intervention on the Isle of Skye late in 1884. Legislation was finally passed in 1886, following the election to Parliament of five Crofters MPs in the wake of the Third Reform Bill.[13] Blind's poem was published just as the Crofters' Holdings (Scotland) Act, modelled on the 1881 Irish Land Act, received royal assent.[14]

The diversity of form and address in *The Heather on Fire* is immediately striking. The framing materials engage directly with contemporary political controversy. They consist of a dedication to Captain Cameron, 'Whose glory it is to have thrown up his place rather than proceed in command of the steamer "Lochiel", which was to convey the police expedition against the Skye crofters in the winter of 1884', a preface which claims a factual basis for the 'atrocities' (p. 1) the poem describes, and notes which excerpt memoirs, analyses, and condemnations of the Clearances.[15] While footnotes to poems were hardly unknown in the context of historical or topical poetry, what is noteworthy here is a sharp disjunction in tone and style (most striking at the beginning) between the poem proper and its apparatus. The poem seems a formally and historically distanced historical artifact telling a universalised or at least decontextualised story of human experience.

On a new page, following a woodblock-style floral illustration that signals a break in the text, are the poem's title and a heading also with decorated capital, 'Duan First'. 'Duan', from Gaelic, was first used in English in 1765 by James MacPherson to designate parts of an epic poem in his alleged translation of the legendary Scots bard Ossian.[16] It aligns Blind's work at once with a highly romanticised and primitivist (if partly manufactured) tradition of poetic discourse. The poem's opening view of a solitary figure reinforces this sense:

> High on a granite boulder, huge in girth,
> Primæval waif that owned a different birth
> From all the rocks on that wild coast, alone,
> Like some grey heron on as grey a stone,
> And full as motionless, there stood a maid,
> Whose sun-browned hand her seaward eyes did shade
> Flinching, as now the sun's auroral motion
> Twinkled in milky ways on the grey heaving ocean.
>
>   (I.i, p. 5)

The imagery, coupled with the ambiguity in the apposition of the initial descriptive phrases, creates a link between the female figure, nature, and a fecundity suggested by the girth of the rock and the heaving sea.

Allusions to the primeval, to the immensely slow processes of geological creation that have produced the landscape, and to the vast operations of the cosmos, along with the extended description, relaxed pace of the metre, and length of the vowels in the rhymes, all contribute to the impression of universality and timelessness, rather than specificity and topicality. The sense of the poem as an archaic account of a timeless people is sustained as the reader proceeds. Although some characters have names, the main figures, Michael and Mary, feel more iconic than individual, and Mary is compared to the Virgin mother. We learn that Rory, the family patriarch, served in the Napoleonic Wars, but only by way of explanation of his infirmity. Familial and social relations, narrowly defined, are the focus of the poem until into the third Duan of four.

Yet *The Heather on Fire* is surrounded by historical precision. The preface recounts how Blind heard from a Scottish woman on a visit to Arran in the summer of 1884 an account of the expulsion of the Glen Sannox people in 1832 by the Duke of Hamilton. The notes detail actual incidents in relation to particular stanzas, although the notes themselves are not signalled in the body of the poem. The poetry, in other words, seems to strive exclusively for what Blind terms the 'thrilling pathos' of the old woman's account, the 'idyll' of her evocation of the lives of the crofters prior to the Clearances (p. 3). An emerging sense of the poem as an elegy for what was, by the time of its publication, understood by many to be the vanishing culture of a people succumbing to the inevitable march of civilization, is apparently confirmed by extended descriptions of nature, the rhythm of Highland life, and of exotic cultural practices such as ceilidhs. In other words, while the preface roundly condemns the way the crofters were 'ruthlessly expelled [from] their native land to make way for sporting grounds rented by merchant princes and American millionaires' (p. 3), economic analysis and political critique intially seem to have been expelled from the body of the poem, which instead offers a generalised Scottish landscape inhabited by representative Crofters.

What is at stake in the negotiation in *The Heather on Fire* between two clusters of associations, the universal, primitive, natural and domestic or familial, on the one hand, and the historically specific, civilised, cultural, and political on the other? The tension between them, I will argue, is closely connected to the poem's linguistic and narrative preoccupation, evident in its opening stanzas, with reproduction, and together they are crucial to Blind's attempt to articulate her vision of the political.

Creation in nature and reproduction in human society are paralleled from the outset of the poem, as its opening illustrates. The narrative is simple: Mary, the maid of the rock, has been affianced for nine years to Michael, a crofter and fisher. The first Duan portrays their meeting upon his return from sea, and their love of the land as they walk to the cottage which shelters his parents. This section concludes with Mary's return to her job—her waged labour an early sign that this is not a nostalgic pastoral idyl—as head of the dairy of 'The lordly mansion of the lord of all that land' (I.xlv, p. 27). Here the simple stanza scheme of four sets of rhyming couplets, which Blind has varied admirably in the preceeding stanzas, becomes inexorably repetitive as she details his property—the glens, pastures, hills, forests, and the birds, wildlife, and fish in stream—culminating in the fact that the lord effectively owns not just the land but the the labour of his tenants:

> For him the hind's interminable toil:
> For him he ploughed and sowed and broke the soil,
> For him the golden harvests would he reap,
> For him would tend the flocks of woolly sheep,
>
> For him would thin the iron-hearted woods,
> For him track deer in snow-blocked solitudes;
> For him the back was bent, and hard the hand,
> For was he not his lord, and lord of all that land?
>
> (I.xlvii, p. 28)

This invocation of greed and a one-way relationship between landlord and tenant follows oppressively, at the conclusion of the first Duan, on the catalogue of nature's bounty and variety.

The second Duan describes in twenty-four stanzas the couple's wedding day and the ceilidh that follows it. There are strong echoes of the egalitarian union of lovers at the conclusion of *Aurora Leigh* (9: 910ff.) in Blind's portrait of Mary's expectations as a bride:

> Ah! dear to her that narrow, grey-thatched home,
> Where she would bide through all the years to come;
> Round which her hopes and memories would entwine
> With fondness, as the tendrilled eglantine
> Clings round a cottage porch; where work and love,
> Like the twin orbs that share the heavens above,
> Would round their lives, and make the days and nights
> Glad with the steady flame of those best household
>   lights.
>
> (II.vi, p. 32)

The first half of the poem, then, represents in pastoral mode the lives of paragons of rural thrift, virtue, and domestic affection; in the second half, political forces intrude to destroy them.

Duan Third takes up the story in the stormy autumn nine years later (this second use of the number nine reinforcing the emphasis on gestation), with a pregnant Mary nursing a sick child, one of four, while Michael is again away fishing. Her daily occupations are interrupted by frantic neighbours announcing fire in the glen from thatched cottages kindled by the agent of the absentee lord. This duan depicts the family precipitously forced from their home, so that Michael's bedridden mother is burning in her bed by the time she is removed, only to die, and the sick child expires that night as they sleep in the open air. The question of a benign providence is raised, in language that parodies that of Biblical parable, as the passivity of these brave stalwarts of the British empire is explained:

> They fly and turn not on the hireling band,
> That unresisting drives them from their land.
> Dowered with the lion's strength, like lambs they go,
> For saith the preacher: 'God will have it so.'
>
> (III.lxiii, p. 73)

The fourth and final Duan describes the horrific aftermath of the firing: the family's refuge in a ruined keep on the cliffs, during a furious storm in which Mary labours, births, and then expires shortly after her newborn; their discovery by the landlord's men; the truncated funeral at which the eldest child dies; the hounding of the crofters to boats. Rory is so overcome by his wife's horrific fate that 'like a village Lear / His eyes rolled maddening' (III.xlvi, p. 65); in his delirium he is (echoing another Shakespearean tragedy) taken for a ghost by Michael in the gale outside the ruined castle. Rory evades the emigration vessel, only to witness the ship containing the remnants of his family wrecked on rocks in the Sound of Sleat. The poem follows this literal miscarriage of the vessel with a final image of death as a form of nurturing and, ironically, of safety from further pain of separation from their beloved land:

> Safe in the deep,
> With their own seas to rock their hearts to sleep,
> The crofters lay: but faithful Rory gave
> His body to the land that had begrudged a grave.
>
> (IV.xlviii; p. 97)

The Heather on Fire is permeated by images of reproduction and miscarriage, nurturing and predation. It thus employs the trope, by then standard in British poetry of famine and protest, of depicting social ills through the sufferings of pregnant or lactating women, helpless children, and the aged or infirm. Speranza's 'The Famine Year', for example, answers the question, 'Pale mothers, wherefore weeping?' with 'Would to God that we were dead— / Our children swoon before us, and we cannot give them bread.'[17] Blind's stress on motherhood exceeds the function of provoking pity and outrage, however. In many respects, it belongs to the tradition in British women's political poetry of articulating a poetic voice out of an emphasis on the generative female body.[18] Mothering permeates Eliza Ogilvy's early work, including *A Book of Highland Minstrelsy* (1846),[19] and informs her call in *Poems of Ten Years* (1854) for a newly politicised poetics. Elizabeth Barrett Browning had incorporated her own reproductive body into the political commentary of *Casa Guidi Windows* (1851), and used the figure of Anita Garibaldi to establish a poetics, both perilous and inspiring, of female political engagement in the maternal body. Yet, indebted as she may be to such predecessors, Blind's emphasis on reproductive processes is more tightly interwoven with contemporary political debate.

As its opening's reference to geological process suggests, the poem stages a dialogue between the human and natural worlds in a decidedly scientific context. Blind's studies of geology had led her at an early age to atheism, for which she was expelled from school,[20] and her framework for understanding the Clearances was decidedly materialist. Blind noted elsewhere that 'the poet's attitude toward, and interpretation of, Nature may be said to undergo continual modification in harmony with the development of religious and scientific thought'.[21] The ascendent theory in her day for explicating the course of human history was the theory of evolution, according to which the reproduction of a species produces random variations in organisms; the processes of competition which result in either survival or death ensure that, as a consequence of 'natural selection', only those variations adapted to their environments are preserved. The centrality of reproduction to both evolutionary theory and *The Heather on Fire* suggests that Blind exploits the former as an interpretive rubric for the Highland Clearances.

The night following Mary's expulsion from her home, her attention is focused on her sick infant held against her pregnant body:

> Mary's care
> Was centered on the child upon her knee,
> Who gasped, convulsed, in his last agony,
> Close to the burden of the life beneath
> Her heart—that battle-field of wrestling life and death.
>
> (III.liv, p. 69)

This is the struggle for survival in relation to environment at its baldest, but its dimensions are not merely physical. The battle-field is ambiguous: the body of the unborn child and perhaps also the mother's womb and her heart are caught up in the struggle. This suggests that the application of theories of nature to the complexities of human culture is hardly a straight-forward matter, and indeed Blind's project in *The Heather on Fire* hinges on the difficulty of that relationship. For as surely as she mocks the notion of the Clearances as the working out of a divinely ordained providence, she describes the events as a travesty rather than a fulfillment of evolutionary process.

Mary has acted according to the dictates of natural selection in choosing to marry and reproduce with a man well adapted to his natural environment. Both she and Michael are handsome, stately, fitted to their habitat and occupations. The vicious factor, whom she spurned as a lover, is by contrast 'A little limping man' (III.xxiv, p. 54). His disability reflects not only the penchant in Victorian literature to associate moral failing with physical deformity, but in the context of Darwinism suggests unfitness. However, he thrives on injustice, and, through him, the inverted social order punishes Mary for her choice, killing the offspring produced by her union with Michael (two of whom are named after their parents, stressing *re*production). The poem throughout draws on traditional Christian imagery, but reverses its values. The eviction of the crofters is represented as the transformation by human agency of paradise into hell; but the angel at the gates is a deformed factor with a burning brand and those burned in hell are innocents like Rory's wife, whose 'fall' cannot be attributed to moral or spiritual failing.

The relationship between poetic text and paratexts strengthens as the narrative develops. The first note attaches to a point in the second Duan which offers a new degree of specificity, albeit one temporally and spatially displaced. Rory describes at length his service as a member of the famed Forty-Second Highland Regiment in Spain during the Napoleonic wars. Blind's note, to Louis Lafond's 1885 *Une crise sociale en Écosse: les Highlands et la question des crofters,* underscores the contribution of Highland men to the national project: 'La population des Crofters, des Highlands et des Iles . . . est une pépinière de bon travailleurs et de bons citoyens pour tout l'empire' (p. 99).[22] Lafond's observation of the suitability of the Gaels for supplying the army and navy seems hardly original enough to offset the potentially alienating effect of citing a foreign expert in a foreign tongue, but the lengthy passage Blind quotes makes explicit her naturalistic perspective, discussing people in terms of habitat and arguing for the outlying regions of Scotland as an ideal nursery ('pépinière') for the workers required to staff the British empire.

The interplay between the particular and the universal in Blind's text as a whole thus starts to come into focus: nineteenth-century naturalistic inquiry looked to the specifics of organisms and their life cycles to reveal larger patterns, clues to universal processes or mechanisms. It moved human reproduction and its consequences—and hence mothering—to the centre of history. The fate of the empire, for Blind, is linked not analogously but metonymically, through a chain of natural causes, to the bodies of women, whose environments and whose labour are crucial to the successful maintenance of culture.

The patterns evident in this human nursery are thus by no means purely natural ones, for the poem represents through the fate of one kinship structure the decisive human destruction of an entire human habitat, a single crofting community, which represents the entire crofting community of Scotland. Part of what is at work here is a realist metonymy emerging from Blind's belief in its political efficacy. In her 1883 monograph *George Eliot,* which defends the extent to which Eliot drew on science and attests to Blind's ease with naturalist, positivist, and other intellectual currents that were so formative for the great prose poet of the 'evolution of society', Blind argued that the novelist had demonstrated the extent to which 'a truthful adherence to nature' placed the artist 'in the very vanguard of social and political reforms; as in familiarising the imagination with the real condition of the people, he [*sic*] did much towards creating that sympathy with their wants, their trials, and their sufferings, which would eventually effect external changes in harmony with this better understanding' (pp. 88, 107). The poet cum scientist can describe a selective sample of organisms that provide insight into general processes, at the same time that the poet cum realist can strive for reform through poetry's established mode of affect by offering individualised objects of sympathy or identification.

Relating the individual to the general is here at least as political as it is natural, which Rory's case underscores as the poem dwells on the irony of the soldier's relation to the state. Personally, Michael's father has suffered a cruel fate:

> His father had come home one winter time
> From some fierce battle waged on fields of Spain,
> Where he and fellows like him helped to gain
> The day for England's king—alas! for him
> That gain was loss indeed:—crippled in life and limb.
>
> (I.xxx, p. 20)

But far from being personal and arbitrary, this is part of a much larger pattern of loss and gain wherein the Highlands gave up thousands of men to fight England's wars and consolidate empire, only to be later repaid by being legally ousted from their homes. Rory boasts: 'Ye'll all have heard / Tell on the Forty-Second? Show us the glen / In Highland or in Island sent not its bonny men!' (II.xvii, p. 37) Just as the opening of the poem indicated that the singular boulder was produced and then (dis-)placed in the landscape by vast geological processes, so too allusion to Britain's wars reveals the population in an apparently isolated and idyllic corner of the world as subject to global politics. This point is intertwined with the climax of the poem's pathos. In the narrative's most startling disjunction, the description of Mary's parturition in the midst of a gale, barely sheltered by the ruined keep, is abruptly checked by Rory, who stumbles in too disoriented to recognise his

own son or realise what is taking place. He embarks on a monologue which tries to reconcile his sense of national identity with what is happening to him:

> So they're burning in the glen,
> But I, ye ken, I'm of the Forty-Secon'!
> I've served my country well as it has me, I'se reckon.'
>
> And therewith burst into a husky song
> Of doughty Highland deeds, and, crazed with wrong,
> Dozed off, nor knew how busy death was there,
> Nor that as his new grandchild felt the air
> And edge of the inhospitable night,
> It shuddered back from life's brink in affright,
> Dragging its mother after.
>
> (IV.xvii-xviii, pp. 82-3)

The jarring interruption of the narrative sequence by Rory's ramblings challenges the reader to reflect on the political ironies at work in the Clearance. Unable in the face of such ideological contradiction to sustain a sense of identity forged in patriotic service, he goes mad.

As the poem mounts towards this twinned physical and ideological crisis, the gulf between poetic centre and surrounding apparatus narrows. The factor echoes his master's self-justifying Malthusian theories[23] when he condemns the crofters as

> Cumbering the ill-used soil they hack and scratch,
> And call it tillage! Silly hens that'd hatch
> Their addled eggs, whether they will or no.
>
> (III.xxv, p. 54)

The poem soon also provides economic analysis: 'But in these latter days men's lives are cheap, / And hardworked Highlanders pay worse than lowland sheep' (III.xxvii, p. 55). The muted dialogue between notes and poetic text thus picks up, both in the poetic language and as the notes become more dense.

Blind's preface addresses the issue of the relationship between the text and historical record briefly but directly:

> I seem to hear many a reader ask whether such atrocities as are described in 'The Heather on Fire' have indeed been committed within the memory of this generation. Let him be assured that this is no fancy picture; that, on the contrary, the author's aim has been to soften some of the worst features of the heart-rending scenes which were of such frequent occurrence during the Highland Clearances. Many of them are too revolting for the purposes of art; for the ferocity shown by some of the factors and ground-officers employed by the landlords in evicting their inoffensive tenantry, can only be matched by the brutal excesses of victorious troops on a foreign soil.
>
> (p. 1)

She alludes only cursorily to contemporary debates, leaving the notes to answer any doubts about historical accuracy. Excerpted entirely from publications about the Clearances, these cite some of the most prominent voices in the fierce debate of the 1880s, ranging from the Napier Commission's 1884 report,[24] to Edinburgh classics professor John Stuart Blackie's *The Scottish Highlanders and the Land Laws: An Historico-Economical Enquiry,*[25] to the eye-witness accounts of Donald Macleod.[26] Blind's support for the details of her narrative includes Macleod's recollection of one expulsion:

> Some old men took to the woods and the rocks, wandering about in a state approaching to or of absolute insanity; and several of them in this situation lived only a few days. Pregnant women were taken in premature labour, and several children did not long survive. . . . I was present at the pulling down and burning of the house of William Chisholme, Badinloskin, in which was lying his wife's mother, an old bedridden woman of nearly one hundred years of age, none of the family being present. . . . Fire was set to the house, and the blankets in which she was carried out were in flames before she could be got out. She was placed in a little shed, and it was with great difficulty they were prevented from firing it also. Within five days she was a corpse.

(p. 110)

As the material from Lafond indicates, however, the eighteen pages of notes balance historical testimony with commentary. One of the lengthiest excerpts is from *Land Nationalisation* by Alfred Russel Wallace, best known now as the man who hurried Darwin into publication of the theory of evolution.[27] A vocal exponent of evolution, Wallace also published influentially on many other issues. He in fact stumbled on the theory of natural selection while reassessing Malthus' work on population, and unlike Darwin he eagerly applied his conclusions as a naturalist to social and religious questions.[28]

As I have already suggested, the insistent imagery of reproduction in *The Heather on Fire* emerges from an evolutionary framework which places the Clearances in the context of imperceptibly slow but irresistible natural processes within which each organism contributes to change. This framework raises questions not only about the relationship between the natural and the social, but also about causality and the possibilities for human agency in political situations such as those the poem laments. Blind's reference to Wallace reveals her poetic strategy as intimately connected to debate over Scottish land reform.

Harriet Beecher Stowe's 1854 defence of the Sutherland landlords who hosted her Highland visit represents their 'Improvements' as 'an almost sublime instance of the benevolent employment of superior wealth and power in shortening the struggles of advancing civilisation'.[29] In the 1880s the Duke of Argyll similarly claimed that the 'old Celtic customs' of land tenure and

use must give way in favour of the settled laws of 'advancing civilisation' but his position as an authority on evolution gave the pronouncement additional force.[30] The debate over land reform in Scotland in fact emerged as one among committed Darwinists. Social Darwinists such as Argyll argued that private property had a natural basis;[31] with Herbert Spencer he opposed government interference to protect weaker, that is, less well adapted, members or groups of society against the operations of a natural social order which could progress solely through the survival of the 'fittest' individuals or races.[32] Wallace, however, considered evolution insufficient to explain people's moral capacities and 'flatly denied that we should allow it to operate in social issues now that man was able . . . to modify his environment, both organic and inorganic, and thus control the forces of nature'.[33] Influenced by Henry George, he revised the theory of value in political economy to place land and labour ahead of capital, becoming a socialist.[34]

Blind's own view emerges from her lecture, published a few months after *The Heather on Fire,* on **'Shelley's View of Nature Contrasted With Darwin's'**. She criticises the lack of 'historic realism' in *Prometheus Bound,* lamenting that Shelley was 'debarred from casting into a poetic mould the modern scientific conception of evolution and the struggle for existence' (p. 18). Such realism, she argued, would depict humanity

> emerging from a semi-brutal, barbarous condition, and continually progressing to higher stages of moral and mental development. For the true conflict consists in man's struggle with the irresponsible forces of Nature, and the victory in his conquest over them, both as regards the subjection of his own lower animal instincts and in his continually growing power through knowledge of turning these elemental forces, that filled his savage progenitors with fear and terror, into the nimblest of servants.

(pp. 18-19)

Thus, although Blind writes as an atheist and Wallace as a spiritualist, they share the conviction that human evolution is as much social as natural, and involves a triumph over rather than adherence to the basic instincts that justify competition and violence in a Social Darwinist model. Three years after *The Heather on Fire,* Blind published another ambitious poem, *The Ascent of Man,* a series of lyrics representing the entire span of human history, from the first inklings of creation when, 'Struck out of dim fluctuant forces and shock of electrical vapour, / Repelled and attracted the atoms flashed mingling in union primeval', to contemporary society with its war, rape and pillage, noisy factories, starving infants, and 'woman's nameless martyrdom'.[35] Wallace contributed a laudatory preface to the second, posthumous, edition a decade later.[36]

In *The Heather on Fire,* although the female body is charged with literal human reproduction—'brooding care' (I.xiv, p. 12)—the imagery of reproduction and nurturing activities applies equally to men. Early on the 'old familiar sights of their own native glen' are as dear to the returning fishermen as 'is her first-born's earliest lisp / To a young mother' (I.v, p. 7). Michael kisses his old mother's face and hair 'As it might be a babe's, with tender care' (I.xxviii, p. 19), and the crofters are later compared to mothers who love best the offspring who give them the most trouble: 'So do these men, matched with wild wind and weather, / Cling to their tumbling burns, bleak moors, and mountain heather' (III.iii, p. 43). On the morning of the eviction, in an extended pastoral passage, both female and male children of the household engage in domestic activities or nurturing. After their expulsion, in their pitiful refuge in the ruined castle, Michael feeds them 'with a mother's tenderness' (IV.viii, p. 78).

Michael is one of the poem's 'patient and laborious men' (I.xix, p. 14), Highlanders who are valorised rather than feminised by repeated association with women's labour, with reproduction, and with nurturing. One of the key differences between Blind's pastoral and an Edenic one lies in her conception of labour. In a Christian context, labour is an undesirable effect of the fall, and women's postlapsarian labour and men's is sharply differentiated. Although her Highlanders by and large engage in a gendered division of labour, in keeping with historical record, Blind seems at pains to dispel the sense that such division is biologically ordained. Women are active partners in the economic activities of the isles, and Michael enjoys a loving equality with Mary, 'faithful partner of his arduous life: / Both toiling late and soon' (III.ii, p. 43). It is as much the waste of salutary labour as the unwarranted human suffering that defines the crime of the Clearances here. When Michael returns from sea to find 'Sore labour's fruits all wasted in a night' (III.lxii, p. 73), both the labour of their hands and the reproductive labour of their bodies have been destroyed.

The tragedy of ***The Heather on Fire*** is the extinction of a community which, although it contains hardship and conflict, and is vulnerable (and possibly culpable) in its patriotism, is a better foundation for the amelioration of society than the individualist, economically rapacious, and at times sadistic order of society represented by the landlord and his agents. ***The Ascent of Man*** lays out what is required for human redemption, when humanist Love,[37] the animating force embedded in evolutionary processes, begs:

> Oh, redeem me from my tiger rages,
> 　Reptile greed, and foul hyæna lust;
> With the hero's deeds, the thoughts of sages,
> 　Sow and fructify this passive dust;
> Drop in dew and healing love of woman
> 　On the bloodstained hands of hungry strife,

> Till there break from passion of the Human
> 　Morning-glory of transfigured life.

> (p. 109)

The sharing of labour, melding of gender roles, and evidence in the Highland men of a nurturing sensibility conventionally associated with women combine within Blind's conceptual framework to suggest that, far from being a primitive or degenerate race, the crofters are an advanced people capable of progressing beyond the slavery to base desires defined by society as masculine.

Poetry for Blind is a major means of transcending the human tendency towards competition and selfishness. ***The Ascent of Man*** characterises it as the highest of the representational arts, one whose creative powers exceed life itself:

> The poet, in whose shaping brain
> Life is created o'er again
> With loftier raptures, loftier pain;
> 　Whose mighty potencies of verse
> 　Move through the plastic Universe,
> And fashion to their strenuous will
> The world that is creating still.

> (p. 54)

It gives tongue to 'silent generations' (p. 54) and allows nations to communicate across time, although the use of the world 'still' here suggests the fragility of the envisioned possibilities intimated elsewhere in Blind's work.

Clearly the displaced, destroyed, and otherwise silenced generations of the Skye crofters motivate ***The Heather on Fire.*** But this poem is also haunted by gendered anxieties about agency and voice. At the centre of the poem is the failed attempt by a woman to intervene in history. After Mary's initial attempt to inspire the sympathy of the factor fails, and he orders her cottage burnt, she is momentarily frozen and 'dumb' (III.xxxviii, p. 61), struck mute. However, she regains presence and voice, resembling a 'warrior queen': 'Cowards!' she cried once more, 'thirst ye for children's blood?' (III.xxxix, p. 61). Her words barely pause the course of events:

> Her regal presence and her flashing eyes,
> Raised as in supplication to the skies,
> Awed even these surly men, who still delayed
> To shove her back, and make a sudden raid
> Upon her cottage;—brutal as they were,
> The motherhood that yearned through her despair
> Awed them a moment—but a moment more
> They'd hustled her aside and tramped towards the door.

> (III.xl, p. 62)

This fleeting moment of agency nevertheless leaves the building in flames, and if the grandmother is almost consumed by them, another creature actually perishes inside the cottage. This is a half-fledged lark rescued and nurtured by the now ailing child, after harvesters' scythes caused the mother to abandon her nest. The bird's fiery death not only suggests the futility of the child's intervention but also metonymically links the trampling of larks' nests by farmer's feet—in which activity the Highlanders are complicit—to the cruel events of the poem, suggesting that human activity may always occur at the cost of 'lower' organisms, of the disruption of mothering, and of the silencing of song. In **'On a Forsaken Lark's Nest'**, a poem published with *The Ascent of Man,* Blind returned to the same scenario, contemplating the 'heartful of song that now will never awaken':

> Poor, pathetic brown eggs! Oh, pulses that never will quicken!
> Music mute in the shell that hath been turned to a tomb!
> Many a sweet human singer, chilled and adversity-stricken,
> Withers benumbed in a world his joy might have helped to illume.

(p. 139)

The Ascent of Man itself contains a parallel image: man's soul 'finding rest nor refuge anywhere, / Seems doomed to be her unborn offspring's grave' (p. 50).

The only imaginative writer among Blind's extensive footnotes is Walter Scott, cited at the moment when the despairing Michael, realising he has no choice but to embark with his remaining children on the ill-fated ship, decides to do so like a man. Stripped of their population, Scott says, 'the Highlands may become the fairy-ground for romance and poetry, or the subject of experiment for the professors of speculation, political and economical' (p. 91). Either eventuality, he implies, is a mockery of pseudo-engagement in the wake of atrocity. Blind's poetic strategy in *The Heather on Fire* initially invokes the first possibility—the tradition of nostalgic lament for a doomed but noble and poetic[38] race—only to dispel it in a nuanced representation of the forces that have depopulated the Highlands. She employs an elevated poetic discourse often understood to convey the universality of the human life cycle and emotions, but interweaves with it other discourses which, with the paratexts invoking the debates over crofting, land reform, and national identity, serve to anchor the poem in a particular history and political analysis. These discourses include the political, the economic, the historical, and the scientific, but operate in the service of an innovative poetics, which, as Isobel Armstrong has argued, is still strongly invested in affect.[39]

Blind's poeticisation of the political seeks to arrive at the ineffable possibilities of the future through a careful account of the past that produced it, charging poetry with a delineation of the delicate historical processes that shape human culture through a dialogue of natural processes and social agency. It thus anticipates Patricia Yaeger's insistence that 'while history-making has its dangers, silence is more dangerous still'. Yaeger draws on Mary O'Brien's *The Politics of Reproduction* to argue that, notwithstanding problems with meta-narratives, feminism requires 'new reproductive narratives so that motherhood, birth, and the unspoken dramas of gestation and parturition will enter the real, will enter history, will be seen as important or "true"'.[40] Blind presents one such strategic narrative by invoking and interrogating the relationship between what Joan W. Scott singles out as two of the major sites of fantasy used to consolidate Western feminist identity: embodied political speech and motherhood.[41] The images of natural reproduction that Blind employs to perform this poetic work imbue apparently insignificant details of human life with the grandeur of cosmic creation, gesturing towards a new kind of historical epic. In using such images to authorise her political poetry, she builds on other writers before her. However, Blind's poetics in *The Heather on Fire* must be understood in relation to the terms in which the late Victorian struggle over land tenure in the Scottish Highlands was debated. What might appear an essentialist poetics founded on a transhistorical biological determinism can be understood as also, and at the same time, an astute literary response to the divergent applications in her time of the theory of evolution to human affairs. Far from anchoring traditional gender roles, Blind's poem attempts to articulate her 'still and mute-born vision' in an innovative poetic mode that challenges the terms in which the Victorians conceived the political: it places women's child-bearing bodies at the centre of history, but hinges the future on a common commitment to nurturing and a more equitable sharing of various forms of labour. Imbued with a sense of the latent power of women's political poetry but equally of its vulnerability in attempting to bring muted possibilities for the future into dialogue with the hostile conditions of the present, *The Heather on Fire* embodies a revisionary evolutionary poetics.

Notes

I would like to thank Ananda Pellerin, Robyn Read, and Laura Stenberg for research assistance, and Charles Davidson, Jennifer Schacker, and Janice Schroeder for helpful advice in connection with this essay.

1. 'Introduction', *A Selection from the Poems of Mathilde Blind,* Symons ed. (London, 1897), pp. v, vi; 'Preface', *The Poetical Works of Mathilde Blind* (London, 1900), p. ix.

2. 'Opinions of the Press', in Mathilde Blind, *The Ascent of Man* (London, 1889), pp. 1, 3.

3. Richard Garnett, 'Memoir', *The Poetical Works of Mathilde Blind* (London, 1900), p. 2.

4. Mathilde Blind as Claude Lake, *Poems* (London, 1867).

5. Mathilde Blind, 'Recollections of Mazzini', *Fortnightly Review* 3078 (May 1891), p. 703.

6. Elizabeth Barrett Browning, *Aurora Leigh,* ed. Margaret Reynolds (Athens, Ohio, 1992), 1: 998-1002, p. 202. Compare also her *Poems before Congress* (1860).

7. Her evocation of George Eliot's own youthful inquiry suggests that Blind revelled in possibilities opened up by scepticism and critique. Mathilde Blind, *George Eliot* (London, 1883), p. 22.

8. Blind, 'Mazzini', p. 706.

9. On the role of gender politics in English middle-class support for Italian nationalism, see Maura O'Connor, *The Romance of Italy and the English Political Imagination* (New York, 1998).

10. Blind, 'Mazzini', p. 703.

11. Mathilde Blind, *The Heather on Fire: A Tale of the Highland Clearances* (London, 1886). Many of Blind's works are available at the Victorian Women Writers Project, Perry Willett general editor, Indiana University: http://www.indiana.edu/~letrs/vwwp/index.html.

12. Garnett, pp. 27-30. Scotland also inspired Blind's *The Prophecy of St Oran* (1881).

13. See Ewan A. Cameron, *Land for the People: The British Government and the Scottish Highlands, c. 1880-1925* (East Linton, 1996); Eric Richards, *The Highland Clearances* (Edinburgh, 2000).

14. The Act received royal assent on 25 June 1886; the *Newcastle Daily Chronicle* reviewed Blind's poem on 3 July. Cameron, *Land,* pp. 37-8; 'Opinions', p. 4.

15. On the conflict in Skye see I. M. M. MacPhail, 'The Skye Military Expedition of 1884-5,' *Transactions of the Gaelic Society of Inverness* 48 (1972-74): 1, pp. 62-94.

16. *The Oxford English Dictionary,* ed. J. A. Simpson and E. S. C. Weiner, 2nd edn (Oxford, 1989), 'Duan'.

17. Jane Francesca Wilde, *Poems by Speranza,* 2nd edn (Glasgow, n.d.), p. 10. Compare *Tuath is Tighearna: Tenants and Landlords, An Anthology of Gaelic Poetry of Social and Political Protest from the Clearances to the Land Agitation (1800-1890),* ed. Donald E. Meek (Edinburgh, 1995).

18. Recent important work on women's political poetry includes Isobel Armstrong's *Victorian Poetry: Poetry, Poetics and Politics* (London, 1993); Tricia Lootens, 'Victorian Poetry and Patriotism', in Joseph Bristow (ed.), *The Cambridge Companion to Victorian Poetry* (Cambridge, 2000), pp. 255-79; plus work on individual poets by critics including Leigh Coral Harris, Antony H. Harrison, Lootens, Esther Schor, and Marjorie Stone.

19. See A. A. Markley, 'Eliza Ogilvy, Highland Minstrelsy, and the Perils of Victorian Motherhood', *Studies in Scottish Literature* 32 (2001): pp. 180-94.

20. Garnett, 'Memoir', p. 8.

21. Mathilde Blind, *Shelley's View of Nature Contrasted with Darwin's* (London, 1886), p. 9.

22. *A Social Crisis in Scotland: The Highlands and the Crofters Question*: 'The population of crofters, of the Highlands and Islands . . . is a nursery for good workers and good citizens for the entire empire.'

23. Mary Jacobus' analysis of Malthus' feminisation of the population problem suggests a related thread of ideological debate in Blind's poem. *First Things: The Maternal Imaginary in Literature, Art, and Psychoanalysis* (New York, 1995), pp. 83-96.

24. *Report of the Commissioners of Inquiry into the Condition of the Crofters and Cottars in the Highlands and Islands of Scotland.* PP 1884 XXXIII-XXXVI.

25. John Stuart Blackie, *The Scottish Highlanders and the Land Laws: An Historico-Economical Enquiry* (London, 1885).

26. Macleod's book first appeared as letters to the Edinburgh *Weekly Chronicle* (see Alexander Mackenzie, *The History of the Highland Clearances* [Inverness, 1883]), then in pamphlet form as *History of the Destitution in Sutherlandshire* (Edinburgh, 1841), then in an expanded edition as *Gloomy Memories in the Highlands of Scotland: Versus Mrs. Harriet Beecher Stowe's Sunny Memories, or, A faithful picture of the extirpation of the Celtic race from the Highlands of Scotland* in Toronto in 1857.

27. Alfred Russel Wallace, *Land Nationalisation: Its Necessity and Its Aims* (London, 1882).

28. Charles H. Smith, ed. and intro., *Alfred Russel Wallace: An Anthology of His Shorter Writings* (Oxford, 1991).

29. Harriet Beecher Stowe, *Sunny Memories of Foreign Lands,* 2 vols (Boston, 1854), 1: 313.

30. George Douglas Campbell, 8th Duke of Argyll, 'A Corrected Picture of the Highlands', *Nineteenth*

Century 1055 (November 1884), p. 690. The article challenges the Napier report. See also 'Isolation, or Survival of the Unfittest', which asks 'who *were* the Hebrideans?' [emphasis mine], answers that they were due to their geographic isolation a throwback culture, and asserts, 'The laws of nature cannot be suspended in favour of any men simply because they speak Gaelic.' *Nineteenth Century* 1641 (November 1889), pp. 13, 33.

31. George Douglas Campbell, 8th Duke of Argyll, 'The Prophet of San Francisco,' *Nineteenth Century* 979 (April 1884), p. 542.

32. Wallace criticised Spencer's views on land reform in 1891. See Smith, p. 511.

33. Harry Clements, *Alfred Russel Wallace: Biologist and Social Reformer* (London, 1983), p. 78.

34. Clements, pp. 165-74, 229. Wallace also supported broadening women's educational and work opportunities.

35. Mathilde Blind, *The Ascent of Man* (London, 1889), pp. 7, 104.

36. Mathilde Blind, *The Ascent of Man,* 2nd edn (London, 1899).

37. This differs from Helen Groth's reading of Christian ideology as central to the poem in 'Victorian Women Poets and Scientific Narratives', in Isobel Armstrong and Virginia Blain (eds), *Women's Poetry, Late Romantic to Late Victorian: Gender and Genre, 1830-1900* (Basingstoke, 1999), p. 336.

38. Compare W. R. Lawson, 'The Poetry and Prose of the Crofter Question', *National Review* 4 (1885), pp. 592-606.

39. Armstrong, *Victorian Poetry,* p. 377.

40. Patricia Yaeger, 'The Poetics of Birth', in Donna C. Stanton (ed.), *Discourses of Sexuality: From Aristotle to AIDS* (Ann Arbor, 1992), pp. 295, 296.

41. Joan W. Scott, 'Fantasy Echo', *Critical Inquiry* 27: 2 (2001), pp. 284-304 (p. 293).

Robert P. Fletcher (essay date winter 2005)

SOURCE: Fletcher, Robert P. "'Heir of All the Universe': Evolutionary Epistemology in Mathilde Blind's *Birds of Passage: Songs of the Orient and Occident*." *Victorian Poetry* 43, no. 4 (winter 2005): 435-53.

[*In the following essay, Fletcher explores Blind's treatment of Eastern culture in* Birds of Passage.]

In the **"Prelude"** to her *Birds of Passage: Songs of the Orient and Occident* (1895), Mathilde Blind tracks an autumn migration of birds in "corporate motion" from "the cliffs of England" to "the sacred Isle of Philæ" in the Nile River near Aswan, Egypt.[1] When this "commonwealth in flight" arrives at its destination some eighteen lines later and perches reverently in the cracks and crevices of the temples and monuments, it unites the "fallen gods of Egypt" with "men's generations" that have "waned and vanished into night" and thus seems to bind Europe and Egypt, Occident and Orient, through the common fate of human transience, symbolized in the "shadows [the birds] cast upon their onward flight." However, the spatio-temporal organization of Blind's panorama—which encompasses Greece, Italy, and "old Egypt's desert"—also retraces an imperial genealogy from present to past, West to East, inverting the conventional plot of western civilization she herself had presented in *The Ascent of Man,* her Darwinian epic (1889). This combination of the bird's eye view and the reverse chronology signals the double discourse of colonialism woven into *Birds of Passage.* On the one hand, like the "Bird of Time" from the *Rubayait of Omar Khayyam,* which appears in the book's epigraph, these birds in their transnational flight would seem to bridge the distance between two cultures in their recognition of *vanitas.* Having arrived inside the "holy halls of Death and Birth," the "gaily twittering swallows," like good tourists, "hush their breath." On the other hand, the migration to Egypt is strangely counterproductive. The birds have traveled from the "falling leaves" of England, past "fair Sicilian . . . meadows," to the Nile "seeking still an ampler light." But instead of this anticipated sunny, warm climate, they find Philæ floating "like some rapt Opium eater's labyrinthine lotos dream," strewn with "twilight-litten" ruins. In other words, the journey ostensibly allegorizes human mortality, but it also emplots the passage from West to East as a fascinating opportunity for the Western subject vicariously to "regress" and, thus, re-inscribes an Orientalist theme.

This discursive double-cross is one indication of how Blind's representations of Egypt, Italy, and England in *Birds of Passage* participate in ideologies of imperialism despite her political radicalism and her usual emphasis in her poetry on liberatory or progressive narratives. In her book *Home and Harem: Nation, Gender, Empire, and the Cultures of Travel,* Interpal Grewal suggests that "rather than debating whether middle-class Englishwomen or working-class men and women in England were anti-imperialist or not," it is more productive to examine "the way they were interpellated as subjects . . . through colonial discourses."[2] Blind's *Birds of Passage* (1895), with its balanced opposition of "Songs of the Orient" and "Songs of the Occident," demonstrates how the subjectivity of an "independent woman" in the Victorian period[3]—or at least the subjectivity constructed in a book of her verse—may be reliant nevertheless on binaries of "East" and "West" fundamental to imperialist ideology and produced through the discourses of romanticism, comparative mythology, evolutionary science, and tourism that Blind weaves into her text.

Blind's radical politics were grounded in her upbringing, developed through education, and expressed throughout her writing. She was step-daughter to Karl Blind, a leader of the Baden insurrection of 1848, and her brother Ferdinand attempted to assassinate Bismarck in 1866, subsequently committing suicide in prison. Her family moved to England after the failure of the revolution, and their home became a gathering place for political exiles, such as Garibaldi and Mazzini. Blind's education included study at a London girls' school, a failed attempt to crash university lectures restricted to men in Zurich, and a solitary walking tour of the Swiss Alps, which she later dramatized in an autobiographical fragment that may have been part of an unfinished second novel. Her writing career also included biographies of George Eliot and Madame Roland, translations of D. F. Strauss's *The Old Faith and the New* and of *The Journal of Marie Bashkirtseff,* and, significantly, editions of Byron and Shelley. Her own poetry, such as the anti-dogmatic **"The Prophecy of Saint Oran"** and *The Heather on Fire: A Tale of the Highland Clearances* (1886), her indictment of the crofter evictions, evidenced her free-thinking and democratic politics. Living for long stretches with Ford Madox Brown's family, Blind was a part of the Pre-Raphaelite circle and friends with the Rossetti brothers and Swinburne. She also socialized with Eleanor Marx, traveled with Mona Caird, and embodied her feminist convictions in sharp-witted verse, such as *Dramas in Miniature,* a volume full of fallen and fatal women in continental settings. Cosmopolitan and widely read, Blind was deeply influenced by Romantic literature and Victorian science, as is shown in both *The Ascent of Man,* with its idealist's pun on Darwin's title, and the lecture she gave comparing the scientist's view of nature with Shelley's. In 1892 and again in 1894, Blind traveled to Egypt on the advice of her doctor in an effort to allay the effects of chronic bronchitis.

While on her second trip to Egypt, Blind requested that her friend Richard Garnett, librarian in the British Museum, send her a copy of Friedrich Max Müller's *Comparative Mythology,* which, she wrote, "would be extremely interesting to have . . . here with the old gods of Egypt confronting one everywhere."[4] Now nearly forgotten but once an influential philologist and Sanskrit scholar at Oxford, Max Müller proposed in his essay a kind of key to all mythologies, which linked Greek/Roman and Egyptian mythologies by tracing the origin of the gods back to sun worship.[5] Müller both insisted that myth "tells us of the story of our own race,

of our own family—nay, of our own selves" and at the same time relegates myths to "the childhood of the human race":

> In our museums we collect the rude playthings of our hero's boyhood, and we try to guess from their colossal features the thoughts of the mind which they once reflected. Many things are still unintelligible to us, and the hieroglyphic language of antiquity records but half of the mind's unconscious intentions. Yet more and more the image of man, in whatever clime we meet him, rises before us, noble and pure from the very beginning: even his errors we learn to understand—even his dreams we begin to interpret.[6]

According to John David Coates, Müller was "reverently interested in spirituality," but he resisted "the whole idea of story or myth in a religious context, as part of a wider distaste for any giving of spiritual experience a local habitation and a name."[7] His ambivalent attitude toward the myths he studied, taking them seriously but needing to explain them away, finds its analogue in Blind's simultaneous fascination with and distancing from an Egypt of tourists and monuments.

Blind's view of Egypt was also shaped by what her friend William Kingdon Clifford termed "evolutionary epistemology," which is central to much her poetry, including her "epic," *The Ascent of Man.* Clifford was a Cambridge mathematician and philosopher who, like Blind, favored metaphysical speculations—attempts to "solve the universe"—grounded in scientific principles. And like Blind, Clifford "waged war on such ecclesiastical systems as seemed . . . to favour obscurantism."[8] Skeptical of religious orthodoxies, he found the source of ethics in the evolutionary development of a "tribal self," arguing in "On the Scientific Basis of Morals" that "those tribes have on the whole survived in which conscience approved such actions as tended to the improvement of men's characters as citizens and therefore to the survival of the tribe."[9] Hence, for Clifford, the moral sense is intuitive because it originates as an inherited characteristic, and the development and decline of civilizations necessarily tell us something of their ethical characters. In "On Some of the Conditions of Mental Development," he sets up an opposition—one that will inform Blind's poetry on West and East-between "races" that can remain plastic, capable of adaptation, and those that "at last . . . will be quite fixed, crystallised, incapable of change" (*Lectures,* p. 69). Like John Stuart Mill, concerned with the "growth of conventionalities," Clifford finds "nations in the East so enslaved by custom that they seem to have lost all power of change except the capability of being destroyed" (p. 71). Clifford's views on religion and the Orient coalesce in his essay on "The Ethics of Religion," where he traces the origin of the crystallized and corrupt Catholic priesthood to the biblical idolaters of Egypt: "The gospel indeed came out of Judea, but the

Church and her dogmas came out of Egypt" (*Lectures*, p. 377). This binary of plasticity and crystallization—reminiscent of Matthew Arnold's Hellenism and Hebraism but grounded now in the language of science—will function as map to Blind as she travels east.

What Müller and Clifford are to Blind as scientific influences, Byron and Shelley are to her as literary influences. I can trace further the ideological implications of these intellectual ties of Blind's by borrowing an opposition Saree Makdisi establishes in *Romantic Imperialism* between the different versions of the Orient he sees in Byron and Shelley.[10] Byron's *Childe Harold's Pilgrimage,* he contends, constructs a version of the Orient as synchronically, disturbingly, and intransigently Other, inassimilable to European history, while Shelley's *Alastor* involves "the invention and spatial production of a certain version of the Orient as Europe's source of origin," and thus supports "the universalizing European claims that time and history are uniform natural 'essences' that point to modernity and to Europe" (p. 146). In Blind's lecture **"Shelley's View of Nature Contrasted with Darwin's,"** which was published privately as a pamphlet in 1886, her opinions of Shelley reveal how her own idealism is interpellated with colonialist assumptions. Contra Makdisi, she sees Shelley's great poem *Prometheus Unbound* as flawed precisely because the poet did not have available to him a developmental model of human history that would have endowed his idealistic vision of the "ultimate triumph of the human mind" with a measure of "historic realism." If he had known Darwin, she argues, Shelley would have preferred an evolutionary to a lapsarian model of history and would have abandoned his Rousseau. In what Virginia Blain calls the "imaginative impressionism" of *The Ascent of Man* (p. 186), Blind herself attempted such a diachronic march from the primeval forest to Western modernity. However, if her thoughts on Shelley and her own evolutionary epic imply that Blind held a view of the Orient as simply a stop on the developmental road to the West, the **"Prelude"** to *Birds of Passage* reminds us that she was also tempted to reverse direction and journey East. In other words, like Byron she could at times imagine a version of the Orient as intriguingly Other and therefore capable of disturbing a complacent vision of the West. What interest me most about *Birds of Passage* are the representational tensions that result from her implicit reliance on these distinct approaches to the East that Makdisi characterizes as Shelleyan and Byronic.

THE POET'S MOBILE SELF

In addition to inheriting constructs of Occident and Orient from Romantic poets, Blind—like her fellow Victorian travelers to Egypt Harriet Martineau and Gertrude Bell—also benefited from "the Romantic conjunction of mobility with freedom" and its construction of the self

through travel (Grewal, p. 172). Grewal argues that both Martineau and Bell escaped their alienation as women at home and demonstrated their equality with the superior English male through their travels and travel writing (pp. 79-80). For *The Athenaeum*'s critic, Blind's poetic venture to the East epitomizes her advancement and uniqueness, in short, her interesting selfhood:

> Few women who have attempted the art of verse have brought with them to the undertaking so wide a culture, so varied an experience, so many keen interests, or have had so rich and exceptional a nature to express. More than most women Miss Blind has lived her own life, has followed the dictates of her own individuality; now singing of the 'Ascent of Man,' now of the crofters. . . . Now, in her present book, she has endeavoured to combine the ecstasy of the poet with the enthusiasm of the traveller, and to bring before English readers, for the first time in English verse, the mystery, the charm, the colour of the East.[11]

Indeed, it is the poet's subjective "vision, intensely personal and intensely sympathetic, of an entirely poetic East" that the critic especially favors, even as he or she notes that "the Egypt of to-day also, if so strange a survival may in any due sense be called contemporary, finds eloquent expression throughout these poems."

East, West, Past, Present, the poet of *Birds of Passage* comfortably traverses all these terrains in language, as Blind comfortably traveled in Egypt under the care of Thomas Cook's steamers and modern tourist hotels, such as the landmark Shepheard's. The book's second lyric, **"Welcome to Egypt,"** depicts the fertility of the contemporary Nile delta, its "interminable crops of wheat and rye"—though not, significantly, the predominant crop, cotton, the cultivation of which, to the exclusion of other staples, the British had encouraged as a source of raw material for their textile mills. It also offers the figure of a live Egyptian, rare in *Birds of Passage,* a "grave Arab" with a "flashing glance" that bespeaks a proprietorship out of step with the actual dominance of the country by the colonizer. He proudly surveys the landscape and assigns a classed, gendered identity to the book's poetic persona, and extends an invitation to the tourist that seems to legitimize as well, one might say, imperial desire: "Lo, this happy day, / My country decks herself in sumptuous green, / And smiling welcome, Lady, bids you stay." The persona of lady traveler remains implicit throughout the volume, but in **"Soul-Drift,"** one of the **"Songs of the Occident"** in the book's second half, the freedom from gendered prohibitions that the traveling Englishwoman enjoys is made explicit through the Romantic discourse of poetic transcendence:

> I LET my soul drift with the thistledown
>   Afloat upon the honeymooning breeze;
> My thoughts about the swelling buds are blown,
>   Blown with the golden dust of flowering trees.

On fleeting gusts of desultory song,
  I let my soul drift out into the Spring;
The Psyche flies and palpitates among
  The palpitating creatures on the wing.

Go, happy Soul! run fluid in the wave
  Vibrate in light, escape thy natal curse;
Go forth no longer as my body-slave
  But as the heir of all the Universe.

The disembodied soul's freedom to traverse from West to East is also the subject of **"Internal Firesides,"** a sonnet about the winter sustenance provided the poet by the "glowing memories" of Eastern travel. The poet retreats from the octave's funereal English landscape, wrapped in a "downy shroud" of snow, to a boat rocked "as on a cradle by the palm-fringed Nile" in the sestet. This representation of Egypt as life-giving and the West as "icy" and "bare" is exceptional in the book, one of those Byronic moments, if you will, where the Orient's difference is attractive as a sign of the dissatisfaction with home and of the poet's enviable familiarity with the exotic, her ability—as another poem, **"On Reading the 'Rubaiyat' of Omar Khayyam in a Kentish Rose Garden,"** would have it—to "translate" the "hieroglyphs" of a foreign culture.

"A Fantasy" takes the mobility of the poet's self to playful extremes, as the lady traveler inhabits a desert romance: "I was an Arab, / I loved my horse; / Swift as an arrow / He swept the course," she imagines, and then four stanzas later, "Free as the wild wind, / Light as a foal; / Ah, there is room there / To stretch one's soul." As Arab horseman, the poet claims now his right to a sexualized Oriental woman, waiting at the expected oasis:

Out of thy Kulleh,
  Fairest and first,
Give me to drink
  Quencher of thirst.

I am athirst, girl;
  Parched with desire,
Love in my bosom
  Burns as a fire.

Green thy oasis,
  Waving with Palms;
Oh, be no niggard,
  Maid, with thy alms.

Kiss me with kisses,
  Buds of thy mouth,
Sweeter than Cassia
  Fresh from the South.

Bind me with tresses,
  Clasp with a curl;
And in caresses
  Stifle me, girl.

I was an Arab
  Ages ago!
Hence this home-sickness
  And all my woe.

Although ironized and reduced, the Byronic Orientalism evident here can still provide the Victorian woman poet a transgressive moment in its provocative fantasy of woman-woman desire and perhaps also in an exhilarating alienation from a Western sense of superiority.

The most significant moments of desire for, and alienation from, an Egyptian Other come, however, in **"The Beautiful Beeshareen Boy,"** a poem noteworthy enough to have attracted the attention of the critics for *The Athenaeum, The Academy,* and *The Bookman.* In her own note accompanying the poem, Blind offers the story her lyric will explore:

> The Beeshareens are a wandering desert tribe of Upper Egypt, reminding one of our Gypsies. Many of them are remarkably handsome, more particularly in childhood. The grace of their movements and charm of manner must strike all travellers on the Nile. The children haunt the shore where boats land, and set up an incessant cry for "backsheesh," and there are few who can resist the winning smiles with which they sweeten their importunities. Conspicuous among the crowd was a lovely boy of sixteen, who attracted the attention of artists and photographers two or three winters ago. He had the elegant proportions of a Tanagra statuette, and was so constantly asked to sit for his portrait that he must have thought that that was the end and aim of all tourists. Finally, he was carried off to the World's Fair with other curiosities of Egypt. When the Beeshareens returned to Assouan he was not amongst them, and rumour says that he got as far as Marseilles, where he utterly vanished.

As what Ali Behdad terms a "belated traveler"—that is, one who arrives when tourism and colonialism have already turned the Orient into familiar territory—Blind finds in the story a literalization of her fear of the disappearing exotic.[12] In the poem itself, this resourceful adolescent becomes an erotic figure of desire—a "Beautiful, black-eyed" and "lithe-limbed" boy with a "Face that finds no maid coy"—an actor in an East primarily, if not entirely, "poetic": "Page for some peerless queen: / Some Orient queen of old, / Sumptuous in woven gold, / Close-clinging fold on fold, / Lightning, with gems between." The poet pursues this "Wild Cupid" in his intoxicating rides through desert and "Fawnlike" dashes through "white-walled town." Shipboard, he is further eroticized and marked off from everyday Egyptians by a "wild mane of jet," his "Curls of rich ebony / Coiled in a coronet," which is far "Better than Felt or Fez."

In the poem's second half, the poet leaves the "lotos dream" of Bedouin campfires behind with the assumption that the Beeshareen boy has remained there. But on a return trip, she finds Aswan "forlorn" without her "pride" and conducts a second search by "riverside" and "Under mimosa trees" without success. The boy's disappearance and her disappointment lead to a shift in tone and purpose, and the poet comes as close as she will to criticizing the colonial regime, satirizing the exploitation of Egypt through the commodification of the boy and everything fashionably Oriental, but, significantly, displacing that criticism onto American commercialism:

> Oh, desert-nurtured Child,
>   How dared they carry thee,
> Far from thy native Wild
>   Across the Western Sea?
> Packed off, poor boy, at last,
>   With many a plaster cast
> Of plinth and pillar vast,
>   And waxen mummies piled!
>
> Ah! just like other ware,
>   For a lump sum or so
> Shipped to the World's great Fair—
>   To big Chicago Show!
> With mythic beasts and things,
> Beetles and bulls with wings,
> And imitation Sphinx,
>   Ranged row on curious row!
>
> Beautiful, black-eyed boy;
>   Ah me! how strange it is
> That thou, the desert's joy,
>   Whom heavenly winds would kiss,
> With Ching and Chang-hwa ware,
> Blue pots and bronzes rare,
> Shouldst now be over there
>   Shown at Porkopolis.
>
> Gone like a lovely dream,
>   Child of the starry smile;
> Gone from the glowing stream
>   Glassing its greenest isle!

To use the *Athenaeum* critic's language, this poem is fascinating for its simultaneous "intensely sympathetic" treatment of colonial exploitation and "intensely personal" vision of the Other. On the one hand, it criticizes explicitly the Western practices that turn Egypt, as Timothy Mitchell phrases it, into an exhibition;[13] on the other hand, its own symbolic use of the Beeshareen boy as figure of desire allows the poet's subjectivity to be re-imagined in the verse. In other words, the independent woman poet identifies with this scholar-gipsy of the East who survives on the margins of, and yet remains aloof from, the structures of Western capitalism.

In another sonnet, **"Sphinx-Money,"** knowledge of the East's true value is, indeed, reserved for the poet-tourist. With "all the morning wonder of a Child" and under the eye of an unappreciative "mute Arab," she hunts fossilized shells among "Pyramids and temple-wrecks," shells that the Bedouins, she tells us, call sphinx-money and that she transmutes to

> poet's gold:
> 'Twill give thee entrance to those rites of old,
> When hundred-gated Thebes, with storied walls,
>   Gleamed o'er her Plain, and vast processions rolled
> To Amon-Ra through Karnak's pillared halls.

Here she exchanges "the Egypt of to-day" for the Egypt of antiquities, and the book's dominant paradigm for representing East and West comes to the fore. If Blind preserves Byron's synchronic, disturbing Orient in the person of the Beeshareen boy, she nevertheless also repeats Shelley's gesture of subsuming the Orient under a diachronic, grand vision of human folly and wisdom. If, according to George Cotterell in *The Academy,* Blind "has penetrated some of [the Orient's] remoter secrets,"[14] through them she re-inscribes a totalizing dichotomy of sublime, inscrutable, and "crystallized" East and beautiful, familiar, and "plastic" West (to cite W. K. Clifford's terms). In doing so, she participates, however inadvertently, in the discursive mechanisms of colonialism.

RE-INSCRIBING THE ORIENT AND OCCIDENT

A measure of both Blind's appreciation for ancient Egyptian culture and the double bind of her placement in the colonial world is her participation in the protests against the proposed Aswan dam project and its threatened destruction of the island of Philæ with its irreplaceable temples and monuments. In *Modernization and British Colonial Rule in Egypt,* Robert L. Tignor describes the arguments over the consequences of the dam's construction:

> The controversy was carried in Europe's leading newspapers and periodicals, with European archeologists almost unanimously opposed to the dam. Although engineers argued that Egypt's present needs were more compelling than the preservation of its ancient monuments, the Egyptian government was hesitant to support this expert opinion in the face of such adverse criticism. "For once and only once, I fear, since we occupied Egypt in 1882," wrote Scott-Moncrieff [the engineer in charge of Egyptian irrigation], "was educated opinion in England and France at one. Both insisted that Philæ should not be drowned." In order to obtain the advice of outside observers, Scott-Moncrieff established an international commission, composed of a French, an English, and an Italian engineer, but their work did not lead to a successful resolution of the problems. In the midst of these difficulties Egypt embarked upon the Sudan campaign, and Cromer feared that funds could not be found for the construction of the dam.
>
> Brushing aside these difficulties, however, Cromer decided in 1898 to give his approval to the project. One of the major reasons was his realization that Egypt would have to increase its revenues if it was to finance the development of the Sudan.[15]

Pierre Loti's book on Egypt bears the subtitle "The Destruction of Philæ," an event which for him is indicative of the colonizers' warped values and lack of taste: on the one hand, they will destroy an ancient treasure in the name of progress by half-submerging it, and on the other they will conduct tours of what little remains.[16] Blind, too, aligned herself with those who protested the sacrifice of the island to modernization. In a letter to Richard Garnett, she claims, "I am just sending off an article on Philæ for the Fortnightly Review. I suppose you would not mind correcting the press for me in case the Editor sends you a proof. The idea of the submersion of this lovely island has preoccupied me a good deal & I have done I could for it [sic]."[17] Unfortunately, the *Fortnightly* seems not to have published the article—at least I have not been able to trace it—for one would like to have seen how Blind framed the issue. An article about Philæ in the *Spectator* by Meredith Townsend that appeared a week before Blind's letter was written begins with an anecdote about Mohammed Ali's supposed plan earlier in the century to destroy the Pyramids for better irrigation (a tragedy averted, Townsend claims, by the wise intervention of Lord Palmerston); it then goes on to argue the folly of any such sacrifice of "what is far more important to mankind than the prosperity of any small nation."[18] The controversy is thereby framed as an opposition of the Western guardians of human knowledge to the self-interest of a backward people. Lost in such an expression of humanist outrage is what Tignor hints at in the passage above: the role of the colonial power and its imperial and commercial interests in the dam's construction. The irrigation the dam was to make possible would increase mainly the cultivation of long-staple cotton, the crop that was the main Egyptian export, bound largely for the textile mills of England. Whether Blind addressed the imperial context for the dam or the needs of the Egyptian economy and people in her article, I have been unable yet to determine. The only mention of Philæ in *Birds of Passage,* though, comes in the **"Prelude,"** a discussion of which began this article, and there her emphasis, like Loti's, is on reverence for the Egypt of the past. With the possible exception of **"The Beautiful Beeshareen Boy,"** however, her poems lack the French writer's bitterness against the modern tourism industry. Indeed, this poet's concentration on the moral lessons to be learned by the visits to various sights seems at times at one with the totalizing discourse of the tourist guide.

Once access is granted her in **"Welcome to Egypt,"** the poet-tourist devotes much of "Songs of the Orient" to deciphering the meanings of the Egyptian monuments, and her efforts produce several rewritings of Shelley's "Ozymandias." Although the sonnet **"The Colossi of the Plain"** comes closest in form to the precursor's text, **"The Tombs of the Kings,"** written, as the *Athenaeum* puts it, in the "chanting measure in which Miss

Blind is at her best" (that is, the meter of the book's **"Prelude"**), most closely approximates Shelley's theme of hubris. But whereas Shelley's traveler has only an iconic sign of the ruler over which to moralize on the vanity of human wishes, in "the mummied Kings of Egypt, wrapped in linen fold on fold," Blind has the rulers themselves, who have turned themselves into perverted symbols of pride. The journey imagined in the poem takes the poet through a land of extremes, from "sulphour hills" of the desert "Where no green thing cast a shadow," to "the Coffin-Hills of Tuat—the Metropolis of Death." This underworld, however, lacks the gothic chill that other travel writers find amidst the mummies. Pierre Loti, for example, is fascinated and repelled by the ghoulish appearance of individuals such as the queen Nsitanebashru, a "dishevelled vampire" whose "implacable ferocity" (p. 56) threatens the traveler's complacent sense of self. Blind's gaze, on the other hand, is directed upon a panorama including not only "the mummied kings of Egypt, pictures of a perished race," who "Lie, [even] of Death forgotten, face by immemorial face," but also a parade of gods on the mausoleum walls, signs, like the mummies, of "the hours and days [that] are passing, and the years and centuries." In aggregate, as presented in the poem, these mummies seem to have no power to disturb; rather, as in "Ozymandias," their folly provides a philosophical reassurance of universal dynamism and the pastness of the past:

> Have they conquered? Oh the pity of those Kings
> within their tombs,
> Locked in stony isolation in those petrifying glooms!
>
> Motionless where all is motion in a rolling Universe,
> Heaven, by answering their prayer, turned it to a
> deadly curse.
>
> Left them fixed where all is fluid in a world of star-
> winged skies;
> Where, in myriad transformations, all things pass and
> nothing dies;
>
> Nothing dies but what is tethered, kept when Time
> would set it free,
> To fulfil Thought's yearning tension upward through
> Eternity.

The poet highlights the contrast between the "divine processionals" of gods "Ibis-headed, jackal-featured, vulture-hooded" on the mausoleum walls and the stagnation of the mummified pharaohs and thus is led to moralize on the willful ignorance of the ancient kings who would defy the motion of the Universe.

In contrast, the poet herself integrates Western mythology into the evolutionary process in the "Songs of the Occident." In **"The Mirror of Diana,"** the poet—drawing on the cultural anthropology of Müller—celebrates the rationalization of myth into a language symbolic of nature. The goddess is still vital, a Queen Moon whose "magic glass of love" is surrounded by white roses and lilies, which in turn are mirrored by the "White rose, white lily of the skies," as "The Moon-flower blossoms in the lake." Ultimately, for the poet the moon goddess is ideal beauty, the Unattainable, an "Ideal set on high" that haunts "the deep reflective mind." The poem's final image of the moon's reflection being dispersed by a "puff of alien wind" and melting "in innumerable rings" figures the current exchange value of Western culture—its semiotic openness, if you will—which has, for Blind, become one more sign of evolutionary process. While the buried gods of Egypt lose their significance for the kings "Pale and passive in their prisons, [who] have conquered, / Chained to death," Diana—thanks to the poet's transformative vision—remains "Elusive in the flux of things."

In **"The Moon of Ramadân,"** that secularizing Western vision is also brought to bear on the historical shift from ancient Egyptian religion to Islam. Despite the various monuments' "mute processionals" of Egyptian gods "wedded to their walls," the poet declares that "Amon's Sun has waned before / The Moon of Ramadân"; even Isis' "white-robed priests who served her shrine / Have turned Mahommedan." Meanwhile, the poet looks to nature—the sunset on the Nile and the rising moon—and moralizes on its indifference toward changing human cultures and beliefs:

> The gods may come, the gods may go,
>   And royal realms change hands;
> But the most ancient Nile will flow,
>   And flood the desert sands;
> And nightly will he glass the stars'
>   Unearthly caravan,
> Nor care if it be Rome's red Mars
>   Or Moon of Ramadân.

Nature's sublime indifference is a corollary to the poet's own superior vision, which is reinforced by her representation of Muslim ritual as a form of idolatry:

> Black outlined on the golden air
>   A turbaned Silhouette,
> The Mueddin invites to prayer
>   From many a Minaret.
> Our dusky boatmen hear the call,
>   And prostrate, man on man,
> They bow, adoring, one and all,
>   The Moon of Ramadân.

In a curious parallel, the poet's own fetishizing of the moon in **"The Mirror of Diana"** is transposed onto Egyptian Muslims. But whereas the poet's nature worship is knowing, the Muslim's is presented here as naive.[19]

The poet's view, moreover, is the Darwinian one. In her poem **"The Desert,"** Blind rewrites Shelley's East, within it emplotting both Darwinian progress from the "Mute spirit of the wilds" to the "grace of god-like Greece" as well as the terrible possibility of degeneration. This is Blind's version of the imperial sublime,[20] and it highlights the double-edged significance of cultural and natural change that so many representations of evolution in late-Victorian literature—from Rider Haggard to H. G. Wells—possess. She finds the "Uncircumscribed, unmeasured, vast" Egyptian desert to be a vestige of evolutionary process: "a land which Nature made / Without a living thing," or better yet, "wreckage of some older world, / Ere children grew, or flowers, / When rocks and hissing stones were hurled / In hot, volcanic showers." Once more, like Shelley's traveler, the poet finds a ruined colossus in the sand that outlasts its creator to bear witness to the progress of passing civilizations:

> And Persia ruled and Palestine;
>   And o'er her violet seas
> Arose, with marble gods divine,
>   The grace of god-like Greece.
> And Rome, the Mistress of the World,
>   Amid her diadem
> Of Eastern Empires set impearled
>   The Scarab's mystic gem.

But, as representative of the desert, this statue, the poem suggests, may have an even more impressive pedigree, having perhaps descended from an unknown race of men and thereby hinting at unknown possibilities of devolution:

> Perchance he has been lying here
>   Since first the world began,
> Poor Titan of some earlier sphere
>   Of prehistoric Man!
> To whom we are as idle flies,
>   That fuss and buzz their day;
> While still immutable he lies,
>   As long ago he lay.

Egypt's desert, then, becomes a land of temporal extremes—signifying by the "wreckage" of its monuments either end of an evolutionary arc—an alternative dimension to the West where "The present . . . becomes the past, / For all futurity." In a gesture typical of "ethnography that denies the Other coevalness"—to use a phrase Behdad adopts from Johannes Fabian (p. 6)—Egypt comes to represent in *Birds of Passage* either a mysterious origin or a terrifying future for a West that the poet identifies with the dynamic present. These polarities have their spatial equivalent in the sublime landscape of the "Songs of the Orient," which is characterized by extremes of temperature and light, the lyrics moving back and forth almost without exception from the darkness of the tombs to the desert's "sun that burns and brands" (**"The Desert,"** l. 5).[21]

In contrast to the extremity of the East, the West of *Birds of Passage* is, by-and-large, marked by temperate weather and lush scenery. The landscapes, whether in

England or Italy, are feminized—beautiful and familiar in counterpoint to the Orient's "empty wilderness." "Maiden meadows" (**"Roman Anemones,"** l. 1) and "fresh lawns" (**"The New Proserpine,"** l. 3) play host, for example, to a "lady sweet," whose "pale, frail hands . . . Gather the spring flowers at our feet, / Fair as some late-born Proserpine" (ll. 5-8). Even the ruins depicted in the "Songs of the Occident" partake of the "growth" associated with the feminized West. In **"On a Torso of Cupid,"** the fragmentary statue—a "poor, dismembered love"—is eulogized by the poet but also naturalized by the "Closely embracing, / Tendrils of clinging [ivy] leaves / Round him enlacing." A nonfinito figure, the significance of which is to be completed by poet and Nature, this "helpless god of old, / Maimed mid the tender / Blossoming white and gold / Of April splendour," is about to be subsumed—"Deep in the daisied sod"—by a burgeoning organic world, when the poet rescinds the sentence: "Nay, broken God of Love, / Still must thou bide above, / While, left for woe or weal, / Thou has a heart to feel." As garden ornament, enhanced by "Nature's sacredness," the god finds its place in the landscape without dominating it, unlike those imposing Egyptian colossi of the plains. Shrouded in ivy, this cupid becomes part of the earth, unlike the unnaturally resistant Egyptian mummies.

The continuing vitality of Western mythologies in the book is best represented by the seven Shakespeare Sonnets at the end of the "Songs of the Occident," so-called not for their form but for their subject matter, the life of the playwright and the sights around Stratford-on-Avon. The poem on **"Anne Hathaway's Cottage"** consecrates the place as holy ground, made seemingly impervious by its association with Shakespeare's language to the evolutionary forces that topple Egyptian monuments:

> To these dear walls, once dear to Shakespeare's eyes,
>   Time's Vandal hand itself has done no wrong;
>   This nestling lattice opened to his song,
> When, with the lark, he bade his love arise
> In words whose strong enchantment never dies—
>   Old as these flowers, and, like them, ever young.

Similarly, an "incommunicable presence," the living spirit of English culture, haunts the church where Shakespeare is buried, his "spirit . . . Pervasive round these old familiar things" leaving the poet with a sense of wonder like that inspired by a beautiful natural phenomenon, the "faint fluid phosphorent rings / On refluent seas."

Finally, in the sonnet called simply **"Shakespeare,"** the works of the playwright, once again epitomizing English culture, become a map to "Blind Nature" herself:

> The world of men, unrolled before our sight,
>   Showed like a map, where stream and waterfall
>   And village-cradling vale and cloud-capped height

> Stand faithfully recorded, great and small;
> For Shakespeare was, and at his touch, with light
> Impartial as the Sun's, revealed the All.

What interests me here is the power of totalization attributed to English culture in both the person of Shakespeare and in the knowledge generated through imperial travel and embodied in cartography. Blind's own taste for a world-framing, epic scope, as evidenced in *The Ascent of Man,* dovetails with the supposed gestures toward cultural and political hegemony admired here.

CONCLUSION

Birds of Passage is a wonderful book of poetry, filled with some of Blind's best verse, and it caps the extraordinary career of a versatile poet capable of both daring and refinement. Her dedication to the craft of poetry is seen in her many epistolary exchanges with Richard Garnett over issues of versification—exchanges in which Garnett often counsels her (often unsuccessfully) to avoid unconventional rhymes and she takes him to task for imprecise imagery. In the introduction to her anthology's selection of Blind's poetry, Virginia Blain cites "the combination of passion and thoughtfulness" in Blind's work that impressed Garnett and other Victorians, before adding her own sense of the "*com*passion" Blind brought to many of her subjects (p. 187). I would contest neither Garnett's nor Blain's admiration, but I would like to reflect a bit further on the role *Birds of Passage* should perhaps have in our understanding of Blind and in our construction of a tradition of Victorian women's poetry.

Most recent commentators on Blind's career say little about her last book of poetry, and, when they do mention it, they seem little concerned with the issues I have been addressing. In her 1993 opus *Victorian Poetry: Poetry, Poetics and Politics,* Isobel Armstrong ends her influential chapter on a separate women's tradition of Victorian poetry with a consideration of Blind's radical challenges to the expressive aesthetics Armstrong sees as defining that poetry in the nineteenth century.[22] Armstrong has little to say, however, about *Birds of Passage,* though her one comment—that for it and other works Blind "ransacked different cultures for material" (p. 375)—is telling. In his extensive and otherwise excellent 1998 *Dictionary of Literary Biography* article on Blind, James Diedrick mentions the importance of **"The Tombs of the Kings"** and notes its resemblance "in spirit" to "Ozymandias," but he remains otherwise silent on the relation between the book and colonial politics.[23]

When we look to the newer anthologies of Victorian women's poetry, both the selections from the book and the accompanying editorial apparatus are significant in what they lack. Leighton and Reynolds' groundbreaking *Victorian Women Poets: An Anthology* (Blackwell, 1995) casts Blind understandably as "a feminist, a revolutionary, a socialist, . . . [and] a sceptic,"[24] but, despite its inclusion of **"The Beautiful Beeshareen Boy,"** it characterizes the poetry of *Birds of Passage* solely through a reference to the "lighthearted" nature of the poem **"A Fantasy."** Blain's anthology is more generous to *Birds of Passage,* including as it does four poems from the volume. Besides **"A Fantasy"** and **"Scarabæus Sisyphus"** (a clever anthropomorphizing of the Egyptian dung-beetle), it reprints two important poems about women: **"Mourning Women"** from "Songs of the Orient" and **"Noonday Rest"** from "Songs of the Occident." The latter is the lyrical portrait of a poor, presumably unmarried mother—"a nameless castaway" asleep on Hampstead Heath with her baby at her breast—while the former is a sonnet that depicts a group of Muslim women as "wretched" because of a supposed Islamic doctrine denying them souls. Indicative of Blind's feminist thought in general and her particular concern about women in circumstances of class and nationality different from her own, the poems—especially when juxtaposed, as in Blain's anthology—critique patriarchal structures of both East and West.

If we read **"Mourning Women,"** however, without noting the vexed mixture of Orientalisms in *Birds of Passage,* we may not understand the poem's significance clearly and may inadvertently reinforce certain of the book's Orientalist motifs. For example, the speaker's sympathy with the Muslim women in the poem depends in part on an ahistorical and totalized understanding of Islam: Blind condemns not the oppression of Egyptian women by an Egyptian male elite of her time which uses certain Islamic traditions and interpretations of sacred text for its misogynist aims, but, rather, the religion of Islam. In other words, Blind, writing in 1895, after a not overly long stay in Egypt, not surprisingly participates in the Orientalist historiography of Islamic women. However, what is surprising is its re-inscription in Blain's footnotes to the poem in her anthology, where she tells the reader "Muslim women clothe themselves in black from head to toe and veil their faces, as a sign of subservience" and asserts ambiguously that a doctrine "that women do not have souls and therefore will be denied entry into paradise" is "believed to be Islamic" (pp. 205-206). Neither of these characterizations of Muslim society and Islamic doctrine is further documented, qualified, or explained, though significant scholarship exists on both the ambiguities of veiling and the spuriousness (and, in fact, imported origin) of the supposedly Islamic denial of spiritual equality to women.[25]

This is neither to contest Blain's insights into Blind's life and career, from which I have learned much, nor to discount either Blind's or Blain's legitimate concerns over the (historically specific) oppression of Muslim women in late nineteenth-century Egypt, but rather to point out the pervasiveness and recalcitrance of Orien-

talist generalizations and oversights in both Victorian culture and our scholarship about it. Given the sonnet's own formal emphasis on the joint cultural/theological grounds for the oppression (that is, the sestet's focus on a Qur'anic basis for the supposed belief), Blind's sympathy with the **"Mourning Women,"** as she calls them, should be separated neither from the mission in much of her work to demythologize systems of religious belief nor from the tendency in *Birds of Passage* to assign Egyptian culture the status of ancient, static, premodern Other. Those artistic aims, as Grewal reminds us, are bound up with Blind's own subjectivity, her place in the colonial world as European, "independent" woman and traveler.

Notes

1. All references are to the online edition of *Birds of Passage: Songs of the Orient and Occident* (1895), edited, transcribed, and encoded by Perry Willet, Victorian Women Writers Project, Library Electronic Text Resource Service (LETRS), Indiana University, Bloomington, IN, January 11, 1996. Available at http://www.indiana.edu/%7Eletrs/vwwp/.

2. Inderpal Grewal, *Home and Harem: Nation, Gender, Empire, and the Cultures of Travel* (Durham: Duke Univ. Press, 1996), p. 13.

3. Virginia Blain, "Mathilde Blind," *Victorian Women Poets: A New Annotated Anthology* (New York: Longman, 2001), p. 187.

4. Letter to Richard Garnett, from Assouan, Egypt, dated January 23, 1894 (British Library Add. MS. 61929, f. 106).

5. For discussions of Müller's thought and influence, see Linda Dowling, "Victorian Oxford and the Science of Language," *PMLA* 97, no. 2 (1982): 160-178; and Gillian Beer, *Darwin's Plots: Evolutionary Narrative in Darwin, George Eliot and Nineteenth-Century Fiction* (Cambridge: Cambridge Univ. Press, 1983), esp. pp. 112-114.

6. Max Müller, *Comparative Mythology, An Essay* (London: Routledge, 1909), pp. 7-9.

7. John David Coates, "Hostility to Myth: Chesteron and His Contemporaries," *Mosaic* 15, no. 4 (1982): 91-105.

8. "William Kingdon Clifford," *Encyclopedia Britannica,* 11th ed. (New York: The Encyclopedia Britannica Co., 1911), p. 508.

9. William Kingdon Clifford, "On the Scientific Basis of Morals," *Lectures and Essays* (London, 1886), p. 297.

10. Saree Makdisi, *Romantic Imperialism: Universal Empire and the Culture of Modernity* (London: Cambridge Univ. Press, 1998).

11. Review of *Birds of Passage, Athenaeum,* July 27, 1895, pp. 121-122.

12. Ali Behdad, *Belated Travelers: Orientalism in the Age of Colonial Dissolution* (Durham: Duke Univ. Press, 1994), pp. 41-43.

13. Timothy Mitchell, *Colonizing Egypt* (Cambridge: Cambridge Univ. Press, 1988).

14. George Cotterell, Review of *Birds of Passage, The Academy,* No. 1223, October 12, 1895, pp. 288-289.

15. Robert L. Tignor, *Modernization and British Colonial Rule in Egypt, 1882-1914* (Princeton: Princeton Univ. Press, 1966), pp. 221-222.

16. Pierre Loti, *Egypt (La Mort De Philæ)*, trans. W. P. Baines (New York: Duffield, 1910).

17. Letter to Richard Garnett, dated March 14, 1894, Luxor Hotel, Egypt (British Library Add. MS. 61929, f. 111).

18. Meredith Townsend, "The Destruction of Philæ," *The Spectator,* v. 72, March 3, 1894, pp. 296-297.

19. In a footnote to the poem Blind insinuates that the hypocrisy of Muslims is notable in their religious rituals:

    The month of Ramadân is the month of fasting, which begins as soon as a Muslim declares that he has seen the new moon. From daybreak to sunset, throughout the month, eating and drinking are absolutely prohibited, but the faithful indemnify themselves by feasting and smoking throughout a great part of the night.

20. On the notion of an imperial sublime, see Sara Suleiri, *The Rhetoric of English India* (Chicago: Univ. of Chicago Press, 1992), esp. chap. 2.

21. The only exception is the introductory "Welcome to Egypt," where the fertility of the Nile delta is emphasized. Note, however, her descriptions of the temperate weather she encountered in Aswan in her letter to Garnett: "The air is lovely here, like a lovely spring day, the sun is shining on golden sands and the broad fans of the palms and the red flags in honour of the Khedive's visit, are fluttering and waving in a fresh northerly breeze" (January 23, 1894; British Library Add. MS. 61929, f. 105).

22. Isobel Armstrong, *Victorian Poetry: Poetry, Poetics and Politics* (London: Routledge, 1993).

23. James Diedrick, "Mathilde Blind," *Dictionary of Literary Biography,* vol. 199, *Victorian Women Poets* (Detroit: Gale Research, 1998), pp. 28-39.

24. Margaret Reynolds, "Mathilde Blind," *Victorian Women Poets: An Anthology* (London: Blackwell, 1995), pp. 454-456.

25. On the spuriousness of an Islamic doctrine that women have no souls, see Barbara Freyer Stowasser, *Women in the Qur'an, Traditions, and Interpretation* (Oxford: Oxford Univ. Press, 1994), esp. chap. 2. On the subtle context-determined meanings of the veil and other elements of dress in Muslim nations, see Fadwa El Guindi, *Veil: Modesty, Privacy, and Resistance* (New York: Berg, 1999).

FURTHER READING

Criticism

Diedrick, James. "'The Hectic Beauty of Decay': Positivist Decadence in Mathilde Blind's Late Poetry." *Victorian Literature and Culture* 34, no. 2 (2006): 631-48.
    Discusses how Blind's interest in positivist science informs her extreme departures from the conceptions of gender identity and world order espoused by her contemporaries.

LaPorte, Charles. "Atheist Prophecy: Mathilde Blind, Constance Naden, and the Victorian Poetess." *Victorian Literature and Culture* 34, no. 2 (2006): 427-41.
    Explores how Blind and her contemporary, Constance Naden, employ a narrative model developed by George Eliot to "reclaim and redeem some of the prominent religious elements of the mid-century poetess tradition."

Rudy, Jason R. "Rapturous Forms: Mathilde Blind's Darwinian Poetics." *Victorian Literature and Culture* 34, no. 2 (2006): 443-59.
    "[E]xamines Blind's complex ideal of rapturous communion from the perspective of evolutionary theory, focusing in particular on Blind's nuanced juxtaposing of poetic form with Darwinian theories of development."

The Brothers Karamazov

Fyodor Dostoevsky

The following entry presents criticism of Dostoevsky's novel *Brat'ya Karamazovy* (1880; *The Brothers Karamazov*) from 1994 to 2007. For further discussion of *The Brothers Karamazov*, see *NCLC,* Volume 43; for discussion of Dostoevsky's complete career, see *NCLC,* Volume 2; for discussion of his novel *Prestuplenie i nakazanie* (*Crime and Punishment*), see *NCLC,* Volumes. 7 and 167; for discussion of his novel *Besy* (*The Possessed*), see *NCLC,* Volume 21; for discussion of his novella *Zapiski iz podpol'ya* (*Notes from Underground*), see *NCLC,* Volume 33; for discussion of his novel *Idiot* (*The Idiot*), see *NCLC,* Volume 119.

INTRODUCTION

Brat'ya Karamazovy (1880; *The Brothers Karamazov*), Dostoevsky's last and, by his own account, greatest work, is widely considered one of the masterpieces of world literature. The novel is commonly regarded as the culmination of Dostoevsky's career and is praised for its formal artistry, thematic complexity, and philosophical profundity. Ostensibly a murder mystery and tale of parricide, *The Brothers Karamazov* relates the experiences of Dmitri, Ivan, and Alyosha, the sons of corrupt landowner Fyodor Karamazov. In telling the story of Fyodor's murder—apparently by Dmitri—and its aftermath, Dostoevsky dramatizes quintessentially modern literary themes such as emotional isolation, uncertainty, disorder, and personal spiritual crisis and focuses upon the problem of maintaining faith in a world filled with evil and suffering. In *The Brothers Karamazov,* Dostoevsky presents the forces of atheism, materialism, nihilism, and socialism at odds with simple Christian piety to illustrate his overarching theme: the achievement of human redemption through acceptance of guilt and suffering.

BIOGRAPHICAL INFORMATION

Scholars have noted parallels between elements of *The Brothers Karamazov* and events in Dostoevsky's life. In 1839, Dostoevsky's father, a severe and dictatorial landowner, was murdered by servants on his estate. The shock of his father's death and Dostoevsky's feelings of guilt regarding the incident affected him deeply; Sigmund Freud, in his *Dostoevsky and Parricide,* maintained that the murder of Dostoevsky's father was the source of the author's epilepsy. Subsequent commentators have disputed this association, pointing out that the first manifestations of Dostoevsky's epilepsy did not appear until a decade after his father's murder, during Dostoevsky's imprisonment at the Omsk Penal Settlement. While exiled at Omsk for his involvement with the Petrashevsky Circle, a political discussion group that advocated utopian socialism, Dostoevsky met a former military officer who had been convicted of killing his father but had remained optimistic and unrepentant throughout his sentence. The man, whose name—Ilinsky—appeared in rough drafts of *The Brothers Karamazov,* was declared innocent ten years after his father's murder. In May, 1878, while he was still in the planning stages of *The Brothers Karamazov,* Dostoevsky's three-year-old son Alyosha died of epilepsy. The fact that his son died of a disease that he inherited from his father again focused Dostoevsky's attention on the issue of guilt between fathers and sons. Overwhelmed by grief and a sense of responsibility for his son's death, Dostoevsky traveled to the Optina Pustyn' monastery and sought guidance from renowned spiritual leader Elder Amvrosy. Following this visit, Dostoevsky returned home and began work on *The Brothers Karamazov.*

PLOT AND MAJOR CHARACTERS

Following a brief exposition of the Karamazov family history, *The Brothers Karamazov* opens in the cell of the monastic Elder Zossima, where all four members of the contentious family have gathered in an attempt to reconcile their differences. During the meeting Dmitri, a dissolute army officer, clashes with his father. The two men are rivals for the affections of a prostitute, Grushenka. The buffoonish Fyodor tells those gathered in the cell of Dmitri's engagement to the beautiful and aristocratic Katerina, his love for Grushenka, and his abuse of one Captain Snegiryov. Dmitri's explodes with fury and a fearful Fyodor is forced to leave with his son Ivan, an atheist and intellectual who, like Dmitri, despises his father, but unlike his brother displays his anger in a quiet, measured, and rational manner. Ivan's anger finds expression in his symbolic poem against authority entitled "The Legend of the Grand Inquisitor" and in his dictum "If God does not exist, everything is permitted." Ivan's words influence Smerdyakov, Fyodor's servant and by all indications illegitimate son, who lights upon this idea and convinces Ivan to go to the town of Chermashnya, leaving Fyodor unattended and vulnerable to attack. Dmitri, who has meanwhile discovered that Grushenka is missing and suspects that she is with his father, grabs a brass pestle and rushes to his father's house. He leaps the back fence and upon encountering Fyodor, feels a rush of revulsion and rage. Dmitri grabs the pestle from his pocket, seemingly intent on killing his father, but instead strikes a servant, Grigory, and flees. Following this incident Dmitri pursues Grushenka, who was not with his father but with a former lover. Dmitri succeeds in regaining Grushenka's affection, but his drunken victory celebration is cut short by the arrival of the police, who arrest him and charge him with the murder of his father. Later, Ivan speaks with Smerdyakov and discovers that the simple-minded servant is his father's true killer. Through his discussions with Smerdyakov, Ivan realizes his own guilt, as the servant merely acted upon what Ivan had told him of his philosophy of total freedom. Ivan suffers a mental collapse, and Alyosha later informs him that Smerdyakov has hanged himself. Dmitri is convicted of murder based on circumstantial evidence and is sentenced to twenty years of hard labor. Dmitri's plans to escape to America, followed by Alyosha's hopeful speech on spiritual rebirth over the grave of Captain Snegiryov's son Ilyusha, form the epilogue to the novel.

MAJOR THEMES

Despite the densely interwoven thematic structure of *The Brothers Karamazov,* critics have agreed that themes of spirituality and faith dominate the novel. Commentators have perceived that Dostoevsky's deep concern with the spiritual crisis of humanity is displayed in the character of Ivan. "The Legend of the Grand Inquisitor," Ivan's symbolic poem, dramatizes the character's defiant rejection of God's universe based on the existence of suffering in the world. In "The Legend" Ivan tells a story, set in sixteenth-century Seville, of the ninety-year-old Grand Inquisitor, who delivers his philosophy of human weakness and his own faithlessness to Jesus Christ, who has returned to Earth and has been arrested by the Inquisitor after performing a miracle. Christ sits silently throughout the exposition; his sole response to the Inquisitor is a simple kiss. Alyosha's reaction upon hearing Ivan's poem is to kiss his brother as Christ kissed the Grand Inquisitor. Critics posit that Dostoevsky intends Alyosha to be the hero of the novel and that Alyosha, along with Zossima and the values that they both espouse—compassion, active love, and human responsibility for suffering—are meant to refute Ivan's skepticism and rebellion. Alyosha's char-

acter also serves as a referent to the so-called "children's theme" of *The Brothers Karamazov.* Through Alyosha's involvement with Snegiryov's son Ilyusha and the gang of boys who torment him, Dostoevsky highlights the suffering of innocents. Critics note that the related themes of integration and reconciliation are prevalent in the novel as well. Dostoevsky explores the divided and alienated nature of the human mind, body, and spirit—personified by Ivan, Dmitri, and Alyosha, respectively—as well as in the psychological torments of pride, jealousy, and guilt that afflict nearly every character in the novel. These divisions are overcome, many scholars assert, by Zossima's reconciling philosophy, which declares that "all are responsible for all."

CRITICAL RECEPTION

Much of the criticism of *The Brothers Karamazov* focuses upon the novel's analysis of the issue of faith and religious experience; in particular, many critics explore the manner in which various philosophical and theological works and traditions informed Dostoevsky's approach to faith and religion in the novel. Some commentators maintain that Dostoevsky's forceful argument for the rejection of God's universe in "The Legend of the Grand Inquisitor" overshadows the word and deeds of Zossima and his deeply Christian philosophy as well as Alyosha's humble speech in favor of spiritual rebirth. Conversely, other scholars hold that the novel's assault on atheism, Western intellectualism, and nihilism are eloquent and sustained, and represent Dostoevsky's theodicy. A parallel line of criticism has been concerned with the formal aspects of the novel and has analyzed its complex narrative structure. The issue of realism in *The Brothers Karamazov* has also garned significant critical commentary. While some critics declare that Dostoevsky's characters, especially those of a spiritual nature such as Alyosha and Zossima, lack verisimilitude, other commentators emphasize what they have assessed as Dostoevsky's blend of literary realism with his own symbolic and spiritual conception of the world. Many critics note that Dostoevsky shuns linear time in the novel and instead allows a multiplicity of narrative voices to the tell the story, often retelling the same event from different perspectives or in light of new information. Some critics have argued that this multiplicity creates a mood of uncertainty and disorder in *The Brothers Karamazov.* Although this perception led some early reviewers to fault the work as disjointed and attacked its narrative dissonance and apparent lack of cohesiveness, many twentieth and twenty-first century critics have since appreciated the novel's plurality of voices as a groundbreaking innovation in the history of novel writing.

PRINCIPAL WORKS

Bednye lyudi [*The Poor Folk*] (novel) 1846

Dvoinik [*The Double: A Poem of St. Petersburg*] (novella) 1846; published in the journal *Otechestven-nye zapiski*

Unizhennye i oskorblennye. Iz zapisok neudavshegosia literatora [*Injury and Insult*] (novel) 1861; published in the journal *Vremia*

Zapiski iz mertvogo doma [*The House of the Dead*] (novel) 1860-62; published in the journals *Russkii mir* and *Vremia*

Zimnie zametki o letnikh vpechatleniiakh [*Winter Notes on Summer Impressions*] (novel) 1863; published in the journal *Vremia*

Zapiski iz podpol'ya [*Notes from Underground*] (novella) 1864; published in the journal *Epokha*

Igrok [*The Gambler*] (novel) 1866

Prestuplenie i nakazanie [*Crime and Punishment*] (novel) 1866; published in the journal *Russkii Vestnik*

Idiot [*The Idiot*] (novel) 1868; published in the journal *Russkii Vestnik*

Vechnyi muzh [*The Eternal Husband*] (novel) 1870; published in the journal *Zaria*

Besy [*The Possessed*] (novel) 1871-72; published in the journal *Russkii Vestnik*

Podrostok [*A Raw Youth*] (novel) 1875; published in the journal *Otechestvennye zapiski*

Dnevnik pisatelya [*The Diary of a Writer*] (essays and short stories) 1876-77, 1880, 1881

Brat'ya Karamazovy [*The Brothers Karamazov*] (novel) 1879-80; published in the journal *Russkii Vestnik*

Polnoe sobranie sochinenii. 14 vols. (novels, essays, and short stories) 1882-83

Pis'ma v chetyrekh tomakh. 4 vols. (letters) 1928

Sobranie Sochinenii. 10 vols. (novels, essays, and short stories) 1956-58

CRITICISM

Gary Rosenshield (essay date summer 1994)

SOURCE: Rosenshield, Gary. "Mystery and Commandment in *The Brothers Karamazov*: Leo Baeck and Fedor Dostoevsky." *Journal of the American Academy of Religion* 62, no. 2 (summer 1994): 483-508.

[*In the following essay, Rosenshield draws parallels between the ideas of Rabbi Leo Baeck and Dostoevsky concerning the "relationship between mystery and commandment," emphasizing Dostoevsky's representation of these ideas in* The Brothers Karamazov.]

It would seem that Leo Baeck, the twentieth-century liberal, rationalist rabbi, would have little in common with Distoevsky, the nineteenth-century Russian Orthodox author of *The Brothers Karamazov.* It is not only that they come from different religious and cultural traditions, but temperamentally they are almost stereotypically polar opposites: Baeck the German, reserved, somewhat distant,[1] Distoevsky the bilious and exuberant Russian. Further, Distoevsky seems to be the embodiment of what Baeck was polemicizing against, the Christianity that he called romantic religion,[2] a religion that "privileged" the ecstatic and the miraculous and elevated faith over ethics, or in Baeck's words, mystery over commandment. Eastern Orthodoxy, in addition, places even greater weight on mystery and the sacraments than do the Western pietistic denominations that Baeck saw as representative of the essence of Christianity.[3] Yet on further inspection, the ideas of Baeck and Dostoevsky on the relationship between mystery and commandment are in some ways so strikingly similar that one feels compelled more closely to examine both Baeck's definition of Judaism and Christianity and Dostoevsky's mystical ethics. Had Baeck misrepresented the relationship of mystery and ethics even in the more mystical forms of Christianity? Or was the prominence of ethics in *The Brothers Karamazov* merely an example of Dostoevsky's heretical divergences from Orthodox practice and doctrine?

In his essay "Mystery and Commandment," Baeck argued that mystery is also essential to Judaism, the classical religion (1981:171-85).[4] In Judaism, however, in contrast to Christianity, mystery does not play an all-encompassing role: it is always balanced by its integration with ethics in the form of the commandment, the means by which mystery is revealed. But it is precisely for Baeck's definition of ideal Judaism that *The Brothers Karamazov* poses its greatest problem; for although the religion of the novel is explicitly grounded in the most ecstatic mystical experience, it manifests itself just as strongly in universal ethical, but freely accepted, imperatives: in commandments. Moreover, in *The Brothers Karamazov,* mystery and commandment are integrally related; they issue one from the other not theoretically, but existentially, dialogically, and creatively. Has Dostoevsky heretically strayed here from the Orthodox mystical tradition? Or has he perhaps given us—in Christian form—one of the most profound existential representations of Baeck's idea, the greatest mystery of all: the dynamic, mutually validating relationship between mystery and commandment?

Before addressing these and related questions, I would like to summarize Baeck's views on the relationship of mystery to ethics in Christianity and Judaism in order to provide the categories that will guide the analysis of the mystico-ethical structure of *The Brothers Karamazov.* Baeck's definition of the essence of Christianity will be taken here not so much as an objective definition—the polemical nature of Baeck's article on Christianity led to inevitable overstatements—but rather as Baeck's method of defining the essence of his ideal Judaism: a Judaism which by the 1920s included mystery as an essential element, but which still remained as passionately as ever committed to commandment.[5]

In "Romantic Religion," Baeck's strategy was to show that at the heart of Christianity lay a doctrine of personal salvation which was based primarily on the ecstatic, mystic experience of faith and a passive, completely dependent sinner. In rejecting commandment and the ethical imperative that goes along with it, Christianity had, like many of the Oriental and Greek religions, relied almost entirely on mystery, on mysticism. Feeling and faith had become the ideal and the ultimate test—faith alone, *sola fide,* and in the extreme not only faith without ethics, but faith against ethics.[6] In romantic religion, Baeck argued, salvation is based on emotional experience, feeling, rapture, transport, the intoxication (the voluptuousness as Novalis put it) of ecstatic vision and the experience of faith, in which the self abandons itself completely to the Absolute. Since sin exists in man by nature and can be eliminated only by the annulment of nature, man is in absolute need of a miracle—grace—without which he is doomed to perdition. Man, powerless and dependent, becomes the object of God's activity, God's work. As Luther said, man should wait for salvation as one paralyzed, *velut paralyticum.* The saved soul is a soul which exists in Greek perfection: completed, rounded off, living in the past, not the future. Since he who has faith is just, justice becomes an action performed on man; man can only be made just. The result comes before the task. The grounds for ethics, the responsible subject, is destroyed, replaced by mystery and miracle. Ethics becomes a supplement. Deeds cannot buy heaven.

Baeck argued not only against the passive nature of the essence of Christianity, which he believed led to an indifference, even antagonism to ethics, but also against what he perceived to be the subtle egoism of a doctrine in which personal salvation becomes the be-all and end-all, in which human action, striving, struggle, achievement, commandment do not play a central role. "Man devoid of commandment is wrapt up in himself and his own salvation." Saints and hermits can become egoists of piety. Baeck's views with regard to salvation are not significantly different from Buber's. One must "begin with oneself, but not end with oneself; to start from oneself, but not to aim at oneself" (Buber:163); the goal is not salvation, but redemption, doing God's work. "Judaism . . . teaches that what a man does now and here with holy intent is no less important, no less true . . . than the life in the world to come" (Buber:174).[7]

Even when Baeck had come to see the importance of mystery to Judaism as well, he nevertheless insisted on

the difference of Jewish mysticism from the mysticism of Christian, Greek, and Oriental religions. Jewish mysticism did not attempt to lose itself in religious experience, in miracle and ecstasy, to seek union with the divine, but was always intimately tied with ethics, with the divine law, with commandment—with ethical monotheism. In Judaism there is an unbridgeable gap between the human and the Divine. One can approach God, speak with God, engage in dialogue with God, imitate God by performing God's commandments, but not become one with God.[8] Yet the genius of Judaism—and of Jewish mysticism—is its ability both to maintain and bridge that gap between God and man by creatively resolving "the conflict between transcendence and immanence" (174), by embracing simultaneously mystery and commandment. "Hence any opposition between mysticism and ethics has no place here [in Judaism] . . . In Judaism, all ethics has its mysticism and all mysticism its ethics" (175). There is no commandment not rooted in mystery, no mystery which does not speak out of commandment. "There is no such thing as a Judaism which is nothing but Kantian philosophy or ethical culture. . . . And the distinctive essence of Judaism is lost, too, where the abundance of its laws may still prevail, but merely as something that is performed, severed from its roots in mystery, void of devotion" (178).

As might be expected from his criticism in "Romantic Religion" of the passivism of Christianity and man's absolute dependence on God, Baeck posits for man in Judaism an active and creative role in the endless redemption of the world in history. Man lives essentially in the future. "The commandment of God is a commandment which leads into the future and involves a mission which, in the words of the Bible, continues 'from generation into generation'" (180). "Redemption here is not redemption from the world, but in the world, consecration of the world, realization of the kingdom of God" (181). This relationship between ethics and mystery, is, moreover, not an abstract formulation, a solution to an intellectual problem (that is a problem confronting all religions, of determining the relationship of ethics and the mystical) but the basis for a set of religious beliefs and practices that Baeck lived, and one that emerged even stronger after having being tested in the ultimate crucible of faith, Nazi Germany.[9]

The literature on the religion of Dostoevsky and his novels is voluminous and partisan: that is, interpretable.[10] Interpretations often reveal as much, if not more, about readers and their agendas than they do about the actual texts. Literary critics, however, have shown that some of the religious views and practices of Father Zosima, the religious ideal in *The Brothers Karamazov,* diverge from Orthodoxy and even owe a great deal to the Western literary tradition. Roger Anderson has shown the mythic and pantheistic side of Father Zosima's religious practices and philosophy (272-289) and

Sven Linnér that Dostoevsky's Father Zosima diverges significantly from the typical Russian *starets* (religious elder), and even from Father Zosima's most widely recognized Russian prototypes (85-111).[11] Linnér also shows that the characterization of Father Zosima follows the models of Rousseau, Hugo, Chateaubriand, and other Western writers as much as it does those of Orthodox hagiography (112-140).[12] Russian Orthodox theologians, thinkers, and critics also are not in accord about Dostoevsky, yet Zenkovsky argues that however much Dostoevsky constituted "a break with the classical formulations of the Church Fathers," his writings were the greatest influence on the Russian Orthodox religious renaissance of the late nineteenth and early twentieth centuries (145).[13]

Most Orthodox theologians, moreover, would agree that the essence of Orthodoxy, as Baeck might say, is at the heart of Dostoevsky's work, and especially *The Brothers Karamazov*. Moreover, *The Brothers Karamazov* provides us with an unusual opportunity for comparative analysis. Mystical experiences are not a common occurrence, to say the least, in nineteenth-century psychological novels, not to speak of great ones. The Dostoevskian novel, however, is radically atypical in that it attempts not only to fuse and integrate diverse and heterogeneous materials but also to establish the validity of the interrelated but disparate worlds of the noumenal and phenomenal.[14] The religious experiences of at least three of the characters in *The Brothers Karamazov*, Father Zosima, Father Zosima's brother, Markel, and Alesha Karamazov, are firmly grounded in mystical experience: in transport, rapture, ecstasy. Moreover, on first inspection, they seem to be the perfect stuff for Baeck's critique of Christianity in "Romantic Religion." In an attempt to avoid adding to numerous generalizations on Dostoevsky's religion, I would like instead to confine myself to a close textual and contextual analysis of several of the actual mystical experiences themselves.[15]

The most detailed description of a specific mystical experience is that of Alesha Karamazov. It is the night of the murder of Alesha's father, Fedor Karamazov. Alesha's spiritual father, Father Zosima, the elder of the monastery at which Alesha is a novice, passed away the night before. Alesha had been asked earlier by Father Zosima to mind his brothers, both of them, for Father Zosima had seen hatred and parricide in both Dmitri's and Ivan's heart. Instead of being with his brothers, who were in most need of his help, Alesha had decided to remain with the dying Father Zosima, who least of all, needed Alesha's attendance or assistance. In fact, after Father Zosima's death, Alesha, whose faith was shaken by the rapid decay of his beloved mentor, had gone to the reputedly dissolute and wicked Grushen'ka to ruin himself because of the shame he felt over the scandal created by the stench of Zosima's rotting body. Alesha venerated Zosima as a saint. According to the

Russian hagiographical tradition, the body of a true saint does not undergo normal decay. But Grushen'ka treats Alesha like a dear friend, she takes compassion on him, and restores his faith.

When he returns to the hermitage, he hears Father Paissy reading about the marriage of Cana of Galilee. He falls down upon his knees before the coffin as though it were a holy shrine and begins to pray almost mechanically. His heart is already overflowing in love and he has an overwhelming sense of light, joy, and the wholeness of things. The words for joy, ecstasy, transport, and light occur over thirty times in some three pages.[16] Alesha imagines he sees Father Zosima as a guest at the marriage feast in Cana. Overwhelmed by his hallucination, Alesha runs outside, falls down on the ground and undergoes what is clearly a mystical experience.

If we study the Cana of Galilee section carefully we see that in many ways Dostoevsky's representation of Alesha's mystical experience coincides quite closely with Baeck's description of the romantic miracle in Christianity. (I omit the first half of the experience having to do with the marriage feast at Cana.)

> The silence of earth seemed to melt into the silence of the heavens. The mystery of earth was one with the mystery of the stars. . . . Alesha stood, gazed, and as though mown down, fell to the ground.
>
> He did not know why he embraced it. He could not have told why he so longed so irresistibly to kiss it, to kiss it all. But he kissed it weeping, sobbing and watering it with his tears, and vowed passionately to love it, to love it forever and ever. "Water the earth with the tears of your joy, and love those tears," echoed in his soul. What was he weeping over? Oh! in his rapture he was weeping even over those stars, which were shining to him from the abyss of space, and "he was not ashamed of that ecstasy." There seemed to be threads from all those innumerable worlds of God, linking his soul to them, and it was trembling all over "in contact with other worlds." He longed to forgive everyone and for everything, and to beg forgiveness. Oh, not for himself, but for all men, for all and for everything. "And others are praying for me too," echoed again in his soul. But with every instant he felt clearly and, as it were, tangibly, that something firm and unshakable as that vault of heaven had entered into his soul. It was as though some idea had seized the sovereignty of his mind—and it was for all his life and forever and ever. He had fallen on the earth a weak youth, but he rose up a resolute champion, and he knew and felt it suddenly at the very moment of his ecstasy. And never, never, all his life long, could Alesha forget that minute. "Someone visited my soul in that hour," he used to say afterwards, with implicit faith in his words.
>
> Within three days he left the monastery in accordance with the words of his elder, who had bidden him to "sojourn in the world."

> (340-341)[17]

What Alesha experienced has been called "cosmic consciousness." William James, in the section on mysticism in his *Varieties of Religious Experience,* cites a number of examples of this phenomenon including one by R. M. Bucke, who coined the term. In all such experiences, the individual enters a state of exultation which is distinctly different from all types of noetic and sensual experiences, it is a form of superconsciousness: when one feels completely at one with the universe and senses that one has acquired the most profound knowledge of the true nature of all things.

R. M. Bucke describes the phenomenon in the following way:

> The prime characteristic of cosmic consciousness is consciousness of the cosmos, that is, of the life and order of the universe. Along with the consciousness of the cosmos there occurs an intellectual enlightenment which alone would place the individual on a new plane of existence—would make him almost a member of a new species. To this is added a state of moral exaltation, an indescribable feeling of elevation, elation and joyousness, and a quickening of the moral sense, which is fully as striking, and more important than is the enhanced intellectual power. With these come what may be called a sense of immortality, a consciousness of eternal life, not a conviction that he shall have this, but the consciousness that he has it already.
>
> (306)

Recounting his own mystical experience, Bucke continues:

> Directly afterward there came upon me a sense of exultation, of immense joyousness accompanied or immediately followed by an intellectual illumination impossible to describe. Among other things, I did not merely come to believe, but I saw the universe is not composed of dead matter, but is, on the contrary, a living Presence; I became conscious in myself of eternal life. It was not a conviction that I would have eternal life, but a consciousness that I possessed eternal life then; I saw that all men are immortal; that the cosmic order is such that without any peradventure all things work together for the good of each and all; that the foundation principle of the world, of all the worlds is what we call love, and the happiness of each and all is in the long run absolutely certain . . . the memory of it and the sense of reality of what it taught has remained during the quarter of a century which has since elapsed. I knew then that what the vision showed was true. . . . I may say that consciousness has never, even during periods of the deepest depression, been lost.
>
> (307)

Equally interesting is the testimony of Malwida von Meysenburg who associates her experience with prayer. Alesha is at prayer when he experiences his transport. In the Eastern Orthodox Church, prayer and the mechanical repetition of prayers is one of the main means of what James calls methodical mysticism, a mysticism which is consciously cultivated.[18]

> I was alone upon the seashore as all these thoughts flow over me, liberating and reconciling . . . I was impelled to kneel down, this time before the illimitable ocean, symbol of the Infinite. I felt that I prayed as I never prayed before and knew now what prayer really is: to return from the solicitude of individuation into the consciousness of unity with all that is, to kneel down as one passes away, and to rise up as one imperishable. Earth, heaven, and sea resounded as in one vast world-encircling harmony.
>
> (304)

The similarity of Bucke's experience to Alesha's is especially striking in its emphasis on "moral exaltation," "more important than the enhanced intellectual power," and on universal harmony in which "all things work for the good of each and all." Alesha senses the "threads from all those innumerable worlds of God, linking his soul to them." Malwida von Meysenburg's testimony not only focuses on the importance of prayer in inducing the mystical state but also echoes the theme of resurrection, of falling down on the earth and rising "up as one insuperable." Alesha, too, "rises up resolute as a champion." Further, there are also several crucial aspects of Alesha's mystical experience that also seem in accordance with Baeck's description of the Christian mystical experience. First, faith descends upon Alesha. He is overcome, overwhelmed by his experience. Though it is a violent experience, it is essentially passive. The Russian says it was "as though he were mown down." The experience is described in terms of transport, ecstasy, rapture, voluptuousness, even seizure—as Alesha finds himself thrown on the ground. One is reminded of the perfect peace and harmony that overtakes Myshkin in *The Idiot* in the aura before the onset of an attack of epilepsy. Further, it seems as though the intensity of the emotion, the transport of the soul "to other worlds," guarantees the validity of the religious experience.

The Brothers Karamazov, of course, is not hagiography, but a nineteenth-century psychological novel. The mystical experience needs to be analyzed in the context of fictional reality, a fact which Dostoevsky himself insists on by linking the experience symbolically, narratologically, and psychologically with almost everything else in the novel. To use the imagery of Alesha's mystical experience itself, there are innumerable threads linking Alesha's experience with the novel's past, present, and future.

First, the mystic experience is directly associated on many planes with the representations and discussions of Christian miracle in the text itself. The supporters of Father Zosima have expected a miracle upon his death confirming his sainthood. The expected miracle does not occur; the body, rather than exuding a pleasing fragrance, decomposes and stinks. There are the disappointment and dismay of Father Zosima's followers, prime among them Alesha, and the joy of his enemies. But as one miracle fails to occur, another one comes to take its place. It occurs in the monastery, where Alesha has returned to pray. Over the dead and stinking body, the windows opened, Father Paissy reads of Christ's first great miracle at the marriage feast in Cana of Galilee. Christ came to the poor and humble and in their joy. It is after all joy, rapture, ecstasy which is the keynote of Alesha's experience, and thus the miracle, the mystery, is in complete accord with it. And behold an even greater miracle occurs in its seeming absence. In Alesha's imagination, Father Zosima has been called to the wedding feast by Christ, and at the feast, he calls out to Alesha reminding him that he has been called, or will be called, too. And the greatest miracle of all is that Alesha is indeed called, for when he rises after the experience, he does so with his faith reborn. He has received a sign. He has, as it were, been resurrected from the dead, taking part, in joy, in the marriage feast of the prefigured heavenly kingdom.

I would like to try to answer, using Baeck's categories, several questions concerning the more purely religious sides of the mystical experiences in *The Brothers Karamazov.* First, just how important are ritual and mystery to Alesha's experience and is the validation of the experience to be found in the rapture, the ecstasy attending the experience itself? Actually there is little religious ritual represented in *The Brothers Karamazov,* and in general rather than emphasizing the importance of ritual, sacrament, miracle, and dogma in the Church, Dostoevsky either passes them over or subjects them to a good deal of criticism. The upholders of asceticism in the monastery and strict adherence to tradition, ritual, and dogma are shown to be engaged in what Baeck would call an egoism of piety, a voluptuousness of abnegation. In contrast to Father Ferapont, Father Zosima seems to regard ritual and dogma, even the sacraments, not nearly as important as man's relation to his fellow man. Father Zosima is even accused by some of his opponents among the monks of abusing the sacraments.[19] In the novel, this is to be sure all malice; on the other hand, Father Zosima is not presented as a champion of sacramental religion. When he speaks of mystery, he speaks of stories, of biblical narratives, of love: one of the greatest of all miracles, for him, is the ability of Job to love again after all had been taken from him. Zosima embraces, to be sure, not a few of the utopian socialist ethical values (universal brotherhood, etc.) of Dostoevsky's earlier years.[20] It is certainly not strict Orthodoxy, but probably Dostoevsky never intended it to be.

The representation of the mystical experience, which at first seems so perfectly to fit Baeck's description of Christian mystery, diverges in several important respects from ecstatic absorption into, or union with, the Divine that Baeck says is especially characteristic of the Eastern mystery religions.[21] Dostoevsky emphasizes

throughout the passage precisely Alesha's ecstasy, joy, rapture, transport and he uses the same words that Father Zosima uses elsewhere to describe the holiest emotions of the Christian experience. But the rapture is first of all in accord with the miracle of Cana of Galilee which Father Paissy is reading. Christ visited the poor and the humble in their hour of joy, and Alesha comes to experience the same joy as though he himself had been invited to the feast, and perhaps that is exactly what he is doing in his imagination: envisioning the joy to come in the Kingdom of God promised by the Resurrection. Eastern Orthodoxy in general places far more emphasis on the glory of the Resurrection of the victorious Christ than on Christ the victim, the suffering of the crucified Christ, the Man of Sorrows, the subject of the *Stabat Mater.* It tends to see the Crucifixion more in terms of the Resurrection, the cross as an emblem of victory. The most dramatic moment in Orthodoxy is the bursting open of the tomb under the pressure of divine life, and Christ triumphant risen from the dead. The "liturgy still enshrines that element of sheer joy in the Resurrection of the Lord that we find in so many of the early Christian writings" (Hammond:20). Particularly striking examples of this joy in Christ's Resurrection are the Easter Sermons of Sergei Bulgakov, who reminds the congregation of the first word of the risen Christ in his appearance to the myrrh-bearing women: "Rejoice" (Schmemann:300-301). To be sure, the joy and ecstasy in the novel are a validation of the experience, but they are in large part motivated by the theology of joy within the text itself and in Eastern Orthodoxy.

The more problematic question regarding the nature of mysticism in *The Brothers Karamazov* is that of absorption into or union with the Divine. According to the Orthodox Church the final goal of all Christians is deification, *theosis.* "For Orthodoxy, man's salvation and redemption mean his deification."[22] Christ prays that we shall be taken up into the Godhead. Athanasius says that God became man so that man could become God. But according to Timothy Ware deification does not mean man becomes God with a capital G. "Union with God means union with the divine energies, not the divine essence: the Orthodox Church, while speaking of deification and union, rejects all forms of pantheism" (237). God's essence is unknowable, we can know him only in the manifestations of his energies: that is, in his creation, his revelation, his actions, his relationship to man. And here Ware attempts to separate Orthodoxy from "Eastern religions" and the charge of mystical fusion and loss of identity. "The mystical union between God and man is a true union, yet in this union Creator and creature do not become fused into a single being. Unlike the eastern religions which teach that man is swallowed up in the deity, Orthodox mystical theology has always insisted that man, however, closely linked to God, retains his full personal identity and integrity.

Man, when deified, remains distinct (though not separate) from God" (237).[23] Underlying the last analogy of course is the Orthodox view of the Trinity in which each member of the Trinity, in its unity, still maintains its personal characteristics.

Alesha's mystical experience is in accord with the above interpretation of union with the divine, although it would be stretching it to say that deification is at the center of Alesha's experience. Dostoevsky says of Alesha that "there seemed to be threads from all those innumerable worlds of God, coming together all at once in his soul, and it was trembling all over in contact with other worlds." What Alesha experiences is not an absorption into the deity, a fusion with the deity, but perhaps a feeling of oneness with all of God's revealed creation, with God's *energies*. This is what causes him to throw himself down on the earth (matter in Orthodoxy will be redeemed in the end, too) and wet it with tears of joy. So, too, in his imagination, he is not deified, but is invited to come to participate in the wedding feast along with Father Zosima, where all, however, seem to have maintained their personal integrities. We may view this entire literary representation of the mystical experience, as well as the entire novel if you will, as a sort of verbal icon, in which the Divine participates through its energies rather than its essence.

But what about the essential point, the relationship between mystery and ethics? At the very height of his mystical experience, the auric moment to speak in Dostoevskian terms, Alesha has a realization, an illumination of the essential truth of all creation, that we are all responsible to each other for everything. He wishes to forgive everyone for everything and to be forgiven by everyone for everything, just as they are at this moment asking him. It is a vision of redeemed mankind, of heaven on earth. But it is also a moral vision, a vision of man's responsibility for his fellow man, of Alesha's personal responsibility for the death of his father, his responsibility to his brothers, his responsibility to love his neighbor as himself: it is the teaching of Father Zosima, but also the Baeckian commandment in Dostoevskian dress.

Here we must abandon Alesha, who soon after his vision leaves the monastery to go out into the world, and work our way back to the mystical experiences of Father Zosima and his elder brother Markel who died of consumption when he was seventeen. Before Markel dies he has visions (brought on, to be sure, by his illness) in which he comes to see not only God, but the necessary relationship between the existence of God and man's relation to his fellow man:

> A marvelous change passed over him, his spirit seemed transformed (267). "Mother, little heart of mine," he said (he had begun using such strange caressing words

at that time), "little heart of mine, my joy, believe me, everyone is really responsible to all men for all men for everything. I don't know how to explain it to you, but I feel it is so, painfully even. And how is it we went on then living, getting angry and not knowing?"

(268)

Here mystery and ethics are inextricably bound, not by necessity, but by mystery. The formula is not Baeckian, but Christian: faith precedes ethics; ethics arises mysteriously but directly from the ground of faith. It is not the Baeckian "Thou shalt love thy neighbor as thyself—I am thy God," but "I am thy God—Thou shalt love thy neighbor as thyself."

But Markel, like Prince Myshkin in **The Idiot,** is a special case. His ecstatic visions are engendered at least in part by his illness. Although illness, and imminent death, can be interpreted, as in Tolstoy, as the essential realities that make possible the vision of truth obscured by daily life, Dostoevsky seems to want to avoid having the epiphanies in **The Brothers Karamazov** conditioned by illness.[24] Thus Father Zosima himself, in contrast to Markel, is in perfect health when, right before a duel, he experiences an epiphany in which are revealed to him the oneness of all creation and its moral correlative: mutual and universal responsibility. Though Zosima and his brother are equally overwhelmed by the same ethical conclusions as a result of their mystical experience, the ground of the mythical experience differs—ethically as well as physically. This is significant because it is Father Zosima, and not his brother, who sets the pattern for the later epiphanies of the Karamazov brothers. Moreover, Zosima's vision is not only a moral one, and one that has profoundly ethical consequences in his later life, it also arises from a profoundly moral ground, from a set of clearly delineated moral and psychological circumstances. From what we know of Father Zosima's life before the duel, he seems, like Dmitri Karamazov before him, to have been little preoccupied with religious questions. It is also clear that Father Zosima bows down before Dmitri at the hermitage because he sees Dmitri as a version of his former self. He had been living, like Dmitri, the life of a rake in the Russian literary tradition, an offshoot of the Byronic Silvio in Pushkin's "The Shot" and Pechorin in Lermontov's "A Hero of Our Time." If he had been living in Kierkegaardian despair, he was one of those who, unlike the Underground Man and Raskol'nikov, were not conscious of it.[25] When Zosima strikes his servant before the duel in a moment of anger, it precipitates a crisis that represents the culmination of a long unconscious psychological-ethical process—as does Dmitri's dream of the starving babes. The preparation for the ground of miracle is long and arduous, full of trial and tribulation. Like the miracle of grace in the Orthodox tradition, the sinner must have been prepared to receive it. There must be a cooperation of man with God. The duel is the final blow, a blow by which the individual awakens to the existential consequences of his decisions, and finds himself responsible not for the life of a loved one, but for that of a rival, or enemy: that is, one whose murder can be rationally, but not existentially, justified. The mystical experience is a miracle, but a miracle psychologically grounded in the past.[26]

To Baeck the relation between the commandment and the Absolute (God) is a mystery, it is not logically, but existentially derived. That following God's commandment one comes to see God is no less a mystery than the meeting of the finite and infinite and the temporal and eternal. That loving one's neighbor as oneself would lead one to the living God is as much a mystery as perhaps the relation between religious experience and ethics must always be. "Jewish piety lives in the paradox, in the polarity with all its tension and compactness. That which is a contradiction in the abstract world of mere theory is made a unity and a whole in the religious consciousness" (Baeck 1981:174). This formulation is perhaps not that distant from the Orthodox mystical doctrine of grace and free will according to Vladimir Lossky:

> Thus grace is not a reward for the merit of human will, as Pelagianism would have it; but no more is it the cause of the "meritorious acts" of free will. For it is not a question of merits but co-operation, of a synergy of the two wills, divine and human, a harmony in which grace bears ever more and more fruit, and is appropriated—"acquired"—by the human person. Grace is the presence of God within us which demands constant effort on our part; these efforts, however, in no way determine grace, nor does grace act upon our liberty as if it were external or foreign to it. This doctrine, faithful to the apophatic spirit of the Eastern tradition, expresses the mystery of the coincidence of grace and human freedom in good works, without recourse to positive and rational terms [which Lossky considers to be the errors of both Pelagius and Augustine; GR].
>
> (1987-98)[27]

That Zosima should have a mystical experience revealing the oneness of all creation is not rationally explainable, but the *ethical* conclusion of the experience of mutual responsibility derives directly from the revelation, the epiphany—that is, the oneness of creation, and the mystical links tying everything to everything else. If the all is one, the commandment of loving one's neighbor as oneself is resolved. The mystical experience remains mystery, but the form of the vision is almost purely ethical. Ethics leads to mystery, mystery leads to commandment, and commandment follows consistently from the vision of the mystical experience.[28] One also must not lose sight here that this moral epiphany is dictated by the ethical system of the novel wherein the principle of mutual responsibility is set against that of license: all is permitted. Dostoevsky remains romantic, founding the revelation of the commandment on mysti-

cal experience (however shaped by previous moral decisions), where the less romantic Baeck sees revelation, the mystery, arising out of the existential *choices* of the commandments. It is also important to stress that in both Baeck and Dostoevsky, the commandment is freely chosen, and that only those who freely choose God's commandment experience true freedom. In *The Brothers Karamazov,* Father Zosima's life and ideas serve as both a defense of a freely chosen faith (Christianity) and an implicit attack against the rationalistic system of the Grand Inquisitor, which starts with absolute freedom and ends with demonic compulsion, imposing its "faith" by manipulating the human need for "miracle, mystery, and authority" (232). Just as "The Russian Monk" constitutes an attempt to give intimations of the proper relationship between mystery and commandment, so **"The Grand Inquisitor"** can be seen, conversely, as Dostoevsky's exposé of the perverted relationship that must exist between mystery and commandment in a rationalist utopia.

But is the mystical experience, and the moral enlightenment that accompanies it, presented in Dostoevsky as an end in itself, as salvation? And if salvation is achieved through miracle, and the ecstasy of miracle is the validation of the miracle, does not the romantic become, through the mystical experience, a completed self, a saved self, who need not proceed further, need not enter into the world? Lossky, when speaking of the Orthodox doctrine of deification, says: "The deification or *theosis* of the creature will be realized in its fullness only in the age to come, after the resurrection of the dead. This deifying union has, nevertheless, to be fulfilled ever more and more even in this present life, through the transformation of our corruptible and depraved nature and by its adaption for eternal life" (196).

But Dostoevsky goes further and suggests the heretical possibility—through mystical experience—of experiencing heaven on earth, an aspect of Dostoevsky's thought which Zenkovsky has characterized as "Christian naturalism" (136-37). Father Zosima's brother explicitly states: "Mother, it's not for grief I'm crying. Though I can't explain it to you, I like to humble myself before them, for I don't know how to love them enough. If I have sinned against anyone, yet all forgive me, too, and that's heaven. Am I not in heaven now?" (268-269). Echoing his brother, Father Zosima says "We alone don't understand that life is a paradise, for we have only to understand that and it will at once be fulfilled in all its beauty, we shall embrace each other and weep" (278-279).[29]

Baeck has spoken of the egoism of salvation. But in *The Brothers Karamazov,* at least novelistically, salvation is not often presented as a goal, and where it is presented as a goal, it is also presented as egoism. Where the monastery becomes a place solely for personal salvation rather than a light unto the world, that is, an instrument for the salvation of *all* souls, it is a perversion of mission. In Russian Orthodox theology, salvation cannot be achieved individually, in separation from the group; personal salvation is possible only as part of the collective. As Khomiakov writes: "We know that when any one of us falls, he falls alone; but no one is saved alone. But he who is saved in the church, is saved as a member of it and in union with all its other members" (*Tserkov'* 67).[30] Father Zosima is explicit on this point (293-294). Father Zosima sends Alesha out into the world not for the salvation of his soul, it seems to me, but to strive and to suffer, to fulfill the commandment. To paraphrase Dostoevsky, man sins most when he does not strive to fulfill the commandment. The saint must live not for the salvation of his own soul, for bliss, for ecstasy. The salvation of the soul is achieved not through desire aimed at the self, but through commitment to others, and only when the self loses consciousness of the self as an "individual," as a self defined essentially as separate from others, only when it realizes itself in its commitment to the other. "Seek no reward, for great is your reward on this earth" (301).

Zosima will later also insist, as do Baeck and Buber, that it is only through the fulfillment of the commandment—active love—that we will come to know God. "If you love everything, you will perceive the divine mystery in things. Once you perceive it, you will begin to comprehend it better every day" (298).

In practice, Father Zosima looks upon his mystical experience, however unique, in no way as final. He does not see the experience as an end but as a gift to challenge man to strive through active love to achieve the ideal revealed in the epiphany.[31] Ecstasy accompanies the vision, but the vision is one that implicitly calls for struggle and commandment. Zosima sees love as a task, as hard and incessant work: "Work without ceasing. If you remember in the night as you go to sleep I have not done what I ought to have done, rise up and do it" (300). "Brother, love is a teacher, but one must know how to acquire it, for it is hard to acquire, it is dearly bought, it is won slowly by long labor. For we must love not only occasionally, for a moment, but forever. Everyone can love occasionally, even the wicked can" (298).[32] Though active love is buttressed by mystery, it is realized only through struggle. If there is any salvation it is not at the moment of the mystical experience at all, but in the actual performance of the commandment that is revealed through it. "There is only one means of personal salvation, then take yourself and make yourself responsible for all man's sins, that is the truth, you know, for as soon as you sincerely make yourself responsible for everything and for all men, you will at once see that it is really so" (299). The twentieth-century liberal rabbi and the nineteenth-century Ortho-

dox novelist are, after all, not so far apart in their understanding of the relationship between mysticism and ethics.

That resemblances should exist, and that Dostoevsky has, in addition, presented one of the greatest demonstrations of Baeck's theological position, is not, however, another mystery. As we have seen, both Baeck and Dostoevsky diverged, in places, significantly from the original sources of their traditions. Baeck had an excellent classical as well as a Jewish education. Further, he was greatly influenced by the neo-Kantian thought of his teacher, Hermann Cohen and various currents of nineteenth and twentieth-century Christian thought. Though Dostoevsky came from an entirely different tradition, he too was a child of his age, and was greatly influenced, as were most Russian Orthodox theologians and thinkers, by Western—and especially—German and French thought. Father Zosima's thought is shot through with undeniably pantheistic, Franciscan, Pietistic, Utopian Socialist, Hegelian historicist and sentimental humanitarian elements.

There are, of course, significant and obvious differences between Baeck and Dostoevsky which I have no wish to minimize. But in the course of their creative work, both set before themselves similar tasks: somehow to preserve, if not reconcile, the mystical and ethical in their world-views. In the first edition of *What is Judaism?* (1905), a polemic with von Harnack's *What is Christianity?*, Baeck presented a strictly ethical Judaism. But in "Mystery and Commandment," we already see Baeck's ardent attempt fully to integrate mystery with ethics into the center of his Judaism. Dostoevsky, too, was engaged in a similar enterprise, one that, moreover, posed a seemingly insuperable dilemma in his preferred form of expression: the psychological realistic novel, a genre far more conducive to the representation of ethical than religious experience. ***The Brothers Karamazov*** marks Dostoevsky's greatest attempt to integrate—in a genre which is by its very nature ironic and deflationary—a positive portrayal of Orthodox mystical experience in relation to ethics.

The similarities between Baeck's and Dostoevsky's projects might also be explained in terms of the intrinsic natures of Judaism and Orthodoxy themselves. To be sure, in the last two centuries in Judaism more and more emphasis has been placed on the role of ethics, on ethical monotheism. Orthodoxy, on the other hand, has always seen mysticism at the very center of the faith and has generally concerned itself with ethics less than most Western Christian denominations.[33] But modern Judaism's increasing flexibility with, and receptivity to, mysticism and Eastern Orthodoxy's less Augustinian understanding of grace and free will make the reconciliation of ethics and mysticism perhaps less problematic for theologians and novelists like Baeck and Dostoevsky. Perhaps its emphasis on *theosis* (the deification of matter or the world)[34] and synergy (the active cooperation of man and God in man's salvation) facilitates the development of an ethics coupled with mysticism. And this seems in fact to be what modern Russian theologians, and Dostoevsky, have done, integrating an ethics into a tradition that does not emphasize ethics but which is not theologically inhospitable to it: deeds in Orthodoxy are seen neither as an obstacle to salvation nor a guarantee of acquiring grace. But perhaps most important, Dostoevsky and Baeck were in the end searching for the same thing, an ethics grounded in the eternal, in the mystery of life (*Lebensgeheimnis*). And it is perhaps not surprising that they both found it in a mystical union of mystery and commandment.

Notes

1. See, for example, the interesting description of Baeck in Walter Laqueur's novel *The Missing Years* (143-145).

2. See Baeck's essay, "Romantic Religion," in *Judaism and Christianity*. The translation is of a revised and expanded version (printed in 1938) of the 1922 essay.

3. Vladimir Lossky, in justifying the title of his work on Orthodoxy, writes: "There is, therefore, no Christian mysticism without theology; but, above all, there is no theology without mysticism. It is not by chance that the tradition of the Eastern Church has reserved the name of 'theologian' particularly for three sacred writers of whom the first is St. John, most 'mystical' of the four Evangelists; the second St. Gregory Nazianzen, writer of contemplative poetry; and the third St. Symeon, called 'the New Theologian,' the singer of union with God. Mysticism is accordingly treated in the present work as the perfecting crown of all theology: as theology *par excellence*" (9). What the Western churches suffer from according to A. S. Khomiakov is the sacrament of rationalism (59). There is, of course, a later (post-Petrine), more Latinate, scholastic, and rationalistic Russian Orthodox tradition (Prokopovich, for example), but obviously this is a tradition that at least Dostoevsky and the most prominent Russian Orthodox thinkers of his time did not embrace.

4. The original "Geheimnis und Gebot" first appeared in *Der Leuchter* (1921-1922:137-53). It is also included in Baeck's *Wege in Judentum: Aufsätze und Reden*.

5. For a discussion of the evolution of Baeck's greater acceptance of mysticism as an integral part of the Jewish tradition, see Altmann; Friedlander (155-189). For two other early essays of Baeck on the role of mysticism in Judaism, see 1933 (90-102). The essays are: "Bedeutung der jüdischen Mystik für unsere Zeit," published in 1923 in *Die Tat,* and "Die Mystik im Judentum" published in 1928 in *Süddeutsche Monatshefte.*

6. The object of attack was Pauline Christianity, specifically certain pietistic Protestant denominations Baeck associated with the romantic Christianity of Schleiermacher in which the self gave itself up entirely, in complete dependence, to the Absolute in the hope of personal salvation, in the hope of God's grace.

7. Further, Buber writes: "One of the main points in which Christianity differs from Judaism is that it makes each man's salvation his highest aim. Judaism regards each man's soul as a serving member of God's creation which, by man's work, is to become the Kingdom of God; thus no soul has its object in itself, in its own salvation" (165).

8. Altmann discusses Baeck's borrowing from Edvard Lehmann, the Danish historian of religion. Baeck argues that the new mysticism Lehmann writes about is really the old Jewish mysticism, in which "God no longer wants his faithful one to claim identity with Him; he desires that in his fear of God he remain himself" (1933:17-18). Even when Baeck comes closest to implying union, he concludes with commandment: "Alle Versenkung in die Gottestiefe ist immer zugleich eine Versenkung in den Willen Gottes, in sein Gebot" (1933:37).

9. Baeck is not without his critics. See, for example, the critical comments on Baeck by Richard Rubenstein (74).

10. On the religion of *The Brothers Karamazov,* see, for example: Romano Guardini (135-239); Berdyaev (188-212); Ivanov (109-166); Hamilton (245-262); E. Solov'ev (47-53); Rozanov; Chaitin (68-87); Gibson (169-208); Sutherland (1976:364-373; 1977); Walsh (161-164); Haim (198-209); Hackel (139-168).

11. For the Orthodox thinker who most criticized the figure of Zosima, see Leont'ev (7:438-48; 9:13, 17).

12. That Dostoevsky's portrait of Zosima borrows from Western models does not invalidate it in terms of Orthodox spirituality. By the middle of the eighteenth century, Russian theologians, elders, and other religious figures were considerably influenced by Western philosophic, religious, and even secular thought. It is thus not surprising to see elements of Western ideas in the works of Russian thinkers and churchmen of this time and after, despite the fact that a strong reaction against positivism in the nineteenth century led to a move-

ment advocating a return to original Orthodox sources. Timothy Ware notes of St. Tikhon of Zadonsk (1724-83), the main prototype of Father Zosima: "A great preacher and a fluent writer, Tikhon is particularly interesting as an example of one who, like most of his contemporaries, borrowed heavily from the West, but who remained at the same time firmly rooted in the classic tradition of Orthodox spirituality" (129). For other Western elements in the characterization of Zosima and in the religious thought of the novel in general, see Terras (29-30, 57, 77-78, 248-50, 252, 258-261).

13. For the most critical view of Father Zosima as an Orthodox monk and of the religion of *The Brothers Karamazov* as Orthodoxy, see Leont'ev (8:193-202). For Leont'ev, even Zola's depictions of monks were much closer to the spirit of true, personal monasticism than Dostoevsky's. Further, he states that the religion of the novel is far more imbued with sentimental, democratic humanism than with true Orthodoxy. Vladimir Solov'ev, a theologian, and Russia's greatest philosopher, also expressed his doubts—in a letter to Leont'ev—about Dostoevsky's religion. See Leont'ev, *Pis'ma* 59. See also Pletnev (289); Gorodetzky. For those emphasizing Dostoevsky's basic adherence to Orthodox thinking and spirituality, see Berdyaev; A. L. Volynskii; Preosviashchennyi; Losskii. Gustafson sees Father Zosima no less than an icon of "the Orthodox view of life" (461).

14. As Guardini points out, Dostoevsky "had the gift to so translate extrahuman existence into human terms that a real human being would appear before us, yet so that the image of that extrahuman element would emerge from it" (101). Terras probably is stating a commonly held view when he writes that *The Brothers Karamazov,* more than any other work of Dostoevsky's, affirms his belief in the reality of mystic experience" (75).

15. By concentrating on these passages, I shall, of necessity, be treating the religion of *The Brothers Karamazov* somewhat "monologically." The mystical in the novel, of course, exists in a polyphonic context, in constant dialogue with other religious points of view—or voices—as well as with more rationalistic voices, such as those of Ivan Karamazov and Dmitri Karamazov's defense lawyer, Fetiukovich, who argue that mysticism should have no place in real life.

16. The image of light is central to Orthodox mysticism. According to Ware, for Hesychasm, the most mystical strain of Orthodoxy, "the culmination of mystical experience was the vision of Divine and Uncreated Light" (75).

17. The English in all translations of Dostoevsky has been revised where necessary on the basis of the Russian texts in Dostoevskii, vol. 14.

18. For the mystical nature of prayer in Orthodoxy, see Ware (310-314); Bulgakov (170-71).

19. This de-emphasis on ritual, dogma and the sacraments has elicited charges by Leont'ev (8:199, 203) and others that Dostoevsky's religion diverges significantly from Orthodoxy and verges in places on eighteenth-century "enlightened" Pietism, Franciscan teachings, and sentimental humanitarian. See also Terras: 249, 251, 258, 259, for citations of specific passages. Among other things, Father Zosima has a Catholic ivory crucifix hanging in his cell (32).

20. This socialist brotherhood has, of course, been transformed by Zosima into a Christian, free communion—and community—of souls. It is the antithesis of the forced, universal socialist "brotherhood" advanced by Ivan in "The Grand Inquisitor."

21. It is difficult to say whether Baeck considered, or would have considered, Eastern Orthodoxy even closer to the Eastern mystery religions than the Western denominations on which he focuses. Altmann writes that Baeck, who was an avid student of all forms of mysticism, recommended to him "Sergius Bulgakov's *The Eastern Church,* a book that has an instructive chapter on *Eastern mysticism*" (24; italics mine).

22. (Ware:236). Von Harnack actually has much harsher words for Greek Orthodoxy than for Judaism. Speaking of the former, he writes: "It was to destroy this sort of religion that Jesus Christ suffered himself to be nailed to the cross" (255). He is especially severe on the Orthodox doctrine of deification, which he holds is "subchristian" and "has scarcely any connexion with the Jesus Christ of the Gospel" (252).

23. However, Vladimir Solov'ev, in his desire for total unity, sometimes comes close to arguing a mystical, pantheistic fusion of the human and divine. "In man the world-soul is inwardly united with the divine Logos in consciousness for the first time, as a pure form of total-unity" (82).

24. James writes that mystical experience can also be induced by drugs and is not unrelated to some pathological conditions and drug induced states (297-302). But in terms of evaluation, as a good pragmatist, James is more concerned with the fruits of the experience than its psychological causes.

25. On the other hand, Zosima carries a Bible with him even during his most dissolute period—a typical Dostoevskian touch.

26. It is typical of Dostoevsky's technique to provide the basis for a psychological interpretation of all the experiences of his characters, even though in many cases psychology is not the real issue. Here, however, Dostoevsky seems to insist on the inextricable tie between experience and miracle.

27. Regarding the mystical relation between mystery and commandment, Buber is quite close to both Baeck and Lossky. "In reality, in Judaism the relation between man's action and God's grace is guarded as a mystery, even as that between human freedom and God's all-knowing, a mystery which is ultimately identical with that of the relation between God and man" (30).

28. This is also basically Zenkovsky's view of Dostoevsky's "mystical ethics" in which "the moral impulses are not determined by feeling, rationality, or reason, but primarily by a living sense of God" (140).

29. Again Dostoevsky is not necessarily equating the feeling that heaven might be achieved immediately on earth with Orthodox dogma. But one suspects that Dostoevsky is trying to have it both ways.

30. This idea, known as *sobornost'* in Russian, was propounded by A. S. Khomiakov (1975). For an English translation, see 1985.

31. For an excellent discussion of the relation between morality and active love in Father Zosima, see Gustafson (461-63).

32. Zosima also, of course, emphasizes the importance of mystery. "Much is hidden from us, but to make up for it we have been given a precious mystic sense of our living bond with other worlds, with the higher heavenly world, and the roots of our feelings are not here but in other worlds" (299).

33. Orthodoxy attempts not to make a distinction between faith and deeds, but sees them almost as a mystical unity. According to Khomiakov, the Church, "aware of her living unity . . . cannot even understand the question whether salvation lies in faith alone of in faith and works together. In her eyes life and truth are one . . ." (Schmemann: 54:55). Baeck writes: ". . . dass sich hier diese beiden Erfahrungen in eine Einheit zusammenschliessen, in einer völligen Einheit erlebt werden . . ." (1933:35).

34. Orthodoxy places much less emphasis on original sin than do most Western Christian denominations.

References

Altmann, Alexander 1973 *Leo Baeck and the Jewish Mystical Tradition.* New York: Leo Baeck Institute.

Anderson, Roger B. 1979 "Mythical Implications of Father Zosima's Religious Teachings." *Slavic Review* 38:2:272-89.

Baeck, Leo *Judaism and Christianity Essays by Leo Baeck.*

1981 Trans. Walter Kaufmann. New York: Antheum.

1933 *Wege in Judentum: Aufsätze und Reden.* Berlin: Schocken.

Berdyaev, Nicholas 1957 "The Grand Inquisitor: Christ and Antichrist." In *Dostoevsky,* 188-212. Trans. by Donald Attwater. New York: Meridian.

Buber, Martin 1958 *Hasidism and Modern Man.* Trans. and Ed. Maurice Friedman. New York: Horizon.

Bulgakov, Sergei 1935 *The Orthodox Church.* London:

Chaitin, Gilber D. 1972 "Religion as Defense: The Structure of *The Brothers Karamazov." Literature and Society* 22:68-87.

Dostoevskii, F. M. 1972-90 *Polnoe sobranie sochinenii.* 30 vols. Leningrad: Nauka.

Dostoevsky, Fyodor 1976 *The Brothers Karamazov.* Trans. by Constance Garnett. New York: Norton.

Friedlander, Albert H. 1968 *Leo Baeck: Teacher of Theresienstadt.* New York: Holt.

Gibson, A. Boyce 1973 "Each and All: The Brothers Karamazov." In *The Religion of Dostoevsky,* 169-208. London: SCM.

Gorodetzky, Nadeja 1938 *The Humiliated Christ in Modern Russian Thought.* London: Society for Promoting Christian Knowledge.

Guardini, Romano 1951 *Religiöse Gestalten in Dostojewskijs Werk: Studien über den Glauben.* München: Kusel.

Gustafson, Richard 1986 *Leo Tolstoy: Resident and Stranger.* Princeton: Princeton University Press.

Hackel, Sergei 1983 "The Religious Dimension: Vision or Evasion? Zosima's "Discourse in *The Brothers Karamazov."* In *New Essays on Dostoyevsky.* Ed. by Malcolm Jones. Cambridge: Cambridge University Press.

Haim, Gordon 1979 "Dostoevsky and Existential Education: Father Zosima as Religious Educator." *Religious Education* 74-2:198-209.

Hamilton, William 1959 "Banished from the Land of Unity: A Study of Dostoevsky's Religious Vision through the Eyes of Ivan and Ayosha Karamazov." *Journal of Religion* 39:245-262.

Hammond, Peter 1956 *The Waters of Marah: The Present State of the Greek Church.* New York: Macmillan.

Harnack, Adolph von 1903 *What is Christianity?* Trans. by Thomas Bailey Saunders. New York: Putnam.

Ivanov, Vyacheslav 1957 "Hagiology." In *Freedom and the Tragic Life: A Study in Dostoevsky,* 142-166. Trans. by Norman Cameron. New York: Noonday.

James, William 1958 *The Varieties of Religious Experience.* New York: Signet.

Khomiakov, A. S. 1977 "On the Western Confessions of Faith." In *Ultimate Questions: An Anthology of Modern Russian Religious Thought,* 31-69. Ed. by Alexander Schmemann. Crestwood: St. Vladimir's Seminary Press.

Khomiakov, A. S. 1985 "The Church Is One." In *Russian and the English Church During the Last Fifty Years,* 192-222. Ed. by W. J. Birbeck London: Ribington.

1975 *Tserkov' odna.* 2nd ed. Montreal: Bratstvo Pren. Iova Pechaeskogo.

Laqueur, Walter 1980 *The Missing Years.* London: Weidenfeld.

Leont'ev, K. N. *Pis'ma Vasiliiu Rozanovu.* Ed. by Nina Karsov.

1981 London: Billing.

1912 *Sobranie sochinenii.* 9 vols. Moscow: Sablin.

Linnér, Sven 1976 *Starets Zosima in The Brothers Karamazov: A Study in the Mimesis of Virtue.* Stockholm: Almquist.

Losskii, N. 1953 *Dostoevskii i ego khristianskoe miroponimanie.* New York: Izdatel'stvo imeni Chekhova.

Lossky, Vladimir 1976 *The Mystical Theology of the Eastern Church.* New York: St. Vladimir's Seminary Press.

Pletnev, R. V. 1929-36 "Serdtsem mudrye: O startsakh u Dostoevskogo." In *O Dostoevskom,* 2:73-92. Ed. by A. L. Bem. Prague: Khudomel.

Preosviashchennyi, Antonii 1921 *Slovar' k tvoreniiam Dostoevskogo: Ne dolzhno otchaiavat'sia.* Sofia: Rossiisko-bolgarskoe knigoizdatel'stvo.

Rozanov, Vasily 1972 *Dostoevsky and the Legend of the Grand Inquisitor.* Trans. by Spencer E. Roberts. Ithaca: Cornell UP.

Rubenstein, Richard L. 1975 *The Cunning of History: The Holocaust and the American Future.* New York: Harper.

Schmemann, Alexander, ed. 1977 *Ultimate Questions: An Anthology of Modern Russian Religious Thought.* New York: St. Vladimir's Seminary Press.

Solov'ev, E. 1971 "Verovanie i vera Ivana Karamazova." *Nauka i religiia* 11:47-53.

Solovyov, Vladimir 1965 "Lectures on Godmanhood." In *Russian Philosophy,* 3:62-84. Ed. by James M. Edie. Chicago: Quadrangle.

Sutherland, Stewart R. 1977 *Atheism and the Rejection of God: Contemporary Philosophy and The Brothers Karamazov.* Oxford: Blackwell.

1976 "Dostoevsky and the Grand Inquisitor: A Study in Atheism." *Yale Review* 66:364-373.

Terras, Victor 1981 *A Karamazov Companion.* Madison, Wisconsin: University of Wisconsin Press.

Volynskii, A. L. 1901 *Tsarstvo Karamazovykh.* St. Petersburg: Stasiulevich.

Walsh, Harry 1977 "The Book of Job and the Dialectic of Theodicy in *The Brothers Karamazov.*" *The South Central Bulletin* 37.4:161-164

Ware, Timothy 1963 *The Orthodox Church.* London: Penguin.

Zenkovsky, V. V. 1962"Dostoevsky's Religious and Philosophical Views." In *Dostoevsky: A Collection of Critical Essays,* 130-145. Ed. René Wellek. Englewood Cliffs: Prentice-Hall.

Paul J. Contino (essay date spring 1995)

SOURCE: Contino, Paul J. "Zosima, Mikhail and Prosaic Confessional Dialogue in Dostoevsky's *Brothers Karamazov.*" *Studies in the Novel* 27, no. 1 (spring 1995): 63-86.

[*In the following essay, Contino illustrates and explains Dostoevsky's use of the "prosaic confessional dialogue" in* The Brothers Karamazov.]

In the first chapter of **The Brothers Karamazov,** the narrator digresses to tell a story:

> I knew a young lady of the "romantic" generation before the last who after some years of an enigmatic passion for a gentleman, whom she might easily have married at any moment, invented insuperable obstacles to their union, and ended by throwing herself one stormy night into a rather deep and rapid river from a high bank, almost a precipice, and so perished, entirely to satisfy her own caprice, and to be like Shakespeare's Ophelia. Indeed, if this precipice, a chosen and favorite spot of hers, had been less picturesque, if there had been a prosaic flat bank in its place, most likely the suicide would never have taken place. This is a fact, and probably there have been not a few similar instances in the last two or three generations of our Russian life.[1]

The narrator suggests strongly that a prosaic setting would have successfully counteracted the solitary, self-dramatizing, and romantic impulse—and the woman would have chosen to live.

The beneficial influence of the prosaic can be located as running throughout **The Brothers Karamazov**—especially in the many scenes of confessional dialogue throughout the novel, the vital importance of which Mikhail Bakhtin emphasizes: Dostoevsky "asserts the impossibility of solitude, the illusory nature of solitude . . . confession is the object of his artistic vision and depiction. He depicts confession . . . in order to show the interdependence of consciousnesses that is revealed during confession. I cannot manage without another, I cannot become myself without another."[2] In each of his major novels, Dostoevsky's confessors—Sonia Marmeladov in **Crime and Punishment,** Prince Myshkin in **The Idiot,** Father Tikhon in **The Possessed,** Alyosha Karamazov and Father Zosima—assist others when they are most violently fractured and self-destructive. The splintered selves of these confessants is often due to their overweening concern about the way they are being perceived by others. The confessor's authority lies in his or her capacity to assist the other toward recovering what Bakhtin calls "the deepest I,"[3] or what might be understood as "the prosaic self." The prosaic self proves capable of free, integral speech and action before others, and the "labor and fortitude" of what Zosima calls "active love" (p. 49). The encounter between Zosima and Mikhail, his "mysterious visitor," offers an exemplary instance of prosaic confessional dialogue.

BAKHTIN AND THE PROSAIC SELF

In *Mikhail Baktin: Creation of a Prosaics,* Gary Saul Morson and Caryl Emerson coin the term "prosaics" "to cover a concept that permeates Bakhtin's work":

> Prosaics encompasses two related, but distinct, concepts. First, as opposed to "poetics," prosaics designates a theory of literature that privileges prose in general and the novel in particular over the poetic genres. Prosaics in the second sense is far broader than theory of literature; it is a form of thinking that presumes the importance of the everyday, the ordinary, the "prosaic."[4]

In its second sense, prosaics is a form of realism. It attends to and accepts the limits and graces embodied in the here and now, the temporal, and suspects the romantic, utopian, and apocalyptic. The concept of the prosaic self extends this understanding of prosaic by integrating what seem to be conflicting strands in Bakhtin's work: his affirmation of both the open and closed in human experience.

On the one hand, and as is commonly accepted, Bakhtin celebrates openness and unfinalizability. He extols Dostoevsky's "new artistic position" in relation to his characters, "a fully realized and thoroughly consistent dialogic position, one that affirms the independence, internal freedom, unfinalizability, and indeterminacy of the hero."[5] On the other hand, in his earlier ethical writings, *Toward a Philosophy of the Act* and "Author and Hero in Aesthetic Activity," Bakhtin stresses the necessity of "finalizing" one's deeds before the eyes of others.[6] In *Act,* for example, he writes: "It is not the content of an obligation that obligates me, but my signature below it—the fact that at one time I acknowledged or undersigned the given acknowledgment."[7] By publicly affixing one's "signature" to what one has done or is doing, one takes responsibility for it before others. The closure such signature brings frees one to move on to other things. Unlike Sartre, Bakhtin sees the finalization with which the other views me as positive: the boundaries of self which I receive from the other give me a sense of self around which I can coalesce. "Biography is bestowed as a gift: I receive it as a gift from others and for others," writes Bakhtin in "Author and Hero."[8] Thus, as Caryl Emerson notes, "[Bakhtin's] other always works to define us in ways we can live with."[9] By signing, and by allowing the other's "authorship" of me by virtue of my signing, I retain a vital tie to the community. This is the tie that Kierkegaard's aesthetic man lacks, as do Dostoevsky's signature-refusers: the Underground Man, Stavrogin, even Prince Myshkin. The no-exit of reality and other people is not infernal for Bakhtin, as it is for Sartre. It is the very place where individual possibility and benevolent community are to be found.

To live prosaically is thus to balance the open and the closed. One remains aware of one's own and the other's capacity to grow, for one's self can never ultimately be reduced to a single deed. At the same time one accepts that one must work and choose amidst the limits and gifts of the everyday—time, place, the existence of other people—to bring potential into reality, to take responsibility before others for what one has done or is doing.[10] It is to have attained a sense of personal identity that might be called a prosaic sense of self. In Dostoevsky's novels, successful confessants achieve such a prosaic self; beneficent, prosaic confessors assist them in doing so.[11]

It should be noted here that Bakhtin did not see the self as a monad, an autonomous Cartesian subjectivity. The self is always involved in dialogue; "to be means to communicate," Bakhtin writes. The self is "nonself-sufficient": "To be means to be for another, and through the other, for oneself. A person has no internal sovereign territory, he is wholly and always on the boundary; looking inside himself, he looks into the eyes of another or with the eyes of another."[12] For Bakhtin, the word one speaks, as utterance, is necessarily a shared word, infused with one's sense of one's listener, the influence of other speakers one has heard in one's life, and the heteroglossia of one's particular social and temporal situation.

A prosaic self integrates an awareness of both personal possibility and personal responsibility amidst others.

When Bakhtin describes "the deepest I" as "the pure, deep I from within oneself,"[13] he may be understood as describing such a self. With his keen awareness of ethical contingencies and the centrifugal energies of dialogue, Bakhtin typically suspects "the pure." But the "pure, deep I" should not be read as a Platonic essence, removed from the material, social, and historical. Rather, the phrase points to a self which has mutually interactive capacities for openness and closure: on the one hand, the self can change, for as long as one is alive one is free and unfinalizable; on the other hand, the self achieves definition and identity through signature, amidst others, in time, for as long as one lives in the world one must use one's freedom to make decisions, to bring closure to one thing to get on with another.

Tellingly, the person who sustains such an integrated, prosaic, "pure" self more successfully and satisfyingly enters into and grows through relationships with others. His sense of an integral self secure, the gazes and words he shares with others do not deteriorate into what Bakhtin calls "sideward glances" and "loopholes." He speaks and listens to the other without cringing in expectation of the other's judgment. The person who lacks such a prosaic sense of self, however, is prone to endlessly seek his identity in externals—most excruciatingly, in the eyes of the other. He desires and seeks self-definition from the other's eyes, but also fears what that definition might be. Simultaneously, he hates himself for seeking such a definition, and the other for imposing it. He lashes back with a willful assertion of his unfinalizability, a perverse assertion of freedom that is unfree in its impulse and compulsion. The lashes prove self-lacerating: fear and hatred dissolve the person's already shaky sense of self, and so spins the "vicious circle" of the sideward glance.

As any reader of his work knows, numerous characters in Dostoevsky's fiction, bereft of a prosaic sense of self, fall into just such a pattern of pathological human relationship. The Underground Man comes quickly to mind. He begins his confession with an initial self-description, a pause, and a second self-description: "I am a sick man . . . I am a spiteful man."[14] He attempts confession by initially offering a realistic, accurate self-description in his first statement: "I am a sick man." In his pause, he casts a "sideward glance" at his listener, the reader of his notes, and anticipates him forming an evaluation of him ("poor man, he needs help"). Unable to rest securely in any stable self-definition, the Underground Man in fact seeks just such an evaluation from the other and, in his pain, pity as well. But at the same time he hates the other for the privileged position from which he offers his or her evaluation and sympathy. He rejects the other, and tries to destroy his need of the other, by insisting that only he himself can speak the final word about himself: "I am a spiteful man." But this final word does not represent a simple signing for his past spiteful actions. It comprises, rather, a "false ultimate word"[15] for again he looks at his listener, and cringes in anticipation. What if his listener should agree and respond, "Yes, you are spiteful"—or nasty, or ugly? If he spies such a response, the Underground Man has a "loophole": he can assert—as he does later—his capacity for sublime and beautiful dreams.

The Underground Man fails to find closure to his torments because he is unwilling to sign his past deeds before another. Signing would entail a simple taking of responsibility for past deeds and a willing acceptance of the future's possibilities: "I have been spiteful in the past, but would like not to be in the future." In Bakhtin's words, "such a soberly prosaic definition [of himself] would presuppose a word without a sideward glance, a word without a loophole."[16] By spurning the prosaic, the Underground Man rejects the possibility of living healthily with others, or of ever changing. He chooses a static existence in a hellish world that is structured as the inverse of the balanced open and closed of the prosaic. Here he is trapped by his dependence upon the other's look, asserting his freedom perversely by ranting that he himself retains the final word about himself, even as he compulsively glances at the other from the corner of his eye. Bakhtin captures the endlessly repetitive quality of the Underground Man's situation by describing him as "caught up in the vicious circle of self-consciousness with a sideward glance":

> The loophole creates a special type of fictive ultimate word about oneself with an unclosed tone to it, obtrusively peering into the other's eyes and demanding from the other a sincere refutation . . . The loophole makes the hero ambiguous and elusive even for himself. In order to break through to his self he hero must travel a very long road.[17]

In the course of *Notes from Underground,* however, the narrator never achieves such a breaking through. In cruelly forsaking Liza, who, in response to his confession, stretches out her arms to him, he renounces his best chance to do so. Unwilling to travel "a very long road" of balancing the open and closed (the metaphor is prosaic; one recalls Zosima's description of active love as "labor and fortitude") he remains in his endless, vicious cycle, scrawling his notes, which an outside editor cuts off arbitrarily.[18]

Other characters in Dostoevsky's fiction, similarly sensitive to the other's judgment, meretriciously employ confession as a means toward self-justification, aggrandizement, or exhibition. In "Dostoevsky and Rousseau: The Morality of Confession Reconsidered," Robin Feuer Miller discusses such spurious, failed confessions in Dostoevsky and uncovers his implicit critique of Rousseau's style of confession in his portrayals of the Underground Man, Nastasya Filippovna's nameday party, and Stavrogin's confession before Tikhon: "In Dostoevsky's canon . . . the literary—bookish—written confession most often tends to be, to seem self-justification, or to aim at shocking the audience. But Dostoevsky does concede that the choice of an audience is important, and successful, genuine confessions do occur—witness Raskolnikov with Sonya, or 'the mysterious visitor' with the elder Zosima, or even the hapless Keller of Myshkin."[19] J. M. Coetzee offers similar observations, and suggests that which makes possible such successful confessions, although he doesn't himself discuss these: "True confession does not come from the sterile monologue of the self, or the dialogue of the self with its own self-doubt, but . . . from faith and grace. It is possible to read **Notes from Underground, The Idiot,** and Stavrogin's confession as a sequence of texts in which Dostoevsky explores the impasses of secular confession, pointing finally to the sacrament of confession as the only road to self-truth."[20] In fact, depictions of the actual sacrament of confession appear rarely, if at all in Dostoevsky's work. Indeed, his most exemplary confessor, Zosima, stands accused by some of "arbitrarily and frivolously degrad[ing] the sacrament of confession" by his attending to the many who come to the monastery "to confess their doubts, their sins, and their sufferings, and [to] ask for counsel and admonition" (p. 22) outside the confessional. Nevertheless, Coetzee's point is close to the mark: in Zosima's meetings with his visitors—and in crucial meetings between Alyosha and his brothers, and Sonia with Raskolnikov—Dostoevsky portrays successful confessional encounter as sacramental; the act emerges as a vehicle of divine grace. Assisted by grace, and a profound attentiveness to the other, the confessor helps the other to recover her or his prosaic self. He or she helps the confessant to step out of the vicious circle of the sideward glance, and to speak with a voice of clarity and resolve. In such help, the confessor brings a particular kind of authority to the encounter.

THE AUTHORITY OF DOSTOEVSKY'S PROSAIC CONFESSOR

The words of the prosaic confessor penetrate and assist in the transformation of the other, and are thus authoritative. This authority is not, however, imposed, subject upon object, from without. Rather, the authority emerges, in part, from the confessor's profound attention toward the other. Bakhtin stresses the "penetrative" quality of the confessor's discourse with the other. In doing so, he adopts Vyacheslav Ivanov's insight into Dostoevsky in *Freedom and the Tragic Life.* According to Ivanov, Dostoevsky envisions the importance of "proniknovenie, which properly means 'intuitive seeing through' or 'spiritual penetration' . . . It is a transcension of the subject. In this state of mind we recognize the other Ego not as our object, but as another subject . . . The spiritual penetration finds its expression in the

unconditional acceptance with our full will and thought of the other-existence—in 'Thou art.'"[21] The confessor's attentiveness toward the other's subjectivity allows him or her to discern the "pure, deep I from within" the confessing speaker. His or her authoritative discourse penetrates and becomes "internally persuasive"[22] for the one who confesses: Sonia's authoritative words penetrate Raskolnikov and help him to find the self that longs for reconciliation with the earth, and the voice with which he will confess his crime.

To be as attentive to another as Sonia is, it is necessary to relinquish the distractions of self-absorption. Simone Weil stresses this in her essay on "School Studies": "The soul empties itself of all its own contents in order to receive into itself the being it is looking at, just as he is, in all his truth. Only he who is capable of attention can do this."[23] Indeed, Ivanov emphasizes such relinquishing or emptying with the Greek word *kenosis*: "If this acceptance of the other-existence is complete; if, with and in this acceptance, the whole substance of my own existence is rendered null and void (*exinanitio, kappa epsilon nu omicron sigma iota*), then the other-existence ceases to be an alien 'Thou'; instead, the 'Thou' becomes another description of my 'Ego.'"[24] *Kenosis,* "emptying out," is a central concept in Christianity, and especially in the Russian Orthodox tradition. In his Letter to the Philippians, St. Paul uses this image of emptying to describe Christ's descent to earth, his incarnation as a common man, and his death on the cross. "Make your own the mind of Christ Jesus," he exhorts,

> Who, being in the form of God,
> did not count equality with God
> something to be grasped.
> But he emptied himself,
> taking the form of a slave,
> becoming as human beings are;
> and being in every way
> like a human being,
> he was humbler yet,
> even to accepting death,
> death on a cross.
> And for this God raised him high,
> and gave him the name which is above all other
>   names;
> so that all beings
> in the heavens, on earth
> and in the underworld,
> should bend the knee at the name of Jesus
> and that every tongue should acknowledge
> Jesus Christ as Lord,
> to the glory of God the Father.
>
> (Phil. 2:5-11)[25]

In *The Russian Religious Mind,* George P. Fedotov stresses the importance of kenotic spirituality in Russian Orthodoxy. He traces the roots of this tradition to two eleventh-century sources: to the cult surrounding the politically motivated murders of the Princes Boris and Gleb, who treated their murderers with humility and "forgiving nonresistance,"[26] and so were canonized as saints; and to the life of Saint Theodosius. Although from a well-off family, Theodosius willingly wore poor clothes, and worked in the fields with the slaves. Later, as a monk, he opened up relations between the monastery and the lay world; he began the long tradition (of which Zosima is exemplary) of monks serving as confessors for lay people. Fedotov writes:

> Theodosius draws his main religious inspiration from the contemplation of the human nature of Christ[,] . . . of His descent to earth . . . In the light of this Christology, one is fully entitled to term the spirituality of Theodosius as "kenotic," using the Pauline word of "kenosis" or emptying of Christ . . . Theodosius himself quotes the Epistle to the Philippians. His word to his mother about Christ who "became poor for our sake" is also Pauline (II Corinthians 8:9) . . . The kenotic idea has its practical expression with Theodosius in three Christian virtues: poverty, humility, and love, in their complete unity as one inseparable whole.[27]

Joseph Frank cites Fedotov, and tells of the great influence saints' lives like that of Theodosius's had on Dostoevsky:

> "In childhood I heard these narratives myself, before I even learned to read" [wrote Dostoevsky]. These stories of the lives of the saints were no doubt steeped in the special spirit of Russian kenoticism—the glorification of passive, completely non-heroic and non-resisting suffering, the suffering of the despised and humiliated Christ—which is so remarkable a feature of the Russian religious tradition.[28]

In their relinquishing of self, and entering into the suffering of the other, Dostoevsky's confessors stem from this tradition and imitate Christ.

If the authority of the confessor's words stems from his or her discerning, kenotic attentiveness to the other, it also stems, for Dostoevsky, from his or her openness to God. The words of Dostoevsky's efficacious confessors reverberate with a tone of divine inspiration. When, for example, Tikhon speaks to Stavrogin for the last time, prophesying his further crime, he "crie[s] in a voice that penetrate[s] the soul."[29] The words penetrate Stavrogin, and, for a moment, he considers deferring his crime. Sonia speaks similarly penetrating words to Raskolnikov, but the effect is longer lasting: "Go to the cross roads, bow down to the people, kiss the earth, for you have sinned against it too, and say aloud to the whole world, 'I am a murderer.'" He "suddenly recall[s]" her words the following day, and the sensation is like "a single spark kindled in his soul and spreading fire through him." He "soften[s]," cries, and falls "to the earth on the spot."[30] At times the confessor's words echo Scripture as when Sonia earlier reads to Raskolnikov the raising of Lazarus from the Gospel of John.

"Penetrated word" aptly translates Bakhtin's term by suggesting its two key dimensions: the word penetrates the one who wishes to confess, but the word itself is penetrated by the authority of God's grace, and is thus sacramental. In Bakhtin's words, the penetrated word "is capable of actively and confidently interfering in the interior dialogue of the other person, helping the person to find his own voice."[31]

Bakhtin offers as illustration Prince Myshkin's admonishment of Nastasya in Part One of *The Idiot.* She has been taunting Rogozhin in Ganya's crowded apartment, provoking violence. She is wearing a mask, as Bakhtin points out: "she is desperately playing out the role of 'fallen woman' . . . [and] Myshkin introduces an almost decisive tone into her interior monologue":

> "Aren't you ashamed? Surely you are not what you are pretending to be now? It isn't possible!" cried Myshkin suddenly with deep and heartfelt reproach.
>
> Nastasya Filippovna was surprised, and smiled, seeming to hide something under her smile. She looked at Ganya, rather confused, and walked out of the drawing-groom. But before reaching the entry, she turned sharply, went quickly up to Nina Alexandrovna, took her hand and raised it to her lips.
>
> "I really am not like this, he is right," she said in a rapid eager whisper, flushing hotly; and turning around, she walked out so quickly that no one had time to realise what she had come back for.[32]

For a moment Nastasya speaks clearly and resolutely, without a mask; she seems "to find her own voice." Caryl Emerson comments on the momentary quality of the penetrated word's effect here—and in general:

> The Prince can, and often does, appeal to one of the voices warring inside another person, and if he reaches an "authentic voice" he can trigger a major moral reversal. But the penetrated word does not last. It can only enter at a specific time and place to work a temporary realization. It is only possible in dialogue, in a specific dialogue with another person; it never accumulates authority and therefore lacks ultimate sovereignty . . . The penetrated word makes authority real, but only for the moment; it remains personal, historical, and conditional.[33]

The penetrated word is a profoundly tactful word. The speaker utters it with a careful attentiveness to the particularity of this person, in this place, at this time. In such tact it is prosaic. But for all its rootedness in the particular moment, Dostoevsky offers instances—especially in *The Brothers Karamazov*—of the way its effects may accrue. The penetrated utterance may take root in memory, and at some future time, assist in one's personal growth. Its capacity to last and accumulate authority depends upon the person who utters it. As Bakhtin points out—and Emerson, too, observes—"never, in the case of Myshkin" is the penetrated word spoken "in a decisive voice . . . A firm and integral monologic discourse is unknown to him too. The internal dialogism of his discourse is just as great and anxiety-ridden as that of the other characters."[34] Nor does Myshkin respect the necessity of signing—the fact that he and others are responsible for their deeds.

Other characters of Dostoevsky do speak in firm and decisive voices and take seriously the necessity of signing. As a result, their words penetrate more deeply, lastingly, and affect the listener not only at the time, but over time. Sonia's "Go to the cross roads" offers one example. In *The Brothers Karamazov*—a novel in which the memory of the deeds and words of others plays such a vital role—Zosima and Alyosha offer further examples. Myshkin flies from the finitude of decision, most tragically fails to choose between Nastasya and Aglaya, refuses to "sign" his choice. He responds to others, especially Nastasya, with a kind of boundless pity; Bakhtin points to his "deep and fundamental horror at speaking a decisive and ultimate word about another person."[35] In fact, his words to Nastasya, cited above, "almost decisive," are as close as he comes to a prosaic approach to another. His words reveal both an appreciation of Nastasya's possibilities—"surely you are not what you are pretending to be now"—and a clear judgment of actions for which she ought to take responsibility: "Aren't you ashamed?" he cries "with deep and heartfelt reproach." He speaks these words in Part One of *The Idiot*. In the four hundred or so pages that follow, Myshkin grows increasingly indecisive. Ultimately, his image emerges as unprosaic; his effect upon others proves violent and tragic.

In contrast to Myshkin, Zosima—and his student Alyosha—are both "realists" (pp. 19-20) and decisive. They respond prosaically to people and situations. As a result, their utterances—sometimes "spoken" in the form of silent gesture: a bow, a blessing, a kiss—seem to accrue beyond their initially penetrative effect upon the other. They speak, in dialogue, amidst the limited, with particular people in particular circumstances. But, because they live prosaically, their words help others to not only find but to some degree sustain their "own voice." They serve as mediating, healing presences for those tempted towards destroying themselves and others.

Zosima and Mikhail

Perhaps the exemplar of the successful confessional dialogue occurs in Book Six of *The Brothers Karamazov,* in which the young Zosima meets Mikhail, his "mysterious visitor," burdened with guilt for a murder he committed fourteen years before. Bakhtin points to this encounter near the conclusion of *Problems of Dos-*

toevsky's Poetics, comments upon the way that it is typical of confessional dialogues but, like most other Dostoevsky commentators, does not give it close attention.

Bakhtin sees confessional dialogues as being "prepared for by the plot, but their culminating points—the peaks of the dialogues—rise above the plot in the abstract sphere of pure relationship, one person to another."[36] Zosima's encounter with Mikhail indeed rises "above the plot" in that it comprises an interpolated section of Book Six, "The Russian Monk," the form and language of which is, as Nathan Rosen observes, inspired by the old Russian genre of "a saint's life (zhitie) . . . not a reliable factual biography, but a sort of dramatized sermon."[37] Mikhail's conversion story, however, connects to the plot of *The Brothers Karamazov* in important ways. In his depiction of an extensive confessional dialogue, Dostoevsky illustrates the way such dialogues can deteriorate, but also how they can develop and culminate in a salutary way. The story emerges as paradigmatic in its portrayal of the interpersonal and in its engagement of the central themes of the novel: How can a scene of violence be transformed into one of reconciliation and peace? How can the confessor be at the same time authoritative und respectful of the freedom of the other? We recall the Grand Inquisitor's assertion that people embrace authority in order to escape the anguish of human freedom. Indeed, the Grand Inquisitor claims that he "love[s] mankind" (p. 237) because he is willing to "save them from the great anxiety and terrible agony they endure at present in making free decisions for them" (p. 240). What is the role of human love before the anguish of another? Can one discern in such situations the workings of divine grace? A close analysis of the encounter between Zosima and Mikhail can serve a heuristic purpose by helping to illuminate the numerous other confessional dialogues that precede and follow it in the novel.

When they first begin their evenings of "stirring and fervent talk" (p. 283), Zosima and Mikhail seem to share a friendship in which each has achieved a prosaic, integral sense of self. Here, and throughout the section, the image of looking reveals much. As Zosima tells Mikhail of his conversion, the looks the men exchange suggest trust, clear-eyed enjoyment, and admiration. Zosima narrates: "All the while he was speaking, I looked him straight in the face and I felt all at once a complete trust in him" (p. 281); "I liked the way he looked at me as he listened" (p. 282). One can perhaps hear in Mikhail's announcement at the end of their first meeting—"I will come to see you again and again" (p. 282)—a healthy acceptance of temporality, of the fact that his growing resolve to confess—to Zosima and then the public—will take time to enact, that there will be, in William Lynch's phrase, "intermediate steps"[38] to take before he reaches that point.

In fact, Mikhail's achievement of an integral self is not firm. He gradually reveals himself to be divided between what Bakhtin calls a "pure I," capable of wishing and acting on that wish, and an "unstable I," which holds a sideward glance upon his listener, Zosima, agonizingly concerned about the way in which Zosima may be looking at him, judging him, and thereby "finalizing" him. Signs of Mikhail's self-division appear even in their early meetings. Mikhail makes his pronouncement that "Paradise lies hidden within all of us" as if looking to Zosima for corroboration: "he was . . . gazing mysteriously at me, as if he were questioning me" (p. 282). And when Zosima reveals his own "bitter" doubts concerning the kingdom of Heaven becoming a "living reality," Mikhail lashes back tauntingly, as if wanting to kick away any pedestal he himself may have placed under Zosima: "What then you don't believe it . . . You preach it and don't believe it yourself" (p. 282).

After a month or so, Mikhail unexpectedly, stammeringly, makes his confession to Zosima: "I . . . do you know . . . I murdered someone." The words that follow further suggest his self-division. On the one hand, his confession to Zosima is a "first step" toward a self-determined, public signing of his deed: "Now I have said [the first word] I feel I've taken the first step and shall go on." On the other hand, the utterance that precedes this reveals Mikhail casting a sideward glance at Zosima: "'You see,' he said with a pale smile, 'how much it cost me to say the first word'" (p. 284). He wants to make sure Zosima sees him in a certain way: not as a murderer, but as self-sacrificing, noble, willing to pay the price.

Mikhail's confession contains what Bakhtin calls a "loophole," and in the weeks that follow, his evening dialogues with Zosima betray the attributes of a vicious circle. He moves back and forth between an integral, "determined" (p. 287) resolve to confess, rooted in "the pure, deep I from within," and an intensifying itch to know the way others are looking or will look at him, visualizing himself "through the eyes of another." His decision to confess publicly, and his visits with Zosima, have been inspired by a healthy perception of the younger man's goodness, as he avows to Zosima: "Looking at you I have made up my mind." But in the same exchange, and in those that follow, his appreciation sours into envy, and his gaze grows jaundiced: "'Looking at you, I reproached myself and envied you,' he said to me almost sullenly" (p. 287). On the night of his first visit, he reveals an especially pained consciousness of the way Zosima may be looking at him: "Every time I come to you, you look at me so inquisitively as though to say, 'He has still not proclaimed!' Wait a bit, don't despise me too much. It's not such an easy thing to do as you would think" (p. 288). In fact, Mikhail increasingly projects his own self-derision onto Zosima;

looks between them have deteriorated so much that at this point, Zosima is "afraid to look at him at all" (p. 288). Like the Underground Man, Mikhail craves approval from the other, even as he hates himself and others for such a craving. His sideward glance anxiously sweeps the public: "will people recognize it, will they appreciate it, will they respect it?" (p. 288). Lynch observes that "a man who is truly wishing does not need an audience."[39] Looking to externals for his identity, Mikhail's internal capacities to wish, resolve, and act grow feeble: "Perhaps I shall not do it at all" (p. 288).

As Mikhail's "pure, deep I from within" grows more elusive, so too does his grasp of his uniquely human gift of freedom, that gift which enables a person to wish, resolve, and act. To be true to himself, he himself must enact his resolution to confess, but he evades signature. He speaks to Zosima, "as though all [the decision] depended on [him]" (p. 287). Finally, his prosaic self crippled, he pleads, "Decide my fate!" (p. 288), and thus flees from his individual freedom by looking to Zosima, the authority, to decide for him.

Zosima responds with a prosaic balance of the open and closed. He authoritatively exhorts Mikhail to enact his deed through signature, and bring his resolve to closure: "Go and proclaim" (p. 288). But the authority of Zosima's presence and utterance, the "closed" dimension of his response to Mikhail, is grounded in openness. His prosaic response enables Mikhail to ultimately embrace the freedom that he sought to flee by his demand.

First of all, Zosima is open toward and respectful of Mikhail's individual freedom. He renounces any will toward omniscience in his relation to Mikhail; he attempts no verbal "ambush," coercive inquisition, or "attack from behind."[40] He keeps a tactful silence when he senses Mikhail "brooding over some plan in his heart": "Perhaps he liked my not showing curiosity about his secret, not seeking to discover it by direct question or by insinuation" (p. 283). He refrains from looking at Mikhail when his visitor is at his most defensive: "far from looking at him with indiscreet curiosity, I was afraid to look at him at all" (p. 288). And he forbears from embracing him at a delicate moment: "I wanted to take him in my arms and kiss him, but I did not dare—his face was contorted and somber" (p. 289). Zosima is deeply attentive toward Mikhail in Simone Weil's sense: "the soul empties itself of all its own contents in order to receive into itself the being it is looking at, in all his truth." Zosima's attention exemplifies kenosis: he empties himself of any egocentric distraction or will to power over Mikhail.[41] Indeed, letting the other be can be understood as a dimension of kenotic attentiveness.[42]

To let the other be, however, is not to detach oneself from the other. Zosima engages in letting Mikhail be, and at the same time, opens himself up to and enters into Mikhail's agonizing situation. Mikhail's weeks of self-division make Zosima's own "heart ache" (p. 287), and his own soul "full of tears" (p. 288). In one moment he inwardly chastises Mikhail for "thinking of other people's respect at such a moment." But, in the same moment, he enters into Mikhail's situation and feels for himself the horror of public confession: "I was aghast, realizing with my heart as well as my mind, what such a resolution meant" (p. 288). Zosima recognizes, however, that Mikhail has himself resolved to confess. This is a crucial point: Zosima not only enters into the pain of Mikhail, he enters into his resolve. After Zosima comes to believe in Mikhail's guilt, and to recognize his "resolution" to confess (pp. 287, 288), he supports that decision as Mikhail's own. Zosima cannot wish for Mikhail; in his live entering[43] into Mikhail's resolve, however, he wishes with him. When Mikhail departs, with "contorted and somber" face, Zosima is "half an hour praying in tears" for his friend, feeling the horror of what Mikhail has "gone to face" and supporting him in his wish to do so (p. 289).

With prayer, finally, we see Zosima's openness to God. He utters his first authoritative exhortation to Mikhail—"Go! . . . 'proclaim it to the world'"—only after he has "sat still and repeated a silent prayer" (p. 287). Later, his "Go and proclaim" (p. 288) comprises a penetrative utterance itself penetrated by the authority of Scripture of which, Zosima states, the Holy Spirit is the author. He shows two passages from the New Testament to Mikhail. The first, from John's Gospel, calls Mikhail to a kenotic death to self in order to find life: "Verily, verily I say unto you, except a corn of wheat fall into the ground and die, it abideth alone: but if it die, it bringeth forth much fruit" (John 12:24). The second passage (Letter to Hebrews 10:31) might be read as a reminder to Mikhail from Zosima that he is not in the hands of his confessor—his confessor holds no such power—but in "the hands of the living God" (pp. 288-89).

Out of his openness, Zosima emerges as authoritative, a living icon of Christ, much like the Christ who remains kenotically silent during the Grand Inquisitor's harangue, and who silently kisses him when he discerns the Inquisitor's longing for a response.[44] Zosima does not impose his word upon Mikhail from above, he utters it on the same level, respectful of Mikhail's freedom to assimilate its authority and find it internally persuasive, if he so chooses. Indeed, Zosima's authority is grounded in his kenotic relation with Mikhail and is thus authentically authoritative.

Zosima's words do not penetrate Mikhail immediately. Although they accrue and are assimilated in time, Mikhail at first rejects them as he rejects their speaker. On the night before Mikhail confesses, he has reached the nadir of a vicious circle. In his first visit, he speaks with integral, prosaic resolve. In the weeks that follow, as he grows increasingly conscious of the way others—his family, the public—may look at him if he does confess, and, most perniciously, of the way Zosima may be looking at him as he defers confessing, his prosaic, "pure, deep I from within"—capable of wish, resolve, and act—disintegrates. His gift of freedom thus grows intolerably burdensome, to the extent that he throws it upon Zosima: "Decide for me!"[45]

As we have seen, the roots of Zosima's authority lie in his refusal to relieve another of his freedom. Such authority stands in sharp contrast to the spurious authority of the Grand Inquisitor.[46] His response, "Go and proclaim," is authentically authoritative because it articulates a deep respect for Mikhail's freedom, and wishes with the resolution Mikhail has already made.

In his weakness, however, Mikhail hears Zosima's words as a willful imposition from without rather than a respectful echo of his own "pure, deep I from within." The hateful visage that soon results recalls that of the Underground Man. In his "Notes," the Underground Man hits upon the truth that human beings will never utterly conform to authority imposed from without, but will always need and assert their freedom, their power to desire and wish: "What man needs is only his independent wishing, whatever that independence may cost, and wherever it may lead. And the devil knows what this wishing. . . ."[47] What the Underground Man never recognizes is that what he calls "independent wishing" is precisely not that. Bereft of a prosaic self, he asserts his individual freedom perversely: thumbing his nose at his listener, his sideward glance cringing in anticipation, endlessly depending upon an external other for his chimeric identity. Thus his despair. William Lynch's fine study of wishing in *Images of Hope* sheds light on this pathology: incapable of authentically wishing, he can only wish against; his capacity for integral will crippled, he can only strike back willfully—at others, and at himself.

So too, at his lowest point, Mikhail. Wishing against Zosima, he profoundly distorts his confessor's authentic, kenotic authority. When Zosima humbly attributes authorship of the Scriptures to the Holy Spirit, Mikhail lashes back, "almost with hatred," "It's easy for you to prate" (p. 289). Although Zosima wishes with Mikhail, Mikhail would strike him down as an opposing power. Respectful of his friend's freedom, Zosima has renounced any impulse toward finalizing Mikhail. But in Mikhail's midnight hour, walking the streets in the darkness, he hates Zosima so much that he can "hardly bear it" (p. 291). He imagines Zosima looking at him condemningly—panoptical,[48] ubiquitous, omniscient: "I thought, 'How can I look him in the face if I don't proclaim my crime?' And if you had been at the other end of the earth, but alive, it would have been all the same, the thought was unendurable that you were alive know-ing everything and condemning me. I hated you as though you were the cause, as though you were to blame for everything" (p. 291). He returns to murder Zosima.

"And the devil knows what this wishing," scrawls the Underground Man, leaving his thought unfinished. The devil indeed knows: Mikhail's murderous intention comprises no real wish, but is willful, and as Lynch aptly observes: "At its worst [willfulness] has all the marks which tradition in the West has always associated with the devil."[49] Mikhail himself will later speak of "the devil in [his] heart." Dostoevsky had profound in-sight into this devil, and termed its perverse assertion of freedom *nadryv,* translated by Garnett as "laceration." Edward Wasiolek explains the derivation of the word and its significance in Dostoevsky's work:

> The word comes from the verb *nadryvat,* which means—apart from its literal meaning of tearing things apart, like paper—"to strain or hurt oneself by lifting something beyond one's strength." To this must be added Dostoevsky's special use of the word to mean a purposeful hurting of oneself, and to this, an explana-tion of the purpose. *Nadryv* is for Dostoevsky a pur-poseful and pleasurable self-hurt . . .
>
> *Nadryv* is for Dostoevsky a primal psychological fact. It is the impulse in the hearts of men that separates one man from another, the impulse we all have to make the world over into the image of our wills . . . From the **Underground Man** on, one of the premises of Dosto-evsky's mature dialectic has been that the Will will subvert the best and highest motives to its own pur-poses. *Nadryv* is Dostoevsky's mature pointing to the psychological impulse that works to corrupt everything to its own purposes.[50]

Indeed, Robert Belknap observes *nadryv*'s "boundary with the diabolic, along the lines of self-annihilation, as well as with the buffoonery, along the lines of irratio-nality."[51] We catch a glimpse of *nadryv* when, after re-citing his tale of the Grand Inquisitor, Ivan encourages his beloved Alyosha to reject him: "will you renounce me for that, yes?" (p. 244). We see Mikhail consumed with *nadryv* as, lost to himself, he distorts Zosima's im-age, and longs to kill his closest friend.

He cannot escape the self-consuming, endless maze of *nadryv* and recover his prosaic self except through an-other; he can "become [himself] only while revealing [himself] for another, through another, and with the help of another."[52] For Mikhail, this other is Zosima, the man he believes he must kill. When he returns to do so, something miraculous happens:

> Suddenly I saw the door open and he came in again. I was surprised.
>
> "Where have you been?" I asked him.
>
> "I think," he said, "I've forgotten something . . . my handkerchief I think . . . Well, even if I've not forgot-ten anything, let me stay a little."

He sat down. I stood over him. "You sit down, too," said he. I sat down. We sat still for two minutes; he looked intently at me and suddenly smiled—I remem-bered that—then he got up, embraced me warmly and kissed me.

> "Remember," he said, "how I came to you a second time. Dost thou hear, remember it!"

(p. 289)

Mikhail has perceived Zosima as objectifying him with an infernal, Sartrean look. But in a moment his own sideward glance is smilingly transformed into a Bube-rian gaze, shared with a "Thou," as "for the first time he addresse[s] [Zosima] with the familiar pronoun."[53]

This moment bears a similarity to that which Lynch de-scribes in a discussion of mutuality in the psychothera-peutic relationship. Defining mutuality as "an interact-ing relationship . . . from which something new and free is born," he points to "the critical moment" in the doctor/patient relationship when, after much work, the patient begins to see the doctor no longer as an enemy but as someone on his or her side: "The patient had felt the constant need to be alert, but now he enters a new and creative passivity, that acts almost without acting, because it now wishes with, not against, and is felt to be wished with by another."[54] Mikhail releases his ever alert sideward glance; he grows attentive to Zosima, sees him "as he is, in all his truth."

It is Zosima's own continuing, kenotic attention toward Mikhail that, in part, inspires this release. He exempli-fies the kenotic in two ways here. First, he symbolically enacts the passage of kenosis as he willingly descends from a position above the other to one of equality: "He sat down. I stood over him. 'You sit down, too,' said he. I sat down." Second, recalling Christ before the Grand Inquisitor, he keeps a profoundly tactful silence and stillness in the two minutes in which Mikhail "look[s] intently" at him.[55]

In the two minutes he spends with Zosima, Mikhail re-covers his prosaic self and his own voice. Before he leaves, he utters something of a confident, penetrated word of his own, as he charges Zosima to "remember!" this second visit. Clearly Zosima does: he specifically recalls Mikhail's smile (p. 289), and concludes his story with the solemn cadence of ritual remembrance: "But every day, to this very day, I remember in my prayer to this day, the servant of God, Mikhail, who suffered so greatly" (p. 291).[56]

The creative mutuality that Zosima and Mikhail share can be understood as the horizontal dimension of the story. But, as Mikhail relates to Zosima, there exists a vertical dimension as well: "The Lord vanquished the devil in my heart. But let me tell you, you were never nearer death" (p. 291). Grace infuses the silent two minutes the two men sit together. The penetrated word—itself infused from above—is spoken by one who wishes with the other, who wishes that the other may find his or her own voice. Grace, as Lynch's commentary helps us see, can be understood in an analogous way:

> The best and the most human part of man is the ability to wish, to say "I wish"; one of the most splendid qualities of the outside world, whether that world be things or God or a teacher or a parent or a doctor, is the ability to communicate help in such a way as to create in others the interior ability to really wish. Grace, therefore, should be understood as the act by which an absolutely outside and free reality communicates an absolutely interior and free existence. The theology of grace has talked mostly of the absolute act and wish of God; it should talk more, as should all of us, of that other absolute to which it is so deeply related, the absolute act and wish of man.[57]

Through the intervention of Zosima and God's grace, Mikhail makes his public confession. And when Mikhail confesses, he accomplishes what he wishes and freely chooses to do. The authentic freedom he enacts, however, differs profoundly from that perverse freedom he would have asserted if he had in fact murdered Zosima.

Dostoevsky depicts two kinds of freedom in *The Brothers Karamazov*: inauthentic and authentic. The inauthentic finds its image in the perverse assertion of will that is *nadryv*. It bespeaks an absence of prosaic self, an endless dependence upon the look of another, if only to spite it, and a scorn of mutuality and relation. Zosima imagines the ultimate, infernal image of this diabolical state:

> Oh, there are some who remain proud and fierce even in hell, in spite of their certain knowledge and contemplation of the absolute truth; here are some fearful ones who have given themselves over to Satan and his proud spirit entirely. For such, hell is voluntary and ever consuming; they are tortured by their own choice. For they have cursed themselves, cursing God and life. They live upon their vindictive pride like a starving man in the desert sucking blood out of his own body. But they are never satisfied, and they refuse forgiveness, they curse God Who calls them. They cannot behold the living God without hatred, and they cry out that the God of life should be annihilated, that God should destroy Himself and His own creation. And they will burn in the fire of their own wrath for ever and yearn for death and annihilation. But they will not attain to death . . .
>
> (p. 302, Dostoevsky's ellipses)

We recall the "hell" that Alyosha sees in Ivan's heart and head (p. 243). In "Rebellion" Ivan asserts: "I would rather remain with my unavenged suffering and unsatisfied indignation, even if I were wrong" (p. 226, Dostoevsky's emphasis). The proud souls in hell know they are wrong: they curse God "in spite of their certain knowledge and contemplation of the absolute truth."

Their assertion of freedom thus wishes against both God and themselves. Willfully, they seal the beneficent loophole of divine forgiveness.[58] Paradoxically, their insistence upon such closure ushers in an infinity of self-consuming pain.

For Dostoevsky, authentic freedom finds its image in Christ.[59] It can be understood as that which integrates the prosaic and the kenotic. In its prosaic dimension, it embraces a sense of personal possibility, and the complementary recognition that one must, among others, enact one's possibilities through choice, creation, and signature. Further, authentic freedom realizes the kenotic in two ways: it recognizes, first, that one is not self-sufficient, but that others necessarily assist one in the work of choosing, creating, and signing; and, second, if one follows the example of Christ, it recognizes that one is called upon to assist others in their work. Christos Yannaras, the distinguished contemporary Orthodox theologian, describes kenosis as "the act of emptying out every element of individual autonomy and self-sufficiency."[60] Mikhail empties himself of self-sufficiency through his attentive looking at the image of the kenotic Zosima—who has himself bowed before his servant, relinquished his gun in a duel, and now sits silently with his friend. Through such a release of self-sufficiency, Mikhail recovers his prosaic self, and enacts his wish by signing his deed before the townspeople and his family. Opening himself to the public, Mikhail enacts a further release of self-sufficiency. No one believes him, but Mikhail lets that be, opening himself further, to "God's mercy" (p. 291). He has "done [his] duty" as he tells Zosima. In so doing, he ends his hell of self-sufficiency—"terrible individualism" (p. 283), as he calls it in the apocalyptic tale which mirrors his own. And he opens up the possibility of "joy and peace" (p. 290) and "love" (p. 291).

We might say that the two dimensions of authentic freedom crystallize in the virtue of humility. Through kenosis, one empties oneself of self-sufficiency to open oneself to the help of another; or, one empties oneself of any egocentric distraction or will to power in order to help another. Both sides of kenosis call for a release from pride—and for humility. So too a prosaic sense of self. On the one hand, one justly perceives one's possibilities; on the other, one recognizes that one canot dwell in a sovereign realm of "maybe." One must, in the end, like Mikhail, just do it. Just doing it—imperfectly, in the sight of others—takes humility. Appropriately, a synonym for "prosaic" is "humble."

Thus Mikhail discovers humility. He enacts the passage of self imaged in the epigraph to *The Brothers Karamazov*: "Verily, verily, I say unto you, except a corn of wheat fall into the ground and die, it abideth alone: but if it die, it bringeth forth much fruit."

Notes

1. Fyodor Dostoevsky, *The Brothers Karamazov,* trans. Constance Garnett, ed. Ralph E. Matlaw (New York: W. W. Norton and Co., 1981), pp. 2-3. All subsequent references are to this edition and will be cited parenthetically in the text.

2. Mikhail Bakhtin, "Toward a Reworking of the Dostoevsky Book (1961)," in *Problems of Dostoevsky's Poetics,* ed. and trans. Caryl Emerson (Minneapolis: Univ. of Minnesota Press, 1984), p. 287, Bakhtin's emphasis.

3. Ibid., p. 294, Bakhtin's emphasis.

4. Gary Saul Morson and Caryl Emerson, *Mikhail Bakhtin: Creation of a Prosaics* (Stanford: Stanford Univ. Press, 1990), p. 15.

5. Bakhtin, *Problems of Dostoevsky's Poetics,* p. 63, Bakhtin's emphasis.

6. The current, popular image of Bakhtin is, in the words of Morson and Emerson, that of "the anarchistic Bakhtin . . . an antinomian, rejoicing, Bakunin-like, in joyful destruction, carnival clowning, and novels-as-loopholes" (*Prosaics,* p. 67). According to the authors, however, "Bakhtin . . . never gave up his commitment to ethical responsibility . . . Generally speaking, Bakhtin was much less concerned with [the] millenarian fantasies and holy foolishness [of carnival world] than with the constraints and responsibilities of everyday living" (p. 67). The prosaic tension and balance between the open and closed present in Bakhtin's work in the 1920s—*Art and Answerability, Toward a Philosophy of the Act,* "Author and Hero in Aesthetic Activity," "The Problem of Content, Material, and Form in Verbal Art"—can be located in the later work as well. In his "Notes Made in 1970-71," for example, he writes: "The better a person understands the degree to which he is externally determined (his substantiality), the closer he comes to understanding and exercising his real freedom." (In *Speech Genres and Other Late Essays,* trans. Vern W. McGee, eds. Caryl Emerson and Michael Holquist [Austin: Univ. of Texas Press, 1986], p. 139).

7. Bakhtin, *Toward a Philosophy of the Act,* trans. Vadim Liapunov, eds. Vadim Liapunov and Michael Holquist (Austin: Univ. of Texas Press, 1993), p. 38.

8. Bakhtin, "Author and Hero in Aesthetic Activity," *Art and Answerability,* trans. Vadim Liapunov, eds. Michael Holquist and Vadim Liapunov (Austin: Univ. of Texas Press, 1990), p. 168.

9. Caryl Emerson, "Problems in Bakhtin's Poetics," *Slavic and East European Journal* 32 (1988): 514.

Earlier in her essay, Emerson quotes the above cited line from Bakhtin's "Author and Hero" (p. 511).

10. In his discussion of the narrative quality of human life in *After Virtue* (2nd ed. Notre Dame: Univ. of Notre Dame Press, 1984), Alasdair MacIntyre locates a similar balance between what he calls the "unpredictable" and the "teleological" character of human life (pp. 215-16).

11. I see this essay as linked to two current, interrelated conversations. The first evinces a resurgent interest in the study of literature as an occasion for ethical reflection. Martha Nussbaum's work offers an especially forthright example. In *Love's Knowledge: Essays on Philosophy and Literature* (New York: Oxford Univ. Press, 1991) she "imagine[s] a future in which our talk about literature will return, increasingly, to a concern with the practical—to the ethical and social questions that give literature its high importance in our lives . . . a future in which literary theory (while not forgetting its many other pursuits) will also join with ethical theory in pursuit of the question, 'How should one live?'" (p. 168). Philosophers such as MacIntyre, Stanley Cavell, and Charles Taylor have also turned to literature in their discussion of ethical issues.

Nussbaum's "concern with the practical" points to the second, related conversation: thinkers like Cavell and Taylor emphasize the role of "the ordinary" in ethical questions. In "Politics as Opposed to What," *The Politics of Interpretation,* ed. W. J. T. Mitchell (Chicago: Univ. of Chicago Press, 1983), Cavell writes of "the appeal to the ordinary . . . as an indictment of metaphysics" (p. 197). In *The Sources of the Self: The Making of the Modern Identity* (Cambridge: Harvard Univ. Press, 1989), Taylor locates "the entire modern development of the affirmation of ordinary life . . . foreshadowed and initiated, in all its facets, in the spirituality of the Reformers" as a crucial underpinning of the modern conception of self (p. 218) I see my own stress upon the importance of the prosaic, as I have worked out the concept by way of Bakhtin, Morson, and Emerson, as apposite to the current ethical discussion and its valuing of the ordinary, the prosaic.

12. Bakhtin, "Reworking," p. 287, Bakhtin's emphasis.

13. Ibid., p. 294, Bakhtin's emphasis.

14. Fyodor Dostoevsky, *Notes from Underground,* trans. Mirra Ginsburg (Toronto: Bantam, 1983), p. 1, ellipsis Dostoevsky's.

15. Bakhtin, "Reworking," p. 294.

16. Bakhtin, *Problems,* p. 232, my emphasis.

17. Ibid., p. 234.

18. In its maneuvers, the Underground Man's confession bears similarities to Stavrogin's with Tikhon in *The Possessed.* As Bakhtin observes: "Stavrogin's confession . . . is deprived of any finalizing force and tends toward that same vicious circle that marked the speech of the Underground Man" (*Problems,* p. 244). For Bakhtin's complex analysis of Stavrogin, see also *Problems,* pp. 242-46, 262-65. For a fine analysis of the Underground Man's trapped situation, see Robert Louis Jackson's chapter, "Aristotelian Movement and Design in Part Two of *Notes from Underground.*" *The Art of Dostoevsky: Deliriums and Nocturnes* (Princeton: Princeton Univ. Press, 1981), pp. 171-88.

19. Robin Feuer Miller, "Dostoevsky and Rousseau: The Morality of Confession Reconsidered" (1979) in *Dostoevsky: New Perspectives,* ed. Robert Louis Jackson (Englewood Cliffs, New Jersey: Prentice Hall, 1984), p. 98.

20. J. M. Coetzee, "Confession and Double Thoughts: Tolstoy, Rousseau, Dostoevsky." *Comparative Literature* 37 (1985): 230. I thank Susan Gallagher for calling this essay to my attention.

21. Vyacheslav Ivanov, *Freedom and the Tragic Life: A Study in Dostoevsky,* trans. Norman Cameron (New York: Noonday, 1959) pp. 26-27.

22. Another Bakhtinian term, from M. M. Bakhtin, "Discourse in the Novel," *The Dialogic Imagination,* trans. Caryl Emerson and Michael Holquist, ed. Michael Holquist (Austin: Univ. of Texas Press, 1981). In this important essay, written in the 1930s while in exile during Stalin's reign of terror, Bakhtin looks with understandable suspicion upon authoritative discourse—even to the point of describing Dostoevsky's portrayals of characters who speak with spiritual authority—for example, Tikhon, Sonia, Zosima—as "hopeless attempts" (p. 344)! In this essay, however, Bakhtin does leave open the possibility of the authoritative discourse of another becoming internally persuasive—and thus integral—for the self: "Both the authority of discourse and its internal persuasiveness may be united in a single word—one that is simultaneously authoritative and internally persuasive—despite the profound differences between these two categories of alien discourse" (p. 342, Bakhtin's emphasis). See also Morson and Emerson, *Prosaics* (pp. 220-21), on the process of "assimilating" another's word.

23. Simone Weil, "Reflections on the Right Use of School Studies with a View to the Love of God," in *Waiting for God,* trans. Emma Craufurd (New York: Harper and Row, 1951), p. 115.

24. Ivanov, *Freedom,* p. 27. For a fine appreciation of Ivanov—his anticipation of Bakhtin and understanding of Dostoevsky—see Robert Louis Jackson's "Vision in His Soul: Vyacheslav I. Ivanov's Dostoevsky" in *Dialogues with Dostoevsky: The Overwhelming Questions* (Stanford: Stanford Univ. Press, 1993).

25. *The New Jerusalem Bible* (Garden City, New York: Doubleday, 1985), emphasis in original.

26. George P. Fedotov, *The Russian Religious Mind* (I) (Cambridge: Harvard Univ. Press, 1946), p. 101.

27. Ibid., pp. 127-28. Katerina Clark and Michael Holquist also cite Fedotov in their discussion of the kenotic tradition in Russian Orthodoxy, and its impact upon the thought of Bakhtin (Mikhail Bakhtin [Cambridge: Harvard Univ. Press, 1984], pp. 84-85).

28. Joseph Frank, *Dostoevsky: The Seeds of Revolt, 1821-1849* (Princeton: Princeton Univ. Press, 1976), p. 48.

29. Fyodor Dostoyevsky, *The Devils,* trans. David Magarshack (Harmondsworth: Penguin, 1953), p. 704.

30. Fyodor Dostoyevsky, *Crime and Punishment,* trans. Constance Garnett (New York: Random House, Modern Library, 1950), pp. 471-72, Dostoevsky's ellipses.

31. Bakhtin, *Problems,* p. 242. In *Images of Hope: Imagination as Healer of the Hopeless* (Notre Dame: Univ. of Notre Dame Press, 1965), William F. Lynch discusses the interactive relationship between personal wishing and interpersonal mutuality. His insights here often parallel Bakhtin's on confession. For example: "In mutuality each of the parties helps the other to become himself" (p. 171).

32. *The Idiot,* Part One, ch. 10, as cited in Bakhtin, *Problems,* p. 242.

33. Caryl Emerson, "The Tolstoy Connection in Bakhtin," in *Rethinking Bakhtin: Extensions and Challenges,* eds. Gary Saul Morson and Caryl Emerson (Evanston: Northwestern Univ. Press, 1989), p. 157.

34. Bakhtin, *Problems,* p. 242.

35. Ibid., p. 242.

36. Ibid., p. 265.

37. Nathan Rosen, "Style and Structure in The Brothers Karamazov" (1971) in *The Brothers Karamazov* (Norton Critical Edition), p. 845.

38. Lynch, *Hope,* p. 180.

39. Ibid., p. 154.

40. Bakhtin, "Reworking," p. 299.

41. Margaret Ziolkowski, in *Hagiography and Modern Russian Literature* (Princeton: Princeton Univ. Press, 1988) sees Zosima's kenotic attitude as exemplary of a crucial strain in the Russian monastic tradition. She writes: "[Zosima's] ability to understand even the most tortured souls is one of the hallmarks of the great kenotics" (p. 162). Harriet Murav, in *Holy Foolishness: Dostoevsky's Novels and the Poetics of Cultural Critique* (Stanford: Stanford Univ. Press, 1992), discusses Zosima (and Mikhail) in the light of the related Russian tradition of the holy fool (pp. 153-60).

42. One thinks here of Heidegger's concept of Gelassenheit, "releasement toward things and openness to the mystery" (*Discourse on Thinking,* trans. John M. Anderson and E. Hans Freund [New York: Harper and Row, 1966], p. 55), although, as is characteristic of his later writings, Heidegger speaks here of a "letting be" toward things, not people. Long before Heidegger, though, Meister Eckhart uses the word to describe one's proper relationship to God: "detachment [Gelassenheit] is receptive to nothing at all except God" (*The Essential Sermons, Commentaries. Treatises, and Defense,* trans. Edmund Colledge, O. S. A. and Bernard McGinn [New York: Paulist Press, 1981], p. 286). I am grateful to David Morgan for pointing this passage out to me.

43. In *Toward a Philosophy of the Act,* Bakhtin develops this concept of "live entering," as Morson and Emerson translate it (*Prosaics,* p. 54). Bakhtin writes (in Vadim Liapunov's translation): "I empathize actively into an individuality and consequently, I do not lose myself completely, nor my unique place outside it, even for a moment . . . Passive empathizing, being-possessed, losing oneself—these have nothing in common with the answerable act/deed of self-abstracting or self-renunciation" (*Act,* pp. 15-16, Bakhtin's emphasis).

44. In *The Illuminating Icon* (Grand Rapids, MI: Eerdmans, 1989), Anthony Ugolnik discusses the importance of the icon in the Orthodox imagination, and observes: "In Orthodox cultures the encounter with God and the flash of insight that conveys religious meaning occur not so often in private reflection as in encounter with another. That encounter is sometimes expressed in dialogue with a spiritual elder or holy individual who has 'absorbed' the Word and can now reflect it. But often the encounter is silent, like the icon itself. It emerges through the act of embrace. To embrace another, even a sinner, is to encounter directly the image of Christ." Ugolnik goes on to point to Sonia, who, "even in her sin, becomes an icon of the Christ whose selflessness she reflects," and to Christ with the Inquisitor (p. 51). See too Harriet Murav, *Holy Foolishness* (pp. 131-34) for a discussion of Dostoevsky's iconic art.

45. Running throughout *The Brothers Karamazov* is this anguished demand upon the confessor to relieve the confessant of the anguish of her or his conscience. Alyosha develops into a prosaic confessor as, at crucial moments, he must face such demands. Katerina Ivanovna, about to commit herself to Dmitri out of laceration, says to Alyosha: "I foresee that your decision, your approval will bring me peace" (p. 172). The next day, Grushenka wants Alyosha to decide how she should respond to the lover who jilted her five years before: "'Decide for me, Alyosha, the time has come, it shall be as you say. Am I to forgive him or not?'" (p. 334). Three months later, on the evening before the trial, Mitya tells Alyosha how his conscience is tormented over the plan for his escape, and claims "'It's your decision that will decide it'" (p. 563). We can trace Alyosha's development as confessor in the way that he responds in each case. In the earliest scene he impulsively attempts to decide for Katerina; later, with Grushenka and Mitya, he has learned to attentively locate the confessants' own choices, and wishes with them.

46. Victor Terras in *A Karamazov Companion* (Madison: Univ. of Wisconsin Press, 1981), cites Roger L. Cox who discerns that the Inquisitor's "authority" is tyranny, his "miracle" sorcery, and his "mystery" mystification (p. 233).

47. Dostoevsky, *Notes from Underground,* pp. 28-29, emphasis and ellipsis Dostoevsky's.

48. In Michel Foucault's sense, when he studies Jeremy Bentham's penitentiary design for surveillance and domination. See *Discipline and Punish,* trans. Alan Sheridan (New York: Vintage, 1979) and "The Eye of Power" in *Power/Knowledge,* trans. and ed. Colin Gordon (New York: Pantheon, 1980), pp. 146-65. Foucault discusses confession in *The History of Sexuality, Volume 1: An Introduction,* trans. Robert Hurley (New York: Vintage, 1978)—but reduces it to a paradigm of power and domination. He writes, for example, that "the agency of domination does not reside in the one who speaks (for it is he who is constrained), but in the one who listens and says nothing: not in the one who knows and answers, but in the one who questions and is not supposed to know. And this discourse of truth finally takes effect, not in the

one who receives it, but in the one from whom it is wrested" (p. 62).

49. Lynch, *Hope,* p. 154.

50. Edward Wasiolek. "*The Brothers Karamazov*: Idea and Technique" (1964), in *The Brothers Karamazov* (Norton Critical Edition), pp. 820-21.

51. Robert L. Belknap, *The Structure of "The Brothers Karamzov"* (Evanston: Northwestern Univ. Press, 1989), pp. 37-38.

52. Bakhtin, "Reworking," p. 287.

53. In *I and Thou* (trans. Ronald Gregor Smith [New York: Scribner's, 19581), Buber uses the image of the gaze to describe authentic dialogue and mutuality: "I and thou take their stand not merely in relation, but also in the solid give-and-take of talk. The moments of relation are here, and only here, bound together by means of the element of the speech in which they are immersed. Here what confronts us has blossomed into the full reality of the Thou. Here alone, then, as reality that cannot be lost, are gazing and being gazed upon, knowing and being known, loving and being loved" (p. 103). Bakhtin was familiar with Buber's work. For a brief comparative study of the two thinkers, see Nina Perlina, "Bakhtin and Buber: Problems of Dialogic Imagination," *Studies in Twentieth Century Literature* 9 (1984): 13-28.

54. Lynch, *Hope,* pp. 169-70.

55. Of Christ's silence with and kiss of the Inquisitor, George Steiner writes: "Christ's refusal to engage in the duel yields a dramatic motif of great majesty and tact," *Tolstov or Dostoevskv* (Chicago: Univ. of Chicago Press, 1985), p. 342. Steiner's concern with tact toward the other is evident in *Real Presences* (Chicago: Univ. of Chicago Press, 1989). The other he writes of here is a work of art, but the analogy he uses to describe such an approach to art is that of "our encounter with the freedom of presence in another human being, or attempts to communicate with that freedom, [which] will always entail approximation" (p. 175): "Where there is *cortesia* between freedoms, a vital distance is kept. A certain reserve persists. Understanding is patiently won and, at all time, provisional. There are questions we do not ask our "caller" (p. 176). Zosima reveals such *courtesia.*

56. See Diane Oenning Thompson's *"The Brothers Karamzov" and the Poetics of Memory* (Cambridge: Cambridge Univ. Press, 1991) for an extensive study of this theme in the novel and its intrinsic relation in Dostoevsky to "the ideal of Christ" (p. 273). I do not here discuss the theme of suffering, so important to *The Brothers Karamazov.* Simply put, Mikhail's growth through suffering, and his clear-eyed recognition of its expiatory quality ("I want to suffer for my sin" [p. 289]), provide part of Dostoevsky's oblique, artistic answer to Ivan's challenge: suffering is meaningful for Mikhail. (I agree with Lynch, in *Images of Faith: An Exploration of the Ironic Imagination* [Notre Dame: Univ. of Notre Dame Press, 1973], p. 149, however, that Ivan's challenge concerning the suffering of innocent children is unanswerable.) Another aspect of Dostoevsky's answer is in his artistic depiction, in the story of Mikhail, of authentic authority, mystery, and miracle. See also Nathan Rosen, "Style and Structure," on this subject.

57. Lynch, *Hope,* p. 157.

58. By pointing to the "forgiveness" offered those in hell, and to "God who calls them," Zosima reveals his sometimes unorthodox views of the afterlife. For Zosima, active love is imaged even in hell (p. 302).

59. Perhaps the most famous example of Dostoevsky's embrace of Christ as the ideal is his letter to N. D. Fonvizina in February-March 1854 in which he writes: "if someone succeeded in proving to me that Christ was outside the truth, and if, indeed, the truth was outside Christ, then I would sooner remain with Christ than with the truth" (*Selected Letters of Fyodor Dostoyevsky,* trans. Andrew R. MacAndrew, eds. Joseph Frank and David I. Goldstein [New Brunswick: Rutgers Univ. Press, 1987], p. 68, Dostoevsky's emphasis). Bakhtin writes of Dostoevsky: "The image of the ideal human being or the image of Christ represents for him the resolution of ideological quests" (*Problems,* p. 97). In *Toward a Philosophy of the Act,* Bakhtin himself sees Christ as a model of the act of self-renunciation and writes: "The world from which Christ has departed will no longer be the world in which he had never existed; it is, in its very principle, a different world" (p. 16). In "Author and Hero in Aesthetic Activity," Bakhtin writes, "For the first time [in Christ], there appeared an infinitely deepened I-for-myself—not a cold I-for-myself, but one of boundless kindness toward the other; an I-for-myself that renders full justice to the other as such, disclosing and affirming the other's axiological distinctiveness in all its fullness" (p. 56, Bakhtin's emphasis). In this essay, Bakhtin writes of the human need for God and refers to three episodes of the New Testament which, Ann Shukman writes, "show human beings calling out to God, or to Christ, from the very depths of the self, those depths in which, as Bakhtin wrote in the same essay, we sense our incompleteness and long for the miracle of new birth" ("Bakhtin's

Tolstoy Prefaces," in *Rethinking Bakhtin,* p. 144). Finally, in his late "Notes Made in 1970-71," in a section on Dostoevsky, Bakhtin writes, "The word as something personal. Christ as truth. I ask him" (*Speech Genres,* p. 148).

60. Christos Yannaras, *The Freedom of Morality* (Crestwood, NY: St. Vladimir's Press, 1984), p. 53. Cited by Caryl Emerson, "Problems in Bakhtin's Poetics," p. 523, n. 22. For an analysis of "authenticity" as being necessarily dialogical, see Charles Taylor, *The Ethics of Authenticity* (Cambridge: Harvard Univ. Press, 1991).

Alexander von Schönborn (essay date 2000)

SOURCE: Schönborn, Alexander von. "Church and State: Dostoevsky and Kant." In *Cold Fusion: Aspects of The German Cultural Presence in Russia,* edited by Gennady Barabtarlo, pp. 126-36. New York: Berghahn, 2000.

[*In the following essay, Schönborn studies the notion of sacrificing freedom to gain peace of mind within the context of "The Grand Inquisitor" chapter of* The Brothers Karamazov *and the philosophy of Immanuel Kant.*]

The title of this essay is the conjunction of what one might view as two truisms. The first of these is that Dostoevsky's main concern throughout his life was with the nature of social order and, more particularly, with its specifications as church and state. The large secondary literature follows Dostoevsky himself in viewing the **"Legend of the Grand Inquisitor"** chapter in *The Brothers Karamazov* (1879-80) as the culmination of his lifelong pertinent ruminations. Thus, to pick but one example, Bruce K. Ward[1] writes in regard to this chapter: "This short writing, considered by him to be the 'culminating point' of *The Brothers Karamazov,* can be regarded as the culmination also of his religious and political thought—his 'final statement' concerning the question of human order." The key phrases here—"culminating point" and "final statement"—are Dostoevsky's own, cited by Ward from a letter to N. A. Liubimov dated 10 May 1879.[2] The second truism leading to the title of this short essay concerns the conjoining of Dostoevsky and Kant. This chapter presents a dispute in regard to the issue of whether freedom or happiness ought to be the highest principle in human affairs. Kant initially raised this question, which has ever since vexed ethicists and thoughtful people generally, reflecting on the standards of their conduct.

I want therefore to look at Dostoevsky's **"Grand Inquisitor"** chapter in the light of Kant's philosophy. In particular, I seek to ascertain how the Cardinal's rejec-

tion of freedom in favor of happiness might be understood in terms of the conceptual resources provided by Kant. The result of this effort is to provide various possibilities of interpretation between which a reader of the rest of the novel and of Dostoevsky's other works will have to decide.

Unfortunately, the secondary literature linking Dostoevsky and Kant is exceedingly sparse. What little there is does not prove helpful. H. Tencler, in his book on the problem of freedom in *The Brathers Karamazov,* mentions Kant once to indicate that what Dostoevsky means by "soul" is what Kant calls "personality."[3] In terms of more extended treatments, there is the work by Ia. Golosovker.[4] Since we know that on 22 February 1854—over a quarter century before the publication of *The Brothers Karamazov*—Dostoevsky wrote to his brother requesting a copy of Kant's *Critique of Pure Reason* (1781), Golosovker plausibly assumes that Dostoevsky read this work. He then treats the relation between Dostoevsky and Kant in terms of the doctrine of "the Antinomy of Pure Reason" as put forth in this work by Kant. Focusing specifically on the Third Antinomy, which is concerned with the theoretical issue of freedom and determinism, Golosovker argues that Dostoevsky rejects Kant's belief that the antinomies are insoluble and uses the character of Ivan in *The Brothers Karamazov* to argue against the critical philosophy. But this reading is not helpful. Not only does Kant not consider the antinomies insoluble, he considers it the singular merit of the critical philosophy that it alone solves them. Moreover, the Third Antinomy is concerned with freedom as a theoretical issue only; it is in Kant's moral and religious texts that freedom is treated as a practical principle, i.e., as a principle of human conduct, and Dostoevsky is clearly interested, in *The Brothers Karamazov,* in the question of how we ought to conduct ourselves. In this arena, Dostoevsky clearly is with Kant, not against him.

To anticipate how I think Dostoevsky sides with Kant, let me summarize my reading of **"The Grand Inquisitor"** chapter in slogan form. In the past, people adhered to the "Divine Command" theory of moral obligation. That theory has, for good reasons, been abandoned and is historically passé. It has been replaced by two more humanistically focused theories of moral obligation: the Kantian account, which defines freedom as autonomy, and the various teleological or consequentialist accounts that make happiness, however defined, the highest principle of morality. The Grand Inquisitor's defense of the latter principle leads to the realization that, when pushed to its extreme in politicized fashion (so characteristic for Dostoevsky), such a consequentialist principle manifests itself as but a secularized version of the Divine Command theory in all its unsavory aspects. This leaves but one viable account, that of freedom as the highest moral principle.

I assume, of course, that Dostoevsky was familiar with Kant's account, an assumption that seems quite reasonable not only in terms of the content of **"The Grand Inquisitor"** chapter, but in view of the following facts. As a very young man, Dostoevsky had already become acquainted with Kant's moral thought through N. Karamzin's (for whom Kant himself apparently summed up the main points of his ethics) *Letters of a Russian Traveler, 1789/90*.[5] Dostoevsky was also a member of the "Society of the Lovers of Wisdom" whose meetings "were concerned almost exclusively with the reading and discussion of modern German philosophers such as Kant, Fichte and Schelling" (17). Finally, various Russian translations of Kant's moral and religious writings were in wide circulation during the second half of Dostoevsky's life.

But let me start at the beginning—the Preface to Ivan's prose poem—which immediately raises a series of questions. Ivan begins by noting that if his story, set in the sixteenth century, had been written at the time of its setting, it would have required a preface "to bring down heavenly powers on earth."[6] Such a preface is then provided. It contains, as its center, a paraphrase of the poem "The Wanderings of Our Lady Through Hell." In it, Our Lady, shocked by what she observes, "bids all the saints, all the martyrs, all the angels and archangels to fall down with her and pray for mercy on all without distinction" (20). She obtains from God a respite from suffering, at which point the sinners cry thankfully from hell, "Thou art *just,* O Lord, in this judgment." With that cry the paraphrase of the poem ends, and Ivan immediately adds again that his "poem would have been of that kind if it had been written at that time" (20), which, of course, it was not. This raises some obvious questions: Why is the Preface there at all, especially in light of the fact that it is clearly historical in a way that no sixteenth-century preface ever was? What is the meaning of that strange cry—strange, given what one might imagine oneself saying under those circumstances—emanating from hell?

Parenthetically, I might note the unfortunate fact that the various major treatments of this famous chapter make no attempt to deal with the Preface. This strikes me as unfortunate because of Dostoevsky's contorted efforts to have it in place and the issues of content it raises. Connected with these omissions is the absence of an adequate account why a sixteenth-century setting was chosen for the story. The typical explanation—a number of examples can be found in a collection edited by J. S. Wasserman[7]—alludes to Dostoevsky's desire to castigate both socialism and Roman Catholicism for attempting the compulsory organization of human happiness and for claims to infallibility thereby required. This seems true enough. But the choice of a sixteenth-century setting makes reference to socialism by anything more than allusions and formulas obviously diffi-

cult. This difficulty could easily have been removed by setting the plot in the present, which would have had the added advantage of possible reference to the pronouncements of the First Vatican Council—*The Brothers Karamazov* was, after all, written in the decade following that Council's proclamation of papal infallibility. Be that as it may, I think that an appropriate consideration of both the Preface and the setting of the Legend provides an answer to R. L. Cox's plaint: "Some, notably Berdyaev, identify Dostoevsky with Christ rather than with the Inquisitor, but they point to no cogent and specific reasons within the chapter itself for doing so."[8]

But how might one interpret that thankful "Thou art *just,* O Lord, in this judgment"? Surely God was not unjust before granting the temporary reprieve from suffering, nor would He have been so without heeding Mary's supplication. I would suggest that the only view of justice on which this cry, under the conditions of its utterance, makes sense is the Divine Command theory of moral obligation. According to that view, to which even such late medieval thinkers as John Duns Scotus and William of Ockham were still partial,[9] "what ultimately makes an action right or wrong is simply its being commanded or forbidden by God and nothing else."[10] If God decrees no respite, then He is just; and if He decrees a respite, then He is just as well, because it is His decree that ipso facto makes something just. Such decrees, like any legal positivism, are accompanied by external sanctions and coercion, as indeed they must be: temporal punishment in this life and in purgatory, eternal reward or punishment in the life to come. Dostoevsky alludes to this view and does so in the distinctive fashion I have indicated to show that this view is no longer a live option. Very few Western philosophers of note have maintained it since late medieval times. Kant in his *Groundwork of the Metaphysic of Morals* (1785)—the most widely read of his ethical works—dismisses it as the very worst of moral theories because it forms "the basis for a moral system which would be in direct opposition to morality."[11]

Dostoevsky is, of course, not interested in the theory of obligation per se but rather in its historical realization, as both the historical character of the Preface and the later, nostalgic allusion by the Inquisitor to "the rigid, ancient law" prior to Christ's initial appearance on earth make clear.[12] It is worthwhile to look for a moment at the Israel of the Old Testament through Kantian eyes, for this community is clearly an instance of the theory I have mentioned above.

Kant distinguishes between state and church on the basis that the former is a civil society bound by coercive laws, while the latter is a civil society bound by noncoercive laws, i.e., moral laws. Legality and morality are not to be conflated. The principle of freedom as governing our maxims—the intentional rules prompting our actions—is the principle of morality. As normative for external legislation, for laws which prescribe actions rather than maxims of actions, the principle of freedom is the highest principle of the state and of its specification of civil rights. In regard to religion, Kant distinguishes between an ecclesiastic faith—convictions resting on statutory laws and on putative historical facts concerning the founding of a church—and a religious faith that is grounded in, and is an extension of, moral practice.

In terms of these distinctions, one would have to say that Israel had no church, but only a theocratically organized state, and that in this state there was no possibility of genuine religious faith, but only of an ecclesiastical faith. True religion was thus not possible in that historical context, given its conception of moral obligation. According to Kant, what God's becoming incarnate symbolically represents, regardless of historical beliefs that may have prompted this insight, is the possibility of genuine morality and hence of true religion. This, in turn, allows for an appropriate distinction between, and a coexistence of, church and state. But if so, then this Israelite realization of the Divine Command theory is as passé historically as the underlying theory of Divine Command. Both have thus yielded the stage—and thus serve quite literally as preface—to the contemporary options discussed by the Grand Inquisitor.

As mentioned, these options are freedom and happiness. They are respectively championed in our chapter by Christ and by the Grand Inquisitor, who is the servant of Satan. Why do freedom and happiness have these particular champions, given that, for example, we do not normally associate happiness with Satan or, more generally, with evil?

Here again Kant is highly instructive. In many of his works, Kant argues that the moral law (formulated, for example, as "Act in such a way that you always treat humanity, whether in your own person or in the person of any other, never simply as a means, but always at the same time as an end"[13] or, as I might put it very simply, "Respect every human being equally") is the expression of our autonomy; we are the source not only of free or self-initiated actions, but also, through practical reason, of the law to which these voluntary actions ought to conform and for the sake of which they ought to be undertaken. The moral law, he further argues, commands that all of our intentions and dispositions conform to it. This entails, since complete fitness of all our intentions to the moral law is defined by him as "holiness," that the moral law requires us to attain holiness. In his *Religion Within the Limits of Reason Alone* (1793), Kant goes on to add that since holiness is originally the trait of divinity, the moral necessity of such holiness in human beings requires us to think of God as

uniting Himself with humanity: God made Flesh. Christ is thus the exemplification and instantiation of the ideal of moral perfection, of a fully autonomous human being. We experience the actuality of this incarnation in moral obligation; how this is possible we do not and cannot understand, though we must believe in the possibility of this incarnation as a postulate of the rationality of our moral life. Religious belief, therefore, is generally an outgrowth of our practice of morality, of the right exercise of our autonomy. As such, genuine religious faith cannot countenance any aspect of ecclesiastical faith that has a destructive impact on practical rationality as the source of our autonomy or on freedom as the genuine foundation of religious faith. On the other hand, any human act not springing from autonomy is morally wrong, even if, viewed externally, it appears to be in accord with the moral law; its principle is one of heteronomy rather than autonomy. When we make a principle of heteronomy the basic reason for our action, we subordinate our autonomous freedom to that principle. Such subordination is the nature of moral and religious evil. Since happiness, as the putative ground of our conduct, is for Kant the paradigmatic instance of an heteronomous principle when this happiness is made the ultimate justification of that conduct, it is easy to see why Satan's man should be cast in the role of the champion of happiness.

Let me now turn to the dialogue itself or, rather, to the Inquisitor's monologue. What are the Inquisitor's charges? I quote:

> I swear, man is weaker and baser by nature than Thou hast believed him! Can he, can he do what Thou didst? By showing him so much respect, Thou didst, as it were, cease to feel for him, for Thou didst ask far too much from him—Thou who hast loved him more than Thyself! Respecting him less, Thou wouldst have asked less of him.[14]

Again, in altered form:

> Thou wouldst not enslave man by a miracle, and didst crave faith given freely, not based on miracle.[15]

> There are three powers, three powers alone, able to conquer and to hold captive forever the conscience of these impotent rebels [i.e., most of humankind] for their happiness—those forces are miracle, mystery, and authority. Thou hast rejected all three and hast set the example for doing so.[16]

In order to understand the Legend, it is important not to cede "miracle, mystery, and authority" to the Inquisitor; after all, the story begins with Christ performing a miracle. As Cox has noted, "the Inquisitor reverses the real situation—he is the one who rejects miracle, mystery, and authority, and proposes to meet man's needs by *magic, mystification,* and *tyranny.*"[17] These Christ does reject. As the Inquisitor notes, "Thou wouldst not deprive man of freedom and didst reject the offer, thinking, what is that freedom worth, if obedience is bought with bread?"[18]

"Bread," in the remark last cited, is the Inquisitor's symbol for happiness, so that his question becomes "What is freedom worth if acting for its sake is motivated by and hence subordinated to happiness?" The answer from Christ's perspective is that, morally and religiously speaking, it is worth nothing at all. But why do I think that the Grand Inquisitor uses "bread" as a synonymous expression for "happiness"? The antonym to "bread" in the story is "hunger." Like Kant, the Inquisitor sees human finitude in terms of empirical needs, deprivations, and the desires for their respective assuaging. The satisfaction of our desires, to the extent that they fit into a coherent whole, is generally the modern Western conception of happiness.

For Kant and Dostoevsky, of course, this is only part of the human condition. A human being is also a being of reason or, in Dostoevsky's terms, a being with a soul, and practical reason—or, more colloquially, will—specifies human ends that set limits qua morality to the intended satisfaction of desire. Our autonomy dictates what we morally ought or ought not to do. Moreover, for Kant, though not for Dostoevsky, autonomy entails as external freedom a body of rights, of civil liberties. Dostoevsky restricts the principle of freedom to internal freedom—having a conscience—and views civil rights only as a historically associated coproduct of what he calls in **The Raw Youth** the "Geneva" idea.

Kant takes the unconditional character of autonomy's demand on us to mean that we can satisfy it. In his famous dictum, "Ought implies can." It is in regard to that "can" that the Inquisitor, on the one hand, and Dostoevsky (with the restriction just mentioned) and Kant, on the other, part company. For the latter, that "can" characterizes every human being as a moral subject, as a "person"; for the former, it characterizes only the strong, the scriptural "elect." Put in terms of the basic human dispositions pertinent to will, which Kant analyzed at the start of his *Religion Within the Limits of Reason Alone,*[19] the Inquisitor believes that all human animals are capable of attaining "humanity"—theoretical rationality, which can also serve desire—but only very few are capable of the exercise of "personality," of being capable of moral accountability or of that respect toward the law of the will that is a sufficient incentive for our power of choice. Put differently, according to the Inquisitor we are all humans, but very few of us are persons in fact. He vacillates about how this fact is to be construed. At times he suggests that the majority of human beings will become premoral children still using the notions of right and wrong and those of heaven and hell as well—even atheists such as the Inquisitor or Robespierre recognize the necessity of the latter notions for social order in situations where the coercive sanctions of positive law are not effective. However, being unable to derive the notions of right and wrong from their own theoretical but also premoral rationality, these

"children" will have to receive them heteronomously. At other times, the Inquisitor suggests that all human beings have moral autonomy—they all have a genuine conscience—but the vast majority choose to give its exercise away without culpability owing to weakness of the will, self-deception, and deception by the state. For example, if being able to ascertain the facts relevant to a moral decision is a necessary condition for the exercise of autonomy, they would lack this condition (à la George Orwell's *1984*).

What are the implications of this profoundly ambiguous characterization of human beings? The Inquisitor has no quarrel with freedom as the highest internal principle in the lives of persons, a relatively tiny subclass of humans. But for the vast majority of humans, freedom in the sense of autonomy cannot be the highest principle of their inner and outer conduct. It is in reference to this human multitude that the Inquisitor declares: "Dost Thou know that the ages will pass, and humanity will proclaim by the lips of their sages that there is no crime, and therefore no sin; there is only hunger?"[20] Universal happiness must, for most of us, take the place of autonomy whose demands we cannot or will not meet.

To say that, for most of us, universal happiness must be the highest principle does not mean, to the Inquisitor, that this principle suffices. As he sagely notes, "without a stable conception of the object of life, man would not consent to go on living, and would rather destroy himself than remain on earth, though he had bread in abundance" (32). Given the modern growth in consciousness of freedom, it will thus be necessary to persuade the human majority that "they will only become free when they renounce their freedom to us and submit to us" (38), so that "people are more persuaded than ever that they have perfect freedom, yet they have brought their freedom to us and laid it humbly at our feet" (26). The freedom thus relinquished cannot be that of autonomy; it must refer to such manifestations of freedom as civil liberties, as the preferential choices of prudence, and as what the Inquisitor himself calls "free thought." (38). The Inquisitor does not mention the devices, beyond simple deception, whereby this persuasion is accomplished. Orwell's *1984* can once again suitably fill in the blanks.

According to the Inquisitor, the quest for universal happiness will initially turn to science for the satisfaction of hunger. But science will prove disappointing. In meeting needs, it generates new ones without a limiting principle so that "freedom and bread enough for all are inconceivable together, for never, never will they be able to share between them!" (38).

It is here that Dostoevsky and Kant part company. Writing the better part of a century after Kant, Dostoevsky might have sought to expand the modern doctrine of civil rights through a deeper understanding of the no-tion of autonomy than Kant's. Indeed, given his consid-erable sensitivity to profound economic inequality and inequity, he might have pointed ahead to the next cen-tury by seeing whether a doctrine of economic rights might be anchored in the principle of freedom as au-tonomy. Instead and as mentioned, Dostoevsky equates the principle of freedom with inner freedom. This forces him, in effect, into ceding the political arena to the In-quisitor. Dostoevsky seems convinced that the indi-vidual pursuit of happiness within the juridical frame-work of a liberal state grounded in a conception of freedom, as envisioned by Kant, can in principle neither satisfy nor contain within moral limits the demand for "the universal happiness of man" (37). More and more state intervention—"socialism"—will be required for building the requisite institutions and, given the dispar-ity of wealth among nations, will finally have to take the form of a single world-state. Moreover, this socialist or communist program will have to be melded with, in Kant's terms, an ecclesiastic faith ascribing omniscience or infallibility, paternalistic benevolence, and benefi-cence to its governing group. For only such can be trusted to distribute bread equitably and to make con-tinuous progress in its maximal availability. (We need only recall here the role of the chocolate rations in Or-well's *1984*.) Only such an ecclesiastical state will be "able to conquer and to hold captive forever the con-science of these impotent rebels for their happiness" (33).

Having relinquished the political realm, Dostoevsky en-visions his alternative social order as a form of Chris-tianity. Specifically, he seems to envision the church as the community of religious faith based on the principle of freedom—Luther's and Kant's "invisible church"[21]—with some monks of the Russian Orthodox community and the Russian commune forming, again in Kant's terms, the visible and true church, representing the in-visible to the extent possible within experience through such marks as freedom, holiness, universality, and depth of redemptive suffering. Dostoevsky calls this visible community "Russian socialism."[22] As Father Zossima urges elsewhere in the novel, the state must become the church! This is not a demand for a true theocracy in op-position to the Inquisitor's illusory one; it is not a de-mand for a current version of ancient Israel. What Zossima demands is "church" as specified above. Dos-toevsky thus seems implicitly committed to what, from a political perspective, might be called a Christian anar-chism. (Perhaps, given Russia under Alexander II's late rule, this provides an additional reason for Christ's si-lence in the **"Grand Inquisitor"** chapter.)

But let me return to the Inquisitor's infallible state. What Dostoevsky means to show through its character-ization by the Inquisitor is that the quest for universal happiness must culminate in a state of affairs that can

only be described as a secularized institutionalization of the Divine Command theory, a humanistic refurbishing of a discredited view and of the practices it entails. The Inquisitor himself comes to this realization when, upon having fully articulated his view, he is nevertheless kissed by Christ in a sign of love and respect. Freedom is the right moral principle, but its demands are, in the Inquisitor's enduring judgment, too stringent for the majority of human beings to meet. In short, he contin-ues to see no alternative except for the Elect. "The kiss glows in his heart, but the old man adheres to his idea."[23]

Notes

1. B. K. Ward, *Dostoyevsky's Critique of the West* (Waterloo, 1986), p. 101.

2. Ibid.

3. H. Tencler, *Das Freiheitsproblem in Brüder Kara-mazov von Dostoevski* (Riga, 1928), p. 26.

4. Ia. E. Golosovker, *Dostoevsky and Kant* (Moscow, 1963).

5. Ward, *Dostoyevsky's Critique of the West,* p. 16, n. 33.

6. F. Dostoevsky, *The Grand Inquisitor on the Na-ture of Man* (Indianapolis, 1948), p. 19.

7. F. Dostoevsky, *The Grand Inquisitor,* ed. J. S. Wasserman (Columbus, 1970).

8. R. L. Cox, "Dostoevsky's Grand Inquisitor," in F. Dostoevsky, *The Grand Inquisitor,* pp. 77-92, here p. 77.

9. A. Fagothey, *Right and Reason* (St. Louis, 1953), p. 111.

10. W. K. Frankena, *Ethics* (Englewood Cliffs, N. J., 1973), p. 28.

11. I. Kant, *Groundwork of the Metaphysics of Morals* (New York, 1956), p. 111.

12. Dostoevsky, *The Grand Inquisitor on the Nature of Man,* pp. 32-33.

13. Kant, *Groundwork of the Metaphysics of Morals,* p. 96.

14. Dostoevsky, *The Grand Inquisitor on the Nature of Man,* p. 35.

15. Ibid., p. 34.

16. Ibid., p. 33.

17. Cox, "Dostoevsky's Grand Inquisitor," p. 79.

18. Dostoevsky, *The Grand Inquisitor on the Nature of Man,* p. 29.

19. I. Kant, *Religion Within the Limits of Reason Alone* (New York, 1934), pp. 21-23.

20. Dostoevsky, *The Grand Inquisitor on the Nature of Man,* p. 29.

21. Tencler, *Das Freiheitsproblem in Brüder Karamazov von Dostoevski,* p. 36.

22. Ward, *Dostoyevsky's Critique of the West,* pp. 179-81.

23. Dostoevsky, *The Grand Inquisitor on the Nature of Man,* p. 45.

William Mills Todd III (essay date 2000)

SOURCE: Todd, William Mills, III. "Storied Selves: Constructing Characters in *The Brothers Karamazov.*" In *Self and Story in Russian History,* edited by Laura Engelstein and Stephanie Sandler, pp. 266-79. Ithaca, N.Y.: Cornell University Press, 2000.

[*In the following essay, Todd offers a scholarly analysis of Dostoevsky's conceptions of the self and narrative in* The Brothers Karamazov.]

For a volume on "self and story" in Russian history, a study of Dostoevsky's last novel, *The Brothers Karamazov (Brat'ia Karamazovy,* 1881), which foregrounds its characters' uses and misuses of narrative as they attempt to understand the extreme possibilities of human behavior, offers many opportunities to reflect on both "self" and "story." In this essay I will outline a reading of the novel that focuses upon the central themes of this volume, illuminating them with modern theories of narrative which share Dostoevsky's own fascination with self and story. To the extent that *The Brothers Karamazov* constitutes not only a reflection on narrative in general but criticism of the kinds of story told by its culture, I will suggest how it can help make us aware of the ways late nineteenth-century Russians told stories. Here I will use modern theories of narrative to discuss the novel's own problematization of narrative, which is itself part of a long tradition in literature and in critical reflection.

Since Greek antiquity selves and stories have been inextricably intertwined in accounts of both "self" (or its rough equivalents) and "story." Our earliest theory of narrative, Aristotle's *Poetics,* may not entertain the notion of "self" in a recognizably modern sense, but it does have to deal with human agency in discussing actions, it does consider the social position of these agents, and it does endow them with character traits.[1] Subsequent theories, such as Propp's, at the very least entertain the first of these hypostases of character, the notion of agency. But most, whether normative or descriptive, will attempt to do more: dictate the types of characters most appropriate to a particular kind of narrative; posit

what makes a character interesting or capable of generating narrative curiosity; study how characters can be constructed in narratives. Our most ornate and brilliant theory of narrative, Roland Barthes' *S/Z,* giving play to myriad critical discourses, jargons, and terms only to be found in a Greek dictionary, nevertheless makes problems of character and human agency central to the working of his five narrative codes.[2] Indeed, reversing the focus on action that has been the rule since Aristotle, Barthes argues that it is this movement of traits toward a proper name, not action, that is the property of narrative.[3] In plainer English, narrative becomes a process of endowing proper names with character. In any event, Barthes preserves and expands Aristotle's understandings of literary personages as agents, characters, and functions of context.

When we move from narrative in general to its principal modern literary manifestation, the novel, we see that theories of the novel are to an even greater degree fixated upon character, emphasizing to a greater degree, as is historically appropriate, issues of individuation and consciousness. Georg Lukács's famous inquiry defines novelistic plotting in terms of the movements and understandings of character: the "outward form" of the novel is the biography of a problematic individual, whose individuality is an end unto itself in a contingent world, while what Lukács calls the "inner form" of the novel is the problematic individual's journey toward self-recognition. "Outward" and "inner" in each case focus upon an individual.[4] Lukács's Russian contemporary, Mikhail Bakhtin, was drawn to and challenged such a conception of the novel, developing a number of different insights about narrative which explode the traditions of plot-oriented Aristotelian poetics. Speech, not action, becomes the center of Bakhtin's focus in his most developed essay, "Discourse in the Novel," and the "speaking person" becomes the novel's hero. But for all of Bakhtin's indifference to plotting in a traditional sense of the ordering of events, the testing or challenging of the hero in his theory of the novel do enter into a sort of master plot, the process of the speaking person's "coming to know his or her own language as it is perceived in someone else's language, coming to know one's own belief system in someone else's system."[5] "Story," in short, has become inconceivable without not just actors or products of cultural contexts but also without "selves," individuated and coherent in varying degrees, depending on the theory in question.

But "self" is scarcely less conceivable without "story" in most modern treatments. Where it once may have been adequate to describe a character by measuring a person against an established norm or by attaching traits to a proper name—no small process of individuation, given that Webster's gives nearly 18,000 trait names[6]—a modern sense of self generally involves development over time. And the depiction of development over time inevitably calls forth narrative, our principal cognitive means, as Louis Mink has put it, for making comprehensive the many successive interrelationships that are composed by a career.[7] Cathy Popkin's paper for this volume shows how medical science of the late nineteenth century used narrative to constitute character according to disciplinary rules. We do not need to rehearse here the many different ways in which our various schools of psychoanalysis and developmental psychology construct, or deconstruct, individuated or integral selves, normative life histories, or case studies. The point is that all do this in story form.

Distinctions suggested by the novel itself aid our inquiry. These distinctions, in narratological terms, address three aspects of the poetics and pragmatics of narrative: the *plot,* the ordering of events and personages; the *narration,* the teller's presentation of events and personages; and the *reception,* the reader's or listener's processing of the story. The first aspect, plot, involves the openness of the story, the play that it allows for the subject's agency, potential, and own definition of self. It also involves the scope of the story: Is it a general account or a particular story? The whole story of the self, or just a part? The second aspect, narration, involves, primarily, distance and engagement: Is the story told with scientific objectivity, from a distance, or with varying kinds of personal involvement (egocentric/selfless) with the object of discourse? A related set of distinctions, ones involving the ideological involvement of the narrator, sets secular discourse against the insights of faith (scientific objectivity/loving empathy). The third aspect of the novel's stories of the self, reception, involves the participation of the listener, for many of these stories are told orally to personages, in their physical presence, making them the objects of dialogue, often heated or abusive.

The Brothers Karamazov, serialized over a two-year period in one of Russia's leading "thick journals" (1879-80), represents a field where Russia's various stories for constituting selves could, and did, confront each other. Or, more precisely, a field within a field, for the thick journals themselves, by bringing together fiction and literary reviews with articles on a variety of historical, scientific, and social-scientific topics, themselves forced confrontations between the discourses of Russia's incipient professions and academic disciplines. We may borrow the prosecutor's simile, "like the sun in a small drop of water," in turn borrowed from Derzhavin, to suggest this process of miniaturization, by which contemporary ways of characterizing the self come together first in the period's popular journals, then in Dostoevsky's last novel.[8] During the two years of serialization alone, *The Russian Herald* (*Russkii vestnik*) sandwiched the installments of *The Brothers Karamazov* among articles, many of them also serialized, on natural and physical science, military history, imperial history

(the Polish and Eastern questions), religion, travel, the law (courts and prison reform), pedagogy, economics, music, art, and literature.[9] Contemporary readers of the novel would have these subjects before their eyes from this journal alone, to say nothing about what they would have encountered in rival thick journals, such as *The Herald of Europe* (*Vestnik Evropy*), *National Annals* (*Otechestvennye zapiski*), *Deed* (*Delo*), and *Russian Wealth* (*Russkoe bogatstvo*). The increasingly popular daily newspapers of the 1870s had come to carry the greater part of court and crime reporting, although Dostoevsky's one-man journal, **Diary of a Writer** (**Dnevnik pisatelia**), treated a number of trials at length as well as many of the social, cultural, and foreign-policy controversies of the time.[10] But Dostoevsky established a further journalistic context for his readers by setting his novel in the postreform late 1860s, when the journals—which then included *The Contemporary* (*Sovremennik*) and the Dostoevsky brothers' *Time* (*Vremia*) and *Epoch* (*Epokha*)—devoted more space to discussion of the judicial reforms as well as to deterministic theories of human development, such as we encounter in the novel in the writings and dialogue of the journalist Rakitin in **The Brothers Karamazov.**

The prosecutor accompanies his simile, however, with a specular metaphor: "in the picture of this fine little family it is as if certain general fundamental elements of our contemporary intellectual society may be glimpsed—oh, not all the elements, and in microscopic view, 'like the sun in a small drop of water,' yet something has been reflected in it."[11] If one must have an optical metaphor, I would prefer "refracted," because it seems that when the novel deals with contemporary ways of storying the self, it does so by bending and ordering them from a particular angle, much as a prism would bend and order the intensities of a stream of light.

Through this prism of novelistic discourse the self becomes indeed storied, not only in the sense of the object and subject of stories, but also by being layered, as in the stories of a house. The personages of the novel become subject to many kinds of story, some literary, some scientific, some social-scientific. But we are never allowed to forget the angles of refraction, that stories are told by someone, to someone, and, instrumentally, for some purpose. This manifest refracting of stories of the self is evident from the opening pages of the novel, the passage "From the Author," which is generally ignored in the critical discourse. Here a sarcastic, maddeningly indefinite author figure presents Alesha, the youngest of the Karamazov brothers, from several different angles: as hero of the novel, as a character possibly not grand enough to play this role, as an indefinite figure, and as an eccentric, a special case, yet one which might represent "the heart of the whole" more than the other people of the era.[12] The author is fussy, hostile, on the edge of that aggressive buffoonery which character-narrators (Fedor, Maksimov, Ivan's devil, the defense attorney) will later adopt, on the edge of that clumsy, excited, at times ungrammatical, discourse that Valentina Vetlovskaia has accurately attributed to the novel's primary narrator.[13] This author figure's only solution to the problems he poses, including those of character, is his refusal to solve them. He makes a mockery of the notion that literature imitates reality by treating both text and reality in terms of senselessness and confusion (*bestoloch'*). Every aspect of the text, he promises, will be either ambiguous or muddled: its genre, both "biography" and novel"; the hero, an unheroic eccentric; and its structure—it begins with a preface the author calls superfluous yet nevertheless includes, and its significance will become clear only from the sequel, which the author does not, of course, include. The reader, assaulted by these equivocations, ambiguities, and muddles, finds him or herself projected, sarcastically, as one who will disagree with the "author," will have to guess at what the author is trying to say, and may even read through to the end, unlike the sixty or so unnamed "Russian critics" who took it upon themselves to review the novel before serialization was completed.[14] As a provocation to the reader, the narrator's own disjointed narrative becomes purposeful. The structure of the book will provide many patterns of repetition to guide the reader, as Robert Belknap has noted, and some of the book's characters, primarily Alesha and Zosima, will successfully "read" the other characters' stories with a measure of insight.[15] But these characters, whose insight is not infallible, will be the closest a reader comes to finding positive models of narrative reception in the text. The other characters, as narrators and listeners to narrative, provide only negative guidance: how *not* to process narrative and how *not* to understand character.

The author figure yields to the primary narrator as the novel opens, but "senselessness and confusion" echo from its opening pages through to the great trial scene in the novel's last book. Not the least of these enigmas concerns character, and the older two brothers, Dmitri and Ivan, represent its greatest mysteries and greatest breadth in the novel, with the principal female characters, Grushenka and Katerina Ivanovna, coming close behind. Dmitri poses the question most extravagantly, characterizing Ivan as a "tomb" and humanity a "riddle" and launching into his own refraction, in extravagantly aesthetic terms, of the spectrum of human capabilities:

> God sets us nothing but riddles. There the shores meet and all contradictions coexist. . . . It's terrible how many mysteries there are! Too many riddles weigh men down on earth. We must solve them as we can, and try to come out of the water with a dry skin. Beauty! I can't bear it that a man of lofty mind and heart begins with the ideal of the Madonna and ends with the ideal of Sodom. What's still more terrifying is that a man

with the ideal of Sodom in his soul does not renounce the ideal of the Madonna, and his heart may be on fire with that ideal, genuinely on fire, just as in his days of youth and innocence. No, man is broad, too broad, indeed. I'd narrow him.[16]

The movement of the novel involves the reader in a quest to resolve these enigmas, as it does the characters. Multiple narrations construct incidents in different ways, indexing the characters with different traits. Dmitri himself will provide the richest examples, as he finds himself, even in the opening parts of the novel, the object of five different narrations of the thrashing of Captain Snegirev: by Fedor, who omits the specific nature of the captain's business; twice by Dmitri, who ignores the captain's lamentable family situation; once by Katerina Ivanovna, who adds the presence of the captain's son, and, finally, in excruciating detail by the captain himself, who adds Dmitri's viciously humiliating offer to fight a duel. Depending on the version, Dmitri comes off as noble officer, brute, or sadist—i.e., as the military equivalent of one who bears the ideal of Madonna or the ideal of Sodom. At the end of the novel, when he is tried for parricide, Dmitri will again be the object of multiple narrations, emerging with a similar range of "selves" from the narratives of lawyers, doctors, and witnesses.

Many of these stories collapse in utter futility; some—for the characters and perhaps for the reader—have the ring of truth. In a novel legendary for its ambiguities and confusion, how are these stories of the self ordered? Which emerge as plausible? By what criteria? Does the novel, adopting the grand ambitions of nineteenth-century science, posit laws by which the self may be known? Probabilities? Possibilities? Or does it, rejecting even the most modest of these conclusions, undermine all the stories by which the self might be known? Who pretends to story the self, by what authority, and how? Some of the answers involve recognizable scientific discourses, at times in the mouths of licensed representatives of Russia's incipient professions (such as lawyers or doctors), at times in the reports of educated laymen (such as the narrator or the journalist-seminarian Rakitin). It is not possible to account for every story told in **The Brothers Karamazov,** but we may essay some observations on these stories' attempts to deal with the characters of the novel.

Among the discourses the novel examines are those in which the observer tries to penetrate the secrets of the self and still, to borrow Dmitri's image, "come out of the water with a dry skin": medicine and "psychology." These attempts range from typification (as in the narrator's learned discussion of the abused women who become "shriekers") to specific diagnoses (the famous Moscow doctor's prescriptions for Iliusha, the court psychiatrists). Such stories told in the absence of the subject may have the ring of plausibility, as when the narrator explains the calming effect of the Eucharist on an hysterical peasant woman:

> The strange and instantaneous healing of the possessed and struggling woman as soon as she was led up to the holy sacrament, which had been explained to me as pretense and even trickery arranged by the "clericals," arose probably in the most natural manner. . . . With a nervous and psychically ill woman, a sort of convulsion of the whole organism inevitably took place at the moment of bowing before the sacrament, aroused by expectation of the inevitable miracle of healing and the fullest belief that it would come to pass; and it did come to pass, though only for a moment.[17]

The narrator's sympathy for the hard lot of rural women, expressed in the philanthropic terms of a socially and culturally superior observer, his eschewal of an easy cynical explanation (a show staged by the clergy), and his rational, psychological account of irrational behavior make this explanation persuasive. At this relatively early point in the novel (Book Two, Chapter Three) we have nothing to contradict either its explanatory power or the narrator's credibility. Indeed, the early chapters feature a number of such commonsensical explanations, which the novel has not yet taught its readers to distrust. The narrator's presentation of Fedor Karamazov's first wife abounds in such explanations: "Adelaida Ivanovna's behavior was without doubt the echo of foreign influences, also the irritation from thought imprisoned. She perhaps wished to display female independence, to go against social conventions, against the despotism of her relatives and family."[18] The reader's subsequent acquaintance with the characters of the novel will reveal the superficiality and inadequacy of such seemingly plausible cultural, social, and psychological explanations.

Indeed, as the novel continues, commonsense psychological explanations become nuanced and undermined. Hysteria, for instance, becomes the property of all classes—and genders—of the novel's characters, and it is far from easily calmed by any treatment. Ultimately, the more rational—and the more scientific or professionalized—the story of sickness, the less adequate it becomes. The old German doctor, Herzenstube, is absolutely helpless as a physician, but his kindness touches Dmitri and is remembered by him. The district doctor, Varvinskii, is fooled by Smerdiakov, Markel's doctor mistakes religious enlightenment for brain fever, the confession of Zosima's mysterious visitor is taken for madness. The famous Moscow doctor's prescriptions for the impoverished Snegirev family create for them an absurd story that is cruelly impossible to live out: travel to Syracuse for Iliusha, to the Caucasus for Nina, to the Caucasus and to Paris for the mother. Medical science reaches the height of absurdity at the trial, where three doctors (Herzenstube, the Moscow special-

ist, and Varvinskii) debate the direction in which Dmitri, if sane, should have looked upon entering the court, to the left, to the right, or straight ahead.[19]

Ultimately the medical narratives, like the psychological ones, are subservient to the legal process, which brings not only the characters but also their stories together in the last, and longest, book of the novel. Here the reader sees that the plots and characters created by the novel's police investigators and attorneys likewise fail to come to grips with the breadth of the novel's personages. The story that the district attorney and his colleagues put together during the preliminary investigation (Book Nine) is based on their assumptions and on Grigorii's faulty evidence as well as on what they can squeeze out of the exhausted, ecstatic Dmitri. It is remarkable for its deductive logic: they have decided that Dmitri is guilty, therefore they will assemble what they need to confirm that the murder is a rational, premeditated act. Dmitri counters their story of him with "his own story," as he calls it, that of an honorable officer who has had some difficulties, but who has not become a thief and who has been saved from murdering his father by his guardian angel. Dmitri's story lacks coherence, to say nothing of the weight of institutional authority, and it cannot counteract the police account of him as a rational killer. A third story of Dmitri's character is constructed during this investigation, however, this time by the narrator with help from the reader's ability to remember previous detail; this emerging story compares the former Dmitri to the one who develops during his ordeals. The new Dmitri still bears the traits of recklessness and impulsiveness but, as is seen in his dream of the baby, has compassion and concern for the suffering of others. His vision occurs toward the end of the interrogation, a process which has a profound moral impact upon him, stripping him of his superiority and his superficial sense of honor, the sense of honor that had, we may recall, led him to invite the helpless Snegirev to challenge him to a duel. As Dmitri is quite literally stripped, he loses his old attachments to life and turns, ever so slowly, toward new ones. It is, after all, hard to feel proud and superior in dirty socks and underwear.

The narratives constructed by the attorneys in the trial only compound the inadequacy of the preliminary investigation by adding the expert testimony of medical science and amateurish social science. Under Russia's recently instituted adversarial system, a trial had become a contest between storytellers, as Dostoevsky had pointed out in his journalistic pieces and demonstrates here, in Book Twelve of *The Brothers Karamazov*. To gain a conviction, the prosecution had to construct an airtight narrative in which some criminal event took place and its willing agent was the defendant. The defense was given a different storytelling task. To create the necessary grain of doubt, it had to break the prosecution's narrative down by showing that there was no criminal event or chain of events, or by showing that even if there was, the defendant was not the agent of these events.

In this trial both attorneys cut corners in their research and argumentation. The form of the story overwhelms its content; fiction-making talent comes to the fore. The narrator, lawyers, and witnesses use, in fact, a variety of literary terms to describe the trial and its arguments: "tragic," "comedy," "scenario," "spectacle," "fiction," "novel," "legend," "drama."[20] The prosecutor begins with the conclusion to the plot (that Dmitri with premeditation killed his father) and builds the story accordingly: this involves dismissing the intelligence, stability, and character of Dmitri's three witnesses (Alesha, Ivan, Grushenka). It involves constructing Dmitri's character to suit the plot and finalizing that character. For the prosecutor to tell us that there is a "real" Dmitri Karamazov ignores Dmitri's development and range of possibilities. Using this fictitious "real Dmitri," the prosecutor in turn shapes the events of the murder plot. This implicates Dmitri in a series of hypothetical actions which, as the reader by now knows, did not take place: Dmitri gradually spending the reserve of money, for instance. As if Dmitri could do such things in small installments! Or Dmitri consciously hiding the remaining 1500 rubles in Mokroe. As if Dmitri could have been concerned with anything but Grushenka at that moment. Ivan, whom the reader has seen undergoing the most profound transformation in the novel, is similarly grist for the prosecutor's mill. We see the prosecutor questioning why Ivan did not immediately come forth to report Smerdiakov's confession. The demands of legal narrative require that the prosecutor make Ivan a calculating, dishonorable slanderer of the dead, not a man wracked with guilt—and the prosecutor does precisely this. Finally, and pivotally, the prosecutor must, ventriloquized by Smerdiakov himself, construct a suitable biography and character for the only plausible alternative murderer, Smerdiakov. And in the prosecutor's "treatise on Somerdiakov" we see him doing just this. The result is a timid, sickly, "naturally honest" Smerdiakov who couldn't possibly have committed the crime that we know by this time he did commit. The prosecutor's loaded words in this treatise—"psychology," "fact," "natural"—conceal the extent to which psychology, fact, and nature are the prosecutor's narrative constructs, constructs that he has assembled in accordance with his needs and institutional requirements, constructs that he has borrowed wholesale from the murderer.

The defense attorney, Fetiukovich, adopts a different narrative strategy and tells a different story, using many of the same acts and actors. But, predictably, he provides different contexts and puts the acts and actors into different chains of events, drawing on different traits to characterize his personages. His institutional role re-quires him to see sudden acts and incoherence where the prosecution sees deliberate thought and action. Thus the "talented" Fetiukovich gives priority to acts and actors as potential plot material, not as products of his need for a particular outcome. He attacks the "whole logic of the prosecution." He dismantles the "combination of facts." And he reverses the psychology of all the characters, drawing on his famous maxim that "psychology is a two-edged weapon." To this end he employs his "talent" for humor, ridicule, and deconstructive logic. He takes each building block of the prosecutor's narrative—each character, each event—and gives it a different spin, a different place in a different story. Countering the dead certainty of the prosecutor's account and its determinism, which is based on notions of both the Karamazovs' heredity and their environment, the wily defense attorney constructs character and action in ways closer to the understandings of the loving Christian figures, Zosima and Alesha, namely, character as open construct and actions as sudden, spontaneous. Thus Fetiukovich makes Smerdiakov a much more clever, complex character than does the prosecutor, and this is, in fact, closer to the truth. Does this make Fetiukovich a spokesman for Dostoevsky? Or does it make him similar to Dostoevsky's greatest liar, General Ivolgin in *The Idiot,* who happened to tell the truth once, by accident? It is probably the latter. Fetiukovich's job is to sow doubt, not to tell the truth. His narrative, like the prosecutor's, is still a fiction, although a more modern, sophisticated one.

As these narratives, ostensibly created in the service of truth and justice, become increasingly a matter of personal competition between the attorneys, as, indeed, the medical experts' testimony had been a matter of personal pride and competition, we must turn to the second of the three aspects of narrative that the novel foregrounds, the teller's role in the story. The defense attorney's own term for the story with which he concludes his speech is "hypothesis"—i.e., an unproven fiction which might capture reality. This is a term that Kolia Krasotkin uses, as does Ivan Karamazov. It implies an intellectual detachment from life, from empathy. And here it becomes a masterpiece of equivocation on Fetiukovich's part. It is not enough for him to discredit the witnesses and to deconstruct the prosecution's story. He must become a romance writer himself. And so he reaches out to argue that there was no robbery and no murder. He must put his talent for rhetoric and casuistry to the ultimate test, to argue before a jury of patriarchal Russians that even if Dmitri murdered his father, it really did not count as parricide, because Fedor had not been a real father to him. One could only call it murder out of "prejudice." Fetiukovich concludes his speech with notions of salvation, penitence, regeneration, and resurrection, but the damage is done. He has been swept away by his talent, and both prosecutor and jury recoil from his flamboyant hypothesis by convicting Dmitri.

It is possible to argue that the defense attorney here is trying to mitigate Dmitri's guilt. Under the postreform judicial procedures, a simple majority of jurors could have called for clemency. But I would argue that Fetiukovich's argument is more a case of ego run amok, of the inspired lying one so often encounters in Dostoevsky's characters. The motives and interests behind his storytelling are clearly competitive and aesthetic. His wildly applauded performance is answered by Dmitri's simple but dignified final statement, in which he refuses to recognize himself in either lawyer's account.

This ineluctably self-interested aspect of the attorneys' stories is but a special case of most of the novel's stories; the teller's egocentricity becomes, paradoxically, most evident in those discourses that pretend to the greatest distance and objectivity. Not only are stories told in the professionalized discourses (medicine, psychology, law), then, limited by the rules of the profession, they are also limited by the vanity, competitiveness, and hostility of the speaker. This holds true for the journalists' discourse as well, that of both Ivan and Rakitin. The "little pictures" of Ivan's attack on God's world, culled from the newspapers, nevertheless are marshaled in an argument the basic aim of which is an attack on Alesha's faith and an attempt, momentarily successful, to seduce him to share in Ivan's unforgiving hostility. Rakitin's explanations in terms of heredity and environment, which so influence the prosecutor, emerge from the novel's refraction as the products of his greed, ambition, and resentment of Ivan. In each case any attempt to tell a truthful story is overshadowed by deeply personal attempts to exercise power or to gain vengeance. This, in turn, further compromises the professional discourses, which already appear inadequate for their rule-bound, limited view of the self.

Much of the dynamism of a Dostoevsky novel, and this one in particular, derives from the third aspect of stories of the self, their reception. Even the most silent listener to a story of the self, Christ before the Grand Inquisitor, makes a gesture of response, the kiss that may signify the forgiveness which undercuts the Grand Inquisitor's argument. The novel's nondivine characters typically respond more violently and vociferously to the storied selves which other characters create for them. From the beginning of the novel to the end, examples abound of these rebellious rejections of another's story—present, past, or future—about oneself. Fedor increases his buffoonery and lying after Zosima proposes to him that he try to stop. Grushenka turns savagely against Katerina Ivanovna because she refused to be the person Katerina Ivanovna wanted her to be; Grushenka refused to play the necessary part in Katerina Ivanovna's dream, as Dmitri astutely and gleefully notes: "She truly fell in love with Grushenka, that is, not with Grushenka, but with her own dream, her own delusion—because it was her own dream, her own delusion."[21] Captain Snegirev

suddenly rejects and tramples a much-needed two-hundred-ruble gift from Katerina Ivanovna at the very moment when Alesha, his interlocutor, unthinkingly inserts himself into a story of the captain's future life, as Alesha subsequently comes to realize.[22] The captain tramples the money in trying to escape precisely that characterization of him which Alesha offers to Lise ("he is a cowardly man and weak in character"). Down to the last pages of the novel, when we see Dmitri railing against Claude Bernard, the famous French physician who was a darling of the journalists of the 1860s for his physiological explanations of human behavior, we see the novel's personages reject any sort of contextualization, any attribution of traits, or any assigned roles in another's narrative. They are quick to insist that these are not the whole story or the true story, and if the story seems too whole or true, they will do something to contradict it or otherwise show its inadequacy. The novel, then, develops a *negative* poetics for stories of the self, which its characters emphatically reject: excessive narratorial distance, egocentric narratorial involvement, rigid master plots, formal rules. Such plot schemes and ways of telling finalize character, they preclude agency and unexpected change on the part of the characters in the narratives, and they fail to allow for the possibility of unexpected change-producing events, such as Dmitri's vision of the baby.

Zosima's teachings, as they are constructed by Alesha in Book Six of the novel, offer an implicit *positive* poetics for the creation of stories that might be acceptable and effective: his teachings about the need for erasing the difference between servants and masters, his teaching about the interconnectedness of all, about the mutual responsibility of all for all, about mysterious seeds from other worlds all imply stories that would lack a hierarchy or distance among teller, subject, and listener; they suggest tellers as open to change and new understanding as the characters they are constructing; they remind us of Yuri Lotman's point that "events" are happenings that did not have to happen.[23]

Alesha's final speech once again adumbrates this positive poetics—indeed, ethics—of narration. It appeals to narrative, making Iliusha's life into an exemplary narrative which might be joined to the future narratives of his own and the boys' lives, and it appeals for narrative, the expression of the memory that will be a moral force not only for these young people, but for Alesha himself. Here Alesha does not, as narrator, separate himself from the events and characters of this concluding story, for to do so would manifest the negative poetics and pragmatics of narration which the novel has so rigorously exposed.

At the same time, however, the world of the novel shows its readers that even this ideal narrative communication, with its open endings and unfinalized characters, can be strenuously resisted by its characters, whose suspicions and fears can lead them to see coercion and fixity. Zosima's life is filled with characters who have accepted stories—Markel, Zosima himself, Zosima's mysterious visitor—but it is not easy even for these parable-like figures to accept the "spiritual, psychological" process of transformation, supported by active love.[24] Of the Karamazov brothers, only Alesha seems to have accepted it by the novel's end. Ivan is suffering from brain fever; Dmitri realizes that his acceptance of grace is at best fragile.

Toward the very beginning of Dostoevsky's writing career, in 1847, his early supporter and critic, Belinsky, wrote: "With us the personality is just beginning to break out of its shell."[25] Dostoevsky's mature writings would show both how difficult it was to break out of that shell, and how inadequately the regnant discourses of his day described the process for personalities who would accept neither the traits, nor the contexts, nor the roles that these discourses assigned them. Stories and selves fit very poorly together in Dostoevsky's novels, which transform learned treatises into fiction, narrators into liars, and listeners into resentful rebels, especially when the stories concern themselves. The more authoritative, rule-governed, and professionalized the narrative, the more likely it is to fail its subject and object, generating in turn new stories. Whether addressing the memorably resilient selves of its characters or turning outward to reflect on history, thought, and culture, *The Brothers Karamazov* never lets its readers forget that stories are never detached, nor disinterested, nor predictably instrumental. Yet the simple fact that Dostoevsky included his critique of narrative within a narrative, a lengthy novel, testifies to the inescapability of storytelling in coming to grips with the elusive self. It also testifies to his hope that teller and reader might, at last, get the story right.

Attention to the terms and debates of narrative theory illuminates the complexities of Dostoevsky's storied selves. Multiple refractions await even the dimmest ray of narrative light. Turning outward from literature and literary theory to Russian history, politics, and culture, Dostoevsky's novel reminds its readers that the stories one tells are part of a process in which the role stories play is neither detached, nor disinterested, nor predictably instrumental.

Notes

1. For a discussion of Aristotle's treatment of character, see Seymour Chatman, *Story and Discourse: Narrative Structure in Fiction and Film* (Ithaca: Cornell University Press, 1978), 108-10.

2. The hermeneutic code, by which enigmas are posed and resolved, clearly deals with problems of human identity; the proairetic code, which gov-

erns actions, presupposes (as in Aristotle and Propp) human actors; the symbolic code organizes character as a function of rhetorical figures and tropes, such as antithesis; the cultural code views character as the product of regnant understandings, such as popular psychology; and the semic code attaches traits to a proper name. See Roland Barthes, *S/Z: An Essay,* trans. Richard Miller (New York: Hill and Wang, 1974).

3. Barthes, *S/Z,* 191.

4. Georg Lukács, *The Theory of the Novel* (Cambridge, Mass.: MIT Press, 1971), 77-80.

5. M. M. Bakhtin, *The Dialogic Imagination: Four Essays,* trans. Caryl Emerson and Michael Holquist (Austin: University of Texas Press, 1981), 365. Cf. Bakhtin's notion of "ideological becoming": the process of selectively assimilating the words of others, of liberating oneself from the authority of another's discourse, 341-48.

6. Chatman, *Story and Discourse,* 125n38.

7. Louis Mink, "Narrative Form as a Cognitive Instrument," in R. Canary and H. Kozicki, ed., *The Writing of History: Literary Form and Historical Understanding* (Madison: University of Wisconsin Press, 1977), 134.

8. F. M. Dostoevskii, *Polnoe sobranie sochinenii v tridtsati tomakh* (Leningrad: Nauka, 1972-90), 15: 125.

9. For a more detailed account of this phenomenon, see William Mills Todd III, "*The Brothers Karamazov* and the Poetics of Serial Publication," *Dostoevsky Studies* 7 (1986): 87-97.

10. For information on Dostoevsky and the court reporting of the time, see David Keily, "*The Brothers Karamazov* and the Fate of Russian Truth: Shifts in the Construction and Interpretation of Narrative After the Judicial Reform of 1864," Ph.D. diss., Harvard University, 1996; also T. C. Karlova, *Dostoevskii i russkii sud* (Kazan: Izdatel'stvo Kazanskogo Universiteta, 1975).

11. Dostoevskii, *Polnoe sobranie sochinenii,* 15: 125.

12. Ibid., 14: 5.

13. V. E. Vetlovskaia, *Poetika romana "Brat'ia Karamazovy"* (Leningrad: Nauka, 1977), 34-39.

14. For a survey of these reviews, see William Mills Todd III, "Contexts of Criticism: Reviewing *The Brothers Karamazov* in 1879," *Stanford Slavic Studies* 4, no. 1 (1991): 293-310.

15. Robert L. Belknap, *The Structure of* The Brothers Karamazov (Evanston: Northwestern University

Press, 1989). On the function of memory in the novel's poetics, see Diane Oenning Thompson, The Brothers Karamazov *and the Poetics of Memory* (Cambridge: Cambridge University Press, 1991).

16. Dostoevskii, *Polnoe sobranie sochinenii,* 14: 104.

17. Ibid., 14: 44.

18. Ibid., 14: 8.

19. Ibid., 15: 103-7.

20. The Russian word *roman* can be translated either as "novel" or as "romance." For an exploration of the storytelling manner of the two attorneys, see W. Wolfgang Holdheim, *Der Justizirrtum als literarische Problematik: vergleichende Analyse eines erzahlerischen Themas* (Berlin: De Gruyter, 1969). A large and growing body of contributions to the "law and literature" movement in legal studies has begun to address problems of legal narrative, although rarely drawing on the full complexity of narrative theory. For an exception, with useful bibliography, see Keily, *"The Brothers Karamazov* and the Fate of Russian Truth."

21. Dostoevskii, *Polnoe sobranie sochinenii,* 14: 143.

22. Ibid., 14: 196.

23. Iu. M. Lotman, *Struktura khudozhestvennogo teksta* (Providence: Brown University Press, 1971), 285.

24. Dostoevskii, *Polnoe sobranie sochinenii,* 14: 175.

25. V. G. Belinskii, *Polnoe sobranie sochinenii v deviati tomakh* (Moscow: Khudozhestvennaia literatura, 1976-82), 9: 682.

Abbreviations

The following abbreviations have been used for archival citations.

GARF: Gosudarstvennyi arkhiv rossiiskoi federatsii [State Archive of the Russian Federation]

GMIR: Gosudarstvennyi muzei istorii religii [State Museum of the History of Religion]

RGALI: Rossiiskii gosudarstvennyi arkhiv literatury i iskusstva [Russian State Archive of Literature and Art]

RGIA: Rossiiskii gosudarstvennyi istoricheskii arkhiv [Russian State Historical Archive]

OR-RGB: Otdel rukopisei, Rossiiskaia gosudarstvennaia biblioteka [Manuscript division, Russian State Library]

RO-BAN: Rukopisnyi otdel, Biblioteka Akademii nauk [Manuscript division, Academy of Sciences Library]

TsGIAM: Tsentral'nyi gosudarstvennyi istoricheskii arkhiv g. Moskvy [Moscow City Central State Historical Archive]

f.: fond [collection]

op.: opis' [inventory]

d.: delo, dela [file or files]

l.: list [sheet]

ll.: listy [sheets]

ob.: oborot [verso]

Vladimir Kantor (essay date fall 2004)

SOURCE: Kantor, Vladimir. "Whom Did the Devil Tempt, and Why? Ivan Karamazov: The Enticements of the 'Russian Path.'" *Russian Studies in Literature* 40, no. 4 (fall 2004): 69-92.

[*In the following essay, which was translated from the original Russian text by Liv Bliss, Kantor studies* The Brothers Karamazov *as a commentary on temptation and a blueprint for an idealized brand of Russian socialism.*]

1. A NOVEL OF TEMPTATIONS

Of all Dostoevsky's novels, **The Brothers Karamazov** has had the greatest social resonance. The explanation for this is, among all else, that two years prior to its publication Dostoevsky had been reaching out directly to the reading public *as a sociopolitical commentator.* As the composer Mikhail Aleksandrovich Aleksandrov recalled: "the readership for **A Writer's Diary** consisted mainly of the intellectual portion of society. . . . Some told Fedor Mikhailovich that they read his **Diary** reverently, as if it were Holy Writ; some looked on him as a spiritual mentor and others as an oracle, asking him to resolve their doubts on several burning questions of the time."[1] The refrain that ran through all Dostoevsky's journalistic commentary was the idea of the special path—the *Russian* path—whereby all the world's cataclysms, and those of Europe in particular, would eventually be smoothed away and a genuinely Christian way of life, which he, preempting Spengler's "German socialism," called "Russian socialism," would be established on earth. That thought never left him, as can be seen from the last issue of his **Diary,** which came out in 1881, after the publication of **The Brothers Karamazov**: "It is not in communism, not in mechanical forms that we find the socialism of the Russian People; they believe that salvation is ultimately to be found only in *worldwide union in the name of Christ.* That is our Russian socialism!"[2]

So his last novel was read as an explication of "the people's truth" and "the Russian path" and as a condemnation of the Russian intelligentsia. And there were, without question, good grounds for viewing it in that way. At the end, in Book XII, the procurator, as if recapitulating the tragedy that has been unfolding before the reader's eyes, offers the following summation: "What, after all, is this Karamazov family, which has gained such an unenviable notoriety throughout Russia? . . . it seems to me that *certain fundamental features of the educated class of today are reflected in this family picture.*" It was understood as saying that the people were to suffer (we recall Mitya's dream of a hungry peasant infant), that the people are with Christ, are holy, while the ideas of the intelligentsia, for all its nobility, are filled with diabolically alluring incitements that culminate in criminal acts. Let us keep in mind that the mental and intellectual excitements of the day made the words of the great writer seem like *the Word of a prophet.*

Meanwhile, historical humor can be derived from the manner in which this novel was perceived, in that the faith in the Russian people that Dostoevsky repeatedly proclaimed coincided with the love for the people professed by the entire Russian intelligentsia. which was profoundly ashamed of the supposed advantages that it enjoyed relative to the people (*education,* for one, which the peasantry valued not at all). It was, however, forgotten that the prophet is the envoy of God and denounces a nation's sins, castigates its faults, but in no way holds out the promise of prosperity to his own people. *While wishing to bless, he oftentimes curses.* It was only to be expected, then, that after a bloody revolution, people would begin to sift through Dostoevsky's oeuvre, looking for any indication that such a catastrophe was in the offing, and to berate him for the illusions that he had fed into the mind of educated society. Reflecting on the ruins of Russia's destiny in an article entitled "The Spirits of the Russian Revolution" [Dukhi russkoi revoliutsii] published in the famous anthology *From the Depths* [*Iz glubiny*], Nikolai Berdiaev summed up the new attitude toward Dostoevsky's oeuvre thus: "Dostoevsky's inclination to truckle to the people came to grief in the Russian revolution. His positive prophesies did not come to pass. But his prophetic insights into Russian enticements are carrying the day."[3]

Those "Russian enticements," the temptations that Russia experienced . . . what does this mean? Vladimir Dal's dictionary defines "to tempt" as "to endeavor to turn a person way from the path of weal and truth."[4] Nations, as well as individuals, can yield to temptation, prime examples of this being Russia and Germany, which were enticed by the Devil onto a hellish path that led to an interminable succession of crimes. The significance of that enticement is that a nation (or a person) comes to identify itself (himself) with the Devil and its

(his) path with the Devil's path, which from that point on is believed to be the only possible way to go—perhaps not a good path but certainly an unavoidable one.

A close reading of **The Brothers Karamazov** will give us no difficulty in understanding that its nerve center, its basic motive force, is the endless temptations that all the novel's characters experience—each on his own level, of course. Grushenka—the "temptress," the "infernal" being, as she is called in the novel—tempts old man Karamazov and Mitya and even Alyosha, when she sits on his knee (after the death of the Elder Zosima). Temptation comes to the Elder Zosima's mysterious visitor and to Zosima himself (the duel). Mitya is tempted by Smerdyakov and Fyodor Pavlovitch to commit murder (Smerdyakov's report of Grushenka's visit to the old man, and the father's insults to the memory of Mitya's dead mother and the withholding of Mitya's maternal inheritance). Ivan tempts Alyosha with stories of suffering children, causing him to make the radically uncharacteristic statement that the perpetrator should be shot. Smerdyakov tempts the young Ilyusha, by persuading him to kill the dog Zhuchka. Grushenka is tempted by her love for her former lover. Katerina Ivanovna experiences a diabolical temptation, when, with the intention of saving Ivan, she destroys Mitya. Smerdyakov is tempted to use stolen money to open up a business in Petersburg. Finally, *the one most beset by temptation is Ivan Karamazov,* who is first tempted by the disorder in the world (working on the assumption that "this world" belongs to God, not to the Devil) and then is directly tempted by Smerdyakov (who seeks his permission to commit patricide) and is treated to a personal visit from the Devil—the very same who, by the latter's own admission, tempted believers with the odor of corruption that emanated from the corpse of the Elder Zosima. It is in Ivan's poem that the Grand Inquisitor recalls how "the wise and mighty spirit in the wilderness" tempted Christ on three separate occasions. In fact, Christ's three temptations create a kind of backdrop for the novel's entire philosophical problem set.

But perhaps the basic temptation for all the novel's characters who are involved in its murder-mystery plot—as, indeed, for all its readers—is the search for old man Karamazov's murderer. Who should be charged with the murder? Who is guilty? Let me repeat that the Russian intelligentsia is usually held to blame, for such is the straightforwardly journalistic conclusion drawn from the mystery plot, in disregard of an extremely complex system of artistic and philosophical concatenations and mirroring of images born of Dostoevsky's "cruel talent."

Let us listen to the opinion of Iakov Golosovker, a remarkable Russian thinker who sought to read the novel not in sociohistorical terms but as something of a philosophical theorem, even discarding the religious and moral evaluations of the characters that so typified Russian neo-religious philosophy and its epigones, and who went on record as saying: "By the author's design, Smerdyakov and the Devil are the two real murderers of Fyodor Pavlovitch. . . . Smerdyakov is the actual, the 'material' murderer, so to speak, and is the alter ego of the Devil, the symbolic murderer, while the Devil is, in turn, the alter ego of Smerdyakov, who has not recognized that he is the only murderer and is in general to blame for the murder."[5] In other words, Golosovker thinks that if one approaches the novel's plot without artifice and prejudice, it becomes evident that "the only one to blame for Fyodor Pavlovitch Karamazov's murder is, by the author's design, none other than the Devil."[6] Consequently it is the Devil who tempts a huge number of the novel's characters—and its readers, too—to take on the function of Divine judgment in indicting the guilty and passing sentence.

We can see, then, that this entire vast novel is structured as a system of coequal temptations experienced to differing degrees by different characters. But why was this theme—the theme of enticement—so important to Dostoevsky? There will scarcely be a short and sweet answer to this question. Let us try to talk it out.

2. Who Is the Usual Target of the Devil's Temptations?

What sense is there in tempting inveterate or—even more so—congenital criminals? In Swedenborg's remarkable understanding, evildoers who are cast down into the realm of darkness and "gnashing of teeth"—that is, denizens of the infernal depths—take pleasure in being where they are and have no wish whatsoever for salvation. Only the righteous who have sinned suffer torment. So the only ones who can be tempted are the righteous, the seekers after a higher, spiritual, moral life. Even the Devil expatiates on this subject. Ivan asks his uninvited nocturnal guest: "Fool! did you ever tempt those holy men who ate locusts and prayed seventeen years in the wilderness till they were overgrown with moss?" And he receives this reply: "My dear fellow, I've done nothing else. One forgets the whole world and all the worlds, and sticks to one such saint, because he is a very precious diamond. One such soul, you know, is sometimes worth a whole constellation. We have our system of reckoning, you know. The conquest is priceless! And some of them, on my word, are [no less developed than you], though you won't believe it. They can contemplate such depths of belief and disbelief at the same moment that sometimes it really seems that they are within a hair-breadth of being 'turned upside down,' as the actor Gorbunov says."

I shall not describe in detail the temptations of sainted zealots of the Church and religious reformers, from St. Anthony to Martin Luther, who were constantly being visited by fiends, including the Devil himself. Satan appeared to Christ in the wilderness. But even if everyone in the novel—this essential microcosm of Russia—is led into temptation, we can hardly imagine that Dostoevsky was holding up the country he adored as the Devil's spawn. Russia is tempted because within its essential self it maintains a kernel of sanctity. Such is the position articulated on a number of occasions by this great Russian writer. Even so, there have been and still are those who, after reading Dostoevsky's novels, have apostrophized Russia as a country that bears the mark of anathema. So let us look now at the novel's most problematic character.

Writing on Dostoevsky's oeuvre in the early twentieth century, the Russian philosopher Sergei Bulgakov noted: "it is more natural to dwell on the work that is, in philosophical and artistic terms, Dostoevsky's greatest act of genius, on *The Brothers Karamazov,* and to select the most philosophically vivid point in that novel—the image of Ivan Karamazov. Of the entire gallery of types in this novel, that image is the closest, the dearest to us, the Russian intelligentsia: we ourselves ache for his sufferings and his desiderata are understandable to us. Moreover, that image elevates us to the dizzying height to which philosophical thought has risen only in the person of its most courageous acolytes."[7]

Who is the chief suspect in the murder, the chief accused, and, simultaneously, the one chiefly tempted? Ivan Karamazov, of course. It is to him, and him alone, that the Devil appears. If our argument that only the righteous are tempted is dismissed, then the upshot is, as it always has been, that Ivan is the novel's manifest and sole vehicle of evil. Thus the Devil presented him to an audience and (we add, getting ahead of ourselves) to himself. And the critics were all the more enthusiastic in taking up the Devil's invective, since the Devil numbers himself among them ("without denial there's no criticism and what would a journal be without a column of criticism?"); he counts himself a colleague of theirs—that is, after a fashion. Even Vasilii Rozanov, who considered himself spiritually and physically close to Dostoevsky, fell for the Devil's provocations with his announcement: "In Ivan, though in a purified form, are concentrated the might of denial and death, the might of evil. Smerdyakov is only its husk, its putrescent off-scourings."[8]

But that is a manifest untruth, for in fact *the Devil senses that Ivan is cut from a different cloth*: "for that is what you are secretly longing for. You'll dine on locusts, you'll wander into the wilderness to save your soul!"

Even so, one contemporary scholar identifies Ivan in all practical terms with the Devil, seeing in him a representative of that demonic world in whose vivid portrayal Dostoevsky was so adept (*The Possessed*): "Ivan's laughter is unquestionably diabolical in nature"; "In tempting his brother, Ivan carries out a diabolical mission. He yet again confirms thereby his proximity to the Devil"; "The 'furious scream' that Ivan emits is the scream of a maniac, a person whom ancient beliefs held to be possessed by a demon"; "And so, listening to Ivan, Alyosha (and the reader) hears the Devil himself"; "A diabolical lie, inimical to people and to life stands behind Ivan's blasphemous 'jokes.'"[9]

That said, the question remains: What sense does it make for the Devil to tempt the Devil?

3. WHO, THEN, IS IVAN?

But if Ivan is not the Devil, then who is he?

Bulgakov was quite clear on this: Ivan is a *Russian intellectual.* Dostoevsky said the same thing, as have all the critics who have written about the novel subsequently. But, remembering the journalistic invective that Dostoevsky constantly directed at the intelligentsia, they naturally looked for only negative traits in the image of Ivan, too. The radicals perceived the novel as a libel against the Russian intelligentsia, whereas after the first and second Russian revolutions [in 1905 and 1917—Ed.] the neo-religious thinkers perceived it *as a warning* about the intelligentsia's negative role. Berdiaev once said something similar, having noticed that the relationship between Ivan and Smerdyakov exemplified the intelligentsia's relationship with the people in revolution, when the latter was seduced by the former. "Dostoevsky foresaw that Smerdyakov would come to hate Ivan *who had taught him atheism and nihilism.* And that is playing out in our day between 'the people' and 'the intelligentsia.' The entire tragedy shared by Ivan and Smerdyakov was a unique symbol of the unfolding tragedy of the Russian revolution."[10]

Even in his journalism, however, Dostoevsky is far from unambiguous.

In *A Writer's Diary* for 1876 he wrote: "[W]e ought to bow down before the People and wait for everything from them, both ideas and the form of those ideas; we must bow down before the People's truth . . . [b]ut, on the other hand, we should bow down only on one condition, and that is a sine qua non: the People must accept much of what we bring with us. We cannot utterly annihilate ourselves before them and their truth, whatever that truth might be. Let that which is ours remain with us; we will not give it up for anything on earth, even, at the very worst, for the joy of unity with the People. If such does not happen, then let us both perish on our separate ways."[11] That little word "we" is highly characteristic, for it tells us that Dostoevsky *fully identified himself with the intelligentsia.*

It is no coincidence that in his notebooks Dostoevsky rated his hero extremely highly: "Iv[an] F[yodorovich] is profound. This is not one of your modern atheists, demonstrating in their unbelief only the narrowness of their worldview and the obtuseness of their obtuse little abilities."[12] It was evidently with good reason that the perspicacious Stepun followed [Dmitri] Merezhkovsky in categorizing Dostoevsky himself as a member of the intelligentsia: "Dostoevsky, who described the intelligentsia so mercilessly in *The Possessed* is, for all that, an intellectual, while Tolstoy is not. The reason for this is that one senses in Dostoevsky's life and work a passionate vested interest in questions pertaining to life in society. It is not coincidental that in his youth he attached himself to the Petrashevskii circle and was sentenced to hard labor."[13]

It follows that what the Elder Zosima says of Ivan Fedorovich's *elevated spirit* also warrants careful consideration. Let us review that conversation. To Ivan's assertion that "There is no virtue if there is no immortality," Zosima replies:

> "You are blessed in believing that, or else most unhappy."
>
> "Why unhappy?" Ivan asked smiling.
>
> "Because, in all probability you don't believe yourself in the immortality of your soul, nor in what you have written yourself in your article on Church Jurisdiction. . . . That question you have not answered, and it is your great grief, for it clamors for an answer."
>
> "But can it be answered by me? Answered in the affirmative?" Ivan went on asking strangely, still looking at the elder with the same inexplicable smile.
>
> "If it can't be decided in the affirmative, it will never be decided in the negative. You know that that is the peculiarity of your heart, and all its suffering is due to it. But thank the Creator who has given you a lofty heart capable of such suffering; of thinking and seeking higher things, for our dwelling is in the heavens. God grant that [the answer will reach your heart] on earth, and may God bless your path."

In any event, this is a testimonial that should not be rejected in favor of what the Devil says, or of Smerdyakov's assurance to Ivan: "You are very clever. You are fond of money, I know that. You like to be respected, too, for you're very proud; you are far too fond of female charms, too, and you mind most of all about living in undisturbed comfort, without having to depend on anyone—that's what you care most about. . . . You are like Fyodor Pavlovitch, you are more like him than any of his children; you've the same soul as he had."

Who should we believe, then: the Elder Zosima or Smerdyakov? The question is not as absurd as it might seem at first glance. An attentive reading of *Karamazov* criticism persuades us that, as a rule, Smerdyakov's opinions are accepted and carry the day. For instance, Valentina Vetlovskaia maintains that, while listening to Ivan, Alyosha is hearing the Devil himself. I can only say that if this is true, then the Devil is a Slavophile, because Ivan sounds thoroughly Slavophilic when he speaks of the decline of Europe, reproaches Catholicism for its totalitarianism, expresses his fear that if there is no God the world will be overrun by anthropophagy, and so on.

This needs to be discussed in somewhat greater detail. I remind the reader of Ivan's oft-quoted words: "I want to travel in Europe, Alyosha, I shall set off from here. And yet I know that I am only going to a graveyard, but it's a most precious graveyard, that's what it is!" Like many Slavophiles—including Dostoevsky's beloved Tiutchev—Ivan wants to go to Europe but describes it as a cemetery. Characteristically enough, even after Ivan's Slavophilic disquisitions, even a modern English scholar attributes to him a Westernizer's dislike of Russia: "Nor does the graveyard of Europe preserve the tombstone over the grave of that long deceased saintly monk. . . . Nor are they the graves of people Ivan has known such as Alyosha visits. They are inert, dead, far-away, without living human associations to his own life. They belong to an alien cultural heritage."[14] We must not, however, forget Alyosha's rebuttal to Ivan, which suggests faith in Europe: "Why, one has to raise up your dead, who perhaps have not died after all." Alyosha—like the Elder Zosima, his spiritual father—sees Christianity as Europe's unifying religion. It is with good reason that Zosima is given the name "Pater Seraphicus" in the novel (a name he shares with St. Francis of Assisi), and the walls of his cell are hung with engravings of Italian masters, "a Catholic cross of ivory, with a Mater Dolorosa embracing it." In addition, Zosima is the one whom Father Ferapont, the fundamentalist monk, hates with all the strength of his simple soul, as an enemy of the traditional "soil-bound" [*pochvennyi*] Orthodoxy. I would say, *pace* the commonly held opinion, that the image of the Elder Zosima depicts a Russian Orthodox ecumenist, while Ivan's image is that of a noble Slavophile extremist reminiscent of Khomiakov or of Dostoevsky himself, who had seen that the "distant West, that land of sacred wonders" is "shrouded in thick darkness" [from an 1835 poem by Khomiakov—Trans.] and that death was advancing on Europe, which had seen in Catholicism a betrayal of Christ's work (Ivan's poem offers a brilliant portrait of the Grand Inquisitor, a Catholic who constructs a unique portent of the totalitarian socialism that was assailing the world). It was the Slavophiles who feared that a disavowal of belief in God would lead to moral degeneration, a conviction also expressed in Ivan's aphorism, "If there is no God, all is permitted." As we are reminded by Sergo Lominadze, it was to Ivan that Dostoevsky

entrusted his idea that it is impossible to construct a happy world on the unhappiness of even one person (on the tear of a child).[15]

Let us also not forget Dostoevsky's own daughter's report that he "depicted himself in Ivan Karamazov."[16] Scholars have frequently waxed ironic over this observation by Liubov' Fedorovna, but it seems to me that her words are worthy of our attention, given the common *intellectual nature* of the writer and his hero. We must bear in mind the number of autobiographical traits that accompany the image of Ivan Karamazov—when, say, Smerdyakov sends Ivan to Chermashnia, the name of the Dostoevsky family's ancestral estate. Or when we realize that Ivan is the novel's only original *writer and thinker,* a man with his own ideas who has penned an article about church and state and composed one poem about a Grand Inquisitor and another entitled "The Geological Cataclysm" ["Geologicheskii perevorot"], which compares the coming social upheavals with a geological archetype. (Herzen, too, used geology as a metaphor for the impending revolution.)[17] The description, in the conversation with the Devil, of what it is like to go to one's own execution ("Thousands of things are unconsciously remembered like that even when people are being taken to execution") and, in the chapter entitled "Rebellion," a throwaway comment from Ivan ("I knew a criminal in prison") speak to events that are not part of the character's own past but did happen to Dostoevsky. It is not simply that he inserted his own experience into the character's life story (neither execution nor penal servitude belonged in the biography of this twenty-three-year-old student); this is, rather, an *unforced admission* on Dostoevsky's part, which lets us know that he is speaking through Ivan.

Dostoevsky has invested in Ivan too much of himself to be able to stand aloof from him. Ivan, for instance, has a "collection" of "factoids." Other similarities notwithstanding, I only note here that Dostoevsky loved and collected facts, too, and quote his famous observation: "Facts. They pass them by. They do not notice."[18] He also spoke of facts that contain plots of Shakespearean proportions—a circumstance that he demonstrated by extracting a great novel in no way inferior to Shakespeare from a primitive crime plot, a criminal "factoid." In a letter to Strakhov, Dostoevsky defended his method of elevating the fact to the level of philosophical and artistic generalization: "I have my own particular view of reality (in art) and what the majority calls almost fantastic and exceptional for me sometimes constitutes the very essence of the real. . . . In every issue of the newspaper you encounter a report containing the most real facts and yet the most bizarre. For our writers, they are fantastic; so they pay them no mind; and yet they are reality because they are *facts*. Who, then, will notice them, elucidate them and record them?"[19] So Dostoevsky was engaged in seeking to discern through the empirical fact the structure of the human universe and human existence, *which calls for an even more attentive scrutiny of the hero's temptations, since they are the author's own.*

But this idea is, as a rule, indignantly rejected, because Dostoevsky is a thinker with a positive ideal, while Ivan is allegedly a *negator,* full of vacillation and doubt and resistant to the world that God has made. We have, however, evidence to the contrary from Dostoevsky himself. In a diary entry for 1881 on the public reaction to his novel, he wrote:

> The blackguards have been badgering me over my UN-EDUCATED and reactionary faith in God. Those block-heads have not even dreamed of a negation of God as powerful as that lodged in the Inquisitor and in the pre-ceding chapter, the reply to which constitutes the whole novel. My belief in God is not that of a fool or a fa-natic. And these people wanted to tell me what's what and laughed at my lack of development. *And their own stupid selves have not even dreamed of a negation as powerful as that through which I have passed.*
>
> ([SMALL CAPS] marks Dostoevsky's emphasis, and italics mine—V. K. [Vladimir Kantor]).[20]

Thus, the negation of God and of the world He made is part of Dostoevsky's own personal experience.

The ultimate outcome for Ivan is therefore, in essence, the ultimate outcome for Dostoevsky—namely, the ex-tent of his ability to come to terms with the racking problem of whether or not *Russia was moving down the path of the just*—which is another way of saying that in the final analysis, the fate of Russia hangs on Ivan Kara-mazov's view, and understanding, of himself. The edu-cated castes did not emerge in Russia without purpose, "for they are educated people, after all, and the last word belongs to them."[21]

4. WHAT AND WHO IS THE DOUBLE IN *THE BROTHERS KARAMAZOV*?

Ivan is always considered in connection with the char-acter who is, as a rule, called his "double." That would be Smerdyakov. Most critics take Smerdyakov to be, in a way, Ivan's direct handiwork—the materialization of his idea, as it were, the idea made real. For instance, the famous Slavophile Orest Miller, one of the first ana-lysts to recognize the novel's metatemporal signifi-cance, wrote, "The unfortunate Smerdyakov, subordi-nating himself blindly to Ivan's ideal . . . committed a crime."[22] That idea has been reiterated by Russian phi-losophers and scholars for more than century. The ex-amples are legion. It is of pivotal importance, however, that in fact this idea was foisted first upon the prosecu-tor, then upon the audience in the novel, then upon the readers, and, finally, upon philosophically minded crit-ics *by Smerdyakov himself*: "At the preliminary inquiry, he told me with hysterical tears how the young Ivan

Karamazov had horrified him by his spiritual audacity. 'Everything in the world is lawful according to him, and nothing must be forbidden in the future—that is what he always taught me.' I believe that idiot was driven out of his mind by this theory [*that he was taught*]."

Apparently, then, Smerdyakov is a blind tool in Ivan's hands, and is therefore his double. But, if one thinks about it, this interpretation of duality is generally dubi-ous. In the tradition of world literature, the double is a character who, you might say, *understudies* the main character, *parasitizes* his external self, his nobility, his lineage, and so on. In short, the double is conspicuously antagonistic and inimical to a character *that the author holds dear* and about whom he cares, for whatever rea-son. Dostoevsky's own villain of that type is found in ***The Double*** [***Dvoinik***], his "Petersburg poem," in the person of Goliadkin Junior, who proved himself more resourceful and decisive and wily and ignoble than Go-liadkin Senior, whom he expunges, outflanks at every turn, and finally drives mad, ending up by having him committed to an insane asylum and taking his place. Such is the bloodthirsty criminal Count Viktorin in E. T. A. Hoffmann's *The Devil's Elixir* [*Die Elixiere des Teufels*], who all but destroys the monk Medardus's soul. Such is the Shadow in Evgenii Shvarts's play of the same name [*Ten'*].

Even when the double is ostensibly the product of the main character's mind, as in Robert Louis Stevenson's *Strange Case of Dr. Jekyll and Mr. Hyde,* he still van-quishes the one who must be called his *parent,* by kill-ing him. But never does he subordinate himself to the main character. That is the law that all doubles follow.

It makes sense to examine Smerdyakov in this context.

Who is Smerdyakov? Above all, we should once more place on record that he is from a different social stra-tum from Ivan and comes, moreover, *from the people* (Berdiaev was right about this). This is suggested by his surname, since Dostoevsky did not assign surnames to his characters on impulse. "Smerdyakov" comes from *smerd',* a medieval word [roughly approximate to "churl"—Trans.] that Dal's dictionary defines as "a member of the rabble, base (by descent), a peasant, a particular grade or caste of slaves, of bondmen; *later,* a serf . . . *The glance of a churl is worse than abuse . . . Where the churl was thinking, God was not there.*"[23] A disdainful upper-class attitude toward the peasantry, the churls, gave rise to the verb *smerdet'* [to stink], meaning to smell like a churl—a word that Dostoevsky used in connection with Smerdyakov's crime, the mur-der of Fyodor Pavlovitch. The careerist seminarian Ra-kitin, speaking with Alyosha about the Elder Zosima's reaction to the Karamazov family's recent visit, even hints, as it were, at the key culprit: "the old man really has a keen nose; he *sniffed* a crime. Your house *stinks* [*smerdit*] of it."

Yet one would think, based on Dostoevsky's ideology, that Smerdyakov should be an especially positive character, particularly because not only his surname but even an authorial comment associates Smerdyakov with the classical Russian archetype of a man of the people:

> There is a remarkable picture by the painter Kramskoy, called *Contemplation.* There is a forest in winter, and on a roadway through the forest, in absolute solitude, stands a peasant in a torn kaftan and bark shoes. He stands, as it were, lost in thought. Yet he is not thinking; he is "contemplating." If anyone [were to] touch him he would start and look at one as though awakening and bewildered. It's true he would come to himself immediately; but if he were asked what he had been thinking about, [standing there,] he would [probably] remember nothing. Yet probably he has, hidden within himself, the impression which had dominated him during the period of contemplation. Those impressions are dear to him and no doubt he hoards them imperceptibly, and even unconsciously. How and why, of course, he does not know either. [Perhaps], after hoarding impressions for many years, [he will suddenly] abandon everything and go off to Jerusalem on a pilgrimage for his soul's salvation, or perhaps he will suddenly set fire to his native village, and perhaps do both. *There are a good many "contemplatives" among the peasantry.* Well, Smerdyakov was probably one of them, and he probably was greedily hoarding up his impressions, hardly knowing why.

On several occasions, however, Smerdyakov declares his hatred of the Russian people ("Can a Russian peasant be said to feel, in comparison with an educated man? He can't be said to have feeling at all, in his ignorance . . . [This rascal of ours *stinks* in his poverty and finds nothing nasty in that.] The Russian people want thrashing"), and speaks of his desire to go into business for himself ("with luck I could open a cafe restaurant [on the] Petrovka, in Moscow"—this being an indication that he wants out of the peasantry). He is a lackey in Ivan's estimation, as reported by Smerdyakov himself: "[H]e said I was a [*noisome (voniuchii)*] *lackey.*" The peasantry is usually mentioned by scholars as a force that intimidated Dostoevsky; your humble author, too, said as much in a long-ago book.[24] But is it so?

Let us not forget that a nice little business was in essence the dream of all peasants, who had but recently broken free from serfdom and endless unpaid drudgery. It was the logical path whereby the entire peasantry would move from the disenfranchisement of servitude to economic independence: some became draymen, others joined builders' cooperatives, yet others opened little stores, and so on. It was with good reason that Dostoevsky brought his almost unconscious (perhaps even conscious!) artistry to bear in narrowing the distance between the familiar word-symbols of his novel: *Smerdyakov* says that the Russian peasant *stinks,* while allowing that he himself is a *noisome* lackey: that is, *the noisome lackey* speaks disdainfully of *the stinking churls* [*smerdiashchie smerdy*], while not considering himself one of them. The situation is somewhat comical, although there really is little humor in it. The historical tragedy here is that Smerdyakov is a representative not simply of the people but of its most advanced and ever-growing subset. He could not care less about higher spirituality (he rejects Gogol, for instance: "'It's all untrue,' mumbled [Smerdyakov], with a grin," and is equally indifferent to Smaragdov's *Universal History* [*Vseobshchaia istoriia*]). He wants nothing to do with the rest of the world, being entirely immersed in his own concerns (a prime hallmark of a person with the limited horizons of an elementary education). His small degree of education has, admittedly, rendered him capable of *contemplation.* But, since none of this is enriched by any over-arching idea, that partiality to contemplation can, as Dostoevsky observes, end up becoming explosively dangerous ("he will suddenly set fire to his native village").

On the one hand, Dostoevsky is fearful: "these same people of little education who have still managed to acquire some culture, even if only poorly and superficially, even if only in a few aspects of their behavior, in a new set of prejudices, or in a new set of clothes— these same people, without exception, began precisely by expressing scorn for their former milieu, their People, and even their religion, sometimes even to the point of hatred."[25] On the other hand, seeing the ongoing and inevitable progress of bringing literacy to the people, he is hopeful: "a solid core has been preserved within our People, a core that will save them from the excesses and aberrations of our culture and will persist even through the process of education which will soon occur, so that the image and form of the Russian People will survive undamaged."[26] (All this appears in one section of Dostoevsky's **Writer's Diary** for April 1876.) The image of Smerdyakov is the test case for the likelihood of preserving the people's truth.

Some historico-theoretical clarifications are in order at this point. The type of Christianity that took shape in Russia after its transition from a land of towns (Novgorodian-Kievan Rus) to a peasant land constituted an acceptance of sorts, with all the attendant repercussions, of the urban religion that had been represented by the Christianity brought to Rus from Byzantium—a religion of the educated, literate strata of society. I remind the reader that the towns of Rus—the palatine and mercantile towns—were the vectors of the new faith, in counterweight to the heathen population of the countryside, and I cite in support of this Max Weber's groundbreaking study: "Christianity . . . began its course as a doctrine of itinerant artisan journeymen. During all periods of its mighty external and internal development *it has been a quite specifically urban, and above all a civic, religion.* This was true during Antiquity, during the Middle Ages, and in Puritanism."[27] This is why the peasantry's emergence from a state of patriarchal ignorance and its exposure to the rudiments of urban education and literacy was such a complex experience for it in religious and metaphysical terms. It was, in essence, a litmus test for the spiritual depth of the Christianity that the people had assimilated.

The literacy and education that were permeating through the people were the logical result of Russia's sociohistorical development. But education, as Chernyshevsky ironically observed, is not a medicine and cannot be swallowed in one draught; hence Russia was doomed to be inundated by undereducated, one-third-educated, and semieducated *Smerdyakovs.* Dostoevsky's own temptation was his faith in the sanctity of the Russian people, and he presents as one of his novel's main characters the peasant, the *churl,* as he will be after he has undergone his imminent and inevitable development.

It is this "undereducated" person who *becomes the double* of the "highly educated" individual. This is where a Russian writer is able to add something substantial to world literature's mature image of the double—namely, a double that proceeds beyond simply parasitizing the main character and using his appearance as a cover for his ignoble motives and deeds, and assumes the role of *tempter* of the main character.

5. THE DOUBLE AS TEMPTER

Smerdyakov's temptation of Ivan is well-considered and purposeful.

Ivan feels that Smerdyakov is not learning from him but is, rather, *studying* him. Dostoevsky conveys with the precision of genius both that effort and the self-satisfaction of an undereducated mind that has made contact with a superior intellect and then has imposed its own understanding of that intellect as if its understanding were definitive and mutually accepted, despite the awkwardness of the situation and the attempts of the superior, educated mind to distance itself from any such understanding:

> Smerdyakov was always inquiring, putting certain indirect but obviously premeditated questions, but what his object was he did not explain, and usually at the most important moment he would break off and [lapse] into silence or pass to another subject. But what finally irritated Ivan most and confirmed his dislike for him was the peculiar, revolting familiarity which Smerdyakov began to show more and more markedly. Not that he forgot himself and was rude; on the contrary, he always spoke very respectfully, yet *he had obviously begun to consider—goodness knows why!—that there was some sort of [grounds for solidarity] between him and Ivan*

Fyodorovitch. He always spoke in a tone *that suggested that those two had some kind of compact, some secret between them,* that had at some time been expressed on both sides, *only known to them and beyond the comprehension of [the mere mortals that swarmed] around them.*

It is interesting that Ivan finds out about the revelations made by Smerdyakov and accidentally overheard by Alyosha, and that they make him oddly agitated (the chapter entitled "The Brothers Make Friends" follows directly after "Smerdyakov with a Guitar"):

> Alyosha rapidly, though *minutely,* described his meeting with Smerdyakov.
>
> Ivan began listening anxiously and *questioned him . . .*
>
> Ivan frowned and pondered.
>
> "Are you frowning on Smerdyakov's account?" asked Alyosha.
>
> "Yes, on his account. [*Devil take him*]."

Something in Ivan's relationship with Smerdyakov has begun to cause him great unease. Although he has not yet guessed exactly what it is, he is already repudiating Smerdyakov as manifest evil ("Devil take him"). But he does not have time to think his unease through, although recently he has begun to notice "a growing feeling that was almost of hatred *for the creature.*" He does not even consider Smerdyakov a person (*the creature!*), but, churl as he may be, Ivan seems bewitched by him. Coming home after his talk with Alyosha in the tavern, Ivan bumps into Smerdyakov and has every intention of passing him by:

> "Get away, [you wretch]. [Why should I spend any time with you, you fool?]" was on the tip of his tongue, but *to his profound astonishment [what fell from the tip of that tongue was something else altogether.]*
>
> "Is my father still asleep, or has he waked?" He asked the question *softly and meekly,* [catching himself unawares] and at once, [*again catching himself unawares,*] sat down on the bench. For an instant *he felt almost frightened;* he remembered it afterward. Smerdyakov stood facing him, his hands behind his back, looking at him *with assurance and almost severity.*

So what is happening here?

It is as though diabolical forces that Ivan is unable to resist are stepping into the action and subordinating his will. Smerdyakov almost forces Ivan to sanction the murder, tempting him with their supposedly unspoken unity and mutual understanding. A villain's classic ploy is to implicate an outside party in a crime, to keep the outsider forever entrammeled in evil. Thus Nechaev (Verkhovensky in *The Possessed*) bound his anarchist cells *with blood.* Ivan is ashamed to flaunt his intellectual superiority before this importunate and rather boorish churl whose pointed cunning he despises. This is why he lies to himself, claiming that he could not care less about the dark hints that the servant is throwing out. The Russian intellectual is ashamed to live. In an article written for *Grazhdanin* in 1873 entitled "Something About Fibs" ["Nechto o vran'e"], Dostoevsky remarked: "Our universal Russian lie insinuates . . . that we are all ashamed of ourselves. Indeed, each of us carries within himself an all but innate shame of ourselves and our own countenances, and scarcely have they appeared in society than all Russian people promptly strive with all due speed and come what may each tries to pass himself off unfailingly as something different, so long as it be not what he really is; each hastens to assume a completely different countenance."[28] God has supposedly enjoined us all not to be ashamed, to be ourselves, but there was nowhere to hide from the greatest falsehood of all—shame before the people for possessing intellectual capacities! One's own depth and educational attainment seemed a criminal luxury in that wicked world, where the erstwhile churl was all at once making the grueling effort to stand up straight and have his say. That, incidentally, is why intellectual youngsters accepted that monster Nechaev, *who spoke for the people* and announced with brazen certitude "the moral unsteadiness of the civilized minority."[29]

The most striking point is that Ivan, a typical intellectual, is unable to determine the reason for his inability to accept the words and the vague desires of *Smerdyakov, the churl.* As a result of their strange, bewitching conversation, full of hints and words left unspoken, Ivan cannot sleep that night: "[A]fter midnight he suddenly had an intense irresistible inclination to go down . . . and beat Smerdyakov. *But if he had been asked why, he could not have given any exact reason,* except perhaps that he loathed the [lackey] as one who had insulted him more gravely than anyone in the world."

So, entirely in the spirit of its Russian archetype, *the intelligentsia could say nothing against the peasantry, victor in the October Revolution and the Civil War,* whose modicum of education had filled it with scorn for the norms of patriarchal life but had also prevented it from accepting the norms of civilized and moral life. If we look at the questionnaires of party and ideological activists recruited in the Stalin (and, for that matter, the Lenin) levy, we will see that *the majority* declared themselves to be of *peasant origin.* It is probably no accident that, once the Smerdyakovs had elbowed their way into power, they began calling all the enemies of their regime *enemies of the people.* But, as we know, the chief enemy was the Russian intelligentsia, whose knowledge and capacities could actually be put to use, although, even so, the engineers and economists, the scholars, scientists, and writers who had done no small service to Soviet power were sooner or later destroyed. The full horror of this is that the intelligentsia went uncomplainingly to the slaughter, for they considered the

new order and their new Smerdyakovian rulers to be their own handiwork. We remember how, in Arthur Koestler's *Darkness at Noon,* it is this that breaks the Old Bolshevik Rubashov (he had given birth to a dictatorship!) when faced by Gletkin the "Neanderthal," who had been recruited into the Cheka in a party levy of candidates from the countryside. But Dostoevsky had already produced a typology that predicted and portrayed this temptation in **The Brothers Karamazov.**

6. IVAN'S GREATEST TEMPTATION

That temptation is, of course, associated with the appearance of the Devil.

Even before the Devil appears, Smerdyakov has Ivan baffled and almost beaten. As early as their second conversation, he is couching his utterances in such a way that Ivan in his confusion accuses himself of the murder, although in strictly legal terms he was in no way complicit in the crime. Smerdyakov is banking on the "profound conscience" of the hero, who tells his fiancée bemusedly, "If it's not Dmitri, but Smerdyakov who's the murderer, I share his guilt, for I put him up to it. *Whether I did, I don't know yet.* But if he is the murderer, and not Dmitri, then, of course, I am the murderer." We see here that Ivan is still vacillating. But what matters to Smerdyakov is to make Ivan not only an accomplice to but the chief perpetrator of the murder, to identify him with earthly evil. In their third, and last, conversation, he hurls this at Ivan: "Here we are face to face; what's the use of going on keeping up a farce to each other? Are you still trying to throw it all on me, to my face? *You murdered him; you are the real murderer, I was only your instrument, your faithful servant, and it was following your words I did it.*" Ivan is staggered: "Did it? Why, did you murder him?" Smerdyakov is persistent: "It was done in a most natural way, following your very words." Even so, there comes a point at which he lets it slip:

> "But can you possibly have thought of all that on the spot?" cried Ivan, overcome with astonishment. *He looked at Smerdyakov again [in fright].*
>
> "Mercy on us! Could anyone think of it all in such a desperate hurry? *It was all thought out beforehand.*"
>
> "Well . . . well, *it was the devil helped you!*" Ivan cried again. "No, you are not a fool, you are far cleverer than I thought."

One cannot help remembering the proverb quoted by Dal in his dictionary: *Where the churl was thinking, God was not there.* Exactly right. God was not there, but the Devil was.

It is no coincidence that whenever Ivan speaks of, or assesses the actions of, Smerdyakov, he invokes the Devil. And hardly has Smerdyakov's active role in the novel ended (through his suicide) when the Devil appears to Ivan.

Here we come up against a striking paradox. Even those who would seek to vindicate Ivan, to declare him innocent of the murder (Sergei Bulgakov, for example: "Indeed, it is not difficult to see that the bloody event in the novel is approaching with fatal strength, that the tragedy is inescapable, and would play out regardless, with no involvement on Ivan's part. Looking at it objectively, Alyosha can be considered as collusive as Ivan"),[30] are, in obedience to the laws of everyday realism, prepared to admit that the Devil is the handiwork of Ivan's illness, his hallucination, his second Self: "Ivan Fyodorovitch's Devil is not a metaphysical Mephistopheles, depicting an abstract principle of evil and irony. This is a product of Ivan's own sick soul, a particle of his own self. Everything that torments Ivan, that he despises in himself and hates, not only in the here and now but also in the past, all that is, as it were, personified in the Devil."[31]

But this conviction is precisely what the Devil wants, and this is precisely the idea he uses to make Ivan suffer: "I sometimes don't see you and don't even hear your voice as I did last time, but I always guess what you are prating, for *it's I, I myself speaking, not you!*" (Dostoevsky's italics—V. K.). It must be made perfectly clear that, as a believing Christian, Dostoevsky was as a matter of course convinced of the existence of evil spirits, and therefore the Devil's cat-and-mouse game with Ivan indicates that Ivan was not only physically but also metaphysically sick. Dostoevsky said on numerous occasions that, although physical illness facilitates contact with other worlds, those are not morbid images but simply what happens when a person's supernatural sensibilities are honed by illness. He called himself a realist in the higher sense of the word—not a crude realist, that is, or a naturalist, but a writer capable of depicting the world in all its fullness, including otherworldly forces.

The Devil mocks Ivan, now trying to dissuade Ivan from believing in him, now seemingly inviting him to accept his reality. "I told you your anecdote you'd forgotten, on purpose, so as to destroy your faith in me completely," he remarks. Then, a couple of minutes later, he is acting as if the details brought to bear on Ivan are realistic, although those details actually have the opposite—in fact, the desired—effect. Ivan exclaims, "You want to get the better of me by realism, to convince me that you exist, but I don't want to believe you exist! I won't believe it!" In other words, he is identifying himself with the Devil, even though he feels that for the sake of his spiritual health he needs to transform the Devil from a particle of his Self into an object outside himself:

> "From the vehemence with which you deny my existence," laughed the gentleman, "I am convinced that you believe in me." . . .

"Not for one minute," cried Ivan furiously. "*But I should like to believe in you,*" he added strangely.

Not long after this, now completely spent, Ivan is complaining to Alyosha: "'Do you know, Alyosha,' Ivan added in an intensely earnest and confidential tone, 'I should be awfully glad to think that it was *he* and not *I*'" (Dostoevsky's italics—V. K.).

The point is that Ivan's lack of belief in the Devil has rendered him unable to contend with the Devil. In his conversation with Ivan, the Devil mentions Mephistopheles and *Luther's inkstand,* representing a literary fact and a historical fact, brought together by a single circumstance: since the evil spirit was outside and apart from the protagonist in each case, both Faust and Luther could stand up in support of their own moral rectitude, grave as that struggle may have been. Here the founding father of the Reformation had this to say: "More than once already he has had me by the gullet, yet has for all that been constrained to release me. But I by experience know how to deal with him. He has beset me so often that I no longer knew if I was alive or dead. He would bring me to such confusion as to cause me to ask myself if God is in this world and to despair completely in the Lord our God."[32] But he struggled, and he won. Nor did Mephistopheles manage to take Faust's soul. As God had foretold, Faust was able, on his own and with no outside help, to resist the Devil's snares and enticements (*Ein guter Mensch, in seinem dunklen Drange / Ist sich des rechten Weges sohl bewußt* ["A good man, through obscurest aspirations / Has still an instinct of the one true way": Goethe's *Faust*—Trans.]).

Ivan's challenge is to prevail against the temptations of Smerdyakov and the Devil, to differentiate himself from them and their works, and in so doing to understand that the sublunary world "lieth in wickedness" [1 John 19:5—Trans.], being guided certainly not by Divine law but by the laws of the Devil, with whom God, too, is locked in combat. Consequently, anyone who desires the betterment of this world must not work against God but must help Him. That is the path Ivan takes in his conversation with Alyosha, when he finally rejects the idea of the Devil as a hallucination and repeats, over and over again, "*he* said." Alyosha understands his brother: "'The anguish of a proud determination[, a profound] conscience!' God, in Whom he disbelieved, and His truth were gaining mastery over his heart, which still refused to submit."

7. WHY IS IT SO IMPORTANT TO DIFFERENTIATE IVAN FROM THE DEVIL?

In compiling his stringent *Laws,* the later Plato allowed himself the observation that "the beginning, which is also a God dwelling in man, preserves all things, if it meet with proper respect from each individual."[33] Each individual—in the ideal, since many will prove incapable—must honor the Divine spirit in him- or herself. But such is the doom of a writer rethinking all the essential natures of being, after which he will be able to see that Divine beginning in his characters beneath the most "coarse crust of materiality" (Vladimir Solov'ev). It is that search for the Divine center in man that distinguishes writers and thinkers of Dostoevsky's caliber from crude realists, naturalists, and those chasing the latest fad. One of the very last things Dostoevsky wrote about himself (shortly before his death) was: "*To find the person in a person with complete realism.* This is a superlatively Russian trait, and in that sense I, of course, am of the people (for the direction I take flows from the depths of the people's Christian spirit), and although I am unknown to the Russian people of the present, I will be known to the Russian people of the future."[34]

The claim that this approach marks a "superlatively Russian trait" is dubious, since Christianity is a world religion, not an expression of narrowly national idiosyncrasies. But the attempt "to find the person in a person"—and "with complete realism" at that—signifies one thing and one thing only: to see the evil and imperfection in the world and in humanity and to depict them relentlessly, while still leaving open the possibility for those who seek to find and those who suffer to be comforted. The writer, moreover, is "unknown (and, let us add, unnecessary) to the Russian people of the present" precisely because the people, like the world, abides in wickedness, overwhelmed by the Smerdyakovs who are rising to power—as Dostoevsky in general recognized. *A Writer's Diary* for 1876 contains the following horrified entry:

> It is as if the very atmosphere contains some sort of intoxicant, a kind of itch of depravity. An unprecedented distortion of ideas has begun among the People, along with a general worship of materialism. In this instance what I mean by materialism is the People's adoration of money and the power of the bag of gold. The notion has suddenly burst forth among the People that a bag of gold now is everything, that it holds every sort of power, and that everything their fathers have told them and taught them hitherto is all nonsense. It would be a great misfortune if this way of thinking should become firmly established among the People, and yet, how else are they to think? . . . The People see and marvel at such might—"They do whatever they like"—and they begin to doubt in spite of themselves. "So that's where the real power is; and that's where it has always been. Just get rich and you can have it all; you can do anything you like." There can be no notion more corrupting than this one. And it is in the very air and gradually is permeating everything.[35]

Behind Dostoevsky's devout belief in the people lurked doubt and secret disbelief. What if the decisive force in Russia were in fact to become the Smerdyakovs? They were going all-out to turn the ideas of the intelligentsia to their own mercenary ends *while speaking of some-*

thing entirely different. As Merab Mamardashvili [Georgian philosopher, 1930-1990—Trans.] was fond of saying when philosophers were accused of laying the groundwork for something untoward, "A philosopher should always tell his practically minded audience, '*I'm sorry, but that's not what I'm talking about.*'"

The peasant insurgents of October 1917 appropriated the intelligentsia's quest in exactly that way. As early as May 1918, the Russian historian and philosopher Georgii Petrovich Fedotov was writing, "For a whole year now, with inexpressible pain, we have beheld the red banner being dragged in the mire, and *hatred, avarice, and concupiscence raging in the name of brotherhood and justice. . . . In the name of socialism, the working masses have been poisoned by the toxin of a genuinely bourgeois, philistine greed.*"[36] There was, of course, not even the slightest trace of the "Orthodox socialism" that was Dostoevsky's dream. But the most terrifying point, as I have already mentioned, was that most of the Russian intelligentsia held themselves to be the accomplices of, and the inspiration behind, this formidable tyranny of the masses, having proved incapable of differentiating themselves from diabolical initiatives, and they threw themselves on the mercy of the plebs triumphant, having been worsted in the Devil's ordeal.

Dostoevsky himself, in drawing the image of Smerdyakov and presenting to us, his readers, *overcame his own temptation to truckle blindly to the people.* But he was seeking the person in a person and searching in the people for the deeply hidden Christian ideal, for "without ideals—that is, without at least some partially defined hopes for something better—our reality will never become better. One can even state positively that there will be nothing but even worse abominations. *In my way of seeing things, at least, there is a chance left*; if things are not attractive now, then with a clear and conscious desire to become better (i.e., with ideals of something better), we may indeed one day collect ourselves and become better."[37]

At that time, unfortunately, the chance remained exactly that—a chance. In his sociopolitical commentary and his novels, Dostoevsky seemed to be calling on his readers to take "the Russian path," but he said nothing about an indispensable condition of any such movement—namely, the ability to look realistically at the world; to trace the course, moment by moment, of God's struggle with the Devil; and hence *to overcome the temptation to take any path immediately after sensing that the Devil or Smerdyakov is becoming one's second Self.* Smerdyakov is indeed the infamous Russian path, just as Hitler was the German path, and so forth. It is worthwhile at this point to quote the disclosures of a Bolshevik with the eloquent name of *Gavriil Il'ich Miasnikov* [Butcher], who murdered Grand Duke Mikhail Aleksandrovich (Russia's last tsar [for a few hours after the abdication of Nicholas II, before he refused the crown—Ed.]). In a boastful brochure entitled "The Philosophy of Murder, Or, Why and How I Killed Mikhail Romanov" [Filosofiia ubiistva, ili pochemu i kak ia ubil Mikhaila Romanova], Miasnikov, among all else, makes the following appeal: "Smerdyakov must be-rehabilitated from the infamies of Dostoevsky by demonstrating the greatness of the Smerdyakovs as they stepped onto the stage of history to join the battle between freedom and oppression and by telling, in passing, the whole truth about the divine enslavers."[38]

Characteristically, the murderer Smerdyakov is also an Orthodox Christian, not only baptized but depicted with profound and penetrating derision on the eve of his suicide (an act that in and of itself leads straight to hell but is aggravated here by the fact that now the guilt for the patricide will fall squarely on Mitya and Ivan) reading *The Sermons of the Holy Father Isaac the Syrian,* a book by a renowned Orthodox thinker. Furthermore, Smerdyakov is a socialist, entirely in the spirit of Lenin's exhortation to "Loot what has been looted!" He is both one and the other and at the same time neither one nor the other—just like our party activists, who eagerly swapped their party cards for crosses when that proved advantageous.

Dostoevsky summoned us to take the ideal path but depicted the danger of the real path. He pointed out to the intelligentsia the responsibility it bears not for its words (since so many different words have been spoken throughout history) but for the ability to separate its words from another's deeds, not to hallow with its words another's evil. That is why it was so important to Dostoevsky to differentiate between Ivan and the Devil: he understood that Russia's fate depended on the success of that differentiation. If those who are *spiritually superior* (and are the focal point for the presently undereducated churl now taking his place in history) impute the evil to themselves, they will in so doing pervert the entire country, the entire people, which will not then go in search *of the hidden ideal and of those righteous ones who preserve that ideal.* Then the people will say that if the spiritually superior are siding with the Devil, everything must indeed be permitted.

Dostoevsky the realist, however, demonstrated *only the potential* for differentiation, leaving the reader with the faint hope of a favorable outcome. In a conversation that takes place between Alyosha and Mitya at the end of the novel, Mitya says: "You know, [brother] Ivan [will surpass] all of us. He ought to live, not us. He will recover." His younger brother (the mouthpiece for the writer's positive ideas) is more circumspect: "'Ivan has a strong constitution, and I, too, believe there's every hope that he will get well,' Alyosha observed *anxiously.*"

As we now know, brother Alyosha's anxiety was not unwarranted. But *The Brothers Karamazov* was not written only for a specific time: its ideas and images are topical even today and will remain so until history is no more. Consequently, the problem that Dostoevsky posed—the problem of temptation—becomes part of the spiritual and intellectual experience of any thinking person who participates in the life of society through the words he utters.

Notes

English translation © 2004 M. E. Sharpe, Inc., from the Russian text © 2002 *Voprosy literatury.* "Kogo i zachem iskushal chert? Ivan Karamazov: soblazny 'russkogo puti,'" *Voprosy literatury,* 2002, no. 2, pp. 157-81.

Translated by Liv Bliss.

Unless noted otherwise, italics in quotations are Kantor's. Notes renumbered for this edition.—Ed.

All quotations are taken, with significant modifications indicated by bracketed text, from the Garnett translation at eserver.org/fiction/brothers-karamazov.txt.—Trans.

1. M. A. Aleksandrov, "Fedor Mikhailovich Dostoevskii v vospominaniiakh tipografskogo naborshchika v 1872-1881 godakh," in *F. M. Dostoevskii v vospominaniiakh sovremennikov* (Moscow, 1990), vol. 2, pp. 280-81.

2. F. M. Dostoevskii, *Polnoe sobranie sochinenii* (Leningrad: Nauka, 1972-90; henceforth *PSS*), vol. 27, p. 19. [English quotations from *A Writer's Diary* are taken from Kenneth Lantz translation (Evanston, IL: Northwestern University Press, 1993-94). The source of this quotation is vol. 2, p. 1351.—Trans.]

3. N. A. Berdiaev, "Dukhi russkoi revoliutsii," in Berdiaev, *O russkikh klassikakh* (Moscow, 1993), p. 96.

4. Vladimir Dal', *Tolkovyi slovar' zhivogo velikorusskogo iazyka* (Moscow, 1981), vol. 2, p. 52.

5. Ia. E. Golosovker, *Dostoevskii i Kant* (Moscow, 1963), p. 23.

6. Ibid., p. 24.

7. S. N. Bulgakov, "Ivan Karamazov kak filosofskii tip," in Bulgakov, *Sochineniia* (Moscow, 1993), vol. 2, p. 17.

8. V. V. Rozanov, "Legenda o velikom inkvizitore F. M. Dostoevskogo," in Rozanov, *Mysli o literature* (Moscow, 1989), p. 78.

9. V. E. Vetlovskaia, *Poetika romana "Brat'ia Karamazovy"* (Leningrad, 1977), pp. 93, 98, 99, 100, 109.

10. Berdiaev, "Dukhi russkoi revoliutsii," p. 95.

11. *PSS,* vol. 22, p. 45 [*Writer's Diary,* vol. 1, pp. 349-50].

12. Ibid., vol. 27, p. 48.

13. F. A. Stepun, "Proletarskaia revoliutsiia i revoliutsionnyi orden russkoi intelligentsii," in Stepun, *Sochineniia* (Moscow, 2000), p. 617.

14. D. E. Tompson, *"Brat'ia Karamazovy" i poetika pamiati* (St. Petersburg, 2000), p. 181. [English quotation from Dianne Oenning Thompson, *The Brothers Karamazov and the Poetics of Memory* (Cambridge: Cambridge University Press, 1991), p. 182.]

15. S. Lominadze, "Slezinka rebenka v kanun XXI veka," *Voprosy literatury,* 2000, no. 1, pp. 334-35.

16. L. F. Dostoevskaia, *Dostoevskii v izobrazhenii ego docheri* (Moscow-Petrograd, 1922), p. 18.

17. This image appeared in Dostoevsky's favorite work by Herzen, *From the Other Shore* [S togo berega] (published in Russia in 1855 and 1858), which he read after serving out his sentence of penal servitude. Compare: "Or is it that you don't see . . . the new barbarians marching to destroy? They are ready; like lava they are stirring heavily underground, in the bowels of the mountains. When the hour strikes, Herculaneum and Pompeii will be wiped out, the good and the bad, the innocent and the guilty will perish side by side. This will not be a judgment, not retribution, but a cataclysm, a total revolution" (A. I. Gertsen, *Sobranie sochinenii* [Moscow, 1955], vol. 6, p. 58) [English quotation from *From the Other Shore and The Russian People and Socialism* (Westport, CT: Hyperion Press, 1981), p. 66—Trans.]. In other words, Ivan's poem also contains echoes of the writer's own experience.

18. *PSS,* vol. 16, p. 329.

19. Ibid., vol. 29, pp. 1, 19.

20. Ibid., vol. 24, p. 48.

21. Ibid., vol. 27, p. 25 [*Writer's Diary,* vol. 2, p. 1358].

22. Orest Miller, *Russkie pisateli posle Gogolia* (St. Petersburg, 1900), vol. 1, p. 264.

23. Dal', *Tolkovyi slovar',* vol. 4, p. 232.

24. See V. K. Kantor, *"Brat'ia Karamazovy" F. Dostoevskogo* (Moscow, 1983), pp. 100-103.

25. *PSS,* vol. 22, p. 115 [*Writer's Diary,* vol. 1, p. 442].

26. Ibid., p. 119 [*Writer's Diary,* vol. 1, p. 447].

27. Max Weber, "Khoziastvennaia etika mirovykh religii," in Weber, *Izbrannoe. Obraz obshchestva* (Moscow, 1994), p. 45. [*Die Wirtschaftsethik der Weltreligionen.* The English quotation is from an uncredited translation under the title *Sociology of World Religions: Introduction* at www.ne.jp/asahi/moriyuki/abukuma/weber/world/intro/world_intro_frame.html.—Trans.]

28. *PSS,* vol. 21, p. 119.

29. [S. G. Nechaev and M. A. Bakunin], "Vzgliad na prezhnee i nyneshnee polozhenie dela," in *Revoliutsionnyi radikalizm v Rossii. Vek deviatnadtsatyi. Dokumental'naia publikatsiia,* ed. E. L. Rudnitskaia (Moscow, 1997), p. 227. Nechaev was not at all embarrassed about his lack of education: "We—that portion of plebeian youth, that is, that had somehow managed to acquire training" ("Izdaniia obshchestva 'Narodnoi raspravy.' No. 1," in *Revoliutsionnyi radikalizm v Rossii,* p. 223).

30. Bulgakov, "Ivan Karamazov kak filosofskii tip," pp. 17-18.

31. Ibid., pp. 18-19.

32. Martin Liuter [Martin Luther], "Zastol'nye besedy" [Table Talk], in *Legenda o doktore Fauste* (Moscow-Leningrad, 1958), pp. 21-22.

33. Platon [Plato], "Zakony" [Laws], in Plato, *Sochineniia* (Moscow, 1944), vol. 4, p. 227 [Book VI—Trans.].

34. *PSS,* vol. 27, p. 65.

35. Ibid., vol. 22, p. 30 [*Writer's Diary,* vol. 1, p. 330].

36. G. P. Fedotov, *Sobranie sochinenii* (Moscow, 1996), vol. 1, p. 101.

37. *PSS,* vol. 22, p. 75 [*Writer's Diary,* vol. 1, p. 388].

38. Quoted from Viktor Topolianskii, "'Velichie Smerdiakovykh': partiinyi otchet ob ubiistve," *Kontinent,* 1999, no. 2 (100), p. 226.

Anne Hruska (essay date summer 2005)

SOURCE: Hruska, Anne. "The Sins of Children in *The Brothers Karamazov*: Serfdom, Hierarchy, and Transcendence." *Christianity and Literature* 54, no. 4 (summer 2005): 471-95.

[*In the following essay, Hruska argues that "the tension between childhood innocence and childhood guilt is" a central theme in* The Brothers Karamazov.]

Near the end of **Crime and Punishment,** in one of the most harrowing passages in all of Dostoevsky's works, Svidrigailov is plagued by a series of nightmares. The last of his dreams is the most horrifying of all: Svid-rigailov dreams that he helps and comforts a miserable five-year-old girl whom he finds sobbing in a corner, hiding from her abusive mother. After he tucks her into bed, she attempts to seduce him, with a "fiery and shameless look" on her "completely unchildlike face." "Ah, cursed girl!" he exclaims, and awakes (*PSS* 6:393; *CP* 509).[1] Soon after, he commits suicide, unable to accept his own inner world where purity cannot exist without being defiled. The little girl of Svidrigailov's dream is the only child in *Crime and Punishment* who could be called anything other than deeply innocent. It is a mark, indeed, of Svidrigailov's own vileness that he is able to imagine this devilish, sexualized child. Children in *Crime and Punishment* are often victims of violence and poverty, but they retain purity and natural empathy—thus Raskolnikov's childhood self in his dream protests against the torture of the horse while the grownups around him are at best indifferent to its sufferings.

The Brothers Karamazov likewise insists on the innocence of children, an idea reiterated throughout the novel. Characters of otherwise opposing viewpoints reinforce the idea that children are pure: Zosima says that children are "sinless, like angels" (*PSS* 14: 289; *BK* 319) while Ivan protests against the suffering of children in part because they "have not eaten [the apple] yet, and are not yet guilty of anything" (*PSS* 14: 216; *BK* 238). The death of the consumptive Ilyusha can be read as an example of just such a suffering innocent. Rimvydas Silbajoris, for example, writes that Ilyusha at the end of the novel is the "symbolic equivalent of the dead Christ" (37), a sinless being who, in dying, helps to redeem those left behind.

But Ilyusha's Christ-like nature is far murkier than it might at first seem. Dostoevsky's thoughts about childhood innocence became more complex between 1866, when *Crime and Punishment* was published, and the late 1870s, when he was writing *The Brothers Karamazov.* Even while *The Brothers Karamazov* insists on the innocence of children, it also undercuts this idea, showing how children can be sinful even while they suffer. Ilyusha is a sinner at the same time that he is Christ-like; suffering leads to cruelty even while it brings the sufferer closer to God.

This article will argue that the tension between childhood innocence and childhood guilt is at the very heart of the novel. Children in *The Brothers Karamazov* are frequent victims of poverty, abuse, and neglect. In this they resemble another category of natural victims, the peasants, who had recently been freed from serfdom. Abused children reflect the historical and personal suffering so many serfs underwent, and the long-term results of that suffering. Among the saddest of these results is that the victims of cruelty go on to perpetuate it,

thus creating more victims and more violence. The novel proposes a solution to the vicious cycle of abuse: people need to be willing not to strive for the top of the hierarchy, but rather to put themselves in the position of historical victims. If everyone becomes like a child or like a serf, then power structures become meaningless and the whole violent system dissolves. *The Brothers Karamazov* offers an understanding of kenosis that takes literally Paul's call to "let the same mind be in you that was in Christ Jesus, who . . . emptied himself, taking the form of a slave, being born in human likeness" (Phil 2: 5-7). Thus kenosis can be a spiritual act with immediate social and political implications.

And yet, the novel also makes it clear that such glorious solution is next to impossible: almost no one is willing to risk such a radical act of humility. Within the world of *The Brothers Karamazov,* the continuing corruption of the innocent is a simple and all but inescapable fact. The hope for lasting change is not for this world but the next, a world where people will overcome their need to have power over others, and where even those who performed acts of cruelty on earth can find, at last, forgiveness and love.

To understand the contradictory nature of innocence in the novel, it helps to begin by looking at Father Zosima's ideas, as expressed in his "Talks and Homilies." Zosima stresses the innocence of children while also revealing the ambiguous nature of that innocence. For Zosima, ideas of innocence tend to be connected with images of abuse and exploitation. Even when proclaiming the natural innocence of children, Zosima also makes it clear that this innocence is continually being corrupted. Shortly before his proclamation that children are "sinless," Zosima relates, "I have even seen ten-year-old children in the factories: frail, sickly, stooped, and already depraved" (*PSS* 14: 289-90; *BK* 319). These children suffer from social and economic circumstances that push them into sin. Zosima tells his listeners:

> Love the animals: God gave them the rudiments of thought and an untroubled joy. Do not trouble it, do not torment them, do not take their joy from them, do not go against God's purpose. Man, do not exalt yourself above the animals: they are sinless, and you, you with your grandeur, fester the earth by your appearance on it, and leave your festering trace behind you—alas, almost every one of us does! Love children especially, for they, too, are sinless, like angels, and live to bring us to tenderness and the purification of our hearts and as a sort of example to us. Woe to him who offends a child.
>
> (*PSS* 14: 289-90; *BK* 319)

Children, Zosima tells us, are like animals—pure and innocent, living examples of purity and of God's love.

Zosima here talks of children as only the victims of abuse, never the perpetrators. But the juxtaposition of animal torture and child abuse in this passage hints at the distressing fact that abuse in the novel is more often than not committed by children themselves. Ilyusha feeds Zhuchka a piece of bread with a pin embedded in it, knowing that she is starving and will swallow it whole. Kolya breaks a goose's neck for a joke. Smerdyakov as a child killed cats and buried them with religious ceremony. Children also torment other children: they throw rocks at each other, taunt, and humiliate each other as a matter of course. Kolya and the other boys isolate Ilyusha socially, mock him, and beat him. Ilyusha stabs Kolya in the thigh with a penknife. Lise Khokhlakova fantasizes about crucifying a five-year-old and eating pineapple compote while delighting in his torments.[2] Lise is the most extreme example—but she is far from the only child in the novel who wants to hurt the defenseless.[3]

The cruelty and vulnerability of children is connected throughout the novel to that of peasants. Literature of the nineteenth century often describes peasants, especially serfs, as being children, or childlike. (The fatherly relationship between the landowner and his serfs could be described as benevolent or abusive, depending on the social views of the writer.) *The Brothers Karamazov* is set in 1866, just five years after the emancipation that freed the serfs yet left them vulnerable to a new form of economic exploitation in the factories.[4] As Zosima describes the peasants, they suffer from the corruption of sin, while simultaneously bearing a redemptive force that will help save Russian society. He explains,

> God knows there is sin among the peasantry, too. . . . The peasants are festering with drink and cannot leave off. And what cruelty towards their families, their wives, even their children, all from drunkenness! I have even seen ten-year-old children in the factories: frail, sickly, stooped, and already depraved. The stuffy workshop, work all the God's day long, depraved talk and wine, wine—is that what the soul of such a still little child needs? He needs sunshine, children's games, bright examples all around, and to be given at least a drop of love. Let there be none of that, monks, let there be no torture of children; rise up and preach it at once, at once! But God will save Russia, for though the simple man is depraved, and can no longer refrain from rank [literally, "stinking"] sin, still he knows that his rank sin is cursed by God, and that he does badly in sinning.

(*PSS* 14: 285-6; *BK* 315)

Zosima's rhetoric moves back and forth between peasant children and adults—the peasantry as a whole is like the depraved but innocent children he describes. And yet, Zosima predicts, just as children are "like angels," so also are the common Russian people blessed with a spiritual faith that will lead them to conquer their sin.

There are other moments in the novel, though, that cast doubt on Zosima's certainty. These moments imply that class differences are eternal, and that just as parents will always be able to abuse and neglect their children, so also will masters be able to exploit their servants. Fyodor Pavlovich—neglectful father extraordinaire— enthuses about the sensual opportunities class structure provides. Gleefully describing his exploits as sexual predator, Fyodor Pavlovich gushes, "It's very nice, indeed, that there have always been and always will be slaves and masters in the world, and so there will always be such a little floor-scrubber and there will always be her master, and after all, that's all you need for happiness in life" (*PSS* 14: 126; *BK* 136). The novel offers a number of examples of this philosophy in action, the most obvious one being Fyodor Pavlovich's rape of Stinking Lizaveta, an act that ultimately leads to her death.

Fetyukovich, the lawyer defending Mitya, offers another such example in his closing speech. He mentions the story of a Finnish servant girl who was discovered to have hidden her pregnancies and killed each of her three children as soon as they were born. The defense lawyer condemns her, comparing her to Fyodor Pavlovich, and exclaims, "Will any of us dare to pronounce over her the sacred name of mother?" (*PSS* 15: 170; *BK* 774). But there are other questions that the lawyer doesn't address—who, for one thing, was the father of these children? Was it not yet another gentleman who thought it very nice indeed that there would always be slaves and masters in the world? Fetyukovich, not surprisingly, doesn't bother to ask these questions; for all his liberal grandstanding, he has no real interest in the downtrodden. But we as readers ought to ask them. Without absolving her, we ought to recognize that the servant girl is on the wrong end of a social hierarchy that makes her defenseless against sexual exploitation. Sadly, her victimization tempts her into horrific cruelty of her own against creatures even more defenseless than she.

Dostoevsky shows throughout *The Brothers Karamazov* that hierarchies create violence. Peasants, children, and animals, as beings at the bottom of the power hierarchy, are most likely to be the objects of that violence—but they're likely to be the perpetrators of it as well. Ivan tells a story in the "Rebellion" chapter that illustrates the ways in which categories of victim and abuser become intertwined. He tells of an eight-year-old boy "in the darkest days of serfdom" (*PSS* 14: 221; *BK* 242), who throws a stone at his master's dog, wounding its paw. As punishment, the boy's master orders that the pack of dogs be set on the boy and tear him to pieces. Readers witness the abuse of two defenseless creatures: first the child harms the dog, and then the dogs kill the child. In telling the story, Ivan mentions that the boy wounded the dog "somehow, while he was playing"—but we know too much about how children play in the novel to be able to assume that the boy wounded the dog by accident. On the contrary, it's very probable that the boy meant to hit the dog, if only to prove that despite his enslavement he still had the power to hurt. The child in this story can be read both as cruel tormentor and as helpless victim, just as the dog is both innocent sufferer and murderous beast. The worst culprit of all, the general who orders the boy killed, goes all but unpunished. Dostoevsky portrays serfdom here as a sort of institutionalized child abuse, implicating not only the boy's master, but all those who passively accept this evil system.[5]

A passage in Dostoevsky's *Diary of a Writer* from 1877 is particularly explicit about serfdom's similarity to both child and animal abuse. Addressing the intellectuals who accuse the peasantry of "brutality", Dostoevsky fumes:

> Do not reproach [the peasantry] for "brutality and ignorance," my wise sirs, because it was you, precisely you, who did nothing for it. On the contrary—you left it two hundred years ago, abandoned it, separated yourselves from it, turned it into a legal entity and an article of quitrent [a financial duty of serfs]. And it grew up, my enlightened sirs, forgotten by you, beaten by you, forced by you like a beast into its den. But Christ was with it, and with Christ alone it lived until the great day twenty years ago, when the northern eagle, fired by the flame of mercy, waved and spread its wings, and shielded it with those wings . . .[6] Yes, there is much brutality in the peasantry, but don't point your finger at it. That brutality is the slime of the centuries—it will be cleaned away.

> (*PSS* 25: 124)

The peasant, then, is sinful—but, Dostoevsky implies, it's not the peasant's fault. A violent or brutal peasant is only acting out the historical wrong that was done to him and generations of his ancestors. The ones who are truly to blame for his brutality are the peasant's educated former masters, who betrayed and abandoned him, treating him like the wild animal he has begun to resemble.

The implication here, that the responsibility for the peasant's brutality rests with someone other than the peasant himself, is an unusual one for Dostoevsky to make. An 1873 passage in *Diary of a Writer,* titled "Environment," argues, with equal passion and in similar terms, exactly the opposite—that peasants must be held to account for their own brutality if they are to be truly free. Again, Dostoevsky places his argument in the context of serfdom; he begins with a description of the difficulites that the recently freed peasants must experience in taking on the responsibilities of serving on a jury, especially given the sympathy toward prisoners traditional in Russian peasant culture. But, Dostoevsky continues, it is critical that the jurors be willing to judge their fellow man, despite the painfulness of such a task, for "truth is higher than your pain" (*PSS* 21: 15). In

particular, Dostoevsky emphasizes, jurors cannot allow themselves to accept the idea that the criminal's environment—his poverty and unhappiness—forced him to commit the crime. He writes,

> In making man responsible, Christianity by that very act acknowledges his freedom. In making man dependent on every mistake in the social structure, the teaching [that environment is all-powerful] brings man to the point of complete freedom from any sort of personal duty, from any sort of independence, brings him to the state of the most loathsome slavery imaginable.

> (*PSS* 21: 16)

Dostoevsky insists that to allow the idea that environment is destiny would be to push the peasantry into a moral bondage that is even worse than the serfdom they recently escaped.

Dostoevsky tells of how such a way of thinking can be used to justify horrific acts of abuse. He expounds in particular on the case of the peasant N. A. Saiapin, who had recently been prosecuted in connection with the death of his wife. Saiapin, Dostoevsky tells us, enjoyed tormenting chickens by holding them upside down by their claws. He used the same technique in beating his wife: he would tie her up, hang her upside-down by her heels, then beat her at luxurious length, delighting in her screams. After all, Dostoevsky comments sarcastically, "the peasant's life is deprived of all aesthetic delights—no music, no theaters, no literary magazines; naturally he needs to fill his life with something" (*PSS* 21: 21). Saiapin's wife committed suicide after one such beating; the peasant was charged with having abused his wife, found guilty but "deserving of leniency" and sentenced to eight months in prison. When those eight months were over, Saiapin was to be able to return to take custody of his young daughter, who had testified against him. "Once again, he'll have someone to hang by the heels," Dostoevsky darkly predicts (*PSS* 21: 22).

Saiapin re-creates the structure of serfdom within his own family. As Dostoevsky imagines him, the peasant bears a strong resemblance to the stereotypical master: "He is tall, very thick-set, strong, blond . . . His body is white and puffy, his movements are slow and self-important, his gaze is fixed; he speaks little and rarely, dropping his words like precious beads, and is himself the first to value them" (*PSS* 21:20). In imprisoning, starving, and beating his wife, one could argue, Saiapin is only mirroring what he and generations of Russian peasants had lived through themselves as serfs, and therefore he cannot be held fully accountable for his crimes. But Dostoevsky explicitly and virulently refutes such an explanation. According to his argument here, the members of the jury who judged Saiapin not fully responsible for his crimes committed an act of cruelty toward his daughter and injustice toward his late wife. They were even unjust to Saiapin himself in allowing him to escape accepting responsibility for his wife's sufferings, an act of penitence that could have led to spiritual purification.

So which is it? Is it the peasant himself who must be held responsible for his brutality, as Dostoevsky argues here? Or is it the fault of those who condemned him to centuries of slavery, as he writes later? In *The Brothers Karamazov,* both sides of the argument are valid. Victims of cruelty often perpetuate that cruelty themselves—a fact that does not absolve them of responsibility but that does encourage readers to look for other bearers of guilt as well.

The contradictory nature of Dostoevsky's thinking on innocence and guilt is apparent in an 1876 passage from *Diary of a Writer*; the imagery and logic in this passage reappears in *The Brothers Karamazov.* Dostoevsky discusses the Kroneberg case, in which a father was accused of having tortured his seven-year old daughter. He uses the image of a cruel and destructive serf-child, to whom he compares the girl's father, as a way of intensifying the reader's sympathy for the Kroneberg girl and the servant woman who tried to protect her. Dostoevsky writes of the servant who, distressed by the child's cries, finally decided to alert the police. In describing her defense of the girl, Dostoevsky writes,

> Do you see that chicken, that lay-hen, standing in front of her chicks and spreading her wings to defend them? These pathetic chickens, defending their chicks, sometimes become almost frightening. In my childhood, in the countryside, I knew one little house-serf boy who horribly loved to torment animals, and particularly loved to kill the chickens himself when they needed to be cooked for the gentry folks' supper. I remember how he'd climb along the straw roof of the threshing barn, and he particularly loved to find sparrows' nests in it: he'd find a nest, and right away begin to tear off the sparrows' heads. Just imagine, this tormenter was horribly afraid of a chicken, when, furiously spreading out her wings, she would stand before us, defending her chicks; he would always hide behind me then.

(*PSS* 22: 62)

Dostoevsky employs the metaphor of the desperate chicken to describe a servant defending an innocent child. And yet the "tormentor" whom the chicken defies, and who so delights in murdering sparrows, is himself both a child and a servant. This rhetoric seems odd—Dostoevsky, so intent on defending the victims of injustice, here seems to be singling out another victim of historical injustice as a perpetrator of cruelty on the defenseless.

The serf boy who torments birds reappears in *The Brothers Karamazov* in the description of Smerdyakov. Smerdyakov is not technically a serf, but his position in the house is that of a servant, and even his name implies servitude. Vladimir Kantor has pointed out that "smerd" can mean not only "stink" but also "rabble," or "serf"; he writes, "The evaluative nuance of the word from which Dostoevsky produced the name Smerdyakov is easy enough to understand, and is linked with Russia's primary evil as most Russian writers saw it: the evil of serfdom" (201).[7] Mitya, in ridiculing the idea that Smerdyakov could have murdered his father, exclaims that Smerdyakov is a "coward" and a "sickly, epileptic, feebleminded chicken, who could be thrashed by an eight-year-old boy" (*PSS* 14: 428; *BK* 475). In this echo of the image from *Diary of a Writer,* Smerdyakov is the chicken, weakly resisting the child's murderous impulses. But surely, at the same time, Smerdyakov can also be read as the serf-boy, taking out his own victimization on animals weaker than himself. In this way Smerdyakov embodies the problem of the cruelty wrought by victims of cruelty. To understand broader questions of guilt and innocence in *The Brothers Karamazov,* it is crucial to understand the victimization of Smerdyakov, and to see how he perpetuates the wrongs done to him.

For most of the twentieth century, scholars consistently read Smerdyakov as uniformly evil. Robert Belknap, in his classic 1967 work *The Structure of The Brothers Karamazov,* sums up Smerdyakov as a "cockroach-crushing, cat-hanging, master-and-self-slaughtering fungus" (71). More recently, Diane Oenning Thompson eloquently details the diabolical elements of Smerdyakov's character, claiming that Smerdyakov, in corrupting the word of God, becomes the embodiment of evil in the novel. She argues, "Smerdyakov's corruption of the collective sacred memory defines his prime evil function in the novel. He is the affirmation of Ivan's "spirit of negation," and is thus unambiguously diabolic" (*Poetics* 136-157, esp. 153-4).

In the last decade, though, there has been an increasing tendency to look for the good in Smerdyakov, and to focus on the ways in which the people around him neglect and betray him. The first scholar to do this was Olga Meerson, in her 1998 study of what she calls Dostoevsky's "taboos"—his indirect challenges of unwritten social laws so absolute that they cannot even be directly mentioned. According to Meerson, the fact that Smerdyakov is one of the Karamazov brothers is the novel's central taboo. The narrator seduces the reader into regarding Smerdyakov with the same contemptuous neglect that he gets from society and from his biological family. For Meerson, *The Brothers Karamazov* is primarily a novel about brotherly responsibility and its failure. In failing to acknowledge Smerdyakov as his brother, Ivan treats him as cruelly as Joseph's brothers treat him, selling him into slavery (a story which the Elder Zosima dwells on during his homilies.) The narrator shows us the abuse and neglect Smerdyakov suffers during his childhood and yet also pushes us as readers to accept it as being somehow within the order of things. The reader who accepts Smerdyakov's plight as natural and just is put in the position of moral responsibility for neglect that the whole society of *The Brothers Karamazov* shares (Meerson 183-209).

Other scholars have built on Meerson's argument. Vladimir Golstein also emphasizes the ways Smerdyakov's family mistreats him. But for Golstein, the primary responsibility for Smerdyakov's wretchedness lies not with his brothers but with his fathers—his neglectful biological father, Fyodor Pavlovich, and his abusive, harsh foster father, Grigory. Both of them, according to Golstein, insist on seeing Smerdyakov as an animal, ignoring the connection to the divine inherent in every living being. Lee D. Johnson also argues for the divine element in Smerdyakov, claiming that Dostoevsky invests him with a profound intuitive spiritual understanding, particularly of the idea of theosis. According to Johnson, Smerdyakov reaches a sort of spiritual epiphany right before his death, coming to a closer understanding of Orthodox ideas of community and the return to Godhead. And yet, tragically, Smerdyakov struggles against and finally rejects his own understanding of divinity.[8]

I think it's important to incorporate both sides of this argument into an understanding of Smerdyakov, to see him as both evil and innocent. In seeing Smerdyakov as victim, we do not need to ignore the diabolic element so consistently associated with him in the novel.[9] In a sense, Smerdyakov does embody evil in that, as the victim of evil, he goes on to create other victims.[10] Smerdyakov is indeed father-and self-slaughtering. He is also, and at the same time, an embodiment of the "wee one" the weeping, starving baby in Mitya's dream. Mitya recognizes both a personal and a communal responsibility for this child, as he joyfully recognizes "that he wanted to do something for them all, so that the wee one will no longer cry, so that the blackened and dried-up mother of the wee one will no longer cry, so that there will be no more tears in anyone from that moment on, and it must be done at once, at once" (*PSS* 14: 457; *BK* 508). Smerdyakov never physically starves, like the wee one, but he is starved in emotional and spiritual terms. He then grows up to revenge himself on the world for his own suffering—tormenting animals, tempting others to sin, destroying his father and finally himself.

Dostoevsky had written of abandoned illegitimate children earlier in his *Diary of a Writer,* describing his visit to an orphanage in terms that strongly foreshadow Smerdyakov. Dostoevsky remarks on the "impudence" of the babies who dare to demand food and attention as if they were normal children with loving families. He writes of his worry about the time

when these children begin to find out that they are worse than everyone, that is that they are not the same kind of children as "those others," but are much worse, and live not at all because they have the right to, but only, so to speak, out of charity? . . . The highest type of them—they will be able to forgive; the others, perhaps, will begin to take vengeance for themselves—on whom, on what—they will never solve that, and they won't understand, but they will take vengeance.

(*PSS* 23:22)

Dostoevsky suggests one possible way to avoid the future vengeance of these illegitimate children: they could be made "communal children," belonging to everyone, with their education to be paid for by the taxpayers.[11]

At Smerdyakov's birth, it briefly looks as though he will become one of these children cared for by all the community. When Grigory first finds the infant Smerdyakov, he sees him as a duty given to him by divine Providence. Grigory calls the baby "God's child-orphan, everyone's kin" (*PSS* 14: 92; *BK* 100). It doesn't last long, though—as soon as he catches Smerdyakov burying a cat, Grigory whips him painfully, and later tells him, "You think you're a human being? . . . You are not a human being, you were begotten of bathhouse slime, that's who you are" (*PSS* 14: 114; *BK* 124). Grigory here not only dehumanizes Smerdyakov but also denies any kinship with him; having previously acted as the boy's father, he here disowns him. The narrator tells us, "Smerdyakov, as it turned out later, could never forgive him for these words"—a sad marker of Smerdyakov's general inability to forgive. But surely the knife cuts both ways. Smerdyakov is learning to be unforgiving from his foster father, who himself fails to forgive Smerdyakov either his birth or his sins. The spiritual lesson of rigidity and abuse continues when Smerdyakov is twelve and Grigory gives him his first lessons on the Scriptures. When Smerdyakov asks the wrong question in the wrong tone, Grigory whacks him across the face; Smerdyakov's first epileptic attack soon follows.[12] Grigory's religious lessons to Smerdyakov involve a false understanding of an unloving, unforgiving God, a God whose power rests on punishment and hierarchy.

Not only does the society of Skotoprigonevsk fail to make Smerdyakov "kin to them all," they abandon him as a community. Smerdyakov's emotional abandonment has to be seen as not just the fault of his biological family or his foster family but of everyone around him because each person allows Smerdyakov to grow up without the "bright examples" and the "drop of love" that Zosima tells us are essential to a child's soul. Alyosha, at the end of the novel, famously tells the boys to preserve a good memory from childhood so that later in their lives they can be guided by it when tempted to do evil. Thompson has shown how this act of remembrance brings people into a communal sacred memory, connecting them to God (*Poetics,* esp. pp. 74-125).[13] Smerdyakov, as far as we can tell, has no such sacred memory to preserve him. Part of the reason, then, for the trials (literal and figurative) that Skotoprigonevsk has to undergo is this communal failure towards the wee one, even in its unappealing guise as Smerdyakov.[14]

Rather than recognize Smerdyakov's human dignity, the other characters of *The Brothers Karamazov* consistently dehumanize him: he's a chicken, an ass, a viper, an insect, a dog. Golstein points out that these names are far from incidental; when the narrator calls Smerdyakov "Balaam's ass," for example, Dostoevsky invites the reader to make the connection with the biblical book of Numbers, and to consider the idea that Smerdyakov sees an angel no one else can see (103-4). I want to argue that Smerdyakov's status as dog is particularly important, both to his own character and to the social ills of the novel. In particular, Smerdyakov is consistently connected in the novel to Zhuchka, the dog he persuades Ilyusha to torment, as, in Kolya's words, a "brutal joke" (*PSS* 14: 480; *BK* 535). Zhuchka helps to connect Smerdyakov to Ilyusha, the quintessential suffering child of the novel. In her apparent resurrection, Zhuchka shows that forgiveness is there for Smerdyakov, as it is there for Ilyusha—if Smerdyakov can allow himself to accept it.

Zhuchka is a creature to inspire pity if there ever was one: she is, Kolya tells us, "a yard dog from the sort of house where they simply never fed her, and she just barked at the wind all day long" (*PSS* 14: 480; *BK* 535). Zhuchka is the very image of a neglected child, and thus another version of Smerdyakov's own self. Smerdyakov is repeatedly associated with dogs in general and Zhuchka in particular. Even Smerdyakov's childhood love of executing cats can be read as another canine attribute. In this context, the devil's remark to Ivan, right after Smerdyakov's suicide, is particularly poignant. Ivan's devil burbles, upon hearing Alyosha's knock, "Open, open to him. There's a blizzard out there, and he's your brother. *Monsieur saitil le temps qu'il fait? C'est a ne pas mettre un chien dehors*" (*PSS* 15: 84; *BK* 650).[15] While Alyosha, Ivan's brother, can come in out of the snowstorm, Smerdyakov, Ivan's other brother, is still trapped in the loveless world he had been abandoned to at his birth. It's weather you wouldn't put a dog outside in—unless it's a stray dog, or an illegitimate brother who doesn't really count. As Mitya exclaims at his trial, on hearing of Smerdyakov's suicide, "A dog's death for a dog!" (*PSS* 15: 94; *BK* 661).

Zhuchka connects Smerdyakov to Ilyusha, the novel's most obvious suffering innocent child. When he first enters the novel, Ilyusha is very similar to Smerdyakov

during his childhood years. While he's crucially privileged in having a loving father, Ilyusha is in many ways a social victim; his poverty forces him into humiliation, disease, and early death. Much like Smerdyakov, Ilyusha begins to act out his misery by tormenting animals, which only intensifies his feelings of worthlessness. These feelings are reinforced by the society around him; Kolya, for example, tells Alyosha "You still don't know what a scoundrel he [Ilyusha] is, Karamazov. Killing's too good for him" (*PSS* 14: 162; *BK* 178). Ilyusha himself seems to be willing to believe that he has no choice but evil because he cannot be forgiven. When Kolya announces to him that he refuses to speak to him any longer, Ilyusha shouts, "I'm going to throw bread with pins in it to all the dogs, all of them, all of them!" (*PSS* 14: 482; *BK* 535). In trying to glory in his role as social and moral outcast, Ilyusha casts himself in the same mold as Smerdyakov and looks to be moving towards a similar outcome. At Ilyusha's first appearance in the novel, we see him throwing stones at the other boys and biting Alyosha ferociously, like a wild beast. Later, Mme. Khokhlakova postulates that Ilyusha might have been rabid: "Your boy was bitten by a rabid dog, and became a rabid boy, and had to bite" (*PSS* 14: 168; *BK* 184). Khokhlakova's remark, for all its silliness, hints at an important idea: that sin and violence can work like rabies, infecting the innocent from outside.[16]

Alyosha's defense of Ilyusha from the other boys seems particularly significant in this context. In a novel where ideas of sin and grace play such important roles, the defense of a sinning outcast from stoning must carry an echo of the moment in the Gospel of John, when Christ defends the woman taken in adultery. In protecting Ilyusha, Alyosha reenacts Christ's defense of the woman and implies a forgiveness that will extend to Ilyusha's crime. Neither Ilyusha nor the other boys are free from the all-infecting sin of cruelty, and thus none has the right to cast the first stone. Alyosha, in protecting the sinning child, offers him a human embodiment of the love and forgiveness of God. This forgiveness is later made flesh in the resurrection of Zhuchka as Perezvon.

In this way, Zhuchka is another version of Lazarus. Olga Meerson has pointed out the ways in which Smerdyakov the neglected brother is connected to Lazarus, the poor man. She brilliantly argues for the significance of a folk poem from the collection of Appollon Grigoriev, a good friend of Dostoevsky. In the poem, Lazarus begs for help from the rich man, whom he calls "brother"; the rich man angrily responds,

> Oh thou, a stinking peasant, the stinking stinker's son,
> How darest thou come to [my] window?
> How darest thou call me brother? . . .

> Here, thy brothers are two mean dogs—
> These are more of thy brethren than me.[17]

As Meerson points out, Smerdyakov, who is denied by his wealthier brothers, and whose very name means "stink," can be read as another version of this humble, stinking Lazarus. Meerson also argues that the poor Lazarus of Christ's parable is connected to Christ's friend, the resurrected Lazarus: both of them stink (from poverty or from decay) and yet both are beloved by God (198). Smerdyakov contains elements of both Lazaruses—both the poor man whose brotherhood is denied and the man who died to rise again through God's miraculous love.

In this way Lazarus, the stinking dog of the folk poem, becomes not just one of the insulted and the injured. The rebirth of the stinking dog Zhuchka has to do not only with life eternal, with sacred memory and the living Word of Christ. It also has to do with the redemption of sin for the penitent, with the possibility that even horrible actions can be undone. Zhuchka becomes living evidence of Christ's power to restore life to what was dead and to forgive even grievous sins. This idea of Christ's resurrective power was central in *Crime and Punishment,* where only acceptance of Christian love can raise Raskolnikov from the living death to which his sin has condemned him. The rebirth of Zhuchka implies that Smerdyakov as well can find spiritual life, even after his physical death.

Zosima discusses a similar idea in his "Talks and Homilies." In speaking on the idea of hell, Zosima exclaims, "Woe to those who have destroyed themselves on earth; woe to the suicides! I think no one can be unhappier than they" (*PSS* 14: 293; *BK* 323). But Zosima also asserts—contradicting Orthodox teachings—that it is permissible to pray for the suicides, for God does not forget them. He tells his listeners that even in hell, the damned are loved and forgiven by the righteous in heaven. Zosima continues, "having accepted the love of the righteous together with the impossibility of requiting it, in this obedience and act of humility they would attain at last a certain image, as it were, of the active love they scorned on earth" (*PSS* 14: 293; *BK* 323). Zosima contradicts Abraham's words in the story of the rich man and Lazarus, that "between you [in hell] and us [in heaven] a great chasm has been fixed, so that those who might want to pass from here to you cannot do so, and no one can cross from there to us" (Luke 16: 26). According to Zosima, Smerdyakov, another version of Lazarus, can find spiritual resurrection even in hell. Perhaps he can be given the onion he was never given in life, a gift of unconditional love that will lead him to redemption. And yet, in order to achieve it, Smerdyakov will need to do one crucial thing that he never did in life—that is, to be truly humble.

In Matthew 18, a passage that is obliquely reflected in *The Brothers Karamazov,* Christ says to his disciples,

> Unless you change and become like children, you will never enter the kingdom of heaven. Whoever becomes humble like this child is the greatest in the kingdom of heaven. Whoever welcomes one such child in my name welcomes me. If any of you put a stumbling block before one of these little ones who believe in me, it would be better for you if a great millstone were fastened around your neck and you were drowned in the depth of the sea.

Children are "the greatest in the kingdom of heaven" not because of their essential innocence, but because of their humility. In fact, Christ emphasizes that children can be tempted to sin and that "occasions for stumbling blocks are bound to come." The crucial difference in the little child, as exemplified by Ilyusha, is the child's ability to humble himself, to sorrow for his own sin, and to suffer for it.

Ilyusha's sufferings at his death are not the result of human cruelty, as they are in the stories Ivan tells of suffering children. Nor are they even primarily the result of his physical pain. Ilyusha is particularly tormented by the idea of his own sin, "the memory of the unfortunate Zhuchka, whom he had tormented to death" (*PSS* 14: 487; *BK* 541). His certainty of the enormity of his own sin makes him believe that he is being killed for it; he tells his father, "I'm sick because I killed Zhuchka, papa; God is punishing me for it" (*PSS* 14: 482; *BK* 536). As Alyosha asserts, "If only we could find that Zhuchka now and show him that she's not dead, that she's alive, he might just be resurrected by the joy of it" (*PSS* 14: 482; *BK* 536). The crucial difference between Smerdyakov and Ilyusha is not as much in the sins that they commit as it is in their relationship to those sins. Ilyusha is saved in large part because of his ability to be "like a little child"—and here that doesn't mean innocence. Rather, it means the ability to be hurt and to suffer, an ability that's always associated with children in *The Brothers Karamazov.* Ilyusha becomes truly like a little child in feeling empathy for the stray dog, rather than exulting in his superiority over her.

Ilyusha humbles himself, becoming one with Zhuchka in her sufferings. In this, he approaches Dostoevsky's kenotic ideal. There has been a great deal already written about the great importance of the kenotic saint both in the Russian religious tradition, and in Dostoevsky's spiritual and artistic understanding.[18] As St. Paul describes kenosis in his letter to the Philippians, Jesus emptied himself, descending from divine form to human in an act of supreme sacrifice. On a far smaller scale, but in a similar way, Ilyusha allows himself to extend his empathy to a stray dog. He empties himself of ego in his willingness to abandon his superior position and feel Zhuchka's pain. In this way, Ilyusha follows Christ in his suffering, in a brave and kenotic act of empathy.

The novel features a number of calls for similar acts of kenotic empathy, for willingness to identify with children, animals, and servants, the lowest beings on the social hierarchy. In addition to his admonition to respect both children and animals, Zosima tells his listeners that they should be willing to abandon their social status and become like servants. He asserts, "The world cannot do without servants, but see to it that your servant is freer in spirit than if he were not a servant" (*PSS* 14: 287-8; *BK* 317). In saying that "the world cannot do without servants," Zosima echoes Fyodor Pavlovich's assertion that "there will always be slaves and masters." Rather than using this truth of inequality as justification for exploitation, Zosima uses it as a reason to take on the duties of a servant himself. He tells his listeners,

> And why can I not be the servant of my servant, and in such wise that he even sees it, and without any pride on my part, or any disbelief on his? Why can my servant not be like my own kin, so that I may finally receive him into my family, and rejoice for it? This may be accomplished even now, but it will serve as the foundation for the magnificent communion of mankind in the future, when a man will not seek servants for himself, and will not wish to turn his fellow men into servants, as now, but, on the contrary, will wish with all his strength to become himself the servant of all, in accordance with the Gospel.

> (*PSS* 14: 288; *BK* 317)

While Fyodor Pavlovich made his child into a servant, Zosima proposes the opposite: people should make servants parts of their families. They should feel empathy with those who serve them and be willing literally to take their places.

Zosima's proposal can also be read as a redemptive way of dealing with the historical wounds of serfdom.[19] Previously, masters neglected and exploited the charges they ought to have protected, forcing them into servitude. But according to Zosima's vision, servitude can become an act of voluntary humility rather than forced humiliation. In becoming servants to everyone, people can truly become like little children, and thus fit to enter the kingdom of heaven. Zosima himself puts his words in the context of serfdom and emancipation, noting that the peasantry has survived "two centuries of slavery" (*PSS* 14: 286; *BK* 316). And yet, Zosima claims, the peasants have retained an inner freedom and understanding of the sacred that will allow them to lead the rest of society to true justice and equality. Thus, as

Zosima puts it, "The stone that the builders rejected has become the cornerstone" (*PSS* 14: 288; *BK* 318; Matthew 21: 42).

But Zosima's vision is ultimately an apocalyptic one. "Many who are last will be first," yes—but only "at the renewal of all things, when the Son of Man sits on his glorious throne" (Matthew 19: 28, 30). As Dostoevsky revealed more clearly in his journalistic writings of the late 1870s, he believed that the Second Coming was approaching, and that Russia, an apparently disintegrating society, would lead the rest of the world to a post-apocalyptic unity.[20] Zosima's words, for all their beauty, do not describe the actual society of Skotoprigonevsk, but rather a vision of what that society could be if it were to devote itself fully to Christ. Zosima's "magnificent communion of mankind in the future" references a heavenly society that can come about only after great suffering and destruction.

Zosima is more explicit about the apocalyptic nature of his ideas in his description of Mikhail, the "mysterious visitor" whom he helped in his youth to confess his crime of murder. Zosima later writes of Mikhail, "I learned much that was useful from him, for he was a man of lofty mind" (*PSS* 14: 275; *BK* 302). Mikhail's spiritual views are in accordance with Zosima's and help to clarify some of the aspects Zosima leaves vague. Mikhail emphasizes the need to live through a period of "horrible isolation" before "heaven on earth, not only in a dream, but in truth" is achieved. He tells Zosima,

> Until one has indeed become the brother of all, there will be no brotherhood . . . But there must needs come a term to this horrible isolation, and everyone will all at once realize how unnaturally they have separated themselves one from another. Such will be the spirit of the time, and they will be astonished that they sat in darkness for so long and did not see the light. *Then the sign of the Son of Man will appear in the heavens . . .* But until then we must keep hold of the banner, and every once in a while, if only individually, a man must suddenly set an example, and draw the soul from its isolation for an act of brotherly communion.

> (*PSS* 14: 275; *BK* 303-304, emphasis mine.)

True, eternal brotherhood, Mikhail emphasizes, is not something that the human world in its current state is capable of. Until the Second Coming of Christ, the most that people can do is attempt individual, temporary, heroic acts of brotherly love.[21]

As the novel shows, fellow feeling with the humble is an excruciatingly difficult act. Acts of kenotic empathy are rare in the novel, and those who commit them are usually just about to die. Zosima, the one exception to this rule, understands that he was cruel in striking his servant only when he is on the brink of being shot in a duel. He survives and continues with his new empathetic knowledge, unlike the other kenotic characters in the novel, who die soon after they reach this level of understanding. Zosima's brother Markel suddenly decides, "let me be the servant of my servants, the same as they are to me," (*PSS* 14: 262; *BK* 289) only when he is dying of consumption. Ilyusha's act of empathy for Zhuchka also comes as he is dying. True sympathy with the downtrodden is something it's almost impossible to sustain in the everyday world. Not even Alyosha is able to understand that Smerdyakov is his brother.

Ivan has one important moment of empathetic suffering along with the suffering children of the world. Robert Louis Jackson has described the "Rebellion" chapter as Ivan's "great lamentation." Ivan's rejection of a world harmony that is based on the suffering of children becomes a philosophical self-laceration; Ivan willfully chooses a world of endless and meaningless suffering over a divine universe built in part on the sufferings of children. And yet, Jackson argues, Ivan in his rebellion suffers along with the children, and therefore along with Christ (319-34). But then, as Ivan himself says, "Christian love is in its kind a miracle impossible on earth" (*PSS* 14: 216; *BK* 237). Ivan proves unable to sustain his sympathy once he moves from theory to practice; despite his beautiful ideas, he behaves with consistent cruelty toward children and the lower classes: Lise, Smerdyakov, and the drunken peasant he pushes down into the snow.[22]

Ivan's tendency to take out his anger on the downtrodden is one he shares with many other characters in the novel. In one particularly poignant moment, toward the end of the novel, the boy Smurov, while crying after Ilyusha's funeral, throws a piece of brick at a passing flock of sparrows. The sparrows are a particularly significant target for Smurov to choose: Ilyusha had requested that his father crumble bread on his grave, "so the sparrows will come, and I'll hear that they've come and be glad that I'm not lying alone" (*PSS* 15: 192; *BK* 771). In his anger and grief, Smurov reestablishes the hierarchy of beings that Ilyusha had briefly managed to dissolve and disrupts his imagined community with the sparrows. The moment is succeeded, though, by a moment of almost pure community, as the end of the novel offers Ilyusha's sin, suffering, and redemption as a path to universal love. Alyosha tells the boys gathered around the stone after Ilyusha's funeral, "never forget how we were once happy here, all of us together, united by such a good and kind feeling that made us, at this time of love for the poor boy, maybe better than we truly are" (*PSS* 15: 195; *BK* 774). He calls upon the boys always to remember Ilyusha's sufferings as they grow up, so as to retain within themselves an element of their childhood selves that will function as a force for good. The boys answer, "We will, we will remember! He was

brave, he was kind!" (*PSS* 15: 196; *BK* 775). Ilyusha's death acts as a solidifier of this childhood community; feelings of sympathy for Ilyusha help connect the boys to each other and to God. For a brief moment, the boys transcend hierarchy, no longer struggling to be older and to establish supremacy over each other. They empty themselves of ego and voluntarily identify themselves with a poor, humiliated, vulnerable child.

The violence against the innocents implied by Smurov's act is overcome by the community of boys united by their memory of Ilyusha. For one fragile moment, the boys form a loving harmony similar to that which Zosima had called for, an earthly reflection of a heavenly society in which all will truly be brothers. The novel also makes it quite clear that this moment can't be expected to last. Alyosha repeatedly advises the boys to fix the moment in their memories as a safeguard against the time when "perhaps we will even become wicked later on, will even be unable to resist a bad action, will laugh at people's tears" (*PSS* 15: 195; *BK* 774). The moment needs to be saved up precisely because it is temporary, a fleeting transcendence of the power hierarchy that pervades the world of *The Brothers Karamazov*. This hierarchy can fully be transcended only in the afterlife. There, Zosima tells us, even the elevation of the righteous in heaven over sinners in hell can be overcome through love and humility. Until then, the novel's end offers a glimpse of a glorious future convergence beyond hierarchy and beyond time, as the world hurtles towards the abyss, and trembles on the brink of salvation.

Notes

1. I am grateful to Paul Contino, Christian Riblet, Carol Flath, and Lynn Patyk for their comments and advice on earlier versions of this article. Quotations from Dostoevsky's works are from the Academy edition of Dostoevsky's complete works. The translations from *Crime and Punishment* and *The Brothers Karamazov* are from the Pevear and Volokhonsky translations of these novels; I have occasionally made some minor changes. The parenthetical citations give references first for the Academy edition, or *Polnoe sobranie sochinenii*, abbreviated as *PSS*. After this follows the page number of the Pevear and Volokhonsky translation; *The Brothers Karamazov* is abbreviated as *BK,* and *Crime and Punishment* as *CP*. Translations from *Diary of a Writer* and *The Count of Monte Cristo* are my own.

2. Dianne Oenning Thomspon reads Lise as a suffering child who moves from good to evil. She writes, "Presenting Lise's condition as one of self-corruption, Dostoevsky shifts the problem of her pathology to the problem of evil inherent in the soul" ("Lise," 293). Thompson argues that Lise is

both "*shalunia*" and "*besionok*"—alternating between joyful child and corrupted sadist.

3. Victor Terras notices the sinfulness of children in *The Brothers Karamazov* as well. He writes, "It is certainly significant that the Devil is not absent from the world of children either: Liza Khokhlakova and Kolia Krasotkin are both in grave danger, she because she is already tainted, and he because he is clearly a double of Ivan Karamazov. Could this be a part of Dostoevsky's strategy to diffuse the power of Ivan Karamazov's charge that God allows innocent children to suffer?" (127).

4. N. Berkovskii argues that *The Brothers Karamazov* shows the relationship between the old wrong of serfdom and the new wrong of rampant capitalism. According to Berkovskii, the two systems are more or less the same thing, leading to equal unfreedom and to the sufferings of the innocent. "Bourgeois violence against human beings becomes identified with the violence of serf-holding—this is the nature of "*karamazovshchina*" (203). I think Berkovskii states the case somewhat too strongly—Dostoevsky does make it clear that emancipation improved things. But I agree with Berkovskii that wealth in the novel can be used as a sort of violence and in this is quite similar to serfdom.

5. Dostoevsky cherished a lifelong hatred for serfdom—indeed, he was sentenced to four years of hard labor for having spoken against serfdom in a secret political circle. Dostoevsky believed that his father had been murdered by his own serfs; Joseph Frank argues that part of Dostoevsky's intense hatred of serfdom came from a feeling of complicity in his father's death because he had been making demands on his father for large sums of money in the year or two before his father died, thus inadvertently making life all the harder for the overworked serfs (81-91). The role of serfdom and emancipation in Dostoevsky's fiction has recently become the subject of some important scholarship. Harriet Murav argues that serfdom and its aftereffects are an integral part of the way Dostoevsky portrays both family and community in *Diary of a Writer*. Murav concentrates on Dostoevsky's discussions of child abuse; she argues that Dostoevsky depicts peasants as akin to suffering children, while also being nurturing parents to the gentry. In his journalism of the late 1870s, Murav shows, Dostoevsky claims that Russia can transcend the abusive Europeanized gentry family to create a new, higher sort of human family, with no further use for boundaries of class (125-55). Susanne Fusso argues that Dostoevsky's later novels can be read as a constant attempt to rewrite

Turgenev's *Fathers and Sons* to more accurately reflect what he saw as the chaos infecting both Russian society and family life. According to Fusso, the idea of responsibility is crucial to the family as Dostoevsky understood it. Serfdom is one of the worst examples of the failure of responsibility; rather than caring for their peasant charges, Dostoevsky's characters exploit them and forget about them, just as Fyodor Pavlovich neglects and exploits his children.

6. The reference here is to Alexander II's 1856 speech announcing the need for an end to serfdom. The official emancipation took place February 19, 1861.

7. Olga Meerson also points out the class meaning of the word "smerd" and notes it is used by characters in the novel to imply that low class people in general and Smerdyakov in particular ought to be excluded from brotherly love (198).

8. Valerii Shevchenko goes even farther, portraying Smerdyakov as a calumniated and heroic figure. He argues that Smerdyakov is innocent of the tormenting of Zhuchka, the murder of his father, and the killing of all but one cat. For Shevchenko, the novel is a tale of Smerdyakov as "insulted and injured," slandered on all sides and finally pushed into confessing a crime he did not commit (82-195). While I agree with some of Shevchenko's points about Smerdyakov's victimization, I disagree with his apparent assumption that if Smerdyakov is a victim, he cannot be guilty of a crime.

9. Modern psychological research on neglected children has shown that children who have grown up without love tend to act very much like Smerdyakov. Daniel Hughes writes that children who have suffered from profound neglect are filled with an all-consuming sense of shame and worthlessness. He writes, "The typical reinforcers of the poorly attached child are not common to most kids. They include being in control of the feelings and behaviors of others and winning every power struggle. These children also love saying 'No!' and maintaining their negative view of themselves and others. They also find it reinforcing to be able to need no one, and to avoid both experiences of reciprocal fun and love, and also having to ask for favors and being praised. . . . [Such children] do not experience remorse for hurting others. They have little empathy for others and little guilt for their behaviors" (39, 68). I find this description amazingly similar to Smerdyakov, and I find it helpful to keep in mind as a way of retaining sympathy for him. As Hughes emphasizes, the unappealing, almost evil children he describes here are in fact not evil in the least but are living a night-

marish, loveless existence because they were deprived of love from birth.

10. Thompson writes that evil, for Dostoevsky, is innate. Smerdyakov is born evil, just as Lise is born with elements of both evil and good within her ("Lise" 293; *Poetics* 142). But my reading of *The Brothers Karamazov* suggests the opposite: evil is not innate in people, but rather is brought about by social realities and human constructions. It only makes sense, for example, that the devil in *The Brothers Karamazov* does not "appear in some sort of red glow, 'in thunder and lightning,' with scorched wings" (*PSS* 15: 81; *BK* 647) but rather as an ordinary man of the social world, a former serf-holder and a neglectful father. The devil is part of the social structure, a structure that creates the sufferings of the innocent, and thus works to perpetuate evil.

11. Shevchenko also notes the failure to make Smerdyakov a "communal child" (101-105).

12. In fact, Johnson argues, Smerdyakov's question (about where the light came from before God created the sun and the moon) is perceptive one, highly important to Orthodox thought.

13. Thompson names Smerdyakov as an abandoned child (161) and discusses how neglect of children is a diabolical act of forgetting that works to rend family and community (*Politics,* 161-171).

14. Here it's helpful to keep in mind V. E. Vetlovskaia's discussion of the "Rebellion" chapter and her polemic with Ivan. Vetlovskaia argues that the crucial mistake Ivan makes in rejecting God's world because it requires the suffering of children is that he fails to understand that there is no sharp dividing line between children and adults. Ivan condemns grownups while claiming to defend children—he does not recognize that, in practice, this approach doesn't work. Suffering children and sinful adults can't be fully separated from each other; Mitya and Grushenka, for example, are sinners and children at the same time (100-122). Smerdyakov himself works as another example of a character who is both grown-up sinner and suffering child.

15. Meerson notes the ambiguous use of "brother" here, which could be read as applying either to Alyosha or to Smerdyakov (192-3).

16. Khokhlakova's remark carries an echo from *The Count of Monte Cristo,* a novel Dostoevsky certainly read. At one point, when about to watch the execution of "a miserable man who murdered the priest who brought him up" (401), the Count explains to his horrified guests that the man deserves no pity. He tells them, "If you heard someone cry

'Mad dog!' you would take your gun, you would run out into the street, you would mercilessly shoot the poor beast, who, after all, was only guilty of having been bitten by another dog, and then doing what was done to him. And yet you pity a man who, without being bitten by another man, has nonetheless killed his benefactor" (436). Dostoevsky, who had come close to death by firing squad, was fascinated by literary depictions of executions (Knapp 66-101) and would have been sure to read this passage with great attention. Later events in the novel disprove the Count's contention that members of the community (and parents in particular) bear no blame for the sins of those who depended on them.

17. Pavel Iakushkin, *Russkie narodnye pesni iz sobraniia Iakushkina,* St. Petersburg, 1865, 45. Translation in Meerson, 190. The Academy edition of Dostoevsky's works also contains a short reference to the song (15: 589).

18. George Fedotov in *The Russian Religious Mind* (1: 94-131) gives a detailed account of the importance of kenosis in early Russian religious thought. Margaret Ziolkowski gives a brief explanation of the kenotic tradition in Russian Orthodoxy, and a summary of Dostoevky's use of it in his works. Ziolkowski points out that Dostoevsky tends to combine the kenotic ideal with nationalism, a somewhat idiosyncratic pairing. My discussion of kenoticism is particularly indebted to Paul Contino, who emphasizes the abandonment of ego needed to connect oneself with another. Contino argues that the kenotic saint is especially evident in the Dostoevskian role of confessor—those, like Sonia in *Crime and Punishment,* Tikhon in *The Demons,* and Zosima in *The Brothers Karamazov,* who are able to follow Christ by emptying themselves of egotism in order to enter into an understanding of the suffering of the confessing sinner.

19. I am grateful to my student, John Cadena (Stanford 2007) for this idea.

20. Gary Saul Morson discusses in detail the apocalyptic passages in *Diary of a Writer* (33-38).

21. This passage carries a reflection of Dostoevky's famous diary entry on Holy Thursday, 1864, while sitting with the body of his first wife. Dostoevsky begins by wondering whether he will see his wife again in the afterlife; he then moves on to a discussion of the impossibility of pure Christian love on earth. If loving one's neighbor as oneself "is the final goal of humankind . . . then it follows that man, in achieving it, completes his existence on earth. Therefore, on earth man is only a developing being, and, it follows, not a final creation, but a transitional one (*PSS* 20: 172-3). Dostoevsky

returned to this idea repeatedly in his subsequent fiction, as Liza Knapp has shown in *The Annihilation of Inertia* (see esp. 14-15, 41-45, 207-16).

22. I am grateful to my student Ilana Lohr-Schmidt (Stanford 2008) for pointing out that Ivan's behavior towards the peasant and towards the bumbling, foolish Mikhailov can be read as acts of violence against the innocent.

Works Cited

Belknap, Robert L. *The Structure of The Brothers Karamazov.* The Hague: Mouton, 1967.

Berkovskii, N. "O "Brat'iakh Karamazovykh."" *Voprosy literatury* 952.3 (1981): 197-213.

Contino, Paul. "Zosima, Mikhail, and Prosaic Confessional Dialogue in Dostoevsky's *Brothers Karamazov.*" *Studies in the Novel* 27: 1 (1995): 63-87.

Dostoevsky, F. M. *The Brothers Karamazov.* Trans. Richard Pevear and Larissa Volokhonsky. New York: Farrar, Straus and Giroux, 1990.

———. *Crime and Punishment.* Trans. Richard Pevear and Larissa Volokhonsky. New York: Random House, 1992.

———. *Polnoe sobranie sochinenii.* Academy edition. 30 vols. Leningrad: Izd. Nauka, 1972-1990.

Dumas, Alexandre. *Le Comte de Monte-Cristo.* Paris: Gallimard, 1981.

Fedotov, George P. *The Russian Religious Mind.* 2 vols. Cambridge: Harvard UP, 1946.

Frank, Joseph. *Dostoevsky: The Seeds of Revolt, 1821-1849.* Princeton: Princeton UP, 1976.

Fusso, Susanne. "Dostoevsky and the Family." *The Cambridge Companion to Dostoevskii.* Ed. W. J. Leatherbarrow. Cambridge: Cambridge UP, 2002. 175-190.

Golstein, Vladimir. "Accidental Families and Surrogate Fathers: Richard, Grigory, and Smerdyakov." *A New Word on The Brothers Karamazov.* Ed. Robert Louis Jackson. Evanston: Northwestern UP, 2004. 90-106.

Hughes, Daniel A. *Building the Bonds of Attachment: Awakening Love in Deeply Troubled Children.* Lanham: Rowman and Littlefield, 1998.

Jackson, Robert Louis. *The Art of Dostoevsky: Deliriums and Nocturnes.* Princeton: Princeton UP, 1981.

Johnson, Lee D. "Struggle for Theosis: Smerdyakov as Would-be Saint." *A New Word on The Brothers Karamazov.* Ed. Robert Louis Jackson. Evanston: Northwestern UP, 2004. 74-89.

Kantor, Vladimir. "Pavel Smerdyakov and Ivan Karamazov: The Problem of Temptation." *Dostoevsky and the Christian Tradition.* Eds. George Pattison and Diane Oenning Thompson. Cambridge: Cambridge UP, 2001. 189-225.

Knapp, Liza. *The Annihilation of Inertia: Dostoevsky and Metaphysics.* Evanston: Northwestern UP, 1996.

Meerson, Olga. *Dostoevsky's Taboos.* Dresden: Dresden UP, 1998.

Morson, Gary Saul. *The Boundaries of Genre: Dostoevsky's Diary of a Writer and the Traditions of Literary Utopia.* Austin: University of Texas Press, 1981.

Murav, Harriet. *Russia's Legal Fictions.* Ann Arbor: U of Michigan P, 1998.

Shevchenko, Valerii. *Dostoevskii: paradoksy tvorchestva.* Moscow: Izd. Ogni, 2004.

Silbajoris, Rimvydas. "The Children in *The Brothers Karamazov.*" *Slavic and East European Journal* 7 (1963): 26-38.

Terras, Victor. *Reading Dostoevsky.* Madison, WI: U of Wisconsin P, 1998.

Thompson, Diane Oenning. *The Brothers Karamazov and the Poetics of Memory.* Cambridge: Cambridge UP, 1991.

———. "Lise Khokhlakova: *shalunia/besionok.*" *O Rus! Studia litteraria slavica in honorem Hugh McLean.* Berkeley: Berkeley Slavic Specialties, 1995. 281-297.

Vetlovskaia, V. E. *Poetika romana "Brat'ia Karamazovy."* Leningrad: Izd. Nauka, 1977.

Ziolkowski, Margaret. "Dostoevsky and the Kenotic Tradition." *Dostoevsky and the Christian Tradition.* Eds. George Pattison and Diane Oenning Thompson. Cambridge: Cambridge UP, 31-40.

Paul J. Contino (essay date 2006)

SOURCE: Contino, Paul J. "'Descend That You May Ascend': Augustine, Dostoevsky, and the Confessions of Ivan Karamazov." In *Augustine and Literature,* edited by Robert P. Kennedy, Kim Paffenroth, and John Doody, pp. 179-214. Lanham, Md.: Lexington Books, 2006.

[*In the following essay, Contino illustrates how* The Brothers Karamazov *is informed by the philosophy of St. Augustine.*]

INTRODUCTION

"On Earth, indeed, we are as it were astray, and if it were not for the precious image of Christ before us, we should be undone and altogether lost, as was the human race before the flood. Much on earth is hidden from us, but to make up for that we have been given a precious mystic sense of our living bond with the other world, with the higher heavenly world, and the roots of our thoughts and feelings are not here but in other worlds."[1] In his indispensable companion to *The Brothers Karamazov*, Victor Terras claims that the latter sentence commences what is "probably the master key to the philosophical interpretation, as well as the structure, of *The Brothers Karamazov*."[2] These words—spoken by Father Zosima at the end of his life—affirm his perception of the spiritual dimension of reality, the way in which "God took seeds from different worlds and sowed them on this earth" (299). I would suggest, however, that the first sentence I quote here—that which emphasizes the salvific presence of Christ's image—offers the "master key" to the novel's theological meaning, and to the Christological pattern of descent and ascent which structures Dostoevsky's greatest and final novel. For in Dostoevsky's vision, the Incarnation itself sows the fruitful seed. Recall the novel's epigraph: "Verily, verily, I say unto you, except a corn of wheat fall into the ground and die, it abideth alone: but if it die, it bringeth forth much fruit" (John 12:24). In the Word made flesh, Jesus descends into our humble, human plot of *humus* or earth; he suffers, dies, rises, ascends to his Father—and brings life to the world. Or, as Jesus says to Nicodemus earlier in John's gospel, in words which Dostoevsky underscored: "And no man hath ascended into heaven, but He that descended out of heaven, even the Son of Man which is in heaven" (John 3:13).[3] This Christological pattern of descent and ascent provides the pattern to which each of the three young Karamazov brothers—Dmitri, Ivan, and Alyosha—eventually conforms in the tortuous course of the novel.

It is also the pattern which the middle-aged Augustine discerns when he recalls his own youthful conversion in the *Confessions*. Through their assertion of pride, the Karamazov brothers and Augustine fall. In penitence, each encounters his creatural limitations and humbly accepts the grace of God. Each then arises (or, in Ivan Karamazov's case, promises to arise) with the capacity to reflect Christ's image to others. A first, necessary descent follows the assertion of pride and the consequent acknowledgement of creatural dependence upon the loving Creator. But, with ascent and recovery of the *imago Dei*, a second and successive descents follow: in the daily practice of what Zosima calls "active love" (49) each reflects the image of the kenotic Christ—who lovingly descended to our earthly state. Here creature reflects Creator in "loving humility" (*Karamazov*, 298), in what Augustine calls the "the charity which builds on the foundation of humility which is Christ Jesus."[4] In their depiction of the human vocation to conform to the Christological pattern of descent and ascent we can discern the deep affinity between Augustine and Dostoevsky, the crucial conceptual link between the two.[5]

KENOSIS: EAST AND WEST

A question immediately arises: Can we draw upon the Latin, Western Augustine to illuminate the theological meanings of Dostoevsky when so many theologically minded commentators locate the novelist within his own Russian Orthodox tradition? As the editors of *Russian Religious Thought* point out: "[The] medieval Russian intellectual culture grew up in isolation from the whole Latin tradition and to a great extent from the classical Greek heritage as well. Aristotle, Augustine, and Aquinas remained largely unknown."[6] In fact, for a number of major, recent Orthodox theologians, Augustine lays the seeds for schism, the eventual split between the Catholic and Orthodox churches in 1054. For Vladimir Lossky, for example, Augustine goes wrong in his fiercely anti-Pelagian insistence upon grace over free will; "[t]he Eastern tradition never separates these two elements: grace and human freedom are manifested simultaneously and cannot be conceived apart from each other."[7] For John Zizioulas, Augustine rightly understands the Holy Spirit as "Communion," but fails to recognize the way in which such a reality transforms ontology and makes it inherently relational.[8] For Christos Yannaras, the "augustinian tradition [sic] . . . taught the autonomy of the intellectual capacity of the individual, and European man claimed in consequence this autonomy by rejecting even the metaphysical reference or bond."[9] Indeed, Yannaras goes so far as to call Augustine "the fount of every distortion and alteration in the Church's truth in the West."[10] For Eastern theologians, Augustine fails to emphasize the reality of human freedom—intrinsic to the human being's creation as *imago Dei*—and our communal need for others.

On the contrary, both freedom and community are vital components in Augustine's thought. As Peter Brown argues, Augustine sees grace and freedom as working together in an integral process of healing: "It is the connection of the two, in a single healing process, that occupies all Augustine's attention: any attempt to dissect such a living relationship, to see a contrast where he saw only a vital interdependence, frankly puzzled him: 'Some men try hard to discover in our will what good is particularly due to ourselves, that owes nothing to God: how they can find this out, I just do not know'" (374).[11] Regarding the necessity of relational, communal support in the life of faith, and the folly of any assertion of individual autonomy, one need only point to the mediatory significance Augustine grants Monica, his mother, and Bishop Ambrose of Milan. On the first page of *Confessions*, for instance, Augustine points to the intermediation of both Christ's Incarnation and Ambrose's pastoral care in his reception of faith: "[My faith] is your gift to me. You breathed it into me by the humanity of your Son, by the ministry of your preacher" (1.1.1).

Eastern insistence upon irremediable theological differences aside, there is little evidence that Dostoevsky himself ever read Augustine. Whereas Lisa Knapp observes that Dostoevsky was "likely to write with an awareness of [both the Augustinian and Rousseauian] models" of "the confessional genre,"[12] (17), she admits:

> Dostoevsky's works do not, as far as I know, contain any overt references to Augustine's *Confessions,* other than a note Dostoevsky made to himself to read Augustine's *Confessions.* The fact that he wanted to read it does not mean that he had never read it before. In any event, it is reasonable to assume that he would have been familiar with the basic structure and the fact that this penitent Christian confession was very different from Rousseau's nonpenitent confession.[13]

Indeed, as Avril Pyman has recently argued, the boundaries between Eastern and Western theological traditions can be overly emphasized, especially in the case of a nineteenth-century novelist who "developed through a process of cross pollination and grafting and translation."[14]

One may speculate about indirect influence. The great seventh-century Eastern theologian Maximus the Confessor has been linked to Dostoevsky's understanding of Christology,[15] and as Jaroslav Pelikan notes, "It would seem highly unlikely that Maximus could have spent such a long time in North Africa without becoming acquainted with the works of its most celebrated Christian thinker, Augustine . . . but we have tantalizingly little evidence that [Maximus] did in fact read Augustine."[16] Less indirectly, one can point to Dostoevsky's younger and ecumenically inclined friend, Vladimir Solovyov, with whom Dostoevsky traveled in his 1878 pilgrimage to Optina Pustyn monastery and whose lectures on divine humanity Dostoevsky attended. In Lecture 6, Solovyov draws on the Trinitarian dimension of Augustinian thought, as found not only in *De Trinitate,* but primarily in the *Confessions* in which, Solovyov writes, "In our spirit, we must differentiate between its simple immediate being (*esse*), its knowledge (*scire*), and its will (*velle*)" (*Lectures,* 94-95).[17]

Being, knowledge, will; mind, knowledge, love; memory, intelligence, will[18]—Trinitarian patterns such as these "run all through the theologically structured account of Augustine's life,"[19] and throughout *The Brothers Karamazov* as well. One can point to numerous examples in Augustine. Three will suffice: On the opening page of *Confessions,* Augustine speaks of the process of "seeking, finding, and praising" God (1.1.1), a pattern which at least one commentator sees as animating the rest of the work.[20] Drawing on 1 John 2:16, Augustine outlines "three chief kinds of wickedness": domination, curiosity, and sensuality (3.8.16). And in his discussion of time, he speaks of the "three aspects of time in the soul": "memory," "immediate awareness," and "expec-tation" (11.20.26). Charles Taylor notes similar "parallels with the Christian doctrine of the Trinity," and cogently observes that for Augustine "man shows himself most clearly as the image of God in his inner self-presence and self-love. It is a kind of knowledge where knower and known are one, coupled with love, which reflects most fully God in our lives. And indeed, the image of the Trinity in us is the process whereby we strive to complete and perfect this self-presence and self-affirmation."[21]

The salient instances of triads in *The Brothers Karamazov*—upon rereadings of the novel they seem to spring up almost everywhere!—are nicely summarized by David S. Cunningham in "*The Brothers Karamazov* as Trinitarian Theology":

> As many commentators have noted, triads dominate the novel. There are three . . . "lacerations" . . . , three 'confessions of an ardent heart', three temptations of Christ (mirrored by the three forces employed by the Inquisitor), three meetings with Smerdyakov, three 'torments of the soul'. The murder and the investigation focuses on Dmitry's need for 3,000 roubles, and the galloping troika invoked at his trial (on three different occasions). Fyodor is murdered by being hit three times with a paperweight weighing about three pounds; the murderer takes from him an envelope (containing 3,000 roubles) which is sealed with 'large red wax seals'—yes, you've guessed—three of them.[22]

One can point to a host of additional affinities. Both *Confessions* and *The Brothers Karamazov* bear a deep intertextual relationship with the Bible and are infused with Scripture. Of course, both Augustine and Dostoevsky loved the Bible, but especially the Gospel of John.[23] Moreover, as in the famous scene of Augustine in the Milan garden "open[ing] the book and read[ing] the first chapter I might find" (8.11.29), Dostoevsky would, from time to time, open the Bible at random for guidance and inspiration.[24] This deep familiarity with Scripture bore fruit in his novels. As Nina Perlina demonstrates, "Biblical narrative, the most authoritative and universal text that has ever existed, engulfs all the individual discoveries made by Dostoevsky's heroes [in *The Brothers Karamazov*]. A figural interpretation of the novel tends to saturate occurrences of everyday life with the spirit of eternity."[25] Perlina draws explicitly upon Erich Auerbach's essay "Figura," which emphasizes Augustine's development of the figural interpretation of Scripture. Grounded in his faith in the Incarnation, Augustine takes "the concrete event, completely preserved as it is, from time and transposes it into a perspective of eternity."[26] Thus, the works of Augustine "creat[e] a whole structure of verbal echoes, linking every part of the Bible."[27] Similarly, *The Brothers Karamazov*'s scriptural resonances and rhymes lend the novel so much of its formal, symphonic beauty.

Indeed, both writers shared a profound appreciation of beauty, and of God as beauty. As Hans Urs von Balthasar writes, "No one has praised God so assiduously as the supreme beauty or attempted so consistently to capture the true and the good with the categories of aesthetics as Augustine in the period during and after his conversion."[28] Much like Dostoevsky, Augustine recognized the beauty of Christ—even in his most radically kenotic state of forsakenness. For Augustine, "a person must love Christ and have pure eyes to see his inner spiritual beauty, because for those who stand at a distance, and certainly for his persecutors, he is veiled to the point of ugliness."[29] So too Dostoevsky, who declared in his 1854 letter to N. D. Fonvizina that he believed "that there is nothing more beautiful . . . more perfect than Christ."[30] As Robert Louis Jackson writes, "the focal point of [Dostoevsky's] vision is ultimately the image of Christ. But it is an aesthetically conceived image. Faith in Christ is faith in embodied form, in an image of beauty, perfection, and transfiguration."[31] In *The Idiot,* the often Christlike Prince Myshkin is quoted as saying "that the world will be saved by beauty,"[32] yet an important influence upon Dostoevsky while he composed that novel was his viewing of Hans Holbein's terrifyingly realistic portrait from 1521, *Dead Christ.*[33]

Devotion to Scripture and to the beauty of the humiliated Christ point to the deepest affinity between Augustine and Dostoevsky: both reveal a profound appreciation of Christ's humility as it is revealed in his kenosis, the self-emptying described by St. Paul in his letter to the Philippians. As Erich Auerbach argues, the Bible's humble style—its *sermo humilis*—aptly weds subject and form. In the *sermo humilis,* "humble everyday things"[34] and language are used in rhetoric concerning the most sublime subjects—God, grace, redemption—and are authorized in doing so by the event of the Incarnation: "*Humilis* is related to *humus,* the soil, and literally means low, low lying, of small stature";[35] "*humilis* became the most important adjective characterizing [Christ's] Incarnation."[36] Further, "the most important passage in this connection is Phil. 2: 7f,"[37] the passage in which St. Paul presents the hymn which celebrates Christ's kenosis or self-emptying. Here is that passage:

> Let the same mind be in you that was in Christ Jesus, who, though he was in the form of God, did not regard equality with God as something to be exploited, but emptied himself, taking the form of a slave, being born in human likeness. And being found in human form, he humbled himself and became obedient to the point of death—even death on a cross. Therefore God also highly exalted him and gave him the name that is above every name, so that at the name of Jesus every knee should bend, in heaven and on earth and under the earth, and every tongue should confess that Jesus Christ is Lord, to the glory of the Father.
>
> (Phil. 2. 5-11)

As Auerbach observes: "The humility of the Incarnation derives its full force from the contrast with Christ's divine nature: man and God, lowly and sublime, *humilis*

et sublimis; both the height and the depth are immeasurable and inconceivable . . ."[38] Such a paradoxical combination of sublime subject and humble style suggested confusion to its audience in antiquity, notably the youthful Augustine: "Most educated pagans regarded the early Christian writings as ludicrous, confused, and abhorrent . . ."[39] But to Christian believers, Christ had poured out any aspirations to divinity to become a person of lowly station, to die as a criminal, and it was *thus* that every knee should bend at the sound of his name.[40]

Few theological concepts in the Russian Orthodox tradition are given as much emphasis as that of Christ's kenosis. In *The Russian Religious Mind,* George P. Fedotov emphasizes the kenotic spirituality evident in the stories of Russian saints like the martyrs Boris and Gleb, and the willing poverty of St. Theodosius: "The kenotic idea has its practical expression with Theodosius in three Christian virtues: poverty, humility, and love, in their complete unity as one inseparable whole."[41] Joseph Frank points to the kenotic example of such saints, whose stories Dostoevsky heard as a child.[42] In an essay on P. A. Florensky, Steven Cassedy writes that "In Russian theology the term ["kenosis"] serves as a sort of negative corollary to incarnation, which emphasizes the divine presence in matter," and that "[f]ew writers had as vivid an intuition of the kenotic principle and its ramifications as did Dostoevsky . . ."[43] As Dostoevsky wrote in 1863, as he kept watch over the body of his first wife, Masha, "Christ entered entirely into humanity, and man strives to transform himself into the *I* of Christ."[44]

In what currently stands as the most influential study of Dostoevsky, *Problems of Dostoevsky's Poetics,* Mikhail Bakhtin draws upon the kenotic insights of Vyacheslav Ivanov to articulate what he sees as Dostoevsky's unique contribution to novelistic form: polyphony, the many voices that he represents in his novels, each of which he respects as free. In his "new artistic position . . . with regard to the hero," Dostoevsky "affirms the independence, internal freedom, unfinalizability, and indeterminacy of the hero. For the author the hero is not 'he' and not 'I' but a fully valid 'Thou,' that is, another and other autonomous 'I' ('Thou art')."[45] The kenotic dimension of this author-character relationship is evident in the first chapter of *The Brothers Karamazov.* The narrator is an ordinary townsperson of Skotoprigonevsk, and recalls events that occurred there thirteen years before. He first describes Fyodor Pavlovich as "an ill-natured buffoon and nothing more" (3), his tone insistent, judgmental. But in the final paragraph of the first chapter, he grows less certain—"But who knows?"—as he describes Fyodor's reaction to his first wife's departure and eventual death:

> Fyodor Pavlovich was drunk when he first heard of his wife's death, and the story is that he ran out into the

street and began shouting with joy, raising his hands to Heaven: "Lord, now lettest Thou Thy servant depart in peace," but others say he wept without restraint like a little child, so much so that people were sorry for him, in spite of the repulsion he inspired. It is quite possible that both versions are true, that he rejoiced at his release, and at the same time wept for her who released him. As a general rule, people, even the wicked, are much more naive and simple-hearted than we suppose. And we ourselves are, too.

(4)

We can observe here the narrator's humility in relation to his reader. As Victor Terras points out, "The narrator's manner is that of a 'conversation with the reader,' and his vocabulary and syntax tend to be those of an oral narrative: sentences and paragraphs are not well-constructed and well-balanced . . ."[46] Robin Feuer Miller describes the narrator as "chatty, often digressive."[47] Nina Perlina describes him as a "meek and resigned narrator, who always feels 'somewhat at a loss,' who is always afraid that his readers are still unconvinced, and constantly doubts whether 'he will succeed in proving' his ideas to the reader."[48] Indeed, the humility of this narrative style—which alternates with a more conventionally omniscient one—harkens back to the *sermo humilis* as described by Auerbach: "accessible to all, descending to all men in loving-kindness, secretly sublime, at one with the whole Christian congregation."[49] The last sentence of the paragraph suggests such "at-oneness," and exhorts his readers to renounce the finalizing impulse the narrator has just relinquished in response to Fyodor.

Here, in his relationship to the character, the loving descent of the narrator is most evident. By pointing to the possibility of the two conflicting responses—histrionic, buffoonish exultation, and authentic, childlike grief—the narrator acknowledges Fyodor's possibilities. He descends from a position of reductive omniscience above Fyodor, to a position in which he can slow down and give him loving attention.[50] Summoning negative capability, he resists an all-too-neat explanation of Fyodor's apparently contradictory behavior, and reveals a respect for the complex "unfinalizability" of this other person, Fyodor Karamazov. In the narrator's "loving descent" from a finalizing position above Fyodor, to an open position beside him—and the other characters in the novel—we can discern an analogy to the kenosis of Christ. Katerina Clark and Michael Holquist first suggested this analogy in their pioneering biography of Bakhtin. In contrast to Flaubert, who situates himself in a controlling distance above his characters, "in the best kenotic tradition, Dostoevsky gives up the privilege of a distinct and higher being to descend into his text, to be among his creatures. Dostoevsky's distinctive image of Christ results in the central role of polyphony in his fiction."[51]

Polyphony can thus be seen as bearing a structural relation to the Augustinian *sermo humilis*. Near the end of *Mimesis,* Auerbach points explicitly to the link between Russian realism like Dostoevsky's, which "conceiv[es] of everyday things in a serious vein," and "the Christian and traditionally patriarchal concept of the creatural dignity of every human individual regardless of social rank and position . . ." He concludes that the Russian novel is "hence . . . fundamentally related rather to old Christian than to modern occidental realism," represented by Balzac, Flaubert, or Zola.[52] Dostoevsky sought to be a "realist in a higher sense," "to find the man [or the human] in a man" and to "depict all the depths of the human soul."[53] I believe that the term "Incarnational realism" aptly describes his novelistic vision of Dostoevsky in *The Brothers Karamazov,* that such realism is evident in the narrator's approach to Fyodor, and that it points to his affinities with Augustine.[54]

DESCENTS AND ASCENTS: *CONFESSIONS* AND *THE BROTHERS KARAMAZOV*

In Book 7 of the *Confessions,* the middle-aged Augustine recalls the agony of his irresolution, his inability to commit himself to the Catholic Christian faith with unity and wholeness of will. In their understanding of God as creating and sustaining spirit, and of evil as an absence of good, the Neoplatonists provide him with an alternative to the self-justifications and contradictions of the Manichees. But the Platonists lack any mention of the Word made flesh or of the kenosis of Christ:

In reading the Platonic books I found expressed in different words, and in a variety of ways, that the Son, "being in the form of the Father did not think it theft to be equal to God", because by nature he is that very thing. But that "he took on himself the form of a servant and emptied himself, was made in the likeness of men and found to behave as a man, and humbled himself being made obedient to death, even the death of the Cross so that God exalted him" from the dead "and gave him a name which is above every name, that at the name of Jesus every knee should bow, of celestial, terrestrial, and infernal beings, and every tongue should confess that Jesus is the Lord in the glory of God the Father" (Phil. 2:6-11)—that these books do not have.

(7.9.14)

As Augustine writes later, addressing the Platonists in the *City of God*: "It can only be that Christ came in humility, and you are proud."[55]

When Augustine follows the proud Platonist path, and wills a solitary ascent to the immutable realm, he falls fast:

[S]tep by step I ascended from bodies to the soul which perceives through the body. . . . But I did not possess the strength to keep my vision fixed. My weakness reasserted itself, and I returned to my customary condition. . . . I sought a way to obtain strength enough to enjoy you; but I did not find it until I embraced 'the mediator between God and man, the man Christ Jesus' (I Tim. 2:5) . . . Your Word, eternal truth, higher than the superior parts of your creation, raises those submissive to him to himself. In the inferior parts he built for himself a humble house of our clay. By this he detaches from themselves those who are willing to be made his subjects and carries them across to himself, healing their swelling and nourishing their love. They are no longer to place confidence in themselves, but rather to become weak by his sharing in our 'coat of skin' (Gen. 3:21). In their weariness they fall prostrate before this divine weakness which rises and lifts them up.

(7.17.23, 7.18.24)

Through the divine kenosis, the Logos descends and takes the weak form of an infant. Thus, paradoxically, God raises all who look upon his image and fall, both in neediness and praise. As Augustine puts it in one of his Christmas sermons, "Human Pride had pressed us so flat that only Divine Humility could raise us up."[56] Or later, in *City of God*: "[I]n a surprising way, there is something in humility to exalt the mind, and something in exaltation to abase it."[57]

Book 8 of *Confessions* depicts this passage of descent and ascent in its first, creatural mode of recognizing sin and accepting the need for grace. No longer a Manichee, Augustine recognizes his responsibility for the habits that have forged the chains of his divided will (8.5.10): "the turning and twisting first this way then that, of a will half wounded, struggling with one part rising up and the other part falling down" (8.7.19). He attempts to will himself to make the final step of conversion: "Inwardly I said to myself, 'Let it be now, let it be now'" (8.11.25). He hears the voice of another, Lady Continence, who exhorts him to relinquish his pride and self-sufficiency and humbly accept the grace of God: "Why are you relying on yourself, only to find yourself unreliable? Cast yourself upon him, do not be afraid. He will not withdraw himself so that you fall. Make the leap without anxiety; he will catch you and heal you'" (8.11.27). Augustine descends. He throws himself "down somehow under a certain figtree," weeps, and hears the voice of a child: "'Pick up and read. Pick up and read.'" He gets up, reads Romans 13, and "it was as if a light of relief from all anxiety flooded into my heart. All of the shadows of doubt were expelled" (8.12.29).

Augustine's conversion is complete. His convalescence will continue until his death,[58] but his descents will be more often marked by charitable service to others, especially in his exegesis of Scripture, modeled for him by Ambrose. Thus Augustine undergoes the passage that he exhorts his readers to take: "Come down so that you can ascend, and make your ascent to God. For it is by climbing against God that you have fallen" (4.12.19).

Book 9 follows the conversion scene with the *Confessions'* most potent image of ascent—at Ostia, with Monica, the woman whose presence and prayers have mediated God's grace for him, Augustine glimpses his paradisal home: "Our minds were lifted up by an ardent affection towards eternal being itself" (9.10.24).

In the "prosaics of conversion"[59] presented in *The Brothers Karamazov,* each of its main characters descends so as to ascend. As with Augustine, recognition of responsibility through the graciously mediatory presence of others, confession, and the exercise of loving humility usher in an experience of paradise: "[I]n truth we are each responsible to all for all, it's only that men don't know this. If they knew it, the world would be a paradise at once" (277). Zosima remembers these words of his brother Markel after recklessly committing himself to a duel and, in frustration, striking his servant Afanasy in the face. Zosima recalls his vicious deed and descends in an agony of shame: "I hid my face in my hands, fell on my bed, and broke into a storm of tears" (277). During an anguished night of penitence, he recognizes Afanasy as "another man, a fellow creature, made in the image and likeness of God" (277). The mediatory memory of Markel's words guides him toward confession: "'Afanasy,' I said, 'I gave you two blows on the face yesterday, forgive me,' . . . I dropped at his feet and bowed my head to the ground. 'Forgive me,' I said" (277).

As he will in his dying gesture, Zosima physically descends to the earth, in a gesture of profound humility. But the descent of the younger man is the first step "on the road" (281) of a new life of service, most tellingly as a confessor who attends kenotically to others.[60] His life culminates in his dying descent, his kiss of the earth, and ascent to paradise: "though suffering, he still looked at [his friends] with a smile, sank slowly from his chair on his knees, then bowed his face to the ground, stretched out his arms and as though in joyful ecstasy, praying and kissing the earth (as he taught), quietly and joyfully gave up his soul to God" (303). Both of Zosima's descents are Christological in form, but differ in the stage of spiritual journey they reflect. The first enacts the necessary descent of the repentant sinner. The second provides an iconic image of what every human sinner is called to become, and what Zosima has become—a saint. The image of the saint, his countenance and form, analogically reflects the salvific image of Christ, and "if it were not for the precious image of Christ before us, we should be undone and altogether lost" (299). Zosima's life and death provide such an iconic image.

Zosima's sacramental image impresses itself upon Alyosha Karamazov, the hero of the novel. In his three-month sojourn, Alyosha increasingly conforms to Christ's image. At his lowest point, after the death of

Zosima and the incarnational indignity of his beloved elder's body emitting an odor of corruption, Alyosha rebels against God's created order, and allows himself to be taken to Grushenka's house where he expects to be seduced. For a moment, haunted by Ivan's words of rebellion, Alyosha willfully relishes a fall into sin. To his surprise, Grushenka's humble attentiveness to his grief provides Alyosha with a Christlike icon that inspires his ascent. He implores the cynical Rakitin to "look at her," and praises Grushenka as a mediator of grace: "'You've raised my soul from the depths'" (329). When he returns to the monastery, Alyosha receives a vision of the risen Zosima alongside the risen Christ.[61] Out again in the open air, he bodily performs the pattern of descent and ascent: "he threw himself down on the earth"; he kisses it, waters it with his tears. "He had fallen on the earth a weak youth, but he rose up a resolute champion" (340-41).[62]

Alyosha can now serve as a "monk in the world" and among those he serves is his brother Dmitri, Grushenka's beloved. Dmitri undergoes his own passage of descent and ascent. After his humiliating interrogation for Fyodor's murder, which he did not commit, Dmitri publicly confesses his many faults and acknowledges his need for grace: "I understand now that such men as I need a blow, a blow of destiny to catch them as with a noose and bind them by a force from without. Never, never should I have risen of myself!" (481). Two months later, he confirms the necessity of his descent and the reality of his ascent to Alyosha: "A new man has risen up in me. He was hidden in me, but would never have come to the surface, if it hadn't been for this blow from heaven" (560). After his trial, he descends again in his capacity for humility: he agrees with Alyosha that whereas he must bear the cross, the path to fruitful sacrifice lies in escape to America and not in Siberia for a crime he has not committed. He must remain with Grushenka who, as she has done for Alyosha—and as Monica for Augustine—mediates God's grace for him.[63]

"THE CROSS NOT THE GALLOWS": IVAN KARAMAZOV'S DESCENT AND ASCENT

What of Ivan Karamazov, the proudest and most tormented of the three brothers?[64] On the surface, the sole kinship between Augustine and Ivan lies in their prodigious intellectual gifts. As a youth, Augustine does not recognize his intellect as a gift: "You know, Lord my God, that quick thinking and capacity for acute analysis are your gift. But that did not move me to offer them in sacrifice to you" (4.16.30). Neither does Ivan acknowledge his intelligence as a gift, although in Ivan's first appearance in the novel, the elder Zosima exhorts him to do so. When Ivan humbly reveals his need for help, and asks Zosima whether he will ever be able to answer the question of faith in the affirmative, Zosima responds

prophetically: "'If it can't be decided in the affirmative, it will never be decided in the negative. You know that that is the peculiarity of your heart, and all its suffering is due to it. But thank the Creator who [has] given you a lofty heart capable of such suffering; of thinking and seeking higher things, for our dwelling is in the heavens. God grant that your heart will attain the answer on earth, and may God bless your path'" (61). Surprisingly, Ivan humbly ascends to receive Zosima's blessing.

But does Ivan sustain the Christological passage of descent and ascent for which this moment plants a seed?[65] Much like the younger Augustine, Ivan is characterized by pride and consequent self-division. Ivan's "affirmative" side is best described by his brother Alyosha in their long conversation at the Metropolis tavern: "you are just a young and fresh and nice boy, green in fact!" Ivan responds "warmly and good-humoredly," and affirms to Alyosha his "thirst for life": "I love the sticky little leaves as they open in spring. I love the blue sky, I love some people, whom one loves you know sometimes without knowing why" (211). Ivan's love for life in its entire sensual splendor recalls the note of childlike wonder struck by the aged Augustine near the end of *City of God*: "How could any description do justice to all these blessings? The manifold diversity of beauty in sky and earth and sea; the abundance of light, and its miraculous loveliness, in sun and moon and stars; the dark shades of woods, the colour and fragrance of flowers; the multitudinous varieties of birds, with their songs and their bright plumage. . . ."[65] For Augustine, the "small physical size of a child" is emblematic of Christ's humility (*Conf.* 1.19.30). When Ivan is at his most childlike, as in this chapter with Alyosha, he reveals his nascent humility, his desire to accept the gracious help of others, and his love of abundant life: "'I don't want to wound my little brother who has been watching me with such expectation for three months. . . . Of course I am just such a little boy as you are . . . I want to be friends with you, Alyosha, for I have no friends and want to try it. Well, only fancy, perhaps I too accept God,' laughed Ivan, 'that's a surprise for you, isn't it'" (215).

Almost from the start of their conversation, however, Ivan reveals a self divided. On the one hand, he voices his humble longing for life and love. On the other, he asserts an antithetical impulse driven by pride, a desire to hurt others and himself. He declares it likely that he will "dash the cup to the ground" when he is thirty and commit suicide. When Alyosha tells Ivan of his beloved Katerina's illness, in one breath he declares that he "must find out" if she is all right, and in another "I won't go at all" (214). When Alyosha asks how the dreadful conflict between their brother Dmitri and their father, Fyodor, will end, Ivan lashes back by evoking Cain, the biblical figure who, for Augustine, ushers in the violence that characterizes the "city of man":[66] "'You are always harping upon it! What have I to do with it? Am I my brother Dmitri's keeper? . . . Well, damn it all, I can't stay here to be their keeper can I?'" (213). Ivan's self-bifurcation is evident the day before when, anticipating violence between his father and Dmitri, he says to Alyosha: "'Be sure, I shall always defend [Fyodor]. But in my wishes I reserve myself full latitude in this case" (131). In Bakhtin's cogent analysis, "Ivan . . . wants his father murdered, but he wants it under the condition that he himself remain not only externally but even *internally* uninvolved in it. He wants the murder to occur as an inevitability of fate, not only *apart from his will,* but in opposition to it."[67] Torturous self-division necessarily follows such conflicting desires. When the brothers part ways after their talk at the Metropolis, Ivan's "wishes" corrode his capacity to keep his promise: in a paralyzed state—one that recalls Augustine just before his conversion—Ivan allows Smerdyakov to manipulate him into leaving town even as he senses the looming violence.

Before Ivan's departure, however, Alyosha plants a seed in Ivan that bears fruit two months later, when he will confess to the court his role in his father's murder. While conversing in the Metropolis, Ivan tells Alyosha he has rejected God's world because he cannot accept any image of harmony and reconciliation founded upon the suffering of innocent children. With savage irony, he regales Alyosha with detailed stories, drawn from the newspapers, of the torture and killing of children. Alyosha responds by correcting Ivan, by passionately reminding him that any future harmony must be founded upon Christ, who is the only "Being [who] can forgive everything, all *and for all,* because he gave his innocent blood for all and everything" (227, italics in original). In the novel's vision, the faithful response to Christ's image is to accept one's responsibility "to all men and for all and everything" (149). The repeated phrase that links both claims—"All and for all"—suggests the synergistic relationship between Christ's sacrifice "for all" and the believer's sacrificial response to that gift. Indeed, in the Orthodox liturgy, which Dostoevsky would certainly have known, the priest elevates the Eucharistic gifts and prays, "Thine own of Thine own we offer unto Thee, on behalf of all and for all."[68] In Dostoevsky's novel, responsibility is encompassing—"for all"—as it is lived out within a fluid reality of interrelations, in which "all is like an ocean, all is flowing and blending; a touch in one place sets up movement at the other end of the earth" (299).[69] To accept and enact such responsibility is to conform to the kenotic pattern of Christ.[70]

Ivan responds to Alyosha with his "poem"-in-process, **"The Grand Inquisitor."** The cardinal rejects Christ because he has laid such an intolerable burden of freedom upon the shoulders of weak humanity. In league with Satan, he offers instead travesties of "miracle,

mystery, and authority." The Inquisitor's insistence that only an ascetic elite can carry the burden of freedom recalls the heresies which Augustine battled most fiercely in the second half of his life, Donatism and Pelagianism.[71] Indeed, Ivan's sympathy with the Inquisitor suggests his own stance of self-sufficiency. But as author, Ivan also creates an image of Christ that, as others have noted, is kenotic.[72] Ivan's Jesus is a loving, suffering servant who opens not his mouth. Christ's single response to the Inquisitor's long tirade is a kiss—and the kiss moves the Inquisitor profoundly. In the place of his univocal condemnation and rejection of Christ, the kiss creates an opening for another voice, a tone of possible, if eventual, acceptance. The Inquisitor's last word to Christ—"Go!"—suggests both rejection and generous release, for he had earlier announced his plan to burn Christ at the stake. The Inquisitor "adheres to his idea" but "the kiss glows in his heart" (243).

So too Ivan, whose poem reveals his creative capacity to imagine both self-annihilating pride (the Inquisitor) and transformative humility (Christ). When Ivan invites the rejection of his beloved brother—"The formula, 'all is lawful,' I won't renounce—will you renounce me for that, yes?"—Alyosha "softly kisse[s] him on the lips" (244). Ivan, "delighted," responds with new resolve, declares his love for Alyosha, and promises to see him before he ever dashes the cup to the ground. But the specter of Cain remains: "And about brother Dmitri too, I ask you specially never speak to me again" (244). As he walks away, toward Smerdyakov, Ivan sways, and "his right shoulder looked lower than his left" (245). We recall Augustine's image of himself, "fruitlessly divided" (2.1.1), "struggling with one part rising up and the other part falling down" (8.8.19).

Ivan wants freedom from responsibility, and thus from his human calling to conform to the pattern of Christ. In his pride and desire to remain blameless, he is akin to Augustine the Manichee, who blamed evil on the "alien nature" of matter: "It flattered my pride to be free of blame and, when I had done something wrong, not to make myself confess to you that you might heal my soul" (*Conf.* 5.10.18). But also like Augustine, Ivan is haunted by "a deep conscience" (622) that torments him when twice, atop the stairs, he hovers with malevolent, finalizing omniscience—unlike the narrator!—and listens to his father "stirring down below" (255-56), when he arrives in Moscow after making his getaway from domestic entanglements (260), and, about three months later, when he learns from Smerdyakov that the lackey has taken his teaching—that if there is no immortality then "all things are lawful" (599)—and run with it by pounding a paperweight into his father's skull.

At the end of his last talk with Smerdyakov, he is finally ready to take responsibility. He solemnly promises to confess his sins, before God and the public in court the next day: "'God sees,' Ivan raised his hand, 'perhaps I, too, was guilty; perhaps I really had a secret desire for my father's . . . death, but I swear I was not as guilty as you think, and perhaps I didn't urge you on at all'" (598). This is one of Ivan's truest, most integral utterances. Ivan is *not* the murderer as Smerdyakov—who denies his own freedom as a creature formed *imago Dei*—accuses him of being.[73] In perhaps the most resonant instance of what Mikhail Bakhtin calls "the penetrated word"—a word whose attentive authority not only penetrates the hearer but is itself penetrated by the authority of the divine word[74]—Alyosha whispers firmly to Ivan: "'It was not you who killed father, not you!'" (569). However, textual echoes again prove revealing: Alyosha repeats the phrase "not you" later that evening, when Ivan attributes to the Devil—with whom he has just been speaking—the idea that conscience is merely a habit to be dropped to allow the man-god to arise: "'It was he who said that, it was he who said that!' 'And not you, not you?' Alyosha could not help shouting, looking frankly at his brother" (620). When paired, Alyosha's two "not yous" can be read as an invitation to Ivan to discern and humbly accept his partial guilt, and to refrain from either of two prideful extremes: taking on all of the blame (a form of pride which denies his shameful tutelage of and manipulation by Smerdyakov) or rejecting acceptance for any of it (as Manicheanism enabled Augustine to do).

Augustine's thought illuminates numerous aspects of Ivan's Devil. First there is the catalyst for the Devil's appearance. After Ivan makes his solemn vow and departs Smerdyakov's with "something like joy . . . springing up in his heart" (600), Ivan saves the life of a drunken peasant he had earlier knocked into the snow and left for dead. "The acknowledgement of dependence, and with it, the capacity to be grateful, does not come easily, in Augustine's opinion."[75] Certainly not for Ivan: after arranging for the peasant's care, Ivan feels no gratitude. He ought to: by again chancing upon the peasant he has just avoided becoming a true murderer; further, for the first time he senses the peace of firm resolve, comparable to Augustine's luminous moment in the garden. Instead, Ivan is filled with self-satisfaction and asserts his complete autonomy: "'I am quite capable of watching myself, by the way,' he thought at the same instant, with still greater satisfaction, 'although they have decided that I am going out of my mind!'" (600).

In reviewing his life, Augustine came to realize "if denial of guilt was the first enemy, self-reliance was the last."[76] By separating "himself" from "them," Ivan corrodes the very foundation of his earlier resolve—an acceptance of his responsibility to others. If there is anything that Ivan ought to do at this point, it is to go straight to the prosecutor's with the information and evidence (the three thousand roubles surrendered by

Smerdyakov) he now has. This thought cuts into Ivan's self-satisfied musings and halts his steps: "Just as he reached his own house he stopped short, asking himself suddenly whether he hadn't better go at once now to the prosecutor and tell him everything. He decided the question by turning back to the house. 'Everything together tomorrow!' he whispered to himself, and, strange to say, almost all his gladness and self-satisfaction passed in one instant" (601). Self-enclosed, Ivan rejects both the subjugating claims of others and the limitations of time. Tomorrow will be too late to save Dmitri. But Ivan is not thinking of Dmitri. He wants his day in court "to say what he had to say boldly and resolutely and 'to justify himself to himself'" (601). Never is Ivan more "Pelagian" than in his desire to achieve his own justification.[77] From an Augustinian view, the consequence of such exalted self-assertion is a plunge into nightmare. As Augustine writes, "Nothing is superior to God; and that is why humility exalts the mind by making it subject to God. Exaltation, in contrast, derives from a fault in character, and spurns subjection for that very reason. Hence it falls away from him who has no superior, and falls lower in consequence."[78] Ivan denies his creatural limitations, even to the extent of self-justification. Hence his midnight visit from the Devil.

As Deborah Martinsen observes, Dostoevsky "sets up a series of implicit comparisons between Christ's incarnation and the devil's. Whereas Christ takes on human form to redeem the sins of the world, Ivan's devil takes on human form to attend a cocktail party" (210).[79] Such "comic contrasts" suggest travesty, a concept implicit in Augustine's conception of evil. Recall Augustine's extended reflection on his youthful theft of the pears, a gratuitous act that he later recognizes as "an assertion of possessing a dim resemblance to omnipotence" (2.6.14). He sees the theft as a travesty of God's power, as opposed to an analogical imitation of his love: "In their perverted way all humanity imitates you . . . and [they] exalt themselves against you. But even by thus imitating you they acknowledge that you are the creator of all nature and so concede that there is no place where they can entirely escape from you" (2.6.14). Augustine's analysis thus reveals perversity as parasitic upon the good. Recognizing in Dostoevsky's depiction of the Devil a travesty of the Incarnation corrects the claims, sometimes made, that Dostoevsky holds a "Manichean" view of equally oppositional good and evil.[80] In fact, as Augustine observes, evil is an absence, with no reality of its own: "The theft itself was a nothing" (2.8.16) for "as long as [things] exist, they are good. Accordingly, whatever things exist are good, and the evil into whose origins I was inquiring is not a substance, for if it were a substance, it would be good. . . . For our God has made 'all things very good' (Gen. 1:31)" (7.12.18). Dostoevsky's vision is similarly nondualistic: as a creature, the Devil was created as good by a superior, loving Creator; in his perversity, the Devil's capacity for good has deteriorated. In fact, the Devil's conflicting claims regarding his reality point up that his aim is to bring Ivan himself to nothing, the attempt at self-annihilation that is suicide.[81] In a travesty of Zosima's blessing, he admits as much: "But hesitation, suspense, conflict between belief and disbelief—is sometimes such torture to a conscientious man, such as you are, that it's better to hang oneself at once. . . . I lead you to belief and disbelief by turns, and I have my motive in it" (612). His motive is to impel Ivan toward the Judas-like path Smerdyakov takes—hanging himself upon the gallows.

"Tomorrow the cross, but not the gallows. No, I won't hang myself" (619), Ivan declares to Alyosha upon his beloved brother's arrival and his tempter's departure. But when Ivan arrives at the court the next day, it's clear that his commitment to the cross—to humbly confessing his involvement in Fyodor's murder—is not wholehearted. He shows up, and this in itself is significant given his earlier exits from social responsibilities. But his condition resembles Augustine's in the garden: his "soul hung back. It refused and had no excuse to offer" (8.7.18). Ivan has been called before the court, but hangs back "owing to an attack of illness or some sort of fit" (650). In retrospect, Augustine sees that "my madness with myself was part of the process of recovering health, and in the agony of death I was coming to life" (8.8.19). Similarly, when Ivan finally walks into the courtroom, "there was an earthy look in [his face], a look like a dying man's" (650). To bear fruit, the corn of wheat must fall to the ground and die.

Like Augustine, Ivan's will is painfully divided, and this division has bodily manifestations. Like Augustine—who "made many physical gestures of the kind men make when they want to achieve something and lack the strength" (8.8.20)—Ivan slowly enters the courtroom, listlessly responds to the questions, then turns to leave "without waiting for permission":

> But after taking four steps he stood still, as though he had reached a decision, smiled slowly, and went back.
>
> "I am like the peasant girl, your excellency . . . you know. How does it go? 'I'll stand up if I like, and I won't if I don't.' They were trying to put on her sarafan to take her to church to be married, and she said, 'I'll stand up if I like, and I won't if I don't.' . . . It's in some book about our folklore."
>
> (651)[82]

He is like Augustine facing his decision: "I was neither willing nor wholly unwilling. So I was in conflict with myself and was dissociated from myself" (8.10.22).

Ivan's comparison, drawn from Russian peasant tradition, reveals the most important link between Augustine's conversion and Ivan's confession: Marriage, in both Orthodox and Catholic tradition, entails not only a mutual exchange of vows, but a gift of grace that undergirds the unity forged in the sacrament. Like any sacrament, it entails free will and the gift of God's grace, a gift beyond the power of the person to control.

Further, in a marriage, grace is mediated by the community. For both Augustine and Ivan, communal mediation proves vital: for Augustine, the words and presence of Monica, Ambrose, and Alypius; for Ivan, the prayers of Katerina (568) and Alyosha, who reflects upon his brother the night before, "'The anguish of a proud determination. A deep conscience!' God, in Whom he disbelieved, and His truth were gaining mastery over his heart, which still refused to submit. . . . 'Either he will rise up in the light of truth, or . . . he'll perish in hate, revenging on himself and on everyone his having served the cause he does not believe in,' Alyosha added bitterly, and again he prayed for Ivan" (622).

In his first resolute utterance before the court, Ivan "rises in the light of truth." He presents the monetary evidence to the president of the court and precisely confesses his culpability: "I got [the money] from Smerdyakov, from the murderer yesterday. . . . I was with him just before he hanged himself. It was he, not my brother, who killed our father. He murdered him, and I incited him to do it. . . . Who doesn't desire his father's death?" (651). The last sentence indicates, however, that Ivan's will remains divided. In the pause suggested by the ellipsis, he casts a sideward glance at the gazing public, feels ashamed, and, in a proud attempt to escape responsibility and judgment, grabs the loophole of rationalization: I'm just like everybody else.[83] The "revenge" that Alyosha feared marks the "contemptuous" and "snarl[ing]" utterances that follow. Yet Ivan does not "perish in hate." Although he is dragged from the courtroom "yell[ing] and scream[ing] something incoherent"—a far cry indeed from the luminous peace Augustine experiences when he reads Romans 13 (*Conf.* 8.12.29)!—Ivan remains, like Augustine, in the process of being healed by grace.

Like Augustine, Ivan is ill, but his final words can be explicated, if not by his interlocutors in court, then by the attentive reader. His words reveal Ivan cooperating with grace, choosing the humility of Christ, the "God-man," and rejecting the pride inherent in his previous aspirations to "mangodhood," his declarations that "all things are lawful." The first shift from pride to humility occurs when Ivan moves from accusation back to confession: "'It's a spectacle they want! "Bread and Circuses." Though I am one to talk! Have you any water? Give me a drink for Christ's sake!' He suddenly clutched his head" (652). In his self-critical pause, Ivan senses the folly of his pride and, albeit angrily, asks for a symbolically suggestive form of help—a drink of water. Terras notes that Russian commentators locate here "a symbol of the 'living water' of faith," and that Ivan "here for the first time invokes the name of Christ."[84] Further, he invokes a promise of Christ that suggests Ivan may be moving from a stance of rebellion to discipleship: "whoever gives even a cup of cold water to one of these little ones in the name of a disciple—truly I tell you, none of these will lose their reward" (Matt. 10.42).[85]

Then, Ivan "confidentially" reveals his belief in the Devil and, implicitly, his desire to believe in God. Here are his final words:

> "He [the devil] is here somewhere, no doubt—under that table with the material evidence on it, perhaps. Where should he sit if not there? You see, listen to me. I told him I don't want to keep quiet, and he talked about the geological cataclysm . . . idiocy! Come, release the monster . . . he's been singing a hymn. That's because his heart is light! It's like a drunken man in the street bawling 'Vanka went to Petersburg,' and I would give a quadrillion quadrillions for two seconds of joy. You don't know me! Oh, how stupid all this business is! Come, take me instead of him! I didn't come for nothing. . . . Why, why is everything so stupid? . . ."
>
> (652)

Here Ivan rejects as "idiocy" his "Geological Cataclysm," the poem in which he had posited the "need to destroy the idea of God in man," so that, "Man will be lifted up by a spirit of Titanic pride and the man-god will appear" (616). He embraces instead an alternative vision, given form in a piece that Ivan composed at seventeen: A deceased atheist refuses to accept the beatific vision "on principle" and is given a purgative prescription "to walk a quadrillion kilometers in the dark" before arriving at "the gate of heaven" and finding "forgiveness" (610). In protest, he lies down for a thousand years, and then begins his walk. The moment he arrives in paradise, he "crie[s] out that those two seconds were quadrillions, raised to the quadrillionth power!" and sings "Hosannah!" (611). Ivan now declares his desire to take this purgative walk: "'I would give a quadrillion quadrillions for two seconds of joy.' 'You don't know me!'" No longer is Ivan so "very fond of being alone" (581). He now intensely wishes to be known by others, which suggests a kenotic emptying of his self-sufficiency. As Christos Yannaras writes: "What God asks of man, existentially alienated and degraded as he is, is an effort, however small, to reject his self-sufficiency, to resist its impulses and to will to live as one loving and loved. . . . It is the kenosis put into practice by Christ as man: the act of emptying out every element of individual autonomy and self-sufficiency and realizing the life of love and communion" (*The Freedom of Morality,* 52-53). Ivan here takes this "first step" of kenosis (*The Freedom of Morality,* 52). Like Mitya singing his "Hymn," he wants to give his life for

another, his innocent brother: "'Come, take me instead of him! I didn't come for nothing. . . . Why, why is everything so stupid?. . . .'"

Ivan sees all as "stupid" because his spiritual and psychological state is shattered. However, he can be understood as suffering less from "a breakdown" than from the experience of being broken down by God. Recall Alyosha's prayerful reflection from the night before: "God in Whom he disbelieved, and His truth were gaining mastery over his heart, which still refused to submit" (622). Like Augustine in the garden, Ivan struggles against, and gradually submits to God's truth. Recall Mitya's words: "A new man is risen up in me. He was hidden in me, but would never have come to the surface, if it hadn't been for this blow from heaven" (560). In Ivan's last tormented words and screams, the reader can discern Ivan's experiencing such a healing, restorative blow, especially given the scriptural echo that concludes the scene.

Ivan tries to gain control, to gather his stupefied wits by "slowly, and as it were reflectively, looking round him again." He is not expecting the bailiff's seizure of his arm:

> "What are you doing?" he cried, staring into the man's face, and suddenly seizing him by the shoulders, he flung him violently to the floor. But the police were on the spot and he was seized. He screamed furiously and all the time he was being removed, he yelled and screamed something incoherent.
>
> (652-53)

Terras notes, "in the original, *zavopil neistovym voplem* is clearly biblical language, bringing to mind the screams of the possessed healed by Jesus and the apostles (e.g., Luke 8:28, Acts 8:7)."[86] With this echo in mind, we can see Ivan's final, frenzied exit as an exorcism, a healing in process, an answer to the prayer of Alyosha (622), and Ivan's own "Give me a drink for Christ's sake." As in Augustine, free will and grace work cooperatively. Ivan's fractured words have enacted a kenotic outpouring of his old, diabolical pride. At the same time, such pride is being emptied by God in the transpiring of a healing exorcism. Ivan does not finally "'perish in hate'" as does Smerdyakov. Fitfully, he opens himself to helping and being helped by others. He thus approaches an imitation of the kenosis imaged by the cross. At the same time, he is visited—brutally, healingly—by the one who hung on that cross.

Like so much in *The Brothers Karamazov,* Ivan's future is left open-ended. Mitya's words—"He will recover" (822)—resonate, but Alyosha seems less sure: "'I too believe there is every hope that he will get well,' Alyosha observed anxiously" (723). At the end, he describes Ivan to the schoolboys as "lying on death's door" (733). No one in the courtroom—not even Aly-osha—has discerned that a healing is taking place. They see a young man descending into "brain fever" and collapse—an apparent evil. So, too, many readers. Vladimir Kantor, for example, writes: "Ivan identifies himself with Smerdyakov and the truth of repentance becomes a demonic farce, definitively confirming Mitya in the murder."[87] Ivan's confession ushers in the evil of Katerina's subsequent testimony, in which she frantically tries to protect Ivan by producing the letter that falsely incriminates Dmitri. Where is God's presence and grace in the midst of this brokenness? This is the question that haunts Alyosha: "Does the spirit of God move above that force [of the raging Karamazovs]?" (202). It is also the question that torments Ivan when he considers the suffering and death of children.

In a thoughtful essay, Caryl Emerson grapples with a version of this question when she considers the pain ushered in by another confession in the novel, that of Mikhail, Zosima's mysterious visitor.[88] Mikhail's family suffers the bitter consequences of his confession and subsequent death. In the short term, his confession may seem senseless, even selfish. But in the long, long term—in what Mikhail Bakhtin called "great time"[89]—evil events or seemingly evil events, may make sense: "Great time is that which enables the imperfectly realized meanings of a thing to stretch out and seek contexts in which they will be 'at home,' not forgotten, sympathetically understood."[90]

But is this to accept an image of harmony, of parallel lines meeting, of an edifice built upon the tears of an innocent child—the suspect theodicy rightly rejected by both Ivan and Alyosha? No. Ivan's non-Euclidean image turns out to be all too rational in its presumptuous claim that suffering will produce harmony; it reduces "great time" to formulaic cause and effect. In the novel, the realities of authoritative miracle and mystery abide. As Emerson points out, great time is "unpremeditated and often unexpected."[91] As Graham Pechey suggests, great time can discern "miracle" and ushers in "the order of grace: the future neither hoped for nor feared but in which our completion as finite beings lies" (cited by Emerson 171). Great time lends form to Augustine's promise in his *Enchiridion*: God, "the supremely Good [can turn] to good account even what is evil" (116). This is the "order of grace" glimpsed by the reader in the final scene of **The Brothers Karamazov**: a Eucharistic community founded upon the memory of a dead child.

For the reader, the ascent to this glimpse arrives after a difficult descent. Such is the demand of Dostoevsky's final novel, composed in the Christological spirit and form memorably voiced by St. Augustine: "Descend that you may ascend, and make your way to God."

Notes

1. Fyodor Dostoevsky, *The Brothers Karamazov*, ed. Ralph Matlaw, trans. Constance Garnett (New York: Norton Critical Edition, 1981), 299.

2. Victor Terras, *A Karamazov Companion: A Commentary on the Genesis, Language, and Style of Dostoevsky's Novel* (1981; repr., Madison: University of Wisconsin Press, 2002), 259.

3. Irina Kirillova, "Dostoevsky's Markings in the Gospel according to St. John," in *Dostoevsky and the Christian Tradition,* ed. George Pattison and Diane Oenning Thompson (Cambridge, UK: Cambridge University Press, 2001), 41-50, notes and comments on this as one of the passages that Dostoevsky marked in his copy of the New Testament (45).

4. St. Augustine, *Confessions* 7.20.26, trans. Henry Chadwick (Oxford, UK: Oxford University Press, 1991). Further references to Augustine in the text are to his *Confessions* and are all from this translation.

5. Dostoevsky's understanding of the salvific image of Christ is grounded in his faith in Christ's Incarnation, his humble acceptance of our human condition, as he writes: "It is not the morality of Christ, not the teachings of Christ that will save the world, but the belief that the word became flesh" (Geir Kjetsaa, *Fyodor Dostoevsky: A Writer's Life,* trans. Siri Hustvedt and David McDuff [New York: Fawcett Columbine, 1987], 223). In Dostoevsky's Orthodox tradition, as in the Catholic tradition, the Incarnation is understood not only as that which atones for human sinfulness, but as that event which makes possible at-one-ment between the human and Divine. Athanasius writes of Christ: "He, indeed, assumed humanity that we might become God" (*On the Incarnation,* trans. Sister Penelope Lawson, C.S.M.V [New York: Macmillan, 1946], 86). As Vladimir Lossky emphasizes, however, although humans are called to sanctification and ultimately deification, they have the freedom to reject that calling: "Man, according to St. Basil, is a creature who has received a commandment to become God. But this commandment is addressed to human freedom, and does not overrule it. As a personal being man can accept the will of God; he can also reject it" (*The Mystical Theology of the Eastern Church* [Crestwood, NY: St. Vladimir's Seminary Press, 1976], 124). Vladimir Soloviev, whom Dostoevsky befriended and whose 1878 lectures on Godmanhood he attended, reprises the doctrine of deification in his thought. Richard Gustafson writes: "The Russian Soloviev . . . made the Eastern Christian doctrine of deification, understood as

both the idealistic and realistic overcoming of division and death, the cornerstone of his theology of Godmanhood" in which "Christ's work [of kenosis] becomes our work too" ("Soloviev's Doctrine of Salvation," in *Russian Religious Thought,* ed. Judith Deutsch Kornblatt and Richard F. Gustafson [Madison: University of Wisconsin Press, 1996], 31-48, at 39). As Marina Kostalevsky has convincingly argued, "Soloviev's thought and personality are directly reflected in *The Brothers Karamazov*" (*Dostoevsky and Soloviev: The Art of Integral Vision* [New Haven, CT: Yale University Press, 1997], 2).

6. Judith Deutsch Kornblatt and Richard F. Gustafson, Introduction to *Russian Religious Thought,* ed. Judith Deutsch Kornblatt and Richard F. Gustafson (Madison: University of Wisconsin Press, 1996), 6.

7. Vladimir Lossky, *The Mystical Theology of the Eastern Church* (Crestwood, NY: St. Vladimir's Seminary Press, 1976), 197.

8. John D. Zizioulas, *Being as Communion: Studies in Personhood and the Church* (1985; repr., Crestwood, NY: St. Vladimir's Seminary Press, 1993), 182.

9. Christos Yannaras, *Elements of Faith: An Introduction to Orthodox Theology* (Edinburgh, UK: T & T Clark, 1991), 160.

10. Christos Yannaras, *The Freedom of Morality* (Crestwood, NY: St. Vladimir's Seminary Press, 1984), 151 n. 10.

11. Peter Brown, *Augustine of Hippo: A Biography* (London: Faber and Faber, 1967), 374. Brown here cites *De Peccatorum meritis et remissione et de baptismo parvulorum* (2.18.28). For a helpful discussion of Augustine's recognition of free will and its relation to grace, see Eleanore Stump, "Augustine and Free Will," in *The Cambridge Companion to Augustine,* ed. Eleonore Stump and Norman Kretzmann (Cambridge, UK: Cambridge University Press, 2001), 124-47. As Don Marshall observes in "The Conversion Scene in Augustine's *Confessions*" (Fletcher Jones Chair of Great Books Inaugural Lecture, Pepperdine University, January 22, 2004): "The conversion dramatizes a subtle and complex interaction between God's action of grace and Augustine's cooperating response" (21).

12. Liza Knapp, *The Annihilation of Inertia: Dostoevsky and Metaphysics* (Evanston, IL: Northwestern University Press, 1996), 17.

13. Knapp, *Annihilation of Inertia,* 233 n. 7. My thanks to Gary Rosenshield for also alerting me to this note to Augustine made by Dostoevsky: "The

note is from about 1875-76 when [Dostoevsky] was writing *A Raw Youth.* Solovyov is mentioned in the same note. But the notes are very random. The note occurs in volume 27, page 113. . . . Dostoevsky did not own any [books] by Augustine" (e-mail communication, April 26, 2004). For other discussions of Dostoevsky which suggest affinities with Augustine, see Rosenshield's "The Realization of the Collective Self: The Rebirth of Religious Autobiography in Dostoevsky's *Notes from the Hours of the Dead*" (*Slavic Review* 50, no. 2 [1991]" 317-27) and Robin Feuer Miller's "Dostoevsky and Rousseau: The Morality of Confession Reconsidered" (1979), repr. in *Dostoevsky: New Perspectives,* ed. Robert Louis Jackson (Englewood Cliffs, NJ: Prentice Hall, 1984), 82-98.

14. Avril Pyman, "Dostoevsky and the Prism of the Orthodox Semiosphere," in *Dostoevsky and the Christian Tradition,* ed. George Pattison and Diane Oenning Thompson (Cambridge, UK: Cambridge University Press, 2001), 103-15, at 105. "Cross-pollination" between East and West can be seen in Dostoevsky's preferences in pictorial art. Icons hold a central place in Orthodox worship. And Dostoevsky owned, for example, "a personal icon of the Mother of God, 'The Joy of All Who Sorrow,' (1874)," a copy of which graces the cover of *Dostoevsky and the Christian Tradition.* But in his study there also hung a print of Raphael's *Sistine Madonna.* Dostoevsky saw the original in Dresden and, according to his wife, Anna, saw in it 'the loftiest revelation of the human spirit.' He could sit for hours in front of this image of the Mother of God (Kjetsaa, *Fyodor Dostoevsky,* 205). In Eastern Orthodox theology, Raphael's status is akin to Augustine's: the Italian Renaissance, which Raphael represents, marks the decisive, deviant turn from the Orthodox iconic tradition. Leonid Ouspensky, for example, describes Raphael's *Madonna del Granduca* as "an individual interpretation or an abstract or more-or-less deteriorated understanding" as opposed to the "truth taught by the Church" in the Orthodox icon of the Virgin (*Theology of the Icon,* vol. 1 and 2, trans. Anthony Gythiel [1978; repr., Crestwood, NY: St. Vladimir's Seminary Press, 1992], 184). In Dostoevsky's novel, Father Zosima reveals an ecumenical visual sensibility similar to his novelistic creator's: In his room hangs "one huge, very ancient icon of the Virgin," but also "a Catholic cross of ivory, with a Mater Dolorosa embracing it, and several foreign engravings from the great Italian artists of past centuries. Next to these costly and artistic engravings were several of the roughest

Russian prints of saints, martyrs, prelates, and so on, such as are sold for a few farthings at all the fairs" (32).

15. Joseph Frank writes: "in one of the few nonpartisan studies of Dostoevsky's Christology, Ryszard Przybylski links his ideas with those of the seventh-century theologian Maximus Confessor. . . . See Ryszard Przybylski, *Dostojewski I 'Przeklete Problemy'* (Warsaw, 1946), 219-46" (*Dostoevsky: The Stir of Liberation, 1860-1865* [Princeton, NJ: Princeton University Press, 1986], 386 n. 6).

16. Jaroslav Pelikan, Introduction to *Maximus Confessor: Selected Writings,* trans. George C. Berthold (New York: Paulist Press, 1985), 1-13, at 3.

17. Vladimir Solovyov [Soloviev], *Lectures on Divine Humanity,* trans. Peter Zouboff, rev. and ed. Boris Jakim (Hudson, NY: Lindisfarne Press, 1995), 94-95. David S. Cunningham, "*The Brothers Karamazov* as Trinitarian Theology," in *Dostoevsky and the Christian Tradition,* ed. George Pattison and Diane Oenning Thompson (Cambridge, UK: Cambridge University Press, 2001), 135-55, writes: "As a number of commentators have noted, the shape of *The Brothers Karamazov* was heavily influenced by Dostoevsky's relationship with Vladimir Solovyov. This relationship may very well have helped to intensify the novelist's fascination with triads and triplicity" (142). Cunningham too points to Solovyov's references to Augustine (143).

18. Charles Taylor notes these latter two triads in his discussion of Augustine in *Sources of the Self: The Making of the Modern Identity* (Cambridge, MA: Harvard University Press, 1989), 137.

19. Garry Wills, *Saint Augustine* (New York: Penguin, 1999), 93.

20. See, for example, Karl Joachim Weintraub, *The Value of the Individual: Self and Circumstance in Autobiography* (Chicago: University of Chicago Press, 1978), who writes, "The self-clarification is steady, but gradual. Seeking-Finding-Praising, these are the never-ending activities of man on earth" (26). Frederick Crossan, "Structure and Meaning in St. Augustine's *Confessions,*" *The Augustinian Tradition,* ed. Gareth B. Matthews (Berkeley: University of California Press, 1999), 27-38, sees the descent/ascent pattern in *Confessions* as itself marked by triads: "[B]ooks 2, 3, and 4 mark stages of descent, so books 6, 7, and 8 mark successive stages of ascent. Moreover, these three stages of descent are structured according to the triad that remained central to Augustine's thought about religion over the course of his life,

from the *De vera religione* to the *Enchiridion.* That triad is found in the scriptural text about the concupiscence of the flesh, the concupiscence of the eyes (i.e., of the mind), and the ambition of this world" (31).

21. Taylor, *Sources of the Self,* 136-37.

22. Cunningham, "*The Brothers Karamazov,*" 142.

23. Thomas Williams, "Biblical Interpretation," in *Cambridge Companion to Augustine,* 59-70, writes: "Perhaps [Augustine's] greatest work on scripture is the *In Joannis evangelium tractatus* (406-22) (the dates are much disputed), a collection of sermons treating the whole of the Gospel. It is a masterly blend of literal and allegorical exegesis, philosophical speculation, moral exhortation, and theological polemic" (60). Irina Kirollova, "Dostoevsky's Markings," observes that in Dostoevsky's copy of the New Testament, "the greatest number of markings comes in the Gospel of St John. . . . There is a direct correlation between the Christological thrust of St John's Gospel, Dostoevsky's lifelong veneration of Christ and the number of markings" (42).

24. Irina Kirillova, "Dostoevsky's Markings," writes: "Dostoevsky's markings [in the New Testament] begin after 1850, the year he was given the book of the Gospels by one of the Decembrist wives, in exile in Tobolsk. It was then that he developed his lifelong habit of not only 'dipping' into the text continuously, but also of opening it at random and seeing providential guidance in the passages that presented themselves in this way" (43).

25. Nina Perlina, *Varieties of Poetic Utterance: Quotation in the Brothers Karamazov* (Lanham, MD: University Press of America, 1985), 13.

26. Erich Auerbach, "Figura," in *Scenes from the Drama of European Literature* (1959; repr. Minneapolis: University of Minnesota Press, 1984), 11-76, at 42. Others employ Auerbach's insights into figural interpretation in discussions of *The Brothers Karamazov.* For example, Diane Oenning Thompson, *The Brothers Karamazov and the Poetics of Memory* (Cambridge, UK: Cambridge University Press, 1991), writes: "For the modern realist there is only this world. But for Dostoevsky, this world, while it never loses its concrete historicity, reflects 'other worlds' which though invisible are just as real as this one, perhaps even more real, worlds which have been revealed in the Bible from which he took his prototypes. And just here is where Auerbach's analysis of figural interpretation proves so illuminating for the poetics of memory in Dostoevsky's last novel" (224). See too Harriet Murav's related discussion of "reca-

pitulation" in *Holy Foolishness: Dostoevsky's Novels and the Poetics of Cultural Critique* (Stanford, CA: Stanford University Press, 1992), 148-69.

27. Brown, *Augustine of Hippo,* 254.

28. Hans Urs von Balthasar, *The Glory of the Lord: A Theological Aesthetics,* vol. 2, *Studies in Theological Style: Clerical Styles,* trans. Andrew Louth, Francis McEonagh, and Brian McNeil, C.R.V., ed. John Riches (San Francisco, Ignatius Press, 1984), 95.

29. Balthasar, *The Glory of the Lord,* 135.

30. Fyodor Dostoevsky, *Selected Letters of Fyodor Dostoyevsky,* ed. Joseph Frank and David I. Goldstein (New Brunswick, NJ: Rutgers University Press, 1987), 68.

31. Robert Louis Jackson, *Dostoevsky's Quest for Form: A Study of His Philosophy of Art,* 2nd ed. Bloomington, IN: Physsandt, 1978), xiv-xv.

32. Fyodor Dostoevsky, *The Idiot,* trans. David Magarshack (New York: Penguin 1955), 394.

33. In the conclusion of his "Letter to Artists" (April 4, 1999, http://www.vatican.va/holy_father/john_paul_ii/letters/documents/hf_jp-ii_let_23041999_artists_en.html [accessed July 15, 2004]), Pope John Paul II juxtaposes Myshkin's words about the salvific potential of beauty with Augustine's famous prayer in *Confessions*: "Late have I known you, beauty so old and so new" (10.27.38). "'Beauty will save the world—two kinds of beauty," Dostoevsky observes, without further explanation in one of his notebooks to *The Idiot.* "The world will become the beauty of Christ," Dostoevsky answers in one of his notes to *The Devils.* Robert Louis Jackson notes these quotations in the best discussion of this subject in *Dostoevsky's Quest for Form*: 40. See also James P. Scanlan's fine *Dostoevsky the Thinker* (Ithaca, NY: Cornell University Press, 2002), chap. 4, "The Logic of Aesthetics."

34. Erich Auerbach, "Sermo humilis," in *Literary Language and Its Public in Late Antiquity and in the Middle Ages,* trans. Ralph Manheim (Princeton, NJ: Princeton University Press, 1965), 27-66, at 37.

35. Auerbach, "Sermo humilis," 39.

36. Auerbach, "Sermo humilis," 40.

37. Auerbach, "Sermo humilis," 41.

38. Auerbach, "Sermo humilis," 43.

39. Auerbach, "Sermo humilis," 45.

40. Before his conversion, Augustine's "inflated conceit shunned the Bible's restraint. . . . I disdained to be a little beginner. Puffed up with pride, I considered myself a mature adult" (3.5.9). After his conversion, Augustine "recognized the 'lowliness' of the Biblical style, which . . . [given the Incarnation] possessed a new and profound sublimity" (Auerbach, "Sermo humilis," 47). Auerbach goes on to describe what might be called the "Augustinian" as opposed to "Augustan aesthetic": "The lowly or humble style is the only medium in which such sublime mysteries can be brought within the reach of men. It constitutes a parallel to the Incarnation, which was also a *humilitas* in the same sense, for men could not have endured the splendor of Christ's divinity. But the Incarnation, as it actually happened on earth, could only be narrated in a lowly and humble style. The birth of Christ in a manger in Bethlehem, his life among fishermen, publicans, and other common men, the passion with its realistic and scandalous episodes—none of this could have been treated appropriately in the lofty oratorical, tragic, or epic style. According to the Augustan esthetic, such matters were worthy, at best, of the lower literary genres. But the lowly style of Scripture encompasses the sublime. Simple, vulgar, and crassly realistic words are employed, the syntax is often colloquial and inelegant; but the sublimity of the subject matter shines through the lowliness, and there is hidden meaning at every turn. . . . The common denominator of this style is its humility" (51-52).

41. George P. Fedotov, *The Russian Religious Mind (I)* (Cambridge, MA: Harvard University Press, 1946), 127-28.

42. Joseph Frank, *Dostoevsky: The Seeds of Revolt, 1821-1849* (Princeton, NJ: Princeton University Press, 1976), 48.

43. Steven Cassedy, "P. A. Florensky and the Celebration of Matter," in *Russian Religious Thought,* 95-111, at 95. Cassedy points specifically to Dostoevsky's recording of these intuitions, "as he kept vigil over the body of his first wife in April of 1864," and wrote of "the highest use [man] can make of his individual person, of the fullness of the development of his self, is, as it were, to annihilate this self. . . ." (96). I would add that by 1880, when he wrote *The Brothers Karamazov,* Dostoevsky no longer saw the human practice of kenosis as self-annihilation but, rather, as the practice of attentive, active love. See also Margaret Ziolkowski, "Dostoevsky and the Kenotic Tradition," in *Dostoevsky and the Christian Tradition,* 31-40.

44. Fyodor Dostoevsky, *The Unpublished Dostoevsky: Diaries and Notebooks,* 3 vol., ed. Carl R. Proffer,

trans. Arline Boyer and David Lapeza (Ann Arbor, MI: Ardis, 1976), 41.

45. Mikhail Bakhtin, *Problems of Dostoevsky's Poetics,* ed. and trans. Caryl Emerson (1963; repr., Minneapolis: University of Minnesota Press, 1984), 63.

46. Terras, *A Karamazov Companion,* 87.

47. Miller, "Dostoevsky and Rousseau," 16.

48. Perlina, *Varieties of Poetic Utterance,* 80. Perlina draws here on Kljuchevsky's scholarly work on hagiographic style.

49. Auerbach, "Sermo humilis," 65.

50. In *Toward a Philosophy of the Act* (trans. and notes Vadim Liapunov, ed. Vadim Liapunov and Michael Holquist [Austin: University of Texas Press, 1993]), Bakhtin writes of the artistic creator's need "to slow down and *linger intently* over an object. . . . Only love is capable of being aesthetically productive . . ." (64, italics in original). In *A Theology of Reading: The Hermeneutics of Love* (Boulder, CO: Westview Press, 2001), Alan Jacobs helpfully links both Bakhtin and Augustine in developing what he calls "the hermeneutics of love."

51. Katerina Clark and Michael Holquist, *Mikhail Bakhtin* (Cambridge, MA: Harvard University Press, 1984), 249.

52. Erich Auerbach, *Mimesis: The Representation of Reality in Western Literature,* trans. Willard R. Trask (Princeton, NJ: Princeton University Press, 1953), 521.

53. Donald Fanger, *Dostoevsky and Romantic Realism* (Cambridge, MA: Harvard University Press, 1965), 215.

54. A similar term is used by at least two current Russian commentators. In his Preface to the 2002 edition of *A Karamazov Companion,* Terras writes of the current critical return in Russia to Dostoevsky's Christian vision: "V. N. Zakharov, competent and energetic leader of this movement, has coined the term *khristianskii realizm* (Christian realism) by which he designates the manner of Dostoevsky's greatest novels" (xx). In her Translator's Afterword to Vladimir Kantor's "Pavel Smerdyakov and Ivan Karamazov: The Problem of Temptation" (trans. Caryl Emerson, in *Dostoevsky and the Christian Tradition,* 189-220), Caryl Emerson identifies what Kantor calls Dostoevsky's "Christian realism" (220).

55. St. Augustine, *City of God* 10.29, trans. Henry Bettenson (New York: Penguin, 1984).

56. St. Augustine, *Sermons to the People,* trans. and ed. William Griffin (New York: Image, 2002), 83.

57. Augustine, *City of God,* 14.13.

58. As Peter Brown, *Augustine of Hippo,* aptly writes, Book 10 of *The Confessions,* in which Augustine looks to his present life in 397 as bishop of Hippo, presents "the self portrait of a convalescent" (177).

59. With this term, I echo John Freccero's *Poetics of Conversion* (*Dante: The Poetics of Conversion,* ed. Rachel Jacoff [Cambridge, MA: Harvard University Press, 1986]), which, especially in its first chapter, "The Prologue Scene," illuminates the Augustinan patterns in Dante's *Commedia.* Freccero's work is utilized in Harriet Murav's illuminating discussion of *The Brothers Karamazov* in *Holy Foolishness.* The term "prosaics" was coined by Gary Saul Morson and Caryl Emerson in *Mikhail Bakhtin: The Creation of a Prosaics* (Stanford, CA: Stanford University Press, 1990). More recently, Morson has employed the term "mythic prosaic" to describe the art of *The Brothers Karamazov* in his "The God of Onions: *The Brothers Karamazov* and the Mythic Prosaic," in *"A New Word" on The Brothers Karamazov,* ed. Robert Louis Jackson (Evanston, IL: Northwestern University Press, 2004), 107-24.

60. For an analysis of Zosima as confessor, see my essay, "Zosima, Mikhail, and Prosaic Confessional Dialogue" in *Studies in the Novel,* 27, no. 1 (Spring 1995): 63-86.

61. Diane Oenning Thompson, "Problems of the Biblical Word in Dostoevsky's Poetics," in *Dostoevsky and the Christian Tradition,* 69-99, aptly claims that Alyosha here "glimps[es] the beatific vision" (93). In her book-length study, *The Brothers Karamazov and the Poetics of Memory,* Thompson draws briefly on Augustine's discussion of memory in the *Confessions* in an analysis of Ivan's forgetting (186). The power of salvific memory, as opposed to destructive forgetting, is a vital theme in *The Brothers Karamazov.*

62. I first understood the significance of this descent/ascent pattern by reading, over twenty years ago, William F. Lynch's discussion of this scene in *Christ and Apollo. The Dimensions of Literary Imagination* (1960; repr., Wilmington, DE: ISI Books, 2004), 40-41.

63. See my essay, "Dostoevsky and the Ethical Relation to the Prisoner," *Renascence* 48, no. 4 (Summer 1996): 259-78, for a detailed defense of Dmitri's decision to escape to America.

64. Smerdyakov is, of course, the fourth, though unacknowledged brother. On Smerdyakov's night-

stand sits a copy of *The Sayings of the Holy Father Isaac the Syrian.* (The "big yellow book" [592] hides the money, but has Smerdyakov left it unread?) One of the seventh-century Isaac's sayings has a remarkably Augustinian ring: "Dive away from sin into yourself and there you will find the steps by which to ascend" (34).

65. Augustine, *City of God,* 22.24.

66. In *City of God,* Augustine writes of Cain: "The first founder of the earthly city was . . . a fratricide, overcome by envy, he slew his own brother, a citizen of the Eternal City, on pilgrimage in this world" (15.5)

67. Bakhtin, *Problems of Dostoevsky's Poetics,* 258.

68. See *The Divine Liturgy According to St. John Chrysostom,* 2nd ed. (South Canaan, PA: St. Tikhon's Seminary Press, 1977), 65. My thanks to Father Steven Belonick of St. Vladimir's Seminary for his help in locating this Eucharistic prayer in the liturgy.

69. For an excellent discussion of Dostoevsky's "Ethics of Altruism" that links his "mystical sense of responsibility" with its "correspondence with the ideal image of Christ, who in the atonement took upon himself the sins of all humanity" (109), see James P. Scanlan's *Dostoevsky the Thinker.*

70. See also pages 277 and 282, in which Zosima repeats this phrase. Mitya's version appears in his "Hymn": "we are all responsible for all" (560). In my reading, the echo of "all for all" implies that in our "intercreatural" relations (Graham Pechey's Augustinian coinage ["Intercultural, Intercreatural: Bakhtin and the uniqueness of 'Literary Seeing,'" in *Bakhtin and his Intellectual Ambience,* ed. Boguslaw Zylko (Gdansk, Poland: Wydawnictwo Uniwersytetu Gdanskiego, 2002]), we cooperatively share in the salvific work of Christ when we take up our responsibility and serve in humble, active love. The notion of the cooperative "fellow worker" is an important one in Orthodox thought. As Timothy (Kallistos) Ware, *The Orthodox Church* (New York: Penguin, 1993), writes: "To describe the relation between the grace of God and human freedom, Orthodoxy uses the term cooperation or synergy (*synergeia*); in Paul's words: 'We are fellow-workers (*synergoi*) with God' (1 Corinthians 3.9)" (221). *The Catechism of the Catholic Church.* (New York: Catholic Book Publishing Company, 1994) understands this relation very similarly and draws on Augustine in its articulation: "God brings to completion in us what he has begun, 'since he who completes his work by cooperating with our will began by working so that we might will it': 'Indeed we also work, but

we are only collaborating with God who works, for his mercy has gone before us. It has gone before us so that we may be healed, and follows us so that once healed, we may be given life; it goes before us so that we may be called, and follows us so that we may be glorified; it goes before us so that we may live devoutly, and follows us so that we may always live with God: for without him we can do nothing.' God's free initiative demands *man's free response,* for God has created man in his own image by conferring on him, along with freedom, the power to know him and love him" (2001-2002). The first imbedded quotation here is from Augustine's *De gratia et libero arbitrio,* 17: PL 44, 901; the second is from Augustine's *De natura et gratia,* 31: PL 44, 264.

71. As Peter Brown, *Augustine of Hippo,* writes: "To [Augustine] it seemed that the new claims made by the Pelagians, that they could achieve a church 'without spot or blemish', merely continued the assertions of the Donatists, that only they belonged to just such a church. He was in no mood to tolerate the *coteries* of 'perfect' Christians, that had sprung up in Sicily and elsewhere under Pelagian influence" (348).

72. See, for example, Terras, *A Karamazov Companion,* 229.

73. For recent analyses which place a strong emphasis upon Smerdyakov's manipulation and culpability, see Kantor, "Pavel Smerdyakov and Ivan Karamazov," in *Dostoevsky and the Christian Tradition,* 189-220, and Marina Kanevskaya, "Smerdyakov and Ivan: Dostoevsky's *The Brothers Karamazov,*" *The Russian Review* 61 (July 2002): 358-76.

74. Bakhtin writes that "the penetrated word . . . is . . . capable of actively and confidently interfering in the interior dialogue of the other person, helping that person to find his own voice" (*Problems of Dostoevsky's Poetics,* 242). I employ Bakhtin's notion of the penetrated word and discuss its kenotic dimension in "Zosima, Mikhail, and Prosaic Confessional Dialogue."

75. Brown, *Augustine of Hippo,* 326.

76. Brown, *Augustine of Hippo,* 176.

77. Regarding this moment, Bakhtin aptly cites an 1877 letter of Dostoevsky to G. A. Kovner: "it is still better if I justify you rather than you justify yourself" (*Problems of Dostoevsky's Poetics,* 257). In his 1961 notes "Toward a Reworking of the Dostoevsky Book," Bakhtin writes, "Justification cannot be self-justification, recognition cannot be self-recognition. I receive my name from others . . . ." (*Problems of Dostoevsky's Poetics,* 288).

78. Augustine, *City of God* 14.13.

79. Deborah Martinsen, *Surprised by Shame: Dostoevsky's Liars and Narrative Exposure* (Columbus: Ohio State University Press, 2003) 210. Martinsen continues: "Whereas Christ suffers mockery and humiliation, Ivan's devil suffers the air's iciness. Whereas Christ is put to death, Ivan's devil catches cold and suffers from rheumatism. These comic contrasts emphasize Christ's transcendence and the devil's worldliness, thereby reflecting the struggle in Ivan's soul between ethical action and earthly desire" (210).

80. Such claims can point, for example, to two moments in the novel: Dmitri's claim to Alyosha that "God and the Devil are fighting [and] the battlefield is the heart of man" (97), and the Devil's claim to Ivan that if he were to "bawl hosannah, . . . the indispensable minus would disappear at once. . . . And that would mean, of course, the end of everything. . . ." (615). Robin Feuer Miller, "Dostoevsky and Rousseau," cites the words of Mikhail, Zosima's mysterious visitor, "The Lord vanquished the devil in my heart" (*BK*, 291) and claims that the words "recall Mitya's and Dostoevky's own attraction to the Manichean heresy" (78). If, however, Dostoevsky understands the Devil as creature, created by a superior, loving Creator, who has fallen through perverse choices (among them, lying), the charge of Manicheism cannot stick. In such a view, God's grace must always be stronger than any power of the Devil, seductive as his temptations may be. A person's will may be divided into warring halves, but that does not mean it is composed of two antithetical natures or substances, as the Manicheans claimed. See *Conf.*, 8.9.21-8.10.24.

81. Book 6 concludes with Zosima's discourse on hell, where like "the starets Leonid, in effect the founder of eldership (*starchestvo*) at Optina Pustyn" (Sergei Hackel, "The Religious Dimension: Vision or Evasion? Zosima's Discourse in *The Brothers Karamazov*," in *New Essays on Dostoevsky*, ed. M. V. Jones and G. Terry [Cambridge, UK: Cambridge University Press, 1983], 139-68, at 156), he prays for those who commit suicide, and reflects upon those who "remain proud and fierce even in hell," who "yearn for death and annihilation. But they will not attain to death. . . ." (302). Evil itself is an absence, but the creature can never annihilate what God has created. In Zosima's unorthodox and provocatively loving view, God continues to love and call the souls in hell (302). Given the image of this divine, loving call-

ing, I cannot agree with Hackel when he argues that "some references to God towards the very end of [Zosima's discourse on hell] hardly compensate for [God's] absence hitherto" (155). For an appreciation of Zosima's words (and Grushenka's apposite legend of "the onion"), see Chapter 3 of Balthasar's *Dare We Hope "That All Men Be Saved"?* (trans. David Kipp and Lothar Krauth [San Francisco: Ignatius Press, 1988]).

Balthasar concludes the chapter with a discussion of Book 21 of *City of God*, which presents Augustine's very different, very closed image of hell, but implicitly suggests a possible bridge between Zosima and Augustine by arguing the "foolish[ness]" of tying "the so incomprehensibly rich and many-sided theology of Augustine down to this single point. If his uncountable thought-provoking ideas do not permit being unified into a consistent system, they are, nevertheless, linked to one another in a living way and point together toward a center that is none other than the heart aflame with love that the saint is repeatedly depicted as holding in his hand. If that is true—and the great Tradition has always seen the great 'Father of the Western world' in this way—then we are not entitled to regard his hard eschatological statements, which grew still harder in his old age, simply as a turning away from his innermost concern" (71).

82. Victor Terras, *A Karamazov Companion*, glosses Ivan's words: "An allusion to the wedding ritual of the Russian peasants, where the bride would go through a routine of wavering between joining her betrothed and refusing to do so"(409).

83. In his analysis of the failed confessional discourse of Dostoevsky's underground man, Bakhtin observes that his "word about himself is not only a word with a sideward glance; it is also . . . a word with a loophole" (*Problems of Dostoevsky's Poetics* 232-33).

84. Terras, *A Karamazov Companion*, 410.

85. Augustine comments on this line in *On Christian Doctrine* 4.18.37, trans. D. W. Robertson, Jr. (Indianapolis: Bobbs-Merrill, 1981): "Unless, perhaps, because a cup of cold water is a small and most insignificant thing, we should also regard as small and most insignificant the promise of the Lord that he who gives such a cup to one of his disciples 'shall not lose his reward'" (145). Hanging upon the cross, Jesus says, "I am thirsty" (John 19.27), which suggests another link between Ivan and Christ. My thanks to Maire Mullins for reminding me of this scriptural passage, and for her helpful editorial suggestions throughout this essay.

86. Terras, *A Karamazov Companion*, 410.

87. Kantor, "Pavel Smerdyakov and Ivan Karamazov," 217.

88. Caryl Emerson, "Zosima's 'Mysterious Visitor': Again Bakhtin on Dostoevsky, and Dostoevsky on Heaven and Hell," in *"A New Word,"* 155-79. Robin Feuer Miller, *The Brothers Karamazov: Worlds of the Novel* (New York: Twayne, 1992), also links Ivan with Mikhail: "Ivan's predicament recalls that of Zosima's mysterious visitor; authentic confessions are rarely believed. The true confession, in earthly terms, usually seems gratuitous and impotent; these are the deceptive earmarks of its unassailable authenticity" (125). Although she develops her argument with different emphases, Miller too sees in Ivan "a spiritual process of recovery" (125).

89. Mikhail Bakhtin, "Toward a Methodology for the Human Sciences," in *Speech Genres and Other Late Essays,* ed. Caryl Emerson and Michael Holquist, trans. Vern W. McGee (Austin: University of Texas Press, 1986), 159-72. In her poem "Sacrifice," Jeanne Murray Walker evokes the semantic sense of "great time": "*Sacrifice* / is slow as a funeral procession / in rush-hour traffic, the sort of word / other words pass, honking . . ." (in *A Deed to the Light* [Urbana: University of Illinois Press, 2004], 17). As Bakhtin writes: "Nothing is absolutely dead: every meaning will have its homecoming festival. The problem of *great time*" ("Methodology," 170).

90. Emerson, "Zosima's 'Mysterious Visitor'," 170.

91. Emerson, "Zosima's 'Mysterious Visitor'," 171.

References

Athanasius, St. *On the Incarnation.* Trans. Sister Penelope Lawson, C.S.M.V. New York: Macmillan, 1946.

Auerbach, Erich. "Figura." In *Scenes from the Drama of European Literature.* Reprint, Minneapolis: University of Minnesota Press, 1984. Pp. 11-76.

———. *Mimesis: The Representation of Reality in Western Literature.* Trans. Willard R. Trask. Princeton, NJ: Princeton University Press, 1953.

———. "Sermo humilis." In *Literary Language and Its Public in Late Antiquity and in the Middle Ages.* Trans. Ralph Manheim. Princeton, NJ: Princeton University Press, 1965. Pp. 27-66.

Augustine, St., *City of God.* Trans. Henry Bettenson. New York: Penguin, 1984.

———. *Confessions.* Trans. Henry Chadwick. Oxford, UK: Oxford University Press, 1991.

———. *Enchiridion on Faith, Hope, and Love.* Trans. J. B. Shaw. Washington, DC: Regenery, 1996.

———. *On Christian Doctrine.* Trans. D. W. Robertson, Jr. Indianapolis: Bobbs-Merrill, 1981.

———. *Sermons to the People.* Trans. and Ed. William Griffin. New York: Image, 2002.

Bakhtin, Mikhail. *Problems of Dostoevsky's Poetics.* Ed. and Trans. Caryl Emerson. 1963. Reprint, Minneapolis: University of Minnesota Press, 1984.

———. "Toward a Methodology for the Human Sciences." In *Speech Genres and Other Late Essays.* Ed. Caryl Emerson and Michael Holquist. Trans. Vern W. McGee. Austin: University of Texas Press, 1986. Pp. 159-72.

———. *Toward a Philosophy of the Act.* Trans and Notes Vadim Liapunov. Ed. Vadim Liapunov and Michael Holquist. Austin: U of Texas P, 1993.

Balthasar, Hans Urs von. *Dare We Hope "That All Men Be Saved"?* Trans. David Kipp and Lothar Krauth. San Francisco: Ignatius Press, 1988.

———. *The Glory of the Lord: A Theological Aesthetics.* Vol. 2, *Studies in Theological Style: Clerical Styles.* Trans. Andrew Louth, Francis McEonagh, and Brian McNeil, C.R.V. Ed. John Riches. San Francisco: Ignatius Press, 1984.

Brown, Peter. *Augustine of Hippo: A Biography.* London: Faber and Faber, 1967.

Cassedy, Steven. "P. A. Florensky and the Celebration of Matter." In *Russian Religious Thought.* Ed. Judith Deutsch Kornblatt and Richard F. Gustafson. Madison: University of Wisconsin Press, 1996. Pp. 95-111.

Catechism of the Catholic Church. New York: Catholic Book Publishing Company, 1994.

Clark, Katerina, and Michael Holquist. *Mikhail Bakhtin.* Cambridge, MA: Harvard University Press, 1984

Contino, Paul J. "Dostoevsky and the Ethical Relation to the Prisoner." *Renascence* 48, no. 4 (Summer 1996): 259-78.

———. "Zosima, Mikhail, and Prosaic Confessional Dialogue" in *Studies in the Novel* 27, no. 1 (Spring 1995): 63-86.

Crossan, Frederick J. "Structure and Meaning in St. Augustine's *Confessions.*" *The Augustinian Tradition.* Ed. Gareth B. Matthews. Berkeley: University of California Press, 1999. Pp. 27-38.

Cunningham, David. "*The Brothers Karamazov* as Trinitarian Theology." In *Dostoevsky and the Christian Tradition.* Ed. George Pattison and Diane Oenning Thompson. Cambridge, UK: Cambridge University Press, 2001. Pp. 135-55.

The Divine Liturgy According to St. John Chrysostom. 2nd ed. South Canaan, PA: St. Tikhon's Seminary Press, 1977.

Dostoevsky, Fyodor. *The Brothers Karamazov.* Ed. Ralph Matlaw. Trans. Constance Garnett. New York: Norton Critical Edition, 1981.

———. *The Idiot.* Trans. David Magarshak. New York: Penguin, 1995.

———. *Selected Letters of Fyodor Dostoevsky.* Ed. Joseph Frank and David I. Goldstein. New Brunswick, NJ: Rutgers University Press, 1987.

———. *The Unpublished Dostoevsky: Diaries and Notebooks.* 3 vols. Ed. Carl R. Proffer. Trans. Arline Boyer and David Lapeza. Ann Arbor, MI: Ardis, 1976.

Emerson, Caryl. Translator's Afterword to *Dostoevsky and the Christian Tradition.* Pp. 220-25.

———. "Zosima's 'Mysterious Visitor': Again Bakhtin on Dostoevsky, and Dostoevsky on Heaven and Hell." In *"A New Word" on The Brothers Karamazov.* Ed. Robert Louis Jackson. Evanston, IL: Northwestern University Press, 2004. Pp. 155-79.

Fanger, Donald. *Dostoevsky and Romantic Realism.* Cambridge, MA: Harvard University Press, 1965.

Fedotov, George P. *The Russian Religious Mind (I).* Cambridge, MA: Harvard University Press, 1946.

Frank, Joseph. *Dostoevsky: The Seeds of Revolt, 1821-1849.* Princeton, NJ: Princeton University Press, 1976.

———. *Dostoevsky: The Years of Ordeal, 1850-1859.* Princeton, NJ: Princeton University Press, 1983.

———. *Dostoevsky: The Stir of Liberation, 1860-1865.* Princeton, NJ: Princeton University Press, 1986.

———. *Dostoevsky: The Miraculous Years, 1865-1871.* Princeton, NJ: Princeton University Press, 1995.

———. *Dostoevsky: The Mantle of the Prophet, 1871-1881.* Princeton, NJ: Princeton University Press, 2002.

Freccero, John. *Dante: The Poetics of Conversion.* Ed. Rachel Jacoff. Cambridge, MA: Harvard University Press, 1986.

Gustafson, Richard F. "Soloviev's Doctrine of Salvation." In *Russian Religious Thought.* Ed. Judith Deutsch Kornblatt and Richard F. Gustafson. Madison: University of Wisconsin Press, 1996. Pp. 31-48.

Hackel, Sergei. "The Religious Dimension: Vision or Evasion? Zosima's Discourse in *The Brothers Karamazov.*" In *New Essays on Dostoevsky.* Ed. M. V. Jones and G. Terry. Cambridge, UK: Cambridge University Press, 1983. Pp. 139-68.

Isaac the Syrian, St. *On Ascetical Life.* Trans. Mary Hansbury. Crestwood, NY: St. Vladimir's Seminary Press, 1989.

Jackson, Robert Louis. *Dostoevsky's Quest for Form: A Study of His Philosophy of Art.* 2nd ed. Bloomington, IN: Physsardt, 1978.

Jacobs, Alan. *A Theology of Reading: The Hermeneutics of Love.* Boulder, CO: Westview Press, 2001.

John Paul II. "Letter of His Holiness Pope John Paul II To Artists." April 4, 1999, http://www.vatican.va/holy_father/john_paul_ii/letters/documents/hf_jp-ii_let_23041999_artists_en.html (accessed July 15, 2004).

Kanevskaya, Marina. "Smerdyakov and Ivan: Dostoevsky's *The Brothers Karamazov.*" *The Russian Review* 61 (July 2002): 358-76.

Kantor, Vladimir. "Pavel Smerdyakov and Ivan Karamazov: The Problem of Temptation." Trans. Caryl Emerson. In *Dostoevsky and the Christian Tradition.* Ed. George Pattison and Diane Oenning Thompson. Cambridge, UK: Cambridge University Press, 2001. Pp. 189-220.

Kirillova, Irina. "Dostoevsky's Markings in the Gospel according to St John." In *Dostoevsky and the Christian Tradition.* Ed. George Pattison and Diane Oenning Thompson. Cambridge, UK: Cambridge University Press, 2001. Pp. 41-50.

Kjetsaa, Geir. *Fyodor Dostoevsky: A Writer's Life.* Trans. Siri Hustvedt and David McDuff. New York: Fawcett Columbine, 1987.

Knapp, Liza. *The Annihilation of Inertia: Dostoevsky and Metaphysics.* Evanston, IL: Northwestern University Press, 1996.

Kornblatt, Judith Deutsch, and Richard F. Gustafson. Introduction to *Russian Religious Thought.* Ed. Judith Deutsch Kornblatt and Richard F. Gustafson. Madison: University of Wisconsin Press, 1996. Pp. 3-24.

Kostalevsky, Marina. *Dostoevsky and Soloviev: The Art of Integral Vision.* New Haven, CT: Yale University Press, 1997.

Lossky, Vladimir. *The Mystical Theology of the Eastern Church.* Crestwood, NY: St. Vladimir's Seminary Press, 1976.

Lynch, S. J., William F. *Christ and Apollo. The Dimensions of Literary Imagination.* 1960. Reprint, Wilmington, DE: ISI Books, 2004.

Marshall, Donald. "The Conversion Scene in Augustine's *Confessions.*" Fletcher Jones Chair of Great Books Inaugural Lecture, Pepperdine University, January 22, 2004.

Martinsen, Deborah. *Surprised by Shame: Dostoevsky's Liars and Narrative Exposure.* Columbus: Ohio State University Press, 2003.

Miller, Robin Feuer. "Dostoevsky and Rousseau: The Morality of Confession Reconsidered." (1979). Reprinted in *Dostoevsky: New Perspectives.* Ed. Robert

Louis Jackson. Englewood Cliffs, NJ: Prentice Hall, 1984. Pp. 82-98.

———. *The Brothers Karamazov: Worlds of the Novel.* New York: Twayne, 1992.

Morson, Gary Saul. "The God of Onions: *The Brothers Karamazov* and the Mythic Prosaic." In *"A New Word" on The Brothers Karamazov.* Ed. Robert Louis Jackson. Evanston, IL: Northwestern University Press, 2004. Pp. 107-24.

Morson, Gary Saul and Caryl Emerson. *Mikhail Bakhtin: Creation of a Prosaics.* Stanford, CA: Stanford University Press, 1990.

Murav, Harriet. *Holy Foolishness: Dostoevsky's Novels and the Poetics of Cultural Critique.* Stanford, CA: Stanford University Press, 1992.

The New Revised Standard Version of the Bible. Oxford. 1991.

Ouspensky, Leonid. *Theology of the Icon.* Vol. 1 and 2. Trans. Anthony Gythiel. 1978. Reprint. Crestwood, NY: St. Vladimir's Seminary Press, 1992.

Pechey, Graham. "Eternity and Modernity: Bakhtin and the Epistemological Sublime." In *Critical Essays on Mikhail Bakhtin.* Ed. Caryl Emerson. Boston: G. K. Hall, 1999. Pp. 355-77.

———. "Intercultural, Intercreatural: Bakhtin and the Uniqueness of 'Literary Seeing.'" In *Bakhtin and his Intellectual Ambience.* Ed. Boguslaw Zylko. Gdansk, Poland: Wydawnictwo Uniwersytetu Gdanskiego, 2002.

Pelikan, Jaroslav. Introduction to *Maximus Confessor: Selected Writings.* Trans. George C. Berthold. New York: Paulist Press, 1985. Pp. 1-13.

Perlina, Nina. *Varieties of Poetic Utterance: Quotation in the Brothers Karamazov.* Lanham, MD: University Press of America, 1985.

Pyman, Avril. "Dostoevsky and the Prism of the Orthodox Semiosphere." In *Dostoevsky and the Christian Tradition.* Ed. George Pattison and Diane Oenning Thompson. Cambridge, UK: Cambridge University Press, 2001. Pp. 103-15.

Rosenshield, Gary. "The Realization of the Collective Self: The Rebirth of Religious Autobiography in Dostoevsky's *Notes from the Hours of the Dead.*" *Slavic Review* 50, no. 2 (1991): 317-27.

Scanlan, James P. *Dostoevsky the Thinker.* Ithaca, NY: Cornell University Press, 2002.

Solovyov [Soloviev], Vladimir. *Lectures on Divine Humanity.* Peter Zouboff. Trans. Boris Jakim. Rev. and Ed. Hudson, NY: Lindisfarne Press, 1995.

Stump, Eleonore. "Augustine on Free Will." In *The Cambridge Companion to Augustine.* Ed. Eleonore

Stump and Norman Kretzmann. Cambridge, UK: Cambridge University Press, 2001. Pp. 124-47.

Taylor, Charles. *Sources of the Self: The Making of the Modern Identity.* Cambridge, MA: Harvard University Press, 1989.

Terras, Victor. *A Karamazov Companion: A Commentary on the Genesis, Language, and Style of Dostoevsky's Novel.* 1981. Reprint, Madison: University of Wisconsin Press, 2002.

Thompson, Diane Oenning. "Problems of the Biblical Word in Dostoevsky's Poetics." In *Dostoevsky and the Christian Tradition.* Ed. George Pattison and Diane Oenning Thompson. Cambridge, UK: Cambridge University Press, 2001. Pp. 69-99.

———. *The Brothers Karamazov and the Poetics of Memory.* Cambridge, UK: Cambridge University Press, 1991.

Walker, Jeanne Murray. "Sacrifice." In *A Deed to the Light.* Urbana: University of Illinois Press, 2004. Pp. 17-18.

Ware, Timothy (Bishop Kallistos of Diokleia). *The Orthodox Church.* New York: Penguin, 1993.

Weintraub, Karl Joachim. *The Value of the Individual: Self and Circumstance in Autobiography.* Chicago: University of Chicago Press: 1978.

Williams, Thomas. "Biblical Interpretation." In *The Cambridge Companion to Augustine.* Ed. Eleonore Stump and Norman Kretzmann. Cambridge, UK: Cambridge University Press, 2001. Pp. 59-70.

Wills, Garry. *Saint Augustine.* New York: Penguin, 1999.

Yannaras, Christos. *Elements of Faith: An Introduction to Orthodox Theology.* Edinburgh, UK: T & T Clark, 1991.

———. *The Freedom of Morality.* Crestwood, NY: St. Vladimir's Seminary Press, 1984.

Ziolkowski, Margaret. "Dostoevsky and the Kenotic Tradition." In *Dostoevsky and the Christian Tradition.* Ed. George Pattison and Diane Oenning Thompson. Cambridge, UK: Cambridge University Press, 2001. Pp. 31-40.

Zizioulas, John D. *Being as Communion: Studies in Personhood and the Church.* 1985. Reprint, Crestwood, NY: St. Vladimir's Seminary Press, 1993.

Stewart Justman (essay date 2006)

SOURCE: Justman, Stewart. "Quixotism in *The Brothers Karamazov.*" In *Literature and Human Equality,* pp. 109-32. Evanston, Ill.: Northwestern University Press, 2006.

[*In the following essay, Justman discusses the tragic-comic parallels between the characters Dmitri Karamazov and Don Quixote.*]

EQUALITY AS A LITERARY PRINCIPLE

If, as M. M. Bakhtin argues, the hero of a novel cannot be "a clerk, a landowner, a merchant, a fiancé, a jealous lover, a father," and nothing more,[1] in the person of Fyodor Pavlovich Karamazov we meet a landowner who "hardly ever lived on his own estate" (7), a businessman who pays no attention to his taverns, a father who more or less forgot the existence of his sons and stands as a kind of antithesis of fatherhood as such, and a possessive lover who does not in fact possess the woman of his affections and probably never could. Neither, however, does *The Brothers Karamazov* itself slot into existing categories. Whether the author's genius was just too original to fit a model or his interest in boundary conditions extended even to boundaries of a literary kind, the fact is that *The Brothers Karamazov* blurs the lines that set off one literary domain from another. It redraws the map of literature; or imagines one where the continents haven't yet drifted apart. In view of its strongly dramatic character, even cataloging *The Brothers Karamazov* as a novel, the most open and least defined of literary forms, is somehow misleading. *Joseph Andrews* is bewilderingly classified by its author as a "comic epic-poem in prose."[2] *The Brothers Karamazov* might be termed a drama in prose, a drama both comic and tragic.

It is of course strictly impossible for narrative to become drama, inasmuch as stage action is not related to the audience but realized in its presence. This impossibility does not daunt an author unwilling to sacrifice either the immediacy of drama or the unlimited range of narrative. Parallel lines do meet, more or less, in *The Brothers Karamazov.* The elementary distinction between drama and narrative loses much of its force in a work where by far the greater part of the telling is done directly by the characters themselves—the only description of the murder comes from the killer—and where the narration is hedged with disclaimers as if to keep it from intervening too positively between the reader and events. Such narration as there is, moreover is deeply infiltrated by the direct speech of the characters. The novel opens conventionally enough, with information about the brothers' childhood—all were abandoned by their father and taken in by others, like the exposed infants of romance—but not until the scandal scene in the elder's cell do we learn of current affairs in the Karamazov family, and then not through narration but direct speech. So knotted and tense is the situation that emerges that it could work itself out in a dozen ways.[3] Much as a character might be endowed with a surplus of potential, the conflict in the Karamazov household is of such intensity that it could drive different novels. We first learn of Dmitri's rivalry with his father, and his disloyalty to his betrothed, in the heat of dialogue.

The foreword to *The Brothers Karamazov* identifies Alyosha as the hero, and it is true that readers enter into a special bond with Alyosha in the sense that we go through the tale in a state of half-perception resembling his own. When Alyosha voices astonishment at Rakitin's prediction of a crime in his household, we may be struck with his lack of perception, but until a moment before we ourselves didn't even know what was going on in that household. Somehow we had gotten several chapters into this great novel before stumbling on the information that father and eldest son happen to be colliding over a certain woman, and two brothers are potentially in conflict over another. When Dmitri makes his passionate confession to Alyosha, neither Alyosha nor the reader knows that he has not in fact told all. No more than Alyosha do we ourselves know what Dmitri means by striking himself on the chest "as though [his] dishonor was lying and being kept precisely there" (156). Alyosha never considers that Smerdyakov might actually be his brother, and indeed Smerdyakov barely enters his field of consciousness, but at the same time readers never really hear from Smerdyakov in the way we do from Dmitri, Ivan, and Alyosha himself. One book of *The Brothers Karamazov* is entitled "Alyosha," another "Dmitri," another "Ivan"; none is entitled "Smerdyakov." It is as if we had been made to partake of Alyosha's own defects of perception. (Had Smerdyakov been treated as a brother, that is, an equal, rather than a menial by the other three, events might have taken a different course.) Denied the comfort of superior knowledge, readers of *The Brothers Karamazov* are in fact placed again and again in a position like that of the least knowing of the brothers. As noted, Alyosha sometimes seems to understand as little of the events crashing and swirling around him as Pierre does of events on the battlefield. "Despite the incessant firing going on there, he had no idea that this was the field of battle" (847). The Karamazov family is a field of battle in its own right, but this is also to say that the conflict has many centers, not just one.

Being so intricate, the drama of the Karamazov household revolves around no one brother exclusively. But while none occupies the central position of a tragic hero, for the title of tragicomic hero of *The Brothers Karamazov* there is only one candidate: Dmitri. In part this means simply that Dmitri, and he alone, possesses a rich mix of tragic and comic qualities. His every word and deed recoiling against him, he finds himself by the middle of the novel in the classically tragic position of one who brings his fate upon himself but whose suffering is in excess of his deserts. At the same time, however, Dmitri is magnificently comic, something akin to a swaggering soldier who blows the bubble of his bravado so large it finally pops.[4] His jealousy alone appears in both tragic and comic lights. Intense suspicion of his own father as a sexual rival renders Dmitri all at once an extreme danger to himself and others and a clownish dupe who sees things that aren't there and misses things that are. Jealousy is a comic passion under whose dominion men sink to base and ludicrous actions like spying, even while consumed with thoughts of their own honor; it is also, in Dmitri's case, a terrible error and a cause of ruin.[5] But as this may already suggest, Dmitri is in fact more than a collection of qualities, some tragic and some the opposite. In him we are reminded of a figure who embodies the tragic and the comic in a profound human unity: Don Quixote. The things Dmitri does under the influence of his passion for Grushenka—his fixed idea, his Dulcinea—can only be described as quixotic. Certainly Dmitri cannot just be labeled a rake, a bully, a military officer, a victim of temporary insanity, or for that matter a specimen of jealousy, all such terms containing some fatal inaccuracy and all of them far too limiting, too "finalizing" as Bakhtin would say. The reason he *can* be labeled a Quixote—himself a man without a role—is precisely the unlimited richness of that great archetype.[6] Don Quixote's preoccupation with relieving distress reappears in the urge "to do something" to relieve human suffering that wells up in Dmitri's powerful dream of the baby following his interrogation (508), and what makes this urge truly quixotic is that it *is* bound up in a dream.

Noble in dreams, foolish in reality, Dmitri earlier in the novel is seized with the idea of turning a piece of bad legal paper into 3,000 roubles—an ambition no less visionary than Parson Adams's hope in *Joseph Andrews* (a work of homage to *Don Quixote*) of getting a hundred pounds for "nine volumes of manuscript sermons."[7] Adams for his part appears in a comic light, the object of jokes and receiver of knocks as well as the voice of benevolence, his indignities reminding us that comedy delights in humiliation. Humiliation also, however, lies at the core of tragic experience: Lear's reduction to a beggar, Ivan Ilych's physical helplessness, Michael Henchard's retreat to a hovel in [Thomas Hardy's novel] *The Mayor of Casterbridge*. There are scenes in *The Brothers Karamazov*, notably Dmitri's interrogation and the taunting of Ivan by his private devil, where humiliation appears in both aspects at once, as though the author sought the common root of the tragic and comic modes. Where Dickens explodes the social distinctions that ground the traditional literary categories of tragedy and comedy, Dostoevsky scrambles those categories themselves (as in Dmitri's tragic antics) while keeping clear of anything that could be mistaken for a program of Jacobinism or political leveling.[8] He prosecutes his argument with tradition in literary, not political terms. In the opinion of Bakhtin, this archconservative was in fact the greatest innovator in the history of the novel.[9] If Bakhtin is correct and Dostoevsky endows his heroes with rights against their own author, and other characters with rights equal to theirs, then in fact he has translated the most incendiary ideal of the French Revolution, the Rights of Man, into literary innovation.[10]

Dostoevsky wrote of the insulted and the injured and entered into a dialogue of differences with those radicals who espoused a social religion of equality. In his vision of a perfect society, ordinary people would freely serve the great like Shakespeare, proving by the act of service that "I am in no way beneath thee in moral worth and that, *as a person,* I am equal to thee."[11] In the words of Father Zosima's brother, "we must all serve each other" (289). Here I am concerned with equality less as a political than a literary principle. If by virtue of being human we cannot be known like objects (as Dostoevsky's friend Strakhov maintained and he himself believed), then *The Brothers Karamazov* ought to be composed accordingly. According to Bakhtin, it is. Dostoevsky's heroes, he says, are in truth the opposite of known quantities—never can it be said of them that "all of you is here, there is nothing more in you, and nothing more to be said about you."[12] I think it is this factor of the unknown, or the incompletely known, that not only distinguishes these heroes from the more transparent characters common to fiction but gives them a resemblance to living persons. But if unknowability belongs to the heroes of *The Brothers Karamazov* as an endowment of their humanity, then not even the author possesses complete insight into them, and if not him, still less us. We read *The Brothers Karamazov,* therefore, not as possessors of superior knowledge (as though we had been let into the councils of the gods) but as novices willing to give up the pride and pretension of knowledge itself. "I am not a doctor," says the narrator of *The Brothers Karamazov* before launching into an account of Ivan's delirium (634).

The argument has been made, and I think made well, that early readers of *War and Peace* offended by its violation of conventional practices came closer to the truth than those today who read the work with no sense of shock.[13] The original readers of *The Brothers Karamazov,* that is, the literate public of Russia, read each successive installment of the novel with rapt attention and great expectation. Today first or second or third-time readers of *The Brothers Karamazov* may come closer to its truth than professional readers who, in retrospect, can discern in the narrative the clear signs of foreshadowing. (Such retrospective prophets remind me of Polyphemus in the *Odyssey,* who after he is blinded by Odysseus remembers the prophecy that he would be blinded by someone of that name.) While the novel was still coming out in serial form, a woman wrote the author asking who the murderer of old Karamazov was. A modern edition of the novel refers to the questioner as a real-life Madame Khokhlakov, as if she were tormented by a featherbrained curiosity. Dostoevsky answered her patiently. In point of fact, all readers of *The Brothers Karamazov* have found and at one time or another still find themselves in the same position as this ridiculed inquirer: the position of not knowing. As Dostoevsky takes the mystery tale to a higher level, so too does *The*

Brothers Karamazov induce the tension of uncertainty not only for the sake of suspense but to dispel in the reader every assurance of superior knowledge and to remind us of our fallibility and our limits. When Ivan tells Alyosha in his famous indictment of divine indifference to human suffering, "I confess in all humility that I can understand nothing of why" the world is arranged as it is (243), his spirit is prosecutorial, his humility a pose. Every reader of *The Brothers Karamazov* experiences the humility of not understanding.

To Dostoevsky the epigraph to *Anna Karenina*—"Vengeance is mine; I will repay"—meant that only God can judge because "only to Him is known the *entire* mystery of this world."[14] Human beings lack knowledge. What is more, if all things were known, faith would lose meaning, inasmuch as faith as Dostoevsky conceives of it means belief in the absence, and without the comforts and assurances, of positive knowledge. Not Dostoevsky but Ivan's creation the Grand Inquisitor makes the argument that Jesus should have proven his divinity to the world so that humanity would know for certain who he was. Later in *The Brothers Karamazov* the jury is unable to credit Dmitri's innocence with all of the evidence on the other side. Dmitri's guilt can be "proven" but not his innocence. As in this case, human knowledge falls short, and by keeping the reader's knowledge always incomplete Dostoevsky remains true to the conditions of human life as he understands them.

Only when the Karamazovs meet in the elder's cell and words fly do we begin to understand the forces at work in the family, and then only in outline. When Alyosha somehow fails to heed his elder's warning to watch over Dmitri, we ourselves lose sight of Dmitri as well. At the point we learn that Dmitri was "unaware . . . of what had happened with" Grushenka, that he "could make nothing out of her intentions," that he knew only in part of the contents of the letter from her former lover (364-65), our own knowledge of these matters is sketchy; and of the money worn on his very chest we know nothing. When, in a jealous fury, Dmitri races to his father's house with a blunt instrument in hand, we do not know Grushenka is not there. On this crucial matter it might be said that we and Dmitri are equals in ignorance. Only well after the fact do we learn from Dmitri that he drank and brawled perhaps "just because unknown ideas were storming within me" (592). They were unknown to us as well. Not until Grushenka opens her heart to Alyosha do we understand why she toys so recklessly with both father and son, and perhaps not even then. If Dostoevsky had been Cervantes, however, we would have known more than the characters themselves.

The Quixotic Dmitri Karamazov

When Pierre in *War and Peace* imagines himself "a sort of Paris possessed of a Helen" (22) as he dreams of marriage to Hélène, he shows an infatuation with romantic illusion that marks him a kind of Quixote, though the smile of irony has been replaced with a bitter grin of negation. Quixotism makes its appearance in *The Brothers Karamazov* as early as the novel's second paragraph, in the story of a romantic who drowned herself as, and because, Ophelia did. (Actually, this version of Ophelia's end is itself a romantic distortion. Ophelia did not hurl herself into a stream.) Where Don Quixote devotes himself to the imitation of imaginary examples, this copyist imitates the Ophelia of her imagination even at the cost of her life. Of the river bank she leaps from, Dostoevsky writes, "If this cliff . . . had not been so picturesque, if it had been merely a flat, prosaic bank, the suicide might not have taken place at all" (8). For Dmitri Karamazov there is no escape from prosaic existence—as is true of Don Quixote as well.

Once caricatured by Turgenev as the "Knight of the Rueful Countenance,"[15] Dostoevsky cites Don Quixote more often than any other literary figure in *A Writer's Diary,* remarking at one point of Cervantes' masterwork, "There is nothing deeper and more powerful in the whole world than this piece of *fiction*. It is still the final and the greatest expression of human thought, the most bitter irony that a human is capable of expressing."[16] The bitterest irony is of course tragic irony, though the comic energy of *Don Quixote,* as well as its disregard of the conventions and formal requirements of tragedy, precludes us from viewing the work as tragic per se. If *Don Quixote* were less tonally ambiguous, it might have seemed to Dostoevsky less profound. It is his striving to realize the ideal on an earth antithetical to the ideal that makes the story of Don Quixote so comic and tragic. Dmitri Karamazov too sees his passion for the ideal crossed and mocked.

> I can't bear it that some man, even with a lofty heart and the highest mind, should start from the ideal of the Madonna and end with the ideal of Sodom. It's even more fearful when someone who already has the ideal of Sodom in his soul does not deny the ideal of Madonna either, and his heart burns with it, verily, verily burns, as in his young, blameless years.
>
> (108)

This passage resonates with a comment in the author's notebook of 1864 that has been identified as "perhaps philosophically the most important line in all his work. . . . 'Man strives on earth toward an ideal that is *contrary* to his nature.'"[17] In the story of the broad-natured Dmitri Karamazov and his longing for the ideal—a story at once intensely ironic and highly ridiculous—a double tonality similar to that of *Don Quixote* is at work.

Smeared with blood (though not his father's), flaunting a suspicious sum of money (also not his father's), Dmitri professes astonishment when arrested for the murder of a man whose life he threatened for all to hear but whom he did not kill after all. If his interrogation, trial, and conviction make for a tale of terrible irony, his belief that fate has somehow conspired against him is nevertheless as ludicrous as Don Quixote's belief that he is being persecuted by magicians. The truth is that one who acts as blindly as Dmitri Karamazov is a fool of comic proportions. One of the great fools of literature, Dmitri is a hero of the ridiculous, blinded by visions of Grushenka and given to the belief that a kind of sorcery is at work against him. "It's a wonder, fantastic!" he exclaims to his captors (479). Quixotic in the complete sense and the subject of a "fate" that is indeed most bitterly ironic, Dmitri finds himself incriminated by his own actions and struggles against his plight in a manner both tragic and ludicrous. As Dr. Johnson notes, it is one thing to read romances, with their "heroes and . . . traitors, deliverers and persecutors," another to read of persons like ourselves, "leveled with the rest of the world."[18] Dmitri, like one who has read too many romances, has visions of deliverance and falls into the delusion that he has been singled out for persecution by the power of the extraordinary. If he really were targeted by the malice of fate, or indeed if he were to walk away scot-free from his own actions, he would have to be some special category of person, subject to conditions that do not apply to humanity in general. Dmitri does not belong to a special category. He has no exemption from the conditions of prosaic existence. He is level with—equal to—his fellow beings, not in a category apart. Says Folly in The Praise of Folly, "I am the only deity who embraces all men equally."[19]

Where Don Quixote belongs to the lowest rank of the Spanish nobility, Dmitri, son of the lowest sort of landowner, demands to be treated under arrest as a man of honor and hopes to serve out a short prison sentence "without loss of the rights of my rank" (567). (That, contrary to his fantastic hopes, the guards "talk down" to him is more than he can bear [763].) Also under interrogation, Dmitri reveals himself, like his Spanish ancestor, as "markedly obsessional, but only on a defined and limited range of matters," the special object of his mania being the rag he wore around his neck containing 1,500 roubles.[20] It is next to impossible for Dmitri to convey to third parties the significance that rag holds for him, destroying as it does his own image of himself as one too uncalculating and romantic to put away one woman's money to finance his escape with another. His Dulcinea, again, is the commoner Grushenka, and much as Don Quixote under the inspiration of romantic ideals is apt to see things that are not, Dmitri can practically see and feel Grushenka in his father's house when she is not there. (Recall, however, that the reader has no more idea than Dmitri that on the critical night she is literally and figuratively somewhere else entirely.) It is his suspicion that Grushenka is with his father that takes him to the house on the night of the murder and

thus makes possible the crime itself. In the comic figure of Don Quixote who nevertheless dramatized for Dostoevsky "the most bitter irony," as well as in his descendant Dmitri, we have an image as it were of the multi-tonality of The Brothers Karamazov.

What could be more extravagantly misguided, more quixotic, than Dmitri's frantic search for the 3,000 roubles that to his brain represents salvation? Though not a knight, Dmitri certainly has a quest, and it takes him first of all to the old merchant Samsonov. As the common-law partner of Grushenka, however, old Samsonov is no more likely than his own father to give Dmitri the means to run off with her, nor is such a classical miser going to send good money after bad by purchasing financial paper from a Dmitri Karamazov. But while Dmitri is on the verge of complete despair, the scene itself takes place at the border of hilarity. From Samsonov's giant of a son to his own mighty but suppressed rage, the entire event is a comedy, if only Dmitri realized it. Perhaps no one but a Dmitri Karamazov would place his hope in the ogre described toward the opening of the scene in all his Dickensian ugliness.[21] And from here Dmitri takes his suit to two others maybe even more improbable than Samsonov himself. As we discover later when the seal of silence is broken and Dmitri reveals the story of the money around his neck, half the magic sum of 3,000 roubles is all this time on his own person. Why then does he seek it at all? Because he is intoxicated with the fantasy of carrying away Grushenka in triumph, which he cannot do on another woman's money. But if standard roles ill suit a true novelistic hero like Dmitri Karamazov, what of a script so standard, a story so overtold (as though it appeared in a thousand old books of knight-errantry) that we wonder how it could take possession of an intelligent brain? In the manner of a Quixote, Dmitri has become enthralled to a fantasy of honor: honorably paying off one woman so that he can chivalrously carry off another. Seeking a sum of money that will purchase his release from Katerina (impossible) and finance his escape with Grushenka, he succeeds only in building up the case against himself in the eyes of the law. In the full quixotic sense of the word, Dmitri's quest for 3,000 roubles is an errand of folly—all the more because his money isn't really needed at all to carry away a woman, Grushenka, who has money of her own in abundance.

While no one is going to mistake Father Zosima for Rousseau, still the elder's indictment of a corrupt and unequal society in which people enslave themselves to superfluous desires is consonant with the sentiments of Rousseau's Discourse on Inequality. "Taking freedom to mean the increase and prompt satisfaction of needs," says Zosima, discussing a world divided into rich and poor,

> [moderns] distort their own nature, for they generate
> many meaningless and foolish desires, habits, and the

most absurd fancies in themselves. They live only for mutual envy, for pleasure-seeking and self-display. To have dinners, horses, carriages, rank, and slaves to serve them is now considered such a necessity that for the sake of it, to satisfy it, they will sacrifice life, honor, the love of mankind.

(313-14)

The young Zosima, a well-regarded military officer, was himself an "absurd creature" full of imaginary notions of honor and precedence (295). Dmitri Karamazov as an officer seems to have been much like this, but even now he acts like Zosima's moderns. Given to display, Dmitri has a theatrical personality, throws ostentatious parties, and, as we saw, is touchy about the privileges of rank, but as revealing as any of these symptoms is his subjection to a "meaningless," "foolish," "absurd" need for money, the idol of the modern world. From one point of view a romantic fantasy, his dream of bearing Grushenka away with his own financial power can also be read as the sort of mania to which men abandon their freedom in a highly class-conscious society, according to Zosima. Zosima describes those so distorted by the world they live in that they do not know what to do with their own freedom. Dmitri seems to have trouble with the freedom he possesses because he is no longer in uniform, and over the course of the novel he succeeds in forfeiting it. Certainly the need driving Dmitri's quest for 3,000 roubles is imaginary; and yet the consequences of the adventure are real enough, as it is cited against him by the authorities as proof that at the time he had no money to speak of, and that the money that appeared in his hands on the night of the murder can therefore only have materialized as a result of the murder. The man who spends the first half of *The Brothers Karamazov* obsessed by a dream later finds himself trapped in a nightmare.

Captivated as he is by the foolish and the absurd, Dmitri, like his great original, Don Quixote, believes himself, or would like to believe himself, a hero in a romance, a lightning rod for the power of the marvelous. If only by portraying Dmitri as one who imagines himself at the mercy of events like the hero of a Greek romance, or subject to the black magic of coincidence like a Don Quixote, *The Brothers Karamazov* takes its place in a tradition inaugurated by *Don Quixote* itself, that of ironizing the romantic foundations of the novel.[22] Dmitri feels that circumstances conspire against him, that he is at the center of a "plot." While there is a certain fractional truth to this, it could more justly be said that the plot of *The Brothers Karamazov* has Dmitri bringing about his own ruin, knotting his own noose; everything he says and does comes back to incriminate him, with an effect at once bitterly ironic and tragically ludicrous. As though Dostoevsky sought to surpass even the irony of Cervantes, he denies Dmitri the escape to the road that he yearns for and that constitutes the very

condition of adventure. In fact, Dmitri's most quixotic delusion may be his fantasy of one day clearing all debts, cutting the bonds of his entanglements, and betaking himself to a new life like Don Quixote taking to the highway. No such escape is possible for Dmitri Karamazov, caught as he is in the humiliating "prosaics" of circumstance.[23] (The very setting of *The Brothers Karamazov* in a miserable small town produces a similarly constricting effect, with high drama reduced to local scandal.) Among the possibilities opened by the promotion of commoners to positions of importance in novels is the commoner enchanted with the delusion of not being an ordinary person at all. Such a commoner is Dmitri, believing as he does that he is at the mercy of fortune and misfortune like someone lost in the magic world of romance.

In a novel that immortalizes the theme of the flight from freedom, Dmitri not only enslaves himself to a purely imaginary need for money but is so oppressed by his own power to act that he dreams of having no such power at all. Even with 1,500 roubles around his neck he acts as though only someone else could solve his money troubles and he himself had no ability to restore that very sum to Katerina. Dmitri's hope that money, and with it redemption, "would somehow fly down to him by itself, from the sky no less" (367) is as quixotic as his hope that Samsonov of all people will be its supplier (or indeed that Katerina would allow Dmitri to buy her off in the first place, in effect selling her honor). The man who tells his interrogators, "I understand now that for men such as I a blow is needed, a blow of fate, to catch them as with a noose and bind them by an external force" (509) is not only oppressed by freedom but thinks of his fate as something that comes down from the sky. Such beliefs might make more sense if Dmitri were the hero of a Greek romance, exposed to the power of the extraordinary, the plaything of fortune and misfortune, one to whom events just happen.[24]

This sort of exposure to the force of events is dramatized by one of the commonplaces of the Greek romance: abduction. Suddenly brigands appear and you are taken. You are no more an agent in your own capture than you were in receiving identity at birth or losing your birth identity—your nobility—by misfortune. In *Daphnis and Chloe* the former is momentarily borne away by pirates, an episode included, it seems, for no other reason than to honor or parody the romance formula. Treating such formulas ironically in the tradition of Cervantes, Dostoevsky reveals Dmitri's image of himself as a special victim of fortune as one more quixotic delusion, and among his most sensational. Considering that Dmitri gets carried away by passion, it may be no wonder that he thinks of himself as a victim like those literally carried away in the Greek romance. Not being at one with himself, he knows otherwise, however, as does the reader.

For our own passions do not act on us like external events. When Dmitri declares that if Grushenka presents herself to his father, he may kill him or he may not, depending on the intensity of the moment, he talks as if he were buffeted by his own passions like a sailor in a squall.[25] Supporting the delusion that his own deeds somehow happen to him, such talk is itself dangerous. When, in the event, Dmitri strikes down not his father but the servant Grigory, the act is narrated as if he himself did not perform it.

> "Parricide!" the old man shouted for the whole neighborhood to hear, but that was all he had time to shout: suddenly he fell as if struck by a thunderbolt. Mitya jumped back down into the garden and bent over the stricken man. There was a brass pestle in Mitya's hand, and he threw it mechanically into the grass.
>
> (394)

It is almost as if the pestle came from the sky and performed the crime "by itself." If the heroes of the Greek romance are subjected to chance (or in the case of *Callirhoe,* Fortune), with Dmitri it is purely a matter of chance whether or not he kills the drunken peasant from whom he hoped to get 3,000 roubles shortly before his encounter with Grigory. "On another occasion Mitya might have killed the fool in a rage, but now he himself became weak as a child" (379). In view of Dmitri's sense that his own actions somehow befall him, it seems poetically just that he should be *un*justly arrested for another's deed.

Once again it is Dmitri's quest for 3,000 roubles that brings out the folly of his belief that he is a plaything of circumstance like someone abducted or delivered— but in any case, removed from the realm of ordinary existence—in an ancient romance. Throughout this sequence Dmitri is possessed by the idea that his very fate rests in the hands of another—first the merchant Samsonov, then the drunken peasant to whom Samsonov refers him as a malicious joke, third the scatterbrained Madame Khokhlakov. "Oh, the irony of fate!" Dmitri exclaims upon finding the peasant "on whom my entire fate now depends" unconscious from drink (376-77). When he approaches Madame Khokhlakov, "at first things seemed to smile on him" (383); then his fortune turns. To the reader it becomes apparent that Dmitri is the victim not of fate or fortune or some persecuting force but his own folly and miscalculation, and finally his very belief that someone else has got to rescue him. Even before we discover that he is wearing 1,500 roubles next to the silver icon Madame Khokhlakov slips around his neck, we sense that Dmitri could hardly have chosen three unlikelier persons on this earth

to hear his suit, that his dream of someone delivering him from his crisis is as vain as his dream of carrying Grushenka far away to begin another life, all debts cleared. When Dmitri puts it to old Samsonov that he (Samsonov) must "choose: me or the monster [that is, his father]" (371), we wonder how it is that Dmitri himself seems to have so little power of action that this misanthrope must be his savior. Dostoevsky allows Dmitri no possibility of a miraculous deliverance, no escape from the net of circumstance, no exemption from the sort of conditions binding equally on all of us. Nor is Dmitri at the mercy of fortune. On the contrary, like his belief that others are plotting against him (390), his notion that he is the plaything of events is both an abdication of his own freedom and a delusion worthy of a Quixote—the error, at once pathetic and ludicrous, of one whose head has been turned by romantic visions. Where Don Quixote bumps into stories about himself, Dmitri is undone by the stories that circulate about him, such as his having spent a full 3,000 roubles at one throw some weeks before the murder: a fiction authored and published by himself.

While the one who does and suffers these things is revealed as the great fool of *The Brothers Karamazov,* his higher yearnings and passionate delusions rouse in us a kind of love for this modern Quixote. In Prince Myshkin, the Idiot, Dostoevsky had indeed created a Quixote, but one too Christlike, as it happened, to call forth laughter and derision as well as pity, wonder, and love in the fully orchestrated manner of Dmitri Karamazov.[26] In Dmitri the contradictory potentials of Don Quixote are richly realized. Like that knight encountering rival versions of himself, in the courtroom Dmitri runs into errant accounts of his own exploits—accounts that all seem true to those who offer them, owing to the many-sidedness of his nature.

Dmitri's own deeds thus come back to haunt him, as they also contribute to the murder of his father in ways he does not and cannot understand at the time. But as I have said, neither can we understand at the time. So intricate is the web of circumstance in *The Brothers Karamazov* that only after the fact do we begin to understand just how Dmitri's actions contributed to the crime, and by then Dmitri is beginning to understand, too. Rather than allowing readers the privilege of higher knowledge, Dostoevsky constructs *The Brothers Karamazov* in such a way that it reminds us continually of what we do not know; and it intimates that incomplete knowledge, in the double form of a liability to error and a capacity for surprise, is a feature of our common humanity. Early in the novel, looking back on his military days, Dmitri tells Alyosha, "I didn't understand a thing then: not until I came here, brother, and even now until these very last present days, maybe even not until today, did I understand anything in all these financial squabbles between me and father" (111). The experience of incomprehension and belated understanding is also dealt to the reader of *The Brothers Karamazov.*

Inasmuch as the full consequences of his actions escape him, Dmitri's story confirms unforgettably the principle that action is risky, both because acts cannot be undone and because their effects pass from our control. This double burden of risk undertaken by one who acts is brought out with great clarity by Hannah Arendt in her discussion of the nature of action itself. It has long been known, she writes, that "he who acts never quite knows what he is doing, that he always becomes 'guilty' of consequences he never intended or even foresaw, [and] that no matter how disastrous and unexpected the consequences of his deed he can never undo it."[27] But if the meaning of an action "never discloses itself to the actor but only to the backward glance of the historian who himself does not act"[28]—which comes close to Tolstoy's doctrine that history can be understood only in retrospect—*The Brothers Karamazov* supplies no such historian, and it is left to us to determine, if we can, exactly how each brother's actions contribute to the Karamazov disaster. For just because of the part each brother plays by act or omission in the murder of their father, all of them stand morally responsible for the crime. Without the complicity of each, the act could not have been committed. In contrast to a "collective guilt" divided into ever smaller pieces as it is shared out among more and more, each of the brothers, then, whatever his "part" (and Dmitri's is large) bears a full measure of moral guilt. If Hamlet famously exceeds the part of the avenger that has been assigned him, the brothers bear a guilt that exceeds their part in the crime, if only because real guilt is not and cannot be fractional in nature. A jury today may find a defendant 42 percent liable for a plaintiff's injuries, but Dostoevsky does not think like that jury and does not subscribe to such Euclidean reckonings.

Then too, even if one who acts does not understand, the "historian" is in no position to look down on those who assume the risks of action. No one ever embraced those risks more fervently than Dmitri Karamazov. If the actor doesn't know what he is doing, then Dmitri must be the actor supreme. Dmitri in truth never knows what he is doing (which is what makes the prosecution's portrayal of him such a caricature). Even when he snatches up a pestle he could hardly say why. Like everything else he does, however, this deed of a moment proves irreversible and "fateful." As his acts pass out of his hands, Dmitri becomes guilty of a murder he did not commit; but as the quotation marks in which Arendt encloses the word "guilty" imply, you cannot be held guilty in a strict legal sense for doing you know not what. The guilt that descends on the actor as the price of his own temerity, the guilt that descends on Dmitri Karamazov for enabling a murder by his own sensational recklessness, can only be moral guilt. As Dmitri's

case is heard in the courtroom, his actions are interpreted in the light of legal categories as ill-fitting as the clothes he was given to cover his nakedness under interrogation. Strangely, these categories too are affiliated with the tradition of romance.

In *Callirhoe,* all of Babylon buzzes with news of the trial of Mithridates on the charge of seduction. "During the thirty days men and women in Persia talked of nothing but this trial, and, to tell the truth, all Babylon became a courthouse" (247). The most sustained episode in *Callirhoe,* the trial scene itself has been judged "much superior in dramatic effect to anything one meets with elsewhere in the Greek romance," the peak moment of the genre.[29] All of Russia seems abuzz over the trial of Dmitri Karamazov. Throwing open the shutters of the Karamazov household, the event is a public spectacle charged with the thrill of revelation and heightened with displays of rhetorical art. (Recall Father Zosima: in a modern society of unequals men live for display.) The trial of Dmitri is a great drama; it is also a circus, a grievous mistake, and a theater of sophistry. As such, it reminds us that the truth passes unnoticed, as Tolstoy, Dickens, and George Eliot might agree.

Romance tends to divide characters into friend and foe, hero and villain, so that "every typical character in romance tends to have his moral opposite confronting him, like black and white pieces in a chess game."[30] It may be in the courtroom that the principle of formal opposition and contest is played out most vividly, as argument meets counterargument. As it happens, the Greek romance not only features legal trials but has certain links to the sophistic tradition that arose alongside the legal culture of ancient Athens and concerned itself with the construction of legal arguments, both pro and contra. By contrast, the clash of point and counterpoint in Dmitri's trial only illustrates the superficial character of the event as a public spectacle, for in a real exchange as Dostoevsky understands it, speakers do not stoop to a detailed refutation of the other's claims. "They never argue over *separate points,* but always over *whole points of view.*"[31] Every last point in the case against Dmitri is argued over.

The Greek romance is sometimes called sophistic, and the courtroom arguments in *The Brothers Karamazov* are certainly that. In his peroration, Dmitri's lawyer rises to a higher rhetorical level even as he discredits all that fails the test of rational analysis, for example, the superstition that even the worst father, even Fyodor Pavlovich Karamazov, deserves the love of his son. Using the incendiary language of rights, the lawyer contends that the son of such a man "has the right henceforth to look upon his father as a stranger and even as his enemy" (746). He proceeds to give a fanciful account of the crime (the kind of tale he himself elsewhere calls a romance) in which unfortunate things happen to Dmitri in the course of killing his father. Dmitri does not author events; they befall him. A pestle finds its way into his hand. At the sight of his father "a feeling of hatred took hold of him involuntarily" (746), under the dominion of which the act of murder took place, if in fact it took place at all. In narrating the event, the one thing the lawyer never quite says is that Dmitri Karamazov actually killed his father:

> But even then the prisoner did not kill—I assert it, I cry it aloud—no, he merely swung the pestle in disgusted indignation, not wishing to kill, not knowing that he would kill. Had it not been for that fatal pestle in his hand, he would perhaps only have beaten his father, and not killed him. He did not know as he ran away whether the old man he had struck down was killed or not. Such a murder is not a murder.
>
> (746-47)

The act here described—a murder that is not a murder, performed by a magic pestle—is sui generis, outside of existing categories. Before his arrest, Dmitri acts as if he himself were outside the limitations binding on an ordinary person.

From the lawyer's account, at any rate, Dmitri emerges as a victim of misfortune, a direct if distant descendant of the storm-tossed figures of romance. But if the meaning of an action reveals itself only in retrospect, still the lawyer claims too much knowledge for himself and leaves Dmitri with too little. However much Dmitri might like to imagine himself the victim of his passions and his star, even he denies that he acted involuntarily, unconsciously, as though in his sleep. Nor is his role in events a simple one. Like his dream of bearing Grushenka away with his own money, which reads both like an innocent if vain romantic fantasy and like the sort of enthralling delusion to which moderns surrender their own freedom according to Zosima, so the story of Dmitri's actions confounds the very categories of guilt and innocence decisive in romance.[32] Of course he is innocent of the murder for which he stands trial, and yet he very nearly fractures Grigory's skull, threatens in writing to do the same to his father, assaults others as well, provides cover for the actual murderer (however unwittingly), and in any case builds up such a mountain of evidence and seeming evidence against himself by his own actions that a reader, even knowing the truth of the matter, can hardly fault the jury for lacking the faith to move the mountain. Where a hero of the Greek romance, who really has been removed from the world of the ordinary, undergoes a series of adventures, Dmitri both authors and suffers his fate. The opposite confronting him in the chess game, like a nemesis, is himself.

A VICTIM OF CIRCUMSTANCE?

In accordance with his aim of deflating human glory, Tolstoy makes the argument in *War and Peace* that an action assumes historical significance only insofar as it merges with other actions in a great fabric of coincidence. Coincidence serves to keep any one action from becoming too important. Only as they receive a kind of accidental support from the actions of others do our deeds become important to history. The murder of the father in *The Brothers Karamazov* really is a joint venture, and an action that none of the sons would probably have performed unassisted, but in this case we have to do not with world-historical events but the drama of a single household, and the role of coincidence is reduced accordingly. In this closely plotted tale coincidences—things that inexplicably, "fatefully," happen to occur together—are for the most part an illusion. The novel is designed, however, so that only in retrospect and upon reflection does their falsity become apparent. In real time, as it were, we do not and cannot know what's what. In the case of the almost simultaneous death of Father Zosima and old Karamazov, we can't be sure even on reflection that the conjunction of events is accidental. Perhaps if Alyosha had been less preoccupied with his dying elder, he would have been able to devote more of himself to preventing a catastrophe in his own household. Again, that Dmitri happened to drag Captain Snegiryov by the beard in the town square just as the schoolboys, including the captain's son, were coming onto the scene (203-4) may be coincidental; but even so, Dmitri is not the victim but if you will the perpetrator of the coincidence, and it is as an eventual consequence of his act of almost unfathomable cruelty that the captain's son, Ilyusha, dies.

Arrested shortly after shedding one man's blood for the murder of another, Dmitri finds himself trapped in what seems to him an evil web of coincidence. His entrapment is and is not a coincidence; mainly not. Exactly how Smerdyakov knew to batter Fyodor Pavlovich's skull with a blunt instrument just as Dmitri battered Grigory, no one can say, but that he used Dmitri as a decoy to deflect attention no one can doubt. Upon analysis, the murder of old Karamazov just after Dmitri's actions have presented Smerdyakov with the perfect cover is no more coincidental than the fact that the events of the novel take place immediately after the brothers happen to assemble for the first time. The elements of a dangerous mixture come together. While *The Brothers Karamazov* does contain its fraction of truly inexplicable coincidences to enrich the mix and add confusion and wonder, by and large the linkages in this work more closely resemble the taut logic of tragedy than the improbabilities of romance. Only in the mind of Dmitri (or the impressions of an amazed reader) are the events enmeshing him "a wonder, an absurdity, an impossibility" (458), as if they took place in what Dmitri calls "an Arabian tale" (116) and he had been specially targeted by the power of misfortune.

An ancient romance like *Callirhoe* or the *Ethiopian Story* turns upon the purest of coincidences: not just love but mutual love at first sight. In the latter work it happens that two persons who are each the epipsyche of the other find themselves in the same place at the same time. "At the moment of meeting" Theagenes and Chariclea "looked and loved, as though the soul of each at the first encounter recognized its fellow and leaped toward that which deserved to belong to it."[33] On this most perfect of coincidences is predicated all the subsequent action of the tale. In a thoroughly ironic rendering of the motif of the meeting of the eyes, Dmitri and Katerina are locked in love/hate from the moment of first sight.

> I saw her sizing me up; it was at the battery commander's, but I didn't go up to her then: I scorn your acquaintance, thought I. I went up to her a bit later on, also at a party; I began talking, she barely looked at me, pressed her contemptuous lips together. Well, thought I, just wait, I'll get my revenge!
>
> (111)

In the scene this leads into, a Dmitri possessed by "the kind of hatred that is only a hair's breadth from love, from the maddest love" (114) hands 5,000 roubles to Katerina without taking sexual advantage of her. Aftershocks of the encounter are felt throughout *The Brothers Karamazov.* What makes the encounter possible in the first place is the accident (which must seem to Dmitri a double godsend at the time) that money from his father has fallen into his hands at the very moment when Katerina's father is desperately in need of money. Truly a coincidence, but one with ironic qualifiers attached. It turns out that Dmitri's thousands come to him only after he signs away his rights to the remainder of his inheritance, another act that returns to haunt him. So too, while the money seems to come to Dmitri of its own accord, it enables him to toy with Katerina of *his* own accord and at his own risk and peril. In the courtroom it is Katerina who destroys Dmitri's last hope. Things seem to fall into place for Dmitri when, by good fortune, money puts Katerina in his power; later all the pieces of the case against him fall into place as well, and Fortune's child becomes misfortune's darling.

Dmitri's rescue of Katerina in the manner of a kind of irregular chivalric hero sets up what must be, next to the commission of the murder just as he flees from the scene, the purest non-coincidence of *The Brothers Karamazov.* A month before the action of the novel begins, Katerina, now rich and betrothed to Dmitri, entrusts him with 3,000 roubles to telegraph to Moscow—this "precisely at that fatal moment" (490) when he has become enchanted with Grushenka. Possibly more than any other single factor, it is the weight of 1,500 roubles of Katerina's money around his neck that drives Dmitri to distraction, to the point that he imagines himself singled out for suffering. While he does not know this at the time (119), there is nothing coincidental about

Katerina's placing in his hands, at just this moment, a sum of money that will enable him to run off with Grushenka if such is his desire. Dmitri is being tempted. He is subject not to the whims of fate or the abstract power of coincidence, not to extraordinary forces that do not afflict his fellow human beings, but to the vengeful will of Katerina Ivanovna, a will roused by his own acts.

By the time Dmitri cries out in open court, "I intended to become an honest man ever after"—as though fairytale endings were possible in life—"precisely at the moment when fate cut me down" (661), his complaint of being a victim of circumstance has taken on a hollow, repetitive sound. (If Ivan were to complain that his father was killed "just at the moment" when he set off for Moscow to begin a new life, he would simply be advertising his own blindness. Only belatedly, however, do both Ivan and the reader unravel the connection between these two events.) Dmitri was struck down by fate after he struck Grigory down, and what drove him to his father's garden in the first place was his obsession with Grushenka, the object of his quixotic fantasy of running away to begin a new and honest life (always assuming his debt of honor to Katerina could be cleared for the sum of 3,000 roubles). Wrongly accused of murder, Dmitri is the victim of such a gross error that he does not always grasp that he is nevertheless responsible for his plight and that the evidence stacked against him measures his own recklessness. The same evidence makes for another ironic, or if you will Cervantesque, comment on romance. In the world of romance, tokens like Odysseus's scar and pin serve to establish identity. In the anti-romance of *The Brothers Karamazov,* the tokens are a pestle and blood-soaked clothing, and what they establish is the false case against Dmitri. That the only exculpatory evidence Dmitri can produce is a story about a rag nowhere to be found, a rag that no one but Alyosha and the reader believe in, a rag that would prove precisely nothing even *if* found, illustrates his desperate position.

Though Dmitri finds himself in the tragic bind of one who undergoes complete humiliation and suffers excessively even as he authors his own ruin, he is nevertheless not "the tragic hero" of *The Brothers Karamazov,* if only because all of this is also true of Ivan. With the public making Dmitri the great focal point of gossip and speculation, it is as if those given to the satisfaction of imaginary needs (as Zosima said) had turned the case into a drama for their own gratification; or as if those addicted to spectacle were entertaining themselves with the spectacle of Dmitri. Why is it that Dmitri fills the role of the central figure of the case so well? According to Bakhtin, a "Ptolemaic" perception of language lacks an appreciation of its "plenitude."[34] It is exactly Dmitri's richness as a character, his plenitude, that makes the different stories or romances circulating about him seem believable to those who credit them. At once reckless and in one "fatal" instance calculating, fanatically suspicious and yet astonishingly naive, innocent and guilty, the man is a cornucopia, distinguished more by the wealth of his traits than by any single trait. And much of that wealth derives from the great exemplar of the tragicomic, Don Quixote, also endowed with both nobility and folly, and also an object of notoriety within his own tale.

DENIAL OF SUPERIOR KNOWLEDGE

When we finally meet the hero in book 5 of the *Odyssey,* he has already consulted Tiresias in the underworld and heard the prophecy of his own homecoming, but of this he gives no sign. Nor, when Calypso releases him, does he have the feeling that the prophet's prediction is at last coming to pass. Why is this? Not because Homer wants to keep us in uncertainty about the hero's chances or because the hero is withholding a secret from us, but simply because the narrative of the *Odyssey* hasn't reached Tiresias yet and so can't refer to his prediction, as it does not refer to any of Odysseus's adventures before his arrival on Calypso's island. When the *Odyssey* finally does come to Tiresias and the hero is told, in effect, that the survival of his crew depends on their leaving the cattle of Helios untouched, he suffers no agonies of suspense. If his crew is made of such poor stuff that their moral strength is uncertain as his is not, by the same token they are beneath a hero's concern. Suspense concerns the unknown, and in this case the unknown are Odysseus's mostly nameless sailing companions dismissed by the poet himself as fools for violating the sun god's decree. In the matter of Dmitri and his 1,500 roubles, everything is otherwise. Before we ourselves come to know of it, he does give signs of the money's existence, at one point even striking himself high on the chest, although we cannot possibly interpret these indications until after the fact. About Dmitri's money affairs Dostoevsky keeps us in the most acute uncertainty. The question is electrified with suspense, all the more because Dmitri keeps his secret from us until it is forced out of him in the course of events. It seems that in order for Dmitri to be the moral equal of his own author, he must have not only the power to speak but the right to remain silent.

Not from the narrator but from Dmitri himself, under the duress of interrogation, do we learn the story of his rag containing 1,500 roubles. Far from knowing more than Dmitri in this matter, Dmitri himself is the source—the only source—of our knowledge. So pronounced is the shift of storytelling responsibility to the persons of the drama in *The Brothers Karamazov* that it gives rise to the impression that these are beings like the author or the reader, outside the narrative itself. On this impression the argument of Bakhtin's remarkable study of Dostoevsky is raised. Dostoevsky's characters,

argues Bakhtin, are the equals of their author, free agents "capable of standing alongside their creator, capable of not agreeing with him and even rebelling against him." Such a work as *The Brothers Karamazov* represents a "*great dialogue* in which characters and author . . . participate with equal rights."[35] That a Dmitri Karamazov is an autonomous being with the power to oppose and surprise his own creator is a proposition that cannot really be demonstrated. You accept it or you don't. Clearly, however, we ourselves enjoy no superiority of knowledge over these characters, depending on them as we do for our information. As though Dostoevsky had revolutionized the device of direct speech that originates in Homer, our knowledge of events in *The Brothers Karamazov* derives very largely from the drama of dialogue. It is the predominance of direct speech in *The Brothers Karamazov* that underwrites our impression that its great characters have burst the frame of narrative. No longer simply placed in a story, they tell their own story. They are not spoken of, so much as they speak in their own right—and keep silence.

In the ironic sense that unauthorized Don Quixotes sprang into being owing to the success of the tales of his earlier exploits, Cervantes' hero as well took on an existence independent of his author. But assuming that Dostoevsky hoped the message of *The Brothers Karamazov* would root and sprout in Russia in accordance with the novel's epigraph—"Verily, verily I say unto you, Except a corn of wheat fall into the ground and die, it abideth alone: but if it die, it bringeth forth much fruit"—then he too thought books could come alive. If quixotism takes life for literature and literature for life, is there not already some trace of this noble malady in Dostoevsky as Bakhtin envisions him—one whose own inventions possessed the rights and privileges of living beings?

An author whose Quixote is fully real to him is himself a Quixote. But if there is something to Bakhtin's idea that Dostoevsky's characters stand equal to him, implying that he does not really possess knowledge superior to theirs in spite of being their creator, then still less does a reader know more than they. This means that for all Dmitri's quixotism, never can a reader survey his folly from a position of superior understanding, as we do continually with Don Quixote himself. Never do we share Don Quixote's mistakes of perception; but often in *The Brothers Karamazov* we see with Dmitri's eyes. In effect Dostoevsky completes what Bakhtin calls the Copernican revolution of modern prose by denying readers the privileged position of observation allowed them even in one of its greatest works.

By analogy, consider the difference between the handling of jealousy in *The Brothers Karamazov* and in *Othello.* (Jealous eyes after all see things, like Don

Quixote.) In an essay on jealousy inserted into the section of the novel devoted to Dmitri's search for 3,000 roubles, Dostoevsky writes:

> Jealousy! "Othello is not jealous, he is trustful," Pushkin observed, and this one observation already testifies to the remarkable depth of our great poet's mind. Othello's soul is simply shattered and his whole world view clouded because *his ideal is destroyed.* Othello will not hide, spy, peep: he is trustful. On the contrary, he had to be led, prompted, roused with great effort to make him even think of betrayal. A truly jealous man is not like that.

> (380)

However revealing this may be as a reading of *Othello,* it does point toward a critical difference between the case of the famous Moor and that of ex-lieutenant Dmitri Karamazov. In Othello's case we, the readers or spectators, know for certain of Desdemona's innocence. Dramatic irony is worked to its highest pitch. Of Grushenka's intentions we have no such knowledge or assurance, nor can we possibly tell that she is playing with the fire of Dmitri's jealousy in order to distract herself from her own troubles, if that is really what she is up to.[36] On the night of the murder we do not even know her whereabouts until Dmitri discovers, too late, that she is miles away. Dmitri's agony is the reader's uncertainty. As for the famous insufficiency of the motives of Othello's tormentor and destroyer Iago, its immediate equivalent in **The Brothers Karamazov** would be the undermotivation of Smerdyakov (who like Iago resents his subordinate position and uses honesty as his pose, at once a villain and a mystery). But Grushenka's motives too, whatever they are, hardly account for the magnitude of her deeds—the detonation of an explosive conflict in the Karamazov household. For that matter, if Fyodor Pavlovich raped an idiot girl in order to impress his friends, as seems likely, the crime far exceeded the triviality of its own motivation. (Is this not what is meant by the "banality of evil" after all—that monstrous actions should arise inexplicably from commonplace motives?) Similarly, Dmitri's humiliation of Captain Snegiryov in the town square, while the captain's son kisses his very hand, is an act of such cruelty that no motive—certainly not the meager available motive of getting even with the captain for being involved somehow with his father—seems capable of "explaining" it. Unlike Iago, then, Smerdyakov is not alone in the drama of **The Brothers Karamazov** in being undermotivated.[37] Indeed, his undermotivation is but a variant of the "surplus of humanness" enjoyed by the major characters of the tale: just as Dmitri can't be reduced to a figure of dissipation or Grushenka to a reformed harlot, so Smerdyakov can't simply be identified as, say, a denied son envious of his brothers, as though this closed the matter. In **The Brothers Karamazov** Iago's lack of transparency becomes something like a general condition, which for the reader means a loss of certainty. As

a close student of *Othello* remarks, we just don't know much about Iago.[38] At this point the contrast between Dostoevsky's procedure and that of Cervantes comes into focus.

Recall the famous "terrifying and never-before-imagined adventure of the windmills" early in *Don Quixote.* The episode begins as follows:

> Just then they came in sight of thirty or forty windmills that rise from that plain, and no sooner did Don Quixote see them than he said to his squire: "Fortune is guiding our affairs better than we ourselves could have wished. Do you see over yonder, friend Sancho, thirty or forty hulking giants?"[39]

The reader never has a chance to enter into Don Quixote's error of perception, that is, to identify the windmills as monstrous enemies. Before he speaks the shapes in the distance are defined to us as windmills. And so it is throughout *Don Quixote.* Never do we partake of Don Quixote's illusions or forego our advantage of perception, though Cervantes beautifully complicates things by making folly so nearly indistinguishable from nobility and by endowing Sancho Panza, who calls a windmill a windmill, with his own generous portion of folly. As Dmitri races from one unlikely candidate to another in a misguided and highly quixotic search for 1,500 roubles, we do not know the critical fact that this amount is all the time around his own neck. Not only are we allowed no advantage in knowledge, we know less than Dmitri at this moment. Not until later do we discover the existence of the 1,500—significantly, from his own lips and no one else's—and only at that point do we begin to understand his earlier frantic actions as a sign of the torment caused by that money, worn around his neck like an amulet of shame. If Dulcinea exists she is a coarse, ill-smelling peasant girl. Dmitri's election of Grushenka as his queen seems ludicrous, but who is to say that she doesn't possess the moral beauty he sees in her? The fact is that Dmitri in his folly and nobility infuses an uncertainty into **The Brothers Karamazov** that does not exist in a world where a thing is either a windmill or a giant.[40] From moment to moment in **The Brothers Karamazov,** even to the end, we never really know what Dmitri will do next, as though the author had loaded him with such an excess of potential that for everything he does there exists a kind of immediate possibility of him doing otherwise (which is also to say that Dmitri is like all of us, only more so). He can be imagined dreading to touch the cursed rag around his neck, tearing it off, dividing it in half, restoring the whole sum to Katerina in an attempt to quit his debt, reverting to Katerina, spending the whole sum in despair, and maybe even casting himself penniless at Grushenka's feet. Except perhaps for his beautiful discourses and spells of lucidity, such unpredictability has no equivalent in Don Quixote. In part because what Dmitri does do is no more probable than what he doesn't, the interrogators, prosecutor, and jury have great difficulty believing his story but no difficulty believing that he killed and robbed his father. (To the deluded prosecutor he seems a man of "resolution, cold-bloodedness, and calculation" [477]—the attributes of Odysseus.) We know better, but earlier in the novel, when he tells Alyosha that he might kill the old man and might not, we find ourselves as readers in the same position of uncertainty before the future as he himself is in.

If Dostoevsky confers on his characters, at least his great characters, rights equal to his own, certainly he also denies readers a position superior to those characters. Only after the fact do we learn of Grushenka's whereabouts on the night of the murder. We make the discovery when Dmitri does. (Indeed, not until the trial, that is, practically at the end of the novel, do we learn Grushenka's surname, Svetlov. We learn it when the narrator does.) Only after the fact do we learn that Dmitri actually had 1,500 roubles on his person as he raced around begging for money. Only after the murder do we ascertain how it was committed, and only then can we begin to piece together each brother's role in that complex event. The very nature of this polyphonic novel as "a work in which several consciousnesses meet as equals and engage in a dialogue that is in principle unfinalizable," that is, endlessly surprising[41]—this in itself seems to dictate that the reader of *The Brothers Karamazov* will possess no marked advantage of knowledge, no immunity to surprise or error, nothing comparable in degree or kind to the privilege of knowing possessed by some and not others in the *Odyssey*. Not until the members of the Karamazov family, minus Smerdyakov, assemble for a "dialogue" in an elder's cell do we discover what is going on in that household; and that state of affairs is so volatile and complicated that no one, not even the actors, can tell what will happen next. Only after the fact (a day later) do we learn what Father Zosima meant by kneeling before Dmitri in his cell, and then only darkly. After the scene in the cell when the cynical Rakitin comments that the Karamazov family "stinks" of crime (78), we have hardly heard of, and have not yet seen, Smerdyakov, whose name carries the epithet "Stinking," so that if Rakitin's choice of words constitutes foreshadowing, it is the kind of foreshadowing that reveals itself only in retrospect. All in all, it seems that Dostoevsky binds the reader by what Tolstoy calls "the rule forbidding us to eat of the fruit of the Tree of Knowledge" (*War and Peace* 1007), and he does so, I believe, to impress upon us the always incomplete nature of our knowledge—the correlate of the "unfinalized" nature of our being.

At a few points in the Shakespeare canon modern editors reassign a speech in the belief that it seems "out of character" for the original speaker. Commenting on this practice, Frank Kermode remarks that "the motive is not a good one, for it assumes that editors already know all they need to about the limits of the character."[42] Reading *The Brothers Karamazov,* we discover that we do not already know all we need to know, and even in retrospect can hardly tell what the "limits" of Dmitri's character may be.

MUCH IS CONCEALED

"Equality is only in man's spiritual dignity," says Zosima (316).[43] By the design of an author who so believes in the equality of souls that, arguably, he endows his heroes with a sort of equality to himself, a reader cannot really enter into those characters without giving up every pretense of superior knowledge. Within the world of *The Brothers Karamazov* itself there is no Tiresias, after all, who knows what lies ahead. Father Zosima bows down to Dmitri because he "seemed to see something terrible" (285) in Dmitri's face—a premonition nothing like Tiresias's road map of the future—and when Alyosha asks the elder to explain himself, he is checked in language that recalls the traditional injunction against thirsting for excessive knowledge: "Do not be curious" (285). (How different is the spirit of his warning from "The Tale of Ill-Advised Curiosity"—an extended fabliau—in *Don Quixote*.) Perhaps in Zosima's admonition lies some hint of the author's reasons for keeping the reader of *The Brothers Karamazov* always in the presence of the unknown. As moderns and especially as children of the Enlightenment, we pride ourselves highly on our knowledge. By now it is an article of secular faith that knowledge liberates, that you cannot really have too much of it, and that anything that impedes the quest for knowledge is a shackle on human progress. As a critic of modern rationalism Dostoevsky can't be expected to go along with such doctrines, and I believe that by divesting readers of *The Brothers Karamazov* of their proudest possession and dearest pretense—their knowledge—he imposes on us something like the awe before the unknown that Father Zosima enjoins on his young disciple. Says Father Zosima, "There is much in the strongest feelings and impulses of our nature that we cannot comprehend while on earth. . . . Much on earth is concealed from us" (320). Exactly who threw the stone that killed the boy Ilyusha, exactly who put the pillow under Dmitri's head following the ordeal of his interrogation is hidden from us. Certainly volume 2 of *The Brothers Karamazov* is hidden from us.

Each of the moderns considered in these pages, whatever his ideology, cautions against the pride of knowledge. To be told that

> in historic events the rule forbidding us to eat of the fruit of the Tree of Knowledge is specially applicable. Only unconscious action bears fruit, and he who plays a part in an historic event never understands its significance
>
> (*War and Peace* 1007)

is to be reminded of traditional prohibitions and to have the pride of knowledge mortified. Those who act, even act well, do not fully know what they do, while those who survey the past with belated knowledge pay for that knowledge with their own insignificance. In *Great Expectations,* the reader who does not know joins the company of Pip, ignorant that Biddy has married Joe; of Herbert, ignorant that Pip has established him in business; of Magwitch, ignorant of Miss Havisham; of Miss Havisham, ignorant that her ward is Magwitch's daughter. Ignorance unites, as though it belonged to our humanity itself. In **The Brothers Karamazov** people may be ignorant or they may just ignore.

Somehow Dmitri manages to ignore the dishonor he does to Katerina by relating the story of her humiliation to Grushenka. Somehow, too, he ignores the evidence that Grushenka's thoughts are not with his father but with her former lover, the Pole:

> Everything was clear as day: he knew about him, he knew everything perfectly well, knew it from Grushenka herself, knew that a month ago a letter had come from him. So for a month, for a whole month this affair had been going on in deep secret from him, up to the present arrival of this new man, and he had not even given him a thought! But how could he, how could he not give him a thought? Why had he simply forgotten about the officer, forgotten the moment he learned of him?
>
> (396)

Similarly, Ivan fails to discern Smerdyakov's ill intentions when he leaves for Moscow and the young Zosima failed to notice that the woman he was interested in was already betrothed. (The young Zosima had a quixotic streak of his own, challenging the woman's husband to a duel not so much because he loved her as because he was enamored of the romantic role he was playing. "Later I perceived and realized that I was perhaps not so greatly in love with her after all" [296].) Such critical lapses of attention—critical because they can alter the direction of a life—suggest that we have no option to abandon the quest to know and fall back on the comforts of "unconscious action." What we need to know, however, may lie in full view. Of his lady friend's betrothal, Father Zosima says, "Almost everyone knew, and I alone knew nothing" (296).[44] Nor is his blindness forever cured by this episode. Of Smerdyakov, the half-brother of his disciple and the ruin of the Karamazov household, Father Zosima appears completely unaware. The wisest person in the novel knows nothing of the most malevolent.

Immediately before affirming that "we must all serve each other" (289), Father Zosima's brother, the inspiration of his conversion, asks how it is that he failed to recognize such a simple principle before *his* conversion: "How is it that I did not know it, that I did not ap-

preciate it before?" (288-89). Readers of **The Brothers Karamazov** ask themselves the same question. Like Zosima himself, they too "know nothing." In *Don Quixote* everyone but the hero, that enthusiast of delusion, can perceive things more or less as they are. In **The Brothers Karamazov** everyone from the sage Zosima to the very reader is liable to the power of error.

Notes

1. Bakhtin, *Dialogic Imagination,* 37.

2. Fielding, *Joseph Andrews,* 25. As Fielding says on his title page, the novel was "Written in Imitation of the Manner of Cervantes, Author of *Don Quixote.*"

3. On the surplus of narrative possibilities, see Morson, *Narrative and Freedom.*

4. Even the theme of sexual rivalry between father and son, fraught as it is with tragic potential, recalls Greek New Comedy. The figures of the soldier and the cook—Smerdyakov's trade—are also ingredients of New Comedy.

5. On the dual nature of jealousy, see E. A. J. Honigmann, introduction to *Othello,* by William Shakespeare, Arden edition (Walton-on-Thames, Eng.: Thomas Nelson & Sons, 1997), 76-77: "Even if Othello were not an older and almost doting husband, jealousy—especially causeless jealousy—was thought ridiculous in itself, a folly deserving laughter, as the bystanders tell us in *The Winter's Tale* (2.1.198; 2.3.128). We do not laugh at either Leontes or Othello, yet the dramatist, a master of emotional chiaroscuro, knew that the conventions of comedy can tone in with tragedy."

6. Auerbach, *Mimesis,* 137.

7. Fielding, *Joseph Andrews,* 86.

8. The portrayal of the downtrodden Captain Snegiryov nevertheless contains a strong indictment of the class system; see 242-43.

9. At least this is Bakhtin's position in *Problems of Dostoevsky's Poetics.* In *The Dialogic Imagination* Dostoevsky is one among many.

10. Bakhtin makes the "rights" argument throughout the early chapters of *Problems of Dostoevsky's Poetics.* According to Bakhtin, the polyphonic author knows no more than his own characters—he renounces the "authorial surplus" (72). Dickens moots the question of authorial surplus by making Pip the "author" of *Great Expectations* and giving him, in that capacity, greater knowledge than he originally had. According to Bakhtin, "Only in the form of a confessional self-utterance, Dostoevsky maintained, could the final word about a person

be given, a word truly adequate to him" (55-56). *Great Expectations* constitutes a confessional utterance.

11. Cited in Frank, *Dostoevsky: The Mantle of the Prophet,* 546.

12. Bakhtin, *Problems of Dostoevsky's Poetics,* 58. It has been said that our humanity itself "entails not having complete insight into the motives and intentions of other people and even into our own," that "knowledge forbidden to us [lies] in the very midst of our existence" (Roger Shattuck, *Forbidden Knowledge* [New York: Harcourt Brace, 1996], 314).

13. Morson, *Hidden in Plain View.*

14. Cited and discussed in Eikhenbaum, *Tolstoi in the Seventies,* 138.

15. Joseph Frank, *Dostoevsky: The Seeds of Revolt, 1821-1849* (Princeton: Princeton University Press, 1976), 168.

16. Fyodor Dostoevsky, *A Writer's Diary, vol. 1, 1873-1876,* trans. Kenneth Lantz (Evanston, Ill.: Northwestern University Press, 1993), 411.

17. Robert Louis Jackson, "Alyosha's Speech at the Stone: 'The Whole Picture,'" in *New Word on "The Brothers Karamazov,"* 249-50.

18. *The Rambler* no. 4.

19. Erasmus, *The Praise of Folly,* trans. Robert M. Adams (New York: Norton, 1989), 48. Speaking of bewilderment and uncertainty, Folly also says, "That's what it is to be a man" (32).

20. Watt, *Myths of Modern Individualism,* 70.

21. "Mitya was also struck by the face of Kuzma Kuzmich, which had become extremely swollen recently: his lower lip, which had always been thick, now looked like a kind of drooping pancake" (*Brothers Karamazov* 369).

22. In the *Odyssey,* the original romance, the hero returns to a palace debauched by the suitors. In *The Brothers Karamazov* the sons return to a house debauched by their father.

23. On "prosaics" see Gary Saul Morson and Caryl Emerson, *Mikhail Bakhtin: Creation of a Prosaics* (Stanford: Stanford University Press, 1990).

24. Compare Bakhtin's discussion of the Greek romance in *The Dialogic Imagination,* 86-110.

25. "I don't know, I don't know . . . Maybe I won't kill him, and maybe I will. I'm afraid that at that moment his face will suddenly become hateful to me" (*Brothers Karamazov* 122).

26. Watt, *Myths of Modern Individualism,* 224-26.

27. Hannah Arendt, *The Human Condition* (Chicago: University of Chicago Press, 1958), 233.

28. Arendt, *Human Condition,* 233.

29. Perry, *Ancient Romances,* 133.

30. Frye, *Anatomy of Criticism,* 195.

31. Bakhtin, *Problems of Dostoevsky's Poetics,* 96.

32. If history, in Tolstoy's judgment, eludes the interpretive grid the historians seek to impose on it (Morson, *Narrative and Freedom,* 157), the story of Dmitri eludes the official procedures used to establish guilt and innocence. The truth seems to flow right through these proceedings without being caught by them, like water running through a net.

33. Heliodorus, *Ethiopian Story,* 70.

34. Bakhtin, *Dialogic Imagination,* 366.

35. Bakhtin, *Problems of Dostoevsky's Poetics,* 6, 71. Compare Iris Murdoch, *Existentialists and Mystics: Writings on Philosophy and Literature* (Harmondsworth, Eng.: Penguin, 1997), 254: "Here, I think, we naturally envisage a relation between the author and his character as if the character could turn around and say to the author, 'You have been unfair to me.'"

36. Not once on Calypso's island or on the way to Ithaca is Odysseus shown consumed with jealousy and suspicion over the suitors. Such is the difference between the romance of the *Odyssey* and the anti-romance, *The Brothers Karamazov.*

37. From the viewpoint of his interrogators, the rag around Dmitri's neck, if it existed, cannot account for the torments he attributes to it—an ironic instance of insufficient motivation.

38. See Honigmann, *Othello,* 31. When, in the first scene of the play, Iago claims that Othello snubbed those who pled for his promotion, we cannot tell if this ever took place, and when, in the last scene, he is asked why he caused such ruin, he refuses to answer.

39. Miguel de Cervantes, *Don Quixote,* trans. Walter Starkie (New York: New American Library, 1964), 98.

40. On Dostoevsky's transcendence of Cervantes, see chapter 11 ("The Ridiculous Man—Beyond Don Quixote") in Robert Louis Jackson, *The Art of Dostoevsky: Deliriums and Nocturnes* (Princeton: Princeton University Press, 1981).

41. Morson and Emerson, *Bakhtin: Creation of a Prosaics,* 238-39.

42. Kermode, *Shakespeare's Language,* 178n.

43. Spiritual equality is to be set against "socialist" equality as defined later in the novel by young Kolya Krasotkin. Socialism, says Kolya, repeating formulas, is "when everyone is equal, everyone has property in common, there are no marriages, and each one has whatever religion and laws he likes, and all the rest" (527). When Alyosha greets him as an equal (538), Kolya responds with the human warmth missing from these words.

44. Compare the words of Father Zosima's brother: "We are all in paradise, but we do not want to know it" (*Brothers Karamazov* 288).

Editions Cited

All works listed are cited by page number in text and notes unless otherwise indicated here.

Chariton. *Callirhoe.* Translated by G. P. Goold. Cambridge, Mass.: Harvard University Press, 1995.

Dickens, Charles. *Great Expectations.* San Francisco: Rinehart, 1948. (Cited by chapter and page numbers.)

Dostoevsky, Fyodor. *The Brothers Karamazov.* Translated by Richard Pevear and Larissa Volokhonsky. San Francisco: North Point, 1990.

Homer. *The Iliad.* Translated by Richmond Lattimore. Chicago: University of Chicago Press, 1961. (Cited by book and line numbers.)

———. *The Odyssey.* Translated by Richmond Lattimore. New York: Harper-Collins, 1991. (Cited by book and line numbers.)

Tolstoy, Leo. *Anna Karenina.* Translated by Richard Pevear and Larissa Volokhonsky. Harmondsworth, Eng.: Penguin, 2000.

———. "The Death of Ivan Ilych." In *Tolstoy's Short Fiction,* edited and translated by Michael R. Katz. New York: Norton, 1991.

———. *War and Peace.* Translated by Louise and Aylmer Maude. Oxford: Oxford University Press, 1991.

Other Works Cited

Auerbach, Erich. *Mimesis: The Representation of Reality in Western Literature.* Translated by Willard Trask. Princeton: Princeton University Press, 1953.

Bakhtin, Mikhail M. *The Dialogic Imagination.* Translated by Caryl Emerson and Michael Holquist. Austin: University of Texas Press, 1981.

———. *Problems of Dostoevsky's Poetics.* Translated by Caryl Emerson. Minneapolis: University of Minnesota Press, 1984.

Fielding, Henry. *Joseph Andrews.* Hammondsworth, Eng.: Penguin, 1985.

Frank, Joseph. *Dostoevsky: The Mantle of the Prophet, 1871-1881.* Princeton: Princeton University Press, 2002.

Frye, Northrop. *Anatomy of Criticism.* New York: Atheneum, 1967.

Heliodorus, *Ethiopian Story.* Translated by Sir Walter Lamb. Rutland, Vt.: Everyman, 1997.

Kermode, Frank. *Shakespeare's Language.* New York: Farrar, Straus, and Giroux, 2000.

Morson, Gary Saul. *Narrative and Freedom: The Shadows of Time.* New Haven: Yale University Press, 1994.

Perry, Ben Edwin. *The Ancient Romances: A Literary-Historical Account of Their Origins.* Berkeley: University of California Press, 1967.

Watt, Ian. *Myths of Modern Individualism: Faust, Don Quixote, Don Juan, Robinson Crusoe.* Cambridge, Eng.: Cambridge University Press, 1997.

Kate Holland (essay date spring 2007)

SOURCE: Holland, Kate. "Novelizing Religious Experience: The Generic Landscape of *The Brothers Karamazov.*" *Slavic Review* 66, no. 1 (spring 2007): 63-81.

[*In the following essay, Holland explores the manner in which the narrative structure of* The Brothers Karamazov *is influenced by religious tradition and folklore.*]

In the chapter of **The Brothers Karamazov** entitled "Cana of Galilee," Fedor Dostoevskii presents the novel theorist with a rich web of problems of interpretation.[1] Alesha Karamazov, returning to the monastery after the death and subsequent putrefaction of his elder Zosima have challenged his faith, hears Father Paissii reading the parable of the miracle of the wedding at Cana. Pondering the meaning of the story, Alesha seems to hear the voice of his departed elder and at once feels his soul become one with the universe, as he falls down to embrace the earth. This representation of Alesha's sudden epiphanic transformation challenges many of the core genre assumptions of novel theory. In this moment the gulf between the problematic individual and his world, which for Georg Lukács was the defining generic principle of the novel, is suddenly closed, as novel gives way to epic.[2] For Mikhail Bakhtin this scene represents the only moment in the whole work when the narrator breaks through the novelistic frame, taking on the tone of a hagiographer.[3] Here Dostoevskii seems to move out of the traditional realm of novelistic narrative into a world of silence, unity, and myth. Narrative is no more, and the novel must end. Yet it does not. This kairotic moment notwithstanding, Alesha goes back out into the world, Fedor Karamazov is murdered, Dmitrii is arrested; the novelistic machinery continues to turn.

"Cana of Galilee" places in sharp relief the dilemmas facing the author who seeks to represent religious experience in novelistic narrative. What happens to the novel when it has closed the gap within which narrative is possible, when it appears to disregard that uncertainty of identity upon which novels themselves are predicated? How will the reader react when, expecting a detective story, he is confronted with a novelistic world that is unashamedly dualistic, balanced precariously between a tangible heaven and hell? At the heart of the generic project of *The Brothers Karamazov* is Dostoevskii's attempt to overcome this creative paradox, to find a way of expressing religious experience within novelistic narrative.

Faced with a novel that insists on the possibility of representing religious experience, critics of *The Brothers Karamazov* have traditionally chosen to focus on only one side of the equation, preferring either to examine it as a novel much like any other while ignoring the generic transgressions, or else to focus on it as a theodicy, a confession of the author, or a philosophical treatise, while turning a blind eye to the issue of novelistic form.[4] A recent rich vein of criticism has begun to address the work's complex generic status, exploring the relationship between its religious message and the formal demands of the novel as a genre. Scholars such as Nina Perlina and Diane Oenning Thompson have examined how the novel's engagement with the authoritative sacred texts of scripture and high religious genres fits with the ambivalence and openendedness that is the hermeneutic legacy of the novelistic form.[5] Like these scholars, I see the question of genre as primary for an understanding of the aesthetic and ethical worldview of *The Brothers Karamazov,* a work that occupies a key position in the generic experimentation that characterized much of Dostoevskii's last decade. I argue that the writer moves away from the fragmentary, centrifugal model of the novel he used in his 1875 work *The Adolescent* and leaves aside the contemporary modes of secular biography and sociology, instead returning to the aesthetic and ethical values of an earlier, more traditional genre system. *The Brothers Karamazov* constitutes an attempt to reveal, transform, and extend the novel's own genre possibilities by engaging with, and borrowing from, the rich generic heritage of Christian legend. Dostoevskii recasts the problem of the reconciliation of the Christian moral paradigm and novelistic narrative within the framework of a trial of genres.

The Brothers Karamazov engages with many different traditions of Christian legend, from the high canonical genre of hagiographic legend to the oral, popular genre of folk legend, from the medieval apocrypha with their roots in early Christian doctrinal anxieties, to nineteenth-century popular legends that unite Christian motifs with the social and political concerns of the Russian peasantry. While previous scholars have discussed the novel's use of hagiographic and apocryphal legend and of different kinds of popular folkloric narrative, there has never been a systematic study of the function of these references, of their relation to one another, or of their connection to the literary, textological, and philological debates of Dostoevskii's time.[6] Dostoevskii does not merely borrow isolated elements from these genres of the legend but models them as authentic worldviews, structuring their aesthetic and ethical differences and dialogic interactions into his novel. An examination of the generic hierarchy of the different legends allows us to trace how their aesthetic and ethical reverberations rock the novel's very narrative structure.

In all its many incarnations, Christian legend has traditionally carried out the function of narrating the spaces between the scriptures, of contextualizing the biblical narratives within the popular imagination, of demonstrating how Christian moral law affects the life of an ordinary believer, and of exploring the narrative implications of Christianity itself.[7] Combining the canonical and noncanonical, high and low, written and oral genres, the generic landscape of legend shares much with the heterogeneous and nonhierarchical generic territory of the novel.

THE LEGEND AS GENRE

The legend is a hybrid genre, which exists at the meeting point of official hagiography, the saints' lives of the Orthodox collections of the *Prolog* and the *Chet'i Minei,* apocryphal literature, and folklore. Even a brief examination of the etymology and nineteenth-century usage of the term *legenda* demonstrates the complicated patchwork of textual traditions and religious and national affiliations that attached themselves to this genre designation. The word entered the Russian language at the turn of the nineteenth century, coming either through French or German from the Medieval Latin *legenda.*[8] It was in frequent use during the first quarter of the century. Pavel Chernykh notes that the word first appeared in a dictionary in 1845.[9] By the 1850s the word had begun to be used interchangeably with the older genre designations *predanie* and *skazanie,* passed down from the Church Slavic, which had previously been used to translate the Latin legenda as well as the Greek equivalents. The entry in Vladimir Dal''s dictionary includes the definition, "sacred legend [*sviashchennoe predanie*]." We see the interchangeability of the genre designations legenda, predanie, skazanie in Grigorii Kushelev-Bezborodko's *Monument to Old Russian Literature,* edited by Nikolai Kostomarov, which is subtitled, "Skazaniia, legendy, povesti, skazki i pritchi."[10]

The genre territory of the legend as understood in the second half of the nineteenth century includes at least three distinctive groups of works: the hagiographic legend, the apocryphal legend, and the folk legend. Although each group is derived from the doctrines of the Orthodox Church, each maintains a very different relationship toward the canonical texts and is governed by a different set of narrative conventions. The hagiographic legend, the *zhitie,* is a high religious genre contained within the Orthodox canon. In the Orthodox tradition it refers to those lives of saints included in the canonical collections of the *Prolog* and the *Chet'i Minei* and arranged according to where the saints' days fell in the Orthodox calendar. The lives within the *Chet'i Minei* were intended to be read silently to oneself, those from the *Prolog* to be read out loud.[11] The most influential hagiographic collection was that compiled by the sixteenth-century Metropolitan of Moscow Makarii. It was the subject of renewed scholarly interest from the 1860s onwards, and a critical edition was undertaken in 1868.[12] Dostoevskii had in his library an 1860-1861 selection of the lives in twelve volumes.[13]

The second group of works comprises the so-called apocryphal legends, written texts that had been rejected by the ecclesiastical authorities and thus remained outside the Orthodox canon. They include Old and New Testament apocrypha, translations from Greek, South Slavic borrowings, and apocrypha originating within the Russian lands. Alongside the "Gospels" of Thomas, Jacob, and Nicodemus and "The Legend of How God Created Adam," exist narratives about the journeys of the Virgin, Christ, and the Apostle Paul into hell. The main collections of apocrypha were those edited by Nikolai Tikhonravov and Aleksandr Pypin, both of which were published in 1863.[14] The 1860s and 1870s saw a flood of interest in the apocrypha on the part of scholars, writers, and even the educated public.[15] Dostoevskii's knowledge of and interest in apocryphal legend is demonstrated through the range of references he makes to apocryphal narratives in **The Brothers Karamazov.**

The third kind of legend is the folk legend, the *narodnaia legenda.* This differs from the other two groups through its oral transmission, and it was at its height much later, in the eighteenth and nineteenth centuries. In the folk legend, motifs, plots, and characters from canonical Orthodox texts including the Bible, the *Prolog* and the *Chet'i Minei* coexist both with supernatural and fantastic elements from the wonder tale and other folk genres and with social themes taken from the lives of its peasant narrators. The first and most important collection of legends was Aleksandr Afanas'ev's *Russian Folk Legends,* collected by the folklorist in northern and western Russia and in Ukraine.[16] The coexistence of pagan and Orthodox beliefs as well as the anticlerical nature of many of the legends led to its banning on the orders of the Holy Synod. The ban notwithstanding, Afanas'ev's collection was read extremely widely in intellectual and literary circles, and many other collections followed in its wake. Dostoevskii's knowledge of Afanas'ev's work is demonstrated by his use of one of the folklorist's Ukrainian folk legends as the prototype for Grushenka's tale of the onion.

Folklorists distinguish the folk legend from the wonder tale by virtue of its religious elements, which tend to vary significantly from Orthodox doctrines.[17] A common theme is that of Christ as *strannik,* wandering the earth in the guise of a beggar in the company of his apostles or saints, coming into contact with peasants, and setting them some kind of moral test. The contradictory relationship between folk legend and the doctrines of organized religion is revealed through its dependence on motifs from apocryphal legend and through its irreverent portrayals of heaven and hell. A common theme the folk legend takes from the apocrypha is a journey into heaven or hell, sometimes both, often undertaken by a conscript on his way back from military service. Heaven becomes tedious because of its lack of alcohol and tobacco, while the conscript is frequently thrown out of hell for building a chapel in which to worship.[18]

The Novel, Legend, and Literary Scholarship

Dostoevskii's use of the genres of the legend in **The Brothers Karamazov** should be viewed in the context of a surge of interest on the part of scholars and writers of the 1860s and 1880s in the relationship between the verbal culture of early Christianity and the medieval period on the one hand, and the genre of the novel on the other. The nineteenth-century philologist Fedor Buslaev was the first Russian scholar to point out the similarities in function and structure between different genres of Christian legend in the medieval period and the novel in his own century. Uniting adventure narratives, family memoirs, and important historical events, hagiographic legends were the novels of their day, claimed Buslaev.[19] Aleksandr Veselovskii, perhaps the greatest Russian philologist of the nineteenth century, wrote extensively on the connections between medieval Byzantine and Russian Christian legends and apocrypha, most notably in a series of articles he wrote on the Christian legend for the journal of the Ministry of National Enlightenment entitled, "Studies in the History of the Development of Christian Legend."[20] In works such as "Monuments of Narrative Literature," he traced a link between medieval narrative genres and the modern novel.[21] This interest resulted in his treatise, "History or Theory of the Novel?" a work of historical poetics and an embryonic theory of the novel.[22]

Dostoevskii's contemporaries had begun to understand the generic peculiarities of the novel in terms of its heterodox ancestry, which derived from neither the classical genres of antiquity, nor the stratified, eighteenth-century genre system, but rather from the complex interplay between the written and oral genres of the Middle Ages, between the strict doctrines of the church and the heterogeneous beliefs of the people. This line of research would be enthusiastically pursued by many novel theorists in the following century, including Mikhail Bakhtin.[23] The philological debates on these diverse kinds of legends taking place in the 1860s and 1870s provide not only the background but also a significant motivating force behind the generic and religious dynamism of *The Brothers Karamazov.* Dostoevskii takes part in contemporary genre debates within the novelistic form, and in that process, structures within his own novel the pre-history of its genre.[24]

In juxtaposing the novel and the legend, Buslaev and Veselovskii were plowing a rich seam of generic parallels. The novel shares with the legend its status as compilation, as container-genre. The medieval hagiographic legend frequently took the form of a series of narratives of differing liturgical and hagiographic genres, which were placed together in an anthology.[25] The Bakhtinian view of the novel as an overarching genre that carries within itself a multiplicity of interpolated genres borrows more from medieval textual tradition than Bakhtin himself ever admitted. *The Brothers Karamazov* makes explicit the parallels between these two apparently wholly different textual traditions. By placing the hagiographic legend of the Life of Zosima alongside the apocryphon of the **"Grand Inquisitor,"** the folk legend of the onion alongside the sacral narrative of Alesha's moral resurrection, Dostoevskii creates his own novelistic compilation in the manner of medieval legend.

Dostoevskii also exploits similarities in the intertextual relationships between the legend and the novel. Both the novel and the legend are engaged in a continual process of dialogue, drawing on a repository of shared themes, motifs, and paradigms. Where hagiographic legends explore the theoretical models of Christianity laid out in scripture and test out ways of living according to the moral precepts of the Bible, apocrypha seek to provide a fresh perspective on the stories from the Bible and the hagiographic legends themselves, while folk legends rework apocryphal visions and recontextualize figures from the Bible and from hagiographic legend in a contemporary rural Russian setting. The canonized St. Georgii becomes the folk hero Egor the Brave, while the Old Testament apocryphal narratives of Solomon the Wise were updated by peasants in the nineteenth century and passed down through the oral tradition.[26] Novels share this process of narrative recycling, taking part in a broader social dialogue, refracting within their own structure previous literary formulations of the themes they address.[27] *The Brothers Karamazov* borrows quotations and motifs from Johann Wolfgang von Goethe, Friedrich Schiller, and Jean-Jacques Rous-

seau, reworks plots from George Sand and Émile Zola, takes part in contemporary debates over crime, biology, the relationship between church and state, education, and legal and governmental reforms.[28] Dostoevskii supplements these parallels, highlighting the similarities in both genres' preoccupation with the tension between the moral paradigms offered by scripture and the chaotic and contradictory worlds which they themselves represent.

Dostoevskii works these differing models into the novel itself through the generic identities of the three Karamazov brothers. Each brother expresses himself within the terms of a different kind of legend, and his ethical identity is revealed along with the generic perspective and worldview of the legend with which he is associated. Alesha experiences a moment of transfiguration modeled according to the conventions of hagiographic legend, and hagiographic discourse flows into the novel itself in the chapter "Cana of Galilee." Ivan borrows from the diverse forms of apocryphal legend for the ideological and aesthetic underpinnings of his "Rebellion" and **"Grand Inquisitor."** And after his arrest and during his incarceration, Dmitrii takes on the ambivalent moral dimensions of the hero of folk legend. Interrogation of these different kinds of legends and their associated worldviews opens up a new perspective, not only onto the relationships between the Karamazovs, but also onto the genre assumptions of the novel itself and its own representation of religious experience.

IVAN AND APOCRYPHAL LEGEND

Ivan Karamazov identifies with the literary form and many of the spiritual and philosophical assumptions of apocryphal legend. His rebellion and *poema* engage with several different Old Russian apocryphal traditions: the apocalyptic tradition; the tradition of God's questioner; the journey through hell; and finally and most obviously, the apocryphal variant of the biblical wilderness temptation narrative. Though often perceived by critics as an essentially modern nihilist-existentialist vision, Ivan's rebellion borrows from a rich tradition of popular religious dissent and heresy dating back to the medieval period, and its spiritual and philosophical foundation within this tradition is reflected in his borrowings from the genre of the apocryphal legend.

Ivan's rebellion consists in his refusal to accept the construction of a world predicated on human suffering. As an expression of spiritual discontent and a plea for an explanation of the ways of God, it engages with the generic tradition of the frequently heretical medieval apocrypha that seek to fill in the spiritual or narrative gaps in the canonical biblical texts. These apocrypha present a biblical character, such as the Mother of God, an apostle or a prophet, who addresses questions either to God or to the Devil. These questions usually concern the afterlife, the fate of souls in heaven and hell, or the events that took place in the period following the Resurrection. To this group belong apocrypha such as "St. Bartholomew's Questions to the Mother of God," "St. Bartholomew's Questions to Jesus," "The Questions of John the Theologian to God on Mountain Tabor," "The Questions of John the Theologian to Abraham about Righteous Souls," "The Questions of John the Theologian to Abraham on Mount Elyon."[29] These apocrypha are often apocalyptic in mode, hence their attribution to John the Theologian, the apostle traditionally perceived as the author of Revelation, the only apocalyptic text in the canonical New Testament.[30] By framing his rebellion within the terms of these medieval apocrypha, Ivan invests it with a powerful spiritual, intellectual, and emotional legitimacy. He is expressing the same doubts with which Christians have been grappling for well over a thousand years: What kind of accounting will there be in the afterlife for the injustices that have taken place on earth?

As Harriet Murav points out, Ivan's narration of his anecdotes on the suffering of children as an explanation of his decision to "return his ticket" provides a symbolic representation of another subgenre of apocryphal narrative, that of the tour of hell.[31] With his graphic description of the children's suffering, Ivan leads Alesha through the circles of hell just as the Archangel Michael leads the Mother of God in the *Mother of God Visits the Torments,* which is a crucial reference narrative for **"Grand Inquisitor."**[32] Byzantine in origin, the apocryphon was transmitted to the Russian lands in a South Slavic translation in the early medieval period and was included by both Tikhonravov and Pypin in their collections.[33] The legend recounts how the Mother of God is led through hell by the Archangel Michael. Touched by the fate of the sinners, especially those who have been consigned to a burning lake and "forgotten by God," she asks God to pardon all those whose suffering she has witnessed. God refuses to release them, pointing to Christ's wounds and asking how he can forgive what has been done to his Son. The Mother of God then asks all the saints and apostles to pray with her for their absolution, and God agrees to a cessation of their torments once a year for the period from Good Friday to Pentecost.

Ivan places the legend as a kind of biblical thematic motif before his "poema," implying that in both its ethical and its generic foundations the *Mother of God* prefigures his own poema.[34] With its presentation of the sufferings of sinners in hell, the apocryphon serves to link Ivan's refusal to accept the sufferings of the innocent and his denial of the necessity of suffering as atonement for original sin in "Rebellion" to the Grand Inquisitor's complete negation of suffering and his subsequent inversion of the Christian moral paradigm. Framed within Ivan's narrative, it is God's intransi-

gence that is stressed, his merciless insistence on the continued sufferings of the sinners as atonement for their persecution of Christ, that finds both its mirror and its antagonist in the obduracy of the Grand Inquisitor. As Ivan paraphrases the plot of the apocryphon for Alesha, he dwells on those forgotten by God. God's plea, "How can I forgive his tormentors," echoes the plea Ivan himself makes to Alesha on behalf of the tortured children. The legend illustrates a suffering that will no longer exist under the rule of the Grand Inquisitor.

Framed within the novel as a whole, however, the legend carries altogether different resonances. When we read it alongside the novel's other narratives of sin, expiation, and redemption, such as Grushenka's tale of the onion and the folk legend about hell told to Ivan by his coachman, then the meaning of the apocryphon is transformed. It functions as an illustration of the infinite mercy of God and of the continuing possibility of moral regeneration, even from within the flames of hellfire itself. The clash of these two framings immediately throws into question the ethical and narrative implications of Ivan's own apocryphal legend.

The "poema" **"Grand Inquisitor"** is scattered with references to apocryphal narratives, as well as to the Revelation of John, which, though canonical, retains more affinity with apocrypha than it does with the rest of the New Testament because of its apocalyptic tone. Though its central metaphor, the devil's three temptations of Christ in the wilderness, is taken from the synoptic Gospels, the "poema" locates itself outside the biblical canon. The Grand Inquisitor's retelling and analysis of the temptation narrative is structured as an apocryphal gospel in its own right, a restructuring of the biblical events from a retrospective perspective.[35] With its vision of a world where the church has thrown in its lot with the devil, **"Grand Inquisitor"** evokes one of the most revolutionary of the medieval heresies, that of the bogomils, which itself played a significant role in the shaping of many medieval Russian apocrypha.[36]

If Ivan starts out as the author of an apocryphon, he ends up as the protagonist of his own apocryphal narrative. The aesthetic and ethical implications of the poema he himself has written determine his subsequent development within the novel. Through Ivan's appropriation of man's freedom, the Grand Inquisitor, and through him, Ivan, forecloses all temporality and choice, and thus all narrative potentiality. Without freedom of choice, there remains nothing to narrate. Through this attack on the concept of individual moral freedom, Ivan lays siege, not only to the foundations of the Christian moral paradigm, but to the foundations of novelistic narrative as well. Himself a novelistic creation, Ivan is implicated in this denial of narrative potentiality. Though Ivan criticizes Christianity for the inevitable universal cycle of suffering that it imposes on his followers, the alternative he offers falls into the same blind determinism. While for Dostoevskii the Orthodox believer it is Ivan's negation of man's moral freedom that undermines his metaphysical vision, for Dostoevskii the novelist it is Ivan's rejection of narrative possibility that in the end leads him into madness.

The ultimate poetic justice is meted out to Ivan in his confrontation with the devil. With the appearance of the "dread spirit," apocryphal legend permeates the novel's own structure, flouting the conventions of the realist novel. Denying the narrative freedom upon which the realist novel relies, Ivan is condemned to wander through his own philosophical hell, to inhabit the fictional world of apocryphal legend, and to lose his sanity along with his individual autonomy. While the novel recoils from the genre implications of Ivan's own apocryphon and his own rebellion is parodied as Enlightenment vaudeville, semantic fragments from his apocryphal subtexts lodge themselves within the novel. His adoption of the form of the apocryphal legend to question the Christian doctrines of original sin, suffering, and expiation is upheld in the novel; it is his answers that are rejected. His apocryphal questions are answered instead within the frame of the novel itself, in the form of a very different genre of legend.

ALESHA AND HAGIOGRAPHIC LEGEND

Alesha is characterized within the terms of a different kind of legend: hagiography. Just as Ivan is transformed from author to subject of his own apocryphal narrative, Alesha begins as hagiographer but ends up as hagiographic hero.[37] Writing the "Life of Zosima," a hagiographic legend that becomes incorporated into the novel's own narrative structure, Alesha begins to model his own worldview according to hagiographic convention, and his faith is challenged as he observes the gap between the novelistic world he inhabits and the hagiographic world he produces in his own work.

Like all hagiographic legend, the "Life" is structured, not by *chronos,* but by *kairos*; it assumes the existence of a kairotic moment, a point of conversion located outside the ordinary human experience of temporality.[38] In this moment, the saint ceases to inhabit the fallen world of flux and fragmentation. Past, present, and future become fused in the experience of oneness with God. This breakdown of temporality proves problematic for the hagiographer, who must find a way of narrating a life touched by the sacred and thus invested with a higher significance. As he lives his life, the future saint is not conscious of the imminence of the moment of conversion, of the moment when he will become aware of his oneness with God, yet once his "Life" is narrated, the hagiographer reorders the events of his life in the light of the kairotic moment.

The moment of conversion in the "Life of Zosima" takes place on the morning when the future elder is pre-

paring to fight his duel. Remembering his violence toward his manservant Afanasii, he recalls his brother Markel's teachings and "suddenly the whole truth appeared to me in its full enlightenment."[39] Zosima's conversion is marked by the bridging of the gap between himself and others, and between himself and God. The sudden revelation that all men are made in the image and likeness of God strips Zosima utterly of the consciousness of the difference between self and other. His transformation is made immediately obvious to those present at the duel; he is forgiven for withdrawing the challenge as soon as it becomes clear that he has ceased to inhabit the social world in any ordinary sense and has begun to realize his monastic vocation.

The difference between the hagiographic and novelistic modes is evident if we compare the narrative of Zosima's duel and the narrative of the mysterious stranger.[40] Even as Zosima describes the events leading up to the challenge, the moment of conversion intrudes. His behavior seems to follow a predetermined pattern, a path toward enlightenment. There is no narrative suspense, no identifiable moment of moral choice, when his conscience could have led him either one way or another. The mysterious stranger on the other hand continually defers his admission of guilt, demonstrating the palpable mechanism of his moral choice.

The hagiographic mode is structured according to a set of assumptions that could not be further from those of the novel. Within the complex web of novelistic structure, every description, every event is subject to a plethora of possible interpretations, whereas in hagiography it corresponds to a single stable interpretation. In the novel repetition implies connection; if characters share a trait or an experience, this is not accidental but rather provides a structural connection that affects the interpretation of the whole. Yet at the same time, each character must also be perceived as the arbiter of his or her own individual fate. The individual's autonomy is continually circumscribed by family and social identifications; biological or genetic motivations in turn are balanced by individual intellectual or moral developments and environmental factors. Novelistic representation must structure this balance between individuality and sameness. If each event in each individual human biography can be simultaneously interpreted as being the result of genetic predisposition, social or environmental factors, and individual choice, each event in hagiographic discourse is subject to a particular law of hagiographic representation and plays a stable and predictable role in the artistic and ideological structure of the whole.

Dostoevskii models the clash between the assumptions of hagiographic and novelistic representation on the level of novelistic structure in the failure of Zosima's body to escape decomposition.[41] As a reader and writer of hagiographic legend, Alesha anticipates the miracle of bodily preservation, and when it fails to take place his faith is shaken. His expectations are shaped by his identification with hagiographic narrative, not merely as a literary and philosophical system, but as lived experience. When life fails to emulate literary convention, he is forced to reassess his entire belief system.

THE ONION

In the chapters "The Onion" and "Cana of Galilee," Dostoevskii offers two different models of moral resurrection. One, Alesha's conversion experience, unfolds according to the conventions of hagiography, offering up a miracle that, suggesting as it does the transcendence of the space of incomprehension separating man from God, leads beyond the realm of novelistic narrative. The other, the complex mutual conversion of Grushenka and Alesha, which finds expression in the folk legend of the onion, suggests a model of resurrection that takes place *within* narrative, can be expressed in narrative, and is fully compatible with the laws of the novelistic universe.

Alesha's spiritual resurrection is a complex process that extends beyond the boundaries of hagiographic representation. His and Grushenka's moral transformations occur simultaneously, and it is impossible to identify which is the instigator of the conversion process. His grief for the elder provides him with, as the narrator announces, his greatest defense against seduction. Grushenka's discovery of the elder's death induces shame in her at her own behavior, yet seduction never appears likely. The complexity and multiplicity of motivations and the impossibility of predicting either Grushenka's or Alesha's behavior foreground an ambiguous kind of conversion, a process rather than a moment, which follows a novelistic rather than hagiographic trajectory.

The onion legend provides the metaphor for the apparent "miracle" of Grushenka's decision not to seduce Alesha, which displaces the failed miracle of Zosima's bodily preservation. In the legend a wicked old woman is given the chance to escape from a fiery lake in hell by her guardian angel, who, remembering her one good deed, digging up an onion for a beggar woman, offers her the onion to pull herself out of hell. When her fellow sinners try to hold onto her legs to get out of the lake, she kicks them back down, the onion breaks, and she is sent careering down into hell. The legend models the central theme of the novel itself: the continuing possibility of moral resurrection at the last possible moment, even from within hell. The onion narrative bears remarkable similarity to one of the variants of a legend published by Afanas'ev in *Russian Folk Legends,* "Christ's Brother."[42]

The onion, a characteristic motif in the folk legend, functions as a familiar symbol of the sustenance and protection offered by the earth. The possibility of escaping from hell is testament to an ethical-religious outlook that offers more compassion and second chances than that of canonical Orthodoxy, but the woman's failure to grasp the moral principle of the onion or to spread her good fortune among the denizens of hell suggests a worldview in which religious principles are tempered by bitter social experience. The onion narrative offers two different conclusions: in the legend the old woman fails the moral test set by her guardian angel, but in the novel itself Grushenka takes the onion and refuses to seduce Alesha, thus beginning her moral regeneration.[43] This "novelistic" miracle is dualistic, bounded by alternative narrative outcomes.

The onion narrative and its novelistic incarnation are juxtaposed to the transcendent miracle of Alesha's spiritual regeneration. Where Alesha's miracle seems to stop narrative in its tracks, Grushenka's miracle regenerates it, opening up a number of alternative plot scenarios. Grushenka has sinned, yet she is on one of many paths to redemption. Far from circumscribing her narrative possibilities, the onion legend opens up narrative vistas for her. It underlines her moral potentiality as it is realized within the structure of the novel: the onion stands as the symbol of her redemption, possible yet not inevitable. Unlike Alesha's kairotic moment, it is a miracle that is realized *within* narrative, enabled by the narration of the legend itself.

In the chapter "Cana of Galilee" Alesha at last experiences the kairotic moment denied him in the hours following Zosima's death. This miracle of oneness with the universe in fact follows precisely the pattern already laid out in the chapter "Elders": the miracle follows the faith, rather than the other way round.[44] Grushenka's transformation is the spiritual and narrative peripetaeia that leads to the moment of conversion. And since Grushenka's own moral potentiality is conveyed through the legend of the onion, then it follows that what appears at first as an affirmation of the hagiographic perspective, is in fact mediated first and foremost by the folk legend.

This redemptive narrative climax is structured by a multilayered hagiographic perspective, by hagiography as popular legend rather than as literary or spiritual system. The novel's brief opening onto the transcendent simultaneously carries within itself a return to the earthly, which we see mirrored in the mechanism of spatial perspective: after Alesha has looked up into the heavens, he returns his gaze immediately to the earth and throws himself on the ground. Thus what has begun as a movement away from the earth, a retreat into the divine, in fact turns out to be the opposite, an embrace of the earth and of the human. In the end it is the onion narrative, rather than the "Life" or "Cana of Galilee," that provides the aesthetic and ethical momentum for the rest of the novel, and it is Mitia, rather than Alesha, who comes to play the role of novelistic hero.

Mitia and Folk Legend

Dmitrii Karamazov appears in the first half of the novel as what Gary Saul Morson has called a generic refugee, a hero in search of a genre.[45] This search is modeled in the structure of the novel itself in the three confessional chapters devoted to Mitia, "Confessions of an Ardent Heart." In the chapter "Confessions of an Ardent Heart in Verse," he locates himself in a world modeled primarily according to Romantic convention, identifying his own "insect sensuality" in Schiller's "Ode to Joy."[46] Yet his understanding of Romanticism is a limited one; he identifies with its outer form, its portrayal of extreme states, of the abyss, and of the duality of beauty, but he is unable to grasp its inner content.

His first meeting with Katerina Ivanovna as related in the following chapter takes place within the terms of the debased romanticism of the French boulevard novel. Yet he inhabits even this generic universe only for a second, before rewriting himself into a tragedy: "You understand the first half: it's a drama and happened there. The second half is a tragedy and will happen here."[47] Mitia occupies the role of tragic hero for much longer, and this is the one the novel itself at first seems to sanction. The suggestion that it is he who will murder Fedor, Zosima's bow to him in the monastery, and his own continual references to the abyss over which he is poised, all serve to bolster the idea that Mitia stands at the center of a tragedy beginning to unfold.

The tragic momentum builds to a climax in Book 8, which provides an account of Dmitrii's frantic attempts to procure the 3,000 rubles he must return to Katerina Ivanovna so that he can clear his name and win Grushenka. Following on from the chapter "Cana of Galilee" and Alesha's moment of revelation, when the narrative perspective breaks free of the boundaries of novelistic time and space and enters into the realm of hagiographic legend, the narrative in Book 8 moves back in time, covering the same two days from Dmitrii's perspective. Repetitions of the word *fate* and its variants alert us to the fact that we are in the realm of tragedy, whose governing principle is fate.

The play between open and closed narrative development comes to a climax at the moment of the murder in Mitia's vacillation over whether or not to murder his father. The ellipses that represent the murder of Fedor Karamazov signify the turn from tragic inevitability to novelistic potentiality. The moment Mitia utters the words "God was watching over me then," the spiral of fate is resisted, the tragic mode exploded.[48] The following moment Mitia knocks down Grigorii Vasil'evich, undercutting any interpretation of this as a second miracle akin to that experienced by Alesha in the previous section. This reminds us that we are in the dominion of the novel, rather than in the realm of salvation literature. The either/or of the tragic mode has been replaced, not by the kairotic time of a conversion narrative, but by the novelistic open field, and there is all to play for.

With the explosion of the tragic mode, Mitia goes once more in search of a genre. The narration of a folk legend by the coachman Andrei at last makes clear Mitia's own generic affiliation. As an ex-soldier, womanizer, and drunkard with a predisposition for violence, Mitia resembles the archetypal hero of folk legend. Up until the murder he is never explicitly connected with the genre; it is Alesha and Grushenka who feel the aesthetic and ethical reverberations of the previous folk legend invoked by Dostoevskii, the legend of the onion. Here the insertion of the folk legend plays a crucial role; it provides a generic model for Mitia's moral choice to not murder his father.

The second half of the novel serves as a trial, not merely of Mitia, but also of genre itself, the search for a form which can explain that missing narrative, and in doing so, provide a literary model for the representation of man and his manifest moral contradictions. In the chapters following the murder, when Mitia's innocence is already clear, the novel demands a reassessment of human potentiality; it suggests a very different image of man from that offered by epic and tragedy. The folk legend Andrei tells Mitia is thus located at a crucial moment in the novel, after the collapse of the previous genre models offered to us. In the light of this collapse, it is able to offer a very different worldview and image of man from those of the "high" literary genres that precede it.

Having failed to find Grushenka, Mitia sets off for Mokroe in a troika driven by the coachman Andrei. In response to Mitia's question whether he believes he will go to hell, Andrei tells him the folk legend:

> You see sir, when the Son of God was crucified on the cross and died, he went straight from the cross to hell and freed all the sinners that were suffering there. And hell groaned, because it thought it wouldn't have any more sinners coming. And the Lord said to hell: "Do not groan, O hell, for all kinds of mighty ones, rulers, great judges and rich men will come to you from all parts, and you will be as full as ever, unto ages of ages, till the time when I come again."[49]

The editors of the Academy Edition reference the legend first of all in terms of the "harrowing of hell" apocrypha where, following the Crucifixion but before the Resurrection, Christ frees sinners from hell.[50] Such apocrypha include "St. Bartholomew's Questions" and "Pilate's Epistle to the Emperor Tiberius," part of the apocryphal gospel of Nicodemus, both included in Pypin's collection.[51] They go on to suggest that the source may be a piece of religious folk poetry.[52] Yet Mitia's response, "a folk legend [*narodnaia legenda*], wonderful," makes the genre of the narrative clear. The motif of a newly resurrected Christ liberating the sinners from hell can be found in one of the folk legends in Afanas'ev's collection, no. 15 "Solomon the Wise."[53] Solomon the Wise is a common character in the folk legends, primarily because of his presence in so many apocrypha.[54] In Afanas'ev's legend, Christ releases all the other sinners from hell, but leaves Solomon there, since he is wise enough to get out on his own initiative. Asked by a devil why he is measuring hell, Solomon replies that he is intending to build a monastery and a church right there in hell. The frightened devil runs to tell Satan, who releases Solomon forthwith.

The legend demonstrates an unexpectedly dualistic attitude toward miracles. Hell is anthropomorphized, groaning as it is emptied of sinners. God here is forced to sympathize with hell, to promise it recompense in the form of the authority figures that will be sent there in their stead. The emptying of hell is, on the one hand, testament to the infinite compassion of Christ, who, even before his Resurrection, redeems the sinners. On the other it demonstrates the enduring existence of hell itself, of the continuation of sin, and of the unchanging nature of the human. This is a profoundly ambivalent model of sin, expiation, and redemption. The sinners are released, not because they have repented, but because of Christ's compassion. In its folk legend incarnation, the miracle of the "harrowing of hell" is built on novelistic rather than eschatological foundations.

The genre of the folk legend fuses the earthly with the divine; though inspired by apocryphal motifs and biblical images, it is grounded in the earth and projects an image of man as greedy and generous, wily and naive, selfish and selfless: as broad as the Karamazovs. Despite its spatial and temporal configurations, its frequent representations of heaven and hell, the folk legend is concerned not with beginnings and ends but with the essentially unchanging cycle of life. It thus provides a way to narrate religious experience within the generic terms of the novel, without impinging upon the novelistic hero's ability to carry on the endless process of self-definition through narrative.

The folk legend provides the model for Mitia's subsequent moral and spiritual development within the novel. The vision of hell instantiated in the folk legend here permeates the novelistic structure. Identifying with the worldview expressed in Andrei's legend, Mitia enters into his own process of redemption. His cross-examination is played out against the background of the model of hell instantiated in the legend. The three chapters that recount his interrogation are entitled "The Soul's Journey through the Torments" after the forty days of torments the soul was forced to endure after death according to popular Orthodox belief.[55]

Just like the torments, the interrogation serves as a moral test for Dmitrii, forcing him to undergo diverse kinds of humiliation, from insults to Grushenka, to being forced to take off all his clothes and disclose his "great secret." With the revelation of the great secret, the interplay of genres at last comes to an end. Mitia's aesthetic and ethical worldview becomes fully delineated, modeled within the generic foundations of the so-called legend of the *ladonka,* Mitia's decision to put aside half of the 3,000 rubles given to him by Katerina Ivanovna in a cloth bag to demonstrate that he is "a scoundrel, not a thief."[56]

Like Grushenka's onion tale and Andrei's legend of the sinners in hell, the cloth bag narrative offers an ambivalent vision of human morality, giving rise to a contradictory set of narrative scenarios. The cloth bag contains only half the money Mitia has taken from Katerina Ivanovna and thus brings to mind the moral depths to which he has sunk. Yet, although the ladonka is half-empty, at the same time it is half-full. While the money remains round his neck he retains on his person the physical, tangible proof of the possibility of moral resurrection; he can go to Katerina Ivanovna and show her that he is not beyond repair; that though fallen, he can still be resurrected.[57]

The cloth bag narrative reveals the novelistic hero's ambivalent relationship toward the Christian moral paradigm. Mitia's actions testify to his awareness of a higher spiritual ideal, his sense of himself as an ethical being bound by moral law. Yet this awareness is tempered by his continuing need to fight against that ethical system, to feel out its limits, and to prove his individuality through transgression. In this he stands apart from both Ivan, who denies absolutely the authority of the Christian moral code, and Alesha, who accepts it wholeheartedly. It is precisely his ability to embody these two antithetical instincts that accords him his status as novelistic hero. The novel finds its subject in the shortfall of these paradigms, in the space between the absolute moral categories of the protagonist's belief system and the untidy reality in which he finds himself. Like Christian legend, it occupies that ambiguous space between scripture and human life, providing the narrative foreground and background for biblical narratives that often seem far removed from the concerns and dilemmas of human society.

Dostoevskii found in the literary form and metaphysical landscape of legend an alternative to the secular subgenres of the novel within which he had been working in the 1870s. In its use of the diverse genres of the legend, ***The Brothers Karamazov*** achieves the status of a work of religious polyphony that navigates the normally tense spaces between doctrinal/canonical Orthodoxy and popular religion. It celebrates Orthodox Christianity not as canon law, as an established set of moral laws that must be followed, but as a rich repository of narrative forms. Legend demonstrates the creativity and literary potentiality contained in religious narrative, in its ability to continually generate new variants. Whether through the Byzantine Lives of Saints that made sacred virtue tangible through its instantiation within the life of an individual, the medieval apocrypha that sought to illuminate the darker corners of the Christian doctrines, or the nineteenth-century folk legends that recast the values of the biblical accounts in the light of the social values of the peasantry, legend has always provided the narrative means by which Christianity has become intelligible to the majority of its followers.

Through its celebration of narrative potentiality, the legend functions as a genre metaphor for the novel itself. Like the legend, the novel takes as its subject the problematic realm between divine law and earthly freedom. It finds its raw materials in the gap between the ideal and the real. ***The Brothers Karamazov*** is concerned with moments of moral suspense, narrative scenarios where characters must measure themselves against absolute moral standards, and with how they will respond to this moment of reckoning. By structuring the generic interplay between hagiography, apocrypha, and folk legend within the central characters of the Karamazov brothers, Dostoevskii was able to provide three competing models of sin, expiation, and redemption. But it is the spirit of the folk legend, crystallized within the narrative of Dmitrii Karamazov, that most closely approaches the ethical and aesthetic assumptions of the novel as a genre.

Notes

I would like to thank those who have read and commented on previous versions of this article, especially Robert Louis Jackson, Vladimir Alexandrov, Harvey Goldblatt, Irina Paperno, and Ilya Kliger, the two anonymous reviewers for *Slavic Review* and Diane Koenker.

1. F. M. Dostoevskii, *Polnoe sobranie sochinenii v tridtsati tomakh,* ed. V. G. Bazanov et al. (hereafter *PSS*) (Leningrad, 1972-1990), 14:328. All English translations are mine.

2. Georg Lukács, *Die Theorie des Romans* (Berlin, 1920), 68-72.

3. Mikhail Bakhtin, *Problemy poetiki Dostoevskogo* (Moscow, 1963), 335.

4. In the first group I have in mind such critics as V. L. Komarovich, B. G. Reizov, and Robert Belknap; in the second Vasilii Rozanov, Nikolai Berdiaev, and a host of contemporary Russian and western critics writing under their influence. V. L. Komarovich, *F. M. Dostojewskij: Die Urgestalt der Brüder Karamasoff: Dostojewskijs Quellen, Entwürfe und Fragmente* (Munich, 1928); B. G.

Reizov, "K istorii zamysla *Brat'ev Karamazovykh*," *Zven'ia* 6 (1936): 545-73; Robert Belknap, *The Structure of* The Brothers Karamazov (The Hague, 1967); V. V. Rozanov, *Legenda o "Velikom inkvizitore" F. M. Dostoevskogo* (St. Petersburg, 1891); N. Berdiaev, *Novoe religioznoe soznanie i obshchestvennost'* (St. Petersburg, 1907); Ellis Sandoz, *Political Apocalypse: A Study of Dostoevsky's Grand Inquisitor* (Baton Rouge, 1971).

5. Nina Perlina, *Varieties of Poetic Utterance: Quotation in* The Brothers Karamazov (Lanham, Md., 1985); Diane Oenning Thompson, The Brothers Karamazov *and the Poetics of Memory* (Cambridge, Eng., 1991).

6. For previous discussions of the role of hagiography in *The Brothers Karamazov,* see V. E. Vetlovskaia, *Poetika Romana "Brat'ia Karamazovy"* (Leningrad, 1977); Jostein Børtnes, "The Function of Hagiography in Dostoevskij's Novels," *Scando-Slavica* 24 (1978): 27-33, Margaret Ziolkowski, *Hagiography and Modern Russian Literature* (Princeton, 1988); A. Opul'skii, *Zhitiia sviatykh v tvorchestve russkikh pisatelei XIX veka* (East Lansing, Mich., 1986); and Thompson, *Brothers Karamazov,* 74-107. On the significance of apocryphal legend, see Harriet Murav, *Holy Foolishness: Dostoevskii's Novels and the Poetics of Cultural Critique* (Stanford, 1992), 140-42; and Perlina, *Varieties of Poetic Utterance,* 82-87. For accounts of Dostoevskii's uses of folk legend in *The Brothers Karamazov,* see George Gibian, "Dostoevskii's Use of Russian Folklore," *Slavic Folklore: A Symposium,* vol. 6 (1956): 230-45; L. M. Lotman, "Romany Dostoevskogo i russkaia legenda," *Realizm russkoi literatury 60-kh godov XIX veka* (Leningrad, 1974), 285-315; Faith Wigzell, "Dostoevskii and the Russian Folk Heritage," in W. J. Leatherbarrow, ed., *The Cambridge Companion to Dostoevskii* (Cambridge, Eng., 2002), 21-46; Thompson, *Brothers Karamazov,* 108-16; and Shawn Kate Elliott, "The Aesthetics of Russian Folk Religion and *The Brothers Karamazov*" (PhD diss., University of California, Berkeley, 1997).

7. For a discussion of the sociological and narrative functions of Christian legends, see Hippolyte Delehaye, *Les Légendes hagiographiques* (Brussels, 1906) and André Jolles, *Einfache Formen* (Halle, 1930).

8. "Legenda," *Tolkovyi slovar' velikogo russkogo iazyka* (Moscow, 1881); Max Vasmer, "Legenda," *Etimologicheskii slovar' russkogo iazyka* (Moscow, 1964).

9. Chernykh notes an early attribution to Aleksandr Pushkin, in a letter to-Petr Pletnev, in which Push-

kin suggests that Pletnev should encourage Zhukovskii to read the *Chet'i Minei,* "especially the legends [*legendy*] about the Kievan wonderworkers." "Legenda," in P. Chernykh, ed., *Istoriko-etimologicheskii slovar'* (Moscow, 1993).

10. *Pamiatniki starinnoi russkoi literatury,* 4 vols., vols. 1, 2, and 4 ed. N. Kostomarov, vol. 3 ed. A. Pypin (St. Petersburg, 1860-1862).

11. Ziolkowski, *Hagiography,* 19.

12. This period also saw the publication of Vasilii Kliuchevskii's groundbreaking work on the historical importance of hagiography, *Drevnerusskiie zhitiia sviatikh kak istoricheskii istochnik* (Moscow, 1871), as well as Nikolai Kostomarov, *Russkaia istoria v zhizneopisaniiakh ee glavnykh deiatelei* (St. Petersburg, 1874), and Archmandrite Ignatii, *Kratkie zhizneopisaniia russkikh sviatykh* (St. Petersburg, 1875).

13. *Izbrannye zhitiia sviatykh, kratko izlozhennye po rukovodstvu Chet'ikh-Minei* (Moscow, 1860-61). See Leonid Grossman, *Biblioteka Dostoevskogo* (Odessa, 1919). This work is number 185 of Grossman's inventory.

14. N. Tikhonravov, ed., *Pamiatniki otrechennoi russkoi literatury* (St. Petersburg, 1863), A. Pypin, ed., "Lozhnye i otrechennye knigi russkoi starinnoi," *Pamiatniki starinnoi russkoi literatury,* vol. 3.

15. See, for instance, A. Pypin, "Drevniaia russkaia literatura. I, Starinnye apokrify. II, Skazanie o khozhdenii bogoroditsy po mukam," *Otechestvennye zapiski* 115 (1857); I. I. Sreznevskii, "Khozhdenie bogoroditsy po mukam," *Izvestiia II imperatorskoi Akademii nauk za 1863 god* (1863); I. Smirnov, "Apokrificheskie skazaniia o Bozhiei Materi i deianiiakh apostolov," *Pravoslavnoe obozrenie* (1873); F. Kerenskii, "Drevnerusskie otrechennye verovaniia i kalandar' Briusa," *Zhurnal Ministerstvo narodnogo prosveshcheniia* (1874).

16. A. N. Afanas'ev, *Narodnye russkie legendy, sobrannye Afananasievym* (Moscow, 1859).

17. Jack V. Haney, "Legends," *An Introduction to the Russian Folktale,* vol. 1 of *The Complete Russian Folktale* (Armonk, N.Y., 1999), 106-8.

18. See, for instance, the variants of the folk legend, "Soldat i smert'," Afanas'ev, *Narodnye russkie legendy,* 122-30.

19. Fedor Buslaev, *Istoricheskie ocherki russkoi narodnoi slovesnosti i iskusstva* (St. Petersburg, 1861), 172.

20. A. Veselovskii, "Opyti po istorii razvitiia khristianskoi legendy," *Zhurnal Ministerstva narodnogo prosveshcheniia* (St. Petersburg, 1875-1877).

21. A. Veselovskii, "Pamiatniki literatury povestvovatel'noi," in A. Galakhov, ed., *Istoriia russkoi slovesnosti, drevnei i novoi,* 2d ed. (St. Petersburg, 1880).

22. A. Veselovskii, "Istoriia ili teoria romana?" and "Iz istorii romana i povesti," *Izdanie otdeleniia russkogo iazyka i slovesnosti* (St. Petersburg, 1886, 1880).

23. Mikhail Bakhtin, "Iz predystorii romannogo slova," *Voprosy literatury i estetiki* (Moscow, 1975), 408-46. Its subtitle, "Towards a Historical Poetics," itself seems to invoke Veselovskii's work. Of all the Russian philologists of the previous generation, only Veselovskii was capable of impressing Bakhtin. See I. Shaitanov, "Aleksandr Veselovskii's Historical Poetics: Genre in Historical Poetics," *New Literary History* 32 (2001): 429-43.

24. Though there is no concrete evidence to show that Dostoevskii read the works of Buslaev, Veselovskii, and Pypin, one work in his library does show similar concerns and preoccupations, namely P. V. Evstaf'ev, *Drevniaia russkaia literatura: Do-Petrovskii period: Ustnaia narodnaia slovesnost'* (St. Petersburg, 1877). This work is no. 115 in Grossman, *Biblioteka Dostoevskogo.* Evstaf'ev's survey discusses the unique cross-breed of medieval oral literature, engendered by the fertile verbal culture of *dvoeverie,* nourished alike by the narrative traditions of Christianity and of pre-Christian beliefs. He draws a line to the oral literature of the nineteenth century, the folk legends and religious poetry still being narrated in villages all across the Russian empire. He discusses the heterogeneous nature of folk legend, quoting at length from one of Afanas'ev's legends. The academic discussion in Evstaf'ev's book may well have resonated with Dostoevskii's own sense of the rich artistic and spiritual sensitivity of the Russian peasantry, and their innate feeling for their own religious and cultural heritage.

25. Vasmer's definition highlights this aspect of the legend: "a collection of liturgical extracts for the daily service." Vasmer, "Legenda," *Etimologicheskii slovar'.*

26. See the discussion of the appropriation and reworking of Christian legend in folkloric contexts in E. V. Anichkov, "Khristianskie legendy v narodnoi peredache," *Istoriia russkoi literatury,* 2 vols. (Moscow, 1908).

27. See Bakhtin's discussion of the novel's emergence from the low parodic versions of high literary genres. Bakhtin, "Iz predystorii romannogo slova," 424-32.

28. On the breadth of the novel's intertextual references, see Robert Belknap, *The Genesis of* The Brothers Karamazov: *The Aesthetics, Ideology, and Psychology of Text Making* (Evanston, 1990), and Reizov, "K istorii zamysla *Brat'ev Karamazovykh*," 559-73.

29. Tikhonravov, ed., *Pamiatniki otrechennoi literatury,* 18, 173, 193, 197; Pypin, ed., "Lozhnye i otrechennye knigi russkoi starinnoi," 109, 113.

30. A. Pypin, "Legendy i apokrify v drevnei russkoi pis'mennosti," *Vestnik Evropy* (1894): 314, 325.

31. Murav, *Holy Foolishness,* 139-40. Also see Pypin, "Drevniaia russkaia literatura."

32. Dostoevskii, *PSS,* 14:225.

33. Tikhonravov, ed., *Pamiatniki otrechennoi literatury,* 23; Pypin, ed., "Lozhnye i otrechennye knigi russkoi starinnoi," 18.

34. See V. E. Vetlovskaia, "Apokrif 'Khozhdenie bogoroditsy po mukam' v *Brat'iakh Karamazovykh* Dostoevskogo," *Dostoevskii i mirovaia kul'tura* 11 (1998): 35-47.

35. In fact Tikhonravov includes two apocryphal accounts of the temptation narrative in his collection "God's Debate with the Devil," and several of the other apocrypha make reference to the same events: Tikhonravov, ed., *Pamiatniki otrechennoi literatury,* 282.

36. The bogomils, medieval dualistic dissenters, believed that the material world was the creation of the devil himself. On the role of the bogomil heresy in the development of Slavic apocrypha, see V. Mil'kov, *Drevnerusskie apokrify* (St. Petersburg, 1999), 92.

37. For a strikingly different analysis of the significance of hagiography in the generic hierarchy of the novel, see Thompson, *Brothers Karamazov,* 74-106.

38. For a discussion of the conflict between kairotic and chronological time and its significance for novelistic narrative, see Frank Kermode, *The Sense of an Ending* (Oxford, 1967), 46-54.

39. Dostoevskii, *PSS,* 14:20.

40. Caryl Emerson sees the episode with the mysterious stranger as a powerfully unresolved moment in the "Life" and a key stage in the transposition of hagiographic to novelistic discourse. Caryl Emerson, "Zosima's 'Mysterious Visitor': Again Bakhtin on Dostoevsky, and Dostoevsky on Heaven and Hell," in Robert Louis Jackson, ed., *A New Word on* The Brothers Karamazov (Evanston, 2004), 155-79.

41. Dostoevskii took the corruption motif from Monk Parfenii's travelogue, as he indicates in a letter to Nikolai Liubimov, his editor: Dostoevskii, *PSS,* 30.2:126. See R. Pletnev, "Dostojevskij und der Hieromonach Parfenij," *Zeitschrift für slavische Philologie* 14 (1937): 30-46.

42. Afanas'ev, "Khristov bratets," *Narodnye russkie legendy,* 130-31. Whether consciously or unconsciously, Dostoevskii hides the origins of the legend. Grushenka calls the onion narrative a tale (*basnia*), and, in a letter to Liubimov, Dostoevskii claims that it was told to him by a peasant woman: Dostoevskii, *PSS,* 14:319, 30.1:126-27. His claim to have heard it for the first time is not backed up by any evidence, and the similarities with Afanas'ev's version are undeniable.

43. Gary Saul Morson makes a similar point in "The God of Onions: *The Brothers Karamazov* and the Mythic Prosaic," in Jackson, ed., *A New Word on* The Brothers Karamazov, 107-24. Also see Sara Smyth, "The 'Lukovka' Legend in *The Brothers Karamazov,*" *Irish Slavonic Studies* 7 (1986): 41-51.

44. Dostoevskii, *PSS,* 14:24-25.

45. Morson coined this term in an essay on *Fathers and Sons,* but he uses it in relation to Alesha's role in *The Brothers Karamazov.* Although all of the Karamazov brothers can be seen as refugees from other kinds of legends, I feel that this description is particularly appropriate for Mitia. Morson, "The God of Onions," 112, 123, see also Morson, "Genre and Hero/Fathers and Sons: Intergeneric Dialogues, Generic Refugees, and the Hidden Prosaic," in Edward J. Brown, Lazar Fleishman, Gregory Freidin, and Richard Schupbach, eds., *Literature, Culture, and Society in the Modern Age, Stanford Slavic Studies* 4, no. 1 (1991): 336-81.

46. Dostoevskii, *PSS,* 14:98.

47. Ibid., 14:103.

48. Ibid., 14:355.

49. Ibid., 14:372.

50. Ibid., 15:575.

51. Pypin, ed., "Lozhnye i otrechennye knigi russkoi starinnoi," 109, 106.

52. The folk poetry mentioned is one of the "Dream of the Virgin" prototypes, of Christ's dialogue with hell. The "Visit of the Mother of God through the Torments" can also obviously be seen as another variant of the "harrowing of hell" narrative.

53. Afanas'ev, *Narodnye russkie legendy,* 53.

54. Pypin, ed., "Lozhnye i otrechennye knigi russkoi starinnoi," 51-71; Tikhonravov, ed., *Pamiatniki otrechennoi literatury,* 254-72. The inclusion of motifs from many different types of apocrypha in folk legends is very characteristic. Old and New Testament apocrypha provided the inspiration for a significant number of the legends recorded by Afanas'ev.

55. In fact Dostoevskii's notebooks for 1877 testify to the fact that one of his creative projects was a poema on the subject of the *sorokovina,* these forty days of torments. Dostoevskii, *PSS,* 17:14.

56. Dostoevskii, *PSS,* 14:444.

57. For a fuller discussion of the cloth bag narrative and its context in the novel, see Kate Holland, "The Legend of the *Ladonka* and the Trial of the Novel," in Jackson, ed., *A New Word on* The Brothers Karamazov, 192-200.

FURTHER READING

Criticism

Ellias, S. "The Burden of Shouldering Identity: A Micro-Essay in Dostoevsky." *Canadian-American Slavic Studies* 36, no. 1-2 (2002): 19-100.

> In-depth examination of the representation and background of Dostoevsky's treatment of the issue of identity in *The Brothers Karamazov.*

Alfred, Lord Tennyson
1809-1892

English poet and playwright.

The following entry provides criticism on Tennyson's works from 2000 to 2007. For further discussion of Tennyson's complete career, see *NCLC,* Volume 30; for discussion of *Idylls of the King,* see *NCLC,* Volume 65; for discussion of *In Memoriam,* see *NCLC,* Volume 115.

INTRODUCTION

Tennyson is widely considered one of the greatest poets to have written in the English language. He was immensely popular during his lifetime, especially in the years following the publication of his lengthy elegiac poem *In Memoriam* (1850). Epitomizing Tennyson's art and thought, this work was embraced by readers as an affirmation of their religious faith amid doubt raised by the scientific discoveries and theories of the time. Queen Victoria declared that she valued *In Memoriam* next to the Bible as a work of consolation, thus contributing to Tennyson's stature as the foremost poet of his generation and the quintessential poetic voice of Victorian England. While many critics have since faulted his poetry as excessively moralistic, Tennyson is universally acclaimed as a uniquely gifted lyricist.

BIOGRAPHICAL INFORMATION

The fourth of twelve children, Tennyson was born in Somersby, Lincolnshire. His father was a rector who maintained his benefice grudgingly as a means of supporting himself and his family. The elder son of a wealthy landowner, he had obtained the rectory when his younger brother was designated as a prospective heir to the family's estate. According to biographers, Tennyson's father responded to his virtual disinheritance by indulging in drugs and alcohol, creating an unstable domestic atmosphere marked by his violent temper. Each of his children suffered to some extent from drug addiction or mental illness, promoting the family's speculation on the "black blood" of the Tennysons, whose history of mental and physical disabilities, epilepsy prominent among them, had become a distressing hallmark of their family heritage. Biographers speculate that the general melancholy expressed in much of Tennyson's verse is rooted in the unhappy environment at Somersby.

Tennyson's first volume of poetry, *Poems by Two Brothers,* included the work of his two elder brothers and was published in 1827. Later that year, Tennyson enrolled at Trinity College, Cambridge, where he won the chancellor's gold medal for his poem *Timbuctoo* in 1829. *Poems, Chiefly Lyrical* (1830) was well received and marked the beginning of Tennyson's literary career; another collection, *Poems,* was published in 1832 but was less favorably reviewed, with many critics praising Tennyson's artistry but objecting to what they perceived as an absence of intellectual substance. This latter volume was published at the urging of Arthur Hallam, a brilliant Cambridge undergraduate who had become Tennyson's closest friend and was an ardent admirer of his poetry. Hallam's enthusiasm was welcomed by Tennyson, whose personal circumstances led to a growing despondency: his father died in 1831, leaving Tennyson's family in debt and forcing his early departure from Trinity College. One of Tennyson's brothers suffered a mental breakdown and was institutionalized, and Tennyson was himself extraordinarily fearful of falling victim to epilepsy or madness. Hallam's untimely death in 1833, which prompted the series of elegies later comprising *In Memoriam,* caused Tennyson to plummet into a deep depression and prompted suicidal thoughts.

For nearly a decade after Hallam's death Tennyson published no poetry. During this period he became engaged to Emily Sellwood, but financial difficulties and Tennyson's persistent anxiety over the condition of his health contributed to the couple's separation. In 1842, yielding to a friend's insistence, Tennyson published his two-volume collection *Poems,* which was virtually unanimously admired by reviewers. That same year an unsuccessful financial venture cost Tennyson nearly everything he owned: he again fell into a deep depression, and required medical treatment. In 1845 Tennyson was granted a government pension in recognition of both his poetic achievement and his financial need. Contributing to his financial stability, the first edition of his narrative poem *The Princess* (1847) sold out within two months of its publication. Tennyson resumed his courtship of Sellwood in 1849, and they were married the following year.

The timely success of *In Memoriam* in 1850 ensured Tennyson's appointment as poet laureate, succeeding William Wordsworth. *Idylls of the King* (1859), considered by Tennyson's contemporaries to be his masterpiece, and *Enoch Arden* (1864), which sold more than forty thousand copies upon publication, increased both Tennyson's popularity and his wealth. Although the dramatic works written later in his career were largely unsuccessful, Tennyson completed several additional collections of poems in the last decade of his life, all of which were well received. In 1883 Tennyson accepted a peerage, becoming the first poet to be so honored strictly upon the basis of literary achievement. Tennyson died in 1892 and was interred in Westminster Abbey.

MAJOR WORKS

Tennyson's first two significant collections, *Poems, Chiefly Lyrical* and *Poems,* were considered by many critics to be of considerable literary merit but lacking meaning or purpose beyond pure artistry. The collection of *Poems* that was published in 1842 included radically revised versions of his best poems from the earlier volumes, and addressed such themes as duty, self-discipline, and the complexities of religious faith, offering what critics considered to be a truer representation of humanity than that depicted in his earlier works. Such poems as "The Palace of Art," "St. Simeon Stylites," "The Two Voices," and "The Vision of Sin" display an attitude of moral determination that characterizes the collection as a whole, examining the conflict between indulgence and morality while expressing the need for social involvement. While many of Tennyson's earlier poems, such as "Recollections of the Arabian Nights" and "The Hesperides" disclose a desire to escape into fantasy, the *Poems* of 1842 demonstrate Tennyson's effort to face reality. *The Princess,* which examined the education of women in Victorian England, was Tennyson's response to critics who urged him to address the major issues of his day. The focus of the poem shifts from the establishment of women's colleges to a more general consideration of what Tennyson regarded as the unnatural attempt of men and women to assume identical roles in society. Many critics assessed Tennyson's treatment of the central question—women's education—to be superficial and representative of what they considered to be a major weakness in his poetry. Nevertheless, *The Princess* was warmly received by the British public, who favored its idealism and celebration of domesticity.

Tennyson's next major work, *In Memoriam,* expressed his personal grief over Hallam's death while examining more generally the nature of death and bereavement in relation to nineteenth-century scientific issues, especially those concerning evolution and the geologic dating of the earth's history, both of which brought into question traditional religious beliefs. Largely regarded as an affirmation of faith, *In Memoriam* was especially valued for its reflections on overcoming bereavement. Comprising 132 sections written over the course of nearly two decades, the poem progresses from despair to joy and concludes with a marriage celebration, symbolically expressing Tennyson's faith in the moral evolution of humanity and reflecting the nineteenth-century ideal of social progress. In his ceremonial role as poet laureate, Tennyson composed such poems as *Ode on the Death of the Duke of Wellington* (1852) and "The Charge of the Light Brigade" (1854), each of which is a celebration of heroism and civic responsibility. The title poem of *Maud, and Other Poems* (1855) is a "monodrama" in which the changing consciousness of the narrator is traced through a series of tragedies that result in his insanity. Confined to an asylum, the protagonist is cured of his madness and asserts his love for humanity by serving his country in the Crimean War. Madness, suicide, familial conflict, shattered love, death and loss, and untempered mammonism, all central concerns in Tennyson's life, are attacked openly and passionately in *Maud,* with war cultivating the spirit of sacrifice and loyalty, virtues which Tennyson felt essential to avert the self-destruction of a selfishly materialistic society.

Tennyson's epic poem *Idylls of the King* followed *Maud* by examining the rise and fall of idealism in society. Tennyson was concerned with what he considered to be a growing tendency toward hedonism in society and an attendant rejection of spiritual values. *Idylls of the King* expresses Tennyson's ideal of the British empire as an exemplar of moral and social order, personified in King Arthur and the other members of the court of Camelot. However, when the adultery committed by Arthur's wife and Lancelot spurs further individual acts of betrayal and corruption, the ensuing disorder destroys the Round Table, symbolizing the effects of moral decay that Tennyson feared. Tennyson completed an enlarged edition of *Idylls of the King* in 1874, and in the decade that followed he focused his efforts on the composition of historical dramas. *Queen Mary* (1875), his first published drama, is regarded by critics as characteristic of a central flaw in all of Tennyson's dramatic works: a lack of familiarity with the limitations of theatrical production. Set changes were frequent and elaborate, and Tennyson's meticulous adherence to detail lessens the play's dramatic impact. Moreover, Tennyson's verse was considered cumbersome and ineffective as dramatic dialogue, and *Queen Mary* was withdrawn after twenty-three performances. Of all of Tennyson's plays, only *The Cup and the Falcon* (1884) and *Becket* (1884) proved commercially successful.

CRITICAL RECEPTION

Although Tennyson was an enormously popular poet, critical response to his works during his lifetime was varied, and largely focused upon whether or not the poet's choice of subject matter was deemed worthy of po-etic expression, rather than on the technical merits of the poetry itself. During the post-World War I era, the works of Tennyson and other Victorian writers were de-rided as part of an overall rejection of the Victorian Age as materialistic, hypocritical, self-satisfied, and narrow-minded. Since the mid-twentieth century, however, Ten-nyson's talent, his role in shaping the literature of his time, and the biographical details of his life have served as the focus of a large body of scholarly work. Not only has Tennyson been viewed as a consummate poet by literary scholars, his works are routinely interpreted as challenging or supporting Victorian social, political, re-ligious, and moral standards, rather than merely echo-ing them. The nature of Tennyson's relationship with Hallam has been a topic of interest to many literary critics and biographers, who point to what they per-ceive as homoerotic elements in *In Memoriam* and other works. Many critics have debated whether the nature of Tennyson's treatment of women, femininity, and wom-en's issues in his poetry—particularly in "The Lady of Shalott," which appeared in his *Poems* of 1832—repre-sents a feminist or anti-feminist stance, and the poet's symbolic representation of religious and scientific is-sues continues to generate critical commentary.

PRINCIPAL WORKS

Poems by Two Brothers [with Frederick and Charles Tennyson] (poetry) 1827

Timbuctoo: A Poem (in Blank Verse) Which Obtained the Chancellor's Gold Medal at the Cambridge Com-mencement (poem) 1829

Poems, Chiefly Lyrical (poetry) 1830

Poems (poetry) 1832

Poems. 2 vols. (poetry) 1842

The Princess: A Medley (poem) 1847

In Memoriam (poem) 1850

Ode on the Death of the Duke of Wellington (poem) 1852

"The Charge of the Light Brigade" (poem) 1854; pub-lished in the journal *The Examiner*

Maud, and Other Poems (poetry) 1855

Idylls of the King (poetry) 1859; enlarged edition, 1874

Enoch Arden, Etc. (poetry) 1864

The Holy Grail, and Other Poems (poetry) 1869

Gareth and Lynette, Etc. (poetry) 1872

Queen Mary: A Drama (verse drama) 1875

Harold: A Drama (verse drama) 1876

Ballads and Other Poems (poetry) 1880

Becket (verse drama) 1884

The Cup and the Falcon (verse drama) 1884

Tiresias, and Other Poems (poetry) 1885

Locksley Hall Sixty Years After, Etc. (poetry) 1886

Demeter, and Other Poems (poetry) 1889

The Death of Oenone, Akbar's Dream, and Other Po-ems (poetry) 1892

The Foresters, Robin Hood and Maid Marian (verse drama) 1892

The Poems of Tennyson [edited by Christopher Ricks] (poetry) 1969

The Letters of Alfred Lord Tennyson. 3 vols. [edited by Cecil Y. Lang and Edgar F. Shannon, Jr.] (letters) 1981-90

CRITICISM

Alisa Clapp-Itnyre (essay date summer 2000)

SOURCE: Clapp-Itnyre, Alisa. "Marginalized Musical Interludes: Tennyson's Critique of Conventionality in *The Princess*." *Victorian Poetry* 38, no. 2 (summer 2000): 227-48.

[*In the following essay, Clapp-Itnyre interprets the mu-sical interludes in* The Princess *as "pivotal feminist commentaries."*]

In 1847, when Alfred Lord Tennyson's *The Princess* was first published, Victorian England was embroiled in a vast array of debates concerning women's role in so-ciety, placed under the canopy term "the Woman Ques-tion." Should women work? What kinds of education should they have? Was marriage to be their sole lot in life? Tennyson's response, couched in this seven-book novel-in-verse, has proven to be a contentious one for his readers then and for critics now. Tennyson's frame story introduces seven college men on holiday who take turns creating an inner story about a medieval princess rebelliously embracing these challenges facing women. Specifically, Princess Ida flees a contracted marriage to a local prince in order to establish a women's university where men are forbidden under penalty of death. But the Prince and two of his men, for love and for the sport of it, disguise themselves as women and invade the Academy, the Prince falling more deeply in love with Ida before they are discovered. When Ida still re-fuses to marry, the Prince's father declares war on her father's kingdom and ultimately the Academy is turned into a hospital for wounded soldiers. Tending to the wounded Prince, the "hard-hearted" Princess relents and eventually agrees to marriage while the Prince's two friends also claim wives from the university. Granted, the Princess espouses powerful feminist rheto-ric throughout the poem, but her eventual marriage leaves nothing but a bad taste in the mouths of many critics. So, while F. B. Pinion praises the ending in that

"Ida eventually recognizes the unnaturalness of feminist militancy," Marion Shaw reads the ending as Ida's "defeat . . . her reclamation into an unredeemed, unaltered marriage relationship."[1] Through these clever young men, Tennyson projects a progressive vision of women's community and educational aspirations but seems compelled to curtail this vision to accommodate the romantic ending of Victorian middle-class ideals. If so, he is not the first writer to fall into this happy-ending trap.

Tennyson's narrative structure, too, tends to confirm conservative interpretations. As described in the frame, the college men at a middle-class luncheon party at Sir Walter Vivian's undertake to tell Princess Ida's story themselves despite the fact that there are numerous women in the audience—"Aunt Elizabeth / And Lilia with the rest, and lady friends / From neighbour seats" (Prol., ll. 96-98).[2] Instead, the men invite the "ladies [to] sing us, if they will, / From time to time, some ballad or a song / To give us breathing-space" so "the women sang / Between the rougher voices of the men, / Like linnets in the pauses of the wind" (Prol., ll. 233-235, 237-239). Marginalized by the male narrators, the women are relegated to "mere" singing. Frank and Dillon note the similarity with Chaucer's *Canterbury Tales*: "Indeed, rules are set down for the passing of story from one speaker to the next. But in Tennyson the men tell the stories and the women sing only the interpolated lyrics. . . . Chaucer's Wife of Bath would obviously find these story-telling laws quite absurd."[3] Certainly, there are troubling gender and genre assumptions in the telling of Princess Ida's story—"embarrassments" as Elaine Jordan calls the poem's "risks and explor[ations with] both gender and genre" (p. 97). By controlling the powerful, novel-like verbal plot, the men imply that, as musical lyrics, these songs are entirely emotive, inarticulate pieces in contrast to the more politically engaging verbal tale. The men insinuate that, because the women lack university training, they cannot handle the more intellectually challenging job of creating the main storyline. Additionally, while the men adopt a mock-heroic, idealistic tone in their story, the women set a more serious, realistic mood with their songs about contemporary domestic issues. Yet this becomes another reason to see the interlude songs as "dull" and "conventional" just as Aunt Elizabeth is seen to be when she suggests the entire story be "Heroic . . . Grave, solemn!" (Prol., ll. 207-208). Clearly, genre and gender assumptions rear ugly heads in this creative collaboration which privileges male discourse and conventions and demotes music, realism, and women accordingly.

The male narrators' unspoken assumptions about gender and genre have, interestingly, tended to be upheld by recent scholarship. A first problem is that, though hailed as immensely poetic, the interlude poems still lose critical interest when compared to those lyrics found within the male narrative: **"Tears, idle tears,"** **"Now sleeps the crimson petal,"** and **"Come down, O Maid."** Some scholars, such as Christopher Ricks, base the achievement of *The Princess* solely on these three lyrics: "a poem which incorporates three of Tennyson's finest lyrics . . . is patently not negligible."[4] Further, when the interlude poems are given critical attention, they are praised for their lyric beauty and consequently anthologized separately,[5] which only reinforces the belief that these lyrics have no bearing on the main storyline of *The Princess*, that female creativity really is marginal entertainment, albeit beautiful. When these songs are actually read for meaning within the context of the main story, they too often are summed up as the women's conservative affirmation of children, domesticity, and wifely experience; as Bernard Bergonzi writes, "With their intensity of feeling and static, self-contained quality, [they] provide emblems of what the feminine nature is conventionally supposed to be."[6] Shaw resents that the women's songs are only about romantic love, a situation which implies that "love is to do with ideality, and not with the practical and social world, and moreover that the subjective mode of expressing that ideality, lyric poetry, likewise belongs to a marginalized and feminine voice" (p. 48). When critics sense a real power to these songs, as when Eve Kosofsky Sedgwick calls them "ravishing lyrics that intersperse the narrative, often at an odd or even subversive angle to what is manifestly supposed to be going on,"[7] they do not closely pursue the implications of this "subversive angle." My study will attempt to do just that: to examine these interlude songs closely as pivotal feminist commentaries. Not only will this process suggest the extent of Tennyson's feminist sympathies in this poem but in his larger poetic scheme, a point which has continued to divide critics.[8]

When determining whether the interlude lyrics merit meaning within the larger story, one must realize that they did not appear in the first edition of the poem; rather, Tennyson added these songs to the third edition (1850) of *The Princess*. Edgar Finley Shannon, Jr., in *Tennyson and the Reviewers*[9] attributes most changes in the third edition to reviewer commentary in the intervening years. He shows that reviewers were most critical of Tennyson's "unpoetical" blank verse and suggests that Tennyson added the lyric poems, "a form in which he was an undoubted master," so as to reaffirm opinions of his poetic ability (p. 139). Shannon also points out that many readers of the first edition seemed to misread Tennyson's intended argument about women's rights: "The *Sun* had felt it necessary to inform its readers that the purpose of *The Princess* was not to satirize women"; still, "seven months later *Tait's Edinburgh Magazine* had perversely declared that the main object of the poem was to combat the desires of women for political equality with men. The poet seems to have been trying in his revised edition to make it clear from the first that he was not belittling his heroine" (pp. 133-

134). Shannon proceeds to examine poetic changes Tennyson made in the poem proper in order to redeem Princess Ida's heroic stature. My argument, however, is that Tennyson attempts to redeem his misread poem less by individual word changes than by adding the interlude songs. As he writes in **A Memoir,** "The songs . . . are the best interpreters of the poem. Before the first edition came out, I deliberated with myself whether I should put songs between separate divisions of the poem; again I thought that the poem would explain itself, but the public did not see the drift."[10] "The drift" which his readers were missing was his true sympathy for contemporary women's struggles. Hallam writes in **A Memoir** that his father reportedly identified housing and education for the poor and the higher education of women as "the two great social questions impending in England" and "the sooner woman finds out, before the great educational movement begins, that 'woman is not undevelopt man, but diverse,' the better it will be for the progress of the world" (p. 249). Too, Hallam recognized that the "six songs were introduced . . . to express more clearly the meaning of 'the medley'" (p. 251), that indeed women are not "undevelopt" but "diverse" from men in their approaches to life and art.

In this study, then, I will argue that Tennyson intended these songs to be the "the meaning of 'the medley'" and the "best interpreters of the poem" because they tell the story that Ida might have told if the women had controlled her story: a more realistic portrait of Victorian women's social roles and creative energies to counter the narrators' parody of women's social and creative aspirations. Firstly, whereas the men mock women's radical political endeavors, the women offer a more sober perspective on women's socio-economic status of the present. Whereas the men relegate the musical genre to an insignificant art form for women, the women resuscitate it into a powerful form of self-expression and aesthetic beauty. Finally, whereas the men use the figure of the child as a metaphoric and metonymic equivalent to woman to demote her, the women heighten this child figure into a symbol of women's futuristic art which is genderless, timeless, and limitless.[11]

From the very beginning, the seven college men and the women of the frame story bring contrasting ideologies to their party on the lawn. Due to the men's class and gender advantage, life has become an intellectual game in which they exchange witty flirtations with Lilia and recount their frolics at college, how "They boated, . . . cricketed, . . . vext the souls of deans; / They rode . . . betted" (Prol., ll. 159-162). Lilia appears to joke too, even carelessly emasculating the statue of Sir Ralph with her scarf. Clearly, though, this gesture shows her vengeful awareness of how many of the men's opportunities are closed to her solely due to her gender. Pointing out that there are thousands of

great women "but convention beats them down," she concludes: "You men have done it: how I hate you all!" (Prol., ll. 128, 130). The men appear to empathize with her feelings, suggesting her idea for a women's university be the source of a group-story, but in their attitude the men continue to treat the task as another college romp. Her aunt begs them for a heroic tale, reminding them that they reside over a tomb and thus the tale should be something "to suit the place, / Heroic, for a hero lies beneath, / Grave, solemn!" (Prol., ll. 206-208). The first-person narrator of the frame and his friend Walter scoff at her, though: Walter "warped his mouth at this / To something so mock-solemn, that I laughed" (Prol., ll. 208-209). The aunt acquiesces with "As you will" (l. 214), and the men take up the story in all its mock-heroic glory.

So, while appearing to embrace Lilia's feminist agenda, the men concurrently mock it. Indeed, **The Princess** is often equated with Shakespeare's *Love's Labor's Lost* (Jordan, pp. 85-87) and studied as an "experiment in comedy" (Thomson, p. 84). The story utilizes cross-dressing; comic characters like Cyril and a villain like Lady Blanche;[12] and not one but three romantic plot-lines—nearly all the ingredients of a Gilbert and Sullivan comic opera which, not surprisingly, did appear in 1884 as *Princess Ida.* But Ida's scenes carry a disproportionate amount of this comedy which ultimately undercuts any of the serious feminist propaganda. Tennyson's attempts to strengthen Ida's heroics in the third edition, as Shannon argues (pp. 133-138), were not conclusive enough to quell contemporary critics' discussions of mode.[13] W. David Shaw, for instance, attributes Ida's character inconsistencies to her intentional alternation "between high epic seriousness and comic plain speaking" (p. 18). I would insist, however, that we remember the narrative rules that Tennyson establishes: the men create and narrate these scenes, thus generating Ida's comic language, foibles, and idiosyncrasies despite the solemn ambitions of the listening women. Thus, the comedy is very intentional in showing male mockery of female ambitions. For instance, upon first welcoming her new "students" (that is, the Prince and his friends) to the Academy, Ida bursts out "are the ladies of your land so tall?" (2.33), and her comic naiveté in not seeing the men under their masks lessens the impact of her next speech in which she describes all the great women of history, leaving us to wonder if these noble women, too, could not have been masquerading men. Similarly, after Psyche's feminist lecture which prophesies "Two heads in council, two beside the hearth" (2.156),[14] the narrators shift to the women of the Academy after lectures are over, recording their grumbling against their constrictive environment: "what was learning unto them? / They wished to marry; they could rule a house; / Men hated learned women" (2.440-442). The narrators suggest that the students' allegiance to the Academy is tenuous at best, possibly enforced, and they would rather fulfill their traditional "womanly" roles. Even Ida has many moments of "womanly" slips: during the narrator's horseride-conversation with Ida, her famous speech defining women's "duty" not as child-rearing but as accomplishing "great deeds" (3.237) ends with funny, "feminine" crying when the narrator pointedly notes that "She bowed as if to veil a noble tear" (3.272). Indeed, the male narrators' creative details provide comedy but also reinforce a view of innate "feminine" behavior even if, with the Princess, it is also "noble."

Throughout, Ida's rhetoric, riddled with awkward royal "we's" and often unintelligible imagery, also diminishes the passion of her weighty orations. In her fervent speech about the future, "that great year of equal mights and rights" (4.56), Ida uses strong language, but once again the narrators mock her ideas by sprinkling her long-winded speech with odd metaphors and imagery ("though the rough kex break / The starred mosaic, and the beard-blown goat / Hang on the shaft, and the wild figtree split / Their monstrous idols"—referring to Babel, 4.59-62). The fact that she so soon afterward careens over the bridge and into the river while making her noble escape from the discovered masqueraders only adds more levity to a scene implicitly tragic: at worst, she nearly loses her life while at best she is on the brink of losing her life's work. (This "drowning scene" is sometimes elaborated on in *Princess Ida* productions to heighten the hysterics and, ultimately, Ida's vulnerability).

In essence, the men create their comedy from a woman's dramatic quest for equal and separate rights, mocking her actions and speech and undermining her influence over her disciples. Especially important to this study is how music plays a key role in the comedic plotline. Even as the women have been relegated to singing "some ballad or song" during the storytelling, the lyrical musical genres in the storyline are typically gendered feminine and, accordingly, demeaned. For instance, Princess Ida's feminist ideology is disseminated in large part by songs which her father King Gama refers to as the "awful odes she wrote": "rhymes / And dismal lyrics, prophesying change / Beyond all reason" (1.137,140-142). Likewise, Ida's organ-playing at the university serves her feminist cause, "rolling through the court / A long melodious thunder to the sound / Of solemn psalms, and silver litanies . . . to call down from Heaven / A blessing on her labors for the world" (2.451-455); but the narrators mockingly refer to the great organ as "almost burst[ing] his pipes / Groaning for power" (2.450). The fact that the organ is gendered male betrays the unease the male narrators feel towards Ida's mastery of music and of men.

After the battle, Ida sings in gratitude that "Our enemies have fallen, have fallen" (6.17), using music now not only to disseminate ideologies but rebellious emotions. However, recall that the male storytellers are orchestrating this once again, and we suddenly see an attempt to show not power but the "unnaturalness" of Ida's actions. After all, war songs are gendered male elsewhere as when the Prince is inspired to do battle: "when first I heard / War-music, felt the blind wildbeast of force, / Whose home is in the sinews of a man, / Stir in me as to strike" (5.255-258). The fact that Ida also sings wild war-songs is yet another proof of her hard-heartedness, her "steel temper," her "lioness" nature, and the doubtful womanhood with which the story's men continually charge her. Further, the uneven meter of this war song (even the first line exemplifies a bumpy iambic hexameter), its ludicrous lyrics ("the fangs / Shall move the stony bases of the world," 6.41-42), and the odd picture, as she sings from the rooftops holding a baby, once again pointedly undermine much of her supremacy over the men she has just defeated and even cast doubt on her aesthetic competence. By including the baby in their description, the male narrators align her with the simplicities of a child and assign her a domestic role instead of her chosen political one. Thus, because of the narrators' mock-heroic tone in describing Ida's appropriation of political music, we see not admiration for but a parody of Ida's "unnatural" zeal.

In the male narrators' scheme, women should be singing love-songs and it is yet another confirmation of Ida's aberrant behavior that she condemns these songs. In the middle of the story, Ida calls for music and a maid sings the famous "Tears, idle tears" song which laments "the days that are no more" and the "lips that are for others" (4.21, 25, 38). Not only does the Princess callously berate the sentimentality of this song—"nor is it / Wiser to weep a true occasion lost" (4.50)—but seems completely ignorant of its aesthetic complexities—"we should cram our ears with wool" (4.47). When the disguised Prince is also asked to contribute a song, he can only sing (in falsetto) a sappy love song he wrote, "O Swallow . . . Fly to her, and pipe and woo her, and make her mine" (4.96-97).[15] This causes the Princess to enter into a diatribe about love songs which "dress the victim to the offering up," where men "play the slave to gain the tyranny" (4.112, 114). An argument important to Ida's egalitarian goals, yes, but the narrators cannot leave it at that for in the next moment gender stereotypes are comically reinscribed. Cyril bursts out into a "careless tavern-catch / Of Moll and Meg, and strange experiences / Unmeet for ladies" which betrays his vulgar, "male" taste (4.139-141).[16] Because of their feminine sensibilities, the women are offended; further, they realize that only a man could have sung such a crude song, and the princes are exposed by their musical taste. With a reinscription of gendered aesthetic taste, gender roles quickly resume, too: the Prince chivalrously rescues Ida from drowning and the women nurse the convalescing soldiers soon after.

By the end, Ida is reading love poems to the Prince on his sickbed, conspicuously of the carpe-diem genre like the Prince's **"Swallow"** song [**"O Swallow, Swallow"**]. But by causing Ida to mouth carpe-diem arguments, the male narrators unintentionally create a scene of great pathos: the Princess is attempting to persuade herself to become the Prince's wife. In prophetic irony, she is now the "victim [being dressed] to the offering up," singing of lilies and shepherdesses being seduced by lovers.

Ida reads **"Now sleeps the crimson petal"** and **"Come down, O maid, from yonder mountain height,"** often anthologized as independent poems. Both are typically explored in terms of their lyricism: see Ricks (pp. 200-204) and Thomson (pp. 103-104) for persuasive close readings. Yet both critics miss the larger narrative context of these lyric poems which are pivotal loci in the story that the male narrators are attempting to conclude. While the speaker of "Now sleeps the crimson petal" attempts to woo his lover to "slip / Into my bosom and be lost in me," the "sleep" of Nature becomes symbolic of death: the cypress no longer waves, the milk-white peacock droops "like a ghost," even the lily folds "her sweetness up, / And slips into the bosom of the lake" (7. 161-174). Becoming "lost" in a love relationship is aligned with an engulfment, even a death or nullification of at least one person's identity. The imagery becomes more sexual, more troublesome in the next poem as a young maid is exhorted by her lover to leave the cold mountain height "so near the Heavens" and come down "for Love is of the valley" (7.180, 183): that is, leave your heaven of cold purity and embrace the lushness of the valley of love. The speaker describes her world in harsh imagery—"blasted pines," "firths of ice," "monstrous ledges" (7.182, 191, 197)—in an effort to coerce her to leave it and join him. What she gains— the "azure *pillars* of the *hearth*" (7.201; my italics)— though connoting shelter and warmth, respectively, also connote phallic and domestic images of oppression, hardly worth relinquishing a near-paradise for as Ida must certainly realize. Sadly, renouncing her feminist songs, Ida must accept men's *carpe-diem* poems and their implications. As Marion Shaw writes, "From being a speaker, Ida becomes a listener, from being a poet she becomes the reader of other (men's) poetry. . . . Ida's eventual silence, passivity and self-doubt are dressed out in the blushings, pallor, sighs, mild eyes and trembling voice which are the conventional attributes of virtuous womanhood" (p. 47).

Often the power of Ida and her compatriots is minimized by equating them both metaphorically and metonymically with children, yet a third of the male story-tellers' ploys to create mock-heroics. Certainly children are central to the men's story proper. Despite Ida's resentment of children, her two teachers Blanche and Psyche both bring children to the university. The men's narrative focuses on the resulting disruptions to the academic life, implying that women cannot both study and mother. After all, though Psyche manages to teach classes with her baby sleeping soundly by her side, greater problems than daycare—indeed the infighting of women and eventual downfall of the Academy—arise from the presence of children. Melissa angers her mother and endangers the entire Academy by playfully keeping the men's secret. And Ida and Psyche's close relationship is permanently damaged when Ida keeps Psyche's baby Aglaïa as punishment for Psyche's betrayal. Psyche's panic is rendered as nearly fatal as she cries to Ida, "'Mine—mine—not yours, / It is not yours, but mine: give me the child' . . . So stood the unhappy mother open-mouthed . . . Red grief and mother's hunger in her eye, / And down dead-heavy sank her curls, and half / The sacred mother's bosom, panting, burst / The laces toward her babe" (6.124-133). Prostrate, sickly, her exposed breasts clearly "revealing" her maternal role to the men about her, Psyche cannot fight her own battle against Ida but is championed by a sickly Cyril who berates Ida as a "Lioness" (6.147). This Solomon-esque fighting over a child confirms Ida as "unnaturally" hard-hearted and selfish and Psyche as pathetically dependent upon men. Arac, watching Ida and Psyche argue, quips: "the woman is so hard / Upon the woman" (6.205-206). The women are thus presented as acting no better than children as they fight, cry, and cringe.

Further, by suggesting Ida's strong feelings for the child, the male narrators attempt to verify her "true," maternal nature, especially as she glides amongst the wounded warriors, carrying the child and tending to their wounds. Inevitably she begins to enact the "women's role" that the Prince's narrow-minded father describes: "The bearing and training of a child / Is woman's wisdom" (5.455-456). Seen with children, the women become equated with their assumed social role and also metonymically associated with children. Princess Ida resents this image of women: "she / Whose name is yoked with children's" (5.407-408). For indeed the men about her constantly portray women as infantile: Gama complains that Ida's songs encourage women's "losing of the child," their child-like behavior (1.140), and the Prince himself, despite his grand speech about helping the Princess with her liberal ideas, still hopes that women will not "lose the childlike in the larger mind" (7.268). Notably, Ida and the Prince's childhood betrothal, like historically real contracts, is legally binding by the simple fact that men assume the grown Ida will, like a child, blindly obey her father's wishes. To be aligned with a babe, the most inarticulate, simple, and helpless of humans, is indeed the issue that these early feminists had to face. As Lilia protests at the beginning, men "love to keep us children!" (Prol., l. 133).

The songs, then, become a means for the listening women to retort to the damaging assumptions about women being created in this "feminist narrative." Free to choose their own tone, they rely on a solemn approach to address the issues that they and other women face in their own time and place. Being relegated to song, they elevate it aesthetically and as a means of transmitting ideologies, even utilizing music-as-power imagery within the songs themselves. And using the child as a symbol for more than women's domestic responsibilities, they suggest the (pro)creative artistry of which women are capable.

Tennyson's portrayal of women's issues in these songs, significantly, follows closely that of actual early-nineteenth-century feminists. Looking at women's reform work of the 1830s and 1840s, Kathryn Gleadle argues that though early feminists (in particular, radical unitarians) advocated greater educational and political roles for women, they "did not promote women purely in those areas where they might achieve like men, but were also keen to herald the particular contribution women might make to society in their capacity as mothers . . . encouraging men to also embrace the caring values of the home."[17] Philippa Levine reiterates that one of the noteworthy goals of "Victorian feminism was its concerted attempt to remould rather than reject marital practice"; attitudes such as Ida's hostility to marriage would not become prominent until the latter decades of the century.[18] What radical women wanted, of course, were more options within the schema of women's domestic work: the choice to reject marriage, or the chance to work publicly while caring for children. Literature became one means of assimilating these two disparate goals as well as promoting the gradually increasing reformist rhetoric of women; Gleadle, in fact, examining writing circles and literary activities of the period, argues the vital part writing played "in the formation of a feminist consciousness" for many women beyond those achieving success like the Brontës (p. 2). I argue elsewhere that women also used music to distribute coded rebellious messages, such as occurs amongst the women's communities of Elizabeth Gaskell's novels.[19] Thus, marriage, child-rearing, and art were readily embraced by early feminists of the 1840s when *The Princess* was written; by showing male reappropriation and mock-exaggeration of such rebellion, Tennyson depicts the often hostile environment of women's struggles; by incorporating women's music as interludes, Tennyson uses women's art to reflect the concerns and realities of many women of the period.

For instance, the first song sung by the women in the audience describes a husband and wife who "fell out" but "kissed again with tears" as they came to the grave of "the child / We lost in other years." The women insert this as a sad reminder of the realities of marital strife and the death of children that accompany the "bliss" of marriage. Too, they contextualize the tragedy within a space foreign to the listeners absorbed in a tale of upper-class nobility: that of the laboring class, the pluckers of "ripened ears," whose poverty no doubt hastens the child's death. This is no dramatic exaggeration for emotive purposes only, not in an age when working-class parents would, on average, lose one in every two children.[20] Lilia and her friends' concern for the working class suggests that they have noted with more concern the arrival of "the multitude" from the Institute whose holiday festivities at Sir Vivian's the frame narrator can only describe as "strange" (Prol., ll. 57, 54). Historically, philanthropy and sheer adventure led more and more middle-class feminists to empathize with the lower classes and "explore beyond the restraining class boundaries" of their experience (Levine, p. 56). Also significant is the inclusion of the father as an equal partner in the strife and grief of this domestic drama, a goal radical unitarians in particular espoused. This portrait of marital strife and child-rearing pains for both genders, then, provides a more solemn expression of domestic experience to counter the extreme, bitter speech of the Princess who, when asked by the Prince if she won't miss "what every woman counts her due, / Love, children, happiness?" replies, "But children die . . . [or] Kill us with pity, break us with ourselves" (3.228-229, 236-241). Coming as it does after the entrance of the Prince and his men into the university, this song seems an ominous comment on the Prince's utopian and upper-class ideals of marriage and parenthood.

The women's second song also invokes a strained familial situation. The women sing a lullaby to a child, "my pretty one," whose father is out to sea; the ballad's wife begs the "wind of the western sea" to "Blow him again to me." This song follows a scene where Phoebe has caught the men in disguise and fears the harsh penalty of death for them should they be caught. Ironically, the university women wish unsuccessfully to have men absent from their world, but the song reminds the audience that all too often husbands are absent and their wives must continually pray for their safe return.

Indeed, though statistics are sketchier in the years up to 1850, after 1850, records show that one in twelve women was a widow as early as ages 35-44, husbands most often dying from work-related accidents on land and at sea (Perkin, p. 132). Historian Joan Perkin also suggests that wife desertion was not uncommon; men often left the country or changed their names to escape caring for the family. By detailing actual accounts of the many widows who found work and raised their children despite the death or absences, Perkin concludes that "many widows showed an amazing capacity for hard work in supporting their families" (p. 138). Lilia and her fellow "feminists" celebrate these accomplishments in the second song.

Given that war between the Prince and Princess' fathers is imminent in the poem proper, the women's fourth and fifth songs remind the men of the hard truth about war: it creates widows more quickly than any other social phenomenon. Lilia, in her "half-possessed" solo (Song 4), describes the man dreaming of his brood about his wife's knee as he steps up to kill the enemy "for thine and thee"—a reminder that soldiers leave families behind. The fifth interlude song expounds on this idea, describing a woman to whom "they brought her warrior dead" and her response to his death. Showing no emotion at first, the balladic wife gives forth a "summer tempest" of tears when realizing that their child is now without a father. No longer the romantic scene of women nursing brave warriors and ultimately falling in love with them, as the men chronicle in the next section about Ida, this song describes the realistic tragedy of war for the women and children left alone. Tennyson, we remember, was the great eulogizer of the military tragedy during the **"Charge of the Light Brigade"** of the Crimean War, a war which took the lives of over 23,000 British husbands, fathers, and sons. Clearly, Tennyson was sensitive to the pains of war and his focus on the loss of life—not this actual military victory during the Battle of Balaklava—smacks of "feminine," not "masculine," concerns.

So these songs revise the men's flippant portrayal of child-rearing and war to reflect more accurately the experiences of nineteenth-century women, solemnizing the mock-heroic tone of the story proper. It seems no coincidence that the men set their story in the medieval past while the women's songs are set in the realistic present. Further, at the heart of the songs' poetics we find impressively progressive ideas concerning gender and discourse—and the power of women's designated genre, music. **"Sweet and low,"** for instance, is a lullaby which invests power in the voice of its singer, the abandoned wife. Crooning her baby to "sleep and rest," her song is full of soft sounds: note the prevalence of "w," "s," "e," and "r" and gentle adjectives— "sweet and low." But then her language takes on the force of harsh consonants ("c" and "b") and verbs— "come" and "breathe and blow." Ultimately, her words are authoritative, commanding the wind to "blow him [her husband] again to me" and assuring the babe that "Father will come to thee soon" (ll. 7, 10). By utilizing an internal rhyme in the line "Rest, rest, on mother's breast" as self-containment to the rhyme pattern, Tennyson suggests the autonomy of the "mother's breast" as she provides both physical and emotional nourishment for her child. But her body is more than a source of sustenance and her singing is more than sleep-inducing, aesthetic prettiness. Like a sorcerer, her voice can control the wind and sea, the moon and "silver sails." Thus, to breathe and to blow—the essential components of music-making, after all—are no longer insignificant actions but potent incentives to action.

The women expound on the power of non-traditional communication more incessantly in their third song, **"The splendor falls on castle walls,"**[21] as a means of reaffirming their non-verbal status in the men's story-telling agenda. Set between two of Ida's witless speeches already discussed concerning "miserable" children and "tyrannic" love songs, this song stands as a testament to women's authentic and beautiful speech, both because it is a lyric poem of great elegance and because it venerates music as an alternatively powerful means of non-verbal speech. As the poem describes, musical sounds produced by horns and bugles paradoxically become clearer as they get thinner. Thus, as they "die in yon rich sky" they "grow for ever and for ever," rolling from soul to soul (ll. 13, 16). What seems insignificant becomes amplified and amplified throughout the ages. And the bugle inspires other natural elements to speak as well: the "snowy summits" give their story while the purple glens "reply." Even light "shakes across the lake" in audible ways. Everywhere the supposedly silent landscape is set to sound by the musical—and, notably, pastoral and not martial—bugles. Claiming musical discourse to which they have been relegated, the women also embrace the pastoral genre classically associated with male shepherd poet/singers. Further, by reinforcing the timeless energy of music, the women subtly reinscribe value to "their" aesthetic form. Even after the men's story is over, they imply, their songs will "grow for ever and for ever."

"Home they brought her warrior dead" shows a woman resisting expected womanly discourse yet embracing tears and motherhood on her own terms. As described earlier, this song depicts a woman's reactions upon learning that her husband has just been killed in battle. This balladic woman threatens traditional female roles by remaining silent and stoic when faced with the corpse of her dead husband. The women around her are amazed: "She must weep or she will die." Neither verbal nor visual stimuli have any effect: the woman can praise him and uncover his face and still she remains unimpassioned. The verbs reiterated in the poem stress conventional expectations: the wife should "swoon," "cry," "weep," "die," "move." Instead, the woman chooses to speak, along with a "tempest" of tears: "Sweet my child, I live for thee" (l. 16). In ending with public speech, she replaces the expected tears and swooning with empowering words of self-worth. Rather than crying or weeping in silent resignation, her grief is as potent and auspicious as a tempest. Rather than caught up in praise for the deeds of her warrior-husband as the other women are ("Then they praised him, soft, and low, / Called him worthy to be loved"), she privileges the unlived life of her child. Thus, rather than ending her life when her husband's has ended, she validates her own worth as a woman and mother. Neither is she coerced into doing so by male authority or guilt-making as occurs in the poem proper. Note Cyril's words to the "half-shrouded" Psyche when Ida has banished her and her friendship: "Yet I pray / Take comfort; live, dear lady, for your child!" (5.76-77). As Margaret Homans points out, there is a difference between "'experts' telling women that wifehood and motherhood is their proper sphere and proper duty" and feminist confirmation of "the origins and the genuinely positive value, for men as well as women, of such female roles as child rearing and such traditional female values as pacifism."[22] Recognizing this, the frame women rewrite the roles of mother and of weeper into vestures of power. They also reinvest humanity in the "hard-hearted," "unfeminine" woman as Princess Ida is so often labeled.

Four of the six interlude songs focus on children. Tennyson acknowledged that "The child is the link thro' the parts as shown in the songs" (*Memoir,* 1:254). Christopher Ricks makes a case for the remaining two poems also being ultimately about children,[23] concluding that Tennyson's belated insertion of these poems "consolidat[es] that aspect of the story which showed the child Aglaïa, and so motherhood, to be the Princess' fatal miscalculation" (p. 194). But I would argue that the prevalence of children in these poems is more than a reminder of women's maternal roles or of Ida's many miscalculations. Because the children are nameless and nearly formless, they are less bodies than symbols of women's creative capacity. Recall the common trope among women artists of the 1840s and 1850s of their art as children, used either as a justification for a public career as Elizabeth Gaskell did, or as a sometimes-resentful, sometimes-satisfactory replacement for the child one lacks, as Elizabeth Barrett Browning's Aurora Leigh contemplates.[24] In Tennyson's songs, not only are children the recipients of musical creativity as in the lullaby song, they become generational extensions of that music as the posterity implied by "Our echoes roll from soul to soul." Like art, the child takes on dimensions of time, becoming a link with the past, its memory uniting estranged parents ("As through the land at eve we went"), and a link with the future, becoming a reason to live for both balladic women deserted by husbands ("Sweet my child, I live for thee"). In an unpublished fragment which Tennyson intended as an interlude poem, he stresses the moral, futuristic importance of the child more vigorously: "O the child so meek and wise, / Who made *us* wise and mild!" (*Memoir,* 1:255).

Noticeably, the children in the songs reside in a futuristic, genderless realm of existence: none is ever identified by gender to be labeled with conventional male-female stereotypes. Similarly, a feminist goal of both the 1840s and the 2000s was and is fluid gender qualities of parents so that both equally share the joys and sorrows of domestic life. Such is described in Tennyson's first poem, "As through the land at eve we went," where the speaker/father mourns as unabashedly as the wife over the loss of their child. As men emote lyrical poetry about domestic sentiments, not the grand heroics of martial music, romance of carpe-diem songs, or even the epic poetry of the story proper, aesthetic genres transcend gender, too.

The final song, however, is a crushing defeat after the optimism presented by the first five songs, though still a revealing statement by the women in attendance. As Ida prepares to soften her heart and "yield herself up" to the Prince, the women sing a tragic song of forced love, **"Ask me no more,"**[25] in which the speaker, presumably a woman, very reluctantly agrees to marry her wooer. The final stanza appears not to be high-minded ideals of love but a simple relenting: "Ask me no more: thy fate and mine are sealed, / I strove against the stream and all in vain; / Let the great river take me to the main. / No more, dear love, for at a touch I yield; / Ask me no more" (ll. 11-15). The woman pleads with her lover to stop asking, to stop speaking to her, repeating this entreaty seven times in the three-stanza poem. She denies her own past speech—"when have I answered thee?"—but feels she must speak now. Rather then commanding the wind as in the first poem, the woman cannot now strive "against the stream." In fact, she becomes the object to be carried by natural forces: "Let the great river take me to the main." Reminiscent of **"Crossing the Bar,"** which Tennyson had yet to write, this poem suggests that like the speaker in that poem, she, too, is close to a symbolic death: her marriage. And this seems entirely a sacrifice to sustain his life—"I will not have thee die!" Unlike the sacrifices of other balladic women made wilingly to save their children, her sacrifice is cast as an unnecessary one made to appease society and a conniving lover—"I love not hollow cheek and faded eye" (l. 6). So, at the brink of her own (apparent) silence, she can merely beg him not to speak anymore. Surely not a flattering response to an impassioned lover like the Prince, this song casts doubt on the "happy ending" envisioned by all the male storytellers. From the women's viewpoint, then, Ida's marriage—and the many like it coerced by men and not truly chosen by women—truly is a defeat.

Thus, all songs—even more than the embedded male songs—tell literal stories, narratives of solemn domestic realities in sharp contrast to the mocking heroics of the story proper. In *Bearing the Word,* Margaret Homans, rewriting Lacanian theory, shows that in linguistic practices "the literal is associated with the feminine, [while] the more highly valued figurative is associated with the masculine" (p. 5). In this schema, the process of child-bearing models the process of "literalization" since "something becomes real that did not exist before . . . the relatively figurative becomes the relatively literal" (p. 26). Attention to children and child-rearing, then, is a significant means of recovering woman's experience and elevating her unique creative abilities, such as this attention to the literal. Of course, Tennyson was not privy to the nineteenth-century woman writer's psyche, but I would propose that his preoccupation with the "feminine" in his poetry suggests his insight into feminine psychological states as well as nineteenth-century women's social issues. Certainly the songs he inserted belatedly—though most often read as figurative lyric poetry—also go far in demonstrating the "literalization" phenomenon of nineteenth-century women's writing. Tennyson shows how even the "masculine" realm of lyric poetry can be augmented by literal, "feminine" energies. No longer songs of carpe-diem seductions masquerading as pastoral idylls, these lyrics literalize women's struggles. But women are not incapable of utilizing symbols, their most potent one being the child who emblematizes a genderless, egalitarian future, a future not now parodied but anticipated as a time when women's marginalized creations like emotive, literal lyrics will come to prominence.

The Princess does yield to marriage at the end of the poem amid general audience approbation. Yet the frame's narrator notes that "something in the ballads which [the women] sang" (Concl., l. 15) gave a "solemn close" to the story. That "something," I would suggest, is the underlying solemnity of women's literal experience. And this solemnity at least transforms the narrator who, in conversation with a friend afterward about the state of the world, concludes: "This fine old world of ours is but a child / Yet in the go-cart. Patience! Give it time / To learn its limbs: there is a hand that guides" (Concl., ll. 77-79). Succinctly restating the world-as-child metaphor which the women have evoked throughout their songs, he can look, as they do, to the real future—not the medieval past—when the world will have overcome "social wrong" (Concl., l. 73). As the men and women of the frame once again engage in a battle over the "mock-heroic" and "true-sublime" genres, the peripheral songs have engaged another, perhaps more influential art form—that of music—and its powerful ability to give voice to women's sublime concerns despite the male-controlled, mock-heroic story proper.

Thus, the women's music becomes an important means of self-recovery and revelation in ***The Princess.*** Tennyson, being read as a conservative applauding the downfall of Princess Ida and her women's university, felt compelled to add these songs three years later to enforce his feminist sympathies. In so doing, Tennyson elevated the "feminine" and "insignificant" genre of musical song in order to recognize the beautiful artistry of which women—in contrast to the men's witless Ida—were truly capable. He also created a solemn, feminist commentary on the men's mock-heroic, romanticized response to "the woman question" by giving voice to women's real experience, including their hope in the

"child" as symbolic of the egalitarian future. Unfortunately for Tennyson, the songs' political relevance has been marginalized by readers even to this day. Clearly, though, these songs suggest a more liberal dimension to this conventionally read poem and poet.

Notes

1. F. B. Pinion, *A Tennyson Companion* (New York: Macmillan, 1984), p. 120, and Marion Shaw, *Alfred Lord Tennyson* (Atlantic Highlands: Humanities Press, 1988), p. 47. Kate Millett expressed an early resentment of patriarchy in the poem: "Under the force of sickbed sympathy, Ida says yes. Now thoroughly in command, the prince abandons the role of invalid. With great assurance he dismisses the subject of education altogether. . . . Ida's college is closed; the prince has co-opted all her theories with the unctuous ingenuity of the doctrine of the separate spheres" (*Sexual Politics* [Garden City: Doubleday, 1970], p. 79). Other feminist critics allow for some liberal qualities to the poem while still lamenting the conservative ending. Isolde Karen Herbert resents the frame characters' "conservative interpretations of potentially rebellious material [e.g., Aunt Elizabeth's feminist propaganda] that anticipates the work's concluding affirmation of the status quo" ("'A Strange Diagonal': Ideology and Enclosure in the Framing Sections of *The Princess* and *The Earthly Paradise*," VP [*Victorian Poetry*] 29 [1991]: 149). Marjorie Stone shows how transvestism, imagery, and other "traditional sexual images . . . have the effect of reconstituting the very gender distinctions that Tennyson elsewhere so subtly questions [in the Prince and Princess' role reversals, for instance]" ("Genre Subversion and Gender Inversion: *The Princess* and *Aurora Leigh*," VP 25 [1987]: 114). Elaine Jordan points out that at least the poem "keeps open a space for something else in the residue of pensiveness in Lilia and Ida: they are not made to utterly accede" (*Alfred Tennyson* [Cambridge: Cambridge Univ. Press, 1988], p. 105).

2. All quotations from *The Princess* come from *The Poems of Tennyson,* ed. Christopher Ricks, vol. 2 (Berkeley: Univ. of California Press, 1987).

3. Katherine Frank and Steve Dillon, "Descriptions of Darkness: Control and Self-Control in Tennyson's *Princess,*" VP 33 (1995): 237.

4. Christopher Ricks, *Tennyson* (Berkeley: Univ. of California Press, 1989), p. 180. Gerhard Joseph, Elaine Jordan, and Herbert Tucker, in particular, have all read these poems as great emotional statements by Tennyson. For instance, Joseph considers "Tears, Idle Tears" "one of the loveliest gems of the language," interpreting it and the Princess'

response as "the dialectic of sorrow and hope within Tennyson during the 1840's" (*Tennysonian Love: The Strange Diagonal* [Minneapolis: Univ. of Minnesota Press, 1969], p. 91). Cleanth Brooks' 1944 close reading of the ambiguity and contradictions in "Tears, Idle Tears" elicited more close readings from Graham Hough (1951) and Leo Spitzer (1952) (all three essays found in *Critical Essays on the Poetry of Tennyson*, ed. John Killham [London: Routledge and Kegan Paul, 1960], pp. 175-203). More recently, Jordan speaks of "Tears, Idle Tears," with its "sensations of rising and sinking, waking and dying, [as] Tennyson's finest evocations of purely aesthetic emotion" (p. 96). Herbert F. Tucker, closely explicating all three poems—lyrics "that have understandably won a wider fame than anything else in the poem"—suggests how each "with an inclusiveness that is highly concentrated and above all things sad, articulates the dialectic of will and surrender infusing the narrative they inhabit" (*Tennyson and the Doom of Romanticism* [Cambridge: Harvard Univ. Press, 1988], pp. 362).

5. See Joseph, who suggests that *The Princess* is "admired today largely . . . for the fragile grace of such songs" (p. 77). Further "critics from Harold Nicolson to Kate Millett have commented on the luminous quality of the songs" (Shaw, p. 48).

6. See Bernard Bergonzi, "Feminism and Femininity in *The Princess*," *The Major Victorian Poets: Reconsiderations*," ed. Isobel Armstrong (London: Routledge and Kegan Paul, 1969), p. 46. According to Alastair W. Thomson, too, the songs lead us to believe that children and motherhood are "the only themes the women know or care about" (*The Poetry of Tennyson* [London: Routledge and Kegan Paul, 1986], p. 98). Millett calls the songs "frank propaganda for hearth and home and these latter morsels of domestic piety are placed in the mouths of the girls who listen" (p. 77).

7. Eve Kosofsky Sedgwick, "Tennyson's Princess: One Bride for Seven Brothers" in *Between Men: English Literature and Male Homosocial Desire* (New York: Columbia Univ. Press, 1985), p. 132. Frank and Dillon also point out that the songs "are always associated with dusk or the nocturnal" and suggest the feminine power, "the blank, empty explanation for the aspect of the feminine that cannot be seen in the masculine light of day" (p. 251). Linda M. Shires allows for both conservative and subversive possibilities, suggesting that though "the content of the lyrics may well be in accord with the thrust of the poem towards domesticating the female's desires . . . a digressive lyric energy still plays against and subverts the

unfolding of the narrative" ("Rereading Tennyson's Gender Politics," in *Victorian Sages and Cultural Discourse: Renegotiating Gender and Power*, ed. Thaïs E. Morgan [New Brunswick: Rutgers Univ. Press, 1990], pp. 46-65), p. 57.

8. Shires catalogs the prevalent views of Tennyson's gender politics, ranging from "too feminine" to "too masculine"; she concludes, "These responses demonstrate that Tennyson—his career and poetic discourse—provides a vexed but fascinating ideological site of contestation for literary critics from 1827 to our own day" (p. 48). I hope to suggest a way of reading Tennyson's gender politics with less ambiguity.

9. Edgar Finley Shannon, Jr., *Tennyson and the Reviewers: A Study of His Literary Reputation and of the Influence of the Critics Upon His Poetry, 1827-1851* (Cambridge: Harvard Univ. Press, 1952).

10. Hallam Tennyson, *Alfred Lord Tennyson: A Memoir by His Son* (New York, 1897), 1:254.

11. I would like to thank my good friend Carol A. Wipf-Miller for urging me to see the importance of the child motif and of the belated insertion of the poems, respectively, in my overall argument.

12. Christopher Ricks points out that though Tennyson avoids villains in most of his works, notably *Idylls of the King*, "poor Lady Blanche is made physically and morally unprepossessing; she is rendered as a petty villain, demeaned to a scapegoat" (*Tennyson*, p. 185). I would add that vilifying Blanche is just one of many ways the male narrators accomplish their unrealistic, misogynistic tale.

13. For discussions on genre tensions between the comic and the heroic in *The Princess*, see Ricks, p. 182; Thomson, p. 87; and W. David Shaw, *Alfred Lord Tennyson: The Poet in an Age of Theory* (New York: Twayne, 1996), pp. 17-24. Even early reviewers criticized the "incongruity . . . of grave and gay" and so Tennyson worked painstakingly to amend this duality in the frame in his third edition (Shannon, p. 123).

14. Bergonzi notes that this ambition "stops short of according women total autonomy, inasmuch as they are still supposed to exist in some kind of inescapable relationship with man" (p. 45), suggesting once again that the men of the frame have no intention of according women total autonomy.

15. See Joseph again for a useful interpretation of this song as "a plea for the integration and interpenetration of the Northern and Southern principles" of the Prince and Princess (p. 96).

16. Stone points to exactly this moment when Cyril "trolls out . . . the song that betrays his masculine identity" as one of several examples of how "the inset story continually questions" the alignment found in the frame "between genre and gender, story as male and song as female" (p. 107). I will suggest that these gender inversions in the inset story pale when compared to the gender subversions of the interlude songs, self-consciously female and powerful.

17. Kathryn Gleadle, *The Early Feminists: Racial Unitarians and the Emergence of the Women's Rights Movements, 1831-51* (New York: St. Martin's, 1995), p. 7.

18. Philippa Levine, *Feminist Lives in Victorian England: Private Roles and Public Commitments* (Oxford: Blackwell, 1990), p. 42. John Killham, *Tennyson and "The Princess": Reflections of an Age,* offers useful, though more dated, discussions of the "feminist controversy in England" prior to Tennyson's poem (London: Athlone, 1958).

19. See Alisa M. Clapp, "The City, the Country, and Communities of Singing Women: Music in the Novels of Elizabeth Gaskell," in *Victorian Urban Settings: Essays on the Nineteenth-Century City and Its Contents,* ed. Debra N. Mancoff and D. J. Trela (New York: Garland, 1996), pp. 114-132.

20. This was the average in Bath between 1839 and 1843, while the middle-class average was one in five children (Joan Perkin, *Victorian Women* [New York: New York Univ. Press, 1995], p. 8. Perkin records that as late as 1899 in Liverpool, the poor lost one in four babies, attributing the cause mainly to chest and stomach diseases in the first weeks of life (p. 8).

21. John Hollander reads this song as a "parable of poetic originality: the allusive echoings rebounding from text to text themselves unroll a fable of perpetuation, new versions of romantic summits, 'old in story,' new in poem" (*The Figure of Echo: A Mode of Allusion in Milton and After* [Berkeley: Univ. of California Press, 1981], p. 130).

22. Margaret Homans, *Bearing the Word: Language and Female Experience in Nineteenth-Century Women's Writing* (Chicago: Univ. of Chicago Press, 1986), p. 28.

23. Ricks writes, "In 'The splendour falls on castle walls,' the line 'Our echoes roll from soul to soul' is partly an invoking of one's posterity. This leaves only the final intercalated song, 'Ask me no more,' which . . . depicts the moment of yielding to passionate love [which] . . . is to precede marriage and children" (p. 186n).

24. Gaskell makes a direct, though veiled, link to her son's death and her writing *Mary Barton* (1848) in its Preface: "Three years ago I became anxious (from circumstances that need not be more fully alluded to) to employ myself in writing a work of fiction"; the novel becomes the new child she "bore" to occupy her domestic attention. The fictional Aurora Leigh frequently compares her verses with unborn children, as when she rips them up and finds "no blood . . . The heart in them was just an embryo's heart / Which never yet had beat" (3.246-248) (Elizabeth Barrett Browning, *Aurora Leigh,* ed. Margaret Reynolds [Athens: Ohio Univ. Press, 1992]).

25. W. David Shaw reads this poem differently than I do, suggesting that Ida is "dying of" love, repeating "the words 'Ask me no more,'" not to tranquilize, but to charge the phrase with more and more feeling" (p. 23).

David G. Riede (essay date autumn 2000)

SOURCE: Riede, David G. "Tennyson's Poetics of Melancholy and the Imperial Imagination." *Studies in English Literature, 1500-1900* 40, no. 4 (autumn 2000): 659-78.

[*In the following essay, Riede illustrates how Tennyson asserts poetic authority using feminine representations of his poetic identity.*]

Ever since Arthur Hallam's early review of Alfred, Lord Tennyson's **Poems,** critics have recognized that Tennyson's early work attempts to establish a kind of poetic authority, and that its characteristic power is grounded in melancholy. The best recent criticism, by Herbert Tucker and Isobel Armstrong, argues that Tennyson was especially eager to establish "poetic authority as such" as an "urgent project [in the] context of a society which seemed on the verge of revolution and lawlessness."[1] It has not been sufficiently recognized, however, that Tennyson's melancholy, usually regarded as an apolitical character trait, is itself a source of authority that draws not only on the intensity of mood, but also on current sexist and colonialist discourses, and upon an idiom of eroticized political imperialism.

Hallam, however, even while denying that Tennyson had a political agenda, noted that the "melancholy which so evidently characterizes the spirit of modern poetry" would ultimately exercise a politically conservative function as "a check acting for conservation against a propulsion toward change." Though Hallam worried that such poetry "in proportion to its depth and truth is likely to have little immediate authority over public opinion," his reference to "depth and truth" suggests that the authority of melancholy proceeds from the depths of the poetic self, and carries with it the truth of feeling that Thomas Carlyle called the "felt indubitable certainty of Experience."[2] Melancholy is a physical sensation and seems therefore unarguably "natural," not ideological, so it is not surprising that generations of critics have seen Tennyson's best and most characteristic poetry as apolitical.

Julia Kristeva has suggested a poetics of melancholy as "the royal way through which humanity transcends the grief" of separation from a supposed lost wholeness of being.[3] Tennyson, indeed, would seem, in Kristeva's terms, to have pioneered "a specific economy of imaginary discourses . . . [that] are constituently very close to depression and at the same time show a necessary shift from depression to possible meaning."[4] These discourses include the transmutation of the *imaginary* into artifice "by the means of prosody, the language beyond language that inserts into the sign the rhythm and alliterations of semiotic processes . . . which unsettles naming and, by building up a plurality of connotations around the sign, affords the subject a chance to imagine the nonmeaning, or the true meaning, of the Thing."[5] Kristeva's attempt to identify a language beyond language is inevitably obscure, but her emphasis on the ability of poetic artifice, and particularly rhythm, to express the truths of melancholy may help to explain the perception most notoriously expressed by T. S. Eliot that, although Tennyson had little of consequence to say, he was "the saddest of all English poets" and thus able to communicate the depths of his being from "the abyss of sorrow" because of his remarkable "technical accomplishment."[6] Tennyson's "abyss of sorrow" is not without ideological significance. His melancholy expresses an erotic blend of pain and pleasure that may be traced to a transgression of gender boundaries in the appropriation of female eroticism and of cultural boundaries in an appropriation of exotic, often "Oriental" eroticism. The most influential Tennysonians of the last generation, Christopher Ricks, Jerome Hamilton Buckley, and A. Dwight Culler, all attempted to disengage the "essential genius" of Tennyson's melancholy from the encumbrance of its historical moment.[7] Culler's view of Tennyson's poetry as the expression of "natural" feeling, however, hints at a reading of Tennyson as an imperialist of the imagination: "Unlike the youthful [John] Keats, Tennyson did not remain silent upon a peak in Darien—rather he plunged volubly into its thickets and claimed province after province for his own."[8] To an extent, Culler anticipates Tucker's argument that Tennyson's characteristic poetry is not explicitly imperialist politically, but that "Tennyson represents dilemmas rather of the Romantic imperial self than of political and cultural empire."[9]

Certainly Tennyson was deeply interested in the possibilities of the Romantic imagination as an imperial selfhood capable of entering into and even appropriating provinces and forms of consciousness initially outside the self. This "negative capability" enabled him to enter into the feelings of the many female figures who are generally thought to represent his own poetic sensibility. The imaginative imperialism here is spelled out at length in Hallam's essay "On Sympathy." Hallam provides a native English version of the Hegelian growth of the individual soul or self as a process of confronting other subjectivities and "absorbing . . . this other being into her universal nature."[10] Hallam's "sympathy," a version of Romantic imperialism, is an emotional process enabling the individual self to avoid solipsism and to achieve some awareness of another's subjectivity. The poet whose "soul transfers at once her own feelings and adopts those of the new-comer" is necessarily expanding the individual self to engage with a historically specific "other," so that when Tennyson is at his most apparently Tennysonian, as in **"Mariana,"** it is usually through identification with, or sympathy with, a specifically female other, as femaleness was constructed in the nineteenth century. Tennyson achieves remarkable affect through his appropriation of female subjectivity in such poems as **"Mariana," "Oenone,"** and even **"The Lady of Shalott,"** though, as Marion Shaw has argued, "the male fantasy of female eroticism which these poems embody, is . . . dangerous."[11] In those poems in which Tennyson seems to gender his own poetic sensibility as feminine, it is within a degrading gender ideology that sees women as more emotional than men, but less rational. Also, since women were by definition excluded from political thought, the adoption of female perspectives made it "natural" to disengage the poetic sensibility from the masculine political concerns of the day. When Hallam sought to praise Tennyson as an emotional poet in his review of ***Poems*** of 1830, he did so by distinguishing between "poets of reflection, such as Wordsworth," and what he characterized as the superior, Tennysonian "Poets of sensation," who possess the "powerful tendency of imagination to a life of immediate sympathy with the external universe."[12] Poets of sensation are implicitly feminized: "Susceptible of the slightest impulse from external nature, their fine organs trembled into emotion at colors, and sounds, and movements, unperceived or unregarded by duller temperaments."[13] Hallam, moreover, was well aware that the poets of sensation, Percy Shelley and Keats, were not ideologically neutral, but that Shelley especially, and Keats by association, were seen as politically radical, even as Jacobinical. So, in a futile attempt to de-fang conservative reviewers, he made a point of extricating Tennyson from the politics associated with sensation: "he has also this advantage over [Keats] and his friend Shelley, that he comes before the public unconnected with any political party or peculiar system of opinions."[14] Even though Hallam recognizes that the poetry of sensation has a possibly democratic tendency because poets of sensation "keep no aristocratic state, apart from the sentiments of society at large; they speak to the hearts of all," he affirms that they are at the top of the human hierarchy so that they "elevate inferior intellects into a higher and purer atmosphere."[15] Hallam even goes so far as to imply that John Milton and William Shakespeare were poets of sensation in England's golden literary age, and that the effect of their writings was nothing less than the construction of national identity, of Englishness itself: "the 'knowledge and power' drawn from reading their works was a part of national existence; it was ours as Englishmen; and amid the flux of generations and customs we retain un-impaired this privilege of intercourse with greatness."[16] Hallam further observes, as did many of his contemporaries, that the golden age of poetry is long gone in the present singularly unpoetic age and, in so doing, he takes the opportunity to position the melancholy Tennyson as a conservative, paradoxically preserving the essential elements of England's greatness by the melancholy spirit of modern poetry: "In the old times the poetic impulse went along with the general impulse of the nation; in these it is a reaction against it, a check acting for conservation against a propulsion towards change."[17]

For Hallam, even melancholy—which is generally thought a primary characteristic of Tennyson's essential genius—is to be regarded as a product of the historical moment and, despite its effeminate form, is ideologically aligned with Burkean conservatism and the preservation of Englishness.[18] Hallam and Tennyson paradoxically arrive at the conservative counterforce to the masculine, muscular spirit of the progressive age by colonizing and appropriating the realm of the "weaker" sex, by constructing a feminized version of the powerful imagination of "Poets of sensation." Both Englishness and the melancholy of Tennyson are cultural constructions brought into being by a remarkable detour through a feminized sensibility. Ultimately, though, it is only a detour, since Tennyson usually turns from the feminized poet figure as somehow transgressive, and returns to the masculine cultural order.

His melancholy exploits the poetic power of dangerous feminine emotional lability and passion that threatens his ideal of masculine self-control and public order and makes use of such elements even as it displaces and controls them. Tennyson's use of feminine personae to represent his poetic sensibility enabled him both to represent erotic longing and to distance himself from what was self-evidently "other." Armstrong has demonstrated that Tennyson's emphasis on feeling, on a poetry of sensation, entailed "putting the feminisation of poetry—and men—at the centre of his project. At least the male appropriation of the feminine suggests an admiration for it."[19] Since female eroticism was threatening to social order and was usually suppressed in middle-class English life and thus unavailable to direct observation let alone sympathetic colonization, it is not surprising that Tennyson drew on the current discourse of Oriental

sensuality both to find sources of erotic, sensual beauty and to push the threat from the center of British bourgeois life.

As Edward Said has compellingly demonstrated, to understand the culture of an imperial nation, we must take into account the relation of that culture to the empire, even, and especially, when the cultural products seem unconcerned with empire. If Said is right, it should not be surprising that Tennyson's centrality as the generally acclaimed greatest poet of his age was made possible in part by his use of the current discourse of Oriental sensuality. Though Tennyson's Orientalist sources are often used to represent or to displace his poetic anxieties, they also provided him with a means to explore otherwise forbidden interests in a feminized eroticism, at least as refracted from **"Fatima"** to **"Mariana"** or from **"A Dream of Fair Women"** to **"The Palace of Art."** Seemingly, what he hesitated to say as a socially concerned masculine poet, he could say within the more detached, even scholarly voice of Orientalist discourse.

A closer look at specific poems in which Tennyson is evidently concerned with his own poetic authority indicates that he constructed a poetic self not only in the terms of the imperial, though feminized, Romantic imagination, but also in terms of explicitly political and cultural imperialism. Frequently, Tennyson's English power is expressed in poems about exploration and discovery, figuring the poet more as a "stout Cortez" than as a Keatsian "chameleon poet" of negative capability.[20] Tennyson could have found the analogy of the poet and the explorer in Keats's sonnet, or in the many Byronic figures such as Childe Harold who cultivate a melancholy poetic sensibility in extensive travels to remote regions, but, as Alan Sinfield has pointed out, he would also have seen the idea of the poet converge with that of the explorer in Washington Irving's *Life and Voyages of Christopher Columbus.* According to Sinfield, the continuity of the explorer with the poet was set up for Tennyson by Irving, who represents Columbus's "poetic temperament" as spreading "a golden and glorious world around him." As Sinfield notes, "Irving insists that 'lofty anticipations . . . elevated Columbus above all mercenary interests—at least for a while' . . . The poetic intrusion initiates the sequence which leads to trading, enslavement, colonization and . . . massacre . . . The poetic spirit is the advance guard of capitalism and imperialism, and cannot escape this involvement."[21]

In **"On Sublimity"** (1827), Tennyson collapses the poetic imagination with the wonder evoked by the literature of voyage and exploration; he finds the Burkean sublime not in Romantic landscapes of the transforming imagination, but in actual exotic, far away wonders of the natural world, literally, as W. D. Paden has pointed out, in the pages of C. C. Clarke's *The Hundred Won-*

ders of the World.[22] Unlike William Wordsworth, for whom the "discerning intellect of man / When wedded to this goodly universe" could find sublime landscapes as a "simple produce of the common day," Tennyson sought the sublime in tales of adventurers and explorers reporting on the wonders of the world, from the more-or-less-familiar Fingal's Cave in the Island of Staffa and the by then well-known "Niagara's flood of matchless might," to the more exotic "stupendous Gungotree," "Cotopaxi's cloud-capt majesty" and "Enormous Chimborazo's naked pride."[23] Another poet might have used Mount Snowden or Mont Blanc, but Tennyson's construction of sublimity called for the remote and exotic or, in the phrase that so influenced his childhood, the "far, far away."[24] Like Keats, but unlike Hernando Cortez, Tennyson's "realms of gold" were literary, but, whereas Keats was discovering the wonders of the literary tradition as he read George Chapman's Homer, Tennyson was exploring the discoveries of Cortez's (actually Francisco Pizarro's, of course) followers in the colonial tradition, reading Antonio de Ulloa's *A Voyage to South America.* In general, as Paden's still-important *Tennyson in Egypt* reveals, the reading that most influenced the poetry of early Tennyson was overwhelmingly constituted of books of exploration and discovery and such Orientalist writings as Claude Savary's *Letters on Egypt,* and the works of Sir William Jones.[25]

Far more important than **"On Sublimity"** in constructing Tennyson's poetic authority was his visionary **"Armageddon"** (written in 1828) and its transformation into the Cambridge prize poem, **"Timbuctoo"** (1829). **"Armageddon"** is an exercise in the visionary mode of the egotistical sublime exaggerated almost to the point of madness. Perhaps the most striking characteristic of this effort to achieve prophetic vision is a representation of the egotistical sublime heightened to a hubristic self-deification. One clear danger of the egotistical sublime is solipsism, a dangerous withdrawal from social involvement that Tennyson would further explore in such poems as **"The Lady of Shalott"** and **"The Palace of Art,"** but which appears in its simplest form here. The irony of the visionary poem is that there is no clear vision—rather, as Daniel Albright has shown, there is only an account of visual distortions produced more or less as a disease of the retina.[26] Even when an angel descends to mediate the vision, the poet is confronted by such overwhelming dazzle that he must close himself up within himself:

> So that with hasty motion I did veil
> My vision with both hands, and saw before me
> Such coloured spots as dance athwart the eyes
> Of those that gaze upon the noonday sun.
>
> (1:73-85, 2.6-9)

Even at the triumphant conclusion of the poem, it is unclear what has been seen or heard outside the self:

> An indefinite pulsation
> Inaudible to outward sense,
>
> . . . . .
>
> As if the great soul of the Universe
> Heaved with tumultuous throbbings on the vast
> Suspense of some grand issue.
>
> (4.29-34)

Not only has full vision not yet been vouchsafed, but even the introductory drum roll may be a solipsistic delusion; both Tucker and Armstrong note that the pulsations may be nothing more than the speaker's own heartbeat, as described earlier, when in "dismal pause . . . I held / My breath and heard the beatings of my heart" (1.111-3).[27] Evidently, one reason why Tennyson could not find poetic authority in the egotistical sublime was that he saw too clearly its inherent danger of solipsistic estrangement from the world—again, a theme more clearly played out in **"The Lady of Shalott"** and **"The Palace of Art."** Arguably, his awareness of the dangers of the egotistical sublime led him away from reliance on his own poetic subjectivity and toward the subject matter offered in books of travel that provided referents outside the self for an otherwise entirely self-absorbed melancholy.

Further, there is, throughout **"Armageddon,"** a sense of transgression, of sin, at the presumptuousness of the prophetic mode. The speaker sees "such ill-omened things / That it were sin almost to look on them" (1.53-4). But, beyond the sinfulness of gazing upon "Obscene, inutterable phantasies," is the more obvious transgression of assuming the visionary perspective of "God's omniscience" (1.107, 2.27). In language that anticipates the soul's hubris in **"The Palace of Art,"** the speaker worships his own sublimity: "in that hour I could have fallen down / Before my own strong soul and worshiped it" (2.49-50). To avoid total incoherence, the poet must move beyond the speaker's foundering in the abyss of the inexpressible, and introduce comprehensible content into the sublime, which he accomplishes by returning to his sources in the literature of exploration and discovery, once again calling upon "Cotopaxi's cloud-capt towers" (line 100) and other wonders to give content to his vision. When Tennyson's father insisted that he submit a poem for the Cambridge prize competition on the theme of Timbuctoo, he transformed the seemingly incongruous **"Armageddon"** for the purpose. **"Armageddon,"** as a visionary poem almost without content, could easily be filled with the content of Tennyson's favorite literature of exploration and discovery. What Tennyson did to transform **"Armageddon"** into **"Timbuctoo"** was to muse on "legends quaint and old" (**"Timbuctoo,"** line 16) of other lost cities that had stirred the European imagination: "divinest Atalantis" and "Imperial Eldorado" (1:187-99, lines 22, 24). And now, when the angel appears, he remains too dazzling to be looked upon but nevertheless offers a very clear vision of the celestial city as beheld by St. John on Patmos. Finally, near the end of the poem, the poet achieves a vision of Timbuctoo, or rather, of a rich Oriental city that he imagines as Timbuctoo. He sees

> The argent streets o' the city, imaging
> The soft inversions of her tremulous Domes,
> Her gardens frequent with the stately Palm,
> Her Pagods hung with music of sweet bells,
> Her obelisks of rangèd Chrysolite,
> Minarets and towers

(lines 227-32)

In **"Timbuctoo,"** however, Tennyson exhibits his distrust of the visionary mode—the speaker recognizes that Atalantis and Eldorado are fables, and that even Timbuctoo, when it is discovered rather than imagined, will lose its luster. Before the eyes of "keen *Discovery*" the "brilliant towers" of the city will dissolve like the visions of Prospero's masque, will

> Darken, and shrink and shiver into huts,
> Black specks amid a waste of dreary sand,
> Low-built, mud-walled, Barbarian settlements.

(lines 240-2)

Despite his recognition that discovery is a way of discrediting the imagination and that actuality always falls short of imagination, Tennyson continued to stimulate his imagination with tales of modern adventure that still provided possibilities of magnificence, possibilities to which "Men clung with yearning Hope which would not die" (line 27). He believed, however, that the poetic sensibility must ultimately be restored to the acceptable world of actualities: Timbuctoo is only imagined as an earthly paradise, and then demoted to sordid actuality as the "Barbarian" huts of an inferior race that evidently need to be "improved" by European discovery and appropriation. In **"Timbuctoo,"** Tennyson pushed the dangerously anarchic sublime from the religious centrality of **"Armageddon"** to the edges of the world and then purged it completely by substituting "keen *Discovery*" for imaginative wonder.

The combination of Tennyson's imaginative longing for wonders at the far edge of the known world with his sense of guilt or transgression remained important in his more mature works. Notoriously, in **"Locksley Hall"** (1842), when the speaker seeks escape from his emotional entanglement and suffocation in England, he displaces discontent with England by imagining a retreat to the vast expanses of the Empire, "some retreat / Deep in yonder shining Orient" (2:118-30, lines 153-4). Better yet, he imagines some far-away island, free of all restraints, "all links of habit—there to wander far away" in "Breadths of tropic shade and palms in cluster, knots of Paradise" (lines 157, 160). Not only does the speaker of **"Locksley Hall"** imagine an earthly paradise waiting to be discovered, but so, of course, do Tennyson's Ul-

ysses, the poet of **"The Hesperides,"** and mariners of **"The Lotos-Eaters."**

Sinfield points out that Tennyson's imaginative flight to the remote edges of the world is a defining quality of the poet who sought imaginative escape from an England less characterized by imagination, beauty, or passion than by the rush for progress characterized in **"Locksley Hall,"** "in this march of mind / In the steamship, in the railway, in the thoughts that shake mankind" (lines 165-6). Sinfield describes the process cogently: "Finding imaginative impetus marginalized theoretically and politically in Britain, he invested it in remote places. Finding himself expected to explore states of mind, he did so by using the people and scenery of remote places, and their impact on Europeans."[28] This is, I think, an accurate account of Tennyson's imaginative activity, but I would suggest also that his flights from the center tend to be associated with transgression, with kinds of experience forbidden to an English gentleman. In fact, the flight from the center is, in itself, a form of transgression in its refusal to participate in the communal life. But, of course, the kinds of transgressive experience Tennyson imagines *are* at the center of British imperial culture—Tennyson only makes them seem marginal, in the same way that Victorian culture generally relegated forbidden experiences to the margins. The notoriety of the speaker's desires in **"Locksley Hall"** is not associated with his desire for a tropical paradise, but with his desire for an unlimited range of specifically sexual passion: "There the passions cramped no longer shall have scope and breathing space; / I will take some savage woman, she shall rear my dusky race" (lines 167-8). The transgressive, imperialist fantasy is, of course, almost immediately rejected, simply because the center *is* more valued than the periphery—or more crudely, because the English and their age of progress are immeasurably superior to the lower races at the far end of empire:

>   I *know* my
> words are wild,
> But I count the gray barbarian lower than the Christian child.
>
> I, to herd with narrow foreheads, vacant of our glorious gains,
> Like a beast with lower pleasures, like a beast with lower pains!
>
> Mated with a squalid savage—what to me were sun or clime?
> I the heir of all the ages

(lines 173-8)

The speaker of **"Locksley Hall"** is not to be simply identified as Tennyson, but elsewhere Tennyson shares this speaker's fantasy of escape from restraint by a detour through some exotic and erotic paradise preceding a return to the center with reinforced belief in its values, especially the value of self-control—a quality that

James Eli Adams has shown is perhaps *the* defining quality of Victorian masculinity.[29]

"Anacaona" (1830), a poem based on material from Irving's biography of Columbus, describes just such an escape in the context of imperial exploration. According to Irving, Anacaona was the beautiful queen of an island paradise who "possessed a genius superior to the generality of her race."[30] Tennyson's poem makes the most of her exotic beauty and setting, and heightens her erotic appeal: she is

> A dark Indian Maiden,
>
> . . . . .
>
> Wantoning in orange groves
> Naked, and dark-limbed, and gay
>
> (1:308-11, lines 1-6)

Though "wantoning" is a rather more loaded term than any authorized by Irving, Tennyson did have ample precedent in Irving for stressing the naked beauty of Anacaona. Irving described the welcome offered the European explorers: "the young women were entirely naked, with merely a fillet round the forehead, their hair falling upon their shoulders. They were beautifully proportioned, their skin smooth and delicate, and their complexion of clear agreeable brown."[31]

According to Irving, however, Anacaona was later killed by the Spaniards and, further, the discovery of this island paradise, so far from the authority and restraints of home, helped tempt the sailors into mutiny against Columbus. Tennyson's poem does not mention any of this, though it introduces a somber, foreboding tone in the last stanza: "never more upon the shore . . . wandered happy Anacaona" (lines 77, 82). Still, despite the tone of foreboding, **"Anacaona"** remains a poem of essentially untroubled erotic fantasy—in this case with no apparent sense of guilty transgression. But Tennyson never published it, giving various unconvincing reasons, but perhaps providing the real reason in an unguarded comment describing "that black b_____ Anacaona and her cocoa-shadowed *coves* of niggers—I cannot have her strolling about the land in this way—it is neither good for her reputation nor mine" (1:308 n). According to Culler, "'**Anacaona**' is perhaps the least ambiguous" of the many poems akin to **"The Lady of Shalott"** in presenting an image of the poet's sensibility; Tennyson "could use [Anacaona] as a symbol of the poet not only because she danced and sang the traditional areytos, or ballads, of her people but also because her name and that of her country were so melodious that Tennyson, weaving them into his rhymes, could make it seem as if she and her island were of music all compact."[32] Given the mutinous behavior of the Spaniards in Tennyson's source, this poem and others like it (conspicuously **"The Lotos-Eaters"**) may be attempting a kind of cultural work comparable to that which

Stephen Greenblatt attributes to *The Tempest.* Greenblatt argues that the discovery of an apparent island paradise by the survivors of the shipwrecked "Sea-Venture" of the Virginia Company led to a crisis of authority, since the temptations to remain in paradise rather than proceed to colonial work were almost overpowering at such an extreme distance from governmental authority. *The Tempest,* he argues, represents Prospero's staging of "salutary anxiety" to bring the mutineers of a similar shipwreck back to a proper respect for authoritative order.[33]

What makes **"The Lotos-Eaters"** and **"Anacaona"** strangely ambiguous works is that the temptations of island paradises are forthrightly shown, but the consequences of loss of order are only hinted at by the shift in tone at the end of **"Anacaona"** and the mariners' blasphemous assertions that they, like the soul in **"The Palace of Art,"** are like gods, observing mortal strife, but disengaged from it. Evidently, at any rate, Tennyson himself regarded **"Anacaona"** as morally compromised. The analogy to Greenblatt's reading of *The Tempest* is strengthened by the echoes of *The Tempest,* particularly of Ariel's song that, as Armstrong has said, "haunts" Tennyson's early poems.[34] Further, like Shakespeare, Tennyson was using narratives of colonial exploration as his source. Certainly Tennyson's relocation of excesses of eroticism to the edges of the imperial world provides a kind of outlet for overflow that might otherwise threaten the orderly authority at the imperial center—quite clearly, in **"Locksley Hall"** the deranged speaker can dissipate his dangerously excessive passions in erotic fantasies of tropical paradises.

In **"Anacaona,"** **"The Lotos-Eaters,"** **"The Hesperides,"** and **"Ulysses,"** Tennyson explores the remote margins of the West, as though determined to refute Wordsworth's assertion that tales of legendary lost cities were "a mere fiction of what never was."[35] Even the discourse about the West was obviously "Orientalist," of course, as indicated by the word "Indians" to represent native Americans, but much more often, Tennyson drew on the burgeoning discourse of explicit Orientalism for his representations of transgressive exotic otherness. In **"Persia"** (1827), for example, he makes poetic capital of Oriental names before warming to his theme of the destruction of Persia at the hands of Alexander:

> Land of bright eye and lofty brow!
>   Whose every gale is balmy breath
>   Of incense from some sunny flower,
> Which on tall hill or valley low,
>
> . . . . .
>
> Sheds perfume.
>
> (1:113-6, lines 1-6)

Persia is personified as an exotically perfumed courtesan, suggesting the effeminacy that made her easy prey to Alexander's armies. Still more significantly, within colonialist ideology, the conquest of the Orient is an Englishman's duty, so the erotic conquest of the Orientalized female is appropriated within the sphere of manly duty. Here, as in **"The Expedition of Nadir Shah into Hindostan"** (1827), which draws on Jones's account of the Persian destruction of the Mogul empire in 1738, Tennyson chronicles the loss of Oriental glory and, implicitly, the concomitant transfer of prestige to the West. The armies of Nadir Shah reduce a paradisal realm to a wasteland: "The land like an Eden before them is fair, / But behind them a wilderness dreary and bare" (1:120-2, lines 19-20). It is worth noting that the displacement of the Mogul empire by an anarchic wasteland opened the door to British expansion in India in the eighteenth century, and also, according to Said, the loss of Oriental greatness seemed to the West to call for a reconstruction of the Orient as a discourse, Orientalism. "To reconstruct a dead or neglected Orient . . . meant that reconstructive precision, science, even imagination could prepare the way for what armies, administrations, and bureaucracies would later do on the ground, in the Orient. In a sense the vindication of Orientalism was not only its intellectual or artistic successes, but its later effectiveness, its usefulness, its authority."[36] Ultimately, Tennyson's many poems on Oriental subjects were doing the same cultural work as the Abbe le Mascrier in the immense *Description de L'Egypte* compiled for Napoleon, though Tennyson was not, of course, so explicit in his political implications. The *Description* reconstituted Egypt as a country that "presents only great memories" and affirms that "[i]t is therefore proper for this country to attract the attention of illustrious princes who rule the destiny of nations."[37]

I do not want to attribute excessively sinister motives to Tennyson, but only to note that his numerous early poems on Oriental subjects inevitably took the tone of the dominant Orientalist discourse of his age. In terms of Tennyson's own poetic development, the most important characteristic of Orientalism is its eroticism. The eroticism that was unsuitable in speaking of the chaste English was, of course, perfectly "natural" in descriptions of the Orient or Oriental women. In **"Thou camest to thy bower my love"** (1827), Tennyson was able to write with uncharacteristic erotic directness because he was drawing heavily on Jones's translation of the erotic poem, the *Gitagovinda* (1:148 n):

> Thy breath was like the sandal-wood that casts a rich
>   perfume,
> Thy blue eyes mocked the lotos in the noon-day of his
>   bloom;
> Thy cheeks were like the beamy flush that gilds the
>   breaking day,
> And in the ambrosia of thy smiles the god of rapture
>   lay.
>
>   (1:148-50, lines 5-8)

"The Lotos-Eaters" was primarily based on a passage describing the idyllic lassitude of a colonialist dream in Irving's *Columbus,* but the lotos itself comes not only from Homer but also from Tennyson's characteristic accounts of Oriental lushness and luxuriance. The full importance of Orientalist eroticism in forming Tennyson's poetic sensibility is especially clear in **"Fatima"** (1832), imitating a poem by Sappho but also influenced by the story of Jemily in Savary's *Letters on Egypt.* Jemily is described as waiting in an agony of passion for a lover who will not come for fear of her husband. Of all of Tennyson's female impersonations, **"Fatima"** is far the most impassioned:

> Last night, when some one spoke his name,
> From my swift blood that went and came
> A thousand little shafts of flame
> Were shivered in my narrow frame.
>   O Love, O fire! once he drew
>   With one long kiss my whole soul through
> My lips, as sunlight drinketh dew.
>
>   (1:417-9, lines 15-21)

Tucker describes **"Fatima"** as a "breakthrough" poem for Tennyson because it expresses an "unabashed will to confrontation."[38] But, it is also a breakthrough because it expresses an unashamed sexual desire, akin to, but more outward than, the suppressed yearnings of **"Mariana,"** and this sexual frankness is made possible for Tennyson by displacing it on to an Oriental subjectivity. Like **"Mariana,"** it is a poem about waiting and facing the alternatives of sexual fulfillment or death, but, in the case of **"Fatima"** much more clearly than of **"Mariana,"** it is explicitly a longing for erotic fulfillment rather than a more spiritual love:

> My whole soul waiting silently,
> All naked in a sultry sky,
> Droops blinded with his shining eye:
> I *will* possess him or will die.
> I will grow round him in his place,
> Grow, live, die looking on his face,
> Die, dying clasped in his embrace.
>
>   (lines 36-42)

"Fatima" is an important poem in our understanding of Tennyson if only because it represents an Oriental other that helps to define the Western subjectivity by contrast, and especially to suggest the energy of suppressed passion in Tennyson's more canonical poems. Similarly, in **"A Dream of Fair Women"**(1832), the eroticism of the poem owes nothing to the apparent inspiration, Geoffrey Chaucer's *Legend of Good Women,* but rather is picked up on another detour into Oriental sensuality via Savary's *Letters on Egypt.* Savary, not Chaucer, stimulated reverie about "hushed seraglios," and Cleopatra, the dominant figure of the poem, owes little to Chaucer's Cleopatra, or even to Shakespeare's, despite her "swarthy cheeks" from *Antony and Cleopatra* (1:479-92, line 36).[39]

Tennyson's representation of Cleopatra is especially striking because it parallels his much-better-known representation of the soul in **"The Palace of Art"** (1832). The soul, generally assumed to represent the evil consequences of living in art, falls from grace by becoming a kind of hubristic inspiration to spiritual anarchy:

> I take possession of man's mind and deed.
>   I care not what the sects may brawl.
> I sit as God holding no form of creed,
>   But contemplating all.
>
>   (1:436-56, lines 209-12)

Cleopatra, in "A Dream of Fair Women" makes an analogous claim: "'I governed men by change, and so I swayed / All moods'" (lines 130-1). The implication is that Tennyson's fear of art detached from social good is in part at least a fear of the eroticism that both attracts and repels him in representations of the Orient.

This interpretation is strengthened by noting that, in its original form, **"A Dream of Fair Women"** was, like **"The Palace of Art,"** a representation of the poetic spirit divorcing itself from the social order. The opening stanzas compared the poet with a balloonist raised high above mankind and, like the soul in **"The Palace of Art,"** or like the Lady of Shalott, viewing mankind from a detached, "aesthetic distance":

> So, lifted high, the Poet at his will
> Lets the great world flit from him, seeing all,
> Higher through secret splendours mounting still,
> Self-poised, nor fears to fall.
>
>   (1:479-80 n)

A still earlier version even more strongly suggests the similarities among the soul's, the poet's, and Cleopatra's ability to be an unmoved mover: "The poet's steadfast soul, poured out in songs, / Unmoved moves all things with exceeding might" (1:480 n). **"A Dream of Fair Women,"** structured like **"The Palace of Art"** as a series of tableaux, seems to have been an earlier or contemporary effort to analyze the dangers of unrestricted art or imagination and seems, moreover, to have seen these dangers as analogous to the dangers represented by Eastern female sensuality and its supposed tyranny over the rational mind. Indeed, some of the influences of Orientalist discourse remain evident in **"The Palace of Art"** itself. Ricks points out that the poem "was probably influenced by Sir William Jones, a favourite of his when young," and that there "are also affinities with George Sandys's account of Egyptian 'Palaces' in his *Travels*" (1:437). But the most obvious Orientalist influence is Samuel Taylor Coleridge's "Kubla Khan," whose "stately pleasure dome" is ostentatiously echoed in the "lordly pleasure-house" of Tennyson's opening line. In the 1832 version, the soul's downfall in the midst of embroideries of "every legend fair /

Which the supreme Caucasian mind / Carved out of Nature for itself" (lines 125-7) was given a somewhat Oriental cast by reference to a mysterious "Asiatic dame": "in her pride" (1:445 n, line 1), the soul beholds in herself

>   Madonna, Ganymede,
> Or the Asiatic dame—
>
> Still changing, as a lighthouse in the night
>   Changeth athwart the gleaming main,
> From red to yellow, yellow to pale white,
>   Then back to red again.
>
>   (1:446 n, lines 7-12)

Whoever the "Asiatic dame" may be, anxiety about the possibly anarchic power of art is here associated with the threat of a disordered, feminized mutability ("*la donna e mobile*") and simultaneously, perhaps, with suggestions of Eastern, specifically Hindu, mysticism. In addition, the moral fable is very clearly of a piece with such Oriental tales as Frances Sheridan's *The History of Nourjahad*, which also teaches that the possession of all imaginable luxuries and beauties leads only to a blasphemous impulse to worship oneself as a God. **"The Palace of Art"** is very much within a European tradition of moral lessons about worldliness cast as eroticized Oriental luxuriance that extends from the chastely somber *Rasselas* to the extraordinary excesses of *Salammbô*.

The clearest example of Tennyson's early uses of Oriental lore to construct and express a poetic sensibility is the poem Hallam cited as characteristic of Tennyson's genius at its best: **"Recollections of the Arabian Nights."** Hallam's praise of the poem, not incidentally, coyly indicates how the source could be simultaneously innocent and expressive of forbidden desires: "Our author," he says, "has, with great judgment, selected our old acquaintance, 'the good Haroun Alraschid,' as the most prominent object of our childish interest, and with him has called up one of those luxurious garden scenes, the account of which, in plain prose, used to make our mouth water for sherbet, since luckily we were too young to think much about Zobeide!"[40] Possibly it was this transgressively erotic mode that inspired Hallam's enigmatic suggestion that modern poets are unlike their great Elizabethan predecessors as repentance is unlike innocence (p. 190).

The poem itself is a colonialist's dream. The fantasy is distanced by setting it in childhood, and the "realms of gold" represented in the poem are, of course, literary realms. Still, the poem indicates that, for Tennyson, the "golden realms" of literature were often very like the "golden realms" dreamed of by imperial conquerors. Besides, as Said has made clear, the Orient only existed for the West as a literary realm, as the discourse of Orientalism. The childhood memories are recalled as a voyage into the Middle East:

And many a sheeny summer-morn,
Adown the Tigris I was borne,
By Bagdat's shrines of fretted gold.

(1:225-31, lines 5-7)

Arabia is, in fact, transformed by the poet into a literal golden realm. Everything he sees is perceived as a treasure: the "costly doors," the "gold glittering" of lamplight, the "broidered sofas," even the natural landscape:

the moon-lit sward
Was damask-work, and deep inlay
Of braided blooms unmown.

(lines 27-9)

The stream is seen as wealth: "diamond rillets" and "crystal arches" all "silver-chiming," the lake covered with "diamond plots," the leaves "rich gold-green," the flowers "studded wide / With disks and tiars," and even the anchor silver (lines 49-51, 82, 63-4). The shallop eventually enters into the palace and harem of Haroun Alraschid, where still greater riches are exhibited, climaxing not in sherbet, as was Hallam's analogy, but in erotic voyeurism:

Then stole I up, and trancedly
Gazed on the Persian girl alone,
Serene with argent-lidded eyes
Amorous, and lashes like to rays
Of darkness, and a brow of pearl
Tressèd with redolent ebony,
In many a dark delicious curl,
Flowing beneath her rose-hued zone.

(lines 133-40)

The scene is reminiscent of Porphyro's voyeurism in Keats's "Eve of St. Agnes," but Tennyson arrives at this expression of erotic desire by a route that takes him like a conqueror through an Eastern version of El Dorado. Once again, Tennyson's "Poetry of sensation" is not an emanation of his autonomous essential genius, but a social construct very much dependent on England's contemporary imperial "mission." As Culler has noted, the final vision of the poem brings the poet face to face with Haroun Al Raschid: "in the 185th tale of *The Arabian Nights,* on which the poem is based, there is nothing the young Prince, who has secretly stolen to an assignation with the Caliph's favorite, would less rather see than the Caliph himself. Yet this is what Tennyson has him do, and so the heady amorous vision dissolves in boyish laughter."[41] The voyeurism, for Culler, is whitewashed by the innocent boyishness of the poet, but one might argue that the apparent complicity of the Caliph, whose eyes laugh "[w]ith merriment of kingly pride," (line 151) suggests a willingness to share his harem, and thus suggests precisely the triangulation of desire that Eve Sedgwick has argued is the paradigm of male homosocial desire in the nineteenth century. Peace is made with the colonial other, and the treaty is ratified by the exchange or sharing of the woman. It is under the approving glance of the Caliph that Tennyson's poetic, erotic, and cultural imperialism are all made acceptable, even "natural" within the hegemonic homosocial and colonialist culture of his day.

Tennyson's later works generally depend less on Orientalist discourse for their inspiration, despite such exceptions as **"Akbar's Dream,"** but they continue to depend upon a representation and simultaneous distancing of emotions and modes of thought perceived as feminine. John Killham has argued, for example, that the "erotic near Eastern setting invented for the Persian girl is carried over" to *The Princess* (1:225 n), and Sedgwick's analysis of *The Princess* has convincingly shown that it represents not female liberation through education, but rather an extreme form of male homosocial bonding through the exchange of women. Even in *In Memoriam,* the authoritative masculine voice is achieved by personifying the poet's emotion, "Sorrow," as female, a weakness that is long indulged, but must eventually be exorcised.

Notes

1. Herbert F. Tucker, *Tennyson and the Doom of Romanticism* (Cambridge MA and London: Harvard Univ. Press, 1988), p. 10; Isobel Armstrong, *Victorian Poetry: Poetry, Poetics, and Politics* (London and New York: Routledge, 1993), p. 49.

2. Arthur Hallam, "On Some of the Characteristics of Modern Poetry, and on the Lyrical Poems of Alfred Tennyson," in *The Writings of Arthur Hallam,* ed. T. H. Vail Motter (New York: Modern Language Association of America, 1943), pp. 182-98, 190; Thomas Carlyle, *Sartor Resartus: The Life and Opinions of Herr Teufelsdröckh,* ed. Charles Frederick Harrold (New York: Odyssey Press, 1937), p. 196.

3. Julia Kristeva, *Black Sun: Depression and Melancholia,* trans. Leon S. Roudiez (New York: Columbia Univ. Press, 1989), p. 100.

4. Ibid.

5. Kristeva, p. 97.

6. T. S. Eliot, "In Memoriam," rprt. in *Tennyson's Poetry,* ed. Robert W. Hill Jr. (New York: W. W. Norton, 1971), pp. 613-20, 620.

7. See Christopher Ricks, *Tennyson,* 2d edn. (London: Macmillan, 1989); Jerome Hamilton Buckley, *Tennyson: The Growth of a Poet* (Cambridge MA: Harvard Univ. Press, 1974); and A. Dwight Culler, *The Poetry of Tennyson* (New Haven and London: Yale Univ. Press, 1977). Ricks, Buckley, and Culler were all following in the tradition of Harold Nicolson, who famously argued that there were

two Tennysons, the melancholy "essential genius" and the official Victorian spokesman. See Nicolson, *Tennyson: Aspects of His Life and Character* (London: Constable, 1970), p. 5.

8. Culler, p. 9.

9. Tucker, p. 28.

10. Hallam, "On Sympathy," in *The Writings of Arthur Hallam,* pp. 133-42, 137.

11. Marion Shaw, *Alfred Lord Tennyson* (New York: Harvester Wheatsheaf, 1988), p. 105.

12. Hallam, "On Some of the Characteristics of Modern Poetry," p. 186.

13. Ibid.

14. Hallam, "On Some of the Characteristics of Modern Poetry," p. 191.

15. Hallam, "On Some of the Characteristics of Modern Poetry," p. 189.

16. Ibid.

17. Hallam, "On Some of the Characteristics of Modern Poetry," p. 190.

18. For a full discussion of Tennyson's contribution to the conception of Englishness, see John Lucas, *England and Englishness: Ideas of Nationhood in English Poetry, 1688-1900* (London: Hogarth Press, 1990), esp. chap. 8, "Tennyson's Great Sirs," pp. 161-80.

19. Armstrong, p. 37.

20. "Stout Cortez" is from John Keats's "On First Looking into Chapman's Homer," line 11, *The Poems of John Keats,* ed. Jack Stillinger (Cambridge MA: Harvard Univ. Press, 1978), p. 64. The phrase "chameleon poet" is from Keats's letter to Richard Woodhouse, 27 October 1818, in *The Letters of John Keats 1814-1821,* 2 vols., ed. Hyder Edward Rollins (Cambridge MA: Harvard Univ. Press, 1958), 1:387.

21. Alan Sinfield, *Alfred Tennyson* (London: Basil Blackwell, 1986), pp. 52-3.

22. W. D. Paden, *Tennyson in Egypt: A Study of the Imagery in His Earlier Work,* Humanistic Studies 27 (Lawrence: Univ. of Kansas, 1942), pp. 24-30.

23. William Wordsworth, *Home at Grasmere,* MS D, lines 805-8 in *Home at Grasmere: Part First, Book First of The Recluse,* ed. Beth Darlington (Ithaca: Cornell Univ. Press, 1977), pp. 35-107; Tennyson, "On Sublimity," in *The Poems of Tennyson,* ed. Christopher Ricks, 2d edn., 3 vols. (Berkeley and Los Angeles: Univ. of California Press, 1987), pp. 85-98, lines 91, 72. All references to Tennyson's poems will be to this edition and hereafter will be cited parenthetically in the text by inclusive page numbers on first reference, line numbers on all references, and stanza numbers where appropriate.

24. Hallam Tennyson, *Alfred Lord Tennyson: A Memoir by His Son,* 2 vols. (1897; rprt. New York: Greenwood Press, 1969), 1:11.

25. Paden, pp. 30-40.

26. Daniel Albright, *Tennyson: The Muses' Tug-of-War* (Charlottesville: Univ. Press of Virginia, 1986), pp. 15-8.

27. See Armstrong, p. 88, and Tucker, p. 48.

28. Sinfield, p. 39.

29. See James Eli Adams, *Dandies and Desert Saints: Styles of Victorian Manhood* (Ithaca: Cornell Univ. Press, 1995).

30. Washington Irving, *The Life and Voyages of Christopher Columbus,* ed. John Harmon McElroy (Boston: Twayne, 1981).

31. Irving, p. 351. Irving himself may have found this passage too racy, and in his abridgment he eliminated references to nakedness and merely said that the women were "beautifully formed." Tennyson would have had less justification for the eroticism of the poem if he had read the version standard for general readers. See Irving, *The Life and Voyages of Christopher Columbus* (abridged by Irving) (London: John Murray, 1830), p. 222.

32. Culler, p. 56.

33. Stephen Greenblatt, "Martial Law in the Land of Cockaigne," *Shakespearean Negotiations: The Circulation of Social Energy in Renaissance England* (Berkeley: Univ. of California Press, 1988), pp. 129-63, 135.

34. Armstrong, p. 58.

35. Wordsworth, *The Recluse,* line 804.

36. Edward Said, *Orientalism* (New York: Random House, 1979), p. 123.

37. Said, Abbe le Mascrier, *Description de L'Egypte,* p. 84.

38. Tucker, p. 145.

39. Tennyson said, "I was thinking of Shakespeare's Cleopatra: 'Think of me / That am with Phoebus' amorous pinches black' (Antony and Cleopatra, I.v.28). Millais has made a mulatto of her in his illustration. I know perfectly well that she was a Greek" (quoted in Ricks, 1:486 n).

40. Hallam, "On Some of the Characteristics of Modern Poetry," p. 192.

41. Culler, p. 32.

Daniel Denecke (essay date winter 2001)

SOURCE: Denecke, Daniel. "The Motivation of Tennyson's Reader: Privacy and the Politics of Literary Ambiguity in *The Princess*." *Victorian Studies* 43, no. 2 (winter 2001): 201-27.

[*In the following essay, Denecke views Tennyson's treatment of various aspects of gender, politics, religion, and identity in* The Princess.]

With the publication of "The Motivation of Tennyson's Weeper," Cleanth Brooks's essay on **"Tears, Idle Tears"** in *The Well Wrought Urn* (1947), a fragment of *The Princess* (1847) appeared at the source of what would become a major debate in English literary criticism between formalists and antiformalists.[1] There, Brooks performed an exemplary close reading of Tennyson's lyric without any analysis of the surrounding text or context, and with no mention of *The Princess* as the place where the lyric gem first appeared before being salvaged from the wreck of the longer poem by later anthologists.[2] If Brooks's essay represents the extreme of formalist discussions of *The Princess,* antiformalist criticism of the poem has tended to ignore the lyrics altogether. Critics such as Eve Kosofsky Sedgwick have sought rather to decode the ideological work performed by the verse-narrative, where a complex interplay of gender and class dynamics reveals the poem to be either a liberal or a conservative political tale of the triumph of domesticity and the consolidation of the state.[3] Even when critics do tackle both the lyrics and the verse-narrative, they frequently maintain the parallel distinction between formalist aesthetic and antiformalist sociological concerns.[4] So Laurence Lerner, in a study of competing ideologies in *The Princess,* writes: "[I]n relating a poem to its society we ought never to ignore what makes it poetry," that is, elements of "pure technique" of sound and image (210). The fact that the lyrics and verse-narrative have attracted two different kinds of critics has blinded both to the extent to which *The Princess* constitutes a defense of poetry, in the sense that it explores the distinctive political effects of lyric and song.

By situating the lyrics within a verse-narrative about women's higher education, Tennyson developed an argument about the political effects of poetry with a degree of sophistication not recognized by either fans of his fine ear or critics of his social agenda. The lyrics serve several public purposes. For example, they serve as strategic techniques for generating group identities,

as forms for the expression of sentiments and ideals that conflict with the demands of group identity, and as public occasions for readers to occupy a space that is irrevocably private. Additions that Tennyson made in 1850 further illustrate his commitment to representing poetry as a public activity. These include a debate in the frame about what form the published version of the verse-narrative should take and a number of new songs which the women in the frame sing to give "breathing space" (Prologue 234) to the men narrating the verse-tale. Throughout the verse-narrative and the frame, then, Tennyson represents the production and reception of poetry as activities that take place within a distinctly public arena. Tennyson's interest in poetry as a public activity has been overlooked by critics like Brooks who have treated extracts such as **"Tears, Idle Tears"** as versions of what we have come to recognize as the "romantic lyric," as expressions of a solitary speaker providing a revelatory account of the self. This way of reading his lyrics reflects the persistence of modernist appraisals of Tennyson as a gifted lyric poet, but an at-best inarticulate, and at-worst insidious social thinker. T. S. Eliot delivered such a divided verdict, for example, when he admiringly shored up lyrical fragments from *The Princess* to conclude *The Waste Land* (1922) but dismissed Tennyson's thought as mere "rumination" (248). And this forked evaluation took its strongest form in W. H. Auden's famous claim that while Tennyson "had the finest ear [. . .] of any English poet; he was also undoubtedly the stupidest" (222).

If Tennyson's insistence on the public uses of lyric should prompt us to resist tendencies to treat extracts from the poem as versions of the romantic lyric, it also provides us with new insight into his political thought. For the lyrics within the poem answer a question that has long puzzled critics grappling with the poem's politics: what causes the poem's heroine to convert from radical feminist to angel in the house? What motivates Princess Ida to renounce her leadership of a separatist, women's education movement and marry the Prince? Though most critics agree that Ida experiences a surge of sentiment or—in Christopher Ricks's words—an "eruption of love" (*Tennyson* [1972] 188) and that the poem's political resolution accurately reflects her interior state, no one has adequately answered the question of what causes this belated recognition of latent desires. In response to these critics, I first suggest that the poems within the poem play a crucial and hitherto neglected role in what appears as Ida's conversion. The lyrics within the verse-narrative and the songs between the parts make it appear that Ida experiences a revelation about her true identity as her interests in radical feminism yield to a desire for domestic bliss. But more importantly, I argue, Tennyson ultimately renders Ida's interior state opaque.

While he could have revealed her true nature in a clear confessional statement, at no point in the verse-narrative does he do so, and I take this to be a strategic decision on Tennyson's part. Moreover, ambiguities within the lyrics continually fail to provide any unequivocal revelation of identity with which Ida as a reader of these lyrics might identify. By celebrating the inaccessibility of private motives that contemporaries like Thackeray and Trollope lamented, Tennyson explicitly broke with the form of the conversion narrative. This may seem counterintuitive, given that critics of Tennyson's politics have been so persistent in reading *The Princess* as a conversion narrative in which political resolution is achieved with the revelation of identity. The final product does not reflect a Tennyson divided between aesthetic aspiration and social concern, as advocates of the time-honored "Two Tennyson" theory maintain and as the division between literary critics would seem to reiterate.[5] Rather, formal ambiguities within the poem reveal two positions on the social effects of poetry between which Tennyson alternates. As a conversion narrative, *The Princess* exhibits his residual concern with securing consensus by coordinating private interests. As a critique of conversion narratives, the poem exhibits Tennyson's emergent attempt to render consensus irrelevant to modern social cohesion and to carve out a space for the private self that is truly private. These two positions correspond to two models of the relation between public and private in the discourse of liberalism. Tennyson's residual position mirrors what critics have characterized as the poet's conservatism or "liberalism," by which they generally mean his insistence that consensus-oriented politics depends upon the compromise of private interests. The emergent position I characterize here reflects another strain in liberalism that celebrates the sanctity of the private individual and defends his or her right to be free from government interference. The purpose of my argument, however, is not merely to identify Tennyson's position with a paradox of liberalism. Rather, I argue that Tennyson's ostensible commitment to privacy for privacy's sake is better understood as an insistence that the political virtues of poetry lie in its celebration of the uncertainty that contemporary authors of social problem literature generally sought to dispel.

One of the most popular and flexible techniques for dispelling such uncertainty was the conversion narrative. The revelation that facilitates an individual's reintegration into the community provided a template for texts that addressed a variety of social questions ranging from Catholic and Jewish emancipation, to the status of women, to the representation of class in the industrial novel. Tennyson's break with conversion narrative conventions in *The Princess* reveals him not just to be interested in women's emancipation and higher education, but, far more generally, to be articulating a defense of poetry in response to one of the dominant problems

of the day: the political coordination of personal beliefs. The problem already loomed large in nineteenth-century debates about religious identity, and such debates provide a crucial backdrop for Tennyson's arguments about gender politics and exclusive state and educational structures. By the time he was composing *The Princess,* the last remaining religious group to be deprived of full citizenship and a place at Oxbridge were Jews. At the heart of mid-century arguments over Jewish emancipation and access to the universities were fundamental disagreements over the separation of church and state, and the desirability of aligning political and public structures with what were increasingly being defined as private religious beliefs. Though contemporary arguments about women's emancipation took a quite different form from arguments about Jewish emancipation, Tennyson explicitly borrowed narrative conventions for treating religious identity and used them as tools for treating gender politics as an identity issue.

More specifically, in his treatment of the Woman Question, Tennyson drew on three literary answers to the Jewish Question: conversion, a liberal critique of conversion, and burlesque. All three involve marriage plots, focus on the political effects of a female character's religious identity, and imagine social cohesion to depend upon a fit between religious belief and social structure. Dating back to Shakespeare's *Merchant of Venice* (1600), conversion narratives imagine national unity to depend in part upon the conversion of a Jewish heroine and her subsequent marriage to a Christian man. In contrast, nineteenth-century liberal critiques of conversion celebrate the Jewish heroine's heroic resistance to conversion efforts, and imagine social cohesion to depend upon the modern recognition that a non-Christian religious identity does not constitute a threat to British national interests. One of the most important examples of such a critique, Walter Scott's *Ivanhoe* (1819), provided an important source for Tennyson's *Princess.* Although a novel like *Ivanhoe* imagines the foundation of the nation-state to depend upon the marriage of Norman Ivanhoe and Saxon Rowena, Scott defines modern social cohesion through Rebecca's heroic resistance to conversion.

Finally, the burlesque on conversion centers on the crypto-Jew, a false convert who uses a Christian persona to gain access to a position of civic power while secretly harboring hidden counter-civic interests.[6] When Benjamin Disraeli's early conversion from Judaism to Christianity enabled him to enter Parliament in 1837, Michael Ragussis notes, the crypto-Jew began to take center stage in British politics and literary culture. Culminating in the novels Trollope published during the height of Disraeli's tenure as Prime Minister (1874-1880), the problem of the *converso,* or crypto-Jew, had already attained a prominent position in Victorian literary politics through Thackeray's burlesques on Scott and Disraeli, published contemporaneously with *The Princess*.[7] His burlesque on *Ivanhoe—Rebecca and Rowena*—appeared in *Fraser's Magazine* in 1846, just a year before the first edition of Tennyson's poem. Here, Ivanhoe marries the Jewish Rebecca rather than the Saxon Rowena but only after Rebecca converts to Christianity.[8] Just as he did in his 1847 burlesque of *Coningsby*, Thackeray dramatizes the anxiety of a nation where a position of public power requires a profession of Christian faith—the anxiety, that is, that one could never verify such oaths by having recourse to another person's interior. As long as a Jew's conversion to Christianity might enable him to enter Oxbridge or Parliament, Thackeray suggests that one must always wonder whether his true allegiance is not to Palestine.

While Tennyson's poem contains a number of prominent allusions to *Ivanhoe*,[9] his position in *The Princess* is much closer to Thackeray's contemporaneous burlesque. Drawing on this rhetoric of conversion and crypto-identity in his representation of Ida,[10] and by substituting Ida's feminism for Rebecca's Judaism, Tennyson signaled that he was entering literary debates about the extent to which social cohesion depended upon aligning private beliefs and public structures. All three of the available positions—conversion, critique, and burlesque—are apparent in some form in Tennyson's poem, and all three define genuine national unity in terms of a fit between personal beliefs and public structures. But the poem is finally reducible neither to a conversion narrative (where personal interests are merely a thing to be overcome) nor to a liberal critique of conversion narratives (where an accommodating political, social, or literary structure comes to register the interests of previously excluded groups). This leaves the burlesque, and I argue that while the poem takes its structure from mid-Victorian satires on conversion, the object of Tennyson's burlesque is not crypto-identity (where a divided self harbors secret counter-civic interests while professing to share common beliefs). The real object of Tennyson's burlesque is rather the notion common to all three modes of addressing the politics of religious identity: the notion that genuine social cohesion depends upon aligning public structures with determinable forms of the private self. In particular, Tennyson attempts to show both that lyric poetry consistently fails to secure such an alignment and that this failure is an occasion for political optimism, not despair.

* * *

Tennyson begins his argument about the political function of lyrics in *The Princess* by portraying poetry as a didactic vehicle designed to have a determinate effect on the private self and thereby to secure a definite political outcome. In so doing, Tennyson establishes the first move in what will be his argument against precisely such an understanding of poetry's political func-

tion. When the Prince visits Ida's father in Part 1, King Gama informs him of the principle upon which the women's college has been founded and notes the central role that poems played in facilitating that mission:

> [. . .] they had but been, she thought,
> As children; they must lose the child, assume
> The woman: then, Sir, awful odes she wrote,
> Too awful, sure, for what they treated of,
> But all she is and does is awful; odes
> About this losing of the child; and rhymes
> And dismal lyrics, prophesying change
> Beyond all reason: these women sang;
> And they that know such things—I sought but peace;
> No critic I—would call them masterpieces:
> They mastered *me*.
>
> (1.135-45)

Ida's father relates with surprising fidelity the nineteenth-century feminist argument for extending the franchise prophetically evoked in Ida's dicate that women "los[e] the child." The phrase epitomizes reactions against those such as James Mill, whose 1820 essay on "Government" argued that women were like children in that their interests were already represented by the male heads of household. Mill and others argued against women's suffrage not because women's interests could be said to conflict with British national interests, but because women's and men's interests were not widely perceived to be sufficiently distinct. In this feudal setting, then, Ida and her community seem to protest simultaneously against two sides of a Victorian double bind: women are excluded from the education that would prepare them for full citizenship because they need not be citizens, and—like the working class—they cannot be granted citizenship yet because they lack the necessary education. On the one hand, Ida and the other community leaders seek to consolidate women as an interest group requiring representation, and on the other, they seek to create the conditions under which educational opportunities are equally, though separately, accessible to women.

Poetry plays a central role in both of these endeavors. In the passage above, we see "odes," "rhymes," and "lyrics" deployed for their affective capacity to consolidate and dissemble particular forms of interest. The poems have two distinct effects. First, they "master" Gama into granting the women use of his summer estate, and thus displace the sovereign's interest in consolidating the nation-state through the marriage of the northern Prince and the southern Princess. At the same time, these poems are designed to instill within women a sense of identity as a group, in conflict with men, which Ida and the other leaders of the movement seek to have represented in a fair political and social structure. Political change is thus already enacted in the top-down sovereignty model that Sedgwick identifies as the paradoxical cause of the feminist community's downfall and the paternal frame's success. Asking the perennial question of what causes the college to crumble at a "mere male touch," Sedgwick points to the combination of this aristocratic social structure and Ida's personal susceptibility to love (126-27). But here, this aristocratic model of social change serves feminism well. And more importantly, we see that it is not a mere female touch at which Gama yields, but rather a mere lyric touch, the dis-interesting effect of literary masterpieces that ultimately serves the political interests of a competing faction. Just as the heroic poems provide a particular form of "assum[ing] the woman," Gama's confession, "[t]hey mastered me," immediately registers a particular personal effect with political ramifications.

Throughout the remainder of ***The Princess,*** Tennyson criticizes such a didactic model for the political use of poetry. He aims his critique at the notion that lyric poems could ensure predetermined political outcomes by having predictable effects on the private self. This becomes clear in the first set of situated lyrics. After learning of Ida's mission, the Prince and his two companions, Florian and Cyril, dress in drag in order to infiltrate the women's college, convert Ida from her errant feminist ways, and win her hand in marriage for the Prince. When the cross-dressed Prince and his companions join Ida and her entourage in Part 4, we are presented with two lyrics: **"Tears, Idle Tears"** and **"O Swallow, Swallow."** Both are subject to Ida's scrutiny, and both fail to meet the aesthetic criteria she establishes in her call for exclusively heroic poems. The first lyric expresses a surge of sentiment in the maid who sings it, while the second represents a strategic attempt on the Prince's part to convert Ida through love poetry. While Ida reprimands the maid for her nostalgic sentiment, she castigates the Prince for his unwitting susceptibility to love poetry's ideological function, by which men "play the slave to gain the tyranny" (4.114).

These two songs represent two political possibilities for lyric poems within ***The Princess*** and provide the framework within which critics continue to understand the author's politics. Tennyson's own rhetorical position and his attempt to facilitate social cohesion are frequently understood in terms of the maid's primordial sentiment or the Prince's affective strategies. Whether the poem's conclusion is interpreted as a political victory for a liberalism of compromise or as a social setback for women, the consensus upon which that conclusion depends is finally the result of either a surge of naturalized sentiment, a persuasive ideological gesture, or a combination of the two. Through Ida's response to each of these lyrics, however, Tennyson already provides a political critique of the lyric as the sentimental effusion of a solitary speaker. Ida attempts to show the maid and the Prince that at such moments they are revealing not their innermost selves but the extent to which their private lives have been constructed by literary conventions that serve insidious political ends.

Tennyson's position on the politics of lyric finally resembles neither the maid's expressive nor the Prince's strategic sentiment. Nor does Tennyson simply side with Ida's critique of sentimental poetry as an instrument that serves to standardize the private self for politically regressive ends. His position lies much closer to a third poem sung by the Prince's companion, Cyril. Cyril sings a burlesque, a "careless, careless tavern-catch / Of Moll and Meg, and strange experiences / Unmeet for ladies" (4.139-41). His burlesque breaks the tension between the heroic poems demanded and the sentimental poems proffered as he makes explicit the running theme of lesbian love, picking up on the homoerotic possibilities of **"O Swallow, Swallow"** and Ida's subsequent confession of love for her "maid of honor" (115-18).[11] Cyril thus mocks the whole situation, but draws particular attention to the absurdities of a cross-dressed Prince attempting to convert a Princess through song and Ida's misrecognition of his strategic attempt as yet another surge of misplaced sentiment. For it is the possibility of such misrecognition that allows Cyril to recognize ambiguities in the earlier lyric and turn them to comic effect.

Most importantly, however, Cyril's burlesque draws attention to the fact that each of the lyrics offered up fails to produce communal bonds. Through Cyril, Tennyson thus criticizes the assumptions that govern Ida's assessment of the two lyrics. Ida assumes that she is in a position to know the private motives that lie behind such lyrics as they issue from the mouths of the maid and the Prince. But while Ida considers the Prince's lyric to reveal his identity as a subjected woman, Cyril's song harps on the discrepancy between the Prince's public persona and his hidden, private motives. Through Cyril, Tennyson answers the failure of Ida's all-too-careful attempt to manufacture a seamless group identity through pre-given aesthetic criteria with a burlesque that renders Ida's response irrelevant to its success. Cyril's song is "careless" not merely because he thoughtlessly blows their cover as cross-dressed men nor because he doesn't care to meet Ida's demands for a didactic poetry geared toward facilitating consensus. Rather, his carelessness anticipates Tennyson's forceful claim that poetry's political virtues lie not in its capacity to facilitate consensus-formation but in its ability to illuminate the potential gap between private identifications and public effects. Cyril's "careless, careless" song thus prepares the way for Tennyson's argument that carelessness is a constitutive feature of modern poetry.

At the end of the poem, Tennyson turns the object of Cyril's burlesque, Ida's failure to consolidate group identity through poetry, into a virtue of the lyric. For

Tennyson defines the lyric, and particularly the lyric featured as a private effusion in a public setting, as a means to carve out a space for the private self that is truly—and impenetrably—private. Because lyrics exchanged in public settings will always be put to unpredictable uses, he maintains, such lyrics finally cordon off a place for the private self that the romantic lyric only affected.

This aspect of his argument is most evident in the major revisions that Tennyson made to the poem after the publication of the first edition and in the final set of situated lyrics. To see how this claim works, we can turn to the interpolated songs that Tennyson added in 1850. He later stated that he added the songs between the parts as a means of addressing the discrepancy between authorial intention and public reception: "The child is the link thro' the parts as shown in the songs which are the best interpreters of the poem. Before the first edition came out, I deliberated with myself whether I should put songs between the separate divisions of the poem; again, I thought the poem would explain itself, but the public did not see the drift" (qtd. in Hallam Tennyson 254). Frustrated with the public's initial tendency to read the poem as either a feminist manifesto or a misogynist satire, Tennyson would seem to have designated these songs the poem's "best interpreters" because they reinforce an interest at odds with Ida's interest. For by foregrounding the centrality of the child, he implies, they explicitly subvert the canonical criteria by which Ida's college was founded, and thus counteract the "odes / About this losing of the child" (1.139-40) which mastered King Gama in the beginning of the verse-narrative. The songs problematically represent Tennyson's residual belief in the poem's capacity to guide its own reception and interpretation at the very moment that he appears to be articulating an argument about the ultimate irrelevance of the particular private motives engaged in particular readings. But while Tennyson's statement may suggest that the interpolated songs could serve to correct the public's misinterpretations, in another sense, it merely shifted the public's burden of interpretation from the verse-narrative onto these songs. And the meaning of these songs is far from self-evident.

On one reading, for example, the last of these songs, **"Ask Me No More,"** simply prophesies the conversion that is completed within the verse-narrative:

> Ask me no more: the moon may draw the sea;
> The cloud may stoop from heaven and take the shape
> With fold to fold, of mountain or of cape;
> But O too fond, when have I answered thee?
> Ask me no more.
>
> Ask me no more: what answer should I give?
> I love not hollow cheek or faded eye:
> Yet, O my friend, I will not have thee die!

> Ask me no more, lest I should bid thee live;
> Ask me no more.

                                              (1-10)

The song leads the speaker through a pattern of conversion, from denial through liberal pity toward assent.[12] Despite the speaker's avowed refusal to answer the addressee in the first stanza, by the end of the song she has given her answer. The third and last stanza, however, describes a turn that is both enacted and averted:

> Ask me no more: thy fate and mine are sealed:
> I strove against the stream and all in vain:
> Let the great river take me to the main:
> No more, dear love, for at a touch I yield;
> Ask me no more.

                                              (11-15)

If the first stanza discourages the addressee because persistence is futile, the last discourages him because his inevitable success is tragic. Although she suggests that her own assent is imminent if he persists in asking, the speaker continues to urge the addressee at the beginning and end of the stanza not to do so. The speaker here thus exhibits a divided self: one part still resisting, while another promises to yield. Rather than simply prophesy Ida's inevitable conversion in the verse-narrative, the lyric lays bare the central problem of her psychological state at the end of the poem as a formal problematic. From one perspective, the speaker appears as a convert, while from another perspective, she appears as a divided subject, a *converso,* simultaneously acknowledging and disavowing the rhetorical efficacy of the addressee's question and, arguably, of lyric itself. If this song is intended to correct public misinterpretation of *The Princess,* it certainly doesn't do so by providing the reader with clear insight into the speaker's inner self.

Such a reading interprets the song's ambiguity as an index to Tennyson's divided politics. A conservative Tennyson wrote the song as a conversion for the speaker from feminist resistance to romantic acquiescence, while the subversive Tennyson inscribed the possibility of a crypto-feminist who never quite caves in. This way of inferring his politics from his commitment to ambiguity, however, depends upon the very alignment of private motive and political cause that he seeks to check through the structure of burlesque. **"Ask Me No More"** underscores Tennyson's critique of such an alignment in the third stanza when the speaker revises her metaphor for rhetorical influence. At the song's pivotal moment, the speaker states: "No more, dear love, for at a touch I yield." To ask is now to "touch," to have an immediate physical effect, just as the tidal influence of convention resisted in the first stanza yields to the irresistible stream and river of the last. But "touch" here retains an elusive quality. The word may metaphorize assent as tactile. But it may also work to remove the process from the realm of consent into the realm of physical influence. The rhetorical status of the question, in other words, might serve to elicit a merely physical response. Like a rhetorical question, the lyric doesn't so much solicit an answer as render one irrelevant. Rather than provide a revelation that the reader could use to interpret Ida's conversion in the verse-narrative, this song exemplifies Tennyson's argument about the lyric as a tool for asking the question of identification, not for answering the question of identity.

The famously ambiguous lyrics that appear at the end of the verse-narrative ("**Now Sleeps the Crimson Petal**" and "**Come Down, O Maid**") continue to exhibit the poet's commitment to creating a space for the private self that does not resolve into a public identity. In both of these lyrics, ambiguity is generated by the relation between the texts that Ida reads over the body of the unconscious and prostrate Prince and the fact that it is never clear with whom Ida identifies. Ambiguities within these final lyrics reveal either Ida the convert or Ida the crypto-feminist, depending upon whether the reader perceives her to be identifying with the addressee or with the speaker. While Marjorie Stone reads the subversive possibilities here as inherently at odds with Tennyson's conservative ideology manifest in the frame, she suggests that within the generic logic of the burlesque, or satire, such subversions are ironically fully compatible with social conservatism. The world is turned upside down in order to secure its status right side up. The lyrics reveal the subversive possibility of a feminist Ida in the manifestly conservative poem. But this is to read even the lyrics' ambiguities as revealing, rather than concealing, Ida's true nature.

By contrast, I read the equivocation of these lyrics as central to Tennyson's contribution to the broad spectrum of Victorian literary-political debates about grounding the legitimacy and origins of the nation-state in *homo credens,* the believing individual. From the etiologies of national identity provided by Scott and Disraeli and Thackeray's burlesques to public discussion over the Test Acts and the secularization of compulsory education, the Victorian concern to align public structures with private beliefs was ubiquitous. With their rhetoric and narrative structures of conversion experienced, resisted, and pretended, the positions taken within these debates shared the assumption that the legitimate nation-state is, or ought to be, founded on and grounded in an unproblematized psychology. Advocates of conversion, its liberal critics, and the mid-Victorian satirists of crypto-conversion all resorted to narrative as a way to produce something like a profession of faith, or an exclusive understanding of the self, whose political ramifications were immediately apparent. Critics like Stone echo this stance by imagining that ambiguities within the lyrics finally reveal two competing identities with immediately apparent political implications.

Like Thackeray's contemporaneous burlesques, but in a more cryptic and less contemptuous political spirit, Tennyson's *Princess* moves in the direction of problematizing psychology, and thus of problematizing the relation between psychology and social formation that many nineteenth-century conversion narratives took for granted. The attribution of a legible interior to Ida, and the accompanying conviction that the political stakes of the poem lie here, is merely a reader's projection. Although one reader may see Ida the convert here, and another might see Ida the *converso,* or crypto-feminist, yet another astute reader such as Stone may see a radical ambiguity in the situated lyric. These options are not psychologized within the verse-narrative—at least not yet. This is not to say that the reader is merely presented with options, however, but rather to argue that Tennyson insists on ambiguity as an index to privacy. Unable to ascertain a private motive outside of the lyric, the reader is unable to discern a clear position from which Ida might be identifying with either of the lyric's possibilities. Tennyson conspicuously denies the reader access to Ida's interior in order to make a case for the lyric that does not require it to arrive at a definitive statement of what its hierarchy of loyalties might be. Moreover, he uses ambiguity to dramatize the independence of political solutions from individual identifications with poetry.

With "**Come Down, O Maid,**" for example, as with the earlier poem, Ida sings "low-toned" (7.208), and may thus be ventriloquizing the Prince and identifying with the addressee and the "maid" who sang "**Tears, Idle Tears.**" Alternately, she may be identifying with the speaker and associating the Prince with the maid, thus converting the prostrate Prince into a legitimate love object. In sum, either Ida tells herself to come down and join the Prince, or she beckons the Prince to come down and join her. In either case, the subversive Ida is submerged, for though there are a variety of possible positions with which Ida can identify here, the possibilities do not present the same option between convert and crypto-feminist present in "**Ask Me No More**" and "**Now Sleeps the Crimson Petal.**" Both options entail Ida's capitulation to the codes of dynastic romance.

If the Prince's earlier attempt in "**O Swallow, Swallow**" failed to convert the Princess, the lyrics Ida sings to herself now seem to effect the conversion by providing her with a revelatory experience. The earlier failure of the lyrics to convert Ida is due to what Sedgwick describes as the trickle-down structure of social change, which operated through a canon of civic models, sanctioned by Ida's narrow aesthetic criteria. Similar in message to "**O Swallow, Swallow,**" but different in its effect on Ida, Part 7's **"Come Down, O Maid"** is closer to **"Now Sleeps the Crimson Petal"** than to the earlier poem because this lyric is not sung by someone Ida assumes to be a social subordinate but rather read by the Princess to herself. Though all of the lyrics have been measured within the community in terms of their social effect of consolidating women's interests, this is the first time that Ida herself experiences a conversion comparable to Gama's experience with lyrics in Part 1. If the pressure of a public assembly had enabled Ida to buttress her feminist convictions in the first half of the poem, this private reading experience would appear to draw out her natural susceptibility to the sentiments of love poetry.

This is to read **"Come Down, O Maid"** as the irrepressible and long-awaited lyric that triumphantly reveals Ida's true identity to herself and to the modern reading audience. Tennyson capitulates to the model of the romantic lyric in the end by using the lyric either to instill or to definitively express Ida's conversion experience. But even this poem firmly challenges our understanding of lyric as an occasion for the revelation of self-identity. The speaker of **"Come Down, O Maid"** is a shepherd who is not necessarily the same man in love with the elevated maid. As in **"O Swallow, Swallow,"** the relationship between the medium and the agent is unclear, and this ambiguity works on several levels. In the social situation, the lyric may prophesy the firm possibility that it is not the Prince but poetry that converts Ida. More importantly, however, the lyric may suggest that it is not Ida, but the poem that registers this conversion. Rather than merely providing Tennyson's reader with a sense of Ida's interiority (as a convert), Tennyson situates the song so as to dramatize the fact that Ida's private identifications remain private. As in the verse-narrative surrounding **"Now Sleeps the Crimson Petal,"** we never have access to Ida's interiority. That is, we never receive confirmation that the conversion is either experienced or resisted, except through three rather external indicators: (1) the change in institutional identity from college to hospital and Ida's subsequent positional change from educator to nurse; (2) the Prince's highly unreliable account of Ida's conversion; and (3) the accumulated series of lyrics that have repeatedly thematized the pattern of conversion. But these very same lyrics may also be said to undermine the rhetorical efficacy that they thematically assert when socially situated by the verse-narrative. Again, for Tennyson, the lyric's primary function is to draw attention to the fact of the inaccessibility of Ida's interior.

This reading of **The Princess** suggests a new way of drawing the old "Two Tennyson" portrait. We see here a Tennyson divided not between aesthetic aspiration and social concern but, rather, between two distinct views on the social effects of poetry. According to tra-

ditional accounts, Tennyson's sources of social cohesion are mired in nature, the unconscious, and latent sentiment. That which had been deprived representation in the college's canon finally erupts as Ida's own repressed nature as Tennyson grounds the verse-narrative's political conclusion in her conversion and the triumph of popular sentiment. It is largely this Tennyson with whom critics have sought to come to grips, variously locating the cause of Ida's conversion in her psychology, body, or nature. If we are to read his defense of poetry along these lines, primordial sentiment emerges triumphant in the form of love poetry, a genre whose efficacy even its staunchest critic is unable to resist. In the verse-narrative, the structure of dynastic romance thus enabled Tennyson to isolate modern social change as a problem of individual will. He figured the reading public as a potential convert, modern liberalism as aristocracy, and the complex project of mid-Victorian social cohesion as dependent upon either the psychological conversion or the rhetorical victory of a few good nobles.

But Tennyson was well aware that such rhetorical strategies could not secure their own efficacy, or ensure the consent of an expansive reading public. It is arguably in response to this problem that he adopted the more radical position, which conformed neither to a simple conversion narrative nor to a liberal celebration of resistance, and took explicit issue with Thackeray's mid-Victorian burlesques on crypto-identity. Strategic, conscious, calculating, and rhetorically adept, the Tennyson that I have argued for gestures toward a definition of authentic selfhood as a rhetorical option available to others, and he did so in the service of a conservative social formation. In **The Princess,** Tennyson suggests neither that lyric poems provide the occasion merely to identify the social position that one already occupies prior to one's experience with poetry, nor that they successfully determine a particular form of private life. Rather, he maintains that lyric ambiguity provides an occasion for privately identifying with positions that do not resolve into public identities. In his defense of lyric and his critique of conversion narrative form, then, Tennyson sought to remove the burden of exemplifying social solutions from the individual. He thus joined the company of a number of prominent publishers, educators, and authors of imaginative literature who have been misunderstood by critics and historians as either ideologues of compromise or technicians of disinterestedness. For the Tennyson we see emerging here embraces a fact that many of his contemporaries lamented—that the modern age is an age of inaccessible private motives.

* * *

Tennyson's argument thus far mirrors liberal efforts to repeal the restrictive legislation that made access to public political and university life dependent upon oaths of allegiance to the Anglican Church. Although Protestant Nonconformists already benefited from Toleration Acts that suspended the legislation, Lord John Russell's proposal to repeal the Test Acts, as one historian puts it, "involved an open abandonment of the principle that membership of the State Church was a prerequisite for full citizenship under the British constitution" (McCord 40). The 1828 repeal marked the beginning of a series of nineteenth-century legislative decisions that rendered religion private by making religious creeds unacceptable bases for active public life.[13] By rendering literary experience private in a similar way, Tennyson acknowledged the extent to which Victorian literary conventions were constantly making a particular form of the individual's private life at best a prerequisite and at worst a substitute for the resolution of political conflicts faced by a British public.

While these conventions took on religious form in literary responses to the Jewish Question, they assumed a secular form in the mid-Victorian industrial novel. And Tennyson's break with such conventions in *The Princess* was as much a break with the ways in which the industrial novel was beginning to take shape as with literary treatments of religious identity. For that genre arguably presented the most dramatic picture of political resolution achieved through a heroine's revelation about her identity. While industrial novels begin by realistically representing the conditions of poverty that lead to working-class violence or radicalism, they tend to resolve the political crises posed by trade unionism or Chartism by shifting the focus from hero to heroine and substituting a sentimental plot for a political one. In Thomas Carlyle's terms, what begins as an inquiry into the "condition" of fathers concludes by unveiling the "disposition" of daughters (326). As Ruth Bernard Yeazell has shown, the industrial novel typically solves its social problem when the heroine experiences a revelation about her true identity. What critics frequently perceive, however, as the industrial novel's insidious substitutions (of heroine for hero, private sentiment for public politics, psychological disposition for physical condition) are in fact the novel's characteristic solutions to the more general problem of political uncertainty. This strategy is particularly evident in Disraeli's *Sybil* (1845). As in Tennyson's *Princess,* a man disguises himself in order to infiltrate an insular community, political resolution appears to hinge on this hero's success in wooing his heroine, and that heroine's recalcitrant private self is conspicuously figured in silences. But in Disraeli's novel, these silences are immediately followed by self-revelations, confessions, and subsequent concessions. Such revelations are typical of the mid-Victorian industrial novel, and serve to emblematize the genre's crucial equation of privacy and political uncertainty. In discussing Mary Barton as among the industrial novel's many heroines who first refuse marriage proposals and then realize their error in the form of a

"clear revelation," Yeazell emphasizes that "to have allowed an interval of narrative time to have elapsed would have been to introduce *an uncertainty of motive and feeling* that the story of Mary Barton cannot afford" (136, emphasis added). Narrative serves to register the heroine's unequivocal self-revelation—to unveil "the passionate secret of her soul" (Gaskell 176-77)—because to allow the reader to entertain doubts about the heroine's private self is to confess the inadequacy of literary texts to provide unequivocal political solutions.

Tennyson thus issued a challenge to contemporary authors of social problem literature. The fact that he weaves allusions to the Jewish Question and the Condition of England Question into his narrative about the Woman Question indicates the extent to which Tennyson recognized the homogeneity of mid-Victorian literary answers to such social problems. By meeting the Jewish Question, the Condition of England Question, and the Woman Question with the same answer—a heroine's revelation about her essential self—social problem novelists revealed their inability to think outside the terms of consensus and sentiment. If such strategies offered ineffective political solutions, they could also be seen to threaten the sanctity of the private self that would become such an obsession for nineteenth-century British liberal philosophers.

Tennyson's refusal to provide such an unequivocal self-revelation for Ida surely marks his refusal to sanction burdening the individual with the task of resolving social solutions and stakes a claim for the sanctity of the private self. But Tennyson finally aims neither merely to criticize the ethical overburdening characteristic of mid-Victorian social problem novels and the culture prophet tradition nor purely to endorse liberal desires to render the private self inviolable. Rather, Ida's opacity marks Tennyson's optimism in the uncertainty that both positions seek to counter. While Tennyson's literary gesture may resemble the repeal of the Test Acts, his stake in obliterating the literary equivalent of an oath—the heroine's private revelation which takes narrative form in a public confession of love—lies in the articulation of what might be called a "weak" defense of literature's political value. If to render an individual's religion private in the repeal of the Test Acts meant to render religion inviolable, Tennyson renders literary experience private in order to emphasize the uncertain relationship between those experiences and political effects.

* * *

Tennyson's optimism toward the kind of political uncertainty that social problem narratives sought to dispel is extended in the frame to *The Princess.* Here, through formal means, he addressed his frustration with reviewers who judged the poem's first edition as a failure because it was either a satire maimed by a residue of tragic heroism or a tragedy tempered with too much satirical bite.[14] By 1850, Tennyson had incorporated the two prongs of this critical response into the poem. He now revised the conclusion to include a debate between the men and women in the modern frame about what the poetically embellished version of the feudal verse-narrative should be. The men call for a burlesque, while the women call for a "true-heroic—true-sublime" Ida (Prologue 20). Once he has concluded the verse-narrative, the narrator in the frame confesses that he has tried to position himself "betwixt both" the male "mockers" and the female "realists." But he fears that, in order "to please them both," he "neither pleased myself nor them" by moving in "a strange diagonal" (Conclusion 25-28). "But Lilia pleased me," he claims, "for she took *no part* / In our dispute" (29-30, emphasis added). Though the interpolated songs are the poem's "best interpreters," Tennyson does inscribe a competent reader within the frame, one whose response to the formally ambiguous poem supersedes the divisive social interests represented by a misguided reading public. Tennyson now shifts our focus from reviewers evaluating the narrator's poem to the narrator's evaluation of Lilia for her superior aesthetic response. Her response pleases the narrator in part because it is nonpartisan; she takes "no part" in the debate. Lilia pleases, in other words, insofar as she refrains from becoming a reviewer, a literary critic who confuses aesthetic and social interests.

Another reason why Lilia gives the narrator pleasure, however, is that she appears to have experienced the tale as rhetorical force. For "the sequel of the tale," presumably the narrative following her intervention in Part 5, "[h]ad *touched* her" (Conclusion 30, 31). The narrator's interpretation of this gesture as "touch" recalls the penultimate line of **"Ask Me No More"** ("No more, dear love, for at a touch I yield"). Just as the term in that song serves to render the speaker's private motives all the more private, the term here indicates a response that is deeply personal only because it remains purely personal. The fact that the narrator here echoes the Prince's treatment of Ida reveals the verse-narrative to be on one level only a symbolic rehearsal of the imminent relationship in the frame between the narrator and Lilia. There is a significant difference, however. Whereas the Prince interprets Ida's silence at the end of the verse-narrative as registering a particular effect (she is converted), the narrator interprets Lilia's silence as merely being moved. In other words, if the Prince defines the sexual contract upon which the consolidation of the nation-state depends as sealed through Ida's consent, the narrator imagines poetry to serve its modern social function insofar as it carves out a space for a privacy that is truly private. Lilia's silence pleases the narrator here not because it represents a partisan conver-

sion, but rather because it serves as a publicly recognizable form of radical privacy. It is true that Lilia alone appears to register the effect of the generic and semantic ambiguities within the verse narrative and lyrics, respectively. *How* ambiguity touches, or motivates, however, is left unanswered. Is Lilia converted from her earlier feminist yearnings that spawned the story, won over into heterosexual romance by the wooing narrator, or does her silence exhibit the introversion of a disappointed or crypto-feminist? Like Ida at the close of the verse-narrative, Lilia's private motives remain pleasingly opaque.

This is not to say that Tennyson's ideal reader—if we read Lilia as such—has internalized a particular form of disinterestedness by appreciating the poem's ambiguity. To see her as such an exemplar of disinterestedness would entail attributing to Lilia a particular form of private response in which she alone transcends the terms of position-taking because she alone perceives that ambiguity requires a new and as yet unarticulated position. Though this is not Tennyson's lesson in **The Princess,** this is precisely the lesson that Isobel Armstrong would wish us to take from Tennyson's poetry. In *Victorian Poetry* (1993), Armstrong calls on critics to recognize what she sees as the preeminent Victorian poetic form, which she dubs the "double poem" (17). Central to Armstrong's project is the desire to rescue ambiguity from its largely ludic status in deconstructive readings and from its relatively negligible status in Marxist and feminist readings. She accuses both Alan Sinfield and Sedgwick, for example, of systematically excluding ambiguity in their readings of an unequivocally reactionary Tennyson. Or when they do confront ambiguity, they divide a poem like **The Princess** into an intended meaning and an unintended meaning, and proceed to show how the text's manifest liberal intentions are subverted by its latent conservative desires. For Armstrong, however, to perceive the poem's ambiguity as an intentional structure is to uncover Tennyson's highly equivocal political position as a "subversive conservative" (41).

Armstrong's account interests me less because she equates Tennyson's literary ambiguity with political equivocation, however, than because her own blend of Marxism and deconstruction produces a defense of poetry that hinges on the reader's affirmation of ambiguity as an ethical imperative. For Armstrong proposes a "way of reading" that not only recognizes ambiguity, but revels in an "endless" oscillation between irresolvable political options (10).[15] "The active reader," she writes,

> is compelled to be internal to the poem's contradictions and recomposes the poem's processes in the act of comprehending them as ideological struggle. There is no end to struggle because there is no end to the cre-

ative constructs and the renewal of content which its energy brings forth.

(13)

This view epitomizes what Tony Bennett has recently criticized as literary criticism's ethicization of politics. According to Bennett, such ways of reading present themselves as means of uncovering the truth about literary objects but are in fact techniques of subjectification, ways of shaping the ethical selves of readers within a "literary-pedagogical apparatus." They are

> dependent on inducting the reader into the socially constructed interior of the text as a space in which to exhibit, not correct readings but a way of reading in relation to norms which, since their essence consists in their capacity for endless revision, can never be precisely specified.

(190)

The "way of reading" that Armstrong recommends, and that Bennett denounces, entails entering into the interior of a text (whatever that might mean) and embarking on a process of endless self-revision. For Armstrong, this is a way of doing justice to texts; for Bennett, it is a way of perpetuating injustice within the classroom. Where Armstrong is primarily concerned with the interpretation of literary texts, Bennett is concerned with the social effects of a regime of interpretation. Where Armstrong imagines a reader compelled by the text's inherent ambiguity, Bennett sees the attraction of such so-called formal features as ambiguity as the misrecognized compulsion of a long-standing institutional regime whose function has been to disseminate a particular form of subjectivity. From Bennett's perspective, then, a critic like Armstrong may intend to produce an active reader attuned to the ambiguous political truths of texts, but the unintended political effect of her way of reading is to produce a passive form of the private self—the subject—whose endless inward turns incapacitate her from exercising political "agency" in a "public arena" (239).

What is striking about Bennett is finally not his suspicion that such ethicized criticism is politically useless, but rather his conviction that criticism has been so thoroughly successful in determining the form of private life. For Bennett imagines that a criticism attuned to literary ambiguity has the unambiguous political consequence of producing a standard form of privacy incompatible with participation in the public arena. Armstrong's hope that the active reader's critical exemplarity might serve to standardize private life in such a way as to disseminate modern subjectivity is matched by Bennett's conviction that it already has. It is for this reason that even Bennett's antidote to criticism—his prescription to get "outside literature"—looks like a strong defense of literary education. Bennett would re-

place the unspecified norms of an interpretive regime with the specified norms of a descriptive criticism because he holds the modern literary lesson virtually accountable for the fall of the public sphere.[16] So concerned to check the ethical burden of literary education's political claims, Bennett loads the literary lesson with a political burden that it could never possibly bear.

Though they provide diametrically opposed accounts of the political value of ambiguity within literary education, both Armstrong and Bennett see ambiguity as an occasion to exercise a particular form of subjectivity, where the reader comes to internalize irresolvable options. In sum, where Armstrong would read Tennyson's lyrical ambiguity as an occasion for reveling in the oscillation between conservative conversion and subversive crypto-feminism, Bennett would read this very oscillation between irresolvable options as the uniquely modern form of conversion: from publicity to privacy, from agency to subjectivity.

In *The Princess,* Tennyson's account of literary ambiguity looks radically different from either Armstrong's or Bennett's accounts precisely because it depends upon acknowledging the privacy of the private self. Tennyson's burlesque, already attuned to the social function of literary ambiguity, criticizes the framework of conversion and subversion within which critics continue to occupy positions on the politics of ambiguity. Far from serving as a modern technique for producing a mass subject, literary ambiguity provided Tennyson with a means of acknowledging the impossibility of standardizing private life through literature—even if we wanted to. Lilia's aesthetic response in *The Princess* is significant not because she properly internalizes contradictions, but because she properly keeps to herself any private identifications she might have, and therefore refrains from using them as sources from which to review the poem. Lilia may look like the perfect example of a reader who internalizes the verse-narrative's ambiguity and thus drops out of public debate. But this is to read her as the Prince reads Ida: that is, as a kind of convert who exemplifies a particular form of the private self. Tennyson's point with Lilia is not to affirm the ethical imperative to oscillate between the generic or semantic ambiguities of the poem, however, but to recommend that private responses remain private. In other words, Tennyson frees the individual from the imperative to exemplify social solutions. Rather than merely exhibit a dramatic conversion from a public to a private self, Tennyson's argument about poetry finally removes the burden of social cohesion from the individual altogether.

In order to make the case most forcefully, however, Tennyson also removes from the individual the burden of participation. The narrator countenances Lilia's alternative to reviewing not simply because she is nonpartisan, but because she is a nonparticipant. Lilia is an odd figure for the ideal reader, then, because her response exhibits the inaccessibility of the private self that Tennyson thematized in the verse-narrative and the lyrics as a position that one should occupy in the public arena. For Tennyson's ideal reader is not a critic at all, but the private reader who displays a commitment to privacy as a viable option within the public arena. The narrator faced with reviews expressing the divisive social interests of a divided reading public implies that such a display of privacy is the only adequate way to assess the poem, the poet, and ultimately poetry itself. Thus Tennyson revises a claim that Arthur Henry Hallam had made in "Some Characteristics of Modern Poetry" (1830). After citing Tennyson's **"Recollections of the Arabian Nights"** (1831) in full, Hallam states: "Criticism will sound but poorly after this; yet we cannot give silent votes" (855). With Lilia, Tennyson suggests that it is because criticism must sound poorly after poetry that a vote for poetry could only take the form of silence.

Notes

I am grateful to Frances Ferguson, Mary Poovey, and Scott Black for their help on this paper.

1. Graham Hough and Leo Spitzer have debated the value of Brooks's close reading method as applied to "Tears, Idle Tears." For the subsequent history of the debate between formalist and antiformalist literary critics, see Baldick.

2. In taking "Tears, Idle Tears" out of the context of *The Princess,* Brooks echoed Edgar Allan Poe's celebration of that lyric in "The Poetic Principle" (1850), where he famously argued that a long poem was "a flat contradiction in terms" because the "elevating excitement of the Soul" which defines true poetry "cannot be sustained" (154, 173).

3. In its most simple form, Tennyson's "liberal argument" is represented in Rod Edmond's *Affairs of the Hearth* (1988): "In a way which is characteristic of the poem as a whole, and recognizable as a familiar kind of liberal argument, all 'extreme' positions, no matter what their ideological content, are held to be similar. From this point of view, Ida and the northern king, feminism and male chauvinism, are identical in lacking the liberal virtues of tolerance and compromise which the poem preempts" (114). For Sedgwick, the Prince is "an authentic liberal" and inhabits an ideological fiction whose structure, "the liberal structure of 'dialectic,'" is expressive of "'mainstream' English Victorian Culture," (123, 118). For a discussion of the unabashedly conservative (Tory, paternal) side of *The Princess,* see Herbert, especially 150-51. At the end of this essay, I address

Isobel Armstrong's account of a politically equivocal Tennyson.

4. Herbert Tucker is a notable exception to this rule. See 351 and following.

5. In brief, the "Two Tennyson" theory is explained by Jerome Buckley as "the struggle in Tennyson between a personal art for art's sake and an art keyed to the interests of nineteenth-century society" (67).

6. This definition of the crypto-Jew refers to the nineteenth-century satirical literary trope. Originally, the crypto-Jew pretended to convert to Christianity in order to evade persecution during the Inquisition. For an interesting and exhaustive perspective on the history of *conversos* during the Spanish Inquisition, see Netanyahu. According to Netanyahu, no amount of conversion on the part of Jews could satisfy an institution whose aim was the elimination not of the Jewish belief but of Jews.

7. Trollope's attack, Ragussis writes, "demonstrates [. . .] the ultimate dilemma of the conversionist plot of Christian culture. The final attack on this culture is aimed not at the stereotypical 'stiff-necked Jew' who cannot be penetrated by Christianity but at the Jew who does in fact convert and thereby gains access to the highest echelons of Christian society" ("Birth" 499). In 1847, Thackeray published *Codlingsby,* yet another antisemitic burlesque. Where Disraeli's *Coningsby* (1844) had sought to drum up sympathy for Jewish emancipation by arguing for the widespread positions of power held by members of this "pure race of the Caucasian organization" (271), Thackeray capitalized on the comedic possibilities of what he saw as Disraeli's vision of a world-power structure inundated with conspiring crypto-Jews. See Ragussis, *Figures.*

8. The young Walter's wish at the end of the poem that the Princess "had not yielded" (Conclusion 5) is thus a wish that Ida had been more like Scott's Rebecca and less like Thackeray's.

9. The statue of Sir Ralph (or Richard I) that prominently marks the poem's beginning, middle, and end clearly would have called up Scott's novel, and the tale of the Countess of Montfort from the chronicle of Sir Ralph that the narrator reads *is* Rebecca's tale.

10. The poem's numerous allusions to historical conversion narratives and Inquisitorial practices include the tale of the Countess of Montfort, the statue of Sir Ralph, a reference to the popular exhibits in the Mechanics' Institute Festival ("And yonder, shrieks and strange experiments / For

which Sir Ralph would have burned them all" [Prologue 228-29]), and the Prince's seizures, which he inherited from a grandfather who burned a sorcerer at the stake, presumably during the Inquisition. One of the most striking of such allusions is to St. Catherine of Alexandria. Here, Tennyson explicitly criticizes the notion that it is necessary to ground concerted political action in shared belief. When Ida's brother Arac recalls having professed allegiance to Ida's cause before representing the women's college in battle, he significantly forgets the name upon which he swears:

> And, right or wrong, I care not: this is all,
> I stand upon her side: she made me swear it—
> 'Sdeath—and with solemn rites by candle-light—
> Swear by St something—I forget her name—
> Her that talked down the fifty wisest men;
> *She* was a princess too [. . .].
>
> (5.280-85)

St. Catherine is famed not for her military prowess but for her ability to resist fifty missionary attempts to convert her, notably, *from* Christianity. Hallam Tennyson's note on this passage explains: "The Emperor Maxentius during his persecution is related to have sent fifty of his wisest men to convert her from Christianity, but she combated and confuted them all" (qtd. in Ricks, *Poems of Tennyson* 259n284). An imminent assault on the women's college is already figured by Ida, "a princess too," in terms of a conversion narrative that must be resisted. The dependence of concerted political action on shared beliefs is emphasized here in the form of oath-taking. The fact that Arac can only remember "St something" in terms of her function and not her name, however, both attenuates the credibility of the oath, and, because Arac's forces do win in the end, calls into question the necessity of making political allegiance depend upon professing allegiance.

11. The situation of the song might suggest to Ida and her maids that the singer is identifying with the swallow—that is, with the messenger, rather than with the speaker. The attendant maids' laughter, however, suggests that they might alternatively interpret the singer as identifying with the speaker (which indeed he is), but doing so as a woman:

> I ceased and all the ladies, each at each,
> Like the Ithacensian suitors in old time,
> Stared with great eyes, and laughed with alien lips,
> And knew not what they meant; for still my voice
> Rang false.
>
> (4.99-103)

The false ring of the Prince's voice, which is often interpreted as his inability to sustain "their treble" (4.74), may also be interpreted as precisely the opposite. In the traditional interpretation, the verse-narrative surrounding "O Swallow, Swallow" constructs an ambivalent relationship between singer and speaker that threatens, through the rising of the body's truth, to collapse into a direct correspondence between speaker and singer. In the alternative reading, however, if "still my voice / Rang false" is taken to mean that the Prince still sang in the "treble" of women, then they may in fact be laughing at the possibility that the speaker is not a man beseeching his loved one but a woman beseeching hers. The embarrassment then would result from a new, homoerotic use of song which follows up on the eroticism with which "Tears, Idle Tears" had ended. Love poetry need not necessarily invoke heterosexuality and the family as Ida maintains. This possibility is reinforced in the Homeric allusion, for the comparison of the attendant women to the "Ithacensian suitors" would establish them in an erotic competition with the Prince (as the disguised Odysseus) for the hand of Princess Ida (as Penelope).

12. For the standard account of this conversion structure as central to Tennyson's poetics, see Buckley.

13. These include Catholic Emancipation in 1829, the "conscience clause" amended to Forster's 1870 Education Act, and the 1871 repeal of the Universities Test Act at Oxford.

14. In an 1848 *Athenaeum* review of the first edition, for example, J. W. Marston wrote a statement about *The Princess* that registers both of these criticisms: "The familiar and conventional impair the earnestness of the ideal:—and what might else have been appreciated as a genial satire loses its force from its juxtaposition to tragic emotion" (qtd. in Ricks, *Tennyson* [1972] 190). On the one hand, Marston seems to align himself with the feminist argument, insofar as the "ideal" is the formal autonomy of the women's university where "convention" is held at bay with much effort. On the other hand, he chastises the poem for failing as a satire where "tragic emotion" intervenes.

15. The options presented in Tennyson's "Mariana" (1830), for example, "can hardly be resolved" (15).

16. A more "progressive literary pedagogy," Bennett states, would depend upon replacing the "*unending* process of ethical self-correction" that New Criticism, deconstruction, and Marxism have inherited from a Romantic aesthetic ideal of a harmonious personality with "exercises, tests and forms of assessment through which readings can be assessed as definitely correct or not in relation to stated and hence debatable criteria" (190). Bennett here draws from Ian Hunter's valuable work

on the genealogy of English in *Culture and Government* (1988).

Works Cited

Armstrong, Isobel. *Victorian Poetry: Poetry, Poetics, and Politics.* London: Routledge, 1993.

Auden, W. H. "Tennyson." *Forewords and Afterwords.* New York: Random House, 1973. 221-32.

Baldick, Chris. *Criticism and Literary Theory, 1890 to the Present.* London: Longman, 1996.

Bennett, Tony. *Outside Literature.* London: Routledge, 1990.

Brooks, Cleanth. *The Well Wrought Urn: Studies in the Structure of Poetry.* London: Methuen, 1968.

Buckley, Jerome Hamilton. *The Victorian Temper.* New York: Vintage, 1964.

Carlyle, Thomas. "Chartism." *The Collected Works.* 1870-87. vol. 10. London: Chapman and Hall, 325-426.

Disraeli, Benjamin. *Coningsby.* New York: Penguin, 1989.

Edmond, Rod. *Affairs of the Hearth: Victorian Narrative Poetry and the Ideology of the Domestic.* London: Routledge, 1988.

Eliot, T. S. "Metaphysical Poets." *Selected Essays.* New York: Harcourt Brace Jovanovich, 1964. 241-50.

Gaskell, Elizabeth. *Mary Barton.* New York: Penguin, 1970.

Graff, Gerald. *Professing Literature: An Institutional History.* Chicago: U of Chicago P, 1987.

Hallam, Arthur Henry. "Some Characteristics of Modern Poetry." Rpt. in *Victorian Poetry and Poetics.* Ed. Walter E. Houghton and G. Robert Stange. New York: Houghton Mifflin, 1959. 848-60.

Herbert, Isolde Karen. "'A Strange Diagonal': Ideology and Enclosure in the Framing Sections of *The Princess* and *The Earthly Paradise.*" *Victorian Poetry* 29.2 (Summer 1991): 145-59.

Hough, Graham. "Tears, Idle Tears." *Hopkins Review* 4 (Spring 1951): 31-6.

Hunter, Ian. *Culture and Government: The Emergence of Literary Education.* Houndsmills: Macmillan, 1988.

Killham, John. *Tennyson and* The Princess: *Reflections of an Age.* London: Athlone, 1958.

Lerner, Laurence. "An Essay on *The Princess.*" *The Victorians.* Ed. Laurence Lerner. New York: Holmes and Meier, 1978. 209-22.

McCord, Norman. *British History, 1815-1906.* Oxford: Oxford UP, 1991.

Mill, James. "Government." *Political Writings.* Ed. Terence Ball. Cambridge: Cambridge UP, 1992. 3-42.

Netanyahu, B. *Toward the Inquisition: Essays on Jewish and Converso History in Late Medieval Spain.* Ithaca: Cornell UP, 1997.

Pecora, Vincent. *Households of the Soul.* Baltimore: Johns Hopkins UP, 1997.

Pitkin, Hannah. *The Concept of Representation.* Berkeley: U of California P, 1967.

Poe, Edgar Allan. "The Poetic Principle." *Complete Poems and Selected Essays.* London: Everyman, 1993. 154-74.

Ragussis, Michael. "Birth of a Nation in Victorian Culture: Spanish Inquisition, the Converted Daughter, and the 'Secret Race.'" *Critical Inquiry* 20 (Spring 1994): 477-508.

———. *Figures of Conversion: "The Jewish Question" and English National Identity.* Durham, NC: Duke UP, 1995.

Ricks, Christopher, ed. *The Poems of Tennyson.* vol. 2. Berkeley: U of California P, 1987.

———. *Tennyson.* New York: Macmillan, 1972.

———, ed. *Tennyson: A Selected Edition.* Berkeley: U of California P, 1989.

Robbins, Bruce. Introduction. *The Phantom Public Sphere.* Ed. Bruce Robbins. Minneapolis: U of Minnesota P, 1993. vii-xxvi.

Sedgwick, Eve Kosofsky. *Between Men: English Literature and Male Homosocial Desire.* New York: Columbia UP, 1985.

Spitzer, Leo. "'Tears, Idle Tears' Again." *Hopkins Review* 5 (Spring 1952): 71-80.

Stone, Marjorie. "Genre Subversion and Gender Inversion: *The Princess* and *Aurora Leigh.*" *Victorian Poetry* 25.2 (Summer 1987): 101-27.

Tennyson, Alfred. *The Princess.* Ricks 1987, 185-296.

Tennyson, Hallam. *Alfred Lord Tennyson: A Memoir, by His Son.* vol. 1. New York: Macmillan, 1897.

Tucker, Herbert. *Tennyson and the Doom of Romanticism.* Cambridge, MA: Harvard UP, 1988.

Yeazell, Ruth Bernard. "Why Political Novels Have Heroines: *Sybil, Mary Barton,* and *Felix Holt.*" *Novel* 60.2 (1985): 126-44.

Michael Hancock (essay date spring 2001)

SOURCE: Hancock, Michael. "The Stones in the Sword: Tennyson's Crown Jewels." *Victorian Poetry* 39, no. 1 (spring 2001): 1-24.

[*In the following essay, Hancock demonstrates Tennyson's use of gems as symbols of imperialism and acquisition in* Idylls of the King.]

Of all the illicit affairs in *The Idylls of the King,* none is more unusual than "bold" Sir Bedivere's relation with Excalibur ("**PA**", l. 207).[1] Commanded to cast the kingdom's founding sword into the lake where it surfaced, the Round Table's first knight finds himself dazzled by the brand's moonlit handle, which "twinkle[s] with diamond sparks, / Myriads of topazlights, and jacinth-work / Of subtlest jewellery" ("**PA**", ll. 224-226).[2] Thinking of how the gems might please "the eyes of many men" by being preserved for posterity "in some treasure-house of mighty kings" ("**PA**", ll. 259, 269), an enthralled Bedivere tries to salvage the sword through disobedience and deceit. Only when Arthur threatens to slay the faithless knight does Bedivere return Excalibur to its source. The precious stones in the sword, as objects of desire, thus become an obstacle almost as difficult to overcome as the very vows that make and break Camelot.

The conversion of Excalibur from sword into stones is hardly an anomaly in the *Idylls.* Tennyson's poem is itself a collection like Arthur's sword, encrusted with a dragon's hoard of jewels. These gems are more than colorful baubles, as they come out of nature to become part of the king's commerce with his wife and knights. As I will explain, the qualities of rarity and reflection that recommend Excalibur's pommel and haft to Bedivere help to distinguish gems as uncommonly precious possessions in the *Idylls.* In fact, these ornaments for person and property become, after the Grail itself, the most sought-after of all objects in Tennyson's Camelot.

Arthur's kingdom, however, is founded on disciplining the body, not on adorning it. The body is, after all, a distraction from "high thought, and amiable words / And courtliness, and the desire of fame, / And love of truth, and all that makes a man" ("**G**," ll. 478-480). Even in Camelot, these masculine ideals typically come into conflict with more worldly matters and material interests, including sexual desire. If women are to be worshipped by chaste love and won "by years of noble deeds" ("**G**," l. 473), then the quest for precious stones would seem to be superfluous, if not actually antagonistic, to Arthur's project of keeping the kingdom together. Yet Tennyson's gems, which articulate the body, become a locus of value recognized and even accumulated by the very king who tries to keep bodies under wraps. Although Arthur expects his bachelor knights to lead celibate lives, he also encourages them to decorate their maiden loves with hard-won gems, making these women's fair charms even more difficult to resist. Because it does not profit Arthur to tempt his Table in some dearly-bought war of "Sense . . . with Soul" ("**To the Queen**," l. 37), the very visible presence of Camelot's stones seems problematic, to say the least.

The virtual absence of gems from the rest of Tennyson's work makes their ubiquity here all the more conspicuous.[3] Yet this is not to say that these jewels are misplaced; indeed, they amass significance by being gathered in this textual treasury. In particular, four prominent collections of Camelot's precious stones—Arthur's gemmed sword, Elaine's pearl sleeve, Lancelot's nine diamonds, and Nestling's ruby carcanet—all emerge as storied objects of desire in the *Idylls.* Although Tennyson borrows the first two of these collections from the *Morte d'Arthur,* his jewels nonetheless provide a model of consumption that Malory only begins to suggest.

Appointed to specific uses, Tennyson's gems obtain symbolic value through their connection to particular owners. As Arjun Appadurai states, however, "Even though from a *theoretical* point of view human actors encode things with significance, from a *methodological* point of view it is the things-in-motion that illuminate their human and social context."[4] To write the social history of Camelot's jewels, then, I will trace how its gems shift in meaning and value as they move from one frame of reference to another. When these collections change hands, they acquire an unexpected agency by being improperly displayed, given, or obtained; used in a manner contrary to custom, conduct, or character, they bring disappointment and even death to those who would make them their own. If, as Walter Benjamin suggests, "the most distinguished trait of a collection will always be its transmissibility,"[5] then Camelot's jewels are defined by the very failure of the transactions in which they figure.

Because Victoria, as queen and collector, had taken possession of many foreign jewels at the height of her reign, Tennyson's gems offer an implicit warning to the monarch about her own acquisitions. In particular, the great diamond of "**Lancelot and Elaine**" speaks directly to Victoria by virtue of its close resemblance to one of her recently acquired Indian jewels. In 1849, English officials in the Punjab seized the famed Lahore Treasury's most prized gem, the 186-carat Koh-i-noor diamond, for the queen, in accordance with the treaty imposed on the teenage Maharajah Dhulip Singh and his regents by the British.[6] This new crown jewel was presented to Victoria in 1850 by the governing East India Company, and it was later featured at the Great Exhibition of 1851 as the epitome of empire's rewards. Despite the conquest symbolized by this celebrated diamond, the Indian Mutiny of 1857 soon made Britain's hold on the stone's native land a tenuous one. When Tennyson decided to make a large diamond the centerpiece of "**Elaine**" only a year later, just after British troops had restored order to India, the idea of a queen who needed to control her possessions was a matter of sovereign interest.[7]

Ultimately, then, Camelot's gems, collected incessantly, afford the so-called poet of empire a rare chance to question the validity and permanence of England's own acquisitions. By portraying gems as fickle forms that often abandon their owners, especially women, Tennyson implicates Queen Victoria's own crown jewels as failed representations of imperial dominion. If England could hardly hold what it had, the suggestion was, it could not afford to obtain even more costly possessions. This reading of the *Idylls* expands our sense of the imperialist anxieties that Tennyson's epic exhibits throughout, revealing greater apprehensions than those expressed in the dedication **"To the Queen."**[8] Moreover, my focus on precious stones in the *Idylls* shows that Tennyson's poetic reflections on material culture were not confined either to "brands" (in the sense of swords and commercial names alike) or to issues of his relation to the Victorian literary marketplace.[9] As vehicles of dissent, Camelot's gems offer Tennyson, in his self-conscious role as poet laureate, a way of voicing concerns about the state without the conspicuous appearance of contradicting his queen.[10] By subtle yet effective means, then, Tennyson attempts in the *Idylls* to make Victoria, as consumer and queen, more aware of the costs of her own possessions in the imperial marketplace.

1

Even as Camelot's gems look forward to Victoria's reign, Tennyson looks back on collecting precious stones during the Middle Ages for his own instruction and inspiration. Inherently attractive and relatively rare, gems were valued, then as now, for their durable looks and scarcity alike.[11] However, of nearly a dozen different kinds of jewels mentioned by Tennyson, only pearls, mostly of a misshapen or dully opaque and worthless variety, are indigenous to Britain.[12] Since gemstones had to be brought at considerable cost to England, usually from the East via Italian ports,[13] they became the special prerogative of those of high social and economic standing. Thus, the wealthy and powerful, from royals and nobles to great ecclesiastics and rich merchants, all accumulated stores of precious and semi-precious stones. Although these exotic gems were sometimes kept as a financial reserve, their main purpose was wear and display, especially on ceremonial occasions.[14]

Hard to come by and highly esteemed, jewels also represented many different aspects of what Krzysztof Pomian refers to as "the other side of the boundary separating the sacred from the secular," or "the invisible" (p. 22). Spatially and temporally distant, the invisible is a timeless, autonomous, and otherworldly, fantastic, or ideal realm articulated through a culture's narratives. This world and its meaning are made materially accessible through "semiophores," or collection pieces, endowed with special significance, which have been removed from everyday use and kept out of the economic circuit (Pomian, pp. 29-34). As Pomian explains, gemstones, as semiophores, are as multifaceted in their

meaning as they are in their appearance. For one, they encapsulate the natural world in all its power and beauty. In Western medieval societies, gems were also variously identified with mythical figures and events, exotic origins, and alimentary powers. Moreover, jewels served to legitimate a specifically male authority. According to Pomian, precious stones, like precious metals,

> were noble and extraordinary substances used to produce or decorate images, reliquaries and more generally everything the king used, including his dishes, clothes, furniture, weapons, armour and regalia, in short, everything which represented either the realm as an undivided whole or else the power and wealth of its sovereign. Put another way, the contents of treasure-houses belonging to kings and princes represented the invisible firstly because of the materials from which they were made, secondly because of the forms they were given, such as the crown, as these were the legacy of an entire tradition, and lastly because they had been acquired from a particular individual and thus constituted a reminder of past events, or else were either very old or came from exotic places.

(Pomian, p. 23)

Despite its apparently comprehensive character, Pomian's reading of jewels as the exclusive province of princes and kings overlooks their intimate association with womanhood in its real and idealized forms, as we see in the *Idylls.* Like the gems on Excalibur's hilt, which come from the Lady of the Lake, virtually all of Camelot's precious stones pass through some woman's hands. Men may handle jewels that are on loan or in transit, but women are the ones who make a lasting impression on Camelot's stones through their traffic in them.

This commerce in gems expresses what Susan M. Pearce describes as a characteristically feminine collecting interest in the female body "and its enhancement and adornment through ornaments."[15] As one of Tennyson's contemporaries observed, women's looks were universally highlighted with precious stones:

> Women . . . wreathe [gems] in their tresses, clasp them round their throats, their arms, their waists, decorate their bosoms, ears, fingers, ankles, and even in some lands, their very toes and nostrils with them; using these sparkling trinkets to attract attention to the charms they deem most worthy of admiration.[16]

Even the fairest maiden could profit from such embellishment, as Enid's mother suggests in **"The Marriage of Geraint."** Although Enid might suffer from her father's loss of fortune, she can still outshine any "great court-lady" by being "set forth at her best" (**"MG"** [**"The Marriage of Geraint"**], ll. 723, 728). It may be that Enid's unadorned beauty first enchants Geraint, but her gowns and gems are what promise to win her lasting acceptance at King Arthur's court.

Throughout the *Idylls,* then, gemstones become identified with the women who own and wear them. In **"Merlin and Vivien,"** the earliest of Tennyson's idylls, "the fair pearl-necklace of the Queen" (l. 449) becomes a supremely treasured possession through its association with Guinevere. When the queen's necklace accidentally "burst[s] in dancing," its pearls are split up, "[s]ome lost, some stolen, some as relics kept," and they subsequently live "dispersedly in many hands" (ll. 450, 451, 455). In a metonymic sense, Guinevere is possessed through these unstrung pearls, which serve as souvenirs of and proxies for her. As Merlin's anecdote of the necklace reminds us, this appropriation of the queen's jewels comes at an additional cost to Guinevere herself: "nevermore the same two sister pearls / Ran down the silken thread to kiss each other / On her white neck" (ll. 452-454). Because Guinevere's serial arrangement of pearls is never restored, her body no longer serves as the privileged site for displaying this special collection. Deprived of a valuable and intimate possession in her crown jewel, Guinevere becomes less of a sight herself. Although the immediate consequences of this loss might appear trifling, the queen's inability to manage her image ultimately helps to bring down Camelot. In fact, Guinevere's broken necklace, which was once as sound as Arthur's kingdom, provides a glimpse of that later, larger dispersal that the queen also precipitates.

Moreover, what happens to Guinevere's pearls points to the pervasive connection between women, jewels, and violence in the *Idylls.* In fact, Camelot is established upon these grounds; the bejeweled Excalibur, "Wrought by the lonely maiden of the Lake" (**"PA,"** l. 272), becomes the very instrument with which Arthur "beat his foemen down" (**"CA"** [**The Coming of Arthur"**], l. 308). In a similar fashion, Arthur's emerald cameo of the Virgin Mary channels divine agency for the king on the battlefield near Castle Gurnion. With this talisman, Arthur becomes a holy warrior, strengthened by divine intercession; in Lancelot's words, "[I]n this heathen war the fire of God / Fills him" (**"LE"** [**"Lancelot and Elaine"**], ll. 314-315). In typical chivalric fashion, Arthur's knights also joust for gems, doing battle to win their ladies precious stones that are literally beyond price. In particular, the champions Lancelot and Tristram brave deadly blows to win jewels for other men's wives. Thus, Tennyson's women authorize male violence through the gems with which they are associated and, at times, equated.

These gems themselves tend to be obtained at a great price, like Lancelot's diamonds, which are "Hard-won and hardly won with bruise and blow" (**"LE,"** l. 1158). Whenever precious stones happen to emerge from heaven or earth in the *Idylls,* Tennyson makes his readers aware of the individual and social costs of these artifacts. As with Victoria's Koh-i-noor, Lancelot's diamonds are said to be the spoils of past fratricide and regicide. The ruby necklace of *The Last Tournament* comes to Camelot at the price of the life of the child who bore it, having been "smitten in mid heaven with mortal cold" (l. 27). Moreover, when the curatorial Bedivere imagines putting Arthur's gemmed sword on exhibit for posterity, he provides a narrative of its production by the Lady of the Lake: "Nine years she wrought it, sitting in the deeps / Upon the hidden bases of the hills" (**"PA,"** ll. 273-274). Although this account of Excalibur's origins does not demystify the sword's "jewels, elfin Urim, on the hilt, / Bewildering heart and eye" (**"CA,"** ll. 298-299), it at least acknowledges the hard labor behind this museum-piece.

In his stories of Camelot's precious stones, then, Tennyson suggests that there is always a price to be paid for them. As acts of exchange give voice to otherwise silent stones in the *Idylls,* those who take what is not theirs through illicit transactions suffer grave consequences. Where gems are given, found, earned, or inherited, the exercise of individual taste becomes for Tennyson a paramount necessity in dealing with these prestigious objects from foreign lands, whether medieval or Victorian.

2

The predominantly royal and female passion for collecting gems in the *Idylls* had its parallel in Victorian England, where the queen herself emerged as an arch-collector of beautiful objects of all kinds. From her childhood, when she assembled, dressed, and played with a large collection of dolls,[17] Victoria showed a great zeal for acquiring everything from exquisite lace to fine art. The many sculptures at Osborne House, the Queen's residence on the Isle of Wight, included portrait busts, copies of classical works, and subject-pieces commissioned from fashionable sculptors of the day, along with a few antique marbles.[18] In painting, Victoria's collecting interests usually followed her husband's progressive tastes. Albert commissioned works from many contemporary painters, including Winterhalter and Landseer, who grew in popularity through the prince consort's patronage (Ames, p. 145). Victoria herself made the more expensive purchases, including early Italian and German paintings, as gifts for Albert, who also gave her works of art.

Victoria received public recognition as a collector and benefactor at the 1851 Crystal Palace exhibition, for which she loaned a number of articles from her own private collections. Nearly three dozen of these items were among the first listed in the exhibition's *Official Illustrated and Descriptive Catalogue,* which describes such royal objects as portraits of Victoria and Albert on Sèvres china; a jewel-case in the cinque-cento style; ornate furniture and domestic decorations, including several elegant carpets; and specimens of Abyssinian cloth-ing, saddlery, jewelry, and arms. Victoria's Indian artifacts on exhibit included several richly adorned canopied seats and ivory palanquins, which helped to capture the splendor and luster of the latest jewel in England's imperial crown.[19]

As Victoria's female counterpart in Camelot, Guinevere handles many of Camelot's jewels, though she manages to accumulate or preserve very few. Whereas Guinevere's loss of her pearls is merely accidental, her later divestments of precious stones are purposeful perfor-mances: she tries to send a message through her gems. The first of these stones are the diamonds of 1859's **"Elaine,"** in which Lancelot tries to complete a unique collection of gems as a gift for the queen. Having won eight crown diamonds in a series of annual jousts, Lan-celot goes after the "central diamond and the last / And largest" (**"LE,"** ll. 73-74). Once he has finished his task, Lancelot plans to "snare" Guinevere's "royal fancy" (**"LE,"** l. 71) with unexpected and unequaled largesse; he will give her the diamonds "all at once" (**"LE,"** l. 70), expecting her love and more in return.

Though Tennyson adopts the device of a diamond joust from Malory (Book xviii, chap. 21), he borrows the great diamond of his idyll from Victoria's own crown collections. By the time of the Exhibition, the story of the Koh-i-noor, which had made its way to England af-ter the annexation of the Punjab, was already well known. When the diamond arrived in England in the summer of 1850, the *Times* devoted a leading article to the history and adventures of this unrivaled jewel. Rec-ognizing the diamond's symbolic importance, the paper announced:

> Her Majesty's steam-sloop Medea has just arrived at Portsmouth, with a freight more precious, in nominal value, than was ever carried from Peru to Cadiz. Major Mackeson, one of her passengers, a meritorious and distinguished officer, brings with him that famous dia-mond of the East called, in the fondness of Asiatic hy-perbole, the Koh-i-noor, or *Mountain of Light,* which, after symbolizing the revolutions of ten generations by its passage from one conqueror to another, comes now, in the third centenary of its discovery, as the forfeit of Oriental faithlessness and the prize of Saxon valour, to the distant shores of England.[20]

As the *Times* noted, this unique trophy of empire car-ried a host of associations with it. First and foremost, the Koh-i-noor seemed to hold "the sovereignty of Hin-dostan" within itself. Over three hundred years, this gem had "pass[ed] in the train of conquest and as the emblem of dominion from Golconda to Delhi, from Delhi to Mushed, from Mushed to Cabul, and from Cabul to Lahore." Everywhere it traveled, the diamond stood out "in lustre, esteem, and value." In England, it was said to be the largest known diamond in the world,

"excepting the somewhat doubtful claims of the Brazil-ian stone among the crown jewels of Portugal," and its worth was estimated at two million pounds. Moreover, since England had obtained this jewel "in virtue of con-quest and sovereignty," this diamond was held to be "a fitting symbol of that supremacy" which Britain had so "fairly" won. Even before the Koh-i-noor was seen at the Crystal Palace by over six million visitors, then, the diamond occupied the Victorian popular imagination as visible proof of England's prosperity and an important symbol of Britain's imperial power.

The diamond's contemporary celebrity is further re-flected in its use by Coventry Patmore as a model for value and virtue in his 1856 bestseller *The Angel in the House*. In the late section entitled "The Koh-i-noor" (Vol. II, Canto VIII), Felix responds to his beloved Honoria's desire "[t]o know what mind [he] most ap-proved" by contrasting "man's hard virtues" with "sweet and womanly" ones.[21] What is most striking about Fe-lix's ideal woman is, according to him, "not that she is wise or good, / But just the thing which I desire" (Patmore, p. 183). Likewise, Patmore's title diamond was valued for how it fulfilled Victorian fantasies of conquest and sovereignty, becoming what the British wanted it to be, if only for a time. When Felix says of his "gentle Mistress," "The more I praised [her] the more she shone" (Patmore, p. 184), he might just as well be speaking of the Koh-i-noor. Both appreciate in value according to what others see in them; in Felix's words, "[A] woman, like the Koh-i-noor, / Mounts to the price that's put on her" (Patmore, p. 185).

However, at the height of Felix's reverie, Patmore hints at the trouble with such exotic possessions. In the sec-tion following "The Koh-i-noor," he writes, "A woman is a foreign land, / Of which, though there he settle young, / A man will ne'er quite understand / The cus-toms, politics, and tongue" (Patmore, p. 186). As Victo-ria was soon to discover, her own diamond, like its na-tive land, could also be a hard mistress. After all, the Hindus from whom the stone was taken believed that it brought disaster upon those who possessed it.[22] Previous owners of the diamond had been variously robbed, be-trayed, blinded, dethroned, imprisoned, and even assas-sinated, giving rise to the diamond's legendary curse.[23] Not long after the Koh-i-noor was presented to Victoria, she was herself attacked and struck on the head by a deranged ex-cavalry lieutenant named Pate; at least one observer blamed this assault on the Queen's unlucky charm.[24] Moreover, in 1860, Charles William King, whose books on precious stones provided source mate-rial for George Eliot and Wilkie Collins,[25] noted that the "usual consequences" of the diamond's possession had been "manifested in the Sepoy revolt, and the all but to-tal loss of India to the British crown" (p. 68).

Because Lancelot's gem is big enough to stand out in the king's costly canopy, it bears more than a passing resemblance to Victoria's jinxed jewel, which was said to have decorated the legendary Peacock Throne of the Moguls, completed by the same emperor who built the Taj Mahal.[26] Like its historical counterpart, Tennyson's fictional diamond is both large and costly; Lancelot's entire collection, of which it is the centerpiece, is valued at "the price of half a realm" ("LE," l. 1157). The treasured gem also adorns a king's crown, matching the Koh-i-noor's use by sultans, monarchs, and emperors in various personal ornaments. In addition, the two stones become gifts fit "for queens, and not for simple maids" ("LE," l. 230).

More important, Lancelot's diamond, like the Koh-i-noor, proves to be an unstable possession, passing through many hands in a series of doomed exchanges. Before Arthur wins his throne, he happens upon the skeleton of a king slain by his brother, along with "a crown / Of diamonds, one in front, and four aside" ("LE," ll. 45-46). Setting the crown on his head, Arthur takes his discovery as a sign that he "likewise shalt be King" (l. 55). Of course, the future king little suspects the mordant irony of this premonition, which portends his own violent passing at his nephew Modred's hands in Camelot's civil war. Later, Lancelot nearly loses his own life in winning the final diamond from this same crown, whose jewels Arthur turns to "public use" as tourney-prizes (l. 60). Moreover, Gawain, "surnamed The Courteous" (l. 553), ruins his good name with the king by mishandling this same stone. Commanded to "take / This diamond, and deliver it, and return" (ll. 543-544) with news of the knight with the red sleeve, Gawain gives up his mission before it is complete, turning the gem over to Elaine, partly as a sign of his own fondness for her.

Gawain's personal appraisal of Lancelot's diamond reveals a distinction between its potential worth as a gift and its supposedly intrinsic value:

> [I]f you love, it will be sweet to give it;
> And if he love, it will be sweet to have it
> From your own hand; and whether he love or not,
> A diamond is a diamond.

(ll. 688-691)

As Gawain suggests, even if Lancelot and Elaine do not share the kind of attachment that would lend meaning to the exchange of this diamond between them, the stone can still circulate at some future date within a personal economy of meaning or according to its fair market value. Gawain's treatment of Lancelot's diamond as a present for Elaine brings to mind not only Victoria's Koh-i-noor, which was bestowed upon her by colonial officials, but also the Queen's many Indian artifacts received as offerings from foreign potentates. Amidst the sumptuous Indian regalia at the Crystal Palace, the carved and jeweled ivory throne given to Victoria by the Rajah of Travancore was admired as a specimen of design, and it received pride of place as Albert's seat during the Exhibition's dazzling closing ceremonies (Breckenridge, pp. 203-204). In addition, the presents of the Nawab Nazim of Moorshedabad included an ivory howdah, fully loaded with elephant trappings, all worked in gold and silver (*Official Catalogue*, 4: 929). Such imperial gifts showed generosity toward the Queen, but they also served as a self-interested display of wealth and power, exhibiting the donor's wealth for all the world to see. Moreover, these gifts invited reciprocation from Victoria, who could be expected to give back even more because of her lofty imperial rank.

Such mutual exchange helped to enhance solidarity among peoples and nations within the British realm, even if it does not do so in the *Idylls,* where gems repeatedly suppose what Susan Pearce calls "an unbecoming degree of intimacy" between giver and recipient (p. 73). The lack of reciprocity in Camelot's gift-exchange signals the failure of jewels, as exemplars of material culture in Tennyson, to validate socially or sexually transgressive relationships and unrequited loves. Thus, in **"Geraint and Enid,"** Earl Doorm's offer of a thickly gemmed gown, like his other unwelcome advances, is met with Enid's refusal rather than her acquiescence. In Elaine's case (**"Lancelot and Elaine"**), her gift of pearls fails to win her the favor of Lancelot's diamond, through which she seeks to possess its proprietor. Although Lancelot is willing to give Elaine anything she desires, save himself, Elaine only wants what she cannot have, and so loses both diamond and knight without recompense or reward. Since Lancelot's gem is destined for Guinevere, Elaine's nightmare about this capricious stone proves prophetic: "some one put this diamond in her hand, / And . . . it was too slippery to be held" (ll. 211-212).

Because of Elaine's pearls, Lancelot's idealized transaction with Guinevere also fails to materialize. By wearing Elaine's pearl sleeve as an accessory to his jousting disguise, Lancelot accumulates surplus meaning for his diamonds and himself. His secret identity earns the fury of his own kinsmen, who ambush and critically wound the "stranger knight" (l. 466) who threatens to outshine their Lancelot. After Lancelot's ruse is discovered, Elaine's pearls speak clearly through Camelot's gossip: "'The maid of Astolat loves Sir Lancelot, / Sir Lancelot loves the maid of Astolat'" (ll. 720-721). Guinevere, of course, is not deaf to these rumors; in fact, she anticipates them, taking Elaine's favor as a sign of Lancelot's devotion to this apparent rival for her affections.

Still, Lancelot invites Guinevere to make use of the meaningful properties with which his labor invests the diamonds. He instructs her to customize them according to her taste:

Take, what I had not won except for you,
These jewels, and make me happy, making them
An armlet for the roundest arm on earth,
Or necklace for a neck to which the swan's
Is tawnier than her cygnet's.

(ll. 1174-78)

The possession ritual Lancelot describes would allow Guinevere to personalize the diamonds, just as Victoria did with the Koh-i-noor by having its setting changed from an armlet into a brooch. In so doing, she made the diamond that had been worn by a long succession of male rulers into a queen's jewel. In Guinevere's case, however, no alteration of form can make her diamonds into what Lancelot wants them to be. To the queen, the stones appear not as a sign of long-suffering devotion, but as a bribe for her affections, which she refuses to ransom any further. Here, the Koh-i-noor's association with Lancelot's large diamond contrasts strongly with its proximity to idealized and faithful married love in Patmore. Cast out of the realm of ideal values, Lancelot's gems become, like the jeweled knight in Percivale's vision, an emblem of mere materialism (**"HG"** [**"The Holy Grail"**], ll. 409-420).

Too late, Lancelot learns that the peril of using a gift as a sign of possession lies in its transmissibility. With a sense of drama and irony, Guinevere lays claim to the diamonds, only to discard them after she has instilled the stones with her own meaning. In a final act of dispossession, Guinevere empties the diamonds of their former significance by handling them with scorn. Like Victoria at her Golden and Diamond Jubilees, Guinevere makes quite a spectacle with her gems. However, this queen's display is a furious and irrevocable gesture:

> she seized,
> And, through the casement standing wide for heat,
> Flung them, and down they flashed, and smote the
>   stream.
> Then from the smitten surface flashed, as it were,
> Diamonds to meet them, and they past away.

(ll. 1225-29)

Guinevere's violence, reminiscent of that used to win her jewels or the Koh-i-noor itself, forces a rupture in the meaning of the diamonds that accompanies their transferal. By discarding the indestructible tokens of Lancelot's love, Guinevere breaks her bond with him. When she lets go of the jewels, Guinevere also robs Lancelot of an important means of expressing his attachment to her supposed rival. In addition, the queen's disposal of the diamonds deprives Lancelot of the hard-won signs of his knightly prowess and, by extension, of his masculinity. Even if, as Clyde de L. Ryals notes, Lancelot has earned the gems "in a honorable combat at a tournament where courtesy and manners prevailed,"[27] he forfeits his title to them by virtue of his infamous conduct toward both king and queen.

Despite the seeming finality of her act, not even the queen herself can decree the ultimate meaning of her diamonds. Once they leave her hands, the diamonds again take on a life of their own, as Harold Littledale noted more than a century ago:

> There is a grim irony of fate in the fulfillment of
>   Elaine's dream when the Queen
> in jealous wrath flings the diamonds into the river.
>   [Elaine's] barge is approach-
> ing, and the vanished gems become an offering to the
>   spirit of the dead maiden.[28]

Indeed, Elaine's ineffable smile seems to mock the thwarted queen as she surrenders her jewels. Though Guinevere attempts to deprive Elaine of Lancelot's diamonds, she all but gives them to her former rival, who symbolically lays claim to the gems. However, in death, as in life, actual possession of these jewels eludes Elaine, who is bereft of Lancelot's diamond, along with her own pearls. Unlike her "pearlgarland[ed]" counterpart in the 1832 **"Lady of Shalott,"** Elaine does not apparel herself in a "crown of white pearl," nor does she clasp "one blinding diamond bright" (ll. 33, 46, 49). Having yielded her treasured gems, Elaine holds only a lily, a sign of her purity, and a letter to Lancelot, asking him for the favor of prayer and burial. Like so many of Camelot's gems, the lost diamonds sink into a literal and textual void, never to be seen again.

Through their linked destinies, Elaine's pearls and Lancelot's diamonds alike emerge as what Jacques T. Godbout terms dangerous or "poisoned" gifts.[29] These either harm the recipient directly, like Snow White's apple, or pose a threat through the connections they offer, like the Trojan horse.[30] Elaine's pearls are tainted as gifts by the surreptitious way in which she offers them to Lancelot, which in turn ruins the value of his gems in Guinevere's eyes:

> What are these?
> Diamonds for me! they had been thrice their worth
> Being your gift, had you not lost your own.
> To loyal hearts the value of all gifts
> Must vary as the giver's.

(ll. 1204-08)

Threatened by Lancelot's gift, Guinevere refuses it, "because to accept it would be to tacitly endorse an unwanted relationship" (Godbout and Caillé, p. 9).[31]

Tennyson's portrayal of Camelot's poisoned gift jewels in **"Lancelot and Elaine"** shows his awareness of the threatening qualities of Victoria's own dangerous diamond, which soon became a burden for the crown. Because the Koh-i-noor was taken from its Indian owner, even its very status as a gift proved to be a lasting source of contention; in 1882, the maharajah who was forced to surrender the diamond petitioned Parliament for its return, without success. Besides its supposed curse, this corporate gift of Britain's former Indian administration made great demands upon its new owner. For one, the Koh-i-noor had to be guarded closely and kept "safelier" than the elusive diamond of Elaine's dream ("LE," l. 217). When Victoria's diamond was exhibited at the Crystal Palace, it was placed within a glass bell-jar, inside what was popularly described as "Mr. Chubb's 'iron cage.'"[32] This intricate London locksmith's invention was meant to protect the Koh-i-noor from the very kind of violence with which it had so recently been won. The exhibition catalogue declared this mechanism, which was on display as a technological wonder, to be impregnable:

> This case . . . contains an arrangement for elevating and depressing the diamond without unlocking. It is considered to be impossible to pick the lock or obtain an entrance into this receptacle.
>
> (3:663)

Rigged to lower the diamond automatically into an iron-and-steel safe upon any threat to the stone, this device was a feat of engineering ingenuity and manufacturing prowess, meant to defeat a would-be thief both physically and intellectually. The challenge and reward presented by these defenses inspired Richard Henry Horne to write a short story for Dickens' *Household Words* about an imaginary attempt to steal the diamond. In what turns out to be a dream, the author's alter-ego, a self-described "private gentleman of small means" who takes great pride in his modest collection of gems, successfully mines the Koh-i-noor by burrowing underneath the Crystal Palace at night and drilling through its renowned safe to gain his prize, only to discover later that "the greatest Treasure of the earth" is a fake (Horne, pp. 436, 441). Despite its whimsy, Horne's story reminded contemporary readers that what was won and kept by force could also be taken by it, thus necessitating constant surveillance.

Moreover, the Koh-i-noor brought with it increased obligations in the costly and difficult administration of expanding regions in India. After the Indian Mutiny had, in one historian's words, "shaken any easy hopes in the steady conversion of non-English peoples to English civilization,"[33] the Koh-i-noor hardly seemed like an ideal representation of imperial dominion. Just as Guinevere believed that she had won Lancelot's diamonds only to lose his heart, Victoria had acquired perhaps the world's greatest gem, only to have its motherland nearly slip through her fingers. Moreover, since the East India Company, which obtained the diamond for the Queen, handed over its administrative duties to the crown in 1858, this colonial possession beckoned to past glory rather than future conquests. Even if Victoria's ownership of the gem seemed like "an appropriate and honourable close to its career" for the writers of the offi-

cial Crystal Palace catalogue (3:696), holding the Koh-i-noor did not necessarily grant Victoria absolute sovereignty over India.

Guinevere's lost diamonds also provide an oblique commentary on some of Victoria's other crown jewels. Early in Victoria's reign, there was a dispute between the Queen and her uncle Cumberland, the King of Hanover, and later with his successor, her blind cousin George, over the Hanoverian crown jewels. Ever since Hanover was made a kingdom at the 1814 Congress of Vienna, George IV and William IV had held these jewels as rulers of both it and Britain. However, as a woman, Victoria was excluded from the Hanoverian throne and its trappings, including the renowned Hanoverian pearls, which had belonged to Catherine de Medici; Mary, Queen of Scots; and even Queen Elizabeth.[34] Despite the crown's efforts to purchase the jewels as early as 1841, no compromise could be reached, due in part to varying appraisals of these treasures. Thus, in 1858, the very year in which "Elaine" was written, Victoria, like Guinevere with her diamonds and pearls, was dispossessed of the jewels, which were surrendered to the Queen's foreign relatives. The throne's failure to hold onto its treasures surprised even the Hanoverian emissary, Count Kielmansegge, who had expected England to come up with the funds necessary to retain the regalia (Ames, p. 132).

Besides being a personal disappointment for the Queen, Victoria's lack of success in keeping the Hanoverian jewels in England was a loss to the nation. Indeed, her surrender of precious objects that had formed part of the English regalia for decades suggested a symbolic relinquishment of power. Even if Victoria's ornaments remained in the family, so to speak, their departure from Britain signaled the inability of the monarchy to maintain its possessions by diplomatic or economic means. As Tennyson was to suggest in "The Last Tournament" of 1871, the jewels of empire, like the Koh-i-noor or even India itself, could not be bought but with blood.

3

Like Lancelot's great diamond, the ruby carcanet won by Tristram in "The Last Tournament" closely resembled one of Victoria's newest crown jewels. The Timur Ruby, which once belonged to the conqueror Tamerlane, had also lately arrived from the Lahore Treasury. Like the Koh-i-noor, the ruby appeared at the Crystal Palace in 1851, but with little fanfare. Whereas the exhibition catalogue devoted a full two pages to the history of Victoria's great diamond, the Timur went unnamed as part of a "short necklace, of four very large spinelle rubies" (4:919).[35] The semi-triangular Timur served as the center and largest of three rubies in the middle of Victoria's carcanet, with a smaller gem on the snap at the back. Even on its own, the Timur was still as visually and historically distinguished as the Koh-i-noor. Weighing over 350 carats, the stone, like its diamond counterpart, had once decorated the fabulous Peacock Throne. Described as "upwards of three fingers in breadth and nearly two in length," the gem was so highly valued that it was long known as the "Tribute of the World" (Wilson, p. 150). Its provenance was even engraved on its surface, though one Mogul emperor, in a memorable gesture of appropriation, had this inscription altered to remove the names of three of the jewel's former owners.[36]

More important, the Timur Ruby had long been a companion piece to the great Koh-i-noor itself. As Eric Bruton has noted, "There is a close historical association between the famous diamond and the great 'ruby' because, although they have been fought over and presented for services rendered, they have remained in common ownership . . . since 1612" (p. 133). Victoria's custodianship of the jewels ensured that this legacy would continue. As the *Edinburgh Review* observed in 1866, the Timur, an "enormous stone, time-honoured in Indian tradition," accompanied the Koh-i-noor "into the possession of Her who is now the Sovereign of India."[37]

With a longer history than even the Koh-i-noor, the Timur Ruby also witnessed more violence than any other storied stone. As Mab Wilson writes, "For close to a millennium it watched the savage games of kings, noted their unconcealed pleasure in cruelty, saw greed that was senseless in its magnitude, patricide, fratricide, torture, and rapine" (p. 146). The Timur's documented past goes back as far as the eleventh century and the Hindu dynasties of Delhi, from where it passed by conquest to successive Muslim sultanates, and from them to the great Tamerlane and his Tartar line. The venerable ruby came by way of Persia as a tribute to the Indian Moguls in 1628, soon after which the Koh-i-noor joined it.[38]

Although Tennyson's ruby carcanet may lack these particulars, it too sees and even occasions great bloodshed as it acquires a sense of agency. Even more than Lancelot's great diamond, the rubies of **"The Last Tournament"** prove to be stubbornly resistant to manipulation, and they earn the character of cursed stones whose very ownership means death. Their path of destruction begins with Nestling's passing, after which the queen tries to redeem "the jewels of this dead innocence" (**"LT"** [**"The Last Tournament"**], l. 31) by making them a tourney-prize. Cursing her lost diamonds, Guinevere assures her husband that the rubies will bring "rosier luck" (l. 45) because of their more propitious origins. However, the blood-red of the rubies fails to remind the queen that these jewels are to be won with violence that she herself commissions.

Far from being the token of purity or talisman of virginity envisioned by Guinevere (ll. 49-50), the rubies become a fitting emblem of the victorious Tristram's perceived transgressions: he is literally caught red-handed, covered in someone else's blood. When Tristram declines to give his prize to some lady on the field, he violates custom and courtesy, adding to his crimes. As Marcel Mauss writes of *taonga* gift exchange among the Maori, "To keep this thing is dangerous, not only because it is illicit to do so, but also because it comes morally, physically, and spiritually, from a[nother] person. . . . [I]t retains a magical and religious hold over the recipient."[39] Even if Tristram owns the jewels, he does not fully possess them because he fails to lay immediate claim to their symbolic properties through timely and appropriate exchange.

Moreover, through their appearance, Tristram's red rubies acquire an ominous association with Pelleas, the ruthless "Red Knight" who travesties Arthur's court and brutalizes the king's knights and subjects. Rather than conveying innocence, then, the jewels begin to carry the taint of sin and death, as Tristram's dream about the ruby necklace shows. Like Elaine's vision of the elusive diamond, Tristram's nightmare focuses on a collection that cannot be held or even preserved. In Tristram's imagination, the two Isolts, his wife and his lover, struggle for possession of the ruby-chain. The women do violence for and to the gems, which melt like "frozen blood" in the queen's intemperate grasp (l. 412), leaving her hand with the same telltale stain that incriminated Tristram. The broken circlet also reflects Tristram's divided love, which is split between the sensual attractions of Queen Isolt and the spiritual ministrations of his wife.[40] Sensing that he has sullied the sacred memory of the innocent infant by tarnishing her jewels,[41] Tristram hears "a rush of eagle's wings, and then / A whimpering of the spirit of the child, / Because the twain had spoiled her carcanet" (ll. 416-418). As one critic has suggested, this subdued protest from beyond the grave shows Tristram's mind "pronouncing judgment upon itself."[42] Because he has not lived up to the spirit of his trophy, Tristram suspects that these gems, like Elaine's diamond, will surely slip away. Tennyson's juxtaposition of this dream with the slaughter of the Red Knight and his followers in a river of blood further foreshadows the misfortune that the matching rubies threaten to bring.

Despite his misgivings, Tristram still attempts to claim the rubies for himself in a divestment ritual dedicated to erasing the meaning associated with their previous owner (McCracken, p. 87). As he shows a consumer's anxiety of influence, Tristram implicitly acknowledges that the personal properties with which an object is invested can persist even after it changes hands. Hoping to free up the jewels' symbolic dimensions for his own use, he carries the stones to Queen Isolt and presents them to her at sunset. Though he does not believe in eternal love or any "inviolable vows" (l. 683), Tristram places the trappings of his disowned ideals in the best light possible to seduce Mark's queen, who is unmoved by Tristram's half-hearted professions of constancy. To redeem the gems, Tristram provides a mystical account of their origins. Calling the rubies "the red fruit / Grown on a magic oak-tree in mid-heaven" (ll. 738-739), Tristram effaces their former owner and her part in the jewels' history and meaning. He then brings the carcanet down to earth and personalizes his prize by identifying the rubies as the fruits of his labor, "won by Tristram as a tourney-prize" (l. 740). By calling the rubies his "last / Love-offering and peace-offering" to Isolt (ll. 741-742), Tristram makes yet another attempt to arbitrate the use and meaning of the carcanet. In a concluding act of appropriation, Tristram tries to take possession of Isolt herself through the necklace, which he flings around her neck.

However, just as Tristram's lips touch Isolt's "jewelLed throat" (l. 745), the rubies symbolically contaminate this transaction, revealing the couple's complicity in sin. As he tries to trade the tokens of "dead innocence" for living vice, Tristram falls victim to his own sexual excesses.[43] Though Mark may not have witnessed his wife's previous transgressions, he catches Isolt and Tristram in the act this time and voids their illicit exchange by striking his rival dead. Thus, Tristram's rubies connect sexual rivals more directly than Lancelot's diamonds; Mark encounters his adversary face-to-face, rather than through his jewels. Though the carcanet's story ends with its owner's life, its malign influence appears to linger on: immediately after Mark kills Tristram, Guinevere flees Arthur's court, precipitating Camelot's final battle.

The immense personal and social costs of Tristram's rubies call to mind a related passage from Tennyson's primary source for **"The Last Tournament."** Sharon Turner's *History of the Anglo-Saxons* records a legend of King Alfred about the discovery of the infant "Nestingum," a foundling abandoned, like his namesake in Tennyson, in a tree, though "dressed in purple, with golden bracelets, the marks of nobility, on his arms."[44] More important, Turner's history also cites King Alfred's translation of a paragraph on jewels from Boethius that could hardly have escaped the poet's notice:

Why should the beauty of gems draw your eyes to them to wonder at them, as I know they do? What is then the nobility of that beauty which is in gems? It is theirs; not yours. At this I am most exceedingly astonished, why you should think this irrational, created good, better than your own excellence: why you should so exceedingly admire these gems, or any of those dead-like things that have not reason; because they can, by no right, deserve that you should wonder at them. Though they be God's creatures, they are not to be

measured with you, because one of two things occurs; either they are not good for you themselves, or but for a little good compared with you. We too much undervalue ourselves when we love that which is inferior to us, and in our power, more than ourselves, or the Lord that has made us and given us all these goods.

(2:26)

As Turner notes in his own more succinct translation of the excerpt, Alfred embellished extensively upon the original. The same could be said of Tennyson, who elaborates upon this passage in **"The Last Tournament"** which serves as an extended admonition against taking material things at face value. In fact, Alfred's translation might provide a fitting postscript to the *Idylls* as a whole, since Tennyson repeatedly portrays gems there as seductive and potentially dangerous objects of uncertain worth.

Moreover, Tristram's attempts to remake Nestling's rubies in his own image mirror Victoria's own extensive efforts to transform the Koh-i-noor for her personal use. In form and setting, the famous diamond had been materially changed since its arrival, taming its foreign aspects and making it seem like more of an English possession. Upon the unaltered diamond's debut at the Great Exhibition, a writer in the *Illustrated London News* commented that the Koh-i-noor was "gigantic but somewhat rough and unhewn" in appearance and even "ungraceful" or awkward in its form.[45] The diamond's lack of polish was attributed to the Eastern predilection for size over looks in gems; Indian tastes were said to consider "the magnitude of too great importance to be submitted to the great reduction necessary to show the beauty of a stone" ("Guide," p. 428). Other cut stones from India at the Crystal Palace were supposed to give visitors an idea of "the rich and lavish magnificence of the East, and also of the barbarous nature of this magnificence, since the gems [were] little altered from the rough state in which they occurred in nature" ("Guide," p. 428). These responses to the Koh-i-noor and its companions reflect the Victorian perception of the East as a diamond in the rough, alluring but yet to be tamed.

As for the Koh-i-noor itself, the diamond was said to lack "the best form for exhibiting its purity and lustre" ("Guide," p. 428). Despite the various and expensive means used for displaying the stone to its best advantage, it came far from satisfying public anticipation, leading to suggestions that the diamond's appearance and value alike had been exaggerated.[46] The *Times* itself had compared the Crystal Palace at its opening to Victoria's diamond in a simile that only increased expectations; as the paper reported, "'The blazing arch of lucid glass' with the bright hot sun flaming on its polished ribs and sides shone like the Koh-i-Noor itself."[47] The letdown exhibition-goers felt at the actual sight of the diamond was great, as Richard Henry Horne observed:

Like everybody else, I have been, of course, to the Great Exposition; and, like everybody else, I was strikingly disappointed by the appearance of the Koh-i-noor. My imagination had portrayed something a million times more dazzling.

(pp. 436-437)

Many at the Crystal Palace who had looked forward to seeing a true "Mountain of Light" mistook the building's great central crystal fountain for the neighboring Koh-i-noor. This confusion suggests how large the gem and its native land loomed in the Victorian imagination.

Although the diamond could not be increased in size, at least it could be made to look more like a British jewel. Thus, in 1852, the Koh-i-noor was painstakingly recut in an operation that was said to have "greatly improved its brilliancy and general appearance, [though] at the expense of more than a third of its weight" (de Barrera, p. 281). As Victorian mineralogist Nevil Story-Maskelyne explained, "So large a stone as the Koh-i-nur could never be endowed with the splendour of a smaller diamond" because "as a stone rises in weight and size above twenty carats it loses proportionally in effect" (p. 248). He added that a simple repolishing of the stone's rounded Indian facets would have done just as well for its appearance. However, not even the Koh-i-noor's loss in weight could rob the diamond of its unique prestige.

In fact, this gem's reputation in its new land began to improve over time. English views of the diamond changed for the better with Victoria's extended ownership of the stone. In an 1882 history of the Koh-i-noor that the queen herself read in manuscript, Edwin W. Streeter assured his British readers that the gem would no longer leave "sorrow and sufferings . . . in its wake":

A strange fatality presided over its early vicissitudes, but its alleged 'uncannie' powers have now ceased to be a subject of apprehension. Its latest history eloquently demonstrates the fact that extended empire is a blessing, just in proportion as it finds hearts and hands willing to fulfil the high duties which increased privilege involves.

(Streeter, pp. 128, 134-135)

With good fortune generally following Victoria at home and abroad, the Koh-i-noor slowly acquired a new character. As Stephen Howarth notes, "Gradually it became an accepted standard that bad luck would befall a man who wore the jewel, while good luck would follow a woman" (p. 143). This rosier version of the Koh-i-noor's talismanic powers derived, in part, from one of the stone's former owners, Shah Soujah, who estimated the stone's value by its good luck, "for it [had] ever been his who [had] conquered his enemies" (qtd. in Story-Maskelyne, p. 232).

However, as both Streeter and Tennyson acknowledged, with Britain's material gains came added responsibility. The ceaseless expansion that the British empire was still experiencing had given it, in India, a throne "in our vast Orient" (**"To the Queen,"** l. 30), of which Victoria became the Empress on May 1, 1876, twenty-five years to the day after the opening of the Crystal Palace. A quarter-century after the Great Exhibition, imperial England, like the "spiritual city and all her spires / And gateways in a glory like one pearl" (**"HG,"** ll. 526-527), still held a promise as great as its "orient," or lustrous iridescence, a pearl's counterpart to a diamond's fire. By placing his queen's jewels at the center of the *Idylls,* Tennyson portrays India and empire as pearls of great price, to be won and worn with caution.

Notes

1. All citations of the poetry are from *The Poems of Tennyson,* ed. Christopher Ricks, 3 vols. (Berkeley: Univ. of California Press, 1987). Abbreviations of the titles of Tennyson's *Idylls* follow the list in *Idylls of the King,* ed. J. M. Gray (New Haven: Yale Univ. Press, 1983), p. 303.

2. Tennyson embellishes considerably upon Malory's description of Excalibur in *Morte d'Arthur,* which merely observes that "the pummel and the haft were all of precious stones" (*The History of the Renowned Prince Arthur, King of Britain; with His Life and Death and All His Glorious Battles. Likewise the Noble Acts and Heroic Deeds of his Valiant Knights of the Round Table,* 2 vols. [London, 1816], xxi 4-5). All future references to Malory are to this edition.

3. Tennyson's *Maud* is a striking exception. Like the *Idylls,* the 1855 poem is deeply ambivalent about gems, which have an idealized connection to beauty and constancy in nature and Maud, but are also associated with the "barbarous opulence" of Maud's brother (l. 352) and the ostentatious display of the speaker's rival in love.

4. Arjun Appadurai, ed., *The Social Life of Things: Commodities in Cultural Perspective* (Cambridge: Cambridge Univ. Press, 1986), p. 5.

5. Walter Benjamin, "Unpacking My Library: A Talk about Book Collecting," in *Illuminations,* ed. Hannah Arendt, trans. Harry Zohn (New York: Schocken Books, 1968), p. 66.

6. Stephen Howarth, *The Koh-i-noor Diamond: The History and the Legend* (London: Quartet Books, 1980), pp. 126-127.

7. Although there is no record of Tennyson's acquaintance with the Koh-i-noor, it seems certain that the poet, with his scientific interests, would have seen the diamond at the Great Exhibition. In

late 1851, Tennyson was living eleven miles outside of London, and he made a special effort to visit his literary acquaintances in the city during this time. Victoria had even offered Tennyson the use of her box at the Exhibition. See Robert Bernard Martin, *Tennyson: The Unquiet Heart* (Oxford: Clarendon Press, 1980), pp. 358, 363. Moreover, Tennyson would probably have read about the jewel in the papers of the day, as he made it his business as poet laureate to keep abreast of foreign and domestic affairs.

8. Recent commentaries on the contribution of the dedicatory "To the Queen" to the imperial framework of the *Idylls* include Ian McGuire, "Epistemology and Empire in *Idylls of the King*," *VP* [*Victorian Poetry*] 30 (1992): 388-391, 396-398; Robin L. Inboden, "The 'Valour of Delicate Women': The Domestication of Political Relations in Tennyson's Laureate Poetry," *VP* 36 (1998): 208-210; and Cecily Devereux, "Canada and the Epilogue to the *Idylls*: 'The Imperial Connection' in 1873," *VP* 36 (1998): 223-245.

9. Gerhard Joseph offers compelling readings of the semiotic significance of Excalibur and other swords in Tennyson's poetry in "Tennyson's Sword: From 'Mungo the American' to *Idylls of the King*," *Sex and Death in Victorian Literature,* ed. Regina Barreca (Bloomington: Indian Univ. Press, 1990), pp. 60-68; "Choosing Tennyson: The Stranger's Hovering Sword," *Tennyson and the Text: The Weaver's Shuttle* (Cambridge: Cambridge Univ. Press, 1992), pp. 191-212; and "Commodifying Tennyson: The Historical Transformation of 'Brand Loyalty,'" *VP* 34 (1996): 133-147. For connections between Tennyson's poetry and the Victorian literary marketplace, see Joseph's "Commodifying Tennyson" and Dino Franco Felluga, "Tennyson's *Idylls,* Pure Poetry, and the Market," *SEL* 37 (1997): 783-803.

10. As Grant McCracken explains, material culture acquires a propagandistic value because it works "in more understated, inapparent ways than language." Even if material culture is limited in its expressive range, the inconspicuousness of its messages permits them "to carry meaning that could not be put more explicitly without the danger of controversy, protest, or refusal" (*Culture and Consumption: New Approaches to the Symbolic Character of Consumer Goods* [Bloomington: Indiana Univ. Press, 1988], pp. 68-69).

11. Susan M. Pearce, *Museums, Objects, and Collections: A Cultural Study* (Washington, D.C.: Smithsonian Institution Press, 1992), p. 33.

12. George Frederick Kunz and Charles Hugh Stevenson, *The Book of the Pearl* (New York: The Century Co., 1908), pp. 166-167.

13. Ronald W. Lightbown, *Mediaeval European Jewellery, with a Catalogue of the Collection in the Victoria & Albert Museum* ([London]: Victoria & Albert Museum, 1992), p. 26.

14. Krzysztof Pomian, *Collectors and Curiosities: Paris and Venice, 1500-1800,* trans. Elizabeth Wiles-Portier ([Cambridge]: Polity Press, 1990), pp. 18-19; Lightbown, *Mediaeval European Jewellery,* pp. 63-64.

15. Susan M. Pearce, *On Collecting: An Investigation into Collecting in the European Tradition* (London: Routledge, 1995), p. 203.

16. A. de Barrera, *Gems and Jewels: Their History, Geography, Chemistry, and Ana, from the Earliest Ages to the Present Time* (London: Richard Bentley, 1860), p. 3.

17. Frances H. Low, "Queen Victoria's Dolls," *Strand Magazine* (September 1892): 222-328. See also Low's *Queen Victoria's Dolls,* illus. Alan Wright (London, 1894).

18. Winslow Ames, *Prince Albert and Victorian Taste* (London: Chapman and Hall, 1967), pp. 133-134.

19. *Official Descriptive and Illustrated Catalogue of the Great Exhibition of the Works of Industry of All Nations,* 5 vols. (London, 1851), 1: 111-112; 3: 847. The exhibition catalogue and its objects portrayed India as the repository of vast and varied animal, vegetable, and mineral wealth, "capable of producing, within its own limits, almost all the useful products of every other quarter of the globe" (4:857). India's catalogue listing at the head of Britain's foreign possessions reflected the central position that it had been given inside the Crystal Palace. For more on the representation of India at the Great Exhibition, see Carol A. Breckenridge, "The Aesthetics and Politics of Colonial Collecting: India at World Fairs," *Comparative Studies in Society and History* 31 (1989): 195-216.

20. ["Major Mackeson Brings Koh-i-noor, the Famous Diamond, to England"], *Times,* July 1, 1850, p. 4.

21. [Coventry Patmore], *The Poems of Coventry Patmore,* ed. Frederick Page (London: Oxford Univ. Press, 1949), p. 183.

22. Rev. C[harles] W[illiam] King, *Antique Gems: Their Origin, Use, and Value as Interpreters of Ancient History; and as Illustrative of Ancient Art* (London, 1860), p. 68.

23. Edwin W. Streeter, *The Great Diamonds of the World: Their History and Romance,* 2nd ed. (London, 1882), pp. 116-135.

24. Stephen Howarth, *The Koh-i-noor Diamond: The History and the Legend* (London: Quartet Books, 1980), p. 142.

25. See Joseph Weisenfarth, "Antique Gems from *Romola* to *Daniel Deronda*," *George Eliot: A Centenary Tribute,* ed. Gordon S. Haight and Rosemary T. VanArsdel (Totowa: Barnes and Noble, 1982), pp. 55-63, and Mark M. Hennelly, Jr., "Detecting Collins' Diamond: From Serpentstone to Moonstone," *NCL* [*Nineteenth-Century Literature*] 39 (1984): 25-47.

26. "The Koh-i-noor, or Mountain of Light," *Chambers's Edinburgh Journal,* July 28, 1849, p. 49.

27. Clyde de L. Ryals, *From the Great Deep: Essays on "Idylls of the King"* (Athens: Ohio Univ. Press, 1967), p. 127.

28. Harold Littledale, *Essays on Lord Tennyson's "Idylls of the King"* (London, 1893), p. 204.

29. Jacques T. Godbout and Alain Caillé, *The World of the Gift,* trans. Donald Winkler (Montreal: McGill-Queen's Univ. Press, 1998), pp. 8-9.

30. Godbout and Caillé, pp. 54, 211; Lewis Hyde, *The Gift: Imagination and the Erotic Life of Property* (New York: Vintage Books, 1983), pp. 72-73.

31. Lancelot's incomplete understanding of gifts contrasts with the relative mastery of the gift by women around him. The superior treatment of gifts by Camelot's women, including Enid, Vivien, Elaine, and Guinevere, supports Godbout's contention that women show special competence in the domain of the gift. According to Godbout, "[W]omen are at the heart of the gift in the domestic sphere. . . . Women are in charge of presents and are at ease in that world. . . . Men are clumsy, embarrassed, often ridiculous, understand the rules of the game poorly, lack subtlety, make blunders" (p. 36). Tennyson's anxieties about the Koh-i-noor show his concern over the diamond as a gift in the public sphere, particularly under the aegis of the state, which Godbout views as inimical to the spirit of the gift (pp. 61-62). See also Godbout and Caillé, pp. 149-167.

32. [Richard Henry Horne], "A Penitent Confession," *Household Words,* August 2, 1851, p. 438.

33. R. K. Webb, *Modern England from the Eighteenth Century to the Present* (London: Unwin Hyman, 1980), p. 356.

34. Mab Wilson, *Gems* (New York: Viking, 1967), p. 138.

35. Spinel rubies differ in color and crystal form from the true or "oriental" ruby. Spinels are generally a vivid scarlet, rose, or poppy-red with octahedral crystals, in contrast with the familiar blood-red color and six-sided prisms of the oriental ruby. See Louis Dieulafait, *Diamonds and Precious Stones: A Popular Account of Gems* (London, 1874), pp. 114-119, and de Barrera, *Gems and Jewels,* pp. 183-185. Of spinels, M. H. Story-Maskelyne states, "Nearly all the large and famous stones that pass under the name of rubies belong to this species" ("Precious Stones," *Edinburgh Review* [July 1866]: 243).

36. Eric Bruton, *Legendary Gems; or, Gems that Made History* (Radnor: Chilton, 1986), pp. 131-132.

37. [M. H. Story-Maskelyne], "Precious Stones," *Edinburgh Review* (July 1866): 243. The Timur Ruby arrived separately from the Koh-i-noor, and it was not presented to the queen until 1851. Eric Bruton writes, "While the famous diamond merited special security arrangements, armed guards, and transport in one of Her Majesty's ships, the Timur Ruby went to London by ordinary transport" (p. 133).

38. Wilson, *Gems,* pp. 146-147; Howarth, *The Koh-i-noor Diamond,* p. 11.

39. Marcel Mauss, *The Gift: Forms and Functions of Exchange in Archaic Societies,* trans. Ian Cunnison (New York: W. W. Norton, 1967), p. 10.

40. James R. Kincaid, *Tennyson's Major Poems: The Comic and Ironic Patterns* (New Haven: Yale Univ. Press, 1975), p. 205.

41. J. M. Gray, *Thro' the Vision of the Night: A Study of Source, Evolution, and Structure in Tennyson's "Idylls of the King"* (Edinburgh: Edinburgh Univ. Press, 1980), p. 116.

42. Walter Nash, qtd. in Gray, p. 116.

43. John R. Reed, *Perception and Design in Tennyson's "Idylls of the King"* (Athens: Ohio Univ. Press, 1969), p. 120.

44. Sharon Turner, *History of the Anglo-Saxons,* 2 vols. (London, 1852), 2:119. According to J. Philip Eggers in *King Arthur's Laureate* (New York: New York Univ. Press, 1971), p. 217, Tennyson owned and read Turner in the 1807 edition.

45. "A Guide to the Great Industrial Exhibition: The Gems," *Illustrated London News,* May 17, 1851, p. 426.

46. "A Lady's Glance at the Exhibition (No. III)," *Illustrated London News,* August 23, 1851, p. 242

47. "The Opening of the Great Exhibition," *Times,* May 2, 1851, pp. 4-5.

Catherine Phillips (essay date fall 2002)

SOURCE: Phillips, Catherine. "'Charades from the Middle Ages'? Tennyson's *Idylls of the King* and the Chivalric Code." *Victorian Poetry* 40, no. 3 (fall 2002): 241-53.

[In the following essay, Phillips offers an alternate, multi-faceted reading of Tennyson's treatment of medieval legend in Idylls of the King.*]*

Writing of Tennyson's **"Morte d'Arthur,"** the first of the books that later became *Idylls of the King,* Leigh Hunt remarked that the poem "treats the modes and feelings of one generation in the style of another, always a thing fatal, unless it be reconciled with something of self-banter in the course of the poem itself. . . . The impossibility of a thorough earnestness must, somehow or other, be self-acknowledged."[1] On the other hand, Gerard Manley Hopkins, who dedicated his life to the most Christian of the ideals in Malory in all its Catholicism, thought that Tennyson had not taken his model seriously enough. In the *Idylls,* Hopkins asserted, Malory's *Morte d'Arthur* had become simply *"Charades from the Middle Ages."*[2] Although the treatment of medieval legend and the uses to which it could be put are well known factors in the Victorian encounter with the Middle Ages, I would like to suggest that Tennyson's place in this debate is slightly different from that which has been understood.

Tennyson began to work on the Arthurian legends in the early 1830s, when he wrote **"The Lady of Shalott," "Sir Lancelot and Queen Guinevere,"** and **"Sir Galahad."** The first version of the **"Morte d'Arthur"** was added in 1842. But he was also experimenting with a larger allegorical framework for the material, either as an epic or a musical masque. Tennyson knew all three of the English editions of Malory's *Le Morte d'Arthur* published in the Romantic period by Wilks, Walker, and Southey. As he worked on into the second half of the century there were more editions: Thomas Wright's of 1858 and James Knowles' popular modernized version of 1862 that went through seven printings by the time of Tennyson's death. Malory was Tennyson's main source because it is the most complete and ordered collection of the legends. However, a fissure runs through *Le Morte d'Arthur* deriving from the amalgamation of two traditions: a British *chanson de geste* strain emphasizing military courage, Christianity, and group loyalty centered on Arthur, and a French *roman courtois* strand focused on Lancelot. In the latter, women's approval motivates the knights to daring deeds, and individual personal qualities are more important. There are also more magical elements. Tennyson knew a number of these earlier English and French versions, and their differences, perhaps unintentionally, remain embedded in his *Idylls of the King.* He also knew an Italian version

of the story of Elaine, which he used for **"The Lady of Shalott"** and, travelling extensively in Wales, he collected local fables. As he used the material more and more, he came increasingly to introduce his own emphasis and even to invent incidents.

"Enid and Nimuë" (Nimuë was later called Vivien) was set up in print but not published in 1857 because of an objection made privately to Tennyson about the explicitness of Nimuë's seduction of Merlin.[3] Gustave Doré, in illustrations to the poem in 1868, pictures Vivien as an exotic swarthy gypsy—middle-eastern in dress and appearance—recalling the epithets applied in Shakespeare's *Antony and Cleopatra* to Cleopatra. A group of four *Idylls of the King*—Enid, Vivien, Elaine, and Guinevere—appeared in 1859, and it was not till 1885 that the full twelve books were complete. So Tennyson worked on the legends for over fifty years.

When Tennyson began his work in the 1830s, the medieval period was already being used for contemporary debate. A. W. N. Pugin's book *Contrasts: A Parallel Between the Noble Edifices of the Middle Ages and the Corresponding Buildings of the Present Day, Showing the Present Decay of Taste* (1836) was not just a scholarly and aesthetic comparison. Pugin showed in contrasting plates, for example, a medieval monastery and a Victorian workhouse as examples of the degradation in charity to the poor. Made two years after the introduction of the widely unpopular law instituting workhouses, this was very much a political statement. Pugin, who converted to Catholicism, naturally turned back to the edifices in which Catholicism had been practiced in England. His construction of a number of chapels and the manufacture of ecclesiastical fittings for other people with similar sympathies contributed to the flourishing of Catholicism in England that culminated in the restoration of the Catholic hierarchy in 1850.

Another related range of associations concerned the idea of chivalry. Richard Hurd's *Letters on Chivalry and Romance* of 1762 was largely responsible for introducing into the Gothic Revival the idea of Chivalry as an institution carried out and represented in the figure of the knight. Hurd understood chivalry as a code of moral behavior of upper-class men that showed "their romantic ideas of justice; their passion for adventures; their eagerness to run succour of the distressed and the pride they took in redressing wrongs and removing grievances"[4] Hurd's *Letters* influenced Thomas Percy, Bishop of Dromore, whose *Reliques of Ancient English Poetry* (1765) became a major source of medieval subjects for nineteenth-century writers and artists. The third volume of Percy's *Reliques* was a collection of "Poems on King Arthur & c." and in the introduction to it Percy stated that although the institution of chivalry postdated King Arthur, the ideas of chivalry were already evident in Arthurian society. Percy's poems, many of them from a medieval manuscript, were accompanied by scholarly essays. One of those influenced by Percy's *Reliques* was Walter Scott, whose *Ivanhoe* (1819) was important in the popularizing of the notions of chivalric behavior that were virtually personified by the protagonist, Wilfred of Ivanhoe. Scott's novel made chivalry a code of behavior to be thought about by the upper-class young men of his own day. Such a link between chivalry and gentlemanly actions was made specific by Kenelm Digby, whose *Broadstone of Honour, or Rules for the Gentlemen of England* (1822) was well known in the Victorian period. It went through a number of editions in successively expanded form. Edward Burne-Jones kept it as bedside reading, and it is the source for his painting *The Merciful Knight* (1863), recognized as one of his most important early works. The subject makes Christian virtue central to the image of knighthood, and Burne-Jones inscribed the essence of the legend on the frame: "Of a Knight who forgave his enemy when he might have destroyed him and how the image of Christ kissed him in token that his acts had pleased God." The painting was exhibited at the Old Water Colour Society in 1864 and was criticized in the *Art Journal* in the following way: "We cannot indeed but fear that such ultra manifestations of medievalism, however well meant, must tend inevitably, though of course unconsciously, to bring ridicule upon truths which we all desire to hold in veneration." The problem was that Burne-Jones took literally what was acceptable to Protestant Britain in a vaguely symbolic form. The setting of the painting in a shrine with a large carved figure of Christ, and the depiction of the miraculous behavior of the statue was entirely too Catholic to be comfortable.[5] This too was a type of response that Tennyson was worried by, inevitably most in the quest for the Holy Grail, of which he wrote: "I doubt whether such a subject as the San Graal could be handled in these days without incurring a charge of irreverence. It would be too much like playing with sacred things" (Ricks, 3:463). The fear might have been as much of a charge of Catholicism as of irreverence. He finally wrote the section in 1868.

There was another contemporary project of relevance to Tennyson's handling of medieval legend. When the old Palace of Westminster was burned down in 1834, British politicians and artists had the opportunity of making a political and nationalist statement in designing the new seat of Parliament.[6] A design competition was won by Charles Barry and A. W. N. Pugin, who produced a symmetrical structure encrusted with Perpendicular ornament, a style that is uniquely British and Medieval in origin. The architects created panels in the Lords' Chamber and in the Queen's Robing Room for frescoes. William Dyce, painter and superintendent of the School of Design, unofficially presided over the painting of the frescoes and completed the first of them in August 1846. He spent a winter in Italy studying fresco style and technique before starting, and *The Baptism of Ethelbert* reflects that Italian influence. Ethelbert was a seventh-century Saxon king of Kent who accepted Christianity. The balanced composition, the power and solidity of the figures, and the arch are all Italianate; specific resemblances can be seen to work by Masaccio and the Vatican Stanza. The other subjects for the Lords' chamber were: *The Spirit of Chivalry, The Spirit of Religion, The Spirit of Justice, Edward III Conferring the Order of the Garter on the Black Prince,* i.e. institutionalizing a code of chivalry, and *Prince Henry Acknowledging the Authority of Chief Justice Gascoyne.* They are paintings that are meant to be inspirational, meant to establish the idea that the power of rulers must be subordinate to justice and Christianity. In comparison with earlier history painting the compositions are slimmed down, with far less scholarly detail. They convey a message meant to be timeless but proudly nationalistic: these, they declare, are the values of the British people.

William Dyce suggested that Malory's *Morte d'Arthur* would provide subjects for the Queen's Robing Room and he was set the project. It was the first major depiction of the Arthurian legend since the Middle Ages. Beginning in the autumn of 1849, Dyce painted *Religion: The Vision of Sir Galahad and his Company.* This was followed by *Generosity: King Arthur Unhorsed Spared by Launcelot* and, in 1852, *Courtesy: Sir Tristram Harping to La Beale Isoud, Mercy: Sir Gawain Swearing to Be Merciful and Never Be Against Ladies* (1854), and *Hospitality: The Admission of Sir Tristram to the Fellowship of the Round Table,* begun in 1859 but which Dyce did not live to complete. There were two other designs but these were abandoned on Dyce's death. The decoration was completed in 1870 by eighteen oak bas-reliefs depicting the lives of Arthur and Sir Galahad. What the Westminster project was intended to convey was a prestigious statement that the ethics portrayed were still viable. But, painted in the nineteenth century, the message seemed to be in an outmoded pictorial language, oblivious to the realities of industrial Britain and prettified so that they were unfaithful to the period they purported to present and to Malory. Dyce had great trouble in finding in the romance incidents that he could use to allegorize the various virtues that were thought relevant in the nineteenth century. One of those suggested, Temperance, he simply had to abandon. He also had to bowdlerize the story, leaving out the earthier details in the scenes depicted, reducing the prominence of Guinevere and avoiding the overtly Catholic symbolism.[7]

In 1850 Dyce, who had taught William Holman Hunt and Millais at the Royal Academy, became a patron to Hunt and, although the general public were not allowed to see the Robing Room frescoes, Dyce, who was pushed for time, held discussions there with Hunt and F. G. Stephens about his commission. Stephens was the first of the Pre-Raphaelite Brotherhood to paint an Arthurian subject and in it was stylistically influenced by the Lords' Chamber frescoes. Stephens' picture, which he intended for an exhibition in Liverpool, was begun in July 1849 but never completed. It is, in what survives of it, clearly a close rendering of the following passage from Tennyson's **"Morte d'Arthur"** as it was published in 1842:

> Him Sir Bedevere
> Remorsefully regarded through his tears,
> And would have spoken, but he found not words,
> Then took with care, and kneeling on one knee,
> O'er both his shoulders drew the languid hands,
> And rising bore him through the place of tombs.
>
> (ll. 170-175)

The **"Morte d'Arthur"** was the first of the poems which Tennyson ultimately shaped into the *Idylls of the King,* where he prefaced it with a longer description of the battles that result in the destruction of the Round Table. Tennyson kept the narrative strand of the tale as it is in Book XXI, Chapter 5 of Malory, although he made one significant change in that Malory's Arthur is buried and Bedevere spends the rest of his life as a monk praying for the King's soul. The last we see of Arthur in Tennyson's version is:

> Thereat once more he[that is Sir Bedevere] moved
>   about, and clomb
> Even to the highest he could climb, and saw,
> Straining his eyes beneath an arch of hand,
> Or thought he saw, the speck that bare the King,
> Down that long water opening on the deep
> Somewhere far off, pass on and on, and go
> From less to less and vanish into light.
> And the new sun rose bringing the new year.
>
> (ll. 462-469)

Whether Arthur is passing to death elsewhere or to Avilion where he will be healed to come again is left deliberately ambiguous. The more hopeful possibility was emphasized when, in incorporating the poem into the *Idylls of the King,* Tennyson altered its title from **"Morte d'Arthur"** to **"The Passing of Arthur."** Tennyson embroidered Malory with descriptions such as the clothing of the arm that catches Excalibur and the carrying of Arthur to the barge (ll. 349-360), which is famous and deservedly so.

Less successfully to my mind, he changed the final exchange between Arthur and Bedivere. In Malory Bedivere calls out to Arthur asking what he is to do left alone among his enemies. Arthur tells Bedivere to fare as best he can; he himself is going to Avilion to try to recover from his wound and if Bedivere hears no more of him he is to pray for Arthur's soul. Tennyson, in the 1842 version, turns Bedivere's question into an epitaph for the Round Table:

> Then loudly cried the bold Sir Bedivere:
> 'Ah! My Lord Arthur, whither shall I go?
> . . . . .
>
> For now I see the true old times are dead,
> When every morning brought a noble chance,
> And every chance brought out a noble knight.
> . . . . .
>
> But now the whole Round Table is dissolved
> Which was an image of the mighty world,
> And I, the last, go forth companionless,
> And the days darken round me, and the years,
> Among new men, strange faces, other minds.'
>
> (ll. 394-406)

Tennyson seems to teeter between claims for the reality of what he has depicted—"an image of the mighty world"—and the suggestion that the pictured world has no connection with the modern one—"I . . . go forth . . . among new men, strange faces, other minds." There is, too, ambiguity as to whether "mighty" refers primarily to a world of mighty beings gone forever or means "the whole world." Arthur's response is surprising:

> And slowly answered Arthur from the barge:
> 'The old order changeth, yielding place to new,
> And God fulfils himself in many ways,
> Lest one good custom should corrupt the world.
> Comfort thyself: what comfort is in me?
> I have lived my life, and that which I have done
> May He within himself make pure! but thou,
> If thou shouldst never see my face again,
> Pray for my soul. More things are wrought by prayer
> Than this world dreams of. Wherefore, let thy voice
> Rise like a fountain for me night and day.
> For what are men better than sheep or goats
> That nourish a blind life within the brain,
> If, knowing God they lift not hands of prayer
> Both for themselves and those who call them friend?
> For so the whole round earth is every way
> Bound by gold chains about the feet of God.'
>
> (ll. 407-423)

"God fulfils Himself in many ways, / Lest one good custom should corrupt the world" is ingenious rationalization, but reads as a disclaimer about the status of the Round Table as an ideal. How could the Round Table "corrupt the world"? John Sterling, in a lengthy review of the 1842 volume in the *Quarterly Review,* commented:

> The miraculous legend of "Excalibur" does not come very near to us, and as reproduced by any modern writer must be a mere ingenious exercise of fancy. The poem, however, is full of distinct and striking description, perfectly expressed; and a tone of mild, dignified sweetness attracts, though it hardly avails to enchant us. The poem might perhaps have made the loss of the magic sword, the death of Arthur, and dissolution of the Round Table, a symbol for the departure from earth of the whole old Gothic world, with its half-pagan, all-poetic faith, and rude yet mystic blazonries.[8]

Tennyson wavers, just as he does in *In Memoriam* over the physical possibilities of faith in the modern world. Arthur fades away with a possibility of return and represents in himself an uncomplicated Christian idealism that Tennyson cannot bear to relinquish. But, as in *In Memoriam*, the more worldly side of his mind knew another reality, which can be seen in the next of the idylls that he wrote, **"Nimuë"** (1856), which was to become **"Merlin and Vivien."**

In Malory the story takes only two pages and is simply the tale of a young woman incessantly pestered by an old man, whom she finally manages to lock up in a cavern. Tennyson also drew on a second, longer version, the *Romance of Merlin*, but even so he added a good deal of substance to the story—Vivien's motivation for her destructiveness, her insidious slander-mongering at Camelot, her methods of beguiling Merlin. As in the **"Morte d'Arthur,"** Tennyson ennobles Merlin, though by doing so he creates a less convincing character. The moral of the story on which Tennyson appears to insist is, as Burne Jones painted it, the folly of an old man beguiled by a femme fatale. Tennyson's Idyll ends:

> Then crying 'I have made his glory mine,'
> And shrieking out 'O fool!' the harlot leapt
> Adown the forest, and the thicket closed
> Behind her, and the forest echoed 'fool.'
>
> (ll. 969-972)

This is a marvellously ambiguous modification to the ending of the *Romance of Merlin*, which remarks, *"quil en fut depuis, et est encore tenu pour fol."* Merlin is a fool for having allowed himself to be beguiled by a woman whose wiles he understood, but she is a fool for her inability to distinguish fame from infamy. What may well strike many readers is more double-edged: if the knights are as pure as Merlin thinks, then how hard it is for them to keep any control over their reputations in the face of gossip such as Vivien spreads far and wide. And secondly, if the worldly Vivien is right, then what is the reality of the Round Table as a model of chivalry? What is "chivalry"? Vivien condemns Arthur for apparently knowing of the relationship between Lancelot and Guinevere and doing nothing about it:

> She answered with a low and chuckling laugh:
> 'Man! is he man at all, who knows and winks?
> Sees what his fair bride is and does, and winks?
> By which the good King means to blind himself,
> And blinds himself and all the Table Round
> To all the foulness that they work. Myself
> Could call him (were it not for womanhood)
> The pretty, popular name such manhood earns,
> Could call him the main cause of all their crime;
> Yea, were he not crowned King, coward, and fool.'
>
> (ll. 778-787)

Her attitude here is endorsed by her earlier scoff at Mark's assertion of Arthur's purity: "This Arthur pure!

/ Great Nature through the flesh herself hath made / Gives him the lie! There is no being pure, / My cherub; saith not Holy Writ the same?" (ll. 49-54). It is in details like this—Vivien's cheekily calling King Mark "my cherub"—that she and the *Idylls* come to life. But it is a life that belongs to Victorian society, not the hierarchy of the Middle Ages. Exactly the same thing is true of Arthur's lines on the subject in the idyll titled **"Guinevere"**:

> I hold that man the worst of public foes
> Who either for his own or children's sake,
> To save his blood from scandal, lets the wife
> Whom he knows false, abide and rule the house:
> For being through his cowardice allowed
> Her station, taken everywhere for pure,
> She like a new disease, unknown to men,
> Creeps, no precaution used, among the crowd,
> Makes wicked lightnings of her eyes, and saps
> The fealty of our friends, and stirs the pulse
> With devil's leaps, and poisons half the young.
> Worst of the worst were that man he that reigns!
> Better the King's waste hearth and aching heart
> Than thou reseated in thy place of light,
> The mockery of my people, and their bane.
>
> (ll. 509-523)

"Guinevere" was probably being written while Augustus Egg was completing *Past and Present*, which was displayed at the Royal Academy in 1858 and proved a popular handling of the theme of the fallen woman. *Past and Present* is a triptych, the first of which depicts the husband's discovery of his wife's infidelity. The scene is a comfortable middle-class sitting room. In the foreground is a woman in Victorian dress lying at her husband's feet, her hands clasped in supplication while he sits back in the chair in consternation and indecision, in his hand an intercepted letter. Beside him, prominently on a table, is an apple, which has been sliced to reveal a rotten core. On the left side in the middle ground are their two well-dressed little daughters building a house of cards. The elder, distracted by her parents, is misplacing a card that will cause the card-house to fall. On the back wall, on either side of a central fireplace, are four pictures. On the left, above a portrait of the wife, is a painting of the expulsion from Eden. On the right, above a portrait of the husband, the painting of a shipwreck. The second and third paintings are night scenes. The second depicts the two girls in adolescence. Having lost their father through his grief, they are depicted in a poor attic, one trying to comfort the other in her despair. The third painting shows the expelled and penniless wife, resting beneath the arches of a bridge by the Thames, the thin legs of her illegitimate child visible beneath her shawl. She is evidently thinking of drowning herself.

The technique that Egg uses of incorporating symbols in naturalistic ways—the house of cards, the pictures, and the apple—is one that Holman Hunt and Ford Mad-dox Brown had used in their paintings reflecting contemporary life such as *The Awakening Conscience* and *Work*. Hunt had learned the style from Hogarth and from Ruskin's praise of Tintoretto's *The Annunciation* in the Scuola di San Rocco, Venice,[9] and it provided an alternative method of allegory.

The parting of Arthur and Guinevere is Tennyson's invention—it has no precedent in Arthurian legend that I am aware of. Tennyson is more sympathetic to Guinevere than Egg to his fallen woman:

> But when the Queen immersed in such a trance,
> And moving through the past unconsciously,
> Came to that point where first she saw the King
> Ride toward her from the city, sighed to find
> Her journey done, glanced at him, thought him cold,
> High, self-contained, and passionless, not like him,
> 'Not like my Lancelot'—while she brooded thus
> And grew half-guilty in her thoughts again,
> There rode an armèd warrior to the doors.
> A murmuring whisper through the nunnery ran,
> Then on a sudden a cry, 'The King.' She sat
> Stiff-stricken, listening; but when armèd feet
> Through the long gallery from the outer doors
> Rang coming, prone from off her seat she fell,
> And grovelled with her face against the floor:
> There with her milkwhite arms and shadowy hair
> She made her face a darkness from the King.

(ll. 398-414)

In 1865 James Archer made an oil sketch which is very much based on Tennyson's description. It shows Guinevere grovelling at the feet of the armed King. In style it is very Pre-Raphaelite with rich colors and careful detail of appropriate armor. However, it is not a subject that one finds in medieval art; style and content are out of keeping with the supposed period of the subject. Art and literature here, however, interact. Tennyson introduces into his poem a vivid description of something that is very much a contemporary issue and that description is then used to make a painting. There is almost nothing in Archer's painting that is not in Tennyson's lines but the choice of the subject has two parents: Tennyson's poem and genre paintings such as Egg's. Both probably borrow from melodrama in the posture they use for the fallen woman. Tennyson incorporates in Arthur's condemnation of Guinevere the same implications of the destructiveness of a wife's infidelity that Augustus Egg had portrayed, and he does so in a way that makes the speech more Victorian than medieval in its language and reference to disease. This seems to me to be a key moment in Tennyson's remaking of the medieval story.

In Malory sexuality has a different, much less destructive role. The rift between Arthur and Lancelot is caused not by a fight over Guinevere but because in rescuing her from the stake, which is the legal penalty for her infidelity, Lancelot accidentally kills two of Gawain's brothers, men whom he would never have injured had he recognized them. Arthur is fully prepared for a reconciliation with Lancelot—after all, as he says, he can get plenty of other queens—but the death of Gawain's brothers makes Gawain Lancelot's implacable enemy and he will not allow Lancelot's reconciliation with the King. Thus develops civil war which enables Modred to effect a coup and destroy the Round Table. So, although sexual activity is far from missing in Malory's pictured world, it is neither the dominant nor underlying sin. It is more accepted and less important.

When in the *Idylls* we hear Arthur's condemnation of Guinevere as the cause of the fall of the Round Table, I think we feel that we are hearing something unjust, something that limits and modifies our opinion of Arthur. Critics such as David Staines think that our reactions are brought about by a miscalculation by Tennyson, an inability to bring Arthur to life: "The poet began his presentation of Camelot with a vivid delineation of reality in the form of Arthur's Queen, and he never managed to create an equally vivid delineation of the ideal within the reality of Arthur."[10] He sees Tennyson as having the didactic purpose of showing how necessary to all periods Arthur's values are. Although I agree with a great deal that Staines says, I would like to suggest that when we look at the *Idylls* as a whole, we see that the fault lies elsewhere, not in imaginative or technical failure but in an irremediable clash of styles, a clash that originated in the two sources of the "Morte d'Arthur" and was aggravated in their developed characteristics in the nineteenth century. The situation that Tennyson depicts, with the actions of Vivien, the failings of knight after knight, cannot simply be blamed on Guinevere. By articulating as many of the Idylls through women's voices as he does, Tennyson allows for counter arguments to those of the chivalric values. Even after the titles were changed, Enid remains the focusing consciousness of the Geraint and Enid stories, and her suffering at the hands of her chivalric knight is underlined. Vivien's cynicism may not be true in all the incidents she suggests but it is compelling. Throughout the *Idylls,* Guinevere the queen is not made a repulsive character but one with whose vivacity, moral struggles, regret, and ultimately with whose courage we can sympathize.

What Tennyson gives us in the work as a whole is a range of vision. While this is clearest in the Idyll of the Holy Grail where each of the knights sees according to his moral state, it is more widely true. There is in the work a whole range of moral response to human relationships: Elaine, whose devotion to Lancelot is the hopeless infatuation of first love; Arthur, whose idealism is seen in **"Guinevere,"** lines 457-480, but who is also shown to be unable to guide or communicate with his wife until it is too late; Lancelot, who is torn apart by conflicting loyalty to Arthur and to Guinevere, a conflict inherent in courtly love. And so on. Each position is voiced by its representative.

What the multiple vision does is to raise and leave unresolved the whole question of a code of moral action in the modern world. Tennyson possessed both an idealism that wanted a code of monogamy, loyalty, and courage, and gifts as an observer of the world around him that produced a less rosy understanding of man's nature. That is why I think that he ultimately found the form of the idylls best fitted to his work and why he was so reluctant to accept the allegorical interpretations of it.[11] Rather than being simply didactic, the poem series is exploratory, which may explain Arthur's remarkable lines in **"The Passing of Arthur,"** "The old order changeth, yielding place to new, / And God fulfils himself in many ways, / Lest one good custom should corrupt the world" (ll. 408-410). This statement simply contradicts an interpretation of Arthur's way as ideal and all else as corrupt. The polyphony of the *Idylls* allows for participation in contemporary debate: the poem displays the chivalric code and Christian values that the decoration of Parliament vaunted but also contains a profound, contemporary understanding of human psychology that was recognized by its various critics. The fissure in the work is not, I would suggest, the result of inadequate technique but the product, as in *In Memoriam,* of a conflict within Tennyson and the Age.

Notes

1. Unsigned review, *Church of England Quarterly Review* (October 1842): xii, 361-376, in John Jump, ed., *Tennyson: The Critical Heritage* (London: Routledge and Kegan Paul, 1967), pp. 132-133.

2. Hopkins to Richard Watson Dixon, February 27—March 3, 1879, *The Correspondence of Gerard Manley Hopkins and Richard Watson Dixon,* ed. C. C. Abbott, 2nd ed. (London: Oxford Univ. Press, 1955), pp. 24-25.

3. James Spedding to Tennyson, July 15, 1856, summarized by Christopher Ricks, headnote to "Merlin and Vivien" in *The Poems of Tennyson,* 3 vols. (Berkeley: Univ. of California Press, 1987), 3:393. All quotations from Tennyson are from this edition.

4. Richard Hurd, *Letters on Chivalry and Romance* (London: H. Frowde, 1911), 3:13. See Debra N. Mancoff, *The Arthurian Revival in Victorian Art* (London: Garland, 1990), pp. 27-64 for an excellent and full account of the movement, on which I am drawing in this section of my article.

5. In the 1860s the Anglican clergy could still lose their livings through too Catholic decoration of the altar or "unwise" conduct of the services. Robert Bridges writes of one such case in a letter to Lionel Muirhead, November 25, 1865, in *The Selected Letters of Robert Bridges,* ed. Donald E. Stanford (Newark: Univ. of Delaware Press, 1983), 1:85-86.

6. See Mancoff, pp. 65-100, for a detailed description of the project.

7. Christine Poulson, *The Quest for the Grail: Arthurian Legend in British Art, 1840-1920* (Manchester: Manchester Univ. Press, 1999), pp. 24-45.

8. John Sterling, *Quarterly Review* (September 1842): lxx, 385-416; the comments on "Morte d'Arthur" are reprinted in *Tennyson: The Critical Heritage,* pp. 119-120.

9. George P. Landow, *Victorian Types, Victorian Shadows* (London: Routledge and Kegan Paul, 1980), pp. 122-123.

10. David Staines, *Tennyson's Camelot: the Idylls of the King and its Medieval Sources* (Waterloo: Wilfrid Laurier Univ. Press, 1982), p. 152.

11. Staines, p. 153, quotes several of Tennyson's protests: "'They have taken my hobby, and ridden it too hard, and have explained some things too allegorically, although there is an allegorical or perhaps rather a parabolic drift in the poem'"; "I hate to be tied down to say, '*This* means *that*' because the thought within the image is much more than any one interpretation" (Hallam Tennyson, *Alfred Lord Tennyson: A Memoir,* 2 vols. [New York, 1897], 2:126-127, 134).

Anna Henchman (essay date spring 2003)

SOURCE: Henchman, Anna. "'The Globe We Groan In': Astronomical Distance and Stellar Decay in *In Memoriam.*" *Victorian Poetry* 41, no. 1 (spring 2003): 29-45.

[*In the following essay, Henchman analyzes how Tennyson's knowledge of astronomy informs* In Memoriam.]

Tennyson scholarship has yet to account for the important connections between the poet's lifelong preoccupation with astronomy and his larger poetic project. Astronomy fascinated Tennyson for its own sake, and also, I will argue, because it exposed a particular set of intellectual problems.[1] Tennyson's tutor at Cambridge (1828-1831) was the natural theologian William Whewell, who went on to write the 1833 Bridgewater Treatise *On Astronomy and General Physics.* Throughout the 1830s and 1840s, Tennyson followed contemporary debates in astronomy. He owned Whewell's *History of the Inductive Sciences from the Earliest to the Present Times* (1837), John Pringle Nichol's popular *Views of the Architecture of the Heavens* (1837), John Herschel's *Preliminary Discourse on the Study of Natural Philosophy* (1830), and Mary Somerville's *On the Connexion of the Physical Sciences* (1835).[2] He also appears to have acquired both Whewell's Bridgewater Treatise and Robert Chambers' *Vestiges of the Natural History of Creation* (1844), which begins with an evolutionary account of the origins of the universe.[3] Later in life, he had his own two-inch telescope at Aldworth and visited more powerful observatories to view double stars, and nebulae such as those in Cassiopeia and Lyra.[4] His friend Norman Lockyer, an innovator in the recent science of spectroscopy,[5] commented that Tennyson's "mind is saturated with astronomy" (Hallam Tennyson, 2:381). In later decades, Tennyson continued to follow developments in the new field of astrophysics, building up a substantial library.[6] He was particularly interested toward the end of his life in "the spectrum analysis of light, and the photographs which reveal starlight in the interstellar spaces where stars were hitherto undreamt of" (Hallam Tennyson, 2:408).

How did Tennyson's interest in astronomy infuse the form and subject matter of his poetry? A. C. Bradley has asserted that Tennyson is "the only one of our great poets . . . to whose habitual way of seeing, imagining, or thinking it makes any real difference that Laplace, or for that matter Copernicus, ever lived."[7] I will argue that what drew Tennyson to astronomy as a poetic resource are the lessons it teaches about the fragile relation between human sensory perception and conceptual ideas.

Astronomy presents peculiar challenges to sensory perception. In astronomical observation, vision has a tendency to distort, whereas in ordinary experience, one depends on vision to judge distances accurately. To do so, Richard Gregory explains, it is "necessary that retinal images should be calibrated against direct measures, such as touching objects or walking towards them and recording the size-change of the eye."[8] Neither is possible when observing celestial bodies. At such distances, vision flattens out what one sees. Astronomy pushes discrepancies between perceptual and conceptual knowledge to their most extreme. Our senses tell us that the sun is a luminous disk that rises and sets, the ground we walk on a solid, stationary expanse. Intellectually we know that what we see is not accurate, but that knowledge does not affect our sensory perception (Gregory, pp. 104, 105). By "perceptual" I mean those mental events based on sensory perception; by "conceptual," simply abstract ideas or beliefs.

While references to astronomy appear in Tennyson's poetry throughout his career, *In Memoriam A. H. H.* shows the most sustained preoccupation with astro-

nomical images and ideas. Tennyson's poetry reveals an unexpected affinity between his work as an elegist and the concerns of the nineteenth-century astronomer. The elegy is famously unprecedented in both its length and in the time it took to write, the seventeen years between Hallam's death in 1833 and the poem's 1850 publication.[9] Its 133 sections address Hallam's death from a remarkable variety of perspectives. The poem encompasses wrenching portraits of different manifestations of grief, attempts at connection with the dead through memory and the imagination, the gradual internalization of the deceased, and philosophical speculations given rise to by death and loss. This essay will suggest an analogy between the unusual form of this elegy, with its disparate sections, and the astronomical technique of parallax, which determines the distance of a star by measuring shifts in its apparent position due to the earth's own revolution round the sun. Parallax works on the principle that accurate perception of a distant object depends on its being observed from two or more disparate positions. Each section of *In Memoriam* acts as a single perspective on Hallam's death. Together they compose a trajectory that stresses the discontinuities in Tennyson's experience, yet it is precisely the range of perspectives that enables the poem to evoke the experience of death with the force and accuracy that it does.

THE NEW STELLAR ASTRONOMY: REFRACTION, FLUX, AND STELLAR DECAY

In Memoriam's astronomical references focus on several contemporary topics: the vast scale of stellar astronomy, astronomical refraction, the nebular hypothesis of the origin of the universe, and the hypothesis' darkest implication: solar and stellar decay. Each involved perceptual distortions; some, like refraction, could be predicted and corrected for, while others, like the constitution of nebulae, could not. More obvious conflicts between the perceptual and the conceptual were as present as they had ever been. While the accuracy of the Copernican model was unquestioned in Tennyson's time, the optical illusions that had deceived centuries of astronomers into believing that the earth was the center of the universe remained in place.

In the decades during which Tennyson was writing *In Memoriam,* the 1830s and 1840s, stellar astronomy was a recent invention.[10] Newton and most eighteenth-century astronomers had conceived of the "fixed stars" as unmoving reference points in the sky against which the motions of the solar system could be charted (Hoskin, p. 185). William Herschel (1738-1822) was the first to map the stellar skies comprehensively. Herschel replaced the symmetrical sphere of fixed stars with shifting astral systems separated by vast tracts of void space, the "waste places" of Section 3 of *In Memoriam.*[11] "How thinly scattered through space are the heavenly bodies," comments Whewell in 1833.[12] Herschel showed the stars to be uniform in neither their structure nor their composition. In the 1830 *Preliminary Discourse* owned by Tennyson, Herschel's son John notes that "it is only since a comparatively recent date . . . that any great attention has been bestowed on the smaller stars."[13] Herschel marvels that the "powerful telescopes" and "delicate instruments" of his time have "disclosed the existence of whole classes of celestial objects."[14] The first half of the nineteenth century saw the discoveries of many of these new celestial types: thousands of nebulae, hundreds of double stars, and the first asteroids (Hoskin, pp. 198-255). Nineteenth-century telescopes are for Tennyson the arms of science, bringing the sky within reach: "Science reaches forth her arms / To feel from world to world, and charms / Her secret from the latest moon" (Sec. 21).

Much of this new data proved difficult to interpret; as we shall see, the question of whether or not the nebulae were gaseous or solid structures was a matter of intense debate from the 1780s until 1864 (Crowe, pp. 144, 145). In other cases, scientific progress was more clear. In 1838, advancements in telescopy enabled Friedrich Wilhelm Bessel finally to measure the distance of a nearby star. Astronomers had been trying for centuries to detect an annual stellar parallax. Bessel showed the star 61 Cygni to be at a distance of 657,700 times the distance between the earth and the sun.[15]

In section 92, Tennyson uses the optical illusion of astronomical refraction for the idea that anticipation can lead one to see something before it actually appears: "such refraction of events / As often rises ere they rise." The poet glossed these lines as follows: "The heavenly bodies are seen above the horizon, by refraction, before they actually rise."[16] He uses a visual distortion in the physical world as a figure for a conceptual distortion of the mind caused by anticipation. Mary Somerville's *On the Connexion of the Physical Sciences*, which Tennyson received for Christmas in 1838, explains the phenomena of refraction.[17] Because the atmosphere inflects rays of light toward the earth, "all the celestial bodies appear to be more elevated than they really are." As a result, "*the stars are seen above the horizon* after they are set" (emphasis mine; Somerville, pp. 171, 172). She extends the effects of refraction to any vision of a distant object: "All we see is through the medium of the atmosphere . . . in consequence of the refractive power of the air, *no distant object is seen in its true position*" (emphasis mine; p. 171). In *In Memoriam,* the distant object that cannot be seen in its true position is Arthur Hallam. An 1839 letter to Tennyson's future wife Emily Sellwood echoes Somerville's passage, and directly applies the phenomena of refraction to the difficulty of knowing other persons:

> The light of this world is too full of refractions for men ever to see one another in their true positions. The

world is better than it is called, but wrong and foolish. The whole framework seems wrong, which in the end shall be found right.[18]

The analogy Tennyson makes here, between a human being and a star or planet, comes up repeatedly in *In Memoriam.* As we will see in the third section of this essay, he compares himself to Venus (Sec. 121); his own past to a "perfect star" (Sec. 24); and human beings to "worlds" (Prologue).

The leap Tennyson makes between the phenomenon of refraction and its epistemological consequences is more surprising. He implies that the distortions of earthly refractions are profound enough to threaten the "whole framework" by which we understand our own experience and other people. He departs significantly from Somerville, who stresses that the distortion involved in refraction is negligible: "no object either in or beyond our atmosphere is seen in its true place. But the deviation is so small in ordinary cases that it causes no inconvenience" (p. 173). For Somerville, refraction is an instance of optical distortion that can be corrected for. Tennyson, by contrast, converts his knowledge of refraction into a more general despair about the limits of human perception. He suggests that the difference between what human beings perceive and the true framework of things may be as dramatic as the other reversals that characterize astronomy. Behind this statement lies the subject of much of *In Memoriam*: the crisis that Tennyson experiences as a result of Hallam's death, leaving him without a spiritual framework.

The idea that the universe was not inherently stable, but existed in a state of constant flux, was one of the most radical implications of stellar astronomy. Most eighteenth-century philosophers had conceived of the solar system as an orderly clock-like mechanism that could run indefinitely (Hoskin, p. 198). Gradually, that conception was broken down. In 1783, the older Herschel detected "a motion of our solar system with respect to the stars."[19] In his 1833 Bridgewater Treatise, Whewell acknowledged a "tendency to indefinite derangement" in the solar system (p. 161). Whewell, writes Isobel Armstrong, was "deeply involved in theorising astronomy in terms of flux. He opened up a world in which the stability of the universe could not be guaranteed."[20] Chambers reflected, "Amongst the orbs, which seem so still and serene to our ordinary perceptions, we now know that there is no such thing as rest" (p. 6). The universe could no longer be viewed as a self-perpetuating structure.

The most widely accepted cosmological model for a universe in flux was "the nebular hypothesis," a name invented by Whewell for a hypothesis first proposed by Immanuel Kant, and then developed by Pierre-Simon de Laplace and William Herschel.[21] Five direct references to this hypothesis appear in *In Memoriam,* and its larger implications are found throughout the poem. The hypothesis was a theory of the origin of the universe proposing that solar systems such as ours were derived from fluid bodies of gas and matter, which gradually shaped themselves into suns, then planets, and moons around those planets. It conceived of celestial bodies like the sun and moon as evolving, introducing vast temporal scales similar to those being conceived of in contemporary geology and biology. One of the implications of this hypothesis was that the sun would eventually burn itself out. Nichol predicts the dissolution of the solar system, admitting that "the system, though strong, is not framed to be everlasting" (p. 105). Whewell goes even further, spelling out the certainty of stellar decay:

> It now appears that the courses of the heavens themselves are not exempt from the universal law of decay; that not only the rocks and the mountains, but the sun and the moon have the sentence 'to end' stamped upon their foreheads. They enjoy no privilege beyond man except a longer respite.
>
> (pp. 202-203)

Early in *In Memoriam,* Tennyson invokes these implications to express the anguish he feels in the wake of Arthur Hallam's sudden death. Through the figure of Sorrow, he articulates the idea that the entire cosmos has become lawless, empty, and moribund:

> O Sorrow, cruel fellowship,
>
> . . . . .
>
> What whispers from thy lying lip?
>
> "The stars," she whispers, "blindly run;
>   A web is woven across the sky;
>   From out waste places comes a cry,
> And murmurs from the dying sun."
>
> (Sec. 3)

Subjective perception and scientific accuracy concur powerfully in this passage. Read outside the context of contemporary astronomical debates, Sorrow's statement could be interpreted as a straightforward instance of pathetic fallacy, of the false projection of human sorrow onto the natural world. The speaker would appear to have generalized his specific grief into a universal despair. This reading would be supported by the fact that Sorrow's statements are discredited as lies before she utters them. Moreover, her claim that the stars run blindly contradicts the poet's ultimate assertion that there is "One God, one law . . . To which the whole creation moves" (Epilogue). Again, the discrepancy between Sorrow's nihilism and the Epilogue's optimism might encourage us to interpret this stanza as a false worldview produced by grief.

Tennyson draws these images of a dying sun, blind stellar motion, and waste places, however, from the very

astronomical discoveries that he himself was convinced were true. Sorrow articulates the poet's worst fears about the physical world, fears drawn directly from his reading in astronomy. The passage's scientific accuracy makes it impossible, therefore, to dismiss this view as merely the subjective misperceptions of a miserable mind. We might expect the two registers—the subjectivity of poetry and the objectivity of science—to be in conflict with one another. But in this passage the two agree. If we are persuaded by their scientific authority, we cannot dismiss Sorrow's bleak assertion as false (see Millhauser, pp. 18-19).

The nebular hypothesis was the subject of heated controversy on three levels: first, there was the nature of the evidence itself; second, the question of what that evidence did or did not prove; and third, what it would mean if the hypothesis turned out to be accurate. Today the accuracy of the hypothesis is undisputed, but in the decades prior to 1864, writes Simon Schaffer, "the nebular hypothesis carried many messages." Schaffer contrasts the contradictory evidence and arguments that William and John Herschel, Nichol, Chambers, and Whewell used to evaluate the accuracy and significance of the hypothesis (p. 131). Tennyson himself possessed several of these competing and mutually contradictory accounts of the nebular hypothesis and would have been poignantly aware of the ambiguity of the data, and of the many different conclusions that astronomers drew from the same information.

The first question, of the evidence, centered on the nature of what appeared to be patches of gaseous matter in bodies like the nebula of Orion. If gaseous nebulae could be proved to exist, they would be strong evidence in support of the hypothesis. William Herschel's discovery of thousands of nebulae appeared to support the theory, but that evidence was complicated by the fact that, as Herschel and his contemporaries developed increasingly powerful telescopes, they often found that what had appeared to be patches of luminous matter could be resolved into individual stars by stronger telescopes. This left the significance of the remaining nebulae ambiguous: was their gaseous state an illusion created by telescopes not yet powerful enough to resolve those patches of matter into stars? Herschel himself changed his mind about the nature of the nebulae (Crowe, p. 144). Initially he assumed that all nebulae were resolvable, but his 1790 discovery of an individual star surrounded by luminous matter, an event Tennyson would have read about in Nichol, made him reconsider his position.[22] Subsequent evidence tended to support the existence of gaseous nebulae, but there were exceptions. In the 1840s, at least two astronomers claimed that their new telescopes had resolved nebulae, including that of Orion, into individual stars (Crowe, pp. 167, 172-174). "The testimony of astronomers about the existence of true nebulosity," Schaffer explains, "was extraordinarily malleable. The stars gave no un-ambiguous lesson" (p. 136).

The implications of the evidence collected were similarly difficult to determine. Nichol's writing acknowledges that the nebula of Orion seems to have been resolved into stars, but does not allow resolution of that nebula to cast doubt on the accuracy of the hypothesis (Schaffer, p. 140). John Herschel, by contrast, "never allowed that true nebulosity implied the truth of the nebular formation of our Solar System," writes Schaffer. Instead, Herschel "insisted that this cosmogony could only be accepted if individual objects were seen condensing, obviously an impossible demand" (Schaffer, p. 137). The significance of the hypothesis was also at issue. Nichol and Chambers used it to argue for a teleological progression in social evolution, while Whewell used it to prove the existence of "an Intelligent Author" (Whewell, p. 189). Tennyson was himself attuned to the arbitrariness of assigning theological significance to scientific data. Months before Hallam's death, the two men looked at moths' wings and gnats' heads through a microscope. Tennyson commented, "Strange that these wonders should draw some men to God and repel others. No more reason in one than in the other" (Hallam Tennyson, 1:102). For Tennyson, Hallam's death and a shifting universe are both facts that lead him to doubt the existence of a universal law, but he stands apart from Whewell, Herschel, and Nichol in his reluctance to extract coherent conclusions out of ambiguous data.

Tennyson's five specific references to the nebular hypothesis reflect the ambiguities surrounding the theory. Two are deeply pessimistic: the first reference occurs in the Prologue: "Our little systems have their day; / They have their day and cease to be" (ll. 17-18); and the second, as we have seen, appears with the "dying sun" of Section 3.[23] Elsewhere, Tennyson casts the theory in a far more positive light. He figures the solar system as a family, describing the evening star, Venus, as the sun's daughter; when she sets with the sun, she falls "into her father's grave" (Sec. 89). This image of the solar system as a family might well have been inspired by metaphors Nichol and Chambers use to describe relations between suns and planets.[24] Nichol describes a "single sun" as "having come . . . from the womb of the Nebulae," while Chambers writes of the "mazy dances of vast families of orbs" in the universe as a whole, and a "true family likeness" among the constituents of our solar system.[25] The poem's final two references to the nebular hypothesis are part of the poem's own evolutionary thrust, in which the universe progresses toward "ever nobler ends," an ideal form of man, of which Hallam is a prototype: "They say, / The solid earth whereon we tread / In tracts of fluent heat began" (Sec. 118). In Section 103, the poet has a vision, in which one maiden chants "the history / Of that great race, which is to be. / And one the shaping of a star."

Certainty about the accuracy of the nebular hypothesis was achieved in Tennyson's lifetime: in 1864, William Huggins used a spectroscope and a telescope to show that the nebula in Draco produced bright-line spectra, proving that it was indeed "not an aggregation of stars, but a luminous gas."[26] But for Tennyson, the debate's larger epistemological implications would outlast the uncertainty surrounding this particular hypothesis.

"LIKE A STAR": STELLIFICATION, ORBING, AND SPLITTING

Tennyson is unique among his contemporaries not perhaps in the extent to which he uses stellar imagery, but in the extent to which he requires that imagery to be consistent with astronomical innovation. Precisely because recent discoveries eluded everyday sensory perception, they were easy enough for poets to overlook. Marilyn Gaull notes, for instance, that while Wordsworth and Keats knew that the stars were in perpetual motion and gradually dying out, each continued to use the stars as symbols of fixity and permanence.[27] In traditional elegies such as Milton's "Lycidas" and Shelley's "Adonais," consolation was achieved only once the poet was able to let go of the deceased's earthly incarnation, and to realize that he had been transported to a better world. One image for such a transformation is the act of stellification, of turning the deceased into a star, as Shelley does to Keats at the end of "Adonais."[28] Tennyson, like Shelley before him, maintains the elegiac convention of figuring the deceased as a star, but, unlike Shelley, revises the convention, drawing on his knowledge of astronomy.

"Adonais" and *In Memoriam* share a number of patterns which suggest that Tennyson was consciously reworking Shelley's use of astronomical imagery. Both poems invoke Urania, the muse of Astronomy, and include the allegorical figure of Sorrow. Both represent grief in celestial terms, as a clouding of the heavens. After Hallam's death, Tennyson finds himself "always under altered skies . . . My prospect and horizon gone" (Sec. 38). He writes that "A rainy cloud possessed the earth" (Sec. 30), eclipsing stars and sun; "clouds . . . drench the morning star" (Sec. 72); "The moon is hid" (Sec. 28); and "ghastly through the drizzling rain / On the bald street breaks the blank day" (Sec. 7). The day of Hallam's death is the day that "blurred the splendour of the sun" (Sec. 72). Both poets associate consolation with an unveiling of the heavens, which, for Shelley, reveals the "immortal stars."

The peculiar sensory qualities of stars make them apt images for an elegy, as the relation between sensory perception and abstract conception is a central elegiac concern. Death forces a conceptual relocation of the deceased's identity. When alive, a person's identity tends to be associated automatically with his or her body. After death, identity shifts primarily to the conceptual realm, to the memories and thoughts of other people. One aspect of the work of mourning performed within an elegy is to enact that transformation from perception to conception. The period between death and burial, to which most elegies confine themselves, constitutes a peculiar time in which the body is still available to sensory perception, but no longer the primary location of the deceased's identity. I believe that the elegiac convention of stellification grows out of stars' unique relation to the perceptual and the conceptual. Stars are just on the cusp of perceptibility; they seem to have neither substance nor dimension, but they can be seen. They provide a reassuring image for the dead: no longer physically present, the deceased remains just accessible to the senses.

In "Adonais," Shelley's stellification of Keats happens twice. First, Keats is welcomed into "the kingless sphere" that awaits his death, part of a Ptolemaic system of concentric spheres. Then, at the end of the poem, the speaker sees in Adonais an unequivocal symbol of immortality:

> burning through the inmost veil of Heaven,
> The soul of Adonais, like a star,
> Beacons from the abode where the Eternal are.
>
> (ll. 493-495)

For Shelley, grief arises out of a misperception that death is a loss, an ending, whereas, in fact, a new form of life continues. Shelley figures death as a "low mist" that obscures the dead from human eyes, but he emphasizes that, seen or unseen from earth, the stars continue to exist. For Shelley, human perception is flawed, but the universe's structure remains constant.

While his stellification of Hallam is less explicit than Shelley's transformation of Keats, Tennyson builds a sustained association between Hallam and the stars. Hallam is addressed as the "happy star" who "O'erlookst the tumult from afar" (Sec. 127) and Tennyson imagines that "Ye watch, like God, the rolling hours / With larger eyes than ours" (Sec. 51). He refers to "The starry clearness of the free" (Sec. 85) and notes, "I seem in star and flower / To feel thee some diffusive power" (Sec. 130). While Tennyson adheres to this elegiac convention, however, he has rethought what it means to compare someone to a star. It is no longer an image of immortality and coherence.

Tennyson's larger revision of stellar imagery appears in the analogies he draws between celestial bodies and human beings. He uses images of stars seen from vast distances to emphasize radical discontinuities in ideas that are commonly expected to be coherent, such as the concept of identity, or the significance of an experience like Hallam's sudden death. In these analogies, one's

present corresponds to a star or planet viewed from its own surface, one's past to a celestial body seen from afar. The poet reminisces, for instance, that when Hallam was alive, "all we met was fair and good, / And all was good that Time could bring" (Sec. 23). But in the next section he stops to question the accuracy of his own statement:

> was the day of my delight
> As pure and perfect as I say?
> The very source and fount of Day
> Is dashed with wandering isles of night.
>
> (Sec. 24)

In this passage, Tennyson evaluates his current perception of his own past by comparing the sun seen from a distance, the "source and fount of Day," to the fact he knows about its surface, that it is "dashed" with enormous "wandering" sunspots.[29]

He realizes that he must inevitably have idealized his memories of life with Hallam, and wonders what the source of that distortion is. Has his grief made him idealize Hallam? Or is it simply that distance itself produces idealized images:

> is it that the haze of grief
> Makes former gladness loom so great?
>
> . . . . .
>
> Or that the past will always win
> A glory from its being far;
> And orb into the perfect star
> We saw not, when we moved therein?
>
> (Sec. 24)

Present experience he compares to the earth as it is seen from its own surface, past experience to a "perfect" point of light, devoid of detail. Neither image is by any means comprehensive. The imagined observer begins on the surface of the planet and rises far above it until he or she can apprehend its roundness. The verb "orb" is carefully chosen to evoke the gradual, yet ultimately dramatic, perceptual shift from the apparent flatness and color of the ground to the apprehension of the roundness of the planet. With distance, the planet appears to contract into a sphere, and then into a dimensionless point, the "perfect star / We saw not, when we moved therein." Time transforms prior experience, life with Hallam, into something both apparently perfect— "the perfect star"—and disturbingly unrecognizable— "We saw not, when we moved therein."

Another instance of orbing celestial bodies occurs in an 1839 letter to Emily Sellwood, in which Tennyson again compares his past and his present, respectively, to a distant planet and the earth he stands on:

> To me often the far-off world seems nearer than the
> present, for in the present is always something unreal

and indistinct, but the other seems a good solid planet, rolling round its green hills and paradises to the harmony of more steadfast laws.[30]

By saying that the "far-off" past seems "nearer" than the present, Tennyson appears to contradict his own metaphor, for it is precisely the distance from the past that makes it seem "a good solid planet" rather than "unreal and indistinct." Nearness here means not proximity, but the point at which a past event is distant enough to come into focus. Only after it is far enough away to be apprehensible to the senses (to be seen as a "solid planet") can it then become comprehensible (understood to be subject to "more steadfast laws"). Some six months after Hallam's death, Tennyson writes to Hallam's father, apologizing that he has been unable thus far to write a tribute to his friend: "I find the object yet is too near me to permit of any very accurate delineation."[31] Where Section 24 explores the distortions of distance, these two letters suggest that proximity likewise blunts perception.

Images of orbing come up repeatedly in ***In Memoriam.*** Sometimes they refer to the earth seen from a celestial perspective, as with the "round of green" of Section 34. In Section 12 we find the speaker mentally "hast[ing] away / O'er ocean-mirrors rounded large" to hover near the ship that carries Hallam's body. Elsewhere the distances are truly astronomical. Section 76 instructs the reader to imagine ascending into space, "so distant in void space that all our firmament would appear to be a needlepoint thence."[32] This passage makes another analogy between space and time, equating "wings of fancy" to the next stanza's "wings of foresight." On an astronomical scale, Tennyson's poem is insignificant, his "songs are vain":

> Take wings of fancy, and ascend,
>   And in a moment set thy face
>   Where all the starry heavens of space
> Are sharpened to a needle's end.
>
> (Sec. 76)

Tennyson requires another extraordinary imaginative act of his reader here—to assume a perspective that shrinks the entire visible sky to the point of a needle.[33] Tennyson's mental manipulation of celestial objects becomes a sophisticated analysis of how one's location radically transforms one's perception of an object.

These images of orbing raise a crucial epistemological problem: can we predict and correct for the distortions of distance and proximity? This problem is as much a source of anxiety to the elegist struggling against the distortions of grief and memory as it is to the astronomer observing nebulae, or determining solar motion by apparent shifts in distant stars. For Tennyson the past seems to "orb into the perfect star," but he is the one

moving forward in time. He uses these images of orbed planets as a figure for looking at oneself as something both apart from, and identical to, oneself.

The schism Tennyson feels between his present and his past takes many forms. Hallam's death creates fissures not only between Tennyson's early life and the fifty-nine years by which he would survive Hallam, but also within himself, in the sequence of contradictory emotions unleashed in him by the loss. Discontinuities in his own identity prompt his use of the discontinuous planet Venus, sometimes evening, sometimes morning star:

> Sweet Hesper-Phosphor, double name
>   For what is one, the first, the last,
>   Thou, like my present and my past,
> Thy place is changed; thou art the same.
>
> (Sec. 121)

Venus' two names stem from an optical phenomenon, the change in Venus' celestial position when it is east or west of the sun. Venus becomes a touchstone for the philosophical problem of how two names can refer to the same object. The planet provides a model of the self that embodies conceptual unity in perceptual fragmentation: "Can calm despair and wild unrest / Be tenants of a single breast?" (Sec. 16).

Images of orbing are part of a lifelong preoccupation with a perceptual experiment Tennyson engages in again and again. The speaker of the 1886 **"Locksley Hall Sixty Years After"** considers the planet Venus and asks:

> Hesper-Venus—were we native to that splendour or in Mars,
> We should see the Globe we groan in, fairest of their evening stars.
>
> Could we dream of wars and carnage, craft and madness, lust and spite,
> Roaring London, raving Paris, in that point of peaceful light?
>
> (ll. 187-190)

This passage imagines an observer gazing at Venus from the earth, then standing on the surface of Venus or Mars and turning back to look at "the Globe we groan in." The earth appears as the "fairest of their evening stars." Neither the tumult of earth as we experience it when we "move therein," nor that "point of peaceful light" seen from afar capture the earth's complete identity. Paris and London are far more exciting in their particularity than are points of light. By extension, the stars as we see them from earth's surface would seem to provide an inadequate insight into *their* particularities. The final couplet poses a question about the capacity of the imagination to attach a complex set of conceptual ideas to an image as disembodied as a point of light: if we could only view the earth from a distance, could we even conceive of the "wars and carnage" it contains? The deep asymmetry between the rich specificity with which Tennyson endows terrestrial life and the peacefulness with which he characterizes the surface of Venus or Mars suggests that the answer to this question may be no. His own inability to imagine perceptual details on another planet suggests that sensory perceptions may have more power over the conceptual mind than one might expect.

Both Tennyson's images of individual celestial bodies and the larger structure of *In Memoriam* provide him with a way to allow conflicting accounts of a single experience—his response to Hallam's death—to stand next to one another without canceling one another out. This gives the elegy's conclusion a peculiar status. Where most elegies mark a relatively straightforward progression from grief to consolation, Tennyson's includes convincing accounts of doubt, grief, and inconsolability which cannot simply be dismissed as mistaken perceptions.

The elegy does mark a progression from conceiving of Hallam as a bodily presence to a more abstract conception of his identity. Early in the poem, Tennyson feels Hallam's loss as a physical absence no longer accessible to his senses. Death makes Tennyson "like to him whose sight is lost" (Sec. 66); death "bore thee where I could not see" (Sec. 22) and "put our lives so far apart / We cannot hear each other speak" (Sec. 82). Only gradually, over many years and many individual sections, does the more abstract conception of Hallam develop: "I felt and feel, though left alone, / His being working in mine own" (Sec. 85). Even then, the poet's conceptual grasp of Hallam's death is not a stable one; like the Copernican system, death is a conceptual idea unsupported by perceptual experience, and thus must be recalled and reasserted again and again.

The status of consolation is similarly contingent in this elegy. Glimpses of consolation, when they come, are depicted in terms of an unveiling of the heavens. When the poet finally overcomes his grief, that psychological progression is expressed in terms of a renewed perception of the universe's eternity and lawfulness. The speaker addresses Hallam as a quasi-celestial presence:

> Oh, wast thou with me, dearest, then,
>   While I rose up against my doom,
>   And yearned to burst the folded gloom,
> To bare the eternal heavens again,
>
> To feel once more, in placid awe,
>   The strong imagination roll
>   A sphere of stars about my soul,
> In all her motion one with law.

                                   (Sec. 122)

This image of a recovered view of the sky has affinities with Shelley's glimpse of the "immortal stars." Yet here the triumphant perception is not presented as a certain fact that the mourner is suddenly able to perceive; its accuracy is as tenuous as the earlier images of an altered sky. Tennyson emphasizes the agency of his "strong imagination" in rolling this "sphere of stars about my soul." The cosmic structure implied by this image—a revolving stellar sphere and a centered universe—has already been discredited by the poem's more rigorous astronomical images. Thus Tennyson's invocation of "the strong imagination" is tantalizingly ambiguous. On the one hand it suggests the power and flexibility that his poetry requires of its readers, the ability, for instance, to shrink the universe to a needlepoint and transport oneself through space. On the other hand "the strong imagination" suggests a mental force with the power to distort accurate perception, the mind's problematic tendency to deceive.

The form of the elegy likewise works against a sense of coherent progression from grief to consolation. Instead, like the astronomical technique of parallax, its structure works on the principle that a single subject position can never produce a complete description of the object. Missing pieces lead one to draw distorted conclusions, and only a plenitude of positions begins to produce something like the truth. Unlike parallactic measurement, the poem does not provide an identifiable answer to the questions it raises. The elegy's epilogue asserts that there is "One God, one law, one element / To which the whole creation moves." Yet the lessons Tennyson takes from astronomy caution against drawing the kind of conclusion upon which an unambiguous consolation depends. These lessons demonstrate not only that perceptions with no emotional valence can be misleading, but more surprisingly, that conceptual ideas are just as subject to emotional distortion as are sensory perceptions. What can be achieved in astronomy through parallax is approximated through the continual array of disparate positions that *In Memoriam* puts forth.

Notes

1. The most comprehensive treatment of Tennyson's knowledge of astronomy is Milton Millhauser, "Fire and Ice: The Influence of Science on Tennyson's Poetry," Tennyson Society Monographs (Lincoln: Tennyson Society, 1971). Two excellent, if brief, accounts of Tennyson and astronomy are Jacob Korg, "Astronomical Imagery in Victorian Poetry," in *Victorian Science and Victorian Values: Literary Perspectives,* ed. James Paradis and Thomas Postlewait (New Brunswick: Rutgers Univ. Press, 1985), pp. 148-153, and A. J. Meadows, *The High Firmament: A Survey of Astronomy in English Literature* (Leicester: Leicester Univ. Press, 1969), pp. 170-176. See also Norman

Lockyer, *Tennyson as a Student and Poet of Nature* (1910; New York: Russell and Russell, [1972]).

2. Records of the books in Tennyson's library come from *Tennyson in Lincoln: A Catalogue of the Collections in the Research Centre,* vol. 1, compiled by Nancie Campbell (Lincoln: Tennyson Society, 1971). Relevant 1830s texts include Nichol (No. 1688), Somerville (No. 2073), and Whewell, *History of the Inductive Sciences* (No. 2322). Eleanor Bustin Mattes writes that Tennyson "seems to have come into possession of J. F. W. Herschel's *A Preliminary Discourse on the Study of Natural Philosophy* in October 1843," *In Memoriam: The Way of a Soul* (New York, Exposition Press, 1951), p. 76. We can be certain that Tennyson had some earlier acquaintance with Herschel's work, as cited in Nichol, Somerville, and Charles Lyell.

3. *The Letters of Alfred Lord Tennyson,* vol. 1, 1821-1850, ed. Cecil Y. Lang and Edgar F. Shannon (Cambridge: Harvard Univ. Press, 1981) gives more evidence of what Tennyson was reading at this time, possibly including Whewell's Bridgewater Treatise. As Whewell was his tutor, we can safely assume familiarity with Whewell's astronomical theories. James A. Secord records Tennyson's acquisition of Chambers in *Victorian Sensation: The Extraordinary Publication, Reception, and Secret Authorship of Vestiges of the Natural History of Creation* (Chicago: Univ. of Chicago Press, 2000), p. 9.

4. Hallam Tennyson, *Alfred Lord Tennyson: A Memoir by His Son,* 2 vols. (1897; New York: Greenwood Press, 1969), 1:384; Lockyer, *Tennyson,* p. 4.

5. Michael Hoskin, *The Cambridge Illustrated History of Astronomy* (New York: Cambridge Univ. Press, 1997), p. 268.

6. Astronomical works Tennyson acquired after 1850 include: Robert Ball, *Story of the Heavens* (1885; No. 488); Richard Proctor, *Half-Hours with the Telescope* (1868; No. 1836) and *Poetry of Astronomy* (1881; No. 1837); Norman Lockyer, *Spectroscopic Observations of the Sun* (1870; No. 1414); William Huggins, *Solar Corona* (1885; No. 1203); Willis Nevins, *Christianity and Astronomy* (1876; No. 1682); William Robinson, *First Chapter of the Bible and Last Chapter of Astronomical Science* (1856; No. 1889); and Alexander Keith Johnston, *School Atlas of Astronomy* (1869; No. 1270).

7. A. C. Bradley, *A Commentary on* In Memoriam (London, 1930), cited in Robert E. Ross's edition of *In Memoriam* (New York: Norton, 1973), p. 95.

8. Richard Langton Gregory, *The Intelligent Eye* (New York: McGraw-Hill, 1970), p. 104.

9. Peter Sacks, *The English Elegy: Studies in the Genre from Spenser to Yeats* (Baltimore: Johns Hopkins Univ. Press, 1985), p. 167.

10. Michael J. Crowe, *Modern Theories of the Universe from Herschel to Hubble* (New York: Dover Publications, 1994), pp. 71-145; and Hoskin, pp. 198-255. Tennyson would have read Nichol, pp. 7, 19.

11. Citations from *In Memoriam* and other poems come from *The Poems of Tennyson,* ed. Christopher Ricks, 3 vols. (Berkeley: Univ. of California Press, 1987). Section number follows in parentheses.

12. William Whewell, *Astronomy and General Physics Considered with Reference to Natural Theology* (London, 1834), p. 274. This edition also bears a title page with the title *The Bridgewater Treatises . . . Treatise III,* Fourth Edition.

13. John Herschel, *Preliminary Discourse on the Study of Natural Philosophy* (London, 1830), p. 279.

14. Herschel, pp. 282-283. Also Somerville, pp. 413-451; Nichol, pp. 7-34; Chambers, pp. 1-6; Whewell's *Inductive Sciences,* 2:268-271; 290-296.

15. Crowe, pp. 152-165. For a contemporary account, see Chambers, p. 3.

16. Tennyson's explanation, cited in Ross, Sec. 92, p. 59, note 2.

17. *Tennyson in Lincoln* lists Somerville's 1837 edition: "on fly-leaf 'A. Tennyson, Xmas Day, 1838'" (No. 2073), 1:95.

18. Tennyson to Emily Sellwood, 1839, extracted in Hallam Tennyson, 2:168.

19. Chambers, p. 3. See also Nichol, p. 57, and Chambers, p. 155.

20. Isobel Armstrong, *Victorian Poetry: Poetry, Poetics and Politics* (New York: Routledge, 1993), p. 42.

21. Simon Schaffer, "The Nebular Hypothesis and the Science of Progress," in *History, Humanity and Evolution,* ed. James R. Moore (New York: Cambridge Univ. Press, 1989), pp. 131-164; Crowe, pp. 76-185; and Secord, pp. 57-59. Schaffer and Secord both record the fact that Whewell coined the term. Tennyson would have read Nichol, pp. 71-115, and Whewell, pp. 159-191.

22. Nichol describes this event, citing William Herschel, pp. 72-73. The citation comes from Her-

schel's 1791 paper "On Nebulous Stars, Properly So Called," excerpted in Crowe, pp. 125-136.

23. Ross mentions only three references to the nebular hypothesis.

24. My thanks to the editors, Gowan Dawson and Sally Shuttleworth, for alerting me to this specific connection between Tennyson's metaphor and those in Nichol and Chambers and for their many other helpful suggestions.

25. Chambers, pp. 17 and 9 respectively; Nichol, pp. 93-94.

26. William Huggins, excerpted in Crowe, p. 187.

27. Marilyn Gaull, "Under Romantic Skies: Astronomy and the Poets," *Wordsworth Circle* 51, no. 1 (1990): 38.

28. See Sacks, pp. 53-55, 162-165, 171.

29. The existence of sunspots had been known for centuries, but John Herschel had measured them in 1836; Somerville, pp. 425-426.

30. Tennyson to Emily Sellwood, 1839, excerpted in Hallam Tennyson, cited in Ricks, 3:156.

31. Tennyson to Henry Hallam, February 14, 1834, *Letters,* 1:108, cited in Ricks, 2:307.

32. Tennyson's explanation, cited in Ross, Sec. 76, p. 45, note 1.

33. A similar image of the firmament viewed from a distance appears in John Milton's *Paradise Lost,* ed. Merritt Y. Hughes (New York: Macmillan, 1962), 2.1046-52, p. 59.

Larry Brunner (essay date fall 2003)

SOURCE: Brunner, Larry. "'I Sit as God': Aestheticism and Repentance in Tennyson's 'The Palace of Art.'" *Renascence* 56, no. 1 (fall 2003): 43-54.

[*In the following essay, Brunner delineates Tennyson's representation of aestheticism and repentance in "The Palace of Art."*]

Alfred Lord Tennyson provides an interesting point of departure for readers of **"The Palace of Art"** by recalling an observation by Archbishop Trench of Dublin when they were undergraduates at Trinity Cambridge: "Tennyson, we cannot live in Art." The poet then observes that the poem is "the embodiment of my own belief that the Godlike life is with man and for man" (Grey and Tennyson 80). This belief is demonstrated by revealing the consequences of life lived in art, life which opposes God and neglects the Godlike life which

affirms and realizes true humanity. To live in art, the poem demonstrates, is to live for selfish delight, which issues not in the Godlike, but in the hellish. Tennyson presents a detailed analysis of prideful and isolated aestheticism and rejects its selfish solitude in favor of art that humbles itself before God and before other people as the objects of God's love.

This early allegory offers insight into a useful generalization about Tennyson as a creative artist: he is seldom satisfied with mere accurate observations of states of mind. He seeks to relate these states to a moral worldview. In **"The Palace of Art"** we see that in this worldview art has a high place, but not the supreme place, of value. Such considerations provide a fundamental approach to understand why Tennyson wrote and why he was so widely read. However, only one significant critical essay on this poem, by Richard Cronin, has appeared in the last decade. Perhaps because **"The Palace of Art"** is a relatively early work, it has not received what may be its due in the attention of contemporary criticism; also, much of that criticism is impatient, for political or cultural reasons, of any assertion of the moral absolutes Tennyson assumes in this poem.

In Tennyson's narrative, the soul of the aesthete—presented as feminine in gender—builds the Palace of Art as a resort for her own selfish solitude: "My soul would live unto herself / In her high palace there" (11-12), action and attitude which "shuts Love out" (prologue 14)—love of both God and man. Speddings, a contemporary reviewer of the poem, offered a telling assessment of this poem's effect and intention, finding that it "represents allegorically the condition of a mind which, in the love of beauty, and the triumphant consciousness of knowledge, and intellectual supremacy, in the intense enjoyment of its own power and glory, has lost sight of its relation to man and God" (quoted in Baum 83). Intellectual pride, expressed in aesthetic arrogance, leads to inevitable judgment. The poem's assumption that God will stand ultimately in judgment upon art and artist (and critic!) has not been well received by some modern critics. Upset by its moralizing close, Tucker for one finds the poem "confused and ultimately compromised" (117). Confusion here is functional, accurately revealing the disharmony and compromise of a life lived for vain indulgence. Baum sees in the poem "the young poet arguing with himself—some say, preaching to himself—about a question which concerns him particularly, the ethics of his profession" (85). The Victorians' special concern about the social function of the artist is clearly in evidence here, but it is perhaps an overstatement to see "argument" here—indeed, that the poem seems excessively "pat" or static may be its greatest flaw. Since the narrator/speaker is giving us a report of completed action from the perspective of a now-received revelation, argument as debate or dialogue is nowhere in evidence. The speaker offers experienced truth, exhortation instead of persuasion.

As the speaker's soul has conceived it, art's function is pure self-realization; "art for art's sake" is really "art for *my* sake"—my pleasure, my fulfillment. Art as such is not reverenced—the soul loves art for what it does, namely providing elegant reasons for intellectual pride to approve of itself. Beauty, knowledge, even perceptions of "good" are meant to function toward self-validation. The aesthete's soul seeks beauty and art for its own effects, its self-justifying "utility," in Benthamite terms.

As the Palace of Art is created by the aesthete's imagination, it offers a landscape in each room to satisfy "every mood of mind . . . gay, or grave, or sweet, or stern," and the soul claims to have achieved "not less than truth designed" (90-92); Tennyson here clearly expects a contrast with truth revealed. The soul's prideful self-sufficiency allows it to claim a "truth" without objective foundation, a self-generated truth that can be designed, built, possessed and so controlled (W. B. Yeats would heartily approve of this notion of truth designed, but Tennyson intends to present its inherent self-defeating futility and falsehood). Designing truth, the soul seeks to "reign . . . apart, a quiet king" (14). This assertion of power and creative control is cheese in the trap which the palace becomes. The prideful assertion grows when the soul asserts not only "truth designed," but finally "not less than life designed" as her own (128). In her pride, the soul asserts her prerogative to design truth, define reality, and thereby design life, as art attains to life. The artist thereby becomes his own creation, the author of life, his own god.

Swollen with pride that invites comparison—compare Ozymandias's "look on my works ye mighty, / And despair"—the soul challenges all with "who shall gaze upon / My palace with unblinded eyes . . . ?" (42). In loving, perhaps fulsome, detail, Tennyson presents the various features of the palace's elegant artifacts. Among these, a mosaic depicts "cycles of the human tale / Of this wide world" (145-147), indicating the cool aesthetic distancing which characterizes the aesthete's approach (compare Yeats's "Cast a cold eye / On life, on death"). The soul affirms her superiority to the human tale, using art to disconnect from the human and prove itself superior to its sufferings (and so to its lessons). Goslee observes: "within her inner searching [the soul] is able to reduce the whole tragedy of human social history to a decorative pattern" (42). This "human tale" displays a panorama of human misery and trial, in which the human is a toiling "beast of burden," "pricked with goad and stings" (149-50). The grotesque and capricious violence of political upheaval is seen as a tiger plays "rolling to and fro / The heads and crowns of

kings" (151-52). An uninvolved and dispassionate philosophic distancing here blocks compassion or the demand for intelligent intervention. Broken strength and frustrated hope appear in the choice plan of the mosaic: "there rose an athlete, strong to break or bind / All force in bonds that might endure" (153-54), but such promising prowess is ever to be cast down and dissipated: "And here once more like some sick man declined / And trusted any cure" (155-56). No cure is found for human mortality in the Palace of Art, but the soul, superior, sees this only as a pleasant melancholy to be tasted but not imbibed, a sadness which could never speak to her *own* condition.

Exultant, superior, the soul in her art has expressed life, contained it, and controlled it. Human experience serves art, art which masters life by giving it aesthetic expression. The soul thrills in her proud transcendence: "Over these she trod" (157), and reaching beyond, "she took her throne" (158). She finally glorifies herself completely, crying "O God-like isolation which art mine" (197), contemptuously dismissing the unwashed mass of humankind as "the darkling droves of swine" (199), living in "filthy sloughs" to "wallow, breed and sleep" (202). Luce identifies the swine as "those humbler human brethren of the plain" (35). Filled with irrational passions, these common masses are driven to the deep by "some brainless devil," recalling the Gadarene swine possessed by demons. The misguided human herd is but fodder for the soul's prideful exaltation of itself above such common rabble. Certainly the palace is shut to such as these; no pearls are to be set before *these* swine!

Having dismissed the rest of humanity as an unwashed herd of pigs, the soul is jarringly content to "prate" of "the moral instinct" and of resurrection "as hers by right of full-accomplish'd Fate" (205-07). Her moral superiority and victory over death are her own destiny, owed to no one. Her foolish chatter betrays the crumbling underpinnings of a foolish and obtuse pride, soon to collapse in fear and dismay. Despite an earlier passing allegiance to "the Great and Wise" (195), the soul claims "possession of man's mind and deed" (209); she assumes a superiority which judges and dismisses every form of faith: "I care not what the sects may brawl. / I sit as God holding no form of creed, / But contemplating all" (210-12). One wonders at the meaning of such contemplation—the Palace offers images of Christ, saints, Hindu gods, myths of various sorts; if no creed is *ever* to command submission, why bother to study them at all? Why should they even interest a soul needing only itself? Contemplating all, yet believing nothing, the soul has no self-knowledge.

The soul delights "all alone . . . to hear her echo'd song" (174-75), and has imagined that her "cycles of the human tale" (146) are "so wrought they will not fail" (148). If they are true indicators of human weakness and futility as well as aspiration and achievement, they must stand in truth. But the soul imagines much more, assuring a protective and immunizing function of art, an ivory tower superiority which cannot fail. But it does, and spectacularly. Immortal poets and wise men appear in portrait—Milton, Shakespeare, Dante, Homer, Plato, Bacon—but they are at last decorations for a fine burial, stifling, enclosed, stagnant. Shaw posits: "If the soul were to become as immaculate and remote as these portraits, it would be dead; and a chill descends whenever we feel behind the poem Tennyson's desolate truth, that for the soul art has become not an affair of life and people, but a tomb" (58). Hughes argues that the poem "is about the possession, the hugging close to oneself, of art, not the process of creation" (87). But in fact both attitudes are undercut by Tennyson's analysis—the Palace becomes an airless trap, enclosed and stifling, but this same palace is also the product of puissant creativity, made on the spot. Creation here is motivated by arrogant self-sufficiency; the romantic trap of solipsism now closes on the speaker. Creativity itself can be corrupted, as C. S. Lewis notes in *The Great Divorce*: "Every poet and musician and artist, but for Grace, is drawn away from love of the thing he tells, to the love of the telling until, down in Deep Hell, they cannot be interested in God at all but only in what they say about Him" (81).

Jordan argues that the expansive description which fills much of the poem was a flaw: "Formal containment was a problem: **'The Palace of Art'** was a series of word-pictures which in spite of its neat quatrains had no necessary limits, no principle of exclusion" (33). But perhaps the medium is the message—an undisciplined mind, moving without constraints of commitment to extra-personal values, must be driven by its own insatiable and confused appetites. The scattered images in the palace really argue a tasteless eclecticism which can only reject whatever does not feed an egocentric pride. The palace's artifacts are, as in Hardy's "The Convergence of the Twain," "jewels in joy designed / To ravish the sensuous mind," and like those on his sunken ship, they come to "lie lightless," "bleared and black and blind" (Ransom 42) in the dark morgue which the palace becomes.

The excessive display of undisciplined decoration offered by the aesthete soul in her palace argues vulgarity of purpose: "Most of the poem is detailed description of the art adorning the building, which sounds rather like Xanadu as constructed by the architect of the Crystal Palace" (Martin 163). As often happens, tastelessness issues in monstrous scale, witness the "huge crag-platform" (5), "ranged ramparts" (6), "royal-rich and wide" in size (20), a "spacious mansion" (234), with "long-sounding corridors" (53), all of which signals the sort of swelling intemperate expansiveness which produces the monstrous vulgarity of Las Vegas casinos. Ri-

chards finds "something corrupt in this widely eclectic taste," recalling the excesses of Browning's Bishop of St. Praxed. The past is to be "rifled and appropriated for self-indulgent delectation." He casts a sidelong shuddering glance at other such "treasure houses" as William Randolph Hearst's monstrous castle, the architectural and decorative muddle at San Simeon, half-seriously observing "Tennyson might have a lot to answer for" (207). The poet, of course, invites judgement of aesthetic excess.

The soul's intention in all this wide-ranging splendor is simply selfish satisfaction, a room for every humor, Star Trek holodecks of aesthetic experience: summer morn for hunting, solitary tract of sand, windy waste, stormy plain with winding river, harvest scene, snowy mountains, English home on dewy pastures. If that were not enough—nothing could be—there is more: "Nor these alone, but every landscape fair / As fit for every mood of mind" (89-90). The palace is the "'locus classicus' of aesthetic escapism," a place to "realize the dreams of . . . imagination" (Richards 206). Sheer delight in imaginative power invests all—even the palace towers have self-moving bells giving "silver sound" (130). In its pleasure house the soul is "well-pleased," abiding "in bliss" amid rooms "fit for every mood" in which no caprice is denied. The soul offers herself "all things fair to sate my various eyes! / O shapes and hues that please me well!" (193-4). Even the gloom beneath is "grateful" (54).

As though to avoid incipient charges of hedonism, the soul venerates wisdom in the Palace of Art, but as images only, not working ideas—the sort of name-dropping portraiture mentioned earlier; but none of their hard-won insights into human experience come into play. Instead, we find gestures—"There was Milton," "Beside him Shakespeare," "And there . . . Dante"—casual pointing-out, the show of wisdom only. The soul, seeking to control these minds in art, pretending to absorb their insights, reveals the shallow dilettantism of the aesthete's approach to life and to art. After the narrator speaks of "truth designed," Christian faith is invoked as a series: "every legend fair" (125), issuing in the claim to "life designed." The palace here anticipates a Paterian religion of art, stirring the aesthetic impulse with no slight hint of self-sacrifice or obedience. The first such stanza reveals "the maid-mother by a crucifix" amid warm pasture beneath branches carved of sardonyx, "smiling babe in arm" (93-96). The odd anachronistic disjuncture of crucifix with mother-and-child indicates the lack of sensitive conviction about the subject; *madonna-cum-crucifix* will not trouble one who does not bother to ponder art's significance but only registers its impressions. Angels rise and descend, as on a Jacob's ladder (143-44), "with interchange of gift," but without the patriarch's realization that he found himself in the presence of God, at the gate of heaven—

the palace offers decorative seraphs, bringing gifts but never judgments. In fact, all the Christian references among the several fair legends seem artifacts only, without a hint of responsive reverence or conviction; after madonna with crucifix, Saint Cecilia sleeps by her organ as an angel watches, followed immediately by Islamic houris, Arthurian myth, a Hindu god, Zeus and Europa, and flying Ganymede. The ordering—or disordering—indicates the casual non-referential quality of conviction in the Palace. A smorgasbord of "every legend fair" of the Caucasian mind is also included (intending all of European culture). This mixture of contradictory allegiances verges on the grotesque and completely undercuts serious responsive faith. As Goslee notes, the "maid mother by a crucifix" allows escape from "any challenge from Jesus's teachings in this conflation of his birth and death" (42).

The palace offers "both luxury and protection" (Kissane 47), gratifying the self-indulgent craving of the soul for a buffer, albeit transparent, from the world outside. The palace is "a worldly pleasure-house," echoing the "stately pleasure dome" of "Kubla Khan," offering aesthetic delight, delicious escape, and no notion that this beauty should aspire to truth; beauty means pleasure alone. Critics have suggested that the disproportionate structure of the poem, two-thirds elaborate description and one-third moral reflection and psychological probing, suggests that Tennyson's true sympathy is with aesthetic withdrawal after all. But this proportion is functional, demonstrating the very imbalance he critiques. The palace must arouse, be elaborately built and furnished, to demonstrate its power to entrap. The prefatory poem prepares us for the coming catastrophe from the start: "he that shuts love out, in turn shall be / Shut out from Love, and on her threshold lie / Howling in outer darkness" (14-16). We anticipate the sudden collapse of the soul's self-sufficiency in this allusion to the casting out of the presumptuous uninvited wedding guest of Matthew 22, thrust into outer darkness.

The soul intends to manipulate and control art on her own terms, holding it at a safe emotional and spiritual distance, avoiding possible personal engagement; art's power to challenge and provoke change is simply set aside. Lionel Trilling notes a parallel tendency in modern literary criticism: "It has taught us how to read certain books; it has not taught us how to engage them. . . . Attributing to literature virtually angelic powers, it has passed the word to the readers of literature that the one thing you do not do when you meet an angel is wrestle with him" (200). The "sinful soul possessed of many gifts" (prologue 3) expresses perfect self-confidence in its own power to "Cast a cold eye / On life, on death" and maintain its unshakable position: "Trust me, in bliss I shall abide / In this great mansion, that is built for me, / So royal-rich and wide" (18-20). This pride goes before destruction, this haughty spirit

rises to fall. It is a telling observation that the faces of "the Great and Wise, / my gods, with whom I dwell" are silent. These mute idols can offer no corrective counsel because the soul is not listening to wisdom. The soul, anticipating Paterian aesthetics, desires a religion of impression, of pleasant visions; it seeks to hold the form of religion but deny the power of it. Although the "riddle of the painful earth" flashes "full oft" through the soul in solitude (213-14), she refuses to find her place in that pain. In Trilling's analysis, the soul maintains critical distance and will not wrestle with this angel, refusing revelation and reality. Instead, exulting in her power, the soul sings her songs alone, enthroned between the oriel windows depicting Plato and Bacon, making a proud trio "of those who know." The irony that these men, among others, were "fountainheads of change" is complete when the soul is seen complacent in stasis, refusing corrective insights, like Tennyson's Lotos Eaters disengaged in cool aestheticism.

The soul's self-satisfied arrogance rises to a height; "Joying to feel herself alive," she declares herself "Lord over Nature, Lord of the visible earth, / Lord of the senses five," all the while "communing with herself" (178-81). Such presumptuous and self-proclaimed lordship invites moral disaster; it precludes communion with God, since God tolerates no rivals and shares his glory with no other. Nature has one Lord only. Unlike God, the soul is indifferent to human welfare or disaster: "Let the world have peace or wars / 'T is all one to me" (182-83). Asserting Lordship, the sinful soul even lights lamps of gemstone "To mimic heaven," recalling the "godlike imitated state" of Satan in *Paradise Lost*: "O God-like isolation which art mine" (197).

The prologue's observation that the soul "did love beauty only" and loves knowledge and good only for their beauty defines an aesthetic impulse so narrow that self-sacrifice, compassion, or altruism are discarded. Seeking only beauty, the soul's hedonistic self-sufficiency "shuts love out"; love needs more than mere self-gratification. The soul maintains "her solemn mirth" (215), knowing that the experience of pleasure must carry the entire meaning of its existence; pleasure here is a very serious business. As C. S. Lewis observed about Walter Pater, the soul must "prepare for pleasure as if it were martyrdom" ("Literature" 10). Ultimately a settled and enervating stasis fills this aesthetic life, as all real ties to others dissolve and the soul collapses into increasing despair. This collapse is anticipated throughout, yet comes suddenly. After three years of thriving and prospering in its enclosed garden of delight, "on the fourth she fell, / like Herod, when the shout was in his ears, / Struck thro' with pangs of hell" (218-220). The soul suddenly faces divine judgment; in Acts 12 Herod accepts godlike elevation, dressed in royal robes and seated on a throne—"I sit as God"—

and he is there destroyed for his pride, eaten by worms. The soul has claimed divinity, sitting on its throne, and is now to receive a redemptive judgment, eaten by despair.

In the gnawing of despair, the soul dreads and loathes the very solitude that had seemed so delicious before. Seeking to save face, she attempts to judge these new emotions, no longer self-controlled, as beneath her, in "scorn of herself" (231). In turn, this mood is replaced by cynical "laughter at her self-scorn" (232), as she vainly musters multiple defenses to maintain self-possession. As the process of judgment continues, the soul is "exiled from eternal God, / Lost to her place and name," and shut up "as in a crumbling tomb, girt round / With blackness as a solid wall" (273-74). Like the universe in Thomas Carlyle's "Everlasting Nay," the palace is becoming "a charnel house with spectres." Attempting to recover poise, the soul reasserts rights of possession—"'What! is not this my place of strength,' she said, / 'My spacious mansion built for me?'" (233-34)—all to no avail. In dark corners of this "place of strength" are "uncertain shapes" (238); these horrors increase, becoming overwhelming: phantasms weeping blood, nightmare shades with hearts aflame, corpses dead three months, standing against the walls. Exiled from God, dying a spiritual death, the sinful soul begins "moulding with the dull earth's moulding sod" (261); its true condition, like the fateful portrait of Dorian Gray, is revealed all unwillingly in the palace's new images of terror, disease, and death.

The tomb, once a palace, now stifles the soul with a growing horror of enclosure: "'No Voice breaks thro' the stillness of this world: / One deep, deep silence all!'" (259-60). No longer "Lord over Nature," "communing with herself" in "Godlike isolation," the soul finds her cool sanctuary dissolving to a sweating hell of loneliness and fear; she herself becomes an "uncertain shape" growing more horrible in the stifling darkness—"A spot of dull stagnation . . . seem'd my soul," cut off from the life and vitality of the outer world: "motions infinite / making for one sure goal" (245-48). Solitude has become fearful loneliness weeping for companionship, the ivory tower a prison cell.

In its misery, the soul's claim to "take possession of man's mind" (209) is especially ironic, since she cannot now control her own thought. "When she would think," God's hand works confusion, dividing completely "the kingdom of her thought," as the "airy hand" wrote "*mene mene*" (225-28), dividing Belshazzar's kingdom in the book of Daniel. "Slothful shame" ensues in the soul's growing self-knowledge, as she hates both life and death, without comfort in either time or eternity, since both are fearful. As a lost soul cast into outer darkness, the soul cries in torment, "I am on fire within" (285). Desperate for rescue, she asks, "What is it that

will take away my sin, / And save me lest I die?" (287-88). Implicit here is the *corrective* intent of these plagues of despair which God has allowed, "Lest she should fail and perish utterly" (221). The soul, renouncing its godlike status, and recognizing its deep need of redemption, realizes at last a merciful judgment. The hideous nightmare loathing issues in reconciliation and truth. Having been "plagued with sore despair," the soul can read the "riddle of the painful earth" with sharp new insight.

By the close, the speaker/narrator of the poem has become intensely self-critical and disillusioned about her entire aesthetic program. That "we cannot live in art," as Trench said to Tennyson, has become fundamental knowledge; mere aestheticism has been displayed, then judged. Smith observes that to say "the moral of the allegory is that a poet must leave his solitary fancy and go to work with his talents in the world of men" is too simple (26); indeed so—the artist must first confront and be confronted by his responsibility to others and to God. The most powerful passages, despite the disparity Smith notes—"fifty-five stanzas for the Palace, one stanza for the cottage" (26)—relate to the consequences of isolation, so distancing the reader from the soul's fatal error. Tennyson has not mistaken his aim. However, Tucker labels Tennyson as "pathological" in the poem, "aesthetically torn," purposing "to blinker his despairing vision and cloak its findings in pious moralities" (118). (Few things are more unpopular now than "pious moralities.") Tucker continues, finding "an extraneous moralism" that "invades the parable to deform its conclusion" (118). But one wonders what else could ensue? Throughout, the poem's aim has been a critique of selfish pride-provoking intellectual display and misuse of art, which Tennyson dislikes as thoroughly as he does asceticism (compare "St. Simeon Stylites"). The poem defines its subject as the experience of a "sinful soul possess'd of many gifts," investing itself in the squandering of those gifts. Buckley observes that the poem records the poet's "reluctant sense of social responsibility" (53). But is it "reluctant"? If anything, the poem embraces a bit too zestfully the resolution of social utility—the pleasure house is not destroyed, and may "perhaps" be inhabited again. No destruction has occurred, only a radical shift of attitudes.

Baum supposes a conflict in Tennyson between "man and God" and art, and perhaps too readily posits that Tennyson's "instincts as a poet were of course all for art" (85). But surely he has other instincts *as a poet*. The point of **"The Palace of Art"** is precisely that art (and the artist) needs engagement with life for either satisfaction or meaning. Tennyson had not reached a point where he needed no audience, either God or man. The poem expresses no brief against art—it attacks selfishness and its stifling limitation of art. Baum complains that Tennyson "made art needlessly odious and selfish and sinful, and in the last stanza took back what he had given" (86). But the poem nowhere attacks art as such—its focus is the soul's improper disengagement from the true concerns of art. Kissane notes that "Tennyson's morbidity made guilt a more or less habitual feeling, but his artist's pride would not let him condemn his handiwork" (49). But this very pride is what the poem *does* condemn. Further, guilt here is not indulged but rather purged. The artist's true greatness is expressed in humility before God and before the example of other great minds and artists. Shaw implies some sort of change of principle as the poem progresses: it was "begun . . . by the Romantic poet of sensuous luxury" only to be "taken over by the Victorian poet . . . critical of escape" (53). But the intention of the poem and its development do not shift from the prologue's assertion that the poem is "a sort of allegory" illustrating the career of "a sinful soul . . . that did love beauty only," finding "he that shuts Love out, in turn shall be / Shut out from Love . . ." (14-15 prologue). Having said that, we must also observe that much of **"The Palace of Art"** shows the pleasure art offers the imagination, the poet's own delight in the creative process. And in the end this delight is not rejected in some puritanical fit—it is affirmed: the palace is not to be torn down. It needs only a new inhabitant, the soul purged of fatal pride and luxury, living there *with* others. Art is placed in its proper context of service to God and love to others; the palace remains—not destroyed, but cherished. In the last stanza, even to the repentant eye, the palace is "so lightly, beautifully built" (294).

An intriguing question is raised by the final few lines of the poem, when the repentant soul, discarding her "royal robes," says, "Make me a cottage in the vale . . . / Where I may mourn and pray" (291-92). Who is addressed here? Is this internal dialogue, as the soul seeks a very different place for spiritual healing, in the vale with people instead of on a splendid rampart above? Or is it in fact a prayer, asking that God's judgment not destroy "my palace towers . . . so lightly, beautifully built"? This seems no demand, but supplication, in the hope that "Perchance I may return with others there / When I have purged my guilt" (295-96). Perhaps the palace may become a real home and a genuine blessing when its delights are *shared*; until then, humility and contrition must seek a simple cottage.

Some critics find this conclusion unsatisfying. Tucker sees Tennyson indulging an "evasion of responsibility, which drains his poem of the moral profundity it wishes to claim" (119), while Ricks calls it "the strangest of all Tennyson's conclusions in which nothing is concluded, a bathos that swallows its poem" (95). I would agree that the poem winds up abruptly, finishing with a jolt, but is this really bathos? What other ending, given the allegory's intention, would seem more appropriate?

Shrug off the soul's despair and desolation? Pull down the palace? Escapist aestheticism is the brunt of attack, the attitude of the soul, not what it has valued. Art is not the dead end, but rather "loving Beauty only." As pretense is discarded with its royal robes, a cottage, an ordinary dwelling, seems fit for prayer, confession, and regeneration, a place to "mourn and pray" (292). The soul seeks reconciliation with God, seeks Reality, not merely static non-referential representations of it.

Smith aptly observes that "This palace is no clay pigeon tossed into the air to be shot down by a virtuous social conscience" (25). Indeed not—it remains treasurable. Yet the issue here is not merely social, but spiritual—the poem offers an analysis of the soul's attitude toward God as well as toward people. "Perchance I may return with others" signals the much altered value of art to the soul, yielding to God's saving intervention "Lest she should fail and perish utterly" (221). But it is also central to the poem's intention that *art* not be cast into the outer darkness, but be redeemed by an attitude open to "the Godlike life . . . with man and for man." The soul had, by claiming to be "godlike," sought to diminish the palpable presence of the real God, in effect making Him one more picture for the Palace gallery, an imaginary god controlled by thought as art.

The soul's journey toward humility and reconciliation must move toward the abnegation represented by the cottage. Fatal solipsism is broken by God's mercy, a gracious, divine judgment which leads the soul outside herself. The soul, in shutting love out, had denied her essential purpose to know God and share His gifts with others. The sinful soul had refused the love of God to love herself alone. Loving "Beauty only," she had in fact loved her own pleasure, seeking to burn with Pater's "hard gemlike flame." Johnson notes, "In **'The Palace of Art,'** unlike **'The Lady of Shalott,'** the reader sympathizes with the external forces which break in on the soul's self-possession" (11). The rescuing discipline seized by the despairing soul is divine mercy, mercy which ultimately affirms and cherishes art, implicitly giving it a place in spiritual culture and the values which enter eternity.

Works Cited

Baum, Paull F. T*ennyson Sixty Years After.* New York: Octagon Books, 1975.

Buckley, Jerome H. *Tennyson: The Growth of a Poet.* Cambridge: Harvard UP, 1961.

Cronin, Richard. "'The Palace of Art' and Tennyson's Cambridge." *Essays in Criticism.* 43.3 (1993): 191-210.

Goslee, David. *Tennyson's Characters.* Iowa City: U of Iowa P, 1989.

Gray, Donald J. and G. B. Tennyson. *Victorian Literature: Poetry.* New York: Macmillan, 1976.

Hughes, Linda K. *The Manyfaced Glass: Tennyson's Dramatic Monologues.* Athens: Ohio UP, 1987.

Johnson, E. D. H. *The Alien Vision of Victorian Poetry.* Hamden, Connecticut: Archon Books, 1963.

Jordan, Elainc. *Alfred Tennyson.* Cambridge: Cambridge UP, 1988.

Kissane, James D. *Alfred Tennyson.* Boston: Twayne, 1970.

Lewis, C. S. "Christianity and Literature," *Christian Reflections.* (1967):10.

————. *The Great Divorce.* New York: Macmillan, 1946.

Luce, Morton. *A Handbook of the Works of Alfred Tennyson.* 1908. Reprint. New York: Franklin, 1970.

Martin, Robert Bernard. *Tennyson: The Unquiet Heart.* New York: Oxford UP, 1980.

Ransom, John Crowe, ed. *Selected Poems of Thomas Hardy.* New York: Collier, 1966.

Richards, Bernard. *English Poetry of the Victorian Period, 1830-1890.* London: Longmans, 1988.

Ricks, Christopher. *Tennyson.* New York: Macmillan, 1972.

Shaw, W. David. *Tennyson's Style.* Ithaca: Cornell UP, 1976.

Smith, Elton Edward. *The Two Voices.* Lincoln: U of Nebraska P, 1964.

Trilling, Lionel. *Beyond Culture: Essays in Literature and Learning.* New York: Harcourt, 1978.

Tucker, Herbert F. *Tennyson and the Dream of Romanticism.* Cambridge: Harvard UP, 1988.

Valerie Purton (essay date November 2003)

SOURCE: Purton, Valerie. "Tennyson and the Figure of Christ." *Tennyson Research Bulletin* 8, no. 2 (November 2003): 85-100.

[*In the following essay, Purton examines Tennyson's treatment of the figure of Christ as "the ideal Other."*]

> 'The Christ I call Christ-like is Sebastian del Piombo's in the National Gallery.'

Tennyson's comment in a discussion with Thomas Carlyle in the 1860s (*Memoir* II, 235), suggests the importance of the figure of Christ as an imaginative paradigm, both to the poet and to the mid-Victorian reading public. I want to examine in this paper the complex ways in which Tennyson and his readers constructed this figure, beginning with the example of the cultural apotheosis of Prince Albert, after his early death in 1861. Tennyson saw the Prince as (in the medieval sense) a 'type' of Christ—a reading he shared of course with Queen Victoria. I shall then consider more generally the anxieties—particularly about gender—evident in the period as to how Christ should be portrayed, to give a cultural context within which to examine Tennyson's presentation of Hallam in *In Memoriam,* both as a Christ-figure and, in Lacanian terms, as the ideal Other. This will lead to a Lacanian re-reading of Tennyson's earliest sonnets to Arthur Hallam. Finally, I shall return to the Sebastian del Piombo painting in the National Gallery, the painting to which Tennyson himself so often, both literally and poetically, returned and attempt to draw together Christian and Lacanian readings.

Tennyson was appointed Poet Laureate in 1850, says Hallam Tennyson, 'owing chiefly to Prince Albert's admiration for *In Memoriam*' (*Memoir* I, 334). It was just over a decade after reading the poem that Prince Albert in death displaced Hallam as its subject, for his royal widow at least. Even Robert Bernard Martin, not noted for his tendency to sentimentalise Tennyson, acknowledges much in common between Poet Laureate and Prince, and suggests as a probability that 'the two men would have become closer . . . on a man-to-man basis', had the Prince not died so young (Martin, 1980, 403-4).

In August 1847 *The Times* noted that the Queen and Prince Albert had visited Tennyson in Esher where he lay ill. Whether true or not, this certainly suggests some informal notice, which culminated in the offering of the Poet Laureateship after Samuel Rogers had declined because, at 87, he felt himself to be 'a shadow so soon to depart'. Tennyson's own fascination with the Prince is shown in a dream he reported the night before the letter arrived containing the Poet Laureate invitation. He dreamt that the Queen and Prince Albert visited him, were extremely kind to him, and that Prince Albert kissed him. 'Very kind and very German' was his gruff awakening disclaimer (Knowles cited in Martin, 351-2)—in much the tone, one imagines, in which he disavowed intimacy with Hallam. 'If anybody thinks I called him 'dearest' in his life, they are much mistaken. I never even called him "dear".' (*Memoir* I, 250). The following year the Tennysons were offered the Queen's Box at the Crystal Palace, Prince Albert being well aware of Tennyson's interest in science. Albert paid an informal visit to Tennyson at Freshwater, (rather inconveniently, just after they had moved in) and later wrote, just like any other admirer of the Great Poet, to ask for an autograph in his own (enclosed) copy of the *Idylls.*

Then in December 1861, at the age of 42, he suddenly died.

Tennyson wrote to the Royal Family, 'I trust that some-how and at some time I may be enabled to speak of Him as He Himself would have wished to be spoken of—surely as gracious and noble and gentle a being as God ever sent among us to be a messenger of good to his creatures' (*Letters,* II, 90). Interestingly, reference to Albert—'He Himself'—are capitalised in this letter (a practice the Queen was to make official) but Tennyson forgets to capitalise God's 'h', the 'H' of 'his creatures'. Within a fortnight of Albert's death, Tennyson had fin-ished the 'Dedication' to his memory for a new edition of the *Idylls* already in the press:

> These to His Memory—since he held them dear,
> Perchance in finding there unconsciously
> Some image of himself—I dedicate,
> I dedicate, I consecrate with tears—
> These Idylls.
>
>   And indeed He seems to me
> Scarce other than my king's ideal knight,
> 'Who reverenced his conscience as his king;
> Who spake no slander, no nor listened to it;
> Who loved one only and who clave to her . . .
>
> . . . all narrow jealousies
> Are silent; we see him as he moved,
> How modest, kind, all-accomplished, wise,
> With what sublime repression of himself,
> And in what limits and how tenderly . . .
>
> . . . through all this tract of years
> Wearing white flower of a blameless life . . .
> . . . a Prince indeed
> Beyond all titles and a household name,
> Hereafter, through all time, Albert the Good.

Tennyson was not the only one to link Albert and King Arthur. As Norman Vance describes it:

> Prince Albert, noble and romantic but also practical and public-spirited, a man of science interested in drains and the Great Exhibition, helped to link essen-tially bourgeois values with the traditions of chivalry. Landseer pained him many times in the robes of medi-eval chivalry. . . .
>
> (Vance, 1985, 20)

Line 6 of the Dedication had originally been, 'Scarce other than my own ideal knight', but Tennyson seems to have been embarrassed by the response to such a personal line and it was altered. Hallam Tennyson's ex-planation is that the idea was already current in society: 'The first reading [he says] . . . was altered because Leslie Stephen and others called King Arthur a portrait of the Prince Consort.' There was inevitably some cyni-cism in reactions to the Dedication. Swinburne sardoni-cally suggested that the central poem of the *Idylls* be retitled 'La Morte D'Albert or Idylls of the Prince Consort' (Jump, 1967, 339).

Meanwhile, in the days immediately after Albert's death, Queen Victoria had been reading and re-reading *In Memoriam,* and apparently the earlier poems too. 'I am like your Mariana now,' she said poignantly to Ten-nyson. She changed the genders in her own copy of *In Memoriam* to fit her own case (changing 'widower' to 'widow' for example, and 'her' to 'his' in section XIII) and took great comfort, she informed Tennyson, in no-ticing that both Albert and Arthur Hallam had blue eyes. 'Next to the Bible *In Memoriam* is my comfort' the Queen famously said, as so often speaking for large numbers of her subjects (Dyson and Tennyson, 1969, 69-70).

At their first meeting after the death Tennyson recorded that,

> I lost my head. I only remember saying to the Queen—big fool that I was—what an excellent King Prince Al-bert would have made. As soon as it was out of my mouth I felt what a blunder I had made. But, happily, it proved to be the very right thing to have said. The Queen replied that that had been a constant sorrow of her life—that she was called to govern, while he who was so worthy of the first place was obliged to take a secondary position.'
>
> (Dyson and Tennyson, 1969, 70)

This sense of inferiority to the lost Beloved in both Vic-toria and Tennyson suggests the notion of worship and returns us to the figure of Christ. The worship of the Prince Consort became a religion to the Queen. Against his stated wish when he was alive, she set about com-missioning statues in towns and cities throughout the land. A Cult of the Prince Consort quickly developed; there was a Tomb, a Cenotaph, there were idealised portraits and monuments which were, to all intends and purposes, shrines. George Gilbert Scott admitted that he designed the Albert Memorial, the most prestigious monument of the Victorian period, 'on the principles of ancient shrines' (Darby and Smith, 1983, 2-6). Tenny-son himself entered into the process eagerly. It was he who seems to have influenced the choice of the sculptor of Prince Albert's statue in the town they both cared for, Cambridge. 'Is there to be a statue of the Prince Consort at Cambridge? If so, don't let it fall into the hands of Marochetti if you can help it. He has neither the gifts nor the influence of Foley or Woolner' (*Letters* II, 296). Tennyson got his way; Foley was given the Cambridge commission and Woolner the equivalent at Oxford. The Queen agonised over the accuracy of each representation—demanding a characteristic look or pose, worrying about the details of dress; modern, Ro-man, formal, informal or perhaps one of the Orders of Chivalry? She seemed to be trying to regain through Art some sense of Presence—to recoup the lost Be-loved in stone as Tennyson endeavoured to recapture Hallam in words in *In Memoriam.*

Mid-Victorian artists engaged in a parallel discourse in representing the figure of Christ, the lost Beloved of the Christian church, and were equally beset by anxiety—an anxiety they expressed in very similar terms here. Here, 'gentleness' was the key word just as it was for Tennyson the key to understanding the Prince. Choice of clothing again was crucial. In 1851, Ford Madox Brown had painted Jesus washing Peter's feet. Christ was originally portrayed semi-nude, but, according to the artist, 'people could not see the poetry of my conception and were shocked by it'—so the figure was eventually clothed. A combination of professional models and friends was used, with Elizabeth Siddal being a model for the head of Christ (Bowness, 1984, 101). In the same year, 1851, William Holman Hunt painted *The Light of the World,* in which the kind, wise figure of the loving Christ stands at the door of the human soul awaiting admittance. This painting caused Hunt enormous problems. His aim was to include both feminine and masculine qualities in the Christ figure and he therefore looked for a virginal female model. In his own words, 'Appreciating the gravity and sweetness of expression possessed by Miss Christina Rossetti, I felt she might make a valuable sitter for the painting of the head . . . She kindly agreed' (Sussman, 1985, 125). Elizabeth Siddal put in an appearance again to sit for the colouring of Christ's face, and there were also male sitters, including Millais and, unexpectedly, Thomas Carlyle whom, as Hunt put it, 'I modelled from, furtively, to secure the male character of the head'. Hunt's anxiety about the mixture of genders he saw in Christ is evident in this wide range of models; despite the noble ideals, however, he seems in the end to have lost his nerve, since to the final version of the face he belatedly added an unambiguous full beard. John Ruskin's response at least was reassuring; he saw the nimbus round Christ's head as 'full of softness . . . yet so powerful'. Ironically, however, Carlyle himself attacked the painting on the grounds of its failure to accord with his ideal of heroic masculinity: 'It is a poor misshapen presentation of the noblest, the brotherliest, and most heroic-minded Being that ever walked on God's earth . . . You should think frankly of His antique heroic soul . . .' (Sussman, 160). Carlyle obviously wanted an all-male hero (he it was who saw Tennyson, typically, as 'a Guardsman spoilt by poetry'). Hunt responded by becoming the all-male artist, trekking alone through the Holy Land and putting his life in danger in order to pain *The Scapegoat.* He returned to the subject of Christ only in 1870, with *The Shadow of the Cross,* for which his models posed on the roof of his house in Jerusalem. There were four sitters whose identities have not been recorded; presumably all were male, considering the following comment from the painter. His anxiety again was about the head: 'I must depend upon this [the head] to shew people the personage it represents, for the originality of the treatment would lead people away from recognising it—yet I want to get into the head too much that is different from the conventional head, which always seems too weak for me' (Bowness, 222). He had obviously internalised the lesson from Carlyle. This young Christ with his well-toned torso is very obviously male. Carlyle, however, was hard to please. Hallam Tennyson's *Notebook* includes the following snippet:

> One day Carlyle was full of Holman Hunt's 'Shadow of the Cross'.
>
> *Carlyle*: I think poor fellow, he painted that picture in a distraction.

It was at this point that Tennyson commented, as he so often did:

> *A. T.*: The Christ I call Christ-like is Sebastian del Piombo's in the National Gallery.

Certainly Tennyson and Queen Victoria were not embarrassed, as the artists were, by any conflict between masculinity and femininity in their lost Beloveds. The figures of Prince Albert and Hallam are not felt to be weakened by being called 'gentle' (indeed, the word is linked to 'gentility' in the sense of noblesse oblige) but are presented rather as potently androgynous, a characteristic the two mourners specifically associate with Christ. Hallam Tennyson reported his father's belief in 'what he called the man/woman in Christ, the union of tenderness and strength' (*Memoir* I, 32n) and records his comment to Frederick Locker-Lampson: 'they [the Materialists] will not easily beat the character of our Lord, that union of man and woman, sweetness and strength' (*Memoir* II, 69). This is much more than the 'Gentle Jesus meek and mild' or Swinburne's 'pale Galilean' who so infuriated the proponents of 'Muscular Christianity'. C. H. Spurgeon in *A Good Start: A Book for Young Men and Women* (1898) takes Carlyle's line to its logical limit:

> When I say that a man in Christ is a man, I mean that, if he be truly in Christ, he is therefore manly. There has got abroad a notion, somehow, that if you become a Christian, you must sink your manliness and turn milksop.
>
> (Spurgeon, 1898, 16, quoted in Vance, 1926)

Tennyson in contrast ignores gender divisions. Many readers have, like Sinfield, noted in **In Memoriam** a 'complex series of slippages of gender' evoking 'the whole gamut of family relationships—father, mother, maiden, lover, children, deserted maiden, wife' and have found this 'baffling' (Sinfield, 1986, 146). It is less baffling if seen in the context of Queen Victoria's anguished account of her husband shortly after his death:

He, my angel—Albert—my life, the life of my life, he was *husband,* father, *mother,* my support, my joy, the light in our deprived home, the best father who ever lived, a blessing to his country . . .

[my italics]

Such deep mourning seems, then, on the evidence of *In Memoriam* and of the Queen's letters to involve a collapse of gender oppositions. Other oppositions also collapse. Tennyson observed in one of his letters to the Queen, 'the dead, though silent, [are] *more alive* than the living'. Life and Death are reversed, then collapse together or fuse as in *In Memoriam* XCV:

> So word by word and line by line,
>   The dead man touched me from the past,
>   And all at once it seemed at last
> The living soul was flashed on mine
>
> And mine in this was wound . . .

Past and Future are reversed and then collapse together:

> Yes less of sorrow lives in me
>   For days of happy commune dead;
>   Less yearning for the friendship fled,
> Than some strong bond which is to be.
>
> (CXVI)

All hinges on Christ seen, like King Arthur, as the Past and Future King:

> Ring out the darkness of the land,
> Ring in the Christ that is to be.
>
> (CVI)

Eventually identity itself dissolves:

> He that died in Holy Land
> Would reach us out the shining hand,
> And take us as a single soul.
>
> (LXXXIV)

This 'unselving' can be read within the Christian discourse familiar to both mourners: they are recognising in their loss the Christ-like qualities of the person lost; they are reminded of the loss of Christ, the permanent stage of absence on this earth brought about by the Fall, the expulsion from Eden. What they are really yearning for, in their collapsing of Time and Gender and Identity is that lost Eden, the lost wholeness with God, that unity which Tennyson finally proposes at the point at which 'we close with all we love, / And all we flow from, soul to soul.' (CXXXI). I would like, however, in an effort to come to a better understanding of both the process and the poetry, to re-read it instead, not in terms of nineteenth-century Christianity, but in terms of the twentieth-century ideas of Jacques Lacan. Even in their own time there were critics ready to castigate both the

monarch and the poet for unhealthy mourning—to see their grief as a love affair with death, a regression from individual responsibility. Lacan provides a theoretical framework for this process. In his terms, both Tennyson and his Queen would be condemned for retreating from the Symbolic to the Imaginary.

Lacan's notion of the move from the Imaginary to the Symbolic begins as a model of child development and becomes a theory of language. The unity of the preverbal child with its mother is ended at the moment when the child sees an image of itself, a mirror image or an older child, and creates from that an idea of selfhood which precipitates it into language and the sense of a separate identity. The mirror image of the ideal Other is thus crucial in the construction of the Self. The process is so perfectly captured in *In Memoriam* XLV that Terry Eagleton has mischievously declared that 'it is obvious from this section that Tennyson has read Lacan's Ecrits' (in Sinfield, 1986, ix):

> The baby new to earth and sky,
>   What time his tender palm is prest
>   Against the circle of the breast,
> Has never thought that 'this is I:'
>
> But as he grows he gathers much,
>   And learns the use of 'I' and 'me',
>   And finds 'I am not what I see,
> And other than the things I touch.'
>
> So rounds he to a separate mind
>   From whence clear memory may begin,
>   As though the frame that binds him in
> His isolation grows defined.

Alan Sinfield's paraphrase of Lacan is useful here.

> When the human baby learns to say 'Me' and 'I' it is only acquiring these designations from someone and somewhere else, from the world which perceives and names it . . . The child does not discover and develop a pre-existing identity, it receives an identity constructed in the world. Initially the infant experiences a sense of wholeness which it derives from the security of the relationship with the mother. The entrance into language and identity is founded on the loss of that imaginary wholeness: the belief that there must be a point of harmony and certainty persists, but attempts to locate it inevitably incorporate the split which they would heal.
>
> (Sinfield, 1986, 67)

In these terms, once the 'point of harmony and certainty' represented both by Hallam and Prince Albert is removed, the process of 'selving' goes into reverse and there is a desperate desire to be unselved, to lose the identity which separates the mourner from the Beloved. This can only be achieved (in Lacanian terms) in a return to the boundless preverbal Imaginary state, the place where it is possible to 'unite with all we loved, / And all we flow from, / Soul to soul.' Malcolm Bowie, in his account of Lacan, gives the following definitions of the Imaginary and the Symbolic which strongly suggest the rival discourses in *In Memoriam* and, I would argue, in Tennyson's poetry in general:

> The Imaginary is the order of mirror images, identifications and reciprocities. It is the dimension of experience in which the individual seeks not simply to placate the Other but to dissolve his otherness by becoming his counterpart . . . the term has a strong pejorative force, and suggests that the subject is seeking, in a wilful and blameworthy fashion, to remove himself from the flux of becoming. The Symbolic order, on the other hand, is often spoken of admiringly. It is the realm of movement rather than fixity and of heterogeneity rather than similarity. It is the realm of language of the unconscious, of an otherness that remains other.

> (Bowie, 1991, 92)

Critics have recognised in different terms the rival discourses in Tennyson's poetry—that debate enacted most clearly in **'The Two Voices'**. Christopher Ricks calls the negative voice 'a suicidal wish for oblivion'. Sinfield sees the positive voice as Tennyson 'wanting desperately to assert an ultimate reality, and to discover a means of apprehending it through poetic language' (Sinfield, 1986, 86), though the stress in his subsequent argument seems to be more on the desperation than on the apprehension. Aidan Day more excitingly opens up the possibility of a parallelism between Lacanian and Christian readings. Writing of *In Memoriam* in 'The Archetype that Waits' he says, 'the ideal Other . . . is to be gained only at the self-contradictory cost of dying out of the self and out of the language in which that self is constituted' (Day, 1992, 83). Tennyson must have been very familiar with the Christian version of this idea, as preached by his father from the pulpit at Somersby: 'He who would gain his life shall lose it and he who would lose his life for my sake, the same shall save it'. Lacan's reading at this point then seems not necessarily inimical to the Christian reading: both posit a lost wholeness, an Imaginary or Edenic state, and a disjunction between the differentiated Symbolic or Fallen domain—though Lacan's reading privileges the letter, rather than the former. In both versions, a Word has to be made Flesh—a mirror set up—between the two spaces. The paradox, of course, in both approaches, is that the more Tennyson argues for Hallam's continued individuality ('I shall know him when we meet'), the more he confirms the separation between them. Articulation of the desire for union itself, as Day argues, splits the speaker 'by his very articulation from the object of his desire' (Day, 1992, 82).

In both Lacanian and Christian thinking, the desire for lost wholeness is a part of the construction of the human subject, part of the human condition. In this sense, Tennyson had 'lost' Hallam before they ever met. Hillis Miller explains it neatly: 'Hallam's death did not generate Tennyson's feeling of loss. Rather, the death gave him an occasion to personify a loss he already felt' (Hillis Miller, 282). The point is effectively made by an examination of some of Tennyson's early sonnets, addressed, according to Ricks, to a Hallam who was very much alive.

> Me my own Fate to lasting sorrow doometh:
> > *Thy* woes are birds of passage, transitory:
> > Thy spirit, *circled with a living glory.*
> In summer still a summer joy resumeth.
> Alone my hopeless melancholy gloometh,
> > Like a lone cypress, through the twilight hoary,
> From an old garden where no flower bloometh,
> > One cypress on an island promontory.
> But yet my lonely spirit follows thine,
> > As round the rolling earth night follows day:
> But yet thy lights on my horizon shine
> > Into my night, when thou art far away.
> I am so dark, alas! And thou so bright,
> When we two meet there's never perfect light.

Composed while Tennyson was still very much under the poetic and personal influence of his father, this sonnet is similar to several of those by George Clayton Tennyson—it is tempting to think of it as having been written in his vicarage garden, the 'old garden' at Somersby. It is a poem about self-definition, beginning with 'Me'—but 'me' is an Object not a Subject, passive not active. Even by the end, the 'I' that has been reached in the penultimate line is only a twilight figure, not able to exist alone, but only as one of a series of binary oppositions. Winter is set against the summer of the Beloved's presence, stasis against movement, loneliness against companionship, night against day. The mixed Petrachan and Shakespearean rhyme scheme (unique in Tennyson's poetry, says Ricks) suggests the pulling of opposites. There is resistance against the iambic rhythm in the effortful opening stresses on lines 1, 2 and 3—'Me', 'Thy', 'Thy' and finally in line 13, 'I', suggesting rhythmically the construction of the speaker's identity only against the Other—from Me to I via Thy. Already the figure of the Beloved is glorified, like the head of Christ ('The nimbus made a very pleasing effect' as Holman Hunt remarked of Christ's halo in his painting of Christ and Peter). Indeed, in *In Memoriam* there are several instances of such silent visual deification, notably in Hallam seeing 'His own vast shadow glory-crowned' (XCVII). Most interestingly, there is already in place the movement of endless loss and desire—the hopelessness of night's continual pursuit of day 'round the rolling earth'—an anticipation of **"Tithonus."** Here already is Tennyson's fascination with liminal states, the notion of the horizon as the ultimate barrier, but one which is in fact unreal, non-existent—

simply the limit of vision. Here too is the movement we find both in **'Tears, Idle Tears'**, with its wonderfully bewildering reversal 'that brings our friends up from the underworld . . .', and in Ulysses's 'untravelled world / Whose margin fades / Forever and forever when I move'. This seems very much in line with the Lacanian notion of the Other as crucial in delimiting the Self—holding out a promise of plenitude and fulfilment but, as the flat and unsuccessful final line suggests, always and inevitably deferred, out of reach.

> When that rank head of evil's tropic day
>> Made floating cloud of floating joy, and cleft
> My shores of life (their freshness steamed away,
>> Nothing but salt and bitter crystals left),
> When in my lonely walks I seemed to be
>> An image of the cursed figtree, set
>> In the brown glen of this Mount Olivet,
> Thy looks, thy words, were . . . and rain to me,
> When all sin-sickened, loathing my disgrace,
>> Far on within the temple of the mind
>>> I seemed to hear God speaking audibly,
> 'Let us go hence'—sometimes a little space,
>> Out of the sphere of God, I dared to find
>>> A shadow and a resting place in thee.

Here is the tropical imagery of **"Armageddon"** and *Timbuctoo*—on this occasion heat representing evil, while the gaze of the Beloved gives coolness and strength. Ricks suggests that the 'sun' which Sir Charles Tennyson blithely supplies to fill the lacuna in line 8 is unlikely, since it reverses the dry heat/wet coolness opposition being set up—but against that could be set the suggestive dissonance of 'sun' and 'sin'. The speaker's guilt and disgrace are perhaps linked with adolescent excess, the springs of joy dried out to 'salt and bitter crystals' through misuse. They do, though, certainly have biblical significance: the cursed figtree' recalls the figtree in Matthew 21, 17-20 that is cursed because it does not bear the fruit that Christ expects, and 'Let us go hence' echoes Christ's words to His disciples as He prepares them for the separation that is about to happen in Jerusalem (John 14, 31) 'Ye have heard how I said unto you, I go away, and come again unto you. If you loved me, you would rejoice, because I said I go unto the Father . . .'

The poem's inside/outside binary is revealing, if complicated: the speaker seems trapped in his own mind—though holy (a temple) it is oppressive being presided over by a very audible God who gives commands reminds us uncomfortably of future separation. The speaker daringly sneaks away from this oppressive heat, 'out of the sphere of God', away from the all-seeing eye, (the 'Word of the Father' for Lacan), to the formlessness of 'a shadow'. The Beloved provides a place of rest from observation and official morality. How far though, can something as intrinsically shifting as a shadow *be* 'a place'? Again the speaker attempts to find closure and safety by fixing the Beloved's identity—a 'resting place in thee'—but the poem is one of clouds and shadows and still marked by an ultimately doomed reaching out for an ultimately insubstantial Other.

Sonnet

> As when with downcast eyes we must and brood,
> And ebb into a former life, or seem
> To lapse far back in some confusèd dream
> To states of mystical similitude;
> If one but speaks or hems or stirs his chair,
> Ever the wonder waxeth more and more,
> So that we say, 'All this hath been before.
> All this hath been, I know not when or where.'
> So, friend, when first I looked upon your face,
> Our thought gave answer each to each, so true—
> Opposed mirrors each reflecting each—
> That though I knew not in what time or place,
> Methought that I had often met with you,
> And either lived in either's heart and speech.

(1832, Ricks, 459)

This sonnet consists of two quatrains with the *In Memoriam* rhyme scheme, followed by an intricate Petrarchan sestet. The epic simile quite conventionally sets up an example which makes the simile seem vividly real before the 'real' subject of the comparison is introduced in line 9. In the sestet the process is reversed: the 'real' first experience is more unreal than the second—a 'déjà vu' experience, undermining past and present, reality and dream, built on images of ebbing and lapsing set against images of flowing and waxing. There is again a 'baffling slippage'—this time in the oppositions set up in the simile. The ebbing is, predictably, into the past, but the waxing is not into the future, but into a dream. There in the sestet are Lacan's mirrors, undermining selfhood even as they apparently reflect it. Two mirrors reflecting each other leave no space for presence at all; they are reflections of reflections—rather like the image of Sir Lancelot which the Lady of Shalott saw doubly refracted 'from the bank and from the river'.

From the evidence of many such poems, Tennyson does seem to use the Christ-like figure of Hallam as an imaginative paradigm for a sense of loss which predates the historical death of Arthur Hallam and is intrinsic to his own self-formation. Lacan would go further and say that this self-formation, though inevitable, is a chimera. There is ultimately no Self to hold on to—in Margaret Reynold's words, for Lacan 'the ego subsists in a world of mirrors, of doubles, of reflected selves where the purpose is at once to differentiate and to endorse, to be separate, and to be the same, in a measuring of subject and object which blurs the boundaries of each' (Reynolds, 2002). Christianity, in contrast, is popularly thought to offer hope precisely because it rests on a conception of a unitary, redeemable Self. Yet it too deconstructs, in its demand for loss of selfhood in Christ: 'He who would gain his life must lose it'. What these apparently opposed accounts of the self, the Christian and the Lacanian, have in common, is the figure of a self that is always incomplete, always reaching out for a wholeness which Lacan believes to be illusory and Christianity believes to have been lost in the Fall, the expulsion from Eden. Both therefore posit an endless cycle of loss and desire.

The attempt to recoup the lost Hallam in language, like Queen Victoria's attempt to recapture Albert in stone is, in both Christian and Lacanian terms, doomed to fail. Tennyson's characteristic melancholy, in Sinfield's opinion, comes from his intermittent recognition of the ultimate inadequacy of language, his realisation that 'the loss of the imaginary wholeness which he associates with the loss of a beloved person coincides with the inability of language quite to restore that imaginary wholeness' (Sinfield, 1992). *In Memoriam* is full of syntactical and metaphorical strategies to over come the problem. In it's dreams, the identity of mourner and mourned are confused (LXVIII) and, in one strange Blakean lyric, LXIX, the speaker even takes Hallam's place as the Christ figure:

> I dreamed there would be Spring no more,
>   That Nature's ancient power was lost:
>   The streets were black with smoke and frost,
> They chattered trifles at the door:
>
> I wandered from the noisy town,
>   I found a wood with thorny boughs:
>   I took the thorns to bind my brows,
> I wore them like a civic crown:
>
> I met with scoffs, I met with scorns
>   From youth and babe and hoary hairs:
>   They called me in the public squares
> The fool that wears the crown of thorns:
>
> They called me fool, they called me child:
>   I found an angel of the night;
>   The voice was low, the look was bright;
> He looked upon my crown and smiled:
>
> He reached the glory of a hand,
>   That seemed to touch it into leaf:
>   The voice was not the voice of grief,
> The words were hard to understand.

The public role of poet here seems necessarily to involve martyrdom—but the real martyrdom is the agony of having only language, not presence, signifiers but no signified. The 'thorns' seem to be the speaker's poor words, sharp and painful because always pointing away from themselves to a reality which they do not contain. Tennyson is characteristically ambiguous about the gender and identity of the 'Divine Thing', though the 'glory

of a hand' suggests an apotheosised Hallam. This angel *can* establish a relationship between thorns and leaves, between words and things; he seems to be a guarantor that there is meaning, presence, behind the poet's poor and inadequate words. What is important here is that the martyred Christ-figure is not Hallam, but the *speaker himself,* the poet as creator, if only for a moment, of presence through words.

The Christian view of the ideal Other is that officially espoused by Tennyson at the end of *In Memoriam*: in Christ, the Beloved is regained in grander form, beyond individuality:

> . . . that friend of mine who lives in God
>
> That God who ever lives and loves
>   Once God, one law, one element,
>   And one far-off divine event
> To which the whole creation moves.

(Epilogue)

The Lacanian view, more bleakly, is that there is no Other to reclaim—nor even properly a unified Self to reclaim it, but only 'floating signifiers'. The Christ-figure, according to this view, is simply the transcendent signifier who *appears* to make meaning. Anxieties about the representations of Christ in art and literature suggest the importance of such a 'point of harmony and certainty', as if the experience of poetry or of painting can momentarily and tantalisingly give a glimpse of presence, of something beyond itself—can, in *In Memoriam*'s terms, bring Lazarus back from the Dead.

I want to return at last to the National Gallery. Hallam Tennyson records that:

> In the summer as children we generally passed through London on our way to Lincolnshire and [inaudible] would take us for a treat to Westminster Abbey, the Zoological gardens, the Tower of London . . . or the National Gallery. In the last he much delighted and would point out us out the excellencies of the different Masters; he always led the way first of all to the 'Raising of Lazarus' by Sebastian del Piombo'.

(*Memoir* I, 371)

The painting was acquired by the original National Gallery at 100 Pall Mall in 1824. Almost certainly, Arthur Hallam and Tennyson visited it together, probably in 1832. It is a massive painting and must, as Leonée Ormond has observed, have had a part to play in the imaginative creation of the 'Lazarus' sections of *In Memoriam,* which were probably the earliest to be written during the following dreadful year. Here the notion of the ideal Other, the heroic figure variously embodied for Tennyson in King Arthur, Prince Albert and Hallam himself, finds visual expression in the commanding figure of Christ, 'The Christ I call Christ-like'. It is easy to read into the face of a likeness to Hallam. Here is the 'manhood fused with female grace' which Tennyson saw in his friend; here is the light shining on 'the brow of Michael Angelo'. Christ is summoning back from the darkness the huge, gauche, dusky-skinned figure of Lazarus, whose form in the composition of the painting balances and completes His own. It is tempting to see this as an emblem of the longed-for reunion, just beyond the scope of *In Memoriam*—Christ, through Hallam, calling his benighted friend back to life. ('I am so dark and thou so bright.') Hallam in death is more than he was in life—he is the transcendent signifier, the guarantor of meaning, the sun whom Tennyson's 'lonely spirit' followed, 'as round the rolling earth night follows day', in those earliest sonnets. And yet, tantalisingly, an opposite and equal reading offers itself. In a balancing movement, Tennyson himself, as artist, becomes the Christ-figure, the one who alone can draw the Beloved, if only for a moment, back from the dead, through Lacan's Mirror, at the intersection of the Imaginary and the Symbolic where, through art, the Word is made Flesh.

Works Cited

Bowie, Malcolm, 1991: *Lacan*. (London: Fontana).

Bowness, Alan, 1984: *The Pre-Raphaelites*. (London: The Tate Gallery).

Darby, Elizabeth and Smith, Nicola, 1983: *The Cult of the Prince Consort*.

Day, Aidan, 1992: 'The Archetype that waits', in *Tennyson: Seven Essays*. Philip Collins ed. (London: Macmillan).

Dyson, Hope and Tennyson, Sir Charles, 1969: *Dear and Honoured Lady*. (London: Macmillan).

Jump, John D. ed., 1967: *Tennyson: the Critical Heritage*. (London: Routledge & Kegan Paul).

Lacan, Jacques, 1977: *Ecrits: A Selection*. (New York: Norton).

Lang, Cecil D. and Shannon, Edgar, 1981-1990: *The Letters of Alfred Lord Tennyson*, 3 vols. (Cambridge, Mass: Harvard University Press). [Abbreviated as *Letters*]

Martin, Robert Bernard, 1980: *Tennyson: The Unquiet Heart*. (Oxford: Faber).

Miller, J. Hillis, 1992: 'Temporary Topographies: Tennyson's Tears'. *Victorian Poetry* 30 (Autumn 1992), pp. 277-89.

Ormond, Leonée, 1989: *Tennyson and the Old Masters*. Tennyson Society.

Occasional Paper No. 7. (Hull: The Tennyson Society).

Reynolds, Margaret, (2002): *Tennyson and Sappho*. Tennyson Society Occasional Paper No. 10. (Lincoln: Tennyson Society)

Ricks, Christopher, 1972: *Tennyson*. (London: Macmillan).

Saville, Julia, 1992: 'The Lady of Shalott: A Lacanian Romance'. *Word and Image* 8:1.

Sinfield, Alan, 1986: *Alfred Tennyson*. (Oxford: Blackwell).

Sussman, Herbert, 1995: *Victorian Masculinities*. (Cambridge: Cambridge University Press).

Poems of Tennyson, 1969: ed. Christopher Ricks (London: Longman). [Includes *Idylls of the King*, abbreviated as *Idylls*.]

Tennyson, Hallam, 1897: *Tennyson: A Memoir*. (London: Macmillan). [Abbreviated as *Memoir*.]

Vance, Norman, 1985: *The Sinews of the Spirit*. (Cambridge: Cambridge University Press).

Weintraub, Stanley, 1997: *Albert: Uncrowned King*. (London: John Murray).

Stephen Ahern (essay date winter 2004)

SOURCE: Ahern, Stephen. "Listening to Guinevere: Female Agency and the Politics of Chivalry in Tennyson's *Idylls*." *Studies in Philology* 101, no. 1 (winter 2004): 88-112.

[*In the following essay, Ahearn asserts that Tennyson's representation of Guinevere, as well as her relationship with King Arthur in the* Idylls, *is a key component in interpreting the author's views on his own society and culture.*]

> Nature, Universe, Destiny, Existence, howsoever we name this grand unnamable Fact in the midst of which we live and struggle, is as a heavenly bride and conquest to the wise and brave, to them who can discern her behests and do them; a destroying fiend to them who cannot.
>
> —Thomas Carlyle, *Past and Present* (1843)

In 1857 Alfred Tennyson printed the first of his *Idylls of the King* under the title **"Enid and Nimüe: The True and the False."**[1] Tennyson's early choice of title indicates much about the treatment of identity and gender in his poem cycle as a whole, for throughout the *Idylls* a model of femininity is elaborated in the terms of truth and falsity. Consistently a woman's essential character is defined according to her degree of loyalty to a male counterpart. She is "true" or "false" insofar as she fulfils the expectations of her lover, who articulates the expectations of her society in general. The women of Arthur's court occupy positions on a spectrum of ethical capacity. Ranging from the madonna figure to the whore figure, from the ever-suffering Enid to the cunning Vivien, the women of the *Idylls* embody aspects of morality in a quintessentially Victorian construction of woman as a symbolic repository of social values.

Largely because of the role he played as poet laureate and cultural sage, Tennyson has often been read as propagating unequivocally the patriarchal assumptions of the Victorian literary and socio-economic establishment. With few exceptions recent critics contend that Tennyson's lyrics reinscribe and thereby reinforce the gender ideology of his time.[2] As Linda M. Shires has suggested, however, Tennyson's relationship to his culture's ideology is more equivocal and complex than critics have noticed.[3] I will argue here that as he updates Arthurian romance to speak to the concerns of contemporary England, Tennyson does not mirror uncritically the sexual politics of his culture. The *Idylls* candidly depicts the problems that result from subscribing to a model of feminine nature that pervaded Victorian thinking. The contradictions of this model appear in stark relief in the epigraph I quote above from *Past and Present,* in which Carlyle invokes a discourse that makes woman the cipher of a given metaphysical conceit—here, Nature, Universe, Destiny, Existence. The problem with such rhetoric becomes evident when abstract qualities are projected onto an actual person. It is of course absurd to construct an individual—let alone half the human population—as the embodiment of a concept as arcane as "the grand unnamable Fact" that gives meaning to human life. Yet such a construction of woman has a long history. Codified initially by the medieval courtly love tradition, the myth of romantic love permeated western literature with a conviction that union with the beloved will enable sexual, emotional, and spiritual fulfillment. The ideal of woman as ennobling influence gained especial force in Tennyson's era, which saw a revival of interest in the culture of chivalry.[4]

Identifications of the beloved with a promise of ennobling self-realization pervade the *Idylls.* Yet throughout the poem cycle there is a pattern of implicit, and at times explicit, criticism of the ways Arthur and his knights exploit the women of Camelot for their own ends. This exploitation follows a common trajectory: the knight idealizes his female counterpart, and when the woman does not live up to the demands such a role dictates, she is blamed for his failure to succeed in the world. Within the allegorical schema of the Grail quest, attainment of the ideal woman becomes, like attainment of the Grail itself, a figure for the fulfillment of desire. In their dealings with the women of Camelot, Arthur's

knights exhibit behavior that ranges from Pelleas's naïve infatuation to Geraint's jealous obsession. These varied responses to womanhood become comprehensible when the knights' actions are read as manifestations of the same passionate yearning. The narrative makes clear that each of these men is driven by a longing for atonement, which is a longing both for the attainment of a unified self and for a submersion of the self in a larger whole. Galahad's declaration as he embraces the Grail vision illustrates the paradoxical nature of this desire: "If I lose myself," he asserts, "I save myself."[5]

These ostensibly antithetical impulses—the search for an individuated identity and the quest for a loss of self—are given form in the *Idylls* in the same gendered terms deployed by Carlyle. Feminine nature is embodied either as the nurturing mother figure who will provide self-completion to the questing male, or as the mysterious femme fatale, agent of the overwhelming forces of nature.[6] This conception of femininity as both the ego-completing energy of creative will and the ego-effacing destructive potency of instinct underlies the delineation of almost every male-female bond in the *Idylls.* The intensity of the consequences faced by each male character varies in direct proportion to how radically he has misrepresented the character and motivations of his female counterpart and has thereby misunderstood the nature of their alliance.

I will focus here on the relationship of Camelot's king and queen. Theirs is the heterosexual bond against which all others are measured in the *Idylls,* and as such their relationship functions as an exemplary case study that dramatizes the mechanics of idealization and disillusion. Because Arthur insists on casting Guinevere as emblematic of his destiny, he fails to fulfil the expectations of the real woman and loses her completely. Tennyson presents Guinevere as an agent in her own right, as a strong character who struggles against a society that typecasts her within narrowly defined boundaries. Because her voice controls large sections of text, she has opportunities to present her own perspective on her lot and thereby to create a sympathetic audience for her version of the events leading up to the fall of Camelot. As a result of this narrative freedom, the story of Guinevere's rebellion against, and eventual capitulation to, her husband's vision of her proper wifely function provides an ambivalent representation of the expectations of patriarchal culture.

Analysis of the relationship of Camelot's royal couple is also, I would argue, the key to reading Tennyson's Arthuriad as commentary on the values of his own society. Tennyson's explicit identification of King Arthur with Prince Albert[7] invites us to read the *Idylls* as an allegory of contemporary manners as much as a mythopoeic meditation on the enduring structures of human experience. What Tennyson called the "parabolic drift" of the poem cycle depends on the articulation of a complex ideology of proper manly and womanly behavior. Camelot's reigning monarchs and mid-nineteenth-century England's own royal couple share a function that is at once emblematic and banal as they stand in both for a vision of ideal chivalry and a vision of ordinary domestic life.[8] Tennyson's epic becomes as a result as much a vehicle to explore his own culture's contradictory opinions on the relation of gender to power as a reiteration of legendary stories obscured by the mists of time.

. . . . .

Young King Arthur hopes that marriage will give him a psychic stability that will help him impose his will in the public world. The interior monologue he delivers when first captivated by Guinevere's beauty exemplifies the kind of Victorian rhetoric that proffers refuge in woman as the palliative to a life spent tossed about by the storms of fortune.[9] Arthur desires to incorporate Guinevere into his life, and thereby attain communion with his emotional and spiritual self. We are told that Arthur "felt / Travail, and throes and agonies of the life / Desiring to be joined with Guinevere" (**"The Coming of Arthur,"** ll. 74-76). A life spent battling heathen hordes is not enough for the angst-ridden monarch. He yearns to be merged with the alter ego who will make him whole:

> What happiness to reign a lonely king,
> Vext—O ye stars that shudder over me,
> O earth that soundest hollow under me,
> Vext with waste dreams? for saving I be joined
> To her that is the fairest under heaven,
> I seem as nothing in the mighty world,
> And cannot will my will, nor work my work
> Wholly, nor make myself in mine own realm
> Victor and lord. But were I joined with her,
> Then might we live together as one life,
> And reigning with one will in everything
> Have power on this dark land to lighten it,
> And power on this dead world to make it live.

(ll. 81-93)

This passage exemplifies the Victorian discourse that constructs the union of a man and a woman as the integration of complementary aspects of human nature, and that celebrates the power of wholeness such an integration will afford the man.[10] Without Guinevere, Arthur feels he has no identity—he is "nothing." Before marriage he is impotent; he "cannot will [his] will, nor work [his] work / Wholly" in the "mighty world" and is thus a failure as a king. In an image that resonates with archetypal symbolism, Arthur believes that were he joined with Guinevere he would gain the strength to effect an illumination of the Christian good over the dark reign of pagan evil. Were he endowed with the vital life-force of "the fairest under heaven" he could exert

"power on this dead world to make it live." His queen would ground his "vext dreams," for she as incarnation of the feminine principle represents for him the fertile powers of the earth. As such, she would provide him the power of emotional strength and stability. Her symbolic role would be like that of the "three fair queens," the "friends / Of Arthur" who at the creation of the Round Table "stood in silence near his throne" and who will return to "help him at his need" (**"The Coming of Arthur,"** ll. 275-78). Guinevere would be a mortal surrogate for the Lady of the Lake, the Goddess figure who gave the king earthly potency in the form of Excalibur, and who "knows a subtler magic than [Merlin's] own" (l. 283).[11] This figuration of Guinevere as the feminine principle of nature is explicit in the description of the joy Arthur's knights experience at his wedding, when "The Sun of May descended on their King, [and] / They gazed on all earth's beauty in their Queen" (ll. 461-62). In this binary opposition, Arthur is identified with the sun—a symbol of imagination and will—while Guinevere embodies the fecund grandeur of nature. The saint who officiates at the ceremony articulates the aspirations of the king when he proclaims: "Reign ye, and live and love, and make the world / Other, and may thy Queen be one with thee" (ll. 471-72).

This benediction betrays more about the workings of Arthur's ill-fated mission than is first apparent. Arthur's obsession, his consuming *idée fixe,* is to impose the order of Christian law onto the natural world. His is the Apollonian realm of art, symbolized by Camelot, "the city built to music." His goal is to subdue the Dionysian forces of nature—symbolized by the imagery of the encroaching wasteland—and thereby to bring the chaos of the wilderness into the controlling domain of his kingship.[12] He does indeed "make the world / Other," but he does it by constructing whatever lies beyond his control as the threatening opposite of all he desires and not by transforming the world as he finds it for any more than a brief time. Arthur, intent on shaping the world in his own image, invests responsibility for his success in the image of ideal womanhood he projects onto his wife.[13] She, too, is the otherness of nature, of emotional intensity and irrational potency, and when she refuses to be cast in the role of avatar of his destiny, Arthur blames her for the failure of his vision.[14] Arthur makes Guinevere the central reference point of his worldview, and when this center does not hold, his world falls apart.

A number of critics have explored the consequences of Arthur's appropriation of Guinevere's gendered identity for his own uses. In his influential article "The Female King: Tennyson's Arthurian Apocalypse," Elliot L. Gilbert shows how "Tennyson's very contemporary poem can be read as an elaborate examination of the advantages and disadvantages and dangers of sexual role reversal, with King Arthur himself playing, in a number of significant ways, the part usually assigned by culture to the woman."[15] Gilbert argues convincingly that the *Idylls* reflect contemporary anxieties about the feminization of history and politics, and concludes that its "central theme" is that "all certainty is impossible for a man who rejects the stability of patrilineal descent and seeks instead to derive his authority from himself, to build a community on the idealization of nature and female energy."[16] Gilbert is probably right about the overall conservative ethos at work in Tennyson's epic, and he is certainly right about the failure of Arthur's self-authorizing vision. Like other critics, however, Gilbert in an important sense "buys into" Arthur's mythology by treating Guinevere as emblem and not as individual. To counter such readings, I want here to consider a perspective that has been consistently overlooked: Guinevere's side of the story. Again, Gilbert's analysis is telling, for he provides the strongest validation I have read of the queen's position when he asserts: "In the end, Guinevere's reality triumphs over Arthur's and Lancelot's abstraction in the *Idylls of the King,* just as her irresistible sexual energy at last defeats her husband's passionlessness."[17] Gilbert then goes on to argue, however, that "this outcome is inevitable"; "Indeed," he concludes, "Tennyson's profoundest insight in the poem may be that nature cannot be courted casually, that the id-like energy of the deep must not be invoked without a full knowledge of how devastating and ultimately uncontrollable that energy can be."[18] Though ostensibly providing a critique attuned to the workings of gender ideology, Gilbert here himself equates woman with "nature" and depicts female sexuality as a "devastating" and "uncontrollable" force that is, he implies, akin to the mob violence of the French Revolution. In the process, he ascribes to Tennyson a position that the evidence of the text does not support.

As recent feminist literary and cultural critics have shown, Tennyson's contemporaries tended to promote an emblematic reading of feminine nature that was disturbing in its implications for a real woman. In her study *Woman and the Demon,* Nina Auerbach details how Victorian "literary iconography gave womanhood virtually exclusive access to spiritual depths and heights."[19] The *Idylls* reflects this view of feminine nature, a view that Merlin articulates when, struggling to defend himself against Vivien's charms, he declares that "men at most differ as Heaven and earth, / But women, worst and best, as Heaven and Hell" (**"Merlin and Vivien,"** ll. 812-13). Guinevere's predicament in the *Idylls* is that she cannot fit into this schema. Unlike Enid and Vivien, she is neither passively submissive to, nor maliciously scornful of, the expectations of her society. Guinevere occupies a position somewhere between these extremes on a spectrum of womanly character. Her situation is literalized when Modred looks over the garden wall and spies "the Queen who sat be-

twixt her best / Enid, and lissome Vivien, of her court / The wiliest and the worst" (**"Guinevere,"** ll. 27-29).

Because Guinevere embodies neither of these extremes, she is caught in a position that is difficult to negotiate. She occupies an unstable middle ground that causes her to experience feelings of self-doubt even as she declares her right to assert an identity free from the symbolic function Arthur imposes on her. The king wants his queen to act as a kind of private-sphere buttress to his public self, as the nurturing anima to his agonistic animus. Her inability to fulfil this role is assumed to be the catalyst of the fall of Camelot. But Guinevere consistently denies responsibility for this failure as she struggles against her society's censure. As a result, she becomes the most balanced and fully human figure in the *Idylls.* This holds true despite her complicity in the defeat of Arthur's quest to impose order on the chaos of the natural world.

The problem with Guinevere is that she does not want to "reign with one will in everything" because that "one will" is Arthur's, not hers. She refuses to play angel of the house, let alone of the castle. The queen chooses instead to rebel against the constraints of her social position by affirming her right to live her life as she desires. Her freedom of choice is limited by the world in which she finds herself, but she has no qualms about asserting her agency in the one arena in which she as a woman of noble stature can exert control—the arena of love. She resists playing muse to what she considers Arthur's project of self-aggrandizement. This resistance is conspicuously expressed in her love for Lancelot.

Guinevere rejects an arid life as paragon of her husband's moral order for the sensual bond she shares with Lancelot. Although Lancelot treats the queen with perhaps too much of the idolatry prescribed by the courtly love code, he does seem to accept her for what she is: a sexual being with a strongly individualist identity. Guinevere repeatedly criticizes Arthur for the austere expectations of his ideal, and for his resulting lack of empathy for the limitations of his subjects. She maintains that he expects too much of those around him, and of herself in particular.

The most developed exposition of her perspective comes during a scene mid-way through the poem cycle in which she and Lancelot are left alone before the annual tournament. The queen criticizes Lancelot for making excuses to miss the joust, and for having possibly intensified the rumors of their adultery that are swirling around Camelot. An indignant Lancelot asks if she has "grown weary of [his] service and devoir" and if she will as a result "Henceforth be truer to [her] faultless lord" (**"Lancelot and Elaine,"** ll. 118-19). Responding with a "little scornful laugh," Guinevere affirms her love for Lancelot and blames her husband for being too pure for mere mortals to bear, saying: "Arthur, my lord, Arthur, the faultless King, / That passionate perfection, my good lord— / But who can gaze upon the Sun in heaven?" (ll. 120-23). Guinevere criticizes her husband for neglecting her and uses the fact that he has never suspected her infidelity as proof that he does not love her. Guinevere then provides one of the strongest indictments of Arthur's dream when she insists that his treatment of her is but one symptom of an all-absorbing egocentrism. His neglect, she argues, stems from the fact that he is "Rapt in this fancy of his Table Round, / And swearing men to vows impossible, / To make them like himself" (ll. 129-31).[20]

The queen further asserts her individualist spirit when, condemning Arthur's pursuit of an ideal of ascetic purity, she tells Lancelot:

> friend, to me
> He is all fault who hath no fault at all:
> For who loves me must have a touch of earth;
> The low sun makes the colour: I am yours,
> Not Arthur's, as ye know, save by the bond.
>
> (ll. 131-35)

Her love, she insists, is something to be given freely to a man worthy of her affection; she is not, her use of possessive pronouns emphasizes, so much chattel transferred to a husband by the convention of the marriage rite. Guinevere here reasserts her passion for Lancelot in the face of the cloud of suspicion and intrigue that is gathering over Camelot. She debunks Arthur's code of chivalry—by which he "honours his own word, / As if it were his God's"—as the fanciful preoccupation of "A moral child without the craft to rule" (ll. 143-45). In a cutting insult to Arthur's manhood, she equates his lack of kingly mettle with his failure as a lover: he must be an incompetent leader, she concludes, "Else had he not lost me" (l. 146).

Guinevere then illustrates her own skill at the "craft" needed for leadership by giving shrewd advice to Lancelot, who is at a loss as to how to rejoin the tournament without risking the king's displeasure. It becomes clear that she exerts control in their relationship when she prefaces her advice with the patronizing comment: "but listen to me, / If I must find you wit" (ll. 146-47). The queen tells Lancelot to join the tournament in disguise, on the pretext of wanting to gain glory without relying on the advantage of his great reputation. Guinevere knows how to play Arthur, because she is aware of his great weakness—his pride. She explains to Lancelot:

> how meek soe'er he seem,
> No keener hunter after glory breathes.
> He loves it in his knights more than himself:
> They prove to him his work.
>
> (ll. 154-57)

Although vengeful peripheral figures such as Mark and Vivien condemn the king's moral code for hypocrisy, Guinevere's comments are the most damning because she is the supposed personification of his ideal. Here she insists that Arthur's ambition is not as altruistic as his subjects believe, that he is motivated by more than a disinterested desire to act as the conduit of Christian enlightenment.

Guinevere is proven wrong in her prediction of Arthur's behavior. When she tells him of Lancelot's triumphant ruse, Arthur is disappointed that Lancelot did not trust his king with the secret he shared with his queen (**"Lancelot and Elaine,"** ll. 585-90). Guinevere's main point is not contradicted, however, because Arthur's pride is indeed wounded because he has been excluded from their conspiracy. For the first time Arthur shows a hint of jealousy concerning his wife's relationship with his greatest knight, a relationship that has captured the imagination and now rouses the suspicions of Arthur's subjects far and wide. According to Guinevere—whose opinion is not disputed in Tennyson's text—Arthur has always been too concerned with his kingly duties to pay much attention to the woman he married. There are in fact few scenes in the *Idylls* shared by Arthur and his queen, a notable omission considering how central their relationship is to the rise and fall of Camelot. The times when they do appear together are marked by the remote demeanor of a king whose attempts to communicate are limited either to perfunctory courtesy or—in the case of their final encounter in the convent—to self-righteous indignation. By contrast, Guinevere and Lancelot share a number of scenes that illustrate the fervent passion they feel for each other.

The most illuminating explication of the nature of their bond comes during the conversation they have in the castle garden. Lancelot recounts his previous night's vision of a "maiden Saint" who stood with a "spiritual lily" in her hand. His response to this dream image of a madonna figure shows the conflict he experiences between the idealized purity his society expects him to desire in a woman and his passion for the less acceptable sensual honesty of a woman like Guinevere. The dramatic pause in his declaration that the image "drew mine eyes—away" emphasizes the initial attraction and ultimate repulsion that this figure exerts on him. As he relates how he turned away from the apparition, he suggests that such a woman would be too "perfect-pure," since the slightest flush of sexual desire on either her "silver face" or on the lily from which a spiritual light emanates would "mar their charm of stainless maidenhood" (**"Balin and Balan,"** ll. 255-63).

Guinevere cuts through the iconographic ambiguity of Lancelot's dream and his implicit criticism of such perfection with a frank assertion of her own down-to-earth philosophy. She declares: "Sweeter to me this garden rose / Deep-hued and many-folded! sweeter still / The wildwood hyacinth and the bloom of May" (ll. 264-66). With luxuriously erotic imagery, the queen here becomes the voice of a sensual naturalism. She asserts the value of domesticated nature ("this garden rose") over ascetic purity (the "spiritual lily"), and of untamed nature over the products of cultivation held captive behind garden walls. Guinevere's manifesto entrances Lancelot—he cannot move his eyes from her face—and the temper of his passion for his queen becomes apparent. He loves her for her sensual honesty and not for her embodiment of some chivalric ideal. His rejection of the madonna of his vision for the earthy queen explains his later lack of interest in Elaine, the "lily maid" of Astolat whose virginal purity is embalmed in a perverse act of ritual suicide.[21]

Neither Lancelot nor Guinevere escapes the social consequences that their spirit of romantic independence provoke. Torn between his love for his queen and his duty as vassal to his king, Lancelot is driven by guilt to undertake an ill-fated Grail quest in the hope of absolution. Guinevere never completely disavows her love for the knight who respects her for her own particular qualities, and not for some ideal he wants her to embody. However, the queen is affected increasingly by the repercussions of her transgressive act. The strength of her society's censure is proven by how deeply she internalizes feelings of culpability for the fall of Arthur's civilization. When Guinevere has a premonition that she cannot escape Modred's determined campaign to track her guilt, the traitorous knight becomes her social conscience. The "Powers that tend the soul" begin to "vex and plague her," and she is gripped by "a vague spiritual fear" that her sin will destroy "all the land" (**"Guinevere,"** ll. 64-81). In desperation she asks Lancelot to leave the court before their adultery becomes public knowledge. He responds that in the safety of his castle he will "hide thee . . . and hold thee with my life against the world" (ll. 111-14). She replies that it is impossible for her to escape the "shame" of her sin, for he cannot "hide me from myself" (ll. 117-18). As Richard A. Sylvia observes, far from gloating over the fate of the fallen queen, Tennyson's narratorial voice here portrays the queen with a measure of sympathy that works to counter Arthur's later denunciation of her "great sin."[22]

Guinevere's malaise is relieved for a time when she receives sanctuary in the convent at Almesbury. At first the anonymous queen finds escape from her guilt in a novice's "babbling heedlessness / Which often lured her from herself" (**"Guinevere,"** ll. 149-50).[23] Soon, however, the novice becomes, like the image of Modred that haunts her dreams, the voice of Guinevere's social conscience. She is a fury who will not let the queen remain in peace. Apparently unaware of Guinevere's identity, the novice relates the story of "the good King and

his wicked Queen" to her weeping sister, singing that it is "too late" to alter what has passed (ll. 164-210). She then says of the queen's sin: "this is all woman's grief, / That *she* is woman, whose disloyal life / Hath wrought confusion in the Table Round" (ll. 216-18). She thereby articulates her society's tendency to impute the guilt of one emblematic woman to the whole of womankind. Like Eve's before her, the queen's single action causes the world to fall from ordered perfection into a state of chaotic nature.

Although the novice plays the role of an impugning Greek chorus, she is a silly figure from the outset. As a result her condemnations of the queen's actions are undercut by her own lack of credibility. As well, the counterpointing of her criticisms with Guinevere's responses allows the queen opportunity to refute the charges of her society. In reply to the novice's blaming "the sinful Queen" for ruining the reputation of all womankind, Guinevere asks herself: "Will the child kill me with her foolish prate?" (l. 223). She then counters the girl's account of the rise and fall of Camelot by saying: "O little maid, shut in by nunnery walls, / What canst thou know of Kings and Tables Round, / Or what of signs and wonders, but the signs / And simple miracles of thy nunnery?" (ll. 225-28).

With her limited imagination and experience, the novice lacks a sophisticated understanding of human behavior. She sees the world in black and white, in terms of the inflexible categories of conventional morality. Her failure to recognize the subtle nuances of individual circumstance is shown by her conclusion that Lancelot could not possess noble character because he is disloyal to his king. Guinevere's "mournful answer" to the ingenue is that outside "narrowing nunnery-walls" judgments about life are never so easy, because the world, with "all its lights / And shadows," is so complex that rigid moral absolutes fail to account for everything that matters (ll. 340-45). The novice is a vacuous character who decries her own verbosity—she cries "Shame on her garrulity garrulously" and says that she is often censured for "her gadding tongue" (ll. 310-11). The novice comes across as a *naif* whose opinions are formulaic repetitions of what she has been told by her father and others. She is the worst kind of gossip, repeating hearsay and harsh ethical verdicts that she herself has never thought through.

The fact that a "babbler" such as the novice and a "subtle beast" (l. 58) such as Modred act as Guinevere's social conscience in these scenes demands that the context, and not just the content, of her subsequent repentance be kept in focus. Guinevere's waverings between her pleasant memories of Lancelot and her attempts to assuage what she calls her "own too-fearful guilt" (l. 368) with assertions of pious regret demonstrate her inability to conform in other than a half-hearted way to her society's demands for expiation. Close analysis of the final scenes at the convent shows the queen's capitulation to be not a genuinely cowed contrition, but the reluctant choice of an ostracized woman who, having above all the shrewd character of a survivor, is presented with no viable alternative for her future.

Immediately after she yells at the novice for criticizing "the sinful Queen," Guinevere muses "surely I repent," since she will no longer think of Lancelot and the "sins that made the past so pleasant to us" (ll. 370-73). The irony of this passage is that her resolution not to revel in thoughts of past sin does not constitute what her accusers would consider much of a penance. In a wonderfully ambiguous use of repetition, the queen says, "I have sworn never to see him more, / To see him more" (ll. 373-74). Her attempt at self-denial is short lived. Even as she makes this affirmation, her "memory from old habit of mind" goes "slipping back upon the golden days" when she first met Lancelot (ll. 375-77). Here her feelings of love trump any desire to make amends for her socially transgressive actions. She remembers her journey to court with Lancelot as a time of Arcadian bliss and contrasts this memory with her first impression of her betrothed, a man she found "cold / High, self-contained, and passionless" (ll. 402-3).

Guinevere's evocation of her first meeting with Lancelot is authoritative because it is the only description we get of this meeting. She controls the narrative with her own version of events, a version gilded with romantic nostalgia. Her memory of pastoral enchantment casts her love affair with Lancelot in intensely personal terms and makes the transgression that springs from this love understandable. As a result, Guinevere's account deflates the rhetoric of those such as the novice who would represent the queen's action in mythopoeic terms as the great sin that precipitated the demise of Arthur's dream of a secular kingdom of Christ. It is also significant that Guinevere's description of her first encounters with Lancelot and Arthur comes immediately before the king's entry onto the scene to confront her. Because Guinevere's reverie, which acts as a kind of self-defense, is the prelude to the king's arrival, it provides the context in which to interpret his long final monologue. Juxtaposed against her charming memories, his speech—a "Denouncing judgement" put forth by a disembodied voice that is "Monotonous and hollow like a Ghost's" (ll. 417-18)—seems the forced harangue of a man who proves himself to be exactly as Guinevere first thought: "cold / High, self-contained."[24]

As Arthur delivers his side of the story while Guinevere "grovels" at his feet, his speech becomes a diatribe on the faithlessness of woman that reveals the misogynistic basis of his chivalric code. He says that he wanted the "fair Order of my Table Round, / . . . To serve as model

for the mighty world," and that he expected his relationship with his queen to serve as a model for his knights' own behavior (ll. 460-62). In language that epitomizes the Victorian construction of woman as edifying moral influence, the king describes how he had conceived of the function of love before his marriage:

> I knew
> Of no more subtle master under heaven
> Than is the maiden passion for a maid,
> Not only to keep down the base in man,
> But teach high thought, and amiable words
> And courtliness, and the desire of fame,
> And love of truth, and all that makes a man.
>
> (ll. 474-80)

The king then says that he had expected Guinevere to conform to this preconceived vision of her wifely role. He wanted her to be a "helpmate" who would sacrifice her own identity to his greater cause (ll. 481-83). Arthur expected his supporters to constitute a body politic subservient to his own ambitions.[25] He saw himself as the "Head" (l. 459) of his vassal lords, and he saw Lancelot as his "right arm" (l. 426). That he desired Guinevere to be his heart becomes clear when he says that because she rejected him for Lancelot, his knights drew "foul ensample from fair names" (l. 487). As a result, he claims: "the loathsome opposite / Of all my heart had destined did obtain, / And all through thee!" (ll. 488-90). Mentioning Lancelot's treachery only in passing, Arthur tells Guinevere: "thou hast spoilt the purpose of my life" (l. 450).[26]

Because Guinevere has failed to embody his ideal, he demonizes her as the inverse—as the "loathsome opposite"—of it. Because she has refused to conform to the submissive wifely role her husband and her society prescribe, she has become not only a threat to social order, but the signifier of all threat to that order. Guinevere's assertion of free will represented by her choice of lover is an example of behavior that shakes the foundations of her patriarchal culture.[27] Arthur dreads the consequences of losing control over his wife. His anxiety is manifested in a fear of female reproductive power. He declares, "Well it is that no child is born of thee," since the destruction she has engendered even while childless is already potent and prolific:

> The children born of thee are sword and fire,
> Red ruin, and the breaking up of laws,
> The craft of kindred and the Godless hosts
> Of heathen swarming o'er the Northern Sea.
>
> (ll. 421-25)

Arthur then voices the most extreme expression in the *Idylls* of the fear of women's sexuality when he says that he "hold[s] that man the worst of public foes" whose "cowardice" permits an adulterous wife to "abide and rule the house." Because she is "taken everywhere for pure" such a woman will, he contends, spread moral contagion to the entire populace:

> She like a new disease, unknown to men,
> Creeps, no precaution used, among the crowd,
> Makes wicked lightnings of her eyes, and saps
> The fealty of our friends, and stirs the pulse
> With devil's leaps, and poisons half the young.
>
> (ll. 509-19)

In this image Arthur equates the virulence of the faithless wife with venereal infection, against which no prophylactic is used because no suspicion of disease exists. He contends that the noxious influence of the fallen woman who is believed to be pure disrupts the social order. Her unregulated sexuality subverts her husband, who cannot control his domestic life and as a result is mocked by his fellow men. Like a vampire, she "saps / The fealty of our friends." She becomes here the serpent-woman, or lamia, who according to legend has the "power to destroy men" by "magically undermining their vitality."[28]

This characterization of Guinevere is, however, both unjust and misplaced. Unlike Vivien, the lamia-figure who styles herself as the nemesis of Arthur's ideal, Guinevere does not actively strive to undermine his authority. At most, she ridicules his dream of order as an egocentric delusion. Her attitude is characterized primarily by a disdainful indifference. But true to the binary logic of his view of female agency, Arthur interprets her indifference as malicious intent. She does not fulfil the symbolic role he has imposed on her, and she has gone so far as to have an affair with his most valiant knight. In Arthur's definition of good and evil, the fallen angel of purity must become an agent of the apocalypse. He imputes this destructive otherness to Guinevere in a way that reveals the distrust of woman's sexuality that underlay the Victorian idealization of an asexual domestic and domesticated femininity.[29] If Guinevere has not surrendered to Arthur's figuration of her as his nurturing epipsyche, then she must signify the beast-like power of instinct and passion that threatens to throw his kingdom back into the anarchy of the wasteland.

As his invective reaches a crescendo, Arthur claims that it would be "Worst of the worst" for a knowing cuckold to reign, and implies that as a result he will soon relinquish his position as sovereign. He says that as a private man he will suffer for the loss of Guinevere, and that, as he sees her now in such a contemptible state, his "vast pity almost makes [him] die" (l. 531). As he prepares to abandon her—proclaiming dramatically, "Yet must I leave thee, woman, to thy shame" (l. 508)—he strives to keep the moral high ground with a declaration of his magnanimity. He blesses her with the

benediction: "I forgive thee, as Eternal God / Forgives" (ll. 541-42). The tone of condescending self-righteousness here is representative of the aloofness Arthur displays throughout his final address to Guinevere. The king's professions of enduring love ring hollow in light of his past neglect of his wife, and they show that even if Arthur ever did love Guinevere for herself, he now can only pity her as the greatest of sinners—as the architect of his doom.

As Steven Dillon observes, Arthur's solemn departure from his queen contrasts with the earlier bittersweet parting of Guinevere from Lancelot, a time when the lovers "kissed, and parted weeping" (**"Guinevere,"** l. 124).[30] As a result, a certain irony underlies the king's final speech and subverts the pious assertions of forgiveness that punctuate his catalog of the consequences of her betrayal. It is a telling indictment of the superficial nature of his attachment when—answering his own question "But how to take last leave of all I loved?"—he describes only her physical attributes in a stock Petrarchan blazon (ll. 543-51). He apostrophizes her "golden hair" and her "imperial-moulded form," and he laments the loss of enjoyment of a "beauty such as never woman wore." His words then reveal in stark terms the economy of possession that underwrites the chivalric ethos, when he says: "I cannot touch thy lips, they are not mine, / But Lancelot's: nay, they never were the King's." Because he is no longer the master of her lips—a metonymic figure for her body as a whole—she is now nothing more than "polluted" flesh to be rejected with disgust.

Arthur then contrasts his own purity with her incontinence, claiming "I was ever virgin save for thee" (l. 554). His assertion cannot be read as wholly credible, however. By mentioning his early sexual experience, the king raises the specter of his youthful incestuous behavior that was a traditional feature of the Arthurian story, one that Tennyson initially considered including in his own version.[31] It is therefore rather suspect when later in this same passage Arthur insists that Modred, who has become his archenemy, is "no kin of mine" (l. 570). Perhaps the king protests too much here, feeling compelled to deny at least implicitly the rumor that his sister's child is his own son. Certainly, by introducing the topic of his premarital sexual experience he raises doubts about his own much-vaunted purity.[32]

With no more than a "Farewell!" Arthur then leaves Guinevere prostrate on the convent floor as he marches off "ghostlike to his doom" (ll. 577, 601). Guinevere is left alone with her husband's accusations ringing in her ears. She again professes her repentance—this time in hyperbolic terms—and again rationalizes away the sense in inflicting suffering on herself. She says:

>   he, the King,
> Called me polluted: shall I kill myself?
> What help in that? I cannot kill my sin,
> If soul be soul; nor can I kill my shame;
> No, nor by living can I live it down.
> The days will grow to weeks, the weeks to months,
> The months will add themselves and make the years,
> The years will roll into the centuries,
> And mine will ever be a name of scorn.
> I must not dwell on that defeat of fame.
> Let the world be; that is but of the world.

                              (ll. 614-24)

Always the pragmatist, Guinevere here sees no use in trying to fight an infamy that will continue to grow regardless of her own contrition. She then fixates on Arthur's suggestion that they may meet again as pure souls in heaven. Guinevere says that her "false voluptuous pride" has prevented her from recognizing her husband as "the highest and most human" of men (ll. 636, 644). She professes repentance, saying "It was my duty to have loved the highest," and "We needs must love the highest when we see it, / Not Lancelot, nor another" (ll. 652-56).

This declaration has been taken at face value by many critics. The reception of her speech has tended to two extremes, both of which result from a failure to see the dramatic irony of the final scene between the king and his queen. Critics tend either to praise the repentance of the fallen queen as a vindication of the truth of Arthur's vision,[33] or to indict Tennyson for making his heroine capitulate to, and thus sustain, the patriarchal hegemony of her culture.[34] I would not want to argue that Tennyson's Guinevere is a model of self-possessed resistance to patriarchy; we need only look at the protagonist of William Morris's *Defence of Guenevere*—published the year before Tennyson's **"Guinevere,"** in 1858—to find a queen who, unlike the at least ostensibly contrite woman of the *Idylls,* retains an assertive self-confidence to the end.[35] However, when put in the context of everything else Tennyson's queen says, her change of heart—which is phrased in the idiom of the king, and not the queen—rings hollow. She says it was her wifely "duty" to have loved her husband, even as she again evokes with sensual imagery her passion for her favorite knight, saying, "I yearned for warmth and colour which I found / In Lancelot" (ll. 642-43). Turning to the novice who has plagued her with condemnations of her sin, Guinevere assumes the demonic role that her society has ascribed to her: "Ye know me then, that wicked one, who broke / The vast design and purpose of the King" (ll. 663-64).

As she declares her intention to live a life of penance, however, Guinevere concentrates on performing the superficial duties expected of her and not once displays what could be read as genuine spiritual torment caused by guilt. She makes clear the attraction convent life holds: she sees it as the only way to escape "the voices crying 'shame'" outside the "narrowing nunnery-walls" (ll. 665-67). She chooses a life of religious seclusion because, abandoned by her husband and shunned by her society, she has no other options. She becomes an example of the fallen woman so ubiquitous in Victorian literature, but her plight is blamed on the idealistic delusions of the king and not on Guinevere's own innate iniquity. She has all along refused to conform to Arthur's vision of her as his literal better half, and in her final capitulation she declines to express any but the most formulaic admissions of guilt. A certain poetic justice attends Guinevere's fate, since her final years are described as a time of relative happiness during which she regains enough social stature to be named abbess of the convent. It is clear, however, that she never fully escapes the censure of a society that anathematizes women who will not conform to its expectations. She finds refuge from the "voices" that come from beyond the walls of her new home, but not from the reproaches of an internalized sense of shame. Only in death, we are told, does she finally "[pass] / To where beyond these voices there is peace" (ll. 691-92).

        . . . . .

Thus Guinevere's capitulation is equivocal. She becomes the kind of Magdalen figure that fascinated a Victorian reading public eager for tales of sin punished and virtue rewarded. Yet in her fallen state she gains a measure of freedom from the model of womanliness that binds a woman of her social position. She has played neither the angelic helpmeet nor the demonic temptress, regardless of Arthur's attempt to cast her as the force that destroys his dream of forging Christian order out of the chaotic realm of nature. It is Arthur who has made the fatal mistake by investing a mortal woman with the powers of transcendent emotional strength, by assuming she could act to anchor his struggle to change the world for good. Most tellingly, Arthur himself finally provides the most forceful statement of the necessary transience of any dream of order in the world. Before the "last dim, weird battle of the west," Bedivere overhears the king lamenting that efforts "to work His will" have been "in vain," that "all whereon I leaned in wife and friend / Is traitor to my peace, and all my realm / Reels back into the beast and is no more" (**"The Passing of Arthur,"** ll. 22-26). In the aftermath of the battle, however, Arthur listens as Bedivere mourns the dissolution of the Round Table fellowship (ll. 394-406). In response, the king, resigned to his fate, wistfully declares: "The old order changeth, yielding place to new, / And God fulfils himself in many ways, / Lest one good custom should corrupt the world" (ll. 408-10).

The *Idylls* closes with an epilogue **"To the Queen"** that strives to efface the skeptical treatment to which Arthur has been subjected throughout the poem cycle. Declaiming in the voice of poet laureate, Tennyson endorses in hyperbolic terms the expansionist, imperialist ethos of Arthur's dream of conquering "many a race and creed" who are desperate for the civilizing influence of Anglo-Saxon culture (l. 10). Like Arthur, however, Tennyson laments the breaking up of empire, and he ends with a wistful comment on the limits of human ambition; "the goal of this great world," he says, "Lies beyond sight" (ll. 59-60). Tennyson blames the decay of Britain's authority on foreign influence—on rumblings of discontent from colonized Canada (ll. 14-17), on "Art with poisonous honey stolen from France" (l. 56). I would argue, however, that as in Arthur's world this decay results from a failure of moral authority at the very core of Tennyson's culture. This problem has been emphasized throughout the *Idylls* themselves by the words and actions of women like Guinevere whose lives are intimately affected by visions of male glory. Tennyson's Guinevere is dramatically stronger, her criticism of Arthur more credible and damaging, and her final repentance more ambivalent than critics have acknowledged. Despite Arthur's closing words to Bedivere and Tennyson's closing address to Queen Victoria, the poem cycle as a whole makes clear that the failure of both societies to model an ideal of community life is not primarily the fault of forces beyond their control. It is, finally, more the fault of a masculinist culture of chivalry that blames women for its own failure to succeed in a mission whose ideals demand not prejudice and hypocrisy, but the equitable treatment of every citizen.

Notes

1. This title was used for a trial run of the poem cycle that Tennyson quickly withdrew from circulation in the face of negative criticism. It was later abandoned when an expanded grouping of idylls was published in 1859. In this later version, "Nimüe" becomes "Vivien." For information about the poem cycle's early publication history, see the headnote to *The Idylls of the King* in *The Poems of Tennyson,* ed. Christopher Ricks, 2nd ed., 3 vols. (Berkeley: University of California Press, 1987), 3:257-62.

2. See, for example: Dino Franco Felluca, "Tennyson's *Idylls,* Pure Poetry, and the Market," *Studies in English Literature* 37 (1997): 783-803; Debra N. Mancoff, "To Take Excalibur: King Arthur and the Construction of Victorian Manhood," in *King Arthur: A Casebook,* ed. Edward Donald Kennedy (New York: Garland, 1996), 257-80; Alan Sinfield, "Tennyson and the Cultural Politics of Prophecy," *ELH* 57 (1990): 175-95, and *Alfred Tennyson* (Oxford: Blackwell, 1986); James Eli

Adams, "Woman Red in Tooth and Claw: Nature and the Feminine in Tennyson and Darwin," *Victorian Studies* 33 (1989): 7-27; Marion Shaw, *Alfred Lord Tennyson* (Atlantic Highlands, NJ: Humanities, 1988); Carol T. Christ, "The Feminine Subject in Victorian Poetry," *ELH* 54 (1987): 385-401, and "Victorian Masculinity and the Angel in the House," in *A Widening Sphere: Changing Roles of Victorian Women,* ed. Martha Vicinus (Bloomington: Indiana University Press, 1977), 146-62.

3. Commenting in general terms on Tennyson's poetry, Shires observes that his "texts subvert gender ideology. . . . Ideological contradictions are obvious in the verse itself" ("Rereading Tennyson's Gender Politics" in *Victorian Sages and Cultural Discourse: Renegotiating Gender and Power,* ed. Thaïs E. Morgan [New Brunswick: Rutgers University Press, 1990], 49).

4. My own investigation here of the politics of chivalry in the *Idylls* is indebted to the rich body of existing scholarship that examines the religious, political, and aesthetic aspects of the medieval revival in England from the late eighteenth century onward. Insightful general studies include: Debra N. Mancoff, *The Return of King Arthur: The Legend through Victorian Eyes* (New York: H. N. Abrams, 1995); Florence S. Boos, ed., *History and Community: Essays in Victorian Medievalism* (New York: Garland, 1992); Raymond Chapman, *The Sense of the Past in Victorian Literature* (London: Croom, 1986); K. L. Morris, *The Image of the Middle Ages in Romantic and Victorian Literature* (Beckenham: Croom, 1984); M. Girouard, *The Return to Camelot: Chivalry and the English Gentleman* (New Haven: Yale University Press, 1981); and Alice Chandler, *A Dream of Order: The Medieval Ideal in Nineteenth-Century English Literature* (Lincoln: University of Nebraska Press, 1970). For Tennyson's particular contribution to the rekindling of interest in Arthurian legend, see: Clinton Machann, "Tennyson's King Arthur and the Violence of Manliness," *Victorian Poetry* 38 (2000): 199-226; Mancoff, "To Take Excalibur: King Arthur and the Construction of Victorian Manhood"; Roger Simpson, *Camelot Regained: The Arthurian Revival and Tennyson, 1800-1849* (Cambridge: D. S. Brewer, 1990); Beverly Taylor and Elisabeth Brewer, *The Return of King Arthur: British and American Arthurian Literature Since 1800* (Cambridge: D. S. Brewer, 1983), especially 68-167; David Staines, *Tennyson's Camelot: "The Idylls of the King" and Its Medieval Sources* (Waterloo, Ontario: Wilfrid Laurier University Press, 1982); Girouard, *The Return to Camelot,*

177-96; and J. Phillip Eggers, *King Arthur's Laureate* (New York: New York University Press, 1971).

5. Alfred Tennyson, "The Holy Grail," *The Idylls of the King,* in *The Poems of Tennyson,* 3:178. All subsequent references to Tennyson's text are to this edition, by idyll title and line number.

6. Tennyson taps into a tradition in western culture that identifies woman with nature. In this configuration the feminine is both the nurturing and healing powers of a benevolent Mother Nature, and the mysterious and terrifying forces of a phenomenal world that acts with cold indifference to the fate of her human (read: male) children. On the history of this trope, see: Carolyn Merchant, *The Death of Nature: Women, Ecology, and the Scientific Revolution* (New York: Harper, 1990), especially the chapters "Nature as Female," 1-41, and "Nature as Disorder: Women and Witches," 127-48; Sherry B. Ortner, "Is Female to Male as Nature is to Culture?" in *Woman, Culture, and Society,* ed. Michelle Z. Rosaldo (Stanford: Stanford University Press, 1974), 67-87; and Simone de Beauvoir, *The Second Sex,* trans. and ed. H. M. Parshley (New York: Vintage, 1989), 144ff.

7. The *Idylls* are framed by a "Dedication" to the memory of the recently deceased Prince Consort—to "Albert the Good" who "seems to me / Scarce other than my king's ideal knight" (ll. 42; 5-6)—and by a closing address "To the Queen," in which the poet laureate insists that his Arthur is modeled on Albert—on "Ideal manhood closed in real man" (l. 38)—and not on the Arthur of legend, the hero of a more "adulterous" time (ll. 39-45).

8. Tennyson's representation of royal function gains particular resonance when read in the context of Queen Victoria's effort to portray herself and Albert both as rulers of empire and as the core of a prototypically bourgeois family unit. For a more general discussion of the role that royal marriages played in modeling bourgeois behavior, see the introduction to Joan Perkin's *Women and Marriage in Nineteenth-Century England* (Chicago: Lyceum, 1989).

9. I am thinking here of the kind of rhetoric exemplified by Peter Gaskell's *The Manufacturing Population of England,* which figures a man's retreat into the domestic sphere as the sole opportunity for withdrawal into an authentic inner self. Of the home, Gaskell rhapsodizes:

> It is here alone that man can develop in their full beauty those affections of the heart which are destined to be, through life, the haven to which he may retire when driven about and persecuted by the storms of fortune. It is here alone it can find refuge . . . it is here that he may hold communion with himself; and it is here and here, alone, that he will be enabled to retain his pride of self.
>
> (*The Manufacturing Population of England, its moral, social, and physical conditions, and the changes which have arisen from the use of steam machinery; with an examination of infant labor* [1833; reprint, New York: Arno Press, 1972], 270).

10. This discourse appears as well in Tennyson's most direct intervention into the contemporary debate regarding the so-called "Woman Question." In his 1847 mock-heroic poem *The Princess,* the narrator-prince is the voice of biological essentialism. Pressing his marriage suit on Princess Ida, the prince claims that a man's "mental breadth" would complement woman's "sweetness" and "moral height," for "either sex alone / Is half itself, and in true marriage lies / Nor equal nor unequal: each fulfils / Defect in each, and always thought in thought, / Purpose in purpose, will in will, they grow, / The single pure and perfect animal, / The two-celled heart beating, with one full stroke, / Life." Having advanced this Platonic notion that love has the power to reunify body and soul, the prince declares that such a bond will return "a statelier Eden back to man" (*The Poems of Tennyson,* 2:242-89). As is the case with King Arthur, the prince cannot be read as the unmediated mouthpiece of Tennyson's own views, for a certain authorial distance from the narrator is maintained throughout the poem.

11. This exchange of power invites a psychoanalytic reading. Carol Christ reads Arthur's desire for Guinevere as pre-Oedipal, suggesting that "intercourse becomes an incorporative fantasy, almost a reversal of the birth process, enabling him to become pregnant and potent in absorbing her" ("Feminine Subject," 394). And Gerhard Joseph provides an interesting discussion of the symbolic significance of the fact that Arthur receives, and then returns, such an obviously phallic token of virility as a sword from such an archetypally feminine source as a lady in a lake. See "Tennyson's Sword: From 'Mungo the American' to *Idylls of the King,*" in *Sex and Death in Victorian Literature,* ed. Regina Barreca (Bloomington: Indiana University Press, 1990), 64-68.

12. I draw here on William Brashear's compelling reading of the *Idylls* in the terms of Nietzsche's opposition of the Apollonian and the Dionysian. See "Tennyson's Tragic Vitalism: *Idylls of the King,*" *Victorian Poetry* 6 (1968): 29-49.

13. Carol Christ in "Victorian Masculinity and the Angel in the House" focuses on the work of Coventry Patmore and Tennyson to demonstrate how this type of projection functions. She argues that Patmore's celebration of unthinking, passive womanliness is in fact a creation of the possibility for escape from the "anxiety and pain" that is the by-product of active, logical, and ambitious manliness. If man can "find and worship a creature that he conceives to be free from [his] conflicting desires, he is able to find some salvation from them" (152). This, Christ proposes, is what underlies the Victorian man's "desire to incorporate a passivity and asexuality he assumed was a woman's natural identity" (159). If this "natural identity" is proven to be false, then hope for "salvation" is doomed; if woman is sexual, so to must man be beast-like (162). Indeed, when Arthur finally realizes that his queen is neither passive nor asexual, he gives up hope of overcoming his greatest fear—that his kingdom will "Reel back into the beast, and be no more" ("The Last Tournament," l. 125).

14. Arthur envisions Guinevere as the inferior half of a Platonic duality in which she is body and he is mind. This hierarchy is implicit in the question Arthur asks himself as he considers marrying Guinevere, who is the "fairest of all flesh on earth": "Shall I not lift her from this land of beasts / Up to my throne, and side by side with me?" ("The Coming of Arthur," ll. 79-80). This identification of Guinevere with a feminized nature does not originate with Tennyson. In his brief but illuminating study of the mythological and archetypal features of the Arthurian tradition, John Matthews identifies as "ancient" a "notion which saw Arthur as inheriting his kingdom through marriage to an earthly representative of the Goddess" (*The Arthurian Tradition* [Shaftesbury, UK: Element, 1989], 6). However, the rhetorical development of this motif in the *Idylls* is typically Victorian in construction, and Tennyson untypically portrays the destructive consequences of Arthur's use of Guinevere in this way.

15. Elliot L. Gilbert, "The Female King: Tennyson's Arthurian Apocalypse" *PMLA* 98 (1983): 865.

16. Ibid., 875.

17. Ibid., 872.

18. Ibid.

19. Nina Auerbach, *Woman and the Demon: The Life of a Victorian Myth* (Cambridge: Harvard University Press, 1982), 58.

20. More telling than Guinevere's indictment is the fact that Merlin, the creative architect of Arthur's dream of order, corroborates her opinion early in the *Idylls*, before any obvious sign of Camelot's moral decay. Speaking to Gareth, Merlin concedes that Arthur binds his knights to vows that are noble but are such that "No man can keep" ("Gareth and Lynette," ll. 248-93). Also revealing is Tristram's declaration to Isolt that he has learned from watching the travails of Arthur's knights that "The vow that binds too strictly snaps itself," and that "being snapt— / We run more counter to the soul thereof / Than had we never sworn" ("The Last Tournament," ll. 652-55). Tristram's principle is demonstrated when the knights like Balin and Pelleas who believe most fervently in Arthur's dream become the most disillusioned and destructive when they discover that their chivalric code is based on fantasy.

A number of critics have explored the troubling implications of the assumptions that underwrite Arthur's dream. Speaking of the king's "solipsistic isolation," for example, Elliot L. Gilbert argues convincingly that it is not Guinevere's adultery but "Arthur's naiveté about the dynamics of the human psyche that dooms his ideal community from the start" ("Female King," 874). Linda M. Shires perhaps best captures the untenable nature of Arthur's position when she writes: "Arthur represents a mixture of both real and ideal and of male and female. He is historically marked as feminine by his sexuality and his position as a cuckold; he is marked as masculine by his aggression in battle, his subordination of women, and his rule as king. His paradoxical goal is to act as a patriarch in a world in which he also seeks to abolish gender difference" ("Patriarchy, Dead Men, and Tennyson's *Idylls of the King*," *Victorian Poetry* 30 [1992]: 409). And Ian McGuire profitably reads the Round Table fellowship as a psychiatric case study of an all-male community caught in a state of arrested development that cannot last: "For Camelot to flourish the Oedipal process must not be successfully completed by Arthur's knights but must rather be suspended indefinitely between the renunciation of the mother and the discovery of the wifely substitute"; as a result, "it is not surprising that Camelot fails as a long-term political entity, relying as it does upon the indefinite extension of the transitional period of male adolescence" ("Epistemology and Empire in *Idylls of the King*," *Victorian Poetry* 30 [1992]: 387).

21. By situating the representation of Elaine's suicide in the context of Victorian culture, Elisabeth Bronfen provides a compelling analysis of her death both as a capitulation to a culture that fetishizes

the female corpse and as an assertion of herself as author of her fate in opposition to the expectations of patriarchal culture. See *Over Her Dead Body: Death, Femininity, and the Aesthetic* (New York: Routledge, 1992), 141-67.

22. Sylvia is, in fact, the only critic to take into account how the several alternative versions of events that frame Arthur's denunciation work to undercut it. Although I find Sylvia's analysis generally compelling, we differ in our readings of Guinevere's final state of mind: whereas he argues that "at the close she, too, sadly espouses her culture's values" (27), as I argue below I read her contrition as equivocal at best. This difference in conclusion stems perhaps from the fact that Sylvia focuses only on the narrative events that precede the king's speech, whereas I factor in as well the ambivalences in the queen's response to his visit. See "Sexual Politics and Narrative Method in Tennyson's 'Guinevere,'" *Victorian Newsletter* 76 (1989): 23-28.

23. Cf. Sylvia, "Sexual Politics and Narrative Method," 25.

24. Tennyson departs here significantly from his primary model for Arthurian legend, Malory's *Morte D'Arthur.* In Malory, Guinevere enters the convent after hearing of Arthur's death and has her only conversation with Lancelot. Tennyson's alteration allows Arthur a chance to present his side of the story while venting his disappointment. However, far from vindicating his anger and justifying his harsh judgment of his wife, Arthur's haughty castigation confirms Guinevere's preceding account of her unfavorable first impression of the king. Response by contemporaries to Arthur's speech was generally positive, although the self-righteous tone of the king's sermon prompted one reviewer to comment that he sounds like a "crowned curate." As well, the fact that R. H. Hutton in 1888 feels compelled to defend Tennyson's Arthur against the "taunt" that he is an "impeccable prig" suggests that such an appraisal was common and defensible enough to merit an extended rebuttal (quoted in *Tennyson: The Critical Heritage,* ed. John D. Jump [New York: Routledge, 1967], 386).

25. Richard D. Mallen profitably explores the political implications of Tennyson's use of such corporate metaphors in "The 'Crowned Republic' of Tennyson's *Idylls of the King,*" *Victorian Poetry* 37 (1999): 275-89.

26. Tennyson's king here is very different from Malory's Arthur, who is much more concerned by the loss of his comrade-in-arms Lancelot than by the loss of his queen, whom he views as easily replaceable.

27. On this point, Marion Shaw lucidly observes that "Guinevere's crime is not that she is deliberately destructive . . . but that she is desirous as well as desirable. . . . Uncontrolled, unlegalized female sexual desire both emasculates men and reduces their manly function; Arthur's 'vast design and purpose' is broken and Lancelot's 'own name shames [him], seeming a reproach'; both men die heirless" (*Alfred Lord Tennyson,* 122).

28. H. R. Hays, *The Dangerous Sex: The Myth of Feminine Evil* (New York: Putnam, 1966), 132. The figure of the lamia, the beautiful woman who changes into a serpent-woman soon after marriage and then devours her husband, is common in many occidental folk and literary traditions. Margaret Hallissy argues that the lamia, a demonic agent possessed of insatiable carnal appetite and the ability to adopt the guises of witch, vampire, and incubus, "embodies male fears of women's changeability" (*Venomous Woman: Fear of the Female in Literature* [New York: Greenwood, 1987], 91). According to Hallissy, the lamia represents the male fear of incorporation into the female, which is a fear of a loss of power that will precipitate a loss of self. Such a loss of self is, indeed, the fate of Merlin at the hands of Vivien. Nina Auerbach in *Woman and the Demon* identifies Vivien as one of many lamia-figures in Victorian literature who "exude a power that withers patriarchs" and who "all find their greatest triumphs in displacing male authorities" (8). She is the archetypal femme fatale, whose mysterious sexuality conquers intellect. With her prophetic pronouncements she is the counterpart of Merlin. She is anarchic, sensual paganism, while he is ascetic Christian order; she is the Dionysian "fiery flood" that overwhelms the "frosty cells" of Apollonian monkishness with the promise of a release from the pain of consciousness (see "Balin and Balan," ll. 434-53). Although Tennyson could be criticized for reinforcing stereotypes of woman's evil in his use of lamia imagery, his portrayal of Vivien precludes any real criticism. Far from being an unsympathetic figure, Vivien gains heroic stature as the embodiment of the forces of nature that necessarily prevail over the transient efforts of individual will.

29. As Mary Poovey observes, the Victorian image of the pure woman appears antithetical to the image that predominated during the previous three centuries, when "woman was consistently represented as the site of willful sexuality and bodily appetite" and was "associated with flesh, desire, and unsocialized, hence susceptible, impulses and passions." See *Uneven Developments: the Ideological*

Work of Gender in Mid-Victorian England (Chicago: University of Chicago Press, 1988), 9-19. Yet this apparent discrepancy is not as inexplicable as it first appears, for implicit in the shrill Victorian insistence on woman's natural innocence is a recognition that alternative modes of being and behavior are possible. In the very creation of an asexual ideal, there was acknowledgment of a need to repress desires smoldering just under the surface in young women by "protecting" them from the public world of corruption. On this point, see Peter T. Cominos, "Innocent Femina Sensualis in Unconscious Conflict" in *Suffer and Be Still: Women in the Victorian Age,* ed. Martha Vicinus (Bloomington: Indiana University Press, 1972), 156.

30. Steven C. Dillon, "Milton and Tennyson's 'Guinevere,'" *ELH* 54 (1987): 152.

31. In the final version of his poem cycle, Tennyson excludes any explicit reference to Arthur's relationship with his half-sister. In so doing, he diverges from the traditional story of the French romances that had come into English literature through Malory and follows instead the accounts familiar to many Victorian readers, the chronicles of Geoffrey of Monmouth and Layamon. Yet Tennyson's initial intention to use Malory's version seems clear, for in an early notebook he jotted down "a genealogy that identified Morgause as 'Arthur's sister' and Mordred as her 'Son by Arthur'" (Eggers, *King Arthur's Laureate,* 11).

32. Algernon Swinburne remarked in 1872 that Tennyson had "lowered and degraded" the Arthurian story by omitting Arthur's incestuous affair with his half-sister. According to Swinburne, this omission erases much of the tragic force of Malory's text and distorts the significance of Guinevere's adultery. She is changed from "a wife unloving and unloved" whose sin can be understood if not condoned, into a "vulgar adultress." Tennyson's excision of the "tragic and exceptional" circumstances of Malory's narrative has the effect, Swinburne fumed, of "reducing Arthur to the level of a wittol, Guinevere to the level of a woman of intrigue, and Lancelot to the level of a 'corespondent'" in a story that is "rather a case for the divorce-court than for poetry" (quoted in *Tennyson: The Critical Heritage,* ed. Jump, 318-19). Swinburne's criticism of Tennyson's treatment is finally less a defense of Guinevere than a diatribe against the "pitiful and ridiculous" figure the laureate creates in the devoted Arthur. According to Swinburne, the king's "besotted blindness" to his wife's adultery makes him an unmanly—and thus an incredible and unsympathetic—hero.

33. See, for example, Stanley J. Solomon, "Tennyson's Paradoxical King," *Victorian Poetry* 1 (1963): 261.

34. See, for example, Shaw, *Alfred Lord Tennyson,* 52-53. In one of the few extended discussions of the "Guinevere" idyll, Margaret Linley stresses the oppositional nature of the queen's new position as a member of a community of women. She notes that because a "profound ambivalence in attitude toward the nature of women's religious orders existed at mid century," Tennyson's contemporaries would have read Guinevere's decision to seek refuge in a convent as more than a simple act of retreat and contrition. As a result, Linley concludes, "her cloistered virtue is ironically as much a further extension of her 'crime' against domestic order and the state as it is a gesture of repentance" ("Sexuality and Nationality in Tennyson's *Idylls of the King,*" *Victorian Poetry* 30 [1992]: 371, 372). Linley also provides a wonderfully subtle analysis of how Arthur inhabits "a variety of shifting subject positions" during his final denunciation of his wife, with the result that his claim to authority is destabilized. Linley goes on, however, to argue that "the fact that Arthur achieves his social mission only as a result of repeated acts of linguistic violence upon Guinevere is displaced by her internalization of the entire system of values, attitudes, and practices which Arthur rehearses at various moments"; according to Linley, Guinevere "demonstrate[s] her consent to submissive oppression" and as a result "Tennyson manages to confine, in spite of the potential subversiveness of his treatment of domestic masculinity, all possible conflicting interests between marriage partners" (374). Although Linley has worked to show the varieties of equivocation at work in this idyll, I would argue that her unequivocal conclusion rather unconvincingly and peremptorily shuts down the many oppositional strategies that counter or at least call into question Arthur's masculinist, imperialist ethos.

35. As Jonathan Freedman notes, Morris's Guenevere refuses to accept blame for the fall of Camelot; she "accuses her accusers, both in the immediate context of the poem, and in the larger, extended context of the Victorian public to which it is addressed" ("Ideological Battleground: Tennyson, Morris, and the Pastness of the Past" in *The Passing of Arthur: New Essays in Arthurian Tradition,* ed. Christopher Baswell and William Sharpe [New York: Garland, 1988], 241). For an overview of other sympathetic Pre-Raphaelite depictions of Guinevere and other Arthurian women, see Carole Silver, "Victorian Spellbinders: Arthurian Women and the Pre-Raphaelite Circle," in *The Passing of Arthur,* ed. Baswell and Sharpe, 249-64.

Anna Jane Barton (essay date fall 2004)

SOURCE: Barton, Anna Jane. "'Eternal Honour to His Name': Tennyson's *Ode on the Death of the Duke of Wellington* and Victorian Memorial Aesthetics." *Victorian Newsletter,* no. 106 (fall 2004): 1-8.

[*In the following essay, Barton explores the circumstances and issues surrounding the negative reception of Tennyson's* Ode on the Death of the Duke of Wellington.]

The death of the Duke of Wellington stamped itself on the national consciousness of nineteenth-century Britain. Wellington and Nelson were the "heroes of the age" but it was Wellington who survied into peacetime, proving himself as "the greatest single argument for Victorian hero worship" "the greatest single argument for Victorian hero worship" (Houghton 309). In mourning for Wellington, the people of Britain had the opportunity to act out their emergent national and cultural identity. Wellington's death provided an occasion for Victoria's nation to describe itself. He was "one of the established institutions of the country . . . as little to be questioned as the existence of St. James's Palace or the action of parliament" (*The Spectator* 18/9/1852), and so to memorialize "England's Duke" was to memorialize the Duke's England. And yet, burdened by an awareness of its own modernity, this Great Exhibition of Grief could never do its subject justice. As one journalist wrote in *The Spectator* "you might as well (to use the phrase in no irreverent sense) seek a biography of gunpowder or of steam, as of that strong-willed English sense of duty which the Duke impersonated among public men" (*Ibid*). The feeling that an occasion so momentous could only be trivialized by public ceremony was strengthened by the Duke's own reputation as a man of silence and of action, who "hated display of any kind" (*Gentleman's Magazine* Oct, 1852). For the two months that followed Wellington's death and culminated with his funeral, an apparently compulsive need to create and produce display through lavish ceremony, public art and pages upon pages of print was countered by a general sense of unease about the pomp and circumstance that were required to memorialize the great Duke.

The protracted debate surrounding the funeral procession and ceremony revolved around this conflict between distaste for lavish public spectacle and the impossibility of producing anything else. The funeral was a pageant of modern Englishness. From the parade of military strength that accompanied the coffin, to the gas lights that were used to illuminate St. Paul's and the mechanical pulley that was used to winch the coffin from the funeral car, to the multitude of people that swarmed into London on the railways to witness the procession, every detail of the event spoke of the new commercial and industrial Empire of which the Duke of Wellington had been a figurehead. The fact that the extensive preparations were barely finished on time and the modern technologies employed were not entirely successful—the funeral car was too heavy and broke down under its own weight, the pulleys used to winch the bier did not work smoothly and the light from the gas lamps was drowned out by the sunlight streaming through the windows of the cathedral—lent the occasion a clumsiness that only served to emphasise its modernity.

The modernity of the funeral provoked an uncomfortable response: "The few great ceremonials, whether local or national, still remaining among us hold there place as relics of the past, not to be lightly interfered with, or approved by, the spirit of our age" (*Illustrated London News* 25/9/1852). One of the event's more generous reviewers, while acknowledging the need for such magnificence, expresses unease about the overt materialism:

> We could not have been content with less than the performance of such a tribute, and yet while it was in progress we felt it was too much . . . That it was an impressive pageant—that it did express a great national idea—that it spoke eloquently the national sentiment in regard to the national man, we all admit; and yet there is a feeling, that the spontaneity, the completeness, the genuineness of the manifestation are abated by the sight of the machinery. It was the real thing, but made to wear the aspect of a getting-up. Enthusiasm wearied itself with its own appliances. The sentiment was overlaid by the timber, the estimates and the plans; the thing was done so handsomely that the material was in excess of the spiritual.
>
> (*The Spectator* 20/11/1852)

The reviewer for *The Examiner* found the ceremony to be a distraction from the serious business of remembrance:

> Reverent thoughts of the dead were in all minds; but necessarily overlaid by thoughts obtruded by the pageantry, they were drawn away from the coffin and passed to the "funeral car drawn by twelve horses, decorated with trophies and heraldic achievements."
>
> (20/11/1852)

And a particularly critical letter to the editor of *The Spectator,* entitled "Funereal and Memorial Aesthetics," describes the "whole proceedings" as "vulgar, overcharged and unnatural" and sees the Duke's funeral as representative of much that was wrong with the England of the day:

> Though Englishmen possess sensibility they suppress it. . . . They are so very practical that they take more interest in the sign than in the signified. By velvet at twelve shillings a yard, and gilding laid on without stint, they express the measure of difference between a hero and a common man.
>
> (20/11/1852)

Each writer suggests that the measure of a hero cannot be found on the rich surfaces of fine ceremony, that it is a thing of depth, beyond the "double gilt, illuminated embroidered and embossed" material language of greatness.

Permanent public memorials to the Duke, were received with a similar scepticism. Two statues had been erected in honor of Wellington while he was still alive: the eighteen foot high naked Achilles, subscribed for and erected to Wellington and his brave companions in arms by their countrywomen had caused a certain amount of laughter.[1] Matthew Cotes Wyatt's bronze statue of the Duke was so unpopular that it was moved from its original site in Hyde Park to Aldershot after his death. In spite of a general feeling that "Colossal statues have rarely produced happy works of art" (*Spectator* 25/20/1852). £23,000, left over from the £100,000 set aside for the cost of the funeral, was used to pay for a national memorial and numerous provincial statues were erected throughout the country.

All of this commentary and criticsm was recorded in the national press.[2] Every day for the two months between the Duke's death and his funeral newspapers published articles about his life, his career and meticulous and endlessly revised accounts of his final hours, until the writing became its own self-perpetuating subject. The press had a strong sense of its role in transforming Wellington into a national institution:

> His attendance at the early service at the Chapel Royal and at the Whitehall sermons, his walk in the park in former years, and of late times his rides to the Horse Guards or the House of Lords, with his servants behind him, are incidents which every newspaper has long chronicled for the information of the country.
>
> (*Gentleman's Magazine* Oct. 1852)

Articles expressed a new confidence in the adequacy of the press to such an important occasIon:

> The press of all parties, in paying tribute to departing greatness, has reviewed the career and the character of the Duke of Wellington with a fairness and a discrimination to which journalism would not have been equal some years before.
>
> (*Spectator* 18/9/1852)

But despite these claims, its extensive involvement might still be felt to be somehow inappropriate:

> It needs all the genuine respect for the memory of the Duke of Wellington to prevent the mass of writing, about the past, present and even future, which floods the journals, in respect to his career, his departure and his funeral, from degenerating into a nuisance; and there can be no doubt that it has already had an inevitable tendency in that direction. Every conceivable phase of his character, all the traits that marked and did

not mark it, are reviewed, not as chance suggests, but systematically, from day to day. A "leading article" about Wellington blocks up one column in each morning journal, as a funeral shutter remains in the window of some West End shopkeeper every day. Society itself joins in the endless talk; seeming to feel that it is bound to show that it appreciates its loss, and forgetting that genuine feelings usually find their own utterance.

> (*Ibid*)

The author of this article, despite his opinion that "genuine respect" and "genuine feelings" are best expressed by not writing and not talking, is unable himself to remain silent. His own contribution to the mass of articles that he considers such a nuisance is just one more example of the dilemma of presentation occasioned by the death of the Duke of Wellington. Moved to use everything available to them in order adequately to respond to the demise of their national hero, the Victorians found that what the technology and culture of their age produced, these massive surfaces of material and print, offended their aesthetic sensibility. Their commitment to sincerity, depth and silence, inherited from previous generations was buried beneath modern surfaces, many of which were perpetuated by anxieties about their own value.

The death of the Duke of Wellington gave not just the nation, but its recently appointed laureate an opportunity to establish a new identity. ***Ode on the Death of the Duke of Wellington,*** Tennyson's first separate publication since he had been appointed laureate in 1850, was not officially a laureate poem—Tennyson received no request from the Queen for its composition—but the connection between national hero and national poet was readily available to reviewers and journalists: "It is fitting" wrote a reviewer for *The Times,* "that the requiem for England's greatest warrior should be hymned by England's laureate." Hence Tennyson's poem was not only a memorial tribute to the Duke, but also the first monument to Tennyson's laureateship. Tennyson expressed something of this in a letter to his Aunt Russell, saying of the ***Ode***: "I wrote it because it was expected of me to write."

The poem was very much a part of the funeral ceremony and the press response. Ten thousand copies were printed for sale on the day of the funeral and the fact that only 6,000 of these were bought can to some extent be explained by the fact that it was reproduced more or less in its entirety in *The Times* the previous day. Although the poem was by no means the critical disaster that Tennyson perceived it to be, it was not an unqualified success. Reviews of the poem express a disappointment and a discomfort very similar to that expressed about the funeral ceremony and press involvement. There is a sense of the potential that the occasion offers—"Of these themes, the ode before us has the most august that ever fell to the chance of poet laureate, one to have wakened emotion in the most humble of minstrels"—a feeling that Tennyson's poem only served to trivialize its occasion—"But Mr. Tennyson seems to have thought otherwise, and regarded the occasion as happily intended to illustrate how readily he could sport with a great subject and reduce its mightiness to the sing-song of indolent rhythm and familiar rhyme"—and that the strained dignity of the poem was incongruous with the hero it celebrated: "Most inappropriate alas! Is this mode of treatment to the topic; for the 'Great Duke' whom he commemorates was the most unaffected of men; and this selfsame method is, of all the methods of verse-writing, the most affected" (*Illustrated London News* 27/11/1852). The only defense is that it is at least in keeping with the elaborate funeral ceremony: "Grand and solemn to the occasion is the poet's simple strain of music that accompanies the funeral pageant to St. Paul's" (*Examiner* 20/11/1852).

Ode on the Death of the Duke of Wellington might also be criticized for its lack of difference from the funeral ceremony and the media circus surrounding it. Even though the newspapers and journals made it part of the "Wellington Literature" that filled their pages by quoting it wholesale in their reviews, what they saw as its failure to stand apart from the mass of print became a subject of their criticism. *The Weekly News and Chronicle* could see little to separate the poem from "dozens of such lines" that had been received by the provincial newspapers over the past three months (20/11/1852) and *The Leader* (20/11/1852) expressed its disappointment that the only thing that caused this ode to "stand eminent" from the "articles and biographies, pamphlets and poems that crowd upon the inattentive public" was Tennyson's name at the bottom (20/11/1852). While feelings of unease about the magnificence of the funeral could be tempered by an understanding that nothing else and nothing less could be done, there was a more specific, more informed view that this was not the way one should do poetry.

The poem's failings were often put down to its being a piece of laureate verse, required by public events rather than inspired by Tennyson's own feelings of loss— "Wherefore did Alfred write this ode? Because he is Poet Laureate? Surely not because the [spirit] within goaded him with that poetic pain that insists on utterance" (*The Leader* 20/11/1852)—and the position of laureate was itself called into question: "Poets Laureate in these material times are veritable objects of pity. To dream dreams, to open cells of sweet sensibility—to order—is now a thing of terror to a man of poetic genius" (*Weekly News and Chronicle* 20/11/1852). This last remark is particularly interesting because it suggests that it is the materialism of the age that unfits it for poetry. Materialism, the word that defined Victorian modernity for this journalist, is placed in opposition to aesthetics.

Patronage confounds poetic sensibility in the same way that the twelve shilling yards of velvet suppressed the sensibility of a nation at the Duke's funeral. Poetry of any worth cannot, therefore, be modern; it must rise above the times or stay behind them, confining itself to the margins in order to retain any worth.

Ironically, it seems to have been Tennyson's own *In Memoriam* that helped to create all the expectations that *Ode on the Death of the Duke of Wellington* disappointed. The reviewer for *The Court Journal* goes so far as to make a direct comparison:

> Alfred Tennyson, who, when really touched by grief, sobbed forth his soul in the touching *In Memoriam*— Alfred Tennyson, as we suppose feeling himself bound, as the public's pensioner, to pay his laudatory tribute to the memory of the public's idol, has written an ode which . . . is very far inferior to anything that has yet fallen from his pen?
>
> (20/11/1852)

It is a comparison that is hard to ignore. *In Memoriam* and *Ode on the Death of the Duke of Wellington* were almost consecutive publications and both poems are written on the occasion of the death of a man named Arthur. This initial similarity makes differences between the poems all the more obvious. The first Arthur, too young to have achieved any public fame when he died, was Tennyson's close personal friend. The poem that mourned him was written and revised over the course of sixteen years and published anonymously with only Hallam's initials printed on the second title page. The second Arthur, living into old age to acquire unparalleled fame was no better known to Tennyson than he was to the public at large. Tennyson wrote his poem to this Arthur in just two months and the published edition bore the names and titles of both himself and the Duke.[3] It is this easy juxtaposition that informed the reception of *Ode on the Death of the Duke of Wellington.* Tennyson's own *In Memoriam* provided the most powerful precedent for modern elegy. *In Memoriam* not only represents the aesthetic from which Tennyson departed when he wrote his ode, it also exemplified and helped to form the public sensibility that was so offended by the whole memorial experiment instigated by Wellington's death: by the funeral, by the press accounts of the man and by Tennyson's own memorial ode.[4]

In a recent essay on the Victorian elegy Seamus Perry locates its emergence "at a specific, late-Romantic moment in history," a moment that was influenced by the inward turn towards the "particular 'I,'" towards uniqueness and sincerity, "so that the testing point for post-Romantic elegy is about the eloquence or the inwardness of poetic language: its public efficacy and address or its personal authenticity" (117-118). Naming Wordsworth as "the most important Romantic presence in

Victorian elegy," Perry cites Wordsworth's "Essays on Epitaphs" in order to illustrate his argument. In these essays Wordsworth's emphasis is not on the meaning of the words that are carved on the tombstone, but on the "slow laborious work" to which the engraven letters "testify" and the unwritten feeling that lies within them, all the more sincere and powerful for its not being bodied forth in language:

> . . . where the internal evidence proves that the writer was moved, in other words where the charm of sincerity lurks in the language of a tombstone and secretly pervades it, there are no errors in style or manner for which it will not be, in some degree, a recompense.
>
> (345)

In Memoriam, with its fragmented collection of four-line stanzas, might be compared to a graveyard in which the few words on each tombstone are only markers for the body that is buried beneath it. To indicate the depth and sincerity of his grief, the speaker constantly draws attention to the inadequacy of words fully to express it: he is no more articulate than "an infant crying in the night," his "large grief" is "given in outline and no more" (V, 9-12). The yew tree that marks out the poem's broken progress fascinates the mourner because he imagines that the roots from which its trunk and branches are "wrapped around the bones" of his friend (II, 4). But, even though it is in closer contact with Hallam than the stone that marks his grave, the mourner is frustrated by the tree's refusal to communicate what is going on beneath it:

> And gazing on thee, sullen tree,
> Sick for thy stubborn hardihood,
> I seem to fail from out my blood
> And grow incorporate into thee.
>
> (II, 13-16)

He wonders that his own life, like that of the tree, can continue after Hallam's death, but, although on the surface his life and work may even signify the opposite of what they mean, they are valuable because their presence marks the loss that they grieve. In this sense, the lyrics that make up Tennyson's elegy are repeated inscriptions of its title: *In Memoriam A. H. H.*[5]

In Wordsworth's third essay on epitaphs he writes:

> The most numerous class of sepulchral inscriptions do indeed record nothing more than the name of the buried person, but that he was born on one day and died on another . . . a Tomb like this is a shrine to which the fancies of a scattered family may repair in pilgrimage; the thoughts of the individuals, without any communication with each other, must oftentimes meet here. Such a frail memorial then is not without its tendency to keep families together; it feeds also local attachment, which is the taproot of the tree of patriotism.
>
> (370)

We hear the echo of these ideas in Section 67 of *In Memoriam*:

> When on my bed the moonlight falls,
> I know that in thy place of rest
> By the broad water of the west,
> There comes a glory on the walls;
> Thy marble bright in dark appears,
> As slowly steals the the silvber flame
> Along the letters of thy name,
> And o'er the number of thy years.
>
> (LCVII, 1-8)

This imaginary pilgrimage to his friend's tomb occurs a number of times throughout *In Memoriam.* The anonymity of the poem's author and the fact that even the name of the person being mourned is reduced to its initials (the initials of an unknown youth) mean that it is a pilgrimage in which any of its readers may join. The initials can be appropriated by any mourner, since they function only as markings for the body beneath: the letters themselves can be substituted by any name, as long as it is that of a person who has been lost and for whom deep grief is felt. In this way, Tennyson manages to express a loss that is no less bitter for being common.

But this account of *In Memoriam* as epitaph can never do justice to such an intricate and lengthy poem. By making explicit the inarticulate depth of his feelings, Tennyson is free to write. Poetry is no more than a "sad mechanic exercise," so divorced from any real expression of grief that it serves as a distraction, numbing the pain that he cannot express. Safe in the knowledge that he can say nothing, Tennyson can say anything and he can do so as many times as he chooses. In so doing he amasses a weight of words that, of course, speaks volumes. Tennyson's compulsion to mark out his grief with poetry, like a prisoner marking out the days of his sentence on the prison wall, results in a rich and eloquent meditation on death informed by the religious, social and scientific debates of the time it was written. Thus, the sequence of voluble silences that make up Tennyson's epitaph, speak the grief of an age and a nation.

This is only one way of explaining the central paradox and great achievement of *In Memoriam* that has been addressed in some way by nearly every critic of the poem. Christopher Ricks describes it as "anonymous but confessional, private but naked" (221); David Shaw writes that, being "both introverted and intellectual" it successfully "transforms the official affirmations of his era into experienced truths" (141) and Alan Sinfield bases his reading of the poem around the figures of "The Linnet and the Artefact," arguing that Tennyson, builds a meaningful and powerful monument out of the unchecked outpourings of a genuine grief (17). But it was T. S. Eliot who first described this paradox in terms of depth and surface. In his essay on *In Memoriam* he writes:

Tennyson's surface, his technical accomplishment, is intimate with his depths: that which we most quickly see about Tennyson is that which moves between the surface and the depths, that which is of slight importance. By looking innocently at the surface, we are now likely to come to the depths, to the abyss of sorrow.[6]

(337)

In other words *In Memoriam* is a poem that effectively communicates the value of silence through its eloquence and of depth through its surfaces.

Many of these critics also argue that the reconciliation of the poem's paradoxical elements is achieved through its, somewhat circuitous, progress: that the movement of *In Memoriam* is upwards and outwards. Herbert F. Tucker provides the best description of this movement. He describes the poem as being at once private and public and argues that the poem works to reconcile the alienated, solipsistic mourner to society. This is not only a personal journey, it also travels forward from the moment in literary history described by Perry, building away from the Romantic traditions that form its foundations:

> The ennobling of *In Memoriam,* the calling of the "high muse" of Romanticism must draw on inward sources; yet the motive for this elevation is felt as a public duty to the poet's "brethren." The elegiac conventions of the poem will entail connecting the silent "deep self" to the self that speaks and reacts with the world . . . and the rapprochement that the poem goes on to seek with the vanished presence of Hallam will be a massive figuration of the poet's own private brooding with public display.
>
> (389)

Tucker describes the process itself, the description of what a thing is through the narrative of what it was and what it has come to be, as "Bildungspoesie." This is as much part of Tennyson's Romantic inheritance as a belief in the incomprehensible depths of real feeling, but Tennyson uses it to move away from that inheritance. By charting this movement as a self-conscious, doubtful and often guilty narrative, he is able to legitimize his arrival at the surface. Like the initials on a gravestone that gain strength and meaning from the life whose end they mark, *In Memoriam* draws much of its success from the traditions that its composition seeks to conclude.

Tucker also observes that this journey is somewhat contrived. The first verses of *In Memoriam* that Tennyson composed were not the ones in which the mourner appears farthest removed from society. His response to Hallam's death was initially social, the sections that reflect upon archetypal figures of mourning were among the first to be written, and it is from these that he withdrew "into a subjective realm of analysis and refine-

ment," ending with a more powerful assertion of where he had begun.[7] The abba stanza form reflects this contrivance, retreating inwards from a first line that is then re-established, strengthened by the two lines which have intervened, in line four. The process that Tennyson describes might then be understood as being played out for the benefit of a late-Romantic readership more than working through his own grief in verse. This is not to say that Tennyson's grief at the loss of his friend was not immense, only that it was ineffable, so utterly beyond words, that a surface response was as accurate as any other and was perhaps more honest, in that it made no attempt to reach the feelings that words could not hope to fathom. It is this surface response, which Tennyson takes up in his composition of *Ode on the Death of the Duke of Wellington,* that I am suggesting corresponds to the material surfaces of the funeral ceremony, the empty signification that was seen in both cases to be so reprehensibly modern.

Reviewers who found themselves disappointed by *Ode on the Death of the Duke of Wellington* in spite of an admiration of Tennyson's work in general, often excused this new poem on the grounds that its author had not had enough time adequately to develop and reflect upon the national sense of bereavement. The review in *The Leader* ends by saying: "Tennyson is said to compose with great slowness and as this ode must have been written hastily, it may have that extenuation" (20/11/1853), and *The Illustrated London News* concludes that:

> The subject must, it is clear, await Mr Tennyson's better mood; must become, perhaps idealized by distance, of time, and then we doubt not that we shall have a fine poem from his pen . . . not hurried by the pressure of circumstances, but a free offering from the soul of the poet.
>
> (27/11/1852)

Their suggestion that, over time, Tennyson might present a more satisfactory offering from his soul offers guidelines for the composition of another *In Memoriam.* To a very limited extent, the predictions of these reviewers were fulfilled. A revised edition of the poem was published the following year and more changes were made to it before its inclusion in *Maud and Other Poems* in 1855. Tennyson's revisions of *Ode on the Death of the Duke of Wellington* have been examined in two articles by Edgar F. Shannon and Christopher Ricks, who observe that some of the alterations make for a poem that is more feeling and less formal. However, they also point out that these changes were made largely in response to the criticism that Tennyson received from the reviews. Ironically, it was in responding to the demands of his late-Romantic readership for spontaneity that Tennyson was writing to order, the very practice that so many of the reviewers had identified as the cause of the poem's failure. But no amount of revision could have transformed the *Ode* into a poem that could be enjoyed by the tastes *In Memoriam* had created.

Tennyson's very first response to the problem of commemorating Wellington is Wordsworthian in every sense. In March 1851, eighteen months before the death of Arthur Wellesley, Tennyson wrote the following letter to Thomas Woolner:

> My dear Woolner,
>
> I had rather let Dr Davy have his own way but since he and you require an opinion, look here is an epitaph on the Duke of Wellington.
>
> > To the memory Of the Duke of Wellington
>
> Who by singular calling and through the special foresight of Almighty God was [raised] up to be the safeguard of the greatest people of the world—who possessing the greatest military genius which the world etc. Won the battle of Waterloo etc etc etc—who was equally great in statesmanship as he was in etc. Now look here, do not the very words Duke of Wellington involve all this?
>
> Is Wordsworth a great poet? Well then, don't let us talk of him as if he were half known
>
> > To the memory of William Wordsworth The Great Poet
>
> Even that seems too much but certainly is much better than the other, far nobler in its simplicity.
>
> (***Letters*** 2:10)

By using the name of the former laureate further to illustrate his point, Tennyson suggests a relationship between the name and fame of military leaders and of poets so that, even in this private letter, concerns about his own posterity are bound up with the Duke's memorial. But his invocation of Wordsworth as part of a discussion about epitaphs also recalls Wordsworth's own comments on epitaphs that commemorate greatness:

> The mighty benefactors of mankind, as they are not only known by their immediate survivors, but will continue to be known familiarly to latest posterity, do not stand in need of biographic sketches, in such a place; nor deliniations of character to individualise them. This is already done by their works, in the memories of men. Their naked names, and a grand comprehension of civic gratitude . . .—these are the only tribute that can here be paid—the only offering that upon such an altar would not be unworthy.
>
> (336)

Tennyson's letter echoes these remarks. The impatient 'etceteras' that punctuate his imaginary epitaph stand in for facts and forms so familiar that they need not be spelled out and anticipate his final proposal that the Duke's name alone would make the best epitaph. The ability of the name to speak for itself is testament to its greatness and Tennyson suggests that allowing it to do so is the only way to give a man such as the Duke of Wellington the honor he deserves.

Such thoughts seem in keeping with *In Memoriam* but wholly incongruous with *Ode on the Death of the Duke of Wellington,* a poem that does such wordy honour to the Duke's name. The fact that Tennyson expressed these ideas in private and then went on to compose his ode a year later is a contradiction that attests not just to his own unease but to the general unease of a nation compelled by the death of their hero to confront a modernity that offended its late-Romantic way of seeing. Tennyson's letter to Woolner places the poet amongst his readership. Like them, his tastes and ways of understanding were to a large extent defined by the Wordsworthian memorial aesthetic of *In Memoriam* and, like them, his sense of "duty" forced him into a poetic experiment that went against the grain. *Ode on the Death of the Duke of Wellington,* then, should not only be read as characteristic of Victorian modernity, a poetic representation of "these material times," but also as a poem painfully aware of its newness, embarrassed by, and with little confidence in, its maginificent surfaces.[8]

Far from the modern development that I have been describing, *Ode on the Death of the Duke of Wellington* seems to be an anachronism that does not fit into literary histories of the elegy or the ode, a step backwards rather than forwards. Jahan Ramazani, in the introduction to his study of the modern elegy, uses Tennyson's ode, the epitome of a traditional elegy, as a point of comparison with the modern works that he is introducing and then goes on to name *In Memoriam* as the first modern elegy, ignoring the fact that this "modern" poem preceded its "traditional" counterpart (2-10). Critics who have charted the history of the ode tend to locate the culmination of its development in the early nineteenth century with Keats and Shelley. *Ode on the Death of the Duke of Wellington* serves only as a postscript: it was a "return to the metrical exemplars of antiquity," a symptom of the intellectual drift of his later poetry towards conservatism (Shuster 279). Paul Fry ignores the poem completely. He makes brief mention of Tennyson's early "apprentice work" before moving straight over to Swinburne. Fry understands that "to write an ode is to honor the company of fools: court hacks, windy curates, triflers with nature, versifiers on milady's fan—laureates. . . . The very word 'ode' has been enough to call down journalistic ridicule from antiquity to the present (10). A poem composed in earnest by just one such laureate does not fit happily into his scheme of development which describes the history of the ode as a sequence of increasingly self-aware performances.

However, Fry describes the form itself in terms that can help to understand how *Ode on the Death of the Duke of Wellington* moves away from the illusory depths of *In Memoriam* and thus establishes its uneasy modernity. As the most formal, elevated and public poetry, the ode is poetry at its farthest remove from the possibility of natural language. He argues that it has therefore become "a form of ontological and vocational doubt," "a proving ground of presentation that boldly attempts to invoke the reality that it would be part of, knowing that, if it were part of that reality, there would be no need to call" (9). Written out of the full knowledge of the inevitable failure of its project, it does not dwell on its inadequacies in an attempt to make up for them; instead it "writes itself hoarse," throwing itself into its doomed project with a masochistic poetic honesty. The superficiality of this formal anachronism enables it to be rewritten and reread as modern in a Victorian context, appropriate, if not appealing to a newly material nation. By composing *Ode on the Death of the Duke of Wellington,* Tennyson takes the form to its farthest extreme, committing himself, without irony, to the surfaces of language that he knows to be inadequate.

Rather than leaving Wellington's name to speak for itself, the ode insistently speaks for the name. The poem may be entitled *Ode on the Death of the Duke of Wellington,* but, after that title, the Duke's name is excluded from the poem. Tennyson prefers to talk about and around it. Wellington is the "Great Duke," the "last great Englishman," the "great world-victor's victor," "England's greatest son." These periphrastic expressions contrive repetitively to assert a greatness that they also imply goes without saying. Everything in the poem is brought back to the name, almost to the exclusion of the Duke himself. The thrice repeated refrain announces that the project of the ode and of the people for whom it would speak is to honor the name of their hero:

> A people's voice, when they rejoice
> At civic realm and pomp and game,
> Attest their great commander's claim
> With honour, honour, honour to him,
> Eternal honour to his name.
>
> (146-50)

Rather than admitting that language can barely scrape the surfaces of identity and loss by leaving the name, like an epitaph, as a marker for what the Duke was, Tennyson uses names that describe and explain. In so doing, he refuses to acknowledge the depths that separate his ode from what it represents. It does not keep a respectful and modest silence, nor does it verbalize silence with the anxiety-ridden language of *In Memoriam.* It is reduced instead to a rhetoric that is at once empty and insistent, a rhetoric of repetitions:

> With honour, honour, honour to him,
> Eternal honour to his name.

The result is a poem that strains under its own wordiness. Its compulsive and cumulative verbal over-reach

works to create immense stretches of verse that draw attention to their own technicality rather than "the brilliance or profundity of their thought" (Pitt 191). Tennyson's reference to the funeral car, "bright . . . with his blazoned deeds" (56) brings his own descriptions of the Duke's life and work to mind so that we can almost see his own poem blazoned across the pall. Even the simplest ideas are endlessly embroidered and elaborated upon. Each section is built around a single thought or statement that is clarified, drawn out, returned to and reiterated. In Section One this process occurs within a single sentence. The poem's opening exhortation: "Let us bury the Great Duke / With an empire's lamentation" is immediately repeated; but, as if the poet was not satisfied that he had used enough words, the "empire's lamentation" is rewritten as "the noise of the mourning of a mighty nation." This "rewrite" is nearly twice as long, the downbeats of "noise," "mourning," "mighty" and "nation" jolt the reader slowly along the line and the mirror symmetry of their initials (n, m, m, n.) draw attention to its wrought artifice. As the poem gains momentum its self-perpetuating sentences, intent on imitating the length of the funeral procession, become longer. Another clause is added and then another; and each compulsive addition is openly displayed to the reader through the use of conjunctions that naively reveal how one clause is simply tacked onto the next, drawing attention to the poet's need always to say just one more thing:

> Let the long long procession go,
> And let the sorrowing crowd about it grow,
> And let the mournful martial music blow;
> The last great Englishman is low.
>
> (15-18)

Tennyson sees Wellington's death was the end of an era. As the "last great Englishman" Wellington takes with him a time that cannot be retrieved, but he also leaves behind a legacy that it is the nation's duty to sustain. This theme is strongest in the 1852 version of the poem; Section Four begins:

> Mourn for to us he seems the last,
> Our sorrow draws but on the golden Past.

In the 1853 version the second line was changed to: "Remembering all his greatness in the Past," so that the absolute split of then and now occasioned by the Duke's death is exchanged for the departed greatness of a single man. The less moderate first version gives greater purpose to the lengthy descriptions of Wellington that follow. The remainder of Section Four draws on journalistic sketches of his character. Wellington was "moderate, resolute" (25), "greatest yet with least pretence" (29), "Rich in saving common sense / And, as the greatest only are, / In his simplicity sublime" (32-4). The reviewers need not have pointed out the disparity between Wellington's character and Tennyson's poetic, as the laureate seems intent on doing it for them. With this remarkably elaborate tribute to simplicity, Tennyson acknowledges the need to move forward, away from a past that, though golden, is nevertheless over, and into the modern present that remains.

Wellington's voice, now silent, is employed by Tennyson as symbol of the late lamented national character. The Duke's language was the deep, wordless language of canon-fire:

> And the volleying canon thunder his loss;
> He knew their voices of old.
> For many a time in many a clime
> His captain's-ear had heard them boom
> Bellowing victory, bellowing doom:
> When he with those deep voices wrought,
> Guarding realms and kings from shame;
> With those deep voices our dead captain taught
> The tyrant, and asserts his claim
> In that dread sound to the great name.
>
> (63-71)

But, however powerful, it will be heard no more: "O friends, our chief state-oracle is mute" (23), "His voice is silent in your council-hall / For ever" (174-5). A different voice, however imperfect, must now be used, to do honour to the name. *Ode on the Death of the Duke of Wellington* attempts to find that voice and speak with it:

> A people's voice! we are a people yet.
> Though all men else their nobler dreams forget,
> Confused by brainless mobs and lawless Powers;
> We have a voice, with which to pay the debt
> Of boundless love and reverence and regret.
>
> (151-5)

But the poem is uneasy about its own procedures. In Section Five, a single line thrice repeated, "Let the bell be tolled," briefly interrupts the momentum of ode and funeral procession as they roll towards St Paul's. The invocation of this wordless sound, the tolling bell, betrays a conviction that the proper indication of the sincerity of grief is the inarticulacy that lies buried beneath this poem's persistent articulations.[9] In Section Nine the poem enjoins silence:

> Peace, his triumph will be sung
> By some yet unmoulded tongue
> Far on in summers that we shall not see:
> Peace, it is a day of pain
> For one about whose patriarchal knee
> Late the little children clung:
> O peace. . . .
>
> (232-238)

As he draws his ode to a close, Tennyson offers consolation to the mourners, but his call upon them to be at peace can also be read as a request, made to himself as

much as to them, to be quiet. The ode seems to split into two voices, one asking for peace, the other unable to stop talking. By this stage the second voice has gained too much momentum to be held to a dignified silence and it moves on to a beautiful profession of faith before it is asked once again to "Hush" as the Duke is committed to the ground. Tennyson is unable to brazen out this moment with words. At the point towards which this whole poem has been moving, his ode recognizes its own inappropriateness and, in the few lines that follow the burial, reach its oddly muted conclusion. It will "speak no more of his renown" and concludes instead with a quiet prayer: "God accept him, Christ receive him" (281). *Ode on the Death of the Duke of Wellington,* then, was not the complete departure from *In Memoriam* that the reviews understood it to be; rather it expands upon the surfaces that *In Memoriam* ventures towards, immersing itself in the material world to which Hallam's mourner is finally reconciled. The self-doubt that runs through *Ode on the Death of the Duke of Wellington,* its embarrassment about its own public magnificence results in the poem being a rather fine poetic failure. Tennyson's lack of confidence in these great surfaces of language that he has created lends them the fragility of a nation and a poet reaching maturity. In the end, *Ode on the Death of the Duke of Wellington* can never be uncoupled from anxieties surrounding the emergent modernity of Victorian Britain. And these are anxieties that persist. A poetic that so perfectly reflects the age in which it is written is distasteful even now and the embarrassment with which Tennyson's ode resonates is our own. Not yet reconciled to an aesthetic made up of the material surfaces of modern culture and still enamored with illusions of depth, we are more likely to regard *Ode on the Death of the Duke of Wellington* as an historical document than a poem: an artifact that confers honour on the name of its subject rather than a work of art that honours the name of the poet.

Notes

1. Benedict Read uses memorial statues of the Duke of Wellington to illustrate the difficulties surrounding public sculpture during the Victorian Period and there are parallels to be drawn between this art form and Tennyson's laureate verse. Read writes that although "as a form of patronage, the public memorial could bring consistently to the sculptor both prestige and success," the artistic integrity of the sculptor was seen to be compromised by the patron and commissioned sculptures suffered strong criticism from the likes of Arnold and F. T. Palgrave. He also comments on the difficulty of memorializing modern subjects as works of art, which, for Victorian sculptors, manifested itself in the question of how to clothe their subjects. The "tight trousers" of contemporary dress were seen as unsuitable costume for sculptures

and contemporary subjects were often presented in classical dress. This is an example of a nineteenth-century squeemishness about its own modern aesthetic that Tennyson had to confront in his composition of his memorial verse. His decision to write a classical ode on a modern subject might be understood as analogous to those sculptors such as Gibson, whose statue of Peel of 1852, is dressed in a toga.

2. Peter W. Sinnema provides a case study of the ways *The Illustrated London News* reported the death and funeral of the Duke of Wellington in the final chapter of *Dynamics of the Pictured Page: Representing the Nation in the Illustrated London News*. He describes its coverage as "sincere but opportunistic" (182). His observation that the pictures of the funeral procession "withhold a glimpse of the funeral car" (195) is particularly pertinent to this discussion because it implies that "the dead hero functions as an alibi for something else," (195) for a celebration of the modernity that enveloped it.

3. "Tennyson's Arthurian psychodrama" by Cecil Y. Lang makes a comparison between these two Arthurs and the *Arthur of Idylls of the King.*

4. In her recent article "Burying the Great Duke: Victorian Mourning and the Funeral of the Duke of Wellington," Cornelia D. J. Paersall examines the Duke's funeral and Tennyson's ode as examples of Victorian cultural anxiety about death and mourning. Her argument focuses on the two-month delay between Wellington's death and burial and describes an unwillingness to commit the dead body to the earth. The pageant and public spectacle, she argues, was a way of keeping him part "of the civic landscape," rescuing it from "the yearning, defiled interior." My argument, which covers the same ground as Pearsall's article would place greater emphasis on on the anxieties about the civic landscape itself, and understand the Duke's death as an unprecedented occasion for the presentation of that landscape, uncomfortably new to the eyes of nineteenth-century Britain.

5. This reading resonates with Isobel Armstrong's discussion of graffiti in *The Radical Aesthetic*. She writes that graffiti does "not have the deciferability of writing. The many sets of initials tell you only that these are initials, just as the dominance of pseudo-words—KOF, UURZ—tells you that you cannot read them. . . . These are anti-words . . . [they] constitute an aggressive barrier to reading" (152).

6. Ideas about surface and depth also form part of Eric Griffiths' discussion of *In Memoriam* and *Maud* (97-170).

7. Without this contrivance the social, or surface poetic is unpalatable even to critics today. I imagine that David Shaw speaks for many readers when he asserts that the Prelude to *In Memoriam* does not work because private truths are too quickly and too easily bodied forth as public sentiment.

8. Valerie Pitt is the only critic I have come across who recognizes Tennyson's laureate verse as trying out a new poetic. She argues that "Tennyson's major problem . . . was that, although there was a body of common sentiment, there was no available poetic with which to express it. . . . Tennyson's laureate verse is not, then, the verse of a complacent poet working in outworn conventions, but the vigorous creation of new forms for a new national consciousness" (195).

9. An addition made to the 1855 version of the *Ode* is worth noting. Between the lines "Let the bell be tolled" and "And the sound of the sorrowing anthem rolled," Tennyson inserted "And a deeper knell in the heart be knolled. This additional line, which gestures towards depths that the poem does not otherwise attempt to fathom, is a capitulation to the critics: a return to the self-conscious poetic of *In Memoriam.*

Works Cited

Armstrong, Isobel. *The Radical Aesthetic*. Blackwell, 2000.

Court Journal. November 20, 1852.

Eliot, T. S. "In Memoriam," in *Selected Essays*. London: Faber & Faber, 1951.

The Examiner. November 20, 1852.

Fry, Paul H. *The Poet's Calling and the English Ode*. New Haven, CT: Yale UP, 1980.

The Gentleman's Magazine. October, 1852.

Griffiths, Eric. *The Printed Voice in Victorian Poetry*. Oxford: Clarendon. 1989.

Houghton, Walter. *The Victorian Frame of Mind 1830-1870*. New Haven: Yale UP, 1957.

Illustrated London News. November 25, 1852.

———. November 27, 1852.

Lang, Cecil Y. "Tennyson's Arthurian Psychodrama." Lincoln: *The Tennyson Society*, 1983.

The Leader. November 20, 1852.

The London Times. November 27, 1852.

Pearsall, Cornelia D. J. "Burying the Great Duke: Victorian Mourning and the Funeral of the Duke of Wellington." *Victorian Literature and Culture* 27:2 (1999): 265-93.

Perry, Seamus. "Elegy," in *A Companion to Victorian Poetry and Poetics.* Eds. Richard Cronin, Alison Chapman and Antony S. Harrison. Oxford: Blackwells, 2002.

Pitt, Valerie. *Tennyson Laureate.* Toronto: U of Toronto P, 1962.

Ramazani, Jahan. *Poetry of Mourning: The Modern Elegy from Hardy to Heany.* Chicago: U of Chicago P, 1994.

Read, Benedict. *Victorian Sculpture.* New Haven & London: Yale UP, 1983: 85.

Ricks, Christopher. *Tennyson.* New York & London: Macmillan, 1972.

Shannon, Edgar F. "The History of a Poem: Tennyson's *Ode on the Death of the Duke of Wellington.*" *Studies in Bibliography* (1960): 149-77.

————, and Christopher Ricks. "A Further History of Tennyson's *Ode on the Death of the Duke of Wellington.* The Manuscript and the Galley Proofs at Lincoln." *Studies in Bibliography* (1979): 125-57.

Shaw, W. David. *Tennyson's Style.* Ithaca, NY: Cornell UP, 1976.

Shuster, George N. *The English Ode from Milton to Keats.* New York: Columbia UP, 1940.

Sinfield, Alan. *The Language of Tennyson's In Memoriam.* Blackwell, 1971.

Sinnema, Peter W. *Dynamics of the Pictured Page: Representing the Nation in the Illustrated London News.* Aldershot: Ashgate, 1998.

The Spectator. September 18, 1852.

————. November 11, 1852.

Tennyson, Alfred Lord. *The Letters of Alfred Lord Tennyson.* 3 vols. Eds. Cecil Y. Lang and Edgar F. Shannon. Oxford: Clarendon, 1982-1990.

Tucker, Herbert F. *Tennyson and the Doom of Romanticism.* Cambridge: Harvard UP, 1988.

Weekly News and Chronicle. November 20, 1852.

Wordsworth, William. *Selected Prose.* Ed. John O'Hayden. New York: Penguin, 1988.

Devon Fisher (essay date 2004)

SOURCE: Fisher, Devon. "In Graceful Service to the Queen (Bee): The Politics of the Hive in Tennyson's *The Princess.*" *Victorians Institute Journal* 32 (2004): 107-28.

[*In the following essay, Fisher illuminates Tennyson's use of bees and hives as symbols of English political and social issues and traditions in* The Princess.]

In an 1848 review of *The Princess,* J. W. Marston concludes that the subjects with which the poem deals "are antagonisms which no art can reconcile" (171). While Marston has in mind the curious mix of medievalism and modernism that permeates the poem, his comment suggests something about the underlying structure of language in *The Princess*—that the sum total of meaning in the poem somehow exceeds what we feel the language should allow. While this sense of overflow could lead us in any number of directions, I am most concerned here with Tennyson's attempt in *The Princess* to explore his own position as a poet within the British state, a position with which he always felt some level of discomfort. Tennyson was so conflicted about accepting the Laurcateship, for instance, that when offered the position in 1850, he composed two letters to the Queen—one accepting the position and the other declining it. I will return to these letters later, but they illustrate just how ambivalent Tennyson was about the idea of service to the state. Like Tennyson's early work, *The Princess* admits these political concerns only indirectly;[1] they are engaged primarily through the tangled gender and power relationships that emerge beneath the ostensible subject of the poem, the question of the place of women in the educational system. One of the strategies that Tennyson employs to structure the multiple ways in which gender, power, and politics converge in *The Princess* is to liken the university to a hive filled with bees. Although the hive offers a traditional, conservative vision of governance, it also provides a space within which the relationships between these multiple discourses fail to hold up as we might expect. The playful banter of the men and women on Sir Walter's lawn initially invites us to accept the smooth functioning of Victorian ideology which seems naturally to align certain categories; the "feminine," for instance, with "domestic," "passive," and a certain type of poetic voice. Within the hive of the university, however, these categories no longer hold, and we see a shifting by which the feminine no longer aligns with other discourses as the Victorian auditors might expect. This categorical reconfiguration allows Tennyson to explore different ways of singing for a Queen and finally to adopt a carefully considered androgynous ideal that encompasses multiple, seemingly contradictory relationships to the Crown. Or, to put it in the terms that Marston used, in *The Princess,* the hive creates antagonisms that Tennyson's art ultimately chooses not to reconcile.[2]

I. RECONSTRUCTING THE HIVE: CLASSICAL AND CONTEMPORARY USAGES

Tennyson certainly was aware of the hive's currency as a vehicle for discussing the relationship between individuals and their government, if only because of Shelley's use of the image in "A Song: 'Men of England'" and in *Queen Mab* (III, 107-118). The radical politics of Shelley's use of the hive, however, deviates from a body of work dating to antiquity that incorporates the figure of speech, work with which Tennyson almost certainly was familiar. Before turning to Tennyson's use of the bee and its hive in **The Princess,** then, I will sketch out how this particular figure of speech was used both historically and in the 1830s and 1840s as a way for the individual to negotiate his relationship with monarchy. My purpose in so doing is not necessarily to suggest a linear relationship of influence on Tennyson (although given his wide reading in the classics and his fascination with entomology, this may well be the case). Instead, by tracing the development of the hive metaphor from antiquity to the early nineteenth century, I will demonstrate that historically the figure of speech had been used as a natural image that portrayed a hierarchical vision of government based on patriarchal authority. Second, by exploring selected beekeeping manuals from the first half of the nineteenth century, I will illustrate how the hive as a metaphor for government had been laid open to multiple interpretations by the late Romantics and early Victorians.[3]

Historically, writers turned to the hive as a powerful way of illustrating the appropriate governance of the state. Although writers as early as Homer developed this metaphor, it was not until the time of the classical Latin writers that it came into its fullest use. In his *Rerum rusticarum libri tres,* for instance, Varro writes that the honeybee is endowed with reason, allowing it to develop the human structures of kingship, government, and community. His vision of the government of the hive is rigidly hierarchical. The bee community follows its king in war and peace, working at all costs to preserve him from harm. Although Varro addresses the concept of the hive purely in the context of natural history, by the time of Virgil the metaphor has been poeticized—we see Virgil incorporating it even more explicitly than Varro in both *The Georgics* and *The Aeneid.* He associates the hive with structures of government, describing it in the fourth *Georgic* as a "miniature state" and claiming that he will "give an account of its fierce-hearted leaders, / Its orderly tribes, their manners, their pursuits, their wars" (2-4). The remainder of the poem elaborates on this government in miniature, one that, like Varro's, depends entirely on the figure of a King whose position in the hive corresponds to that of the male head of state. So rigidly hierarchical is Virgil's bee-society, in fact, that if the King dies, the community dissolves. Within this hierarchy, Virgil locates a utopian vision, claiming that the bees are the only creatures that live in an idealized community.

These Latin writers offer a metaphor of the hive that relies on the proximity of the king bee to the literal male head of the state in such a way that meaning naturally attaches to the metaphor. And, although by the time of Chaucer, writers were aware of the biological fact that the head of the hive was female, the Latin metaphor,

centered on a king, continued through the English Renaissance. Shakespeare, for instance, employs the idea of a king bee in *Henry V* as a naturalized image for the monarchy and the British state; bees are creatures that teach "The act of order to a peopled kingdom. / They have a king, and officers of sorts, / Where some like magistrates correct at home" (1.2.336-338). The Victorians were quick to note this oddity; in his study of entomology based on Shakespeare's plays, Robert Patterson observes Shakespeare's use of the classical idea of the king, writing that "It is the queen bee, you are aware, that seems to regulate the industry and preserve the equilibrium of the denizens of the hive; and to her, Shakspeare [sic], like the ancients, invariably applies a male epithet" (115). Shakespeare's appropriation of the hive metaphor as illustration of a kingship, however, jars with the obvious political reality that England was in fact governed by a Queen at the time of the writing of *Henry V.*

By the early eighteenth century, the work of the metaphor had moved in two different directions to accommodate the disjunction between the sex of the queen bee and the fact that the English monarchy was headed exclusively by men in the years following Elizabeth I. Charles Butler's *The Feminine Monarchy; Or the History of Bees; Shewing Their Admirable Nature and Property* (1704) simply reserves the metaphor for the Queenship, using it as a means to discuss the life of Elizabeth I. The other strategy available to writers was to shift the focus of the metaphor away from the head of the state. Bernard Mandeville's *Fable of the Bees* (1705), published only a year after Butler's *The Feminine Monarchy,* opens with a description of the hive's government:

> No Bees had better Government,
> More Fickleness, or less Content.
> They were not Slaves to Tyranny,
> Nor ruled by wild Democracy;
> But Kings, that could not wrong, because
> Their Power was circumscrib'd by Laws.
>
> (7-12)

Although Mandeville maintains the idea of the "king bee" that the classical writers had developed, the question of whether the head of the hive is a King or a Queen is subordinate to the real issue—the question of how a limited monarchy maintains an appropriate balance between the King or Queen and a body of laws. In the 1714 "Preface" to the fable, Mandeville explicitly makes this point, writing that the nation represented by the hive must be "a large, rich and warlike nation that is happily governed by a limited monarchy." Mandeville's use of the hive is part of a shift in the focus of the metaphor away from the monarch and onto the *structure* of English government as a hierarchical institution. The result is that the tenor of the metaphor separates from the vehicle, yielding a breach that becomes increasingly realized during the Hanoverian dynasty. By the early Romantic period, the gap between the thing meant and the thing said was wide enough that the hive as metaphor came under increased scrutiny as a means of defining British society. Thus in the proliferation of beekeeping manuals in the early nineteenth century, the different representations of the hive became a point of interrogation of both the hierarchical nature of the monarchy and the gendered language that had historically been used to describe that hierarchy.

Some of those who wrote on the subject of bees in the early nineteenth century held onto vestiges of the hive's use as a metaphor for the monarchy. Thomas Nutt's *Practical Directions for the Management of Honeybees* (1832), for instance, suggests reform for the monarchy but ultimately maintains the hierarchical structure of the British government. As he describes the state in terms of the hive, Nutt relegates the English worker to a position analogous to that of the worker bee. In his 1832 dedication of the book to Queen Adelaide, Nutt expresses his hopes that she will improve the condition of the worker, declaring that "here is a sort of analogical propriety in dedicating to Your Gracious Majesty this work, the leading feature of which is Humanity to Honey Bees" (5). Nutt, though, never explicitly defines this analogical relationship. Clearly he intends a one to one correlation—the hive has a queen just as England has a Queen. By couching the issue of the English labor force in terms of the hive, though, Nutt must appeal to the maternal nature of the Queen rather than directly to the political power of the King. He pleads for Adelaide to use her "fostering and influential Patronage" (presumably with the King) to ensure that the bees are treated well. This rhetoric hinges on a modification of the classical use of the hive metaphor, for Nutt maintains a hierarchical vision of government headed by the king even as he suggests that the King must allow himself to be guided by the feminine instinct of the Queen.

In the political climate of the years following the publication of *Practical Directions for the Management of Honeybees,* the hive as a metaphor for government became increasingly less applicable. During the 1830s and 1840s with the various Reform Bills, the Chartist movement, and the seemingly inevitable movement towards reform in which the seat of power shifted from the monarch to Parliament, the rigid hierarchy of the hive was no longer pertinent. Facing these dilemmas, many early Victorians simply shifted the terms of the metaphor away from the political. One potential way to rewrite the politics of the hive was to go a step further even than Nutt, focusing so exclusively on the Queen's maternal nature that she became politically powerless. Perhaps the most interesting example of this use of the hive is William Cotton's "A Short and Simple Letter to Cottagers." In the first edition, published in 1838, Cot-

ton makes little of the typical associations of the hive with government. In 1842, though, he reprinted the letter as part of a larger collection titled *My Bee Book.* In this reprinting, Cotton includes on the first page a drawing titled "A Queen Laying Eggs." The drawing consists of a hexagonal design representing a cell of the honeycomb in which a queen bee is surrounded by twenty-four worker bees. Written just above the queen bee are the words "Long live the queen and all the royal family." Although Cotton's drawing does place the queen at the center of the hive's activity, the text surrounding the image delineates a purely maternal function for the queen. The message of the drawing is quite clear—the queen's express purpose is the production of a royal family. Cotton uses the drawing, then, to defuse the potentially disturbing power of the hive's monarch by transmuting the political nature of Queenship into the safer image of the Queen as mother. Ultimately, Cotton seems far more anxious at the idea of a female monarch than he does at the prospect of the crumbling of the hierarchical British system of government. Another strategy employed by the Victorians was to shift the tenor of the metaphor from politics to economics as does Matthew Pile, whose *Bee Cultivator's Assistant* (1838) was published in the year after Victoria's accession. In it, Pile writes that "the order and harmony there displayed [in the hive], fills us with surprise, we there behold as it were a manufactory, where there are frequently many thousands of industrious artisans engaged in manifold labours, which are so admirably displayed by the acquirement of their riches" (ix). Pile effects a critical shift in the terms of the metaphor here, for when he ties the hive to industry, Victoria's place in the structure that the hive represents is recognizable only in its absence.

Although some Victorians tried to recast the hive metaphor in terms of economics or maternity, others simply ignored its historical use as a metaphor for the political system. Samuel Bagster, Jr., for instance, directly refuses to acknowledge the historical use of the metaphor. He writes "A common error in most of the old authors was a repeated introduction of political allusions. I have avoided such extraneous matter, as much from a conviction of its entire uselessness in such as work as this, as from a personal dislike I entertain to such discussions" (xi-xii). The vehemence with which Bagster denies the applicability of the hive metaphor to contemporary government points to his underlying motivations. As the son of a Baptist publisher and as a Baptist himself, Bagster's refusal to admit the monarch as the head of the hive reflects his opposition to the monarch's position as head of the Church. Moreover, it seems likely that Bagster's refusal to acknowledge the hive as a metaphor for government stems as well from his political affiliations. Both Bagster's Baptist heritage and his involvement in the abolition movement suggest that he favored a more egalitarian form of government than the hive metaphor permits.[4]

Although each of the writers I have discussed so far approaches the hive in a different way, each uses the metaphor to position himself in relation to the state. In recent years, Cristopher Hollingsworth has explored the hive as a theoretical construct by which this positioning occurs. For him, the hive becomes a figure that can be manipulated by the writer. He defines it as such: "I mean the word 'Hive' more abstractly, to signify a mental structure that informs any representation that implicitly or explicitly, defines the individual and the social order in relation to each other" (ix). Hollingsworth bases his argument that the hive becomes a structure that defines individuals and societies on a diachronic view of the metaphor. He goes on to claim that the figure of speech obtains its power not through direct influence but through meaning accumulated over time. Such a view of this particular figure of speech, however, allows it to function only as an abstract principle. As I turn to Tennyson, I hope to retain Hollingsworth's view of the hive as a metaphor that has become an image of the hierarchy of monarchy in the abstract over the course of several thousand years. However, I also hope to draw in contemporary usages of the metaphor to suggest that like his contemporaries, Tennyson used the hive as an imaginary space in which to define his own relationship to the Queen.

II. "As Bees about their Queen": The University as Hive

References to bees and the hive appear repeatedly in *The Princess,* particularly at crucial moments in the Prince's development. The first of these references occurs when the Prince first speaks of Ida, declaring that he wears her picture and a tress of her hair around his neck and that "around them both / Sweet thoughts would swarm as bees about their Queen" (I, 38-39).[5] From the earliest moments in the poem the narrator establishes Ida as a queen among bees. This sort of imagery reappears when the Prince meets Ida for the first time; she uses the metaphor to describe the university, telling the Prince, Cyril, and Florian that the new arrivals "press in from all the provinces / And fill the hive" (II, 81-84). Later in the poem, the Prince continues to employ this language. Again at a crucial moment—the point at which Ida discovers that he is indeed male—he recalls that "Across the woods, and less from Indian craft / Than beelike instinct hiveward, [I] found at length / The garden portals" (IV, 180-182). Similarly, when Ida later confronts the Prince regarding his intrusion, she refers to him and his friends as "wasps in our good hive" (IV, 514). The narrative closes with yet more apian imagery. As the university crumbles in front of Ida, she sees at various points "the swarm / Of fe-

male whisperers" and "swarms of men / Darkening her female field" (VI 335-336, VII 18-19). And in the final and perhaps most recognized instance of bee imagery, Ida ends her pastoral song "Come down, O maid, from yonder mountain height" with the "murmuring of innumerable bees" (VII, 207). The language of bees and their hive thus appears at crucial moments in the text, creating a sustained association of the University with the hive.

In presenting the university as a hive ruled by a woman, Tennyson allows his thought to be shaped by the metaphor that his fellow Victorians (such as Bagster) resisted. The meaning of the metaphor for Tennyson, though, is anything but clear. On the one hand, he turns to the hive with all of its diachronic significance as a way of structuring Ida's kingdom. With this usage of the metaphor, Tennyson invests Ida with all of those qualities that the Victorians would have associated with the masculine sphere. On the other hand, Tennyson's usage of the metaphor also admits all of the doubts about the monarchy that are attached to contemporary portrayals of the hive. The hive thus forces a realignment of all the categories that Victorian ideology tries to link together so seamlessly. Linda Shires has argued that despite the poem's gesture towards heterosexual marriage, "radical gender constructions do remain in play, exceeding the stability of a hermeneutic closure, which attempts to suppress differences"(55). Shires' point is important, for if the gender constructions of the poem remain in play, so too does the resulting confusion of all the other discourses attached to those gender constructions. Thus by examining the reconfiguration of gender expectations within the hive, we are able to see how Tennyson ultimately embraces ambivalence and ambiguity as the most acceptable way of locating himself between the radical politics of the hive and the conservative ideology of the surrounding frame.

In *The Honey Bee* (1827), Edward Bevan offers a description of the relationships between bees and the hive that is particularly useful when considering Tennyson's use of the metaphor:

> Contrary to what occurs in the human species and in other parts of the animal creation, among bees, the females alone exhibit activity, skill, diligence, and courage, whilst the males take no part whatever in the labours of the community, but are idle, cowardly and inactive, and possess not the usual offensive weapon of their species. The only way in which the drones promote the welfare of the society is a sexual one; and I shall endeavour to show, in the course of this chapter, that they serve no other purpose than that of impregnating such of the young queens as may lead forth swarms in the season, or be raised to the sovereignty of the parent hive.
>
> (5)

Bevan's description anticipates in many ways the Victorian idea of the separate spheres with one very notable exception—within the hive, gender roles are entirely reversed. The female takes on a role that is active, public, and in service to the community. The male, on the other hand, adopts a domestic role, avoiding the public conflict of warfare and serving the community primarily through the act of reproduction.

Tennyson's association of the university with the hive functions like Bevan's description of the hive in that it foregrounds these confused, inverted gender relationships. The space that Ida occupies as queen becomes contested as competing demands force their way onto her. Within the context of the university, Ida's role is a masculine one; as the head of a political system, she ventures into a role that had traditionally been reserved for men. The language that the narrative voice uses to define this role reflects this entrance into the male sphere; Psyche describes the project of the university in this way—"she [Ida] has founded; they [the women at the university] must build" (II, 129). Statements like this explicitly define Ida's role as Queen as one that crosses over into industry, politics, and governance—all things that conflict with traditional perceptions of women's roles, perceptions that Ida learns to defy from Blanche and Psyche (I, 135-145). At the same time, however, the very fact of her biological sex foists on Ida all of the demands of motherhood, and although she tries to resist these, her insistence that she "lose the child" (I, 136) suggests that traditional roles for women always compete in her mind with the more public, intellectual guise that she takes on in the university.

If the narrative voice positions Ida as the monarch, the queen of the hive, he imposes upon the Prince the position of a drone in the community. Throughout the text, we see the male Prince pushed into a feminine space. He is initially described as "blue-eyed, and fair in face, . . . With lengths of yellow ringlet, like a girl" (I, 1-3). Later in the poem, Ida suggests that the Prince "seems no better than a girl; / As girls were once" (III, 202-203), and indeed, in the argument that follows it is the Prince—not Ida—who argues for the virtues of motherhood. Even in the traditionally masculine pursuit of war, the Prince fails miserably; in the single conflict in which he engages, he is quickly unhorsed and defeated. His primary function in society is, as Terry Eagleton has suggested, a sexual one (77); his union with Ida ensures the fulfillment of the marriage contract established by his father which facilitates the reproduction of the state much as the drone's only purpose is to reproduce the structure of the hive through his union with the Queen. The Prince's quest becomes—whether through war or through love—that of impregnating the young queen to ensure the reproduction of the state, and the success or failure of his quest depends largely on how well he navigates the confused and inverted

gender relationships within the hive. And—most importantly for Tennyson himself—the path through the hive lies in language in general and poetic language specifically.

At the very heart of *The Princess* is the issue of language and how it functions within the hive. In order for the Prince to be successful in his efforts to woo Ida, he must find a poetic language that takes into account several factors—his position as a man attempting to seduce a woman, his position as a subject in relationship to a monarch, and Ida's own resistance to being assimilated into any language that he knows. Initially, the Prince approaches Ida with the traditional language of love. She notes this language and insists that it has no place inside her university. When the Prince sings his own praises, she responds that "We scarcely thought in our own hall to hear / This barren verbiage, current among men, / Light coin, the tinsel clink of compliment" (II, 39-41). Thus upon the Prince's first arrival at Ida's university, he proceeds by way of the language to which he is accustomed. This model, however, fails immediately, for while it accounts for the discourse of traditionally structured male-female relationships, it also draws from an ancient metaphor in which the Prince is destined to become the king bee, replacing Ida as monarch. Thus it cannot account for the power dynamic existing between Ida as monarch and Prince as subject within the walls of the university, nor is it a language to which Ida will submit. The Prince, however, is a ready (but not particularly apt) pupil; within a short time he has learned that the terms by which he initially seeks to describe the relationship between himself and Ida cannot work. He responds to this failure of one mode of discourse by turning to another, as when Ida later asks him for a song appropriate for her and her maids. The Prince responds with **"O Swallow, Swallow, flying, flying South,"** a sickly sweet and sentimental poem that Ida rejects, describing it as a "mere love-poem" (IV, 108). The Prince describes himself as singing in a way that is "maidenlike as far / As [he] could ape their treble" (IV, 73-74). Here the Prince attempts to speak in a voice that he has learned is "feminine" and that he assumes is the sort of voice that the Princess expects from her subjects in the university. If at first his song was masculine and thus unable to capture the entirety of his relationship with Ida, here too his poetic voice is untenable. By "aping" the feminine, the Prince once again fails to recognize that his very conception of the category "feminine" cannot hold Ida's role as ruler of a community; the result once again is a voice that fails to please a queen, for "still [his] voice rang false" (IV, 103).

In addition to providing much of the comic effect of the poem, this confusion of discourses highlights Tennyson's struggle at this point in his career—the difficulties of singing for a Queen. If the Prince manages only to display his desire to win the heart of the Princess through his song, Ida's response represents a very different approach to poetry fitting for the female monarch. She adopts a poetic voice that accommodates her place as queen within the hive:

> But great is song
> Used to great ends: ourself have often tried
> Valkyrian hymns, or into rhythm have dashed
> The passion of the prophetess; for song
> Is duer unto freedom, force and growth
> Of spirit than to junketing and love.
>
> (IV, 119-124)

What Ida recognizes here is the power of text, which can both enslave women through its construction of the very norms and expectations that the Prince's song expresses or be used for more liberating ends. By contrasting the Valkyrian hymn and the passion of the prophetess with the sentimental sweetness of **"O Swallow, swallow,"** Ida reconfigures the expectations of poetry written in celebration of the queen, for her own celebratory verse engages with the patently political—freedom, force, and growth of spirit.[6] Ida's own vision of poetry, then, stands in stark contrast to that of the Prince in that it is neither "barren verbiage" nor "mere-love song"; it is a poetry that reinforces her own position as the Queen of her hive.

Within the framework of the narrative, the resolution (or lack thereof) of these opposed visions of poetic language depends heavily on our interpretation of a prophecy made by the Lady Psyche. In a lecture given to the students at the university, Psyche elaborates a vision of a woman-led world. She notes that though few and far between, there have been great women in the past—Joan of Arc, Sappho, Elizabeth, and Ida herself. This vision of a woman-led society, though, is a temporary one. Psyche quickly becomes prophetic, predicting that

> 'everywhere
> Two heads in council, two beside the hearth,
> Two in the tangled business of the world,
> Two in the liberal offices of life,
> Two plummets dropt for one to sound the abyss
> Of science, and the secrets of the mind. . . .'
>
> (II, 155-160)

In this prophetic vision of an ideal society, woman no longer needs to assert her sole primacy, and the hive metaphor dissolves because of an emerging equality predicated upon the union of masculine and feminine. Significantly, Psyche's vision incorporates male and female into both the domestic sphere and the political. When, later in the poem, the Prince approaches Ida with the idea of marriage, he takes up a very similar sort of language, proposing to her that "either sex alone / Is half itself, and in true marriage lies / Nor equal, nor unequal: each fulfills / Defect in each" (VII, 283-286).

Ida responds by asking him "What woman taught you this?" (VII, 291). The answer, it seems, is the Lady Psyche, and having learned from her and from his experience within the hive, the Prince finally approaches Ida with a language of equality. As Beverly Taylor has pointed out, faced with the Prince's final call for a relationship based on equality, we are left with two choices—that he is sincere or that he is blatantly lying (15). Like Taylor, I accept the Prince's words as sincere and genuine. If he is, the proposed marriage becomes the fulfillment of Psyche's vision as two heads join together to govern both hearth and throne, and presumably, the two visions of poetic language represented by the drone and the queen come to stand in a relationship of equality.

Reading the marriage between the Prince and the Princess in this way, though, only intensifies the confusion of discourses that has typified the narrative. If through marriage the inequalities in the relationship between male and female are dissolved, then so too are all of the other inequalities in the different discourses attached to the figures of the Prince and Princess. This conclusion implies that in order to discover a true poetic voice, both the Prince and Ida must remove themselves from the terms of the hive metaphor within which they had tried to structure their relationship. For the Prince specifically, this restructuring requires that he and Ida be equal, and Ida accordingly assumes a position of equality both in marriage and in government.[7] The hive as a description of government thus ceases to function at the end, for the hierarchy implied by the very terms of the metaphor cannot be sustained given the equalizing forces of marriage. In the same way, the battle over appropriate poetic voice for a queen necessarily ends with a truce; the feminine voice that the Prince learns stands now in equal relation to the masculine voice performed by Ida.

III. The "Strange Diagonal"

Within the central narrative of **The Princess,** then, two distinct poetic voices emerge—the masculine voice demanded by Ida and the feminine voice in which the Prince sings. These two voices remain separate in the narrative; we never see the consummation of the marriage that might allow the two to merge.[8] Only in the Conclusion does the narrator attempt to accommodate both of these voices. Jerome McGann suggests that the conclusion of **The Princess** is perhaps the clearest example of what he calls Tennyson's "aesthetics of reconciliations," an aesthetic "not merely designed to accommodate different views and alternate readings, but that actively anticipated these differences—that (as it were) called out to them, and that offered Victorian readers a place where they would find their differences reconciled" (179). What McGann identifies as an aesthetic generated from Tennyson's relationship to the publishing industry, however, holds equally true for Tennyson himself, for just as the poem accommodates multiple interpretations from its audience, so too does it afford Tennyson multiple subject positions within which to locate his own poetic voice.

The central narrative of *The Princess* identifies two primary modes of poetic discourse, the one a masculinized voice associated with Ida and her call for an active, political poetry, the other the feminized voice of the Prince that Ida rejects. Significantly, these two voices represent the different modes of poetry to which Tennyson felt himself pulled as a poet in relation to the state. On the one hand, throughout the late 1840s, Tennyson was drawn towards a political verse that corresponds to the types of songs that Ida suggests are appropriate for a monarch. In 1846, he received a pension from the Crown that caused him no small level of anxiety. Tennyson felt intuitively that by accepting the favor of the government he was allowing himself to be interpellated by an ideology that would require a political verse aligned with the conservative structure of the monarchy. In a series of letters following his acceptance of the pension, Tennyson affirms that he can still critique the government; his claims, though, serve only to foreground his own anxiety that he must now produce the sort of political verse required for the Queen. Writing to Thomas Hardwicke Rawnsley, Tennyson explains

> Peel tells me that I need not by it be fettered in the public expression of any opinion that I choose to take up so if I take a pique against the Queen or the court or Peel himself I may, if I will, bully them with as much freedom though not perhaps quite so *gracefully* as if I were still unpensioned. Something in that word pension sticks in my gizzard: it is only the name and perhaps would smell sweeter by some other.

> (*Letters* 247, my emphasis)

Tennyson's concern with the gracefulness with which he can remain detached from the Queen and the government reveals his own uneasiness at being placed in a position of debt to the crown. His hesitancy to engage with the political becomes even more explicit the next year. In March of 1847, William Whewell, the Master of Trinity College, proposed that Tennyson should compose an ode for the occasion of the Prince Consort's installation as Chancellor of the University. He declined. In his letter to Whewell, he writes "Household affection to my old College and filial regard to the University I have [. . .] neither am I without loyal touches towards Queens and Princes, but for all that the ode is more than I dare pledge myself to accomplish" (272-73). Here Tennyson establishes for himself a stance that places him at a distance from the monarchy, acknowledging his debt to the Crown while still refusing to have his poetic project dictated by the demands of the state.

At the same time, however, Tennyson was equally pulled towards a Romantic lyricism that several of his contemporaries derided as excessively feminine. In 1846, just as Tennyson began serious work on *The Princess,* Edward Bulwer-Lytton published "The New Timon" in which he derided Peel's decision to bestow a pension on "School Miss Alfred" (51).[9] Bulwer-Lytton claims for his own verse that "No tawdry grace shall womanize my pen" (50), and he goes on to decry the womanish qualities of British Romanticism with which he associates Tennyson, declaring that his own poetry will have none of

> the mock-bird's modish tune,
> The jingling medley of purloin'd conceits,
> Outbabying Wordsworth, and outglittering Keats,
> Where all the airs of patchwork-pastoral chime
> To drowsy ears in Tennysonian rhyme.

> (51)

Bulwer-Lytton's "womanizing" of Tennyson echoes a common complaint about his verse—that its Keatsian qualities made it vapid and without substance.[10] Yet Bulwer-Lytton's critique registers at multiple levels, much as language does in *The Princess.* Having dismissed Tennyson's verse as "womanish," he goes on to draw clear parallels between the feminized Romantic lyric and ineffective politics, chastising Peel because he "plump[s] the puling Muse . . . [and] pensions Tennyson, while starving a Knowles" (52). Bulwer-Lytton's characterization of Tennyson in *The New Timon* demonstrates the extent to which different discourses of gender coding and politics merge; the gender-coded language with which Bulwer-Lytton attacks Tennyson shifts smoothly into the language of politics and the accusation that Peel and by extension Victoria herself have embraced the womanish poetry of Tennyson at the expense of the somehow more legitimate and mannish verse that *should* celebrate Britain's monarchy.

The solution that Tennyson works out to these competing demands is also the one worked out in the frame to the central narrative of *The Princess.* In a statement cited by virtually every critic of the poem, Tennyson famously remarks that the intercalary songs between the sections are the key to the poem (H. Tennyson 254). What exactly he may have meant by this certainly is open to debate. However, if we consider that both the imagery of the hive and the end of the love story inside the frame speak to questions about a gendered poetics, the songs inserted between the sections of the poem may offer some hint as to the resolution of the two seemingly incompatible voices of the narrative. All of these songs, the narrator tells us, are sung by the women "between the rougher voices of the men" (Prologue, 257). Yet Tennyson goes to great pains to establish that the entirety of the project comes from the mouth of a single poet. In the Prologue, the narrator claims "here I give the story and the songs" (259), and in the epilogue, he recalls that "the words are mostly mine" (Conclusion, 3). This last claim can be read in two ways. It may be that the narrator confesses here that he has had some help, that this is a communal effort despite his claims to the contrary. This seems unlikely, however, when several lines later the central question becomes "how to bind the scattered scheme of seven / Together in one sheaf" (Conclusion, 8-9). Instead, the claim that it is "mostly" his seems to me an act of appropriation; the narrator has so taken over the story and the songs that they no longer can be said to belong to the other men and women involved in the first telling of the tale. Instead, the narrator so completely learns to adopt both voices in the text—that of the narrative demanded by the queen and the feminine lyric to which the drone aspires—that we as readers simply do not question that we hear the songs as the women would have sung them. Ultimately, the narrator's voice becomes that of the worker bee"—that androgynous ideal that exists somewhere between the drone and the Queen. From this position somewhere in between the men who demand a mock heroic gigantesque and the women who wish for the "true-heroic, true-sublime" the narrator moves "as in a strange diagonal," somehow able to traverse with ease the lines of gendered language.

This in-between space from which the narrator speaks remains a profoundly disturbing aspect of the text, for the narrator's refusal to align himself with either the feminine poetic voice or the masculine also calls into question traditional understandings of government as represented by the hive metaphor and points towards a society in which the monarch's position is purely that of a figurehead. Lest we miss the point that this in-between space carries direct political implications, the narrator records for us the diatribe delivered by his college friend. In this speech, the college friend contrasts his vision of Britain with that of France. In contrast to the French, whose governmental system has crumbled with "mock heroics" stranger than the ones that the students have just created, the English are presented as ordered, structured, and efficient. In response to this political invective, the narrator calms his friend and suggests the value of the poet's own place as a worker within English society. He tells his friend to have patience, for

> ourselves are full
> Of social wrong; and maybe wildest dreams
> Are but the needful preludes of the truth:
>
> . . . . .
>
> This fine old world of ours is but a child
> Yet in the go-cart. Patience! Give it time
> To learn its limbs: there is a hand that guides.
>
> (Conclusion, 72-79)

The end, then, is a beginning, and the narrator suggests the importance of his own role as a poet in guiding a new English society. If the medley sung by seven friends and the six women who listen becomes, when transformed by the poet, the "prelude of the truth," then we must assume that the hand that will guide the nation as it rights the social wrong and as it continues to develop is that of the Poet himself. The honey-combed structure of *The Princess,* with the solid walls of the epic narrative interspersed with the sweet honey of the lyric, becomes the product built by the worker bee—the poet whose guiding hand and voice will shape the building of the British Empire. In the end, this role for the poet is only suggested. The narrator refuses to embrace fully the position of the guiding hand that would displace both monarchy and social hierarchy, and although the scene closes with a gentle satire of Sir Walter and his guano pamphlets, it also capitulates to the rights of the aristocracy and praises them for the generosity of welcoming the commoners to their estates several times during the year. As the poem closes, we are left with a vision similar to the one of "radical conservatism" that Isobel Armstrong locates in Tennyson's early poetry (56); the narrator dwells somewhere between the radical politics of the hive and the conservative ideology of Sir Walter.

If the pension and the expectations that he would produce a certain type of poetry stuck in Tennyson's gizzard in 1846 and 1847, he seems to have reached a quite different conclusion by 1850. Just four years after his anxiety at accepting a pension and only three years after declining Whewell's invitation, Tennyson accepted the Laureateship, the most politically demanding post available to him as a poet. He writes to Sophia Elmhirst that "I would rather not have been made Laureate if I could have helped it: but I was told by those who know these matters that being already in receipt of a pension I could not *gracefully* decline the Queen's offer. As for writing court odes except upon express command from Headquarters, that I shall not do. Pretty things they are likely to be" (343). As in 1846, Tennyson expresses concern at his position within the Victorian state, recognizing that a refusal of the Laureateship will be seen as a graceless act yet also desiring the individual autonomy that would be impossible as Laureate. The crucial difference in 1850, though, is that Tennyson accepts the invitation to pen verse for the monarchy. I do not mean to imply that he embraced wholeheartedly his new position as Laureate. On the contrary, the two different letters that Tennyson composed in response to the Queen's offer suggest just how deeply felt was his ambivalence toward the idea of poetic service to the state. What I am interested in, though, is not Tennyson's feeling about the position but the course of action that he took. Between 1846 and 1850 Tennyson's position in relation to the Crown shifts from a refusal to engage with the political event of the Prince Consort's installation as Chancellor to an acceptance—however reluctant it may have been—of the Laureateship.

The Princess, a text written in the years between Whewell's request and Tennyson's acceptance of the Laureateship, is fundamental to understanding this shift in perspectives, for it is Tennyson's final public statement of a strategy of ambivalence and accommodation before he accepted the Laureateship in 1850. Antony Harrison has suggested that throughout his career as Poet Laureate, Tennyson "manipulated a variety of cultural discourses in order to fashion not only poems but also a poetic self, sometimes with seductive explosions of beauty, often with ringing declamations of prophetic authority, but most characteristically with bursts of strategic ambivalence" (45). Certainly in his public performances as Laureate, we see Tennyson making such declamations in poems that are quite clearly written in service to the British throne, poems like **"Ode on the Death of the Duke of Wellington"** and **"The Charge of the Light Brigade."** At the same time, however, Tennyson continued to embrace the personal intimacy of the lyric mode, composing poems like **"Flower in the Crannied Wall"** and **"Hendecasyllabics"** in which he playfully describes himself as "some rare little rose, a piece of inmost / Horticultural art, or half coquette-like / Maiden, not to be greeted unbenignly" (19-21). And as Harrison suggests, at his best Tennyson held these voices in a near-perfect tension, as in the *Idylls of the King* or in his description of Arthur Hallam as "manhood fused with female grace" (*In Memoriam,* CIX, 17). Tennyson's voice as Laureate—like the voice of the narrator of *The Princess*—accommodates both Ida's Valkyrian hymn and the Prince's sentimental lyric by turning to a carefully considered androgyny that hovers somewhere in the space between the competing ideologies represented by the two different modes of poetic discourse. As it turns out, the voice of the worker bee is not a voice that fails to please anyone as the narrator worries (*Princess,* Conclusion, 25). Instead, the voice of the worker bee as it is developed in *The Princess* is the only voice that can please anyone, and it is to this voice that Tennyson turns as he sings in graceful service to the Queen.[12]

Notes

1. For more on the indirectness of Tennyson's early verse, I direct readers to Isobel Armstrong whose characterization of Tennyson's "aesthetics of ambiguity" has been influential in the shaping of my argument.

2. One of the chief difficulties with *The Princess* is our own need to try to reconcile what Tennyson leaves ambiguous. One approach has been to read the poem as a piece of political conservatism that inadvertently admits some current of liberal feminism through the person of Ida. This sort of read-

ing has led to a wide range of interpretations, from Eagleton's psychoanalytic approach to the text as a reinforcement of masculine hegemony, to Sedgwick's reading of the poem as a triumph of conservative values expressed through the homosocial bonds between men, to Gail Turley Houston's more recent discussion of *The Princess* as a text that ultimately holds to a representation of gender and sexuality in strictly binary terms in which "masculinity is defined against its opposite—the feminine" (77). Alternatively, the poem has (less frequently) been read as a piece of progressive feminist propaganda written by a poet who ultimately could not escape his own conservatism. Isobel Armstrong suggests, for instance, that the poem is a "feminist tract" (111) while Beverly Taylor writes that it "eludes and subverts Victorian gender stereotypes" even as it registers coded Victorian gender norms (14). Even Alan Sinfield's provocative reading of Tennyson forces us into choosing one of these positions as "the preferred version of reality which constitutes the author's project" (8).

3. Limitations of space prohibit me from exploring the use of the hive as fully as I could. I have chosen to examine scientific discourse because it is here that the hive emerges most explicitly as political metaphor. We must remember, however, that this sort of figurative language was certainly not limited to the scientific community. Indeed, Gail Turley Houston has offered a wonderfully suggestive reading of two non-scientific uses of this metaphor as a way of discussing the potential problems inherent when the monarchy is headed by a woman. The fact that her illustrations include Mrs. Trimmer's *Fabulous Histories* (1794) and George Cruikshank's etching "The British Beehive" (1840) suggests that the hive held currency as a sort of political allegory over a significant period of time in the nineteenth century.

4. I base this suggestion in part on the general political affiliations of Baptists in the early nineteenth century. For more on this, see G. I. T. Machin.

5. All references to poems by Tennyson are taken from the taken from Christopher Ricks' *Tennyson: A Selected Edition.* Citations will be given as line numbers or, in the case of *The Princess,* as section number followed by line number.

6. It is worth noting that we see enacted here the same forces that set the university into motion; Ida's version of song echoes the "rhymes / and dismal lyrics, prophesying change / Beyond all reason" (I, 140-142) that initially persuaded her father to grant her land for the university.

7. This conflation of gender and politics in the terms of a single metaphor is, I believe, the source of

much of the disagreement over *The Princess*. If we read the conclusion of the narrative strictly in terms of gender politics, the result is troubling, for Ida must sacrifice a position of power in order to enter into the marriage contract. From this perspective, the Prince's language of equality is simply cover for the elevation of his male authority and the lessening of Ida's female authority. On the other hand, read in terms of politics, this language of equality is a radically liberal proposition in which the queen and her subject voluntarily enter into what is presented as a democratic relationship. Recognizing that both of these perspectives are presented through the same language accounts for the multiple reactions to the text as well as to the fact that the different values presented in *The Princess* may be fundamentally unresolvable.

8. One could argue that Ida's voicing of the lyrics "Now Sleeps the Crimson Petal" and "Come down O Maid" represents a realignment of the feminine with the sentimental lyric mode and thus a capitulation to the ideologies that sustain the institution of marriage outside the university. It seems to me, however, that two things work against this reading of the lyrics. First, these poems are not Ida's voice; she reads them from a volume of poems from her own land. More importantly, both of these lyrics claim a male speaker speaking in the same mode with which the Prince approached Ida. We thus see Ida voicing a male speaker who in turn speaks in what *The Princess* has already identified as a feminized mode of poetry. As Ida considers her response to the Prince, these lyrics seem to me to only highlight the final play of gender roles with which the narrative of *The Princess* closes.

9. Because the reprint edition of *The New Timon* does not include line numbers, all references to it are given as page numbers.

10. See for instance John Wilson Croker's review of the 1832 volume and Leigh Hunt's comments on the 1842 *Poems*. Even Arthur Hallam's 1830 review of *Poems, Chiefly Lyrical* draws these sorts of connections between Tennyson and Keats, although Hallam presents this association in terms much more positive than Croker, Hunt, or Bulwer-Lytton.

11. To be perfectly clear, Tennyson does not use this term of the narrative voice; it is, however, an apt extension of the hive imagery that captures perfectly the nature of the narrator's poetic accomplishments.

12. As a final note, readers may be interested to know that all of the language of the honeybee and its hive is dropped in Gilbert and Sullivan's operatic rendition of *The Princess*.

Works Cited

Armstrong, Isobel. *Victorian Poetry: Poetry, Poetics, and Politics*. New York: Routledge, 1993.

Bagster, Samuel. *The Management of Bees. With a Description of the "Ladies' Safety Hive."* London, 1834.

Bevan, Edward. *The Honey-bee: Its Natural History, Physiology and Management*. London, 1827.

Butler, Charles. *The Feminine Monarchy; or the History of Bees; Shewing Their Admirable Nature and Property*. London, 1704.

Cotton, William Charles. *A Short and Simple Letter to Cottagers*. Oxford, 1838.

———. *My Bee Book*. London, 1842.

Eagleton, Terry. "Tennyson: Politics and Sexuality in *The Princess* and *In Memoriam*." *Tennyson*. Ed. Rebecca Stott. New York: Longman, 1996. 76-86.

Harrison, Antony H. *Victorian Poets and the Politics of Culture: Discourse and Ideology*. Charlottesville: U P of Virginia, 1998.

Hollingsworth, Cristopher. *Poetics of the Hive: the Insect Metaphor in Literature*. Iowa City: U of Iowa P, 2001.

Houston, Gail Turley. *Royalties: the Queen and Victorian Writers*. Charlottesville: U P of Virginia, 1999.

Lytton, Edward Bulwer. "The New Timon." *The New Timon, The Heptalogia, Disgust: A Dramatic Dialogue*. Eds. William E. Fredeman, Ira Bruce Nadel and John F. Stasny. New York: Garland, 1986.

Machin, G. I. T. *Politics and the Churches in Great Britain, 1832-1868*. Oxford: Clarendon P, 1977.

Mandeville, Bernard. *The Fable of the Bees: or, Private Vices Publick Benefits*. London, 1714.

Marston, J. W. "*The Princess* [1847]." *Tennyson: The Critical Heritage*. 1848. Ed. John D. Jump. London: Routledge & Kegan Paul, 1967. 166-71.

McGann, Jerome J. *The Beauty of Inflections: Literary Investigations in Historical Method and Theory*. Oxford: Clarendon, 1985.

Nutt, Thomas. *Practical Directions for the Management of Honey Bees, Upon an Improved and Humane plan, by which the Lives of Bees May Be Preserved, and Abundance of Honey of a Superior Quality May Be Obtained*. 7th ed. Wisbech, 1848.

Patterson, Robert. *Letters on the Natural History of the Insects Mentioned in Shakspeare's Plays: with Incidental Notices of the Entomology of Ireland*. London, 1838.

Pile, Matthew. *The Bee Cultivator's Assistant, or, A New and Complete Discovery in the Management of Bees*. Gateshead, 1838.

Sedgwick, Eve Kosofsky. "Tennyson's Princess: One Bride for Seven Brothers." *Tennyson.* Ed. Rebecca Stott. New York: Longman, 1996. 181-96.

Shakespeare, William. *King Henry V.* Ed. Andrew Gurr. Cambridge: Cambridge UP, 1992.

Shires, Linda M. "Rereading Tennyson's Gender Politics." *Victorian Sages and Cultural Discourse: Renegotiating Gender and Power.* Ed. Thaïs Morgan. New Brunswick: Rutgers UP, 1990. 46-65.

Sinfield, Alan. *Alfred Tennyson.* Oxford: B. Blackwell, 1986.

Taylor, Beverly. "'School Miss Alfred' and 'Materfamilias': Female Sexuality and Poetic Voice in *The Princess* and *Aurora Leigh.*" *Gender and Discourse in Victorian Literature and Art.* Ed. Antony H. Harrison and Beverly Taylor. DeKalb: Northern Illinois U P, 1992. 5-29.

Tennyson, Alfred. *The Letters of Alfred Lord Tennyson.* Ed. Cecil Y. Lang and Edgar F. Shannon. Vol. 1. Cambridge: Harvard U P, 1981.

———. *Tennyson: a Selected Edition.* Ed. Christopher Ricks. Harlow: Longman, 1989.

Tennyson, Hallam. *Alfred Lord Tennyson: a Memoir.* New York: Greenwood, 1969.

Varro, Marcus Terentius. *The Three Books of M. Terentius Varro Concerning Agriculture.* Trans. T. Owen, Oxford, 1800.

Virgil. *The Georgics.* Trans. Robert Wells. Manchester: Carcanet New Press, 1982.

Kathryn Ledbetter (essay date spring 2005)

SOURCE: Ledbetter, Kathryn. "Protesting Success: Tennyson's 'Indecent Exposure' in the Periodicals." *Victorian Poetry* 43, no. 1 (spring 2005): 53-73.

[*In the following essay, Ledbetter considers the implications of the relatively large number of Tennyson's poems that were published—in periodicals, rather than in book form—in 1868.*]

Five poems in seven periodicals comprised Tennyson's entire list of publications for the year 1868: **"The Victim"** in *Good Words* (January 1); **"The Spiteful Letter"** in *Once a Week* (January 4); **"Wages"** in *Macmillan's Magazine* (February); **"1865-1866"** in *Every Saturday* (U.S., February 22) and *Good Words* (March); and **"Lucretius"** in *Macmillan's Magazine* (May) and *Every Saturday* (U.S., May 2). The output worried Swinburne, who pleaded to Lord Houghton: "Cannot you, as a friend of Mr. Tennyson prevent his making such a hideous exhibition of himself as he has been doing for the last three months? I thought there was a law against 'indecent exposure'?"[1] Such attitudes suggest that periodicals generally published inferior literature, and that writers whose works appeared in them devalued both literary quality and reputation through unsophisticated exposure in the mass media. Tennyson outwardly concurred, repeatedly claiming to hate publishing in periodicals. He typically returned a negative answer to editors' requests, as in this letter to an unidentified correspondent on May 25, 1859: "It is so contrary to the wont of my whole life to write in Magazines that I cannot accept your proposal, but I will become your subscriber—at least for a year."[2] Upon learning that Thackeray was to be the editor of a new monthly magazine, the *Cornhill,* Tennyson wrote to him on November 6, 1859:

> I am sorry that you have engaged for any quantity of money to let your brains be sucked periodically by Smith, Elder and co.: not that I don't like Smith . . . but that so great an artist as you are should go to work after this fashion. Whenever you feel your brains as the "remainder biscuit" or indeed whenever you will, come over to me and take a blow on these downs where the air as Keats said is "worth sixpence a pint."
>
> (*Letters,* 2:245)

He tells American publisher James Ripley Osgood, who may have been soliciting poems for any of the publications owned by Ticknor and Fields (April 4, 1867): "I am not in the habit of inserting poems in the English Magazines, and why should I in the American?—particularly as in this unhappy condition of international Copyright law the English Magazines would immediately pirate any thing of mine in yours" (*Letters,* 2:457 and n.).

In spite of Tennyson's frequent public complaints about periodicals, from his first adolescent contributions of **"Timbuctoo"** to the *Cambridge Chronicle and Journal* (July 10, 1829) and early poetry for literary annuals (*The Gem,* 1831; *Friendship's Offering,* 1832 and 1833; *Yorkshire Literary Annual,* 1832; *The Keepsake,* 1837; and *The Tribute,* 1837), periodicals brought Tennyson exposure to new readers, improved his financial status with increasingly higher fees, and, later when he became Poet Laureate and literary celebrity, provided him with an outlet for trumpeting opinions on his latest political cause. Indeed, Tennyson's entire career is inseparable from a dependence on the very format he supposedly hated, and generations of scholars have largely ignored or devalued important contexts provided by periodicals, misled by Tennyson's protestations and prejudice against the genre. Tennyson and Victorian periodicals were partners and interdependent commodities, sharing in the profits, the popularity, and the proliferation of culture.

Yet scholars continue to speculate about Tennyson's occasion for comparatively prolific periodical publications in 1868. For example, Charles Tennyson suggests that "feeling uneasy at his long lack of contact with the public, and not yet ready with enough work for a new volume, he published a series of poems (the fruits of his increased activity) in periodicals."[3] Alternately, Robert Bernard Martin cites the fear of financial distress caused by the recent purchase of Aldworth and plans for a new house. According to Martin, Tennyson was also

> genuinely worried about the dry season of his creativity, which sometimes made it seem possible there would never be another volume of poetry. It was common gossip at the time that Tennyson's day would soon be over, and the publication of these poems was an answer to the rumours, asserting that the old master had lost neither his inspiration nor his cunning.
>
> (p. 476)

Publication in periodicals would solve his money worries, as well as any insecurities about creativity. June Steffensen Hagen, whose important book about Tennyson's publishing history curiously omits significant discussion of Tennyson's appearance in periodicals, notes that Tennyson's troubled relationship with Moxon's manager J. Bertrand Payne was aggravated in 1867 by the discovery that the firm had been collecting copyright infringement fees from the Religious Tract Society and others without his approval or benefit; Tennyson complained: "I could not accept anything from God nor I think can I directly or indirectly."[4] Payne's highly commercial style was reminiscent of that of literary annuals' editors whom Tennyson found offensive early in his career.[5] In 1864, when Tennyson suggested a working-class edition of **Enoch Arden,** Payne had expanded Tennyson's idea of a cheap series of sixpenny parts by producing a somewhat elaborate five-shilling anthology. Although the volume brought Tennyson well over £5700 and confirmed his role as the "Poet of the People," Tennyson felt that he had been "persuaded, against his will, to issue the volume in a more ornamental style than his severe taste generally admitted" (Charles Tennyson, p. 354). As with periodical publication, Tennyson's populist desire to reach a mass audience conflicted with his own elitist, romantic notions of poetry. Ironically, the machinery of commercial production that gave Tennyson the cash needed to purchase Aldworth forced him into a material code that offended what he believed to be the cultural aesthetic obvious within his own poetic, personal, and public persona. Whether his concessions to periodicals were motivated by money, friendly favors, or calculated business moves, Tennyson's "severe taste" consistently clashed with an urge to be a popular (and financially successful) poet; thus the appearance of Tennyson's poetry in Victorian

periodicals sometimes betrays his professed aims and invites potential cultural contexts that can distinctively shape our reading of his art.

Tennyson's outward excuses for consenting to periodicals were friendship or money. Frustrations with Payne and fear of the company's financial collapse caused him to seek a new publisher in Alexander Strahan, owner of *Good Words* from 1860 to 1911. Martin notes Tennyson's temporary solution: "To sell his poems to periodicals was to ensure their publication without having to deal with Payne," thus solving the financial problems as well as the disagreements with Payne (p. 477). For some time Strahan had been courting Tennyson, who wrote to Emily Tennyson on November 14, 1868, "Strahan dined here yesterday and has not the least doubt that he can make the £4000 per annum (which he promised me). . . . Strahan asserts that he makes a clear profit of £7000 a year by *Good Words* alone, and that my business would bring no end of grist to his mill" (**Letters,** 2:506). Publication in Strahan's periodical proved to be a good business move for Tennyson, and Strahan paved a clear path by offering Tennyson the extraordinary fee of £700 for a single poem, **"The Victim."**

Such practical concerns do not seem evident, however, in Tennyson's correspondence about his involvement with *Good Words*. At the fringes of his contribution was an earlier request from the Duchess of Argyll on December 12, 1863:

> I should make Norman Macleod extremely grateful if I could persuade you to send him something for "Good Words"—and I should like to please him, as I think him an excellent Man. He has not asked me to do this. You know it is the best of all the Cheap periodicals, and you should be glad to help it. They are printing 1,500,000—for next year!
>
> (**Letters,** 2:346n)

The invitation mixes personal loyalty to the Duchess, sentiment for *Good Words* editor Macleod, and the inevitability of commercial success. Yet Tennyson characteristically refused, writing to the Duchess on December 26, 1863, "I dare say 'Good Words' is a very meritorious and very popular publication but, you see my feeling is against writing in Magazines. 'Why then did you'—I know the argument against me, but what I put in the Cornhill were things sui generis, experiments which I wished to try with the public" (**Letters,** 2:346). Tennyson's excuse seems valid, for his December 1863 *Cornhill* poems were indeed experimental, but Thackeray's recruitment efforts for this first volume of the *Cornhill* also included an appeal to friendship, while Thackeray's publisher George Smith surpassed any desire for experiment or friendly relations by offering Tennyson 5,000 guineas to publish his poetry in the *Cornhill* for three years. Here, as in *Good Words,* money would become the subtext to friendship, ultimately convincing Tennyson to publish in the periodical in spite of his proclaimed hatred for the commercial product.

The Duchess further promotes *Good Words* to Tennyson on October 3, 1867, saying that her husband the Duke had "written a good deal" for *Good Words,* which had paid him "very well" and "is read by thousands" (**Letters,** 2:346n). Personal appeal, promises of mass readership, a calculated business move with a new publisher, and high fees combined to make *Good Words* an irresistible proposition for the reluctant poet, who writes to the Duchess of Argyll on November 4, 1867:

> You need not have thanked me for you know I was ungracious enough to refuse you—and as to Dr. MacLeod—(though there was such a pathos in his letter enclosed to me by Strahan that it bore me down) I gave in to his wish against the grain: perhaps indeed for that I ought to be thanked more not less—but as far as you are concerned—I can't see that you owe me anything but objurgation. Now I am . . . afraid to think what I have done . . . for my one answer to all applicants is no longer usable.
>
> (**Letters,** 2:470-471)

Of course his one answer was that he hated to publish in magazines and periodicals, but it rarely worked, not just because other friends would make pitiful appeals, but also because he could not refuse good money and exposure to the mass reading audiences that could be reached in periodicals.

Emily Tennyson had approved of her husband's contribution of **"Tithonus"** to the *Cornhill* in 1860, writing to Margaret Gatty on January 23, "I hope there will be one thing at all events in the *Cornhill Magazine* this month which you will like—Ally's '*Tithonus,*' a companion poem to '*Ulysses.*' 75,000 Mr. Smith said have been published for this month and were nearly sold when he wrote some days ago."[6] Nevertheless, Emily did not approve of Tennyson's dealings with *Good Words* in 1868 when it appeared that Tennyson would suffer from the year's overexposure in the periodicals, as she explains to Gatty on October 7, 1868:

> In an evil hour if we look only to the consequences to himself, he yielded to the entreaties of friends that he would do what he could to relieve Mr. Norman Macleod's mind of anxiety during his Indian Mission [**"The Victim"**], then his friend Mr. Grove would be hurt if refused [**"Lucretius"** and **"Wages"**], then his printers must have something and so he heaped up abuse to himself by giving such little things as he had by him [**"The Spiteful Letter"**], and then another friend for charity [Christopher Ricks suggests **"1865-1866"**] but you will quite understand that this is very different from writing something at their request. This, to save his life he could not do worthily unless the fit were upon him.
>
> (**Letters,** 2:504-505)

Money was Emily's concern about Tennyson's *Good Words* commitment; she preferred volume publication to the periodical. Emily writes to Tennyson about future publications (November 20, 1868): "Pray do not let the poems go into 'Good Words.' . . . [W]hen it is taken into consideration that **Enoch Arden** in one year brought in about £6000 it is perfectly absurd to think of £700. . . . I do entirely object not only on these grounds but on the ground of the unpleasant position it puts thee in with regard to other magazines" (*The Letters of Emily Tennyson,* p. 227). Here Tennyson's publications in the periodicals become contextualized in a mire of sympathy for editors and publishers, a practical need for commercial appeal, and elitist professions of exclusivity, coloring perceptions of quality and meaning.

Emily's narrow vision did not perceive the importance of Tennyson's contributions to such periodicals as *Good Words* beyond the bottom line. They also frequently demonstrate a thorough integration with the aesthetic and literary community of women writers. For instance, the idea for **"The Victim"** came from Charlotte Yonge's *A Book of Golden Deeds.*[7] Tennyson had long been writing in context with women readers and writers, enough to inspire criticism from Edward Bulwer-Lytton in 1864 when he derided Tennyson as "a poet adapted to a mixed audience of school-girls and Oxford dons."[8] Harold Nicolson recalls yet an earlier complaint in Lytton's *The New Timon* (1846) about Tennyson's "School-Miss Alfred" style.[9] The aesthetic considered traditionally feminine, and therefore distastefully sentimental to these critics, involved themes and expressions of the heart, usually involving women characters or domestic situations. **"The Victim"** clearly encodes the domestic ideology that ennobled women for sacrificial display. Yet the poem, as contextualized in *Good Words,* a periodical designed for Sunday reading, also provides evidence that woman's role in such incidents of martyrdom serves to counter, rather than confirm, religious aims by questioning the authority and benevolence of the church, and the fact that women readers sometimes disapproved of Scottish preacher and *Good Words* editor Norman Macleod's secular approach merely adds ironic context.

Macleod was publisher Alexander Strahan's choice for the magazine's first editor when it began as an eight-page weekly in 1860. Sally Mitchell notes that "contributors to more intellectual magazines tended to sneer at *Good Words,*" but the publication "records the literature of respectable bourgeois England" and, "during its best years in the 1870s, regularly sold between 80,000 and 130,000 copies per issue, which was more than any other monthly of that time."[10] According to Mitchell, "Their intention was to produce a periodical that would have as much variety as secular magazines and yet retain a distinctively Christian spirit, so that it could provide Sunday reading without insulting intelligent adults" (p. 145). Within a year, the publication's format had changed to a monthly, and its religious focus relaxed through the ensuing years to include more secular articles and fiction than religious readings. Macleod monitored his magazine and its contributors carefully for high standards of Christian morality. Nevertheless, readers often complained. To one such woman critic, he wrote:

> It must surely be acknowledged that the periodical, so far as its mere "secular" element is concerned, may be admitted as a respectable and a worthy visitor of a Christian family on at least six days in the week? And if so, why not take the visitor by the throat, say at 11.55 on Saturday night, just at the moment when he is being transformed into a dangerous intruder, and incarcerate him till he becomes once more respectable at 12.5 [sic] on Monday morning?[11]

Macleod's liberal approach often rankled readers, but Mitchell defines *Good Words* as a significant literary document because the fiction it printed was "the fiction accepted for family reading by the broad mass of respectable, churchgoing people in the Victorian middle class" (p. 145). The "distinctively Christian spirit" prevailed until its later years.

"The Victim" concerns a legend from Yonge's *Golden Deeds* that intrigued Tennyson. The Eversley Edition of Tennyson's poems records him as noting "I read the story in Miss Yonge's *Golden Deeds*, and made it Scandinavian."[12] The tale is included in a series titled "The Devotion of the Decii, B.C. 339." It tells of a "heathen monarch who was bidden by his priests to appease the supposed wrath of his gods by the sacrifice of the being dearest to him," his son. (Yonge, p. 63). The monarch's wife dies in the son's place "with a last look of exceeding joy at her husband's love and her son's safety." Yonge writes that "human sacrifices are of course accursed, and even the better sort of heathens viewed them with horror; but the voluntary confronting of death, even at the call of a distorted presage of future atonement, required qualities that were perhaps the highest that could be exercised among those who were devoid of the light of truth" (pp. 63-64). In Tennyson's poem, a priest prays to the gods Thor and Odin for relief from famine and plague afflicting his people, promising the life of the country's dearest soul. His prayers bring no relief while "the Priesthood moan'd."[13] Eventually "it seemed that an answer came": to sacrifice the life dearest to the king. The priest goes to find the king but first comes upon the queen and their eight-year-old son. Assuming that this boy who "seem'd a victim due to the priest" must be dearest to the king, thus the sacrifice needed to placate the gods, the priest takes him away. When the boy's grief-stricken mother later asks the king who is dearest, the king avoids the challenge, saying, "'what use to answer now? / For now the Priest

has judged for me'" (p. 18). Meanwhile, "the Priest was happy, / His victim won." In the last moments, just as the knife comes down to kill the boy, the mother intervenes at the altar stone and receives the knife into her breast, "shrieking '*I* am his dearest, I— / *I* am his dearest!'" (p. 18). The priest is just as happy with this sacrifice as with the other; apparently any sacrifice will satisfy him, and whoever dies proves that the gods have answered any question about which one should be martyred. Tennyson uses the word "seemed" in stanzas II and III to indicate the priest's justification for any apparent answer to his prayer, suggesting that he is simply reaching for signs without believing that the gods are listening.

The priest's fearful, ambivalent attitude toward the fate of whomever should be chosen for the sacrifice appears irresponsible and cruel. He has no more concern for the suffering of the king's family than he has clarity about any guidance from the gods. The anger of the gods created the famine, according to the people's belief, but they do not respond to pleas for mercy. The priest's exultation at murdering the child seems eerily sadistic, even in light of the country's desperate situation. In a poem about a pagan society, these details may serve to affirm the righteousness of Christianity to Victorian readers; yet Tennyson's priest, perhaps forgiven for his para-Christian Scandinavian culture, gives us little confidence in church leaders or in knowing God's will, as He leaves people adrift to depend only upon their own action and values.

A similar ideological conflict caused Macleod to reject Anthony Trollope's novel *Rachel Ray* in 1863 because of "Trollope's often caustic attacks on the clergy's role as society's moral guardians," according to Mark W. Turner[14]:

> *Rachel Ray* demonstrates Trollope's own ethical system in which the need for individuals, and women particularly, to become their own moral guardians is more important than following the strict advice of the pastoral adviser who is probably somewhat hypocritical anyway. Unless he was prepared to promote a value system which undermined the eminence and influence of the clergy, MacLeod had to reject *Rachel Ray*.
>
> (p. 57)

Meaning in Tennyson's poem is more ambivalent than in Trollope's novel and Tennyson was the greater literary celebrity, thus no controversy ensued as with Trollope. Tennyson's characterization of the queen first with evangelical notions of woman's sacrificial domestic role as wife and mother, but other ambiguities and questions remain. Had the king privately confessed his preference to his wife for the son over the mother, causing her to choose a suicidal sacrifice that would soothe her pride by placing her in the position of "saving" her country, as well as her son? The possibility suggests that the woman's love (and domestic ideology) has been betrayed. Without such speculation, the woman remains the poem's heroic figure; she alone serves everyone in the poem by martyring herself for love of her country, husband, and child. As in many other poems, Tennyson sets up a textual dialogue aimed at pleasing the middle-class woman reader. He also confirms Yonge's dedication to female sacrifice, condoning suicide as a righteous martyrdom.

The accompanying illustration by A. Boyd Houghton and engraved by Thomas Dalziel provides yet another interpretation of Tennyson's poem. J. Hillis Miller theorizes that "a picture and a text juxtaposed will always have different meanings or logoi. They will conflict irreconcilably with one another, since they are different signs, just as would two different sentences side by side, or two different pictures. Only the same can mean the same."[15] In this way, the periodicals featuring illustrated Tennyson poems create new meanings that have not been explored. The full-page *Good Words* illustration of **"The Victim"** depicts a dark scene at the altar-stone with a grizzled priest's knife raised over a bound and naked boy who clings to his mother. She looks to the heavens as she opens the bodice of her dress to expose a well-shaped breast to the knife. The husband/father/king looks away as if hiding his eyes, while he holds onto the wife's hand. In Tennyson's poem the wife "sprang alone," away from her husband who, with better reflexes, might have tried to pull her back from the knife. But Houghton's illustration portrays him looking away, as if he is allowing his wife's sacrifice to occur. In this context, the woman stands between the boy and his father, both literally and symbolically, for the patriarchy and kingly line must survive long after the woman has served her purpose in childbearing. This martyrdom is far less optimistic than if the wife had chosen the powerful role as savior to the people.

A testament to the poem's potential for popularity with women readers is its appearance in the women's periodical *The Queen: The Lady's Newspaper* (January 11, 1868), uncatalogued by Tennyson scholars. Launched by Samuel Beeton in 1861 and merged with *The Lady's Newspaper* in 1863, *The Queen* was a quarto sixpenny weekly packed with illustrated fashions, embroidery patterns, travel essays, and articles about social events, music, books, flowers, and domestic hints. According to Margaret Beetham:

> The ladies' newspaper above all produced femininity as a text available for reading. The masculine reader might engage with this femininity only as an object of his gaze. The feminine reader, however, not only read but used her reading to reproduce herself as another feminine text, available in turn to other knowledgeable readers.[16]

As with literary annuals earlier in the century, Tennyson's poetry becomes contextualized as feminine through his appearance in a woman's periodical. *Queen* editor Helen Lowe most certainly pirated **"The Victim"** from *Good Words* a week after its original publication. Here it appears in ironic display (without the illustration) as the sole offering under the lighthearted column title "The Wise, the Witty, and the Beautiful." The poem's theme is anything but witty or beautiful, but, positioned above a book review feature titled "Gleanings from New Books," **"The Victim"** places Tennyson's work in the *Queen*'s literary offerings as something new and significant for a proper lady's cultural awareness, while the poem thematically ennobles the publication's domestic focus. The page features article reprints, such as "Platonic Women," from the *Saturday Review,* which delineates how attitudes toward women could fulfill "the dreams of her favourite philosopher," Plato.[17] The author describes with amused tone the challenges confronting a professor teaching women students at a "Ladies' College" and concludes that woman does have equality in warfare, but the battle is fought at home:

> Woman alone keeps up the private family warfare which in the earlier stages of society required all the energies of man. It is a field from which man has completely retired, and which would be left wholly vacant were it not occupied by woman. . . . The Platonic woman of to-day may not march to the field or storm the breach, but she is unequalled in outmanoeuvring a rival, in forcing an entrance into society, in massacring an enemy's reputation, in carrying off matrimonial spoil.
>
> (p. 37)

This description contextualizes the wife in Tennyson's poem. Although the ironic tone de-sentimentalizes the poetic situation and characterizes women as somewhat shallow, the ideology of woman as savior in "Platonic Woman" also uplifts the woman in Tennyson's poem as a heroic warrior against a dysfunctional priesthood, an ineffective patriarchy, and a society desperately needing her martyrdom. Tennyson thus becomes once again a poet for all people, not just men.

Two months after **"The Victim"** appeared, Tennyson published another poem in *Good Words,* **"1865-1866."** The poem reflects a particularly windy season in 1865 when Tennyson complained to Francis Turner Palgrave, "What a season! The wind is roaring here like thunder, and all my ilexes rolling and whitening. Indeed we have had whole weeks of wind" (*Letters,* 2:427). As he is being tossed about by the "roaring and blowing of the winds" brought by the old and new years, the fisherman who narrates the poem expresses doubt about the future, asking the New Year whether the years ahead offer

"aught that is worth the knowing?
Science enough and exploring,
Wanderers coming and going,
Matter enough for deploring,
But aught that is worth the knowing?"[18]

A full-page illustration drawn by Lord Frederic Leighton and engraved by the Dalziel brothers frames the poem's text on page 144 of the March issue and faces an additional illustration (unlisted in the *Good Words* index) on the next page, engraved and probably drawn by Thomas Dalziel, meant to correspond with the other image and the poem. Leighton's frame depicts a fisherman standing at his post in front of a tower wall, blown about by winds coming from the two bodiless heads of the old and new years, demonstrating the roaring winds described in the poem. Seasonal bells strung upon wires at the top of the tower ring out the old year and ring in the new, while the fisherman holds a sprig of holly next to a fire that blows violently out of its grate. In sharp contrast, the fisherman in the darker engraving on the opposite page calmly smokes his pipe as he looks out toward a troubled ocean and foreboding skies from the guard post at the top of a castle tower, as if to represent the future in Tennyson's poetic philosophy. Although the poem provides no answers to the poet's questioning, if the fisherman of the first page is blown about by the anxieties of scientific theories and strange new explorations in the past, the fisherman of the second regards the turmoil from his post behind England's powerful protective fortress, a symbol of the empire's longstanding history of strength and security, ensuring a safe future, but not answering the question of what is worth knowing.

The Dalziel brothers had a longstanding relationship with Alexander Strahan from the 1860s through the 1880s, engraving many of his books and other publications, and Strahan appointed them to control the illustrations for *Good Words* in 1862. George Somes Layard credits the publication with having inaugurated the era of wood-engraved book illustration, and the Dalziel brothers engraved a large proportion of these fine illustrations in its most successful years.[19] Writing in 1901, the brothers Dalziel asserted that *Good Words,* "considering the period of its advent, was equal to anything that has yet been done at that price, and, if measured by the distinguished artists and brilliant writers of whose work it was composed, it is a question whether any of the more recent magazines would equal it in actual merit" (p. 158). Nevertheless, Leighton's artwork displeased Hallam Tennyson, who wrote that the poem was "ruined by the absurd illustrations."[20] The Poet Laureate's experience with Moxon's *Illustrated Edition* of 1857 had been less than satisfying, and he seldom approved of visual representations of his poems. According to Robert Bernard Martin, Tennyson "disliked having artists distort his words" and took the artists "sternly to task if any of their illustrations contained a single detail that could not be plainly justified by the words of the poems" (p. 414). Lorraine Janzen Kooistra further explains Tennyson's problem with illustrations in Moxon's edition:

> What the poet was really protesting against was the right of the reader to interpret and envision a train of associations sparked by the images and situations in his text. It is for this reason that illustrated poetry in the latter part of the nineteenth century becomes so important for understanding poetic (con)texts. Illustration offers the student of Victorian literature a material trace of contemporary readers' responses to a poem, not only in the pictures themselves, but also in the critical reviews assessing the pictures in relation to their poems.[21]

Kooistra notes that Tennyson, as "(after Longfellow) . . . the period's most illustrated poet," was a "reluctant collaborator at best, and a subversive one at worst" (p. 394). He knew the importance of images to his readers and eventually accepted the unstable visual rhetoric of his work as a necessary evil, especially when he began to reap the financial rewards from reissues illustrated by Arthur Hughes and Gustave Doré in this same period. By 1875, indeed, Tennyson himself approached Julia Margaret Cameron with the idea of creating photographic illustrations for the two-volume 1875 edition of *Idylls of the King.* Marylu Hill shows that Tennyson "took an active interest in the choice of appropriate models for the Arthurian characters, going so far as to debate with Cameron in a public space over a young and visibly embarrassed bishop as to whether or not he would be a good Lancelot."[22]

In spite of Tennyson's criticism of the illustrations for **"1865-1866,"** the two image texts inform the poem with a surprisingly Tennysonian interpretation, confirming his conservative notions of a powerful England. Although **"1865-1866"** was not reprinted in a volume of Tennyson's poems in book form until Ricks's complete edition, Tennyson sent it to his American publisher James Fields, who published it in *Every Saturday* (February 22, 1868). Fields would eventually pay Tennyson £500 to get copies of poems before their publication in England (Martin, p. 502). **"1865-1866"** appears in *Every Saturday* without illustrations at the end of the issue below a longer poem by Robert Buchanan, with significantly less fanfare than it received in *Good Words.*

Tennyson's inconsistency about whether to refuse to publish in periodicals invited a stream of requests from friends and literary professionals for contributions. On March 20, 1861 he writes to Anna Maria Hall, founding editor of the *St. James's Magazine,* which would begin publication the following month, "I regret that I cannot have the pleasure of sending you a Poem for your Magazine as I have refused and been obliged to refuse similar requests even from personal friends, such requests having become too numerous to grant" (*Letters,* 2:272-273). By 1868 he had undoubtedly written scores of such refusals, possibly receiving scores of irate responses that we shall never read because of Hallam Tennyson's careful assignment of much Tennyson correspondence to the fire after his death. Tennyson hints at such letters when he writes to William Bradbury upon returning the proofs for **"On A Spiteful Letter"** for publication in the January 4 issue of *Once a Week,* "It is quite correctly printed and I expect will bring upon me more spiteful letters. It is no particular letter to which I allude: *I have had dozens of them* from one quarter or another" (*Letters,* 2:473). This particular poem reflects Tennyson's hatred of literary feuds, but *Once a Week* was a publication "born in controversy," according to Jerold J. Savory.[23] Bradbury and Evans introduced the periodical on July 2, 1859, after a quarrel with their erstwhile partner Charles Dickens over the publication of *Household Words.* Dickens split from the team and started *All the Year Round,* while Bradbury and Evans competed with Dickens by initiating *Once A Week,* featuring a higher priced, better quality publication illustrated by artists from their *Punch* staff, such as John Millais, John Tenniel, and Hablot K. Browne. Tennyson's contribution to its early issues on July 16, 1859, **"The Grandmother's Apology,"** undoubtedly added fuel to the competition.

The poet in **"On A Spiteful Letter"** responds to an anonymous letter writer with acrimonious complaints: "Greater than I—isn't that your cry? / And I shall live to see it. / Well, if it be so, so it is, you know; / And if it be so—so be it!"[24] The repetition of "so" implies "So what?" in an effective sarcasm that puts the letter writer in his place. The poem evokes a weary tone, a soul worn out with complaints and public criticism: "O faded leaf, isn't fame as brief? / What room is here for a hater? / Yet the yellow leaf hates the greener leaf, / For it hangs one moment later" (p. 13). As a feature in an issue inaugurating the new year and placed above a hopeful article about "New Year's Day Vows," Tennyson's poem seems jaded. Yet, ironically, 1868 would be an eventful year for his career, and increasing fame would only bring more conflicts between Tennyson, his public, and his publishers.

Another magazine whose owners would later be Tennyson's future publishers was *Macmillan's Magazine* (1859-1907), begun as the brainchild of Alexander Macmillan and frequenters (including Tennyson, Herbert Spencer, F. D. Maurice, T. H. Huxley, Francis Palgrave, William Allingham, and Coventry Patmore) of Thursday evening social events that came to be known as "tobacco parliaments" at Macmillan's office. Influenced

by the recent publication of Tennyson's *Idylls of the King,* Macmillan called his group "The Round Table" and considered giving the magazine the same title. Macmillan hoped that Tennyson would contribute to his new periodical and wrote to James MacLehose on October 6, 1859, after a satisfying visit with Tennyson at Cambridge:

> Don't whisper it to a soul, as it may after all come to nothing, but I am in hopes of a poem from Tennyson. . . . He said several times he wished we were his publishers, but he was so tied that he could not move at present. . . . My hope for Tennyson's poem is a half promise he made when he was in Cambridge, which I mean to try and clinch—if I can do it without obtrusiveness—when I am with him.[25]

According to George J. Worth, Macmillan's hopes were partially realized when Tennyson contributed **"Sea Dreams"** in the January 1860 issue, but the poem "did not have the dramatic effect on the fortunes of the *Magazine* that Macmillan had hoped for."[26] The year 1868 marked his reappearance in *Macmillan's* with two poems, **"Wages"** in February and **"Lucretius"** in May.

Macmillan's new editor George Grove sought out Tennyson for the magazine in 1867, and "was piqued that Alexander Strahan and the Reverend Norman Macleod . . . had successfully anticipated him," according to Edgar F. Shannon, Jr.[27] Grove writes to Macmillan on December 23, 1867:

> I have got a little poem from A. T.—at last Mrs. Tennyson sent it today for the January No. with an injunction that if too late I was to send it back and I should have it again—This of course I have done. 2 verses very pretty and strong, a sort of pendant to *the Will* [sic]. ("O well for him") [**"Wages"**] It came very nicely and gratefully on my disappointment about Good Words.[28]

After seeing an advertisement of *Good Words* featuring Tennyson's contribution, Grove wrote to Macmillan a few days later (December 28, 1867) that "A. T. is making himself very common: I notice a poem announced by him for Good Words" (Shannon, p. 149). Thus Grove set out for Farringford to expand his request and received a commitment for an additional poem, **"Lucretius,"** at £300. Grove's persistence demonstrates once again the aggressive business tactics of Victorian periodicals editors that Tennyson hated, but he gave in to a friendly appeal and a generous monetary arrangement.

"Wages" met with enthusiastic approval by Macmillan, who praised the poem as a "very noble and true idea fitly expressed," while Grove said, "There is enough in these 10 lines for a whole No." (Shannon, p. 150). Thematically, the poem reflects Tennyson's concern about immortality. According to Martin, Tennyson became increasingly troubled about morality in England, and the whole problem was intimately connected with his growing preoccupation with religion and the old duality of spirit and matter that had perplexed him for so long. . . . [I]t was essential for him to believe in an afterlife in order to believe in morality in this world. Repeatedly he told his friends that if there were no afterlife he would jump into the Seine or the Thames, put his head in the oven, take poison, or fire a pistol at his own temple.

(p. 482)

The same intensity evident in this anecdote appears in the *Macmillan's* poem, as the poet hopes for the "glory of going on" after death, making earthly glories and virtue worthwhile. The two-stanza poem is unimpressive in itself, but as a commercial token printed in a popular Victorian periodical and offered in good faith toward the poet's professional future with the periodical's publisher and editor, it becomes a significant cultural document; it displays Tennyson in the mainstream of Victorian society, while ensuring future publishing agreements with Macmillan.

The text of **"Lucretius"** and its publication history are far more complex and have become a textbook example of how publishers prudishly protected their readers, although Worth claims that "Macmillan's interventions in the textual histories of these works were not grounded primarily in his squeamishness" (p. 39). Edgar F. Shannon, Jr. expertly summarizes the contexts, critical reception, and textual variations of this poem in his 1981 study titled "The Publication of Tennyson's 'Lucretius'"; he demonstrates how comprehensive studies such as his "supply significant insights into the poet's personality and method of composition and into the human relationships among author, publisher, editor, and wife" (p. 147). Previously unpublished letters reproduced in Shannon's article provide evidence of Tennyson's attitudes about his periodical publications in 1868 and help to focus my discussion. Tennyson's experience with publishers of *Macmillan's* and *Every Saturday* typify the continuing contentious relationship between creators of literature and their material product discussed in this essay; authors who wished to reap the financial rewards of new markets could not avoid their commercially aggressive business partners and the uncontrollable texts that came into the public domain in mass-produced Victorian periodicals, in spite of payments, copyrights, lawyers, contracts, manuscripts, and authorial wishes.

Immediately after Tennyson committed **"Wages"** and **"Lucretius"** to George Grove in January 1868, he began to have doubts about publishing **"Lucretius"** in the magazine. He sent Macmillan the poem with the understanding that it was to go thenceforth to Boston for dual publication in Ticknor & Fields's periodical in the United States, *The Atlantic Monthly,* the only American

firm to pay English poets (Martin, p. 404). Tennyson hoped to cash in on extravagant profits extended to Dickens (a generous £2,000) for "some slight essays" published in the firm's periodical (*Letters,* 2:479); yet Tennyson remained concerned that **"Lucretius"** would be pirated and sent an alternate poem, **"God spake out of the skies"**: "With respect to the Lucretius I am staggered by what I hear from good authority. That if I publish in a serial I virtually give up my copyright & any one has a right to republish me. Really if this be so I must decline giving it to your Magazine however unwillingly" (2:477). Macmillan sought legal counsel about his parameters with copyright violations and wrote to Grove on January 14, 1868: "[There is] no doubt that we have a perfect right to prevent the Journals from copying the poem entire, and I will do it. . . . It is only a bad custom, in no sense a right that has led to this sort of elaborate plundery" (Shannon, p. 151). With this assurance and after an additional concession to the Tennysons for the right to republish **"Lucretius"** in volume format within twelve months, breaking their contractual agreement on this detail, Grove and Macmillan thought they would receive Tennyson's manuscript on deadline.

However, additional problems arose when Francis Turner Palgrave and Edmund Lushington disapproved of the poem's publication in a magazine; Macmillan evidently pleaded to Palgrave not to interfere. Yet Tennyson remained reluctant. Grove wrote to Macmillan: "He WILL not let us have the Lucretius—Strahan's plaeds [pleadings] and Dallas's advertizments, added to Payne's and E. Lushingtons dissuasions have frightened him [sic]. . . . I confess to being VERY MUCH VEXT, but I fear he is immoveable" (Shannon, p. 154). Tennyson decided at the last moment against letting Macmillan publish **"Lucretius,"** evidently because of pressures from Strahan, who had just outbid Macmillan for Tennyson's signature on a publishing contract. Moxon's Payne continued to be troublesome, and an advertising campaign promoting Tennyson's January contribution to *Once a Week,* conducted by the magazine's editor E. S. Dallas, was far too commercial for Tennyson's taste. Emily Tennyson indicates their hatred of publicity in her *Journal* on March 10, 1868: "Very much annoyed by Mr. Payne who cannot understand our love of absolute simplicity in advertisement & business arrangements so that we may be free to take thankfully what comes in this way. Be it much or little. What grieves me is that his love of excitement may mislead the public as to A. who has nothing to do with these matters."[29] Emily wanted Tennyson to appear simple before his public and free from the crass implications of commercialization; she writes to Thomas Woolner on March 10, 1868: "What I do really care for is that my Ally should stand before the world in his own child-like simplicity."[30] Advertising should be conservatively tasteful and plain, so that Alfred would not "appear a mere low, cunning tradesman" (p. 218). Any noble protection of Tennyson's image by Emily is informed by her consistently aggressive attempts to get maximum fees for his poetry, whether it appeared in periodicals or volume format; his image was partly her product.

By early February 1868, future and former publishers, editors, critics, and loyal supporters were badgering Tennyson so much that he froze all commitments. Macmillan wrote this last-minute, desperate personal appeal to Lushington on February 3:

> [Tennyson] has given us a short poem and promised a longer one—**"Lucretius."** Indeed we actually have it in type. He now wishes to recal it; two motives chiefly operate with him as I understand: one, that other magazine publishers have dragged his name into vulgar publicity, the other that you disapprove of it. Now whatever other publishers have done, we have not been guilty in this respect, our advertisements have been unostentatious, not sensational. . . . Now I promise that there will be no vulgar advertisements, and remind you that our Magazine is in no sense a sensational magazine & never has been. . . . [T]he appearance of this poem in a Scholarly magazine like ours would I am sure in no way do him injury.
>
> (Shannon, pp. 154-155)

The letter is a shrewd appeal to Lushington's sense of scholarly sophistication, while settling Emily's fear of vulgar commerciality.

Tennyson's poem appeared in the May issue after much textual adjustment. Tennyson was enmeshed in a specific moment of publishing history; it may have seemed for him a somewhat frantic three-month period in 1868, but the 1860s were an excitingly innovative decade when Victorian periodicals reached a point of popularity never before achieved. Publication in fine intellectual magazines such as the long-running *Macmillan's,* the literary *Cornhill* (whose first issue sold 120,000 in 1859), and less expensive publications such as *Good Words* and *Once a Week,* featuring illustrations by notable artists and engravers, were not the poor business choices for Tennyson that his friends and wife often claimed. These were commercial products of the unavoidable new world of mass readership. The financial business intimidated and confused Tennyson as much as his well-meaning friends. According to Herbert F. Tucker, **"Lucretius"** and other Tennyson poems articulate the "doom of Romanticism": "Tennyson's theme and imagery gravitate toward some inevitable ground in the power of God, the drift of nature, or a psychic fixation upon the days that are no more"[31]; I would further add that Tennyson himself was caught in a divide. To aggressively engage the marketplace meant that he must publish in Victorian periodicals. Yet his romantic fixation caused him to seek solace in publishing genres and methods of the past, however unrealistic and inappropriate for his present.

The irony of publishing **"Lucretius"** in *Macmillan's* is that the poem, according to Christopher Ricks, "compacts three of Tennyson's horrors: at erotic madness, at a Godless world, and at a juggernaut universe";[32] all three seem valid responses to the confusing swirl of competitive business tactics and aggressive marketing of Victorian periodicals that caused Tennyson to recoil, along with an uncontrollable growth in mass readerships that threatened tradition and social control, and a commodity culture that devalued the need for moral value in favor of materialism. As Daniel Albright claims:

> Tennyson intended the poem as an indictment of an age that found no true sacredness in things, an age that saw the gods only as figments of philosophers or pornographers. . . . "Lucretius," like "Balin and Balan," investigates the decay of mythology: as myths lose their efficacy they become fairy tales to amuse children, or, Vico-fashion, the halting attempts of primitive man, incapable of abstraction, to explain natural phenomena with his impoverished vocabulary.[33]

Yet the poem invites the very conflict that its author feared. **"Lucretius"** is a dramatic monologue about the loss of control over erotic desires and represents Tennyson's critique of materialism and agnosticism; the subject of the monologue is Roman poet and philosopher Lucretius, author of *De Rerum Natura,* a book explaining the material philosophy of Epicurus that structures Tennyson's poem. The poem explicitly describes the loss of sexual control by Lucretius, whose wife has poisoned his drink with an aphrodisiac. The description challenged Macmillan to remove passages he feared too seductive for his readers; most famous of the many changes Tennyson made for Macmillan is the following description of an Oread quoted from *Every Saturday,* reinserted by Tennyson for the American edition because "they are not so squeamish as we are" (*Letters,* 2:483): "how the sun delights / To glance and shift about her slippery sides / And rosy knees, and supple roundedness, / And budded bosom-peaks."[34] The description is mild by today's standards, but it does evoke a visual image of ripe sexuality, and the poem provides an intense character study of a man overcome by the sensual and whirling toward suicide. Yet George Worth offers an additional explanation of Macmillan's concern, claiming that the poem's history "indicates that more was involved in this curtailment than mere prudery, for example Macmillan's acceptance of Tennyson's request that the poem be set up in larger-than-usual type, a change that appeared to Macmillan to call for some condensation" (p. 41). Worth further states that we must not "dismiss Macmillan as a spokesman for Mrs. Grundy; on the contrary, he deplored Grundyism as a serious obstacle to the appreciation of Tennyson's poetry" (p. 42). Worth's assessment reminds us that unscholarly attachments to traditional interpretations of nineteenth-century literary history overlook more valuable perspectives that place poetry in its proper context as a material product with commodity status, in conflict and cooperation with market, publisher, and author demands.

As if to make an example of the uncontrollable forces of the marketplace, Tennyson's poem was not delivered to James Fields in America until March 17, and he could not make the deadlines for the *Atlantic Monthly*. Fields writes: "We printed it in our 'every Saturday,' and it was immediately cribbed all over the country and printed in magazines and newspapers. It was a great disappointment to us not to have it for the Atlantic, but we did the next best thing left us and put it into the weekly" (Shannon, p. 168). Regardless of their attempts to avoid piracy, **"Lucretius"** became a regular feature in periodicals throughout the United States in 1868.

By March Tennyson was receiving warnings from friends such as Benjamin Jowett, who writes on March 8, 1868: "Don't write any more in Magazines if you can help: indeed, it is a goodnatured mistake and will do you harm. The Magazine-writers say, 'Art thou become as one of us?' etc." (**Letters**, 2:484). Tennyson would not publish again in periodicals until 1871, but the exposure he received through periodical publications in 1868 would produce more than generous fees. Tennyson managed to restore his creative confidence, arrange profitable publication agreements in England and America, participate in the initiation and growth of illustrated periodicals of the Victorian era, and continue to cultivate women readers.

In spite of elitist concerns for preferred genres of publication, the quality of Tennyson's poetry did not deteriorate because of periodical publication, nor did he send inferior poems to periodicals. Rather, Tennyson's reputation merely increased as readers who might never purchase a volume of poetry read his work in the context of *Good Words* and many other such publications throughout the Victorian era, and we should avoid sharing in the critical misjudgment of casually viewing periodical publications as occasional lines cast off as favors; if a list of the poems published in periodicals during Tennyson's lifetime appears uneven, it merely represents the instability of all creativity, regardless of its mode of display. The pages of Victorian periodicals provide contexts to Tennyson's poetry that richly serve out desire to know more about his relationship to Victorian culture and literature.

Notes

1. Robert Bernard Martin, *Tennyson: The Unquiet Heart* (New York: Oxford Univ. Press, 1980), p. 476.

2. *The Letters of Alfred Lord Tennyson*, ed. Cecil Y. Lang and Edgar F. Shannon, Jr., 3 vols. (Oxford: Clarendon Press, 1987), 2:225.

3. Charles Tennyson, *Alfred Tennyson* (New: York, Macmillan, 1949), p. 374.

4. Qtd. in June Steffensen Hagen, *Tennyson and His Publishers* (University Park: Pennsylvania State Univ. Press, 1979), p. 115.

5. See Kathryn Ledbetter, "'BeGemmed and BeAmuletted': Tennyson and Those 'Vapid' Gift Books," *VP* 34 (Summer 1996): 235-245.

6. *The Letters of Emily Tennyson,* ed. James O. Hoge (University Park: Pennsylvania Univ. Press, 1974), p. 145.

7. Yonge wrote to Macmillan on July 1, 1865: "I hear Tennyson is thinking of founding a poem on the story of Odin's Sacrifice in the Golden Deeds" (qtd. in Jenny Stratford, "Tennyson's 'The Victim' and Charlotte Yonge's *A Book of Golden Deeds of all Times and All Lands,* 1864," *The Library* 5th ser. 31, no. 2 [June 1976]: 1401-42). However, there is no tale about Odin in Yonge's book. The tale Tennyson adapts appears in the context of classical Greece as part of "The Devotion of the Decii," from *A Book of Golden Deeds of All Times and All Lands* (Cambridge, 1865), pp. 62-63. See also Christopher Ricks, ed., The Poems of Tennyson, 3 vols. (Berkeley: Univ. of California Press), 2:694

8. Qtd. in The Earl of Lytton, *The Life of Edward Bulwer First Lord Lytton,* 2 vols. (London: Macmillan, 1913), 2:430.

9. Harold Nicholson, *Tennyson: Aspects of His Life, Character and Poetry* (London: Constable, 1923), p. 103.

10. Sally Mitchell, "Good Words," *British Literary Magazines: The Victorian and Edwardian Age, 1837-1913,* ed. Alvin Sullivan (Westport, Connecticut: Greenwood Press, 1984), p. 145.

11. Qtd. in Alexander Strahan, "Norman Macleod," *The Contemporary Review* 20 (1872): 294.

12. *The Works of Tennyson,* ed. Hallam Tennyson, 9 vols. (London: 1908), 2:375.

13. Alfred Tennyson, "The Victim," *Good Words* for 1868 (January 1, 1868): 17.

14. Mark W. Turner, *Trollope and the Magazines: Gendered Issues in Mid-Victorian Britain* (New York: St. Martin's Press, 2000), p. 51.

15. J. Hillis Miller, *Illustration* (Cambridge: Harvard Univ. Press, 1992), p. 95.

16. Margaret Beetham, *A Magazine of Her Own? Domesticity and Desire in the Woman's Magazine, 1800-1914* (New York: Routledge, 1996), p. 91.

17. Anonymous, "Platonic Women (From the *Saturday Review*)," *The Queen, the Lady's Newspaper* (January 11, 1868): 37.

18. Alfred Tennyson, "1865-1866," *Good Words* for 1868 (March 1, 1868): 144.

19. The Brothers Dalziel [George and Edward Dalziel], *The Brothers Dalziel: A Record of Work 1840-1890* (1901; repr., Frome, Wiltshire: Butler & Tanner,1978), p. 23.

20. Qtd. in Ricks, 2:691n.

21. Lorraine Janzen Kooistra, "Poetry and Illustration," *A Companion to Victorian Poetry,* ed. Richard Cronin, Alison Chapman, and Antony H. Harrison (Oxford: Blackwell, 2002), p. 401.

22. Marylu Hill, "'Shadowing Sense at war with Soul': Julia Margaret Cameron's Photographic Illustrations of Tennyson's *Idylls of the King*," *VP* 40 (Winter 2002): 446.

23. Jerold J. Savory, "Once A Week," *British Literary Magazines: The Victorian and Edwardian Age, 1837-1913,* ed. Alvin Sullivan (Westport, Connecticut: Greenwood Press, 1984), p. 287.

24. Alfred Tennyson, "On A Spiteful Letter," *Once A Week* (January 4, 1868): 13.

25. Charles L. Graves, *Life and Letters of Alexander Macmillan* (London: Macmillan, 1910), pp. 133-134.

26. George J. Worth, *Macmillan's Magazine, 1859-1907: "No Flippancy or Abuse Allowed"* (Burlington, Vermont: Ashgate, 2003), p. 21.

27. Edgar F. Shannon, Jr., "The Publication of Tennyson's 'Lucretius,'" *SB* 34 (1981): 148-149.

28. Qtd. in Shannon, "Publication," p. 149.

29. Emily Tennyson, *Lady Tennyson's Journal,* ed. James O. Hoge (Charlottesville: Univ. Press of Virginia, 1981), p. 272.

30. Emily Tennyson, *Letters,* p. 218.

31. Herbert F. Tucker, *Tennyson and the Doom of Romanticism* (Cambridge: Harvard Univ. Press, 1988), p. 13.

32. Christopher Ricks, *Tennyson* (New York, Macmillan, 1972), pp. 290-291.

33. Daniel Albright, *Tennyson: The Muses' Tug-of-War* (Charlottesville: Univ. Press of Virginia), p. 144.

34. Alfred Tennyson, "Lucretius," *Every Saturday* (May 2, 1868): 576.

Helen Small (essay date November 2005)

SOURCE: Small, Helen. "Tennyson and Late Style." *Tennyson Research Bulletin* 8, no. 4 (November 2005): 226-50.

[*In the following essay, Small uses Tennyson's poem "Tiresias" to illustrate how the author's "late style"—the nature of his writings at the end of his career—both conforms to and deviates from the critical conception of "late style" in general.*]

Late style, as Theodor Adorno described it, is antagonistic. Its practitioner is unseduced by the standard judgments and values of his or her time and place. Unseduced too by any hope of transcendence. Such art, exemplified for Adorno by Beethoven, does not seek harmony, or elegance, or aesthetic resolution; it does not lead to a unified 'whole'; rather, it 'tear[s works] apart in time'—'perhaps', he added (but sceptically), 'in order to preserve them for the eternal. In the history of art, late works are the catastrophes' (Adorno, 1964, 126).

Adorno's account of late style has been influential in literary and cultural criticism of the past ten years or so, largely thanks to the work of Edward Said, whose book on the subject was left unfinished at his death in 2004 (Said, 1988; 2003; 2004). In a series of essays on (among others) Benjamin Britten, Thomas Mann, Henrik Ibsen, and Giuseppe Tomasi di Lampedusa, Said extended Adorno's work on Beethoven into a wider consideration of literature as well as music. For Said 'late style' meant something subtly different from what it was for Adorno. 'Lateness', in Adorno's essays, designated an aesthetic style or manner more than a stage of life: it was the name he gave to the valid response of artistic form to capitalism, and though the proximity of the artist to the end of his or her life was seen as its prompt, it is not clear that for Adorno the connection to time of life had to be more than symbolic. Said, by contrast, insisted upon a literal connection to ageing, the decay of bodily powers, the onset of ill health, acknowledging his autobiographical reasons for doing so (his own proximity to death). To be consciously near the end of one's time induces 'tragic self-awareness', he wrote—and the pathos of that claim marks a subtle difference between his humanism and Adorno's stringently post-humanist thinking. In Said's account, late style is, for all its refusal of harmony and wholeness, integrated temperamentally and aesthetically by the force of its anger, its alienation, its anticipatory mourning.

Tennyson's writing in old age—specifically, the last four volumes of poetry: *Tiresias and Other Poems* (1885), *Locksley Hall Sixty Years After* (1886), *Demeter and Other Poems* (1889), and the posthumously published *Death of Œnone, Akbar's Dream, and Other Poems* (1892)[1]—has not played much part so far in the debate about late style. Indeed, reading Tennyson in connection with that debate is of value, I want to argue, not because the poems he wrote in his seventies and eighties are exemplary of late style as Adorno and Said defined it, but because, on the contrary, their descriptions are intriguingly unsuited to Tennyson—though the antagonistic stance he adopted on some social and political questions in those decades might lead one to expect otherwise. I cannot, in the space of this argument, give a full account of Tennysonian late style, but I want to offer, through a general discussion of these last volumes, then a closer reading of one poem (the title work of *Tiresias and Other Poems*), a description of Tennyson's late writings as an effort to define a style in and of old age which embraced exactly that hope of transcendence repudiated by Adorno and Said, while also striving not to be defined exclusively or pre-emptively by it. In part the description I am about to give overlaps with familiar descriptions of Tennyson's verse, especially the often perceived conflict between lyric and narrative modes (and, relatedly, between different kinds of claim to poetic authority). But it also, I hope, opens out new terrain for discussion both of Tennyson and of the concept of late style.

There is plenty of evidence that, in his last years, Tennyson felt himself sometimes at odds with the world around him, and that he had moments (more than moments) of rancour and alienation, particularly on the subject of Gladstone and the defence of the empire.[2] More than one visitor to Aldworth and Farringford in the 1880s found him out of temper with the times and (in Jerome Buckley's words) 'full of large apocalyptic fears more social than strictly political' (Buckley, 1960, 228; see also Horsman, 1953, 283). He was capable of Yeatsian rage against the diminishing powers of his body in old age while the mind remained (as if in mockery) unbowed. Yet, like Yeats, he seemed at other times possessed of an ample Wordsworthian calm—grateful for the gift of a long life, inhabiting the role of 'the old Poet' with grace and pleasure (Tennyson, 1990, III, 428).

'The old Poet' was a self-description he adopted willingly, and he was aware of, and by turns vexed and amused by, the desire of many of his readers to have him fit their preconceived ideas of what an 'old Poet' should sound like. He was pleased (naturally enough) when his continuing poetic powers were recognised and celebrated. Hallam Tennyson records that, when *Demeter and Other Poems* appeared, in Tennyson's 81st year, 'The general tone of criticism was gratifying, and to the effect that the poems were wonderful productions for a man of fourscore years, that they were especially remarkable for rhythm and strength, and close-packed diction, and that there was throughout a trustful peace

and resignation in the evening of life, which touched the heart of the "great public"' (Tennyson, 1990, II, 363). Tennyson evidently felt the attraction of the idea that there are specific virtues proper to the different periods of a man's life, and felt the desirability of those virtues being expressed through poetry. He wrote in 1883 to advise a working man, contemplating poetry as a profession, that poetry 'should be the flower and fruit of a man's life, in whatever stage of it, to be a worthy offering to the world' (Tennyson, 1990, III, 247). He also put on record his identification with Ulysses' view that in old age, 'Though much is taken, much abides', and 'ere the end / Some work of noble note, may yet be done' (**'Ulysses'**, ll.65, 51-52). But he resisted attempts to turn him into a Ciceronian example to the nation,[3] declining Benjamin Jowett's suggestion that he write a poem on the 'Happiness of Old Age' (Tennyson, 1897, II, 372), and rebelling against the conventional blandishments that came from all quarters as he entered his eighties. 'I am sick of [it]', he protested vehemently on his 80th birthday, '—all this fulsome adulation makes me miserable and inclined to vomit morally' (Tennyson, 1990, III, 399).

This distaste for moral sentimentalism about old age was, no doubt, temperamental in part, but it also had a serious philosophical basis. Perhaps the most obvious element in that philosophy came from Tennyson's experience of so many premature deaths during his lifetime: his view of the good life reserved little in the way of special value for a length of life. 'In more of life true life no more', as he put it in *In Memoriam* (XXVI, l.11). His Christianity was an influence here: the promise of an eternal life, next to which 'Our life on earth is but a span' (**'Why Should We Weep for Those that Die?'**, l.10; Tennyson, 1827, 16), its duration therefore of little account. His reading of evolutionary theory, much written about in recent years, was also pertinent—that sense, in *In Memoriam,* of 'songs and deeds and lives, [lying] / Foreshortened in the tract of time. (LXXVII, ll.3-4); or what one of the poems in *Demeter* describes more agitatedly as human life being 'Swallow'd in Vastness' (**'Vastness'**, III.3; Tennyson, 1889, 41-47 (46)). But in several respects the most important reference point for Tennyson's intellectual outlook on old age is Lucretius's *De Rerum Natura,* the one philosophical work with which we know Tennyson to have been intimately familiar, and which explicitly argues against valuing a long life over a short life.

Tennyson's copy of his friend Hugh Munro's 1864 translation of Lucretius is now in the Tennyson Research Centre in Lincoln, together with his earlier, perhaps undergraduate copy of Wakefield's 1796-7 edition (1821), and his father's copies of the Creech (1695) and Wakefield editions.[4] There are pencil underlinings and marginal notes in Tennyson's hand throughout the Munro edition, against both the Latin and the English texts, but they are more than usually heavy in book III where Lucretius presents his reasons for considering the soul, as well as the body, to be mortal. Among the passages marked up is one in which Lucretius enlists old age to support his case: 'you must admit the soul to be mortal', he writes,

> since changed so completely throughout the frame it loses its former life and sense. Then too, in what way will it be able to grow in strength uniformly with its al-lotted body and reach the coveted flower of age, unless it shall be its partner at its first beginning? or what means it by passing out from the limbs when decayed with age (*senectis*)? Does it fear to remain shut up in a crumbling body, fear that its tenement, worn out by protracted length of days, bury it in its ruins?[5]

Tennyson did not explicitly object, as he did in several of the surrounding paragraphs, but one can assume that he found the reasoning as false as he did Lucretius's other arguments against the immortality of the soul.

By contrast, he makes no hostile interventions when Lucretius puts his case against regarding death as an evil. (This is the most famous section of the *De Rerum Natura,* still discussed respectfully by philosophers today.) Lucretius's first and best remembered argument is that our death cannot be a misfortune for us because we do not know of it: where death is, we are not. His second is specific to duration of life. We have no reason, he says, to value a long life over a short life if we consider life in the scale of eternity: given that we shall be dead for eternity, the earliness or lateness of our dying should not matter to us (Lucretius, 1992, 253-75 [III, 830-1097]). The argument can be seen as overlapping with the Christian consolation for death in youth, and with the evolutionary description of historical time extending vastly beyond human history, though it is distinct from both. It is noticeable (but has not I think been noted before) that when Tennyson attacked Epicurean materialism in the dramatic monologue **'Lucretius'** (1868) this was the one major omission from his celebratedly full account of Lucretian thinking. He did not touch it, we can assume, because he considered it to be true.

But if old age was not, in Tennyson's view, a necessary component of a good life, that does not mean that it was without value—or that writing in old age did not present distinctive opportunities and problems for a poet. The late volumes, especially the two wider-ranging selections, *Tiresias* and *Demeter,* indicate a desire to put himself before his public quite explicitly as an old poet—but on his own terms. As selections, they lack the tight coherence of, say, Yeats's *The Tower,* which conducts an extended argument with the world, with old age, and with poetry itself. They are, in larger measure, what came to hand and was deemed finished enough for publication, some of it dating back decades

and being polished up for the occasion. Even so, *Tiresias and Other Poems* shows signs of having been consciously shaped at a very late stage, to give prominence to the issue of the poet's age. Tennyson reordered its contents extensively in revised proofs so as to group it more clearly by genre than in the first proof: the dramatic monologues now came first, after the volume's dedication to Robert Browning, then **'Balin and Balan'** (the last composed of the *Idylls of the King*), a small group of militaristic poems (**'The Charge of the Heavy Brigade',** with dedicatory lines to General Huxley, and, by way of epilogue, a dialogue poem defending the poet's militarism); then a set of epitaphs, a number of epistolary poems to individuals, an elegy for Tennyson's brother Charles, and a dedicatory poem for Charles's verses; a savage satiric blast against Froude's biography of Carlyle; three slight lyrical pieces; one drinking song, showing the strain of its rewriting as a birthday poem for Queen Victoria; and two poems assessing his relationship to classical writers (Tennyson, 1885a and b). At the very end he placed **'Book-Making'**, moving it from its original location at the front of the volume, and retitling it by its first line, **'Old Poets Foster'd Under Friendlier Skies'.** That change, plus the alteration of **'The Ancient Mystic'** to **'The Ancient Sage',** then **'The Old Seer',** then back to **'The Ancient Sage',** suggests that he wanted this volume to be more obviously, but not too harpingly, about old age, and about poetic voice in old age. The change of title also shows Tennyson wrestling with the troublesome ambiguity of 'old' in its adjectival form: its compounding, not always helpfully, of 'antique' and 'former' and 'old in years'. **'The Old Seer'** became **'The Ancient Sage'** in part, presumably, to escape duplication with **'Old Poets',** but in part also because 'ancient' places the emphasis a little more firmly on 'from days gone by'. **'Old Poets',** now the final poem in the collection, makes a clearer reference to Tennyson's own age—not without risk of self-sentimentalisation.

As a collection, *Locksley Hall Sixty Years After* does not reward the same kind of bibliographic description, containing only three poems: the title dramatic monologue, **'The Fleet',** a poem in defence of the navy, an occasional poem on the **'Opening of the Indian and Colonial Exhibition by the Queen',** and the verse drama *The Promise of May. Demeter,* however, contains twenty-eight poems, and although the first twenty-five are ordered neither generically, nor (it would seem) thematically, the final three seem intended to be read as a sequence: **'The Oak',** an elegantly spare poem in trisyllables on the theme of old age, followed by **'In Memoriam—William George Ward',** and finally **'Crossing the Bar'.** Together they describe a progress from praise of old age (defined, via **'The Oak',** as pared back, native, English strength), through an elegy for the dead (not a private act of mourning here, but public homage to a great man), to end with the hymn thanking God for Tennyson's recovery from severe illness in 1889 and looking forward to the transition from life to eternity. ('**Crossing the Bar**' should, Tennyson told Hallam, be 'at the end of all [collected] editions of my poems' thereafter (Tennyson, 1897, II, 367)). *Œnone*, the posthumously published selection of new work which Tennyson saw through the press in the last weeks of his life, follows a similar ordering principle, but—as with *Tiresias*—the detailed shaping of the order of contents came very late in the process.

Over five successive sets of proofs (Tennyson, 1892b), Tennyson gradually rearranged the volume. The major changes came in the last two sets of revises, where he removed some of the slighter poems ('**Pearl**', '**To Sleep!**', and '**The Bee and the Flower**') and created an order similar to that of *Tiresias* (dedicatory poems; dramatic monologues; topical poems about science, social issues, politics; historical poems; one poem about poetry and critics), but, most importantly, created a final set of poems in which, read as a sequence, faith wins out over doubt. The closing poem, written on the death of the Duke of Clarence and Avondale earlier that year, is also implicitly an elegy for himself. In the final proof he deleted the date of composition, encouraging that wider application. Its last line, replacing a series of earlier last lines avowing faith in God and the afterlife, makes this poem more clearly than any of the earlier choices for ending the volume ('**Faith**', '**God and the Universe**') Tennyson in full civic voice, the Poet Laureate, close to death, directing his readers to respond to his death as they should to all deaths, including, when the time comes, their own: 'Mourn in hope!'

Most readers of these last volumes will, however, be struck less by the evidence of their having been shaped to reflect the coming to an end of the poet's life, and to affirm his religious faith, than by the sheer variety of styles they include. One could say that they are *merely* eclectic, and there would be some truth in the criticism. In *Tiresias,* for example, two of the dramatic monologues—'**The Wreck**' (a poem about a woman's loveless marriage, adultery, shipwreck at sea, and miraculous rescue through the intervention of her dying baby daughter) and '**Tomorrow**' (a sub-Walter Scott poem about love-madness, in what purports to be Hiberno-English)—are dramatically overwrought to the point of bathos, while '**The Spinster's Sweet-Arts**' manages to be both twee and weirdly caustic. But even the weaker poems ('**Tomorrow**', or '**Riflemen, form!**', in *Demeter*) earn their place as a demonstration of range and flexibility of voice in old age. And in part that demonstration was necessary to Tennyson not so much because of any external pressure on 'the old Poet' to be narrower than he was (calmer, more resigned to the prospect of death, more inclined to metaphysics than to worldly matters), but because he himself had so often written of

old age in terms which threatened to restrict his late style. Over the course of his career, he had repeatedly used old speakers—men not women—to define a poetic voice which, had he identified himself with it in old age, could have outranked or entirely excluded other voices and other purposes for poetry which he also valued.[6] The idealisation of old age involved was not so much moral (in his dramatic verse he was often disparaging of old age) as rhetorical.[7]

'**The Passing of Arthur**' (written in 1869), defines this 'late' voice in its opening lines:

> That story which the bold Sir Bedivere,
> First made and latest left of all the knights,
> Told, when the man was no more than a voice
> In the white winter of his age, to those
> With whom he dwelt, new faces, other minds.

Here, old age matters less as lived experience than as the kind of speech it makes available to the poet (who need not himself be old). This is speech as near purified utterance, speech that has come as close as possible to being divorced from the constraints of mortality (the literal whiteness of hair is metaphorised into the whiteness of winter). Though his function within the *Idylls* is to convey the narrative, the man who in late age has become 'no more than a voice' simultaneously presses drama as far as it can go towards lyric, in the sense of pure sound, his words seeming to float free of their speaker.[8] The word 'old' does not appear in these lines, being instead sublimated into other words: 'bold', 'told'. (The echoing of that syllable through so much of Tennyson's writing suggests that it had, even free of the association with age, a special acoustic appeal for him (gold, wold, rolled, fold . . .). 'Latest left' more openly alters the issue of physical age into one, rather, of historical persistence. The old Bedivere is also given nothing in the way of personality or character beyond his name, and an epithet which belonged to his youth and which he carries now only by way of courtesy. Like the 'man wellnigh a hundred winters old' who passes down the legend of the Holy Grail (*Holy Grail,* 1.85), like Merlin, and Bleys, the 'old man' without 'a sensual wish' from whom Merlin first learned the secrets of magic ('**Merlin and Vivien**', 1.626), old Bedivere is one of the guardians of the Arthurian stories, their magic, their 'vision of an ideal Arthur'.[9] Age seems to constitute almost a sufficient claim to be a bearer of that myth, his near disembodied state allowing the voice alone to bring into the present moment a time alien to his audience and (something the poem is oddly ready to concede) perhaps of little relevance to them. What urgency do Bedivere's words have for 'new faces, other minds'?

The depiction of Bedivere in '**The Passing of Arthur**' suggests that in early and even in middle career, Tennyson was happy to relinquish any larger or more direct claim to authority born of long experience. In the later poems, by contrast, one can see him asserting that claim as a matter of social, political and historical moment. In **'Locksley Hall Sixty Years After',** for example, the speaker has gained with the passing of the years a historical significance independent of anything he has done with his life. Even the garrulousness and querulousness of his old age escape their ostensible function in self-satire (the later speaker's rejection of his immature self from the first **'Locksley Hall'**) to diagnose the state of the nation: 'I myself have often babbled doubtless of a foolish past; / Babble, babble; our old England may go down in babble at last' (ll.7-8). Charles Tennyson recorded his father's hope that together these works would be considered 'two of the most historically interesting of his poems, as descriptive of the tone of the age at two distant periods of his life': 'his life' being, ambiguously, both the poet's and the speaker's life, though Tennyson tried to resist the conflation. Bulwer-Lytton's praise of the poem placed less emphasis less on distance and change and much more on the holistic impression given by the single life. 'The old lover of **"Locksley Hall"'**, he wrote, to a friend,

> is exactly what the young man must have become, without any changes of character by force of time and experience, if he had grown with the growth of his age.— For that reason alone, the poem in its entirety has a peculiar historical importance as the impersonation of the emotional life of a whole generation.

> (quoted in *Memoir*, II, 330)

In this reading, longevity makes for representativeness: having lived so long, the speaker comes to stand for the spirit of his age. The logic is emotional, not rational, and it tips Bulwer-Lytton's account of the poem over into a self-sentimentalisation and self-aggrandisement of which both the dramatic monologue form and Tennyson himself had been warier. It could be right only if the whole generation failed to be changed by time and experience.

One consequence of Tennyson's looking to reclaim more robustness and more of a stylistic range for the old voice in his late years is that the mythic and magical powers with which the old were often associated in earlier poems are in the main eschewed in the late works. Even in the earlier poems, the depiction of old men was sometimes indicative of doubts over the kind of remote, bardic, poetic utterance for which they were vehicles. Thomas Marks notes that in **'Merlin and Vivien',** written when Tennyson was in his forties, the age and senility of the magician signal the weakness of poetry which aims only to enchant:

> the faint defects of age wrinkle the physical figure of Merlin in this poem and flag the obsolescence of what he represents—his muttered words are 'half-suffocated in the hoary fell / And many wintered fleece of throat

and chin' (ll.839-40). . . . Far from manifesting any supernatural powers, the bardic enchanter's language fails to deflect either Vivien's persistent entreaties or, eventually, 'that small charm of feature mine' (l.75)— let alone charm her; his spells are the antiquated 'spels' of the itinerant story-teller: 'I once was looking for a magic week . . .', 'There lived a king in the most Eastern East . . .' Authority melts from Merlin, as unconvincing narratives substitute for lyrical charms.

> (Marks, 2005, 29)

For Marks, Merlin's age is symptomatic of a 'crisis between lyric and narrative modes', as Tennyson rejects, in narrative terms, the lyricism associated with the Romantic magus, but preserves the weakened linguistic and syntactic remnants of lyric poetry's charms (its sinuous repetitions, its reliance on symbols rather than story) (Marks, 2005; see also Stevenson, 1980). It is a reading which admits of politicisation in line with Matthew Reynolds's argument that **'Merlin and Vivien'** is evidence of a desire not to sacrifice the political imperative of nation-building through myth and the production of linguistic stability to mere musicality (Reynolds, 2005, 246-73). But Marks's interpretation is of special interest here because it raises the question of whether this contest between the different forms of authority available through poetry was not itself altered by Tennyson's experience of ageing: that is, whether he was not readier to deprive the old of all but the most mythic or vatic forms of power at a point when he was not yet himself old—and was correspondingly keen to reinforce their claim to authority once he was, himself, the Old Poet.

This desire to widen and reinforce the voices available to old age in his late years is a major, perhaps the major, component Tennyson's late style. The sheer variety of styles espoused in his last volumes, and especially the variety of their use of the dramatic monologue and dialogue forms, stem in large part from a desire not to be confined to 'late style' as he himself had defined it: not to be limited to his own unbodied isolation of the old voice, while also not *refuting* that ideal. In the late, often bizarrely feverish dramatic monologues—most of them having to do with death, and with faith lost and then miraculously restored, or faith scorned but at the last triumphant—one can see the extreme results of that desire. **'Happy: The Leper's Bride'** is perhaps the most startling case. In this long dramatic monologue a bride addresses her husband, ravaged by leprosy and about to undergo quasi-burial by the medieval church:

> I loved you first when young and fair, but now I love
>   you most;
> The fairest flesh at last is filth on which the worm will
>   feast
>
> . . . . .
>
> And once I worshipt all too well this creature of decay,

For Age will chink the face, and Death will freeze the
   supplest
   limbs—

(ll.30-32, 45-46)

It is not the most successful but it may be the most striking case of Tennyson using the dramatic monologue form to speak *about* old age while not speaking *from* old age, and doing so in order at once to attack and to preserve the idea of the old voice speaking from the outer limit of embodied, mortal life. 'Chink' is an old verbal form, an early modern usage meaning 'To open in cracks or clefts, to crack' (*OED* v. 2). Here it has the effect of turning the body into mere matter. Language and body alike degrade as 'fairest flesh' turns alliteratively to 'filth' and 'feast'. In some respects this is where Tennyson comes closest to 'late style' as Adorno and Said thought of it: in a lexis and tone, at least, that eschews harmony and elegance, even though metrical and verse form remain tightly controlled. But words, like the leper's flesh, can become grotesque here because the poem is repudiating the physical world, the flesh, and the beauty of words, in order to raise up love, compassion, and faith in God above them. Taking advantage of the dramatic monologue's licence to extend his style, Tennyson at once defiles his own earlier idealisation of old age and leaves it untouched: still imaginable as pure voice rather than material body. In so doing, he requires of his readers a reconsideration of the term 'late style' to allow for a plurality of styles in which range of poetic practice is not sacrificed to any single notion of 'late voice'.

As I indicated at the beginning of this argument, there is not room here to consider more than one of Tennyson's late poems in detail. **'Tiresias'** is the title poem of Tennyson's fourth to last selection. A dramatic monologue, it took first place in the volume, prefaced by a dedicatory poem to Edward FitzGerald and followed by an epilogue written soon after the preface, when Tennyson learned that FitzGerald had died before receiving this birthday gift from a fellow poet, friend, and contemporary. I have chosen the *Tiresias* volume in part for the reasons already given: because there is evidence that it was shaped, more carefully than the others, with a view to foregrounding the issue of the poet's old age. I have also chosen it because, as a draft of the volume's dedication (now in the Lincoln archive) reveals, Tennyson thought at the time that it was likely to be his last publication. 'To Robert Browning', the draft reads '. . . / I dedicate this which is probably / My last volume of poems'. (In pencil it is corrected to the text which appeared in print: 'I dedicate this volume with affection'.) At 76 Tennyson was suffering from failing eyesight, fearing he would go blind. The death of FitzGerald, only a year older than himself, and a man whose poetic career had been closely connected with his own, seems to have made him newly conscious that his own end might be near.

'Tiresias' itself is, however, a problematic choice with regard to late style. In 1976 D. F. Goslee speculated persuasively that its composition spanned 50 years of Tennyson's life, the first 8 lines being written in 1833 before Hallam's death, the next 79 lines just after Hallam's death that year, and the remaining text in 1883 (Goslee, 1976). This is part of my reason for choosing it. In **'Tiresias'** one can see Tennyson going back to an earlier, indeed very early style, and reconsidering it, twice over, in terms of its appropriateness for him now in old age. It is also a poem which posits a direct *conflict* between old age and youth—a conflict at once dramatic, ethical and stylistic. It is not alone in this (**'The Ancient Sage'**, for example, does the same thing), but nowhere else is there a straight confrontation between an early Tennysonian style and what he was starting to define consciously in this period as the possibilities of late style.

'I wish I were as in the years of old', 'Tiresias' begins. The latent ambiguity of that opening unfolds in the succeeding lines, where the blind old seer's desire to be back in the time before the Gods turned their anger against Cadmus and his heirs is revealed more clearly as a desire also to be young and sighted and avid for knowledge again:

> I wish I were as in the years of old
> While yet the blessed daylight made itself
> Ruddy thro' both the roofs of sight, and woke
> These eyes, now dull, but then so keen to seek
> The meanings ambushed under all they saw.

(Tennyson, 1885b, ll. 1-5)

For all the retrospective longing of the first line, here something has gone awry with nostalgia. The wish to be as one was is constrained, even rendered null, by knowledge of what one's then future, now lived through, has brought, and by implication what it would bring again were the past restored. The image of waking—dawn light showing red through the lids of the eyes and rousing the sleeper—carries with it inevitable comparison with 'eyes, now dull': Tiresias' eyes, blinded by Pallas Athene; Tennyson's eyes, failing in old age. This pressure exerted on the past by knowledge of that past's future infects the poem also at the level of sound: the assonantal élan of 'keen to seek / The meanings' halted acoustically at 'ambushed'. Grammatically, too, the ambiguity of agency in 'meanings ambushed' makes the young man's ardour for knowledge inseparable from the thought of a later Tiresias, 'ambushed' by a goddess 'in a secret olive grove'.

'Tiresias' is not the only poem in which Tennyson depicted old age as involving a widening gap between the power of prophecy, strengthened by long experience, and the power to alter the future. *Idylls of the King* (most obviously in **'Merlin and Vivien'**), the Epilogue to 'The Heavy Brigade', 'To Virgil', 'The Dead Prophet', and even (notoriously) his ode celebrating the golden jubilee of Queen Victoria register a gap between the power to see and the power to affect. But 'Tiresias' is unlike most of the late poems in the tone of grievance with which the poet/seer expresses his own ineffectuality. The dramatic monologue's register, and often its idiom, are here distinctly closer to Yeatsian rage than to Wordsworthian calm. 'Who ever turn'd upon his heel to hear / My warning?', Tiresias asks, bitterly, rhetorically, of his listener, Menœceus, son of Creon. 'Speak the truth that no man may believe', was the goddess's curse, and his life's experience has borne it out: 'To me / No power' (1.56-7), 'no power on Fate' (1.62), '[my] power hath work'd no good . . . And these blind hands were useless' (ll.76-77). His warnings of 'famine, plague, / Shrine-shattering earthquake, fire, flood, thunderbolt, / And angers of the Gods for evil done / And expiation lack'd' have ever met with 'unbelief' (ll.58-62). 'To cast wise words among the multitude', he tells Menœceus, in a metaphor which deals out scorn for the multitude and scorn for his own condition in equal measure, 'Was flinging fruit to lions' (ll.65-6).

Uncharacteristic of Tennyson's late published poems in the avidity of its anger, 'Tiresias' is also atypical (though not unique) in presenting a direct and dramatic confrontation between the powerlessness of old age and the envied potency of youth. And yet, this is the point at which one must ask how far the role of *senex iratus* is a calculated rhetorical stance on Tiresias' part, designed to place maximum pressure on Menœceus to act as the aged seer/poet is unable to act. Tiresias' aim is to persuade Menœceus that he must sacrifice his young life if the destruction of Thebes is to be averted. If he does so, the god Arês, 'whose one bliss / Is war, and human sacrifice' (ll.108-9) will relent. Behind this plea to the young man, some of the poem's first readers would have recognised Tennyson, at 74, castigating the Liberal government of his day for its decision to reduce the size and power of the British navy, imperilling (as he thought) the security of nation and empire, and exposing both to 'tyranny' as great as that which threatened Thebes. If Menœceus gives up his life, Tiresias promises, the gods will be kind. The young man's reward will be the unrivalled power of 'example' that belongs to all those who risk death to protect the lives of others—of maidens, wives, mothers, babes and 'oldest age' (ll.100-102):

> No sound is breathed so potent to coerce,
> And to conciliate, as their names who dare
> For that sweet mother land which gave them birth
> Nobly to do, nobly to die. Their names,
> Graven on memorial columns, are a song
> Heard in the future; few, but more than wall
> And rampart, their examples reach a hand
> Far thro' all years, and everywhere they meet

> And kindle generous purpose, and the strength
> To mould it into action pure as theirs.

(ll.116-25)

The 'daring' of death is, in the context, coercively euphemistic. To die is for Menœceus not a risk but a guarantee—the act required of him by the god. The prospects of a young man contemplating a career in the late nineteenth-century British navy were not quite so dire, but, read as allegory, the poem exaggerates, rather than mitigates, the dangers. It puts the modern case entirely in terms of the glory of dying for one's country, repeating, almost exactly, the elegiac militarism of 'The Charge of the Light Brigade' from thirty-one years earlier: 'Their's but to do and die'; 'Nobly to do, nobly to die'. 'Tiresias' forges, through parataxis, not an option but an equation of the two statements. Similarly, the active verbs of 'meet / And kindle generous purpose' come close to dishonesty, identifying a power that will be exercised only posthumously, by one's name rather than by oneself.

If there is something discomfiting in the image of the old man urging the young man to his death, it is not a discomfort the poem seeks to avoid or even to mitigate. Tiresias urges, but he also threatens, and in terms which, by playing on the association of the word 'venerable' with the old, seem to deny the young man, should he shirk what is required of him, a good old age. 'Fairer thy fate than mine', he tells Menœceus, 'if life's best end / Be to end well!', but, 'thou refusing this, / Unvenerable will thy memory be' (ll.126-28). Behind Tiresias one hears that great classical precedent, so familiar to Tennyson's first audience that he did not need to name it: the old king Priam, bewailing the fate he foresees for himself, to be torn to pieces by 'ravening dogs at [his] own gates' rather than dying nobly in battle like his son Hector.[10]

Tiresias' predicament, however, is not Priam's. He has never been a warrior. Since he was gifted, and cursed, with insight, his power has rested on, and been limited to, the power to persuade. When he presses heroism on Menœceus, and when Tennyson, through him, presses upon the young men of England the glory of giving up their lives for their country, one can fairly suspect both men of a measure of duplicity about the nature of their power. 'Let thine own hand strike / Thy youthful pulses into rest and quench / The red God's anger', Tiresias urges (ll.151-53), and his words, contrary to all his earlier claims to powerlessness, are potent. The young man departs, leaving 'one warm tear' upon Tiresias' 'useless hand' (ll.159-60). 'Useless' is an adjective too far: the hand may be 'useless' in so far as the god requires another's hand to act, but the word too unabashedly exploits the weakness of age as a weapon of persuasion.

Left musing alone Tiresias is neither quite elegiac nor triumphalist—or rather, he is both, but not in the ways one might expect. 'He will achieve his greatness' is his short, dismissive statement on Menœceus. Tiresias now turns to envisage an afterlife for himself which has little if anything to do with the heroic future for which the young man's sacrifice may be preparing the way. The future he imagines is less an afterlife than a restoration, in the most generalised and gestural terms, of the heroic culture of 'the years of old'. Past and future coalesce at last to the glory of the seer/poet:

> But for me,
> I would that I were gather'd to my rest,
> And mingled with the famous kings of old,
> On whom about their ocean-islands[11] flash
> The faces of the Gods—the wise man's word,
> Here trampled by the populace underfoot,
> There crown'd with worship—and these eyes will find
> The men I knew, and watch the chariot whirl
> About the goal again, and hunters race
> The shadowy lion, and the warrior-kings,
> In height and prowess more than human, strive
> Again for glory, while the golden lyre
> Is ever sounding in heroic ears
> Heroic hymns, and every way the vales
> Wind, clouded with the grateful incense-fume
> Of those who mix all odour to the Gods
> On one far height in one far-shining fire.
>
> (ll.161-77)

The note of grievance is still there ('the wise man's word / now trampled by the populace underfoot'), but it is rapidly assuaged by the rising cadences and intensive repetitions of the final lines. Tennyson seems at this point to have suffered a bad case of what Edna Longley once called 'last stanza itch', or its non-stanzaic equivalent: rhetoric swelling at the expense of its content as the poem seeks a conclusion. The grateful incense fume makes its way downwards through every vale in questionable obedience to the laws of physics, and also at some expense to Tiresias' character. (If this were Browning one could be more confident that it was an intentional effect of the dramatic monologue form.) Tiresias' hopes for the hereafter seem to imply a return to his youthful state, or image of it, watching with the clear eyes of his youth the 'chariot whirl', but they do not involve any resumption of the physical strength of youth—a strength he has admired in others rather than cultivating in himself. He longs, even now, not to act but to see, without penalty, those great men of yore whose humanity was touched with divinity; to watch their strivings after glory, and (the note of grievance again) to have his wise man's word honoured—more than honoured: 'crowned with worship'. He would wish to be, by implication, a king among kings, a half-divine presence mingling freely with the half-divine heroes of the past.

If this were all there was to 'Tiresias' it would be a significant but not especially strong example of Tennyson's last published work—a poem whose weaknesses justify Christopher Ricks's exclusion of it from the one-volume *Selected Edition* of Tennyson's verse, invoking the precedent of Hallam Tennyson's *Tennyson and His Friends* (1897) (Ricks, Preface to Tennyson, 1987, xviii). But 'Tiresias' is of much more interest for a consideration of Tennyson's late style than that editorial judgement would suggest. The prefatory dedication to FitzGerald told the first readers of that poem that 'Tiresias' was an early work, retrieved by Tennyson's son from 'some forgotten book of mine / With sallow scraps of manuscript / And dating many a year ago', and intended to remind FitzGerald of their 'younger London days':

> I send a birthday line
> [. . .] which you will take
> My Fitz, and welcome, as I know
>   Less for its own than for the sake
> Of one recalling gracious times,
>   When, in our younger London days,
> You found some merit in my rhymes,
>   And I more pleasure in your praise.
>
> (ll.45-46)

The modesty topos here repeats (or, for the reader, anticipates) the dramatic monologue's nostalgia for a time in youth when merit was recognised, but it does so without 'Tiresias'' air of complaint. This is not to say that the dedication to FitzGerald is without tonal angularities. The opening lines mock the slightly older man's strict vegetarianism, recalling a visit to FitzGerald's home many years earlier when 'for ten long weeks' Tennyson 'tried [his] table of Pythagoras', and found the lack of meat went to his head. I 'seem'd at first', Tennyson recalls, '"a thing enskied" / (As Shakespeare has it) airy-light / To float above the ways of men' (ll.14-18). (The tongue in cheek reference is to *Measure for Measure* (I.iv) where Lucio, whose sincerity may be doubted, praises Isabella's renunciation of the world.) 'None can say / That Lenten fare makes Lenten thought' (ll.29-30), a more placatory Tennyson goes on, and praises FitzGerald's much-admired translation of the *Rubáiyát*: 'I know no version done / In English more divinely well' (ll.33-34).

Were the dedication the sole addition in 1883 to 'Tiresias,' it would cast a softening light on the dramatic monologue, toning down its dramatisation of an old man's anger with the more friendly intimacies of the letter form. The older Tennyson's taking for granted that complaint can be a licensed kind of banter between friends, the texture of a friendship of many years standing, modifies the monologue's air of grievance. But only by contrast. The dedication, remaining in effect a separate poem (and published as such by Hallam Tennyson and by Ricks), does not directly challenge the dramatic monologue's irritation at the unregardedness of an old man's wisdom, or the sense of entitlement behind that irritation. A more sceptical reading would point out that the dedication to FitzGerald is not quite free of one-upmanship on several scores: on the greater virtue, and warmer pleasures, of eating meat, on being (as Tennyson mistakenly thought) a year younger; perhaps also on being recognised as the greater poet (is there perhaps something ungenerous about praising the *Rubáiyát* as the best translation Tennyson knows of in English?).[12]

FitzGerald's death on 14 June, possibly the same day the lines were written, left that bantering tone uncomfortably exposed. ('I had written a poem to him within the last week', Tennyson told Frederick Pollock on 17 June '—a dedication—which he will never see' (Tennyson, 1990, III, 247).) In the following days Tennyson returned to **'Tiresias',** and penned an epilogue in a new key entirely: thirty-two lines of alternately rhyming verse. (The dedication has the same metre and rhyme scheme; **'Tiresias'** itself is in blank verse.) Picking up and repeating the last line of the dramatic monologue, 'One height and one far-shining fire', the epilogue takes a hard look at the rhetoric of what would have been his last gift to his friend. FitzGerald, Tennyson imagines, would have read the ending of **'Tiresias'** with healthy scepticism of its last-stanza inflation:

> And while I fancied that my friend
> For this brief idyll would require
>   A less diffuse and opulent end,
> And would defend his judgment well,
>   If I should deem it over nice—
> The tolling of his funeral bell
>   Broke on my Pagan Paradise,
> And mixt the dreams of classic times,
>   And all the phantoms of the dream,
> With present grief, and made the rhymes,
>   That miss'd his living welcome, seem
> Like would-be guests an hour too late,
>   Who down the highway moving on
> With easy laughter find the gate
>   Is bolted, and the master gone.
> Gone into darkness, that full light
>   Of friendship! past, in sleep, away
> By night, into the deeper night!
>
> (ll.57-88)

Tacitly rebuking the inadequate generosity of the dedicatory poem to FitzGerald, these lines also, more intensively, rework the imagery of **'Tiresias'** to make of it an elegy for a fellow poet in old age. They imagine an argument left waiting to be had between the two, in which FitzGerald is retrospectively accorded the right of 'judgement' and the power to 'defend' it 'well'. His dying makes his imagined judgement a more serious challenge, pulling Tennyson's doubts about the quality of **'Tiresias'** to the surface.[13] The earlier rhymes of **'Tiresias'** do indeed sound naïve: too young, too confident of their own welcome, and (the praise for FitzGerald is unqualified here) they have missed their appointment with the 'master', letting the full light of his friendship, like the light of Tiresias' eyes, go 'into

darkness'. No dawn will waken FitzGerald again, he having passed, in an image which pointedly reverses the opening lines of the monologue, into 'deeper night'.

But, here again for a second time, Tennyson checks himself rhetorically, once again repeating his own last line with a leaven of scepticism: 'The deeper night?' The ultimate consolations of *In Memoriam*'s Christianity and of a progressivist optimism are at hand, now, to correct the earlier too-easy recourse to literary cliché and to a pagan ideal that envisaged the afterlife only as a return to the past:

> The deeper night? A clearer day
> Than our poor twilight dawn on earth—
>   If night, what barren toil to be!
> What life, so maim'd by night, were worth
>   Our living out? Not mine to me
> Remembering all the golden hours
>   Now silent, and so many dead,
> And him the last; and laying flowers,
>   This wreath, above his honour'd head,
> And praying that, when I from hence
>   Shall fade with him into the unknown,
> My close of life's experience
>   May prove as peaceful as his own.
>
> (ll.57-88)

Tiresias' blindness is recast here, perhaps unconsciously on Tennyson's part, as a symbol of the life without faith in an afterlife. With these lines the old poet directly rejects the paganism of the dramatic monologue, which his revisions had left essentially untouched. 'What life, so maim'd by night, were worth / Our living out?' Such an existence would, like Tiresias', have as its best recourse only the memory of 'golden hours / Now silent, and so many dead'. Its power of insight into the future would be, like this seer-poet's, only reiterative knowledge of the past—the heavy caesuras pulling life and poetry alike towards silence. Instead of this, Tennyson holds out the hope of 'the unknown' that lies ahead, and into which FitzGerald, he trusts, has gone before—not through war, or bloodshed, and not to the militaristic 'Paradise' of **'Tiresias',** but peacefully to the 'unknown' but 'clearer day' that is the Christian afterlife.

In the full text of **'Tiresias'** one thus sees late style not as antagonism, but as a conscious chastening of the posturing antagonisms of an earlier style. In the epilogue Tennyson is asking himself the question he had failed to ask in the dedication to FitzGerald: why this poem, with its unjustified grievances about the powerlessness of the aged poet-seer, should have been the one he chose to retrieve out of (one assumes) many others. There is, of course, a convivial relaxedness about the dedicatory lines: by offering an old poem, they are recalling the early days of a long friendship to FitzGerald, but they also suggest Tennyson conserving his energies in old age. They may even suggest that, in old age, the question of one's style can be a more relaxed matter than it was for an ambitious young poet trying to make a powerful and 'useful' voice for himself. Late Tennyson is, as I have been arguing, a consciously heterogeneous thing, incorporating, and keeping in play, many 'earlier' styles, and **'Tiresias'** is a particularly good example of that, weighted as it is with self-quotation, self-allusion, and self-echo. Several of these references backward and forward to poems written before and after its first composition are identified in Christopher Ricks's notes to the Longman edition, but there are many more, including the repetition of Bedivere's 'story [. . .] told [. . .] in the white winter of his age' reprised as Tiresias' 'tale [. . .] told to me / [. . .] by age as winter-white as mine is now'. This compôting of his own styles makes the poem dense with the sense of Tennyson's self-observation in old age: attempting, it may be, to redeem the poem's style with his own later voice, but also failing, or refusing, to write entirely afresh. The epilogue marks a stronger rebuke to himself, no longer content (in the light of FitzGerald's death) with his younger self's imagining of the Old Poet as an exilic figure, his power to persuade at odds with his power to enforce, or his own partial efforts to repair the verses. It knows the narcissism of the dramatic monologue's imagined antagonism in old age, and holds it culpable also, in the coda, for failing to take seriously its power to direct the reader towards transcendence.

One might fairly ask why a poet not always loathe to revise or reject his work in old age when he found it not up to scratch, should have chosen to publish **'Tiresias'** at all: why not rework it thoroughly, reduce its 'opulence', recast its militarism in a more honest vein? Clearly Tennyson wanted the process of the poem's writing, and then its reconsideration, to be seen as such: he wanted the reader to see him going back not once but twice in his seventies to reconsider the question of old age and poetic voice. **'Tiresias',** for Tennyson, was something like what 'The Circus Animals' Desertion' would be for Yeats much later: an announcement of a new stylistic self-consciousness in old age that is not a retirement from the world, but a re-engagement with it.

Notes

This essay is the revised text of a lecture given to the Annual Meeting of the Tennyson Society, at Lincoln on 4 June 2005. I am grateful to Marion Shaw, Kathleen Jefferson and the Society for their kind invitation. References to Tennyson's poems are to *The Poems of Tennyson,* 2nd edn., 3 vols., ed. by Christopher Ricks (Harlow: Longman, 1987) unless there is reason to cite the original editions.

1. I am excluding the relatively weak verse drama *The Foresters* (1892).

2. 'He hates the modern radicals', Arthur Hardinge reported in 1888: 'he has lost any admiration he may have had for Gladstone, and if he expresses an occasional belief in human or social progress it is a very frigid and doubtful profession of faith. But the old impulsive character of the man is there. . . . In him one sees the two natures in conflict—the impulsive, hopeful, sanguine believer in progress of former days, and the timid Conservative of the present who fears the tendency of modern times and is inclined to look at everything from a very narrow point of view.' (Tennyson, 1990, III, 370).

3. For Cicero's famous Stoic account of old age, see Cicero, 'De Senectute/On Old Age', in Cicero, 1971.

4. An 1807 printing of Creech and 1813 printing of Wakefield, both unmarked by any reader.

5. *Tit. Lucreti Cari. De Rerum Natura. Libri Sex,* with a translation and notes by H. A. J. Munro, 2 vols. (Cambridge: Deighton Bell Co., 1864), I, 138 (III, 771-75). Tennyson underlined *'senectis'* in the Latin, and put a vertical mark in the margin against the first two lines of the English translation: 'granting this so, you must admit . . . sense. Then'.

6. There are poems written in the voices of old women—'The Grandmother', and 'Spinster-Arts'—but they do not present the old voice in the manner described here, fitting instead with the more febrile style of the late dramatic monologues.

7. Maud's father, for example, whose age seems more monitory than realistic: 'that old man, now lord of the broad estate and the Hall, / Dropt off gorged from a scheme that had left us flaccid and drained' (*Maud,* I. 19-20); or the dwarf, 'vicious, old and irritable' in 'The Marriage of Geraint' (l.194); or the old man in 'The Vision of Sin' who hails the group at the ruined inn and bids them drink to Death ('Vision of Sin', IV).

8. 'Tithonus' is of course the extreme expression of that yearning in extreme age to leave the body behind entirely—though, as many critics have noted, the poem deprives him of the classical myth's consolation, metamorphosis into a grasshopper.

9. Tennyson, quoted by Ricks (Tennyson, 1987, III, 671).

10. Homer, *The Iliad,* Book 22, 59-6; trans. Samuel Butler (1898, repr. 1995, 338); I also borrow here from. E. V. Rieu's translation (1950, 398). The lines are sometimes dismissed as being 'late'. See Jasper Griffin, 1980, 117.

11. Revised by Tennyson to 'islets' in 1888.

12. E. H. Whinfield's competing translation had been published the previous year.

13. Goslee discerns in the process of Tennyson's revisions a 'progressive alienation from its "opulent tone", from the world-view it embodies, and finally even from the figure who utters it'. Quoted by Ricks; Tennyson, 1987, III, 623.

Works Cited

Adorno, Theodor W., 1964. 'Spätstil Beethovens', in *Moments Musicaux: Neu Gedruckte Aufsätze 1928-1962* (Frankfurt am Main: Suhrkamp Verlag); repr. as 'Text 3: Beethoven's Late Style' in *Beethoven: The Philosophy of Music: Fragments and Texts,* ed. Rolf Tiedemann, trans. Edmund Jephcott. Cambridge: Polity Press.

Buckley, Jerome H. 1960. *Tennyson: The Growth of a Poet.* Cambridge, MA: Harvard University Press.

Cicero, Marcus Tullius, 1923. *De Senectute; De Amicitia; De Divinatione/On Old Age; On Friendship; On Divination,* tr. W. A. Falconer, Loeb Classical Library. Cambridge, MA: Harvard University Press.

Goslee, David F., 1976. 'Three Stages of Tennyson's 'Tiresias', *JEGP (Journal of English and German Philology)* 75, 154-67.

Griffin, Jasper, 1980. *Homer on Life and Death.* Oxford: Clarendon Press.

Homer, 1898. *The Iliad,* Book 22, 59-6; tr. Samuel Butler, repr. 1995. New York: Barnes and Noble.

Horsman, E. A. (ed.), 1953. *The Diary of Alfred Domett, 1872-1885.* London: Geoffrey Cumberlege and Oxford University Press.

Lucretius Carus, Titus, 1695. *Titi Lucretii Cari De rerum natura libri sex,* with commentary and notes by Thomas Creech (Oxford). George Clayton Tennyson's copy, Tennyson Research Centre, Lincoln Public Library.

Lucretius Carus, Titus, 1796-97. *T. Lucretii Cari de rerum natura libros sex,* comm. illustr., et cum animadversionibus R. Bentleii aliorum subinde miscuit G. Wakefield (London). George Clayton Tennyson's copy, Tennyson Research Centre, Lincoln Public Library.

Lucretius Carus, Titus, 1821. *T. Lucretii Cari, De rerum natura, libri sex,* ed. Gilbert Wakefield (London: Rodwell et Martin [etc.]). Tennyson's copy, Tennyson Research Centre, Lincoln Public Library.

Lucretius Carus, Titus, 1864. *Tit. Lucreti Cari. De Rerum Natura. Libri Sex,* with a trans. and notes by H. A. J. Munro, 2 vols (Cambridge: Deighton Bell Co.). Tennyson's copy, with his annotations, Tennyson Research Centre, Lincoln Public Library.

Lucretius, 1992. *De Rerum Natura,* with an English translation by Martin Ferguson Smith, Loeb Classical Library, rev. ed. 1972. Cambridge, MA: Harvard University Press.

Marks, Thomas, 2005. "A Sort of Magic": Enchantment and Disenchantment in Victorian Poetry', unpublished MSt dissertation (University of Oxford).

Reynolds, Matthew, 2001. *The Realms of Verse 1830-1870: English Poetry in a Time of Nation-Building.* Oxford: Oxford University Press.

Said, Edward, 1988. 'Late Styles: Yeats and Decolonization', in *The Edward Said Reader,* ed. Moustafa Bayoumi and Andrew Rubin (2000), 291-313. New York: Vintage Books.

Said, Edward, 2003. 'Untimely Meditations', *The Nation,* 14 August.

Said, Edward, 2004. 'Thoughts on Late Style', *London Review of Books* 26/15 (5 August).

Stevenson, Caroline Barnes, 1980. 'Druids, Bards, and Tennyson's Merlin', *Victorian Newsletter* 57, 14-23.

Tennyson, Alfred, Lord, 1870. *The Holy Grail and Other Poems.* London: Strahan and Co.

Tennyson, Alfred, Lord, 1885a. Revised proofs of *Tiresias and Other Poems* (London: Macmillan and Co.). Tennyson Research Centre, Lincoln Public Library, P92, Cat. 4288.

Tennyson, Alfred, Lord, 1885b. *Tiresias and Other Poems.* London: Macmillan and Co.

Tennyson, Alfred, Lord, 1886. *Locksley Hall Sixty Years After.* London: Macmillan and Co.

Tennyson, Alfred, Lord, 1889. *Demeter and Other Poems.* London: Macmillan and Co.

Tennyson, Alfred, Lord, 1892a. *The Foresters.* London: Macmillan and Co.

Tennyson, Alfred, Lord, 1892b. Proofs and four revises of *Death of Œnone, Akbar's Dream, and Other Poems* (London: Macmillan and Co.). Tennyson Research Centre, Lincoln Public Library, P74, P75, P76, P77, P78, Cat. 3893.

Tennyson, Alfred, Lord, 1892c. *Death of Œnone, Akbar's Dream, and Other Poems.* London: Macmillan and Co.

Tennyson, Alfred, Lord, 1987. *The Poems of Tennyson,* 2nd edn, 3 vols, ed. Christopher Ricks. London: Longman.

Tennyson, Alfred, Lord, 1990. *The Letters of Alfred Lord Tennyson,* ed. Cecil Y. Lang and Edgar F. Shannon, Jr, 3 vols. Oxford: Clarendon Press.

Tennyson, A. and C., 1827. *Poems by Two Brothers.* London: Simpkin & Marshall; Louth, J. & J. Jackson.

Tennyson, Hallam, Lord, 1897. *Alfred Lord Tennyson, A Memoir,* by his son, 2 vols. London: Macmillan and Co.

Woodward, Kathleen, 1993. "Late Theory, Late Style: Loss and Renewal in Freud and Barthes," *Aging & Gender in Literature: Studies in Creativity,* ed. Anne Wyatt-Brown and Janice Rossen, 82-101. Charlottesville: University of Virginia Press.

Devon Fisher (essay date winter 2006)

SOURCE: Fisher, Devon. "Spurring an Imitative Will: The Canonization of Arthur Hallam." *Christianity and Literature* 55, no. 2 (winter 2006): 221-44.

[*In the following essay, Fisher explores how in* In Memoriam *Tennyson "draws from the religious debates of the day to effect a secular canonization, placing the memory of Arthur Hallam into a form that demands the imitation of an entire culture."*]

T. S. Eliot observes of Tennyson's *In Memoriam* that "its faith is a poor thing, but its doubt is a very intense experience" (200-201). Earlier in the same essay, he compares the poem to "the concentrated diary of a man confessing himself" (196). Together, these statements create the image of a poet struggling to give meaning to life by articulating the enormous pain of doubt and grief. Considered in this way, the very personal qualities of *In Memoriam* transform the reader into a sort of literary eavesdropper, and the sheer pathos of Tennyson's grief feels slightly embarrassing—as if it were something we should not be seeing.[1] Tennyson's poem, however, cannot be read only as a record of private grief, as recent critics have reminded us.[2] Indeed, even Eliot's comparison of the poem to a diary reminds us that the very act of articulation places memory into the public sphere, for a diary, despite the intensely personal feelings it may contain, always exists to be read by others.[3] Modern sociologists have even questioned whether any act of articulating memory can be considered "personal" at all. Eviatar Zerubavel, for instance, builds on the idea of collective memory proposed by Maurice Halbwachs to suggest that "It was language that freed human memory from having to be stored exclusively in individuals' brains" (5). If the pathos of *In Memoriam* begins with "no language but a cry" (54, 20) trapped within Tennyson's own mind, the act of committing Hallam's memory to writing ultimately transfers that memory into a public arena where it becomes something altogether different from the inarticulate cry of personal grief.[4]

Pierre Nora has identified the first half of the nineteenth century as a time characterized by the loss of collective memory, which he defines as "memory without a past that ceaselessly reinvents tradition, linking the history of its ancestors to the undifferentiated time of heroes, origins, and myth" (8). Although Nora writes specifically of French history, his comments speak as well to a process that occurred in Victorian England. Chartism, electoral reform, and various Church reforms together signaled a break in any smooth narrative of English history. In response to these ruptures, Victorians countered with efforts to reestablish a collective memory as Nora defines it. Thomas Carlyle tried to reconnect England with its heroes and its origins by arguing in *On Heroes, Hero-Worship, and the Heroic in History* (1841) and in *Past and Present* (1843) that the only way to proceed into the future was by correctly understanding the past; as he puts it in *Past and Present,* the greatest threat to Victorian England was that the past was "sacrilegiously mishandled; effaced, and what is worse, defaced!" (239). In its own way, the Oxford Movement attempted a similar re-creation of English memory, hoping to locate in the ancient Catholic Church an origin that would preserve the continuity of the English Church despite the recent repeals of the Test and Corporation Acts and the admission of Roman Catholics to the government. Tennyson holds a secure place as one of the chief poetic voices in this effort to repair the breaches in history by giving voice to the past. Unlike Carlyle and Newman, Tennyson seeks not so much to establish a historical chain connecting the past to the present as to recreate the past in the present and by so doing to shape the future. James W. Hood has argued that *In Memoriam*'s "most shocking attribute" is its claim to creative power: it "does not merely remember a dead friend; the poem enshrines him permanently as a much grander figure than he could have been had he lived" (118). I wish to take seriously this idea that the poem "enshrines" Hallam, recognizing, as Hood reminds us to, that Tennyson crafted the poem in a specific historical moment in which the language of religion permeated Victorian culture. With *In Memoriam,* Tennyson draws from the religious debates of the day to effect a secular canonization, placing the memory of Arthur Hallam into a form that demands the imitation of an entire culture.[5] By creating a secularized version of the saint out of Arthur Hallam, however, Tennyson raises vexing questions about how England will move from the present into the future.

Tennyson's response to Roman Catholicism during these years proves difficult to pin down. On the one hand, Edward FitzGerald's description of Tennyson reading **"St. Simeon Stylites"** with "grotesque Grimness" (quoted in Ricks 542) has been taken as indicative of a deep antipathy to Catholic asceticism. On the other, Bernard Aspinwall has suggested that Tennyson nearly followed John Henry Newman into the arms of the Roman Catholic Church. Aspinwall supports this position with the letters of Robert Monteith who writes "'Mr. Tennyson finds beauty and consolation in the B[lessed]

Sacrament and the Intercession of the Saints, but has endless difficulties and perturbations'" (208). The absence of any such sentiment in Tennyson's letters and journals suggests that Tennyson's "endless difficulties and perturbations" may have been indifference to or outright rejection of transubstantiation and the intercession of the saints as theological doctrine. The point that Tennyson (unlike some of his contemporaries) found beauty in these forms, however, deserves further consideration, for nearly twenty years before Monteith's letter, Arthur Hallam had expressed similar sentiments in his essay "The Influence of Italian Upon English Literature" (1831). In this relatively short tract (twenty-nine pages as originally published), Hallam examines first why Italian became the dominant language of the Renaissance and second how that influence infiltrated English literature in the work of Chaucer and Shakespeare. He identifies two key reasons for the prominence of the Italian language—its geographic proximity to the classical Latin writers and its connection to Roman Catholicism. It is with the second of these that I am primarily concerned.

Early in the essay, Hallam notes the connection between Roman Catholicism and the appearance of a tradition of courtly love:

> The inordinate esteem for chastity; the solemnity attached to conventual vows; the interest taken in those fair saints, on whom the Church had conferred beatitude . . . above all the worship of the Virgin, the Queen of Heaven . . . these articles of a most unscriptural, but very beautiful mythology, could not be established in general belief without investing the feminine character with ideal splendour and loveliness.
>
> (219)

Here Hallam indicates that Catholicism gets the form correct but invests it with inappropriate content; he finds beauty in the saints and in the Catholic "worship of the Virgin" but recognizes the incompatibility of the theology with his own. Later in the essay as he explores the link between Catholicism and the emergence of a full-fledged European Renaissance literature, Hallam speaks in similar terms, noting: "the splendors and pomps of the daily worship; the music and the incense, and the beautiful saints and the tombs of the martyrs—what strong hold must they have taken on the feelings of every Italian!" (224). Hallam was quite taken with the splendor of Roman Catholic ritual even as he resisted the impulse to embrace such forms as signifiers of religious faith. Instead, what emerges, as Gerhard Joseph has shown, is a Christian Platonism that embraces the love spoken of here but directs it neither toward Mary nor the saints but toward women in general who become, as it were, conduits to God (62-63). Where Joseph argues that in *In Memoriam* Tennyson imports this model and directs erotic love toward Hallam in an effort to reach God, I contend that Tennyson maintains

the form of the saint but secularizes it, presenting Hallam as a figure who inspires civic rather than spiritual virtue.

If Hallam's writings presented the canonized saint to Tennyson as an aesthetic form, the purpose of which was primarily to contain beauty, the cultural debates surrounding the saints in the 1820s through the 1840s would have suggested to him the power that the form has in shaping the cultural understanding of the past and, implicitly, of the future. As the Church of England grappled in the 1830s and 1840s with the Oxford Movement and the resurgence of Roman Catholicism, the saints occupied a curious place in the collective memory, for the figures canonized in the Roman tradition also held important places in English ecclesiastical history. Looking back at this time period, John Henry Newman would write that the veneration of the saints and the homage paid to the Virgin Mary were the two greatest obstacles to his conversion (*Apologia* 121). Others shared Newman's reluctance to accept what they perceived as the Roman practice of worshiping the saints, many linking the canonized figures to the ancient pantheon. An anonymous reviewer in the *Eclectic Review* suggests a close link between the invocation of saints and "Pagan demonolatry" (Rev. of *An Inquiry* 26), and the travel writer Charlotte Eaton, upon seeing the Church of St. Martina, exclaimed that "the saint herself is no other than the blustering god [Mars] in petticoats" (1:310). As these attacks suggest, the saints became one of the defining markers of difference between Anglicanism[6] and Roman Catholicism, a difference that implies variant narratives of history leading to the present and implying different trajectories for the future.

Before turning to the text of *In Memoriam* to consider how these two uses of the saint converge in Tennyson's work, we must pause to consider how Anglicans understood the process of canonization. In an 1837 sermon included in a collection titled *Ten Sermons on the Principal Errors of the Church of Rome,* the Rev. John Jones, incumbent of St. Andrew's Church in Liverpool, offers this explanation of how the process of canonization came about:

> About the same era [fifth century] we first meet with indications of "a superstitious veneration for the memory of departed saints." But it was not till after a further lapse of two or three hundred years that we find the Popes presuming to canonize deceased persons, and to constitute them intercessors with God in behalf of all who might devoutly crave their assistance.
>
> (20)

Although Jones was an evangelical himself, the rhetoric he uses describing the Pope's assumption of the authority to canonize reflects opinions held by Anglican churchmen in the 1830s. I quote Jones not because Tennyson was necessarily familiar with his sermon but because his understanding of canonization reflects the cultural understanding of what had to occur for someone to be considered a saint. Canonization is a performative act; the saint is canonized because someone utters the words effecting the canonization. Moreover, the act must be performed by someone who in fact has the authority to do so. The difference between "she is such a saint" uttered in everyday conversation and "she is such a saint" issued by the Vatican is immense. Incidentally, these are the grounds upon which Jones dismisses the Roman practice of canonization; he boldly asserts that the Pope simply does not have the authority to perform the act. Finally, for the canonization to be of any value, either the significance of the act must be explained, or the act must occur in a culture that has an *a priori* understanding of the process.

In his sermon, Jones focuses on the moment of canonization, and he thus omits any discussion of other aspects of sainthood, most notably the question of the role of relics. Others, however, took up the relationship between the material body and the spiritual qualities of the saints at length. Although theologians and preachers frequently took the relics of the saints as subjects for their meditations, the Victorians most often encountered the idea that a fixation on the physical remains could ultimately lead to God himself in the popular travel narratives of the time. To turn to just one of the many examples available, Hobart Seymour writes of his attendance at Mass at the Church of the Holy Cross of Jerusalem in Rome where the Bishop paraded relics before those in attendance. In his extensive list, Seymour includes the finger of St. Thomas, the ashes of St. Lawrence, a piece of the head of John the Baptist, and numerous other teeth, knees, fingers, bones, and knuckles (3). For Seymour and countless other Victorians, the journey to Rome became a way of engaging with what they perceived as a Roman Catholic fetishization of the body.

In *In Memoriam,* Tennyson begins the process of canonization not with the actual performative act that Jones describes (this will be delayed until the mid-point of the poem) but with a careful consideration of his own relationship to Hallam's material remains. Darrel Mansell has argued that Tennyson's near obsession with Hallam's physical and literary remains stems from the elegiac convention that the author must obliterate the subject of his poem in order to surpass his rival's poetic skill. Yet in a text that Mansell himself calls a "poem of hagiographic reverence" (98),[7] Hallam's remains also serve as the object of an erotic, spiritual devotion to the dead that the Victorians associated with Roman Catholicism.

In the "fair ship" poems, Tennyson draws what is essentially a poetic travel narrative to its logical end, the returning of the traveler to his native land. He generates the effect of these poems partially by juxtaposing the expectation of the traveler's return with the reality that nothing more than a corpse arrives on the ship. However, a careful consideration of the language used in these lyrics suggests that, like his contemporaries, Tennyson treats the journey to Italy as an encounter with an Other whose mark is inscribed on Hallam's corpse both by the encounter and by the poet's pen.[8] Thus when he first imagines the vessel carrying the body from Italy to England, he imagines it carrying remains that signify something more than just a material corpse:

> Fair ship, that from the Italian shore
> > Sailest the placid ocean-plains
> > With my lost Arthur's loved remains,
> Spread thy full wings, and waft him o'er.
> So draw him home to those that mourn
> > In vain; a favourable speed
> > Ruffle thy mirror'd mast, and lead
> Thro' prosperous floods his holy urn.
>
> (9, 1-8)

As with much of *In Memoriam,* the language used here is that of excess.[9] To speak of "loved remains" is to establish a relationship with the corpse. This is not merely a case in which the poet projects onto the empty body all that he has known of Hallam. Tennyson describes his friend as "lost Arthur," and the desire to grasp the loved remains is but one example of what Herbert Tucker describes as a need to seize "what is emphatically not Hallam" (380). Furthermore, as Tucker goes on to point out, just two poems later, Tennyson contrasts the natural calm of the ocean with the "dead calm in that noble breast / Which heaves but with the heaving deep" (11,19-20), achieving an almost horrific statement of how thoroughly absent Arthur Hallam's life is from his remains (383).

Only by investing the relationship with the corpse with the language of holiness does Tennyson rescue this lyric and others like it (notably lyric 18 where Tennyson imagines that he throws himself onto Hallam's corpse and "breathing through his lips impart[s] / The life that almost dies in me") from a gruesome necrophilia. What the ship bears from Italy is no mere corpse; instead, it holds a "holy urn" that carries "precious relics . . . / The dust of him I shall not see / Til all my widowed race be run" (17,18-20). Michael Tomko argues that Tennyson's "appeal to an avowed idolatry of Hallam [is] not in the name of religion but re-anatomization" (125). We must not, however, overlook the specifically religious idiom that Tennyson chooses. Relics, those material objects that "offer us a remarkably vivid, quasi-tangible contact with the past" (Zerubavel 44), hold forth for Tennyson some sort of spiritual contact with his dead friend. His language transforms the mortal remains of Arthur Hallam into something far more than dust or even a re-anatomized corpse, and the body becomes both a tangible reminder that Hallam continues to exist and an object towards which eroticized devotion can be directed in the expectation that an appropriate relationship to the material can ultimately yield a higher truth.[10] What exactly that higher truth will be remains to be defined in the poem—Tennyson will try out several different possibilities—but here it is enough that he has begun the process of canonizing Hallam by investing his physical remains with the spiritual power held by the relics that religious pamphlets, sermons, and travel narratives regularly set before the Victorians.

Over the next twenty lyrics, the poet resituates his relationship to Hallam, directing his feelings away from the corpse and onto the Being that the body implies. In a series of lyrics beginning with poem 41, Tennyson works within several different schemas to pinpoint precisely what Hallam can do after his death. Each of these positions encapsulates an argument about the soul from contemporary theology (Culler 169-175), and although Tennyson finds a certain appeal in these arguments, with poem 48, he backs carefully away from each, claiming that

> If these brief lays, of Sorrow born,
> > Were taken to be such as closed
> > Grave doubts and answers here proposed,
> Then these were such as men might scorn.
>
> (1-4)

The individual poems, he claims, do not intend to express theological truth, nor do they aspire to any certain answer as to the soul's state after death.

Almost immediately after this renunciation of certain answers, however, the poet offers the words of lyric 50, one of the most moving lyrics of the entire sequence and one that most completely expresses a conviction that Hallam can and will continue to intervene as a mediatory presence in the poet's life. A. Dwight Culler takes this poem as the low point of *In Memoriam,* the point at which the text "collapses into its darkest and most poignant moan" (176). This particular lyric certainly does initiate one of the darkest sections of the poem, but I question whether Tennyson intended it to be quite as dark as Culler reads it. Instead, I read the poem as a preparatory prayer as Tennyson begins his brief journey through the bleak vision of the world expressed in poems 51-56. The repeated "Be near me when" of each stanza implies a future tense, an anticipation of darkness—both the literal darkness of doubt and death and the darkness of the coming lyrics in which Tennyson will face his greatest fears regarding Hallam's absence, the existence of God, and the function of Nature. What remains unclear, however, is to whom this prayer is addressed. One possibility, of course, is that Tennyson intends a conventional prayer to God, and indeed, the ambiguity of the poem fully al-

lows for this reading. In my reading of the poem, however, Hallam himself serves as the audience for this prayer. Although Tennyson leaves lyric 50 ambiguous, lyric 51 clarifies the relationship between the speaker and the auditor. Tennyson refers us back to lyric 50 with the simple question "Do we indeed desire the dead / Should still be near us at our side?" (51, 1-2). Not only does this question suggest that the speaker has desired the presence of the dead, the phrasing ("be near us") repeats that of lyric 50, implying a direct connection between Hallam (who is "the dead" of lyric 51) and the auditor of the narrator's prayer.

If indeed the prayer of lyric 50 is addressed to Hallam, the poem serves as an invocation of Tennyson's friend as proof against a coming darkness. This invocation, however, assigns to Hallam a role that places him beyond the accepted bounds of the Anglican understanding of the dead:

> Be near me when my faith is dry,
> > And men the flies of latter spring,
> > That lay their eggs, and sting and sing
> And weave their petty cells and die.
> Be near me when I fade away,
> > To point the term of human strife,
> > And on the low dark verge of life
> The twilight of eternal day.
>
> (9-16)

In these lines we see Tennyson trying out one way of relating to his dead friend; he places Hallam in the position of the Catholic saint, a mediator who aids his faith and guides him into the afterlife. Even the Tractarians whose theology approached nearer to Rome than any of the other groups within the Church of England noted the danger of the sort of invocation that Tennyson offers here. In his definition of the *Via Media,* for instance, Newman specifically identifies the "direct invocation of Saints" as a "dangerous practice, as tending to give, often actually giving, to creatures the honour and reliance due to the Creator alone" ("Via Media" 12). Although Tennyson does not specifically name Hallam a saint, the language of veneration and invocation places the poem, to say the least, on shaky theological ground.

The seven poems following lyric 50 crescendo to poem 56. In the intervening verses Tennyson ponders whether he would want Hallam to know him in his current state (51), whether he can love Hallam properly (52), whether life progresses onward to a higher goal (54), and whether life continues after death (55). With poem 56, the most intense doubt of *In Memoriam* comes to a head when science and theology collide in Tennyson's effort to make sense of Hallam's death. Here the desire to believe that Hallam maintains some sort of individuality after death battles the fear that he was but one of the many inferior types chosen seemingly without reason for extinction by Nature. Tennyson uses a musical analogy to capture this dynamic. In the presence of Nature "red in tooth and claw" (15) humanity can only feel like a "discord" (21). Even the dinosaurs "that tare each other in their slime / Were mellow music match'd with him [humanity]" (23-24). The profound fear that human life in general and Hallam's life specifically amount to little more than a heap of dust engenders nothing but discordant noise, yet even in the face of this doubt, Tennyson continues to turn to Hallam as evidence of something higher. "O for thy voice to soothe and bless!" (26), he writes; the desire—still unfulfilled, perhaps—for Hallam's voice to lend harmony to the discord caused by Nature becomes Tennyson's reason for proceeding.

The lyric following this point of deepest doubt serves as a transitional poem in *In Memoriam,* for in it, Tennyson declares his own authority for canonizing Hallam. Having given voice to his fear that the ending of the human body may also be the ending of human existence, Tennyson glances backward to assert that his invocation of Hallam in lyric 50 was well founded:

> Peace; come away: the song of woe
> > Is after all an earthly song:
> > Peace; come away: we do him wrong
> To sing so wildly: let us go.
> Come; let us go: your cheeks are pale;
> > But half my life I leave behind:
> > Methinks my friend is richly shrined;
> But I shall pass; my work will fail.
>
> (1-8)

The songs of woe—both the songs of doubt that he sings and the discordant sounds of Nature—are of an earthly sort, and Tennyson realizes that a higher kind of song is in order. As he wills to move beyond the questioning doubt of the previous lyrics, he returns to the same sort of language that he used in lyric 50, making the seemingly offhanded comment that "Methinks my friend is richly *shrined.*" The *Oxford English Dictionary* offers several denotations for this word, most of which relate to concepts of sainthood. Adjectivally, the word means "contained in a shrine," and the only recorded instances refer specifically to a patron saint. As a verb, definitions available to Tennyson include "to enclose (relics) in a shrine, to provide (a saint or deity) with a shrine or sanctuary"; "to venerate or proclaim . . . as a saint"; "to canonize"; and "to enshrine in one's heart or thoughts." This declaration that Hallam has been shrined is of utmost importance in *In Memoriam.* Tennyson could mean simply that the memory of Hallam remains enshrined in his thoughts. This reading, however, overlooks the religious language that occurs earlier in the poem, specifically the reference to Hallam as a man "half-Divine" (14, 10) and to his body as "precious relics" (17, 18) and as "sacred dust" (21, 22). Considered in light of this earlier language, Tennyson's claim that his friend is "richly shrined" may refer to the

physical structures at the parish church of St. Andrew in Clevedon that enclose Hallam's corpse.[11] Beyond this literal meaning, however, when Tennyson claims that Hallam has been shrined, he himself utters the performative that effects the canonization of his friend. Furthermore, the multiple possibilities of the word "shrine" move the canonization out of the poet's mind and into the public domain. To shrine is to enclose or to house, and the text of *In Memoriam* thus proclaims itself to be the visible monument that serves as the public reminder of Hallam's continued presence and influence on British society. Lyric 57 thus simultaneously declares Hallam to have been canonized and authorizes itself in that performative act. From this point, Tennyson begins the process of interpreting the canonization declared by lyric 57 and of demonstrating how Hallam's perpetual presence can shape the course of the entire nation.

Having canonized his friend in the first half of *In Memoriam,* Tennyson finds himself in something of a dilemma. If Hallam intervenes in Victorian culture as a spiritual guide and mediator, then the poem borders on heresy, for it is in the Roman tradition that the saints maintained this sort of autonomy. The orthodox understanding of the dead in the Church of England, however, denies the very individuality that Tennyson hopes to preserve. The High Churchman Walter Farquhar Hook addresses the Anglican view of the dead in a sermon delivered on All Saints' Day in 1849. He poses the question of what Anglicans mean when they speak of saints, and his answer follows:

> All, then, who die in the Lord, enter at once into blessedness and rest; though absent from the body, they are present with the Lord: in the very act of their justification, they hear their Lord say to them, "To-day shalt thou be with Me in Paradise." They are just men, men justified by their faith, made perfect by the Holy Spirit; they are Saints.
>
> (15)

Hook's definition removes all hierarchy from the saints by relegating all Christians to an equal position. For Tennyson to write of Hallam in these terms would be to admit that Hallam's life had no more significance than any other. He resolves this dilemma by maintaining the individualized identity of Arthur Hallam afforded by the Roman concept of sainthood but interpreting the canonization in secular terms.[12]

Having gone through multiple crises of doubt and nearly as many reaffirmations of faith, in poems 109-113, Tennyson finally defines how a secularized version of a saint works. Poem 109 offers up what some readers have recognized as perhaps the most cogent picture of Hallam in the poem. Culler, for instance, suggests that

> We are now getting for the first time an account of the qualities of the man whom we have, for a hundred sec-

tions, been lamenting. But [it] is only now that the poet can talk about him objectively—about his social and intellectual qualities, particularly about the wisdom he represented.

(184-185)

The poet's memory of Hallam seems anything but objective, however. Instead, it is a hagiographic memory of the man that seeks to demonstrate exactly how he will shape the future of English society. Hallam puts doubt to rest not by any supernatural, god-like power, but by the sheer force of "seraphic intellect" and "Impassion'd logic." Tennyson conjures before us an idealized version of Arthur Hallam as a man who demonstrates

> A love of freedom rarely felt,
>   Of freedom in her regal seat
>   Of England; not the schoolboy heat,
> The blind hysterics of the Celt.

(109, 13-16)

The first line of this quatrain exalts the love of freedom as one of the characteristics of the exemplar that Tennyson has created of Hallam. The second and third lines qualify the idea of freedom, locating it as something that belongs within the geo-political boundaries of the English state. Somehow—and Tennyson does not clearly define how this comes to be—Hallam synecdochically represents the entirety of British freedom and liberty.

Tennyson's point in cataloging these virtues appears only in the final quatrain. Here the narrator reasserts his own authority over memory, but in so doing, he illustrates a paradox that Nietzsche identifies as inherent in the effort of what he calls the "monumental historian" to find exemplars in the past. Tennyson's solace in this lyric and over the course of *In Memoriam* is "the knowledge that the great thing existed and was therefore possible, and so may be possible again" (Nietzsche 14). Yet even as Tennyson sets Hallam before us as the exemplar whose virtue must be repeated, the reality of Arthur Hallam fades from view. Nietzsche suggests that the search for exemplars fails because "if it [the past] is to give us strength . . . the individuality of the past [must be] forced into a general formula and all the sharp angles broken off for the sake of correspondence" (14). For Arthur Hallam to serve as an exemplar of civic virtue, he must be refashioned by the poet and forced into a myth of the repeatable. In the final quatrain of lyric 109, the narrator defines what will happen if the past does not serve the present:

> All these have been, and thee mine eyes
>   Have look'd on: if they look'd in vain,
>   My shame is greater who remain,
> Nor let thy wisdom make me wise.

(21-24)

By stating that "all these have been," Tennyson asserts an impossible past, claiming reality for the highly idealized portrait of Hallam that precedes these lines. At the same time, he identifies the cost of failing to recognize the repeatability of the past as a tremendous burden of shame.

In many ways, the next poem in the sequence (110—"Thy converse drew us with delight") seems simply to restate 109. Once again, Tennyson catalogs his friend's qualities, and as before, he defines Hallam's life in terms of civic virtue: Hallam's conversation becomes a beacon for those who listen to him (presumably the Cambridge Apostles); the mildness of his nature disarms both pride and, in a Miltonic gesture, the serpent himself; and sternness, flippancy, and foolishness all melt away in his presence. Two things, however, distinguish 110 from 109. The first occurs in the opening line—"Thy converse drew us with delight." This idea pulls Tennyson in two directions. As in 109, he looks backwards to assert his own control over the ravages of time, but these words also direct Tennyson's attention outward into a public sphere that does not exist in 109. Hallam's intellect receives an audience who, if they ignore his virtues, also deserve the ignominy that the narrator calls down upon himself in 109. This audience disappears from the text in line 13, but the presence of others suggests that Hallam's civic virtues have become a shaping force for the collective rather than serving only as a private model for the narrator.

The second important difference between 109 and 110 is that the latter defines what will happen when the audience succeeds in repeating the past. Tennyson declares that a "vague desire / That spurs an imitative will" (110, 19-20) arises out of love for Hallam. This final line seems an important one for, as Susan Shatto and Marion Shaw note, Tennyson adapted it from "Young is the grief I entertain," a lyric he subsequently dropped from *In Memoriam* (Shatto and Shaw 269). Structurally, "Young is the grief I entertain" is the exact opposite of 110. In it, the "imitative will" is not spurred by memory but by overwhelming grief: "Yet grief deserves a nobler name. / She spurs an imitative will" (5-6). When Tennyson moves this phrase to the end of 110, however, it functions quite differently. In the context of 110, it is not the grief occasioned by Hallam's absence that spurs the poet to imitation but the love generated by his presence felt through memory. In addition, this memory bears on the implied audience of the poem, those same people who sat in rapt attention listening to Hallam speak. The poet thus asserts his own authority over the memory of the figure who now intervenes not only in his own life but also in the lives of his contemporaries.

With poem 113, Tennyson carries forward the argument that Hallam's presence in the collective memory will help to determine the future course of the British Empire. In a spectacularly bold poetic maneuver, he projects the memory of his dead friend into the future, declaring what Hallam would have become had he lived. Tennyson's vision of the future suggests a deep-seated fear of the changes occurring in Victorian culture. The poet imagines a world in which various forces converge, where "licensed boldness" may gather force,

> Becoming, when the time has birth,
>   A lever to uplift the earth
> And roll it in another course,
> With thousand shocks that come and go,
>   With agonies, with energies,
>   With overthrowings, and with cries,
> And undulations to and fro.
>
> (14-20)

Here, Tennyson defines a social order threatened by a chaotic and catastrophic break from its own past; he imagines the end of a society that "had long assured the transmission and conservation of collectively remembered values" (Nora 7). Tennyson fails to specify precisely what forces occasion this rupture, but surely he has in mind lyric 21, a poem in which an imagined traveler critiques "private sorrow's barren song" (14) for its inability to address science, Chartism, and implicitly the crisis of faith that they engender. Perhaps ironically, in lyric 113 private sorrow's barren song now projects Hallam into the collective mind as an example of how memory might yield a conservative response to the upheaval occasioned by mass social change. In order for Hallam's death to have meaning, to afford a response both to the vision of a mechanized world devoid of God's presence and to the chaos brought about by Reform efforts, it must be transformed by the authority of the poet. Hallam must be canonized, changed into a perpetual presence who intervenes in Tennyson's world through the text of the poem. Only after the poet has wrestled with the concern that death may be the end of existence can he come to the point of declaring not only what Hallam was, but where that memory naturally leads:

> A life in civic action warm,
>   A soul on highest mission sent,
>   A potent voice of Parliament,
> A pillar steadfast in the storm.
>
> (113, 9-12)

Hallam inhabits the text, and by the authority of the poet he becomes all of this and more. Shaw and Shatto write of this passage that "The idea is: 'I may grow wise as a result of my sorrow, but you had wisdom in such abundance that it would have benefited not only myself, but also the entire nation in its coming troubles'" (270). Immortalized in the text and made a part of the collective memory of Victorian England, Hallam will benefit the nation in its coming trouble, for his presence demands an imitation that counters the forces that eventually lead to chaos.[13]

As Isobel Armstrong has pointed out, one of the tasks of *In Memoriam* is to "research into history and culture" by "[researching] into what remains of both geological and human 'remains'" (257). Lyrics 110-113 push even beyond "research" into the history and culture of a nation. Indeed, these lyrics posit that the very future of the British nation depends on remembering Arthur Hallam as the idealized figure that Tennyson creates in the poem. To this point, I have been tracing only one of several strategies that Tennyson uses to shape Hallam's memory, and if the strategy of canonization were the only way that Tennyson had to imagine how Hallam's life and death might bear on the collective memory, *In Memoriam* would offer simple, straightforward, deeply conservative politics. Canonization explicitly calls for a continuous repetition of the past, a repetition that assimilates all difference and resists the idea of forward progress. As such, it perpetuates a vision of the past that, as Michel Foucault has argued, attempts to guarantee the viability of the subject but ultimately creates a history that is, "for the subject in question, a place of rest, certainty, reconciliation, a place of tranquillized sleep" (14). The chaos that troubles *In Memoriam* endangers the subject; social and technological changes threaten to erase identity, and Nature itself seems to proclaim humans to be disposable. The canonization process holds these forces at bay by insisting that the past—or at least the idealized version of the past proclaimed by the person performing the canonization—continues to live on and replicate itself in the present. At the same time, however, it leaves the subject unable to move, caught up in the infinitely repeatable and so lulled to sleep.

In Memoriam, however, resists such an easy categorization as a conservative poem. The text ultimately does not offer any coherent vision of progress, but readers have sensed that the poem is not entirely written in service to conservative ideology.[14] Instead, multiple ways of framing Hallam's death that emerge in the poem pull the text in various directions simultaneously. Poem 63 of *In Memoriam* perhaps most clearly illustrates the point of conflict between the two different narrative strategies that Tennyson employs as he presents Hallam to the reading public:

> Yet pity for a horse o'er-driven,
>   And love in which my hound has part,
>   Can hang no weight upon my heart
> In its assumptions up to heaven;
> And I am so much more than these,
>   As thou, perchance, art more than I,
>   And yet I spare them sympathy,
> And I would set their pains at ease.
> So mayst thou watch me where I weep,
>   As, unto vaster motions bound,
>   The circuits of thine orbit round
> A higher height, a deeper deep.
>
> (1-12)

The point of the lyric can be defined analogically: *beasts: Tennyson:: Tennyson: Hallam.*

The first set of these terms sets up a narrative of progress that appears repeatedly in *In Memoriam,* for the relationship between the poet and the beasts fits into the framework afforded Tennyson both by pre-Darwinian evolutionary rhetoric and by the language of Christian typology. Where in lyrics 55 and 56 the scientific evidence of evolution creates tremendous doubt, here it logically provides a vision of progress, for the analogy between the beasts, Tennyson, and Arthur Hallam suggests the possibility of motion toward something that is both different and better in nature. This evolutionary rhetoric is closely allied with Christian typology in that both frameworks locate in the lower form of life the anticipation of the higher. Lyric 63 would thus seem to presage both the "working out the beast" of 118 and the "one far-off divine event, / To which the whole creation moves" of the Conclusion.

Yet even within this single lyric Tennyson refuses to commit himself entirely to a narrative of progress in which the motion of the human soul through different and better states parallels the motion of the human race. The word "perchance" hints at Tennyson's discomfort with the analogical structure set forth by lyric 63. This discomfort stems from the realization of the tremendous distance between the two friends if the terms of the analogy hold. Ultimately, Tennyson cannot bring himself to assert that Hallam is as different from himself as he is different from the beasts. Instead, he draws on a narrative of expansion captured by the rhetoric of sainthood in which the soul always remains recognizable as what it was in life. In this narrative, Hallam's soul expands to ever larger versions of itself, but the essence of his being never changes. Thus in the final quatrain, Tennyson fails to define the progress of the soul as the first half of the poem leads us to expect. Rather than changing in essence, the soul moves in widening circles, entering ever higher states while forever remaining recognizable as the same thing it was in life. This narrative of expansion thus remains deeply conservative, projecting into the future what amounts to little more than a larger version of the past. While both narratives anticipate progress, they define progress differently—the one open to and even welcoming change, the other insisting that progress entails creating ever larger and better versions of a static past.

Isobel Armstrong has rightly pointed out that what I am calling the narrative of progress in *In Memoriam* is itself a conservative strategy (260). At issue, however, is not whether Tennyson is a conservative poet. Instead, the question is whether Tennyson's conservatism seeks only to preserve the past or whether it can accommodate meaningful social change. Arguing that Tennyson's language opens the poem to an acceptance of "disembodied alterity," Julian Wolfreys notes that Tennyson repeatedly figures change using the paradoxical formula "from ___ to ___" ("from more to more," "from world to world," etc.) where both terms in the equation are identical (65-66). This formula, woven throughout *In Memoriam,* implies both geographical and temporal change yet "complete[s] the phrase by a kind of figural palindrome, so that the motion appears to recirculate, to return to its beginning point, to disrupt and thus paradoxically double itself in its own process" (64). In this repeated grammatical construction, Tennyson captures the dynamic of progress and conservation. Moreover, in the closing lyrics of *In Memoriam,* he extends the grammatical structure structure to the person of Arthur Hallam himself, arguing in effect that progress for England will involve a motion from Arthur Hallam to Arthur Hallam. In poem 128 Tennyson writes

> The love that rose on stronger wings,
>   Unpalsied when he met with Death,
>   Is comrade of the lesser faith
> That sees the course of human things.
>
>   (1-4)

Here the narrative of expansion created by the vertical motion of the soul is comrade to the narrative of progress that looks toward the future. The poem links the faith inspired by Hallam's canonization (the narrative of expansion) with the narrative of history that predicts the forward progress of the British Empire through time. The result is neither the pure conservative thought implied by the act of canonizing Arthur Hallam, nor a radical break from the past associated with the Chartist and Reform movements. Instead, by yoking together these two different responses to history, Tennyson charts a middle course (although one that always leans more towards stasis than to radical change—the forward-looking vision is the "lesser comrade" to the preservationist tendencies represented by the soul's vertical motion). The resulting vision of progressive conservatism ultimately allows for the gradual perfection and changing of the civic body only as it remembers and emulates the virtues that *In Memoriam* has attributed to Arthur Hallam.

This progressive conservatism finds its fullest expression in the epithalamium that ends *In Memoriam.* Here Tennyson makes transparent the process by which Arthur Hallam's life attains meaning after having been shrined in the public memory. As Tennyson begins the wedding song, he recalls the intervening years between Hallam's death and Cecilia Tennyson's marriage to Edmund Lushington:

> Nor have I felt so much of bliss
>   Since first he told me that he loved
>   A daughter of our house; nor proved
> Since that dark day a day like this;
> Tho' I since then have numbere'd o'er

> Some thrice three years: they went and
> came,
> Remade the blood and changed the frame,
> And yet is love not less, but more.
>
> ("Epilogue," 5-12)

Lines 9-12 find a natural image that captures the competing narratives of progress and expansion that I find at the heart of *In Memoriam.* The body replaces itself seemingly *ad infinitum* as cells die and regenerate. The material body of the present differs radically from the material body from just nine years earlier; it has been remade into something entirely new and different from what it once was. The self contained by that body, however, does not change in essence; it merely expands. The full implications of this way of thinking climax as Tennyson describes Lushington:

> thou art worthy; full of power;
> As gentle; liberal-minded, great,
> Consistent; wearing all that weight
> Of learning lightly like a flower.
>
> (37-40)

Lushington's wedding to Cecilia provides a fitting conclusion to Tennyson's canonization of Hallam because Lushington embodies the pattern of emulation that Tennyson identifies as the means by which England will progress into the future. In a sense, Lushington fulfills the promise of *In Memoriam* because he follows the example set by Hallam, and by doing so he repeats the values that Hallam represents. Because Tennyson can paint Lushington in these terms, the wedding takes on the appearance of the body renewing itself; the love between the happy couple reproduces the same structure that began with Hallam's declaration of love for Emily Tennyson.

Epithalamium naturally leads to the most visible, tangible form of progress through the procreative act, and as the poem closes, Tennyson imagines how the offspring of Edmund Lushington and Cecilia Tennyson might lead into the future. The child serves as a "closer link / betwixt us and the crowning race" (127-28), and procreation establishes a chain from the present into the future. That future, however, remains inextricably bound with the past that Tennyson has created through his memories, and the society that he envisions will be peopled with those who look for all intents and purposes exactly like Arthur Hallam:

> For all we thought and loved and did,
> And hoped, and suffer'd, is but seed
> Of what in them is flower and fruit;
> Whereof the man, that with me trod
> This planet, was a noble type
> Appearing ere the times were ripe.
>
> (134-39)

The agricultural image illustrates Tennyson's vision of progress. If English society in the 1840s is the seed of a higher and better society of which Hallam is an early representative, then future progress occurs through the replication of something that has already happened. The "one far-off divine event, / To which the whole creation moves" (143-44) becomes an expansion through the civic body of the virtues that Hallam has already exemplified, a collective movement towards the virtues of the past that Tennyson has idealized in the poem.

Canonizing an individual necessarily asserts that a collective body should remember an individual as a moral exemplar, a figure whose virtues shape the future by requiring repetition through imitation. In some respects, canonization as Tennyson uses it participates in a larger Victorian cult of the hero. Tennyson, however, adopts a very specific use of the past that differentiates his thought from that of someone like Thomas Carlyle. If we accept Foucault's claim that Nietzsche was one of the prime movers in reorganizing our conception of history (14), then Nietzsche himself, as one who looked back from a close distance, may offer the best lens through which to understand Tennyson and his contemporaries. In his effort to repair history, Carlyle adopts what Nietzsche calls an "antiquarian" mode of history that takes comfort in finding its origins deep in the past; they find meaning in "the feeling of the tree that clings to its roots [and] the happiness of knowing one's growth to be not merely arbitrary and fortuitous but the inheritance, the fruit and blossom, of a past that does not merely justify but crowns the present" (Nietzsche 19).[15] Tennyson in contrast adopts Nietzsche's monumental mode of history, seeking not so much to find origins but to create exemplars for the benefit of Victorian England.

One of the images that Carlyle uses to describe his use of history is the river: "The poorest Day that passes over us is the conflux of two Eternities; it is made up of currents that issue from the remotest Past, and flow onwards into the remotest Future" ("Signs of the Times" 441). In an antiquarian mode, Carlyle's historian seeks properly to understand the past as a continual flow of greatness from hero to hero. In contrast, Tennyson speaks as Nietzsche's monumental historian, and the source of the river that is the past is of far less importance than Tennyson's own remaking of that source. For Tennyson, secularizing the form of sainthood and canonizing Arthur Hallam as an exemplar of civic virtue become a way of asserting his own authority to remake the past for the present and by so doing to shape the collective memory and guide British society into the future. Canonization, however, does not represent the only method by which Tennyson attempted to shape the collective mind of British society (although it does reappear, most notably in the **"Ode on the Death of the Duke of Wellington"** where the hagiographic rhetoric is perhaps even more pronounced than in the tribute to Arthur Hallam). We also see Tennyson making extensive use, for instance, of legend, most obviously in **"The Epic/Morte D'Arthur"** and the various editions of the *Idylls of the King.* The canonization of Arthur Hallam, then, forms but one piece in a larger project of shaping the collective memory by creating exemplars whose virtues, when idealized and molded by the poet, counter forces of radical social upheaval by offering a vision of progressive conservatism—a motion into the future that proceeds by way of the poet's re-creation of the past. Through the memory of these moral exemplars, Tennyson spurs the imitative will not only of himself but of his entire culture.[16]

Notes

1. Alan Sinfield recognizes this quality of the poem, referring to Hallam as "Arthur" in order to "avoid suppressing the intimacy of the poem" (*Alfred Tennyson* 117).

2. Michael Tomko, for instance, reads *In Memoriam* not "as a journal, a grief observed, but as a text offering an explanation and an interpretation, to the nation" (114). Similarly, Kirstie Blair analyzes the poem as potentially both healing the nation by assuaging Victoria's grief over the death of the Prince Consort and harming it by allowing the Queen to dwell excessively on her grief.

3. For a further discussion of the possibility of a "private diary," I refer readers to Avishai Margalit (157-59).

4. All references to *In Memoriam* are from the Shatto and Shaw edition. Citations will be given in text with stanza number followed by line numbers.

5. Although itself not a pastoral elegy, *In Memoriam* engages extensively with the conventions of that poetic form. Ian H. C. Kennedy reminds us that Tennyson uses the conventions of the genre, "subverting and exploding the existing forms so that he can re-mold them into the new shapes he needs to express himself and his times" (351). The secular canonization that I will be describing is one way in which Tennyson extends the typical apotheosis that occurs in the pastoral elegy; it is both counterpart to and rewriting of the convention of elevating the deceased to the heavens as a star (a tradition which, as Anna Henchman notes, also finds its way into *In Memoriam* [41-42]).

6. I use the term "Anglican" guardedly throughout this article to represent the wide range of theological positions that fell under the authority of the Established Church. I recognize that many of the people to whom I apply this blanket term would not readily have accepted it.

7. It is worth noting that the publication of Hallam's literary remains was typical. During the time be-

tween Hallam's death in 1832 and the publication of *In Memoriam,* the *Remains* of Coleridge, Hazlitt, Hurrell Froude, and a host of other less recognizable figures made their way into print.

8. The fear that Rome would somehow be left as a trace on the body of the English was quite common in the travel narratives of the time; as just one example, Selena Martin asks whether it is possible to live among the Italian Catholics "without catching some contamination?" (309). Although published five years before Hallam's death, Martin's question anticipates similar responses to Roman Catholicism in the travel narratives of the 1830s and 1840s.

9. Alan Sinfield discusses the excess of the language of *In Memoriam* at some length in chapters 2 and 3 of *The Language of Tennyson's* In Memoriam.

10. By describing Hallam's corpse in language inflected with the rhetoric of sainthood, Tennyson places his relationship with his friend in a long-standing tradition of eroticized devotion associated with the saints, and recognizing this language may contribute to the ongoing discussion of Tennyson's sexuality—see Craft, Nunokawa, and Kolb among others. Unfortunately, limitations of space prohibit me from pursuing that line of inquiry here.

11. Darrel Mansell has written at some length about the Tennyson's misuse and misrepresentation of the actual church in which Hallam's body lies.

12. My intent here and elsewhere is not to call into question Tennyson's response to Anglican theology as a whole; instead, I am suggesting that Tennyson secularizes the Roman Catholic response to the dead because Anglican theology (as Hook's sermon illustrates) offers no response suitable to Tennyson's needs. For a fuller discussion of Tennyson's vacillation between orthodox and heterodox theology see Tucker.

13. For an alternate reading of stanzas 109-113, I refer readers to Sinfield (*Alfred Tennyson,* 119-23). Sinfield argues that Tennyson is left with "no political programme" because the "earthly Hallam" fails to achieve bourgeois goals in Parliament (121-22), a reading of the poems that fails, I think, to account for the impact that Arthur has on the collective memory both within the text and (as Tennyson hopes) in Victorian culture.

14. Sinfield (*The Language of Tennyson's* In Memoriam) and Armstrong address the incoherence of the social vision of *In Memoriam* at length. Sinfield reads the poem as a necessarily incoherent picture of the future whereas Armstrong attributes the confused qualities of the texts to its status as a massive "double poem" (256).

15. Nietzsche's words here could be taken almost directly from Carlyle, whose invocation of Tree Igdrasil in *On Heroes* provides an apt metaphor of an organic historical growth (19).

16. I would like to thank Beverly Taylor, John McGowan, Antony H. Harrison, Jeanne Moskal, and William Harmon for reading early drafts of this article. In addition, I would like to thank Brent Kinser who has contributed greatly to my understanding of Thomas Carlyle. The comments of anonymous reviewers for *Christianity & Literature* have greatly shaped this article, and I am grateful for their insights.

Works Cited

Armstrong, Isobel. *Victorian Poetry: Poetry, Poetics, and Politics.* London: Routledge, 1993.

Aspinwall, Bernard. "Did Tennyson Consider Joining the Catholic Church in 1849?" *Notes and Queries* 27 (1980): 208-9.

Blair, Kirstie. "'Touching Hearts': Queen Victoria and the Curative Properties of *In Memoriam*." *Tennyson Research Bulletin* 7 (2001): 246-54.

Carlyle, Thomas. *On Heroes, Hero-Worship, and the Heroic in History.* 1841. Eds. Michael K. Goldberg, Joel J. Brattin, and Mark Engel. Berkeley: U of California P, 1993.

———. *Past and Present.* 1843. Ed. Richard D. Altick. New York: New York UP, 1977.

———. "Signs of the Times." *Edinburgh Review* 49 (1829): 439-59.

Craft, Christopher. "'Descend, Touch and Enter': Tennyson's Strange Manner of Address." *Genders* 1 (1988): 83-101.

Culler, A. Dwight. *The Poetry of Tennyson.* New Haven: Yale UP, 1977.

Eaton, Charlotte. *Rome in the Nineteenth Century: Containing a Complete Account of the Ruins of the Ancient City, the Remains of the Middle Ages and the Monuments of Modern Times: With Remarks on the Fine Arts, on the State of Society, and on the Religious Ceremonies, Manners and Customs of the Modern Romans: In a Series of Letters Written During a Residence at Rome in the Years 1817 and 1818.* 4th ed. 3 vols. Edinburgh, 1826.

Eliot, T. S. "In Memoriam." *Essays Ancient and Modern.* New York: Harcourt, Brace, 1936. 186-203.

Foucault, Michel. *The Archaeology of Knowledge.* Trans. A. M. Sheridan Smith. New York: Pantheon, 1972.

Hallam, Arthur. "The Influence of Italian Upon English Literature." *The Writings of Arthur Hallam.* Ed. T. H. Vail Motter. New York: Modern Language Association, 1943. 213-33.

Henchman, Anna. "'The Globe We Groan In': Astronomical Distance and Stellar Decay in *In Memoriam*." *Victorian Poetry* 41 (2003): 29-45.

Hood, James W. *Divining Desire: Tennyson and the Poetics of Transcendence.* Aldershot: Ashgate, 2000.

Hook, Walter Farquhar. *The Nonentity of Romish Saints and the Inanity of Romish Ordinances.* London, 1849.

Jones, John. "Popery a Novelty, and the Religion of the Reformed Church of England the Religion of Jesus Christ and His Apostles." *Ten Sermons on the Principal Errors of the Church of Rome: Preached in St. Andrew's Church, Liverpool.* Ed. James Haldane Stewart and Robert Peddler Buddicom. Liverpool, 1837. 1-23.

Joseph, Gerhard. *Tennysonian Love; the Strange Diagonal.* Minneapolis: U of Minnesota P, 1969.

Kennedy, Ian H. C. "*In Memoriam* and the Tradition of the Pastoral Elegy." *Victorian Poetry* 15 (1977): 351-66.

Kolb, Jack. "Hallam, Tennyson, Homosexuality and the Critics." *Philological Quarterly* 79 (2000): 365-96.

Mansell, Darrel. "Displacing Hallam's Tomb in Tennyson's *In Memoriam*." *Victorian Poetry* 36 (1998): 97-111.

Margalit, Avishai. *The Ethics of Memory.* Cambridge: Harvard UP, 2002.

Martin, Selena. *Narrative of a three years' residence in Italy, 1819-1822. With Illustrations of the Present State of Religion in that Country.* London, 1828.

Newman, John Henry. *Apologia Pro Vita Sua.* Ed. David J. DeLaura. New York: W. W. Norton, 1968.

———. "Via Media No. 1." *Tracts for the Times* 38 (1839): 1-12.

Nietzsche, Friedrich. *The Use and Abuse of History.* 2nd Revised Ed. Trans. Adrian Collins. New York: Liberal Arts, 1957.

Nora, Pierre. "Between Memory and History: *Les Lieux de Mémoire*." *Representations* 26 (1989): 7-24.

Nunokawa, Jeff. "*In Memoriam* and the Extinction of the Homosexual." *English Literary History* 58 (1991): 427-38.

Rev. of *An Inquiry into the Principal Points of Difference, Real or Imaginary, Between the Two Churches*, by David O'Croly. *Eclectic Review* 15 (1836): 1-29.

Ricks, Christopher, ed. *The Poems of Tennyson.* London: Longmans, 1969.

Seymour, Hobart. *A Public Exhibition of Relics at Rome, in a Letter from the Rev. M. Hobart Seymour to the Rev. Edward Nangle, M.A.* N.p., [1845?].

Shatto, Susan, and Marian Shaw. Commentary. *In Memoriam.* By Alfred Tennyson. Oxford: Clarendon, 1982. 157-302.

"Shrined." *The Oxford English Dictionary.* Online ed. 12 Dec. 2004.

Sinfield, Alan. *Alfred Tennyson.* Oxford: Blackwell, 1986.

———. *The Language of Tennyson's In Memoriam.* Oxford: Blackwell, 1971.

Tennyson, Alfred. *In Memoriam.* Ed. Susan Shatto and Marion Shaw. Oxford: Clarendon, 1982.

Tomko, Michael. "Varieties of Geological Experience: Religion, Body, and Spirit in Tennyson's *In Memoriam* and Lyell's *Principles of Geology.*" *Victorian Poetry.* 42.2 (2004): 113-33.

Tucker, Herbert F. *Tennyson and the Doom of Romanticism.* Cambridge: Harvard UP, 1988.

Wolfreys, Julian. "The Matter of Faith: Incarnation and Incorporation in Tennyson's *In Memoriam. Writing the Bodies of Christ: The Church from Carlyle to Derrida.* Ed. John Schad. Burlington: Ashgate, 2001. 59-74.

Zerubavel, Eviatar. *Time Maps: Collective Memory and the Social Shape of the Past.* Chicago: U of Chicago P, 2003.

Anna Jane Barton (essay date summer 2006)

SOURCE: Barton, Anna Jane. "'What Profits Me My Name?' The Aesthetic Potential of the Commodified Name in *Lancelot and Elaine.*" *Victorian Poetry* 44, no. 2 (summer 2006): 135-52.

[*In the following essay, Barton reads "Lancelot and Elaine" as Tennyson's reflection upon his own name and identity from the vantage point of a well-established, famous poet.*]

A kind of waking trance I have frequently had, quite up from boyhood, when I have been all alone. This has generally come upon me thro' repeating my own name two or three times to myself silently, til all at once, as it were out of the intensity of the consciousness of individuality, the individuality itself seemed to dissolve and fade away into boundless being, and this not a confused state, but the clearest of the clearest, the surest of the surest, the weirdest of the weirdest, utterly beyond words, where death was an almost laughable impossibility, the loss of personality (if so it were) seeming no extinction but the only true life.[1]

Tennyson's ability to put himself into a trance through the repetition of his own name is one of a number of autobiographical vignettes incorporated by his son into the first biography of the poet. By describing the dissolution of individuality into "boundless being," he consciously sets up a poetic that is hard to resist. A name, as the verbal and textual signifier of individual consciousness, works paradoxically as both the link and the barrier between inner self and external reality, figuring the self in the world and announcing its difference. Rather than removing the name so that he might dissolve into reality, the poet's solution to this paradox is to dwell upon it, making his name the site at which he is able to experience the "only true life." Through lyrical repetition, Tennyson's name is charmed into poetry, and it is poetry, figured by the name of Victoria's laureate, which provides a place in which a state "utterly beyond words" might be achieved.

There is much worth exploring in this piece of poetic mysticism, but what the poet fails to specify, and therefore what is most interesting, is what name he used. His story, which insists on the invocation of the name, fails to invoke the name that is at its center. The name that is not mentioned must, of course, be "Tennyson," but it is not until the alternatives are considered that it becomes clear how heavily the anecdote relies upon this assumption. In boyhood—when his waking trances began—"Tennyson" would not have been the name by which the poet was called. First the name of his father, then of his family collectively and also the name by which his eldest brother is most likely to have been known, "Tennyson" would have been anything but the signifier of the poet's individual personality, and it is far more probable that he would have been known to himself and others as "Alfred." But with "Alfred" at its center, the story does not work; the impressive weight and gentle lyricism of "Tennyson" finds a poor substitute in the insubstantial gallop achieved by the repetition of "Alfred" (and even "Alfred Tennyson" is awkward and unsatisfactory in this context). In one sense this is not important, and I am not interested in quibbling over the biographical facts of a story that has been most useful to critics (and to Tennyson himself) as illustrative of his poetic thought. However, rather than substituting "Alfred" for "Tennyson," it is more interesting to leave this story intact and to reconsider it as one which can only have been constructed and understood retrospectively by a poet who had already made a name for himself. It might be expected that for a poet's name to become a material, marketable product would be restrictive to the growth of the poet: there might be an expectation that the poet should work according to the criteria by which he made his name; and the existence of poet as brand name would certainly seem to compromise the value of art as separate from and above the utilitarian world of commerce.[2] However, the story of Tennyson's trances suggests that the opposite is the case. It is the existence of "Tennyson" as commodity—a household name—that allows it to assume its place, unspoken, at the center of his story. Its material status goes hand in hand with its disappearance from the narrative in a manner that reflects the loss of self through insistence on the material signifier of the self that the narrative describes. The name remains a site of potential aesthetic experience, but it does so only because it is both poetic signifier and material commodity.

In *The Radical Aesthetic* Isobel Armstrong attempts to renegotiate the category of the aesthetic, making a strong argument for its value in and beyond the field of cultural production. Addressing Marxist attacks on the aesthetic, she describes how aesthetic value, far from being separate from and irrelevant to material economy, relies absolutely on the systems of production from which "pure art" would disassociate itself and identifies the Victorian Period as one during which "the interdependence of intellectual and aesthetic culture, money and privilege was glaringly obvious."[3] Her argument focuses on the dependence of art on labor, concluding that "a 'pure' theory of art could arise only because mind is given status in a society which can use other people's bodies in vicarious labour" (p. 163). She suggests that, far from being a burden to the economy on which it depends, the "anti-economy" of the aesthetic (with its restricted production, circulation, and consumption) provides a vital space where the world of economy and commodity with which it has a material link, might refigure itself. In the same way that other people's bodies provide the economic opportunity for the aesthetic to set up its anti-economy, so the material commodity of Tennyson's brand name provided the laureate with a secure site within which he could dissolve himself into the aesthetic.

Armstrong's attempt to define the way this site functions has greatly influenced my reading of **"Lancelot and Elaine"** and is worth a brief summary. Her understanding of the aesthetic centers around the idea of play, which she describes as "a form of knowledge itself. Interactive, sensuous, epistemologically charged" (p. 37). "Play is a transitional stage between the situational constraints of childhood and the freedom of the adult" (p. 39). This "transitional stage" is the time during which the child, having been separated from its mother and the total subjectivity of infancy, learns to negotiate its subjectivity within the objective world.[4] In order to cope with the separation that marks the end of its infancy a child invests a material object with the subjective significance of its recently invaded "inner reality." This "transitional object, a thing of paradox, neither subject not object, opens up a third space, the site of play" (Armstrong, p. 39). This is essentially Tennyson's anecdote told in reverse: where the child is forced to move out into the objective world, Tennyson seeks to move back into a universal subjectivity. The paradox

that defines the transitional object of play is the same as the one through which Tennyson's name functions, separating and linking subjective and objective. It is the material status of the transitional object that makes it able to function as a site of aesthetic production.

Tennyson's own interest in names and naming provides numerous opportunities for an exploration of the ways in which his name enabled him to work. In **"Lancelot and Elaine"** he recycles the story of his boyhood trances into a simile for the experience of Elaine's father as he gazes upon the face of his dying daughter:

> As when we dwell upon a word we know,
> Repeating, till the word we know so well
> Becomes a wonder, and we know not why,
> So dwelt her father on her face, and thought
> 'Is this Elaine?'[5]

It is not surprising that Tennyson's anecdote about his own name found its way into the idyll the most preoccupied with the significance of names; however it is not only the subject matter that brings the one story to bear upon the other, but also a sympathy between the material and therefore aesthetic circumstances of the production of each.

The poem has been largely ignored by critical discussion of names and naming in favor of its predecessor **"The Lady of Shalott."** Readings of this poem tend to identify the lady's name as one of the prisons from which she is ultimately unable to escape, figuring it (contrary to what I have been suggesting) as restrictive and oppressive, and often relating this to latent anxieties within the Tennysonian poetic. Rather than contrasting my understanding of Tennyson's commodified poetic with these readings that identify Tennyson as caught up in anxieties surrounding his name, I think it is possible to understand both as products of the same aesthetic economy. **"Lancelot and Elaine,"** read as Tennyson's retelling of **"The Lady of Shalott"** at a point in his career when his name was no longer a source of anxiety but a secure creative space, suggests ways in which poetry might work within the material commodity of a name.

Writing in *Tennyson's Fixations,* his Lacanian study of Tennyson's early poetry, Matthew Rowlinson provides a coherent explanation of the way in which name and space work through **"The Lady of Shalott"**:

> I suggest that this whispered name, the name by which the Lady is known which is still not her name, is the curse under which she lives. For no one's name is really their own; Lacan's dictum has it that by virtue of the proper name, the subject is a slave of a discourse in a universal movement of which it already exists at birth. The poem signals this fact by giving the Lady the name of a place; by making her naming a *placing* of the subject in a space that precedes it. And the consti-

tution of this space as difference, as well as being the burden of the Lady's curse, is in effect that of the poem, in which the repeated rhyme "*Shalott/Camelot*" determines the whole scene of its representation.[6]

The Lady's name, more so than anything else, is what figures her for and conceals her from Camelot. By dwelling upon that name, or more specifically within it—climbing into a boat which has her name written on the prow—she is carried out into the world from which that name has kept her hidden. But this Camelot is not the location of "the only true life," but another world of hollow signs and signifiers and so the Lady's action proves fatal. As the boat travels down the river into the city, the Lady is reduced to the empty corpse of her name. Ann C. Colley recognizes this dilemma as Tennyson's own when she writes:

> It is as if Tennyson were attempting to use the poem as a vessel to rescue himself and his reader from an enclosed and image-bound landscape and move into a recognition of the non-representational. But, as much as he repeats the Lady's name, allows the sound of the refrain to resound, and, in the manner of the ancient sage, lets the poem revolve in itself, he cannot push the poem into a "Nameless" state.[7]

Colley places **"The Lady of Shalott"** in opposition to Tennyson's own experience of the "Nameless" (which he also reproduced in verse in **"The Ancient Sage"**[8]), the implication being that the poem is unable to achieve the vision of "the only true life" that Tennyson and the sage experienced through their trances. She understands **"The Lady of Shalott"** as exemplary of the irreconcilable paradox of poetry, which has always already failed in its attempt to reach a "Nameless" state by virtue of the "mortal limits" of the rhymes and words that are its materials: "The most that the poem, Tennyson, and the reader can do is dip 'into the abysm' beneath the rhyming shadow world" (p. 377). By referring to Tennyson's anecdote as a description of what **"The Lady of Shalott"** is unable to achieve, Colley provides an opportunity for comparison with **"Lancelot and Elaine,"** which is able to incorporate the very anecdote that is beyond the reach of its precursor poem.

The description of the Lord of Astolat gazing upon his daughter's face in **"Lancelot and Elaine"** forms interesting parallels with Lancelot's reaction to the Lady's corpse in the concluding lines of **"The Lady of Shalott"**:

> But Lancelot mused a little space;
> He said: 'She has a lovely face;
> God in his mercy lend her grace,
> The Lady of Shalott.'

> (ll. 168-171)

Read with the later poem in mind, the absence of the anecdotal simile becomes significant. Although Lancelot's attention to the Lady is singled out as more atten-tive than the superstitious horror of the residents of Camelot: "And they crossed themselves for fear, / All the knights at Camelot: / *But* Lancelot" [my italics], the result of his musings is disappointing. His bland observation, "She has a lovely face," is a conscious deflation suggesting that when Lancelot looks on the Lady's face and sees nothing more than her face, his gaze is somehow inadequate. He must call upon God to lend to her name and body the grace that his gaze is unable to supply. In **"Lancelot and Elaine"** the simile replaces Lancelot's appeal to God and participates in a transfiguration that precedes her death. It spills out into the narrative so that by dwelling upon the face as if it were a word, it is a word—his daughter's name—that becomes a wonder to the Lord of Astolat. He finds and loses her name in her face. The reader witnesses this loss in the Lord's question: "Is this Elaine?" This wondering invocation of her name releases Elaine from herself, whereas Lancelot's final naming of the Lady merely bows to the requirements of the poem's lyric refrain and imprisons the Lady within both name and poem. From this one example of Tennyson's altered approach towards his Lady and her name in the later poem, we can begin to see how **"The Lady of Shalott"** might be understood as expressing more specific anxieties within the historical context of its composition and publication.

"The Lady of Shalott" was included in Tennyson's *Poems* of 1832, the second volume of poems to be published under his name (his very first publication had been *Poems by Two Brothers* in 1827, which offered only the initials of each brother as a clue to the identity of the writer). That name was yet to provide any guarantee of material success and his publisher, Edward Moxon, required that he underwrite the publication costs. This was common practice for the publication of single-author poetry collections in the nineteenth century regardless of the notoriety of the poet. In *The Economy of Literary Form* Lee Erickson describes how the declining market for poetry contributed to the formation of the anti-economy of aesthetic production explored by Armstrong.[9] Removed from the economic sphere, poetry was forced to adopt a defensive value system by which its lack of success as a material commodity became indicative of its aesthetic worth. Tennyson's use of names and naming in **"The Lady of Shalott"** is an expression of his ambivalent relationship with his own name as poet, at the start of his career in this emergent cultural environment. On the one hand it conveys a need for his name to be made and known in order that he might escape from the shadows of which he is "half sick." But he is only "half sick," because on the other hand it communicates an anxiety, inspired by the aesthetic anti-economy which so influenced poetry in the nineteenth century, that by establishing his name he will undermine its aesthetic value and it will become a commodity from which he cannot escape. Anxiety triumphs in this earlier poem, transforming the two names—the name of the Lady and her poet—into a site where, as explained by Rowlinson and Colley, poetry itself is found to be inadequate.

In 1859, when **"Elaine"** was first published (Lancelot's name did not appear in the title until 1885), Tennyson's name had achieved the cultural, national, and commercial status that characterized the latter part of his career. Supporters of his poetry were dubbed "Tennysonians,"[10] his appointment as Victoria's laureate meant that his name carried the impressive weight of the Establishment at large, and the poetry to which he gave his name was guaranteed a degree of commercial success. Gerhard Joseph, in an article entitled "Commodifying Tennyson: The Historical Transformation of 'Brand Loyalty,'" examines the laureate's name as "brand." He uses Macmillan's inclusion of an edition of Tennyson's poems in their "net book" scheme as evidence that Tennyson was the first poet whose name was employed as a commercial brand. He then goes on to chart the evolution of the word "brand" from its medieval sense "as a non-commodifiable object/sign, one that is incommensurable and inalienable" that makes up Tennyson's understanding of Excalibur (Arthur's brand) in his *Idylls,* to the "Victorian sense of an author as consumable brand good" to which Tennyson himself was subject.[11] He writes:

> In the wake of such a development, we tend to experience even our most serious authors as products of the various entrepreneurial and professional activities that have combined to represent them rather than as figures prior to, figures somehow independent of such branded representations.
>
> (p. 141)

By tracing "the construction of the literary commodity against its medieval backformation," Joseph makes Tennyson an exemplary participant in Victorian cultural consumerism. His article provides convincing evidence for Tennyson's dependence on his name and although he suggests that the priority and independence of his work from that name is an ideal myth, he is not otherwise concerned with the poetic born of this commodification. **"Lancelot and Elaine,"** as a poem that occurs under the brands of Excalibur and Tennyson, exploits this poetic to the full and in doing so explores reflexively its confinement within the name of its author.

"Lancelot and Elaine" is all about names and naming. Taking up the story in Malory in which Lancelot, the knight whose name is most famous in and beyond Camelot, exchanges his shield for that of an unknown knight and adopts the favor of a lady in order to enter a tournament as an anonymous competitor, Tennyson builds it into a story in which both Lancelot and Elaine are doomed by their anonymity. His most significant addition to the plot is the history of the diamonds for which the tournament is fought:

> For Arthur, long before they crowned him King,
> Roving the trackless realms of Lyonesse,
> Had found a glen, grey boulder and black tarn.
> A horror lived about that tarn, and clave
> Like its own mists to all the mountain side:
> For here two brothers, one a king, had met
> And fought together; but their names were lost;
> And each had slain his brother at a blow
> And he, that once was king, had on a crown
> Of diamonds, one in front and four aside.
>
> (ll. 34-42)

Arthur steps on the king's skull in the dark, rescues the crown, and places it on his head. On doing so he hears voices murmuring, "Lo, thou likewise shall be king" (l. 55). Every year Arthur offers one of the diamonds from this crown as the tournament prize. Lancelot, having won the first four jewels in previous years, rides incognito to win the last of the diamonds from the crown of "the nameless king." The detail of the king's anonymity is stressed, not only by becoming the title by which he is known, but also through its apparently clumsy insertion into this narrative. It reads as a non-sequitur, patched into the narrative sequence with a redundant conjunction. However, this piece of poor narrative fluency indicates Tennyson's insistence on the inclusion of the king's namelessness and might even be understood to lend a precarious narrative power to this otherwise insignificant piece of plot. Tennyson is stating that the names of both brothers are lost to Arthur and to the reader, but his positioning of this refusal-to-name between the battle and the death means that the anonymity of the brothers is conferred on them as they fight, so that the death of each brother at the hands of the other seems almost to rely on their names having been lost to one another. We are encouraged to read these lines as signifying something like this: "For here two brothers, one a king, had met and fought together; but their names were lost; And *so* each had slain his brother at a blow." This, then, is an echo of the story of **"Balin and Balan,"** the brother knights who fight to the death because they fail to recognize each other. The weighty implications of name-loss in that idyll are brought to bear directly upon **"Lancelot and Elaine."**

Elaine's name is not lost; it is never enough in her possession for her to be able to lose it. Her failure to fully establish herself makes the games she plays vulnerable to corruption and causes them to descend into a fatal pathology. Her precarious relationship with her name is established at the very beginning of the poem:

> Elaine the fair, Elaine the lovable,
> Elaine, the lily maid of Astolat,
> High in her chamber up a tower to the east
> Guarded the sacred shield of Lancelot.
>
> (ll. 1-4)

This triple invocation works as a response to an unspoken question about this heroine's identity. Narrating the story of his "waking trance" Tennyson did not need to state his name even once; in contrast the poem's narrator needs to say "Elaine" three times, each time supplying a qualifying piece of information, before he is able to begin his narrative. Elaine has not made her name her own, it is so insubstantial that it must be coupled with the name of her home before it is sufficient to bring her into being. Like **"The Lady of Shalott,"** this name, "the name by which the lady is known that is still not her name, is the curse under which she lives," but in this later poem the emphasis has shifted from the curse of a name, to the curse of a name that is not one's own.

When she next appears in the poem her name is again qualified by home and parentage:

> And close behind them stept the lily maid
> Elaine, his daughter: mother of the house
> There was not.
>
> (ll. 175-177)

Elaine, her father, and brothers are introduced to Lancelot as a family, but the absent wife and mother serves to unsettle her identity within that unit. The enjambment of the clause that informs of the mother's absence encourages us to misread the passage and to make Elaine both daughter and mother of the house. Her name, which should separate her from her mother, conflates their identities, destabilizing her objective existence and becoming an unsafe place for her to play.

In its unstable state, Elaine's name is readily available as the plaything of others. It becomes an object of genial speculation in the conversation of Sir Torre and Sir Lancelot:

> 'And you shall win this diamond,—as I hear
> It is a fair large diamond,—if ye may,
> And yield it to this maiden, if ye will.'
> 'A fair large diamond,' added plain Sir Torre,
> 'Such be for queens and not for simple maids.'
> Then she, who held her eyes upon the ground,
> Elaine, and heard her name so tost about,
> Flushed slightly at the slight disparagement.
>
> (ll. 226-233)

Again her name must be stated: so insignificant has her presence been in the preceding exchange between Lancelot and his new acquaintances that there is a danger of her disappearing altogether. This lack of physical substance becomes her defining characteristic; the lily white of her purity doubles as a ghostly pallor. The sound of her name brings her some brief color (color that is only ever lent to her by the attentions of somebody else: she blushes when addressed by Lancelot and when kissed by her brother), but her discomfort at its use in such games makes her no less vulnerable. It is following this acknowledgement of her dangerous anonymity that she gazes upon Lancelot and so falls in love with him:

> the lily maid Elaine,
> Won by the mellow voice before she looked,
> Lifted her eyes, and read his lineaments.
>
> . . . . .
>
> Marred as he was, he seemed the goodliest man
> That ever among ladies ate in hall,
> And noblest, when she lifted up her eyes.
> However marred, of more than twice her years,
> Seamed with an ancient swordcut on the cheek,
> And bruised and bronzed, she lifted up her eyes
> And loved him, with that love that was her doom.
>
> (ll. 241-259)

The ambiguity of line 253 reveals the reason for her attraction. Elaine does not love Lancelot in spite of his markedness, as the line initially suggests (i.e., "Even though he was marred, he seemed") but because of it ("Thus marred, he seemed"). It is this that her gaze and the gaze of the poem dwells upon, the marks on his flesh that spell out his substantial existence, that are the opposite of Elaine's own youthful pallor. Through her rapt attention to Lancelot's physicality, Elaine is able to bring life to him:

> And all night long his face before her lived,
> As when a painter, poring on a face,
> Divinely through all hindrance finds the man
> Behind it, and so paints him that his face,
> The shape and colour of a mind and life,
> Lives for his children, ever at its best
> And fullest; so the face before her lived.
>
> (ll. 329-335)

This extended simile is another retelling of the story of Tennyson's trances: rapt attention to the material surface of an object brings knowledge of the life beyond it. In this instance Elaine becomes the artist whose love, in the form of her devoted gaze, brings truth to her art.[12]

However, in the absence of Lancelot and without even the knowledge of his name Elaine can move no further than the world of signs and symbols. The paradoxical nature of the transitional object comes into play and what should have been her link with the "outer" world becomes a barrier against it. Armstrong writes: "The transitional object can be part of a continuum which includes madness. . . . When the transitional stage goes badly the toleration of anxiety and ambiguity passes over into fetishizing and persecution" (p. 40). The object in question is Lancelot's shield, left behind with Elaine in order to achieve his own anonymity as he jousts for the diamond of the nameless king.[13] Elaine's gaze is transferred from the lines that mark Lancelot's face to the symbolic text of his decorated shield:

> read the naked shield,
> Now guessed a hidden meaning in his arms,
> Now made a pretty history to herself

Of every dint a sword had beaten in it

    . . . . .

. . . so she lived in fantasy.

(ll. 16-27)

Thus she involves herself in the transitional play of the aesthetic, linking subjectivity to objectivity through the material sign. But Elaine's game is unsafe and her imagination transforms the communal language of the shield's crest into her own personal fantasy.

Elaine then comes to fetishize the shield, building sign upon sign:

Then fearing rust or soilure fashioned for it
A case of silk, and braided thereupon
All the devices blazoned on the shield
In their own tinct, and added of her wit,
A border fantasy of branch and flower.

(ll. 7-11)

Rather than integrating her into a society in which signs form the basis of communal knowledge, her repetitive attentions to the shield possess it for the subjective self that she can no longer escape. Distancing herself from her home and family, she closets herself away with it in her tower chamber:

           day by day,
Leaving her household and good father, climbed
That eastern tower, and entering barred her door.

(ll. 13-15)

Her play has become anti-social and, as such, it fails to provide a constructive transition into a mature reality. When Lancelot leaves a second time, taking his shield with him, Elaine remains isolated within her subjective fantasy:

  So in her tower alone the maiden sat:
His very shield was gone; only the case,
Her own poor work, her empty labour, left.
But still she heard him, still his picture formed
And grew between her and the pictured wall.

(ll. 982-986)

By leaving his shield in Astolat while he competes in the tournament, Lancelot seals his own fate as well as that of Elaine.[14] Lancelot seeks anonymity in an ill-conceived attempt to escape from the world of the sign with which he has become dissatisfied. His dissatisfaction stems from Guinevere who leads him to believe that his name is working to threaten his integrity and that he must therefore compete against it in order to re-establish a reality beyond the sign. However, at the outset Lancelot has confidence in the civilized community of names in which he lives. Reasoning Guinevere out of her fear that their affair will be suspected if he re-

mains with her rather than accompanying Arthur to the tournament, he gives examples of the safe association of their names:

        many a bard, without offence,
Has linked our names together in his lay,
Lancelot, the flower of bravery, Guinevere,
The pearl of beauty: and our knights at feast
Have pledged this union, while the King
Would listen smiling.

(ll. 111-116)

The bard's song, though not repeated for the reader, offers an example of a social lyric that would tell the story of Camelot to itself and so repeat itself into being within its community of listeners. The union of Lancelot and Guinevere's names within these songs and in the formal pledges of the knights offers a reality to which their subjects can aspire.[15] Lancelot recognizes Camelot, under the benign auspices of Arthur, to be a world within which names function constructively.

This Camelot, having evolved from the Camelot of **"The Lady of Shalott"** into a city whose material signs construct a living reality, is a site of communal play.[16] Like the tournaments it hosts, the games played within it can only work creatively by adhering to certain rules. As Armstrong has pointed out, rules are an essential part of what enables play to function in a social context (p. 39). By deceiving the king and pursuing an illicit affair with Guinevere, Lancelot has broken the rules of the game that ensured his name's safety.

His behavior breeds gossip, and it is the use of their names in this informal insidious language that the Queen fears:

'Why go ye not to these fair jousts? The knights
Are half of them our enemies, and the crowd
Will murmur, "Lo the shameless ones, who take
Their pastime now the trustfull King is gone!"'

(ll. 98-101)

In contrast to the public songs and pledges, these private utterances, unsanctioned by Camelot, are unsafe. Later in the narrative, when news of Lancelot and Elaine reaches Camelot, gossip is again the cause of the queen's distress: "All ears were pricked at once, all tongues were loosed: / 'The maid of Astolat loves Sir Lancelot, / Sir Lancelot loves the maid of Astolat'" (ll. 719-721). On this occasion its dangerous name games are exposed. Taking advantage of the verbal similarity of "Astolat" and "Lancelot," the names of subject and object are exchanged in a simple but pernicious word play. The misuse of names signals a threat to the form and function of the society that they have built.

Having acknowledged the power of this word play and determined that Lancelot cannot stay with her, Guinever comes up with an expedient motive for Lancelot's late arrival at the tournament:

'we hear it said
That men go down before your spear at a touch,
But knowing you are Lancelot; your great name,
This conquers: hide it therefore; go unknown.'

(ll. 147-150)

By accepting her false pretext, Lancelot takes on Guinevere's guilty fear of names. He departs abruptly, "Wroth at himself. Not willing to be known" (l. 159). His anonymity is linked with his shame and self-hatred rather than a desire for "gain of purer glory" as Guinevere later claims (l. 584). As he rejects his name and leaves in search of the diamond of the nameless king, Lancelot does not free himself from the deceptive signifiers that held his subjective self captive from reality, rather he exiles himself from the secure site within which he had been able to play out his existence.

On first meeting him, the Lord of Astolat asks for the two names that Lancelot has recently left behind: "'Whence comest thou, my guest, and by what name / Livest between the lips?'" His plain questions establish Astolat as another stronghold of the name. In contrast, Lancelot's sibylline response reveals the semantic crisis into which his anonymity has led him:

'Known am I, and of Arthur's hall, and known,
What I by mere mischance have brought, my shield.
But since I go to joust as one unknown
At Camelot for the diamond, ask me not,
Hereafter ye shall know me—and the shield—
I pray you lend me one, if such you have,
Blank, or at least with some device not mine.'

(ll. 187-193)

In this tortuous mumble, Lancelot grapples with the absence of his name; his stammering demonstrates the uncomfortable loss of the signifier.

He regains his eloquence when asked by Lavaine to 'tell . . . Of Arthur's glorious wars' (l. 284). Lancelot's response is written by Tennyson as reported speech, and the voices of poet and knight combine in a beautiful passage of poetry composed out of names:

And Lancelot spoke
And answered him at full, as having been
With Arthur in the fight which all day long
Rang by the white mouth of the violent Glem;
And in the four loud battles by the shore
Of Dunglas; that on Bassa; then the war
That thundered in and out the gloomy skirts
Of Celidon the forest; and again
By castle Gurnion . . .

. . . . .

And at Caerleon had he helped his lord,
When the strong neighings of the wild white Horse
Set every gilded parapet shuddering;
And up in Agned-Cathregonion too,
And down the waste sand-shores of Trath Treroit.

(ll. 284-300)

Proof of Arthur's power is provided by this epic list; Camelot is revealed as having been founded on a poetic of names. Within this poetic Lancelot can speak freely and well, comfortable with the exotic names that have become real to him through numerous retellings of the legend of his king's rise to power.[17] But he fails to understand the importance of the story he tells and distances himself still further from its poetic by giving up his shield, material symbol of his name and the protection it offers, in exchange for the shield of Sir Torre. He then accepts Elaine's favor as further defence against recognition. Thus, armed with a blank shield and wearing the red sleeve of an anonymous maiden, he departs for Camelot.

In the tournament Lancelot is brought down by the name he has rejected. The tourney-field is a playground made up of the material signifiers of helms and shields and so Lancelot's separation from his name becomes a threat to his life.[18] On two occasions Lancelot's identity is suspected, first by his family—"and one said to the other, 'Lo! / What is he? I do not mean the force alone— / The grace and versatility of the man! / Is it not Lancelot?'"—and then by Arthur, "'So great a knight as we have seen today / He seemed to me another Lancelot— / Yea, twenty times I thought him Lancelot'" (ll.468-471, 531-533). But his blank shield and Elaine's red sleeve present to them a more certain reality than the deeds that hint at his identity. His deeds are such that he at first seems to prove himself without need of his name—"little need to speak, / Of Lancelot in his glory!" (ll. 461-462)—to have fought through to the "purer glory" of a reality beyond the sign. But he is eventually brought down by an attack from his own family:

a fury seized them all,
A fiery family passion for the name
Of Lancelot, and a glory one with theirs

. . . . .

. . . so they overbore
Sir Lancelot and his charger, and a spear
Pricked sharply his own cuirass, and the head
Pierced through his side.

(ll. 475-489)

The knight's name behaves like a weapon against its subject. Lancelot having been diminished by the lack of it, it proves more than his equal: he is wounded not so much by his brothers but by the power of his own name.

Lancelot's final soliloquy is an unsuccessful rendition of Tennyson's own encounter with his name:

Why did the King dwell on my name to me?
Mine own name shames me, seeming a reproach

. . . . .

For what am I? what profits me my name
Of greatest knight? I fought for it, and have it:
Pleasure to have it, none; to lose it, pain
Now grown part of me: but what use in it?

(ll. 1391-1405)

Dwelt upon by Arthur, it cannot "become a wonder" or a divine link to the "only true life"; instead it is a failed signifier, a burdening reminder of his own failure to live up to the reality that it offered. As such it cannot perform its lyric function and Lancelot is left obsessively pacing about his name, unable to move beyond it.

The pathology into which Elaine has fallen is communicated in a fatal lyric. She becomes a poet, and the song that she composes, "The Song of Love and Death," works to confuse its two subjects through a kind of mournful word play that confounds its own logic and causes the death of the singer:[19]

'Sweet love, that seems not made to fade away,
Sweet death, that seems to make us loveless clay,
I know not which is sweeter, no, not I.

'I fain would follow love, if that could be;
I needs must follow death, who calls for me;
Call and I follow, I follow! Let me die.'

(ll. 1006-11)

The obsessive repetition of "love" and "death" forms an instance in lyric poetry of the pathological dwelling on the signifier that characterizes Elaine's relationship with Lancelot's shield. Like Lancelot, Elaine fails to replicate successfully Tennyson's waking trance. She lacks the material security of Tennyson's name and the charmed possibilities offered by its lyrical repetition. Where Tennyson attains a glimpse of "the only true life," from which he then returns, Elaine sings herself to death.

Like Tennyson, it is only retrospectively that Lancelot and Elaine begin to be reconciled to the named poetic from which their story is constructed. The poem's last lines predict Lancelot's return to a right relationship with his name:

So groaned Sir Lancelot in his remorseful pain,
Not knowing he would die a holy man.

(ll. 1417-18)

This brief assurance of redemption seems redundant to the story that has been told, weakening its impact by revealing its effect on Lancelot to be temporary. As such the story becomes another game, played from the material security of Lancelot's legendary name, a security that, in these final lines, Tennyson reveals to be comparable to that of his own. His holiness implies a dissolution of self that might make his death a "laughable impossibility" that will in turn be preserved by his name.

In death, Elaine's name achieves the material substance that enables it to exist as poetry:

Then Arthur spake among them, 'Let her tomb
Be costly, and her image thereupon,
And let the shield of Lancelot at her feet
Be carven, and her lily in her hand.
And let the story of her dolorous voyage
For all true hearts be blazoned on her tomb
In letters gold and azure!'

(ll. 1328-34)

Her tomb, the solid artifact of her name, lends her the significance that she was unable to achieve in life. Her name, and the words and symbols that now belong to it, are carved in stone. Elaine's posthumous fame allows Tennyson to play within her name in the way that she herself could not. In **"The Lady of Shalott"** the fate of the Lady mirrored Tennyson's own anxieties about his anonymity; by the time he comes to write **"Lancelot and Elaine"** he is able to approach the same story retrospectively, from the material security of his established status. Her story is still in some sense his own, and in his ability to tell it he has the advantage over both his hero and heroine, living through his name to the point at which he is able to reflect playfully upon it, creating a poetic by repeating his own name to himself.

Notes

1. Cited by Hallam Lord Tennyson in *Tennyson, A Memoir,* 2 vols. (London, 1897), 1:320.

2. In his article, "Tennyson's *Idylls,* Pure Poetry and the Market," *SEL* 37 (1997): 783-803, Dino Franco Felluga writes, "'Pure Poetry' was defined by both its advocates and its persecutors as going against market concerns and the governing logic of nineteenth century society—political economy" (p. 783). Although my understanding of "Lancelot and Elaine" diverges from his reading of the *Idylls* as a partially successful attempt to accommodate the "real" within the "ideal," Felluga gives a relevant insight into the way that poetry was viewed by Victorian commercial society.

3. Isobel Armstrong, *The Radical Aesthetic* (London: Blackwell, 2000), p. 3.

4. Armstrong bases her understanding of play as defined by D. W. Winnicott in *Playing and Reality* (London: Routledge, 1992), who writes, "On the basis of playing is built the whole of man's experimental experience. No longer are we either extrovert or introvert. We experience life in the area of transitional phenomena, in the exciting interweave of subjectivity and objective observation, and in an area that is intermediate between the inner reality of the individual and the shared reality of the world that is external to individuals" (p. 64).

5. "Lancelot and Elaine," ll. 1020-24. *The Poems of Tennyson,* ed. Christopher Ricks, 3 vols. (Berkeley: Univ. of California Press, 1987).

6. Matthew Rowlinson, *Tennyson's Fixations, Psychoanalysis and the Topics of the Early Poetry* (Univ. Press of Virginia, 1994), p. 82.

7. Ann C. Colley, "The Quest for the 'Nameless' in Tennyson's 'The Lady of Shalott,'" *VP* 23 (Winter 1985): 377-378.

8. Tennyson's description of his boyhood trances in "The Ancient Sage" transcribes his anecdote more exactly:

> And more, my son! for more than once when I
> Sat all alone, revolving in myself
> The word that is the symbol of myself,
> The mortal limit of the Self was loosed,
> And past into the Nameless, as a cloud
> Melts into Heaven. I touched my limbs, the limbs
> Were strange not mine—and yet no shade of doubt,
> But utter clearness, and through loss of Self
> The gain of such large life as matched with ours
> Were Sun to spark—unshadowable in words,
> Themselves but shadows of a shadow-world.
>
> (ll. 229-239)

Tennyson also provides a footnote to the poem: "This is also a personal experience I have had more than once." The passage in "Lancelot and Elaine" is more circumspect and its relationship to Tennyson's experience has not been recognized. However, its similarity to the lines in "The Ancient Sage" can be seen to strengthen its own links to the original anecdote and the two passages together suggest the significance of the trances to Tennyson's poetic thought.

9. Lee Erickson, *The Economy of Literary Form, English Literature and the Industrialization of Publishing 1800-1850* (Baltimore: Johns Hopkins Univ. Press, 1996).

10. In an unsigned article, published in the *National Review* in October 1859, Walter Bagehot wrote: "Everybody admires Tennyson now; but to admire him fifteen years or so ago, was to be a 'Tennysonian'" (*Tennyson, The Critical Heritage,* ed. John D. Jump [New York: Routledge, 1967], p. 216).

11. Gerhard Joseph, "Commodifying Tennyson: The Historical Transformation of 'Brand Loyalty,'" *VP* 34 (1996): 134.

12. The truth of Elaine's love is revealed to Lancelot through a similar reading of the surface of her face:

> his large black eyes,
> Yet larger through his leanness, dwelt upon her,

Till all her heart's sad secret blazed itself
In the heart's colours on her simple face.

(ll. 829-833)

Lancelot's attentive gaze is then repeated by Elaine's father as he dwells on the face of his dying daughter.

13. For a detailed account of the symbolic significance of shields in Arthurian England, see Michael J. O'Shea, "Armorial Bearings in *The Idylls of the King,*" *VP* 21 (1983): 393-402.

14. Margaret Homans addresses Lancelot's relationship with his name in her article "Tennyson and the Spaces of Life," *ELH* (1979): 693-709. She writes: "He [Lancelot] has created a name for himself as much as Arthur creates Pelleas as part of his Order, but the reputation of a knight called Lancelot, who wears Lancelot's armor and wields his sword, is no longer connected to the man himself" (p. 703). See also O'Shea, p. 400 for an account of Lancelot's heraldic anonymity.

15. In *Through the Vision of the Night: A Study of Source, Evolution and Structure in Tennyson's* Idylls of the King (Edinburgh: Edinburgh Univ. Press, 1980), J. M. Gray incorporates the *Idylls'* songs into his evolutionary model: "Each song seems to grow from its context while enlarging it" (p. 100). His argument provides an interesting comparison between the ways that Arthur's Camelot and Victoria's England constructed themselves.

16. The existence of Tennyson's Camelot as a place of transition is an interesting one that has been taken up by a number of critics. Homans writes: "Between 'from the great deep' and 'to the great deep' Arthur must widen for himself a space to live. He must wedge a discontinuity between origins and aims, between past and present" (p. 694) and in "Epistemology and Empire in *The Idylls of the King,*" *VP* 30 (1992): 387-400, Ian McGuire argues, as I do about Elaine's death, that Camelot's failure is inevitable, "relying as it does on the indefinite extension of the transitional period of male adolescence" (p. 387). When talking about the *Idylls* in relation to the age in which he was living, Tennyson himself is recorded as having said: "All ages are ages of transition, but this is an awful moment of transition" (*Memoir,* 1:317).

17. In an article entitled "Tennysonian Topography," *Leeds Studies in English* 18 (1987): 55-69, W. Nash addresses Tennyson's use of place names in the *Idylls.* He argues that Tennyson is less specific than Malory in his description of Arthurian geography, freeing it from "toponymic reference" because "there is no part of speech more limited and

concrete in reference than the proper noun. A name exclusively denotes and in doing so excludes the mysteries and multiplicities of association. . . . For this reason the proper noun is per se anti-poetic" (p. 68). His view replicates the anxieties about names that I have associated with Tennyson's earlier career and his argument provides a useful counter to my own. Whereas he describes the free play of poetry as providing an escape from names, I would suggest that, just as Tennyson's narratives play within the multiplicitous and mysterious names of Arthurian England, the free play of poetry is most successfully achieved within and as part of names and naming.

18. In Malory, the jousting knights challenge each other to "play" and tournaments function throughout the *Idylls* as creative games, sporting conflict that nonetheless effect the chivalric structure of Camelot. In *The Fall of Camelot* (Cambridge, Massachusetts: Belknap Press, 1973), John D. Rosenburg relates these games to Tennyson's poetry: "The only sharply defined feature is the harsh consonantal clash of the words themselves" (p. 97).

19. It is interesting to compare Elaine's death song with the song of Vivien in the preceding idyll:

> In Love, if Love be Love, if Love be ours,
> Faith and unfaith can ne'er be equal powers:
> Unfaith in aught is want of faith in all.
>
> ("Merlin and Vivien," ll. 385-387)

In the same way that Elaine riddles herself into her own death, Vivien attempts to play Merlin into her power. Each song achieves its faulty logic from an over-zealous dwelling on the signifier, again suggesting how the lyric might easily descend into unhealthy pathology.

Noelle Bowles (essay date summer 2007)

SOURCE: Bowles, Noelle. "Tennyson's *Idylls of the King* and Anglican Authority." *Christianity and Literature* 56, no. 4 (summer 2007): 573-94.

[*In the following essay, Bowles asserts that in* Idylls of the King *Tennyson argues in favor of the primacy of the authority of the Anglican church.*]

> In my judgment, an epic poem must either be national or mundane. As to Arthur, you could not by any means make a poem national to Englishmen. What have we to do with him?
>
> —Samuel Taylor Coleridge, 1833

> The Arthurian Romance has every recommendation that should win its way to the homage of a great poet. It is national: it is Christian.
>
> —William E. Gladstone, 1859

From our vantage point in the twenty-first century, we may be tempted to nod along with Gladstone and puzzle over Coleridge's rejection of Arthur as a national icon, for King Arthur is, at least in popular consciousness, a symbol of early medieval England.[1] Coleridge, however, was not so far amiss in his assessment as we might at first imagine. Welsh legends translated into French, co-opted by the Germans, rendered from the French into English and passed down over centuries is an odd road for a "national" myth of England to travel. The path is further complicated when we consider ethnicity and religion and their place in Arthurian legend. There is certainly a curious paradox in Victorian medievalism wherein a presumably Celtic Arthur serves as a quintessentially "English" hero battling Saxon invaders—the same sort of Saxons, it must be noted, who sat upon nineteenth-century England's throne as the Saxe-von-Coburgs and with whose preconquest racial heritage the Victorian English citizenry were encouraged to identify.[2] Arthur and his court are, moreover, if not pagan then at least Roman Catholic—the sole Christian faith in early England. We cannot fault Coleridge if the nationalist connection between a Celtic Catholic Arthur and a Protestant Anglo-Saxon nineteenth-century populace were not readily apparent. Yet something happened between the years of Coleridge's assessment and Gladstone's pronouncement that transformed culturally problematic Welsh legends into icons for Anglican nationalism, and that something was Alfred Lord Tennyson's *Idylls of the King.*

Of course, Tennyson was not solely responsible for nineteenth-century Britain's love of the medieval or even the Arthurian. Three editions of Malory's *Le Morte D'Arthur*[3] as well as the popularity of Sir Walter Scott's *Ivanhoe* (1819) and the emerging popularity of Gothic revival architecture helped fuel Victorian England's fascination with myth and medieval British history.[4] Yet the essentially Catholic nature of the mythic Arthur's faith remained a problem. For instance, artist William Dyce faced trouble in 1848 when, in designing frescoes for the Queen's Robing Room in the New Palace at Westminster, he chose Arthurian themes but needed to find a way to negotiate between "heresy or any endorsement of Catholicism" (Mancoff 451) in the representation of the Grail quest images. Raymond Chapman notes that "[m]edievalism was a strong weapon for the renascent Roman Catholics but it could be two-edged for Anglicans who claimed apostolic continuity without Roman obedience"[5] (*Sense of the Past* 40-41). Tennyson handles this blade carefully and, throughout the composition and expansion of the *Idylls of the King,* maneuvers the myth in such a way as to construct a past in which England, not Rome, reigned as the beacon of divine guidance and moral superiority.

Tennyson's negotiation of the religious conflict implicit between medieval images and settings and contemporary Protestantism relies upon British literary precedence. In this literary history, we find that the legends of King Arthur support English independence from the influences of Rome in two interesting ways. First, the legends assert through mytho-history a freedom from continental religious influence that predates even Henry VIII's break with the Church of Rome. Secondly, Arthurian legends lend the English monarchy spiritual authority equivalent or (depending on the representation) even superior to that of the pope.

The argument of British ecclesiastic autonomy upon which the *Idylls* builds has a history at least as ancient as Geoffrey of Monmouth's *Historia Regum Britanniae* (c. 1136). The revisions within Tennyson's *Idylls,* in many ways, represent the accumulation of changes that began with England's earliest sources. For example, in examining the nationalistic implications of European myths, we find that, while the French tales of Charlemagne's victory over Rome in 800 A.D. depicted a once conquered people's victory over their oppressors, Geoffrey's *Historia* portrays Arthur's army "decisively destroying the entire force of the Roman Lucius in France in the sixth century, long before Charlemagne" (Hieatt 174). Arthur's mythical battle scores three points simultaneously: his actions free England from the tyranny of Rome, conquer the conqueror, and also "predate" the accomplishments of Charlemagne in a kind of one-upmanship of historical legitimacy and national pride. More than 300 years later, in Malory's *Le Morte D'Arthur* (1485), the same concern for English dominance prevails. According to Malory, Arthur not only refuses to pay tribute to Rome but rides forth into battle against the emperor Lucius, slays him, and sacks Rome. Arthur becomes head of the English church (as did Henry VIII), divinely appointed and answerable to no one but God and, occasionally, the Archbishop of Canterbury whom he has appointed.

Yet in both these previous texts specific religions play only a minor role; Geoffrey's *Historia,* for example, combines the druidic sorcery of Merlin, Arthur's wizardly advisors, and the Christian virtues of Arthur's knights without indicating that such a combination might create conflict between characters or their philosophies. Ecclesiastic characters in Geoffrey's work and later in Malory's primarily act either to advise or to give religious sanction to an investiture or declaration of war. Although Arthur makes war on Rome in these early narratives, he does not war specifically on the pope; however, the advent of Protestantism and England's break with the Church of Rome led to interesting transformations in Arthurian legends upon which Tennyson's *Idylls* build.

Protestant English authors who chose Arthur as a subject were faced with a character that, in previous textual incarnations, was a Catholic even if specific religious practices remained textually vague. In order to legitimize Arthur's divine right to rule and simultaneously deny papal authority over the English monarchy, Arthur was often granted qualities of spiritual leadership at least equivalent to those of the pope. Sir Richard Blackmore's *Prince Arthur* (1695), for instance, represents Arthur as defender of Christian Protestantism and connects Catholicism with Satan and Rome. In this work, the author makes no effort to conceal his political agenda; Blackmore's work celebrates the restoration of Protestantism by William III, after James II's attempt to re-establish Catholic supremacy (Jenkins 183). In *Prince Arthur,* Arthur becomes a kind of pope himself, for Blackmore endows him with a direct understanding of God's will:

> [. . .] wise instruction, and discourse Divine,
> from God-like Arthur's Mouth, by Heaven inspired;
> That all their Breasts with sacred Passions fired.
> Great were his Thoughts, strong and sublime his Sense
> Of Heaven's Decrees, Foreknowledge, Providence.[6]
>
> (l. 13)

The Arthur of this passage has no need of religious guidance from any source outside himself. Blackmore's hero serves as his nation's conduit to the divine because, through him and his understanding of "heaven's decrees, foreknowledge, providence," England's struggles are blessed by God.

One hundred and seventy-four years later, Tennyson's *Idylls* reworked the same theme as Blackmore but in a subtler manner. As poet laureate (1850), "Tennyson himself held a court appointment that aligned him with the State to which the Anglican Church was wedded" (Hughes 417). Though his personal beliefs may have varied from that of the orthodox Broad Church Anglicanism of Queen Victoria,[7] the sympathies expressed in the *Idylls* remain firmly with the Anglican Church and the authority of the Protestant monarchy. In Tennyson's *Idylls,* Arthur is closely identified with Christ, and it is a connection that grows stronger as the poet revised and expanded his project. To best examine the development of the epic's religious implications and their relation to nineteenth-century Anglican concerns, it is necessary to consider the *Idylls* in the chronological order of their composition and publication.

The first of the published poems that later became a part of the *Idylls*[8] was **"Mort d'Arthur"** (1842), which was revised and expanded in the 1869 collection as **"The Passing of Arthur."**[9] Tennyson had the poem in manuscript form in 1835,[10] and in *The Epic* (1838), wherein the poem exists as a framed narrative, we see clear evidence of Tennyson's early interest in linking the redemptive qualities of Arthur and Christ's stories. *The Epic* opens on a Christmas Eve gathering of friends who regret that "all the old honor had from Christmas gone" (7). Among them is a parson "harping on the church-commissioners, / Now hawking at geology[11] and schism" (15-16). The parson's comments regarding the church commissioners refers to the Ecclesiastical Commission formed in 1835 to deal with the often gross discrepancies of income among those men serving the Anglican community (Bowen 19) and reveals Tennyson's awareness of the conflicts besetting the church.

In 1833, only a few years before the manuscript composition of the poem, the political upheaval surrounding the sale of preferments[12] and salary inequalities threatened to split the church from within, hence the reference to "schism," while Dissenters' complaints regarding their political exclusion[13] threatened the stability of the church from without. So serious were the problems that Tennyson's grandfather "had given up urging him to take Orders, having become fearful of the threat of disestablishment" (Charles Tennyson 136). It is during this turmoil that Tennyson composes a poem that presents its readers with the redemptive possibility of myth and, at least within the poets' construction, Arthur's link to Christ as well as to contemporary authority.

The self-effacing and insecure poet figure within *The Epic,* Everard Hall, has burned his Arthurian epic because he feels it bears little relevance to modern times. One of his comrades has, however, rescued one of the books from the fire's flame and reads **"Mort d'Arthur"** to the gathering. The parson, ironically, sleeps through the reading of the poem, awaking only upon its conclusion, thereby missing the tale's potential for restoring "all the old honor" (7) of Christmas whose loss he previously mourned. It is our narrator who goes to bed and dreams of

> King Arthur, like a modern gentleman
> Of stateliest port; and all the people cried,
> "Arthur is come again: he cannot die."
> Then those that stood upon the hills behind
> Repeated—"Come again, and thrice as fair;"
> And, further inland, voices echoed—"Come
> With all good things, and war shall be no more."
> At this a hundred bells began to peal,
> That with the sound I woke, and heard indeed
> The clear church-bells ring in the Christmas morn.
>
> (73-82)

In the speaker's dream, Arthur becomes the prince of peace, a modern gentleman, and Christ's second coming. The poem strongly implies that the past can redeem the present and provides a positive answer to *The Epic* poet's disparagement of his work when he asks "why should any man / Remodel models?" (37-38). Within the framed poem of **"Mort d'Arthur,"** Bedivere asserts that Arthur's reign had brought such hopes as "have not been since the light that led / The holy Elders with the gift of myrrh" (400-01).[14] Prior to his removal from the shores of England, Arthur's parting advice to Bedivere is to pray, and he tells his knight that "the whole round earth is every way / Bound by gold chains about the feet of God" (422-23). While readers may experience greater pathos if they connect Arthur's death with Christ's sacrifice, the parallel between the two figures contains ecclesiastic and political ramifications of specific relevance to Victorian Anglicanism.

The ecclesiastic power structure of Tennyson's Camelot surely resonated with mid-nineteenth-century Anglicans: a church linked to a monarch and the monarch linked to Christ creates a powerful symbolic association between myth, hereditary monarchy, and the state religion. Lest we suppose that the Arthur / Christ parallel and its implications were lost on the readers who first saw the *Idylls* publication, we have only to look to William E. Gladstone's reaction in the *Quarterly Review,* October 1859:

> The life of our Savior, in its external aspect, was that of a teacher. It was in principle a model for all, but it left space and scope for adaptations to the lay life of Christians in general, such as those by whom the everyday business of the world is to be carried on. It remained for man to make his best endeavour to exhibit the great model on its terrestrial side, in its contact with the world. Here is the true source of that new and noble cycle which the middle ages have handed down to us in duality of form, but with a nearly identical substance, under the royal scepters of Arthur in England and of Charlemagne in France.
>
> (qtd. in Jump 250)

Yet, unlike Christ, Arthur is a savior for the British only, and Gladstone does not miss the national significance of the *Idylls,* remarking that "the Arthurian Romance has every recommendation that should win its way to the homage of a great poet. It is national; it is Christian" (qtd. in Jump 250). Although Gladstone qualifies his remark, stating "though highly national, [the legend] is universal" (250) in its appeal to human nature, there remains in the minds of its English admirers an ethnic exclusivity about the very essence of the myth, which neither time nor language penetrate; the legends of Charlemagne and Arthur, though similar, remain separate. In 1860, following the success of the first *Idylls,* Carolyn Fox[15] records Tennyson's "firm belief in [Arthur] as an historical personage" (Tennyson, *The Letters* 2: 267), though she also notes that Tennyson "found great difficulty in reconstructing the character, in connecting modern with ancient feeling in representing the ideal king." Her observations lend weight to the assertion that Tennyson consciously desired to create in his Arthur an ideal conflation of past and present. Fox's additional comment that "the Welsh claim Arthur as their own, but Tennyson gives all his votes to us"[16] clearly welcomes Arthur as a national English hero. Yet Tennyson's Arthur is no simple allegory for English nationalism; indeed, Gladstone's praise of the work as "national" and "Christian" marks the very spiritual and temporal conflicts with which the *Idylls* engage. The Anglican desire for an identification between ruler, nation, and faith becomes apparent in examining the strains under which the mid-Victorian Church of England existed.

Erosion of Anglican power began, as Walter L. Arnstein notes, long before Queen Victoria took the throne, but there were three central issues in mid-century that occupied a great deal of public and political attention. The first was the growing schism between the evangelical leanings of Low Church Anglicans and the increasingly Catholic practices of those who followed the High Church ritualists. Cardinal John Henry Newman's conversion to Roman Catholicism in 1845 spawned fears that ritualist practices would lead a large number of Anglicans to Roman Catholicism. In the spring of 1850, Benjamin Disraeli, then a member of Parliament, seemed to foresee some of the conflict that was to beleaguer parliamentary action on religious practice for the better part of the century. In an April 22 letter to Lady Londonderry, he wrote:

> The Church question[17] has scarcely commenced and may, before a very short time, effect some startling consequences. It pervades all classes—literally from the palace to the cottage. Gracious Majesty much excited, and clapped her hands with joy, when the critical decision of the Privy Council, against the Bishop of Exeter,[18] was announced to her.
>
> (*Letters* 5: 319)

The "church question" became further heated with the introduction of a second and incendiary issue: expansion of Roman Catholicism in England.

In September of 1850, Pope Pius IX appointed Nicholas Wiseman as Archbishop of Westminster and issued a papal bull to re-establish Catholic sees in England. The Pope's action became known as the "papal aggression," and it infuriated Queen Victoria who saw it as a usurpation of her temporal and spiritual authority. Regarding Cardinal Wiseman's appointment, Disraeli wrote on November 8, 1850, that "[t]he people are very much alarmed in this country. Even the peasants think they are going to be burned alive—taken up to Smithfield instead of their pigs" (*Letters* 5: 369). Tennyson's *Britons, Guard Your Own* (1852) invokes anti-Catholicism to rouse public support for an active militia in case the Catholic Louis Napoleon should invade England, and the poem expresses fears similar to those noted by Disraeli. Tennyson tells his readers that

> Rome's dearest daughter now is captive France,
> The Jesuit laughs, and reckoning on his chance,
> Would, unrelenting,
> Kill all dissenting.
>
> (31-34)

The image of sinister Jesuits plotting the destruction of dissenting Protestants clearly represents the sort of anti-Catholic hysteria that dominated the public consciousness. The poem details "lying priests" (8) controlling the public vote through their influence at the pulpit, and Tennyson demonizes Louis Napoleon through purely religious terms: "The Pope has bless'd him; / The Church caress'd him" (3-4). The poem does, as Hill notes, reveal the poet's "super-patriotism" and "his strong anti-Catholic prejudice" (n. 5 198). In addition to the real or perceived threat presented by Catholicism, the Church of England continued to face opposition from Nonconformists whose ire concerning church-rates had only strengthened over the years.

This conflict formed the third major source of contention for the Anglican Church and reaffirmed the battle line between those who supported state religion and those who sought its abolition. The Anti-State Church Association, founded in 1844 by Edward Miall, editor of *The Nonconformist,* whose members were primarily Baptists and Congregationalists (Watts 546), changed its name to the Society for the Liberation of Religion of State Patronage and Control (aka Liberation Society) in 1853 to garner more members and funds for the express purposes of lobbying sympathetic MPs, increasing the number of Dissenters on the election roles, and electing Nonconformist MPs (568). By the decade's end the conflict was framed as a matter of survival by those loyal to the Anglican Church. As Watts informs us,

> In July 1859 Samuel Morley and Dr C. J. Foster, chairmen of the Liberation Society's parliamentary committee, found difficulty in denying before a select committee of the House of Lords that the campaign for the abolition of church rates was but a step on the road to the disestablishment of the Church of England, and their evasive replies provided welcome ammunition for the defenders of church rates. Church Defence Associations sprang up throughout the country; in February 1860 the majority for Trelawny's abolition bill fell to 29; in December Disraeli in a speech in his Buckinghamshire constituency urged Churchmen to redouble their efforts to save church rates.
>
> (578)

Although Tennyson's first collection of *Idylls* was published nine years after the initial religious turmoil that marked the beginning of the decade, the internecine conflict of the Anglican Church combined with the incursion of Roman Catholicism and Nonconformist agitation for the abolition of state sanctioned religion certainly informed Tennyson's representation of Anglican faith and authority in his epic poem.

Though Arthur's realm and power are fading when he speaks to his queen in **"Guinevere"** (1859), Tennyson's king sets forth the conditions under which his kingdom flourished:

I made them lay their hands in mine and swear
To reverence the King, as if he were
Their conscience, and their conscience as their King,
To break the heathen and uphold the Christ.

(464-467)

The "King" here, as in other *Idylls,* is indeterminate, perhaps Arthur, perhaps Christ. Yet whichever interpretation we favor, the underlying theme is one of vassal obedience to one's lord. The emphasis upon conscience addresses evangelical Christianity, whether Low Church or Nonconformist, and its reliance upon the conscience, in conjunction with scripture, for determining moral behavior. Here, Tennyson substitutes individual conscience for vassal reliance upon a king, who then substitutes for Christ. To uphold the Christ, individuals ought to properly consign their conscience to a king who can successfully realize the assembly's collective vision. In his discussion of this quote, Anthony Harrison remarks, "Quite obviously, it valorizes Christianity as, implicitly, the exclusive domain of truth and honor. In the political arena it promulgates an alliance between monarchy and religion (conscience) that sanctions imperialism ('to break the heathen')" (223). Arthur's vow builds on an earlier conception of loyalty expressed by Bedivere in **"Mort d'Arthur"** when he says, "Deep harm to disobey, / Seeing obedience is the bond of rule" (261-62); Arthur's words in **"Guinevere"** do, as Harrison states, support the alliance between church and state, and this connection strengthens as Tennyson developed his epic.

The composition of the *Idylls* was not without difficulties, however, and Tennyson paused in continuing his epic for nearly ten years.[19] Hallam Tennyson's *Memoir* tells us that "[i]n spite of the public applause he did not rush headlong into the other **'Idylls of the King,'** although he had carried a more or less perfected scheme of them in his head over thirty years. For one thing, he did not consider that the time was ripe" (2: 125). According to Hallam, his father worried about three things particularly: one, marring the effect of the current edition in which readers encounter a "ghost-like passing away of the King" (126) at the end of **"Guinevere"**; two, fearing to mar the present quality with works that might be less artistic; and "[t]he third was, to give it in Tennyson's own words, 'I doubt whether such a subject as the San Graal could be handled in these days without incurring a charge of irreverence. It would be too much like playing with sacred things'" (126). Though Tennyson may have been working through a creative block, there were also powerful religious controversies building that certainly may have given the poet pause in his epic design.

The *Idylls* with its "medieval setting and descriptions of medieval ritual, then, would in the late 1860s have implicitly invoked Roman Catholicism, Newman's conversion, and the controversial practice of ritualism in selected congregations of the Anglican Church" (Hughes 425). This possibility is also noted by Catherine Phillips who suggests that "the fear might have been as much a charge of Catholicism as of irreverence." Yet there were also events immediately following the *Idylls* publication in 1859 that further complicated the perception of faith in Victorian society as well as Tennyson's artistic vision. A brief examination of the circumstances strongly indicates that he did not simply put the *Idylls* aside while awaiting inspiration.

In late January of 1861, Benjamin Jowett[20] writes that Tennyson

> sometimes talks of going on with "King Arthur." For my own part I hope he won't; he has made as much of it as the subject admits. Twenty years ago he formed a scheme for an epic poem on "King Arthur" in ten books; it is perhaps fortunate for himself that circumstances have prevented the completion of it.
>
> (*Letters* 2: 271)

Jowett's lack of enthusiasm for a continuation of revised mythology is hardly surprising considering that he faced public and private censure for his essay "On Interpretation of Scripture," which appeared in *Essays and Reviews* (1860). Jowett's contribution "urged the free critical study of the Bible 'like any other book'" (Altholz 50) and suggested that, rather than being the divine word of God, the text is open to influences of history and that it contains no one forever fixed truth. In this letter, Jowett sounds much like the earlier voice of Everard Hall who wonders at the wisdom of bringing the past into the present, especially in light of historical and scientific realities. However, Tennyson did clearly understand his work on Arthurian legend as a product of his time and place. In a letter to his publisher, he objects to a critic's assessment, writing:

> I can't conceive of how the Grail M. M.[21] mentions can be treated by a poet of the 13th century from a similar point of view to mine, who write in the 19th, but if so, I am rather sorry for it, as I rather piqued myself on my originality of treatment.
>
> (Hallam Tennyson 61-62)

The Grail and its legend had, by the time Tennyson began to compose his second set of *Idylls,* long been the subject of poetry, literature, and art, so his hesitation regarding his composition of the Grail might seem like a poor excuse were we not to consider the contemporary religious controversies that then beset the Anglican Church. His "doubt whether such a subject as the San Graal could be handled in these days without incurring a charge of irreverence" reveals his awareness of and sensitivity to the religious and political conflicts that were tearing at the power structure of the Church of England. As product of its time, the 1869 *Idylls* in general and **"The Holy Grail"** in particular balance theological skepticism and spiritual vision, forging a path between unreflective faith and atheistic dissolution.

"The Holy Grail" separates England from the continent, and hence Catholicism, and supports Anglican authority through its representation of the knights' quest for the sacred object. The Grail is a powerful relic, the search for which is possible only in England and the acquisition of which triggers corporeal transportation directly to heaven, a feat previously possible only for prophets, saints, and Christ. In Tennyson's version, Percivale's destiny is to watch Galahad's rapture: "thrice above [Galahad] all the heavens / Open'd and blazed with thunder such as seem'd / Shoutings of all the sons of God" (507-509). During Galahad's ascension, Percivale has a vision of the city of heaven and a star shining above it which is "the Holy Grail / Which never eyes on earth again shall see" (531-532). Thus Tennyson grants divine vision and corporeal rapture to England's mythic founders while simultaneously withholding the possibility of such vision and transport from anyone else. If those on earth shall never again see the Grail, subsequent quests for the object are pointless, no matter where or by whom they are conducted.

The representation of the Grail as a symbol attainable only on English soil and by English knights makes the Grail an inherently English symbol, providing additional authority to the Anglican Church. The existence of, and quest for, the Holy Grail undermine the spiritual authority of Rome, for to seek outside the experience of the Catholic Church for spiritual guidance or salvation is sacrilegious at best, heretical at worst. Through the legend of the Holy Grail, England, and by extension its church and monarch, gains a divine approval that denies the need for any external religious authority.

While Arthurian legend provides the English a unified cultural and religious front in relation to other nations and faiths, in terms of England's internal religious politics, it would be a mistake to interpret **"The Holy Grail"** as uniformly supportive of religious ecstasy and personal quests for divine inspiration; in fact, Tennyson is cautious in advocating the merits of spiritual pilgrimages and holy visions. Learning that his knights have all sworn themselves to the quest, Arthur tells Galahad, "for such / As thou art is the vision, not for these" (293-94), indicating his other knights. Through Arthur's qualification of appropriate callings, Tennyson indicates that not all quests are for all people, especially not those for divine objects or insight.

Within **"The Holy Grail,"** Tennyson is careful about the religious and historical aspects of the legend. When Ambrosius refers to Joseph of Arimathea, he tells us that he knows of Joseph's coming into England and founding a church in a swamp near Glastonbury but of the Grail "these books of ours, but seem / Mute of this miracle, far as I have read" (65-66). And later, when Percivale has told the edited version of his adventures, Ambrosius remarks that "These ancient books—and

they would win thee—teem, / Only I find not there this Holy Grail, / With miracles and marvels like to these" (541-43). Tennyson thus maintains the apocryphal nature of the grail legend. In this way, **"The Holy Grail"** treads a narrow path between denial of Roman Catholic authority and denial of the validity of individual interpretation favored by the evangelical Dissenters and Low Church Anglicans. To allow too much freedom in the search for expression of religious feeling would undermine Anglican power and the bishops' authority to interpret the scriptures to their congregations and might further be seen as a concession to evangelical Dissenters. Although Tennyson himself voiced no direct opinion on controversial religious matters (evangelical or otherwise) and counted among his friends Dissenters, Anglicans, and Catholics,[22] his religious conservatism is apparent in Arthur's condemnation of the Grail quest as one which will leave his knights following "wandering fires / Lost in the quagmire!" (318-19). Religious vision in this poem is valuable for only the very few; for the rest, it indicates an irresponsible abdication of duty. As Arthur hears the adventures of his knights returned from their quest, he remarks that they have "left human wrongs to right themselves" (893) in their quest for personal encounters with the divine. Ambrosius echoes Arthur's thoughts[23] about one's appropriate role in society and tells Percivale of the joy he takes in knowing and serving his small community and advises him to "rejoice, small man, in this small world of mine" (559). The common lives of common men, the hermit suggests, is where most of us find what joy life offers.

The poem's other visionary, Percivale's sister, also stands as a caution against following one's visions—or perhaps another's—too far. On first examination, a holy woman so dedicated to prayer and fasting that she is blessed with divine visions seems a harmless enough figure. Indeed, if such devotion can reveal the Grail, we might be led to see convents as a positive force. Yet a closer look reveals that hers is a faith of displacement. Blocked from marriage by a love gone wrong, she takes up the veil and sublimates her sexual desires and "pray'd and fasted, till the sun / Shone, and the wind blew, thro' her" (98-99) in order to induce her visions. William E. Buckler sees her as an occult figure who enchants Galahad into her vision (55). In such a role, she becomes another of the *Idylls'* rejected women who work the undoing of the Round Table. But there is another possibility for Tennyson's depiction of her, and it has historical implications within the Anglican Church.

High Church ritualist parishes and priests sanctioned and sponsored the formation of monastic orders, and Anglican sisterhoods were the earliest of these communities. The year 1846 saw the establishment of the Sisterhood of the Holy Cross, and Anglican sisterhoods continued to grow throughout the remainder of the century. W. S. F. Pickering informs us that in "the early days of Anglo-Catholicism the emergence of religious orders heaped on followers of the Catholic revival as much hostility from ardent Protestants as did the ritualization of Anglican services" (131). Such a reaction is hardly surprising because Broad and Low Church Anglicans as well as Nonconformists would have seen such behavior as further evidence that ritualists were, as one Oxford clergyman noted, trying to "bring the Church of England to Rome by the furtive introduction . . . of Romish practices and observances" (qtd. in Bentley 28). Concern—indeed, one might say paranoia—about these sisterhoods, their nature and influence upon women prompted Parliamentary action. In 1851, The Religious Houses Bill, had it passed, "would have allowed Justices of the Peace to make inquiries after any woman suspected of being held against her will in a convent. H. E. Lacy, MP for Bodmin, sponsored this private bill on the grounds that he failed to understand how several hundred women in England could possibly lead contented lives in convents" (Wallis 10). Anxiety regarding Anglican sisterhoods did not die down as the groups proved their social usefulness;[24] in fact, Charles Newdigate Newdegate, Esquire, MP for Warwickshire, proposed a bill in 1871 that called "for the suppression of monasteries and nunneries" (Bentley 73). Though Newdegate's proposal as well as the furor surrounding the Public Worship Regulation Act of 1874 lie outside the composition timeline of the poems examined here, these issues were hotly debated in the decades during which Tennyson composed the ***Idylls.***

If we consider the public agitation over women's religious houses as part of our reading of **"The Holy Grail"** the young nun's obsessive and unhealthy search for holy visions takes on specific political significance. Percivale's sister, the poem heavily implies, does not enter the convent because she feels specially called to do so but rather because religious aestheticism permits her to bury rejection in visions that allow her to bind a man, Galahad, to her spiritually if not physically. Representing the nun as a "victim of unrequited love who enters a nunnery on the rebound" (Hughes 415), Tennyson creates such qualifiers regarding her motivation that readers are discouraged from condoning her choice of vocation.

Indeed, as Hughes's argument suggests, her visions may be hallucinations designed to complement her confessor's interest in the legend (428). Through Percivale's narrative, we are told that the priest hoped the "Holy Grail would come again" (92) to "heal the world of all their wickedness" (94). Although his hope is compassionate in nature, his relationship to and influence upon Percivale's sister falls in line with anti-Catholic and antiritualist thinking wherein "[n]ovelists and pamphleteers told horrific stories of how unscrupulous priests abused the confessional to gain power over their penitents, even to win the allegiance of women away from their husbands" (Chapman, *Faith* 173). Though the confessor has no such nefarious designs as are popular in contemporary fiction, he gives her little guidance when she asks if the Grail might come to her "by prayer and fasting" (96). He tells her that he does not know, and his statement that her "heart is pure as snow" (97) prompts her to engage in behavior that is clearly self-destructive. The implicit critique is that his role as her confessor, while presumably benevolent, in fact, does her great harm.

The nature and degree of personal spiritual interpretation was a politically volatile subject in mid-nineteenth-century England because evangelical Nonconformists, who favored the idea that the scriptures ought to be one's sole moral authority, were gaining considerable influence over religious and political issues. Margaret Ann Crowther informs us that "the religious census of 1851, although highly inaccurate in detail, revealed that . . . of population of nearly eighteen million in England and Wales, over five and a quarter million did not attend any form of religious worship, . . . and in the remaining worshippers the number of Dissenters almost equaled the number of Anglicans" (219). With the decline in membership, the rising popularity of dissenting congregations, and the political agitation of the Liberation Society, the Church of England was justifiably fearful of losing its control over the colleges and ecclesiastic education, its representation in Parliament, and its acknowledgment as the national, state religion.

Although Tennyson makes devotion to visionary causes highly suspect, the epic encourages unquestioning devotion to the crown and, by implication, the Church of England. When, for example, Arthur's knights swear fealty to him in **"The Coming of Arthur"** (1869), his speech creates in them a mirror image of himself:

> From eye to eye thro' all their Order flash
> A momentary likeness of the King;
> And ere it left their faces, thro' the cross
> And those around it and the Crucified,
> Down from the casement over Arthur smote
> Flame color, vert, and azure, in three rays.
>
> (269-274)

The knights are momentarily king-like, and the juxtaposition of Arthur with the cross and "the Crucified" blends the figure of Arthur with that of Christ. Thus, exactly which king the knights resemble—the King of Heaven or of England—becomes difficult to discern, deliberately so. The "King" in this passage functions both as Arthur and as Christ. In Tennyson's poem, the radiance of Christ's figure in the glass mingles with Arthur's own light, suggesting that Tennyson's Arthur does not rule merely in the name of Christ but as an embodiment of Christ. Such symbolism furthers the Anglican contention that the person who heads the kingdom and hence the Anglican Church does so with God's special blessing.

Moreover, the poem rejects Roman authority that, in Tennyson's version, is Catholic rather than pagan. When Arthur's knights cant against the Roman lords who appear to demand tribute, they ask if "Rome or Heathen rule in Arthur's realm" (484). The distinction is significant because the question indicates that Rome is other than "heathen," and, if not heathen, Rome must necessarily be Catholic; therefore, Arthur's response defies both the temporal authority of the lords and the spiritual authority of the Pope. His knights will follow him rather than anyone else because, as they tell us, "God hath told the King a secret word" (488). Tennyson's Arthur holds direct authority from God, and the knights resolve that: "The King will follow Christ, and we the King, / In whom high God hath breathed a secret thing" (499-500). Central to the revisionist mythology the *Idylls* represents is the assertion that, since Arthur's time, England had never really been a vassal of Catholic Rome, either theologically or militarily.

Tennyson emphasizes the parallel between Arthur and Christ yet again in the revision of **"Mort d'Arthur"** into **"The Passing of Arthur."**[25] Here, we first hear Arthur speak as he meditates upon the fall of his kingdom, and his cry—"My God, thou hast forgotten me in my death! / Nay—God my Christ—I pass but shall not die" (28-29)—evokes Christ's despair on the cross (Matt. 27:46), and, like Christ, whose second coming the Christian faith anticipates, Arthur, too, is predicted to return from the dead; Sir Bedivere tells the reader that "He passes to be king among the dead, / And after healing of his grievous wound / He comes again" (**"The Passing of Arthur"** 449-51). Like Christ, too, Arthur is betrayed, first by the people whom he has ruled, and secondly, though temporarily, by Bedivere.

In **"The Passing of Arthur,"** Bedivere directs the brunt of his disgust at those who have been led astray from Arthur's vision and leadership. The poem's heavy use of Arthur/Christ symbolism suggests that the betrayal may be spiritual as well as temporal. Bedivere tells Arthur that with Modred are

> [. . .] many of thy people, and knights
> Once thine, whom thou hast loved, but grosser grown
> Than heathen, spitting at their vows and thee.
> Right well in heart they know thee for the King.
>
> (60-63)

From the perspective of the throne regarding the ritualist controversies, defections of Anglican leaders to Catholicism, and anti-establishment efforts of Nonconformists, the betrayal comes from within. Before his fight with Modred, Arthur defines the members of his house as "they who sware my vows, / Yea, even while they brake them, own'd me king" (157-58) and the lines reflect the schism of authority within the Anglican Church where ritualist congregations were simulta-

neously members and renegades. Though Tennyson was silent on the specific issue of the Nonconformist desire for the separation of church and state, it is worth noting that these lines were composed little more than a year after the passage of Gladstone's 1868 bills for the Abolition of Compulsory Church Rates and the Disestablishment of the Church of Ireland (Watts 590).

Bedivere's betrayal, born of his unwillingness to part with Arthur or his symbols, is less severe, and he redeems himself in his final obedience to his king's command that he cast Excalibur into the lake. Christopher Hodgkins notes the ecclesiastical and political implications of the scene and writes that

> once Bedivere casts the sword away, the emergence of the mystic, receiving hand from the lake seems to reconfirm a divine presence that reconfers divine blessing on some future British holy warrior. Here again is the old myth of authorizing humility; an ancestral act of surrender empowers the heirs to rule. The mystic hand points to Victorian Britain and the kind of renewed "faith" that will be necessary if its empire is to survive and thrive.
>
> (208)

There are, of course, many sorts of faith, but Tennyson frequently linked faith specifically with Anglicanism and the conservative order of church and state. In discussing parliamentary events of 1884, Charles Tennyson states, "The talk about the disestablishment of the Anglican Church caused him the gravest apprehension, for he felt that this would prelude the fall of much that was greatest and best in England" (478). The accuracy of Charles Tennyson's view is supported in *Locksley Hall Sixty Years After* (1886), where we also see the same parallels that Hodgkins reveals regarding **"The Passing of Arthur."** As the poem's speaker considers the further extensions of the vote and increasing rule by the masses, he laments that this will "[b]ring the old dark ages back without the faith, without the hope, / Break the State, the Church, the Throne, and roll their ruins down / the slope" (137-38). The ideology of the *Idylls* counters such changes by encouraging nineteenth-century readers to conclude that since the religious and political traditions of England had stood the country in good stead from such an ancient past, those same traditions were no less viable and valuable in their own time. Through links with divinity—the Christ-like king and England's ties to the Grail—the British monarchy and the Church of England gained an additional degree of reverence and inviolability. Implicit in Tennyson's *Idylls* is the assertion that any usurpation of power of the authority from Queen Victoria or the Anglican Church was, if not unthinkable, at least spiritually suspect.

Notes

1. See films *King Arthur* (2004), which imagines Arthur as the bridge between Roman and Saxon

civilizations, and *First Knight* (1995) wherein Arthur stands as a defender of truth, justice, and the British way.

2. The Victorian elevation of Saxon rather than Celtic heritage may be found in Thomas Carlyle's *On Heroes, Hero-Worship, and the Heroic in History* (1841) and *Past and Present* (1843), which present the English as the inheritors of the noble characteristics of Saxon and Nordic ancestors. John Beddoe's, *The Races of Britain: A Contribution to the Anthropology of Western Europe* contains a chart—the "index of nigrescence"—that shows the whitest sections of the British Isles as those whose population has primarily Saxon or Viking ancestry. Also see Clare Simmons, *Reversing the Conquest: History and Myth in Nineteenth-Century British Literature,* for a detailed examination of Victorian interest in Saxon culture and heritage.

3. Richard Barber notes that "[f]or English speaking readers, the publication of three editions of Malory's *Morte D'Arthur* in 1816 and 1817 reopened the gates of Arthurian legend" (262).

4. Mark Girourard's *Return to Camelot: Chivalry and the English Gentleman* gives a thorough review of the pervasive influence of medievalism on English culture.

5. The "renascent Roman Catholics" to whom Chapman refers are those English citizens whose civil rights were restored with the Catholic Emancipation Act of 1829. However, Chapman also refers to the Oxford movement as the "Catholic movement within the Church of England" (*Sense* 40). The terms can be confusing because Anglo-Catholicism is used interchangeably with the Oxford Movement, Tractarianism, and High Church ritualism. See W. S. F. Pickering (17-24) for a concise discussion of the difference and historical progression of the terms.

6. Archaic spellings and contractions have been standardized for easier reading.

7. Tennyson was one of the founders of the Metaphysical Society in 1869: however, he resigned his membership in 1879, having attended only eleven meetings (Hallam Tennyson *Memoir* 2: 170).

8. There are other "Arthurian" poems, most notably "The Lady of Shalott" (1842), "Sir Galahad" (1842), and "Merlin and the Gleam" (1889), that are not part of the epic sequence Tennyson imagined for the *Idylls.*

9. References to and citations from Tennyson's poetry are from Robert. W. Hill Jr.'s edition of *Tennyson's Poetry: Authoritative Texts, Juvenilia and Early Responses Criticism* unless otherwise noted.

10. In his footnotes to *The Epic,* Hill explains the history of the poem's composition and Tennyson's desire to create a larger epic in which the work would belong (81-82). "Mort d'Arthur" as referenced here appears in Hill's edition as lines 170-444 of the revised and expanded poem "The Passing of Arthur" (Hill 82). In this essay, the original title "Mort d'Arthur" is used to indicate the first publication of these lines (both within *The Epic* and later as an individual poem) in order to locate the poem within the development of Tennyson's ideological and artistic framework.

11. The reference to geology reveals Tennyson's awareness of Charles Lyell's *Principles of Geology,* which, as Hill notes, was "one of the major contributions to the 'new' science which challenged the Biblical interpretation of creation" (n.7 81).

12. Bowen's *The Idea of the Victorian Church* provides examples of advertised sales of ecclesiastical livings (12-13).

13. Watts explains Dissenting grievances as

> the frequent refusal of clergymen to allow the bodies of Dissenters to be buried in parish graveyards; the liability of Dissenting chapels to demands for the poor rate when parish churches were exempt; the refusal of the courts to accept the validity of Dissenting baptismal and birth registers in the absence of a civil registry of births and deaths; the forcing of Dissenters, apart from Quakers, to submit to the rites of the Church of England for marriage; and the levying on Dissenters of church rates for the support of the established church.
>
> (455)

14. The lines here are printed in Hill's edition as part of the revised and expanded *The Passing of Arthur* and not as they first appeared as part of *The Epic.*

15. The text here, as cited in Tennyson's *Letters* by Lang and Shannon, comes from Carolyn Fox's *Memories of Old Friends,* 349-51. Her father, Robert Were Fox, geologist and scientific writer, was one of Tennyson's friends, and Carolyn Fox was well acquainted with him and other preeminent figures such as John Stuart Mill, and Thomas Carlyle. Lang and Shannon note, "she knew everyone" (*Letters* n.1 226).

16. Fox's comment regarding Arthur's national identity should not be understood as an endorsement on her part of any religious affiliation for the legendary king, for her own family was Quaker.

17. The "Church question" is the conflict between Low, Broad, and High Church Anglicans, and in the Gorham case, the question centered around

who would have final authority over ecclesiastic courts and interpretation of religious doctrine.

18. The decision against the Bishop of Exeter refers to the then famous Gorham case wherein the Bishop of Exeter denied the induction of Rev. G. C. Gorham into the living he had been promised on the basis that the bishop found Gorham's views on baptism to be too overtly Calvinist. Gorham had appealed his decision from the Arches Court of Canterbury to the Judicial Committee of the Privy Council. This court, however, was secular, and its ruling strongly implied that the Crown had final authority over matters of doctrine. Thus, the ruling against the bishop was a victory for Low and Broad Church Anglicans who objected to High Church interpretation of the articles of faith.

19. The 1859 edition of the *Idylls* included "Mort d'Arthur," "Merlin and Vivien," "Geraint and Enid," "Guinevere," and "Lancelot and Elaine." The poems gained a supplemental dedication to Prince Albert in 1862, but no other poems were added until 1869. The publication in print is dated 1870 because the expanded edition came out in late December 1869.

20. Benjamin Jowett was one of seven contributors to *Essays and Reviews* (1860) which "changed the Church of England (and probably modern theology) forever" (McKenna 51). Tennyson remained one of Jowett's friends and supporters in the aftermath of the essay's publication, earning the poet Jowett's deep gratitude (Charles Tennyson 331).

21. M. M. is Max Müller, Professor of Comparative Philology at Oxford and a noted religious scholar. In his letter, Tennyson also requests his publisher to discover if Max Müller will forward "the name of the book, which contains all the Medieval literature about the Grail" (Hallam Tennyson 62), he promises to read it even if he has to translate it from the German. Tennyson's offer here indicates his skepticism that there is a single text in which all lore is contained.

22. Tennyson was on cordial terms with George Eliot, Charles Kingsley, and Cardinal Newman.

23. Whether Ambrosius foreshadows or echoes Arthur's sentiments depends, to some degree, on how we wish to read the sequence of events. Ambrosius's remarks, made long after the fall of Camelot, occur sandwiched between Arthur's comments regarding for whom such quests are appropriate but before we learn of Arthur's final assessment of the quest.

24. Anglican sisters often performed social services such as working in shelters for abandoned women,

caring for the poor, and visiting hospitals. For example, St. John's House (est. 1848) was an Anglican sisterhood devoted to nursing. Pickering notes that the Devonport Sisters helped nurse soldiers during the Crimean War (1854-1856) under the guidance of Florence Nightingale (130-31).

25. "The Coming of Arthur" was composed in the winter of 1868-69 and completed in September of 1869, and *Mort d'Arthur* revised and expanded to "The Passing of Arthur" in September 1869 (Hill 287); therefore, the composition of "The Coming of Arthur" predates that of "The Passing of Arthur."

Works Cited

Altholz, Josef L. "A Tale of Two Controversies: Darwinism in the Debate over 'Essays and Reviews.'" *Church History* 63 (1994): 50-59.

Arnstein, Walter L., "Queen Victoria and the Challenge of Roman Catholicism." *The Historian* 58.2 (1996). *Questia.* 24 May 2006 <http://www.questia.com/PM.qst?a=o & d=5000335283>.

Barber, Richard. *The Holy Grail: Imagination and Belief.* Cambridge, MA: Harvard UP, 2004.

Beddoe, John. *The Races of Britain: A Contribution to the Anthropology of Western Europe.* 1885. London: Hutchinson, 1971.

Bentley, James. *Ritualism and Politics in Victorian Britain: The Attempt to Legislate for Belief.* Oxford: Oxford UP, 1978.

Blackmore, Richard. *Prince Arthur.* 1695. Yorkshire: Scholar, 1971.

Bowen, Desmond. *The Idea of the Victorian Church.* Montreal: McGill UP, 1968.

Buckler, William E. *Man and His Myths: Tennyson's Idylls of the King in Critical Context.* New York: New York UP, 1984.

Carlyle, Thomas. *Past and Present.* New York: Wiley and Putnam, 1847.

———. *On Heroes, Hero-Worship, and the Heroic in History.* 1841. Berkeley: University of California Press, 1993.

Chapman, Raymond. *Faith and Revolt: Studies in the Literary Influence of the Oxford Movement.* London: Weidenfeld and Nicolson, 1970.

———. *The Sense of the Past in Victorian Literature.* New York: St. Martin's, 1986.

Crowther, Margaret Ann. *Church Embattled: Religious Controversy in Mid-Victorian England.* Hamden: Archon, 1970.

Disraeli, Benjamin. *Letters.* Ed. M. G. Wiebe et al. Vol. 5. Toronto: U of Toronto P, 1982.

First Knight. Dir. Jerry Zucker. Perf. Sean Connery, Richard Geer, Julia Ormond. Columbia Pictures, 1995.

Fox, Carolyn. *Memories of Old Friends.* Philadelphia: Lippincott, 1884.

Geoffrey of Monmouth. *Historia Regum Britanniae.* Trans. Sebastian Evans and Rev. Charles W. Dunn. New York: Dutton, 1958.

Girourard, Mark. *Return to Camelot: Chivalry and the English Gentleman.* New Haven: Yale UP, 1981.

Harrison, Anthony H. "Medievalism and the Ideologies of Victorian Poetry." *Medievalism in England.* Ed. Leslie J. Workman. Cambridge: Brewer, 1992. 219-34.

Hieatt, Kent A. "The Passing of Arthur in Malory, Spenser, and Shakespeare: The Avoidance of Closure." *The Passing of Arthur: New Essays in Arthurian Tradition.* Ed. Christopher Baswell and William Sharpe. New York: Garland, 1988. 173-92.

Hill, Robert W. Jr., ed. *Tennyson's Poetry: Authoritative Texts, Juvenilia and Early Responses Criticism.* New York: W. W. Norton, 1971.

Hodgkins, Christopher. *Reforming Empire: Protestant Colonialism and Conscience in British Literature.* Columbia, MO: U of Missouri P, 2002. *Questia.* 30 May 2006 <http://www.questia.com/PM.qst?a=o & d=109323746>.

Hughes, Linda K. "Scandals in Faith and Gender in Tennyson's Grail Poems." *The Grail: a Casebook.* Ed. Dhira B. Mahoney. New York: Garland, 2000. 415-45.

Jenkins, Elizabeth. *The Mystery of King Arthur.* New York: Dorset, 1990.

Jowett, Benjamin. "On Interpretation of Scripture." *Essays and Reviews* 1860. 10 Feb. 2007 <http://lachlan.bluehaze.com.au/1860-essays-reviews/index.html>.

Jump, John D., ed. *Tennyson: The Critical Heritage.* New York: Routledge & K. Paul, 1967.

King Arthur. Dir. Antoine Fuqua. Perf. Clive Owen, Keira Knightley. Touchstone Pictures, 2004.

Malory, Sir Thomas. *Le Morte D'Arthur* (1485). New York: Random House, 1993.

Mancoff, Debra N. "'Pure Heart and Clean Hands': The Victorian and the Grail." *The Grail: a Casebook.* Ed. Dhira B. Mahoney. New York: Garland, 2000. 447-64.

McKenna, Joseph H. "Honesty in Theology?" *Heythrop Journal.* 42 (2001): 50-65.

Phillips, Catherine. "Charades from the Middle Ages? Tennyson's Idylls of the King and the Chivalric Code."

Victorian Poetry 40.3 (2002). *Questia.* 31 May 2006 <http://www.questia.com/PM.qst?a=o & d=5000673636>.

Pickering, W. S. F. *Anglo-Catholicism: A Study in Religious Ambiguity.* London: Routledge, 1989.

Simmons, Clare. *Reversing the Conquest: History and Myth in Nineteenth-Century British Literature.* New Brunswick: Rutgers UP, 1990.

Tennyson, Alfred, Lord. *Tennyson's Poetry: Authoritative Texts, Juvenilia and Early Responses Criticism.* Ed. Robert. W. Hill, Jr. New York: Norton, 1971.

——. *The Letters.* Ed. Cecil Y. Lang and Edgar F. Shannon Jr. 2 vols. Cambridge: Harvard UP, 1981 and 1987.

Tennyson, Charles. *Alfred Tennyson.* London: Macmillan, 1949. *Questia.* 3 Feb. 2007 <http://www.questia.com/PM.qst?a=o & d=57038971>.

Tennyson, Hallam. *Alfred Lord Tennyson: A Memoir.* Vol. 2. New York: Greenwood, 1969. *Questia.* 24 May 2006 <http://www.questia.com/PM.qst?a=0$d=102947504>.

Wallis, Frank. "Anti-Catholicism in Mid-Victorian Britain." *Journal of Religion and Society* 7 (2005). 30 May 2006 <http://moses.creighton.edu/JRS/2005/2005-6.html>.

Watts, Michael R. *The Dissenters.* Vol. 2. Oxford: Clarendon, 1995.

John Hughes (essay date summer 2007)

SOURCE: Hughes, John. "'Hang There Like Fruit, My Soul': Tennyson's Feminine Imaginings." *Victorian Poetry* 45, no. 2 (summer 2007): 95-115.

[*In the following essay, Hughes presents an analysis of the significance of Tennyson's masculine and feminine sensibilities in the author's poetry.*]

Tennyson, we know, was buried with a copy of *Cymbeline* (as well as various wreaths, and roses from Emily), and in the days before his death on October 5, 1892, he repeatedly asked for the relevant volume, laying it "face down" on the page where Posthumous is reconciled with Imogen, and pressing down with his hand so "heavily" that the spine cracked:[1]

> Hang there like fruit, my soul,
> Till the tree die!

Hallam reports his dying father as trying unsuccessfully to read this passage ("which he always called the tenderest lines in Shakespeare") before uttering the sentence "I have opened it,"[2] and then speaking "his last words, a farewell blessing, to my mother and myself."[3] Hallam's account is understandably edited and stylized, but it was clearly an impressive scene.[4] Dr. Dabbs was more unrestrained in drawing out those elements of the poet's passing that lent themselves to a literary apotheosis. The Laureate dies with the majesty of his own King Arthur, and grips his Shakespeare as if it were his passport to the pantheon:

> On the bed a figure of breathing marble, flooded and bathed in the light of a full moon streaming through the oriel window; his hand clasping the Shakespeare which he had asked for but recently, and which he kept by him to the end; the moonlight, the majestic figure as he lay there, "drawing thicker breath," irresistibly brought to our minds his own **"Passing of Arthur."**
>
> (*Memoir,* 2:428-429)

Dabbs's account is stagey and dated, but it is the private, rather than the public, aspect of the scene that is intriguing. Specifically, what did the play, and its final scene mean to Tennyson as he approached death? It is well known that the urgency of his reiterated request for the *Cymbeline* distressed his family who were alarmed by his response to reading some words from it on October 3, whereupon he told the doctor that "now he was convinced of his approaching death" (Martin, p. 581). Turning to the end of the play, we remember Imogen, restored to Posthumous after a period when they had been lost to each other, and when, her life threatened, she had had to brave exile from her sex and her family. Disguising herself as a male, she had entered a wilderness, and all but died, undergoing an episode of death-in-life, and a form of burial, before in the miraculous way of the later plays, she reveals herself and is restored to him.

In what follows, I take this scene as providing a kind of template, a symbolic narrative, that offers a model whereby we can think about what can be called the co-existence, entwinement, and alternation, in Tennyson's imagination, of male and female personae. Broadly, I will hazard a hypothesis that Tennyson's works, like his life and career as a whole, aspired to ultimately masculine positionings of self, but that his work was always animated by an encrypted but constitutive dimension of (what is best called) feminine sensibility that yearned, like Imogen—against hope and experience, as it were—for self-revelation or expression.[5] My argument will be that this unfolding of femininity manifests itself in fundamental (if intermittent and often dissimilated) ways in Tennyson's poetry, largely in so far as an individual work projects an identity with, or as, its central female figure. Of course, as an obvious case like **"Mariana"** makes clear, this distinction is not a simple one, but it usefully allows me to explore two related but different kinds of case which I will use to frame my argument.[6]

In the former, as I shall describe it, romance reveals a form of entranced symbiosis where difference between the masculine hero and a female other is suspended or transcended; and in the latter, the imagining of female identity is more directly enacted or voiced, entailing a conversion of gender. In this context, we can speculate that death represented itself for Tennyson as an opening as well as an ending, a crossing of the bar, where an alienating and constricting male disguise, compulsory for survival, can be miraculously discarded, as for Imogen, whose buried self is revealed at the end of the play.

So Anthony Hecht muses over **"Now sleeps the Crimson Petal,"** and how Tennyson's scrupulousness over words could allow him to use the pronoun "she" in the sixth line for the male peacock, though he also notes within the poem "a deliberate and conscious shift from the masculine to the feminine posture of the mind."[7] In terms of this discussion, a close reading could grapple with the cryptic conjurations of perspective in the lyric, and the opalescent swathes of its language, to demonstrate indeed how its exotic diction (and its cancelling of everyday logic) serves to release a waking dream of female embodiment, one in which what is male may be held or may be lost:

> "Now folds the lily all her sweetness up,
> And slips into the bosom of the lake;
> So fold thyself, my dearest, thou, and slip
> Into my bosom, and be lost in me."
>
> (*The Princess,* 7. 171-174)

One could multiply critical readings that have turned over the seemingly unfathomable riddles of gender in this poem (for instance by tying it more explicitly to Princess Ida than Hecht seems to do).[8] However, what does appear unequivocal, if uncontentious and characteristic, about this lyric for my purposes is the subordination of the masculine self who is eclipsed by the poet's need to make the text a medium for an imagined female self-expression. If Tennyson's work is indeed riven by the tension between the alternating claims of the public masculine and the private feminine voices within the poetry, it is nonetheless the aesthetic triumph of a poem like **"Now Sleeps the Crimson Petal"** that its enchantments can overcome the mere double-binds and contradictions of experience. Thus, the scenario and language of the poem conspire to accommodate the simultaneous necessity and impossibility of enacting this captive, exiled, subterranean, part of the self, this immured and proscribed female element.

Clearly, too, in arguing that these two aspects of the self, male and female, are separate but in constant circulation in Tennyson's work, my account intersects with, and recapitulates, many observations made about issues of gender and sexuality within it, from the earliest comments of celebrated contemporaries (such as Bulwer, Christopher North, J. W. Croker, Manley Hopkins, Charles Kingsley, and Alfred Austin),[9] to more recent and influential discussions (by critics such as Kate Millett, Christopher Ricks, Alan Sinfield, Carol Christ, Christopher Craft, Marjorie Stone, Marion Shaw, Catherine Maxwell, James W. Hood, and James Eli Adams).[10] At the same time, these discussions appear to me to be often hampered by proceeding in terms of a series of competing and ultimately inadequate vocabularies. The either/ors—of homosexuality, bisexuality, and androgyny—that have held sway in Tennyson studies are inadequate to the complexity and dynamics of a case that is better subsumed (so my argument tends) under the rubric of what we are learning to call the transgendered.[11]

Closer to this emphasis would be Richard Cronin's remark, of the early Tennyson, that he wrote "quite uninhibitedly as a woman," though one needs to acknowledge here that Cronin rather collapses the insight by interpreting this as a career move, and so a cultural matter. For Cronin, "writing as a woman" ultimately was a strategic mode by which Tennyson responded, adapted, to the predominantly femininized values of poetry in the 1830s.[12] In what follows, I shall argue that it remained a central component in Tennyson's literary imagination, and evident in many major texts, even as it took often circuitous routes, and was increasingly subject, as Cronin also hints, to self-censorship and disguise. My aim is twofold: to account in plausible ways for a key dynamic that underlies the distinctive aesthetic values and modes of individuation, even temporality, operative in Tennyson's work, and to offer a heuristic contention that removes many of the creases, dead-ends, and shortcomings that bedevil critical discussions of gender and sexuality within it.

I

Much, then, in Tennyson criticism needs to be acknowledged, but also reinflected, in so far as it anticipates, or just stops short of, the case being made here. Alan Sinfield, one of Tennyson's subtlest and most probing critics, cites the notorious reviews of *In Memoriam*—the declaration that "these touching lines evidently come from the full heart of the widow of a military man," and the *Times* reviewer (in this case mindful of Tennyson's authorship), who commented on the verses, "but who would not give them a feminine application?"[13] More broadly, Sinfield has argued, regarding the unselfconsciousness of Tennyson's earliest poems, that Tennyson in later life wished "to distance himself from the effeminacy which previously he had dared," a response to critics' increasing habit of reading through the text to what Allon White called the text's "'real origin' . . . the psycho-physiology of the author" (Sinfield, p. 152). However, a defensive self-consciousness may have set

in much earlier, and with Tennyson's legendary hypersensitivity to reviewers ("I remember everything that has been said against me, and forget all the rest"[14]) a function of anxieties about how people might perceive the gendering of his poetic voice, not least given the oft-noted dominance, as Marjorie Stone put it, in "Tennyson's early works" of "female figures and points of view" (Stone, p. 130). In a broader sense, Edgar Finley Shannon's fifty-year-old study offers powerful evidence for "the part played by the reviewers in Tennyson's ten years' silence from 1832 to 1842, in the revisions and suppressions of the poems of his first two independent volumes, and in the style and subject matter of the new poems published in 1842."[15]

Certainly, from the 1830s and 1840s onward, Tennyson was continually retreating from the insinuations of his critics (not to mention the explicit abuse of a Croker or a Bulwer), that his inspiration was lacking, as the *Athenaeum* reviewer put it, in "the manly courage, the cheerful faith and hope," appropriate to a poet of the time.[16] One can interpret much of his subsequent career as involving turn, as directed, "from the fanciful and the pretty to ideas and themes more concerned with the interests of the day and closer to the hearts of men."[17] Whatever the relative merits of these explanations, and the need for more detailed exposition, one can remark, for instance, that longer poems like *The Princess, Maud, Locksley Hall, The Lover's Tale,* or *Enoch Arden* (and even *In Memoriam*) move narratively towards an eventual, though troubled, reconfirmation of masculinity. In this section, I will consider some representative cases which end with such belated figurations of male selfhood. At the same time, I want to explore the ways in which, contrarily, these poems turn in essential ways on registering moments and events where female alter-egos trigger various sorts of passage outside of the felt constraints of male identity. At this point, it is necessary to acknowledge the connections here with Carol Christ's depiction of Tennyson's poetry as finding its inspiration in "an erotic theft through which the male incorporates a power he locates in the female" (an argument that anticipates elements in Catherine Maxwell's more recent work).[18] Christ indicates how the scenography of many Tennyson poems stages the ambivalent encounter of a male figure with the woman whose power he appropriates. So, Tiresias yearns "for larger glimpses of that more than man," stealing a forbidden glance at Pallas Athene bathing, and then receives the curse of blindness and the gift of prophesy. As Christ puts it, such a stolen access to the feminine "at once organizes the poet's being and threatens to dissolve it" (Christ, p. 386). In terms of my more specific focus on the way love is staged in key narrative poems, one can similarly consider how the male figures find through the central events of love and passion, and the influence of the female, an access to a vitality and reciprocity that is otherwise impossible. However necessary this influence is, by the same token its withdrawal is annihilating, confirming the powerlessness and subjection of the male. So, these poems tend to revert to those eventual, hollowed-out manifestations of masculinity that are the lot of those who discover themselves blighted by a lost contact with the feminine.

In terms of the phenomenology of this, one notices recurrently how the writing works in ways that defeat a simple model of subject and object, as of male and female. To begin with, the relationship takes shape as the wholesale dependence and passivity of the male protagonist or speaker before the key female figure, as in the very early **"Eleänore."** "Tranced" and "rapt," the poet is "overpowered" and "as nothing," before his sovereign female muse. Faced by her stellar and solar powers, the poet seeks his own vanishing point, converting the poem into a kind of mirror, wherein he can enjoy, be lost in, her reflected image as studiedly as she might herself.[19] "[I]n ecstasies," he stands aside, awaiting the unfoldings and radiations of her beauty, so that the whole poem seems an effect of the illumination of "thy large eyes, imperial Eleänore":

5

I stand before thee, Eleänore;
   I see thy beauty gradually unfold,
Daily and hourly, more and more.
   I muse, as in a trance, the while
     Slowly, as from a cloud of gold,
Comes out thy deep ambrosial smile.
I muse, as in a trance, whene'er
   The languors of thy love-deep eyes
Float on to me. I would I were
     So tranced, so rapt in ecstasies,
To stand apart, and to adore,
Gazing on thee for evermore,
Serene, imperial Eleänore!

6

Sometimes, with most intensity
Gazing, I seem to see
Thought folded over thought, smiling asleep,
Slowly awakened, grow so full and deep
In thy large eyes, that, overpowered quite,
I cannot veil, or droop my sight,
But am as nothing in its light:
As though a star, in inmost heaven set,
   Ev'n while we gaze on it,
Should slowly round his orb, and slowly grow
To a full face, there like a sun remain
Fixed-then as slowly fade again,
   And draw itself to what it was before;
     So full, so deep, so slow,
      Thought seems to come and go
   In thy large eyes, imperial Eleänore.

(ll. 69-97)

Eleänore's physical individuality is the condition of the language that embodies itself in embodying her. The logic of the poem is that her beauty is coveted more

than it is desired, the poet seeking through a kind of self-hypnotic self-surrender to participate vicariously in, and to record, the manifestations of her beauty as they pass into the language.[20]

In a more celebrated case like *The Lover's Tale* a similar merging with the female, and a comparable dependence and disposability of male identity, are played out, though obviously in a more narrative and dramatic fashion. Julian, the worshipful male, finds himself at the end cast out of the "land of love" into which he had earlier been introduced through his surrender to Camilla:

Through the rocks we wound:

The great pine shook with lonely sounds of joy
That came on the sea-wind. As mountain streams
Our bloods ran free: the sunshine seemed to brood
More warmly on the heart than on the brow.
We often paused, and, looking back, we saw
The clefts and openings in the mountains filled
With the blue valley and the glistening brooks,
And all the low dark groves, a land of love!

(I.317-325)

The inclusive "we" marks an affective world where distinctions of identity do not count, because all the elements of nature and scene enter into a joyful fluidity and commutability of identity—the pine commerces with the sea-wind, the mountain clefts reveal the beauty of the valley and brooks, and blood runs in the veins as freely as the mountain streams. So too, the sunshine is a spiritual as well as a physical influence, felt more in the heart than "on the brow" (a phrase that itself encompasses inner and outer: in the mind, as well as on the head). In such ways, Tennyson's lyrical mode reveals itself as one where joy or pleasure overcome, suspend, potentially conflictual oppositions and separations.

Of course, by the end of the poem the sanity and equilibrium of the male figure is threatened by the loss of the beloved, and can only be restored when he has heroically renounced both her and "his native land" (IV. 384). In the process, he undergoes an exile mirrored in the parallel-plot of **Maud,** where the protagonist also effectively loses the beloved who shared his childhood, and who always embodied his hopes. In **Maud,** the speaker's incipient hysteria and "jealous dread" (I.330) are confirmed by the poem's melodrama. However, earlier too, his isolation and paranoia had been for a time replaced by the various intermezzos and duets of love:

For a breeze of morning moves,
   And the planet of Love is on high,
Beginning to faint in the light that she loves
   On a bed of daffodil sky,
To faint in the light of the sun that she loves,
   To faint in his light, and to die.

(I.856-861)

The hanging participle ("Beginning") and the pronoun ("she") release multiple amorous possibilities and latent senses. Between dawn and day, identity is occluded and emergent, but also unimportant, because everything sings the same tune. Who is beginning to faint: the breeze? The planet of Love? Who is the "she" who loves: is it Maud, the planet of love? It does not matter because indetermination here is again not contradictory nor nebulous, but a radiant function of inclusive possibility, of enhanced individuation. As in *A Lover's Tale* this harmonious mobility of qualities and identity is again a property of "Love" itself, and is given sonically in the beautiful lilting cadence and repetitions of the stanza's close (and pictorially in that image of the star fading into a greater, encompassing light, "on a bed of daffodil sky"). In these last lines, an anapestic suggestion interplays with the iambic element, before taking over the poem. Lilting, lapping effects of sound prolong the "fainting" of the fading star of love, before providing a dying fall, a soft landing, for the stanza, as it comes to a prolonged anticipation of the demise of this moment, so gentle that it seems less a death than a pleasure.

Love in these extracts, indeed, is less an event in a life than the occurrence or advent of life itself, for someone who will otherwise be returned to a state of death-in-life. So these poems turn regretfully, and seemingly inevitably, from the contacts with femininity which have been staged through these occasions of love. Masculine subjectivity, then, is often reclaimed in Tennyson's work on the far side of lyrical intensities, but in stricken forms that scarcely seem worth possessing. In terms of these narrative poems, it certainly seems that a contact and participation with the feminine is a temptation or enthralment that is conditioned by the poverty of available forms of masculine identity, but which cannot be sustained in lived experience. Accordingly, masculine self-consciousness is eventually revealed as a function of a bereft, fixated, and isolated self, as it is for Ulysses, Simeon Stylites, Tithon, Tiresias, or Lucretius (or for many of the very earliest Byronic protagonists of the juvenilia) for whom also endurance, anchorism, bitter fatalism, stoicism, or the longing for death are the only possible responses to the blights of fate.

The Princess, of course, is an interesting case here, for the unusually affirmative variations it plays on the theme of gender difference. The eventual accommodations of the tale are a correlative of the socio-political vision that the poem projects, as it ties up romance with the feminism that was, as critics have pointed out, summarized in the 1832 version of **"A Dream of Fair Women"**:[21]

> In every land I thought that, more or less,
>   The stronger sterner nature overbore
> The softer, uncontrolled by gentleness
>   And selfish evermore.

> And whether there were any means whereby,
>   In some far aftertime, the gentler mind
> Might reassure its just and full degree
>   Of rule among mankind.

(*Poems,* 1:481)

The ameliorating logic of reconciliation and containment in *The Princess* extends between genders and genres, as Marjorie Stone has argued, to imagined resolutions of the divisions between the classes, and within the self (Stone, pp. 101-127). The poem, however, rather than imagining such comings together, ends with them, rather than with the male figure's mournful sense of their absence. In other respects, the poem obeys the logic of connection and inspiration operative in the other poem. Here too, the male depends—symbiotically or parasitically, as it were—on female influences to bring him to life and to expression. As in *Maud, Enoch Arden,* or *A Lover's Tale,* the poem's affective drama turns not on progressive choices or radical individual or collective action, but on what is literally a "passion of the past," a childhood love/betrothal:

>   Now it chanced that I had been
> While life was yet in bud and blade, betrothed
> To one, a neighbouring Princess: she to me
> Was proxy-wedded with a bootless calf
> At eight years old; and still from time to time
> Came murmurs of her beauty from the South,
> And of her brethren, youths of puissance;
> And still I wore her picture by my heart,
> And one dark tress; and all around them both
> Sweet thoughts would swarm as bees about their
>   queen.

(I.30-39)

The pattern of masculine subjection that is entailed here is articulated in a different, though related, form by the Prince:

>   now,
> Given back to life, to life indeed, through thee,
> Indeed I love.

(VII.323-325)

Certainly, too, the events of the poem demonstrate again that happiness and individual expression for men are contingent, and within the woman's gift: only through his needful indissociability from her can he find himself and his world. Indeed, to describe the common patterns here (where love is dramatized through moments of self-forgetful, reclusive, togetherness; where lovers mirror each other; where difference is bracketed; where common traits are elicited and emancipated by a female figure who also embodies them, and from whom they proceed; where the loss of the female is imagined as burial or exile) is virtually to describe the story of *The Princess.* Here men even go so far as to disguise themselves as women to infiltrate the female domain and find love.

One can also briefly point to those moments in Tennyson's life and work where the emptiness of masculinity surfaces (albeit often in necessarily disguised ways) as longing, envy, resentment, or despair. Much of his own uncertainty with women demonstrably involved a disabling ambivalence, a compound of masculine self-uncertainty, need, and instinctive avoidance. This insecurity seems to underlie many poems addressed to women, from **"Lilian"** or **"Adeline,"** to **"Lady Clara Vere de Vere,"** where so much in the poems' factitious heartiness or moralism or religiosity seems inadvertently to hint at the vertiginous sexual panic, self-alienation, and resentful emotional dependence behind the brittle male front. Jane Carlyle commented on Tennyson's unease with, even defensive contempt for, women (Martin, p. 284), and his oddly asexual and "inert" feeling for Rosa Baring appears again to manifest this general lack of conviction (Martin, p. 219). One can ponder tales of the variety of ways in which he recoiled from female self-displays, and conversely, the relief with which he would embrace forms of self-denial or sublimation (in life as in poems like **"Isabel," "The Lord of Burleigh," "St. Agnes' Eve," "The Beggar-Maid,"** and **"Geraint and Enid"**), or forms of sexual remorse (as in **"The May Queen"** or **"Guinevere"**). So, as a youth, Tennyson would often have to leave a dance to sit beneath the stairs or the stars, so profound were the sadness and feelings of dissociation stirred up in him (Martin, p. 84). As a young man, he avoided a display of female nakedness with another apostle, and as a middle-aged man, he rushed out of the box at the ballet, so overwhelmed was he at the scantily clad dancers (Martin, p. 481). At times, indeed, Tennyson's shyness, insecurity, and censoriousness in relation to women could even be unpleasant, as in his rudeness to Mrs. Norton the beautiful and *"déclassé"* novelist, separated from her husband, whom he met at Rogers' house in 1845 (Martin, pp. 283-284).

More speculative, perhaps, is the sense that these responses derived from a painful sense of the unattainability of female physicality (whether one reads this unattainability as sexual timorousness, as envy, or as both). In this context, one can ponder again whether many of Tennyson's abiding imaginative passions were not fundamentally expressions of that part of himself that desired to escape from the prison of masculine embodiment—his passions for the "far, far away," for the past, for death, for the fluid media of wind and water, his susceptibility to seizures and desire for those "waking trances" that led him into a participation with a "boundless being" transcending the accidents of personality, his fixation on living burial, and so on. From this viewpoint, the flailing reaction against his individual fate can plausibly be read as a literal, as well as familial, reaction to what Martin calls his "dread that one day he would be like his father," the sense even that it was the feminine from which he was fatefully excluded (p. 25).

II

"But do we too need to speak bluntly?" asks Christopher Ricks, Tennyson's least blunt critic. "Is Tennyson's love for Hallam a homosexual love?"[22] Perhaps we should rather ask, can we speak bluntly, since even a critic like Christopher Craft who answers this question broadly in the affirmative, has to develop an account of such sinuous (and surely self-defeating) subtlety. Craft takes his cue from Edward Carpenter's remark, that *In Memoriam* involves a certain reserve, which Craft glosses as Tennyson's "strategic equivocation" on the issue. Writes Craft:

> *In Memoriam* is more than a machine for the sublimation, management, or erasure of male homosexual desire. It is, rather, the site of a continuing problematization: a problematization not merely of desire between men but also of the desire, very urgent in the elegy, to speak it.[23]

Barbarous as Craft's terminology and formulations can appear, one can only admire the ingenuity of his argument: homosexual desire is transformed through elegy into a spiritualized form. In other words, such love is socially acceptable, but only in heaven, and only without bodies. And yet, as Christopher Ricks suggests, why should we not trust Tennyson's own remarks and their tone, in so far as they suggest that there was no homosexual relationship between Tennyson and Hallam, and perhaps no homosexual desire as such (*Tennyson,* pp. 203-209)? Nonetheless, the title of Craft's essay, "'Descend, and Touch, and Enter': Tennyson's Strange Manner of Address," trades on the sense that this is scarcely how heterosexual males speak, and Ricks admits the line to be "disconcert[ing]" (p. 205). What Ricks implies is that what is involved here is rather a transposition of gender (p. 205),[24] as is clearly the case in the manuscript version where Tennyson's speaker in Section 93 implores Hallam: "Stoop soul and touch me: wed me: hear / The wish too strong for words to name" (ll. 13-14).[25] The change of gender is again clearly evident when he writes of himself as being "like some poor girl whose heart is set / On one whose rank exceeds her own," or "of my spirit as of a wife" (60.3-4; 97.8). Ricks explores—without endorsing—the possibility that Tennyson might here be merging his own identity and loss with Emily's, but this seems implausible, unless there was a sense in which they were felt to be identical to start with (and Ricks appears obliquely to concede that this is implausible). Should we read such moments as a strategic dissimilation of self, or what Sinfield calls a "confusion of gender categories" (Sinfield, p. 136)? The difficulty with this, however, seems to be that the unguarded nature of these lyrics make them seem among the most intimate in the poem, moments again of unfolding or revelation, where an emergent female affectivity or voice shapes consciousness. This is not a confusion of gender categories, but a shift in gender positions.

A more striking (if also potentially more ambiguous) example would be Section 103, a seemingly pivotal moment in *In Memoriam* (both in the poem and in the process of bereavement), where the poet "dreamed a vision of the dead" (l. 3). Throughout the poem, he describes himself as with women, though the speaker's gender identity remains equivocal, the language of the passage leaving it uncertain whether he is merely among women or one identified with them: "I dwelt within a hall / And maidens with me" (103.5-6). The undecidability of such questions can be seen perhaps as part of the entranced atmosphere. In this poem daytime facts are surprised, the dead live again, enhanced, and crimson clouds appear, mirrored, like islands in the water; all desires can be inclusively taken up, all disagreements and grievances banished (according to the now familiar aesthetic logic), in the music that sweeps out of "sheet and shroud":

> The man we loved was there on deck,
>   And thrice as large as man he bent
>   To greet us. Up the side I went,
> And fell in silence on his neck:
>
> Whereat those maidens with one mind
>   Bewailed their lot; I did them wrong:
>   'We served thee here,' they said, 'so long,
> And wilt thou leave us now behind?'
>
> So rapt I was, they could not win
>   An answer from my lips, but he
>   Replying, 'Enter likewise ye
> And go with us:' they entered in.
>
> And while the wind began to sweep
>   A music out of sheet and shroud,
>   We steered her toward a crimson cloud
> That landlike slept along the deep.
>
>   (103.41-56)

My argument, then, is that the only way in which the various standards of this discussion can be acknowledged without contradiction is in fact to suspect the validity of the categorizations that are largely at work in the debates about gender and sexuality in Tennyson criticism. Sinfield articulates the problem that critics have faced, "It is not that Tennyson is revealed to have 'homosexual tendencies'—that would enable us to pigeon-hole him—but that there is no proper fit to be achieved with received discourses" (p. 145). In terms of the convergences of different lines of argument that I am suggesting, Tennyson indeed was not a homosexual male, nor was he "androgynous," nor was he drawn to a "blurring" or "inversion" or "transgression" of gender differences (even if *The Princess* does appear at times to investigate what a future might be like that was open to new kinds of gender identity and association). Rather, his imagination was essentially animated by an intra-psychic drama of identification, a rapt or fearful fascination with female figures that was itself predicated on

the surest sense of sexual difference (such as Tennyson possessed throughout his life), but that aspired, in its most extreme form, to an imagined change of gender.[26]

Whatever we make of the dreamt encounter in section 103, and its biographical actuality, the poem's scenario and temporality—as it arranges itself around an expressive interval between life and death—is very typical of Tennyson, and in these respects the lyric can be taken as indicating Tennyson's status as the great poet of suspension without finality: of the "art of the penultimate" in Ricks's phrase (*Tennyson*, p. 45). Yet there is an important difference too, since Ricks's discussion points to an art that is configured around prolonged but essentially hopeless moments of longing, as with many of the other great poems composed after Hallam's death—**"Ulysses," "St. Simeon Stylites," "Tithon,"** or **"Tiresias."** Section 103, on the contrary, is a poem that is possessed by a profound sense of expressive release and satisfaction of a kind deeply uncharacteristic of Tennyson (though its scenario of miraculous dissolution of dissension, and rapt sense of miraculous beauty is similar in mood and technique to so many poems). Indeed, as Ricks intimates, this prevailing sense of life as hopeless detention, of the impossibility of happiness and fulfilment, preceded the death of Hallam that became its greatest occasion. Ricks suggests that consciousness for Tennyson was accursed, exiled from happiness from the beginning. Tennyson's location of happiness in the past was perhaps an attempt to "stifle the other possibility: that a sorrow's crown of sorrow is not having any happier things to remember":

> He was a very truthful man, and he had a simple and most honourable conception of what truth consisted in. But he had too a desperate wish to believe that somewhere in his childhood there had been joy. . . . What is deeper in Tennyson, a poignant recognition that happiness may not have been lost but may rather have never been possessed. . . . Had all pleasant things gone before in Tennyson's earlier life, or had they gone before he was ever born?
>
>   (*Tennyson*, pp. 14-15)

However, if there never was happiness, it is equally true of much of Tennyson's poetry that there never will be. Indeed, the loss of the past can be seen as secondary to, conditioned by, this deeper and less remarked sense, of the loss of a future: the sense that he was exiled from happiness not because it was taken from him from the beginning, in the past, but because it was never available to him as a future. From this point of view, the turning to the past is only superficially mournful, and secretes consolatory fantasies, of a time when identity, particularly gender identity, was not dictated by social consciousness, as with the two children in **"Dualisms"**:

> Two children lovelier than Love adown the lea are singing,

> As they gambol, lilygarlands ever stringing:
> > Both in blosmwhite silk are frocked:
> Like, unlike, they roam together
> Under a summervault of golden weather;
> Like, unlike, they sing together
> > Side by Side,
> MidMay's darling goldenlocked,
> Summer's tanling diamondeyed.

(ll. 14-22)

The reiterated myth of childhood joy in Tennyson is also specifically one where child and mother were bound together, before the knowledge and partitions of gender had come into being. So too, for Tennyson, the birth of consciousness in childhood seems impressed by this sense of precluded expression, marking him out as an individual and poet for whom hope is impossible in this life, and for whom life is an interval to be stoically endured.

"The Lotos-Eaters," though a very different poem, nonetheless also explores comparable ways of eluding the constraints of adult male consciousness. Where masculine subjectivity is merely anticipated in **"Dualisms,"** though, it is truer to say that it is suspended in **"The Lotos-Eaters."** James Eli Adams has shown how the poem dramatizes a renunciation of Victorian forms of masculinity (and its key linkages to the worlds of imperial and industrial striving, and of domestic and moral obligation).[27] For my purposes, I would add too that the poem reveals that the price paid for such an existence is the loss of identity itself, and the meaningful imbrication of time and selfhood on which it depends. In **"The Lotos-Eaters,"** self has nowhere to go, and no time to become, stalled as it is in the charmed circle of the present. This is registered in the poem's melancholy undertow: its sense that the dream of a life of purely aesthetic and sensory pleasure, of endless yieldings, is shadowed by a contrary sense that such an existence of pure immediacy is an Hegelian nightmare of endless self-postponement. Seeing, hearing, tasting, touching have become a way of life rather than transitory, productive, moments of subjective renewal: "Only to hear and see the far-off sparkling brine, / Only to hear were sweet, stretched out beneath the pine" (ll. 143-144).

The reiterated "only" catches the longing for a paradise of ease and plenty, but it also harbors something of Enoch Arden's sense of his island life as unendurable. In the final section, I want to examine further these issues of temporality and subjectivity in relation to overtly feminine self-incarnations in Tennyson's work.

III

Three of Tennyson's finest recent critics, Matthew Rowlinson, Isobel Armstrong, and Robert Douglas-Fairhurst, have 'similarly explored the inwardness of Tennyson's poetry with its art of the interval, of a time between times. Within his fascinating discussion of influence, sympathy, and Tennyson's "passion of the past," Douglas-Fairhurst asserts that "the abiding in the transient is not only what Tennyson describes but also what he achieves."[28] Tennyson's methods of composition similarly betray a principle of continual provisionality and reanimation, a dedication to the "incomplete achievement, or achieved incompleteness" (p. 182) of individual poems. His art would disavow that the past has passed, and so that the future will similarly close up the present. It denies ending, stopping, parting, dying, and is dedicated—even in the turnings and returnings of the light brigade—to rotating perpetually on its own axes of repetition and transition: "In the resolute transformations of his poetry, as in the impassioned yearning of his religious faith, 'the dead are not dead but alive'" (Douglas-Fairhurst, p. 185).

Rather differently, Matthew Rowlinson has pondered the kinds of expressive impasse figured repeatedly in Tennyson's work. His brilliant reading of **"Mariana,"** for instance, brings out its representativeness for early Tennyson, and how the characteristic temporality and linguistic traits of the poems make them work as expressive analogues of the protagonists' quandaries, of lives lived as endless repetition and/or endless suspension, "pending an outcome that may never arise."[29] Interweaving Lacan and de Man, his book yields many insights in its argument for the pre-eminence of allegory as the appropriate trope for the "untimely" mode of Tennysonian textuality (p. 2). In **"Mariana,"** Rowlinson acknowledges the poem's displacement from the lyric values of voice and music (with which he shows it has often been associated), so that the poem can only be seen as an enactment of its own status as intertextual echo: "In **'Mariana'**, the place of the poem's music and breath is elsewhere, in texts constituted, as de Man would have it, in 'pure anteriority'" (p. 99).

For Rowlinson, Tennyson's early work is an aesthetic auto-meditation of the most rigorous kind, an allegorical reflection through its own dramas and language on the poet's intractable exile from the expressive values and desires associated with lyric poetry. On this reading, Mariana drawing the casement curtain and sighing as she glances "athwart the glooming flats" (l. 20), like the shrieking mouse behind "the mouldering wainscot" (l. 64), or the "blue fly" singing all day "in the pane" (l. 63), could be construed as offering an allegory of reading, an image of the poet's inescapable, painful epistemological dilemma as he finds his language endlessly provokes possibilities of an outside—of association, expression, and reference—only to confound them. The poem on this reading imprisons the reader within an endless, fatal, interval. At best we gain a skeptical distance, as if the transparent glass can also at moments become a reflective surface that reveals its own status as barrier, lure, illusion. For Rowlinson, Tennyson's poems display the twin transcendental structures of figuration and the Symbolic Order that produce consciousness as, respectively, ironic repetition or lack.

And yet, one wants to ask, why Tennyson's fixations? Rowlinson's theoretical apparatus does not in practice impede the focus on Tennyson's poetic individuality—on the contrary, his book is immensely subtle and revealing—but its axiomatic approach ultimately cannot distinguish Tennyson's own fixations from those of each and every linguistically constituted subject. For Mariana in her moated grange must we read the signifier in the symbolic order, or the untimely reader in the structure of allegory? An alternative mode of reading emerges in Isobel Armstrong's influential work, which offers a distinctive way of reconceiving Tennyson. For Armstrong, **"Mariana"** genuinely escapes stasis and solipsism. The poem is dynamic because of the way it interrogates as well as expresses Mariana's alienation, and it is social because this interrogation connects the poem to the outside world of nineteenth-century history, culture, and ideology. On this level, the poem's descriptions, its rendering of detail and setting, reveal to the reader not just what Mariana is feeling but also why. The concentric enclosures of landscape, moat, grange, casement, curtain for Armstrong are not simply symbolic equivalents of the heroine's trapped world of feeling, but also images of the essentially external, socialized constraints that have shaped her feminine consciousness as pure, hopeless interiority. The moated grange is a psychic prison, but one whose provenance in this reading of the poem derives from a patriarchal order whose constraints are inescapable, but also historically accidental and transformable. In this way, Mariana lives her endlessly detained affectivity, while the poem, as "a double poem," makes possible a symptomatic reading, through which this critical distance, and visions of an alternative future, can emerge:

> The poignant expression of exclusion to which Mariana's state gives rise, and which is reiterated in the marking of barriers—the moat itself, the gate with clinking latch, the curtained casement, the hinged doors—is simultaneously an analysis of the hypersensitive hysteria induced by the coercion of sexual taboo. These are hymenal taboos, which Mariana is induced, by a cultural consensus which is hidden from her, to experience as her own condition. Hidden from her, but not from the poem, the barriers are man-made, cunningly constructed through the material fabric of the house she inhabits, the enclosed spaces in which she is confined. It is the narrative voice which describes these spaces, not Mariana as speaker.[30]

So too, Armstrong suggests, the reflexive dimensions of **"Mariana"** accommodate an identity between Mariana and the poet's own condition as a post-Romantic poet abandoned at the secluded periphery of nineteenth-century life.

These readings share a common focus on Mariana's situation, but they read it in different ways. Where one could construe the "pane" in Rowlinson's terms as representing a seemingly universal and intractable linguistic-subjective predicament, one could see it in relation to Armstrong's argument, and its twin emphases on lyric and critique, as representing a barrier that is no less inescapable and invisible, since it represents the imprisoning condition, the glass wall so to speak, of female subjectification under nineteenth-century patriarchy. However, this is a situation that is crucially open to a different future. My aim in prolonging this discussion of these exemplary readings of the poem is not to adjudicate or chart a path between them, but to ask whether these explanations plausibly correspond to the reader's sense of the affective dimensions of this and other Tennyson poems? Is this a poem animated ultimately by epistemological, feminist, or cultural issues? Is it these which bind the poet and underlie the poem? On my own reading Mariana, caught up in her own mere virtuality, her unappeased and incessant longing, is an expressive projection, or phantasm, of Tennyson himself, and of those intractable, impossible longings for feminine self-expression that surface through the verse. John Ashbery once commented on "The broken sheds looked sad and strange" as one of the most "wonderfully and weirdly attractive" lines in English poetry.[31] Certainly, the uncanny magnetism of the line can be linked to the larger sense in the poem that the identity positions of poet, reader, Mariana, like the distinctions between past and present, are subject to radically destabilizing kinds of mirroring, transfer, and echoing, in this poem where the sad and strange figure on the page incarnates and reflects aspects of the affective life of the poet.

And so, of course, one can broaden and generalize this account, to describe many such female protagonists in Tennyson's work, whose impeded and yearning predicaments can be taken in this way as externalisations, projections of Tennyson's own inviolable imaginative need for female self-expression. Like the swan singing her "jubilant" but "'eddying song" (**"The Dying Swan,"** ll. 28, 42), the desire is at once irrepressible, but also necessarily transient, fated, circumscribed, and solitary. The early poetry, in particular, abounds in such female figures—Oenone, the Lady of Shalott, Fatima, the Mermaid, the female soul in **"The Palace of Art."** So he made the celebrated remark, of the poems of 1830, of "all these ladies" who "evolved, like the camel, from my own consciousness," women too like **"Claribel," "Isabel," "Lilian," "Adeline," "To Madeline"** and others, perhaps including Oriana in **"The Ballad of Oriana."** Tennyson's words suggest how the consciousness of the youthful poet was possessed by these female figures, in ways that defy the barriers of subject and object. As Marion Shaw has indicated,

Each woman offers the opportunity for a poetic exercise in which Tennyson could both practise his technique and also display attitudes, explore moods and indulge in fancies. They belong particularly to the undergraduate phase of Tennyson's career, the apprentice work of a young poet, interesting and slightly puzzling in that there are so many. They suggest an obsessional concern with women not only as objects to be written about but also as subjective states to be entered into.[32]

In this piece, I have sought to show how this direct and manifold engagement with women and female sensibility continues to operate throughout Tennyson's career, in complex, often covert, ways. Critics have often noted the young poet's more or less conscious imaginative connection with feminine experience, but less considered are the ways in which such a dynamic may underlie his later modes, even when his work ostensibly pursues a viable masculine voice, or when it seeks to "frame and contextualize his 'ladies,'" in Shaw's phrase, and to incorporate them into more narrative and moralizing treatments.

Notes

1. See Robert Martin, *Tennyson: The Unquiet Heart* (New York: Oxford Univ. Press, 1980), p. 581.

2. Hallam Tennyson, *Alfred Lord Tennyson: A Memoir,* 2 vols. (London, 1897), 2:427-428. Hallam says that the words might have referred to the book, or to "one of his last poems" and he cites the last two lines of the following extract from the 1892 poem, "God and the Universe":

   'Spirit, nearing yon dark portal at the limit of thy human state,
   Fear not thou the hidden purpose of that Power which alone is great,
   Nor the myriad world, His shadow, nor the silent Opener of the Gate.'

   (Christopher Ricks, ed., *The Poems of Tennyson,* 3 vols. [Berkeley: Univ. of California Press, 1987], 3:251; further citations are from this text)

3. Norman Page, ed., *Tennyson: Interviews and Recollections* (London: Macmillan, 1983), p. 195.

4. The contrary account here would be that of Hallam's wife, Audrey, who opposed Hallam's account that his father's dying words were "Hallam, Hallam" and (to Emily) "God bless you, my joy" by claiming that "it was almost impossible to make out more than a word here and there of what he said owing greatly I think to his having no teeth in" (Martin, p. 581).

5. In making this argument, I should make it clear that I am largely sidestepping the critical vocabularies that tend to assimilate these issues of gender identity to wider discussions of its cultural or social constructedness (as in James Eli Adams' *Dandies and Desert Saints: Styles of Victorian Masculinity* [Ithaca: Cornell Univ. Press, 1995]), or to an ontology of performance (as in Judith Butler's *Gender Trouble: Feminism and the Subversion of Identity* [New York: Routledge, 1990]). The emphasis here is rather on the coexistence in Tennyson's mind and work of male and female selves, and his continual search for socially tenable forms of masculine identity and self-integration. With respect to those moments and movements feminine self-imagining that I am describing, the conception comes closer to Jay Prosser's emphasis on the somatic, corporeal, and affective aspects of experiencing the body and self as eluding the material sex (*Second Skins: The Body Narratives of Transsexuality* [New York: Columbia Univ. Press, 1983]).

6. This description is broad enough to allow me to acknowledge Carol Christ's argument that Tennyson's poems find their condition in an emancipating (though threatening) aesthetic or amorous participation in the beauty, power, and self-possession of a female muse. See her much-cited essay, "The Feminine Subject in Victorian Poetry," *ELH* 54 (1987): 385-401. This argument, and its important differences from this one, though, will be taken up later.

7. Anthony Hecht, "On Alfred, Lord Tennyson," in *Poetry Speaks,* ed. Elise Paschen and Presson Mosby (Illinois: Sourcebooks, 2001), p. 4.

8. Marjorie Stone does identify the lyric far more closely with Ida and her reading of it, but Stone's discussion is complementary all the same, since it too turns on the constant "gender reversals," the interchange of "male" and "female images" within the poem, so that, for instance, "We might ask of these final four lines: 'Who is metaphorically entering whom?'" ("Genre Subversion and Gender Inversion: *The Princess* and *Aurora Leigh,*" *VP* 25 [1987]: 109).

9. The critical literature on these topics is a study in its own right, and one can broadly contrast the candor and insight of these later discussions with the earlier tendency to more or less veiled, bemused, and unsympathetic imputations of effeminacy or homosexuality. The key references, are the following: Edward Bulwer, "The Faults of Recent Poets," *New Monthly Magazine* 37 (January 1833): 69-74; John Wilson or "Christopher North," Review of *Poems, Chiefly Lyrical, Blackwood's Edinburgh Magazine* 31 (May 1832): 721-741; J. W. Croker, Review of *Poems* in the *Quarterly Review* (April 1833), repr. in *Tennyson: The Critical Heritage,* ed. John Jump (New York: Barnes and

Noble, 1967), pp. 66-83; Manley Hopkins, Review of *Poems, 1842* and *The Princess, Times,* October 12, 1848, p. 3; Charles Kingsley, Review of *Poems, 1842* and *The Princess,* in *Fraser's Magazine* 42 (September 1850): 245-255; and Alfred Austin, "Mr. Swinburne," repr. in *Swinburne: The Critical Heritage,* ed. Clyde K. Hyder (London: Routledge and Kegan Paul, 1970), pp. 92-111.

10. References to the relevant works by these writers will be made in the course of the discussion.

11. While acknowledging that this is scarcely a new emphasis, I would argue that it has rarely drawn a sustained treatment in proportion to its importance. Clearly, though, my account intersects, for example, with points made inimitably by Kate Millett about *The Princess*: "In his early poetry, Tennyson was fond of describing his own moods through lilylike maidens, Shalott, Mariana, etc. But in *The Princess* the fable becomes something of a case history of the poet's own problems of sexual identity. The prince who tells the story is not promising material—an epileptic with long golden curls who goes about in drag, and sings falsetto while courting. Tennyson veers between identifying with this paragon and the princess herself, also a poet, whose fierce desire for learning makes her a passionate and fairly commanding spirit" (*Sexual Politics* [London: Abacus, 1971], pp. 76-77).

Perhaps closer to the account developed here, would be John Killham's sense of Tennyson's "feminine streak" ("Tennyson and Fitzgerald," in *The Victorians,* ed. Arthur Pollard [London: Penguin, 1970], p. 273), or the influential approach of a critic like Lionel Stevenson (Jungian terminology notwithstanding), who saw the early Tennyson's female protagonists as incarnations of his female *anima* ("The 'High-Born Maiden' Symbol in Tennyson," in *Critical Essays on the Poetry of Tennyson,* ed. John Killham [London: Routledge and Kegan Paul, 1960], pp. 126-136).

12. Richard Cronin, *Romantic Victorians: English Literature, 1824-1840* (New York: Palgrave, 2002), p. 107. Cronin's assimilation of Tennyson's feminine identifications with a cultural climate interestingly intersects with Carol Christ's argument (p. 386) concerning Alfred Austin's remarks in 1869, though her emphasis is more marked by the sense of a guilty male appropriation of a distinctively female creative power:

13. Alan Sinfield, *Alfred Tennyson* (Oxford: Basil Blackwell, 1986), p. 143.

14. *Observer,* September 18, 1842, p. 3.

15. Edgar Finley Shannon, Jr., *Tennyson and the Reviewers* (Cambridge: Harvard Univ. Press, 1952), p. 33.

16. *Athenaeum,* April 6, 1844, p. 318. Many of these reviewers clearly anticipate themes in Isobel Armstrong's influential conception of Tennyson's revisions, in citing how Tennyson sought to overcome what were perceived as his langorous tendencies to song, introspection, and "memories of the past," and his need to show how poetry might engage with the world, and "social injustice" (in another phrase from the *Athenaeum* review).

17. Shannon, p. 46. His book, or the *Critical Heritage* volume, indicate how pervasive were these directives.

18. Like Christ, Catherine Maxwell has much to say about the feminine voices and figures in Tennyson's work, and the dependence of his imagination on what she sees as specifically female sources of power. However, the stakes of her argument are broader than Christ's, and less tied than mine to the specifics of Tennyson's individuality: she assimilates the relevant features of Tennyson's work to her description of the conditions of a post-Miltonic lyric tradition in which poetry is essentially and ambivalently associated with feminization, and where the male poet necessarily has to undergo a symbolic castration, through which he gains access to the powers of a female sublime. Such a characterization of Tennyson, taking him as a representative, even paradigmatic, figure in a male canon, though, clearly proceeds along radically different lines from my discussion, for reasons given more fully in footnote 4 above. See Catherine Maxwell, *The Female Sublime from Milton to Swinburne* (Manchester: Manchester Univ. Press, 2001).

19. This description of the poem, I realize, makes it sound similar to the stanza in 'The Miller's Daughter" where the narrator, his thoughts turning to love, peers into the water:

> And there a vision caught my eye;
> The reflex of a beauteous form,
>   A glowing arm, a gleaming neck,
> As when a sunbeam wavers warm,
>   Within the dark and dimpled beck.
>
> (ll. 76-80)

20. James W. Hood argues that such celebrations of female beauty subsume the erotic within a "poetics of transcendence." Physical desire is aestheticized, and transmuted, to figure the endlessly renewed ecstasies of a Dantean eternity of devotion. Thus, Hood says of "Eleänore" and "Madeline," for instance, that the poems stage and sustain an

infinite "suspension between longing and fulfil-ment" (*Divining Desire: Tennyson and the Poetics of Transcendence* [Aldershot: Ashgate, 2000], p. 44)

Hood's account of the characteristic temporality of Tennyson's poems, his contention that the eroti-cism, and engagement with femininity, in the po-etry go beyond simply its expressions of male sexual desire relate to my argument. Similarly, his account of the drive for transcendence in Tenny-son's work connects to my description of Tenny-son's sense of wordly existence as exile.

21. Christopher Ricks and John Killham have com-mented on the ways this passage anticipates the feminism of *The Princess.* See, for instance, Ricks, *Poems,* 2: 186.

22. Christopher Ricks, *Tennyson,* 2nd ed. (London: Palgrave 1989), p. 205. Hereafter cited as *Tenny-son.*

23. Christopher Craft, "'Descend and Touch and Enter': Tennyson's Strange Manner of Address," *Genders* 1 (Spring 1988): 85.

24. See *Tennyson,* pp. 180-219 particularly, for the full discussion of these areas that seemingly adopts a careful implication as its *modus operandi.*

25. Hood convincingly argues that it is implausible to believe that "the wish too strong for words to name" would be a homosexual one, given that Tennyson and his friends (as Ricks has also pointed out in the pages cited in footnote 35) of-ten did talk and write relatively freely about such passions (p. 113).

26. The account I am developing here is not inconsis-tent with his genuine—if mute and convoluted—forms of attraction to, and feeling for, women.

27. James Eli Adams has cogently demonstrated the ways in which "masculine discipline," asceticism, and self-mastery, and a public dedication to progress, industry, and culture coexist (both in Tennyson and in Victorian literary culture at large) with antagonistic dreams of a life of self-indulgent escape, and particularly here "fantasies of escape to a tropical paradise" (p. 111). His book has much to say about Tennyson's "feminine identification" in *In Memoriam,* in particular, and the poem's "extreme questioning of gender" (p. 51) as it in-corporates and gives voice to what Adams sees as explicitly female vocalizations of inner suffering.

28. Robert Douglas-Fairhurst, *Victorian Afterlives: The Shaping of Influence in Nineteenth-Century Literature* (Oxford: Oxford Univ. Press, 2002), p. 183.

29. Matthew Rowlinson, *Tennyson's Fixations: Psy-choanalysis and the Topics of the Early Poetry* (Charlottesville: Univ. of Virginia Press, 1994), p. 3.

30. Isobel Armstrong, *Victorian Poetry* (New York: Routledge, 1993), p. 13.

31. John Ashbery, review of Mark Ford's first poetry collection, *Landlocked, PN Review* (January/February, 1993): 63.

32. Marion Shaw, *Alfred Lord Tennyson* (Hemel Hempstead: Harvester, 1988), p. 75.

FURTHER READING

Criticism

Batchelor, John. "Alfred Tennyson: Problems of Biog-raphy." *Yearbook of English Studies* 36, no. 2 (2006): 78-95.
    Declares that a contextual, biographical reading of Tennyson's works provides essential information for interpreting them.

Campbell, Matthew. "Letting the Past Be Past: The En-glish Poet and the Irish Poem." *Victorian Literature and Culture* 32, no. 1 (2004): 63-82.
    Discusses how Celtic elements inform Tennyson's poetry and result in a transformed, hybrid English-Irish lyric form.

Demoor, Marysa. "'His Way Is thro' Chaos and the Bottomless and Pathless': The Gender of Madness in Alfred Tennyson's Poetry." *Neophilologus* 86, no. 2 (April 2002): 325-35.
    Studies the connection between madness and gen-der in Tennyson's poetry.

Leighton, Angela. "Touching Forms: Tennyson and Aes-theticism." *Tennyson Research Bulletin* 7, no. 5 (November 2001): 223-38.
    Argues that "Tennyson, consciously or uncon-sciously, offers the nineteenth century one of its most memorable, sensuous, aestheticist voices."

Platizky, Roger S. "'Like Dull Narcotics, Numbing Pain': Speculations on Tennyson and Opium." *Victorian Poetry* 40, no. 2 (summer 2002): 209-15.
    Brief article that speculates on Tennyson's aversion to opium.

Sherwood, Marion. "'Mr. Tennyson's Singular Genius': The Reception of *Poems* (1832)." *Tennyson Research Bulletin* 8, no. 4 (November 2005): 251-69.

Surveys Tennyson's contemporaries' critical reaction to his 1832 collection of poetry.

Talbot, John. "Tennyson's Alcaics: Greek and Latin Prosody and the Invention of English Meters." *Studies in Philology* 101, no. 2 (spring 2004): 200-31.

Provides a detailed analysis of Tennyson's use of the alcaic metrical pattern, including the author's adaptation of the form and some Classical Greek and Latin alcaic poetry.

Young-Zook, Monica M. "Sons and Lovers: Tennyson's Fraternal Paternity." *Victorian Literature and Culture* 33, no. 2 (2005): 451-66.

Maintains that "Tennyson's poetry is distinctly representative of a nineteenth-century problem in paternal representation that resulted from a gradual national shift in social structures from paternalistic hierarchies to committees and professional brotherhoods."

Additional coverage of Tennyson's life and career is contained in the following sources published by Gale: *Authors and Artists for Young Adults,* **Vol. 50;** *British Writers,* **Vol. 4;** *Concise Dictionary of British Literary Biography,* **1832-1890;** *Dictionary of Literary Biography,* **Vol. 32;** *DISCovering Authors; DISCovering Authors: British; DISCovering Authors: Canadian; DISCovering Authors Modules: Most-studied Authors* **and** *Poets; DISCovering Authors 3.0; Exploring Poetry; Literature Resource Center; Nineteenth-Century Literature Criticism,* **Vols. 30, 65, 115;** *Poetry Criticism,* **Vol. 6;** *Poetry for Students,* **Vols. 1, 2, 4, 11, 15, 19;** *Poets: American and British; Reference Guide to English Literature,* **Ed. 2;** *Twayne's English Authors; World Literature and Its Times,* **Vol. 4;** *World Literature Criticism;* **and** *World Poets.*

How to Use This Index

The main references

> Calvino, Italo
> 1923-1985 .... CLC 5, 8, 11, 22, 33, 39,
> 73; SSC 3, 48

list all author entries in the following Gale Literary Criticism series:

AAL = *Asian American Literature*
BG = *The Beat Generation: A Gale Critical Companion*
BLC = *Black Literature Criticism*
BLCS = *Black Literature Criticism Supplement*
CLC = *Contemporary Literary Criticism*
CLR = *Children's Literature Review*
CMLC = *Classical and Medieval Literature Criticism*
DC = *Drama Criticism*
FL = *Feminism in Literature: A Gale Critical Companion*
GL = *Gothic Literature: A Gale Critical Companion*
HLC = *Hispanic Literature Criticism*
HLCS = *Hispanic Literature Criticism Supplement*
HR = *Harlem Renaissance: A Gale Critical Companion*
LC = *Literature Criticism from 1400 to 1800*
NCLC = *Nineteenth-Century Literature Criticism*
NNAL = *Native North American Literature*
PC = *Poetry Criticism*
SSC = *Short Story Criticism*
TCLC = *Twentieth-Century Literary Criticism*
WLC = *World Literature Criticism, 1500 to the Present*
WLCS = *World Literature Criticism Supplement*

The cross-references

> See also CA 85-88, 116; CANR 23, 61;
> DAM NOV; DLB 196; EW 13; MTCW 1, 2;
> RGSF 2; RGWL 2; SFW 4; SSFS 12

list all author entries in the following Gale biographical and literary sources:

AAYA = *Authors & Artists for Young Adults*
AFAW = *African American Writers*
AFW = *African Writers*
AITN = *Authors in the News*
AMW = *American Writers*
AMWR = *American Writers Retrospective Supplement*
AMWS = *American Writers Supplement*
ANW = *American Nature Writers*
AW = *Ancient Writers*
BEST = *Bestsellers*
BPFB = *Beacham's Encyclopedia of Popular Fiction: Biography and Resources*
BRW = *British Writers*
BRWS = *British Writers Supplement*
BW = *Black Writers*
BYA = *Beacham's Guide to Literature for Young Adults*
CA = *Contemporary Authors*
CAAS = *Contemporary Authors Autobiography Series*
CABS = *Contemporary Authors Bibliographical Series*
CAD = *Contemporary American Dramatists*
CANR = *Contemporary Authors New Revision Series*
CAP = *Contemporary Authors Permanent Series*
CBD = *Contemporary British Dramatists*
CCA = *Contemporary Canadian Authors*
CD = *Contemporary Dramatists*
CDALB = *Concise Dictionary of American Literary Biography*

CDALBS = *Concise Dictionary of American Literary Biography Supplement*
CDBLB = *Concise Dictionary of British Literary Biography*
CMW = *St. James Guide to Crime & Mystery Writers*
CN = *Contemporary Novelists*
CP = *Contemporary Poets*
CPW = *Contemporary Popular Writers*
CSW = *Contemporary Southern Writers*
CWD = *Contemporary Women Dramatists*
CWP = *Contemporary Women Poets*
CWRI = *St. James Guide to Children's Writers*
CWW = *Contemporary World Writers*
DA = *DISCovering Authors*
DA3 = *DISCovering Authors 3.0*
DAB = *DISCovering Authors: British Edition*
DAC = *DISCovering Authors: Canadian Edition*
DAM = *DISCovering Authors: Modules*
   DRAM: *Dramatists Module;* **MST:** *Most-studied Authors Module;*
   MULT: *Multicultural Authors Module;* **NOV:** *Novelists Module;*
   POET: *Poets Module;* **POP:** *Popular Fiction and Genre Authors Module*
DFS = *Drama for Students*
DLB = *Dictionary of Literary Biography*
DLBD = *Dictionary of Literary Biography Documentary Series*
DLBY = *Dictionary of Literary Biography Yearbook*
DNFS = *Literature of Developing Nations for Students*
EFS = *Epics for Students*
EXPN = *Exploring Novels*
EXPP = *Exploring Poetry*
EXPS = *Exploring Short Stories*
EW = *European Writers*
FANT = *St. James Guide to Fantasy Writers*
FW = *Feminist Writers*
GFL = *Guide to French Literature,* Beginnings to 1789, 1798 to the Present
GLL = *Gay and Lesbian Literature*
HGG = *St. James Guide to Horror, Ghost & Gothic Writers*
HW = *Hispanic Writers*
IDFW = *International Dictionary of Films and Filmmakers: Writers and Production Artists*
IDTP = *International Dictionary of Theatre: Playwrights*
LAIT = *Literature and Its Times*
LAW = *Latin American Writers*
JRDA = *Junior DISCovering Authors*
MAICYA = *Major Authors and Illustrators for Children and Young Adults*
MAICYAS = *Major Authors and Illustrators for Children and Young Adults Supplement*
MAWW = *Modern American Women Writers*
MJW = *Modern Japanese Writers*
MTCW = *Major 20th-Century Writers*
NCFS = *Nonfiction Classics for Students*
NFS = *Novels for Students*
PAB = *Poets: American and British*
PFS = *Poetry for Students*
RGAL = *Reference Guide to American Literature*
RGEL = *Reference Guide to English Literature*
RGSF = *Reference Guide to Short Fiction*
RGWL = *Reference Guide to World Literature*
RHW = *Twentieth-Century Romance and Historical Writers*
SAAS = *Something about the Author Autobiography Series*
SATA = *Something about the Author*
SFW = *St. James Guide to Science Fiction Writers*
SSFS = *Short Stories for Students*
TCWW = *Twentieth-Century Western Writers*
WLIT = *World Literature and Its Times*
WP = *World Poets*
YABC = *Yesterday's Authors of Books for Children*
YAW = *St. James Guide to Young Adult Writers*

Literary Criticism Series
Cumulative Author Index

5, 165, 342; EWL 3; MAL 5; MTCW 1,
2; PFS 19; RGAL 4; TCLE 1:1

Ammons, Archie Randolph
See Ammons, A.R.

Amo, Tauraatua i
See Adams, Henry (Brooks)

Amory, Thomas 1691(?)-1788 .... **LC 48**
See also DLB 39

Anand, Mulk Raj 1905-2004 ..... **CLC 23, 93, 237**
See also CA 65-68; 231; CANR 32, 64; CN
1, 2, 3, 4, 5, 6, 7; DAM NOV; DLB 323;
EWL 3; MTCW 1, 2; MTFW 2005; RGSF
2

Anatol
See Schnitzler, Arthur

Anaximander c. 611B.C.-c.
546B.C. .... **CMLC 22**

Anaya, Rudolfo A. 1937- . CLC 23, 148, 255;
HLC 1
See also AAYA 20; BYA 13; CA 45-48;
CAAS 4; CANR 1, 32, 51, 124, 169; CLR
129; CN 4, 5, 6, 7; DAM MULT, NOV;
DLB 82, 206, 278; HW 1; LAIT 4; LLW;
MAL 5; MTCW 1, 2; MTFW 2005; NFS
12; RGAL 4; RGSF 2; TCWW 2; WLIT
1

Anaya, Rudolpho Alfonso
See Anaya, Rudolfo A.

Andersen, Hans Christian
1805-1875 .... NCLC 7, 79; SSC 6, 56;
WLC 1
See also AAYA 57; CLR 6, 113; DA; DA3;
DAB; DAC; DAM MST, POP; EW 6;
MAICYA 1, 2; RGSF 2; RGWL 2, 3;
SATA 100; TWA; WCH; YABC 1

Anderson, C. Farley
See Mencken, H(enry) L(ouis); Nathan,
George Jean

Anderson, Jessica (Margaret) Queale
1916- .... **CLC 37**
See also CA 9-12R; CANR 4, 62; CN 4, 5,
6, 7; DLB 325

Anderson, Jon (Victor) 1940- .... **CLC 9**
See also CA 25-28R; CANR 20; CP 1, 3, 4,
5; DAM POET

Anderson, Lindsay (Gordon)
1923-1994 .... **CLC 20**
See also CA 125; 128; 146; CANR 77

Anderson, Maxwell 1888-1959 .... **TCLC 2, 144**
See also CA 105; 152; DAM DRAM; DFS
16, 20; DLB 7, 228; MAL 5; MTCW 2;
MTFW 2005; RGAL 4

Anderson, Poul 1926-2001 .... **CLC 15**
See also AAYA 5, 34; BPFB 1; BYA 6, 8,
9; CA 1-4R; 181; 199; CAAE 181; CAAS
2; CANR 2, 15, 34, 64, 110; CLR 58;
DLB 8; FANT; INT CANR-15; MTCW 1,
2; MTFW 2005; SATA 90; SATA-Brief
39; SATA-Essay 106; SCFW 1, 2; SFW
4; SUFW 1, 2

Anderson, Robert (Woodruff)
1917- .... **CLC 23**
See also AITN 1; CA 21-24R; CANR 32;
CD 6; DAM DRAM; DLB 7; LAIT 5

Anderson, Roberta Joan
See Mitchell, Joni

Anderson, Sherwood 1876-1941 ... SSC 1, 46,
91; TCLC 1, 10, 24, 123; WLC 1
See also AAYA 30; AMW; AMWC 2; BPFB
1; CA 104; 121; CDALB
1917-1929; DA; DA3; DAB; DAC; DAM
MST, NOV; DLB 4, 9, 86; DLBD 1; EWL
3; EXPS; GLL 2; MAL 5; MTCW 1, 2;
MTFW 2005; NFS 4; RGAL 4; RGSF 2;
SSFS 4, 10, 11; TUS

Anderson, Wes 1969- .... **CLC 227**
See also CA 214

Andier, Pierre
See Desnos, Robert

Andouard
See Giraudoux, Jean(-Hippolyte)

Andrade, Carlos Drummond de ..... **CLC 18**
See Drummond de Andrade, Carlos
See also EWL 3; RGWL 2, 3

Andrade, Mario de .... **TCLC 43**
See de Andrade, Mario
See also DLB 307; EWL 3; LAW; RGWL
2, 3; WLIT 1

Andreae, Johann V(alentin)
1586-1654 .... **LC 32**
See also DLB 164

Andreas Capellanus fl. c. 1185- .... **CMLC 45**
See also DLB 208

Andreas-Salome, Lou 1861-1937 ... **TCLC 56**
See also CA 178; DLB 66

Andreev, Leonid
See Andreyev, Leonid (Nikolaevich)
See also DLB 295; EWL 3

Andress, Lesley
See Sanders, Lawrence

Andrewes, Lancelot 1555-1626 .... **LC 5**
See also DLB 151, 172

Andrews, Cicily Fairfield
See West, Rebecca

Andrews, Elton V.
See Pohl, Frederik

Andrews, Peter
See Soderbergh, Steven

Andrews, Raymond 1934-1991 .... **BLC 2:1**
See also BW 2; CA 81-84; 136; CANR 15,
42

Andreyev, Leonid (Nikolaevich)
1871-1919 .... **TCLC 3**
See Andreev, Leonid
See also CA 104; 185

Andric, Ivo 1892-1975 .... CLC 8; SSC 36;
TCLC 135
See also CA 81-84; 57-60; CANR 43, 60;
CDWLB 4; DLB 147, 329; EW 11; EWL
3; MTCW 1; RGSF 2; RGWL 2, 3

Androvar
See Prado (Calvo), Pedro

Angela of Foligno 1248(?)-1309 .... **CMLC 76**

Angelique, Pierre
See Bataille, Georges

Angell, Roger 1920- .... **CLC 26**
See also CA 57-60; CANR 13, 44, 70, 144;
DLB 171, 185

Angelou, Maya 1928- ...... BLC 1:1; CLC 12,
35, 64, 77, 155; PC 32; WLCS
See also AAYA 7, 20; AMWS 4; BPFB 1;
BW 2, 3; BYA 2; CA 65-68; CANR 19,
42, 65, 111, 133; CDALBS; CLR 53; CP
4, 5, 6, 7; CPW; CSW; CWP; DA; DA3;
DAB; DAC; DAM MST, MULT, POET,
POP; DLB 38; EWL 3; EXPN; EXPP; FL
1:5; LAIT 4; MAICYA 2; MAICYAS 1;
MAL 5; MBL; MTCW 1, 2; MTFW 2005;
NCFS 2; NFS 2; PFS 2, 3; RGAL 4;
SATA 49, 136; TCLE 1:1; WYA; YAW

Angouleme, Marguerite d'
See de Navarre, Marguerite

Anna Comnena 1083-1153 .... **CMLC 25**

Annensky, Innokentii Fedorovich
See Annensky, Innokenty (Fyodorovich)
See also DLB 295

Annensky, Innokenty (Fyodorovich)
1856-1909 .... **TCLC 14**
See also CA 110; 155; EWL 3

Annunzio, Gabriele d'
See D'Annunzio, Gabriele

Anodos
See Coleridge, Mary E(lizabeth)

Anon, Charles Robert
See Pessoa, Fernando (Antonio Nogueira)

Anouilh, Jean 1910-1987 ..... CLC 1, 3, 8, 13,
40, 50; DC 8, 21; TCLC 195
See also AAYA 67; CA 17-20R; 123; CANR
32; DAM DRAM; DFS 9, 10, 19; DLB
321; EW 13; EWL 3; GFL 1789 to the
Present; MTCW 1, 2; MTFW 2005;
RGWL 2, 3; TWA

Ansa, Tina McElroy 1949- .... **BLC 2:1**
See also BW 2; CA 142; CANR 143; CSW

Anselm of Canterbury
1033(?)-1109 .... **CMLC 67**
See also DLB 115

Anthony, Florence
See Ai

Anthony, John
See Ciardi, John (Anthony)

Anthony, Peter
See Shaffer, Anthony; Shaffer, Peter

Anthony, Piers 1934- .... **CLC 35**
See also AAYA 11, 48; BYA 7; CA 200;
CAAE 200; CANR 28, 56, 73, 102, 133;
CLR 118; CPW; DAM POP; DLB 8;
FANT; MAICYA 2; MAICYAS 1; MTCW
1, 2; MTFW 2005; SAAS 22; SATA 84,
129; SATA-Essay 129; SFW 4; SUFW 1,
2; YAW

Anthony, Susan B(rownell)
1820-1906 .... **TCLC 84**
See also CA 211; FW

Antiphon c. 480B.C.-c. 411B.C. .... **CMLC 55**

Antoine, Marc
See Proust, (Valentin-Louis-George-Eugene)
Marcel

Antoninus, Brother
See Everson, William (Oliver)
See also CP 1

Antonioni, Michelangelo
1912-2007 .... CLC 20, 144, 259
See also CA 73-76; 262; CANR 45, 77

Antschel, Paul 1920-1970
See Celan, Paul
See also CA 85-88; CANR 33, 61; MTCW
1; PFS 21

Anwar, Chairil 1922-1949 .... **TCLC 22**
See Chairil Anwar
See also CA 121; 219; RGWL 3

Anyidoho, Kofi 1947- .... **BLC 2:1**
See also BW 3; CA 178; CP 5, 6, 7; DLB
157; EWL 3

Anzaldua, Gloria (Evanjelina)
1942-2004 .... CLC 200; HLCS 1
See also CA 175; 227; CSW; CWP; DLB
122; FW; LLW; RGAL 4; SATA-Obit 154

Apess, William 1798-1839(?) .... NCLC 73;
NNAL
See also DAM MULT; DLB 175, 243

Apollinaire, Guillaume 1880-1918 .... PC 7;
TCLC 3, 8, 51
See Kostrowitzki, Wilhelm Apollinaris de
See also CA 152; DAM POET; DLB 258,
321; EW 9; EWL 3; GFL 1789 to the
Present; MTCW 2; PFS 24; RGWL 2, 3;
TWA; WP

Apollonius of Rhodes
See Apollonius Rhodius
See also AW 1; RGWL 2, 3

Apollonius Rhodius c. 300B.C.-c.
220B.C. .... **CMLC 28**
See Apollonius of Rhodes
See also DLB 176

Appelfeld, Aharon 1932- ... CLC 23, 47; SSC 42
See also CA 112; 133; CANR 86, 160;
CWW 2; DLB 299; EWL 3; RGHL;
RGSF 2; WLIT 6

Appelfeld, Aron
See Appelfeld, Aharon

Apple, Max (Isaac) 1941- .... **CLC 9, 33; SSC 50**
See also AMWS 17; CA 81-84; CANR 19, 54; DLB 130

Appleman, Philip (Dean) 1926- .... **CLC 51**
See also CA 13-16R; CAAS 18; CANR 6, 29, 56

Appleton, Lawrence
See Lovecraft, H. P.

Apteryx
See Eliot, T(homas) S(tearns)

Apuleius, (Lucius Madaurensis) c. 125-c. 164 .... **CMLC 1, 84**
See also AW 2; CDWLB 1; DLB 211; RGWL 2, 3; SUFW; WLIT 8

Aquin, Hubert 1929-1977 .... **CLC 15**
See also CA 105; DLB 53; EWL 3

Aquinas, Thomas 1224(?)-1274 ..... **CMLC 33**
See also DLB 115; EW 1; TWA

Aragon, Louis 1897-1982 .... **CLC 3, 22; TCLC 123**
See also CA 69-72; 108; CANR 28, 71; DAM NOV, POET; DLB 72, 258; EW 11; EWL 3; GFL 1789 to the Present; GLL 2; LMFS 2; MTCW 1, 2; RGWL 2, 3

Arany, Janos 1817-1882 .... **NCLC 34**

Aranyos, Kakay 1847-1910
See Mikszath, Kalman

Aratus of Soli c. 315B.C.-c. 240B.C. .... **CMLC 64**
See also DLB 176

Arbuthnot, John 1667-1735 .... **LC 1**
See also DLB 101

Archer, Herbert Winslow
See Mencken, H(enry) L(ouis)

Archer, Jeffrey 1940- .... **CLC 28**
See also AAYA 16; BEST 89:3; BPFB 1; CA 77-80; CANR 22, 52, 95, 136; CPW; DA3; DAM POP; INT CANR-22; MTFW 2005

Archer, Jeffrey Howard
See Archer, Jeffrey

Archer, Jules 1915- .... **CLC 12**
See also CA 9-12R; CANR 6, 69; SAAS 5; SATA 4, 85

Archer, Lee
See Ellison, Harlan

Archilochus c. 7th cent. B.C.- .... **CMLC 44**
See also DLB 176

Ard, William
See Jakes, John

Arden, John 1930- .... **CLC 6, 13, 15**
See also BRWS 2; CA 13-16R; CAAS 4; CANR 31, 65, 67, 124; CBD; CD 5, 6; DAM DRAM; DFS 9; DLB 13, 245; EWL 3; MTCW 1

Arenas, Reinaldo 1943-1990 .. **CLC 41; HLC 1; TCLC 191**
See also CA 124; 128; 133; CANR 73, 106; DAM MULT; DLB 145; EWL 3; GLL 2; HW 1; LAW; LAWS 1; MTCW 2; MTFW 2005; RGSF 2; RGWL 3; WLIT 1

Arendt, Hannah 1906-1975 .... **CLC 66, 98; TCLC 193**
See also CA 17-20R; 61-64; CANR 26, 60, 172; DLB 242; MTCW 1, 2

Aretino, Pietro 1492-1556 .... **LC 12**
See also RGWL 2, 3

Arghezi, Tudor .... **CLC 80**
See Theodorescu, Ion N.
See also CA 167; CDWLB 4; DLB 220; EWL 3

Arguedas, Jose Maria 1911-1969 .... **CLC 10, 18; HLCS 1; TCLC 147**
See also CA 89-92; CANR 73; DLB 113; EWL 3; HW 1; LAW; RGWL 2, 3; WLIT 1

Argueta, Manlio 1936- .... **CLC 31**
See also CA 131; CANR 73; CWW 2; DLB 145; EWL 3; HW 1; RGWL 3

Arias, Ron 1941- .... **HLC 1**
See also CA 131; CANR 81, 136; DAM MULT; DLB 82; HW 1, 2; MTCW 2; MTFW 2005

Ariosto, Lodovico
See Ariosto, Ludovico
See also WLIT 7

Ariosto, Ludovico 1474-1533 ... **LC 6, 87; PC 42**
See Ariosto, Lodovico
See also EW 2; RGWL 2, 3

Aristides
See Epstein, Joseph

Aristophanes 450B.C.-385B.C. .... **CMLC 4, 51; DC 2; WLCS**
See also AW 1; CDWLB 1; DA; DA3; DAB; DAC; DAM DRAM, MST; DFS 10; DLB 176; LMFS 1; RGWL 2, 3; TWA; WLIT 8

Aristotle 384B.C.-322B.C. .... **CMLC 31; WLCS**
See also AW 1; CDWLB 1; DA; DA3; DAB; DAC; DAM MST; DLB 176; RGWL 2, 3; TWA; WLIT 8

Arlt, Roberto (Godofredo Christophersen) 1900-1942 .... **HLC 1; TCLC 29**
See also CA 123; 131; CANR 67; DAM MULT; DLB 305; EWL 3; HW 1, 2; IDTP; LAW

Armah, Ayi Kwei 1939- . **BLC 1:1, 2:1; CLC 5, 33, 136**
See also AFW; BRWS 10; BW 1; CA 61-64; CANR 21, 64; CDWLB 3; CN 1, 2, 3, 4, 5, 6, 7; DAM MULT, POET; DLB 117; EWL 3; MTCW 1; WLIT 2

Armatrading, Joan 1950- .... **CLC 17**
See also CA 114; 186

Armin, Robert 1568(?)-1615(?) .... **LC 120**

Armitage, Frank
See Carpenter, John (Howard)

Armstrong, Jeannette (C.) 1948- .... **NNAL**
See also CA 149; CCA 1; CN 6, 7; DAC; DLB 334; SATA 102

Arnette, Robert
See Silverberg, Robert

Arnim, Achim von (Ludwig Joachim von Arnim) 1781-1831 .. **NCLC 5, 159; SSC 29**
See also DLB 90

Arnim, Bettina von 1785-1859 ...... **NCLC 38, 123**
See also DLB 90; RGWL 2, 3

Arnold, Matthew 1822-1888 ..... **NCLC 6, 29, 89, 126; PC 5; WLC 1**
See also BRW 5; CDBLB 1832-1890; DA; DAB; DAC; DAM MST, POET; DLB 32, 57; EXPP; PAB; PFS 2; TEA; WP

Arnold, Thomas 1795-1842 .... **NCLC 18**
See also DLB 55

Arnow, Harriette (Louisa) Simpson 1908-1986 ...... **CLC 2, 7, 18; TCLC 196**
See also BPFB 1; CA 9-12R; 118; CANR 14; CN 2, 3, 4; DLB 6; FW; MTCW 1, 2; RHW; SATA 42; SATA-Obit 47

Arouet, Francois-Marie
See Voltaire

Arp, Hans
See Arp, Jean

Arp, Jean 1887-1966 .... **CLC 5; TCLC 115**
See also CA 81-84; 25-28R; CANR 42, 77; EW 10

Arrabal
See Arrabal, Fernando

Arrabal (Teran), Fernando
See Arrabal, Fernando
See also CWW 2

Arrabal, Fernando 1932- ... **CLC 2, 9, 18, 58**
See Arrabal (Teran), Fernando
See also CA 9-12R; CANR 15; DLB 321; EWL 3; LMFS 2

Arreola, Juan Jose 1918-2001 .... **CLC 147; HLC 1; SSC 38**
See also CA 113; 131; 200; CANR 81; CWW 2; DAM MULT; DLB 113; DNFS 2; EWL 3; HW 1, 2; LAW; RGSF 2

Arrian c. 89(?)-c. 155(?) .... **CMLC 43**
See also DLB 176

Arrick, Fran .... **CLC 30**
See Gaberman, Judie Angell
See also BYA 6

Arley, Richmond
See Delany, Samuel R., Jr.

Artaud, Antonin (Marie Joseph) 1896-1948 .... **DC 14; TCLC 3, 36**
See also CA 104; 149; DA3; DAM DRAM; DFS 22; DLB 258; EW 11; EWL 3; GFL 1789 to the Present; MTCW 2; MTFW 2005; RGWL 2, 3

Arthur, Ruth M(abel) 1905-1979 ..... **CLC 12**
See also CA 9-12R; 85-88; CANR 4; CWRI 5; SATA 7, 26

Artsybashev, Mikhail (Petrovich) 1878-1927 .... **TCLC 31**
See also CA 170; DLB 295

Arundel, Honor (Morfydd) 1919-1973 .... **CLC 17**
See also CA 21-22; 41-44R; CAP 2; CLR 35; CWRI 5; SATA 4; SATA-Obit 24

Arzner, Dorothy 1900-1979 .... **CLC 98**

Asch, Sholem 1880-1957 .... **TCLC 3**
See also CA 105; DLB 333; EWL 3; GLL 2; RGHL

Ascham, Roger 1516(?)-1568 .... **LC 101**
See also DLB 236

Ash, Shalom
See Asch, Sholem

Ashbery, John 1927- ... **CLC 2, 3, 4, 6, 9, 13, 15, 25, 41, 77, 125, 221; PC 26**
See also AMWS 3; CA 5-8R; CANR 9, 37, 66, 102, 132, 170; CP 1, 2, 3, 4, 5, 6, 7; DA3; DAM POET; DLB 5, 165; DLBY 1981; EWL 3; GLL 1; INT CANR-9; MAL 5; MTCW 1, 2; MTFW 2005; PAB; PFS 11, 28; RGAL 4; TCLE 1:1; WP

Ashbery, John Lawrence
See Ashbery, John

Ashbridge, Elizabeth 1713-1755 .... **LC 147**
See also DLB 200

Ashdown, Clifford
See Freeman, R(ichard) Austin

Ashe, Gordon
See Creasey, John

Ashton-Warner, Sylvia (Constance) 1908-1984 .... **CLC 19**
See also CA 69-72; 112; CANR 29; CN 1, 2, 3; MTCW 1, 2

Asimov, Isaac 1920-1992 ..... **CLC 1, 3, 9, 19, 26, 76, 92**
See also AAYA 13; BEST 90:2; BPFB 1; BYA 4, 6, 7, 9; CA 1-4R; 137; CANR 2, 19, 36, 60, 125; CLR 12, 79; CMW 4; CN 1, 2, 3, 4, 5; CPW; DA3; DAM POP; DLB 8; DLBY 1992; INT CANR-19; JRDA; LAIT 5; LMFS 2; MAICYA 1, 2; MAL 5; MTCW 1, 2; MTFW 2005; RGAL 4; SATA 1, 26, 74; SCFW 1, 2; SFW 4; SSFS 17; TUS; YAW

Askew, Anne 1521(?)-1546 .... **LC 81**
See also DLB 136

Assis, Joaquim Maria Machado de
See Machado de Assis, Joaquim Maria

Astell, Mary 1666-1731 .... **LC 68**
See also DLB 252, 336; FW

Beattie, James 1735-1803 .... **NCLC 25**
See also DLB 109

Beauchamp, Kathleen Mansfield 1888-1923
See Mansfield, Katherine
See also CA 104; 134; DA; DA3; DAC;
DAM MST; MTCW 2; TEA

Beaumarchais, Pierre-Augustin Caron de
1732-1799 .... **DC 4; LC 61**
See also DAM DRAM; DFS 14, 16; DLB
313; EW 4; GFL Beginnings to 1789;
RGWL 2, 3

Beaumont, Francis 1584(?)-1616 .. **DC 6; LC 33**
See also BRW 2; CDBLB Before 1660;
DLB 58; TEA

Beauvoir, Simone de 1908-1986 .... **CLC 1, 2, 4, 8, 14, 31, 44, 50, 71, 124; SSC 35; WLC 1**
See also BPFB 1; CA 9-12R; 118; CANR
28, 61; DA; DA3; DAB; DAC; DAM
MST, NOV; DLB 72; DLBY 1986; EW
12; EWL 3; FL 1:5; FW; GFL 1789 to the
Present; LMFS 2; MTCW 1, 2; MTFW
2005; RGSF 2; RGWL 2, 3; TWA

Beauvoir, Simone Lucie Ernestine Marie Bertrand de
See Beauvoir, Simone de

Becker, Carl (Lotus) 1873-1945 ..... **TCLC 63**
See also CA 157; DLB 17

Becker, Jurek 1937-1997 .... **CLC 7, 19**
See also CA 85-88; 157; CANR 60, 117;
CWW 2; DLB 75, 299; EWL 3; RGHL

Becker, Walter 1950- .... **CLC 26**

Becket, Thomas a 1118(?)-1170 .... **CMLC 83**

Beckett, Samuel 1906-1989 ... **CLC 1, 2, 3, 4, 6, 9, 10, 11, 14, 18, 29, 57, 59, 83; DC 22; SSC 16, 74; TCLC 145; WLC 1**
See also BRWC 2; BRWR 1; BRWS 1; CA
5-8R; 130; CANR 33, 61; CBD; CDBLB
1945-1960; CN 1, 2, 3, 4; CP 1, 2, 3, 4;
DA; DA3; DAB; DAC; DAM DRAM,
MST, NOV; DFS 2, 7, 18; DLB 13, 15,
233, 319, 321, 329; DLBY 1990; EWL 3;
GFL 1789 to the Present; LATS 1:2;
LMFS 2; MTCW 1, 2; MTFW 2005;
RGSF 2; RGWL 2, 3; SSFS 15; TEA;
WLIT 4

Beckford, William 1760-1844 .... **NCLC 16**
See also BRW 3; DLB 39, 213; GL 2; HGG;
LMFS 1; SUFW

Beckham, Barry (Earl) 1944- .... **BLC 1:1**
See also BW 1; CA 29-32R; CANR 26, 62;
CN 1, 2, 3, 4, 5, 6; DAM MULT; DLB 33

Beckman, Gunnel 1910- .... **CLC 26**
See also CA 33-36R; CANR 15, 114; CLR
25; MAICYA 1, 2; SAAS 9; SATA 6

Becque, Henri 1837-1899 .... **DC 21; NCLC 3**
See also DLB 192; GFL 1789 to the Present

Becquer, Gustavo Adolfo
1836-1870 .... **HLCS 1; NCLC 106**
See also DAM MULT

Beddoes, Thomas Lovell 1803-1849 .. **DC 15; NCLC 3, 154**
See also BRWS 11; DLB 96

Bede c. 673-735 .... **CMLC 20**
See also DLB 146; TEA

Bedford, Denton R. 1907-(?) .... **NNAL**

Bedford, Donald F.
See Fearing, Kenneth (Flexner)

Beecher, Catharine Esther
1800-1878 .... **NCLC 30**
See also DLB 1, 243

Beecher, John 1904-1980 .... **CLC 6**
See also AITN 1; CA 5-8R; 105; CANR 8;
CP 1, 2, 3

Beer, Johann 1655-1700 .... **LC 5**
See also DLB 168

Beer, Patricia 1924- .... **CLC 58**
See also CA 61-64; 183; CANR 13, 46; CP
1, 2, 3, 4, 5, 6; CWP; DLB 40; FW

Beerbohm, Max
See Beerbohm, (Henry) Max(imilian)

Beerbohm, (Henry) Max(imilian)
1872-1956 .... **TCLC 1, 24**
See also BRWS 2; CA 104; 154; CANR 79;
DLB 34, 100; FANT; MTCW 2

Beer-Hofmann, Richard
1866-1945 .... **TCLC 60**
See also CA 160; DLB 81

Beg, Shemus
See Stephens, James

Begiebing, Robert J(ohn) 1946- .... **CLC 70**
See also CA 122; CANR 40, 88

Begley, Louis 1933- .... **CLC 197**
See also CA 140; CANR 98, 176; DLB 299;
RGHL; TCLE 1:1

Behan, Brendan (Francis)
1923-1964 .... **CLC 1, 8, 11, 15, 79**
See also BRWS 2; CA 73-76; CANR 33,
121; CBD; CDBLB 1945-1960; DAM
DRAM; DFS 7; DLB 13, 233; EWL 3;
MTCW 1, 2

Behn, Aphra 1640(?)-1689 .. **DC 4; LC 1, 30, 42, 135; PC 13, 88; WLC 1**
See also BRWS 3; DA; DA3; DAB; DAC;
DAM DRAM, MST, NOV, POET; DFS
16, 24; DLB 39, 80, 131; FW; TEA;
WLIT 3

Behrman, S(amuel) N(athaniel)
1893-1973 .... **CLC 40**
See also CA 13-16; 45-48; CAD; CAP 1;
DLB 7, 44; IDFW 3; MAL 5; RGAL 4

Bekederemo, J. P. Clark
See Clark Bekederemo, J.P.
See also CD 6

Belasco, David 1853-1931 .... **TCLC 3**
See also CA 104; 168; DLB 7; MAL 5;
RGAL 4

Belcheva, Elisaveta Lyubomirova
1893-1991 .... **CLC 10**
See Bagryana, Elisaveta

Beldone, Phil "Cheech"
See Ellison, Harlan

Beleno
See Azuela, Mariano

Belinski, Vissarion Grigoryevich
1811-1848 .... **NCLC 5**
See also DLB 198

Belitt, Ben 1911- .... **CLC 22**
See also CA 13-16R; CAAS 4; CANR 7,
77; CP 1, 2, 3, 4, 5, 6; DLB 5

Belknap, Jeremy 1744-1798 .... **LC 115**
See also DLB 30, 37

Bell, Gertrude (Margaret Lowthian)
1868-1926 .... **TCLC 67**
See also CA 167; CANR 110; DLB 174

Bell, J. Freeman
See Zangwill, Israel

Bell, James Madison 1826-1902 ..... **BLC 1:1; TCLC 43**
See also BW 1; CA 122; 124; DAM MULT;
DLB 50

Bell, Madison Smartt 1957- ..... **CLC 41, 102, 223**
See also AMWS 10; BPFB 1; CA 111; 183;
CAAE 183; CANR 28, 54, 73, 134, 176;
CN 5, 6, 7; CSW; DLB 218, 278; MTCW
2; MTFW 2005

Bell, Marvin (Hartley) 1937- ...... **CLC 8, 31; PC 79**
See also CA 21-24R; CAAS 14; CANR 59,
102; CP 1, 2, 3, 4, 5, 6, 7; DAM POET;
DLB 5; MAL 5; MTCW 1; PFS 25

Bell, W. L. D.
See Mencken, H(enry) L(ouis)

Bellamy, Atwood C.
See Mencken, H(enry) L(ouis)

Bellamy, Edward 1850-1898 ..... **NCLC 4, 86, 147**
See also DLB 12; NFS 15; RGAL 4; SFW 4

Belli, Gioconda 1948- .... **HLCS 1**
See also CA 152; CANR 143; CWW 2;
DLB 290; EWL 3; RGWL 3

Bellin, Edward J.
See Kuttner, Henry

Bello, Andres 1781-1865 .... **NCLC 131**
See also LAW

Belloc, (Joseph) Hilaire (Pierre Sebastien Rene Swanton) 1870-1953 .... **PC 24; TCLC 7, 18**
See also CA 106; 152; CLR 102; CWRI 5;
DAM POET; DLB 19, 100, 141, 174;
EWL 3; MTCW 2; MTFW 2005; SATA
112; WCH; YABC 1

Belloc, Joseph Peter Rene Hilaire
See Belloc, (Joseph) Hilaire (Pierre Sebastien Rene Swanton)

Belloc, Joseph Pierre Hilaire
See Belloc, (Joseph) Hilaire (Pierre Sebastien Rene Swanton)

Belloc, M. A.
See Lowndes, Marie Adelaide (Belloc)

Belloc-Lowndes, Mrs.
See Lowndes, Marie Adelaide (Belloc)

Bellow, Saul 1915-2005 ...... **CLC 1, 2, 3, 6, 8, 10, 13, 15, 25, 33, 34, 63, 79, 190, 200; SSC 14, 101; WLC 1**
See also AITN 2; AMW; AMWC 2; AMWR
2; BEST 89:3; BPFB 1; CA 5-8R; 238;
CABS 1; CANR 29, 53, 95, 132; CDALB
1941-1968; CN 1, 2, 3, 4, 5, 6, 7; DA;
DA3; DAB; DAC; DAM MST, NOV,
POP; DLB 2, 28, 299, 329; DLBD 3;
DLBY 1982; EWL 3; MAL 5; MTCW 1,
2; MTFW 2005; NFS 4, 14, 26; RGAL 4;
RGHL; RGSF 2; SSFS 12, 22; TUS

Belser, Reimond Karel Maria de 1929-
See Ruyslinck, Ward
See also CA 152

Bely, Andrey .... **PC 11; TCLC 7**
See Bugayev, Boris Nikolayevich
See also DLB 295; EW 9; EWL 3

Belyi, Andrei
See Bugayev, Boris Nikolayevich
See also RGWL 2, 3

Bembo, Pietro 1470-1547 .... **LC 79**
See also RGWL 2, 3

Benary, Margot
See Benary-Isbert, Margot

Benary-Isbert, Margot 1889-1979 .... **CLC 12**
See also CA 5-8R; 89-92; CANR 4, 72;
CLR 12; MAICYA 1, 2; SATA 2; SATA-
Obit 21

Benavente (y Martinez), Jacinto
1866-1954 .... **DC 26; HLCS 1; TCLC 3**
See also CA 106; 131; CANR 81; DAM
DRAM, MULT; DLB 329; EWL 3; GLL
2; HW 1, 2; MTCW 1, 2

Benchley, Peter 1940-2006 .... **CLC 4, 8**
See also AAYA 14; AITN 2; BPFB 1; CA
17-20R; 248; CANR 12, 35, 66, 115;
CPW; DAM NOV, POP; HGG; MTCW 1,
2; MTFW 2005; SATA 3, 89, 164

Benchley, Peter Bradford
See Benchley, Peter

Benchley, Robert (Charles)
1889-1945 .... **TCLC 1, 55**
See also CA 105; 153; DLB 11; MAL 5;
RGAL 4

Benda, Julien 1867-1956 .... **TCLC 60**
See also CA 120; 154; GFL 1789 to the
Present

Berryman, John 1914-1972 ... **CLC 1, 2, 3, 4, 6, 8, 10, 13, 25, 62; PC 64**
See also AMW; CA 13-16; 33-36R; CABS 2; CANR 35; CAP 1; CDALB 1941-1968; CP 1; DAM POET; DLB 48; EWL 3; MAL 5; MTCW 1, 2; MTFW 2005; PAB; PFS 27; RGAL 4; WP

Bertolucci, Bernardo 1940- ...... **CLC 16, 157**
See also CA 106; CANR 125

Berton, Pierre (Francis de Marigny) 1920-2004 .... **CLC 104**
See also CA 1-4R; 233; CANR 2, 56, 144; CPW; DLB 68; SATA 99; SATA-Obit 158

Bertrand, Aloysius 1807-1841 .... **NCLC 31**
See Bertrand, Louis oAloysiusc

Bertrand, Louis oAloysiusc
See Bertrand, Aloysius
See also DLB 217

Bertran de Born c. 1140-1215 .... **CMLC 5**

Besant, Annie (Wood) 1847-1933 ..... **TCLC 9**
See also CA 105; 185

Bessie, Alvah 1904-1985 .... **CLC 23**
See also CA 5-8R; 116; CANR 2, 80; DLB 26

Bestuzhev, Aleksandr Aleksandrovich 1797-1837 .... **NCLC 131**
See also DLB 198

Bethlen, T.D.
See Silverberg, Robert

Beti, Mongo .... **BLC 1:1; CLC 27**
See Biyidi, Alexandre
See also AFW; CANR 79; DAM MULT; EWL 3; WLIT 2

Betjeman, John 1906-1984 ...... **CLC 2, 6, 10, 34, 43; PC 75**
See also BRW 7; CA 9-12R; 112; CANR 33, 56; CDBLB 1945-1960; CP 1, 2, 3; DA3; DAB; DAM MST, POET; DLB 20; DLBY 1984; EWL 3; MTCW 1, 2

Bettelheim, Bruno 1903-1990 .... **CLC 79; TCLC 143**
See also CA 81-84; 131; CANR 23, 61; DA3; MTCW 1, 2; RGHL

Betti, Ugo 1892-1953 .... **TCLC 5**
See also CA 104; 155; EWL 3; RGWL 2, 3

Betts, Doris (Waugh) 1932- ..... **CLC 3, 6, 28; SSC 45**
See also CA 13-16R; CANR 9, 66, 77; CN 6, 7; CSW; DLB 218; DLBY 1982; INT CANR-9; RGAL 4

Bevan, Alistair
See Roberts, Keith (John Kingston)

Bey, Pilaff
See Douglas, (George) Norman

Beyala, Calixthe 1961- .... **BLC 2:1**
See also EWL 3

Bialik, Chaim Nachman 1873-1934 .... **TCLC 25, 201**
See Bialik, Hayyim Nahman
See also CA 170; EWL 3

Bialik, Hayyim Nahman
See Bialik, Chaim Nachman
See also WLIT 6

Bickerstaff, Isaac
See Swift, Jonathan

Bidart, Frank 1939- .... **CLC 33**
See also AMWS 15; CA 140; CANR 106; CP 5, 6, 7; PFS 26

Bienek, Horst 1930- .... **CLC 7, 11**
See also CA 73-76; DLB 75

Bierce, Ambrose (Gwinett) 1842-1914(?) ..... **SSC 9, 72; TCLC 1, 7, 44; WLC 1**
See also AAYA 55; AMW; BYA 11; CA 104; 139; CANR 78; CDALB 1865-1917; DA; DA3; DAC; DAM MST; DLB 11, 12, 23, 71, 74, 186; EWL 3; EXPS; HGG; LAIT 2; MAL 5; RGAL 4; RGSF 2; SSFS 9; SUFW 1

Biggers, Earl Derr 1884-1933 .... **TCLC 65**
See also CA 108; 153; DLB 306

Billiken, Bud
See Motley, Willard (Francis)

Billings, Josh
See Shaw, Henry Wheeler

Billington, (Lady) Rachel (Mary) 1942- .... **CLC 43**
See also AITN 2; CA 33-36R; CANR 44; CN 4, 5, 6, 7

Binchy, Maeve 1940- .... **CLC 153**
See also BEST 90:1; BPFB 1; CA 127; 134; CANR 50, 96, 134; CN 5, 6, 7; CPW; DA3; DAM POP; DLB 319; INT CA-134; MTCW 2; MTFW 2005; RHW

Binyon, T(imothy) J(ohn) 1936-2004 .... **CLC 34**
See also CA 111; 232; CANR 28, 140

Bion 335B.C.-245B.C. .... **CMLC 39**

Bioy Casares, Adolfo 1914-1999 ... **CLC 4, 8, 13, 88; HLC 1; SSC 17, 102**
See Casares, Adolfo Bioy; Miranda, Javier; Sacastru, Martin
See also CA 29-32R; 177; CANR 19, 43, 66; CWW 2; DAM MULT; DLB 113; EWL 3; HW 1, 2; LAW; MTCW 1, 2; MTFW 2005

Birch, Allison .... **CLC 65**

Bird, Cordwainer
See Ellison, Harlan

Bird, Robert Montgomery 1806-1854 .... **NCLC 1, 197**
See also DLB 202; RGAL 4

Birdwell, Cleo
See DeLillo, Don

Birkerts, Sven 1951- .... **CLC 116**
See also CA 128; 133, 176; CAAE 176; CAAS 29; CANR 151; INT CA-133

Birney, (Alfred) Earle 1904-1995 .. **CLC 1, 4, 6, 11; PC 52**
See also CA 1-4R; CANR 5, 20; CN 1, 2, 3, 4; CP 1, 2, 3, 4, 5, 6; DAC; DAM MST, POET; DLB 88; MTCW 1; PFS 8; RGEL 2

Biruni, al 973-1048(?) .... **CMLC 28**

Bishop, Elizabeth 1911-1979 ... **CLC 1, 4, 9, 13, 15, 32; PC 3, 34; TCLC 121**
See also AMWR 2; AMWS 1; CA 5-8R; 89-92; CABS 2; CANR 26, 61, 108; CDALB 1968-1988; CP 1, 2, 3; DA; DA3; DAC; DAM MST, POET; DLB 5, 169; EWL 3; GLL 2; MAL 5; MBL; MTCW 1, 2; PAB; PFS 6, 12, 27; RGAL 4; SATA-Obit 24; TUS; WP

Bishop, John 1935- .... **CLC 10**
See also CA 105

Bishop, John Peale 1892-1944 ..... **TCLC 103**
See also CA 107; 155; DLB 4, 9, 45; MAL 5; RGAL 4

Bissett, Bill 1939- .... **CLC 18; PC 14**
See also CA 69-72; CAAS 19; CANR 15; CCA 1; CP 1, 2, 3, 4, 5, 6, 7; DLB 53; MTCW 1

Bissoondath, Neil 1955- .... **CLC 120**
See also CA 136; CANR 123, 165; CN 6, 7; DAC

Bissoondath, Neil Devindra
See Bissoondath, Neil

Bitov, Andrei (Georgievich) 1937- ... **CLC 57**
See also CA 142; DLB 302

Biyidi, Alexandre 1932-
See Beti, Mongo
See also BW 1, 3; CA 114; 124; CANR 81; DA3; MTCW 1, 2

Bjarme, Brynjolf
See Ibsen, Henrik (Johan)

Bjoernson, Bjoernstjerne (Martinius) 1832-1910 .... **TCLC 7, 37**
See also CA 104

Black, Benjamin
See Banville, John

Black, Robert
See Holdstock, Robert

Blackburn, Paul 1926-1971 .... **CLC 9, 43**
See also BG 1:2; CA 81-84; 33-36R; CANR 34; CP 1; DLB 16; DLBY 1981

Black Elk 1863-1950 .... **NNAL; TCLC 33**
See also CA 144; DAM MULT; MTCW 2; MTFW 2005; WP

Black Hawk 1767-1838 .... **NNAL**

Black Hobart
See Sanders, (James) Ed(ward)

Blacklin, Malcolm
See Chambers, Aidan

Blackmore, R(ichard) D(oddridge) 1825-1900 .... **TCLC 27**
See also CA 120; DLB 18; RGEL 2

Blackmur, R(ichard) P(almer) 1904-1965 .... **CLC 2, 24**
See also AMWS 2; CA 11-12; 25-28R; CANR 71; CAP 1; DLB 63; EWL 3; MAL 5

Black Tarantula
See Acker, Kathy

Blackwood, Algernon 1869-1951 .... **SSC 107; TCLC 5**
See also AAYA 78; CA 105; 150; CANR 169; DLB 153, 156, 178; HGG; SUFW 1

Blackwood, Algernon Henry
See Blackwood, Algernon

Blackwood, Caroline (Maureen) 1931-1996 .... **CLC 6, 9, 100**
See also BRWS 9; CA 85-88; 151; CANR 32, 61, 65; CN 3, 4, 5, 6; DLB 14, 207; HGG; MTCW 1

Blade, Alexander
See Hamilton, Edmond; Silverberg, Robert

Blaga, Lucian 1895-1961 .... **CLC 75**
See also CA 157; DLB 220; EWL 3

Blair, Eric (Arthur) 1903-1950 .... **TCLC 123**
See Orwell, George
See also CA 104; 132; DA; DA3; DAB; DAC; DAM MST, NOV; MTCW 1, 2; MTFW 2005; SATA 29

Blair, Hugh 1718-1800 .... **NCLC 75**

Blais, Marie-Claire 1939- .... **CLC 2, 4, 6, 13, 22**
See also CA 21-24R; CAAS 4; CANR 38, 75, 93; CWW 2; DAC; DAM MST; DLB 53; EWL 3; FW; MTCW 1, 2; MTFW 2005; TWA

Blaise, Clark 1940- .... **CLC 29, 261**
See also AITN 2; CA 53-56, 231; CAAE 231; CAAS 3; CANR 5, 66, 106; CN 4, 5, 6, 7; DLB 53; RGSF 2

Blake, Fairley
See De Voto, Bernard (Augustine)

Blake, Nicholas
See Day Lewis, C(ecil)
See also DLB 77; MSW

Blake, Sterling
See Benford, Gregory

Blake, William 1757-1827 . **NCLC 13, 37, 57, 127, 173, 190, 201; PC 12, 63; WLC 1**
See also AAYA 47; BRW 3; BRWR 1; CD-BLB 1789-1832; CLR 52; DA; DA3; DAB; DAC; DAM MST, POET; DLB 93, 163; EXPP; LATS 1:1; LMFS 1; MAI-CYA 1, 2; PAB; PFS 2, 12, 24; SATA 30; TEA; WCH; WLIT 3; WP

Blanchot, Maurice 1907-2003 .... **CLC 135**
See also CA 117; 144; 213; CANR 138; DLB 72, 296; EWL 3

Blasco Ibanez, Vicente 1867-1928 . **TCLC 12**
See Ibanez, Vicente Blasco
See also BPFB 1; CA 110; 131; CANR 81; DA3; DAM NOV; EW 8; EWL 3; HW 1, 2; MTCW 1

Borel, Petrus 1809-1859 .... **NCLC 41**
See also DLB 119; GFL 1789 to the Present

Borges, Jorge Luis 1899-1986 ... **CLC 1, 2, 3, 4, 6, 8, 9, 10, 13, 19, 44, 48, 83; HLC 1; PC 22, 32; SSC 4, 41, 100; TCLC 109; WLC 1**
See also AAYA 26; BPFB 1; CA 21-24R; CANR 19, 33, 75, 105, 133; CDWLB 3; DA; DA3; DAB; DAC; DAM MST, MULT; DLB 113, 283; DLBY 1986; DNFS 1, 2; EWL 3; HW 1, 2; LAW; LMFS 2; MSW; MTCW 1, 2; MTFW 2005; PFS 27; RGHL; RGSF 2; RGWL 2, 3; SFW 4; SSFS 17; TWA; WLIT 1

Borne, Ludwig 1786-1837 .... **NCLC 193**
See also DLB 90

Borowski, Tadeusz 1922-1951 .... **SSC 48; TCLC 9**
See also CA 106; 154; CDWLB 4; DLB 215; EWL 3; RGHL; RGSF 2; RGWL 3; SSFS 13

Borrow, George (Henry)
1803-1881 .... **NCLC 9**
See also BRWS 12; DLB 21, 55, 166

Bosch (Gavino), Juan 1909-2001 ..... **HLCS 1**
See also CA 151; 204; DAM MST, MULT; DLB 145; HW 1, 2

Bosman, Herman Charles
1905-1951 .... **TCLC 49**
See Malan, Herman
See also CA 160; DLB 225; RGSF 2

Bosschere, Jean de 1878(?)-1953 ... **TCLC 19**
See also CA 115; 186

Boswell, James 1740-1795 ... **LC 4, 50; WLC 1**
See also BRW 3; CDBLB 1660-1789; DA; DAB; DAC; DAM MST; DLB 104, 142; TEA; WLIT 3

Bottomley, Gordon 1874-1948 ..... **TCLC 107**
See also CA 120; 192; DLB 10

Bottoms, David 1949- .... **CLC 53**
See also CA 105; CANR 22; CSW; DLB 120; DLBY 1983

Boucicault, Dion 1820-1890 .... **NCLC 41**
See also DLB 344

Boucolon, Maryse
See Conde, Maryse

Bourcicault, Dion
See Boucicault, Dion

Bourdieu, Pierre 1930-2002 .... **CLC 198**
See also CA 130; 204

Bourget, Paul (Charles Joseph)
1852-1935 .... **TCLC 12**
See also CA 107; 196; DLB 123; GFL 1789 to the Present

Bourjaily, Vance (Nye) 1922- .... **CLC 8, 62**
See also CA 1-4R; CAAS 1; CANR 2, 72; CN 1, 2, 3, 4, 5, 6, 7; DLB 2, 143; MAL 5

Bourne, Randolph S(illiman)
1886-1918 .... **TCLC 16**
See also AMW; CA 117; 155; DLB 63; MAL 5

Boursiquot, Dionysius
See Boucicault, Dion

Bova, Ben 1932- .... **CLC 45**
See also AAYA 16; CA 5-8R; CAAS 18; CANR 11, 56, 94, 111, 157; CLR 3, 96; DLBY 1981; INT CANR-11; MAICYA 1, 2; MTCW 1; SATA 6, 68, 133; SFW 4

Bova, Benjamin William
See Bova, Ben

Bowen, Elizabeth (Dorothea Cole)
1899-1973 . **CLC 1, 3, 6, 11, 15, 22, 118; SSC 3, 28, 66; TCLC 148**
See also BRWS 2; CA 17-18; 41-44R; CANR 35, 105; CAP 2; CDBLB 1945-1960; CN 1; DA3; DAM NOV; DLB 15,

162; EWL 3; EXPS; FW; HGG; MTCW 1, 2; MTFW 2005; NFS 13; RGSF 2; SSFS 5, 22; SUFW 1; TEA; WLIT 4

Bowering, George 1935- .... **CLC 15, 47**
See also CA 21-24R; CAAS 16; CANR 10; CN 7; CP 1, 2, 3, 4, 5, 6, 7; DLB 53

Bowering, Marilyn R(uthe) 1949- .... **CLC 32**
See also CA 101; CANR 49; CP 4, 5, 6, 7; CWP; DLB 334

Bowers, Edgar 1924-2000 .... **CLC 9**
See also CA 5-8R; 188; CANR 24; CP 1, 2, 3, 4, 5, 6, 7; CSW; DLB 5

Bowers, Mrs. J. Milton 1842-1914
See Bierce, Ambrose (Gwinett)

Bowie, David .... **CLC 17**
See Jones, David Robert

Bowles, Jane (Sydney) 1917-1973 ..... **CLC 3, 68**
See Bowles, Jane Auer
See also CA 19-20; 41-44R; CAP 2; CN 1; MAL 5

Bowles, Jane Auer
See Bowles, Jane (Sydney)
See also EWL 3

Bowles, Paul 1910-1999 ..... **CLC 1, 2, 19, 53; SSC 3, 98; TCLC 209**
See also AMWS 4; CA 1-4R; 186; CAAS 1; CANR 1, 19, 50, 75; CN 1, 2, 3, 4, 5, 6; DA3; DLB 5, 6, 218; EWL 3; MAL 5; MTCW 1, 2; MTFW 2005; RGAL 4; SSFS 17

Bowles, William Lisle 1762-1850 . **NCLC 103**
See also DLB 93

Box, Edgar
See Vidal, Gore

Boyd, James 1888-1944 .... **TCLC 115**
See also CA 186; DLB 9; DLBD 16; RGAL 4; RHW

Boyd, Nancy
See Millay, Edna St. Vincent
See also GLL 1

Boyd, Thomas (Alexander)
1898-1935 .... **TCLC 111**
See also CA 111; 183; DLB 9; DLBD 16, 316

Boyd, William 1952- .... **CLC 28, 53, 70**
See also CA 114; 120; CANR 51, 71, 131, 174; CN 4, 5, 6, 7; DLB 231

Boyesen, Hjalmar Hjorth
1848-1895 .... **NCLC 135**
See also DLB 12, 71; DLBD 13; RGAL 4

Boyle, Kay 1902-1992 .... **CLC 1, 5, 19, 58, 121; SSC 5, 102**
See also CA 13-16R; 140; CAAS 1; CANR 29, 61, 110; CN 1, 2, 3, 4, 5; CP 1, 2, 3, 4, 5; DLB 4, 9, 48, 86; DLBY 1993; EWL 3; MAL 5; MTCW 1, 2; MTFW 2005; RGAL 4; RGSF 2; SSFS 10, 13, 14

Boyle, Mark
See Kienzle, William X.

Boyle, Patrick 1905-1982 .... **CLC 19**
See also CA 127

Boyle, T. C.
See Boyle, T. Coraghessan
See also AMWS 8

Boyle, T. Coraghessan 1948- ..... **CLC 36, 55, 90; SSC 16**
See Boyle, T. C.
See also AAYA 47; BEST 90:4; BPFB 1; CA 120; CANR 44, 76, 89, 132; CN 6, 7; CPW; DA3; DAM POP; DLB 218, 278; DLBY 1986; EWL 3; MAL 5; MTCW 2; MTFW 2005; SSFS 13, 19

Boz
See Dickens, Charles (John Huffam)

Brackenridge, Hugh Henry
1748-1816 .... **NCLC 7**
See also DLB 11, 37; RGAL 4

Bradbury, Edward P.
See Moorcock, Michael
See also MTCW 2

Bradbury, Malcolm (Stanley)
1932-2000 .... **CLC 32, 61**
See also CA 1-4R; CANR 1, 33, 91, 98, 137; CN 1, 2, 3, 4, 5, 6, 7; CP 1; DA3; DAM NOV; DLB 14, 207; EWL 3; MTCW 1, 2; MTFW 2005

Bradbury, Ray 1920- ... **CLC 1, 3, 10, 15, 42, 98, 235; SSC 29, 53; WLC 1**
See also AAYA 15; AITN 1, 2; AMWS 4; BPFB 1; BYA 4, 5, 11; CA 1-4R; CANR 2, 30, 75, 125; CDALB 1968-1988; CN 1, 2, 3, 4, 5, 6, 7; CPW; DA; DA3; DAB; DAC; DAM MST, NOV, POP; DLB 2, 8; EXPN; EXPS; HGG; LAIT 3, 5; LATS 1:2; LMFS 2; MAL 5; MTCW 1, 2; MTFW 2005; NFS 1, 22; RGAL 4; RGSF 2; SATA 11, 64, 123; SCFW 1, 2; SFW 4; SSFS 1, 20; SUFW 1, 2; TUS; YAW

Braddon, Mary Elizabeth
1837-1915 .... **TCLC 111**
See also BRWS 8; CA 108; 179; CMW 4; DLB 18, 70, 156; HGG

Bradfield, Scott 1955- .... **SSC 65**
See also CA 147; CANR 90; HGG; SUFW 2

Bradfield, Scott Michael
See Bradfield, Scott

Bradford, Gamaliel 1863-1932 .... **TCLC 36**
See also CA 160; DLB 17

Bradford, William 1590-1657 .... **LC 64**
See also DLB 24, 30; RGAL 4

Bradley, David, Jr. 1950- ...... **BLC 1:1; CLC 23, 118**
See also BW 1, 3; CA 104; CANR 26, 81; CN 4, 5, 6, 7; DAM MULT; DLB 33

Bradley, David Henry, Jr.
See Bradley, David, Jr.

Bradley, John Ed 1958- .... **CLC 55**
See also CA 139; CANR 99; CN 6, 7; CSW

Bradley, John Edmund, Jr.
See Bradley, John Ed

Bradley, Marion Zimmer
1930-1999 .... **CLC 30**
See Chapman, Lee; Dexter, John; Gardner, Miriam; Ives, Morgan; Rivers, Elfrida
See also AAYA 40; BPFB 1; CA 57-60; 185; CAAS 10; CANR 7, 31, 51, 75, 107; CPW; DA3; DAM POP; DLB 8; FANT; FW; MTCW 1, 2; MTFW 2005; SATA 90, 139; SATA-Obit 116; SFW 4; SUFW 2; YAW

Bradshaw, John 1933- .... **CLC 70**
See also CA 138; CANR 61

Bradstreet, Anne 1612(?)-1672 .... **LC 4, 30, 130; PC 10**
See also AMWS 1; CDALB 1640-1865; DA; DA3; DAC; DAM MST, POET; DLB 24; EXPP; FW; PFS 6; RGAL 4; TUS; WP

Brady, Joan 1939- .... **CLC 86**
See also CA 141

Bragg, Melvyn 1939- .... **CLC 10**
See also BEST 89:3; CA 57-60; CANR 10, 48, 89, 158; CN 1, 2, 3, 4, 5, 6, 7; DLB 14, 271; RHW

Brahe, Tycho 1546-1601 .... **LC 45**
See also DLB 300

Braine, John (Gerard) 1922-1986 . **CLC 1, 3, 41**
See also CA 1-4R; 120; CANR 1, 33; CDBLB 1945-1960; CN 1, 2, 3, 4; DLB 15; DLBY 1986; EWL 3; MTCW 1

Braithwaite, William Stanley (Beaumont)
1878-1962 ...... **BLC 1:1; HR 1:2; PC 52**
See also BW 1; CA 125; DAM MULT; DLB 50, 54; MAL 5

Butor, Michel (Marie Francois)
1926- .... **CLC 1, 3, 8, 11, 15, 161**
See also CA 9-12R; CANR 33, 66; CWW
2; DLB 83; EW 13; EWL 3; GFL 1789 to
the Present; MTCW 1, 2; MTFW 2005

Butts, Mary 1890(?)-1937 .... **TCLC 77**
See also CA 148; DLB 240

Buxton, Ralph
See Silverstein, Alvin; Silverstein, Virginia
B(arbara Opshelor)

Buzo, Alex
See Buzo, Alexander (John)
See also DLB 289

Buzo, Alexander (John) 1944- .... **CLC 61**
See also CA 97-100; CANR 17, 39, 69; CD
5, 6

Buzzati, Dino 1906-1972 .... **CLC 36**
See also CA 160; 33-36R; DLB 177; RGWL
2, 3; SFW 4

Byars, Betsy 1928- .... **CLC 35**
See also AAYA 19; BYA 3; CA 33-36R,
183; CAAE 183; CANR 18, 36, 57, 102,
148; CLR 1, 16, 72; DLB 52; INT CANR-
18; JRDA; MAICYA 1, 2; MAICYAS 1;
MTCW 1; SAAS 1; SATA 4, 46, 80, 163;
SATA-Essay 108; WYA; YAW

Byars, Betsy Cromer
See Byars, Betsy

Byatt, Antonia Susan Drabble
See Byatt, A.S.

Byatt, A.S. 1936- .... **CLC 19, 65, 136, 223;
SSC 91**
See also BPFB 1; BRWC 2; BRWS 4; CA
13-16R; CANR 13, 33, 50, 75, 96, 133;
CN 1, 2, 3, 4, 5, 6; DA3; DAM NOV,
POP; DLB 14, 194, 319, 326; EWL 3;
MTCW 1, 2; MTFW 2005; RGSF 2;
RHW; SSFS 26; TEA

Byrd, William II 1674-1744 .... **LC 112**
See also DLB 24, 140; RGAL 4

Byrne, David 1952- .... **CLC 26**
See also CA 127

Byrne, John Keyes 1926-
See Leonard, Hugh
See also CA 102; CANR 78, 140; INT CA-
102

Byron, George Gordon (Noel)
1788-1824 .... **DC 24; NCLC 2, 12, 109,
149; PC 16; WLC 1**
See also AAYA 64; BRW 4; BRWC 2; CD-
BLB 1789-1832; DA; DA3; DAB; DAC;
DAM MST, POET; DLB 96, 110; EXPP;
LMFS 1; PAB; PFS 1, 14; RGEL 2; TEA;
WLIT 3; WP

Byron, Robert 1905-1941 .... **TCLC 67**
See also CA 160; DLB 195

C. 3. 3.
See Wilde, Oscar

Caballero, Fernan 1796-1877 .... **NCLC 10**

Cabell, Branch
See Cabell, James Branch

Cabell, James Branch 1879-1958 .... **TCLC 6**
See also CA 105; 152; DLB 9, 78; FANT;
MAL 5; MTCW 2; RGAL 4; SUFW 1

Cabeza de Vaca, Alvar Nunez
1490-1557(?) .... **LC 61**

Cable, George Washington
1844-1925 .... **SSC 4; TCLC 4**
See also CA 104; 155; DLB 12, 74; DLBD
13; RGAL 4; TUS

Cabral de Melo Neto, Joao
1920-1999 .... **CLC 76**
See Melo Neto, Joao Cabral de
See also CA 151; DAM MULT; DLB 307;
LAW; LAWS 1

Cabrera Infante, G. 1929-2005 ... **CLC 5, 25,
45, 120; HLC 1; SSC 39**
See also CA 85-88; 236; CANR 29, 65, 110;
CDWLB 3; CWW 2; DA3; DAM MULT;
DLB 113; EWL 3; HW 1, 2; LAW; LAWS
1; MTCW 1, 2; MTFW 2005; RGSF 2;
WLIT 1

Cabrera Infante, Guillermo
See Cabrera Infante, G.

Cade, Toni
See Bambara, Toni Cade

Cadmus and Harmonia
See Buchan, John

Caedmon fl. 658-680 .... **CMLC 7**
See also DLB 146

Caeiro, Alberto
See Pessoa, Fernando (Antonio Nogueira)

Caesar, Julius .... **CMLC 47**
See Julius Caesar
See also AW 1; RGWL 2, 3; WLIT 8

Cage, John (Milton), (Jr.)
1912-1992 .... **CLC 41; PC 58**
See also CA 13-16R; 169; CANR 9, 78;
DLB 193; INT CANR-9; TCLE 1:1

Cahan, Abraham 1860-1951 .... **TCLC 71**
See also CA 108; 154; DLB 9, 25, 28; MAL
5; RGAL 4

Cain, G.
See Cabrera Infante, G.

Cain, Guillermo
See Cabrera Infante, G.

Cain, James M(allahan) 1892-1977 .. **CLC 3,
11, 28**
See also AITN 1; BPFB 1; CA 17-20R; 73-
76; CANR 8, 34, 61; CMW 4; CN 1, 2;
DLB 226; EWL 3; MAL 5; MSW; MTCW
1; RGAL 4

Caine, Hall 1853-1931 .... **TCLC 97**
See also RHW

Caine, Mark
See Raphael, Frederic (Michael)

Calasso, Roberto 1941- .... **CLC 81**
See also CA 143; CANR 89

Calderon de la Barca, Pedro
1600-1681 . **DC 3; HLCS 1; LC 23, 136**
See also DFS 23; EW 2; RGWL 2, 3; TWA

Caldwell, Erskine 1903-1987 ... **CLC 1, 8, 14,
50, 60; SSC 19; TCLC 117**
See also AITN 1; AMW; BPFB 1; CA 1-4R;
121; CAAS 1; CANR 2, 33; CN 1, 2, 3,
4; DA3; DAM NOV; DLB 9, 86; EWL 3;
MAL 5; MTCW 1, 2; MTFW 2005;
RGAL 4; RGSF 2; TUS

Caldwell, (Janet Miriam) Taylor (Holland)
1900-1985 .... **CLC 2, 28, 39**
See also BPFB 1; CA 5-8R; 116; CANR 5;
DA3; DAM NOV, POP; DLBD 17;
MTCW 2; RHW

Calhoun, John Caldwell
1782-1850 .... **NCLC 15**
See also DLB 3, 248

Calisher, Hortense 1911- ..... **CLC 2, 4, 8, 38,
134; SSC 15**
See also CA 1-4R; CANR 1, 22, 117; CN
1, 2, 3, 4, 5, 6, 7; DA3; DAM NOV; DLB
2, 218; INT CANR-22; MAL 5; MTCW
1, 2; MTFW 2005; RGAL 4; RGSF 2

Callaghan, Morley Edward
1903-1990 ..... **CLC 3, 14, 41, 65; TCLC
145**
See also CA 9-12R; 132; CANR 33, 73;
CN 1, 2, 3, 4; DAC; DAM MST; DLB
68; EWL 3; MTCW 1, 2; MTFW 2005;
RGEL 2; RGSF 2; SSFS 19

Callimachus c. 305B.C.-c.
240B.C. .... **CMLC 18**
See also AW 1; DLB 176; RGWL 2, 3

Calvin, Jean
See Calvin, John
See also DLB 327; GFL Beginnings to 1789

Calvin, John 1509-1564 .... **LC 37**
See Calvin, Jean

Calvino, Italo 1923-1985 .... **CLC 5, 8, 11, 22,
33, 39, 73; SSC 3, 48; TCLC 183**
See also AAYA 58; CA 85-88; 116; CANR
23, 61, 132; DAM NOV; DLB 196; EW
13; EWL 3; MTCW 1, 2; MTFW 2005;
RGHL; RGSF 2; RGWL 2, 3; SFW 4;
SSFS 12; WLIT 7

Camara Laye
See Laye, Camara
See also EWL 3

Camden, William 1551-1623 .... **LC 77**
See also DLB 172

Cameron, Carey 1952- .... **CLC 59**
See also CA 135

Cameron, Peter 1959- .... **CLC 44**
See also AMWS 12; CA 125; CANR 50,
117; DLB 234; GLL 2

Camoens, Luis Vaz de 1524(?)-1580
See Camoes, Luis de
See also EW 2

Camoes, Luis de 1524(?)-1580 . **HLCS 1; LC
62; PC 31**
See Camoens, Luis Vaz de
See also DLB 287; RGWL 2, 3

Camp, Madeleine L'Engle
See L'Engle, Madeleine

Campana, Dino 1885-1932 .... **TCLC 20**
See also CA 117; 246; DLB 114; EWL 3

Campanella, Tommaso 1568-1639 .... **LC 32**
See also RGWL 2, 3

Campbell, Bebe Moore 1950-2006 . **BLC 2:1;
CLC 246**
See also AAYA 26; BW 2, 3; CA 139; 254;
CANR 81, 134; DLB 227; MTCW 2;
MTFW 2005

Campbell, John Ramsey
See Campbell, Ramsey

Campbell, John W(ood, Jr.)
1910-1971 .... **CLC 32**
See also CA 21-22; 29-32R; CANR 34;
CAP 2; DLB 8; MTCW 1; SCFW 1, 2;
SFW 4

Campbell, Joseph 1904-1987 .... **CLC 69;
TCLC 140**
See also AAYA 3, 66; BEST 89:2; CA 1-4R;
124; CANR 3, 28, 61, 107; DA3; MTCW
1, 2

Campbell, Maria 1940- .... **CLC 85; NNAL**
See also CA 102; CANR 54; CCA 1; DAC

Campbell, Ramsey 1946- ... **CLC 42; SSC 19**
See also AAYA 51; CA 57-60, 228; CAAE
228; CANR 7, 102, 171; DLB 261; HGG;
INT CANR-7; SUFW 1, 2

Campbell, (Ignatius) Roy (Dunnachie)
1901-1957 .... **TCLC 5**
See also AFW; CA 104; 155; DLB 20, 225;
EWL 3; MTCW 2; RGEL 2

Campbell, Thomas 1777-1844 .... **NCLC 19**
See also DLB 93, 144; RGEL 2

Campbell, Wilfred .... **TCLC 9**
See Campbell, William

Campbell, William 1858(?)-1918
See Campbell, Wilfred
See also CA 106; DLB 92

Campbell, William Edward March
1893-1954
See March, William
See also CA 108

Campion, Jane 1954- .... **CLC 95, 229**
See also AAYA 33; CA 138; CANR 87

Campion, Thomas 1567-1620 . **LC 78; PC 87**
See also CDBLB Before 1660; DAM POET;
DLB 58, 172; RGEL 2

De Palma, Brian Russell
See De Palma, Brian
de Pizan, Christine
See Christine de Pizan
See also FL 1:1
De Quincey, Thomas 1785-1859 ..... **NCLC 4, 87, 198**
See also BRW 4; CDBLB 1789-1832; DLB 110, 144; RGEL 2
Deren, Eleanora 1908(?)-1961
See Deren, Maya
See also CA 192; 111
Deren, Maya .... **CLC 16, 102**
See Deren, Eleanora
Derleth, August (William)
1909-1971 .... **CLC 31**
See also BPFB 1; BYA 9, 10; CA 1-4R; 29-32R; CANR 4; CMW 4; CN 1; DLB 9; DLBD 17; HGG; SATA 5; SUFW 1
Der Nister 1884-1950 .... **TCLC 56**
See Nister, Der
de Routisie, Albert
See Aragon, Louis
Derrida, Jacques 1930-2004 ...... **CLC 24, 87, 225**
See also CA 124; 127; 232; CANR 76, 98, 133; DLB 242; EWL 3; LMFS 2; MTCW 2; TWA
Derry Down Derry
See Lear, Edward
Dersonnes, Jacques
See Simenon, Georges (Jacques Christian)
Der Stricker c. 1190-c. 1250 .... **CMLC 75**
See also DLB 138
Desai, Anita 1937- .... **CLC 19, 37, 97, 175**
See also BRWS 5; CA 81-84; CANR 33, 53, 95, 133; CN 1, 2, 3, 4, 5, 6, 7; CWRI 5; DA3; DAB; DAM NOV; DLB 271, 323; DNFS 2; EWL 3; FW; MTCW 1, 2; MTFW 2005; SATA 63, 126
Desai, Kiran 1971- .... **CLC 119**
See also BYA 16; CA 171; CANR 127
de Saint-Luc, Jean
See Glassco, John
de Saint Roman, Arnaud
See Aragon, Louis
Desbordes-Valmore, Marceline
1786-1859 .... **NCLC 97**
See also DLB 217
Descartes, Rene 1596-1650 .... **LC 20, 35, 150**
See also DLB 268; EW 3; GFL Beginnings to 1789
Deschamps, Eustache 1340(?)-1404 .. **LC 103**
See also DLB 208
De Sica, Vittorio 1901(?)-1974 .... **CLC 20**
See also CA 117
Desnos, Robert 1900-1945 .... **TCLC 22**
See also CA 121; 151; CANR 107; DLB 258; EWL 3; LMFS 2
Destouches, Louis-Ferdinand
1894-1961 .... **CLC 9, 15**
See Celine, Louis-Ferdinand
See also CA 85-88; CANR 28; MTCW 1
de Tolignac, Gaston
See Griffith, D.W.
Deutsch, Babette 1895-1982 .... **CLC 18**
See also BYA 3; CA 1-4R; 108; CANR 4, 79; CP 1, 2, 3; DLB 45; SATA 1; SATA-Obit 33
Devenant, William 1606-1649 .... **LC 13**
Devkota, Laxmiprasad 1909-1959 . **TCLC 23**
See also CA 123
De Voto, Bernard (Augustine)
1897-1955 .... **TCLC 29**
See also CA 113; 160; DLB 9, 256; MAL 5; TCWW 1, 2

De Vries, Peter 1910-1993 ..... **CLC 1, 2, 3, 7, 10, 28, 46**
See also CA 17-20R; 142; CANR 41; CN 1, 2, 3, 4, 5; DAM NOV; DLB 6; DLBY 1982; MAL 5; MTCW 1, 2; MTFW 2005
Dewey, John 1859-1952 .... **TCLC 95**
See also CA 114; 170; CANR 144; DLB 246, 270; RGAL 4
Dexter, John
See Bradley, Marion Zimmer
See also GLL 1
Dexter, Martin
See Faust, Frederick (Schiller)
Dexter, Pete 1943- .... **CLC 34, 55**
See also BEST 89:2; CA 127; 131; CANR 129; CPW; DAM POP; INT CA-131; MAL 5; MTCW 1; MTFW 2005
Diamano, Silmang
See Senghor, Leopold Sedar
Diamant, Anita 1951- .... **CLC 239**
See also CA 145; CANR 126
Diamond, Neil 1941- .... **CLC 30**
See also CA 108
Diaz, Junot 1968- .... **CLC 258**
See also BYA 12; CA 161; CANR 119, 183; LLW; SSFS 20
Diaz del Castillo, Bernal c. 1496-1584 .... **HLCS 1; LC 31**
See also DLB 318; LAW
di Bassetto, Corno
See Shaw, George Bernard
Dick, Philip K. 1928-1982 ... **CLC 10, 30, 72; SSC 57**
See also AAYA 24; BPFB 1; BYA 11; CA 49-52; 106; CANR 2, 16, 132; CN 2, 3; CPW; DA3; DAM NOV, POP; DLB 8; MTCW 1, 2; MTFW 2005; NFS 5, 26; SCFW 1, 2; SFW 4
Dick, Philip Kindred
See Dick, Philip K.
Dickens, Charles (John Huffam)
1812-1870 .... **NCLC 3, 8, 18, 26, 37, 50, 86, 105, 113, 161, 187; SSC 17, 49, 88; WLC 2**
See also AAYA 23; BRW 5; BRWC 1, 2; BYA 1, 2, 3, 13, 14; CDBLB 1832-1890; CLR 95; CMW 4; DA; DA3; DAB; DAC; DAM MST, NOV; DLB 21, 55, 70, 159, 166; EXPN; GL 2; HGG; JRDA; LAIT 1, 2; LATS 1:1; LMFS 1; MAICYA 1, 2; NFS 4, 5, 10, 14, 20, 25; RGEL 2; RGSF 2; SATA 15; SUFW 1; TEA; WCH; WLIT 4; WYA
Dickey, James (Lafayette)
1923-1997 ..... **CLC 1, 2, 4, 7, 10, 15, 47, 109; PC 40; TCLC 151**
See also AAYA 50; AITN 1, 2; AMWS 4; BPFB 1; CA 9-12R; 156; CABS 2; CANR 10, 48, 61, 105; CDALB 1968-1988; CP 1, 2, 3, 4, 5, 6; CPW; CSW; DA3; DAM NOV, POET, POP; DLB 5, 193, 342; DLBD 7; DLBY 1982, 1993, 1996, 1997, 1998; EWL 3; INT CANR-10; MAL 5; MTCW 1, 2; NFS 9; PFS 6, 11; RGAL 4; TUS
Dickey, William 1928-1994 .... **CLC 3, 28**
See also CA 9-12R; 145; CANR 24, 79; CP 1, 2, 3, 4; DLB 5
Dickinson, Charles 1951- .... **CLC 49**
See also CA 128; CANR 141
Dickinson, Emily (Elizabeth)
1830-1886 ..... **NCLC 21, 77, 171; PC 1; WLC 2**
See also AAYA 22; AMW; AMWR 1; CDALB 1865-1917; DA; DA3; DAB; DAC; DAM MST, POET; DLB 1, 243; EXPP; FL 1:3; MBL; PAB; PFS 1, 2, 3, 4, 5, 6, 8, 10, 11, 13, 16, 28; RGAL 4; SATA 29; TUS; WP; WYA

Dickinson, Mrs. Herbert Ward
See Phelps, Elizabeth Stuart
Dickinson, Peter (Malcolm de Brissac)
1927- .... **CLC 12, 35**
See also AAYA 9, 49; BYA 5; CA 41-44R; CANR 31, 58, 88, 134; CLR 29, 125; CMW 4; DLB 87, 161, 276; JRDA; MAICYA 1, 2; SATA 5, 62, 95, 150; SFW 4; WYA; YAW
Dickinson, Carr
See Carr, John Dickson
Dickson, Carter
See Carr, John Dickson
Diderot, Denis 1713-1784 .... **LC 26, 126**
See also DLB 313; EW 4; GFL Beginnings to 1789; LMFS 1; RGWL 2, 3
Didion, Joan 1934- . **CLC 1, 3, 8, 14, 32, 129**
See also AITN 1; AMWS 4; CA 5-8R; CANR 14, 52, 76, 125, 174; CDALB 1968-1988; CN 2, 3, 4, 5, 6, 7; DA3; DAM NOV; DLB 2, 173, 185; DLBY 1981, 1986; EWL 3; MAL 5; MBL; MTCW 1, 2; MTFW 2005; NFS 3; RGAL 4; TCLE 1:1; TCWW 2; TUS
di Donato, Pietro 1911-1992 .... **TCLC 159**
See also CA 101; 136; DLB 9
Dietrich, Robert
See Hunt, E. Howard
Difusa, Pati
See Almodovar, Pedro
Dillard, Annie 1945- ...... **CLC 9, 60, 115, 216**
See also AAYA 6, 43; AMWS 6; ANW; CA 49-52; CANR 3, 43, 62, 90, 125; DA3; DAM NOV; DLB 275, 278; DLBY 1980; LAIT 4, 5; MAL 5; MTCW 1, 2; MTFW 2005; NCFS 1; RGAL 4; SATA 10, 140; TCLE 1:1; TUS
Dillard, R(ichard) H(enry) W(ilde)
1937- .... **CLC 5**
See also CA 21-24R; CAAS 7; CANR 10; CP 2, 3, 4, 5, 6, 7; CSW; DLB 5, 244
Dillon, Eilis 1920-1994 .... **CLC 17**
See also CA 9-12R; 182; 147; CAAE 182; CAAS 3; CANR 4, 38, 78; CLR 26; MAICYA 1, 2; MAICYAS 1; SATA 2, 74; SATA-Essay 105; SATA-Obit 83; YAW
Dimont, Penelope
See Mortimer, Penelope (Ruth)
Dinesen, Isak ..... **CLC 10, 29, 95; SSC 7, 75**
See Blixen, Karen (Christentze Dinesen)
See also EW 10; EWL 3; EXPS; FW; GL 2; HGG; LAIT 3; MTCW 1; NCFS 2; NFS 9; RGSF 2; RGWL 2, 3; SSFS 3, 6, 13; WLIT 2
Ding Ling .... **CLC 68**
See Chiang, Pin-chin
See also DLB 328; RGWL 3
Diodorus Siculus c. 90B.C.-c. 31B.C. .... **CMLC 88**
Diphusa, Patty
See Almodovar, Pedro
Disch, Thomas M. 1940- .... **CLC 7, 36**
See Disch, Tom
See also AAYA 17; BPFB 1; CA 21-24R; CAAS 4; CANR 17, 36, 54, 89; CLR 18; CP 5, 6, 7; DA3; DLB 8; HGG; MAICYA 1, 2; MTCW 1, 2; MTFW 2005; SAAS 15; SATA 92; SCFW 1, 2; SFW 4; SUFW 2
Disch, Thomas Michael
See Disch, Thomas M.
Disch, Tom
See Disch, Thomas M.
See also DLB 282
d'Isly, Georges
See Simenon, Georges (Jacques Christian)
Disraeli, Benjamin 1804-1881 ... **NCLC 2, 39, 79**
See also BRW 4; DLB 21, 55; RGEL 2

Dowson, Ernest (Christopher)
1867-1900 .... **TCLC 4**
See also CA 105; 150; DLB 19, 135; RGEL
2

Doyle, A. Conan
See Doyle, Sir Arthur Conan

Doyle, Sir Arthur Conan
1859-1930 ..... **SSC 12, 83, 95; TCLC 7;
WLC 2**
See Conan Doyle, Arthur
See also AAYA 14; BRWS 2; CA 104; 122;
CANR 131; CDBLB 1890-1914; CLR
106; CMW 4; DA; DA3; DAB; DAC;
DAM MST, NOV; DLB 18, 70, 156, 178;
EXPS; HGG; LAIT 2; MSW; MTCW 1,
2; MTFW 2005; RGEL 2; RGSF 2; RHW;
SATA 24; SCFW 1, 2; SFW 4; SSFS 2;
TEA; WCH; WLIT 4; WYA; YAW

Doyle, Conan
See Doyle, Sir Arthur Conan

Doyle, John
See Graves, Robert

Doyle, Roddy 1958- .... **CLC 81, 178**
See also AAYA 14; BRWS 5; CA 143;
CANR 73, 128, 168; CN 6, 7; DA3; DLB
194, 326; MTCW 2; MTFW 2005

Doyle, Sir A. Conan
See Doyle, Sir Arthur Conan

Dr. A
See Asimov, Isaac; Silverstein, Alvin; Silverstein, Virginia B(arbara Opshelor)

Drabble, Margaret 1939- ...... **CLC 2, 3, 5, 8,
10, 22, 53, 129**
See also BRWS 4; CA 13-16R; CANR 18,
35, 63, 112, 131, 174; CDBLB 1960 to
Present; CN 1, 2, 3, 4, 5, 6, 7; CPW; DA3;
DAB; DAC; DAM MST, NOV, POP;
DLB 14, 155, 231; EWL 3; FW; MTCW
1, 2; MTFW 2005; RGEL 2; SATA 48;
TEA

Drakulic, Slavenka 1949- .... **CLC 173**
See also CA 144; CANR 92

Drakulic-Ilic, Slavenka
See Drakulic, Slavenka

Drapier, M. B.
See Swift, Jonathan

Drayham, James
See Mencken, H(enry) L(ouis)

Drayton, Michael 1563-1631 .... **LC 8**
See also DAM POET; DLB 121; RGEL 2

Dreadstone, Carl
See Campbell, Ramsey

Dreiser, Theodore 1871-1945 .... **SSC 30, 114;
TCLC 10, 18, 35, 83; WLC 2**
See also AMW; AMWC 2; AMWR 2; BYA
15, 16; CA 106; 132; CDALB 1865-1917;
DA; DA3; DAC; DAM MST, NOV; DLB
9, 12, 102, 137; DLBD 1; EWL 3; LAIT
2; LMFS 2; MAL 5; MTCW 1, 2; MTFW
2005; NFS 8, 17; RGAL 4; TUS

Dreiser, Theodore Herman Albert
See Dreiser, Theodore

Drexler, Rosalyn 1926- .... **CLC 2, 6**
See also CA 81-84; CAD; CANR 68, 124;
CD 5, 6; CWD; MAL 5

Dreyer, Carl Theodor 1889-1968 ...... **CLC 16**
See also CA 116

Drieu la Rochelle, Pierre
1893-1945 .... **TCLC 21**
See also CA 117; 250; DLB 72; EWL 3;
GFL 1789 to the Present

Drieu la Rochelle, Pierre-Eugene 1893-1945
See Drieu la Rochelle, Pierre

Drinkwater, John 1882-1937 .... **TCLC 57**
See also CA 109; 149; DLB 10, 19, 149;
RGEL 2

Drop Shot
See Cable, George Washington

Droste-Hulshoff, Annette Freiin von
1797-1848 .... **NCLC 3, 133**
See also CDWLB 2; DLB 133; RGSF 2;
RGWL 2, 3

Drummond, Walter
See Silverberg, Robert

Drummond, William Henry
1854-1907 .... **TCLC 25**
See also CA 160; DLB 92

Drummond de Andrade, Carlos
1902-1987 .... **CLC 18; TCLC 139**
See Andrade, Carlos Drummond de
See also CA 132; 123; DLB 307; LAW

Drummond of Hawthornden, William
1585-1649 .... **LC 83**
See also DLB 121, 213; RGEL 2

Drury, Allen (Stuart) 1918-1998 .... **CLC 37**
See also CA 57-60; 170; CANR 18, 52; CN
1, 2, 3, 4, 5, 6; INT CANR-18

Druse, Eleanor
See King, Stephen

Dryden, John 1631-1700 ..... **DC 3; LC 3, 21,
115; PC 25; WLC 2**
See also BRW 2; CDBLB 1660-1789; DA;
DAB; DAC; DAM DRAM, MST, POET;
DLB 80, 101, 131; EXPP; IDTP; LMFS
1; RGEL 2; TEA; WLIT 3

du Bellay, Joachim 1524-1560 .... **LC 92**
See also DLB 327; GFL Beginnings to
1789; RGWL 2, 3

Duberman, Martin 1930- .... **CLC 8**
See also CA 1-4R; CAD; CANR 2, 63, 137,
174; CD 5, 6

Dubie, Norman (Evans) 1945- .... **CLC 36**
See also CA 69-72; CANR 12, 115; CP 3,
4, 5, 6, 7; DLB 120; PFS 12

Du Bois, W(illiam) E(dward) B(urghardt)
1868-1963 .. **BLC 1:1; CLC 1, 2, 13, 64,
96; HR 1:2; TCLC 169; WLC 2**
See also AAYA 40; AFAW 1, 2; AMWC 1;
AMWS 2; BW 1, 3; CA 85-88; CANR
34, 82, 132; CDALB 1865-1917; DA;
DA3; DAC; DAM MST, MULT, NOV;
DLB 47, 50, 91, 246, 284; EWL 3; EXPP;
LAIT 2; LMFS 2; MAL 5; MTCW 1, 2;
MTFW 2005; NCFS 1; PFS 13; RGAL 4;
SATA 42

Dubus, Andre 1936-1999 ..... **CLC 13, 36, 97;
SSC 15**
See also AMWS 7; CA 21-24R; 177; CANR
17; CN 5, 6; CSW; DLB 130; INT CANR-
17; RGAL 4; SSFS 10; TCLE 1:1

Duca Minimo
See D'Annunzio, Gabriele

Ducharme, Rejean 1941- .... **CLC 74**
See also CA 165; DLB 60

du Chatelet, Emilie 1706-1749 .... **LC 96**
See Chatelet, Gabrielle-Emilie Du

Duchen, Claire .... **CLC 65**

Duck, Stephen 1705(?)-1756 .... **PC 89**
See also DLB 95; RGEL 2

Duclos, Charles Pinot- 1704-1772 .... **LC 1**
See also GFL Beginnings to 1789

Ducornet, Erica 1943-
See Ducornet, Rikki
See also CA 37-40R; CANR 14, 34, 54, 82;
SATA 7

Ducornet, Rikki .... **CLC 232**
See Ducornet, Erica

Dudek, Louis 1918-2001 .... **CLC 11, 19**
See also CA 45-48; 215; CAAS 14; CANR
1; CP 1, 2, 3, 4, 5, 6, 7; DLB 88

Duerrenmatt, Friedrich 1921-1990 ... **CLC 1,
4, 8, 11, 15, 43, 102**
See Durrenmatt, Friedrich
See also CA 17-20R; CANR 33; CMW 4;
DAM DRAM; DLB 69, 124; MTCW 1, 2

Duffy, Bruce 1953(?)- .... **CLC 50**
See also CA 172

Duffy, Maureen (Patricia) 1933- ...... **CLC 37**
See also CA 25-28R; CANR 33, 68; CBD;
CN 1, 2, 3, 4, 5, 6, 7; CP 5, 6, 7; CWD;
CWP; DFS 15; DLB 14, 310; FW; MTCW
1

Du Fu
See Tu Fu
See also RGWL 2, 3

Dugan, Alan 1923-2003 .... **CLC 2, 6**
See also CA 81-84; 220; CANR 119; CP 1,
2, 3, 4, 5, 6, 7; DLB 5; MAL 5; PFS 10

du Gard, Roger Martin
See Martin du Gard, Roger

Duhamel, Georges 1884-1966 .... **CLC 8**
See also CA 81-84; 25-28R; CANR 35;
DLB 65; EWL 3; GFL 1789 to the
Present; MTCW 1

du Hault, Jean
See Grindel, Eugene

Dujardin, Edouard (Emile Louis)
1861-1949 .... **TCLC 13**
See also CA 109; DLB 123

Duke, Raoul
See Thompson, Hunter S.

Dulles, John Foster 1888-1959 .... **TCLC 72**
See also CA 115; 149

Dumas, Alexandre (pere)
1802-1870 .... **NCLC 11, 71; WLC 2**
See also AAYA 22; BYA 3; CLR 134; DA;
DA3; DAB; DAC; DAM MST, NOV;
DLB 119, 192; EW 6; GFL 1789 to the
Present; LAIT 1, 2; NFS 14, 19; RGWL
2, 3; SATA 18; TWA; WCH

Dumas, Alexandre (fils) 1824-1895 ...... **DC 1;
NCLC 9**
See also DLB 192; GFL 1789 to the Present;
RGWL 2, 3

Dumas, Claudine
See Malzberg, Barry N(athaniel)

Dumas, Henry L. 1934-1968 . **BLC 2:1; CLC
6, 62; SSC 107**
See also BW 1; CA 85-88; DLB 41; RGAL
4

du Maurier, Daphne 1907-1989 .. **CLC 6, 11,
59; SSC 18; TCLC 209**
See also AAYA 37; BPFB 1; BRWS 3; CA
5-8R; 128; CANR 6, 55; CMW 4; CN 1,
2, 3, 4; CPW; DA3; DAB; DAC; DAM
MST, POP; DLB 191; GL 2; HGG; LAIT
3; MSW; MTCW 1, 2; NFS 12; RGEL 2;
RGSF 2; RHW; SATA 27; SATA-Obit 60;
SSFS 14, 16; TEA

Du Maurier, George 1834-1896 ..... **NCLC 86**
See also DLB 153, 178; RGEL 2

Dunbar, Paul Laurence
1872-1906 .... **BLC 1:1; PC 5; SSC 8;
TCLC 2, 12; WLC 2**
See also AAYA 75; AFAW 1, 2; AMWS 2;
BW 1, 3; CA 104; 124; CANR 79;
CDALB 1865-1917; DA; DA3; DAC;
DAM MST, MULT, POET; DLB 50, 54,
78; EXPP; MAL 5; RGAL 4; SATA 34

Dunbar, William 1460(?)-1520(?) .... **LC 20;
PC 67**
See also BRWS 8; DLB 132, 146; RGEL 2

Dunbar-Nelson, Alice .... **HR 1:2**
See Nelson, Alice Ruth Moore Dunbar

Duncan, Dora Angela
See Duncan, Isadora

Duncan, Isadora 1877(?)-1927 .... **TCLC 68**
See also CA 118; 149

Duncan, Lois 1934- .... **CLC 26**
See also AAYA 4, 34; BYA 6, 8; CA 1-4R;
CANR 2, 23, 36, 111; CLR 29, 129;
JRDA; MAICYA 1, 2; MAICYAS 1;
MTFW 2005; SAAS 2; SATA 1, 36, 75,
133, 141; SATA-Essay 141; WYA; YAW

Duncan, Robert 1919-1988 ... **CLC 1, 2, 4, 7, 15, 41, 55; PC 2, 75**
See also BG 1:2; CA 9-12R; 124; CANR 28, 62; CP 1, 2, 3, 4; DAM POET; DLB 5, 16, 193; EWL 3; MAL 5; MTCW 1, 2; MTFW 2005; PFS 13; RGAL 4; WP

Duncan, Sara Jeannette
1861-1922 .... **TCLC 60**
See also CA 157; DLB 92

Dunlap, William 1766-1839 .... **NCLC 2**
See also DLB 30, 37, 59; RGAL 4

Dunn, Douglas (Eaglesham) 1942- .... **CLC 6, 40**
See also BRWS 10; CA 45-48; CANR 2, 33, 126; CP 1, 2, 3, 4, 5, 6, 7; DLB 40; MTCW 1

Dunn, Katherine 1945- .... **CLC 71**
See also CA 33-36R; CANR 72; HGG; MTCW 2; MTFW 2005

Dunn, Stephen 1939- .... **CLC 36, 206**
See also AMWS 11; CA 33-36R; CANR 12, 48, 53, 105; CP 3, 4, 5, 6, 7; DLB 105; PFS 21

Dunn, Stephen Elliott
See Dunn, Stephen

Dunne, Finley Peter 1867-1936 ...... **TCLC 28**
See also CA 108; 178; DLB 11, 23; RGAL 4

Dunne, John Gregory 1932-2003 ..... **CLC 28**
See also CA 25-28R; 222; CANR 14, 50; CN 5, 6, 7; DLBY 1980

Dunsany, Lord .... **TCLC 2, 59**
See Dunsany, Edward John Moreton Drax Plunkett
See also DLB 77, 153, 156, 255; FANT; IDTP; RGEL 2; SFW 4; SUFW 1

Dunsany, Edward John Moreton Drax Plunkett 1878-1957
See Dunsany, Lord
See also CA 104; 148; DLB 10; MTCW 2

Duns Scotus, John 1266(?)-1308 ... **CMLC 59**
See also DLB 115

du Perry, Jean
See Simenon, Georges (Jacques Christian)

Durang, Christopher 1949- .... **CLC 27, 38**
See also CA 105; CAD; CANR 50, 76, 130; CD 5, 6; MTCW 2; MTFW 2005

Durang, Christopher Ferdinand
See Durang, Christopher

Duras, Claire de 1777-1832 .... **NCLC 154**

Duras, Marguerite 1914-1996 . **CLC 3, 6, 11, 20, 34, 40, 68, 100; SSC 40**
See also BPFB 1; CA 25-28R; 151; CANR 50; CWW 2; DFS 21; DLB 83, 321; EWL 3; FL 1:5; GFL 1789 to the Present; IDFW 4; MTCW 1, 2; RGWL 2, 3; TWA

Durban, (Rosa) Pam 1947- .... **CLC 39**
See also CA 123; CANR 98; CSW

Durcan, Paul 1944- .... **CLC 43, 70**
See also CA 134; CANR 123; CP 1, 5, 6, 7; DAM POET; EWL 3

d'Urfe, Honore
See Urfe, Honore d'

Durfey, Thomas 1653-1723 .... **LC 94**
See also DLB 80; RGEL 2

Durkheim, Emile 1858-1917 .... **TCLC 55**
See also CA 249

Durrell, Lawrence (George)
1912-1990 ..... **CLC 1, 4, 6, 8, 13, 27, 41**
See also BPFB 1; BRWS 1; CA 9-12R; 132; CANR 40, 77; CDBLB 1945-1960; CN 1, 2, 3, 4; CP 1, 2, 3, 4, 5; DAM NOV; DLB 15, 27, 204; DLBY 1990; EWL 3; MTCW 1, 2; RGEL 2; SFW 4; TEA

Durrenmatt, Friedrich
See Duerrenmatt, Friedrich
See also CDWLB 2; EW 13; EWL 3; RGHL; RGWL 2, 3

Dutt, Michael Madhusudan
1824-1873 .... **NCLC 118**

Dutt, Toru 1856-1877 .... **NCLC 29**
See also DLB 240

Dwight, Timothy 1752-1817 .... **NCLC 13**
See also DLB 37; RGAL 4

Dworkin, Andrea 1946-2005 ..... **CLC 43, 123**
See also CA 77-80; 238; CAAS 21; CANR 16, 39, 76, 96; FL 1:5; FW; GLL 1; INT CANR-16; MTCW 1, 2; MTFW 2005

Dwyer, Deanna
See Koontz, Dean R.

Dwyer, K.R.
See Koontz, Dean R.

Dybek, Stuart 1942- .... **CLC 114; SSC 55**
See also CA 97-100; CANR 39; DLB 130; SSFS 23

Dye, Richard
See De Voto, Bernard (Augustine)

Dyer, Geoff 1958- .... **CLC 149**
See also CA 125; CANR 88

Dyer, George 1755-1841 .... **NCLC 129**
See also DLB 93

Dylan, Bob 1941- .... **CLC 3, 4, 6, 12, 77; PC 37**
See also CA 41-44R; CANR 108; CP 1, 2, 3, 4, 5, 6, 7; DLB 16

Dyson, John 1943- .... **CLC 70**
See also CA 144

Dzyubin, Eduard Georgievich 1895-1934
See Bagritsky, Eduard
See also CA 170

E. V. L.
See Lucas, E(dward) V(errall)

Eagleton, Terence (Francis) 1943- .. **CLC 63, 132**
See also CA 57-60; CANR 7, 23, 68, 115; DLB 242; LMFS 2; MTCW 1, 2; MTFW 2005

Eagleton, Terry
See Eagleton, Terence (Francis)

Early, Jack
See Scoppettone, Sandra
See also GLL 1

East, Michael
See West, Morris L(anglo)

Eastaway, Edward
See Thomas, (Philip) Edward

Eastlake, William (Derry)
1917-1997 .... **CLC 8**
See also CA 5-8R; 158; CAAS 1; CANR 5, 63; CN 1, 2, 3, 4, 5; DLB 6, 206; INT CANR-5; MAL 5; TCWW 1, 2

Eastman, Charles A(lexander)
1858-1939 .... **NNAL; TCLC 55**
See also CA 179; CANR 91; DAM MULT; DLB 175; YABC 1

Eaton, Edith Maude 1865-1914 .... **AAL**
See Far, Sui Sin
See also CA 154; DLB 221, 312; FW

Eaton, (Lillie) Winnifred 1875-1954 .... **AAL**
See also CA 217; DLB 221, 312; RGAL 4

Eberhart, Richard 1904-2005 ...... **CLC 3, 11, 19, 56; PC 76**
See also AMW; CA 1-4R; 240; CANR 2, 125; CDALB 1941-1968; CP 1, 2, 3, 4, 5, 6, 7; DAM POET; DLB 48; MAL 5; MTCW 1; RGAL 4

Eberhart, Richard Ghormley
See Eberhart, Richard

Eberstadt, Fernanda 1960- .... **CLC 39**
See also CA 136; CANR 69, 128

Ebner, Margaret c. 1291-1351 ...... **CMLC 98**

Echegaray (y Eizaguirre), Jose (Maria Waldo) 1832-1916 .... **HLCS 1; TCLC 4**
See also CA 104; CANR 32; DLB 329; EWL 3; HW 1; MTCW 1

Echeverria, (Jose) Esteban (Antonino)
1805-1851 .... **NCLC 18**
See also LAW

Echo
See Proust, (Valentin-Louis-George-Eugene) Marcel

Eckert, Allan W. 1931- .... **CLC 17**
See also AAYA 18; BYA 2; CA 13-16R; CANR 14, 45; INT CANR-14; MAICYA 2; MAICYAS 1; SAAS 21; SATA 29, 91; SATA-Brief 27

Eckhart, Meister 1260(?)-1327(?) .. **CMLC 9, 80**
See also DLB 115; LMFS 1

Eckman, F. R.
See de Hartog, Jan

Eco, Umberto 1932- .... **CLC 28, 60, 142, 248**
See also BEST 90:1; BPFB 1; CA 77-80; CANR 12, 33, 55, 110, 131; CPW; CWW 2; DA3; DAM NOV, POP; DLB 196, 242; EWL 3; MSW; MTCW 1, 2; MTFW 2005; NFS 22; RGWL 3; WLIT 7

Eddison, E(ric) R(ucker)
1882-1945 .... **TCLC 15**
See also CA 109; 156; DLB 255; FANT; SFW 4; SUFW 1

Eddy, Mary (Ann Morse) Baker
1821-1910 .... **TCLC 71**
See also CA 113; 174

Edel, (Joseph) Leon 1907-1997 .. **CLC 29, 34**
See also CA 1-4R; 161; CANR 1, 22, 112; DLB 103; INT CANR-22

Eden, Emily 1797-1869 .... **NCLC 10**

Edgar, David 1948- .... **CLC 42**
See also CA 57-60; CANR 12, 61, 112; CBD; CD 5, 6; DAM DRAM; DFS 15; DLB 13, 233; MTCW 1

Edgerton, Clyde (Carlyle) 1944- ...... **CLC 39**
See also AAYA 17; CA 118; 134; CANR 64, 125; CN 7; CSW; DLB 278; INT CA-134; TCLE 1:1; YAW

Edgeworth, Maria 1768-1849 ... **NCLC 1, 51, 158; SSC 86**
See also BRWS 3; DLB 116, 159, 163; FL 1:3; FW; RGEL 2; SATA 21; TEA; WLIT 3

Edmonds, Paul
See Kuttner, Henry

Edmonds, Walter D(umaux)
1903-1998 .... **CLC 35**
See also BYA 2; CA 5-8R; CANR 2; CWRI 5; DLB 9; LAIT 1; MAICYA 1, 2; MAL 5; RHW; SAAS 4; SATA 1, 27; SATA-Obit 99

Edmondson, Wallace
See Ellison, Harlan

Edson, Margaret 1961- ...... **CLC 199; DC 24**
See also CA 190; DFS 13; DLB 266

Edson, Russell 1935- .... **CLC 13**
See also CA 33-36R; CANR 115; CP 2, 3, 4, 5, 6, 7; DLB 244; WP

Edwards, Bronwen Elizabeth
See Rose, Wendy

Edwards, G(erald) B(asil)
1899-1976 .... **CLC 25**
See also CA 201; 110

Edwards, Gus 1939- .... **CLC 43**
See also CA 108; INT CA-108

Edwards, Jonathan 1703-1758 .... **LC 7, 54**
See also AMW; DA; DAC; DAM MST; DLB 24, 270; RGAL 4; TUS

Edwards, Sarah Pierpont 1710-1758 .. **LC 87**
See also DLB 200

Efron, Marina Ivanovna Tsvetaeva
See Tsvetaeva (Efron), Marina (Ivanovna)

Egeria fl. 4th cent. - .... **CMLC 70**

Eggers, Dave 1970- .... **CLC 241**
See also AAYA 56; CA 198; CANR 138; MTFW 2005

Emecheta, Buchi 1944- ... **BLC 1:2; CLC 14, 48, 128, 214**
See also AAYA 67; AFW; BW 2, 3; CA 81-84; CANR 27, 81, 126; CDWLB 3; CN 4, 5, 6, 7; CWRI 5; DA3; DAM MULT; DLB 117; EWL 3; FL 1:5; FW; MTCW 1, 2; MTFW 2005; NFS 12, 14; SATA 66; WLIT 2

Emerson, Mary Moody
1774-1863 .... **NCLC 66**

Emerson, Ralph Waldo 1803-1882 . **NCLC 1, 38, 98; PC 18; WLC 2**
See also AAYA 60; AMW; ANW; CDALB 1640-1865; DA; DA3; DAB; DAC; DAM MST, POET; DLB 1, 59, 73, 183, 223, 270; EXPP; LAIT 2; LMFS 1; NCFS 3; PFS 4, 17; RGAL 4; TUS; WP

Eminem 1972- .... **CLC 226**
See also CA 245

Eminescu, Mihail 1850-1889 .. **NCLC 33, 131**

Empedocles 5th cent. B.C.- .... **CMLC 50**
See also DLB 176

Empson, William 1906-1984 ... **CLC 3, 8, 19, 33, 34**
See also BRWS 2; CA 17-20R; 112; CANR 31, 61; CP 1, 2, 3; DLB 20; EWL 3; MTCW 1, 2; RGEL 2

Enchi, Fumiko (Ueda) 1905-1986 ..... **CLC 31**
See Enchi Fumiko
See also CA 129; 121; FW; MJW

Enchi Fumiko
See Enchi, Fumiko (Ueda)
See also DLB 182; EWL 3

Ende, Michael (Andreas Helmuth)
1929-1995 .... **CLC 31**
See also BYA 5; CA 118; 124; 149; CANR 36, 110; CLR 14, 138; DLB 75; MAICYA 1, 2; MAICYAS 1; SATA 61, 130; SATA-Brief 42; SATA-Obit 86

Endo, Shusaku 1923-1996 ..... **CLC 7, 14, 19, 54, 99; SSC 48; TCLC 152**
See Endo Shusaku
See also CA 29-32R; 153; CANR 21, 54, 131; DA3; DAM NOV; MTCW 1, 2; MTFW 2005; RGSF 2; RGWL 2, 3

Endo Shusaku
See Endo, Shusaku
See also CWW 2; DLB 182; EWL 3

Engel, Marian 1933-1985 .... **CLC 36; TCLC 137**
See also CA 25-28R; CANR 12; CN 2, 3; DLB 53; FW; INT CANR-12

Engelhardt, Frederick
See Hubbard, L. Ron

Engels, Friedrich 1820-1895 .. **NCLC 85, 114**
See also DLB 129; LATS 1:1

Enquist, Per Olov 1934- .... **CLC 257**
See also CA 109; 193; CANR 155; CWW 2; DLB 257; EWL 3

Enright, D(ennis) J(oseph)
1920-2002 .... **CLC 4, 8, 31**
See also CA 1-4R; 211; CANR 1, 42, 83; CN 1, 2; CP 1, 2, 3, 4, 5, 6, 7; DLB 27; EWL 3; SATA 25; SATA-Obit 140

Ensler, Eve 1953- .... **CLC 212**
See also CA 172; CANR 126, 163; DFS 23

Enzensberger, Hans Magnus
1929- .... **CLC 43; PC 28**
See also CA 116; 119; CANR 103; CWW 2; EWL 3

Ephron, Nora 1941- .... **CLC 17, 31**
See also AAYA 35; AITN 2; CA 65-68; CANR 12, 39, 83, 161; DFS 22

Epicurus 341B.C.-270B.C. .... **CMLC 21**
See also DLB 176

Epinay, Louise d' 1726-1783 .... **LC 138**
See also DLB 313

Epsilon
See Betjeman, John

Epstein, Daniel Mark 1948- .... **CLC 7**
See also CA 49-52; CANR 2, 53, 90

Epstein, Jacob 1956- .... **CLC 19**
See also CA 114

Epstein, Jean 1897-1953 .... **TCLC 92**

Epstein, Joseph 1937- .... **CLC 39, 204**
See also AMWS 14; CA 112; 119; CANR 50, 65, 117, 164

Epstein, Leslie 1938- .... **CLC 27**
See also AMWS 12; CA 73-76, 215; CAAE 215; CAAS 12; CANR 23, 69, 162; DLB 299; RGHL

Equiano, Olaudah 1745(?)-1797 ..... **BLC 1:2; LC 16, 143**
See also AFAW 1, 2; CDWLB 3; DAM MULT; DLB 37, 50; WLIT 2

Erasmus, Desiderius 1469(?)-1536 ..... **LC 16, 93**
See also DLB 136; EW 2; LMFS 1; RGWL 2, 3; TWA

Erdman, Paul E. 1932-2007 .... **CLC 25**
See also AITN 1; CA 61-64; 259; CANR 13, 43, 84

Erdman, Paul Emil
See Erdman, Paul E.

Erdrich, Karen Louise
See Erdrich, Louise

Erdrich, Louise 1954- .... **CLC 39, 54, 120, 176; NNAL; PC 52**
See also AAYA 10, 47; AMWS 4; BEST 89:1; BPFB 1; CA 114; CANR 41, 62, 118, 138; CDALBS; CN 5, 6, 7; CP 6, 7; CPW; CWP; DA3; DAM MULT, NOV, POP; DLB 152, 175, 206; EWL 3; EXPP; FL 1:5; LAIT 5; LATS 1:2; MAL 5; MTCW 1, 2; MTFW 2005; NFS 5; PFS 14; RGAL 4; SATA 94, 141; SSFS 14, 22; TCWW 2

Erenburg, Ilya (Grigoryevich)
See Ehrenburg, Ilya (Grigoryevich)

Erickson, Stephen Michael
See Erickson, Steve

Erickson, Steve 1950- .... **CLC 64**
See also CA 129; CANR 60, 68, 136; MTFW 2005; SFW 4; SUFW 2

Erickson, Walter
See Fast, Howard

Ericson, Walter
See Fast, Howard

Eriksson, Buntel
See Bergman, Ingmar

Eriugena, John Scottus c.
810-877 .... **CMLC 65**
See also DLB 115

Ernaux, Annie 1940- .... **CLC 88, 184**
See also CA 147; CANR 93; MTFW 2005; NCFS 3, 5

Erskine, John 1879-1951 .... **TCLC 84**
See also CA 112; 159; DLB 9, 102; FANT

Erwin, Will
See Eisner, Will

Eschenbach, Wolfram von
See von Eschenbach, Wolfram
See also RGWL 3

Eseki, Bruno
See Mphahlele, Ezekiel

Esenin, S.A.
See Esenin, Sergei
See also EWL 3

Esenin, Sergei 1895-1925 .... **TCLC 4**
See Esenin, S.A.
See also CA 104; RGWL 2, 3

Esenin, Sergei Aleksandrovich
See Esenin, Sergei

Eshleman, Clayton 1935- .... **CLC 7**
See also CA 33-36R, 212; CAAE 212; CAAS 6; CANR 93; CP 1, 2, 3, 4, 5, 6, 7; DLB 5

Espada, Martin 1957- .... **PC 74**
See also CA 159; CANR 80; CP 7; EXPP; LLW; MAL 5; PFS 13, 16

Espriella, Don Manuel Alvarez
See Southey, Robert

Espriu, Salvador 1913-1985 .... **CLC 9**
See also CA 154; 115; DLB 134; EWL 3

Espronceda, Jose de 1808-1842 ..... **NCLC 39**

Esquivel, Laura 1950(?)- ... **CLC 141; HLCS 1**
See also AAYA 29; CA 143; CANR 68, 113, 161; DA3; DNFS 2; LAIT 3; LMFS 2; MTCW 2; MTFW 2005; NFS 5; WLIT 1

Esse, James
See Stephens, James

Esterbrook, Tom
See Hubbard, L. Ron

Esterhazy, Peter 1950- .... **CLC 251**
See also CA 140; CANR 137; CDWLB 4; CWW 2; DLB 232; EWL 3; RGWL 3

Estleman, Loren D. 1952- .... **CLC 48**
See also AAYA 27; CA 85-88; CANR 27, 74, 139, 177; CMW 4; CPW; DA3; DAM NOV, POP; DLB 226; INT CANR-27; MTCW 1, 2; MTFW 2005; TCWW 1, 2

Etherege, Sir George 1636-1692 . **DC 23; LC 78**
See also BRW 2; DAM DRAM; DLB 80; PAB; RGEL 2

Euclid 306B.C.-283B.C. .... **CMLC 25**

Eugenides, Jeffrey 1960- .... **CLC 81, 212**
See also AAYA 51; CA 144; CANR 120; MTFW 2005; NFS 24

Euripides c. 484B.C.-406B.C. .... **CMLC 23, 51; DC 4; WLCS**
See also AW 1; CDWLB 1; DA; DA3; DAB; DAC; DAM DRAM, MST; DFS 1, 4, 6, 25; DLB 176; LAIT 1; LMFS 1; RGWL 2, 3; WLIT 8

Eusebius c. 263-c. 339 .... **CMLC 103**

Evan, Evin
See Faust, Frederick (Schiller)

Evans, Caradoc 1878-1945 ... **SSC 43; TCLC 85**
See also DLB 162

Evans, Evan
See Faust, Frederick (Schiller)

Evans, Marian
See Eliot, George

Evans, Mary Ann
See Eliot, George
See also NFS 20

Evarts, Esther
See Benson, Sally

Evelyn, John 1620-1706 .... **LC 144**
See also BRW 2; RGEL 2

Everett, Percival
See Everett, Percival L.
See also CANR 179; CSW

Everett, Percival L. 1956- .... **CLC 57**
See Everett, Percival
See also BW 2; CA 129; CANR 94, 134; CN 7; MTFW 2005

Everson, R(onald) G(ilmour)
1903-1992 .... **CLC 27**
See also CA 17-20R; CP 1, 2, 3, 4; DLB 88

Everson, William (Oliver)
1912-1994 .... **CLC 1, 5, 14**
See Antoninus, Brother
See also BG 1:2; CA 9-12R; 145; CANR 20; CP 2, 3, 4, 5; DLB 5, 16, 212; MTCW 1

Evtushenko, Evgenii Aleksandrovich
See Yevtushenko, Yevgeny (Alexandrovich)
See also CWW 2; RGWL 2, 3

Godwin, Gail 1937- ...... **CLC 5, 8, 22, 31, 69, 125**
See also BPFB 2; CA 29-32R; CANR 15, 43, 69, 132; CN 3, 4, 5, 6, 7; CPW; CSW; DA3; DAM POP; DLB 6, 234; INT CANR-15; MAL 5; MTCW 1, 2; MTFW 2005

Godwin, Gail Kathleen
See Godwin, Gail

Godwin, William 1756-1836 .. **NCLC 14, 130**
See also CDBLB 1789-1832; CMW 4; DLB 39, 104, 142, 158, 163, 262, 336; GL 2; HGG; RGEL 2

Goebbels, Josef
See Goebbels, (Paul) Joseph

Goebbels, (Paul) Joseph
1897-1945 .... **TCLC 68**
See also CA 115; 148

Goebbels, Joseph Paul
See Goebbels, (Paul) Joseph

Goethe, Johann Wolfgang von
1749-1832 . **DC 20; NCLC 4, 22, 34, 90, 154; PC 5; SSC 38; WLC 3**
See also CDWLB 2; DA; DA3; DAB; DAC; DAM DRAM, MST, POET; DLB 94; EW 5; GL 2; LATS 1; LMFS 1:1; RGWL 2, 3; TWA

Gogarty, Oliver St. John
1878-1957 .... **TCLC 15**
See also CA 109; 150; DLB 15, 19; RGEL 2

Gogol, Nikolai (Vasilyevich)
1809-1852 .... **DC 1; NCLC 5, 15, 31, 162; SSC 4, 29, 52; WLC 3**
See also DA; DAB; DAC; DAM DRAM, MST; DFS 12; DLB 198; EW 6; EXPS; RGSF 2; RGWL 2, 3; SSFS 7; TWA

Goines, Donald 1937(?)-1974 .... **BLC 1:2; CLC 80**
See also AITN 1; BW 1, 3; CA 124; 114; CANR 82; CMW 4; DA3; DAM MULT, POP; DLB 33

Gold, Herbert 1924- ... **CLC 4, 7, 14, 42, 152**
See also CA 9-12R; CANR 17, 45, 125; CN 1, 2, 3, 4, 5, 6, 7; DLB 2; DLBY 1981; MAL 5

Goldbarth, Albert 1948- .... **CLC 5, 38**
See also AMWS 12; CA 53-56; CANR 6, 40; CP 3, 4, 5, 6, 7; DLB 120

Goldberg, Anatol 1910-1982 .... **CLC 34**
See also CA 131; 117

Goldemberg, Isaac 1945- .... **CLC 52**
See also CA 69-72; CAAS 12; CANR 11, 32; EWL 3; HW 1; WLIT 1

Golding, Arthur 1536-1606 .... **LC 101**
See also DLB 136

Golding, William 1911-1993 . **CLC 1, 2, 3, 8, 10, 17, 27, 58, 81; WLC 3**
See also AAYA 5, 44; BPFB 2; BRWR 1; BRWS 1; BYA 2; CA 5-8R; 141; CANR 13, 33, 54; CD 5; CDBLB 1945-1960; CLR 94; 130; CN 1, 2, 3, 4; DA; DA3; DAB; DAC; DAM MST, NOV; DLB 15, 100, 255, 326, 330; EWL 3; EXPN; HGG; LAIT 4; MTCW 1, 2; MTFW 2005; NFS 2; RGEL 2; RHW; SFW 4; TEA; WLIT 4; YAW

Golding, William Gerald
See Golding, William

Goldman, Emma 1869-1940 .... **TCLC 13**
See also CA 110; 150; DLB 221; FW; RGAL 4; TUS

Goldman, Francisco 1954- .... **CLC 76**
See also CA 162

Goldman, William 1931- .... **CLC 1, 48**
See also BPFB 2; CA 9-12R; CANR 29, 69, 106; CN 1, 2, 3, 4, 5, 6, 7; DLB 44; FANT; IDFW 3, 4

Goldman, William W.
See Goldman, William

Goldmann, Lucien 1913-1970 .... **CLC 24**
See also CA 25-28; CAP 2

Goldoni, Carlo 1707-1793 .... **LC 4, 152**
See also DAM DRAM; EW 4; RGWL 2, 3; WLIT 7

Goldsberry, Steven 1949- .... **CLC 34**
See also CA 131

Goldsmith, Oliver 1730(?)-1774 .... **DC 8; LC 2, 48, 122; PC 77; WLC 3**
See also BRW 3; CDBLB 1660-1789; DA; DAB; DAC; DAM DRAM, MST, NOV, POET; DFS 1; DLB 39, 89, 104, 109, 142, 336; IDTP; RGEL 2; SATA 26; TEA; WLIT 3

Goldsmith, Peter
See Priestley, J(ohn) B(oynton)

Goldstein, Rebecca 1950- .... **CLC 239**
See also CA 144; CANR 99, 165; TCLE 1:1

Goldstein, Rebecca Newberger
See Goldstein, Rebecca

Gombrowicz, Witold 1904-1969 .... **CLC 4, 7, 11, 49**
See also CA 19-20; 25-28R; CANR 105; CAP 2; CDWLB 4; DAM DRAM; DLB 215; EW 12; EWL 3; RGWL 2, 3; TWA

Gomez de Avellaneda, Gertrudis
1814-1873 .... **NCLC 111**
See also LAW

Gomez de la Serna, Ramon
1888-1963 .... **CLC 9**
See also CA 153; 116; CANR 79; EWL 3; HW 1, 2

Goncharov, Ivan Alexandrovich
1812-1891 .... **NCLC 1, 63**
See also DLB 238; EW 6; RGWL 2, 3

Goncourt, Edmond (Louis Antoine Huot) de
1822-1896 .... **NCLC 7**
See also DLB 123; EW 7; GFL 1789 to the Present; RGWL 2, 3

Goncourt, Jules (Alfred Huot) de
1830-1870 .... **NCLC 7**
See also DLB 123; EW 7; GFL 1789 to the Present; RGWL 2, 3

Gongora (y Argote), Luis de
1561-1627 .... **LC 72**
See also RGWL 2, 3

Gontier, Fernande 19(?)- .... **CLC 50**

Gonzalez Martinez, Enrique
See Gonzalez Martinez, Enrique
See also DLB 290

Gonzalez Martinez, Enrique
1871-1952 .... **TCLC 72**
See Gonzalez Martinez, Enrique
See also CA 166; CANR 81; EWL 3; HW 1, 2

Goodison, Lorna 1947- .... **BLC 2:2; PC 36**
See also CA 142; CANR 88; CP 5, 6, 7; CWP; DLB 157; EWL 3; PFS 25

Goodman, Allegra 1967- .... **CLC 241**
See also CA 204; CANR 162; DLB 244

Goodman, Paul 1911-1972 ..... **CLC 1, 2, 4, 7**
See also CA 19-20; 37-40R; CAD; CANR 34; CAP 2; CN 1; DLB 130, 246; MAL 5; MTCW 1; RGAL 4

Goodweather, Hartley
See King, Thomas

GoodWeather, Hartley
See King, Thomas

Googe, Barnabe 1540-1594 .... **LC 94**
See also DLB 132; RGEL 2

Gordimer, Nadine 1923- ...... **CLC 3, 5, 7, 10, 18, 33, 51, 70, 123, 160, 161; SSC 17, 80; WLCS**
See also AAYA 39; AFW; BRWS 2; CA 5-8R; CANR 3, 28, 56, 88, 131; CN 1, 2, 3, 4, 5, 6, 7; DA; DA3; DAB; DAC; DAM MST, NOV; DLB 225, 326, 330; EWL 3; EXPS; INT CANR-28; LATS 1:2; MTCW 1, 2; MTFW 2005; NFS 4; RGEL 2; RGSF 2; SSFS 2, 14, 19; TWA; WLIT 2; YAW

Gordon, Adam Lindsay
1833-1870 .... **NCLC 21**
See also DLB 230

Gordon, Caroline 1895-1981 . **CLC 6, 13, 29, 83; SSC 15**
See also AMW; CA 11-12; 103; CANR 36; CAP 1; CN 1, 2; DLB 4, 9, 102; DLBD 17; DLBY 1981; EWL 3; MAL 5; MTCW 1, 2; MTFW 2005; RGAL 4; RGSF 2

Gordon, Charles William 1860-1937
See Connor, Ralph
See also CA 109

Gordon, Mary 1949- .. **CLC 13, 22, 128, 216; SSC 59**
See also AMWS 4; BPFB 2; CA 102; CANR 44, 92, 154, 179; CN 4, 5, 6, 7; DLB 6; DLBY 1981; FW; INT CA-102; MAL 5; MTCW 1

Gordon, Mary Catherine
See Gordon, Mary

Gordon, N. J.
See Bosman, Herman Charles

Gordon, Sol 1923- .... **CLC 26**
See also CA 53-56; CANR 4; SATA 11

Gordone, Charles 1925-1995 .... **BLC 2:2; CLC 1, 4; DC 8**
See also BW 1, 3; CA 93-96; 180; 150; CAAE 180; CAD; CANR 55; DAM DRAM; DLB 7; INT CA-93-96; MTCW 1

Gore, Catherine 1800-1861 .... **NCLC 65**
See also DLB 116, 344; RGEL 2

Gorenko, Anna Andreevna
See Akhmatova, Anna

Gorky, Maxim .... **SSC 28; TCLC 8; WLC 3**
See Peshkov, Alexei Maximovich
See also DAB; DFS 9; DLB 295; EW 8; EWL 3; TWA

Goryan, Sirak
See Saroyan, William

Gosse, Edmund (William)
1849-1928 .... **TCLC 28**
See also CA 117; DLB 57, 144, 184; RGEL 2

Gotlieb, Phyllis (Fay Bloom) 1926- .. **CLC 18**
See also CA 13-16R; CANR 7, 135; CN 7; CP 1, 2, 3, 4; DLB 88, 251; SFW 4

Gottesman, S. D.
See Kornbluth, C(yril) M.; Pohl, Frederik

Gottfried von Strassburg fl. c.
1170-1215 .... **CMLC 10, 96**
See also CDWLB 2; DLB 138; EW 1; RGWL 2, 3

Gotthelf, Jeremias 1797-1854 .... **NCLC 117**
See also DLB 133; RGWL 2, 3

Gottschalk, Laura Riding
See Jackson, Laura (Riding)

Gould, Lois 1932(?)-2002 .... **CLC 4, 10**
See also CA 77-80; 208; CANR 29; MTCW 1

Gould, Stephen Jay 1941-2002 .... **CLC 163**
See also AAYA 26; BEST 90:2; CA 77-80; 205; CANR 10, 27, 56, 75, 125; CPW; INT CANR-27; MTCW 1, 2; MTFW 2005

Gourmont, Remy(-Marie-Charles) de
1858-1915 .... **TCLC 17**
See also CA 109; 150; GFL 1789 to the Present; MTCW 2

Gournay, Marie le Jars de
See de Gournay, Marie le Jars

Govier, Katherine 1948- .... **CLC 51**
See also CA 101; CANR 18, 40, 128; CCA 1

Gower, John c. 1330-1408 .... **LC 76; PC 59**
See also BRW 1; DLB 146; RGEL 2

Guiraldes, Ricardo (Guillermo)
1886-1927 .... **TCLC 39**
See also CA 131; EWL 3; HW 1; LAW;
MTCW 1

Gumilev, Nikolai (Stepanovich)
1886-1921 .... **TCLC 60**
See Gumilyov, Nikolay Stepanovich
See also CA 165; DLB 295

Gumilyov, Nikolay Stepanovich
See Gumilev, Nikolai (Stepanovich)
See also EWL 3

Gump, P. Q.
See Card, Orson Scott

Gunesekera, Romesh 1954- .... **CLC 91**
See also BRWS 10; CA 159; CANR 140,
172; CN 6, 7; DLB 267, 323

Gunn, Bill .... **CLC 5**
See Gunn, William Harrison
See also DLB 38

Gunn, Thom(son William)
1929-2004 . **CLC 3, 6, 18, 32, 81; PC 26**
See also BRWS 4; CA 17-20R; 227; CANR
9, 33, 116; CDBLB 1960 to Present; CP
1, 2, 3, 4, 5, 6, 7; DAM POET; DLB 27;
INT CANR-33; MTCW 1; PFS 9; RGEL
2

Gunn, William Harrison 1934(?)-1989
See Gunn, Bill
See also AITN 1; BW 1, 3; CA 13-16R;
128; CANR 12, 25, 76

Gunn Allen, Paula
See Allen, Paula Gunn

Gunnars, Kristjana 1948- .... **CLC 69**
See also CA 113; CCA 1; CP 6, 7; CWP;
DLB 60

Gunter, Erich
See Eich, Gunter

Gurdjieff, G(eorgei) I(vanovich)
1877(?)-1949 .... **TCLC 71**
See also CA 157

Gurganus, Allan 1947- .... **CLC 70**
See also BEST 90:1; CA 135; CANR 114;
CN 6, 7; CPW; CSW; DAM POP; GLL 1

Gurney, A. R.
See Gurney, A(lbert) R(amsdell), Jr.
See also DLB 266

Gurney, A(lbert) R(amsdell), Jr.
1930- .... **CLC 32, 50, 54**
See Gurney, A. R.
See also AMWS 5; CA 77-80; CAD; CANR
32, 64, 121; CD 5, 6; DAM DRAM; EWL
3

Gurney, Ivor (Bertie) 1890-1937 ... **TCLC 33**
See also BRW 6; CA 167; DLBY 2002;
PAB; RGEL 2

Gurney, Peter
See Gurney, A(lbert) R(amsdell), Jr.

Guro, Elena (Genrikhovna)
1877-1913 .... **TCLC 56**
See also DLB 295

Gustafson, James M(oody) 1925- ... **CLC 100**
See also CA 25-28R; CANR 37

Gustafson, Ralph (Barker)
1909-1995 .... **CLC 36**
See also CA 21-24R; CANR 8, 45, 84; CP
1, 2, 3, 4, 5, 6; DLB 88; RGEL 2

Gut, Gom
See Simenon, Georges (Jacques Christian)

Guterson, David 1956- .... **CLC 91**
See also CA 132; CANR 73, 126; CN 7;
DLB 292; MTCW 2; MTFW 2005; NFS
13

Guthrie, A(lfred) B(ertram), Jr.
1901-1991 .... **CLC 23**
See also CA 57-60; 134; CANR 24; CN 1,
2, 3; DLB 6, 212; MAL 5; SATA 62;
SATA-Obit 67; TCWW 1, 2

Guthrie, Isobel
See Grieve, C(hristopher) M(urray)

Guthrie, Woodrow Wilson 1912-1967
See Guthrie, Woody
See also CA 113; 93-96

Guthrie, Woody .... **CLC 35**
See Guthrie, Woodrow Wilson
See also DLB 303; LAIT 3

Gutierrez Najera, Manuel
1859-1895 .... **HLCS 2; NCLC 133**
See also DLB 290; LAW

Guy, Rosa (Cuthbert) 1925- .... **CLC 26**
See also AAYA 4, 37; BW 2; CA 17-20R;
CANR 14, 34, 83; CLR 13, 137; DLB 33;
DNFS 1; JRDA; MAICYA 1, 2; SATA 14,
62, 122; YAW

Gwendolyn
See Bennett, (Enoch) Arnold

H. D. .... **CLC 3, 8, 14, 31, 34, 73; PC 5**
See Doolittle, Hilda
See also FL 1:5

H. de V.
See Buchan, John

Haavikko, Paavo Juhani 1931- .. **CLC 18, 34**
See also CA 106; CWW 2; EWL 3

Habbema, Koos
See Heijermans, Herman

Habermas, Juergen 1929- .... **CLC 104**
See also CA 109; CANR 85, 162; DLB 242

Habermas, Jurgen
See Habermas, Juergen

Hacker, Marilyn 1942- ...... **CLC 5, 9, 23, 72, 91; PC 47**
See also CA 77-80; CANR 68, 129; CP 3,
4, 5, 6, 7; CWP; DAM POET; DLB 120,
282; FW; GLL 2; MAL 5; PFS 19

Hadewijch of Antwerp fl. 1250- ... **CMLC 61**
See also RGWL 3

Hadrian 76-138 .... **CMLC 52**

Haeckel, Ernst Heinrich (Philipp August)
1834-1919 .... **TCLC 83**
See also CA 157

Hafiz c. 1326-1389(?) .... **CMLC 34**
See also RGWL 2, 3; WLIT 6

Hagedorn, Jessica T(arahata)
1949- .... **CLC 185**
See also CA 139; CANR 69; CWP; DLB
312; RGAL 4

Haggard, H(enry) Rider
1856-1925 .... **TCLC 11**
See also BRWS 3; BYA 4, 5; CA 108; 148;
CANR 112; DLB 70, 156, 174, 178;
FANT; LMFS 1; MTCW 2; RGEL 2;
RHW; SATA 16; SCFW 1, 2; SFW 4;
SUFW 1; WLIT 4

Hagiosy, L.
See Larbaud, Valery (Nicolas)

Hagiwara, Sakutaro 1886-1942 .... **PC 18; TCLC 60**
See Hagiwara Sakutaro
See also CA 154; RGWL 3

Hagiwara Sakutaro
See Hagiwara, Sakutaro
See also EWL 3

Haig, Fenil
See Ford, Ford Madox

Haig-Brown, Roderick (Langmere)
1908-1976 .... **CLC 21**
See also CA 5-8R; 69-72; CANR 4, 38, 83;
CLR 31; CWRI 5; DLB 88; MAICYA 1,
2; SATA 12; TCWW 2

Haight, Rip
See Carpenter, John (Howard)

Haij, Vera
See Jansson, Tove (Marika)

Hailey, Arthur 1920-2004 .... **CLC 5**
See also AITN 2; BEST 90:3; BPFB 2; CA
1-4R; 233; CANR 2, 36, 75; CCA 1; CN
1, 2, 3, 4, 5, 6, 7; CPW; DAM NOV, POP;
DLB 88; DLBY 1982; MTCW 1, 2;
MTFW 2005

Hailey, Elizabeth Forsythe 1938- ..... **CLC 40**
See also CA 93-96, 188; CAAE 188; CAAS
1; CANR 15, 48; INT CANR-15

Haines, John (Meade) 1924- .... **CLC 58**
See also AMWS 12; CA 17-20R; CANR
13, 34; CP 1, 2, 3, 4, 5; CSW; DLB 5,
212; TCLE 1:1

Ha Jin 1956- .... **CLC 109, 262**
See Jin, Xuefei
See also CA 152; CANR 91, 130; DLB 244,
292; MTFW 2005; NFS 25; SSFS 17

Hakluyt, Richard 1552-1616 .... **LC 31**
See also DLB 136; RGEL 2

Haldeman, Joe 1943- .... **CLC 61**
See also AAYA 38; CA 53-56, 179; CAAE
179; CAAS 25; CANR 6, 70, 72, 130,
171; DLB 8; INT CANR-6; SCFW 2;
SFW 4

Haldeman, Joe William
See Haldeman, Joe

Hale, Janet Campbell 1947- .... **NNAL**
See also CA 49-52; CANR 45, 75; DAM
MULT; DLB 175; MTCW 2; MTFW 2005

Hale, Sarah Josepha (Buell)
1788-1879 .... **NCLC 75**
See also DLB 1, 42, 73, 243

Halevy, Elie 1870-1937 .... **TCLC 104**

Haley, Alex(ander Murray Palmer)
1921-1992 ...... **BLC 1:2; CLC 8, 12, 76; TCLC 147**
See also AAYA 26; BPFB 2; BW 2, 3; CA
77-80; 136; CANR 61; CDALBS; CPW;
CSW; DA; DA3; DAB; DAC; DAM MST,
MULT, POP; DLB 38; LAIT 5; MTCW
1, 2; NFS 9

Haliburton, Thomas Chandler
1796-1865 .... **NCLC 15, 149**
See also DLB 11, 99; RGEL 2; RGSF 2

Hall, Donald 1928- ... **CLC 1, 13, 37, 59, 151, 240; PC 70**
See also AAYA 63; CA 5-8R; CAAS 7;
CANR 2, 44, 64, 106, 133; CP 1, 2, 3, 4,
5, 6, 7; DAM POET; DLB 5, 342; MAL
5; MTCW 2; MTFW 2005; RGAL 4;
SATA 23, 97

Hall, Donald Andrew, Jr.
See Hall, Donald

Hall, Frederic Sauser
See Sauser-Hall, Frederic

Hall, James
See Kuttner, Henry

Hall, James Norman 1887-1951 ..... **TCLC 23**
See also CA 123; 173; LAIT 1; RHW 1;
SATA 21

Hall, Joseph 1574-1656 .... **LC 91**
See also DLB 121, 151; RGEL 2

Hall, Marguerite Radclyffe
See Hall, Radclyffe

Hall, Radclyffe 1880-1943 .... **TCLC 12**
See also BRWS 6; CA 110; 150; CANR 83;
DLB 191; MTCW 2; MTFW 2005; RGEL
2; RHW

Hall, Rodney 1935- .... **CLC 51**
See also CA 109; CANR 69; CN 6, 7; CP
1, 2, 3, 4, 5, 6, 7; DLB 289

Hallam, Arthur Henry
1811-1833 .... **NCLC 110**
See also DLB 32

Halldor Laxness .... **CLC 25**
See Gudjonsson, Halldor Kiljan
See also DLB 293; EW 12; EWL 3; RGWL
2, 3

Halleck, Fitz-Greene 1790-1867 .... **NCLC 47**
See also DLB 3, 250; RGAL 4

Halliday, Michael
See Creasey, John

Halpern, Daniel 1945- .... **CLC 14**
See also CA 33-36R; CANR 93, 174; CP 3,
4, 5, 6, 7

Hamburger, Michael 1924-2007 ... **CLC 5, 14**
See also CA 5-8R, 196; 261; CAAE 196; CAAS 4; CANR 2, 47; CP 1, 2, 3, 4, 5, 6, 7; DLB 27
Hamburger, Michael Peter Leopold
See Hamburger, Michael
Hamill, Pete 1935- .... **CLC 10, 261**
See also CA 25-28R; CANR 18, 71, 127, 180
Hamill, William Peter
See Hamill, Pete
Hamilton, Alexander 1712-1756 .... **LC 150**
See also DLB 31
Hamilton, Alexander 1755(?)-1804 .... **NCLC 49**
See also DLB 37
Hamilton, Clive
See Lewis, C.S.
Hamilton, Edmond 1904-1977 .... **CLC 1**
See also CA 1-4R; CANR 3, 84; DLB 8; SATA 118; SFW 4
Hamilton, Elizabeth 1758-1816 ... **NCLC 153**
See also DLB 116, 158
Hamilton, Eugene (Jacob) Lee
See Lee-Hamilton, Eugene (Jacob)
Hamilton, Franklin
See Silverberg, Robert
Hamilton, Gail
See Corcoran, Barbara (Asenath)
Hamilton, (Robert) Ian 1938-2001 . **CLC 191**
See also CA 106; 203; CANR 41, 67; CP 1, 2, 3, 4, 5, 6, 7; DLB 40, 155
Hamilton, Jane 1957- .... **CLC 179**
See also CA 147; CANR 85, 128; CN 7; MTFW 2005
Hamilton, Mollie
See Kaye, M.M.
Hamilton, (Anthony Walter) Patrick 1904-1962 .... **CLC 51**
See also CA 176; 113; DLB 10, 191
Hamilton, Virginia 1936-2002 .... **CLC 26**
See also AAYA 2, 21; BW 2, 3; BYA 1, 2, 8; CA 25-28R; 206; CANR 20, 37, 73, 126; CLR 1, 11, 40, 127; DAM MULT; DLB 33, 52; DLBY 2001; INT CANR-20; JRDA; LAIT 5; MAICYA 1, 2; MAICYAS 1; MTCW 1, 2; MTFW 2005; SATA 4, 56, 79, 123; SATA-Obit 132; WYA; YAW
Hammett, (Samuel) Dashiell 1894-1961 .... **CLC 3, 5, 10, 19, 47; SSC 17; TCLC 187**
See also AAYA 59; AITN 1; AMWS 4; BPFB 2; CA 81-84; CANR 42; CDALB 1929-1941; CMW 4; DA3; DLB 226, 280; DLBD 6; DLBY 1996; EWL 3; LAIT 3; MAL 5; MSW; MTCW 1, 2; MTFW 2005; NFS 21; RGAL 4; RGSF 2; TUS
Hammon, Jupiter 1720(?)-1800(?) . **BLC 1:2; NCLC 5; PC 16**
See also DAM MULT, POET; DLB 31, 50
Hammond, Keith
See Kuttner, Henry
Hamner, Earl (Henry), Jr. 1923- ...... **CLC 12**
See also AITN 2; CA 73-76; DLB 6
Hampton, Christopher 1946- .... **CLC 4**
See also CA 25-28R; CD 5, 6; DLB 13; MTCW 1
Hampton, Christopher James
See Hampton, Christopher
Hamsun, Knut ..... **TCLC 2, 14, 49, 151, 203**
See Pedersen, Knut
See also DLB 297, 330; EW 8; EWL 3; RGWL 2, 3

Handke, Peter 1942- .... **CLC 5, 8, 10, 15, 38, 134; DC 17**
See also CA 77-80; CANR 33, 75, 104, 133, 180; CWW 2; DAM DRAM, NOV; DLB 85, 124; EWL 3; MTCW 1, 2; MTFW 2005; TWA
Handy, W(illiam) C(hristopher) 1873-1958 .... **TCLC 97**
See also BW 3; CA 121; 167
Hanley, James 1901-1985 ..... **CLC 3, 5, 8, 13**
See also CA 73-76; 117; CANR 36; CBD; CN 1, 2, 3; DLB 191; EWL 3; MTCW 1; RGEL 2
Hannah, Barry 1942- .. **CLC 23, 38, 90; SSC 94**
See also BPFB 2; CA 108; 110; CANR 43, 68, 113; CN 4, 5, 6, 7; CSW; DLB 6, 234; INT CA-110; MTCW 1; RGSF 2
Hannon, Ezra
See Hunter, Evan
Hansberry, Lorraine (Vivian) 1930-1965 ... **BLC 1:2, 2:2; CLC 17, 62; DC 2; TCLC 192**
See also AAYA 25; AFAW 1, 2; AMWS 4; BW 1, 3; CA 109; 25-28R; CABS 3; CAD; CANR 58; CDALB 1941-1968; CWD; DA; DA3; DAB; DAC; DAM DRAM, MST, MULT; DFS 2; DLB 7, 38; EWL 3; FL 1:6; FW; LAIT 4; MAL 5; MTCW 1, 2; MTFW 2005; RGAL 4; TUS
Hansen, Joseph 1923-2004 .... **CLC 38**
See Brock, Rose; Colton, James
See also BPFB 2; CA 29-32R; 233; CAAS 17; CANR 16, 44, 66, 125; CMW 4; DLB 226; GLL 1; INT CANR-16
Hansen, Karen V. 1955- .... **CLC 65**
See also CA 149; CANR 102
Hansen, Martin A(lfred) 1909-1955 .... **TCLC 32**
See also CA 167; DLB 214; EWL 3
Hanson, Kenneth O(stlin) 1922- .... **CLC 13**
See also CA 53-56; CANR 7; CP 1, 2, 3, 4, 5
Hardwick, Elizabeth 1916-2007 .... **CLC 13**
See also AMWS 3; CA 5-8R; 267; CANR 3, 32, 70, 100, 139; CN 4, 5, 6; CSW; DA3; DAM NOV; DLB 6; MBL; MTCW 1, 2; MTFW 2005; TCLE 1:1
Hardwick, Elizabeth Bruce
See Hardwick, Elizabeth
Hardwick, Elizabeth Bruce
See Hardwick, Elizabeth
Hardy, Thomas 1840-1928 . **PC 8; SSC 2, 60, 113; TCLC 4, 10, 18, 32, 48, 53, 72, 143, 153; WLC 3**
See also AAYA 69; BRW 6; BRWC 1, 2; BRWR 1; CA 104; 123; CDBLB 1890-1914; DA; DA3; DAB; DAC; DAM MST, NOV, POET; DLB 18, 19, 135, 284; EWL 3; EXPN; EXPP; LAIT 2; MTCW 1, 2; MTFW 2005; NFS 3, 11, 15, 19; PFS 3, 4, 18; RGEL 2; RGSF 2; TEA; WLIT 4
Hare, David 1947- . **CLC 29, 58, 136; DC 26**
See also BRWS 4; CA 97-100; CANR 39, 91; CBD; CD 5, 6; DFS 4, 7, 16; DLB 13, 310; MTCW 1; TEA
Harewood, John
See Van Druten, John (William)
Harford, Henry
See Hudson, W(illiam) H(enry)
Hargrave, Leonie
See Disch, Thomas M.
Hariri, Al- al-Qasim ibn 'Ali Abu Muhammad al-Basri
See al-Hariri, al-Qasim ibn 'Ali Abu Muhammad al-Basri

Harjo, Joy 1951- ..... **CLC 83; NNAL; PC 27**
See also AMWS 12; CA 114; CANR 35, 67, 91, 129; CP 6, 7; CWP; DAM MULT; DLB 120, 175, 342; EWL 3; MTCW 2; MTFW 2005; PFS 15; RGAL 4
Harlan, Louis R(udolph) 1922- .... **CLC 34**
See also CA 21-24R; CANR 25, 55, 80
Harling, Robert 1951(?)- .... **CLC 53**
See also CA 147
Harmon, William (Ruth) 1938- .... **CLC 38**
See also CA 33-36R; CANR 14, 32, 35; SATA 65
Harper, F. E. W.
See Harper, Frances Ellen Watkins
Harper, Frances E. W.
See Harper, Frances Ellen Watkins
Harper, Frances E. Watkins
See Harper, Frances Ellen Watkins
Harper, Frances Ellen
See Harper, Frances Ellen Watkins
Harper, Frances Ellen Watkins 1825-1911 .. **BLC 1:2; PC 21; TCLC 14**
See also AFAW 1, 2; BW 1, 3; CA 111; 125; CANR 79; DAM MULT, POET; DLB 50, 221; MBL; RGAL 4
Harper, Michael S(teven) 1938- ..... **BLC 2:2; CLC 7, 22**
See also AFAW 2; BW 1; CA 33-36R; 224; CAAE 224; CANR 24, 108; CP 2, 3, 4, 5, 6, 7; DLB 41; RGAL 4; TCLE 1:1
Harper, Mrs. F. E. W.
See Harper, Frances Ellen Watkins
Harpur, Charles 1813-1868 .... **NCLC 114**
See also DLB 230; RGEL 2
Harris, Christie
See Harris, Christie (Lucy) Irwin
Harris, Christie (Lucy) Irwin 1907-2002 .... **CLC 12**
See also CA 5-8R; CANR 6, 83; CLR 47; DLB 88; JRDA; MAICYA 1, 2; SAAS 10; SATA 6, 74; SATA-Essay 116
Harris, Frank 1856-1931 .... **TCLC 24**
See also CA 109; 150; CANR 80; DLB 156, 197; RGEL 2
Harris, George Washington 1814-1869 .... **NCLC 23, 165**
See also DLB 3, 11, 248; RGAL 4
Harris, Joel Chandler 1848-1908 ..... **SSC 19, 103; TCLC 2**
See also CA 104; 137; CANR 80; CLR 49, 128; DLB 11, 23, 42, 78, 91; LAIT 2; MAICYA 1, 2; RGSF 2; SATA 100; WCH; YABC 1
Harris, John (Wyndham Parkes Lucas) Beynon 1903-1969
See Wyndham, John
See also CA 102; 89-92; CANR 84; SATA 118; SFW 4
Harris, MacDonald .... **CLC 9**
See Heiney, Donald (William)
Harris, Mark 1922-2007 .... **CLC 19**
See also CA 5-8R; 260; CAAS 3; CANR 2, 55, 83; CN 1, 2, 3, 4, 5, 6, 7; DLB 2; DLBY 1980
Harris, Norman .... **CLC 65**
Harris, (Theodore) Wilson 1921- ... **BLC 2:2; CLC 25, 159**
See also BRWS 5; BW 2, 3; CA 65-68; CAAS 16; CANR 11, 27, 69, 114; CD-WLB 3; CN 1, 2, 3, 4, 5, 6, 7; CP 1, 2, 3, 4, 5, 6, 7; DLB 117; EWL 3; MTCW 1; RGEL 2
Harrison, Barbara Grizzuti 1934-2002 .... **CLC 144**
See also CA 77-80; 205; CANR 15, 48; INT CANR-15

Hecht, Anthony (Evan) 1923-2004 .... **CLC 8, 13, 19; PC 70**
See also AMWS 10; CA 9-12R; 232; CANR 6, 108; CP 1, 2, 3, 4, 5, 6, 7; DAM POET; DLB 5, 169; EWL 3; PFS 6; WP

Hecht, Ben 1894-1964 ..... **CLC 8; TCLC 101**
See also CA 85-88; DFS 9; DLB 7, 9, 25, 26, 28, 86; FANT; IDFW 3, 4; RGAL 4

Hedayat, Sadeq 1903-1951 .... **TCLC 21**
See also CA 120; EWL 3; RGSF 2

Hegel, Georg Wilhelm Friedrich
1770-1831 .... **NCLC 46, 151**
See also DLB 90; TWA

Heidegger, Martin 1889-1976 .... **CLC 24**
See also CA 81-84; 65-68; CANR 34; DLB 296; MTCW 1, 2; MTFW 2005

Heidenstam, (Carl Gustaf) Verner von
1859-1940 .... **TCLC 5**
See also CA 104; DLB 330

Heidi Louise
See Erdrich, Louise

Heifner, Jack 1946- .... **CLC 11**
See also CA 105; CANR 47

Heijermans, Herman 1864-1924 .... **TCLC 24**
See also CA 123; EWL 3

Heilbrun, Carolyn G(old)
1926-2003 .... **CLC 25, 173**
See Cross, Amanda
See also CA 45-48; 220; CANR 1, 28, 58, 94; FW

Hein, Christoph 1944- .... **CLC 154**
See also CA 158; CANR 108; CDWLB 2; CWW 2; DLB 124

Heine, Heinrich 1797-1856 .... **NCLC 4, 54, 147; PC 25**
See also CDWLB 2; DLB 90; EW 5; RGWL 2, 3; TWA

Heinemann, Larry 1944- .... **CLC 50**
See also CA 110; CAAS 21; CANR 31, 81, 156; DLBD 9; INT CANR-31

Heinemann, Larry Curtiss
See Heinemann, Larry

Heiney, Donald (William) 1921-1993
See Harris, MacDonald
See also CA 1-4R; 142; CANR 3, 58; FANT

Heinlein, Robert A. 1907-1988 .. **CLC 1, 3, 8, 14, 26, 55; SSC 55**
See also AAYA 17; BPFB 2; BYA 4, 13; CA 1-4R; 125; CANR 1, 20, 53; CLR 75; CN 1, 2, 3, 4; CPW; DA3; DAM POP; DLB 8; EXPS; JRDA; LAIT 5; LMFS 2; MAICYA 1, 2; MTCW 1, 2; MTFW 2005; RGAL 4; SATA 9, 69; SATA-Obit 56; SCFW 1, 2; SFW 4; SSFS 7; YAW

Heldris of Cornwall fl. 13th cent.
- .... **CMLC 97**

Helforth, John
See Doolittle, Hilda

Heliodorus fl. 3rd cent. - .... **CMLC 52**
See also WLIT 8

Hellenhofferu, Vojtech Kapristian z
See Hasek, Jaroslav (Matej Frantisek)

Heller, Joseph 1923-1999 . **CLC 1, 3, 5, 8, 11, 36, 63; TCLC 131, 151; WLC 3**
See also AAYA 24; AITN 1; AMWS 4; BPFB 2; BYA 1; CA 5-8R; 187; CABS 1; CANR 8, 42, 66, 126; CN 1, 2, 3, 4, 5, 6; CPW; DA; DA3; DAB; DAC; DAM MST, NOV, POP; DLB 2, 28, 227; DLBY 1980, 2002; EWL 3; EXPN; INT CANR-8; LAIT 4; MAL 5; MTCW 1, 2; MTFW 2005; NFS 1; RGAL 4; TUS; YAW

Hellman, Lillian 1905-1984 . **CLC 2, 4, 8, 14, 18, 34, 44, 52; DC 1; TCLC 119**
See also AAYA 47; AITN 1, 2; AMWS 1; CA 13-16R; 112; CAD; CANR 33; CWD; DA3; DAM DRAM; DFS 1, 3, 14; DLB

7, 228; DLBY 1984; EWL 3; FL 1:6; FW; LAIT 3; MAL 5; MBL; MTCW 1, 2; MTFW 2005; RGAL 4; TUS

Helprin, Mark 1947- .... **CLC 7, 10, 22, 32**
See also CA 81-84; CANR 47, 64, 124; CDALBS; CN 7; CPW; DA3; DAM NOV, POP; DLB 335; DLBY 1985; FANT; MAL 5; MTCW 1, 2; MTFW 2005; SSFS 25; SUFW 2

Helvetius, Claude-Adrien 1715-1771 .. **LC 26**
See also DLB 313

Helyar, Jane Penelope Josephine 1933-
See Poole, Josephine
See also CA 21-24R; CANR 10, 26; CWRI 5; SATA 82, 138; SATA-Essay 138

Hemans, Felicia 1793-1835 ...... **NCLC 29, 71**
See also DLB 96; RGEL 2

Hemingway, Ernest (Miller)
1899-1961 .... **CLC 1, 3, 6, 8, 10, 13, 19, 30, 34, 39, 41, 44, 50, 61, 80; SSC 1, 25, 36, 40, 63; TCLC 115, 203; WLC 3**
See also AAYA 19; AMW; AMWC 1; AMWR 1; BPFB 2; BYA 2, 3, 13, 15; CA 77-80; CANR 34; CDALB 1917-1929; DA; DA3; DAB; DAC; DAM MST, NOV; DLB 4, 9, 102, 210, 308, 316, 330; DLBD 1, 15, 16; DLBY 1981, 1987, 1996, 1998; EWL 3; EXPN; EXPS; LAIT 3, 4; LATS 1:1; MAL 5; MTCW 1, 2; MTFW 2005; NFS 1, 5, 6, 14; RGAL 4; RGSF 2; SSFS 17; TUS; WYA

Hempel, Amy 1951- .... **CLC 39**
See also CA 118; 137; CANR 70, 166; DA3; DLB 218; EXPS; MTCW 2; MTFW 2005; SSFS 2

Henderson, F. C.
See Mencken, H(enry) L(ouis)

Henderson, Sylvia
See Ashton-Warner, Sylvia (Constance)

Henderson, Zenna (Chlarson)
1917-1983 .... **SSC 29**
See also CA 1-4R; 133; CANR 1, 84; DLB 8; SATA 5; SFW 4

Henkin, Joshua 1964- .... **CLC 119**
See also CA 161

Henley, Beth .... **CLC 23, 255; DC 6, 14**
See Henley, Elizabeth Becker
See also AAYA 70; CABS 3; CAD; CD 5, 6; CSW; CWD; DFS 2, 21; DLBY 1986; FW

Henley, Elizabeth Becker 1952-
See Henley, Beth
See also CA 107; CANR 32, 73, 140; DA3; DAM DRAM, MST; MTCW 1, 2; MTFW 2005

Henley, William Ernest 1849-1903 .. **TCLC 8**
See also CA 105; 234; DLB 19; RGEL 2

Hennissart, Martha 1929-
See Lathen, Emma
See also CA 85-88; CANR 64

Henry VIII 1491-1547 .... **LC 10**
See also DLB 132

Henry, O. .... **SSC 5, 49, 114; TCLC 1, 19; WLC 3**
See Porter, William Sydney
See also AAYA 41; AMWS 2; EXPS; MAL 5; RGAL 4; RGSF 2; SSFS 2, 18; TCWW 1, 2

Henry, Patrick 1736-1799 .... **LC 25**
See also LAIT 1

Henryson, Robert 1430(?)-1506(?) ..... **LC 20, 110; PC 65**
See also BRWS 7; DLB 146; RGEL 2

Henschke, Alfred
See Klabund

Henson, Lance 1944- .... **NNAL**
See also CA 146; DLB 175

Hentoff, Nat(han Irving) 1925- .... **CLC 26**
See also AAYA 4, 42; BYA 6; CA 1-4R; CAAS 6; CANR 5, 25, 77, 114; CLR 1, 52; INT CANR-25; JRDA; MAICYA 1, 2; SATA 42, 69, 133; SATA-Brief 27; WYA; YAW

Heppenstall, (John) Rayner
1911-1981 .... **CLC 10**
See also CA 1-4R; 103; CANR 29; CN 1, 2; CP 1, 2, 3; EWL 3

Heraclitus c. 540B.C.-c. 450B.C. ... **CMLC 22**
See also DLB 176

Herbert, Frank 1920-1986 ... **CLC 12, 23, 35, 44, 85**
See also AAYA 21; BPFB 2; BYA 4, 14; CA 53-56; 118; CANR 5, 43; CDALBS; CPW; DAM POP; DLB 8; INT CANR-5; LAIT 5; MTCW 1, 2; MTFW 2005; NFS 17; SATA 9, 37; SATA-Obit 47; SCFW 1, 2; SFW 4; YAW

Herbert, George 1593-1633 . **LC 24, 121; PC 4**
See also BRW 2; BRWR 2; CDBLB Before 1660; DAB; DAM POET; DLB 126; EXPP; PFS 25; RGEL 2; TEA; WP

Herbert, Zbigniew 1924-1998 ..... **CLC 9, 43; PC 50; TCLC 168**
See also CA 89-92; 169; CANR 36, 74, 177; CDWLB 4; CWW 2; DAM POET; DLB 232; EWL 3; MTCW 1; PFS 22

Herbst, Josephine (Frey)
1897-1969 .... **CLC 34**
See also CA 5-8R; 25-28R; DLB 9

Herder, Johann Gottfried von
1744-1803 .... **NCLC 8, 186**
See also DLB 97; EW 4; TWA

Heredia, Jose Maria 1803-1839 .... **HLCS 2**
See also LAW

Hergesheimer, Joseph 1880-1954 ... **TCLC 11**
See also CA 109; 194; DLB 102, 9; RGAL 4

Herlihy, James Leo 1927-1993 .... **CLC 6**
See also CA 1-4R; 143; CAD; CANR 2; CN 1, 2, 3, 4, 5

Herman, William
See Bierce, Ambrose (Gwinett)

Hermogenes fl. c. 175- .... **CMLC 6**

Hernandez, Jose 1834-1886 .... **NCLC 17**
See also LAW; RGWL 2, 3; WLIT 1

Herodotus c. 484B.C.-c. 420B.C. .. **CMLC 17**
See also AW 1; CDWLB 1; DLB 176; RGWL 2, 3; TWA; WLIT 8

Herr, Michael 1940(?)- .... **CLC 231**
See also CA 89-92; CANR 68, 142; DLB 185; MTCW 1

Herrick, Robert 1591-1674 .. **LC 13, 145; PC 9**
See also BRW 2; BRWC 2; DA; DAB; DAC; DAM MST, POP; DLB 126; EXPP; PFS 13; RGAL 4; RGEL 2; TEA; WP

Herring, Guilles
See Somerville, Edith Oenone

Herriot, James 1916-1995 .... **CLC 12**
See Wight, James Alfred
See also AAYA 1, 54; BPFB 2; CA 148; CANR 40; CLR 80; CPW; DAM POP; LAIT 3; MAICYA 2; MAICYAS 1; MTCW 2; SATA 86, 135; TEA; YAW

Herris, Violet
See Hunt, Violet

Herrmann, Dorothy 1941- .... **CLC 44**
See also CA 107

Herrmann, Taffy
See Herrmann, Dorothy

Hersey, John 1914-1993 .. **CLC 1, 2, 7, 9, 40, 81, 97**
See also AAYA 29; BPFB 2; CA 17-20R; 140; CANR 33; CDALBS; CN 1, 2, 3, 4, 5; CPW; DAM POP; DLB 6, 185, 278, 299; MAL 5; MTCW 1, 2; MTFW 2005; RGHL; SATA 25; SATA-Obit 76; TUS

Hoch, Edward D. 1930-2008
See Queen, Ellery
See also CA 29-32R; CANR 11, 27, 51, 97; CMW 4; DLB 306; SFW 4

Hochhuth, Rolf 1931- .... **CLC 4, 11, 18**
See also CA 5-8R; CANR 33, 75, 136; CWW 2; DAM DRAM; DLB 124; EWL 3; MTCW 1, 2; MTFW 2005; RGHL

Hochman, Sandra 1936- .... **CLC 3, 8**
See also CA 5-8R; CP 1, 2, 3, 4, 5; DLB 5

Hochwaelder, Fritz 1911-1986 .... **CLC 36**
See Hochwalder, Fritz
See also CA 29-32R; 120; CANR 42; DAM DRAM; MTCW 1; RGWL 3

Hochwalder, Fritz
See Hochwaelder, Fritz
See also EWL 3; RGWL 2

Hocking, Mary (Eunice) 1921- .... **CLC 13**
See also CA 101; CANR 18, 40

Hodge, Merle 1944- .... **BLC 2:2**
See also EWL 3

Hodgins, Jack 1938- .... **CLC 23**
See also CA 93-96; CN 4, 5, 6, 7; DLB 60

Hodgson, William Hope
1877(?)-1918 .... **TCLC 13**
See also CA 111; 164; CMW 4; DLB 70, 153, 156, 178; HGG; MTCW 2; SFW 4; SUFW 1

Hoeg, Peter 1957- .... **CLC 95, 156**
See also CA 151; CANR 75; CMW 4; DA3; DLB 214; EWL 3; MTCW 2; MTFW 2005; NFS 17; RGWL 3; SSFS 18

Hoffman, Alice 1952- .... **CLC 51**
See also AAYA 37; AMWS 10; CA 77-80; CANR 34, 66, 100, 138, 170; CN 4, 5, 6, 7; CPW; DAM NOV; DLB 292; MAL 5; MTCW 1, 2; MTFW 2005; TCLE 1:1

Hoffman, Daniel (Gerard) 1923- . **CLC 6, 13, 23**
See also CA 1-4R; CANR 4, 142; CP 1, 2, 3, 4, 5, 6, 7; DLB 5; TCLE 1:1

Hoffman, Eva 1945- .... **CLC 182**
See also AMWS 16; CA 132; CANR 146

Hoffman, Stanley 1944- .... **CLC 5**
See also CA 77-80

Hoffman, William 1925- .... **CLC 141**
See also CA 21-24R; CANR 9, 103; CSW; DLB 234; TCLE 1:1

Hoffman, William M.
See Hoffman, William M(oses)
See also CAD; CD 5, 6

Hoffman, William M(oses) 1939- ..... **CLC 40**
See Hoffman, William M.
See also CA 57-60; CANR 11, 71

Hoffmann, E(rnst) T(heodor) A(madeus)
1776-1822 ..... **NCLC 2, 183; SSC 13, 92**
See also CDWLB 2; CLR 133; DLB 90; EW 5; GL 2; RGSF 2; RGWL 2, 3; SATA 27; SUFW 1; WCH

Hofmann, Gert 1931-1993 .... **CLC 54**
See also CA 128; CANR 145; EWL 3; RGHL

Hofmannsthal, Hugo von 1874-1929 ... **DC 4; TCLC 11**
See also CA 106; 153; CDWLB 2; DAM DRAM; DFS 17; DLB 81, 118; EW 9; EWL 3; RGWL 2, 3

Hogan, Linda 1947- ..... **CLC 73; NNAL; PC 35**
See also AMWS 4; ANW; BYA 12; CA 120, 226; CAAE 226; CANR 45, 73, 129; CWP; DAM MULT; DLB 175; SATA 132; TCWW 2

Hogarth, Charles
See Creasey, John

Hogarth, Emmett
See Polonsky, Abraham (Lincoln)

Hogarth, William 1697-1764 .... **LC 112**
See also AAYA 56

Hogg, James 1770-1835 .... **NCLC 4, 109**
See also BRWS 10; DLB 93, 116, 159; GL 2; HGG; RGEL 2; SUFW 1

Holbach, Paul-Henri Thiry
1723-1789 .... **LC 14**
See also DLB 313

Holberg, Ludvig 1684-1754 .... **LC 6**
See also DLB 300; RGWL 2, 3

Holcroft, Thomas 1745-1809 .... **NCLC 85**
See also DLB 39, 89, 158; RGEL 2

Holden, Ursula 1921- .... **CLC 18**
See also CA 101; CAAS 8; CANR 22

Holderlin, (Johann Christian) Friedrich
1770-1843 .... **NCLC 16, 187; PC 4**
See also CDWLB 2; DLB 90; EW 5; RGWL 2, 3

Holding, James (Clark Carlisle, Jr.)
1907-1997
See Queen, Ellery
See also CA 25-28R; SATA 3

Holdstock, Robert 1948- .... **CLC 39**
See also CA 131; CANR 81; DLB 261; FANT; HGG; SFW 4; SUFW 2

Holdstock, Robert P.
See Holdstock, Robert

Holinshed, Raphael fl. 1580- .... **LC 69**
See also DLB 167; RGEL 2

Holland, Isabelle (Christian)
1920-2002 .... **CLC 21**
See also AAYA 11, 64; CA 21-24R; 205; CAAE 181; CANR 10, 25, 47; CLR 57; CWRI 5; JRDA; LAIT 4; MAICYA 1, 2; SATA 8, 70; SATA-Essay 103; SATA-Obit 132; WYA

Holland, Marcus
See Caldwell, (Janet Miriam) Taylor (Holland)

Hollander, John 1929- .... **CLC 2, 5, 8, 14**
See also CA 1-4R; CANR 1, 52, 136; CP 1, 2, 3, 4, 5, 6, 7; DLB 5; MAL 5; SATA 13

Hollander, Paul
See Silverberg, Robert

Holleran, Andrew .... **CLC 38**
See Garber, Eric
See also CA 144; GLL 1

Holley, Marietta 1836(?)-1926 .... **TCLC 99**
See also CA 118; DLB 11; FL 1:3

Hollinghurst, Alan 1954- .... **CLC 55, 91**
See also BRWS 10; CA 114; CN 5, 6, 7; DLB 207, 326; GLL 1

Hollis, Jim
See Summers, Hollis (Spurgeon, Jr.)

Holly, Buddy 1936-1959 .... **TCLC 65**
See also CA 213

Holmes, Gordon
See Shiel, M(atthew) P(hipps)

Holmes, John
See Souster, (Holmes) Raymond

Holmes, John Clellon 1926-1988 ...... **CLC 56**
See also BG 1:2; CA 9-12R; 125; CANR 4; CN 1, 2, 3, 4; DLB 16, 237

Holmes, Oliver Wendell, Jr.
1841-1935 .... **TCLC 77**
See also CA 114; 186

Holmes, Oliver Wendell
1809-1894 .... **NCLC 14, 81; PC 71**
See also AMWS 1; CDALB 1640-1865; DLB 1, 189, 235; EXPP; PFS 24; RGAL 4; SATA 34

Holmes, Raymond
See Souster, (Holmes) Raymond

Holt, Victoria
See Hibbert, Eleanor Alice Burford
See also BPFB 2

Holub, Miroslav 1923-1998 .... **CLC 4**
See also CA 21-24R; 169; CANR 10; CDWLB 4; CWW 2; DLB 232; EWL 3; RGWL 3

Holz, Detlev
See Benjamin, Walter

Homer c. 8th cent. B.C.- .... **CMLC 1, 16, 61; PC 23; WLCS**
See also AW 1; CDWLB 1; DA; DA3; DAB; DAC; DAM MST, POET; DLB 176; EFS 1; LAIT 1; LMFS 1; RGWL 2, 3; TWA; WLIT 8; WP

Hong, Maxine Ting Ting
See Kingston, Maxine Hong

Hongo, Garrett Kaoru 1951- .... **PC 23**
See also CA 133; CAAS 22; CP 5, 6, 7; DLB 120, 312; EWL 3; EXPP; PFS 25; RGAL 4

Honig, Edwin 1919- .... **CLC 33**
See also CA 5-8R; CAAS 8; CANR 4, 45, 144; CP 1, 2, 3, 4, 5, 6, 7; DLB 5

Hood, Hugh (John Blagdon) 1928- . **CLC 15, 28; SSC 42**
See also CA 49-52; CAAS 17; CANR 1, 33, 87; CN 1, 2, 3, 4, 5, 6, 7; DLB 53; RGSF 2

Hood, Thomas 1799-1845 .... **NCLC 16**
See also BRW 4; DLB 96; RGEL 2

Hooker, (Peter) Jeremy 1941- .... **CLC 43**
See also CA 77-80; CANR 22; CP 2, 3, 4, 5, 6, 7; DLB 40

Hooker, Richard 1554-1600 .... **LC 95**
See also BRW 1; DLB 132; RGEL 2

Hooker, Thomas 1586-1647 .... **LC 137**
See also DLB 24

hooks, bell 1952(?)- .... **BLCS; CLC 94**
See also BW 2; CA 143; CANR 87, 126; DLB 246; MTCW 2; MTFW 2005; SATA 115, 170

Hooper, Johnson Jones
1815-1862 .... **NCLC 177**
See also DLB 3, 11, 248; RGAL 4

Hope, A(lec) D(erwent) 1907-2000 .... **CLC 3, 51; PC 56**
See also BRWS 7; CA 21-24R; 188; CANR 33, 74; CP 1, 2, 3, 4, 5; DLB 289; EWL 3; MTCW 1, 2; MTFW 2005; PFS 8; RGEL 2

Hope, Anthony 1863-1933 .... **TCLC 83**
See also CA 157; DLB 153, 156; RGEL 2; RHW

Hope, Brian
See Creasey, John

Hope, Christopher 1944- .... **CLC 52**
See also AFW; CA 106; CANR 47, 101, 177; CN 4, 5, 6, 7; DLB 225; SATA 62

Hope, Christopher David Tully
See Hope, Christopher

Hopkins, Gerard Manley
1844-1889 .... **NCLC 17, 189; PC 15; WLC 3**
See also BRW 5; BRWR 2; CDBLB 1890-1914; DA; DA3; DAB; DAC; DAM MST, POET; DLB 35, 57; EXPP; PAB; PFS 26; RGEL 2; TEA; WP

Hopkins, John (Richard) 1931-1998 .. **CLC 4**
See also CA 85-88; 169; CBD; CD 5, 6

Hopkins, Pauline Elizabeth
1859-1930 .... **BLC 1:2; TCLC 28**
See also AFAW 2; BW 2, 3; CA 141; CANR 82; DAM MULT; DLB 50

Hopkinson, Francis 1737-1791 .... **LC 25**
See also DLB 31; RGAL 4

Hopley-Woolrich, Cornell George 1903-1968
See Woolrich, Cornell
See also CA 13-14; CANR 58, 156; CAP 1; CMW 4; DLB 226; MTCW 2

Horace 65B.C.-8B.C. .... **CMLC 39; PC 46**
See also AW 2; CDWLB 1; DLB 211; RGWL 2, 3; WLIT 8

Horatio
See Proust, (Valentin-Louis-George-Eugene) Marcel

Jameson, Fredric 1934- .... **CLC 142**
See also CA 196; CANR 169; DLB 67;
LMFS 2

Jameson, Fredric R.
See Jameson, Fredric

James VI of Scotland 1566-1625 .... **LC 109**
See also DLB 151, 172

Jami, Nur al-Din 'Abd al-Rahman
1414-1492 .... **LC 9**

Jammes, Francis 1868-1938 .... **TCLC 75**
See also CA 198; EWL 3; GFL 1789 to the
Present

Jandl, Ernst 1925-2000 .... **CLC 34**
See also CA 200; EWL 3

Janowitz, Tama 1957- .... **CLC 43, 145**
See also CA 106; CANR 52, 89, 129; CN
5, 6, 7; CPW; DAM POP; DLB 292;
MTFW 2005

Jansson, Tove (Marika) 1914-2001 ... **SSC 96**
See also CA 17-20R; 196; CANR 38, 118;
CLR 2, 125; CWW 2; DLB 257; EWL 3;
MAICYA 1, 2; RGSF 2; SATA 3, 41

Japrisot, Sebastien 1931- .... **CLC 90**
See Rossi, Jean-Baptiste
See also CMW 4; NFS 18

Jarrell, Randall 1914-1965 .... **CLC 1, 2, 6, 9,
13, 49; PC 41; TCLC 177**
See also AMW; BYA 5; CA 5-8R; 25-28R;
CABS 2; CANR 6, 34; CDALB 1941-
1968; CLR 6, 111; CWRI 5; DAM POET;
DLB 48, 52; EWL 3; EXPP; MAICYA 1,
2; MAL 5; MTCW 1, 2; PAB; PFS 2;
RGAL 4; SATA 7

Jarry, Alfred 1873-1907 .... **SSC 20; TCLC 2,
14, 147**
See also CA 104; 153; DA3; DAM DRAM;
DFS 8; DLB 192, 258; EW 9; EWL 3;
GFL 1789 to the Present; RGWL 2, 3;
TWA

Jarvis, E.K.
See Ellison, Harlan; Silverberg, Robert

Jawien, Andrzej
See John Paul II, Pope

Jaynes, Roderick
See Coen, Ethan

Jeake, Samuel, Jr.
See Aiken, Conrad (Potter)

Jean Paul 1763-1825 .... **NCLC 7**

Jefferies, (John) Richard
1848-1887 .... **NCLC 47**
See also DLB 98, 141; RGEL 2; SATA 16;
SFW 4

Jeffers, John Robinson
See Jeffers, Robinson

Jeffers, Robinson 1887-1962 .... **CLC 2, 3, 11,
15, 54; PC 17; WLC 3**
See also AMWS 2; CA 85-88; CANR 35;
CDALB 1917-1929; DA; DAC; DAM
MST, POET; DLB 45, 212, 342; EWL 3;
MAL 5; MTCW 1, 2; MTFW 2005; PAB;
PFS 3, 4; RGAL 4

Jefferson, Janet
See Mencken, H(enry) L(ouis)

Jefferson, Thomas 1743-1826 . **NCLC 11, 103**
See also AAYA 54; ANW; CDALB 1640-
1865; DA3; DLB 31, 183; LAIT 1; RGAL
4

Jeffrey, Francis 1773-1850 .... **NCLC 33**
See Francis, Lord Jeffrey

Jelakowitch, Ivan
See Heijermans, Herman

Jelinek, Elfriede 1946- .... **CLC 169**
See also AAYA 68; CA 154; CANR 169;
DLB 85, 330; FW

Jellicoe, (Patricia) Ann 1927- .... **CLC 27**
See also CA 85-88; CBD; CD 5, 6; CWD;
CWRI 5; DLB 13, 233; FW

Jelloun, Tahar ben
See Ben Jelloun, Tahar

Jemyma
See Holley, Marietta

Jen, Gish .... **AAL; CLC 70, 198, 260**
See Jen, Lillian
See also AMWC 2; CN 7; DLB 312

Jen, Lillian 1955-
See Jen, Gish
See also CA 135; CANR 89, 130

Jenkins, (John) Robin 1912- .... **CLC 52**
See also CA 1-4R; CANR 1, 135; CN 1, 2,
3, 4, 5, 6, 7; DLB 14, 271

Jennings, Elizabeth (Joan)
1926-2001 .... **CLC 5, 14, 131**
See also BRWS 5; CA 61-64; 200; CAAS
5; CANR 8, 39, 66, 127; CP 1, 2, 3, 4, 5,
6, 7; CWP; DLB 27; EWL 3; MTCW 1;
SATA 66

Jennings, Waylon 1937-2002 .... **CLC 21**

Jensen, Johannes V(ilhelm)
1873-1950 .... **TCLC 41**
See also CA 170; DLB 214, 330; EWL 3;
RGWL 3

Jensen, Laura (Linnea) 1948- .... **CLC 37**
See also CA 103

Jerome, Saint 345-420 .... **CMLC 30**
See also RGWL 3

Jerome, Jerome K(lapka)
1859-1927 .... **TCLC 23**
See also CA 119; 177; DLB 10, 34, 135;
RGEL 2

Jerrold, Douglas William
1803-1857 .... **NCLC 2**
See also DLB 158, 159, 344; RGEL 2

Jewett, (Theodora) Sarah Orne
1849-1909 . **SSC 6, 44, 110; TCLC 1, 22**
See also AAYA 76; AMW; AMWC 2;
AMWR 2; CA 108; 127; CANR 71; DLB
12, 74, 221; EXPS; FL 1:3; FW; MAL 5;
MBL; NFS 15; RGAL 4; RGSF 2; SATA
15; SSFS 4

Jewsbury, Geraldine (Endsor)
1812-1880 .... **NCLC 22**
See also DLB 21

Jhabvala, Ruth Prawer 1927- . **CLC 4, 8, 29,
94, 138; SSC 91**
See also BRWS 5; CA 1-4R; CANR 2, 29,
51, 74, 91, 128; CN 1, 2, 3, 4, 5, 6, 7;
DAB; DAM NOV; DLB 139, 194, 323,
326; EWL 3; IDFW 3, 4; INT CANR-29;
MTCW 1, 2; MTFW 2005; RGSF 2;
RGWL 2; RHW; TEA

Jibran, Kahlil
See Gibran, Kahlil

Jibran, Khalil
See Gibran, Kahlil

Jiles, Paulette 1943- .... **CLC 13, 58**
See also CA 101; CANR 70, 124, 170; CP
5; CWP

Jimenez (Mantecon), Juan Ramon
1881-1958 .... **HLC 1; PC 7; TCLC 4,
183**
See also CA 104; 131; CANR 74; DAM
MULT, POET; DLB 134, 330; EW 9;
EWL 3; HW 1; MTCW 1, 2; MTFW
2005; RGWL 2, 3

Jimenez, Ramon
See Jimenez (Mantecon), Juan Ramon

Jimenez Mantecon, Juan
See Jimenez (Mantecon), Juan Ramon

Jin, Ba 1904-2005
See Pa Chin
See also CA 244; CWW 2; DLB 328

Jin, Xuefei
See Ha Jin

Jodelle, Etienne 1532-1573 .... **LC 119**
See also DLB 327; GFL Beginnings to 1789

Joel, Billy .... **CLC 26**
See Joel, William Martin

Joel, William Martin 1949-
See Joel, Billy
See also CA 108

John, St.
See John of Damascus, St.

John of Damascus, St. c.
675-749 .... **CMLC 27, 95**

John of Salisbury c. 1115-1180 ..... **CMLC 63**

John of the Cross, St. 1542-1591 .... **LC 18,
146**
See also RGWL 2, 3

John Paul II, Pope 1920-2005 .... **CLC 128**
See also CA 106; 133; 238

Johnson, B(ryan) S(tanley William)
1933-1973 .... **CLC 6, 9**
See also CA 9-12R; 53-56; CANR 9; CN 1;
CP 1, 2; DLB 14, 40; EWL 3; RGEL 2

Johnson, Benjamin F., of Boone
See Riley, James Whitcomb

Johnson, Charles (Richard) 1948- . **BLC 1:2,
2:2; CLC 7, 51, 65, 163**
See also AFAW 2; AMWS 6; BW 2, 3; CA
116; CAAS 18; CANR 42, 66, 82, 129;
CN 5, 6, 7; DAM MULT; DLB 33, 278;
MAL 5; MTCW 2; MTFW 2005; RGAL
4; SSFS 16

Johnson, Charles S(purgeon)
1893-1956 .... **HR 1:3**
See also BW 1, 3; CA 125; CANR 82; DLB
51, 91

Johnson, Denis 1949- . **CLC 52, 160; SSC 56**
See also CA 117; 121; CANR 71, 99, 178;
CN 4, 5, 6, 7; DLB 120

Johnson, Diane 1934- ...... **CLC 5, 13, 48, 244**
See also BPFB 2; CA 41-44R; CANR 17,
40, 62, 95, 155; CN 4, 5, 6, 7; DLBY
1980; INT CANR-17; MTCW 1

Johnson, E(mily) Pauline 1861-1913 . **NNAL**
See also CA 150; CCA 1; DAC; DAM
MULT; DLB 92, 175; TCWW 2

Johnson, Eyvind (Olof Verner)
1900-1976 .... **CLC 14**
See also CA 73-76; 69-72; CANR 34, 101;
DLB 259, 330; EW 12; EWL 3

Johnson, Fenton 1888-1958 .... **BLC 1:2**
See also BW 1; CA 118; 124; DAM MULT;
DLB 45, 50

Johnson, Georgia Douglas (Camp)
1880-1966 .... **HR 1:3**
See also BW 1; CA 125; DLB 51, 249; WP

Johnson, Helene 1907-1995 .... **HR 1:3**
See also CA 181; DLB 51; WP

Johnson, J. R.
See James, C(yril) L(ionel) R(obert)

Johnson, James Weldon
1871-1938 .... **BLC 1:2; HR 1:3; PC 24;
TCLC 3, 19, 175**
See also AAYA 73; AFAW 1, 2; BW 1, 3;
CA 104; 125; CANR 82; CDALB 1917-
1929; CLR 32; DA3; DAM MULT, POET;
DLB 51; EWL 3; EXPP; LMFS 2; MAL
5; MTCW 1, 2; MTFW 2005; NFS 22;
PFS 1; RGAL 4; SATA 31; TUS

Johnson, Joyce 1935- .... **CLC 58**
See also BG 1:3; CA 125; 129; CANR 102

Johnson, Judith (Emlyn) 1936- .... **CLC 7, 15**
See Sherwin, Judith Johnson
See also CA 25-28R; 153; CANR 34; CP 6,
7

Johnson, Lionel (Pigot)
1867-1902 .... **TCLC 19**
See also CA 117; 209; DLB 19; RGEL 2

Johnson, Marguerite Annie
See Angelou, Maya

Johnson, Mel
See Malzberg, Barry N(athaniel)

Justice, Donald 1925-2004 ... **CLC 6, 19, 102;**
   PC 64
   See also AMWS 7; CA 5-8R; 230; CANR
   26, 54, 74, 121, 122, 169; CP 1, 2, 3, 4,
   5, 6, 7; CSW; DAM POET; DLBY 1983;
   EWL 3; INT CANR-26; MAL 5; MTCW
   2; PFS 14; TCLE 1:1
Justice, Donald Rodney
   See Justice, Donald
Juvenal c. 60-c. 130 .... **CMLC 8**
   See also AW 2; CDWLB 1; DLB 211;
   RGWL 2, 3; WLIT 8
Juvenis
   See Bourne, Randolph S(illiman)
K., Alice
   See Knapp, Caroline
Kabakov, Sasha .... **CLC 59**
Kabir 1398(?)-1448(?) .... **LC 109; PC 56**
   See also RGWL 2, 3
Kacew, Romain 1914-1980
   See Gary, Romain
   See also CA 108; 102
Kadare, Ismail 1936- .... **CLC 52, 190**
   See also CA 161; CANR 165; EWL 3;
   RGWL 3
Kadohata, Cynthia 1956(?)- ..... **CLC 59, 122**
   See also AAYA 71; CA 140; CANR 124;
   CLR 121; SATA 155, 180
Kafka, Franz 1883-1924 ... **SSC 5, 29, 35, 60;**
   TCLC 2, 6, 13, 29, 47, 53, 112, 179;
   WLC 3
   See also AAYA 31; BPFB 2; CA 105; 126;
   CDWLB 2; DA; DA3; DAB; DAC; DAM
   MST, NOV; DLB 81; EW 9; EWL 3;
   EXPS; LATS 1:1; LMFS 2; MTCW 1, 2;
   MTFW 2005; NFS 7; RGSF 2; RGWL 2,
   3; SFW 4; SSFS 3, 7, 12; TWA
Kafu
   See Nagai, Sokichi
   See also MJW
Kahanovitch, Pinchas
   See Der Nister
Kahanovitsch, Pinkhes
   See Der Nister
Kahanovitsh, Pinkhes
   See Der Nister
Kahn, Roger 1927- .... **CLC 30**
   See also CA 25-28R; CANR 44, 69, 152;
   DLB 171; SATA 37
Kain, Saul
   See Sassoon, Siegfried (Lorraine)
Kaiser, Georg 1878-1945 .... **TCLC 9**
   See also CA 106; 190; CDWLB 2; DLB
   124; EWL 3; LMFS 2; RGWL 2, 3
Kaledin, Sergei .... **CLC 59**
Kaletski, Alexander 1946- .... **CLC 39**
   See also CA 118; 143
Kalidasa fl. c. 400-455 .... **CMLC 9; PC 22**
   See also RGWL 2, 3
Kallman, Chester (Simon)
   1921-1975 .... **CLC 2**
   See also CA 45-48; 53-56; CANR 3; CP 1,
   2
Kaminsky, Melvin .... **CLC 12, 217**
   See Brooks, Mel
   See also AAYA 13, 48; DLB 26
Kaminsky, Stuart M. 1934- .... **CLC 59**
   See also CA 73-76; CANR 29, 53, 89, 161;
   CMW 4
Kaminsky, Stuart Melvin
   See Kaminsky, Stuart M.
Kamo no Chomei 1153(?)-1216 .... **CMLC 66**
   See also DLB 203
Kamo no Nagaakira
   See Kamo no Chomei
Kandinsky, Wassily 1866-1944 .... **TCLC 92**
   See also AAYA 64; CA 118; 155
Kane, Francis
   See Robbins, Harold

Kane, Henry 1918-
   See Queen, Ellery
   See also CA 156; CMW 4
Kane, Paul
   See Simon, Paul
Kane, Sarah 1971-1999 .... **DC 31**
   See also BRWS 8; CA 190; CD 5, 6; DLB
   310
Kanin, Garson 1912-1999 .... **CLC 22**
   See also AITN 1; CA 5-8R; 177; CAD;
   CANR 7, 78; DLB 7; IDFW 3, 4
Kaniuk, Yoram 1930- .... **CLC 19**
   See also CA 134; DLB 299; RGHL
Kant, Immanuel 1724-1804 ..... **NCLC 27, 67**
   See also DLB 94
Kantor, MacKinlay 1904-1977 .... **CLC 7**
   See also CA 61-64; 73-76; CANR 60, 63;
   CN 1, 2; DLB 9, 102; MAL 5; MTCW 2;
   RHW; TCWW 1, 2
Kanze Motokiyo
   See Zeami
Kaplan, David Michael 1946- .... **CLC 50**
   See also CA 187
Kaplan, James 1951- .... **CLC 59**
   See also CA 135; CANR 121
Karadzic, Vuk Stefanovic
   1787-1864 .... **NCLC 115**
   See also CDWLB 4; DLB 147
Karageorge, Michael
   See Anderson, Poul
Karamzin, Nikolai Mikhailovich
   1766-1826 .... **NCLC 3, 173**
   See also DLB 150; RGSF 2
Karapanou, Margarita 1946- .... **CLC 13**
   See also CA 101
Karinthy, Frigyes 1887-1938 .... **TCLC 47**
   See also CA 170; DLB 215; EWL 3
Karl, Frederick R(obert)
   1927-2004 .... **CLC 34**
   See also CA 5-8R; 226; CANR 3, 44, 143
Karr, Mary 1955- .... **CLC 188**
   See also AMWS 11; CA 151; CANR 100;
   MTFW 2005; NCFS 5
Kastel, Warren
   See Silverberg, Robert
Kataev, Evgeny Petrovich 1903-1942
   See Petrov, Evgeny
   See also CA 120
Kataphusin
   See Ruskin, John
Katz, Steve 1935- .... **CLC 47**
   See also CA 25-28R; CAAS 14, 64; CANR
   12; CN 4, 5, 6, 7; DLBY 1983
Kauffman, Janet 1945- .... **CLC 42**
   See also CA 117; CANR 43, 84; DLB 218;
   DLBY 1986
Kaufman, Bob (Garnell)
   1925-1986 .... **CLC 49; PC 74**
   See also BG 1:3; BW 1; CA 41-44R; 118;
   CANR 22; CP 1; DLB 16, 41
Kaufman, George S. 1889-1961 ...... **CLC 38;**
   DC 17
   See also CA 108; 93-96; DAM DRAM;
   DFS 1, 10; DLB 7; INT CA-108; MTCW
   2; MTFW 2005; RGAL 4; TUS
Kaufman, Moises 1964- .... **DC 26**
   See also CA 211; DFS 22; MTFW 2005
Kaufman, Sue .... **CLC 3, 8**
   See Barondess, Sue K(aufman)
Kavafis, Konstantinos Petrou 1863-1933
   See Cavafy, C(onstantine) P(eter)
   See also CA 104
Kavan, Anna 1901-1968 .... **CLC 5, 13, 82**
   See also BRWS 7; CA 5-8R; CANR 6, 57;
   DLB 255; MTCW 1; RGEL 2; SFW 4
Kavanagh, Dan
   See Barnes, Julian

Kavanagh, Julie 1952- .... **CLC 119**
   See also CA 163
Kavanagh, Patrick (Joseph)
   1904-1967 .... **CLC 22; PC 33**
   See also BRWS 7; CA 123; 25-28R; DLB
   15, 20; EWL 3; MTCW 1; RGEL 2
Kawabata, Yasunari 1899-1972 ..... **CLC 2, 5,**
   9, 18, 107; SSC 17
   See Kawabata Yasunari
   See also CA 93-96; 33-36R; CANR 88;
   DAM MULT; DLB 330; MJW; MTCW 2;
   MTFW 2005; RGSF 2; RGWL 2, 3
Kawabata Yasunari
   See Kawabata, Yasunari
   See also DLB 180; EWL 3
Kaye, Mary Margaret
   See Kaye, M.M.
Kaye, M.M. 1908-2004 .... **CLC 28**
   See also CA 89-92; 223; CANR 24, 60, 102,
   142; MTCW 1, 2; MTFW 2005; RHW;
   SATA 62; SATA-Obit 152
Kaye, Mollie
   See Kaye, M.M.
Kaye-Smith, Sheila 1887-1956 .... **TCLC 20**
   See also CA 118; 203; DLB 36
Kaymor, Patrice Maguilene
   See Senghor, Leopold Sedar
Kazakov, Iurii Pavlovich
   See Kazakov, Yuri Pavlovich
   See also DLB 302
Kazakov, Yuri Pavlovich 1927-1982 . **SSC 43**
   See Kazakov, Iurii Pavlovich; Kazakov,
   Yury
   See also CA 5-8R; CANR 36; MTCW 1;
   RGSF 2
Kazakov, Yury
   See Kazakov, Yuri Pavlovich
   See also EWL 3
Kazan, Elia 1909-2003 .... **CLC 6, 16, 63**
   See also CA 21-24R; 220; CANR 32, 78
Kazantzakis, Nikos 1883(?)-1957 .... **TCLC 2,**
   5, 33, 181
   See also BPFB 2; CA 105; 132; DA3; EW
   9; EWL 3; MTCW 1, 2; MTFW 2005;
   RGWL 2, 3
Kazin, Alfred 1915-1998 ..... **CLC 34, 38, 119**
   See also AMWS 8; CA 1-4R; CAAS 7;
   CANR 1, 45, 79; DLB 67; EWL 3
Keane, Mary Nesta (Skrine) 1904-1996
   See Keane, Molly
   See also CA 108; 114; 151; RHW
Keane, Molly .... **CLC 31**
   See Keane, Mary Nesta (Skrine)
   See also CN 5, 6; INT CA-114; TCLE 1:1
Keates, Jonathan 1946(?)- .... **CLC 34**
   See also CA 163; CANR 126
Keaton, Buster 1895-1966 .... **CLC 20**
   See also CA 194
Keats, John 1795-1821 ...... **NCLC 8, 73, 121;**
   PC 1; WLC 3
   See also AAYA 58; BRW 4; BRWR 1; CD-
   BLB 1789-1832; DA; DA3; DAB; DAC;
   DAM MST, POET; DLB 96, 110; EXPP;
   LMFS 1; PAB; PFS 1, 2, 3, 9, 17; RGEL
   2; TEA; WLIT 3; WP
Keble, John 1792-1866 .... **NCLC 87**
   See also DLB 32, 55; RGEL 2
Keene, Donald 1922- .... **CLC 34**
   See also CA 1-4R; CANR 5, 119
Keillor, Garrison 1942- ..... **CLC 40, 115, 222**
   See also AAYA 2, 62; AMWS 16; BEST
   89:3; BPFB 2; CA 111; 117; CANR 36,
   59, 124, 180; CPW; DA3; DAM POP;
   DLBY 1987; EWL 3; MTCW 1, 2; MTFW
   2005; SATA 58; TUS
Keith, Carlos
   See Lewton, Val
Keith, Michael
   See Hubbard, L. Ron

Koch, Christopher
  See Koch, C(hristopher) J(ohn)
Koch, Kenneth 1925-2002 .... CLC 5, 8, 44;
  PC 80
  See also AMWS 15; CA 1-4R; 207; CAD;
    CANR 6, 36, 57, 97, 131; CD 5, 6; CP 1,
    2, 3, 4, 5, 6, 7; DAM POET; DLB 5; INT
    CANR-36; MAL 5; MTCW 2; MTFW
    2005; PFS 20; SATA 65; WP
Kochanowski, Jan 1530-1584 .... LC 10
  See also RGWL 2, 3
Kock, Charles Paul de 1794-1871 . NCLC 16
Koda Rohan
  See Koda Shigeyuki
Koda Rohan
  See Koda Shigeyuki
Koda Shigeyuki 1867-1947 .... TCLC 22
  See also CA 121; 183; DLB 180
Koestler, Arthur 1905-1983 ... CLC 1, 3, 6, 8,
  15, 33
  See also BRWS 1; CA 1-4R; 109; CANR 1,
    33; CDBLB 1945-1960; CN 1, 2, 3;
    DLBY 1983; EWL 3; MTCW 1, 2; MTFW
    2005; NFS 19; RGEL 2
Kogawa, Joy Nozomi 1935- ..... CLC 78, 129,
  262
  See also AAYA 47; CA 101; CANR 19, 62,
    126; CN 6, 7; CP 1; CWP; DAC; DAM
    MST, MULT; DLB 334; FW; MTCW 2;
    MTFW 2005; NFS 3; SATA 99
Kohout, Pavel 1928- .... CLC 13
  See also CA 45-48; CANR 3
Koizumi, Yakumo
  See Hearn, (Patricio) Lafcadio (Tessima
    Carlos)
Kolmar, Gertrud 1894-1943 .... TCLC 40
  See also CA 167; EWL 3; RGHL
Komunyakaa, Yusef 1947- . BLC 2:2; BLCS;
  CLC 86, 94, 207; PC 51
  See also AFAW 2; AMWS 13; CA 147;
    CANR 83, 164; CP 6, 7; CSW; DLB 120;
    EWL 3; PFS 5, 20; RGAL 4
Konigsberg, Alan Stewart
  See Allen, Woody
Konrad, George
  See Konrad, Gyorgy
Konrad, George
  See Konrad, Gyorgy
Konrad, Gyorgy 1933- .... CLC 4, 10, 73
  See also CA 85-88; CANR 97, 171; CD-
    WLB 4; CWW 2; DLB 232; EWL 3
Konwicki, Tadeusz 1926- .... CLC 8, 28, 54,
  117
  See also CA 101; CAAS 9; CANR 39, 59;
    CWW 2; DLB 232; EWL 3; IDFW 3;
    MTCW 1
Koontz, Dean
  See Koontz, Dean R.
Koontz, Dean R. 1945- .... CLC 78, 206
  See also AAYA 9, 31; BEST 89:3, 90:2; CA
    108; CANR 19, 36, 52, 95, 138, 176;
    CMW 4; CPW; DA3; DAM NOV, POP;
    DLB 292; HGG; MTCW 1; MTFW 2005;
    SATA 92, 165; SFW 4; SUFW 2; YAW
Koontz, Dean Ray
  See Koontz, Dean R.
Kopernik, Mikolaj
  See Copernicus, Nicolaus
Kopit, Arthur (Lee) 1937- ...... CLC 1, 18, 33
  See also AITN 1; CA 81-84; CABS 3;
    CAD; CD 5, 6; DAM DRAM; DFS 7, 14,
    24; DLB 7; MAL 5; MTCW 1; RGAL 4
Kopitar, Jernej (Bartholomaus)
  1780-1844 .... NCLC 117
Kops, Bernard 1926- .... CLC 4
  See also CA 5-8R; CANR 84, 159; CBD;
    CN 1, 2, 3, 4, 5, 6, 7; CP 1, 2, 3, 4, 5, 6,
    7; DLB 13; RGHL

Kornbluth, C(yril) M. 1923-1958 .... TCLC 8
  See also CA 105; 160; DLB 8; SCFW 1, 2;
    SFW 4
Korolenko, V.G.
  See Korolenko, Vladimir G.
Korolenko, Vladimir
  See Korolenko, Vladimir G.
Korolenko, Vladimir G.
  1853-1921 .... TCLC 22
  See also CA 121; DLB 277
Korolenko, Vladimir Galaktionovich
  See Korolenko, Vladimir G.
Korzybski, Alfred (Habdank Skarbek)
  1879-1950 .... TCLC 61
  See also CA 123; 160
Kosinski, Jerzy 1933-1991 ..... CLC 1, 2, 3, 6,
  10, 15, 53, 70
  See also AMWS 7; BPFB 2; CA 17-20R;
    134; CANR 9, 46; CN 1, 2, 3, 4; DA3;
    DAM NOV; DLB 2, 299; DLBY 1982;
    EWL 3; HGG; MAL 5; MTCW 1, 2;
    MTFW 2005; NFS 12; RGAL 4; RGHL;
    TUS
Kostelanetz, Richard (Cory) 1940- .. CLC 28
  See also CA 13-16R; CAAS 8; CANR 38,
    77; CN 4, 5, 6; CP 2, 3, 4, 5, 6, 7
Kostrowitzki, Wilhelm Apollinaris de
  1880-1918
  See Apollinaire, Guillaume
  See also CA 104
Kotlowitz, Robert 1924- .... CLC 4
  See also CA 33-36R; CANR 36
Kotzebue, August (Friedrich Ferdinand) von
  1761-1819 .... NCLC 25
  See also DLB 94
Kotzwinkle, William 1938- ..... CLC 5, 14, 35
  See also BPFB 2; CA 45-48; CANR 3, 44,
    84, 129; CLR 6; CN 7; DLB 173; FANT;
    MAICYA 1, 2; SATA 24, 70, 146; SFW
    4; SUFW 2; YAW
Kowna, Stancy
  See Szymborska, Wislawa
Kozol, Jonathan 1936- .... CLC 17
  See also AAYA 46; CA 61-64; CANR 16,
    45, 96, 178; MTFW 2005
Kozoll, Michael 1940(?)- .... CLC 35
Krakauer, Jon 1954- .... CLC 248
  See also AAYA 24; BYA 9; CA 153; CANR
    131; MTFW 2005; SATA 108
Kramer, Kathryn 19(?)- .... CLC 34
Kramer, Larry 1935- .... CLC 42; DC 8
  See also CA 124; 126; CANR 60, 132;
    DAM POP; DLB 249; GLL 1
Krasicki, Ignacy 1735-1801 .... NCLC 8
Krasinski, Zygmunt 1812-1859 .... NCLC 4
  See also RGWL 2, 3
Kraus, Karl 1874-1936 .... TCLC 5
  See also CA 104; 216; DLB 118; EWL 3
Kreve (Mickevicius), Vincas
  1882-1954 .... TCLC 27
  See also CA 170; DLB 220; EWL 3
Kristeva, Julia 1941- .... CLC 77, 140
  See also CA 154; CANR 99, 173; DLB 242;
    EWL 3; FW; LMFS 2
Kristofferson, Kris 1936- .... CLC 26
  See also CA 104
Krizanc, John 1956- .... CLC 57
  See also CA 187
Krleza, Miroslav 1893-1981 .... CLC 8, 114
  See also CA 97-100; 105; CANR 50; CD-
    WLB 4; DLB 147; EW 11; RGWL 2, 3
Kroetsch, Robert (Paul) 1927- .... CLC 5, 23,
  57, 132
  See also CA 17-20R; CANR 8, 38; CCA 1;
    CN 2, 3, 4, 5, 6, 7; CP 6, 7; DAC; DAM
    POET; DLB 53; MTCW 1
Kroetz, Franz
  See Kroetz, Franz Xaver

Kroetz, Franz Xaver 1946- .... CLC 41
  See also CA 130; CANR 142; CWW 2;
    EWL 3
Kroker, Arthur (W.) 1945- .... CLC 77
  See also CA 161
Kroniuk, Lisa
  See Berton, Pierre (Francis de Marigny)
Kropotkin, Peter (Alekseevich)
  1842-1921 .... TCLC 36
  See Kropotkin, Petr Alekseevich
  See also CA 119; 219
Kropotkin, Petr Alekseevich
  See Kropotkin, Peter (Alekseevich)
  See also DLB 277
Krotkov, Yuri 1917-1981 .... CLC 19
  See also CA 102
Krumb
  See Crumb, R.
Krumgold, Joseph (Quincy)
  1908-1980 .... CLC 12
  See also BYA 1, 2; CA 9-12R; 101; CANR
    7; MAICYA 1, 2; SATA 1, 48; SATA-Obit
    23; YAW
Krumwitz
  See Crumb, R.
Krutch, Joseph Wood 1893-1970 ..... CLC 24
  See also ANW; CA 1-4R; 25-28R; CANR
    4; DLB 63, 206, 275
Krutzch, Gus
  See Eliot, T(homas) S(tearns)
Krylov, Ivan Andreevich
  1768(?)-1844 .... NCLC 1
  See also DLB 150
Kubin, Alfred (Leopold Isidor)
  1877-1959 .... TCLC 23
  See also CA 112; 149; CANR 104; DLB 81
Kubrick, Stanley 1928-1999 .... CLC 16;
  TCLC 112
  See also AAYA 30; CA 81-84; 177; CANR
    33; DLB 26
Kumin, Maxine 1925- .... CLC 5, 13, 28, 164;
  PC 15
  See also AITN 2; AMWS 4; ANW; CA
    1-4R; 271; CAAE 271; CAAS 8; CANR
    1, 21, 69, 115, 140; CP 2, 3, 4, 5, 6, 7;
    CWP; DA3; DAM POET; DLB 5; EWL
    3; EXPP; MTCW 1, 2; MTFW 2005;
    PAB; PFS 18; SATA 12
Kundera, Milan 1929- . CLC 4, 9, 19, 32, 68,
  115, 135, 234; SSC 24
  See also AAYA 2, 62; BPFB 2; CA 85-88;
    CANR 19, 52, 74, 144; CDWLB 4; CWW
    2; DA3; DAM NOV; DLB 232; EW 13;
    EWL 3; MTCW 1, 2; MTFW 2005; NFS
    18, 27; RGSF 2; RGWL 3; SSFS 10
Kunene, Mazisi 1930-2006 .... CLC 85
  See also BW 1, 3; CA 125; 252; CANR 81;
    CP 1, 6, 7; DLB 117
Kunene, Mazisi Raymond
  See Kunene, Mazisi
Kunene, Mazisi Raymond Fakazi Mngoni
  See Kunene, Mazisi
Kung, Hans .... CLC 130
  See Kung, Hans
Kung, Hans 1928-
  See Kung, Hans
  See also CA 53-56; CANR 66, 134; MTCW
    1, 2; MTFW 2005
Kunikida Doppo 1869(?)-1908
  See Doppo, Kunikida
  See also DLB 180; EWL 3
Kunitz, Stanley 1905-2006 ..... CLC 6, 11, 14,
  148; PC 19
  See also AMWS 3; CA 41-44R; 250; CANR
    26, 57, 98; CP 1, 2, 3, 4, 5, 6, 7; DA3;
    DLB 48; INT CANR-26; MAL 5; MTCW
    1, 2; MTFW 2005; PFS 11; RGAL 4
Kunitz, Stanley Jasspon
  See Kunitz, Stanley

Leopardi, (Conte) Giacomo
1798-1837 .... **NCLC 22, 129; PC 37**
See also EW 5; RGWL 2, 3; WLIT 7; WP
Le Reveler
See Artaud, Antonin (Marie Joseph)
Lerman, Eleanor 1952- .... **CLC 9**
See also CA 85-88; CANR 69, 124
Lerman, Rhoda 1936- .... **CLC 56**
See also CA 49-52; CANR 70
Lermontov, Mikhail Iur'evich
See Lermontov, Mikhail Yuryevich
See also DLB 205
Lermontov, Mikhail Yuryevich
1814-1841 .... **NCLC 5, 47, 126; PC 18**
See Lermontov, Mikhail Iur'evich
See also EW 6; RGWL 2, 3; TWA
Leroux, Gaston 1868-1927 .... **TCLC 25**
See also CA 108; 136; CANR 69; CMW 4;
MTFW 2005; NFS 20; SATA 65
Lesage, Alain-Rene 1668-1747 .... **LC 2, 28**
See also DLB 313; EW 3; GFL Beginnings
to 1789; RGWL 2, 3
Leskov, N(ikolai) S(emenovich) 1831-1895
See Leskov, Nikolai (Semyonovich)
Leskov, Nikolai (Semyonovich)
1831-1895 ... **NCLC 25, 174; SSC 34, 96**
See Leskov, Nikolai Semenovich
Leskov, Nikolai Semenovich
See Leskov, Nikolai (Semyonovich)
See also DLB 238
Lesser, Milton
See Marlowe, Stephen
Lessing, Doris 1919- .. **CLC 1, 2, 3, 6, 10, 15,**
22, 40, 94, 170, 254; SSC 6, 61; WLCS
See also AAYA 57; AFW; BRWS 1; CA
9-12R; CAAS 14; CANR 33, 54, 76, 122,
179; CBD; CD 5, 6; CDBLB 1960 to
Present; CN 1, 2, 3, 4, 5, 6, 7; CWD; DA;
DA3; DAB; DAC; DAM MST, NOV;
DFS 20; DLB 15, 139; DLBY 1985; EWL
3; EXPS; FL 1:6; FW; LAIT 4; MTCW 1,
2; MTFW 2005; NFS 27; RGEL 2; RGSF
2; SFW 4; SSFS 1, 12, 20, 26; TEA;
WLIT 2, 4
Lessing, Doris May
See Lessing, Doris
Lessing, Gotthold Ephraim
1729-1781 .... **DC 26; LC 8, 124**
See also CDWLB 2; DLB 97; EW 4; RGWL
2, 3
Lester, Julius 1939- .... **BLC 2:2**
See also AAYA 12, 51; BW 2; BYA 3, 9,
11, 12; CA 17-20R; CANR 8, 23, 43, 129,
174; CLR 2, 41; JRDA; MAICYA 1, 2;
MAICYAS 1; MTFW 2005; SATA 12, 74,
112, 157; YAW
Lester, Richard 1932- .... **CLC 20**
Levenson, Jay .... **CLC 70**
Lever, Charles (James)
1806-1872 .... **NCLC 23**
See also DLB 21; RGEL 2
Leverson, Ada Esther
1862(?)-1933(?) .... **TCLC 18**
See Elaine
See also CA 117; 202; DLB 153; RGEL 2
Levertov, Denise 1923-1997 .. **CLC 1, 2, 3, 5,**
8, 15, 28, 66; PC 11
See also AMWS 3; CA 1-4R, 178; 163;
CAAE 178; CAAS 19; CANR 3, 29, 50,
108; CDALBS; CP 1, 2, 3, 4, 5, 6; CWP;
DAM POET; DLB 5, 165, 342; EWL 3;
EXPP; FW; INT CANR-29; MAL 5;
MTCW 1, 2; PAB; PFS 7, 17; RGAL 4;
RGHL; TUS; WP
Levi, Carlo 1902-1975 .... **TCLC 125**
See also CA 65-68; 53-56; CANR 10; EWL
3; RGWL 2, 3
Levi, Jonathan .... **CLC 76**
See also CA 197

Levi, Peter (Chad Tigar)
1931-2000 .... **CLC 41**
See also CA 5-8R; 187; CANR 34, 80; CP
1, 2, 3, 4, 5, 6, 7; DLB 40
Levi, Primo 1919-1987 ...... **CLC 37, 50; SSC**
12; TCLC 109
See also CA 13-16R; 122; CANR 12, 33,
61, 70, 132, 171; DLB 177, 299; EWL 3;
MTCW 1, 2; MTFW 2005; RGHL;
RGWL 2, 3; WLIT 7
Levin, Ira 1929-2007 .... **CLC 3, 6**
See also CA 21-24R; 266; CANR 17, 44,
74, 139; CMW 4; CN 1, 2, 3, 4, 5, 6, 7;
CPW; DA3; DAM POP; HGG; MTCW 1,
2; MTFW 2005; SATA 66; SATA-Obit
187; SFW 4
Levin, Ira Marvin
See Levin, Ira
Levin, Ira Marvin
See Levin, Ira
Levin, Meyer 1905-1981 .... **CLC 7**
See also AITN 1; CA 9-12R; 104; CANR
15; CN 1, 2, 3; DAM POP; DLB 9, 28;
DLBY 1981; MAL 5; RGHL; SATA 21;
SATA-Obit 27
Levine, Albert Norman
See Levine, Norman
See also CN 7
Levine, Norman 1923-2005 .... **CLC 54**
See Levine, Albert Norman
See also CA 73-76; 240; CAAS 23; CANR
14, 70; CN 1, 2, 3, 4, 5, 6; CP 1; DLB 88
Levine, Norman Albert
See Levine, Norman
Levine, Philip 1928- .. **CLC 2, 4, 5, 9, 14, 33,**
118; PC 22
See also AMWS 5; CA 9-12R; CANR 9,
37, 52, 116, 156; CP 1, 2, 3, 4, 5, 6, 7;
DAM POET; DLB 5; EWL 3; MAL 5;
PFS 8
Levinson, Deirdre 1931- .... **CLC 49**
See also CA 73-76; CANR 70
Levi-Strauss, Claude 1908- .... **CLC 38**
See also CA 1-4R; CANR 6, 32, 57; DLB
242; EWL 3; GFL 1789 to the Present;
MTCW 1, 2; TWA
Levitin, Sonia (Wolff) 1934- .... **CLC 17**
See also AAYA 13, 48; CA 29-32R; CANR
14, 32, 79; CLR 53; JRDA; MAICYA 1,
2; SAAS 2; SATA 4, 68, 119, 131; SATA-
Essay 131; YAW
Levon, O. U.
See Kesey, Ken
Levy, Amy 1861-1889 .... **NCLC 59**
See also DLB 156, 240
Lewes, George Henry 1817-1878 ... **NCLC 25**
See also DLB 55, 144
Lewis, Alun 1915-1944 .... **SSC 40; TCLC 3**
See also BRW 7; CA 104; 188; DLB 20,
162; PAB; RGEL 2
Lewis, C. Day
See Day Lewis, C(ecil)
See also CN 1
Lewis, Cecil Day
See Day Lewis, C(ecil)
Lewis, Clive Staples
See Lewis, C.S.
Lewis, C.S. 1898-1963 ... **CLC 1, 3, 6, 14, 27,**
124; WLC 4
See also AAYA 3, 39; BPFB 2; BRWS 3;
BYA 15, 16; CA 81-84; CANR 33, 71,
132; CDBLB 1945-1960; CLR 3, 27, 109;
CWRI 5; DA; DA3; DAB; DAC; DAM
MST, NOV, POP; DLB 15, 100, 160, 255;
EWL 3; FANT; JRDA; LMFS 2; MAI-
CYA 1, 2; MTCW 1, 2; MTFW 2005;
NFS 24; RGEL 2; SATA 13, 100; SCFW
1, 2; SFW 4; SUFW 1; TEA; WCH;
WYA; YAW

Lewis, Janet 1899-1998 .... **CLC 41**
See Winters, Janet Lewis
See also CA 9-12R; 172; CANR 29, 63;
CAP 1; CN 1, 2, 3, 4, 5, 6; DLBY 1987;
RHW; TCWW 2
Lewis, Matthew Gregory
1775-1818 .... **NCLC 11, 62**
See also DLB 39, 158, 178; GL 3; HGG;
LMFS 1; RGEL 2; SUFW
Lewis, (Harry) Sinclair 1885-1951 . **TCLC 4,**
13, 23, 39; WLC 4
See also AMW; AMWC 1; BPFB 2; CA
104; 133; CANR 132; CDALB 1917-
1929; DA; DA3; DAB; DAC; DAM MST,
NOV; DLB 9, 102, 284, 331; DLBD 1;
EWL 3; LAIT 3; MAL 5; MTCW 1, 2;
MTFW 2005; NFS 15, 19, 22; RGAL 4;
TUS
Lewis, (Percy) Wyndham
1884(?)-1957 .. **SSC 34; TCLC 2, 9, 104**
See also AAYA 77; BRW 7; CA 104; 157;
DLB 15; EWL 3; FANT; MTCW 2;
MTFW 2005; RGEL 2
Lewisohn, Ludwig 1883-1955 .... **TCLC 19**
See also CA 107; 203; DLB 4, 9, 28, 102;
MAL 5
Lewton, Val 1904-1951 .... **TCLC 76**
See also CA 199; IDFW 3, 4
Leyner, Mark 1956- .... **CLC 92**
See also CA 110; CANR 28, 53; DA3; DLB
292; MTFW 2005
Leyton, E.K.
See Campbell, Ramsey
Lezama Lima, Jose 1910-1976 .... **CLC 4, 10,**
101; HLCS 2
See also CA 77-80; CANR 71; DAM
MULT; DLB 113, 283; EWL 3; HW 1, 2;
LAW; RGWL 2, 3
L'Heureux, John (Clarke) 1934- ...... **CLC 52**
See also CA 13-16R; CANR 23, 45, 88; CP
1, 2, 3, 4; DLB 244
Li Ch'ing-chao 1081(?)-1141(?) .... **CMLC 71**
Liddell, C. H.
See Kuttner, Henry
Lie, Jonas (Lauritz Idemil)
1833-1908(?) .... **TCLC 5**
See also CA 115
Lieber, Joel 1937-1971 .... **CLC 6**
See also CA 73-76; 29-32R
Lieber, Stanley Martin
See Lee, Stan
Lieberman, Laurence (James)
1935- .... **CLC 4, 36**
See also CA 17-20R; CANR 8, 36, 89; CP
1, 2, 3, 4, 5, 6, 7
Lieh Tzu fl. 7th cent. B.C.-5th cent.
B.C. .... **CMLC 27**
Lieksman, Anders
See Haavikko, Paavo Juhani
Lifton, Robert Jay 1926- .... **CLC 67**
See also CA 17-20R; CANR 27, 78, 161;
INT CANR-27; SATA 66
Lightfoot, Gordon 1938- .... **CLC 26**
See also CA 109; 242
Lightfoot, Gordon Meredith
See Lightfoot, Gordon
Lightman, Alan P. 1948- .... **CLC 81**
See also CA 141; CANR 63, 105, 138, 178;
MTFW 2005
Lightman, Alan Paige
See Lightman, Alan P.
Ligotti, Thomas (Robert) 1953- ...... **CLC 44;**
SSC 16
See also CA 123; CANR 49, 135; HGG;
SUFW 2
Li Ho 791-817 .... **PC 13**
Li Ju-chen c. 1763-c. 1830 .... **NCLC 137**
Liking, Werewere .... **BLC 2:2**
See Werewere Liking; Werewere Liking

Lilar, Francoise
  See Mallet-Joris, Francoise
Liliencron, Detlev
  See Liliencron, Detlev von
Liliencron, Detlev von 1844-1909 .. **TCLC 18**
  See also CA 117
Liliencron, Friedrich Adolf Axel Detlev von
  See Liliencron, Detlev von
Liliencron, Friedrich Detlev von
  See Liliencron, Detlev von
Lille, Alain de
  See Alain de Lille
Lillo, George 1691-1739 .... **LC 131**
  See also DLB 84; RGEL 2
Lilly, William 1602-1681 .... **LC 27**
Lima, Jose Lezama
  See Lezama Lima, Jose
Lima Barreto, Afonso Henrique de
  1881-1922 .... **TCLC 23**
  See Lima Barreto, Afonso Henriques de
  See also CA 117; 181; LAW
Lima Barreto, Afonso Henriques de
  See Lima Barreto, Afonso Henrique de
  See also DLB 307
Limonov, Eduard
  See Limonov, Edward
  See also DLB 317
Limonov, Edward 1944- .... **CLC 67**
  See Limonov, Eduard
  See also CA 137
Lin, Frank
  See Atherton, Gertrude (Franklin Horn)
Lin, Yutang 1895-1976 .... **TCLC 149**
  See also CA 45-48; 65-68; CANR 2; RGAL
  4
Lincoln, Abraham 1809-1865 .... **NCLC 18,
  201**
  See also LAIT 2
Lind, Jakov 1927-2007 ... **CLC 1, 2, 4, 27, 82**
  See also CA 9-12R; 257; CAAS 4; CANR
  7; DLB 299; EWL 3; RGHL
Lindbergh, Anne Morrow
  1906-2001 .... **CLC 82**
  See also BPFB 2; CA 17-20R; 193; CANR
  16, 73; DAM NOV; MTCW 1, 2; MTFW
  2005; SATA 33; SATA-Obit 125; TUS
Lindsay, David 1878(?)-1945 .... **TCLC 15**
  See also CA 113; 187; DLB 255; FANT;
  SFW 4; SUFW 1
Lindsay, (Nicholas) Vachel
  1879-1931 .... **PC 23; TCLC 17; WLC 4**
  See also AMWS 1; CA 114; 135; CANR
  79; CDALB 1865-1917; DA; DA3; DAC;
  DAM MST, POET; DLB 54; EWL 3;
  EXPP; MAL 5; RGAL 4; SATA 40; WP
Linke-Poot
  See Doeblin, Alfred
Linney, Romulus 1930- .... **CLC 51**
  See also CA 1-4R; CAD; CANR 40, 44,
  79; CD 5, 6; CSW; RGAL 4
Linton, Eliza Lynn 1822-1898 .... **NCLC 41**
  See also DLB 18
Li Po 701-763 .... **CMLC 2, 86; PC 29**
  See also PFS 20; WP
Lippard, George 1822-1854 .... **NCLC 198**
  See also DLB 202
Lipsius, Justus 1547-1606 .... **LC 16**
Lipsyte, Robert 1938- .... **CLC 21**
  See also AAYA 7, 45; CA 17-20R; CANR
  8, 57, 146; CLR 23, 76; DA; DAC; DAM
  MST, NOV; JRDA; LAIT 5; MAICYA 1,
  2; SATA 5, 68, 113, 161; WYA; YAW
Lipsyte, Robert Michael
  See Lipsyte, Robert
Lish, Gordon 1934- .... **CLC 45; SSC 18**
  See also CA 113; 117; CANR 79, 151; DLB
  130; INT CA-117

Lish, Gordon Jay
  See Lish, Gordon
Lispector, Clarice 1925(?)-1977 .... **CLC 43;
  HLCS 2; SSC 34, 96**
  See also CA 139; 116; CANR 71; CDWLB
  3; DLB 113, 307; DNFS 1; EWL 3; FW;
  HW 2; LAW; RGSF 2; RGWL 2, 3; WLIT
  1
Liszt, Franz 1811-1886 .... **NCLC 199**
Littell, Robert 1935(?)- .... **CLC 42**
  See also CA 109; 112; CANR 64, 115, 162;
  CMW 4
Little, Malcolm 1925-1965
  See Malcolm X
  See also BW 1, 3; CA 125; 111; CANR 82;
  DA; DA3; DAB; DAC; DAM MST,
  MULT; MTCW 1, 2; MTFW 2005
Littlewit, Humphrey Gent.
  See Lovecraft, H. P.
Litwos
  See Sienkiewicz, Henryk (Adam Alexander
  Pius)
Liu, E. 1857-1909 .... **TCLC 15**
  See also CA 115; 190; DLB 328
Lively, Penelope 1933- .... **CLC 32, 50**
  See also BPFB 2; CA 41-44R; CANR 29,
  67, 79, 131, 172; CLR 7; CN 5, 6, 7;
  CWRI 5; DAM NOV; DLB 14, 161, 207,
  326; FANT; JRDA; MAICYA 1, 2;
  MTCW 1, 2; MTFW 2005; SATA 7, 60,
  101, 164; TEA
Lively, Penelope Margaret
  See Lively, Penelope
Livesay, Dorothy (Kathleen)
  1909-1996 .... **CLC 4, 15, 79**
  See also AITN 2; CA 25-28R; CAAS 8;
  CANR 36, 67; CP 1, 2, 3, 4, 5; DAC;
  DAM MST, POET; DLB 68; FW; MTCW
  1; RGEL 2; TWA
Livius Andronicus c. 284B.C.-c.
  204B.C. .... **CMLC 102**
Livy c. 59B.C.-c. 12 .... **CMLC 11**
  See also AW 2; CDWLB 1; DLB 211;
  RGWL 2, 3; WLIT 8
Lizardi, Jose Joaquin Fernandez de
  1776-1827 .... **NCLC 30**
  See also LAW
Llewellyn, Richard
  See Llewellyn Lloyd, Richard Dafydd Viv-
  ian
  See also DLB 15
Llewellyn Lloyd, Richard Dafydd Vivian
  1906-1983 .... **CLC 7, 80**
  See Llewellyn, Richard
  See also CA 53-56; 111; CANR 7, 71;
  SATA 11; SATA-Obit 37
Llosa, Jorge Mario Pedro Vargas
  See Vargas Llosa, Mario
  See also RGWL 3
Llosa, Mario Vargas
  See Vargas Llosa, Mario
Lloyd, Manda
  See Mander, (Mary) Jane
Lloyd Webber, Andrew 1948-
  See Webber, Andrew Lloyd
  See also AAYA 1, 38; CA 116; 149; DAM
  DRAM; SATA 56
Llull, Ramon c. 1235-c. 1316 .... **CMLC 12**
Lobb, Ebenezer
  See Upward, Allen
Locke, Alain (Le Roy)
  1886-1954 .... **BLCS; HR 1:3; TCLC 43**
  See also AMWS 14; BW 1, 3; CA 106; 124;
  CANR 79; DLB 51; LMFS 2; MAL 5;
  RGAL 4
Locke, John 1632-1704 .... **LC 7, 35, 135**
  See also DLB 31, 101, 213, 252; RGEL 2;
  WLIT 3

Locke-Elliott, Sumner
  See Elliott, Sumner Locke
Lockhart, John Gibson 1794-1854 .. **NCLC 6**
  See also DLB 110, 116, 144
Lockridge, Ross (Franklin), Jr.
  1914-1948 .... **TCLC 111**
  See also CA 108; 145; CANR 79; DLB 143;
  DLBY 1980; MAL 5; RGAL 4; RHW
Lockwood, Robert
  See Johnson, Robert
Lodge, David 1935- .... **CLC 36, 141**
  See also BEST 90:1; BRWS 4; CA 17-20R;
  CANR 19, 53, 92, 139; CN 1, 2, 3, 4, 5,
  6, 7; CPW; DAM POP; DLB 14, 194;
  EWL 3; INT CANR-19; MTCW 1, 2;
  MTFW 2005
Lodge, Thomas 1558-1625 .... **LC 41**
  See also DLB 172; RGEL 2
Loewinsohn, Ron(ald William)
  1937- .... **CLC 52**
  See also CA 25-28R; CANR 71; CP 1, 2, 3,
  4
Logan, Jake
  See Smith, Martin Cruz
Logan, John (Burton) 1923-1987 .... **CLC 5**
  See also CA 77-80; 124; CANR 45; CP 1,
  2, 3, 4; DLB 5
Lo Kuan-chung 1330(?)-1400(?) .... **LC 12**
Lomax, Pearl
  See Cleage, Pearl
Lomax, Pearl Cleage
  See Cleage, Pearl
Lombard, Nap
  See Johnson, Pamela Hansford
Lombard, Peter 1100(?)-1160(?) ... **CMLC 72**
Lombino, Salvatore
  See Hunter, Evan
London, Jack 1876-1916 .. **SSC 4, 49; TCLC
  9, 15, 39; WLC 4**
  See London, John Griffith
  See also AAYA 13; AITN 2; AMW; BPFB
  2; BYA 4, 13; CDALB 1865-1917; CLR
  108; DLB 8, 12, 78, 212; EWL 3; EXPS;
  LAIT 3; MAL 5; NFS 8; RGAL 4; RGSF
  2; SATA 18; SFW 4; SSFS 7; TCWW 1,
  2; TUS; WYA; YAW
London, John Griffith 1876-1916
  See London, Jack
  See also AAYA 75; CA 110; 119; CANR
  73; DA; DA3; DAB; DAC; DAM MST,
  NOV; JRDA; MAICYA 1, 2; MTCW 1,
  2; MTFW 2005; NFS 19
Long, Emmett
  See Leonard, Elmore
Longbaugh, Harry
  See Goldman, William
Longfellow, Henry Wadsworth
  1807-1882 .... **NCLC 2, 45, 101, 103; PC
  30; WLCS**
  See also AMW; AMWR 2; CDALB 1640-
  1865; CLR 99; DA; DA3; DAB; DAC;
  DAM MST, POET; DLB 1, 59, 235;
  EXPP; PAB; PFS 2, 7, 17; RGAL 4;
  SATA 19; TUS; WP
Longinus c. 1st cent. - .... **CMLC 27**
  See also AW 2; DLB 176
Longley, Michael 1939- .... **CLC 29**
  See also BRWS 8; CA 102; CP 1, 2, 3, 4, 5,
  6, 7; DLB 40
Longstreet, Augustus Baldwin
  1790-1870 .... **NCLC 159**
  See also DLB 3, 11, 74, 248; RGAL 4
Longus fl. c. 2nd cent. - .... **CMLC 7**
Longway, A. Hugh
  See Lang, Andrew
Lonnbohm, Armas Eino Leopold 1878-1926
  See Leino, Eino
  See also CA 123

Lonnrot, Elias 1802-1884 .... **NCLC 53**
  See also EFS 1
Lonsdale, Roger .... **CLC 65**
Lopate, Phillip 1943- .... **CLC 29**
  See also CA 97-100; CANR 88, 157; DLBY
    1980; INT CA-97-100
Lopez, Barry (Holstun) 1945- .... **CLC 70**
  See also AAYA 9, 63; ANW; CA 65-68;
    CANR 7, 23, 47, 68, 92; DLB 256, 275,
    335; INT CANR-7, CANR-23; MTCW 1;
    RGAL 4; SATA 67
Lopez de Mendoza, Inigo
  See Santillana, Inigo Lopez de Mendoza,
    Marques de
Lopez Portillo (y Pacheco), Jose
    1920-2004 .... **CLC 46**
  See also CA 129; 224; HW 1
Lopez y Fuentes, Gregorio
    1897(?)-1966 .... **CLC 32**
  See also CA 131; EWL 3; HW 1
Lorca, Federico Garcia .... **TCLC 197**
  See Garcia Lorca, Federico
  See also DFS 4; EW 11; PFS 20; RGWL 2,
    3; WP
Lord, Audre
  See Lorde, Audre
  See also EWL 3
Lord, Bette Bao 1938- .... **AAL; CLC 23**
  See also BEST 90:3; BPFB 2; CA 107;
    CANR 41, 79; INT CA-107; SATA 58
Lord Auch
  See Bataille, Georges
Lord Brooke
  See Greville, Fulke
Lord Byron
  See Byron, George Gordon (Noel)
Lorde, Audre 1934-1992 .... **BLC 1:2, 2:2;**
    CLC 18, 71; PC 12; TCLC 173
  See Domini, Rey; Lord, Audre
  See also AFAW 1, 2; BW 1, 3; CA 25-28R;
    142; CANR 16, 26, 46, 82; CP 2, 3, 4, 5;
    DA3; DAM MULT, POET; DLB 41; FW;
    MAL 5; MTCW 1, 2; MTFW 2005; PFS
    16; RGAL 4
Lorde, Audre Geraldine
  See Lorde, Audre
Lord Houghton
  See Milnes, Richard Monckton
Lord Jeffrey
  See Jeffrey, Francis
Loreaux, Nichol .... **CLC 65**
Lorenzini, Carlo 1826-1890
  See Collodi, Carlo
  See also MAICYA 1, 2; SATA 29, 100
Lorenzo, Heberto Padilla
  See Padilla (Lorenzo), Heberto
Loris
  See Hofmannsthal, Hugo von
Loti, Pierre .... **TCLC 11**
  See Viaud, (Louis Marie) Julien
  See also DLB 123; GFL 1789 to the Present
Lou, Henri
  See Andreas-Salome, Lou
Louie, David Wong 1954- .... **CLC 70**
  See also CA 139; CANR 120
Louis, Adrian C. .... **NNAL**
  See also CA 223
Louis, Father M.
  See Merton, Thomas (James)
Louise, Heidi
  See Erdrich, Louise
Lovecraft, H. P. 1890-1937 .... **SSC 3, 52;**
    TCLC 4, 22
  See also AAYA 14; BPFB 2; CA 104; 133;
    CANR 106; DA3; DAM POP; HGG;
    MTCW 1, 2; MTFW 2005; RGAL 4;
    SCFW 1, 2; SFW 4; SUFW
Lovecraft, Howard Phillips
  See Lovecraft, H. P.

Lovelace, Earl 1935- .... **CLC 51**
  See also BW 2; CA 77-80; CANR 41, 72,
    114; CD 5, 6; CDWLB 3; CN 1, 2, 3, 4,
    5, 6, 7; DLB 125; EWL 3; MTCW 1
Lovelace, Richard 1618-1657 . **LC 24; PC 69**
  See also BRW 2; DLB 131; EXPP; PAB;
    RGEL 2
Low, Penelope Margaret
  See Lively, Penelope
Lowe, Pardee 1904- .... **AAL**
Lowell, Amy 1874-1925 ... **PC 13; TCLC 1, 8**
  See also AAYA 57; AMW; CA 104; 151;
    DAM POET; DLB 54, 140; EWL 3;
    EXPP; LMFS 2; MAL 5; MBL; MTCW
    2; MTFW 2005; RGAL 4; TUS
Lowell, James Russell 1819-1891 ... **NCLC 2,**
    90
  See also AMWS 1; CDALB 1640-1865;
    DLB 1, 11, 64, 79, 189, 235; RGAL 4
Lowell, Robert (Traill Spence, Jr.)
    1917-1977 .... **CLC 1, 2, 3, 4, 5, 8, 9, 11,**
    15, 37, 124; PC 3; WLC 4
  See also AMW; AMWC 2; AMWR 2; CA
    9-12R; 73-76; CABS 2; CAD; CANR 26,
    60; CDALBS; CP 1, 2; DA; DA3; DAB;
    DAC; DAM MST, NOV; DLB 5, 169;
    EWL 3; MAL 5; MTCW 1, 2; MTFW
    2005; PAB; PFS 6, 7; RGAL 4; WP
Lowenthal, Michael 1969- .... **CLC 119**
  See also CA 150; CANR 115, 164
Lowenthal, Michael Francis
  See Lowenthal, Michael
Lowndes, Marie Adelaide (Belloc)
    1868-1947 .... **TCLC 12**
  See also CA 107; CMW 4; DLB 70; RHW
Lowry, (Clarence) Malcolm
    1909-1957 .... **SSC 31; TCLC 6, 40**
  See also BPFB 2; BRWS 3; CA 105; 131;
    CANR 62, 105; CDBLB 1945-1960; DLB
    15; EWL 3; MTCW 1, 2; MTFW 2005;
    RGEL 2
Lowry, Mina Gertrude 1882-1966
  See Loy, Mina
  See also CA 113
Lowry, Sam
  See Soderbergh, Steven
Loxsmith, John
  See Brunner, John (Kilian Houston)
Loy, Mina .... **CLC 28; PC 16**
  See Lowry, Mina Gertrude
  See also DAM POET; DLB 4, 54; PFS 20
Loyson-Bridet
  See Schwob, Marcel (Mayer Andre)
Lucan 39-65 .... **CMLC 33**
  See also AW 2; DLB 211; EFS 2; RGWL 2,
    3
Lucas, Craig 1951- .... **CLC 64**
  See also CA 137; CAD; CANR 71, 109,
    142; CD 5, 6; GLL 2; MTFW 2005
Lucas, E(dward) V(errall)
    1868-1938 .... **TCLC 73**
  See also CA 176; DLB 98, 149, 153; SATA
    20
Lucas, George 1944- .... **CLC 16, 252**
  See also AAYA 1, 23; CA 77-80; CANR
    30; SATA 56
Lucas, Hans
  See Godard, Jean-Luc
Lucas, Victoria
  See Plath, Sylvia
Lucian c. 125-c. 180 .... **CMLC 32**
  See also AW 2; DLB 176; RGWL 2, 3
Lucilius c. 180B.C.-102B.C. .... **CMLC 82**
  See also DLB 211
Lucretius c. 94B.C.-c. 49B.C. .... **CMLC 48**
  See also AW 2; CDWLB 1; DLB 211; EFS
    2; RGWL 2, 3; WLIT 8

Ludlam, Charles 1943-1987 .... **CLC 46, 50**
  See also CA 85-88; 122; CAD; CANR 72,
    86; DLB 266
Ludlum, Robert 1927-2001 .... **CLC 22, 43**
  See also AAYA 10, 59; BEST 89:1, 90:3;
    BPFB 2; CA 33-36R; 195; CANR 25, 41,
    68, 105, 131; CMW 4; CPW; DA3; DAM
    NOV, POP; DLBY 1982; MSW; MTCW
    1, 2; MTFW 2005
Ludwig, Ken 1950- .... **CLC 60**
  See also CA 195; CAD; CD 6
Ludwig, Otto 1813-1865 .... **NCLC 4**
  See also DLB 129
Lugones, Leopoldo 1874-1938 .... **HLCS 2;**
    TCLC 15
  See also CA 116; 131; CANR 104; DLB
    283; EWL 3; HW 1; LAW
Lu Hsun .... **SSC 20; TCLC 3**
  See Shu-Jen, Chou
  See also EWL 3
Lukacs, George .... **CLC 24**
  See Lukacs, Gyorgy (Szegeny von)
Lukacs, Gyorgy (Szegeny von) 1885-1971
  See Lukacs, George
  See also CA 101; 29-32R; CANR 62; CD-
    WLB 4; DLB 215, 242; EW 10; EWL 3;
    MTCW 1, 2
Luke, Peter (Ambrose Cyprian)
    1919-1995 .... **CLC 38**
  See also CA 81-84; 147; CANR 72; CBD;
    CD 5, 6; DLB 13
Lunar, Dennis
  See Mungo, Raymond
Lurie, Alison 1926- ..... **CLC 4, 5, 18, 39, 175**
  See also BPFB 2; CA 1-4R; CANR 2, 17,
    50, 88; CN 1, 2, 3, 4, 5, 6, 7; DLB 2;
    MAL 5; MTCW 1; NFS 24; SATA 46,
    112; TCLE 1:1
Lustig, Arnost 1926- .... **CLC 56**
  See also AAYA 3; CA 69-72; CANR 47,
    102; CWW 2; DLB 232, 299; EWL 3;
    RGHL; SATA 56
Luther, Martin 1483-1546 .... **LC 9, 37, 150**
  See also CDWLB 2; DLB 179; EW 2;
    RGWL 2, 3
Luxemburg, Rosa 1870(?)-1919 ..... **TCLC 63**
  See also CA 118
Luzi, Mario (Egidio Vincenzo)
    1914-2005 .... **CLC 13**
  See also CA 61-64; 236; CANR 9, 70;
    CWW 2; DLB 128; EWL 3
L'vov, Arkady .... **CLC 59**
Lydgate, John c. 1370-1450(?) .... **LC 81**
  See also BRW 1; DLB 146; RGEL 2
Lyly, John 1554(?)-1606 .... **DC 7; LC 41**
  See also BRW 1; DAM DRAM; DLB 62,
    167; RGEL 2
L'Ymagier
  See Gourmont, Remy(-Marie-Charles) de
Lynch, B. Suarez
  See Borges, Jorge Luis
Lynch, David 1946- .... **CLC 66, 162**
  See also AAYA 55; CA 124; 129; CANR
    111
Lynch, David Keith
  See Lynch, David
Lynch, James
  See Andreyev, Leonid (Nikolaevich)
Lyndsay, Sir David 1485-1555 .... **LC 20**
  See also RGEL 2
Lynn, Kenneth S(chuyler)
    1923-2001 .... **CLC 50**
  See also CA 1-4R; 196; CANR 3, 27, 65
Lynx
  See West, Rebecca
Lyons, Marcus
  See Blish, James (Benjamin)

McCabe, Patrick 1955- .... **CLC 133**
    See also BRWS 9; CA 130; CANR 50, 90,
    168; CN 6, 7; DLB 194

McCaffrey, Anne 1926- .... **CLC 17**
    See also AAYA 6, 34; AITN 2; BEST 89:2;
    BPFB 2; BYA 5; CA 25-28R, 227; CAAE
    227; CANR 15, 35, 55, 96, 169; CLR 49,
    130; CPW; DA3; DAM NOV, POP; DLB
    8; JRDA; MAICYA 1, 2; MTCW 1, 2;
    MTFW 2005; SAAS 11; SATA 8, 70, 116,
    152; SATA-Essay 152; SFW 4; SUFW 2;
    WYA; YAW

McCaffrey, Anne Inez
    See McCaffrey, Anne

McCall, Nathan 1955(?)- .... **CLC 86**
    See also AAYA 59; BW 3; CA 146; CANR
    88

McCann, Arthur
    See Campbell, John W(ood, Jr.)

McCann, Edson
    See Pohl, Frederik

McCarthy, Charles
    See McCarthy, Cormac

McCarthy, Charles, Jr.
    See McCarthy, Cormac

McCarthy, Cormac 1933- .... **CLC 4, 57, 101,**
    204
    See also AAYA 41; AMWS 8; BPFB 2; CA
    13-16R; CANR 10, 42, 69, 101, 161, 171;
    CN 6, 7; CPW; CSW; DA3; DAM POP;
    DLB 6, 143, 256; EWL 3; LATS 1:2;
    MAL 5; MTCW 2; MTFW 2005; TCLE
    1:2; TCWW 2

McCarthy, Mary (Therese)
    1912-1989 .. **CLC 1, 3, 5, 14, 24, 39, 59;**
    SSC 24
    See also AMW; BPFB 2; CA 5-8R; 129;
    CANR 16, 50, 64; CN 1, 2, 3, 4; DA3;
    DLB 2; DLBY 1981; EWL 3; FW; INT
    CANR-16; MAL 5; MBL; MTCW 1, 2;
    MTFW 2005; RGAL 4; TUS

McCartney, James Paul
    See McCartney, Paul

McCartney, Paul 1942- .... **CLC 12, 35**
    See also CA 146; CANR 111

McCauley, Stephen (D.) 1955- .... **CLC 50**
    See also CA 141

McClaren, Peter .... **CLC 70**

McClure, Michael (Thomas) 1932- ... **CLC 6,**
    10
    See also BG 1:3; CA 21-24R; CAD; CANR
    17, 46, 77, 131; CD 5, 6; CP 1, 2, 3, 4, 5,
    6, 7; DLB 16; WP

McCorkle, Jill (Collins) 1958- .... **CLC 51**
    See also CA 121; CANR 113; CSW; DLB
    234; DLBY 1987; SSFS 24

McCourt, Frank 1930- .... **CLC 109**
    See also AAYA 61; AMWS 12; CA 157;
    CANR 97, 138; MTFW 2005; NCFS 1

McCourt, James 1941- .... **CLC 5**
    See also CA 57-60; CANR 98, 152

McCourt, Malachy 1931- .... **CLC 119**
    See also SATA 126

McCoy, Edmund
    See Gardner, John

McCoy, Horace (Stanley)
    1897-1955 .... **TCLC 28**
    See also AMWS 13; CA 108; 155; CMW 4;
    DLB 9

McCrae, John 1872-1918 .... **TCLC 12**
    See also CA 109; DLB 92; PFS 5

McCreigh, James
    See Pohl, Frederik

McCullers, (Lula) Carson (Smith)
    1917-1967 .... **CLC 1, 4, 10, 12, 48, 100;**
    SSC 9, 24, 99; TCLC 155; WLC 4
    See also AAYA 21; AMW; AMWC 2; BPFB
    2; CA 5-8R; 25-28R; CABS 1, 3; CANR
    18, 132; CDALB 1941-1968; DA; DA3;

DAB; DAC; DAM MST, NOV; DFS 5,
18; DLB 2, 7, 173, 228; EWL 3; EXPS;
FW; GLL 1; LAIT 3, 4; MAL 5; MBL;
MTCW 1, 2; MTFW 2005; NFS 6, 13;
RGAL 4; RGSF 2; SATA 27; SSFS 5;
TUS; YAW

McCulloch, John Tyler
    See Burroughs, Edgar Rice

McCullough, Colleen 1937- ...... **CLC 27, 107**
    See also AAYA 36; BPFB 2; CA 81-84;
    CANR 17, 46, 67, 98, 139; CPW; DA3;
    DAM NOV, POP; MTCW 1, 2; MTFW
    2005; RHW

McCunn, Ruthanne Lum 1946- .... **AAL**
    See also CA 119; CANR 43, 96; DLB 312;
    LAIT 2; SATA 63

McDermott, Alice 1953- .... **CLC 90**
    See also CA 109; CANR 40, 90, 126; CN
    7; DLB 292; MTFW 2005; NFS 23

McElroy, Joseph 1930- .... **CLC 5, 47**
    See also CA 17-20R; CANR 149; CN 3, 4,
    5, 6, 7

McElroy, Joseph Prince
    See McElroy, Joseph

McEwan, Ian 1948- ... **CLC 13, 66, 169; SSC**
    106
    See also BEST 90:4; BRWS 4; CA 61-64;
    CANR 14, 41, 69, 87, 132, 179; CN 3, 4,
    5, 6, 7; DAM NOV; DLB 14, 194, 319,
    326; HGG; MTCW 1, 2; MTFW 2005;
    RGSF 2; SUFW 2; TEA

McFadden, David 1940- .... **CLC 48**
    See also CA 104; CP 1, 2, 3, 4, 5, 6, 7; DLB
    60; INT CA-104

McFarland, Dennis 1950- .... **CLC 65**
    See also CA 165; CANR 110, 179

McGahern, John 1934-2006 .... **CLC 5, 9, 48,**
    156; SSC 17
    See also CA 17-20R; 249; CANR 29, 68,
    113; CN 1, 2, 3, 4, 5, 6, 7; DLB 14, 231,
    319; MTCW 1

McGinley, Patrick (Anthony) 1937- . **CLC 41**
    See also CA 120; 127; CANR 56; INT CA-
    127

McGinley, Phyllis 1905-1978 .... **CLC 14**
    See also CA 9-12R; 77-80; CANR 19; CP
    1, 2; CWRI 5; DLB 11, 48; MAL 5; PFS
    9, 13; SATA 2, 44; SATA-Obit 24

McGinniss, Joe 1942- .... **CLC 32**
    See also AITN 2; BEST 89:2; CA 25-28R;
    CANR 26, 70, 152; CPW; DLB 185; INT
    CANR-26

McGivern, Maureen Daly
    See Daly, Maureen

McGivern, Maureen Patricia Daly
    See Daly, Maureen

McGrath, Patrick 1950- .... **CLC 55**
    See also CA 136; CANR 65, 148; CN 5, 6,
    7; DLB 231; HGG; SUFW 2

McGrath, Thomas (Matthew)
    1916-1990 .... **CLC 28, 59**
    See also AMWS 10; CA 9-12R; 132; CANR
    6, 33, 95; CP 1, 2, 3, 4, 5; DAM POET;
    MAL 5; MTCW 1; SATA 41; SATA-Obit
    66

McGuane, Thomas 1939- .. **CLC 3, 7, 18, 45,**
    127
    See also AITN 2; BPFB 2; CA 49-52;
    CANR 5, 24, 49, 94, 164; CN 2, 3, 4, 5,
    6, 7; DLB 2, 212; DLBY 1980; EWL 3;
    INT CANR-24; MAL 5; MTCW 1;
    MTFW 2005; TCWW 1, 2

McGuane, Thomas Francis III
    See McGuane, Thomas

McGuckian, Medbh 1950- .... **CLC 48, 174;**
    PC 27
    See also BRWS 5; CA 143; CP 4, 5, 6, 7;
    CWP; DAM POET; DLB 40

McHale, Tom 1942(?)-1982 .... **CLC 3, 5**
    See also AITN 1; CA 77-80; 106; CN 1, 2,
    3

McHugh, Heather 1948- .... **PC 61**
    See also CA 69-72; CANR 11, 28, 55, 92;
    CP 4, 5, 6, 7; CWP; PFS 24

McIlvanney, William 1936- .... **CLC 42**
    See also CA 25-28R; CANR 61; CMW 4;
    DLB 14, 207

McIlwraith, Maureen Mollie Hunter
    See Hunter, Mollie
    See also SATA 2

McInerney, Jay 1955- .... **CLC 34, 112**
    See also AAYA 18; BPFB 2; CA 116; 123;
    CANR 45, 68, 116, 176; CN 5, 6, 7; CPW;
    DA3; DAM POP; DLB 292; INT CA-123;
    MAL 5; MTCW 2; MTFW 2005

McIntyre, Vonda N. 1948- .... **CLC 18**
    See also CA 81-84; CANR 17, 34, 69;
    MTCW 1; SFW 4; YAW

McIntyre, Vonda Neel
    See McIntyre, Vonda N.

McKay, Claude .... **BLC 1:3; HR 1:3; PC 2;**
    TCLC 7, 41; WLC 4
    See McKay, Festus Claudius
    See also AFAW 1, 2; AMWS 10; DAB;
    DLB 4, 45, 51, 117; EWL 3; EXPP; GLL
    2; LAIT 3; LMFS 2; MAL 5; PAB; PFS
    4; RGAL 4; WP

McKay, Festus Claudius 1889-1948
    See McKay, Claude
    See also BW 1, 3; CA 104; 124; CANR 73;
    DA; DAC; DAM MST, MULT, NOV,
    POET; MTCW 1, 2; MTFW 2005; TUS

McKuen, Rod 1933- .... **CLC 1, 3**
    See also AITN 1; CA 41-44R; CANR 40;
    CP 1

McLoughlin, R. B.
    See Mencken, H(enry) L(ouis)

McLuhan, (Herbert) Marshall
    1911-1980 .... **CLC 37, 83**
    See also CA 9-12R; 102; CANR 12, 34, 61;
    DLB 88; INT CANR-12; MTCW 1, 2;
    MTFW 2005

McManus, Declan Patrick Aloysius
    See Costello, Elvis

McMillan, Terry 1951- .. **BLCS; CLC 50, 61,**
    112
    See also AAYA 21; AMWS 13; BPFB 2;
    BW 2, 3; CA 140; CANR 60, 104, 131;
    CN 7; CPW; DA3; DAM MULT, NOV,
    POP; MAL 5; MTCW 2; MTFW 2005;
    RGAL 4; YAW

McMurtry, Larry 1936- .... **CLC 2, 3, 7, 11,**
    27, 44, 127, 250
    See also AAYA 15; AITN 2; AMWS 5;
    BEST 89:2; BPFB 2; CA 5-8R; CANR
    19, 43, 64, 103, 170; CDALB 1968-1988;
    CN 2, 3, 4, 5, 6, 7; CPW; CSW; DA3;
    DAM NOV, POP; DLB 2, 143, 256;
    DLBY 1980, 1987; EWL 3; MAL 5;
    MTCW 1, 2; MTFW 2005; RGAL 4;
    TCWW 1, 2

McMurtry, Larry Jeff
    See McMurtry, Larry

McNally, Terrence 1939- ... **CLC 4, 7, 41, 91,**
    252; DC 27
    See also AAYA 62; AMWS 13; CA 45-48;
    CAD; CANR 2, 56, 116; CD 5, 6; DA3;
    DAM DRAM; DFS 16, 19; DLB 7, 249;
    EWL 3; GLL 1; MTCW 2; MTFW 2005

McNally, Thomas Michael
    See McNally, T.M.

McNally, T.M. 1961- .... **CLC 82**
    See also CA 246

McNamer, Deirdre 1950- .... **CLC 70**
    See also CA 188; CANR 163

McNeal, Tom .... **CLC 119**
    See also CA 252

Morand, Paul 1888-1976 .... **CLC 41; SSC 22**
See also CA 184; 69-72; DLB 65; EWL 3
Morante, Elsa 1918-1985 .... **CLC 8, 47**
See also CA 85-88; 117; CANR 35; DLB
177; EWL 3; MTCW 1, 2; MTFW 2005;
RGHL; RGWL 2, 3; WLIT 7
Moravia, Alberto .... **CLC 2, 7, 11, 27, 46;
SSC 26**
See Pincherle, Alberto
See also DLB 177; EW 12; EWL 3; MTCW
2; RGSF 2; RGWL 2, 3; WLIT 7
Morck, Paul
See Rolvaag, O.E.
More, Hannah 1745-1833 ...... **NCLC 27, 141**
See also DLB 107, 109, 116, 158; RGEL 2
More, Henry 1614-1687 .... **LC 9**
See also DLB 126, 252
More, Sir Thomas 1478(?)-1535 ... **LC 10, 32,
140**
See also BRWC 1; BRWS 7; DLB 136, 281;
LMFS 1; RGEL 2; TEA
Moreas, Jean .... **TCLC 18**
See Papadiamantopoulos, Johannes
See also GFL 1789 to the Present
Moreton, Andrew Esq.
See Defoe, Daniel
Moreton, Lee
See Boucicault, Dion
Morgan, Berry 1919-2002 .... **CLC 6**
See also CA 49-52; 208; DLB 6
Morgan, Claire
See Highsmith, Patricia
See also GLL 1
Morgan, Edwin 1920- .... **CLC 31**
See also BRWS 9; CA 5-8R; CANR 3, 43,
90; CP 1, 2, 3, 4, 5, 6, 7; DLB 27
Morgan, Edwin George
See Morgan, Edwin
Morgan, (George) Frederick
1922-2004 .... **CLC 23**
See also CA 17-20R; 224; CANR 21, 144;
CP 2, 3, 4, 5, 6, 7
Morgan, Harriet
See Mencken, H(enry) L(ouis)
Morgan, Jane
See Cooper, James Fenimore
Morgan, Janet 1945- .... **CLC 39**
See also CA 65-68
Morgan, Lady 1776(?)-1859 .... **NCLC 29**
See also DLB 116, 158; RGEL 2
Morgan, Robin (Evonne) 1941- .... **CLC 2**
See also CA 69-72; CANR 29, 68; FW;
GLL 2; MTCW 1; SATA 80
Morgan, Scott
See Kuttner, Henry
Morgan, Seth 1949(?)-1990 .... **CLC 65**
See also CA 185; 132
**Morgenstern, Christian (Otto Josef
Wolfgang)** 1871-1914 .... **TCLC 8**
See also CA 105; 191; EWL 3
Morgenstern, S.
See Goldman, William
Mori, Rintaro
See Mori Ogai
See also CA 110
Mori, Toshio 1910-1980 .... **AAL; SSC 83**
See also CA 116; 244; DLB 312; RGSF 2
Moricz, Zsigmond 1879-1942 .... **TCLC 33**
See also CA 165; DLB 215; EWL 3
Morike, Eduard (Friedrich)
1804-1875 .... **NCLC 10, 201**
See also DLB 133; RGWL 2, 3
Mori Ogai 1862-1922 .... **TCLC 14**
See Ogai
See also CA 164; DLB 180; EWL 3; RGWL
3; TWA
Moritz, Karl Philipp 1756-1793 .... **LC 2**
See also DLB 94

Morland, Peter Henry
See Faust, Frederick (Schiller)
Morley, Christopher (Darlington)
1890-1957 .... **TCLC 87**
See also CA 112; 213; DLB 9; MAL 5;
RGAL 4
Morren, Theophil
See Hofmannsthal, Hugo von
Morris, Bill 1952- .... **CLC 76**
See also CA 225
Morris, Julian
See West, Morris L(anglo)
Morris, Steveland Judkins (?)-
See Wonder, Stevie
Morris, William 1834-1896 . **NCLC 4; PC 55**
See also BRW 5; CDBLB 1832-1890; DLB
18, 35, 57, 156, 178, 184; FANT; RGEL
2; SFW 4; SUFW
Morris, Wright (Marion) 1910-1998 . **CLC 1,
3, 7, 18, 37; TCLC 107**
See also AMW; CA 9-12R; 167; CANR 21,
81; CN 1, 2, 3, 4, 5, 6; DLB 2, 206, 218;
DLBY 1981; EWL 3; MAL 5; MTCW 1,
2; MTFW 2005; RGAL 4; TCWW 1, 2
Morrison, Arthur 1863-1945 .... **SSC 40;
TCLC 72**
See also CA 120; 157; CMW 4; DLB 70,
135, 197; RGEL 2
Morrison, Chloe Anthony Wofford
See Morrison, Toni
Morrison, James Douglas 1943-1971
See Morrison, Jim
See also CA 73-76; CANR 40
Morrison, Jim .... **CLC 17**
See Morrison, James Douglas
Morrison, John Gordon 1904-1998 ... **SSC 93**
See also CA 103; CANR 92; DLB 260
Morrison, Toni 1931- . **BLC 1:3, 2:3; CLC 4,
10, 22, 55, 81, 87, 173, 194; WLC 4**
See also AAYA 1, 22, 61; AFAW 1, 2;
AMWC 1; AMWS 3; BPFB 2; BW 2, 3;
CA 29-32R; CANR 27, 42, 67, 113, 124;
CDALB 1968-1988; CLR 99; CN 3, 4, 5,
6, 7; CPW; DA; DA3; DAB; DAC; DAM
MST, MULT, NOV, POP; DLB 6, 33, 143,
331; DLBY 1981; EWL 3; EXPN; FL 1:6;
FW; GL 3; LAIT 2, 4; LATS 1:2; LMFS
2; MAL 5; MBL; MTCW 1, 2; MTFW
2005; NFS 1, 6, 8, 14; RGAL 4; RHW;
SATA 57, 144; SSFS 5; TCLE 1:2; TUS;
YAW
Morrison, Van 1945- .... **CLC 21**
See also CA 116; 168
Morrissy, Mary 1957- .... **CLC 99**
See also CA 205; DLB 267
Mortimer, John 1923- .... **CLC 28, 43**
See also CA 13-16R; CANR 21, 69, 109,
172; CBD; CD 5, 6; CDBLB 1960 to
Present; CMW 4; CN 5, 6, 7; CPW; DA3;
DAM DRAM, POP; DLB 13, 245, 271;
INT CANR-21; MSW; MTCW 1, 2;
MTFW 2005; RGEL 2
Mortimer, John Clifford
See Mortimer, John
Mortimer, Penelope (Ruth)
1918-1999 .... **CLC 5**
See also CA 57-60; 187; CANR 45, 88; CN
1, 2, 3, 4, 5, 6
Mortimer, Sir John
See Mortimer, John
Morton, Anthony
See Creasey, John
Morton, Thomas 1579(?)-1647(?) .... **LC 72**
See also DLB 24; RGEL 2
Mosca, Gaetano 1858-1941 .... **TCLC 75**
Moses, Daniel David 1952- .... **NNAL**
See also CA 186; CANR 160; DLB 334
Mosher, Howard Frank 1943- .... **CLC 62**
See also CA 139; CANR 65, 115

Mosley, Nicholas 1923- .... **CLC 43, 70**
See also CA 69-72; CANR 41, 60, 108, 158;
CN 1, 2, 3, 4, 5, 6, 7; DLB 14, 207
Mosley, Walter 1952- .... **BLCS; CLC 97, 184**
See also AAYA 57; AMWS 13; BPFB 2;
BW 2; CA 142; CANR 57, 92, 136, 172;
CMW 4; CN 7; CPW; DA3; DAM MULT,
POP; DLB 306; MSW; MTCW 2; MTFW
2005
Moss, Howard 1922-1987 . **CLC 7, 14, 45, 50**
See also CA 1-4R; 123; CANR 1, 44; CP 1,
2, 3, 4; DAM POET; DLB 5
Mossgiel, Rab
See Burns, Robert
Motion, Andrew 1952- .... **CLC 47**
See also BRWS 7; CA 146; CANR 90, 142;
CP 4, 5, 6, 7; DLB 40; MTFW 2005
Motion, Andrew Peter
See Motion, Andrew
Motley, Willard (Francis)
1909-1965 .... **CLC 18**
See also AMWS 17; BW 1; CA 117; 106;
CANR 88; DLB 76, 143
Motoori, Norinaga 1730-1801 .... **NCLC 45**
Mott, Michael (Charles Alston)
1930- .... **CLC 15, 34**
See also CA 5-8R; CAAS 7; CANR 7, 29
Mountain Wolf Woman 1884-1960 . **CLC 92;
NNAL**
See also CA 144; CANR 90
Moure, Erin 1955- .... **CLC 88**
See also CA 113; CP 5, 6, 7; CWP; DLB
60
Mourning Dove 1885(?)-1936 .... **NNAL**
See also CA 144; CANR 90; DAM MULT;
DLB 175, 221
Mowat, Farley 1921- .... **CLC 26**
See also AAYA 1, 50; BYA 2; CA 1-4R;
CANR 4, 24, 42, 68, 108; CLR 20; CPW;
DAC; DAM MST; DLB 68; INT CANR-
24; JRDA; MAICYA 1, 2; MTCW 1, 2;
MTFW 2005; SATA 3, 55; YAW
Mowat, Farley McGill
See Mowat, Farley
Mowatt, Anna Cora 1819-1870 ..... **NCLC 74**
See also RGAL 4
Mo Yan .... **CLC 257**
See Moye, Guan
Moye, Guan 1956(?)-
See Mo Yan
See also CA 201
Moyers, Bill 1934- .... **CLC 74**
See also AITN 2; CA 61-64; CANR 31, 52,
148
Mphahlele, Es'kia
See Mphahlele, Ezekiel
See also AFW; CDWLB 3; CN 4, 5, 6; DLB
125, 225; RGSF 2; SSFS 11
Mphahlele, Ezekiel 1919- ...... **BLC 1:3; CLC
25, 133**
See Mphahlele, Es'kia
See also BW 2, 3; CA 81-84; CANR 26,
76; CN 1, 2, 3; DA3; DAM MULT; EWL
3; MTCW 2; MTFW 2005; SATA 119
Mqhayi, S(amuel) E(dward) K(rune Loliwe)
1875-1945 .... **BLC 1:3; TCLC 25**
See also CA 153; CANR 87; DAM MULT
Mrozek, Slawomir 1930- .... **CLC 3, 13**
See also CA 13-16R; CAAS 10; CANR 29;
CDWLB 4; CWW 2; DLB 232; EWL 3;
MTCW 1
Mrs. Belloc-Lowndes
See Lowndes, Marie Adelaide (Belloc)
Mrs. Fairstar
See Horne, Richard Henry Hengist
M'Taggart, John M'Taggart Ellis
See McTaggart, John McTaggart Ellis
Mtwa, Percy (?)- .... **CLC 47**
See also CD 6

Nashe, Thomas 1567-1601(?) . **LC 41, 89; PC 82**
See also DLB 167; RGEL 2
Nathan, Daniel
See Dannay, Frederic
Nathan, George Jean 1882-1958 .... **TCLC 18**
See Hatteras, Owen
See also CA 114; 169; DLB 137; MAL 5
Natsume, Kinnosuke
See Natsume, Soseki
Natsume, Soseki 1867-1916 .... **TCLC 2, 10**
See Natsume Soseki; Soseki
See also CA 104; 195; RGWL 2, 3; TWA
Natsume Soseki
See Natsume, Soseki
See also DLB 180; EWL 3
Natti, (Mary) Lee 1919-
See Kingman, Lee
See also CA 5-8R; CANR 2
Navarre, Marguerite de
See de Navarre, Marguerite
Naylor, Gloria 1950- . **BLC 1:3; CLC 28, 52, 156, 261; WLCS**
See also AAYA 6, 39; AFAW 1, 2; AMWS 8; BW 2, 3; CA 107; CANR 27, 51, 74, 130; CN 4, 5, 6, 7; CPW; DA; DA3; DAC; DAM MST, MULT, NOV, POP; DLB 173; EWL 3; FW; MAL 5; MTCW 1, 2; MTFW 2005; NFS 4, 7; RGAL 4; TCLE 1:2; TUS
Neal, John 1793-1876 .... **NCLC 161**
See also DLB 1, 59, 243; FW; RGAL 4
Neff, Debra .... **CLC 59**
Neihardt, John Gneisenau
1881-1973 .... **CLC 32**
See also CA 13-14; CANR 65; CAP 1; DLB 9, 54, 256; LAIT 2; TCWW 1, 2
Nekrasov, Nikolai Alekseevich
1821-1878 .... **NCLC 11**
See also DLB 277
Nelligan, Emile 1879-1941 .... **TCLC 14**
See also CA 114; 204; DLB 92; EWL 3
Nelson, Willie 1933- .... **CLC 17**
See also CA 107; CANR 114, 178
Nemerov, Howard 1920-1991 .... **CLC 2, 6, 9, 36; PC 24; TCLC 124**
See also AMW; CA 1-4R; 134; CABS 2; CANR 1, 27, 53; CN 1, 2, 3; CP 1, 2, 3, 4, 5; DAM POET; DLB 5, 6; DLBY 1983; EWL 3; INT CANR-27; MAL 5; MTCW 1, 2; MTFW 2005; PFS 10, 14; RGAL 4
Nepos, Cornelius c. 99B.C.-c.
24B.C. .... **CMLC 89**
See also DLB 211
Neruda, Pablo 1904-1973 .. **CLC 1, 2, 5, 7, 9, 28, 62; HLC 2; PC 4, 64; WLC 4**
See also CA 19-20; 45-48; CANR 131; CAP 2; DA; DA3; DAB; DAC; DAM MST, MULT, POET; DLB 283, 331; DNFS 2; EWL 3; HW 1; LAW; MTCW 1, 2; MTFW 2005; PFS 11, 28; RGWL 2, 3; TWA; WLIT 1; WP
Nerval, Gerard de 1808-1855 ... **NCLC 1, 67; PC 13; SSC 18**
See also DLB 217; EW 6; GFL 1789 to the Present; RGSF 2; RGWL 2, 3
Nervo, (Jose) Amado (Ruiz de)
1870-1919 .... **HLCS 2; TCLC 11**
See also CA 109; 131; DLB 290; EWL 3; HW 1; LAW
Nesbit, Malcolm
See Chester, Alfred
Nessi, Pio Baroja y
See Baroja, Pio
Nestroy, Johann 1801-1862 .... **NCLC 42**
See also DLB 133; RGWL 2, 3
Netterville, Luke
See O'Grady, Standish (James)

Neufeld, John (Arthur) 1938- .... **CLC 17**
See also AAYA 11; CA 25-28R; CANR 11, 37, 56; CLR 52; MAICYA 1, 2; SAAS 3; SATA 6, 81, 131; SATA-Essay 131; YAW
Neumann, Alfred 1895-1952 .... **TCLC 100**
See also CA 183; DLB 56
Neumann, Ferenc
See Molnar, Ferenc
Neville, Emily Cheney 1919- .... **CLC 12**
See also BYA 2; CA 5-8R; CANR 3, 37, 85; JRDA; MAICYA 1, 2; SAAS 2; SATA 1; YAW
Newbound, Bernard Slade 1930-
See Slade, Bernard
See also CA 81-84; CANR 49; CD 5; DAM DRAM
Newby, P(ercy) H(oward)
1918-1997 .... **CLC 2, 13**
See also CA 5-8R; 161; CANR 32, 67; CN 1, 2, 3, 4, 5, 6; DAM NOV; DLB 15, 326; MTCW 1; RGEL 2
Newcastle
See Cavendish, Margaret Lucas
Newlove, Donald 1928- .... **CLC 6**
See also CA 29-32R; CANR 25
Newlove, John (Herbert) 1938- .... **CLC 14**
See also CA 21-24R; CANR 9, 25; CP 1, 2, 3, 4, 5, 6, 7
Newman, Charles 1938-2006 .... **CLC 2, 8**
See also CA 21-24R; 249; CANR 84; CN 3, 4, 5, 6
Newman, Charles Hamilton
See Newman, Charles
Newman, Edwin (Harold) 1919- ...... **CLC 14**
See also AITN 1; CA 69-72; CANR 5
Newman, John Henry 1801-1890 . **NCLC 38, 99**
See also BRWS 7; DLB 18, 32, 55; RGEL 2
Newton, (Sir) Isaac 1642-1727 ...... **LC 35, 53**
See also DLB 252
Newton, Suzanne 1936- .... **CLC 35**
See also BYA 7; CA 41-44R; CANR 14; JRDA; SATA 5, 77
New York Dept. of Ed. .... **CLC 70**
Nexo, Martin Andersen
1869-1954 .... **TCLC 43**
See also CA 202; DLB 214; EWL 3
Nezval, Vitezslav 1900-1958 .... **TCLC 44**
See also CA 123; CDWLB 4; DLB 215; EWL 3
Ng, Fae Myenne 1957(?)- .... **CLC 81**
See also BYA 11; CA 146
Ngcobo, Lauretta 1931- .... **BLC 2:3**
See also CA 165
Ngema, Mbongeni 1955- .... **CLC 57**
See also BW 2; CA 143; CANR 84; CD 5, 6
Ngugi, James T. .... **CLC 3, 7, 13, 182**
See Ngugi wa Thiong'o
See also CN 1, 2
Ngugi, James Thiong'o
See Ngugi wa Thiong'o
Ngugi wa Thiong'o 1938- .... **BLC 1:3, 2:3; CLC 36, 182**
See Ngugi, James T.
See also AFW; BRWS 8; BW 2; CA 81-84; CANR 27, 58, 164; CD 3, 4, 5, 6, 7; CDWLB 3; DAM MULT, NOV; DLB 125; DNFS 2; EWL 3; MTCW 1, 2; MTFW 2005; RGEL 2; WWE 1
Niatum, Duane 1938- .... **NNAL**
See also CA 41-44R; CANR 21, 45, 83; DLB 175
Nichol, B(arrie) P(hillip) 1944-1988 . **CLC 18**
See also CA 53-56; CP 1, 2, 3, 4; DLB 53; SATA 66
Nicholas of Cusa 1401-1464 .... **LC 80**
See also DLB 115

Nichols, John 1940- .... **CLC 38**
See also AMWS 13; CA 9-12R, 190; CAAE 190; CAAS 2; CANR 6, 70, 121; DLBY 1982; LATS 1:2; MTFW 2005; TCWW 1, 2
Nichols, Leigh
See Koontz, Dean R.
Nichols, Peter (Richard) 1927- .... **CLC 5, 36, 65**
See also CA 104; CANR 33, 86; CBD; CD 5, 6; DLB 13, 245; MTCW 1
Nicholson, Linda .... **CLC 65**
Ni Chuilleanain, Eilean 1942- .... **PC 34**
See also CA 126; CANR 53, 83; CP 5, 6, 7; CWP; DLB 40
Nicolas, F. R. E.
See Freeling, Nicolas
Niedecker, Lorine 1903-1970 ..... **CLC 10, 42; PC 42**
See also CA 25-28; CAP 2; DAM POET; DLB 48
Nietzsche, Friedrich (Wilhelm)
1844-1900 .... **TCLC 10, 18, 55**
See also CA 107; 121; CDWLB 2; DLB 129; EW 7; RGWL 2, 3; TWA
Nievo, Ippolito 1831-1861 .... **NCLC 22**
Nightingale, Anne Redmon 1943-
See Redmon, Anne
See also CA 103
Nightingale, Florence 1820-1910 ... **TCLC 85**
See also CA 188; DLB 166
Nijo Yoshimoto 1320-1388 .... **CMLC 49**
See also DLB 203
Nik. T. O.
See Annensky, Innokenty (Fyodorovich)
Nin, Anais 1903-1977 ..... **CLC 1, 4, 8, 11, 14, 60, 127; SSC 10**
See also AITN 2; AMWS 10; BPFB 2; CA 13-16R; 69-72; CANR 22, 53; CN 1, 2; DAM NOV, POP; DLB 2, 4, 152; EWL 3; GLL 2; MAL 5; MBL; MTCW 1, 2; MTFW 2005; RGAL 4; RGSF 2
Nisbet, Robert A(lexander)
1913-1996 .... **TCLC 117**
See also CA 25-28R; 153; CANR 17; INT CANR-17
Nishida, Kitaro 1870-1945 .... **TCLC 83**
Nishiwaki, Junzaburo 1894-1982 .... **PC 15**
See Junzaburo, Nishiwaki
See also CA 194; 107; MJW; RGWL 3
Nissenson, Hugh 1933- .... **CLC 4, 9**
See also CA 17-20R; CANR 27, 108, 151; CN 5, 6; DLB 28, 335
Nister, Der
See Der Nister
See also DLB 333; EWL 3
Niven, Larry 1938-
See Niven, Laurence VanCott
See also CA 21-24R, 207; CAAE 207; CAAS 12; CANR 14, 44, 66, 113, 155; CPW; DAM POP; MTCW 1, 2; SATA 95, 171; SFW 4
Niven, Laurence VanCott .... **CLC 8**
See Niven, Larry
See also AAYA 27; BPFB 2; BYA 10; DLB 8; SCFW 1, 2
Nixon, Agnes Eckhardt 1927- .... **CLC 21**
See also CA 110
Nizan, Paul 1905-1940 .... **TCLC 40**
See also CA 161; DLB 72; EWL 3; GFL 1789 to the Present
Nkosi, Lewis 1936- .... **BLC 1:3; CLC 45**
See also BW 1, 3; CA 65-68; CANR 27, 81; CBD; CD 5, 6; DAM MULT; DLB 157, 225; WWE 1
Nodier, (Jean) Charles (Emmanuel)
1780-1844 .... **NCLC 19**
See also DLB 119; GFL 1789 to the Present
Noguchi, Yone 1875-1947 .... **TCLC 80**

Osborne, Dorothy 1627-1695 .... **LC 141**
Osborne, George
See Silverberg, Robert
Osborne, John 1929-1994 .... **CLC 1, 2, 5, 11, 45; TCLC 153; WLC 4**
See also BRWS 1; CA 13-16R; 147; CANR 21, 56; CBD; CDBLB 1945-1960; DA; DAB; DAC; DAM DRAM, MST; DFS 4, 19, 24; DLB 13; EWL 3; MTCW 1, 2; MTFW 2005; RGEL 2
Osborne, Lawrence 1958- .... **CLC 50**
See also CA 189; CANR 152
Osbourne, Lloyd 1868-1947 .... **TCLC 93**
Osgood, Frances Sargent
1811-1850 .... **NCLC 141**
See also DLB 250
Oshima, Nagisa 1932- .... **CLC 20**
See also CA 116; 121; CANR 78
Oskison, John Milton
1874-1947 .... **NNAL; TCLC 35**
See also CA 144; CANR 84; DAM MULT; DLB 175
Ossian c. 3rd cent. - .... **CMLC 28**
See Macpherson, James
Ossoli, Sarah Margaret (Fuller)
1810-1850 .... **NCLC 5, 50**
See Fuller, Margaret
See also CDALB 1640-1865; DLB 1, 59, 73; FW; LMFS 1; SATA 25
Ostriker, Alicia 1937- .... **CLC 132**
See also CA 25-28R; CAAS 24; CANR 10, 30, 62, 99, 167; CWP; DLB 120; EXPP; PFS 19, 26
Ostriker, Alicia Suskin
See Ostriker, Alicia
Ostrovsky, Aleksandr Nikolaevich
See Ostrovsky, Alexander
See also DLB 277
Ostrovsky, Alexander 1823-1886 .. **NCLC 30, 57**
See Ostrovsky, Aleksandr Nikolaevich
Osundare, Niyi 1947- .... **BLC 2:3**
See also AFW; BW 3; CA 176; CDWLB 3; CP 7; DLB 157
Otero, Blas de 1916-1979 .... **CLC 11**
See also CA 89-92; DLB 134; EWL 3
O'Trigger, Sir Lucius
See Horne, Richard Henry Hengist
Otto, Rudolf 1869-1937 .... **TCLC 85**
Otto, Whitney 1955- .... **CLC 70**
See also CA 140; CANR 120
Otway, Thomas 1652-1685 ... **DC 24; LC 106**
See also DAM DRAM; DLB 80; RGEL 2
Ouida .... **TCLC 43**
See De La Ramee, Marie Louise
See also DLB 18, 156; RGEL 2
Ouologuem, Yambo 1940- .... **CLC 146**
See also CA 111; 176
Ousmane, Sembene 1923-2007 .... **BLC 1:3, 2:3; CLC 66**
See also AFW; BW 1, 3; CA 117; 125; 261; CANR 81; CWW 2; EWL 3; MTCW 1; WLIT 2
Ovid 43B.C.-17 .... **CMLC 7; PC 2**
See also AW; CDWLB 1; DA3; DAM POET; DLB 211; PFS 22; RGWL 2, 3; WLIT 8; WP
Owen, Hugh
See Faust, Frederick (Schiller)
Owen, Wilfred (Edward Salter)
1893-1918 ... **PC 19; TCLC 5, 27; WLC 4**
See also BRW 6; CA 104; 141; CDBLB 1914-1945; DA; DAB; DAC; DAM MST, POET; DLB 20; EWL 3; EXPP; MTCW 2; MTFW 2005; PFS 10; RGEL 2; WLIT 4

Owens, Louis (Dean) 1948-2002 .... **NNAL**
See also CA 137, 179; 207; CAAE 179; CAAS 24; CANR 71
Owens, Rochelle 1936- .... **CLC 8**
See also CA 17-20R; CAAS 2; CAD; CANR 39; CD 5, 6; CP 1, 2, 3, 4, 5, 6, 7; CWD; CWP
Oz, Amos 1939- ...... **CLC 5, 8, 11, 27, 33, 54; SSC 66**
See also CA 53-56; CANR 27, 47, 65, 113, 138, 175; CWW 2; DAM NOV; EWL 3; MTCW 1, 2; MTFW 2005; RGHL; RGSF 2; RGWL 3; WLIT 6
Ozick, Cynthia 1928- . **CLC 3, 7, 28, 62, 155, 262; SSC 15, 60**
See also AMWS 5; BEST 90:1; CA 17-20R; CANR 23, 58, 116, 160; CN 3, 4, 5, 6, 7; CPW; DA3; DAM NOV, POP; DLB 28, 152, 299; DLBY 1982; EWL 3; EXPS; INT CANR-23; MAL 5; MTCW 1, 2; MTFW 2005; RGAL 4; RGHL; RGSF 2; SSFS 3, 12, 22
Ozu, Yasujiro 1903-1963 .... **CLC 16**
See also CA 112
Pabst, G. W. 1885-1967 .... **TCLC 127**
Pacheco, C.
See Pessoa, Fernando (Antonio Nogueira)
Pacheco, Jose Emilio 1939- .... **HLC 2**
See also CA 111; 131; CANR 65; CWW 2; DAM MULT; DLB 290; EWL 3; HW 1, 2; RGSF 2
Pa Chin .... **CLC 18**
See Jin, Ba
See also EWL 3
Pack, Robert 1929- .... **CLC 13**
See also CA 1-4R; CANR 3, 44, 82; CP 1, 2, 3, 4, 5, 6, 7; DLB 5; SATA 118
Packer, Vin
See Meaker, Marijane
Padgett, Lewis
See Kuttner, Henry
Padilla (Lorenzo), Heberto
1932-2000 .... **CLC 38**
See also AITN 1; CA 123; 131; 189; CWW 2; EWL 3; HW 1
Page, James Patrick 1944-
See Page, Jimmy
See also CA 204
Page, Jimmy 1944- .... **CLC 12**
See Page, James Patrick
Page, Louise 1955- .... **CLC 40**
See also CA 140; CANR 76; CBD; CD 5, 6; CWD; DLB 233
Page, P(atricia) K(athleen) 1916- ...... **CLC 7, 18; PC 12**
See Cape, Judith
See also CA 53-56; CANR 4, 22, 65; CP 1, 2, 3, 4, 5, 6, 7; DAC; DAM MST; DLB 68; MTCW 1; RGEL 2
Page, Stanton
See Fuller, Henry Blake
Page, Thomas Nelson 1853-1922 .... **SSC 23**
See also CA 118; 177; DLB 12, 78; DLBD 13; RGAL 4
Pagels, Elaine
See Pagels, Elaine Hiesey
Pagels, Elaine Hiesey 1943- .... **CLC 104**
See also CA 45-48; CANR 2, 24, 51, 151; FW; NCFS 4
Paget, Violet 1856-1935
See Lee, Vernon
See also CA 104; 166; GLL 1; HGG
Paget-Lowe, Henry
See Lovecraft, H. P.
Paglia, Camille 1947- .... **CLC 68**
See also CA 140; CANR 72, 139; CPW; FW; GLL 2; MTCW 2; MTFW 2005

Pagnol, Marcel (Paul)
1895-1974 .... **TCLC 208**
See also CA 128; 49-52; DLB 321; EWL 3; GFL 1789 to the Present; MTCW 1; RGWL 2, 3
Paige, Richard
See Koontz, Dean R.
Paine, Thomas 1737-1809 .... **NCLC 62**
See also AMWS 1; CDALB 1640-1865; DLB 31, 43, 73, 158; LAIT 1; RGAL 4; RGEL 2; TUS
Pakenham, Antonia
See Fraser, Antonia
Palamas, Costis
See Palamas, Kostes
Palamas, Kostes 1859-1943 .... **TCLC 5**
See Palamas, Kostis
See also CA 105; 190; RGWL 2, 3
Palamas, Kostis
See Palamas, Kostes
See also EWL 3
Palazzeschi, Aldo 1885-1974 .... **CLC 11**
See also CA 89-92; 53-56; DLB 114, 264; EWL 3
Pales Matos, Luis 1898-1959 .... **HLCS 2**
See Pales Matos, Luis
See also DLB 290; HW 1; LAW
Paley, Grace 1922-2007 ... **CLC 4, 6, 37, 140; SSC 8**
See also AMWS 6; CA 25-28R; 263; CANR 13, 46, 74, 118; CN 2, 3, 4, 5, 6, 7; CPW; DA3; DAM POP; DLB 28, 218; EWL 3; EXPS; FW; INT CANR-13; MAL 5; MBL; MTCW 1, 2; MTFW 2005; RGAL 4; RGSF 2; SSFS 3, 20
Paley, Grace Goodside
See Paley, Grace
Palin, Michael (Edward) 1943- .... **CLC 21**
See Monty Python
See also CA 107; CANR 35, 109; SATA 67
Palliser, Charles 1947- .... **CLC 65**
See also CA 136; CANR 76; CN 5, 6, 7
Palma, Ricardo 1833-1919 .... **TCLC 29**
See also CA 168; LAW
Pamuk, Orhan 1952- .... **CLC 185**
See also CA 142; CANR 75, 127, 172; CWW 2; NFS 27; WLIT 6
Pancake, Breece Dexter 1952-1979
See Pancake, Breece D'J
See also CA 123; 109
Pancake, Breece D'J .... **CLC 29; SSC 61**
See Pancake, Breece Dexter
See also DLB 130
Panchenko, Nikolai .... **CLC 59**
Pankhurst, Emmeline (Goulden)
1858-1928 .... **TCLC 100**
See also CA 116; FW
Panko, Rudy
See Gogol, Nikolai (Vasilyevich)
Papadiamantis, Alexandros
1851-1911 .... **TCLC 29**
See also CA 168; EWL 3
Papadiamantopoulos, Johannes 1856-1910
See Moreas, Jean
See also CA 117; 242
Papini, Giovanni 1881-1956 .... **TCLC 22**
See also CA 121; 180; DLB 264
Paracelsus 1493-1541 .... **LC 14**
See also DLB 179
Parasol, Peter
See Stevens, Wallace
Pardo Bazan, Emilia 1851-1921 .... **SSC 30; TCLC 189**
See also EWL 3; FW; RGSF 2; RGWL 2, 3
Paredes, Americo 1915-1999 .... **PC 83**
See also CA 37-40R; 179; DLB 209; EXPP; HW 1
Pareto, Vilfredo 1848-1923 .... **TCLC 69**
See also CA 175

Paretsky, Sara 1947- .... **CLC 135**
See also AAYA 30; BEST 90:3; CA 125;
129; CANR 59, 95; CMW 4; CPW; DA3;
DAM POP; DLB 306; INT CA-129;
MSW; RGAL 4

Paretsky, Sara N.
See Paretsky, Sara

Parfenie, Maria
See Codrescu, Andrei

Parini, Jay (Lee) 1948- .... **CLC 54, 133**
See also CA 97-100, 229; CAAE 229;
CAAS 16; CANR 32, 87

Park, Jordan
See Kornbluth, C(yril) M.; Pohl, Frederik

Park, Robert E(zra) 1864-1944 ..... **TCLC 73**
See also CA 122; 165

Parker, Bert
See Ellison, Harlan

Parker, Dorothy (Rothschild)
1893-1967 . **CLC 15, 68; PC 28; SSC 2,
101; TCLC 143**
See also AMWS 9; CA 19-20; 25-28R; CAP
2; DA3; DAM POET; DLB 11, 45, 86;
EXPP; FW; MAL 5; MBL; MTCW 1, 2;
MTFW 2005; PFS 18; RGAL 4; RGSF 2;
TUS

Parker, Robert B. 1932- .... **CLC 27**
See also AAYA 28; BEST 89:4; BPFB 3;
CA 49-52; CANR 1, 26, 52, 89, 128, 165;
CMW 4; CPW; DAM NOV, POP; DLB
306; INT CANR-26; MSW; MTCW 1;
MTFW 2005

Parker, Robert Brown
See Parker, Robert B.

Parker, Theodore 1810-1860 .... **NCLC 186**
See also DLB 1, 235

Parkin, Frank 1940- .... **CLC 43**
See also CA 147

Parkman, Francis, Jr. 1823-1893 .. **NCLC 12**
See also AMWS 2; DLB 1, 30, 183, 186,
235; RGAL 4

Parks, Gordon 1912-2006 . **BLC 1:3; CLC 1,
16**
See also AAYA 36; AITN 2; BW 2, 3; CA
41-44R; 249; CANR 26, 66, 145; DA3;
DAM MULT; DLB 33; MTCW 2; MTFW
2005; SATA 8, 108; SATA-Obit 175

Parks, Suzan-Lori 1964(?)- ..... **BLC 2:3; DC
23**
See also AAYA 55; CA 201; CAD; CD 5,
6; CWD; DFS 22; DLB 341; RGAL 4

Parks, Tim(othy Harold) 1954- ...... **CLC 147**
See also CA 126; 131; CANR 77, 144; CN
7; DLB 231; INT CA-131

Parmenides c. 515B.C.-c.
450B.C. .... **CMLC 22**
See also DLB 176

Parnell, Thomas 1679-1718 .... **LC 3**
See also DLB 95; RGEL 2

Parr, Catherine c. 1513(?)-1548 .... **LC 86**
See also DLB 136

Parra, Nicanor 1914- ... **CLC 2, 102; HLC 2;
PC 39**
See also CA 85-88; CANR 32; CWW 2;
DAM MULT; DLB 283; EWL 3; HW 1;
LAW; MTCW 1

Parra Sanojo, Ana Teresa de la
1890-1936 .... **HLCS 2**
See de la Parra, (Ana) Teresa (Sonojo)
See also LAW

Parrish, Mary Frances
See Fisher, M(ary) F(rances) K(ennedy)

Parshchikov, Aleksei 1954- .... **CLC 59**
See Parshchikov, Aleksei Maksimovich

Parshchikov, Aleksei Maksimovich
See Parshchikov, Aleksei
See also DLB 285

Parson, Professor
See Coleridge, Samuel Taylor

Parson Lot
See Kingsley, Charles

Parton, Sara Payson Willis
1811-1872 .... **NCLC 86**
See also DLB 43, 74, 239

Partridge, Anthony
See Oppenheim, E(dward) Phillips

Pascal, Blaise 1623-1662 .... **LC 35**
See also DLB 268; EW 3; GFL Beginnings
to 1789; RGWL 2, 3; TWA

Pascoli, Giovanni 1855-1912 .... **TCLC 45**
See also CA 170; EW 7; EWL 3

Pasolini, Pier Paolo 1922-1975 .. **CLC 20, 37,
106; PC 17**
See also CA 93-96; 61-64; CANR 63; DLB
128, 177; EWL 3; MTCW 1; RGWL 2, 3

Pasquini
See Silone, Ignazio

Pastan, Linda (Olenik) 1932- .... **CLC 27**
See also CA 61-64; CANR 18, 40, 61, 113;
CP 3, 4, 5, 6, 7; CSW; CWP; DAM
POET; DLB 5; PFS 8, 25

Pasternak, Boris 1890-1960 ... **CLC 7, 10, 18,
63; PC 6; SSC 31; TCLC 188; WLC 4**
See also BPFB 3; CA 127; 116; DA; DA3;
DAB; DAC; DAM MST, NOV, POET;
DLB 302, 331; EW 10; MTCW 1, 2;
MTFW 2005; NFS 26; RGSF 2; RGWL
2, 3; TWA; WP

Patchen, Kenneth 1911-1972 .... **CLC 1, 2, 18**
See also BG 1:3; CA 1-4R; 33-36R; CANR
3, 35; CN 1; CP 1; DAM POET; DLB 16,
48; EWL 3; MAL 5; MTCW 1; RGAL 4

Patchett, Ann 1963- .... **CLC 244**
See also AAYA 69; AMWS 12; CA 139;
CANR 64, 110, 167; MTFW 2005

Pater, Walter (Horatio) 1839-1894 . **NCLC 7,
90, 159**
See also BRW 5; CDBLB 1832-1890; DLB
57, 156; RGEL 2; TEA

Paterson, A(ndrew) B(arton)
1864-1941 .... **TCLC 32**
See also CA 155; DLB 230; RGEL 2; SATA
97

Paterson, Banjo
See Paterson, A(ndrew) B(arton)

Paterson, Katherine 1932- .... **CLC 12, 30**
See also AAYA 1, 31; BYA 1, 2, 7; CA 21-
24R; CANR 28, 59, 111, 173; CLR 7, 50,
127; CWRI 5; DLB 52; JRDA; LAIT 4;
MAICYA 1, 2; MAICYAS 1; MTCW 1;
SATA 13, 53, 92, 133; WYA; YAW

Paterson, Katherine Womeldorf
See Paterson, Katherine

Patmore, Coventry Kersey Dighton
1823-1896 .... **NCLC 9; PC 59**
See also DLB 35, 98; RGEL 2; TEA

Paton, Alan 1903-1988 ..... **CLC 4, 10, 25, 55,
106; TCLC 165; WLC 4**
See also AAYA 26; AFW; BPFB 3; BRWS
2; BYA 1; CA 13-16; 125; CANR 22;
CAP 1; CN 1, 2, 3, 4; DA; DA3; DAB;
DAC; DAM MST, NOV; DLB 225;
DLBD 17; EWL 3; EXPN; LAIT 4;
MTCW 1, 2; MTFW 2005; NFS 3, 12;
RGEL 2; SATA 11; SATA-Obit 56; TWA;
WLIT 2; WWE 1

Paton Walsh, Gillian
See Paton Walsh, Jill
See also AAYA 47; BYA 1, 8

Paton Walsh, Jill 1937- .... **CLC 35**
See Paton Walsh, Gillian; Walsh, Jill Paton
See also AAYA 11; CA 262; CAAE 262;
CANR 38, 83, 158; CLR 2, 65; DLB 161;
JRDA; MAICYA 1, 2; SAAS 3; SATA 4,
72, 109, 190; SATA-Essay 190; YAW

Patsauq, Markoosie 1942- .... **NNAL**
See also CA 101; CLR 23; CWRI 5; DAM
MULT

Patterson, (Horace) Orlando (Lloyd)
1940- .... **BLCS**
See also BW 1; CA 65-68; CANR 27, 84;
CN 1, 2, 3, 4, 5, 6

Patton, George S(mith), Jr.
1885-1945 .... **TCLC 79**
See also CA 189

Paulding, James Kirke 1778-1860 ... **NCLC 2**
See also DLB 3, 59, 74, 250; RGAL 4

Paulin, Thomas Neilson
See Paulin, Tom

Paulin, Tom 1949- .... **CLC 37, 177**
See also CA 123; 128; CANR 98; CP 3, 4,
5, 6, 7; DLB 40

Pausanias c. 1st cent. - .... **CMLC 36**

Paustovsky, Konstantin (Georgievich)
1892-1968 .... **CLC 40**
See also CA 93-96; 25-28R; DLB 272;
EWL 3

Pavese, Cesare 1908-1950 .... **PC 13; SSC 19;
TCLC 3**
See also CA 104; 169; DLB 128, 177; EW
12; EWL 3; PFS 20; RGSF 2; RGWL 2,
3; TWA; WLIT 7

Pavic, Milorad 1929- .... **CLC 60**
See also CA 136; CDWLB 4; CWW 2; DLB
181; EWL 3; RGWL 3

Pavlov, Ivan Petrovich 1849-1936 . **TCLC 91**
See also CA 118; 180

Pavlova, Karolina Karlovna
1807-1893 .... **NCLC 138**
See also DLB 205

Payne, Alan
See Jakes, John

Payne, Rachel Ann
See Jakes, John

Paz, Gil
See Lugones, Leopoldo

Paz, Octavio 1914-1998 . **CLC 3, 4, 6, 10, 19,
51, 65, 119; HLC 2; PC 1, 48; TCLC
211; WLC 4**
See also AAYA 50; CA 73-76; 165; CANR
32, 65, 104; CWW 2; DA; DA3; DAB;
DAC; DAM MST, MULT, POET; DLB
290, 331; DLBY 1990, 1998; DNFS 1;
EWL 3; HW 1, 2; LAW; LAWS 1; MTCW
1, 2; MTFW 2005; PFS 18; RGWL 2, 3;
SSFS 13; TWA; WLIT 1

p'Bitek, Okot 1931-1982 . **BLC 1:3; CLC 96;
TCLC 149**
See also AFW; BW 2, 3; CA 124; 107;
CANR 82; CP 1, 2, 3; DAM MULT; DLB
125; EWL 3; MTCW 1, 2; MTFW 2005;
RGEL 2; WLIT 2

Peabody, Elizabeth Palmer
1804-1894 .... **NCLC 169**
See also DLB 1, 223

Peacham, Henry 1578-1644(?) .... **LC 119**
See also DLB 151

Peacock, Molly 1947- .... **CLC 60**
See also CA 103, 262; CAAE 262; CAAS
21; CANR 52, 84; CP 5, 6, 7; CWP; DLB
120, 282

Peacock, Thomas Love
1785-1866 .... **NCLC 22; PC 87**
See also BRW 4; DLB 96, 116; RGEL 2;
RGSF 2

Peake, Mervyn 1911-1968 .... **CLC 7, 54**
See also CA 5-8R; 25-28R; CANR 3; DLB
15, 160, 255; FANT; MTCW 1; RGEL 2;
SATA 23; SFW 4

Pearce, Philippa 1920-2006
See Christie, Philippa
See also CA 5-8R; 255; CANR 4, 109;
CWRI 5; FANT; MAICYA 2; SATA-Obit
179

Pearl, Eric
See Elman, Richard (Martin)

Phillips, Robert (Schaeffer) 1938- .... **CLC 28**
See also CA 17-20R; CAAS 13; CANR 8; DLB 105

Phillips, Ward
See Lovecraft, H. P.

Philo c. 20B.C.-c. 50 .... **CMLC 100**
See also DLB 176

Philostratus, Flavius c. 179-c. 244 .... **CMLC 62**

Piccolo, Lucio 1901-1969 .... **CLC 13**
See also CA 97-100; DLB 114; EWL 3

Pickthall, Marjorie L(owry) C(hristie) 1883-1922 .... **TCLC 21**
See also CA 107; DLB 92

Pico della Mirandola, Giovanni 1463-1494 .... **LC 15**
See also LMFS 1

Piercy, Marge 1936- .... **CLC 3, 6, 14, 18, 27, 62, 128; PC 29**
See also BPFB 3; CA 21-24R, 187; CAAE 187; CAAS 1; CANR 13, 43, 66, 111; CN 3, 4, 5, 6, 7; CP 1, 2, 3, 4, 5, 6, 7; CWP; DLB 120, 227; EXPP; FW; MAL 5; MTCW 1, 2; MTFW 2005; PFS 9, 22; SFW 4

Piers, Robert
See Anthony, Piers

Pieyre de Mandiargues, Andre 1909-1991
See Mandiargues, Andre Pieyre de
See also CA 103; 136; CANR 22, 82; EWL 3; GFL 1789 to the Present

Pilnyak, Boris 1894-1938 . **SSC 48; TCLC 23**
See Vogau, Boris Andreyevich
See also EWL 3

Pinchback, Eugene
See Toomer, Jean

Pincherle, Alberto 1907-1990 ...... **CLC 11, 18**
See Moravia, Alberto
See also CA 25-28R; 132; CANR 33, 63, 142; DAM NOV; MTCW 1; MTFW 2005

Pinckney, Darryl 1953- .... **CLC 76**
See also BW 2, 3; CA 143; CANR 79

Pindar 518(?)B.C.-438(?)B.C. .... **CMLC 12; PC 19**
See also AW 1; CDWLB 1; DLB 176; RGWL 2

Pineda, Cecile 1942- .... **CLC 39**
See also CA 118; DLB 209

Pinero, Arthur Wing 1855-1934 .... **TCLC 32**
See also CA 110; 153; DAM DRAM; DLB 10, 344; RGEL 2

Pinero, Miguel (Antonio Gomez) 1946-1988 .... **CLC 4, 55**
See also CA 61-64; 125; CAD; CANR 29, 90; DLB 266; HW 1; LLW

Pinget, Robert 1919-1997 .... **CLC 7, 13, 37**
See also CA 85-88; 160; CWW 2; DLB 83; EWL 3; GFL 1789 to the Present

Pink Floyd
See Barrett, (Roger) Syd; Gilmour, David; Mason, Nick; Waters, Roger; Wright, Rick

Pinkney, Edward 1802-1828 .... **NCLC 31**
See also DLB 248

Pinkwater, D. Manus
See Pinkwater, Daniel Manus

Pinkwater, Daniel
See Pinkwater, Daniel Manus

Pinkwater, Daniel M.
See Pinkwater, Daniel Manus

Pinkwater, Daniel Manus 1941- .... **CLC 35**
See also AAYA 1, 46; BYA 9; CA 29-32R; CANR 12, 38, 89, 143; CLR 4; CSW; FANT; JRDA; MAICYA 1, 2; SAAS 3; SATA 8, 46, 76, 114, 158; SFW 4; YAW

Pinkwater, Manus
See Pinkwater, Daniel Manus

Pinsky, Robert 1940- .... **CLC 9, 19, 38, 94, 121, 216; PC 27**
See also AMWS 6; CA 29-32R; CAAS 4; CANR 58, 97, 138, 177; CP 3, 4, 5, 6, 7; DA3; DAM POET; DLBY 1982, 1998; MAL 5; MTCW 2; MTFW 2005; PFS 18; RGAL 4; TCLE 1:2

Pinta, Harold
See Pinter, Harold

Pinter, Harold 1930- .. **CLC 1, 3, 6, 9, 11, 15, 27, 58, 73, 199; DC 15; WLC 4**
See also BRWR 1; BRWS 1; CA 5-8R; CANR 33, 65, 112, 145; CBD; CD 5, 6; CDBLB 1960 to Present; CP 1; DA; DA3; DAB; DAC; DAM DRAM, MST; DFS 3, 5, 7, 14, 25; DLB 13, 310, 331; EWL 3; IDFW 3, 4; LMFS 2; MTCW 1, 2; MTFW 2005; RGEL 2; RGHL; TEA

Piozzi, Hester Lynch (Thrale) 1741-1821 .... **NCLC 57**
See also DLB 104, 142

Pirandello, Luigi 1867-1936 .. **DC 5; SSC 22; TCLC 4, 29, 172; WLC 4**
See also CA 104; 153; CANR 103; DA; DA3; DAB; DAC; DAM DRAM, MST; DFS 4, 9; DLB 264, 331; EW 8; EWL 3; MTCW 2; MTFW 2005; RGSF 2; RGWL 2, 3; WLIT 7

Pirsig, Robert M(aynard) 1928- ... **CLC 4, 6, 73**
See also CA 53-56; CANR 42, 74; CPW 1; DA3; DAM POP; MTCW 1, 2; MTFW 2005; SATA 39

Pisan, Christine de
See Christine de Pizan

Pisarev, Dmitrii Ivanovich
See Pisarev, Dmitry Ivanovich
See also DLB 277

Pisarev, Dmitry Ivanovich 1840-1868 .... **NCLC 25**
See Pisarev, Dmitrii Ivanovich

Pix, Mary (Griffith) 1666-1709 ..... **LC 8, 149**
See also DLB 80

Pixerecourt, (Rene Charles) Guilbert de 1773-1844 .... **NCLC 39**
See also DLB 192; GFL 1789 to the Present

Plaatje, Sol(omon) T(shekisho) 1878-1932 .... **BLCS; TCLC 73**
See also BW 2, 3; CA 141; CANR 79; DLB 125, 225

Plaidy, Jean
See Hibbert, Eleanor Alice Burford

Planche, James Robinson 1796-1880 .... **NCLC 42**
See also RGEL 2

Plant, Robert 1948- .... **CLC 12**

Plante, David 1940- .... **CLC 7, 23, 38**
See also CA 37-40R; CANR 12, 36, 58, 82, 152; CN 2, 3, 4, 5, 6, 7; DAM NOV; DLBY 1983; INT CANR-12; MTCW 1

Plante, David Robert
See Plante, David

Plath, Sylvia 1932-1963 ..... **CLC 1, 2, 3, 5, 9, 11, 14, 17, 50, 51, 62, 111; PC 1, 37; WLC 4**
See also AAYA 13; AMWR 2; AMWS 1; BPFB 3; CA 19-20; CANR 34, 101; CAP 2; CDALB 1941-1968; DA; DA3; DAB; DAC; DAM MST, POET; DLB 5, 6, 152; EWL 3; EXPN; EXPP; FL 1:6; FW; LAIT 4; MAL 5; MBL; MTCW 1, 2; MTFW 2005; NFS 1; PAB; PFS 1, 15, 28; RGAL 4; SATA 96; TUS; WP; YAW

Plato c. 428B.C.-347B.C. .... **CMLC 8, 75, 98; WLCS**
See also AW 1; CDWLB 1; DA; DA3; DAB; DAC; DAM MST; DLB 176; LAIT 1; LATS 1:1; RGWL 2, 3; WLIT 8

Platonov, Andrei
See Klimentov, Andrei Platonovich

Platonov, Andrei Platonovich
See Klimentov, Andrei Platonovich
See also DLB 272

Platonov, Andrey Platonovich
See Klimentov, Andrei Platonovich
See also EWL 3

Platt, Kin 1911- .... **CLC 26**
See also AAYA 11; CA 17-20R; CANR 11; JRDA; SAAS 17; SATA 21, 86; WYA

Plautus c. 254B.C.-c. 184B.C. .... **CMLC 24, 92; DC 6**
See also AW 1; CDWLB 1; DLB 211; RGWL 2, 3; WLIT 8

Plick et Plock
See Simenon, Georges (Jacques Christian)

Plieksans, Janis
See Rainis, Janis

Plimpton, George 1927-2003 .... **CLC 36**
See also AITN 1; AMWS 16; CA 21-24R; 224; CANR 32, 70, 103, 133; DLB 185, 241; MTCW 1, 2; MTFW 2005; SATA 10; SATA-Obit 150

Pliny the Elder c. 23-79 .... **CMLC 23**
See also DLB 211

Pliny the Younger c. 61-c. 112 ...... **CMLC 62**
See also AW 2; DLB 211

Plomer, William Charles Franklin 1903-1973 .... **CLC 4, 8**
See also AFW; BRWS 11; CA 21-22; CANR 34; CAP 2; CN 1; CP 1, 2; DLB 20, 162, 191, 225; EWL 3; MTCW 1; RGEL 2; RGSF 2; SATA 24

Plotinus 204-270 .... **CMLC 46**
See also CDWLB 1; DLB 176

Plowman, Piers
See Kavanagh, Patrick (Joseph)

Plum, J.
See Wodehouse, P(elham) G(renville)

Plumly, Stanley (Ross) 1939- .... **CLC 33**
See also CA 108; 110; CANR 97; CP 3, 4, 5, 6, 7; DLB 5, 193; INT CA-110

Plumpe, Friedrich Wilhelm
See Murnau, F.W.

Plutarch c. 46-c. 120 .... **CMLC 60**
See also AW 2; CDWLB 1; DLB 176; RGWL 2, 3; TWA; WLIT 8

Po Chu-i 772-846 .... **CMLC 24**

Podhoretz, Norman 1930- .... **CLC 189**
See also AMWS 8; CA 9-12R; CANR 7, 78, 135, 179

Poe, Edgar Allan 1809-1849 ..... **NCLC 1, 16, 55, 78, 94, 97, 117; PC 1, 54; SSC 1, 22, 34, 35, 54, 88, 111; WLC 4**
See also AAYA 14; AMW; AMWC 1; AMWR 2; BPFB 3; BYA 5, 11; CDALB 1640-1865; CMW 4; DA; DA3; DAB; DAC; DAM MST, POET; DLB 3, 59, 73, 74, 248, 254; EXPP; EXPS; GL 3; HGG; LAIT 2; LATS 1:1; LMFS 1; MSW; PAB; PFS 1, 3, 9; RGAL 4; RGSF 2; SATA 23; SCFW 1, 2; SFW 4; SSFS 2, 4, 7, 8, 16, 26; SUFW; TUS; WP; WYA

Poet of Titchfield Street, The
See Pound, Ezra (Weston Loomis)

Poggio Bracciolini, Gian Francesco 1380-1459 .... **LC 125**

Pohl, Frederik 1919- .... **CLC 18; SSC 25**
See also AAYA 24; CA 61-64, 188; CAAE 188; CAAS 1; CANR 11, 37, 81, 140; CN 1, 2, 3, 4, 5, 6; DLB 8; INT CANR-11; MTCW 1, 2; MTFW 2005; SATA 24; SCFW 1, 2; SFW 4

Poirier, Louis
See Gracq, Julien

Poitier, Sidney 1927- .... **CLC 26**
See also AAYA 60; BW 1; CA 117; CANR 94

Pokagon, Simon 1830-1899 .... **NNAL**
See also DAM MULT

Schneider, Leonard Alfred 1925-1966
   See Bruce, Lenny
   See also CA 89-92
Schnitzler, Arthur 1862-1931 ..... **DC 17; SSC 15, 61; TCLC 4**
   See also CA 104; CDWLB 2; DLB 81, 118; EW 8; EWL 3; RGSF 2; RGWL 2, 3
Schoenberg, Arnold Franz Walter 1874-1951 .... **TCLC 75**
   See also CA 109; 188
Schonberg, Arnold
   See Schoenberg, Arnold Franz Walter
Schopenhauer, Arthur 1788-1860 . **NCLC 51, 157**
   See also DLB 90; EW 5
Schor, Sandra (M.) 1932(?)-1990 ..... **CLC 65**
   See also CA 132
Schorer, Mark 1908-1977 .... **CLC 9**
   See also CA 5-8R; 73-76; CANR 7; CN 1, 2; DLB 103
Schrader, Paul (Joseph) 1946- . **CLC 26, 212**
   See also CA 37-40R; CANR 41; DLB 44
Schreber, Daniel 1842-1911 .... **TCLC 123**
Schreiner, Olive (Emilie Albertina) 1855-1920 .... **TCLC 9**
   See also AFW; BRWS 2; CA 105; 154; DLB 18, 156, 190, 225; EWL 3; FW; RGEL 2; TWA; WLIT 2; WWE 1
Schulberg, Budd 1914- .... **CLC 7, 48**
   See also BPFB 3; CA 25-28R; CANR 19, 87, 178; CN 1, 2, 3, 4, 5, 6, 7; DLB 6, 26, 28; DLBY 1981, 2001; MAL 5
Schulberg, Budd Wilson
   See Schulberg, Budd
Schulman, Arnold
   See Trumbo, Dalton
Schulz, Bruno 1892-1942 .. **SSC 13; TCLC 5, 51**
   See also CA 115; 123; CANR 86; CDWLB 4; DLB 215; EWL 3; MTCW 2; MTFW 2005; RGSF 2; RGWL 2, 3
Schulz, Charles M. 1922-2000 .... **CLC 12**
   See also AAYA 39; CA 9-12R; 187; CANR 6, 132; INT CANR-6; MTFW 2005; SATA 10; SATA-Obit 118
Schulz, Charles Monroe
   See Schulz, Charles M.
Schumacher, E(rnst) F(riedrich) 1911-1977 .... **CLC 80**
   See also CA 81-84; 73-76; CANR 34, 85
Schumann, Robert 1810-1856 ...... **NCLC 143**
Schuyler, George Samuel 1895-1977 . **HR 1:3**
   See also BW 2; CA 81-84; 73-76; CANR 42; DLB 29, 51
Schuyler, James Marcus 1923-1991 .. **CLC 5, 23; PC 88**
   See also CA 101; 134; CP 1, 2, 3, 4, 5; DAM POET; DLB 5, 169; EWL 3; INT CA-101; MAL 5; WP
Schwartz, Delmore (David) 1913-1966 . **CLC 2, 4, 10, 45, 87; PC 8; SSC 105**
   See also AMWS 2; CA 17-18; 25-28R; CANR 35; CAP 2; DLB 28, 48; EWL 3; MAL 5; MTCW 1, 2; MTFW 2005; PAB; RGAL 4; TUS
Schwartz, Ernst
   See Ozu, Yasujiro
Schwartz, John Burnham 1965- .... **CLC 59**
   See also CA 132; CANR 116
Schwartz, Lynne Sharon 1939- .... **CLC 31**
   See also CA 103; CANR 44, 89, 160; DLB 218; MTCW 2; MTFW 2005
Schwartz, Muriel A.
   See Eliot, T(homas) S(tearns)
Schwarz-Bart, Andre 1928-2006 .... **CLC 2, 4**
   See also CA 89-92; 253; CANR 109; DLB 299; RGHL

Schwarz-Bart, Simone 1938- . **BLCS; CLC 7**
   See also BW 2; CA 97-100; CANR 117; EWL 3
Schwerner, Armand 1927-1999 .... **PC 42**
   See also CA 9-12R; 179; CANR 50, 85; CP 2, 3, 4, 5, 6; DLB 165
Schwitters, Kurt (Hermann Edward Karl Julius) 1887-1948 .... **TCLC 95**
   See also CA 158
Schwob, Marcel (Mayer Andre) 1867-1905 .... **TCLC 20**
   See also CA 117; 168; DLB 123; GFL 1789 to the Present
Sciascia, Leonardo 1921-1989 .. **CLC 8, 9, 41**
   See also CA 85-88; 130; CANR 35; DLB 177; EWL 3; MTCW 1; RGWL 2, 3
Scoppettone, Sandra 1936- .... **CLC 26**
   See Early, Jack
   See also AAYA 11, 65; BYA 8; CA 5-8R; CANR 41, 73, 157; GLL 1; MAICYA 2; MAICYAS 1; SATA 9, 92; WYA; YAW
Scorsese, Martin 1942- .... **CLC 20, 89, 207**
   See also AAYA 38; CA 110; 114; CANR 46, 85
Scotland, Jay
   See Jakes, John
Scott, Duncan Campbell 1862-1947 .... **TCLC 6**
   See also CA 104; 153; DAC; DLB 92; RGEL 2
Scott, Evelyn 1893-1963 .... **CLC 43**
   See also CA 104; 112; CANR 64; DLB 9, 48; RHW
Scott, F(rancis) R(eginald) 1899-1985 .... **CLC 22**
   See also CA 101; 114; CANR 87; CP 1, 2, 3, 4; DLB 88; INT CA-101; RGEL 2
Scott, Frank
   See Scott, F(rancis) R(eginald)
Scott, Joan .... **CLC 65**
Scott, Joanna 1960- .... **CLC 50**
   See also AMWS 17; CA 126; CANR 53, 92, 168
Scott, Joanna Jeanne
   See Scott, Joanna
Scott, Paul (Mark) 1920-1978 ...... **CLC 9, 60**
   See also BRWS 1; CA 81-84; 77-80; CANR 33; CN 1, 2; DLB 14, 207, 326; EWL 3; MTCW 1; RGEL 2; RHW; WWE 1
Scott, Ridley 1937- .... **CLC 183**
   See also AAYA 13, 43
Scott, Sarah 1723-1795 .... **LC 44**
   See also DLB 39
Scott, Sir Walter 1771-1832 .... **NCLC 15, 69, 110; PC 13; SSC 32; WLC 5**
   See also AAYA 22; BRW 4; BYA 2; CD-BLB 1789-1832; DA; DAB; DAC; DAM MST, NOV, POET; DLB 93, 107, 116, 144, 159; GL 3; HGG; LAIT 1; RGEL 2; RGSF 2; SSFS 10; SUFW 1; TEA; WLIT 3; YABC 2
Scribe, (Augustin) Eugene 1791-1861 . **DC 5; NCLC 16**
   See also DAM DRAM; DLB 192; GFL 1789 to the Present; RGWL 2, 3
Scrum, R.
   See Crumb, R.
Scudery, Georges de 1601-1667 .... **LC 75**
   See also GFL Beginnings to 1789
Scudery, Madeleine de 1607-1701 .. **LC 2, 58**
   See also DLB 268; GFL Beginnings to 1789
Scum
   See Crumb, R.
Scumbag, Little Bobby
   See Crumb, R.
Seabrook, John
   See Hubbard, L. Ron

Seacole, Mary Jane Grant 1805-1881 .... **NCLC 147**
   See also DLB 166
Sealy, I(rwin) Allan 1951- .... **CLC 55**
   See also CA 136; CN 6, 7
Search, Alexander
   See Pessoa, Fernando (Antonio Nogueira)
Sebald, W(infried) G(eorg) 1944-2001 .... **CLC 194**
   See also BRWS 8; CA 159; 202; CANR 98; MTFW 2005; RGHL
Sebastian, Lee
   See Silverberg, Robert
Sebastian Owl
   See Thompson, Hunter S.
Sebestyen, Igen
   See Sebestyen, Ouida
Sebestyen, Ouida 1924- .... **CLC 30**
   See also AAYA 8; BYA 7; CA 107; CANR 40, 114; CLR 17; JRDA; MAICYA 1, 2; SAAS 10; SATA 39, 140; WYA; YAW
Sebold, Alice 1963(?)- .... **CLC 193**
   See also AAYA 56; CA 203; MTFW 2005
Second Duke of Buckingham
   See Villiers, George
Secundus, H. Scriblerus
   See Fielding, Henry
Sedges, John
   See Buck, Pearl S(ydenstricker)
Sedgwick, Catharine Maria 1789-1867 .... **NCLC 19, 98**
   See also DLB 1, 74, 183, 239, 243, 254; FL 1:3; RGAL 4
Sedulius Scottus 9th cent. -c. 874 .. **CMLC 86**
Seebohm, Victoria
   See Glendinning, Victoria
Seelye, John (Douglas) 1931- .... **CLC 7**
   See also CA 97-100; CANR 70; INT CA-97-100; TCWW 1, 2
Seferiades, Giorgos Stylianou 1900-1971
   See Seferis, George
   See also CA 5-8R; 33-36R; CANR 5, 36; MTCW 1
Seferis, George .... **CLC 5, 11; PC 66**
   See Seferiades, Giorgos Stylianou
   See also DLB 332; EW 12; EWL 3; RGWL 2, 3
Segal, Erich (Wolf) 1937- .... **CLC 3, 10**
   See also BEST 89:1; BPFB 3; CA 25-28R; CANR 20, 36, 65, 113; CPW; DAM POP; DLBY 1986; INT CANR-20; MTCW 1
Seger, Bob 1945- .... **CLC 35**
Seghers, Anna .... **CLC 7**
   See Radvanyi, Netty
   See also CDWLB 2; DLB 69; EWL 3
Seidel, Frederick 1936- .... **CLC 18**
   See also CA 13-16R; CANR 8, 99, 180; CP 1, 2, 3, 4, 5, 6, 7; DLBY 1984
Seidel, Frederick Lewis
   See Seidel, Frederick
Seifert, Jaroslav 1901-1986 . **CLC 34, 44, 93; PC 47**
   See also CA 127; CDWLB 4; DLB 215, 332; EWL 3; MTCW 1, 2
Sei Shonagon c. 966-1017(?) ..... **CMLC 6, 89**
Sejour, Victor 1817-1874 .... **DC 10**
   See also DLB 50
Sejour Marcou et Ferrand, Juan Victor
   See Sejour, Victor
Selby, Hubert, Jr. 1928-2004 ..... **CLC 1, 2, 4, 8; SSC 20**
   See also CA 13-16R; 226; CANR 33, 85; CN 1, 2, 3, 4, 5, 6, 7; DLB 2, 227; MAL 5
Selzer, Richard 1928- .... **CLC 74**
   See also CA 65-68; CANR 14, 106
Sembene, Ousmane
   See Ousmane, Sembene

Summers, (Alphonsus Joseph-Mary Augustus) Montague
1880-1948 .... **TCLC 16**
See also CA 118; 163

Sumner, Gordon Matthew .... **CLC 26**
See Police, The; Sting

Sun Tzu c. 400B.C.-c. 320B.C. ...... **CMLC 56**

Surrey, Henry Howard 1517-1574 ... **LC 121; PC 59**
See also BRW 1; RGEL 2

Surtees, Robert Smith 1805-1864 .. **NCLC 14**
See also DLB 21; RGEL 2

Susann, Jacqueline 1921-1974 .... **CLC 3**
See also AITN 1; BPFB 3; CA 65-68; 53-56; MTCW 1, 2

Su Shi
See Su Shih
See also RGWL 2, 3

Su Shih 1036-1101 .... **CMLC 15**
See Su Shi

Suskind, Patrick .... **CLC 182**
See Sueskind, Patrick
See also BPFB 3; CA 145; CWW 2

Suso, Heinrich c. 1295-1366 .... **CMLC 87**

Sutcliff, Rosemary 1920-1992 .... **CLC 26**
See also AAYA 10; BYA 1, 4; CA 5-8R; 139; CANR 37; CLR 1, 37, 138; CPW; DAB; DAC; DAM MST, POP; JRDA; LATS 1:1; MAICYA 1, 2; MAICYAS 1; RHW; SATA 6, 44, 78; SATA-Obit 73; WYA; YAW

Sutherland, Efua (Theodora Morgue)
1924-1996 .... **BLC 2:3**
See also AFW; BW 1; CA 105; CWD; DLB 117; EWL 3; IDTP; SATA 25

Sutro, Alfred 1863-1933 .... **TCLC 6**
See also CA 105; 185; DLB 10; RGEL 2

Sutton, Henry
See Slavitt, David R.

Suzuki, D. T.
See Suzuki, Daisetz Teitaro

Suzuki, Daisetz T.
See Suzuki, Daisetz Teitaro

Suzuki, Daisetz Teitaro
1870-1966 .... **TCLC 109**
See also CA 121; 111; MTCW 1, 2; MTFW 2005

Suzuki, Teitaro
See Suzuki, Daisetz Teitaro

Svevo, Italo .... **SSC 25; TCLC 2, 35**
See Schmitz, Aron Hector
See also DLB 264; EW 8; EWL 3; RGWL 2, 3; WLIT 7

Swados, Elizabeth 1951- .... **CLC 12**
See also CA 97-100; CANR 49, 163; INT CA-97-100

Swados, Elizabeth A.
See Swados, Elizabeth

Swados, Harvey 1920-1972 .... **CLC 5**
See also CA 5-8R; 37-40R; CANR 6; CN 1; DLB 2, 335; MAL 5

Swados, Liz
See Swados, Elizabeth

Swan, Gladys 1934- .... **CLC 69**
See also CA 101; CANR 17, 39; TCLE 1:2

Swanson, Logan
See Matheson, Richard

Swarthout, Glendon (Fred)
1918-1992 .... **CLC 35**
See also AAYA 55; CA 1-4R; 139; CANR 1, 47; CN 1, 2, 3, 4, 5; LAIT 5; SATA 26; TCWW 1, 2; YAW

Swedenborg, Emanuel 1688-1772 ..... **LC 105**

Sweet, Sarah C.
See Jewett, (Theodora) Sarah Orne

Swenson, May 1919-1989 ...... **CLC 4, 14, 61, 106; PC 14**
See also AMWS 4; CA 5-8R; 130; CANR 36, 61, 131; CP 1, 2, 3, 4; DA; DAB; DAC; DAM MST, POET; DLB 5; EXPP; GLL 2; MAL 5; MTCW 1, 2; MTFW 2005; PFS 16; SATA 15; WP

Swift, Augustus
See Lovecraft, H. P.

Swift, Graham 1949- .... **CLC 41, 88, 233**
See also BRWC 2; BRWS 5; CA 117; 122; CANR 46, 71, 128; CN 4, 5, 6, 7; DLB 194, 326; MTCW 2; MTFW 2005; NFS 18; RGSF 2

Swift, Jonathan 1667-1745 ..... **LC 1, 42, 101; PC 9; WLC 6**
See also AAYA 41; BRW 3; BRWC 1; BRWR 1; BYA 5, 14; CDBLB 1660-1789; CLR 53; DA; DA3; DAB; DAC; DAM MST, NOV, POET; DLB 39, 95, 101; EXPN; LAIT 1; NFS 6; PFS 27; RGEL 2; SATA 19; TEA; WCH; WLIT 3

Swinburne, Algernon Charles
1837-1909 ... **PC 24; TCLC 8, 36; WLC 6**
See also BRW 5; CA 105; 140; CDBLB 1832-1890; DA; DA3; DAB; DAC; DAM MST, POET; DLB 35, 57; PAB; RGEL 2; TEA

Swinfen, Ann .... **CLC 34**
See also CA 202

Swinnerton, Frank (Arthur)
1884-1982 .... **CLC 31**
See also CA 202; 108; CN 1, 2, 3; DLB 34

Swinnerton, Frank Arthur
1884-1982 .... **CLC 31**
See also CA 108; DLB 34

Swithen, John
See King, Stephen

Sylvia
See Ashton-Warner, Sylvia (Constance)

Symmes, Robert Edward
See Duncan, Robert

Symonds, John Addington
1840-1893 .... **NCLC 34**
See also DLB 57, 144

Symons, Arthur 1865-1945 .... **TCLC 11**
See also CA 107; 189; DLB 19, 57, 149; RGEL 2

Symons, Julian (Gustave)
1912-1994 .... **CLC 2, 14, 32**
See also CA 49-52; 147; CAAS 3; CANR 3, 33, 59; CMW 4; CN 1, 2, 3, 4, 5; CP 1, 3, 4; DLB 87, 155; DLBY 1992; MSW; MTCW 1

Synge, (Edmund) J(ohn) M(illington)
1871-1909 .... **DC 2; TCLC 6, 37**
See also BRW 6; BRWR 1; CA 104; 141; CDBLB 1890-1914; DAM DRAM; DFS 18; DLB 10, 19; EWL 3; RGEL 2; TEA; WLIT 4

Syruc, J.
See Milosz, Czeslaw

Szirtes, George 1948- .... **CLC 46; PC 51**
See also CA 109; CANR 27, 61, 117; CP 4, 5, 6, 7

Szymborska, Wislawa 1923- ... **CLC 99, 190; PC 44**
See also AAYA 76; CA 154; CANR 91, 133; CDWLB 4; CWP; CWW 2; DA3; DLB 232, 332; DLBY 1996; EWL 3; MTCW 2; MTFW 2005; PFS 15, 27; RGHL; RGWL 3

T. O., Nik
See Annensky, Innokenty (Fyodorovich)

Tabori, George 1914-2007 .... **CLC 19**
See also CA 49-52; 262; CANR 4, 69; CBD; CD 5, 6; DLB 245; RGHL

Tacitus c. 55-c. 117 .... **CMLC 56**
See also AW 2; CDWLB 1; DLB 211; RGWL 2, 3; WLIT 8

Tadjo, Veronique 1955- .... **BLC 2:3**
See also EWL 3

Tagore, Rabindranath 1861-1941 .... **PC 8; SSC 48; TCLC 3, 53**
See also CA 104; 120; DA3; DAM DRAM, POET; DLB 323, 332; EWL 3; MTCW 1, 2; MTFW 2005; PFS 18; RGEL 2; RGSF 2; RGWL 2, 3; TWA

Taine, Hippolyte Adolphe
1828-1893 .... **NCLC 15**
See also EW 7; GFL 1789 to the Present

Talayesva, Don C. 1890-(?) .... **NNAL**

Talese, Gay 1932- .... **CLC 37, 232**
See also AITN 1; AMWS 17; CA 1-4R; CANR 9, 58, 137, 177; DLB 185; INT CANR-9; MTCW 1, 2; MTFW 2005

Tallent, Elizabeth 1954- .... **CLC 45**
See also CA 117; CANR 72; DLB 130

Tallmountain, Mary 1918-1997 .... **NNAL**
See also CA 146; 161; DLB 193

Tally, Ted 1952- .... **CLC 42**
See also CA 120; 124; CAD; CANR 125; CD 5, 6; INT CA-124

Talvik, Heiti 1904-1947 .... **TCLC 87**
See also EWL 3

Tamayo y Baus, Manuel
1829-1898 .... **NCLC 1**

Tammsaare, A(nton) H(ansen)
1878-1940 .... **TCLC 27**
See also CA 164; CDWLB 4; DLB 220; EWL 3

Tam'si, Tchicaya U
See Tchicaya, Gerald Felix

Tan, Amy 1952- ..... **AAL; CLC 59, 120, 151, 257**
See also AAYA 9, 48; AMWS 10; BEST 89:3; BPFB 3; CA 136; CANR 54, 105, 132; CDALBS; CN 5, 6, 7; CPW 1; DA3; DAM MULT, NOV, POP; DLB 173, 312; EXPN; FL 1:6; FW; LAIT 3, 5; MAL 5; MTCW 2; MTFW 2005; NFS 1, 13, 16; RGAL 4; SATA 75; SSFS 9; YAW

Tandem, Carl Felix
See Spitteler, Carl

Tandem, Felix
See Spitteler, Carl

Tanizaki, Jun'ichiro 1886-1965 ... **CLC 8, 14, 28; SSC 21**
See Tanizaki Jun'ichiro
See also CA 93-96; 25-28R; MJW; MTCW 2; MTFW 2005; RGSF 2; RGWL 2

Tanizaki Jun'ichiro
See Tanizaki, Jun'ichiro
See also DLB 180; EWL 3

Tannen, Deborah 1945- .... **CLC 206**
See also CA 118; CANR 95

Tannen, Deborah Frances
See Tannen, Deborah

Tanner, William
See Amis, Kingsley

Tante, Dilly
See Kunitz, Stanley

Tao Lao
See Storni, Alfonsina

Tapahonso, Luci 1953- .... **NNAL; PC 65**
See also CA 145; CANR 72, 127; DLB 175

Tarantino, Quentin (Jerome)
1963- .... **CLC 125, 230**
See also AAYA 58; CA 171; CANR 125

Tarassoff, Lev
See Troyat, Henri

Tarbell, Ida M(inerva) 1857-1944 . **TCLC 40**
See also CA 122; 181; DLB 47

Tardieu d'Esclavelles, Louise-Florence-Petronille
See Epinay, Louise d'

Author Index

Tsushima, Shuji 1909-1948
See Dazai Osamu
See also CA 107

Tsvetaeva (Efron), Marina (Ivanovna)
1892-1941 .... **PC 14; TCLC 7, 35**
See also CA 104; 128; CANR 73; DLB 295;
EW 11; MTCW 1, 2; RGWL 2, 3

Tuck, Lily 1938- .... **CLC 70**
See also AAYA 74; CA 139; CANR 90

Tuckerman, Frederick Goddard
1821-1873 .... **PC 85**
See also DLB 243; RGAL 4

Tu Fu 712-770 .... **PC 9**
See Du Fu
See also DAM MULT; TWA; WP

Tunis, John R(oberts) 1889-1975 ..... **CLC 12**
See also BYA 1; CA 61-64; CANR 62; DLB
22, 171; JRDA; MAICYA 1, 2; SATA 37;
SATA-Brief 30; YAW

Tuohy, Frank .... **CLC 37**
See Tuohy, John Francis
See also CN 1, 2, 3, 4, 5, 6, 7; DLB 14,
139

Tuohy, John Francis 1925-
See Tuohy, Frank
See also CA 5-8R; 178; CANR 3, 47

Turco, Lewis (Putnam) 1934- .... **CLC 11, 63**
See also CA 13-16R; CAAS 22; CANR 24,
51; CP 1, 2, 3, 4, 5, 6, 7; DLBY 1984;
TCLE 1:2

Turgenev, Ivan (Sergeevich)
1818-1883 ..... **DC 7; NCLC 21, 37, 122;
SSC 7, 57; WLC 6**
See also AAYA 58; DA; DAB; DAC; DAM
MST, NOV; DFS 6; DLB 238, 284; EW
6; LATS 1:1; NFS 16; RGSF 2; RGWL 2,
3; TWA

Turgot, Anne-Robert-Jacques
1727-1781 .... **LC 26**
See also DLB 314

Turner, Frederick 1943- .... **CLC 48**
See also CA 73-76, 227; CAAE 227; CAAS
10; CANR 12, 30, 56; DLB 40, 282

Turton, James
See Crace, Jim

Tutu, Desmond M(pilo) 1931- .... **BLC 1:3;
CLC 80**
See also BW 1, 3; CA 125; CANR 67, 81;
DAM MULT

Tutuola, Amos 1920-1997 .... **BLC 1:3, 2:3;
CLC 5, 14, 29; TCLC 188**
See also AAYA 76; AFW; BW 2, 3; CA
9-12R; 159; CANR 27, 66; CDWLB 3;
CN 1, 2, 3, 4, 5, 6; DA3; DAM MULT;
DLB 125; DNFS 2; EWL 3; MTCW 1, 2;
MTFW 2005; RGEL 2; WLIT 2

Twain, Mark .... **SSC 6, 26, 34, 87; TCLC 6,
12, 19, 36, 48, 59, 161, 185; WLC 6**
See Clemens, Samuel Langhorne
See also AAYA 20; AMW; AMWC 1; BPFB
3; BYA 2, 3, 11, 14; CLR 58, 60, 66; DLB
11, 343; EXPN; EXPS; FANT; LAIT 2;
MAL 5; NCFS 4; NFS 1, 6; RGAL 4;
RGSF 2; SFW 4; SSFS 1, 7, 16, 21;
SUFW; TUS; WCH; WYA; YAW

Tyler, Anne 1941- . **CLC 7, 11, 18, 28, 44, 59,
103, 205**
See also AAYA 18, 60; AMWS 4; BEST
89:1; BPFB 3; BYA 12; CA 9-12R; CANR
11, 33, 53, 109, 132, 168; CDALBS; CN
1, 2, 3, 4, 5, 6, 7; CPW; CSW; DAM
NOV, POP; DLB 6, 143; DLBY 1982;
EWL 3; EXPN; LATS 1:2; MAL 5; MBL;
MTCW 1, 2; MTFW 2005; NFS 2, 7, 10;
RGAL 4; SATA 7, 90, 173; SSFS 17;
TCLE 1:2; TUS; YAW

Tyler, Royall 1757-1826 .... **NCLC 3**
See also DLB 37; RGAL 4

Tynan, Katharine 1861-1931 .... **TCLC 3**
See also CA 104; 167; DLB 153, 240; FW

Tyndale, William c. 1484-1536 .... **LC 103**
See also DLB 132

Tyutchev, Fyodor 1803-1873 .... **NCLC 34**

Tzara, Tristan 1896-1963 .... **CLC 47; PC 27;
TCLC 168**
See also CA 153; 89-92; DAM POET; EWL
3; MTCW 2

Uc de Saint Circ c. 1190B.C.-13th cent.
B.C. .... **CMLC 102**

Uchida, Yoshiko 1921-1992 .... **AAL**
See also AAYA 16; BYA 2, 3; CA 13-16R;
139; CANR 6, 22, 47, 61; CDALBS; CLR
6, 56; CWRI 5; DLB 312; JRDA; MAI-
CYA 1, 2; MTCW 1, 2; MTFW 2005;
NFS 26; SAAS 1; SATA 1, 53; SATA-Obit
72

Udall, Nicholas 1504-1556 .... **LC 84**
See also DLB 62; RGEL 2

Ueda Akinari 1734-1809 .... **NCLC 131**

Uhry, Alfred 1936- .... **CLC 55; DC 28**
See also CA 127; 133; CAD; CANR 112;
CD 5, 6; CSW; DA3; DAM DRAM, POP;
DFS 11, 15; INT CA-133; MTFW 2005

Ulf, Haervd
See Strindberg, (Johan) August

Ulf, Harved
See Strindberg, (Johan) August

Ulibarri, Sabine R(eyes)
1919-2003 .... **CLC 83; HLCS 2**
See also CA 131; 214; CANR 81; DAM
MULT; DLB 82; HW 1, 2; RGSF 2

Unamuno (y Jugo), Miguel de
1864-1936 .. **HLC 2; SSC 11, 69; TCLC
2, 9, 148**
See also CA 104; 131; CANR 81; DAM
MULT, NOV; DLB 108, 322; EW 8; EWL
3; HW 1, 2; MTCW 1, 2; MTFW 2005;
RGSF 2; RGWL 2, 3; SSFS 20; TWA

Uncle Shelby
See Silverstein, Shel

Undercliffe, Errol
See Campbell, Ramsey

Underwood, Miles
See Glassco, John

Undset, Sigrid 1882-1949 .... **TCLC 3, 197;
WLC 6**
See also AAYA 77; CA 104; 129; DA; DA3;
DAB; DAC; DAM MST, NOV; DLB 293,
332; EW 9; EWL 3; FW; MTCW 1, 2;
MTFW 2005; RGWL 2, 3

Ungaretti, Giuseppe 1888-1970 ... **CLC 7, 11,
15; PC 57; TCLC 200**
See also CA 19-20; 25-28R; CAP 2; DLB
114; EW 10; EWL 3; PFS 20; RGWL 2,
3; WLIT 7

Unger, Douglas 1952- .... **CLC 34**
See also CA 130; CANR 94, 155

Unsworth, Barry 1930- .... **CLC 76, 127**
See also BRWS 7; CA 25-28R; CANR 30,
54, 125, 171; CN 6, 7; DLB 194, 326

Unsworth, Barry Forster
See Unsworth, Barry

Updike, John 1932- . **CLC 1, 2, 3, 5, 7, 9, 13,
15, 23, 34, 43, 70, 139, 214; PC 90;
SSC 13, 27, 103; WLC 6**
See also AAYA 36; AMW; AMWC 1;
AMWR 1; BPFB 3; BYA 12; CA 1-4R;
CABS 1; CANR 4, 33, 51, 94, 133;
CDALB 1968-1988; CN 1, 2, 3, 4, 5, 6,
7; CP 1, 2, 3, 4, 5, 6, 7; CPW 1; DA;
DA3; DAB; DAC; DAM MST, NOV,
POET, POP; DLB 2, 5, 143, 218, 227;
DLBD 3; DLBY 1980, 1982, 1997; EWL
3; EXPP; HGG; MAL 5; MTCW 1, 2;
MTFW 2005; NFS 12, 24; RGAL 4;
RGSF 2; SSFS 3, 19; TUS

Updike, John Hoyer
See Updike, John

Upshaw, Margaret Mitchell
See Mitchell, Margaret (Munnerlyn)

Upton, Mark
See Sanders, Lawrence

Upward, Allen 1863-1926 .... **TCLC 85**
See also CA 117; 187; DLB 36

Urdang, Constance (Henriette)
1922-1996 .... **CLC 47**
See also CA 21-24R; CANR 9, 24; CP 1, 2,
3, 4, 5, 6; CWP

Urfe, Honore d' 1567(?)-1625 .... **LC 132**
See also DLB 268; GFL Beginnings to
1789; RGWL 2, 3

Uriel, Henry
See Faust, Frederick (Schiller)

Uris, Leon 1924-2003 .... **CLC 7, 32**
See also AITN 1, 2; BEST 89:2; BPFB 3;
CA 1-4R; 217; CANR 1, 40, 65, 123; CN
1, 2, 3, 4, 5, 6; CPW 1; DA3; DAM NOV,
POP; MTCW 1, 2; MTFW 2005; RGHL;
SATA 49; SATA-Obit 146

Urista (Heredia), Alberto (Baltazar)
1947- .... **HLCS 1**
See Alurista
See also CA 182; CANR 2, 32; HW 1

Urmuz
See Codrescu, Andrei

Urquhart, Guy
See McAlmon, Robert (Menzies)

Urquhart, Jane 1949- .... **CLC 90, 242**
See also CA 113; CANR 32, 68, 116, 157;
CCA 1; DAC; DLB 334

Usigli, Rodolfo 1905-1979 .... **HLCS 1**
See also CA 131; DLB 305; EWL 3; HW 1;
LAW

Usk, Thomas (?)-1388 .... **CMLC 76**
See also DLB 146

Ustinov, Peter (Alexander)
1921-2004 .... **CLC 1**
See also AITN 1; CA 13-16R; 225; CANR
25, 51; CBD; CD 5, 6; DLB 13; MTCW
2

U Tam'si, Gerald Felix Tchicaya
See Tchicaya, Gerald Felix

U Tam'si, Tchicaya
See Tchicaya, Gerald Felix

Vachss, Andrew 1942- .... **CLC 106**
See also CA 118, 214; CAAE 214; CANR
44, 95, 153; CMW 4

Vachss, Andrew H.
See Vachss, Andrew

Vachss, Andrew Henry
See Vachss, Andrew

Vaculik, Ludvik 1926- .... **CLC 7**
See also CA 53-56; CANR 72; CWW 2;
DLB 232; EWL 3

Vaihinger, Hans 1852-1933 .... **TCLC 71**
See also CA 116; 166

Valdez, Luis (Miguel) 1940- ..... **CLC 84; DC
10; HLC 2**
See also CA 101; CAD; CANR 32, 81; CD
5, 6; DAM MULT; DFS 5; DLB 122;
EWL 3; HW 1; LAIT 4; LLW

Valenzuela, Luisa 1938- .... **CLC 31, 104;
HLCS 2; SSC 14, 82**
See also CA 101; CANR 32, 65, 123; CD-
WLB 3; CWW 2; DAM MULT; DLB 113;
EWL 3; FW; HW 1, 2; LAW; RGSF 2;
RGWL 3

Valera y Alcala-Galiano, Juan
1824-1905 .... **TCLC 10**
See also CA 106

Valerius Maximus .... **CMLC 64**
See also DLB 211

Valery, (Ambroise) Paul (Toussaint Jules)
1871-1945 .... **PC 9; TCLC 4, 15**
See also CA 104; 122; DA3; DAM POET;
DLB 258; EW 8; EWL 3; GFL 1789 to
the Present; MTCW 1, 2; MTFW 2005;
RGWL 2, 3; TWA

Valle-Inclan, Ramon (Maria) del
1866-1936 .... **HLC 2; TCLC 5**
See del Valle-Inclan, Ramon (Maria)
See also CA 106; 153; CANR 80; DAM
MULT; DLB 134; EW 8; EWL 3; HW 2;
RGSF 2; RGWL 2, 3

Vallejo, Antonio Buero
See Buero Vallejo, Antonio

Vallejo, Cesar (Abraham)
1892-1938 .... **HLC 2; TCLC 3, 56**
See also CA 105; 153; DAM MULT; DLB
290; EWL 3; HW 1; LAW; PFS 26;
RGWL 2, 3

Valles, Jules 1832-1885 .... **NCLC 71**
See also DLB 123; GFL 1789 to the Present

Vallette, Marguerite Eymery
1860-1953 .... **TCLC 67**
See Rachilde
See also CA 182; DLB 123, 192

Valle Y Pena, Ramon del
See Valle-Inclan, Ramon (Maria) del

Van Ash, Cay 1918-1994 .... **CLC 34**
See also CA 220

Vanbrugh, Sir John 1664-1726 .... **LC 21**
See also BRW 2; DAM DRAM; DLB 80;
IDTP; RGEL 2

Van Campen, Karl
See Campbell, John W(ood, Jr.)

Vance, Gerald
See Silverberg, Robert

Vance, Jack 1916-
See Queen, Ellery; Vance, John Holbrook
See also CA 29-32R; CANR 17, 65, 154;
CMW 4; MTCW 1

Vance, John Holbrook .... **CLC 35**
See Vance, Jack
See also DLB 8; FANT; SCFW 1, 2; SFW
4; SUFW 1, 2

Van Den Bogarde, Derek Jules Gaspard
Ulric Niven 1921-1999 .... **CLC 14**
See Bogarde, Dirk
See also CA 77-80; 179

Vandenburgh, Jane .... **CLC 59**
See also CA 168

Vanderhaeghe, Guy 1951- .... **CLC 41**
See also BPFB 3; CA 113; CANR 72, 145;
CN 7; DLB 334

van der Post, Laurens (Jan)
1906-1996 .... **CLC 5**
See also AFW; CA 5-8R; 155; CANR 35;
CN 1, 2, 3, 4, 5, 6; DLB 204; RGEL 2

van de Wetering, Janwillem
1931-2008 .... **CLC 47**
See also CA 49-52; CANR 4, 62, 90; CMW
4

Van Dine, S. S. .... **TCLC 23**
See Wright, Willard Huntington
See also DLB 306; MSW

Van Doren, Carl (Clinton)
1885-1950 .... **TCLC 18**
See also CA 111; 168

Van Doren, Mark 1894-1972 .... **CLC 6, 10**
See also CA 1-4R; 37-40R; CANR 3; CN
1; CP 1; DLB 45, 284, 335; MAL 5;
MTCW 1, 2; RGAL 4

Van Druten, John (William)
1901-1957 .... **TCLC 2**
See also CA 104; 161; DLB 10; MAL 5;
RGAL 4

Van Duyn, Mona 1921-2004 .... **CLC 3, 7, 63,
116**
See also CA 9-12R; 234; CANR 7, 38, 60,
116; CP 1, 2, 3, 4, 5, 6, 7; CWP; DAM
POET; DLB 5; MAL 5; MTFW 2005;
PFS 20

Van Dyne, Edith
See Baum, L(yman) Frank

van Herk, Aritha 1954- .... **CLC 249**
See also CA 101; CANR 94; DLB 334

van Itallie, Jean-Claude 1936- .... **CLC 3**
See also CA 45-48; CAAS 2; CAD; CANR
1, 48; CD 5, 6; DLB 7

Van Loot, Cornelius Obenchain
See Roberts, Kenneth (Lewis)

van Ostaijen, Paul 1896-1928 .... **TCLC 33**
See also CA 163

Van Peebles, Melvin 1932- .... **CLC 2, 20**
See also BW 2, 3; CA 85-88; CANR 27,
67, 82; DAM MULT

van Schendel, Arthur(-Francois-Emile)
1874-1946 .... **TCLC 56**
See also EWL 3

Vansittart, Peter 1920- .... **CLC 42**
See also CA 1-4R; CANR 3, 49, 90; CN 4,
5, 6, 7; RHW

Van Vechten, Carl 1880-1964 ... **CLC 33; HR
1:3**
See also AMWS 2; CA 183; 89-92; DLB 4,
9, 51; RGAL 4

van Vogt, A(lfred) E(lton) 1912-2000 . **CLC 1**
See also BPFB 3; BYA 13, 14; CA 21-24R;
190; CANR 28; DLB 8, 251; SATA 14;
SATA-Obit 124; SCFW 1, 2; SFW 4

Vara, Madeleine
See Jackson, Laura (Riding)

Varda, Agnes 1928- .... **CLC 16**
See also CA 116; 122

Vargas Llosa, Jorge Mario Pedro
See Vargas Llosa, Mario

Vargas Llosa, Mario 1936- .. **CLC 3, 6, 9, 10,
15, 31, 42, 85, 181; HLC 2**
See Llosa, Jorge Mario Pedro Vargas
See also BPFB 3; CA 73-76; CANR 18, 32,
42, 67, 116, 140, 173; CDWLB 3; CWW
2; DA; DA3; DAB; DAC; DAM MST,
MULT, NOV; DLB 145; DNFS 2; EWL
3; HW 1, 2; LAIT 5; LATS 1:2; LAW;
LAWS 1; MTCW 1, 2; MTFW 2005;
RGWL 2; SSFS 14; TWA; WLIT 1

Varnhagen von Ense, Rahel
1771-1833 .... **NCLC 130**
See also DLB 90

Vasari, Giorgio 1511-1574 .... **LC 114**

Vasilikos, Vasiles
See Vassilikos, Vassilis

Vasiliu, George
See Bacovia, George

Vasiliu, Gheorghe
See Bacovia, George
See also CA 123; 189

Vassa, Gustavus
See Equiano, Olaudah

Vassilikos, Vassilis 1933- .... **CLC 4, 8**
See also CA 81-84; CANR 75, 149; EWL 3

Vaughan, Henry 1621-1695 .... **LC 27; PC 81**
See also BRW 2; DLB 131; PAB; RGEL 2

Vaughn, Stephanie .... **CLC 62**

Vazov, Ivan (Minchov) 1850-1921 . **TCLC 25**
See also CA 121; 167; CDWLB 4; DLB
147

Veblen, Thorstein B(unde)
1857-1929 .... **TCLC 31**
See also AMWS 1; CA 115; 165; DLB 246;
MAL 5

Vega, Lope de 1562-1635 ... **HLCS 2; LC 23,
119**
See also EW 2; RGWL 2, 3

Veldeke, Heinrich von c. 1145-c.
1190 .... **CMLC 85**

Vendler, Helen (Hennessy) 1933- ... **CLC 138**
See also CA 41-44R; CANR 25, 72, 136;
MTCW 1, 2; MTFW 2005

Venison, Alfred
See Pound, Ezra (Weston Loomis)

Ventsel, Elena Sergeevna 1907-2002
See Grekova, I.
See also CA 154

Verdi, Marie de
See Mencken, H(enry) L(ouis)

Verdu, Matilde
See Cela, Camilo Jose

Verga, Giovanni (Carmelo)
1840-1922 .... **SSC 21, 87; TCLC 3**
See also CA 104; 123; CANR 101; EW 7;
EWL 3; RGSF 2; RGWL 2, 3; WLIT 7

Vergil 70B.C.-19B.C. .. **CMLC 9, 40, 101; PC
12; WLCS**
See Virgil
See also AW 2; DA; DA3; DAB; DAC;
DAM MST, POET; EFS 1; LMFS 1

Vergil, Polydore c. 1470-1555 .... **LC 108**
See also DLB 132

Verhaeren, Emile (Adolphe Gustave)
1855-1916 .... **TCLC 12**
See also CA 109; EWL 3; GFL 1789 to the
Present

Verlaine, Paul (Marie) 1844-1896 .. **NCLC 2,
51; PC 2, 32**
See also DAM POET; DLB 217; EW 7;
GFL 1789 to the Present; LMFS 2; RGWL
2, 3; TWA

Verne, Jules (Gabriel) 1828-1905 ... **TCLC 6,
52**
See also AAYA 16; BYA 4; CA 110; 131;
CLR 88; DA3; DLB 123; GFL 1789 to
the Present; JRDA; LAIT 2; LMFS 2;
MAICYA 1, 2; MTFW 2005; RGWL 2, 3;
SATA 21; SCFW 1, 2; SFW 4; TWA;
WCH

Verus, Marcus Annius
See Aurelius, Marcus

Very, Jones 1813-1880 .... **NCLC 9; PC 86**
See also DLB 1, 243; RGAL 4

Vesaas, Tarjei 1897-1970 .... **CLC 48**
See also CA 190; 29-32R; DLB 297; EW
11; EWL 3; RGWL 3

Vialis, Gaston
See Simenon, Georges (Jacques Christian)

Vian, Boris 1920-1959(?) .... **TCLC 9**
See also CA 106; 164; CANR 111; DLB
72, 321; EWL 3; GFL 1789 to the Present;
MTCW 2; RGWL 2, 3

Viaud, (Louis Marie) Julien 1850-1923
See Loti, Pierre
See also CA 107

Vicar, Henry
See Felsen, Henry Gregor

Vicente, Gil 1465-c. 1536 .... **LC 99**
See also DLB 318; IDTP; RGWL 2, 3

Vicker, Angus
See Felsen, Henry Gregor

Vico, Giambattista .... **LC 138**
See Vico, Giovanni Battista
See also WLIT 7

Vico, Giovanni Battista 1668-1744
See Vico, Giambattista
See also EW 3

Vidal, Eugene Luther Gore
See Vidal, Gore

Vidal, Gore 1925- ...... **CLC 2, 4, 6, 8, 10, 22,
33, 72, 142**
See also AAYA 64; AITN 1; AMWS 4;
BEST 90:2; BPFB 3; CA 5-8R; CAD;
CANR 13, 45, 65, 100, 132, 167; CD 5,
6; CDALBS; CN 1, 2, 3, 4, 5, 6, 7; CPW;
DA3; DAM NOV, POP; DFS 2; DLB 6,

152; EWL 3; GLL 1; INT CANR-13; MAL 5; MTCW 1, 2; MTFW 2005; RGAL 4; RHW; TUS

Viereck, Peter 1916-2006 .... **CLC 4; PC 27**
See also CA 1-4R; 250; CANR 1, 47; CP 1, 2, 3, 4, 5, 6, 7; DLB 5; MAL 5; PFS 9, 14

Viereck, Peter Robert Edwin
See Viereck, Peter

Vigny, Alfred (Victor) de
1797-1863 .... **NCLC 7, 102; PC 26**
See also DAM POET; DLB 119, 192, 217; EW 5; GFL 1789 to the Present; RGWL 2, 3

Vilakazi, Benedict Wallet
1906-1947 .... **TCLC 37**
See also CA 168

Vile, Curt
See Moore, Alan

Villa, Jose Garcia 1914-1997 ... **AAL; PC 22; TCLC 176**
See also CA 25-28R; CANR 12, 118; CP 1, 2, 3, 4; DLB 312; EWL 3; EXPP

Villard, Oswald Garrison
1872-1949 .... **TCLC 160**
See also CA 113; 162; DLB 25, 91

Villarreal, Jose Antonio 1924- .... **HLC 2**
See also CA 133; CANR 93; DAM MULT; DLB 82; HW 1; LAIT 4; RGAL 4

Villaurrutia, Xavier 1903-1950 ...... **TCLC 80**
See also CA 192; EWL 3; HW 1; LAW

Villaverde, Cirilo 1812-1894 .... **NCLC 121**
See also LAW

Villehardouin, Geoffroi de
1150(?)-1218(?) .... **CMLC 38**

Villiers, George 1628-1687 .... **LC 107**
See also DLB 80; RGEL 2

Villiers de l'Isle Adam, Jean Marie Mathias Philippe Auguste 1838-1889 ... **NCLC 3; SSC 14**
See also DLB 123, 192; GFL 1789 to the Present; RGSF 2

Villon, Francois 1431-1463(?) . **LC 62; PC 13**
See also DLB 208; EW 2; RGWL 2, 3; TWA

Vine, Barbara .... **CLC 50**
See Rendell, Ruth
See also BEST 90:4

Vinge, Joan (Carol) D(ennison)
1948- .... **CLC 30; SSC 24**
See also AAYA 32; BPFB 3; CA 93-96; CANR 72; SATA 36, 113; SFW 4; YAW

Viola, Herman J(oseph) 1938- .... **CLC 70**
See also CA 61-64; CANR 8, 23, 48, 91; SATA 126

Violis, G.
See Simenon, Georges (Jacques Christian)

Viramontes, Helena Maria 1954- .... **HLCS 2**
See also CA 159; DLB 122; HW 2; LLW

Virgil
See Vergil
See also CDWLB 1; DLB 211; LAIT 1; RGWL 2, 3; WLIT 8; WP

Visconti, Luchino 1906-1976 .... **CLC 16**
See also CA 81-84; 65-68; CANR 39

Vitry, Jacques de
See Jacques de Vitry

Vittorini, Elio 1908-1966 .... **CLC 6, 9, 14**
See also CA 133; 25-28R; DLB 264; EW 12; EWL 3; RGWL 2, 3

Vivekananda, Swami 1863-1902 .... **TCLC 88**

Vizenor, Gerald Robert 1934- .... **CLC 103; NNAL**
See also CA 13-16R, 205; CAAE 205; CAAS 22; CANR 5, 21, 44, 67; DAM MULT; DLB 175, 227; MTCW 2; MTFW 2005; TCWW 2

Vizinczey, Stephen 1933- .... **CLC 40**
See also CA 128; CCA 1; INT CA-128

Vliet, R(ussell) G(ordon)
1929-1984 .... **CLC 22**
See also CA 37-40R; 112; CANR 18; CP 2, 3

Vogau, Boris Andreyevich 1894-1938
See Pilnyak, Boris
See also CA 123; 218

Vogel, Paula A. 1951- .... **CLC 76; DC 19**
See also CA 108; CAD; CANR 119, 140; CD 5, 6; CWD; DFS 14; DLB 341; MTFW 2005; RGAL 4

Voigt, Cynthia 1942- .... **CLC 30**
See also AAYA 3, 30; BYA 1, 3, 6, 7, 8; CA 106; CANR 18, 37, 40, 94, 145; CLR 13, 48; INT CANR-18; JRDA; LAIT 5; MAICYA 1, 2; MAICYAS 1; MTFW 2005; SATA 48, 79, 116, 160; SATA-Brief 33; WYA; YAW

Voigt, Ellen Bryant 1943- .... **CLC 54**
See also CA 69-72; CANR 11, 29, 55, 115, 171; CP 5, 6, 7; CSW; CWP; DLB 120; PFS 23

Voinovich, Vladimir 1932- .. **CLC 10, 49, 147**
See also CA 81-84; CAAS 12; CANR 33, 67, 150; CWW 2; DLB 302; MTCW 1

Voinovich, Vladimir Nikolaevich
See Voinovich, Vladimir

Vollmann, William T. 1959- ...... **CLC 89, 227**
See also AMWS 17; CA 134; CANR 67, 116; CN 7; CPW; DA3; DAM NOV, POP; MTCW 2; MTFW 2005

Voloshinov, V. N.
See Bakhtin, Mikhail Mikhailovich

Voltaire 1694-1778 .. **LC 14, 79, 110; SSC 12, 112; WLC 6**
See also BYA 13; DA; DA3; DAB; DAC; DAM DRAM, MST; DLB 314; EW 4; GFL Beginnings to 1789; LATS 1:1; LMFS 1; NFS 7; RGWL 2, 3; TWA

von Aschendrof, Baron Ignatz
See Ford, Ford Madox

von Chamisso, Adelbert
See Chamisso, Adelbert von

von Daeniken, Erich 1935- .... **CLC 30**
See also AITN 1; CA 37-40R; CANR 17, 44

von Daniken, Erich
See von Daeniken, Erich

von Eschenbach, Wolfram c. 1170-c. 1220 .... **CMLC 5**
See Eschenbach, Wolfram von
See also CDWLB 2; DLB 138; EW 1; RGWL 2

von Hartmann, Eduard
1842-1906 .... **TCLC 96**

von Hayek, Friedrich August
See Hayek, F(riedrich) A(ugust von)

von Heidenstam, (Carl Gustaf) Verner
See Heidenstam, (Carl Gustaf) Verner von

von Heyse, Paul (Johann Ludwig)
See Heyse, Paul (Johann Ludwig von)

von Hofmannsthal, Hugo
See Hofmannsthal, Hugo von

von Horvath, Odon
See von Horvath, Odon

von Horvath, Odon
See von Horvath, Odon

von Horvath, Odon 1901-1938 .... **TCLC 45**
See von Horvath, Oedoen
See also CA 118; 194; DLB 85, 124; RGWL 2, 3

von Horvath, Oedoen
See von Horvath, Odon
See also CA 184

von Kleist, Heinrich
See Kleist, Heinrich von

Vonnegut, Kurt, Jr.
See Vonnegut, Kurt

Vonnegut, Kurt 1922-2007 .... **CLC 1, 2, 3, 4, 5, 8, 12, 22, 40, 60, 111, 212, 254; SSC 8; WLC 6**
See also AAYA 6, 44; AITN 1; AMWS 2; BEST 90:4; BPFB 3; BYA 3, 14; CA 1-4R; 259; CANR 1, 25, 49, 75, 92; CDALB 1968-1988; CN 1, 2, 3, 4, 5, 6, 7; CPW 1; DA; DA3; DAB; DAC; DAM MST, NOV, POP; DLB 2, 8, 152; DLBD 3; DLBY 1980; EWL 3; EXPN; EXPS; LAIT 4; LMFS 2; MAL 5; MTCW 1, 2; MTFW 2005; NFS 3; RGAL 4; SCFW; SFW 4; SSFS 5; TUS; YAW

Von Rachen, Kurt
See Hubbard, L. Ron

von Sternberg, Josef
See Sternberg, Josef von

Vorster, Gordon 1924- .... **CLC 34**
See also CA 133

Vosce, Trudie
See Ozick, Cynthia

Voznesensky, Andrei (Andreievich)
1933- .... **CLC 1, 15, 57**
See Voznesensky, Andrey
See also CA 89-92; CANR 37; CWW 2; DAM POET; MTCW 1

Voznesensky, Andrey
See Voznesensky, Andrei (Andreievich)
See also EWL 3

Wace, Robert c. 1100-c. 1175 .... **CMLC 55**
See also DLB 146

Waddington, Miriam 1917-2004 .... **CLC 28**
See also CA 21-24R; 225; CANR 12, 30; CCA 1; CP 1, 2, 3, 4, 5, 6, 7; DLB 68

Wagman, Fredrica 1937- .... **CLC 7**
See also CA 97-100; CANR 166; INT CA-97-100

Wagner, Linda W.
See Wagner-Martin, Linda (C.)

Wagner, Linda Welshimer
See Wagner-Martin, Linda (C.)

Wagner, Richard 1813-1883 ..... **NCLC 9, 119**
See also DLB 129; EW 6

Wagner-Martin, Linda (C.) 1936- .... **CLC 50**
See also CA 159; CANR 135

Wagoner, David (Russell) 1926- .... **CLC 3, 5, 15; PC 33**
See also AMWS 9; CA 1-4R; CAAS 3; CANR 2, 71; CN 1, 2, 3, 4, 5, 6, 7; CP 1, 2, 3, 4, 5, 6, 7; DLB 5, 256; SATA 14; TCWW 1, 2

Wah, Fred(erick James) 1939- .... **CLC 44**
See also CA 107; 141; CP 1, 6, 7; DLB 60

Wahloo, Per 1926-1975 .... **CLC 7**
See also BPFB 3; CA 61-64; CANR 73; CMW 4; MSW

Wahloo, Peter
See Wahloo, Per

Wain, John (Barrington) 1925-1994 . **CLC 2, 11, 15, 46**
See also CA 5-8R; 145; CAAS 4; CANR 23, 54; CDBLB 1960 to Present; CN 1, 2, 3, 4, 5; CP 1, 2, 3, 4, 5; DLB 15, 27, 139, 155; EWL 3; MTCW 1, 2; MTFW 2005

Wajda, Andrzej 1926- .... **CLC 16, 219**
See also CA 102

Wakefield, Dan 1932- .... **CLC 7**
See also CA 21-24R, 211; CAAE 211; CAAS 7; CN 4, 5, 6, 7

Wakefield, Herbert Russell
1888-1965 .... **TCLC 120**
See also CA 5-8R; CANR 77; HGG; SUFW

Wakoski, Diane 1937- ...... **CLC 2, 4, 7, 9, 11, 40; PC 15**
See also CA 13-16R, 216; CAAE 216; CAAS 1; CANR 9, 60, 106; CP 1, 2, 3, 4, 5, 6, 7; CWP; DAM POET; DLB 5; INT CANR-9; MAL 5; MTCW 2; MTFW 2005

Wiebe, Rudy Henry
See Wiebe, Rudy
Wieland, Christoph Martin
1733-1813 .... **NCLC 17, 177**
See also DLB 97; EW 4; LMFS 1; RGWL
2, 3
Wiene, Robert 1881-1938 .... **TCLC 56**
Wieners, John 1934- .... **CLC 7**
See also BG 1:3; CA 13-16R; CP 1, 2, 3, 4,
5, 6, 7; DLB 16; WP
Wiesel, Elie 1928- ...... **CLC 3, 5, 11, 37, 165;**
WLCS
See also AAYA 7, 54; AITN 1; CA 5-8R;
CAAS 4; CANR 8, 40, 65, 125; CDALBS;
CWW 2; DA; DA3; DAB; DAC; DAM
MST, NOV; DLB 83, 299; DLBY 1987;
EWL 3; INT CANR-8; LAIT 4; MTCW
1, 2; MTFW 2005; NCFS 4; NFS 4;
RGHL; RGWL 3; SATA 56; YAW
Wiesel, Eliezer
See Wiesel, Elie
Wiggins, Marianne 1947- .... **CLC 57**
See also AAYA 70; BEST 89:3; CA 130;
CANR 60, 139, 180; CN 7; DLB 335
Wigglesworth, Michael 1631-1705 .... **LC 106**
See also DLB 24; RGAL 4
Wiggs, Susan .... **CLC 70**
See also CA 201; CANR 173
Wight, James Alfred 1916-1995
See Herriot, James
See also CA 77-80; SATA 55; SATA-Brief
44
Wilbur, Richard 1921- .. **CLC 3, 6, 9, 14, 53,**
110; PC 51
See also AAYA 72; AMWS 3; CA 1-4R;
CABS 2; CANR 2, 29, 76, 93, 139;
CDALBS; CP 1, 2, 3, 4, 5, 6, 7; DA;
DAB; DAC; DAM MST, POET; DLB 5,
169; EWL 3; EXPP; INT CANR-29;
MAL 5; MTCW 1, 2; MTFW 2005; PAB;
PFS 11, 12, 16; RGAL 4; SATA 9, 108;
WP
Wilbur, Richard Purdy
See Wilbur, Richard
Wild, Peter 1940- .... **CLC 14**
See also CA 37-40R; CP 1, 2, 3, 4, 5, 6, 7;
DLB 5
Wilde, Oscar 1854(?)-1900 ... **DC 17; SSC 11,**
77; TCLC 1, 8, 23, 41, 175; WLC 6
See also AAYA 49; BRW 5; BRWC 1, 2;
BRWR 2; BYA 15; CA 104; 119; CANR
112; CDBLB 1890-1914; CLR 114; DA;
DA3; DAB; DAC; DAM DRAM, MST,
NOV; DFS 4, 8, 9, 21; DLB 10, 19, 34,
57, 141, 156, 190, 344; EXPS; FANT; GL
3; LATS 1:1; NFS 20; RGEL 2; RGSF 2;
SATA 24; SSFS 7; SUFW; TEA; WCH;
WLIT 4
Wilde, Oscar Fingal O'Flahertie Willis
See Wilde, Oscar
Wilder, Billy .... **CLC 20**
See Wilder, Samuel
See also AAYA 66; DLB 26
Wilder, Samuel 1906-2002
See Wilder, Billy
See also CA 89-92; 205
Wilder, Stephen
See Marlowe, Stephen
Wilder, Thornton (Niven)
1897-1975 .. **CLC 1, 5, 6, 10, 15, 35, 82;**
DC 1, 24; WLC 6
See also AAYA 29; AITN 2; AMW; CA 13-
16R; 61-64; CAD; CANR 40, 132;
CDALBS; CN 1, 2; DA; DA3; DAB;
DAC; DAM DRAM, MST, NOV; DFS 1,
4, 16; DLB 4, 7, 9, 228; DLBY 1997;
EWL 3; LAIT 3; MAL 5; MTCW 1, 2;
MTFW 2005; NFS 24; RGAL 4; RHW;
WYAS 1

Wilding, Michael 1942- ...... **CLC 73; SSC 50**
See also CA 104; CANR 24, 49, 106; CN
4, 5, 6, 7; DLB 325; RGSF 2
Wiley, Richard 1944- .... **CLC 44**
See also CA 121; 129; CANR 71
Wilhelm, Kate .... **CLC 7**
See Wilhelm, Katie
See also AAYA 20; BYA 16; CAAS 5; DLB
8; INT CANR-17; SCFW 2
Wilhelm, Katie 1928-
See Wilhelm, Kate
See also CA 37-40R; CANR 17, 36, 60, 94;
MTCW 1; SFW 4
Wilkins, Mary
See Freeman, Mary E(leanor) Wilkins
Willard, Nancy 1936- .... **CLC 7, 37**
See also BYA 5; CA 89-92; CANR 10, 39,
68, 107, 152, 183; CLR 5; CP 2, 3, 4, 5;
CWP; CWRI 5; DLB 5, 52; FANT; MAI-
CYA 1, 2; MTCW 1; SATA 37, 71, 127,
191; SATA-Brief 30; SUFW 2; TCLE 1:2
William of Malmesbury c. 1090B.C.-c.
1140B.C. .... **CMLC 57**
William of Moerbeke c. 1215-c.
1286 .... **CMLC 91**
William of Ockham 1290-1349 ..... **CMLC 32**
Williams, Ben Ames 1889-1953 ..... **TCLC 89**
See also CA 183; DLB 102
Williams, Charles
See Collier, James Lincoln
Williams, Charles (Walter Stansby)
1886-1945 .... **TCLC 1, 11**
See also BRWS 9; CA 104; 163; DLB 100,
153, 255; FANT; RGEL 2; SUFW 1
Williams, C.K. 1936- .... **CLC 33, 56, 148**
See also CA 37-40R; CAAS 26; CANR 57,
106; CP 1, 2, 3, 4, 5, 6, 7; DAM POET;
DLB 5; MAL 5
Williams, Ella Gwendolen Rees
See Rhys, Jean
Williams, (George) Emlyn
1905-1987 .... **CLC 15**
See also CA 104; 123; CANR 36; DAM
DRAM; DLB 10, 77; IDTP; MTCW 1
Williams, Hank 1923-1953 .... **TCLC 81**
See Williams, Hiram King
Williams, Helen Maria
1761-1827 .... **NCLC 135**
See also DLB 158
Williams, Hiram Hank
See Williams, Hank
Williams, Hiram King
See Williams, Hank
See also CA 188
Williams, Hugo (Mordaunt) 1942- ... **CLC 42**
See also CA 17-20R; CANR 45, 119; CP 1,
2, 3, 4, 5, 6, 7; DLB 40
Williams, J. Walker
See Wodehouse, P(elham) G(renville)
Williams, John A(lfred) 1925- .... **BLC 1:3;**
CLC 5, 13
See also AFAW 2; BW 2, 3; CA 53-56; 195;
CAAE 195; CAAS 3; CANR 6, 26, 51,
118; CN 1, 2, 3, 4, 5, 6, 7; CSW; DAM
MULT; DLB 2, 33; EWL 3; INT CANR-6;
MAL 5; RGAL 4; SFW 4
Williams, Jonathan 1929-2008 .... **CLC 13**
See also CA 9-12R; 270; CAAS 12; CANR
8, 108; CP 1, 2, 3, 4, 5, 6, 7; DLB 5
Williams, Jonathan Chamberlain
See Williams, Jonathan
Williams, Joy 1944- .... **CLC 31**
See also CA 41-44R; CANR 22, 48, 97,
168; DLB 335; SSFS 25
Williams, Norman 1952- .... **CLC 39**
See also CA 118
Williams, Roger 1603(?)-1683 .... **LC 129**
See also DLB 24

Williams, Sherley Anne
1944-1999 .... **BLC 1:3; CLC 89**
See also AFAW 2; BW 2, 3; CA 73-76; 185;
CANR 25, 82; DAM MULT, POET; DLB
41; INT CANR-25; SATA 78; SATA-Obit
116
Williams, Shirley
See Williams, Sherley Anne
Williams, Tennessee 1911-1983 . **CLC 1, 2, 5,**
7, 8, 11, 15, 19, 30, 39, 45, 71, 111; DC
4; SSC 81; WLC 6
See also AAYA 31; AITN 1, 2; AMW;
AMWC 1; CA 5-8R; 108; CABS 3; CAD;
CANR 31, 132, 174; CDALB 1941-1968;
CN 1, 2, 3; DA; DA3; DAB; DAC; DAM
DRAM, MST; DFS 17; DLB 7, 341;
DLBD 4; DLBY 1983; EWL 3; GLL 1;
LAIT 4; LATS 1:2; MAL 5; MTCW 1, 2;
MTFW 2005; RGAL 4; TUS
Williams, Thomas (Alonzo)
1926-1990 .... **CLC 14**
See also CA 1-4R; 132; CANR 2
Williams, Thomas Lanier
See Williams, Tennessee
Williams, William C.
See Williams, William Carlos
Williams, William Carlos
1883-1963 .... **CLC 1, 2, 5, 9, 13, 22, 42,**
67; PC 7; SSC 31; WLC 6
See also AAYA 46; AMW; AMWR 1; CA
89-92; CANR 34; CDALB 1917-1929;
DA; DA3; DAB; DAC; DAM MST,
POET; DLB 4, 16, 54, 86; EWL 3; EXPP;
MAL 5; MTCW 1, 2; MTFW 2005; NCFS
4; PAB; PFS 1, 6, 11; RGAL 4; RGSF 2;
TUS; WP
Williamson, David (Keith) 1942- ..... **CLC 56**
See also CA 103; CANR 41; CD 5, 6; DLB
289
Williamson, Jack .... **CLC 29**
See Williamson, John Stewart
See also CAAS 8; DLB 8; SCFW 1, 2
Williamson, John Stewart 1908-2006
See Williamson, Jack
See also AAYA 76; CA 17-20R; 255; CANR
23, 70, 153; SFW 4
Willie, Frederick
See Lovecraft, H. P.
Willingham, Calder (Baynard, Jr.)
1922-1995 .... **CLC 5, 51**
See also CA 5-8R; 147; CANR 3; CN 1, 2,
3, 4, 5; CSW; DLB 2, 44; IDFW 3, 4;
MTCW 1
Willis, Charles
See Clarke, Arthur C.
Willis, Nathaniel Parker
1806-1867 .... **NCLC 194**
See also DLB 3, 59, 73, 74, 183, 250;
DLBD 13; RGAL 4
Willy
See Colette, (Sidonie-Gabrielle)
Willy, Colette
See Colette, (Sidonie-Gabrielle)
See also GLL 1
Wilmot, John 1647-1680 .... **LC 75; PC 66**
See Rochester
See also BRW 2; DLB 131; PAB
Wilson, A.N. 1950- .... **CLC 33**
See also BRWS 6; CA 112; 122; CANR
156; CN 4, 5, 6, 7; DLB 14, 155, 194;
MTCW 2
Wilson, Andrew Norman
See Wilson, A.N.
Wilson, Angus (Frank Johnstone)
1913-1991 . **CLC 2, 3, 5, 25, 34; SSC 21**
See also BRWS 1; CA 5-8R; 134; CANR
21; CN 1, 2, 3, 4; DLB 15, 139, 155;
EWL 3; MTCW 1, 2; MTFW 2005; RGEL
2; RGSF 2

Woolf, (Adeline) Virginia 1882-1941 .. SSC 7, 79; TCLC 1, 5, 20, 43, 56, 101, 123, 128; WLC 6
See also AAYA 44; BPFB 3; BRW 7; BRWC 2; BRWR 1; CA 104; 130; CANR 64, 132; CDBLB 1914-1945; DA; DA3; DAB; DAC; DAM MST, NOV; DLB 36, 100, 162; DLBD 10; EWL 3; EXPS; FL 1:6; FW; LAIT 3; LATS 1:1; LMFS 2; MTCW 1, 2; MTFW 2005; NCFS 2; NFS 8, 12; RGEL 2; RGSF 2; SSFS 4, 12; TEA; WLIT 4

Woollcott, Alexander (Humphreys) 1887-1943 .... TCLC 5
See also CA 105; 161; DLB 29

Woolman, John 1720-1772 .... LC 155
See also DLB 31

Woolrich, Cornell .... CLC 77
See Hopley-Woolrich, Cornell George
See also MSW

Woolson, Constance Fenimore 1840-1894 .... NCLC 82; SSC 90
See also DLB 12, 74, 189, 221; RGAL 4

Wordsworth, Dorothy 1771-1855 . NCLC 25, 138
See also DLB 107

Wordsworth, William 1770-1850 .. NCLC 12, 38, 111, 166; PC 4, 67; WLC 6
See also AAYA 70; BRW 4; BRWC 1; CD-BLB 1789-1832; DA; DA3; DAB; DAC; DAM MST, POET; DLB 93, 107; EXPP; LATS 1:1; LMFS 1; PAB; PFS 2; RGEL 2; TEA; WLIT 3; WP

Wotton, Sir Henry 1568-1639 .... LC 68
See also DLB 121; RGEL 2

Wouk, Herman 1915- .... CLC 1, 9, 38
See also BPFB 2, 3; CA 5-8R; CANR 6, 33, 67, 146; CDALBS; CN 1, 2, 3, 4, 5, 6; CPW; DA3; DAM NOV, POP; DLBY 1982; INT CANR-6; LAIT 4; MAL 5; MTCW 1, 2; MTFW 2005; NFS 7; TUS

Wright, Charles 1935- ... CLC 6, 13, 28, 119, 146
See also AMWS 5; CA 29-32R; CAAS 7; CANR 23, 36, 62, 88, 135, 180; CP 3, 4, 5, 6, 7; DLB 165; DLBY 1982; EWL 3; MTCW 1, 2; MTFW 2005; PFS 10

Wright, Charles Penzel, Jr.
See Wright, Charles

Wright, Charles Stevenson 1932- .. BLC 1:3; CLC 49
See also BW 1; CA 9-12R; CANR 26; CN 1, 2, 3, 4, 5, 6, 7; DAM MULT, POET; DLB 33

Wright, Frances 1795-1852 .... NCLC 74
See also DLB 73

Wright, Frank Lloyd 1867-1959 .... TCLC 95
See also AAYA 33; CA 174

Wright, Harold Bell 1872-1944 .... TCLC 183
See also BPFB 3; CA 110; DLB 9; TCWW 2

Wright, Jack R.
See Harris, Mark

Wright, James (Arlington) 1927-1980 .... CLC 3, 5, 10, 28; PC 36
See also AITN 2; AMWS 3; CA 49-52; 97-100; CANR 4, 34, 64; CDALBS; CP 1, 2; DAM POET; DLB 5, 169, 342; EWL 3; EXPP; MAL 5; MTCW 1, 2; MTFW 2005; PFS 7, 8; RGAL 4; TUS; WP

Wright, Judith 1915-2000 ... CLC 11, 53; PC 14
See also CA 13-16R; 188; CANR 31, 76, 93; CP 1, 2, 3, 4, 5, 6, 7; CWP; DLB 260; EWL 3; MTCW 1, 2; MTFW 2005; PFS 8; RGEL 2; SATA 14; SATA-Obit 121

Wright, L(aurali) R. 1939- .... CLC 44
See also CA 138; CMW 4

Wright, Richard (Nathaniel) 1908-1960 ...... BLC 1:3; CLC 1, 3, 4, 9, 14, 21, 48, 74; SSC 2, 109; TCLC 136, 180; WLC 6
See also AAYA 5, 42; AFAW 1, 2; AMW; BPFB 3; BW 1; BYA 2; CA 108; CANR 64; CDALB 1929-1941; DA; DA3; DAB; DAC; DAM MST, MULT, NOV; DLB 76, 102; DLBD 2; EWL 3; EXPN; LAIT 3, 4; MAL 5; MTCW 1, 2; MTFW 2005; NCFS 1; NFS 1, 7; RGAL 4; RGSF 2; SSFS 3, 9, 15, 20; TUS; YAW

Wright, Richard B. 1937- .... CLC 6
See also CA 85-88; CANR 120; DLB 53

Wright, Richard Bruce
See Wright, Richard B.

Wright, Rick 1945- .... CLC 35

Wright, Rowland
See Wells, Carolyn

Wright, Stephen 1946- .... CLC 33
See also CA 237

Wright, Willard Huntington 1888-1939
See Van Dine, S. S.
See also CA 115; 189; CMW 4; DLBD 16

Wright, William 1930- .... CLC 44
See also CA 53-56; CANR 7, 23, 154

Wroth, Lady Mary 1587-1653(?) .... LC 30, 139; PC 38
See also DLB 121

Wu Ch'eng-en 1500(?)-1582(?) .... LC 7

Wu Ching-tzu 1701-1754 .... LC 2

Wulfstan c. 10th cent. -1023 .... CMLC 59

Wurlitzer, Rudolph 1938(?)- ...... CLC 2, 4, 15
See also CA 85-88; CN 4, 5, 6, 7; DLB 173

Wyatt, Sir Thomas c. 1503-1542 . LC 70; PC 27
See also BRW 1; DLB 132; EXPP; PFS 25; RGEL 2; TEA

Wycherley, William 1640-1716 .... LC 8, 21, 102, 136
See also BRW 2; CDBLB 1660-1789; DAM DRAM; DLB 80; RGEL 2

Wyclif, John c. 1330-1384 .... CMLC 70
See also DLB 146

Wylie, Elinor (Morton Hoyt) 1885-1928 .... PC 23; TCLC 8
See also AMWS 1; CA 105; 162; DLB 9, 45; EXPP; MAL 5; RGAL 4

Wylie, Philip (Gordon) 1902-1971 ... CLC 43
See also CA 21-22; 33-36R; CAP 2; CN 1; DLB 9; SFW 4

Wyndham, John .... CLC 19
See Harris, John (Wyndham Parkes Lucas) Beynon
See also BRWS 13; DLB 255; SCFW 1, 2

Wyss, Johann David Von 1743-1818 .... NCLC 10
See also CLR 92; JRDA; MAICYA 1, 2; SATA 29; SATA-Brief 27

Xenophon c. 430B.C.-c. 354B.C. ... CMLC 17
See also AW 1; DLB 176; RGWL 2, 3; WLIT 8

Xingjian, Gao 1940-
See Gao Xingjian
See also CA 193; DFS 21; DLB 330; RGWL 3

Yakamochi 718-785 .... CMLC 45; PC 48

Yakumo Koizumi
See Hearn, (Patricio) Lafcadio (Tessima Carlos)

Yamada, Mitsuye (May) 1923- .... PC 44
See also CA 77-80

Yamamoto, Hisaye 1921- .... AAL; SSC 34
See also CA 214; DAM MULT; DLB 312; LAIT 4; SSFS 14

Yamauchi, Wakako 1924- .... AAL
See also CA 214; DLB 312

Yanez, Jose Donoso
See Donoso (Yanez), Jose

Yanovsky, Basile S.
See Yanovsky, V(assily) S(emenovich)

Yanovsky, V(assily) S(emenovich) 1906-1989 .... CLC 2, 18
See also CA 97-100; 129

Yates, Richard 1926-1992 .... CLC 7, 8, 23
See also AMWS 11; CA 5-8R; 139; CANR 10, 43; CN 1, 2, 3, 4, 5; DLB 2, 234; DLBY 1981, 1992; INT CANR-10; SSFS 24

Yau, John 1950- .... PC 61
See also CA 154; CANR 89; CP 4, 5, 6, 7; DLB 234, 312; PFS 26

Yearsley, Ann 1753-1806 .... NCLC 174
See also DLB 109

Yeats, W. B.
See Yeats, William Butler

Yeats, William Butler 1865-1939 . PC 20, 51; TCLC 1, 11, 18, 31, 93, 116; WLC 6
See also AAYA 48; BRW 6; BRWR 1; CA 104; 127; CANR 45; CDBLB 1890-1914; DA; DA3; DAB; DAC; DAM DRAM, MST, POET; DLB 10, 19, 98, 156, 332; EWL 3; EXPP; MTCW 1, 2; MTFW 2005; NCFS 3; PAB; PFS 1, 2, 5, 7, 13, 15; RGEL 2; TEA; WLIT 4; WP

Yehoshua, A.B. 1936- .... CLC 13, 31, 243
See also CA 33-36R; CANR 43, 90, 145; CWW 2; EWL 3; RGHL; RGSF 2; RGWL 3; WLIT 6

Yehoshua, Abraham B.
See Yehoshua, A.B.

Yellow Bird
See Ridge, John Rollin

Yep, Laurence 1948- .... CLC 35
See also AAYA 5, 31; BYA 7; CA 49-52; CANR 1, 46, 92, 161; CLR 3, 17, 54, 132; DLB 52, 312; FANT; JRDA; MAICYA 1, 2; MAICYAS 1; SATA 7, 69, 123, 176; WYA; YAW

Yep, Laurence Michael
See Yep, Laurence

Yerby, Frank G(arvin) 1916-1991 . BLC 1:3; CLC 1, 7, 22
See also BPFB 3; BW 1, 3; CA 9-12R; 136; CANR 16, 52; CN 1, 2, 3, 4, 5; DAM MULT; DLB 76; INT CANR-16; MTCW 1; RGAL 4; RHW

Yesenin, Sergei Aleksandrovich
See Esenin, Sergei

Yevtushenko, Yevgeny (Alexandrovich) 1933- ...... CLC 1, 3, 13, 26, 51, 126; PC 40
See Evtushenko, Evgenii Aleksandrovich
See also CA 81-84; CANR 33, 54; DAM POET; EWL 3; MTCW 1; RGHL

Yezierska, Anzia 1885(?)-1970 .... CLC 46; TCLC 205
See also CA 126; 89-92; DLB 28, 221; FW; MTCW 1; RGAL 4; SSFS 15

Yglesias, Helen 1915-2008 .... CLC 7, 22
See also CA 37-40R; 272; CAAS 20; CANR 15, 65, 95; CN 4, 5, 6, 7; INT CANR-15; MTCW 1

Yokomitsu, Riichi 1898-1947 .... TCLC 47
See also CA 170; EWL 3

Yolen, Jane 1939- .... CLC 256
See also AAYA 4, 22; BPFB 3; BYA 9, 10, 11, 14, 16; CA 13-16R; CANR 11, 29, 56, 91, 126; CLR 4, 44; CWRI 5; DLB 52; FANT; INT CANR-29; JRDA; MAICYA 1, 2; MTFW 2005; SAAS 1; SATA 4, 40, 75, 112, 158; SATA-Essay 111; SFW 4; SUFW 2; WYA; YAW

Yonge, Charlotte (Mary) 1823-1901 .... TCLC 48
See also CA 109; 163; DLB 18, 163; RGEL 2; SATA 17; WCH

York, Jeremy
See Creasey, John

York, Simon
See Heinlein, Robert A.
Yorke, Henry Vincent 1905-1974 ..... **CLC 13**
See Green, Henry
See also CA 85-88; 49-52
Yosano, Akiko 1878-1942 ... **PC 11; TCLC 59**
See also CA 161; EWL 3; RGWL 3
Yoshimoto, Banana .... **CLC 84**
See Yoshimoto, Mahoko
See also AAYA 50; NFS 7
Yoshimoto, Mahoko 1964-
See Yoshimoto, Banana
See also CA 144; CANR 98, 160; SSFS 16
Young, Al(bert James) 1939- .... **BLC 1:3;**
CLC 19
See also BW 2, 3; CA 29-32R; CANR 26,
65, 109; CN 2, 3, 4, 5, 6, 7; CP 1, 2, 3, 4,
5, 6, 7; DAM MULT; DLB 33
Young, Andrew (John) 1885-1971 ...... **CLC 5**
See also CA 5-8R; CANR 7, 29; CP 1;
RGEL 2
Young, Collier
See Bloch, Robert (Albert)
Young, Edward 1683-1765 .... **LC 3, 40**
See also DLB 95; RGEL 2
Young, Marguerite (Vivian)
1909-1995 .... **CLC 82**
See also CA 13-16; 150; CAP 1; CN 1, 2,
3, 4, 5, 6
Young, Neil 1945- .... **CLC 17**
See also CA 110; CCA 1
Young Bear, Ray A. 1950- ... **CLC 94; NNAL**
See also CA 146; DAM MULT; DLB 175;
MAL 5
Yourcenar, Marguerite 1903-1987 ... **CLC 19,**
38, 50, 87; TCLC 193
See also BPFB 3; CA 69-72; CANR 23, 60,
93; DAM NOV; DLB 72; DLBY 1988;
EW 12; EWL 3; GFL 1789 to the Present;
GLL 1; MTCW 1, 2; MTFW 2005;
RGWL 2, 3
Yuan, Chu 340(?)B.C.-278(?)B.C. . **CMLC 36**
Yurick, Sol 1925- .... **CLC 6**
See also CA 13-16R; CANR 25; CN 1, 2,
3, 4, 5, 6, 7; MAL 5
Zabolotsky, Nikolai Alekseevich
1903-1958 .... **TCLC 52**
See Zabolotsky, Nikolay Alekseevich
See also CA 116; 164
Zabolotsky, Nikolay Alekseevich
See Zabolotsky, Nikolai Alekseevich
See also EWL 3
Zagajewski, Adam 1945- .... **PC 27**
See also CA 186; DLB 232; EWL 3; PFS
25
Zalygin, Sergei -2000 .... **CLC 59**
Zalygin, Sergei (Pavlovich)
1913-2000 .... **CLC 59**
See also DLB 302
Zamiatin, Evgenii
See Zamyatin, Evgeny Ivanovich
See also RGSF 2; RGWL 2, 3
Zamiatin, Evgenii Ivanovich
See Zamyatin, Evgeny Ivanovich
See also DLB 272

Zamiatin, Yevgenii
See Zamyatin, Evgeny Ivanovich
Zamora, Bernice (B. Ortiz) 1938- .. **CLC 89;**
HLC 2
See also CA 151; CANR 80; DAM MULT;
DLB 82; HW 1, 2
Zamyatin, Evgeny Ivanovich
1884-1937 .... **SSC 89; TCLC 8, 37**
See Zamiatin, Evgenii; Zamiatin, Evgenii
Ivanovich; Zamyatin, Yevgeny Ivanovich
See also CA 105; 166; SFW 4
Zamyatin, Yevgeny Ivanovich
See Zamyatin, Evgeny Ivanovich
See also EW 10; EWL 3
Zangwill, Israel 1864-1926 ... **SSC 44; TCLC**
16
See also CA 109; 167; CMW 4; DLB 10,
135, 197; RGEL 2
Zanzotto, Andrea 1921- .... **PC 65**
See also CA 208; CWW 2; DLB 128; EWL
3
Zappa, Francis Vincent, Jr. 1940-1993
See Zappa, Frank
See also CA 108; 143; CANR 57
Zappa, Frank .... **CLC 17**
See Zappa, Francis Vincent, Jr.
Zaturenska, Marya 1902-1982 ..... **CLC 6, 11**
See also CA 13-16R; 105; CANR 22; CP 1,
2, 3
Zayas y Sotomayor, Maria de 1590-c.
1661 .... **LC 102; SSC 94**
See also RGSF 2
Zeami 1363-1443 .... **DC 7; LC 86**
See also DLB 203; RGWL 2, 3
Zelazny, Roger 1937-1995 .... **CLC 21**
See also AAYA 7, 68; BPFB 3; CA 21-24R;
148; CANR 26, 60; CN 6; DLB 8; FANT;
MTCW 1, 2; MTFW 2005; SATA 57;
SATA-Brief 39; SCFW 1, 2; SFW 4;
SUFW 1, 2
Zephaniah, Benjamin 1958- .... **BLC 2:3**
See also CA 147; CANR 103, 156, 177; CP
5, 6, 7; SATA 86, 140, 189
Zhang Ailing
See Chang, Eileen
Zhdanov, Andrei Alexandrovich
1896-1948 .... **TCLC 18**
See also CA 117; 167
Zhukovsky, Vasilii Andreevich
See Zhukovsky, Vasily (Andreevich)
See also DLB 205
Zhukovsky, Vasily (Andreevich)
1783-1852 .... **NCLC 35**
See Zhukovsky, Vasilii Andreevich
Ziegenhagen, Eric .... **CLC 55**
Zimmer, Jill Schary
See Robinson, Jill
Zimmerman, Robert
See Dylan, Bob
Zindel, Paul 1936-2003 ...... **CLC 6, 26; DC 5**
See also AAYA 2, 37; BYA 2, 3, 8, 11, 14;
CA 73-76; 213; CAD; CANR 31, 65, 108;
CD 5, 6; CDALBS; CLR 3, 45, 85; DA;
DA3; DAB; DAC; DAM DRAM, MST,
NOV; DFS 12; DLB 7, 52; JRDA; LAIT

5; MAICYA 1, 2; MTCW 1, 2; MTFW
2005; NFS 14; SATA 16, 58, 102; SATA-
Obit 142; WYA; YAW
Zinger, Yisroel-Yehoyshue
See Singer, Israel Joshua
Zinger, Yitskhok
See Singer, Isaac Bashevis
Zinn, Howard 1922- .... **CLC 199**
See also CA 1-4R; CANR 2, 33, 90, 159
Zinov'Ev, A.A.
See Zinoviev, Alexander
Zinov'ev, Aleksandr
See Zinoviev, Alexander
See also DLB 302
Zinoviev, Alexander 1922-2006 .... **CLC 19**
See Zinov'ev, Aleksandr
See also CA 116; 133; 250; CAAS 10
Zinoviev, Alexander Aleksandrovich
See Zinoviev, Alexander
Zizek, Slavoj 1949- .... **CLC 188**
See also CA 201; CANR 171; MTFW 2005
Zobel, Joseph 1915-2006 .... **BLC 2:3**
Zoilus
See Lovecraft, H. P.
Zola, Emile (Edouard Charles Antoine)
1840-1902 ...... **SSC 109; TCLC 1, 6, 21,**
41; WLC 6
See also CA 104; 138; DA; DA3; DAB;
DAC; DAM MST, NOV; DLB 123; EW
7; GFL 1789 to the Present; IDTP; LMFS
1, 2; RGWL 2; TWA
Zoline, Pamela 1941- .... **CLC 62**
See also CA 161; SFW 4
Zoroaster 628(?)B.C.-551(?)B.C. ... **CMLC 40**
Zorrilla y Moral, Jose 1817-1893 .... **NCLC 6**
Zoshchenko, Mikhail 1895-1958 ...... **SSC 15;**
TCLC 15
See also CA 115; 160; EWL 3; RGSF 2;
RGWL 3
Zoshchenko, Mikhail Mikhailovich
See Zoshchenko, Mikhail
Zuckmayer, Carl 1896-1977 .... **CLC 18;**
TCLC 191
See also CA 69-72; DLB 56, 124; EWL 3;
RGWL 2, 3
Zuk, Georges
See Skelton, Robin
See also CCA 1
Zukofsky, Louis 1904-1978 ... **CLC 1, 2, 4, 7,**
11, 18; PC 11
See also AMWS 3; CA 9-12R; 77-80;
CANR 39; CP 1, 2; DAM POET; DLB 5,
165; EWL 3; MAL 5; MTCW 1; RGAL 4
Zweig, Arnold 1887-1968 .... **TCLC 199**
See also CA 189; 115; DLB 66; EWL 3
Zweig, Paul 1935-1984 .... **CLC 34, 42**
See also CA 85-88; 113
Zweig, Stefan 1881-1942 .... **TCLC 17**
See also CA 112; 170; DLB 81, 118; EWL
3; RGHL
Zwingli, Huldreich 1484-1531 .... **LC 37**
See also DLB 179

Literary Criticism Series
Cumulative Topic Index

This index lists all topic entries in Gale's *Children's Literature Review* (CLR), *Classical and Medieval Literature Criticism* (CMLC), *Contemporary Literary Criticism* (CLC), *Drama Criticism* (DC), *Literature Criticism from 1400 to 1800* (LC), *Nineteenth-Century Literature Criticism* (NCLC), *Short Story Criticism* (SSC), and *Twentieth-Century Literary Criticism* (TCLC). The index also lists topic entries in the Gale Critical Companion Collection, which includes the following publications: *The Beat Generation* (BG), *Feminism in Literature* (FL), *Gothic Literature* (GL), and *Harlem Renaissance* (HR).

Topic Index

Topic Index

Topic Index

Topic Index

Topic Index

NCLC Cumulative Nationality Index

Nationality Index

NCLC-202 Title Index

ISBN-13: 978-1-4144-2133-9
ISBN-10: 1-4144-2133-8

90000